ACCOUNTING PRINCIPLES

THIRD EDITION

JERRY J. WEYGANDT Ph.D., C.P.A.

Arthur Andersen Alumni Professor of Accounting
University of Wisconsin
Madison, Wisconsin

DONALD E. KIESO Ph.D., C.P.A.

KPMG Peat Marwick Professor of Accountancy
Northern Illinois University
DeKalb, Illinois

WALTER G. KELL Ph.D., C.P.A.

Professor Emeritus of Accounting
University of Michigan
Ann Arbor, Michigan

ACCOUNTING PRINCIPLES

 JOHN WILEY & SONS, INC.

New York ▪ Chichester ▪ Brisbane ▪ Toronto ▪ Singapore

Cover Photo   Thomas Lindley/FPG International

Executive Editor   Michael Reynolds
Supplements Editor   Marinita Timban
Supplements Compositor   Donna Kieso
Director of Development   Johnna Barto
Developmental Editor   Ann Torbert
Senior Marketing Manager   Susan Elbe
Marketing Manager   Karen Allman
Senior Production Supervisor   Katharine Rubin
Text Designer   Sheila Granda
Cover Designer   Madelyn Lesure
Manufacturing Manager   Andrea Price
Photo Researcher   Jennifer Atkins
Illustration   Anna Melhorn

This book was set in 10.5/12 Palatino by Waldman Graphics, Inc. and printed
and bound by Von Hoffmann Press. The cover was printed by Phoenix Color Corp.

Recognizing the importance of preserving what has been written, it is
a policy of John Wiley & Sons, Inc. to have books of enduring value
published in the United States printed on acid-free paper, and we exert
our best efforts to that end.

Library of Congress Cataloging in Publication Data

Weygandt, Jerry J.
    Accounting principles / Jerry J. Weygandt, Donald E. Kieso, Walter
G. Kell.—3rd ed.
      p. cm.
    Includes index.
    ISBN 0-471-57064-8
    1. Accounting.   I. Kieso, Donald E.   II. Kell, Walter Gerry,
1921–   .   III. Title.
    HF5635.W524 1992b   92-41815
    657—dc20   CIP

Printed in the United States of America

10 9 8 7 6 5 4

Dedicated to
our teachers—from whom we learned
and
our students—from whom we continue to learn

and to our families,
most especially our wives
Enid
Donna
Linda

ABOUT THE AUTHORS

Jerry J. Weygandt, Ph.D., CPA, is Arthur Andersen Alumni Professor of Accounting at the University of Wisconsin-Madison. He holds a Ph.D. in accounting from the University of Illinois. Articles by Professor Weygandt have appeared in the *Accounting Review, Journal of Accounting Research,* the *Journal of Accountancy,* and other professional journals. These articles have examined such financial reporting issues as accounting for price-level adjustments, pensions, convertible securities, stock option contracts, and interim reports. He is a member of the American Accounting Association, the American Institute of Certified Public Accountants, and the Wisconsin Society of Certified Public Accountants. He has served on numerous committees of the American Accounting Association and as a member of the editorial board of the *Accounting Review.* In addition, he is actively involved with the American Institute of Certified Public Accountants and has been a member of the Accounting Standards Executive Committee (AcSEC) of that organization. He has served as a consultant to a number of businesses and state agencies on financial reporting issues and served on the FASB task force that examined the reporting issues related to "accounting for income taxes." Professor Weygandt has received the Chancellor's Award for Excellence in Teaching; he also has served as Secretary-Treasurer of the American Accounting Association. Recently he received the Wisconsin Institute of CPA's Outstanding Educator's Award.

Donald E. Kieso, Ph.D., CPA, received his bachelors degree from Aurora University and his doctorate in accounting from the University of Illinois. He has served as chairman of the Department of Accountancy and is currently the Peat Marwick Professor of Accountancy at Northern Illinois University. He has public accounting experience with Price Waterhouse & Co. (San Francisco and Chicago) and Arthur Andersen & Co. (Chicago) and research experience with the Research Division of the American Institute of Certified Public Accountants (New York). He has done postdoctorate work as a Visiting Scholar at the University of California at Berkeley and is a recipient of NIU's Teaching Excellence Award and the Executive MBA Golden Apple Teaching Award. Professor Kieso is the author of other accounting and business books and is a member of the American Accounting Association, the American Institute of Certified Public Accountants, the Financial Executives Institute, and the Illinois CPA Society. He has served as a member of the Board of Directors of the Illinois CPA Society, the Board of Governors of the American Accounting Association's Administrators of Accounting Programs Group, the AACSB's Accounting Accreditation and Visitation Committees, the State of Illinois Comptroller's Commission, as Secretary-Treasurer of the Federation of Schools of Accountancy, and as Secretary-Treasurer of the American Accounting Association. Professor Kieso is currently serving as a member of the Board of Directors of Aurora University, the chairman of the AAA/AECC Liaison Committee, the National Accounting Education Change Commission, and committees of the Illinois CPA Society. In 1988 he received the Outstanding Accounting Educator Award from the Illinois CPA Society, and in 1992 he received the FSA's Joseph A. Silvoso Award of Merit and the NIU Foundation's Humanitarian Award for Service to Higher Education.

Walter G. Kell, Ph.D., CPA, received his doctorate in accounting from the University of Illinois. He is Professor Emeritus of Accounting at the University of Michigan, where he has served as Chairman of the Department of Accounting.

He also has served as the Chairman of the Accounting Department of Syracuse University. He has been an active member of the American Institute of Certified Public Accountants and has served on its Committee on Auditing Procedure (predecessor to the Auditing Standards Board) and Auditing Standards Advisory Council. He is a past president of the American Accounting Association. Professor Kell has been a consulting editor and co-editor of the *Accountant's Handbook* and is the co-author of an auditing textbook. He is a member of the Michigan Association of Certified Public Accountants and has served on its Committee on Accounting and Auditing Procedures and Board of Directors. In 1986 Profesor Kell received the Association's Distinguished Service Award because of his significant contributions to the public accounting profession. He recently served as a member and chairman of the CPA Examination Review Board of the National Association of State Boards of Accountancy.

TO THE STUDENT

Welcome to your first course in accounting! We have good news for you. This textbook has been specifically designed to make your first accounting experience meaningful and interesting. You will be using a textbook that has met the test of the marketplace in previous editions. Each chapter contains special features that show you how accounting really works, and how you can use these features as a guide in studying each chapter. These features are highlighted below. We wish you every success in your first course in accounting.

Features that Show You How Accounting Really Works

- Whether you realize it or not, accounting is a part of your life *right now*! Each chapter opens with a **Chapter-Opening Vignette**, a true story that shows you accounting in action on a college campus. These real-life scenarios will help you understand how accounting relates to your own life, and the role accounting plays in all our lives.
- **Accounting in Action** boxes within each chapter show you how real companies put accounting to work. You'll get special insight into business, ethics, and international problems and challenges real accountants face, and the role accounting plays in dealing with these issues.
- One of the most important tools in accounting is the computer. **Technology in Action** boxes show you how computers are continuing to revolutionize accounting, and how they are used in accounting practice today. These boxes will also give you some idea of what the future holds.

Features that Guide You as You Study Each Chapter

- Before you begin a chapter, you'll see a **Concepts for Review** box that lists concepts and skills that you've encountered in previous chapters, and that you will see in the chapter to come. If you review these concepts before you start reading the chapter, the new material will be easier to understand. The page numbers after each concept in the box tell you where to turn to review any concepts you aren't clear about.
- You'll also find a list of **Study Objectives** at the beginning of each chapter. They tell you what you should be able to do after completing the chapter. For example, you might be asked to explain a concept, identify the steps to perform a particular computation, or interpret a type of statement. This helps you focus your attention on what you're expected to learn from the chapter right up front.
- To make sure you stay on track, each chapter includes **Before You Go On** sections. These sections appear in the middle of the text, and ask you to stop and answer a few brief questions before you continue reading. That way, you can check to make sure that you thoroughly understand each concept as it is being developed.
- Sometimes the theoretical discussion of a concept needs to be reinforced. To help you in such cases, your text includes **Helpful Hints** in the margins. These notes help to clarify the particular concept under discussion.
- **Summary of Study Objectives** appears at the end of each chapter. The Study Objectives listed at the beginning are now repeated with complete answers.

This ensures that you understand exactly what you are expected to know once you've completed the chapter.

- In this course you will be required to solve numerous exercises and problems. To give you some help, each chapter includes **Demonstration Problems**. You'll see how particular kinds of problems are solved in a step-by-step manner. You will also get lots of helpful hints to avoid common pitfalls.
- Accounting includes a lot of terms and concepts that will be unfamiliar to you at first. Each chapter includes an **End-of-Chapter Glossary** that defines all the major terms that were introduced in the chapter, so you can quickly refresh your memory as you study.

Features that Show You How You're Doing as You Go Along

- An important element of successful study is knowing how you're doing so far. **Self-Study Questions** in each chapter allow you to check yourself so you'll know which topics you have mastered and which are giving you trouble. These multiple-choice questions are answered at the end of the chapter.
- **Brief Exercises** help you build your confidence and test your basic skills. Each brief exercise focuses on *one* of the study objectives listed at the beginning of the chapter.
- **Broadening Your Perspective** is a section at the end of every chapter that lets you put it all together. This section contains a Critical Thinking Case tied to the chapter-opening vignette, a Financial Reporting Problem, a Decision Case, and an Ethical Case. All of these cases let you integrate and coordinate all the concepts you've encountered in the chapter. In addition, they give you an opportunity to improve your communication skills.

All these features have been carefully interwoven to make the study of accounting as easy as possible for you. If you take advantage of the study features, we are confident that you will be pleased with your performance in accounting principles.

Special Supplements that Help You Get the Best Grade You Can

Working Papers, Volume I: Chapters 1–14 and Volume II: Chapters 14–28

These partially completed accounting forms can be used in all end-of-chapter exercises, problems, and cases. They show you how to correctly set up solution formats.

Student Study Guide, Volume I: Chapters 1–14 and Volume II: Chapters 14–28

This item provides a comprehensive review of accounting! In addition to guiding you through chapter content and the Study Objectives, it gives you additional opportunities to practice your knowledge and skills. Each chapter includes: Study Tips, a Chapter Review consisting of 20–30 key points, a Demonstration Problem linked to study objectives in the textbook, and much more.

Self-Study Problems/Solutions Book

This tutorial is designed to improve your ability in solving accounting principles homework assignments and examination questions. It also provides additional insights and tips on how to study accounting.

Career Supplement

This valuable resource introduces you to the opportunities available in business for people with an accounting background. It gives a broad perspective of accounting and its many applications in business and presents various career paths.

Practice Sets

Practice sets expose you to a real-world simulation of maintaining a complete set of books for a business. You'll find that practice sets reinforce the concepts and procedures learned in each chapter of the textbook, and show you how they are all brought together to generate the accounting information that is essential in assessing the financial position and operating results of a company. The practice sets are:

Campus Cycle Shop: A Business Papers Practice Set
Heritage Home Furniture
Olympic Mowers Co.

General Ledger

An exciting new software supplement developed for the Third Edition, it allows you to solve selected end-of-chapter problems on a computer. It also allows you to do the Campus Cycle Shop and Heritage Home Furniture practice sets on a computer.

Solving Principles of Accounting Problems Using Lotus 1-2-3

These electronic spreadsheets (templates) allow you to complete selected end-of-chapter exercises and problems using Lotus 1-2-3.

Computerized Study Guide

Microstudy is designed to reinforce the material and problems in the Student Study Guides I and II. It offers students both extensive review information and hundreds of self-testing questions from every chapter in the text. You can select from a number of self-study options including: chapter summaries; chapter learning objectives; and multiple choice questions. The multiple choice section of Microstudy offers explanations of why the wrong choices are not correct.

Jerry J. Weygandt
Donald E. Kieso
Walter J. Kell

HOW TO USE THE STUDY AIDS IN THIS BOOK

CONCEPTS FOR REVIEW

Before studying this chapter, you should know or, if necessary, review:

a. *How to prepare a work sheet. (Ch. 4, p. 133–7)*
b. *How to close revenue, expense, and drawing accounts. (Ch. 4, p. 139–42)*
c. *The steps in the accounting cycle. (Ch. 4, p. 146–7)*

2. Study Objectives
Provide a learning framework and appear at beginning of chapter and in main body of the text where addressed.

CHAPTER 5

ACCOUNTING FOR MERCHANDISING OPERATIONS

Study Objectives

After studying this chapter, you should be able to:

1. Identify the components in measuring net income in a merchandising company.

2. Explain the entries for sales revenues.

3. State the steps in determining cost of goods sold.

4. Explain the computation and importance of gross profit.

5. Identify the unique features of the income statement for a merchandising company.

6. Explain the steps in the accounting cycle for a merchandising company.

7. Distinguish between a multiple-step and a single-step income statement.

L*arry Martin is in charge of procuring textbooks for the Washington State University bookstore in Pullman, Washington. The bookstore sells about $4 million in textbooks each year. The average inventory at any point in time is 2,500 titles.*

Mr. Martin's big challenge is to order enough books to satisfy demand—but not too many. For example, say a course historically has sold 75 books. He'll order 85 to be on the safe side. The reason: if he orders short, he'll have to order additional books by second-day air express—which is expensive and cuts into profits. If Martin orders too many, the publisher won't accept for return more than 20% of his original order.

Of course, returns occur all the time, especially when students drop courses during the first week of class. If the returned books are in "new and resellable" condition, the publisher will accept return of such books and issue Mr. Martin a credit memo.

1. Concepts for Review
List accounting concepts you need to know in order to comprehend the topics discussed in the chapter. Gives page references if you need to review before reading the chapter.

3. Chapter Opening Vignettes
Help you understand how accounting topics relate to campus life through real-life scenarios.

4. Accounting in Action
Presents insights into business, ethics, and international problems faced by accountants.

5. Technology in Action
Shows how computers are one of the most important tools to the accountant and users of accounting information.

6. Color Illustrations
Use color as a pedagogical tool to enhance understanding and learning.

---

184   CHAPTER 5 • *Accounting for Merchandising Operations*

Accounting in Action • *Business Insight*

How high is too high? Returns can become so high that it is questionable whether sales revenue should have been recognized in the first place. An example of high returns is Florafax International Inc., a floral supply company, which was alleged to ship its product without customer authorization on 10 holiday occasions, including 8,562 shipments of its product to customers for Mother's Day and 6,575 for Secretary's Day. The return rate on these shipments went as high as 69% of sales. As one employee noted: "products went out the front door and came in the back door."

An offshoot of high returns is "channel stuffing." In channel stuffing, the seller "sells" its product by providing substantial inducement to buy. Although this helps the sellers' revenue in the short run, the long term can be devastating when the merchandise bought remains on the purchasers' shelves for a long period of time.

Sales Returns and Allowances is a **contra revenue account** to Sales. The normal balance of Sales Returns and Allowances is a debit. A contra account is used, instead of debiting Sales, to disclose the amount of sales returns and allowances in the accounts and in the income statement. Disclosure of this information is important to management: excessive returns and allowances suggest inferior merchandise, inefficiencies in filling orders, errors in billing customers, and mistakes in delivery or shipment of the goods. Moreover, a debit directly to Sales would obscure the relative importance of sales returns and allowances as a percentage of sales. It also could distort _____ different accounting periods.

Sales Discounts

The terms of a credit sale may include an _____ discount, to the customer for prompt paym_____ offers advantages to both parties. The pur_____ to convert the accounts receivable into cas_____

The credit terms specify the amount a_____ They also indicate the length of time in w_____ the full invoice price. In the sales invoice i_____ n/30, which is read "two-ten, net thirty."_____ may be taken on the invoice price (less an_____ made within 10 days of the invoice date_____ invoice price less any returns or allowance_____ Alternatively, the discount period may e_____ following the month in which the sale occ_____ month) means that a 1% discount is avail_____ first 10 days of the next month.

When the seller elects not to offer a cas_____ terms will specify only the maximum tim_____ For example, the time period may be state_____

When cash discounts are taken by c_____ counts. To illustrate, assume Chelsea Vide_____ (Sales $3,800 less Sales Returns and Allow_____ the discount period. The cash discount is $_____ cash paid by Chelsea is $3,430 ($3,500 − $_____ by Highpoint Electronic on May 15, the er_____

Helpful hint The term "net" in "net 30" means the remaining amount due after subtracting any sales returns and allowances and partial payments.

---

188   CHAPTER 5 • *Accounting for Merchandising Operations*

Alternatively, passing up the discount may be viewed as **paying an interest rate of 2%** for the use of $3,500 for 20 days. This is the equivalent of an annual interest rate of 36% (2% × 360/20).[2] Obviously, it would be better for Chelsea Video to borrow at prevailing bank interest rates of 8–12% than to lose the discount.

So as not to miss purchase discounts, unpaid invoices should be filed by due dates. For example, Chelsea Video should have a file folder dated May 14 in which all bills to be paid on this date are filed. This procedure helps the purchaser remember the discount date. It also prevents early payment of bills and maximizes the time that available cash can be used for other business purposes.

Technology in Action

In many computer systems, the purchase of goods and the subsequent payment are closely linked. The due date, discount terms, and discount date are entered into the system along with the account names and dollar amounts. When the data have been entered and approved, the system can automatically generate payment checks by the discount date to take advantage of any discounts offered. Such a level of automation may not be necessary for a small firm with only 10 to 20 suppliers. The advantages of such a system quickly surface, though, when hundreds of suppliers are used on a continuous basis, as is the case with many large retailers.

Freight Costs

The sales agreement should indicate whether the seller or the buyer is to pay the cost of transporting the goods to the buyer's place of business. When a common carrier such as a railroad, trucking company, or airline is used, the transportation company prepares a freight bill (often called a bill of lading) in accordance with the sales agreement. Freight terms are expressed as either **FOB shipping point** or **FOB destination**. The letters FOB mean **free on board**. Thus, FOB shipping _____ at goods are placed free on board the carrier by the seller, and _____ s the freight costs. Conversely, FOB destination means that the _____ ed free on board at the buyer's place of business, and the seller _____ t. For example, the sales invoice in Illustration 5-2 on page 182 _____ reight is FOB shipping point. Thus, the buyer (Chelsea Video Inc.) _____ t charges.

_____ purchaser directly incurs the freight costs, the account Freight-in _____ tion-in) is debited. For example, if upon delivery of the goods on _____ Video Inc. pays Acme Freight Company $150 for freight charges, _____ helsea's books is:

_____t-in	150	
_____h		150
_____o record payment of freight, terms FOB shipping		
_____oint)		

_____, Freight-in is a temporary account whose normal balance is a _____ **in is part of cost of goods purchased.** The reason is that cost of _____ ed should include any freight charges necessary to bring the goods

_____use 360 days rather than 365.

Sales Revenue • 181

earning sales revenue. Examples of operating expenses are sales salaries, advertising expense, and insurance expense. The income measurement process for a merchandising company may be diagrammed as shown in Illustration 5-1.

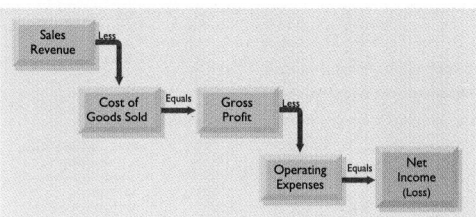

ILLUSTRATION 5-1

Income measurement process for a merchandising company

The operating expenses of a merchandising company include many of the expenses found in a service enterprise. Hence, this chapter focuses primarily on the recording of sales revenues and the related cost of goods sold that produce gross profit.

Sales Revenue

In accordance with the revenue recognition principle, sales revenues, like service revenues, are recorded when earned. Typically, sales revenues are earned when the goods are transferred from the seller to the buyer. At this point, the sales transaction is completed and the sales price is established.

Sales may be made on credit or for cash. Department stores such as J.C. Penney and Sears have significant amounts of both types of sales. Grocery stores such as Safeway and Kroger normally have cash sales. Wholesalers generally sell most goods on credit. Every sales transaction should be supported by a **business**

Study Objective 2

Explain the entries for sales revenues.

7. Before You Go On

Serves as a learning check. If you cannot answer these questions, you should reread the prior section(s) before continuing.

Statement Presentation

As contra revenue accounts, sales returns and allowances and sales discounts are deducted from sales in the income statement to arrive at net sales. The sales revenues section of the income statement based on assumed data for Highpoint Electronic is as follows:

ILLUSTRATION 5-4

Statement presentation of sales revenues section

HIGHPOINT ELECTRONIC, INC. Partial Income Statement		
Sales revenues		
Sales		$480,000
Less: Sales returns and allowances	$12,000	
Sales discounts	8,000	20,000
Net sales		$460,000

This presentation discloses the significant aspects of the company's principal revenue producing activities.

Before You Go On . . .

1. How do the components in measuring net income in a merchandising company differ from those in a service enterprise?

2. What entries are made to record sales, sales returns and allowances, and sales discounts?

3. How are sales and contra revenue accounts reported in the income statement?

(2) The form is simpler and easier to read than the multiple-step fo work problems, the single-step form of income statement should when it is specifically requested.

Accounting in Action · *Business Insight*

Walgreen Co., Munsingwear, Inc., and Black and Decker are among many compa multiple-step form of income statement. Companies that use the single-step General Electric, and Goodyear Tire & Rubber. The PepsiCo income statemen the appendix at the end of this textbook. In a recent survey of 600 of the larg the United States, 368 employed the multiple-step form and 232 employed the si statement format.

Before You Go On . . .

1. What features are found in the income statement of a merchandising comp in the income statement of a service enterprise?

2. How is the beginning and ending merchandise inventory shown in a wor

3. What are nonoperating activities and how are they reported in the income

4. How does a single-step income statement differ from a multiple-step inco

Cost of Goods Sold

As you learned earlier in this chapter, the second factor in measuring net income in a merchandising company is the cost of goods sold. The cost of goods sold may be determined each time a sale occurs or at the end of an accounting period. To make the determination when the sale occurs, a company uses a perpetual inventory system. Under this system, detailed records of the cost of each inventory item are maintained and continuously show the inventory that should be on hand. For example, a Ford dealership will have separate inventory records for each Escort, Tempo, Taurus, and Thunderbird. When a car is sold, its cost is

Study Objective 3

State the steps in determining cost of goods sold.

Summary of Study Objectives

1. *Identify the components in measuring net income in a merchandising company.* The major components in measuring net income in a merchandising company are sales revenue, cost of goods sold, and operating expenses.

2. *Explain the entries for sales revenues.* In recording sales revenues, entries are required for (a) cash and credit sales, (b) sales returns and allowances, and (c) sales discounts.

3. *State the steps in determining cost of goods sold.* The steps in determining cost of goods sold are (a) recording the purchase of merchandise, (b) determining the cost of goods purchased, and (c) determining the cost of goods on hand at the beginning and end of the accounting period.

4. *Explain the computation and importance of gross profit.* Gross profit is computed by subtracting cost of goods sold from net sales. Gross profit represents the merchandising profit of a company, and the

amount and trend of gross profit is closely watched by management and other interested parties.

5. *Identify the unique features of the income statement for a merchandising company.* The income statement for a merchandising company contains three sections: sales revenues, cost of goods sold, and operating expenses.

6. *Explain the steps in the accounting cycle for a merchandising company.* Each of the required steps in the accounting cycle for a service enterprise applies to a merchandi company. A work sheet is again on optional st

7. *Distingu step income* ment show come inclu step incom two catego is determi

8. Marginal Notations of Study Objectives

Signal where objectives listed at beginning of chapter are discussed in context. End-of-chapter exercise and problem material is also keyed to study objectives.

APPENDIX C   Adjusting Entry Method for Merchandise Inventory

Study Objective

After studying Appendix C you should be able to:

8. *Explain how the adjusting entry method is used in the work sheet.*

As stated in this chapter, the change between the beginning and ending inventory balances may be made through adjusting entries rather than through closing entries. Some favor this method because they believe that changes in merchandise inventory should receive the same accounting treatment as changes in the cost of supplies on hand between two points in time. The adjusting entry method is just as acceptable as the closing entry method, and it accomplishes the same objective.

The adjusting entry method affects several steps in the accounting cycle, beginning with the use of a work sheet. Again, these effects are explained and illustrated using Highpoint Electronic as an example.

Using a Work Sheet

In Illustration C-1, you will see a work sheet similar to the work sheet presented in the chapter (Illustration 5-12). The major difference in these two work sheets relates to merchandise inventory. In Illustration C-1, the accounting for merchandise inventory uses the adjusting entry method. In Illustration 5-12, the closing entry method was used. The unique accounts for the adjusting entry method are shown in capital letters in red.

Technology in Action

The adjusting entry method is used in most computerized systems since the programming logic involved is more straightforward. That is, in a computerized system, the command to close the books will close all the temporary accounts to Income Summary. However, if the inventory has not been adjusted, it will not be up-to-date and therefore a misstatement can occur. Some accountants favor the adjusting entry method in manual systems as well.

9. End-of-Chapter Appendix

Addresses topics considered optional by some instructors.

(2) The form is simpler and easier to read than the multiple-step form. For homework problems, the single-step form of income statement should be used only when it is specifically requested.

 Accounting in Action   *Business Insight*

Walgreen Co., Munsingwear, Inc., and Black and Decker are among many companies that use the multiple-step form of income statement. Companies that use the single-step include PepsiCo, General Electric, and Goodyear Tire & Rubber. The PepsiCo income statement is illustrated in the appendix at the end of this textbook. In a recent survey of 600 of the largest companies in the United States, 368 employed the multiple-step form and 232 employed the single-step income statement format.

Before You Go On . . .

1. What features are found in the income statement of a merchandising company that are not in the income statement of a service enterprise?

2. How is the beginning and ending merchandise inventory shown in a work sheet?

3. What are nonoperating activities and how are they reported in the income statement?

4. How does a single-step income statement differ from a multiple-step income statement?

Summary of Study Objectives

1. *Identify the components in measuring net income in a merchandising company.* The major components in measuring net income in a merchandising company are sales revenue, cost of goods sold, and operating expenses.

2. *Explain the entries for sales revenues.* In recording sales revenues, entries are required for (a) cash and credit sales, (b) sales returns and allowances, and (c) sales discounts.

3. *State the steps in determining cost of goods sold.* The steps in determining cost of goods sold are (a) recording the purchase of merchandise, (b) determining the cost of goods purchased, and (c) determining the cost of goods on hand at the beginning and end of the accounting period.

4. *Explain the computation and importance of gross profit.* Gross profit is computed by subtracting cost of goods sold from net sales. Gross profit represents the merchandising profit of a company, and the

amount and trend of gross profit is closely watched by management and other interested parties.

5. *Identify the unique features of the income statement for a merchandising company.* The income statement for a merchandising company contains three sections: sales revenues, cost of goods sold, and operating expenses.

6. *Explain the steps in the accounting cycle for a merchandising company.* Each of the required steps in the accounting cycle for a service enterprise applies to a merchandising company. A work sheet is again an optional step.

7. *Distinguish between a multiple-step and a single-step income statement.* A multiple-step income statement shows numerous steps in determining net income including nonoperating sections. In a single-step income statement all data are classified under two categories, revenues or expenses, and net income is determined by one step.

10. Summary of Study Objectives
Repeats study objectives with brief summary to ensure your understanding.

GLOSSARY

Administrative expenses · Expenses relating to general operating activities such as personnel management, accounting, and store security. (p. 202).

Cost of goods available for sale · The sum of the beginning merchandise inventory plus the cost of goods purchased. (p. 191).

Cost of goods purchased · The sum of net purchases plus freight-in. (p. 189).

Cost of goods sold · The total cost of merchandise sold during the period, determined by subtracting ending inventory from the cost of goods available for sale. (p. 180).

Credit memorandum · A document issued by a seller to inform a customer that a credit has been made to the customer's account receivable for a sales return or allowance. (p. 183).

Debit memorandum · A document issued by a buyer to inform a seller that a debit has been made to the seller's account because of unsatisfactory merchandise. (p. 186).

FOB destination · Freight terms indicating that the goods will be placed free on board at the buyer's place of business, and the seller pays the freight costs. (p. 188).

FOB shipping point · Freight terms indicating that goods are placed free on board the carrier by the seller, and the buyer pays the freight costs. (p. 188).

Gross profit · The excess of net sales over the cost of goods sold. (p. 180).

Income from operations · Income from a company's principal operating activity determined by subtracting cost of goods sold and operating expenses from net sales. (p. 201).

Multiple-step income statement · An income statement that shows numerous steps in determining net income (or net loss), including operating and nonoperating sections. (p. 200).

Net purchases · Purchases less purchase returns and allowances and purchase discounts. (p. 189).

Net sales · Sales less sales returns and allowances and sales discounts. (p. 185).

Operating expenses · Expenses incurred in the process of earning sales revenues that are deducted from gross profit in the income statement. (p. 180).

Other expenses and losses · A nonoperating section of the income statement that shows expenses from auxiliary operations and losses unrelated to the company's operations. (p. 200).

Other revenues and gains · A nonoperating section of the income statement that shows revenues from auxiliary operations and gains unrelated to the company's operations. (p. 200).

Periodic inventory system · An inventory system in which detailed records are not maintained and the cost of goods sold is determined only at the end of an accounting period. (p. 186).

Perpetual inventory system · A detailed inventory system in which the cost of each inventory item is maintained and the records continuously show the inventory that should be on hand. (p. 185).

Purchase discount · A cash discount claimed by a buyer for prompt payment of a balance due. (p. 187).

Purchase invoice · A document that supports each credit purchase. (p. 186).

Sales discount · A reduction given by a seller for prompt payment of a credit sale. (p. 184).

Sales invoice · A document that provides support for credit sales. (p. 181).

Sales revenue · Primary source of revenue in a merchandising company. (p. 180).

Selling expenses · Expenses associated with the making of sales. (p. 202).

Single-step income statement · An income statement that shows only one step in determining net income (or net loss). (p. 202).

11. Glossary
Reviews all the new accounting terms introduced in chapter and provides page reference.

made to the customer's account receivable for a sales return or allowance. (p. 183).

Debit memorandum · A document issued by a buyer to inform a seller that a debit has been made to the seller's account because of unsatisfactory merchandise. (p. 186).

FOB destination · Freight terms indicating that the goods will be placed free on board at the buyer's place of business, and the seller pays the freight costs. (p. 188).

FOB shipping point · Freight terms indicating that goods are placed free on board the carrier by the seller, and the buyer pays the freight costs. (p. 188).

Gross profit · The excess of net sales over the cost of goods sold. (p. 180).

Income from operations · Income from a company's principal operating activity determined by subtracting cost of goods sold and operating expenses from net sales. (p. 201).

Multiple-step income statement · An income statement that shows numerous steps in determining net income (or net loss), including operating and nonoperating sections. (p. 200).

Net purchases · Purchases less purchase returns and allowances and purchase discounts. (p. 189).

which detailed records are not maintained and the cost of goods sold is determined only at the end of an accounting period. (p. 186).

Perpetual inventory system · A detailed inventory system in which the cost of each inventory item is maintained and the records continuously show the inventory that should be on hand. (p. 185).

Purchase discount · A cash discount claimed by a buyer for prompt payment of a balance due. (p. 187).

Purchase invoice · A document that supports each credit purchase. (p. 186).

Sales discount · A reduction given by a seller for prompt payment of a credit sale. (p. 184).

Sales invoice · A document that provides support for credit sales. (p. 181).

Sales revenue · Primary source of revenue in a merchandising company. (p. 180).

Selling expenses · Expenses associated with the making of sales. (p. 202).

Single-step income statement · An income statement that shows only one step in determining net income (or net loss). (p. 202).

DEMONSTRATION PROBLEM

The adjusted trial balance columns of the work sheet for the year ended December 31, 1993, for the Dykstra Company are as follows:

Debit		Credit	
Cash	$ 14,500	Accumulated Depreciation	$ 18,000
Accounts Receivable	11,100	Notes Payable	25,000
Merchandise Inventory	32,000	Accounts Payable	10,600
Prepaid Insurance	2,500	Gene Dykstra, Capital	81,000
Store Equipment	95,000	Sales	520,000

12. Demonstration Problems
Provide a sample problem before you begin homework.

209

Gene Dykstra, Drawing	12,000	Purchase Returns and Allowances	9,600
Sales Returns and Allowances	6,700	Purchase Discounts	7,200
Sales Discounts	5,000	Interest Revenue	2,500
Purchases	352,000		$673,900
Freight-in	8,400		
Freight-out	7,600		
Advertising Expense	12,000		
Store Salaries Expense	56,000		
Utilities Expense	18,000		
Rent Expense	24,000		
Depreciation Expense	9,000		
Insurance Expense	4,500		
Interest Expense	3,600		
	$673,900		

Instructions

(a) Enter the adjusted trial balance data on a work sheet. Complete the work sheet assuming that ending merchandise inventory is $29,000.

(b) Prepare an income statement assuming the Dykstra Company does not use subgroupings for operating expenses.

Solution to Demonstration Problem

(a)

DYKSTRA COMPANY
Work Sheet
For the Year Ended December 31, 1993

13. Solutions
Show you how the problem should be solved.

Account Titles	Adjusted Trial Balance		Income Statement		Balance Sheet	
	Dr.	Cr.	Dr.	Cr.	Dr.	Cr.
Cash	14,500				14,500	
Accounts Receivable	11,100				11,100	
Merchandise Inventory	32,000		32,000	29,000	29,000	
Prepaid Insurance	2,500				2,500	
Store Equipment	95,000				95,000	
Accumulated Depreciation		18,000				18,000
Notes Payable		25,000				25,000
Accounts Payable		10,600				10,600
Gene Dykstra, Capital		81,000				81,000
Gene Dykstra, Drawing	12,000				12,000	
Sales		520,000		520,000		
Sales Returns and Allowances	6,700		6,700			
Sales Discounts	5,000		5,000			
Purchases	352,000		352,000			
Purchase Returns and Allowances		9,600		9,600		
Purchase Discounts		7,200		7,200		
Freight-in	8,400		8,400			
Freight-out	7,600		7,600			
Advertising Expense	12,000		12,000			
Store Salaries Expense	56,000		56,000			
Utilities Expense	18,000		18,000			
Rent Expense	24,000		24,000			
Depreciation Expense	9,000		9,000			
Insurance Expense	4,500		4,500			
Interest Expense	3,600		3,600			
Interest Revenue		2,500		2,500		
Totals	673,900	673,900	538,800	568,300	164,100	134,600
Net Income			29,500			29,500
Totals			568,300	568,300	164,100	164,100

Helpful hint

1. Make sure in the adjusted trial balance that debits and credits are equal before transferring amounts to the income statement and balance sheet columns.

2. Transfer all amounts in the adjusted trial balance to either the income statement or balance sheet columns.

3. The merchandise inventory reported in the adjusted trial balance is the beginning inventory.

4. Record the ending inventory by debiting the balance sheet column and crediting the the income statement column.

5. The net income or net loss is the reconciling item in both the income statement and the balance sheet columns.

14. Helpful Hints
Give tips for avoiding common pitfalls.

210 CHAPTER 5 ▪ *Accounting for Merchandising Operations*

(b)

DYKSTRA COMPANY
Income Statement
For the Year Ended December 31, 1993

Helpful hint

1. In preparing the income statement, remember that the key components are net sales, cost of goods sold, gross profit, total operating expenses, and net income (loss). These components are reported in the right-hand column of the income statement.
2. The most difficult computation is cost of goods sold. Think of beginning inventory + cost of goods purchased − ending inventory = cost of goods sold.
3. Nonoperating items follow income from operations.

Sales revenues			
Sales			$520,000
Less: Sales returns and allowances		$ 6,700	
Sales discounts		5,000	11,700
Net sales			508,300
Cost of goods sold			
Inventory, January 1		32,000	
Purchases	$352,000		
Less: Purchase returns and allowances	$9,600		
Purchase discounts	7,200	16,800	
Net purchases		335,200	
Add: Freight-in		8,400	
Cost of goods purchased		343,600	
Cost of goods available for sale		375,600	
Inventory, December 31		29,000	
Cost of goods sold			346,600
Gross profit			161,700
Operating expenses			
Store salaries expense		56,000	
Rent expense		24,000	
Utilities expense		18,000	
Advertising expense		12,000	
Depreciation expense		9,000	
Freight-out		7,600	
Insurance expense		4,500	
Total operating expenses			131,100
Income from operations			30,600
Other revenues and gains			
Interest revenue		2,500	
Other expenses and losses			
Interest expense		3,600	1,100
Net income			$ 29,500

*Note: All **asterisked** Questions, Exercises, and Problems relate to material contained in the Appendix to this chapter.

SELF-STUDY QUESTIONS

Answers are at the end of the chapter.

(S.O. 1) 1. Gross profit will result if:
a. operating expenses are less than net income.
b. sales revenues are greater than operating expenses.
c. operating expenses are greater than cost of goods sold.
d. sales revenues are greater than cost of goods sold.

(S.O. 2) 2. The sales accounts that normally have a debit balance are:
a. sales.
b. sales returns and allowances.
c. sales discounts.
d. both (b) and (c).

3. A credit sale of $850 is made on June 13, terms 2/10, net/30, on which a return of $50 is granted on June 16. The amount received as payment in full on June 23 is: (S.O. 2)
a. $833.
b. $800.
c. $784.
d. $850.

4. When goods are purchased for resale by a company: (S.O. 3)
a. purchases on account are debited to Merchandise Inventory.

15. Self-Study Questions

Present an opportunity to check your knowledge of important topics in a practice test. Answers are included on last page of chapter. (Self-study Questions keyed to Study Objectives.)

c. operating income section.
d. a sales revenue section.

9. In a work sheet, ending merchandise inventory is shown in the following columns (assuming the closing entry method is used): (S.O. 6)
a. Adjusted trial balance credit and balance sheet debit.
b. Income statement debit and balance sheet debit.
c. Income statement credit and adjusted trial balance debit.
d. Income statement credit and balance sheet debit.

10. In a single-step income statement: (S.O. 7)
a. gross profit is reported.
b. sales revenues and other revenues and gains are reported in the revenues section of the income statement.
c. cost of goods sold is not reported.
d. operating income is separately reported.

*11. In using the adjusting entry method to prepare a work sheet: (S.O. 8)
a. financial statements can be prepared only after closing entries are made.
b. changes in merchandise inventory are made in the adjustments columns of the work sheet.
c. ending inventory appears only in the balance sheet debit column.
d. beginning inventory is not reported on the trial balance before adjustment.

inventory is $50,000, cost of goods sold is:
a. $390,000.
b. $370,000.
c. $330,000.
d. $420,000.

(S.O. 4) 7. If sales revenues are $400,000, cost of goods sold is $250,000, and operating expenses are $60,000, the gross profit is:
a. $90,000.
b. $150,000.
c. $340,000.
d. $400,000.

(S.O. 5) 8. The income statement for a merchandising company shows each of the following features *except*:
a. gross profit.
b. cost of goods sold.

16. Questions

Allow you to explain your understanding of concepts and relationships covered in the chapter.

QUESTIONS

1. How does income measurement differ between a merchandising company and a service company?

2. Cisco Systems has sales revenue of $100,000, cost of goods sold of $60,000, and operating expenses of $20,000. What is its gross profit?

3. Joan Collins believes revenues from credit sales may be earned before they are collected in cash. Do you agree? Explain.

4. (a) What is the primary source document for recording (1) cash sales, (2) credit sales, and (3) sales returns and allowances? (b) Using XXs for amounts, give the journal entry for each of the transactions in part (a).

5. A credit sale is made on July 10 for $700, terms 2/10, n/30. On July 12, $50 of goods are returned for credit. Give the journal entry on July 19 to record the receipt of the balance due within the discount period.

6. Identify the accounts that are added to or deducted from purchases to determine the cost

15. Prepare the closing entries for the merchandise inventory account, assuming a beginning inventory of $54,000 and an ending inventory of $57,000.

16. What merchandising account, or accounts, will appear in the post-closing trial balance?

17. Identify the sections of a multiple-step income statement that relate to (a) operating activities, and (b) nonoperating activities.

18. Distinguish between the types of functional groupings of operating expenses. What problem is created by these groupings?

19. How does the single-step form of income statement differ from the multiple-step form?

*20. Beginning inventory is $72,000 and ending inventory is $79,000. Assuming a work sheet is used with adjusting entries for merchandise inventory:
(a) What amount will appear in the balance sheet debit column for merchandise inventory?
(b) What amounts will appear in the adjustments debit and credit columns for Income Summary?

BRIEF EXERCISES

Compute missing amounts in determining net income.
(S.O. 1)

BE5-1 Presented below are the components in C. Sheen Company's income statement. Determine the missing amounts.

	Sales	Cost of Goods Sold	Gross Profit	Operating Expenses	Net Income
(a)	$75,000	?	$43,500	?	$10,800
(b)	$108,000	$63,000	?	?	29,500
(c)	?	$71,900	$109,600	$39,500	?

Journalize sales transactions.
(S.O. 2)

BE5-2 Prepare the journal entries to record the following transactions on H. Hunter Company's books.

700,000 of merchandise to B. Streisand Company,

...urned $130,000 of the merchandise purchased on

...ved the balance due from B. Streisand Company.

...pare the journal entries to record these transac-

...lowing information for the month ended October
...es $100,000, Sales discounts $5,000, Sales returns
...venues section of the income statement based on

...y has the following account balances: Purchases
...$11,000, Purchase Discounts $8,000, and Freight-
...(b) cost of goods purchased.

BE5-5, and also that K. Bassinger Company has
...ntory of $90,000, and net sales of $630,000. Deter-
...goods sold and gross profit.

...e work sheet presented in the chapter.

...sted Trial ...Balance		Income Statement		Balance Sheet	
	Cr.	Dr.	Cr.	Dr.	Cr.

...ppear on the work sheet (a) cash, (b) beginning
...inventory.
...xample

...sted trial balance debit column; and Balance sheet
debit column.

*BE5-8 Using the information from BE5-7, indicate how these items are presented on the work sheet if the adjusting entry method illustrated in Appendix C is used.

BE5-9 A. Hall Company has the following merchandise account balances: Sales $180,000, Sales Discounts $2,000, Purchases $120,000, Purchase Returns and Allowances $1,000. In addition, it has a beginning inventory of $40,000 and an ending inventory of $30,000. Prepare the entries to record the closing of these items to Income Summary.

BE5-10 Explain where each of the following items would appear on (1) a multiple-step income statement and on (2) a single-step income statement: (a) gain on sale of equipment, (b) casualty loss from vandalism, and (c) cost of goods sold.

Prepare sales revenue section of income statement.
(S.O. 2)

Journalize purchases transactions.
(S.O. 3)

Compute net purchases and cost of goods purchased.
(S.O. 3)

Compute cost of goods sold and gross profit.
(S.O. 3, 4)

Identify work sheet columns for selecting accounts.
(S.O. 6)

Adjusting entry method.
(S.O. 8)

Prepare closing entries for merchandise accounts.
(S.O. 6)

Contrast presentation in multiple-step and single-step income statements.
(S.O. 7)

EXERCISES

Journalize sales transactions.
(S.O. 2)

E5-1 Presented below are the following transactions related to C. Eastwood Company.

1. On December 3, C. Eastwood Company sold $400,000 of merchandise to R. Gere Co., terms 2/10, n/30, FOB shipping point.
2. On December 8, R. Gere Co. was granted an allowance of $60,000 for merchandise purchased on December 3.
3. On December 13, C. Eastwood Company received the balance due from R. Gere Co.

Instructions
(a) Prepare the journal entries to record these transactions on the books of C. Eastwood Company.
(b) Assume that C. Eastwood Company received the balance due from R. Gere Co. on Jan-

17. Brief Exercises

Help you to build your confidence in your basic skills and knowledge by focusing on one of the Study Objectives listed at the beginning of the chapter. (Brief Exercises keyed to Study Objectives.)

---

uary 2 of the following year instead of December 13. Prepare the journal entry to record the receipt of payment on January 2.

Journalize purchases transactions.
(S.O. 3)

E5-2 Presented below is the following information related to N. Nolte Co.

1. On April 5, purchased merchandise from D. DeVito Company for $18,000 terms 2/10, net/30, FOB shipping point.
2. On April 6 paid freight costs of $100 on merchandise purchased from D. DeVito.
3. On April 7, purchased equipment on account for $26,000.
4. On April 8, returned damaged merchandise to D. DeVito Company and was granted a $3,000 allowance.
5. On April 15 paid the amount due to D. DeVito Company in full.

Instructions
(a) Prepare the journal entries to record these transactions on the books of N. Nolte Co.
(b) Assume that N. Nolte Co. paid the balance due to D. DeVito Company on May 4 instead of April 15. Prepare the journal entry to record this payment.

Prepare sales revenues section and closing entries.
(S.O. 2, 5, 6)

E5-3 The adjusted trial balance of the S. Connery Company shows the following data pertaining to sales at the end of its fiscal year October 31: Sales $900,000, Freight-out $12,000, Sales Returns and Allowances $24,000, and Sales Discounts $13,000.

Instructions
(a) Prepare the sales revenues section of the income statement.
(b) Prepare separate closing entries for (1) sales, and (2) the contra accounts to sales.

Prepare purchase entries and closing entries.
(S.O. 3, 6)

E5-4 On June 10, L. Dern Company purchased $5,000 of merchandise from the R. Duvall Company FOB shipping point, terms 2/10, n/30. L. Dern pays the freight costs of $200 on June 11. Damaged goods totaling $300 are returned to R. Duvall for credit on June 12. On June 19, L. Dern pays R. Duvall Company in full, less the purchase discount.

Instructions
(a) Prepare separate entries for each transaction.
(b) Prepare separate closing entries on June 30 for the temporary accounts with (1) debit balances, and (2) credit balances.

Prepare cost of goods sold section and closing entries.
(S.O. 3, 6)

E5-5 The trial balance of the R. Williams Company at the end of its fiscal year, August 31, 1995 includes the following accounts: Merchandise Inventory $17,200, Purchases $142,400, Sales $190,000, Freight-in $4,000, Sales Returns and Allowances $3,000, Freight-out $1,000, and Purchase Returns and Allowances $2,000. The ending merchandise inventory is $28,000.

Instructions
(a) Prepare a cost of goods sold section for the year ending August 31.
(b) Prepare the closing entries for all accounts.
(c) Post the closing entries to Merchandise Inventory.

18. Exercises

Allow you to continue building your confidence by gradually increasing the skills, understanding, and time involved. (Exercises keyed to Study Objectives.)

Identify work sheet columns using adjusting entry method.
(S.O. 8)

*E5–11 The J. Candy Company prepares adjusting entries for merchandise inventory at the end of the accounting period. On January 1, the balance in Merchandise Inventory is $27,500 and the inventory on hand at December 31 is $34,700.

Instructions

(a) Determine the amounts and the work sheet columns in which merchandise inventory will appear.

(b) Journalize the adjusting entries for merchandise inventory at December 31.

PROBLEMS

Journalize, post, and prepare partial income statement.
(S.O. 2, 3, 4, 5)

P5–1 The Dorn Hardware Store completed the following merchandising transactions in the month of May. At the beginning of May, the ledger of Dorn showed Cash of $5,000 and S. Dorn, Capital of $5,000.

May 1 Purchased merchandise on account from Depot Wholesale Supply $5,000, terms 2/10, n/30.
  2 Sold merchandise on account $4,000, terms 2/10, n/30.
  5 Received credit from Depot Wholesale Supply for merchandise returned $200.
  9 Received collections in full, less discounts, from customers billed on sales of $4,000 on May 2.
 10 Paid Depot Wholesale Supply in full, less discount.
 11 Purchased supplies for cash $900.
 12 Purchased merchandise for cash $2,400.
 15 Received refund for poor quality merchandise from supplier on cash purchase $230.
 17 Purchased merchandise from Harlow Distributors $1,900, FOB shipping point, terms 2/10, n/30.
 19 Paid freight on May 17 purchase $250.
 24 Sold merchandise for cash $6,200.
 25 Purchased merchandise from Horicon Inc. $1,000, FOB destination, terms 2/10, n/30.
 27 Paid Harlow Distributors in full, less discount.
 29 Made refunds to cash customers for defective merchandise $80.
 31 Sold merchandise on account $1,600, terms n/30.

Dorn Hardware's chart of accounts includes the following: No. 101 Cash, No. 112 Accounts Receivable, No. 120 Merchandise Inventory, No. 126 Supplies, No. 201 Accounts Payable, No. 301 S. Dorn, Capital, No. 401 Sales, No. 412 Sales Returns and Allowances, No. 414 Sales Discounts, No. 510 Purchases, No. 512 Purchase Returns and Allowances, No. 514 Purchase Discounts, No. 516 Freight-in.

Instructions

(a) Journalize the transactions.

(b) Enter the beginning cash and capital balances and post the transactions. (Use J1 for the journal reference.)

(c) Prepare an income statement through gross profit for the month of May 1993, assuming ending inventory is $2,400, and no beginning inventory.

Journalize, post, and prepare trial balance and partial income statement.
(S.O. 2, 3, 4, 5)

P5–2 John Clark, a former professional golf star, operates the pro shop at the Pelican Bay Golf Course. At the beginning of the current season on April 1, the ledger of Clark's Pro Shop showed Cash $2,500, Merchandise Inventory $3,500, and J. Clark, Capital $6,000. The following transactions were completed during April.

19. Problems

Stress the applications of concepts presented in the chapter. Keyed to multiple Study Objectives to guide your homework. (Problems keyed to Study Objectives.)

...erations

...ance of Global Enterprises for the year ending December 31, 1993 is shown

GLOBAL ENTERPRISES
Trial Balance
December 31, 1993

	Debit	Credit
	$ 14,000	
...eceivable	27,600	
...e Inventory	27,500	
...urance	1,800	
...ment	42,000	
...ed Depreciation—Store Equipment		$ 9,000
...ayable		31,200
..., Capital		50,300
		238,500
...s and Allowances	3,600	
...unts	4,900	
	172,000	
	5,000	
...eturns and Allowances		1,200
...iscounts		2,000
...ense	27,700	
...ense	6,100	
	$332,200	$332,200

...e inventory on hand at December 31, $38,600.
...pired $800.
...n expense, $3,000.
...y uses the adjusting entry method for merchandise inventory.

Instructions

(a) Enter the trial balance on a work sheet and complete the work sheet using the adjusting entry method.

(b) Journalize the adjusting entries.

(c) Prepare the closing entries.

(d) Post the entries in (b) and (c) to Merchandise Inventory, and Income Summary.

ALTERNATE PROBLEMS

Journalize, post, and prepare a partial income statement.
(S.O. 2, 3, 4, 5)

P5–1A The Midvale Distributing Company completed the following merchandising transactions in the month of April. At the beginning of April, the ledger of Midvale showed cash of $9,000 and S. Midvale capital of $9,000.

Apr. 2 Purchased merchandise on account from Kentucky Supply Co. $4,900, terms 2/10, n/30.
  4 Sold merchandise on account $5,000, FOB destination, terms 2/10, n/30.
  5 Paid $200 freight on April 4 sale.
  6 Received credit from Kentucky Supply Co. for merchandise returned $300.
 11 Paid Kentucky Supply Co. in full, less discount.
 13 Received collections in full, less discounts, from customers billed on April 4.
 14 Purchased merchandise for cash $4,400.
 16 Received refund from supplier on cash purchase of April 14, $500.

 18 Purchased merchandise from Pigeon Distributors $4,200, FOB... terms 2/10, n/30.
 20 Paid freight on April 18 purchase $100.
 23 Sold merchandise for cash $6,400.
 26 Purchased merchandise for cash $2,300.
 27 Paid Pigeon Distributors in full, less discount.
 29 Made refunds to cash customers for defective merchandise $9...
 30 Sold merchandise on account $3,700, terms n/30.

Midvale Company's chart of accounts includes the following: No. 101 Ca... Receivable, No. 120 Merchandise Inventory, No. 201 Accounts Payable... Capital, No. 401 Sales, No. 412 Sales Returns and Allowances, No. 414... 510 Purchases, No. 512 Purchase Returns and Allowances, No. 514 Pur... 516 Freight-in, and No. 644 Freight-out.

Instructions

(a) Journalize the transactions.

(b) Enter the beginning cash balances and post the transactions (Us... reference).

(c) Prepare the income statement through gross profit for the month of... ending inventory is $8,700, and no beginning inventory.

P5–2A John William, a former professional tennis star, operates the tennis shop at the Jackson Tennis Club. At the beginning of the current season, the ledger of William's Tennis Shop showed Cash $2,500, Merchandise Inventory $1,700, and J. William, Capital $4,200. The following transactions were completed during April.

Journalize, post, and prepare a trial balance and partial income statement.
(S.O. 2, 3, 4, 5)

Apr. 4 Purchased racquets and balls from Robert Co. $640 FOB shipping point, terms 3/10, n/30.
  6 Paid freight on Robert purchase $40.
  8 Sold merchandise to members $900, terms n/30.
 10 Received credit of $40 from Robert Co. for a damaged racquet that was returned.
 11 Purchased tennis shoes from King Sports, Inc. for cash, $300.
 13 Paid Robert Co. in full.
 14 Purchased tennis shirts and shorts from Events Sportswear, $700, FOB shipping point, terms 2/10, n/60.
 15 Received cash refund of $50 from King Sports, Inc. for damaged merchandise that was returned.
 17 Paid freight on Events Sportswear purchase $30.
 18 Sold merchandise to members, $800, terms n/30.
 20 Received $500 in cash from members in settlement of their accounts.
 21 Paid Events Sportswear in full.
 27 Granted credit of $30 to members for tennis clothing that did not fit.
 30 Sold merchandise to members $900, terms n/30.
 30 Received cash payments on account from members, $500.

20. Alternate Problems

Provide additional opportunities to apply concepts learned in chapter. (Alternate problems keyed to Study Objectives.)

21. General Ledger Problems

icons identify selected problems that can be solved using the new General Ledger Software.

22. Spreadsheet Problems

[S] icons identify selected exercises and problems that can be solved using Solving Principles of Accounting Problems Using Lotus 1-2-3.

23. Broadening Your Perspective

Helps you to pull together various concepts covered in the chapter and apply them to real-life business decisions.

24. Financial Reporting Case

Familiarizes you with the format, content, and uses of financial statements prepared by major U.S. companies.

25. Decision Case

Builds your decision-making skills by analyzing accounting information in a less structured situation. Provides practice in your writing skills.

---

224   CHAPTER 5 ▪ *Accounting for Merchandising Operations*

Prepare correct multiple-step and single-step income statements.
(S.O. 5, 7)

[S]

P5–5A A part-time bookkeeper prepared the following income statement for the Porter Company for the year ending December 31, 1993.

PORTER COMPANY
Income Statement
December 31, 1993

Revenues		
Sales		$702,000
Less: Freight-in	$ 17,200	
Discounts	4,100	21,300
Net sales		680,700
Other revenues (net)		300
Total revenues		681,000
Expenses		
Purchases	470,000	
Selling expenses	100,000	
Administrative expenses	50,000	
W. Porter, Drawings	12,000	
Total expenses		632,000
Net income		$ 49,000

As an experienced, knowledgeable accountant you review the statement and determine the following facts:

1. Sales includes $10,000 of deposits from customers for future sales orders.
2. Discounts consist of purchase discounts earned $7,200 and sales discounts granted $11,300.
3. Other revenues contains two items: interest expense $5,000 and interest revenue $5,300.
4. Purchases includes freight-out $14,000 less purchase returns and allowances $9,000.
5. Ending merchandise inventory increased $20,000 from a beginning inventory of $35,000.
6. Selling expenses consist of sales salaries $76,000, advertising $10,000, depreciation on store equipment $7,500, and sales commissions expense $6,500.
7. Administrative expenses consist of office salaries $19,000, utilities expense $8,000, rent expense $16,000, and insurance expense $7,000. Insurance expense includes $1,200 of insurance applicable to 1994.

Instructions
(a) Prepare a correct detailed multiple-step income statement.
(b) Prepare a correct condensed single-step income statement.

*B*roadening Your Perspective

FINANCIAL REPORTING PROBLEM

Bob Evans Farms, Inc. operates 273 restaurants in 16 states and produces fresh and fully cooked sausage products, fresh salads, and related products distributed to grocery stores in the Midwest, Southwest, and Southeast. For a recent three-year period, Bob Evans Farms reported the following selected income statement data (in millions of dollars):

	1992	1991	1990
Sales	$556.3	$501.3	$454.3
Cost of goods sold	424.3	388.3	357.7
Selling and administrative expenses	72.0	60.3	54.7
Net income	39.3	35.8	27.7

Decision Case ▪ 225

...an of the board and CEO made the following

...and fiscal year 1993 well under way, I am in an ...ny. Sales are up, profits up, morale is high, ...ne to be at Bob Evans Farms."

...nd in net profits from year to year for the three

...ny's gross profit rate make to the improved earn-

...income to net sales in each of the three years?

DECISION CASE

Three years ago, Kathy Paul and her brother-in-law John Paul opened Paul's Department Store. For the first two years, business was good, but the following condensed income results for 1993 were disappointing.

PAUL'S DEPARTMENT STORE
Income Statement
For the Year Ended December 31, 1993

Net sales		$700,000
Cost of goods sold		546,000
Gross profit		154,000
Operating expenses		
Selling expenses	$100,000	
Administrative expenses	25,000	125,000
Net income		$ 29,000

Kathy believes the problem lies in the relatively low gross profit rate (gross profit divided by net sales) of 22%. John believes the problem is that operating expenses are too high.

Kathy thinks the gross profit rate can be improved by making both of the following changes: (1) increase average selling prices by 17%; this increase is expected to lower sales volume so that total sales will increase only 6%. (2) buy merchandise in larger quantities and take all purchase discounts; these changes are expected to increase the gross profit rate by 3%. Kathy does not anticipate that these changes will have any effect on operating expenses.

John thinks expenses can be cut by making both of the following changes: (1) cut 1993 sales salaries of $60,000 in half and give sales personnel a commission of 2% of net sales. (2) reduce store deliveries to one day per week rather than twice a week; this change will reduce 1993 delivery expenses of $30,000 by 45%. John feels that these changes will not have any effect on net sales.

Kathy and John come to you for help in deciding the best way to improve net income.

Instructions
(a) Prepare a condensed income statement for 1994 assuming (1) Kathy's changes are implemented and (2) John's ideas are adopted.
(b) What is your recommendation to Kathy and John?
(c) Prepare a condensed income statement for 1994 assuming both sets of proposed changes are made.

26. Critical Thinking Case
Allows you to apply the concepts learned in the chapter by answering questions that refer back to the Chapter Opening Vignette.

27. Ethical Case
Presents a situation and asks you to reflect on ethical issues typically encountered by an accountant.

28. Answers to Self-Study Questions
Provide feedback on your understanding of concepts through your answers to the Self-Study Questions.

---

226   CHAPTER 5 ▪ *Accounting for Merchandising Operations*

CRITICAL THINKING CASE

Think back to the vignette about the Washington State University bookstore at the beginning of the chapter and answer the following questions:

1. What kind of inventory system is being used in the bookstore? Why?
2. What entry, if any, would the WSU bookstore make when ordering books? When books are received? When returning books? When allowing the students to return books? When purchasing used books from students?
3. How often is it necessary for Larry Martin to take a physical inventory? Why is it necessary to take an inventory? For the inventory taken in September, does Larry need both quantities and costs? Explain.

ETHICAL CASE

Edna Pelzer was just hired as the assistant treasurer of Yorkshire Stores, a specialty chain store company consisting of nine retail stores concentrated in one metropolitan area. Among other things, the payment of all invoices is centralized in one of the departments Edna will manage. Her primary responsibility is to maintain the company's high credit rating by paying all bills when due and to take advantage of all cash discounts. Jamie Caterino, the former assistant treasurer, who has been promoted to treasurer, is training Edna in her new duties. He instructs Edna that she is to continue the practice of preparing all checks "net of discount" and dating the checks the last day of the discount period. "But," Jamie continues, "we always hold the checks at least four days beyond the discount period before mailing them. That way we get another four days of interest on our money. Most of our creditors need our business and don't complain. And, if they scream about our missing the discount period, we blame it on the mail room or the post office. We've only lost one discount out of every hundred we take that way. I think everybody does it. By the way, welcome to our team!"

Instructions
(a) What are the ethical considerations in this case?
(b) Who are the stakeholders that are harmed or benefitted in this situation?
(c) Should Edna continue the practice started by Jamie? Does she have any choice?

Answers to Self-Study Questions
1. d   2. d   3. c   4. c   5. a   6. b   7. b   8. c   9. d   10. b
11. b

BRIEF CONTENTS

CONTENTS

CHAPTER 7 ▪ *Internal Control and Cash*   275

CHAPTER 8 ▪ *Accounting for Receivables*   323

CHAPTER 9 ▪ *Inventories*   357

CHAPTER 10 ▪ *Plant Assets: Acquisition and Depreciation*   397

CHAPTER 11 ▪ *Plant Asset Disposals, Natural Resources,* . *and Intangible Assets*   433

CHAPTER 12 ▪ *Current Liabilities and Payroll Accounting* 467

CHAPTER 13 ▪ *Accounting Principles* 509

CHAPTER 14 ▪ *Accounting for Partnerships* 547

CHAPTER 15 ▪ *Corporations: Organization and Capital Stock Transactions*   585

CHAPTER 16 ▪ *Corporations: Dividends, Retained Earnings, and Income Reporting*   625

CHAPTER 20 ▪ *Financial Statement Analysis*   809

CHAPTER 21 ▪ *Managerial Accounting*   855

THE ROLE OF ACCOUNTING IN SOCIETY

One purpose in writing this text is to help you understand the basic principles of accounting. Another purpose is to help you understand how accounting affects and is affected by its environment. The role of accounting in society is a vital one—to provide information that will help individuals make sound economic decisions. The type of information to be provided, its quantity and its quality, is determined by societal needs and pressures. To better understand these needs and pressures, examples of issues that affect accounting are provided throughout the text. Three of the most important issues are ethics, internationalization, and computer technology.

Ethics

Ethical behavior is necessary for the business world to function in an orderly manner. Imagine trying to carry on a business, trying to perform an audit, trying to invest money, if you could not depend on the individuals you deal with to be honest. If managers, customers, investors, co-workers, and creditors all consistently lied, it would be impossible for effective communication and economic activity to occur. Information would have no credibility.

Fortunately, most individuals in business are ethical, bright, and hard working. However, in some situations public officials, business executives, and respected leaders act in an unethical manner. For instance, Citicorp fired the president and senior executives of a credit-card-processing division for allegedly overstating revenues; American Express fired several executives for failing to write-off customer accounts declared bankrupt in accordance with company policy; Sears was accused of widespread customer overcharging on car repairs; Alamo Rent A Car refunded $3 million to customers who were overcharged for repair costs to damaged rental cars. As one business leader noted: "We are all embarrassed by the events that make the Wall Street Journal read like the Police Gazette."

Ethics and ethical dilemmas abound in daily life, both privately and professionally. Many of the conflicts you encounter in the classroom, in your dormitory, in your part-time job, and in your personal relationships have ethical dimensions not dissimilar to those you will encounter in your work after graduation. How you respond in ethical situations affects how you are perceived by others, how you feel about yourself, and how others respond to you. In the end, ethical behavior affects the quality of your life and that of society.

As a business manager, professional practitioner, entrepreneur, or skilled employee you must appreciate the importance of recognizing ethical dilemmas, analyze the consequences involved, and rationally select among alternative courses of action. Doing the right thing, making the right decision, is not always easy. Right is not always evident. The pressures "to bend the rules," "to play the game," "to just ignore it" can be considerable. Ethical decisions are more difficult because a public consensus has not emerged to formulate a comprehensive ethical system that provides guidelines in making all ethical judgments.

Ethical Cases

Applying ethics and being ethical is necessary and possible. To sensitize you to ethical situations and to give you practice at solving ethical dilemmas, an Ethical Case simulating a business situation is provided at the end of each chapter. You should apply the following steps in the process of analyzing these Ethical Cases.

1. **Recognize an ethical situation and the ethical issues involved.** Your personal ethics and your sensitivity to others will assist you in identifying ethical situations and issues. Professional ethics and specific business codes exist to provide guidance in some business situations.

2. **Move toward an ethical resolution by identifying and analyzing the principle elements in the situation.** Identify the stakeholders (the affected persons or groups) that may be harmed or benefited. Ask the question: What are the responsibilities and obligations of the parties involved?

3. **Identify the alternatives and weigh the impact of each alternative on various stakeholders.** Select the best or most ethical alternative considering all the consequences. Some ethical situations involve one right answer; and what must be done is to identify the one right answer. Other

ethical situations involve more than one right answer; these situations require an evaluation of each and a selection of the best or most ethical alternative.

In the business world, the process of ethical sensitivity, identification of the stakeholders, and selection among alternatives can be complicated by pressures. These pressures may take the form of time pressures, job pressures, financial pressures, personal pressures, peer pressures, and so on.

Internationalization

The world of business is international. For the 100 largest U.S.-based multinational businesses, foreign revenues in 1990 grew 15% while their U.S. sales grew only 4.5%. The foreign operations of these giant companies is now about 40% of their total revenues. Exxon Corporation, for instance, generated 74% of its revenues overseas in 1990. McDonald's, in 1991, for the first time, opened more restaurants overseas than in the United States: 427 abroad, compared with just 188 in the United States. More than ever before, for a U.S. corporation to grow, it must have a global perspective. To even maintain their U.S. market share, all companies must be prepared to compete with foreign competition.

With both commerce and capital crossing borders at an accelerated pace, attention is focusing on the significance of a growing obstacle. That obstacle is one of language. But not, as might be expected, the spoken or written languages of the world of nations. It is the language of finance and commerce—*accounting*. Many nations of the world have their own individual rules of accounting, sufficient to the specific needs of their own commerce and the maturity of their industry. In some cases, the principles and practices that guide the preparation of financial statements in various countries can be so different as to defy comparability. The result is that business managers and financiers in one country, attempting to understand the financial statements of a business in another country, may be at a serious loss to comprehend or use information vital to their needs.

Twenty years ago, this lack of uniform accounting principles was merely an inconvenience. But today, as more business is done internationally, as more capital crosses borders, as more investors seek investment opportunities in other countries, as more managers of international companies attempt to understand the performance of foreign divisions, the problem of diverse accounting standards has become more acute.

International Insight

As a result, the state of international accounting and reporting is changing. Our purpose in this textbook is to sensitize you to some of these changes by introducing international issues and problems where appropriate. For example, Chapter 13 includes a special section entitled, Accounting Principles and International Operations. In addition, international insights are given in some of the Accounting in Action vignettes.

Computer Technology

Those individuals who experienced the arrival of the first personal computer were probably confused and uncertain as to its potential impact. Today that impact is pervasive and irreversible—computer technology has revolutionized our lives and will continue to do so. The impact on the business environment is no less dramatic.

The use of the computer for word processing, data base management, spreadsheet analysis, telecommunications, desktop publishing, electronic mail, and problem solving are now commonplace. Many routine tasks that before involved large amounts of manual labor are now computerized. As an example, automated billing systems are now generally used to increase the speed and accuracy of computations and the flow of paper work. Computers have revolutionized many manufacturing processes. The use of industrial robots, computer aided designs, computer aided manufacturing, statistical process controls, and so on may be found in small as well as large business.

Technology in Action

You will not become a computer expert by reading this text. But, a number of computer exercises and problems (indicated by special icons) are provided so that you can enhance your computer skills. In addition, vignettes entitled Technology in Action provide insight into how the computer is used in an accounting setting.

Summary

The role of accounting in society is to provide information to help individuals make sound economic decisions. The type of information to be provided, its quantity and its quality, are affected by societal needs and pressures. Elements of the economic environment that affect the flow and quality of financial information are ethics, internationalization, and computer technology.

CHAPTER 1

CHARACTERISTICS AND BASIC CONCEPTS OF ACCOUNTING

Study Objectives

After studying this chapter, you should be able to:

1. Explain the meaning of accounting.

2. Identify the users and uses of accounting.

3. Know the major career paths of accountants.

4. Explain the meaning of generally accepted accounting principles and the cost principle.

5. Explain the meaning of the economic entity assumption and the monetary unit assumption.

6. State the basic accounting equation and explain the meaning of assets, liabilities, and owner's equity.

7. Analyze the effect of business transactions on the basic accounting equation.

8. Prepare an income statement, owner's equity statement, and balance sheet.

F
or Alan Bambeck, a senior majoring in accounting at Ohio State University, practical experience has made his studies ever more valuable. Back in high school, he worked with his father, a self-employed accountant, during breaks from school. More recently, he has become the treasurer of a student accounting organization on campus, Beta Alpha Psi.

Bambeck, who plans to take the November 1993 CPA Examination, says a big part of his job as treasurer of Beta Alpha Psi is to collect dues. Each student pays an initiation fee of $56 plus quarterly dues of $5. The initiation fee is easy to collect because a student can't become a member without paying it. Collecting quarterly dues is more difficult. "I have to get after people as the quarter comes to a close," says Bambeck. "Some people are really hard to get hold of." The money is used for meetings with companies, social activities, supplies, and so forth.

"After I collect the money, I write it up in a cash receipts book," he says. And, *"any checks that I write have to be recorded in a cash disbursements book, which organizes the expenditures by category."* On April 30, at the end of the fiscal year, Bambeck prepares an income statement, a balance sheet, and a cash flow statement. These are three very important financial statements that you'll learn about in Chapter 1 and subsequent chapters. The national office of Beta Alpha Psi requires the statements to be audited by a certified public accounting firm.

So, Bambeck deals with cash receipts and disbursements, dues collections, preparing financial statements, and audits. Does he use a computer? *"No,"* says Bambeck, who doesn't own one yet. *"But, I'm looking forward to the day that I get my personal computer and I can let it do the recording and reports preparation."*

In a recent major study of business education in this country, a survey of undergraduate business school alumni indicated that accounting had been of most use in their careers to date.[1] It is therefore not surprising to find that accounting is one of the most popular fields of study in colleges and universities and one of the fastest-growing professions. **The reason for this growth is quite simple: accounting is the financial information system that provides relevant financial information to every person who owns or uses economic resources or otherwise engages in economic activity.**

Regardless of one's pursuits or occupation, the need for financial information is inescapable. Such common activities as earning a living, spending money, buying on credit, making investments, paying taxes—not to mention managing a business—involve receiving, using, or dispensing financial information. Accounting is ingrained in our society and is vital to our economic system.

What Is Accounting?

Study Objective 1

Explain the meaning of accounting.

As a financial information system, accounting is the process of **identifying, measuring, recording,** and **communicating** the economic events of an organization (business or nonbusiness) to interested users of the information. The sale of goods by J. C. Penney Company, the rendering of services by American Telephone & Telegraph, the payment of wages by Ford Motor Company, and the collection of Beta Alpha Psi dues by Alan Bambeck in the opening vignette are examples of economic events. The first part of the process—**identifying**—involves **selecting those events that are considered evidence of economic activity relevant to a particular organization.**

---

[1]Lyman W. Porter and Lawrence T. McKibben, *Management Education and Development—Drift or Thrust into the 21st Century* (New York: McGraw-Hill Book Company, 1988), p. 71.

Once identified, the economic events (called transactions by accountants) must be measured in financial terms, that is, quantified in dollars and cents. If the event cannot be quantified in monetary terms, it is not considered part of the company's financial information system. The measurement function thereby eliminates some significant events (such as the appointment of a new company president) because they lack measurability in financial terms.

Once measured in dollars and cents, the events are recorded to provide a permanent history of the financial activities of the organization. **Recording consists of keeping a chronological diary of measured events in an orderly and systematic manner.** In recording, the accountant also classifies and summarizes these events.

Technology in Action

With the phenomenal growth in computers, more and more record keeping is being performed electronically. Businesses, small as well as large, are finding that through the use of the computer the entire recording process has become more efficient. However it is important to know the procedures used in a manual system to understand the operations a computer performs.

Throughout this textbook you will find computer notes highlighted like this. These notes are designed to show how computer technology is used in accounting and business.

This identifying, measuring, and recording activity is meaningless unless the information is **communicated** to interested users. **The information is communicated through the preparation and distribution of accounting reports, the most common of which are called financial statements.** To make the reported financial information meaningful, accountants describe and report the recorded data in a standardized manner. Information resulting from similar transactions is accumulated and totaled. Such data are said to be reported in the aggregate. For example, all sales transactions of Apple Computer are accumulated over a certain period of time and reported as one amount in the financial statements of Apple Computer. By presenting the recorded data in the aggregate, the accounting process simplifies a multitude of transactions and renders a series of activities understandable and meaningful.

Accountants report financial information on a periodic basis, that is, at regular intervals. The frequency of communicating varies according to the needs of the intended user of the data and the nature of the information reported. For example, the company's treasurer may request daily reports of cash, the sales manager may require weekly reports of sales, and the president may desire monthly reports of operations as a whole. In contrast, annual statements of financial position and results of operations may suffice for investors and governmental agencies.

A vital element in the communication process is the accountant's ability and responsibility to **interpret** the reported information. **Interpretation involves analyzing and explaining the uses, meaning, and limitations of reported data.** Through ratios, percentages, graphs, and charts, significant financial trends and relationships are reported to the users of financial reports. See the specimen financial statements and accompanying notes and graphs of PepsiCo. Inc. provided in Appendix L.

The accounting process as discussed may be diagrammed as follows:

ILLUSTRATION 1-1

Accounting process

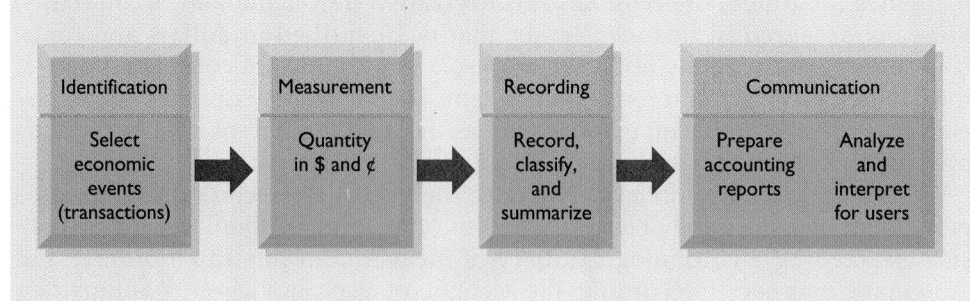

Accounting should consider the needs of the users of financial information. As a consequence, you should know who these users are and something about their needs for information.

Users and Uses of Accounting Data

Study Objective 2

Identify the users and uses of accounting.

Because it communicates financial information about a business enterprise, accounting is often called "the language of business." As indicated, the information that a specific user needs depends upon the kinds of decisions that user makes. The differences in the decisions divide the users into two broad groups: (1) **internal users, those who manage the business (officers and other decision makers),** and (2) **external users, those outside the business who have either a present or potential direct financial interest (investors and creditors) or an indirect financial interest (taxing authorities, regulatory agencies, labor unions, customers, and economic planners).** The relationship of these users to the accounting process and to one another is diagrammed in Illustration 1-2.

Internal Users

Management at all levels uses accounting information in planning, controlling, and evaluating business operations. To perform these functions, managers need detailed information on a timely basis. For example, the managers of a company might ask:

Is cash sufficient to pay our debts?
Are customers paying their bills promptly?
What is the cost of manufacturing each unit of product?
What costs exceed budget?
Can we afford to give employee pay raises this year?
Which product line is the most profitable?
How much money must be borrowed to expand the factory?

To assist management in answering these questions, accounting provides internal reports. Examples include financial comparisons of operating alternatives, projections of income from new sales campaigns, and forecasts of cash needs for the next year. In addition, statements on the financial position and results of operations of the entire business are prepared.

External Users—Direct Interest

Investors (owners) judge the wisdom of buying, holding, or selling their financial interests on the basis of accounting data. **Creditors** (suppliers and bankers) eval-

ILLUSTRATION 1-2

Users of accounting information

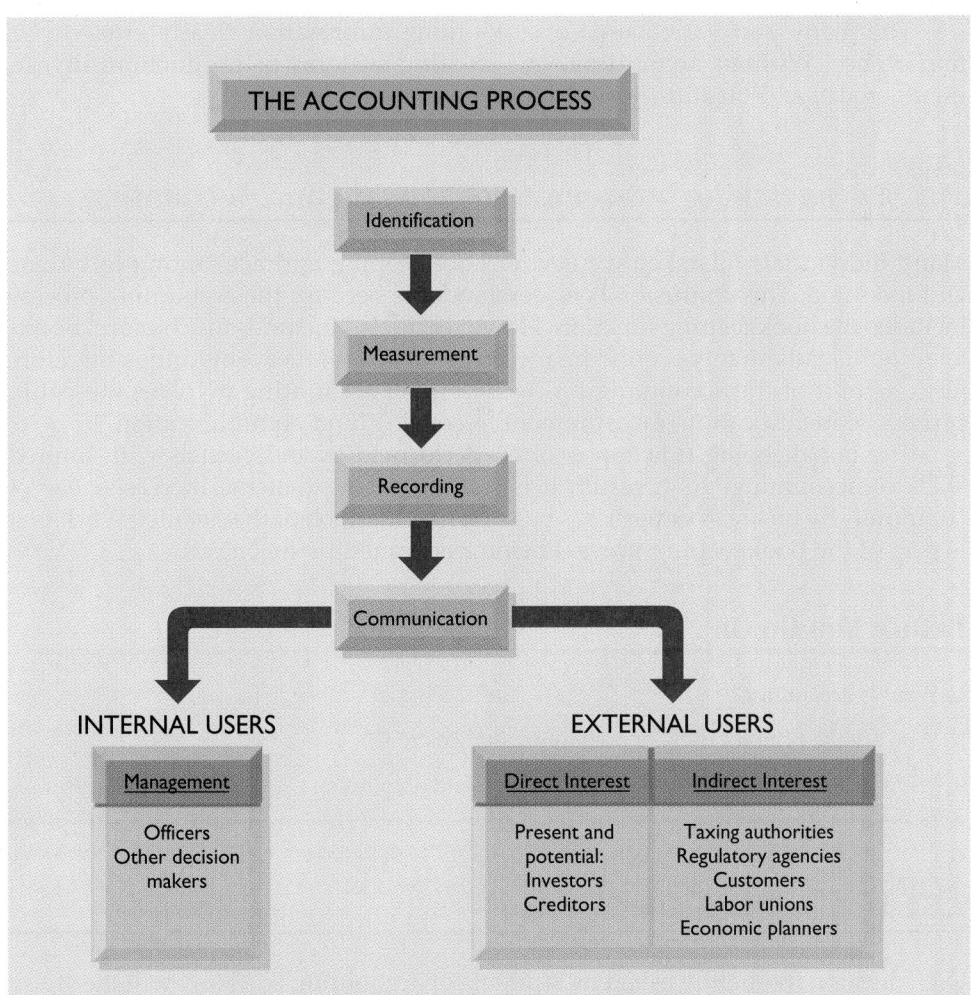

uate the risks of granting credit or lending money on the basis of the accounting information obtained about a particular business. Some of the questions asked by investors and creditors about a company might be:

Is the company earning satisfactory income?

How does the company compare in size and profitability with competitors?

Will the company be able to pay its debts as they come due?

Are interest payments and dividends protected by an adequate inflow of cash from operations?

External Users—Indirect Interest

The information needs and questions of those with indirect financial interests vary considerably. **Taxing authorities** (such as the Internal Revenue Service) want to know if the company complies with the tax laws. **Regulatory agencies** (such as the Securities and Exchange Commission or the Federal Trade Commission) want to know if the company is operating within prescribed rules. **Customers** are interested in whether a company will continue to honor product warranties and otherwise support its product lines. **Labor unions** want to know if the company has the ability to pay increased wages and benefits. **Economic planners** use accounting information to analyze and forecast economic activity.

The many and varied uses of accounting information clearly attest to its importance. **Without accounting, our existing systems of production, investment, credit, and taxation would be seriously impaired.**

Distinguishing between Bookkeeping and Accounting

Many individuals mistakenly consider bookkeeping and accounting to be one and the same. This confusion is understandable because the accounting process includes the bookkeeping function. However, it also includes much more. Bookkeeping usually involves only the recording of economic events and is therefore just one part of the accounting process. In total, **accounting** involves the entire process of identification, measurement, recording, and communication.

The bookkeeping function is often performed by individuals with limited skills in accounting. As a result, it is not surprising that the increased use of computers by business enterprises has resulted in much of the detailed work that is part of the bookkeeping process being performed by machines.

Before You Go On . . .

1. What is accounting?

2. Who are the primary users of accounting information?

3. What is the difference between bookkeeping and accounting?

The Accounting Profession

One question frequently asked by students of accounting is, "How will the study of accounting help me?" Perhaps the easiest way to answer that question is to provide some illustrations. For example, numerous studies confirm the fact that a strong background in accounting is extremely helpful in every business endeavor. One study indicated that many chief executive officers of the largest companies in the United States have a background in the accounting and finance area.

A background in accounting is also helpful in many nonbusiness fields of interest. For example, governmental officials use accounting information to estimate how well programs are working and whether tax dollars are being spent efficiently. Members of the legal profession use accounting data in tax, fraud, and antitrust cases and in determining compliance with governmental regulation. Bankers and investment brokers use accounting information in making investment and other financial decisions. In short, a sound background in accounting will be extremely valuable to you, whatever field of study or career you ultimately select.

A second question often asked by students is, "What would I do if I became an accountant?" The answer is that accountants apply their expertise in three major areas—public accounting, private accounting, and not-for-profit accounting.

Public Accounting

In public accounting, the accountant offers expert service to the general public in much the same way that a doctor serves patients and a lawyer serves clients.

The mark of excellence in public accounting is associated with a license to practice as a certified public accountant (CPA). Like his or her counterparts in medicine and law, the CPA must fulfill certain education and experience requirements and pass a rigorous examination. Many CPAs work independently as a single proprietor; many others work for public accounting firms that vary greatly in size and scope of services. The largest CPA firms are worldwide partnerships with over a thousand partners, more than 20,000 professional staff, and offices in every major city in the world. Such big firms are necessary because their clients are so huge, complex, and international in operation.

Accounting in Action · *Business Insight*

The six largest U.S. public accounting firms, referred to as the "Big Six," employ approximately 12% of the 280,000 CPAs and audit the financial statements of nearly 85% of the 2,600 largest companies. The 1990 U.S. revenues and some of the major clients of the "Big Six" CPA firms are as follows:

	U.S. REVENUES (1990, IN BILLIONS)	MAJOR CLIENTS
Arthur Andersen & Co.	$2.28	Texaco, GTE, Georgia Pacific
Ernst & Young	2.24	Coca Cola, American Express, Mobil Oil
Deloitte and Touche	1.92	General Motors, Merrill Lynch, Sears Roebuck
Peat Marwick and Main (KPMG)	1.82	PepsiCo, General Electric, Citicorp
Coopers & Lybrand	1.40	CBS, AT&T, Ford
Price Waterhouse & Co.	1.20	IBM, du Pont, Walt Disney

Throughout this textbook, you will find Accounting in Action examples highlighted like this. These examples illustrate important and interesting information as it relates to actual accounting situations in business.

As a public accountant, an individual may perform one or more of the following services.

Auditing

A major portion of public accounting practice is involved with **auditing**. In this area, the CPA examines the financial statements of companies and expresses an opinion as to the fairness of presentation. A favorable opinion (called an **unqualified** or **clean** opinion) means that the financial statements may be relied on by investors, creditors, and other interested parties in making decisions about the company. Audited financial statements are required for all companies whose securities are traded on national securities exchanges.

An auditing firm has many clients. For example, one beginning auditor noted, "My assignments in my first year included such diverse enterprises as a large family-owned farming operation, a city government, an international plastics manufacturer, a land developer, a small newspaper, and a telephone company." An audit generally takes anywhere from a few days to several months.

Taxation

Another major area of public accounting is the field of taxation. The work performed by tax specialists includes tax advice and planning, preparing tax returns, and representing clients before governmental agencies such as the Internal Revenue Service. Questions such as the following are often answered by the tax accountant:

1. How will the acquisition of a company affect the client's tax status?
2. How can estate planning minimize estate and inheritance taxes?
3. What are the tax advantages of setting up a company in Switzerland?
4. What tax planning strategies can be used to save for college tuition?

Management Consulting

Because public accountants have financial training and expertise, they often are asked for management advice. In fact, recent surveys indicate that the accounting profession does more consulting than any other professional group.[2] Financial planning and control and the development of accounting and computer systems are important areas of management consulting. Other areas are organizational design, financial forecasting, total quality management, and mergers and acquisitions. Questions addressed by management consultants are:

1. What type of security system should be employed in the data processing area?
2. How can hospitals continue to provide high-quality service in light of reduced governmental support?
3. What are the options open to a package delivery company threatened by electronic mail?

Management consulting ranges from the installation of basic accounting systems to helping companies determine whether they should use the space shuttle for high-tech research.

Private Accounting

Many accountants are employees of business enterprises. Often referred to as private (or managerial) accountants, they perform many different activities within the company. The controller, who supervises the accounting activities, is regarded as the principal accounting officer of the company. As indicated earlier, individuals well versed in the accounting discipline are frequently members of the top management team.

The private accountant may be involved in:

1. **Cost accounting**—determining the cost of producing specific products.
2. **Budgeting**—assisting management in quantifying goals concerning revenues, costs of goods sold, and operating expenses.
3. **General accounting**—recording daily transactions and preparing financial statements and related information.
4. **Accounting information systems**—designing both manual and computerized data processing systems.
5. **Tax accounting**—preparing tax returns and engaging in tax planning for the company.

---

[2]For example, *Forbes* magazine noted that seven of the largest management consulting companies are public accounting firms, and the largest management consulting company is a public accounting firm.

6. Internal auditing—reviewing the company's operations to determine compliance with management policies and evaluating the efficiency of operations.

From the above, it can be observed that within a specific company, private accountants perform as wide a variety of duties as the public accountant.

A certificate in management accounting (CMA) is awarded to individuals who demonstrate expertise in areas of management accounting by passing an examination covering accounting and related disciplines. In addition, a certificate in internal auditing (CIA) is issued to individuals who have demonstrated competence in this field.

Not-For-Profit Accounting

The need for sound financial reporting and control by not-for-profit organizations is imperative. Such organizations include governmental units, foundations, hospitals, unions, educational organizations, and charities. For example, the near bankruptcies of a number of our large cities, such as New York and Cleveland, demonstrate the need for sound financial information to avert these situations. In addition, the influence of not-for-profit organizations is very significant and continues to grow. It has been recently estimated that there are more than 500,000 not-for-profit organizations in the United States.

Governmental

Local, state, and federal governmental units have a high demand for individuals skilled in accounting. Users of governmental financial reports, such as legislators, citizens, employees, and creditors must have adequate financial information to measure the financial health and the efficiency of governmental units. As a result, many different types of governmental agencies employ accountants. At the federal level, the largest employers of accountants include the Internal Revenue Service, the General Accounting Office, the Federal Bureau of Investigation, and the Securities and Exchange Commission.

Nongovernmental

In addition to government, many other organizations such as the United Way, the Ford Foundation, and the Red Cross attempt to provide socially desirable

Accounting in Action · *Ethical Insight*

Help Wanted: Forensic CPAs

Tom Taylor used to pack a .357 magnum; now he pushes a pencil. Taylor, 37, for two years an FBI agent, is a forensic accountant, somebody who sniffs through company books to ferret out white-collar crime.

Demand for this service has surged in the past few years. A recruiter for San Diego's Robert Half International says the headhunting firm placed about 100 such snoops in 1989. This year (1990) he'll be looking for more than 1,000.

Qualifications: a CPA with FBI, IRS, or similar government experience. (For all its macho image, the FBI has long hired mostly accountants and lawyers as agents.)

Source: Fortune, February 10, 1992.

and necessary goods or services. Donors to these organizations need information about how well the organization has met its objectives and whether continued support is justified. Managers and governing bodies of these organizations, as well as all hospitals, colleges, and universities, must make many decisions about the allocation of money. To support these decisions, they need reports that compare budgeted and actual revenue and expenditures.

Accounting as a Career

Typical accounting positions or career paths in the fields of public accounting and private accounting are shown in Illustration 1-4. The salaries at each of the echelons for both career paths are somewhat comparable. A comparison of salaries in the accounting field for private and public accountants is shown in Illustration 1-3:

ILLUSTRATION 1-3

Earnings in the Accounting Field

	Size of Company/Firm	
	Medium	**Large**
Private Accountants		
Entry-level	$23,600 to $26,400	$24,200 to $27,600
Senior accountant	$34,800 to $42,200	$36,700 to $44,200
Manager	$40,700 to $46,700	$44,000 to $66,000
Public Accountants		
Entry-level	$22,600 to $25,900	$24,400 to $27,700
Senior auditor	$34,100 to $44,900	$34,500 to $40,300
Manager	$41,100 to $58,400	$42,400 to $67,600
Source: Robert Half Salary Guide 1991.		

Most of these salaries are increased 5 to 10% if an individual is a CPA or CMA or has a graduate degree. In private accounting, accountants often reach such positions as controller, treasurer, vice president of finance—even chairman of the board. In public accounting, accountants generally move to a partner position. Positions above manager in private and public accounting often earn in excess of $100,000, with substantial potential for even more. It is not uncommon for managers and senior accountants of CPA firms to move from public accounting to similar or higher positions in private accounting.[3]

---

[3]Information about specific careers in accounting may be obtained from the following professional organizations: American Institute of Certified Public Accountants (AICPA), 1211 Avenue of the Americas, New York, NY 10036; Association of Government Accountants (AGA), 2200 Mount Vernon Ave., Alexandria, VA 22301; Institute of Certified Management Accountants, 10 Paragon Drive, Montvale, NJ 07654-1760; Institute of Internal Auditors (IIA), 249 Maitland Ave., Altamonte Springs, FL 32701.

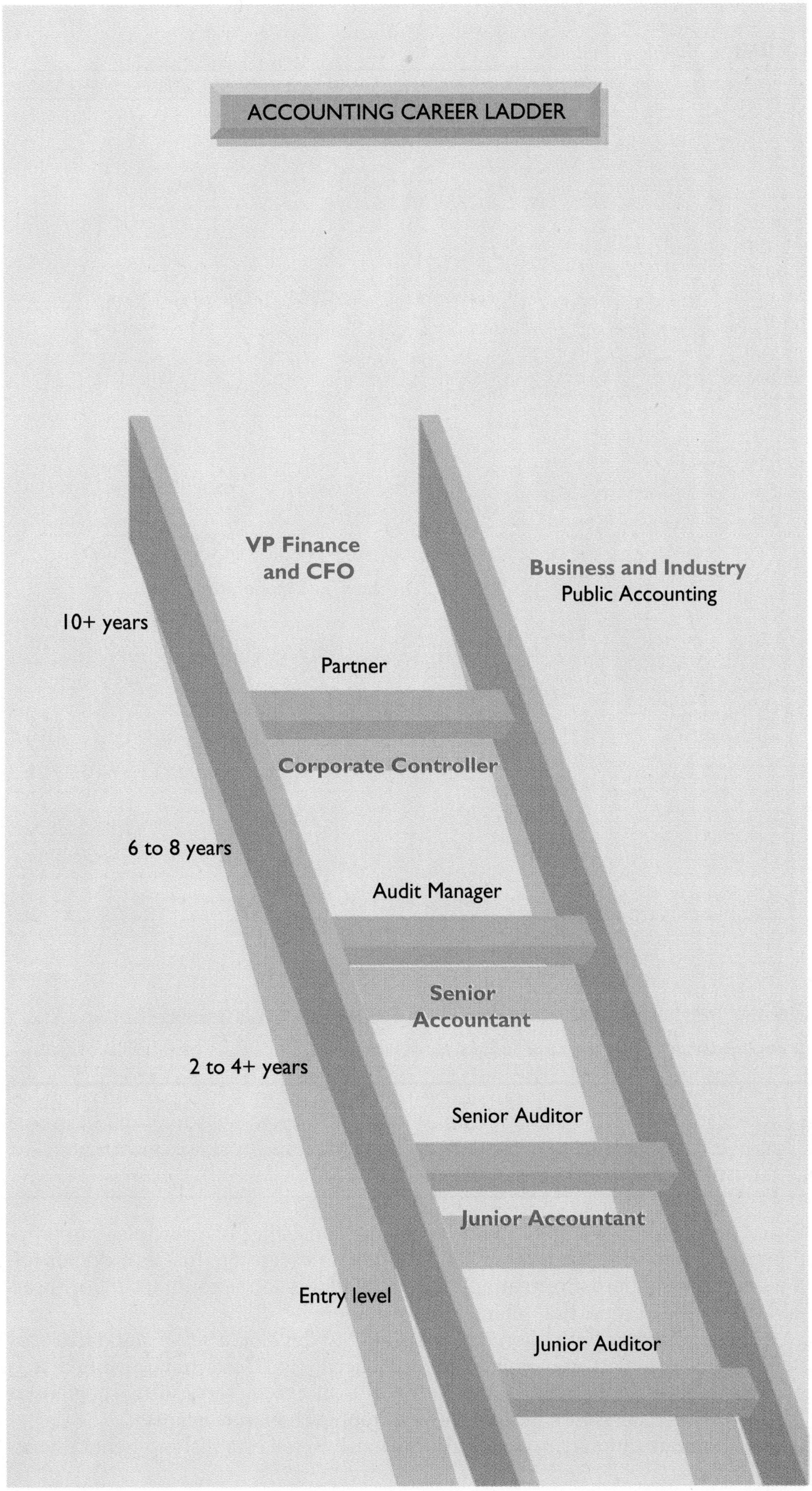

ILLUSTRATION 1-4

Career paths in public and private accounting

Source: After College, October/November 1991.

ACCOUNTING CAREER LADDER

VP Finance and CFO

Business and Industry
Public Accounting

10+ years

Partner

Corporate Controller

6 to 8 years

Audit Manager

Senior Accountant

2 to 4+ years

Senior Auditor

Junior Accountant

Entry level

Junior Auditor

Accounting in Action · *Business Insight*

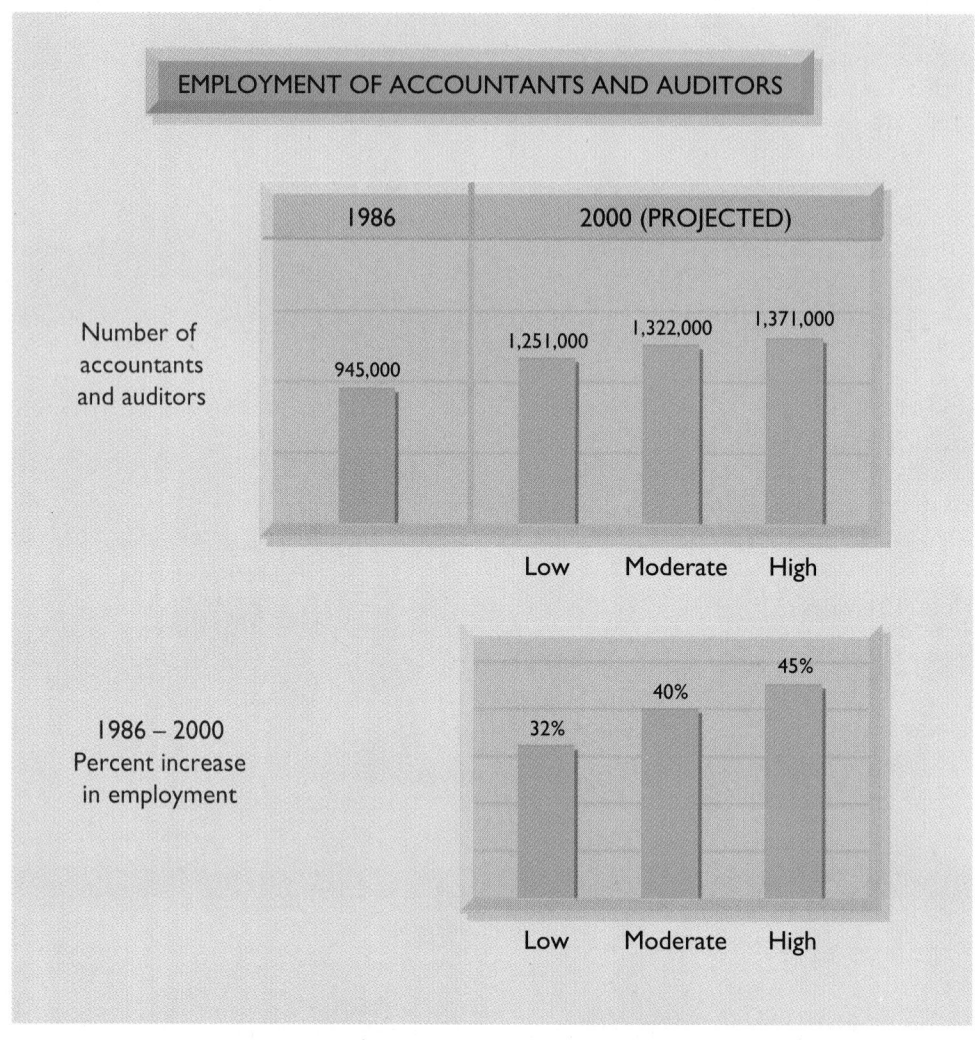

The low, moderate, and high categories indicate the government's projection.

Source: Projections 2000, Bureau of Labor Statistics, March 1988.

Generally Accepted Accounting Principles

Study Objective 4

Explain the meaning of generally accepted accounting principles and the cost principle.

Every profession develops a body of theory consisting of principles, assumptions, concepts, and standards. Accounting is no exception. Just as a doctor follows certain standards in treating a patient's illness, an accountant follows certain standards in reporting financial information.

The accounting profession has attempted to develop a set of standards that is generally accepted and universally practiced. Its efforts have resulted in a common set of standards called **generally accepted accounting principles (GAAP)**. These standards indicate how to report economic events.

Two organizations are primarily responsible for establishing generally accepted accounting principles. The first, the Financial Accounting Standards Board (FASB), is a private organization that establishes broad reporting standards of general applicability as well as specific accounting rules. The second, the Securities and Exchange Commission (SEC), is a governmental agency that requires companies filing financial reports with it to follow generally accepted accounting principles. In situations where no principles exist, the SEC often mandates that certain guidelines be used. In general, the FASB and the SEC work hand in hand to assure that timely and useful financial principles are developed.

One important principle is the cost principle, which states that assets should be recorded at their cost. **Cost is the value exchanged at the time something is acquired.** If you buy a house today, the cost is the amount you pay for it, say $100,000. If you sell the house in two years for $120,000, the sales price is its **market value**—the value determined by the market for homes at that time. At the time of acquisition, cost and fair market value are the same. In subsequent periods, cost and fair market value may vary, **but the accountant continues to use the cost amount**.

For example, at one time, Greyhound Corporation had 128 bus stations nationwide that cost approximately $200 million. The current market value of the stations is approximately $1 billion. Under the cost principle, the bus stations are recorded and reported at $200 million, not $1 billion. Until the bus stations are actually sold, market values are considered too subjective.

Cost has an important advantage over other valuations: it is reliable. Cost is definite and verifiable. The values exchanged at the time something is acquired generally can be objectively measured. The characteristics of objectivity and verifiability are of great importance to those who use accounting information. To rely on the information supplied, users must know that the information is based on fact. By using cost as the basis for record keeping and reporting, accountants can best provide objective and verifiable data in their reports. Other generally accepted principles will be discussed in subsequent chapters.

Assumptions

In developing generally accepted accounting principles, accountants must make certain basic assumptions. These assumptions provide a foundation for the accounting process. Two main assumptions are the **economic entity assumption** and the **monetary unit assumption**.

Economic Entity Assumption

An economic entity can be any organization or unit in society. It may be a business enterprise (such as General Electric Company), a governmental unit (such as the state of Ohio), a municipality (such as Seattle), a school district (such as St. Louis District 48), or a social organization such as a church (Southern Baptist), a fraternity (Theta Chi), or a sorority (Chi Omega). The economic entity assumption states that economic events can be identified with a particular unit of accountability. This assumption requires that the activities of the entity be kept separate and distinct from (1) the activities of its owner and (2) all other economic entities. To illustrate, if Sally Rider, owner of Sally's Boutique, charges any of her personal living costs as expenses of the Boutique, the economic entity assumption is violated. Similarly, the economic entity assumption assumes that the activities of McDonald's, Wendy's, and Burger King can each be segregated into separate economic entities for accounting purposes.

Study Objective 5

State the basic accounting equation and explain the meaning of assets, liabilities, and owner's equity.

Accounting in Action · *Ethical Insight*

Consider how the economic entity assumption was violated in the following situation. An IRS investigation uncovered a scheme used by Mr. Aldo Gucci, owner of the international Gucci retail stores, to divert cash from the business to personal accounts. "Gucci Shops issued checks payable to 'Gucci,' supposedly to pay for expenses of acquiring merchandise through a buying office in Italy. But the checks were deposited in Mr. Gucci's personal bank accounts and divided among him and other family members."

The Wall Street Journal, January 20, 1986.

Although the economic entity assumption can be applied to any unit of accountability, we will generally discuss it in relation to a business enterprise, which may be organized as a proprietorship, partnership, or corporation.

Proprietorship

A business owned by one person is generally a proprietorship. The owner is often the manager/operator of the business. Small service-type businesses (barber shops, law offices, plumbing companies, and auto repair shops), farms, and small retail stores (antique shops, clothing stores, and book stores) are often sole proprietorships. **Usually only a limited amount of money (capital) is necessary to start in business, and the owner receives any profits, suffers any losses, and is personally liable for all debts of the business.** Although there is no legal distinction between the business as an economic unit and the owner, the records of the business activities are kept separate from the personal records and activities of the owner. Although sole proprietorships represent the largest number of businesses in the United States, they are typically the smallest in size and volume of business.

Partnership

A business owned by two or more persons associated as partners is a partnership. In most respects a partnership is similar to a sole proprietorship except that more than one owner is involved. When a partnership is created, an agreement (written or oral) should set forth such terms as initial investment of each partner, duties of each partner, division of net income (or net loss), and settlement to be made upon death or withdrawal of a partner. Each partner generally has unlimited personal liability for the debts of the partnership. **Like a proprietorship, for accounting purposes the partnership affairs must be kept separate from the personal activities of the partners.** Partnerships are often used to organize retail and service-type businesses, including professional practices (lawyers, doctors, architects, and certified public accountants).

Corporation

A business organized as a separate legal entity under state corporation law and having ownership divided into transferable shares of stock is called a corporation. The holders of the shares (stockholders) **enjoy limited liability;** they are not personally liable for the debts of the corporate entity. Stockholders **may transfer all or part of their shares to other investors at any time** (i.e., sell their shares in the securities market). The ease with which ownership can change adds to the attractiveness of investing in a corporation. Because ownership can be transferred without dissolving the corporation, the corporation **enjoys an unlimited life**.

Although the combined number of proprietorships and partnerships in the United States is more than five times the number of corporations, the revenue produced by corporations is eight times greater. Most of the largest enterprises in the United States—for example, Exxon, General Motors, Sears Roebuck, Citicorp, and Pacific Gas and Electric—are corporations.

Monetary Unit Assumption

The monetary unit assumption requires that only transaction data that can be expressed in terms of money be included in the accounting records of the economic entity. Because money is the commonly used medium of exchange, this assumption enables accounting to quantify (measure) the economic event. The monetary unit assumption is vital to applying the cost principle discussed earlier. This assumption prevents such relevant information as the health of the owner, the quality of service, and the morale of employees from being included in the accounting records because they cannot be quantified in terms of money.

An important corollary to the monetary unit assumption is the added assumption that the unit of measure remains sufficiently constant over time. However, the assumption of a stable monetary unit has been challenged because of the significant decline in the purchasing power of the dollar. For example, what used to cost $1.00 in 1960, now costs approximately $4.00 in 1993, an increase of fourfold. In such situations, adding, subtracting, or comparing 1960 dollars with 1993 dollars is highly questionable. The profession has recognized this problem and encourages companies to disclose the effects of changing prices.

Before You Go On . . .

1. What are the major service areas in public accounting? In private accounting? In not-for-profit accounting?

2. What are generally accepted accounting principles? Give an example of an accounting principle.

3. Explain the economic entity and the monetary unit assumptions.

Basic Accounting Equation

Assets are resources owned by a business. **Equities** are rights or claims against these resources. Thus, a company that has $300,000 of assets also has $300,000 of claims against these assets. This relationship can be shown in equation form as follows:

Equities may be further subdivided into two categories: claims of creditors and claims of owners. Claims of creditors are called **liabilities**. Claims of owners are called **owner's equity**. The equation above is then expanded as follows:

ILLUSTRATION 1-6

The basic accounting equation

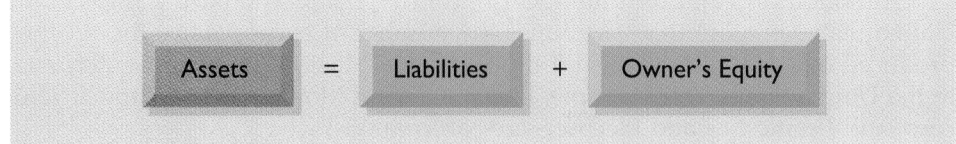

This equation is referred to as the basic accounting equation. Assets must equal the sum of liabilities and owner's equity. Because creditor's claims are paid before ownership claims if a business is liquidated, liabilities are shown before owner's equity in the basic accounting equation.

The accounting equation applies to all economic entities regardless of size, nature of business, or form of business organization. Thus, it applies to a small proprietorship such as a corner grocery store as well as to a giant corporation such as AT&T. The equation provides the underlying framework for recording and summarizing the economic events of a business enterprise.

Assets

As indicated above, assets are resources owned by a business. Thus, they are the things of value used in carrying out such activities as production, consumption, and exchange. The common characteristic possessed by all assets is "service potential" or "future economic benefit." That is, the common characteristic is the capacity to provide future services or benefits to the entities that use them. In a business enterprise, that service potential or future economic benefit eventually results in cash inflows (receipts) to the enterprise.

For example, the enterprise Campus Pizza owns a delivery truck that provides economic benefits because it is used in delivering pizzas. Other assets of Campus Pizza are tables, chairs, jukebox, cash register, oven, mugs and silverware, and, of course, cash.

Liabilities

Liabilities are creditorship claims on total assets. Put more simply, **liabilities are existing debts and obligations**. For example, businesses of all sizes and degrees of success usually find it necessary to borrow money and to purchase merchandise on credit. Campus Pizza, for instance, purchases cheese, sausage, flour, and beverages on credit from suppliers; these obligations are called **accounts payable**. Additionally, Campus Pizza has a **note payable** to First National Bank for the money borrowed to purchase its delivery truck. Campus Pizza may also have **wages payable** to employees, and **sales and real estate taxes payable** to the local government. Persons or entities to whom Campus Pizza owes money are called **creditors**.

Most claims of creditors attach to **total** enterprise assets rather than to the specific assets provided by the creditor. In the event of nonpayment, creditors may legally force the liquidation of a business. In that case, the law requires that creditor claims be paid before ownership claims.

Owner's Equity

The ownership claim on total assets is known as owner's equity. It is equal to total assets minus total liabilities. Here is why: The assets of a business are supplied or claimed by either creditors or owners. To determine what belongs to owners, we therefore subtract creditors' claims—the liabilities—from assets. The remainder—owner's equity—is the owner's claim on the assets of the business. Since the claims of creditors take precedence over ownership claims, the latter are often referred to as **residual equity**.

In proprietorships, the principal subdivisions of owner's equity are capital, drawings, revenues, and expenses.

Capital

Capital is the term used to describe the owner's investment in the business. **An investment made in the business increases capital.** It follows that total owner's equity increases as well.

Drawings

An owner may withdraw cash or other assets during the accounting period for personal use. These withdrawals could directly decrease capital. However, it is generally considered preferable to use a separate classification referred to as drawings to determine the total withdrawals for the accounting period. **Drawings decrease total owner's equity.**

Revenues

Revenues are the gross increase in owner's equity resulting from business activities entered into for the purpose of earning income. Generally, revenues result from the sale of merchandise, the performance of services, the rental of property, and the lending of money.

Revenues usually result in an increase in an asset. They may arise from different sources and are identified by various names depending on the nature of the business. Campus Pizza, for instance, has two categories of sales revenues—pizza sales and beverage sales. Other titles for and sources of revenue common to many businesses are: sales, fees, services, commissions, interest, dividends, royalties, and rent.

Helpful hint The effect of revenues is positive—an increase in assets, an increase in owner's equity or a decrease in liabilities.

Expenses

Expenses are the cost of assets consumed or services used in the process of earning revenue. **Expenses are the decreases in owner's equity that result from operating the business.** Expenses represent actual or expected cash outflows (payments). Like revenues, expenses take many forms and are identified by various names depending on the type of asset consumed or service used. For example, Campus Pizza recognizes the following types of expenses: cost of ingredients (meat, flour, cheese, tomato paste, mushrooms, etc.); cost of beverages; wages expense; utility expense (electric, gas, and water expense); telephone expense; delivery expense (gasoline, repairs, licenses, etc.); supplies expense (napkins, detergents, aprons, etc.); rent expense; interest expense; and property tax expense.

Helpful hint The effect of expenses is negative—a decrease in assets, a decrease in owner's equity, or an increase in liabilities.

In summary, the principal sources (increases) of owner's equity are (1) investments by owners and (2) revenues from business operations. In contrast, reductions in owner's equity are a result of (1) withdrawals of assets by owners and (2) expenses. Net income results when revenues exceed expenses; conversely, a net loss occurs when expenses exceed revenues.

These relationships are shown in Illustration 1-7.

Relationships among subdivisions of owner's equity

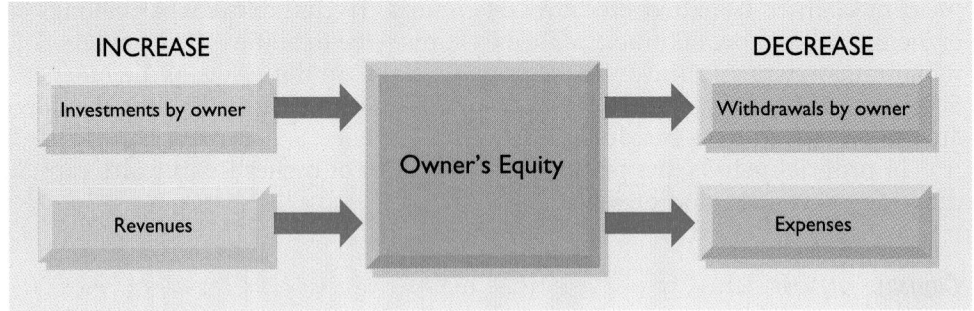

Transactions

Study Objective 7

Analyze the effect of business transactions on the basic accounting equation.

Helpful hint Transactions are events that cause a change in individual assets, liabilities, or one of the subdivisions of owner's equity.

Transactions (often referred to as business transactions) are the economic events of the enterprise recorded by accountants. Transactions may be identified as external or internal. **External transactions involve economic events between the company and some outside enterprise or party.** For example, for Campus Pizza the purchase of cooking equipment from a supplier, the payment of monthly rent to the landlord, and the sale of pizzas to customers are external transactions. **Internal transactions are economic events that occur entirely within one company.** The use of office supplies illustrates this type of transaction for Campus Pizza.

A company may carry on many activities that do not in themselves represent business transactions. Hiring employees, answering the telephone, talking with customers, and placing an order for merchandise with a supplier are examples. Some of these activities, however, may lead to a business transaction: employees will earn wages, and merchandise will be delivered by the supplier. Each transaction must be analyzed in terms of its effect on the components of the basic accounting equation. This analysis must identify the specific items affected and the amount of the change in each item.

Since the equality of the basic equation must be preserved, each transaction must have a dual effect on the equation. For example, if an individual asset is increased, there must be a corresponding:

1. Decrease in another asset, or
2. Increase in a specific liability, or
3. Increase in owner's equity.

It follows that two or more items could be affected when an asset is increased. For example, as one asset is increased, another asset could decrease and a specific liability could increase. Note also that any change in an individual liability or ownership claim is subject to similar analysis.

Analysis of Transactions

The analysis of transactions in terms of the basic accounting equation can be observed by studying the following examples of business transactions for a new computer programming business during its first month of operations.

TRANSACTION (1). INVESTMENT BY OWNER. Ray Neal decides to open a computer programming service in a campus community. On September 1, 1993, he invests $15,000 cash in the business, which is named Softbyte. This transaction results in an equal increase in assets and owner's equity. In this case, there is an increase in the asset Cash, $15,000, and an equal increase in the owner's equity, R. Neal,

Capital, $15,000. The effect of this transaction on the basic equation is:

		Assets	=	Liabilities	+	Owner's Equity	
						R. Neal,	
		Cash	=			Capital	
(1)		+$15,000	=			+$15,000	Investment

Observe that the equality of the basic equation has been maintained. Note also that the source of the increase in owner's equity is indicated. Capital investments by the owner do not represent revenues; they are excluded in determining net income.

TRANSACTION (2). PURCHASE OF EQUIPMENT FOR CASH. Computer equipment is purchased for $7,000 cash. This transaction results in an equal increase and decrease in total assets. The composition of assets, however, is changed: Cash is decreased $7,000, and the asset Equipment is increased $7,000. Both the specific effect of this transaction and the cumulative effect of the first two transactions are:

		Assets			=	Liabilities	+	Owner's Equity
								R. Neal
		Cash	+	Equipment	=			Capital
	Old Bal.	$15,000						$15,000
(2)		−7,000		+$7,000				
	New Bal.	$ 8,000	+	$7,000	=			$15,000
			$15,000					

Observe that total assets are still $15,000 and Neal's equity also remains at $15,000, the amount of his original investment.

TRANSACTION (3). PURCHASE OF SUPPLIES ON CREDIT. Softbyte purchases computer paper and other supplies expected to last several months from Acme Supply Company for $1,600. Acme Company agrees to allow Softbyte to pay this bill in October, a month later. This transaction is often referred to as a purchase on account or a credit purchase. Assets are increased by this transaction because of the expected future benefits of using the paper and supplies, and liabilities are increased by the amount due Acme Company. The asset Supplies is increased $1,600, and the liability Accounts Payable is increased by the same amount. The effect on the equation is:

		Assets					=	Liabilities	+	Owner's Equity
								Accounts		R. Neal,
		Cash	+	Supplies	+	Equipment	=	Payable	+	Capital
	Old. Bal.	$8,000				$7,000				$15,000
(3)				+$1,600				+$1,600		
	New Bal.	$8,000	+	$1,600	+	$7,000	=	$1,600	+	$15,000
			$16,600						$16,600		

Total assets are now $16,600. This total is matched by a $1,600 creditor's claim and a $15,000 ownership claim.

TRANSACTION (4). SERVICES RENDERED FOR CASH. Softbyte receives $1,200 cash from customers for programming services. This transaction represents the principal revenue-producing activity of Softbyte. Recall that revenue increases owner's equity. Both assets and owner's equity are then increased. In this case, Cash is increased $1,200, and R. Neal, Capital, is increased $1,200. The new balances in the equation are:

		Assets			=	Liabilities	+	Owner's Equity	
						Accounts		R. Neal,	
	Cash	+	Supplies	+	Equipment =	Payable	+	Capital	
Old Bal.	$8,000		$1,600		$7,000	$1,600		$15,000	
(4)	+1,200							+1,200	Service Revenue
New Bal.	$9,200	+	$1,600	+	$7,000	=	$1,600	+	$16,200	
			$17,800				$17,800			

The two sides of the equation balance at $17,800. Note that owner's equity is increased when revenues are earned. The source of the increase in owner's equity is indicated as service revenue. Service revenue is included in determining Softbyte's net income.

TRANSACTION (5). PURCHASE OF ADVERTISING ON CREDIT. Softbyte receives a bill for $250 from the *Daily News* for advertising the opening of its business but postpones payment of the bill until a later date. This transaction results in an increase in liabilities and a decrease in owner's equity. The specific items involved are Accounts Payable and R. Neal, Capital. The effect on the equation is:

		Assets			=	Liabilities	+	Owner's Equity	
						Accounts		R. Neal,	
	Cash	+	Supplies	+	Equipment =	Payable	+	Capital	
Old Bal.	$9,200		$1,600		$7,000	$1,600		$16,200	
(5)						+250		−250	Advertising Expense
New Bal.	$9,200	+	$1,600	+	$7,000	=	$1,850	+	$15,950	
			$17,800				$17,800			

The two sides of the equation still balance at $17,800. Observe that owner's equity is decreased when the expense is incurred, and the specific cause of the decrease is noted. Expenses do not have to be paid in cash at the time they are incurred. When payment is made at a later date, the liability Accounts Payable will be decreased and the asset Cash will be decreased [see Transaction (9)]. The cost of advertising is considered an expense as opposed to an asset because the benefits have been used. This expense is included in determining net income.

TRANSACTION (6). SERVICES RENDERED FOR CASH AND CREDIT. Softbyte provides programming services of $3,500 for customers. Cash amounting to $1,500 is received from customers, and the balance of $2,000 is billed to customers on account. This transaction results in an equal increase in assets and owner's equity. Three specific items are affected: Cash is increased $1,500; Accounts Receivable is increased $2,000; and R. Neal, Capital, is increased $3,500. The new balances are as follows:

		Assets				= Liabilities +	Owner's Equity	
			Accounts				Accounts	R. Neal,
		Cash +	Receivable +	Supplies +	Equipment =	Payable +	Capital	
	Old Bal.	$9,200		$1,600	$7,000	$1,850	$15,950	
(6)		+1,500	+2,000				+3,500	Service Revenue
	New Bal.	$10,700 +	$2,000 +	$1,600 +	$7,000 =	$1,850 +	$19,450	
			$21,300				$21,300	

Remember that owner's equity is increased when revenues are earned. The inflow of assets resulting from the earnings of revenues does not have to be in the form of cash. When collections on account are received at a later date, Cash will be increased and Accounts Receivable will be decreased [see Transaction (10)]. The terms Fees Receivable instead of Accounts Receivable and Fees Earned instead of Service Revenue are often used when services are provided on account.

TRANSACTION (7). PAYMENT OF EXPENSES. Expenses paid in cash for September are store rent, $600, salaries of employees, $900, and utilities, $200. These payments result in an equal decrease in assets and owner's equity. Cash is decreased $1,700 and R. Neal, Capital is decreased by the same amount. The effect of these payments on the equation is:

			Assets				= Liabilities +	Owner's Equity	
			Accounts				Accounts	R. Neal,
		Cash +	Receivable +	Supplies +	Equipment =	Payable +	Capital	
	Old Bal.	$10,700	$2,000	$1,600	$7,000	$1,850	$19,450	
(7)		−1,700					−600	Rent Expense
							−900	Salaries Expense
							−200	Utilities Expense
	New Bal.	$9,000 +	$2,000 +	$1,600 +	$7,000 =	$1,850 +	$17,750	
			$19,600				$19,600	

The two sides of the equation now balance at $19,600. Three lines are required in the analysis to indicate the types of expenses that have been incurred.

TRANSACTION (8). RECOGNITION OF SUPPLIES USED. A count of supplies on September 30 indicates that $400 of supplies have been used in developing software for clients. The cost of supplies used is an expense that decreases assets and owner's equity. Specifically this transaction decreases the asset Supplies $400 and decreases R. Neal, Capital $400. The new balances in the equation are:

			Assets				= Liabilities +	Owner's Equity	
			Accounts				Accounts	R. Neal,
		Cash +	Receivable +	Supplies +	Equipment =	Payable +	Capital	
	Old Bal.	$9,000	$2,000	$1,600	$7,000	$1,850	$17,750	
(8)				−400			−400	Supplies Expense
	New Bal.	$9,000 +	$2,000 +	$1,200 +	$7,000 =	$1,850 +	$17,350	
			$19,200				$19,200	

Here, as in previous examples, the cause of the decrease in owner's equity is indicated.

TRANSACTION (9). PAYMENT OF ACCOUNTS PAYABLE. Softbyte pays its *Daily News* advertising bill of $250 in cash. In analyzing the effect of this transaction, we must recall that the bill has previously been recorded in Transaction (5) as an increase in Accounts Payable and a decrease in owner's equity. Thus, this payment "on account" decreases both assets and liabilities. In this case, the asset Cash and the liability Accounts Payable are decreased by $250. The effect of this transaction on the equation is:

		Cash	+	Accounts Receivable	+	Supplies	+	Equipment	=	Accounts Payable	+	R. Neal, Capital
		Assets							=	**Liabilities**	+	**Owner's Equity**
(9)	Old Bal.	$9,000		$2,000		$1,200		$7,000		$1,850		$17,350
		−250								−250		
	New Bal.	$8,750	+	$2,000	+	$1,200	+	$7,000	=	$1,600	+	$17,350
				$18,950							$18,950	

Observe that the payment of a liability related to an expense that has previously been incurred does not affect owner's equity.

TRANSACTION (10). RECEIPT OF CASH ON ACCOUNT. The sum of $600 in cash is received from customers who have previously been billed for services in Transaction (6). This transaction does not change total assets, but it changes the composition of Softbyte's assets. Cash is increased $600 and Accounts Receivable is decreased $600. The new balances are:

		Cash	+	Accounts Receivable	+	Supplies	+	Equipment	=	Accounts Payable	+	R. Neal, Capital
		Assets							=	**Liabilities**	+	**Owner's Equity**
(10)	Old Bal.	$8,750		$2,000		$1,200		$7,000		$1,600		$17,350
		+600		−600								
	New Bal.	$9,350	+	$1,400	+	$1,200	+	$7,000	=	$1,600	+	$17,350
				$18,950							$18,950	

Note that a collection on account for services previously billed and recorded does not affect owner's equity. Revenue was already recorded in Transaction (6) and should not be recorded again.

TRANSACTION (11). WITHDRAWAL OF CASH BY OWNER. Ray Neal withdraws $1,300 in cash from the business for his personal use. This transaction results in an equal decrease in assets and owner's equity. Thus, both Cash and R. Neal, Capital are decreased $1,300, as shown below:

		Cash	+	Accounts Receivable	+	Supplies	+	Equipment	=	Accounts Payable	+	R. Neal, Capital	
		Assets							=	**Liabilities**	+	**Owner's Equity**	
(11)	Old Bal.	$9,350		$1,400		$1,200		$7,000		$1,600		$17,350	
		−1,300										−1,300	Drawings
	New Bal.	$8,050	+	$1,400	+	$1,200	+	$7,000	=	$1,600	+	$16,050	
				$17,650							$17,650		

Observe that the effect of a cash withdrawal by the owner is the opposite of the effect of a capital investment by the owner. **Owner's drawings do not represent expenses.** Like owner's capital investment, they are not included in determining net income.

Summary of Transactions

The transactions of Softbyte are summarized in Illustration 1-8 to show their cumulative effect on the basic accounting equation. The transaction number, the specific effects of the transaction, and the balances after each transaction are indicated. The illustration demonstrates a number of significant facts:

1. Each transaction must be analyzed in terms of its effect on:
   a. the three components of the basic accounting equation.
   b. specific types (kinds) of items within each component.
2. The two sides of the equation must always be equal.
3. The causes of each change in the owner's claim on assets must be indicated in the owner's equity column.

ILLUSTRATION 1-8

Tabular summary of Softbyte transactions

Transaction	Cash	+	Accounts Receivable	+	Supplies	+	Equipment	=	Accounts Payable	+	R. Neal, Capital	
(1)	+$15,000										+$15,000	Investment
(2)	−7,000						+$7,000					
	8,000	+					7,000	=			15,000	
(3)					+$1,600				+$1,600			
	8,000	+			1,600	+	7,000	=	1,600	+	15,000	
(4)	+1,200										+1,200	Service Revenue
	9,200	+			1,600	+	7,000	=	1,600	+	16,200	
(5)									+250		−250	Advertising Expense
	9,200	+			1,600	+	7,000	=	1,850	+	15,950	
(6)	+1,500	+	+$2,000								+3,500	Service Revenue
	10,700	+	2,000	+	1,600	+	7,000	=	1,850	+	19,450	
(7)	−1,700										−600	Rent Expense
											−900	Salaries Expense
											−200	Utilities Expense
	9,000	+	2,000	+	1,600	+	7,000	=	1,850	+	17,750	
(8)					−400						−400	Supplies Expense
	9,000	+	2,000	+	1,200	+	7,000	=	1,850	+	17,350	
(9)	−250								−250			
	8,750	+	2,000	+	1,200	+	7,000	=	1,600	+	17,350	
(10)	+600		−600									
	9,350	+	1,400	+	1,200	+	7,000	=	1,600	+	17,350	
(11)	−1,300										−1,300	Drawings
	$ 8,050	+	$1,400	+	$1,200	+	$7,000	=	$1,600	+	$16,050	

$17,650 $17,650

✐inancial Statements

Study Objective 8

Prepare an income statement, owner's equity statement, and balance sheet.

Three financial statements are prepared from the summarized accounting data:

1. An income statement presents the revenues and expenses and resulting net income or net loss of a company for a specific period of time.
2. An owner's equity statement summarizes the changes in owner's equity for a specific period of time.
3. A balance sheet reports the assets, liabilities, and owner's equity of a business enterprise at a specific date.

Each statement provides management, owners, and other interested parties with relevant financial data. The financial statements of Softbyte and their inter-relationships are shown in Illustration 1-9. The statements are interrelated: **(1) Net income of $2,350 shown on the income statement is added to the beginning balance of owner's capital in the owner's equity statement. (2) Owner's capital of $16,050 at the end of the reporting period shown in the owner's equity statement is reported on the balance sheet.**

Helpful hint The income statement, owner's equity statement, and statement of cash flows are all for a period of time whereas the balance sheet is for a point in time.

A fourth statement, a statement of cash flows, is also prepared. It primarily summarizes information concerning the cash inflows (receipts) and outflows (payments) during the period. This statement will be discussed and illustrated in Chapter 19.

Additionally, every set of financial statements is accompanied by explanatory notes and supporting schedules that are an integral part of the statements. Examples of these notes and schedules are illustrated in later chapters of this textbook.

Be sure to carefully examine the format and content of each statement. The essential features of each are briefly described in the following sections.

Income Statement

The income statement for Softbyte is prepared from the data appearing in the owner's equity column of Illustration 1-8. The heading of the statement identifies the company, the type of statement, and the time period covered by the statement. Note that the primary focus of the income statement is on reporting the success or profitability of the company's operations over a specified period of time. To indicate that it applies for a period of time, the income statement is dated "For the Month Ended September 30, 1993."

✐ccounting in Action · *International Insight*

Although we may take the computation of net income for granted, in Russia such measurements are less common. As noted recently in a financial magazine one Russian was asked, "What is net income?" He responded, "We don't have that concept here." Then, after huddling with his colleagues he explained that although he thinks he understands the concept, he isn't comfortable with it.

Because the income statement summarizes the results of operations, it is often referred to as an operating statement. Revenues are listed first, followed by expenses. Finally net income (or net loss) is determined. Although practice varies considerably on this matter, we have chosen in our illustrations and solutions to homework to list expenses in order of magnitude. Alternative formats for the income statement will be considered in later chapters.

Note that investment and withdrawal transactions between the owner and the business are not included in the measurement of net income. For example, the withdrawal by Ray Neal of cash from Softbyte was not regarded as a business expense, as explained earlier. This type of transaction is considered a reduction of the owner's equity in the enterprise.

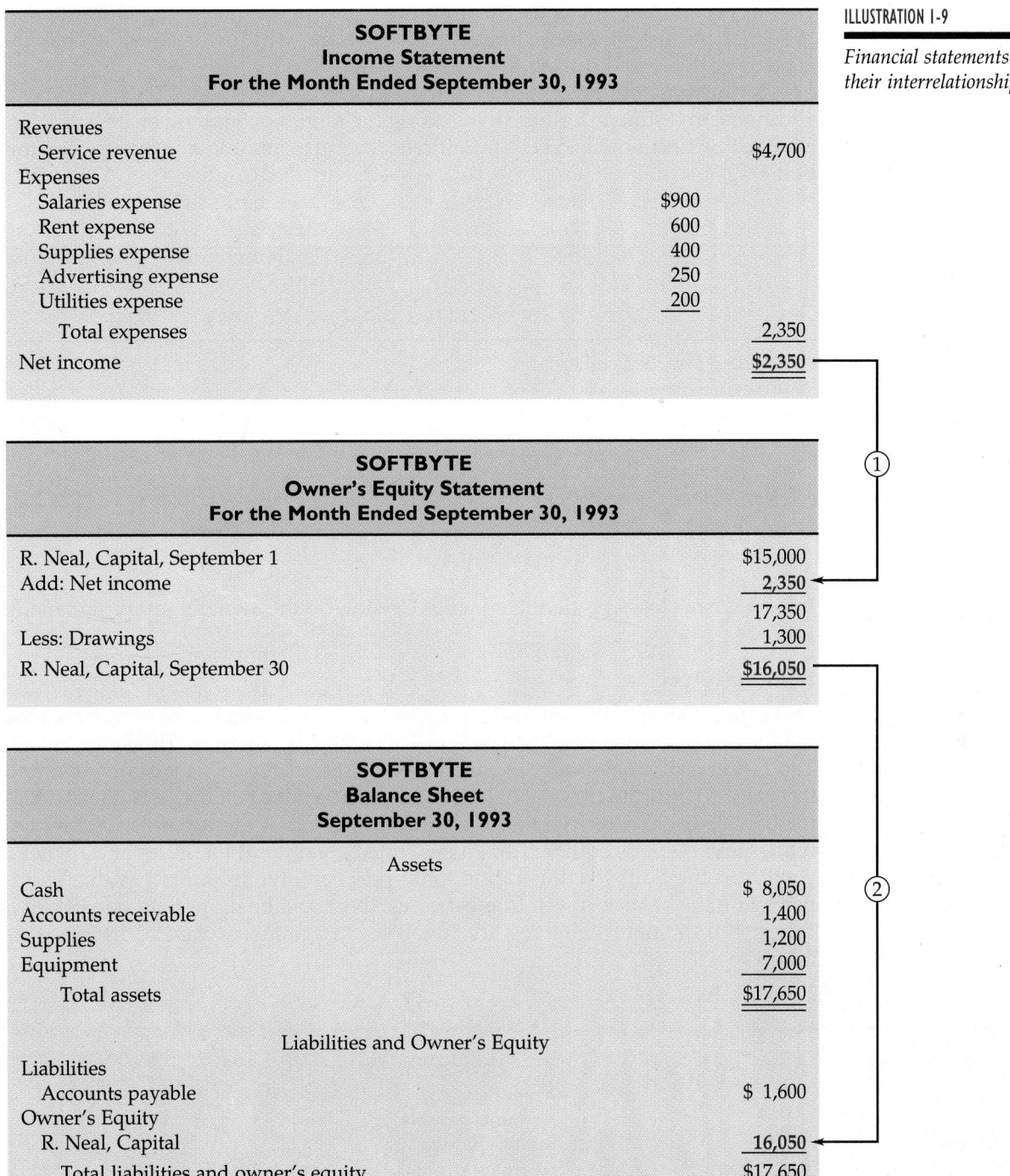

ILLUSTRATION 1-9

Financial statements and their interrelationships

SOFTBYTE
Income Statement
For the Month Ended September 30, 1993

Revenues		
Service revenue		$4,700
Expenses		
Salaries expense	$900	
Rent expense	600	
Supplies expense	400	
Advertising expense	250	
Utilities expense	200	
Total expenses		2,350
Net income		$2,350

SOFTBYTE
Owner's Equity Statement
For the Month Ended September 30, 1993

R. Neal, Capital, September 1	$15,000
Add: Net income	2,350
	17,350
Less: Drawings	1,300
R. Neal, Capital, September 30	$16,050

SOFTBYTE
Balance Sheet
September 30, 1993

Assets	
Cash	$ 8,050
Accounts receivable	1,400
Supplies	1,200
Equipment	7,000
Total assets	$17,650

Liabilities and Owner's Equity	
Liabilities	
Accounts payable	$ 1,600
Owner's Equity	
R. Neal, Capital	16,050
Total liabilities and owner's equity	$17,650

Owner's Equity Statement

Data for the preparation of the owner's equity statement are obtained from the owner's equity column of the tabular summary (Illustration 1-8) and from the income statement. The heading of this statement identifies the company, the type of statement, and the time period covered by the statement. The time period is the same as that covered by the income statement and therefore is dated "For the Month Ended September 30, 1993." The beginning capital amount is shown on the first line of the statement. Then, the owner's additional investments, net income, and the owner's drawings are identified in the statement. The owner's ending capital amount is the final amount on the statement. The information provided by this statement indicates the reasons why owner's equity has increased or decreased during the period.

To illustrate the presentation in the owner's equity statement of an owner's additional investment, assume that during the month of September 1993, R. Neal invested an additional $5,000 in Softbyte. The presentation appears in Illustration 1-10.

ILLUSTRATION 1-10

Presentation of additional investment

SOFTBYTE		
Owner's Equity Statement		
For the Month Ended September 30, 1993		
R. Neal, Capital, September 1		$15,000
Add: Additional investment	$5,000	
Net income	2,350	7,350
		22,350
Less: Drawings		1,300
R. Neal, Capital, September 30		$21,050

If there is a net loss, it is deducted with drawings in the owner's equity statement.

Balance Sheet

The balance sheet for Softbyte is prepared from the column headings and the month-end data shown in the last line of the tabular summary (Illustration 1-8). The heading of a balance sheet must identify the company, the statement, and the date. To indicate that the balance sheet is at a specific date, it is dated "September 30, 1993." Observe that the assets are listed at the top, followed by liabilities and owner's equity. Total assets must equal total liabilities and owner's equity. In the Softbyte illustration, only one liability, accounts payable, is reported on the balance sheet. In most cases, there will be more than one liability. When two or more liabilities are involved, a customary way of listing is as follows:

ILLUSTRATION 1-11

Presentation of liabilities

Liabilities	
Notes payable	$10,000
Accounts payable	63,000
Salaries payable	18,000
Total liabilities	$91,000

The balance sheet is like a snapshot of the company's financial condition at a specific moment in time (usually the month-end or year-end). It is frequently called the statement of financial position.

Before You Go On . . .

1. What is the basic accounting equation?

2. What are assets, liabilities, and owner's equity? Give some examples.

3. What are the balance sheet, income statement, and statement of owner's equity?

Summary of Study Objectives

1. *Explain the meaning of accounting.* Accounting is the process of identifying, measuring, recording, and communicating the economic events of an organization (business or nonbusiness) to interested users of the information.

2. *Identify the users and uses of accounting.* The major users and uses of accounting are: (a) Management uses accounting information in planning, controlling, and evaluating business operations. (b) Investors (owners) judge the wisdom of buying, holding, or selling their financial interests on the basis of accounting data. (c) Creditors (suppliers and bankers) evaluate the risks of granting credit or lending money to particular businesses on the basis of the accounting information obtained about those businesses. Other groups with an indirect interest are taxing authorities, regulatory agencies, customers, labor unions, and economic planners.

3. *Know the major career paths of accountants.* The major career paths in accounting are public accounting, private accounting, and not-for-profit accounting.

4. *Explain the meaning of generally accepted accounting principles and the cost principle.* Generally accepted accounting principles are a common set of standards used by accountants. One important principle is the cost principle, which states that assets should be recorded at their cost.

5. *Explain the meaning of the economic entity assumption and the monetary unit assumption.* The economic entity assumption states that economic events can be identified with a particular unit of accountability. The monetary unit assumption requires that only transaction data capable of being expressed in terms of money be included in the accounting records of the economic entity.

6. *State the basic accounting equation and explain the meaning of assets, liabilities, and owner's equity.* The basic accounting equation is:

Assets = Liabilities + Owner's Equity

Assets are resources owned by a business. Liabilities are creditorship claims on total assets. Owner's equity is the ownership claim on total assets. It is often referred to as residual equity.

7. *Analyze the effect of business transactions on the basic accounting equation.* Each business transaction must have a dual effect on the accounting equation. For example, if an individual asset is increased, there must be a corresponding (1) decrease in another asset, or (2) increase in a specific liability, or (3) increase in owner's equity.

8. *Prepare an income statement, owner's equity statement, and balance sheet.* An income statement presents the revenues and expenses of a company for a specified period of time. An owner's equity statement summarizes the changes in owner's equity that have occurred during a given period of time. A balance sheet reports the assets, liabilities, and owner's equity of a business at a specific date.

GLOSSARY

Accounting · The process of identifying, measuring, recording, and communicating the economic events of an organization to interested users of the information. (p. 2).

Assets · Resources owned by a business. (p. 16).

Auditing · The examination of financial statements by a certified public accountant in order to express an opinion on their fairness. (p. 7).

Balance sheet · A financial statement that reports the assets, liabilities, and owner's equity at a specific date. (p. 24).

Basic accounting equation · Assets = Liabilities + Owner's equity. (p. 16).

Bookkeeping · A part of accounting that involves only the recording of economic events (p. 6).

Capital · Owner's investment in the business. (p. 17).

Corporation · A business organized as a separate legal entity under state corporation law having ownership divided into transferable shares of stock. (p. 14).

Cost principle · An accounting principle that states that assets should be recorded at their cost. (p. 13).

Drawings · Withdrawal of cash or other assets from an unincorporated business for the personal use of the owner(s). (p. 17).

Economic entity assumption · An assumption that economic events can be identified with a particular unit of accountability. (p. 13).

Expenses · The cost of assets consumed or services used in the process of earning revenue. (p. 17).

Financial Accounting Standards Board (FASB) · A private organization that establishes generally accepted accounting principles. (p. 13).

Generally accepted accounting principles (GAAP) · A common set of standards that indicate how to report economic events. (p. 12).

Income statement · A financial statement that presents the revenues and expenses and resulting net income or net loss of a company for a specific period of time. (p. 24).

Liabilities · Creditorship claims on total assets. (p. 16).

Management consulting · An area of public accounting involving financial planning and control and the development of accounting and computer systems. (p. 8).

Monetary unit assumption · An assumption stating that only transaction data that can be expressed in terms of money be included in the accounting records of the economic entity. (p. 15).

Net income · The excess of revenues over expenses. (p. 17).

Net loss · The excess of expenses over revenues. (p. 17).

Operating statement · Another name for the income statement. (p. 24).

Owner's equity · The ownership claim on total assets. (p. 16).

Owner's equity statement · A financial statement that summarizes the changes in owner's equity for a specific period of time. (p. 24).

Partnership · An association of two or more persons to carry on as co-owners of a business for profit. (p. 14).

Private (or managerial) accounting · An area of accounting within a company that involves such activities as cost accounting, budgeting, and accounting information systems. (p. 8).

Proprietorship · A business owned by one person. (p. 14).

Public accounting · An area of accounting in which the accountant offers expert service to the general public. (p. 6).

Revenues · The gross increase in owner's equity resulting from business activities entered into for the purpose of earning income. (p. 17).

Securities and Exchange Commission (SEC) · A governmental agency that requires companies to file financial reports in accordance with generally accepted accounting principles. (p. 13).

Statement of cash flows · A financial statement that provides information about the cash inflows (receipts) and cash outflows (payments) of an entity during a period. (p. 24).

Statement of financial position · Another name for the balance sheet. (p. 26).

Taxation · An area of public accounting involving tax advice, tax planning, and preparing tax returns. (p. 8).

Transactions · The economic events of the enterprise recorded by accountants. (p. 18).

DEMONSTRATION PROBLEM

Mary Malone opens her own law office on July 1, 1993. During the first month of operations, the following transactions occurred:

1. Invested $10,000 in cash in the law practice.
2. Paid $800 for July rent on office space.
3. Purchased office equipment on account, $3,000.
4. Rendered legal services to clients for cash, $1,500. (use Fees Earned)
5. Borrowed $700 cash from a bank on a note payable.
6. Rendered legal services to client on account, $2,000.
7. Paid monthly expenses: salaries, $500; utilities, $300; and telephone, $100.

Instructions
(a) Prepare a tabular summary of the transactions.
(b) Prepare the financial statements at July 31 for Mary Malone, Attorney at Law.

Solution to Demonstration Problem

(a)

Trans-action	Cash	+	Accounts Receivable	+	Equipment	=	Notes Payable	+	Accounts Payable	+	Mary Malone, Capital	
(1)	+$10,000										+$10,000	Investment
(2)	−800										−800	Rent Expense
	9,200					=					9,200	
(3)					+$3,000				+$3,000			
	9,200	+			3,000	=			3,000	+	9,200	
(4)	+1,500										+1,500	Fees Earned
	10,700	+			3,000	=			3,000	+	10,700	
(5)	+700						+$700					
	11,400	+			3,000	=	700	+	3,000	+	10,700	
(6)			+$2,000								+2,000	Fees Earned
	11,400 +		2,000	+	3,000	=	700	+	3,000	+	12,700	
(7)	−900										−500	Salaries Expense
											−300	Utilities Expense
											−100	Telephone Expense
	$10,500 +		$2,000	+	$3,000	=	$700	+	$3,000	+	$11,800	

(b)

MARY MALONE
Attorney at Law
Income Statement
For the Month Ended July 31, 1993

Revenues		
Fees earned		$3,500
Expenses		
Rent expense	$800	
Salaries expense	500	
Utilities expense	300	
Telephone expense	100	
Total expenses		1,700
Net income		$1,800

Helpful hints
1. Remember that assets must equal liabilities and owner's equity after each transaction.
2. Investments and revenues increase owner's equity.
3. Withdrawals and expenses decrease owner's equity.
4. The income statement shows revenues and expenses for a period of time.
5. The owner's equity statement shows the changes in owner's equity for a period of time.
6. The balance sheet reports assets, liabilities, and owner's equity at a specific date.

MARY MALONE
Attorney at Law
Owner's Equity Statement
For the Month Ended July 31, 1993

Mary Malone, Capital, July 1	$10,000
Add: Net income	1,800
Mary Malone, Capital, July 31	$11,800

MARY MALONE
Attorney at Law
Balance Sheet
July 31, 1993

· Assets

Cash	$10,500
Accounts receivable	2,000
Equipment	3,000
Total assets	$15,500

Liabilities and Owner's Equity

Liabilities	
Notes payable	$ 700
Accounts payable	3,000
Total liabilities	3,700
Owner's Equity	
Mary Malone, Capital	11,800
Total liabilities and owner's equity	$15,500

SELF-STUDY QUESTIONS

Answers are at the end of the chapter.

(S.O. 1)   1. The accounting process does *not* include:
  a. identification
  b. verification
  c. recording
  d. communication

(S.O. 2)   2. One of the following statements about users of accounting information is *incorrect*. The incorrect statement is:
  a. Management is considered an internal user.
  b. Taxing authorities are considered external users.
  c. Present creditors are considered external users.
  d. Regulatory authorities are considered internal users.

(S.O. 3)   3. The public accountant generally provides the following services:
  a. auditing, taxation, and management consulting.
  b. auditing, budgeting, and management consulting.
  c. auditing, budgeting, and cost accounting.
  d. internal auditing, budgeting, and management consulting.

4. The cost principle states that: (S.O. 4)
  a. assets should be recorded at cost and adjusted when the market value changes.
  b. activities of an entity be kept separate and distinct from its owner.
  c. assets should be recorded at their cost.
  d. only transaction data capable of being expressed in terms of money be included in the accounting records.

5. Which of the following statements about   (S.O. 5) basic assumptions is *incorrect*?
  a. Basic assumptions are the same as accounting principles.
  b. The economic entity assumption states that there should be a particular unit of accountability.
  c. The monetary unit assumption enables accounting to measure economic events.

d. An important corollary to the monetary unit assumption is the stable monetary unit assumption.

(S.O. 6) 6. Net income will result during a time period when:
   a. assets exceed liabilities.
   b. assets exceed revenues.
   c. expenses exceed revenues.
   d. revenues exceed expenses.

(S.O. 7) 7. The effects on the basic accounting equation of performing services on account are:
   a. increase assets and decrease owner's equity.
   b. increase assets and increase owner's equity.
   c. increase assets and increase liabilities.
   d. increase liabilities and increase owner's equity.

(S.O..7) 8. As of December 31, 1993, Stoneland Company has assets of $3,500 and owner's equity of $2,000. What are the liabilities for Stoneland Company as of December 31, 1993?
   a. $1,500.
   b. $1,000.
   c. $2,500.
   d. $2,000.

9. Genesis Company buys a $900 machine on credit. This transaction will affect the: (S.O. 8)
   a. income statement only.
   b. balance sheet only.
   c. income statement and owner's equity statement only.
   d. income statement, owner's equity statement, and balance sheet.

10. The financial statement that reports assets, liabilities, and owner's equity is the: (S.O. 8)
   a. income statement.
   b. owner's equity statement.
   c. balance sheet.
   d. cash flow statement.

QUESTIONS

1. Two students are discussing the possibility of entering business school. One student remarked that she had heard that the accounting field has grown substantially. Is she right? Discuss.

2. Describe the steps in the accounting process.

3. Two broad sets of users need accounting information. Identify these two sets of users and give examples of each.

4. Which is a broader term, bookkeeping or accounting? Explain.

5. Distinguish among public, private, and not-for-profit accounting.

6. Treadway Travel Agency purchased land for $25,000 on December 10, 1993. At December 31, 1993, the land's value has increased to $33,000. What amount should be reported for land on Treadway's balance sheet at December 31, 1993? Explain.

7. What is the economic entity assumption?

8. What are the three basic forms of business organizations for profit-oriented enterprises?

9. Martha Rose is the owner of a successful printing shop. Recently her business has been increasing, and Martha has been thinking about changing the organization of her business from a proprietorship to a corporation. Discuss some of the advantages Martha would enjoy if she were to incorporate her business.

10. What is the monetary unit assumption? What impact does inflation have on the monetary unit assumption?

11. What is the basic accounting equation?

12. Define the terms assets, liabilities, and owner's equity. What are the subdivisions of owner's equity?

13. Which of the following items are liabilities of Kool-Jewelry Stores?
(a) Cash.   (d) Accounts receivable.   (g) Salaries payable.
(b) Drawings.   (e) Supplies.   (h) Service revenue.
(c) Accounts payable.   (f) Equipment.   (i) Rent expense.

14. Can a business enter into a transaction in which only the left side of the basic accounting equation is affected? If so, give an example.

15. Are the following events recorded in the accounting records? Explain your answer in each case.
(a) Supplies are purchased on account.
(b) The owner of the company dies.
(c) An employee is fired.
(d) The owner of the business withdraws cash from the business for personal use.

16. Listed below are some items found in the financial statements of Ruth Weber, M.D. Indicate in which financial statement(s) the following items would appear.
(a) Advertising expense.   (d) Cash.
(b) Equipment.   (e) Ruth Weber, Capital.
(c) Service revenue.   (f) Wages payable.

17. In February of 1993, Paul Jones invested an additional $5,000 in his business, Jones's Pharmacy, which is organized as a proprietorship. Jones's accountant, Donna Wortham, recorded this receipt as an increase in cash and revenues. Is this treatment appropriate? Why or why not?

18. A company's net income appears directly on the income statement and the owner's equity statement, and it is included indirectly in the company's balance sheet. Do you agree? Explain.

19. Hernandez Enterprises had a capital balance of $138,000 at the beginning of the period. At the end of the accounting period, the capital balance was $198,000.
(a) Assuming no additional investment or withdrawals during the period, what is the net income for the period?
(b) Assuming an additional investment of $13,000 but no withdrawals during the period, what is the net income for the period?

20. Indicate how the following business transactions affect the basic accounting equation.
(a) Paid cash for janitorial services.   (c) Invested cash in the business.
(b) Purchased equipment for cash.   (d) Paid an accounts payable in full.

21. Summarized operations for the Cora L. King Co. for the month of July are as follows:

Revenues earned: for cash $45,000; on account $80,000.

Expenses incurred: for cash $26,000; on account $40,000.

Indicate for Cora L. King Co. (a) the total revenues, (b) the total expenses, and (c) net income for the month of July.

BRIEF EXERCISES

Basic accounting equation.
(S.O. 6)

BE1–1 Presented below is the basic accounting equation. Determine the missing amounts:

	Assets	=	Liabilities	+	Owner's Equity
(a)	$90,000		$60,000		?
(b)	?		$48,000		$70,000
(c)	$94,000		?		$72,000

Basic accounting equation.
(S.O. 6)

BE1–2 Given the accounting equation, answer each of the following questions:

1. The liabilities of Logan Company are $90,000 and the owner's equity is $260,000. What is the amount of Logan Company's total assets?

2. The total assets of Potter Company are $170,000 and its owner's equity is $90,000. What is the amount of its total liabilities?

3. The total assets of Warren Co. are $700,000 and its liabilities are equal to one half of its total assets. What is the amount of Warren Co.'s owner's equity?

BE1–3 At the beginning of the year, Samson Company had total assets of $700,000 and total liabilities of $500,000. Answer the following questions:

1. If total assets increased $150,000 during the year and total liabilities decreased $80,000, what is the amount of owner's equity at the end of the year?

2. During the year, total liabilities increased $100,000 and owner's equity decreased $70,000. What is the amount of total assets at the end of the year?

3. If total assets decreased $90,000 and owner's equity increased $120,000 during the year, what is the amount of total liabilities at the end of the year?

BE1–4 Presented below are three business transactions. On a sheet of paper, list the letters a, b, c with columns for assets, liabilities, and owner's equity. For each column, indicate whether the transactions increased (+), decreased (−) or had no effect (NE) on assets, liabilities, and owner's equity:

(a) Expenses paid in cash.

(b) Received cash for providing a service.

(c) Purchased supplies on account.

BE1–5 Follow the same format as BE1-4 above. Determine the effect on assets, liabilities, and owner's equity of the following three transactions:

(a) Invested cash in the business.

(b) Received cash from a customer who had previously been billed for services provided.

(c) Withdrawal of cash by owner.

BE1–6 Classify each of the following items as owner's capital (C), owner's drawing (D), revenue (R), or expense (E).

____ Advertising expense	____ T. Quick, Capital
____ Commission revenue	____ T. Quick, Drawing
____ Insurance expense	____ Rent expense
____ Salaries expense	____ Utilities expense

BE1–7 Presented below are three transactions. Mark each transaction as affecting owner's investment (I), owner's drawings (D), revenue (R), expense (E), or not affecting owner's equity (NOE):

____ Received cash for services performed

____ Paid cash to purchase equipment

____ Paid accounts payable

BE1–8 In alphabetical order below are balance sheet items for Widget Company at December 31, 1993. Sally Fried is the owner of Widget Company. Prepare a balance sheet, following the format of Illustration 1-9.

Accounts payable	$90,000
Accounts receivable	$80,000
Cash	$41,500
Sally Fried, Capital	$31,500

BE1–9 Indicate whether each of the following items is an asset (A), liability (L), or part of owner's equity (OE).

____ Cash	____ Office supplies
____ Salaries payable	____ B. Jones, Capital
____ Equipment	____ Notes payable

BE1–10 Indicate whether the following items would appear on the income statement (IS), balance sheet (BS), or owner's equity statement (OE).

____ Notes payable	____ Cash
____ Advertising expense	____ Accounts receivable
____ R. Harrison, Capital	

EXERCISES

Classify accounts as assets, liabilities, and owner's equity.
(S.O. 6)

E1–1   The Star Cleaners has the following balance sheet items:

Accounts payable	Accounts receivable
Cash	Notes payable
Cleaning equipment	Salaries payable
Cleaning supplies	H. Star, Capital

Instructions
Classify each item as an asset, liability, or owner's equity.

Analyze the effect of transactions.
(S.O. 6, 7)

E1–2   Selected transactions for Dale's Lawn Care Company are listed below:

1. Made cash investment to start business.
2. Paid monthly rent.
3. Purchased equipment on account.
4. Billed customers for services performed.
5. Withdrew cash for owner's personal use.
6. Received cash from customers billed in (4).
7. Incurred utilities expenses on account.
8. Purchased additional equipment for cash.
9. Received cash from customers when service was rendered.

Instructions
List the numbers of the above transactions and describe the effect of each transaction on assets, liabilities, and owner's equity. For example, the first answer is: (1) Increase in assets and increase in owner's equity.

Analyze the effect of transactions on assets, liabilities, and owner's equity.
(S.O. 6, 7)

E1–3   Wilcox Computer Timeshare Company entered into the following transactions during May 1993.

1. Paid $4,000 cash for May rent on storage space.
2. Purchased computer terminals for $19,000 from Digital Equipment on account.
3. Received $15,000 cash from customers for contracts billed in April.
4. Provided computer services to Brieske Construction Company for $3,000 cash.
5. Paid Southern States Power Co. $11,000 cash for energy usage in May.
6. T. Wilcox invested an additional $32,000 in the business.
7. Paid Digital Equipment for the terminals purchased in (2) above.
8. Incurred advertising expense for May of $1,000 on account.

Instructions
Indicate with the appropriate letter whether each of the transactions above results in:

(a) an increase in assets and a decrease in assets.
(b) an increase in assets and an increase in owner's equity.
(c) an increase in assets and an increase in liabilities.
(d) a decrease in assets and a decrease in owner's equity.
(e) a decrease in assets and a decrease in liabilities.
(f) an increase in liabilities and a decrease in owner's equity.
(g) an increase in owner's equity and a decrease in liabilities.

Analyze transactions and compute net income.
(S.O. 7)

E1–4   A tabular analysis of the transactions made by Roberto Mendez & Co., a certified public accounting firm, for the month of August is shown below. Each increase and decrease in capital is explained.

	Cash	+	Accounts Receivable	+	Supplies	+	Office Equipment	=	Accounts Payable	+	R. Mendez Capital	
1.	+$15,000										+$15,000	Investment
2.	− 750				+$750							
3.	−2,000						+$5,000		+$3,000			

	Cash +	Accounts Receivable +	Supplies +	Office Equipment =	Accounts Payable +	R. Mendez Capital	
4.	+4,600	+3,400				+8,000	Fees Earned
5.	−1,500				−1,500		
6.	−1,000					−1,000	Drawings
7.	− 650					− 650	Rent Expense
8.	+ 450	−450					
9.	−2,900					−2,900	Salaries Expense
10.					+ 500	− 500	Utilities Expense

Instructions

(a) Describe each transaction that occurred for the month.

(b) Determine how much capital increased for the month.

(c) Compute the amount of net income for the month.

E1–5 The tabular analysis of transactions for Roberto Mendez & Co. is presented in E1–4.

Prepare an income statement and owner's equity statement.
(S.O. 8)

Instructions

Prepare an income statement and an owner's equity statement for August and a balance sheet at August 31, 1993.

E1–6 The Hilga Company had the following assets and liabilities on the dates indicated:

Determine net income (or loss).
(S.O. 7)

December 31	Total Assets	Total Liabilities
1993	$380,000	$250,000
1994	$460,000	$310,000
1995	$590,000	$400,000

Hilga began business on January 1, 1993, with a capital investment of $100,000.

Instructions

From an analysis of the change in owner's equity during the year, compute the net income (or loss) for:

(a) 1993, assuming Hilga's drawings were $25,000 for the year.

(b) 1994, assuming Hilga made an additional investment of $50,000 and had no drawings in 1994.

(c) 1995, assuming Hilga made an additional investment of $10,000 and had drawings of $20,000 in 1995.

E1–7 Two items are omitted from each of the following summaries of balance sheet and income statement data for two proprietorships for the year 1993, Kate Nelson, CPA, and Mystery Enterprises.

Analyze financial statements items.
(S.O. 6, 7)

	Kate Nelson, CPA	Mystery Enterprises
Beginning of year:		
Total assets	$ 90,000	$130,000
Total liabilities	80,000	(c)
Total owner's equity	(a)	95,000
End of year:		
Total assets	160,000	180,000
Total liabilities	120,000	50,000
Total owner's equity	40,000	130,000
Changes during year in owner's equity:		
Additional investment	(b)	25,000
Drawings	22,000	(d)
Total revenues	215,000	100,000
Total expenses	165,000	80,000

Instructions

Determine the missing amounts.

Prepare income statement and owner's equity statement.
(S.O. 8)

E1–8 The following information relates to Tone Loc Co. for the year 1993.

Tone Loc, Capital, January 1, 1993	$45,000	Advertising expense	1,600
Tone Loc, Drawing, during 1993	5,000	Rent expense	8,000
Fees earned	50,000	Supplies expense	2,600
Salaries expense	28,000	Utilities expense	3,100

Instructions
After analyzing the data, prepare an income statement and an owner's equity statement for the year ending December 31, 1993.

Correct an incorrectly prepared balance sheet.
(S.O. 8)

E1–9 Karen Lucas is the bookkeeper for Starr Company. Karen has been trying to get the balance sheet of Starr Company to balance. Starr's balance sheet is as follows:

STARR COMPANY
Balance Sheet
December 31, 1993

Assets		Liabilities	
Cash	$16,500	Accounts payable	$18,000
Supplies	8,000	Accounts receivable	(10,000)
Equipment	46,000	Starr, Capital	69,500
Starr, Drawing	7,000	Total liabilities and	
Total assets	$77,500	owner's equity	$77,500

Instructions
Prepare a correct balance sheet.

Compute net income and prepare a balance sheet.
(S.O. 8)

E1–10 Rick Smead is the sole owner of Safari Park, a public camping ground near the Lake Mead National Recreation Area. Rick has compiled the following financial information as of December 31, 1993.

Revenues during 1993—camping fees	$147,000	Market value of equipment	140,000
Revenues during 1993—general store	40,000	Notes payable	60,000
Accounts payable	11,000	Expenses during 1993	152,000
Cash on hand	7,000	Supplies on hand	2,500
Original cost of equipment	115,500		

Instructions
(a) Determine Rick Smead's net income from Safari Park for 1993.

(b) Prepare a balance sheet for Safari Park as of December 31, 1993.

Prepare an income statement.
(S.O. 8)

E1–11 Presented below is financial information related to the 1993 operations of the Sanibel Cruise Company.

Boat rental expense	$ 90,000
Property tax expense (on dock facilities)	10,000
Salaries expense	142,000
Advertising expense	3,500
Ticket revenue	325,000

Instructions
Prepare the 1993 income statement for the Sanibel Cruise Company.

Prepare an owner's equity statement.
(S.O. 8)

E1–12 Presented below is information related to the single proprietorship of Grace Van Owen, attorney.

Legal fees earned—1993	$380,000
Total expenses—1993	205,000
Assets, January 1, 1993	85,000
Liabilities, January 1, 1993	62,000
Assets, December 31, 1993	92,000
Liabilities, December 31, 1993	70,000
Drawings—1993	?

Instructions
Prepare the 1993 owner's equity statement for Grace Van Owen's legal practice.

PROBLEMS

P1-1 On April 1, Laura Izon established the Izon Travel Agency. The following transactions were completed during the month:

Analyze transactions and compute net income.
(S.O. 6, 7)

1. Invested $20,000 cash in Corner State Bank in the name of the agency.
2. Paid $400 cash for April office rent.
3. Purchased office equipment for $2,500 cash.
4. Incurred $300 of advertising costs in the Chicago Tribune, on account.
5. Paid $600 cash for office supplies.
6. Earned $9,000 for services rendered: Cash of $1,000 is received from customers, and the balance of $8,000 is billed to customers on account.
7. Withdrew $200 cash for personal use by Izon.
8. Paid Chicago Tribune amount due in transaction (4).
9. Paid employees' salaries, $1,200.
10. A count of supplies indicates that $450 of supplies have been used.
11. Cash of $8,000 is received from customers who have previously been billed in transaction (6).

Instructions

(a) Prepare a tabular analysis of the transactions using the following column headings: Cash, Accounts Receivable, Supplies, Office Equipment, Accounts Payable, and Laura Izon, Capital.

(b) From an analysis of the column, Laura Izon, Capital, compute the net income or net loss for April.

P1-2 Ivan Pagan opened a law office, Ivan Pagan, Attorney at Law, on July 1, 1993. On July 31, the balance sheet showed Cash $4,000, Accounts Receivable $1,500, Supplies $500, Office Equipment $5,000, Accounts Payable $4,200, and Ivan Pagan, Capital, $6,800. During August the following transactions occurred:

Analyze transactions and prepare income statement and owner's equity statement.
(S.O. 6, 7, 8)

1. Collected $1,400 of accounts receivable.
2. Paid $2,700 cash on accounts payable.
3. Earned fees of $6,400, of which $3,000 is collected in cash and the balance is due in September.
4. Purchased additional office equipment for $1,000, paying $400 in cash and the balance on account.
5. Paid salaries $1,500, rent for August $900, and advertising expenses $350.
6. Used $300 of supplies in August.
7. Withdrew $550 in cash for personal use.
8. Received $1,000 from Standard Federal Bank—money borrowed on a note payable.
9. Incurred utility expenses for month on account, $250.

Instructions

(a) Prepare a tabular analysis of the August transactions beginning with July 31 balances. The column heading should be as follows: Cash + Accounts Receivable + Supplies + Office Equipment = Notes Payable + Accounts Payable + Ivan Pagan, Capital.

(b) Prepare an income statement for August, an owner's equity statement for August, and a balance sheet at August 31.

P1-3 On June 1, Clarice Thiessen started Natural Cosmetics Co., a company that provides individual skin care treatment to clients at their residence, by investing $26,200 cash in the business. Following are the assets and liabilities of the company at June 30 and the revenues and expenses for the month of June.

Prepare income statement, owner's equity statement, and balance sheet.
(S.O. 8)

Cash	$12,000	Notes Payable	$13,000
Accounts Receivable	3,000	Accounts Payable	1,200
Fees Earned	6,500	Supplies Expense	1,200
Cosmetic Supplies on Hand	2,400	Gas and Oil Expense	800
Advertising Expense	500	Utilities Expense	300
Equipment	25,000		

Clarice made no additional investment in June, but withdrew $1,700 in cash for personal use during the month.

Instructions

(a) Prepare an income statement and owner's equity statement for the month of June and a balance sheet at June 30, 1993.

(b) Prepare an income statement and owner's equity statement for June assuming cosmetic supplies on hand at June 30 were $8,000 and a total of $4,600 of supplies were used.

Prepare income statement and owner's equity statement.
(S.O. 8)

P1–4   Michael Foland organized the Foland Consulting Co. on March 1, 1993. The owner's equity column of the tabular summary for the month of March contained the following recorded data:

Transaction	Amount	Description
(1)	$15,000	Investment
(4)	750	Rent expense
(6)	3,250	Fees earned
(8)	400	Advertising expense
(11)	1,000	Salaries expense
(12)	2,100	Fees earned
(15)	250	Utilities expense
(18)	500	Drawings
(20)	3,200	Fees earned
(22)	200	Repair expense
(24)	1,000	Advertising expense
(27)	250	Drawings
(29)	1,100	Fees earned
(32)	900	Salaries expense
(34)	200	Supplies expense
(36)	150	Utilities expense

All data were properly recorded except the following:

In transaction (22), $150 of the repair expense was applicable to Michael Foland's personal residence.

In transaction (36), $80 was applicable to repairs on business property.

Instructions

(a) Prepare an income statement for the month of March.

(b) Prepare an owner's equity statement for March.

Determine financial statement amounts and prepare owner's equity statements.
(S.O. 7, 8)

P1–5   Financial statement information about four different companies is as follows:

	Sanchez Company	Roberts Company	Stein Company	Walker Company
January 1, 1993:				
Assets	$ 80,000	$100,000	(g)	$150,000
Liabilities	50,000	(d)	75,000	(j)
Owner's equity	(a)	60,000	45,000	90,000
December 31, 1993:				
Assets	(b)	130,000	180,000	(k)
Liabilities	55,000	62,000	(h)	80,000
Owner's equity	45,000	(e)	110,000	145,000
Owner's equity changes in year:				
Additional investment	(c)	8,000	10,000	15,000
Drawings	15,000	(f)	12,000	10,000
Total revenues	350,000	400,000	(i)	500,000
Total expenses	330,000	385,000	360,000	(l)

Instructions

(a) Determine the missing amounts.

(b) Prepare the owner's equity statement for Sanchez Company.

(c) Explain the sequence for preparing financial statements and the interrelationship of the owner's equity statement to the income statement and balance sheet.

ALTERNATE PROBLEMS

P1–1A Bob's Repair Shop was started on May 1 by Robert Haar. A summary of May transactions is presented below.

Analyze transactions and compute net income.
(S.O. 6, 7)

1. Invested $15,000 cash in the Fox Valley Bank in the name of the business.
2. Purchased equipment for $5,000 cash.
3. Paid $400 cash for May office rent.
4. Paid $500 cash for barber supplies.
5. Incurred $250 of advertising costs in the Beacon News on account.
6. Received $4,100 in cash from customers for repair service.
7. Withdrew $500 for personal use by Haar.
8. Used $150 of supplies.
9. Paid part-time employee salaries $1,000.
10. Paid utility bills $140.
11. Provided repair service on account to customers, $200.
12. Collected cash of $150 for services billed in transaction (11).

Instructions

(a) Prepare a tabular analysis of the transactions, using the following column headings: Cash, Accounts Receivable, Supplies, Equipment, Accounts Payable, and Robert Haar, Capital. Revenue is called service revenue.

(b) From an analysis of the column, Robert Haar, Capital, compute the net income or net loss for May.

P1–2A Donna Cook opened a veterinary business in Hills, Iowa, on August 1. On August 31, the balance sheet showed Cash $9,000, Accounts Receivable $1,700, Supplies $600, Office Equipment $6,000, Accounts Payable $3,600, and D. Cook, Capital, $13,700. During September the following transactions occurred:

Analyze transactions and prepare income statement and owner's equity statement.
(S.O. 6, 7, 8)

1. Paid $3,100 cash on accounts payable.
2. Collected $1,300 of accounts receivable.
3. Purchased additional office equipment for $2,100, paying $800 in cash and the balance on account.
4. Earned fees of $5,900, of which $2,500 is paid in cash and the balance is due in October.
5. Used $350 of supplies in September.
6. Withdrew $600 for personal use.
7. Paid salaries $700, rent for September $900, and advertising expense $100.
8. Incurred utility expenses for month on account, $170.
9. Received $8,000 from Hilldale Bank—money borrowed on a note payable.

Instructions

(a) Prepare a tabular analysis of the September transactions beginning with August 31 balances. The column headings should be as follows: Cash + Accounts Receivable + Supplies + Office Equipment = Notes Payable + Accounts Payable + Donna Cook, Capital.

(b) Prepare an income statement for September, an owner's equity statement for September, and a balance sheet at September 30.

Prepare income statement, owner's equity statement, and balance sheet.
(S.O. 8)

P1–3A On May 1, Steve Hubert started Skyline Flying School, a company that provides flying lessons to would-be pilots, by investing $45,000 cash in the business. Following are the assets and liabilities of the company on May 31, 1993, and the revenues and expenses for the month of May.

Cash	$ 8,000	Notes Payable	$30,000
Accounts Receivable	7,000	Rent Expense	1,200
Equipment	64,000	Repair Expense	400
Fees Earned	9,600	Fuel Expense	2,200
Advertising Expense	500	Insurance Expense	400
		Accounts Payable	800

Steve Hubert made no additional investment in May, but he withdrew $1,700 in cash for personal use.

Instructions

(a) Prepare an income statement and owner's equity statement for the month of May and a balance sheet at May 31.

(b) Prepare an income statement and owner's equity statement for May assuming the following data are not included above: (1) $800 of fees were earned and billed but not collected at May 31, and (2) $5,300 of fuel expense was incurred but not paid.

Prepare income statement and owner's equity statement.
(S.O. 8)

P1–4A   Presented below are the November 1993 transactions that affected the owner's equity account of the P. Swender Co.

Transaction	Amount	Description
(7)	$ 700	Property tax expense
(9)	6,000	Service revenue
(10)	350	Supplies expense
(13)	4,000	Wage expense
(16)	300	Utilities expense
(18)	1,250	Rent expense
(19)	450	Advertising expense
(22)	2,000	Service revenue
(23)	800	Drawing, P. Swender
(25)	600	Repair expense
(27)	400	Auto expense
(31)	9,000	Service revenue
(32)	1,800	Drawing, P. Swender
(33)	4,000	Wage expense
(34)	500	Utilities expense

In reviewing the account, Mr. Swender realized that his new bookkeeper had made the following errors:

Transaction (23) was actually a drawing of $1,000 by P. Swender.

Transaction (27) was a disbursement for work on P. Swender's family car.

Instructions

(a) Prepare an income statement for the month of November.

(b) Prepare a statement of owner's equity for November, assuming that P. Swender's beginning equity balance was $9,500 on November 1.

Determine financial statement amounts and prepare owner's equity statements.
(S.O. 7, 8)

P1–5A   Financial statement information about four different companies is as follows:

	Ashe Company	Salizar Company	Danforth Company	Johnson Company
January 1, 1993:				
Assets	$ 90,000	$110,000	(g)	$160,000
Liabilities	50,000	(d)	75,000	(j)
Owner's equity	(a)	60,000	55,000	90,000
December 31, 1993:				
Assets	(b)	150,000	200,000	(k)
Liabilities	55,000	65,000	(h)	80,000
Owner's equity	58,000	(e)	130,000	170,000

	Ashe Company	Salizar Company	Danforth Company	Johnson Company
Owner's equity changes in year:				
Additional investment	(c)	15,000	10,000	15,000
Drawings	25,000	(f)	14,000	20,000
Total revenues	350,000	420,000	(i)	520,000
Total expenses	320,000	385,000	350,000	(l)

Instructions

(a) Determine the missing amounts.

(b) Prepare the owner's equity statement for Salizar Company.

(c) Explain the sequence for preparing financial statements and the interrelationship of the owner's equity statement to the income statement and balance sheet.

Broadening Your Perspective

FINANCIAL REPORTING PROBLEM

The actual financial statements of PepsiCo, Inc., as presented in the company's 1991 Annual Report, are contained in Appendix L (at the back of the textbook). Refer to PepsiCo's financial statements and answer the following questions:

1. What were PepsiCo's total assets at December 28, 1991? At December 29, 1990?

2. How much cash (and cash equivalents) did PepsiCo have on December 28, 1991?

3. What amount of accounts payable did PepsiCo report on December 28, 1991? On December 29, 1990?

4. What were PepsiCo's net sales in 1989? In 1990? In 1991?

5. What is the amount of the change in PepsiCo's net income from 1990 to 1991?

6. The accounting equation is: Assets = Liabilities + Owner's Equity. Replacing the words in that equation with dollar amounts, what is PepsiCo's accounting equation at December 28, 1991? (Hint: Owner's equity is equivalent to shareholders' equity.)

DECISION CASE

Betsy and Bill King, local golf stars, opened the Parbuster Driving Range on March 1, 1993, by investing $10,000 of their cash savings in the business. A caddy shack was constructed for cash at a cost of $4,000 and $800 was spent on golf balls and golf clubs. The Kings leased five acres of land at a cost of $1,000 per month and paid the first month's rent. During the first month, advertising costs totaled $750 of which $150 was unpaid at March 31, and $400 was paid to members of the high school golf team for retrieving golf balls. All fees from customers were deposited in the company's bank account. On March 15, Betsy and Bill withdrew a total of $700 in cash for personal living expenses. A $100 utility bill was received on March 31 but it was not paid. On March 31, the balance in the company's bank account was $8,650.

Betsy and Bill thought they had a pretty good first month of operations. However, their estimates of profitability ranged from a loss of $1,350 to net income of $3,200.

Instructions

(a) How could the Kings have concluded that the business operated at a loss of $1,350? Was this a valid basis on which to determine net income?

(b) How could the Kings have concluded that the business operated at a net income of $3,200? (Hint: Prepare a balance sheet at March 31.) Was this a valid basis on which to determine net income?

(c) Without preparing an income statement, determine the actual net income for March.

(d) What were the fees earned in March?

CRITICAL THINKING CASE

Refer back to the story at the beginning of the chapter about Alan Bambeck, senior at Ohio State University.

1. Alan Bambeck prepares an income statement for the year ended April 30. Why do you think the year end is April 30 and not December 31 or some other date? What is your best guess as to the items that appear on the Beta Alpha Psi income statement prepared by Alan?

2. Alan Bambeck prepares a balance sheet as of April 30. On that date, what items, if any, do you think appear on the Beta Alpha Psi balance sheet?

3. How might the Beta Alpha Psi financial statements prepared by Alan Bambeck be used? What is the purpose of having an audit by a CPA firm?

4. What other campus or university related organizations or enterprises at your school maintain accounting records and prepare financial statements? What use is made of the financial statements?

ETHICAL CASE

After numerous campus interviews, Joe Catmus, a senior at Great Eastern College, receives two office interview invitations from the Baltimore offices of two large firms. Both firms offer to cover his out-of-pocket expenses (travel, hotel, and meal). He schedules the interviews for both firms on the same day, one in the morning and one in the afternoon. At the conclusion of each interview, he submits to both firms his total out-of-pocket expenses for the trip to Baltimore, $244: mileage $70 (280 miles at $.25), hotel $120, meals $36, parking and tolls $18, for a total of $244. He believes this approach is appropriate. If he had made two trips, his cost would have been two times $244. He is also certain that neither firm knew he had visited the other on that same trip. Within ten days Joe receives two checks in the mail, each in the amount of $244.

Instructions

(a) Who are the stakeholders (affected parties) in this situation?

(b) What are the ethical issues in this case?

(c) What would you do in this situation?

Answers to Self-Study Questions
1. b   2. d   3. a   4. c   5. a   6. d   7. b   8. a   9. b   10. c

CONCEPTS FOR REVIEW

Before studying this chapter, you should know or, if necessary, review:

a. *What are assets, liabilities, owner's capital, owner's drawings, revenues, and expenses. (Ch. 1, p. 16-7)*

b. *Why assets equal liabilities plus owner's equity. (Ch. 1, p. 15-6)*

c. *What transactions are and how they affect the basic accounting equation. (Ch. 1, p. 18-23)*

CHAPTER 2

THE RECORDING PROCESS

Study Objectives

After studying this chapter, you should be able to:

1. *Explain what an account is and how it helps in the recording process.*

2. *Define debits and credits and explain how they are used to record business transactions.*

3. *Identify the basic steps in the recording process.*

4. *Explain what a journal is and how it helps in the recording process.*

5. *Explain what a ledger is and how it helps in the recording process.*

6. *Explain what posting is and how it helps in the recording process.*

7. *Prepare a trial balance and explain its purposes.*

G*abriella Torres of San Diego learned how to record transactions on a computer before she took her first course in accounting. The reason: by day, she manages the office of Diabetes & Endocrine Associates, a medical practice with an office located near San Diego State University. The doctors' office uses a computer package which makes recording transactions "quite easy." In 1988, Gabriella began her college career at night and hopes to graduate with an accounting degree— and then sit for the CPA exam—in 1994. "The doctors have really been accommodating to my school schedule."*

Working during the day allows Gabriella to bring a real-world perspective to the classroom. In turn, studying accounting and business subjects at night makes her job easier. She is in charge of paying the bills, making sure the bank statement reconciles with the checkbook, hiring office staff, preparing patient bills, and maintaining accounts receivable. "I really love my job," she says, which is one reason she prefers to work days and go to school at night.

Taking her first accounting course helped her understand how the journal entries, the accounts, and financial statements fit together. Unlike doing homework assignments, though, the computer catches some of her errors. "It won't let you proceed from one accounting entry to the next unless the entry's debits and credits balance," she says. In fact, there are no "books" at all, just diskettes and printouts.

As you read Chapter 2, think about what accounts Gabriella might have in her general ledger for the medical practice.

In Chapter 1, we analyzed business transactions in terms of the accounting equation, and presented the cumulative effects of these transactions in tabular form. Imagine Apple Computer using that same tabular format to keep track of every one of its transactions. In a single day, Apple probably engages in many thousands of business transactions. To record each transaction this way would be impractical, expensive, and unnecessary.

As a result, accountants have developed a set of procedures that make it possible to record the transaction data easily. To illustrate these procedures, an example of a manual accounting system is used in this chapter. Each of the individual steps in the recording process will be examined.

Technology in Action

Computerized and manual accounting systems basically parallel one another. Most of the procedures are handled by electronic circuitry in computerized systems. They seem to occur invisibly. To fully comprehend how computerized systems operate, it is, therefore, necessary to illustrate and understand manual approaches for processing accounting data.

The Account

Study Objective 1

Explain what an account is and how it helps in the recording process.

An **account** is an individual accounting record of increases and decreases in specific asset, liability, and owner's equity items. For example, in Softbyte (discussed in Chapter 1) there would be separate accounts for Cash, Accounts Receivable, Accounts Payable, Service Revenue, Salaries Expense, and so on. In its simplest form, an account consists of three parts: (1) the title of the account, (2) a left or debit side, and (3) a right or credit side. Because the alignment of these parts of an account often resembles the letter T, it is referred to as a **T account**. The basic form of an account is shown in Illustration 2-1.

ILLUSTRATION 2-1

Basic form of account

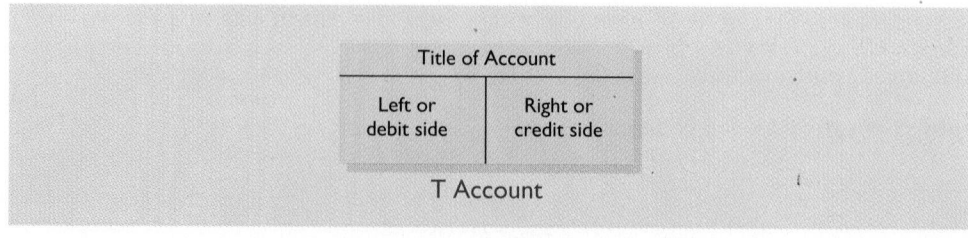

Title of Account	
Left or debit side	Right or credit side

T Account

This form of account will be used often throughout this book to explain basic accounting relationships.

Debits and Credits

The terms debit and credit mean left and right, respectively. They are commonly abbreviated as Dr. for debit and Cr. for credit.[1] These terms do not mean increase or decrease. The terms debit and credit are used repeatedly in the recording process. For example, the act of entering an amount on the left side of an account is called **debiting** the account, and making an entry on the right side is **crediting** the account. When the totals of the two sides are compared, an account will have a **debit balance** if the total of the debit amounts exceeds the credits. Conversely, an account will have a **credit balance** if the credit amounts exceed the debits.

The procedure of having debits on the left and credits on the right is an accounting custom or rule. Accountants could function just as well if debits and credits were reversed. However, the custom of having debits on the left side of an account and credits on the right side (like the custom of driving on the right-hand side of the road) has been adopted in the United States. **This rule applies to all accounts.**

The procedure of recording debits and credits in an account is shown in Illustration 2-2 for the cash transactions of Softbyte. The data are taken from the cash column of the tabular summary in Illustration 1-8.

Study Objective 2

Define debits and credits and explain how they are used to record business transactions.

Helpful hint Think of the terms debit and credit solely as directional signals. Debit—use the left side of the account; credit—use the right side.

ILLUSTRATION 2-2

Tabular summary compared to account form

Tabular Summary		Account Form		
Cash			**Cash**	
$15,000			$15,000	7,000
–7,000			1,200	1,700
1,200			1,500	250
1,500			600	1,300
–1,700		Balance	8,050	
–250				
600				
–1,300				
$ 8,050				

Every positive item in the tabular summary represents a receipt of cash; every negative amount constitutes a payment of cash. However, in the account form the increases in cash are recorded as debits, and decreases in cash are recorded as credits. Having increases on one side and decreases on the other helps in determining the totals of each side of the account and the balance in the account. The account balance, a debit of $8,050, in this case, is shown on the appropriate side, as illustrated.

Debit and Credit Procedure

In Chapter 1 you learned the effect of a transaction on the basic accounting equation. Remember that each transaction must affect two or more accounts if

Helpful hint Debits must equal credits for each transaction.

---

[1]These abbreviations come from the Latin words *debere* (Dr.) and *credere* (Cr.).

the basic accounting equation is to remain in balance. In other words, debits must equal credits in the accounts for each transaction. The equality of debits and credits provides the basis for the double-entry system of recording transactions (sometimes referred to as double-entry bookkeeping).

Under the universally used double-entry system, the dual (two-sided) effect of each transaction is recorded in appropriate accounts. This system provides a logical method for recording transactions. It also offers a means of proving the accuracy of the recorded amounts. If every transaction is recorded with equal debits and credits, then the sum of all the debits to the accounts must equal the sum of all the credits.

The double-entry system for determining the equality of the accounting equation is much more efficient than the plus/minus procedure used in Chapter 1. There, it was necessary after each transaction to compare total assets with total liabilities and owner's equity to determine the equality of the two sides of the accounting equation.

Assets and Liabilities

In the Softbyte illustration earlier in this chapter, increases in cash—an asset— were entered on the left side, and decreases in cash were entered on the right side. It follows that if both sides of the basic equation (assets = liabilities + owner's equity) must be equal, then increases in liabilities must be entered on the right or credit side. Similarly, decreases in liabilities must be entered on the left or debit side. The effects that debit and credit entries have on assets and liabilities are summarized as follows:

ILLUSTRATION 2-3

Debit and credit effect— assets and liabilities

Debits	Credits
Increase assets	Decrease assets
Decrease liabilities	Increase liabilities

Debits to a specific asset account should exceed the credits to that account, and credits to a liability account should exceed debits to that account. Thus, asset accounts normally show debit balances, and liability accounts normally show credit balances. The normal balances may be diagrammed as follows:

ILLUSTRATION 2-4

Normal balances—assets and liabilities

Helpful hint The normal balance for an account is always the same as the increase side.

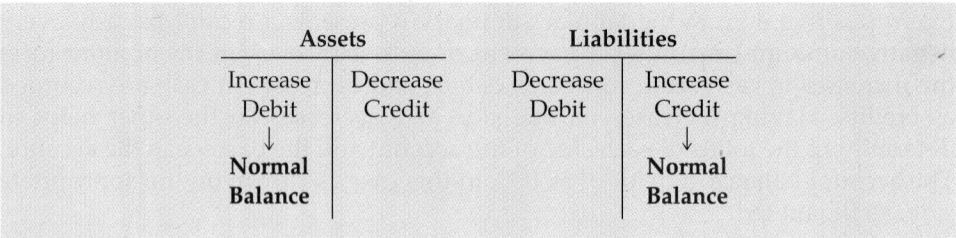

An awareness of the normal balance in an account may help you when you are trying to trace errors. For example, a credit balance in an asset account such as Land and a debit balance in a liability account such as Wages Payable would indicate errors in recording. Occasionally, however, an abnormal balance may be correct. The Cash account, for example, will have a credit balance when a company has overdrawn its bank balance (i.e., written a "bad" check).

Accounting in Action ▪ *Ethical Insight*

Abnormal balances in cash are apparently commonplace in Washington, D.C. For the fiscal year ended June 1990, there were 8,331 overdrafts (credit balances in cash accounts) by U.S. Representatives of their accounts at the House bank. Over a 39-month period, 355 current and former members had about 20,000 overdrafts, some in six figures. The House bank was closed in early 1992. As the 1992 election approached, many representatives were concerned that this ethics scandal might affect adversely their chances for re-election.

Owner's Equity

As indicated in Chapter 1, there are four subdivisions of owner's equity: capital, drawings, revenues, and expenses. In a double-entry system, accounts are kept for each of these subdivisions as explained below.

CAPITAL. The capital account is used to determine the owner's investment in the business. The capital account is increased by credits and decreased by debits. For example, when cash is invested in the business, cash is debited and capital is credited. Conversely, owner's capital is debited when the owner's investment in the business is reduced.

The rules of debit and credit for the owner's capital account are stated as follows:

Debits	**Credits**
Decrease capital	Increase capital

ILLUSTRATION 2-5

Debit and credit effect—owner's capital

The normal balance in this account may be diagrammed as follows:

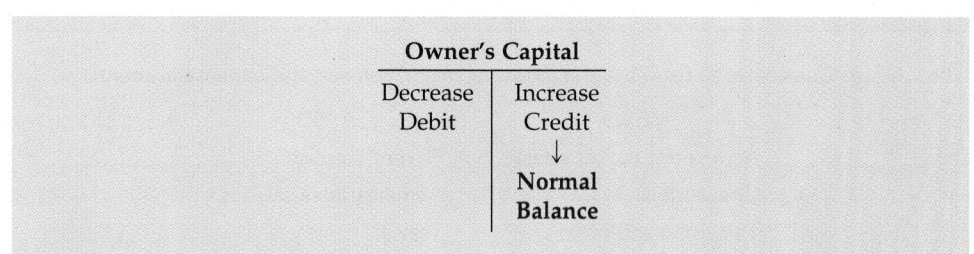

Owner's Capital

Decrease Debit	Increase Credit
	↓
	Normal Balance

ILLUSTRATION 2-6

Normal balance—owner's capital

Helpful hint The rules for debit and credit and the normal balance of owner's capital are the same as for liabilities.

DRAWINGS. An owner may withdraw cash or other assets for personal use. Withdrawals could be debited directly to owner's capital to indicate a decrease in capital. However, it is preferable to establish a separate account, referred to as the owner's drawing account, in order to determine the total withdrawals for the accounting period. **The drawing account is a subdivision of the owner's capital account. It is not an income statement account like revenues and expenses.** Owner's drawing is increased by debits and decreased by credits. Normally, the drawing account will have a debit balance. The rules of debit and credit for the drawing account are stated as follows:

ILLUSTRATION 2-7

Debit and credit effect—owner's drawing

Debits	Credits
Increase owner's drawing	Decrease owner's drawing

The normal balance may be diagrammed as follows:

ILLUSTRATION 2-8

Normal balance—owner's drawing

Owner's Drawing

Increase Debit ↓ Normal Balance	Decrease Credit

Observe that the effect of debits and credits and the normal balance of owner's drawing are exactly the reverse of those relating to owner's capital.

Revenues and Expenses

Helpful hint Because revenues increase owner's capital, a revenue account has the same debit and credit rules as does the capital account. Conversely, expenses have the opposite effect.

When revenues are earned, owner's capital is increased. Revenues are a subdivision of owner's capital that provides information as to why owner's capital increased. Accordingly, **the effect of debits and credits on revenue accounts is identical to their effect on owner's capital**. Revenue accounts are increased by credits and decreased by debits.

On the other hand, expenses decrease owner's capital. As a result, expenses are recorded by debits. Since expenses are the negative factor in the computation of net income, and revenues are the positive factor, it is logical that the increase and decrease sides of expense accounts should be the reverse of revenue accounts. Thus, expense accounts are increased by debits and decreased by credits.

Accounting in Action · *Business Insight*

The Chicago Cubs baseball team has the following major revenue and expense accounts:

REVENUES	EXPENSES
Admissions (ticket sales)	Players' salaries
Concessions	Administrative salaries
Television and radio	Travel
Advertising	Ballpark maintenance

The effect of debits and credits on revenues and expenses may be stated as follows:

ILLUSTRATION 2-9

Debit and credit effect—revenues and expenses

Debits	Credits
Decrease revenues	Increase revenues
Increase expenses	Decrease expenses

Credits to revenue accounts should exceed the debits, and debits to expense accounts should exceed credits. Thus, revenue accounts normally show credit balances and expense accounts normally show debit balances. The normal balances may be diagrammed as follows:

ILLUSTRATION 2-10

Normal balances—revenues and expenses

Revenues		Expenses	
Decrease Debit	Increase Credit	Increase Debit	Decrease Credit
	↓	↓	
	Normal Balance	Normal Balance	

Technology in Action

In automated systems, the computer is programmed to flag these normal balance exceptions and to print out error or exception reports. In manual systems, careful visual inspection of the accounts is required to detect normal balance problems.

Expansion of Basic Equation

You have already learned the basic accounting equation. Illustration 2-11 expands this equation to show the accounts that comprise owner's equity. In addition, the debit/credit rules and effects on each type of account are illustrated. Study this diagram carefully. It will help you understand the fundamentals of the double-entry system. Like the basic equation, the expanded basic equation must be in balance (total debits equal total credits).

ILLUSTRATION 2-11

Expanded basic equation and debit/credit rules and effects

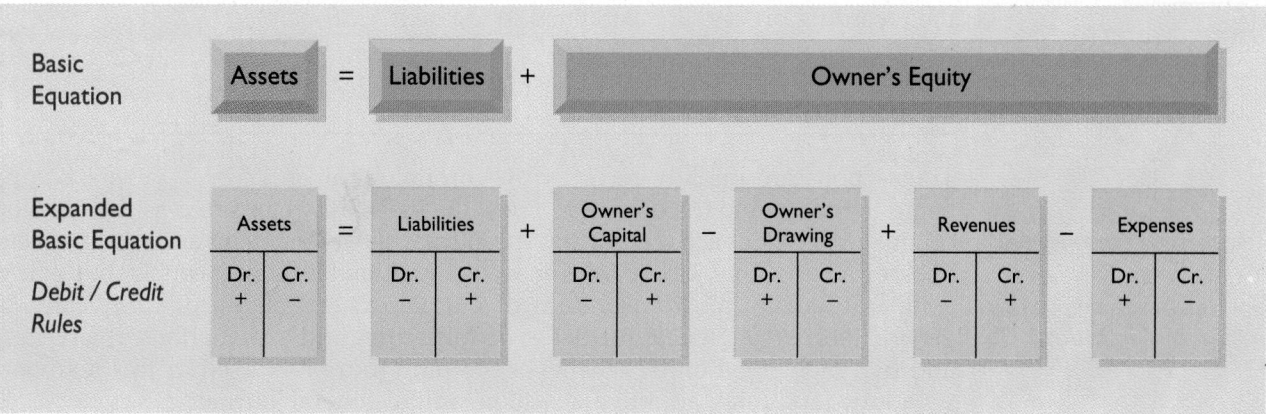

All investments by the owner are credited directly to Owner's Capital.

Before You Go On . . .

1. What is the rule for debits and credits?

2. What are the debit and credit effects on assets, liabilities, and owner's capital?

3. What are the debit and credit effects on revenues, expenses, and owner's drawings?

4. What are the normal balances for individual asset, liability, and owner's equity accounts?

Steps in the Recording Process

Study Objective 3

Identify the basic steps in the recording process.

Although it is possible to enter transaction information directly into the accounts, few businesses do so. In practically every business, the basic steps in the recording process are:

1. Analyze each transaction in terms of its effect on the accounts.
2. Enter the transaction information in a journal (book of original entry).
3. Transfer the journal information to the appropriate accounts in the ledger (book of accounts).

The actual sequence of events begins with the transaction. Evidence of the transaction is obtained in the form of a business document, such as a sales slip, a check, a bill, or a cash register tape. This evidence is analyzed to determine the effect of the transaction on specific accounts. The transaction is then entered in the journal. Finally, the journal entry is transferred to the designated accounts in the ledger. The sequence of events in the recording process can be diagrammed as follows:

ILLUSTRATION 2-12

The recording process

The basic steps in the recording process occur repeatedly in every business enterprise. The analysis of transactions has already been illustrated, and further examples of this step will be given in this and later chapters. The other steps in the recording process are explained in the next sections.

The Journal

Study Objective 4

Explain what a journal is and how it helps in the recording process.

Transactions are initially recorded in chronological order in a journal before being transferred to the accounts. Thus, the journal is referred to as the book of original entry. For each transaction the journal shows the debit and credit effects on specific accounts. Companies may use various kinds of journals, but every company has the most basic form of journal, a general journal. Typically, a general journal has spaces for dates, account titles and explanations, references, and two money columns. Whenever the term journal is used in this textbook without a modifying adjective, it will mean the general journal.

The journal makes several significant contributions to the recording process:

1. It discloses in one place the complete effect of a transaction.
2. It provides a chronological record of transactions.
3. It helps to prevent or locate errors because the debit and credit amounts for each entry can be readily compared.

Journalizing

Entering transaction data in the journal is known as journalizing. Separate journal entries are made for each transaction. A complete entry consists of: (1) the date of the transaction, (2) the accounts and amounts to be debited and credited, and (3) a brief explanation of the transaction.

To illustrate the technique of journalizing, the first two transactions of Softbyte are journalized in Illustration 2-13 using the first page (J1) of the general journal. These transactions were: September 1, Ray Neal invested $15,000 cash in the business, and computer equipment was purchased for $7,000 cash.

GENERAL JOURNAL				J1
Date	Account Titles and Explanation	Ref.	Debit	Credit
1993 Sept. 1	Cash		15,000	
	R. Neal, Capital			15,000
	(Invested cash in business)			
1	Computer Equipment		7,000	
	Cash			7,000
	(Purchased equipment for cash)			

ILLUSTRATION 2-13

Technique of journalizing

The standard form and content of journal entries are as follows:

1. The date of the transaction is entered in the Date column. The date recorded should include the year, month, and day of the transaction.
2. The debit account title is entered first at the extreme left margin of the column headed Account Titles and Explanation. The credit account title is then indented and entered. The indentation decreases the possibility of switching the debit and credit amounts.
3. The amounts for the debits are recorded in the Debit (left) money column and the amounts for the credits are recorded in the Credit (right) money column.
4. A brief explanation of the transaction is given.
5. A space is left between journal entries. The blank space separates individual journal entries and makes the entire journal easier to read.
6. The column entitled Ref. (which stands for reference) is left blank at the time the journal entry is made. The Reference column is used later when the journal entries are transferred to the ledger accounts. At that time, the ledger account number is placed in the Reference column to indicate where the amount in the journal entry was transferred.

It is important to use correct and specific account titles in journalizing. Since most accounts appear later in the financial statements, erroneous account titles lead to incorrect financial statements. Some flexibility exists initially in selecting account titles. The main criterion is that each title must appropriately describe the content of the account. For example, the account title used for the cost of delivery trucks may be Delivery Equipment, Delivery Trucks, or Trucks. Once a specific title has been chosen, all subsequent transactions involving the account should be recorded under that account title.[2]

If an entry involves only two accounts, one debit and one credit, it is considered a simple entry. For some transactions, however, it may be necessary to use more than two accounts in journalizing. Imagine, for example, the numerous accounts needed by General Electric to record the acquisition of all the assets and liabilities of RCA in what was one of the largest mergers ever completed. When three or more accounts are required in one journal entry, the entry is referred to as a compound entry. To illustrate, assume that on July 1, Butler Company purchases a delivery truck costing $14,000 by paying $8,000 cash and the balance on account (to be paid at a later date). The entry is as follows:

ILLUSTRATION 2-14

Compound journal entry

GENERAL JOURNAL					J1
Date	Account Titles and Explanation	Ref.	Debit	Credit
1993 July 1	Delivery Equipment		14,000	
	Cash			8,000
	Accounts Payable			6,000
	(Purchased truck for cash with balance on account)			

In a compound entry, it is important to determine that the total debit and credit amounts are equal. Also, the standard format requires that all debits be listed before the credits are listed.

The Ledger

The entire group of accounts maintained by a company is referred to collectively as the ledger. The ledger keeps in one place all the information about changes in specific account balances.

Companies may use various kinds of ledgers, but every company has a general ledger. A general ledger contains all the assets, liabilities, and owner's equity accounts, as shown in Illustration 2-15. A business can use a looseleaf binder or card file for the ledger with each account kept on a separate sheet or card. Whenever the term ledger is used in this textbook without a modifying adjective, it will mean the general ledger.

The ledger should be arranged in statement order beginning with the balance sheet accounts. First in order are the asset accounts, followed by liability accounts, owner's capital, drawings, revenues, and expenses. Each account is numbered for easier identification.

The information in the ledger provides management with the balances in various accounts. For example, the Cash account enables management to determine the amount of cash that is available to meet current obligations. Amounts due from customers and the amounts owed to creditors can be determined by examining the Accounts Receivable and Accounts Payable accounts, respectively.

---

[2]In homework problems, when specific account titles are given, they should be used. When account titles are not given, you may select account titles that identify the nature and content of each account. The account titles used in journalizing should not contain explanations such as Cash Paid or Cash Received.

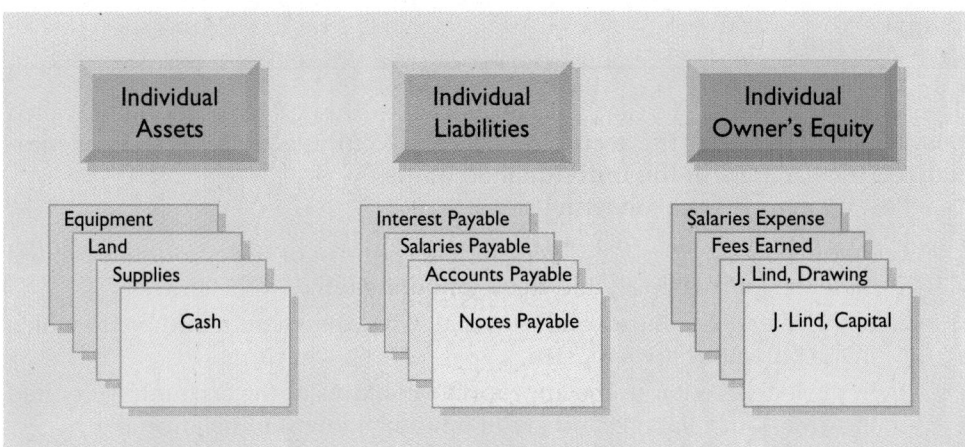

ILLUSTRATION 2-15

The general ledger

Standard Form of Account

The simple T-account form of an account used in an accounting textbook is often very useful for illustration and analysis purposes. However, in practice, the account forms used in ledgers are much more structured. A form widely used in a manual system is shown in Illustration 2-16 using assumed data from a cash account.

ILLUSTRATION 2-16

Three-column form of account

CASH					No. 10
Date	Explanation	Ref.	Debit	Credit	Balance
1993					
June 1			25,000		25,000
2				8,000	17,000
3			4,200		21,200
9			7,500		28,700
17				11,700	17,000
20				250	16,750
30				7,300	9,450

This form has three money columns—debit, credit, and balance. The balance in the account is determined after each transaction. Thus, this form is often called the three-column form of account. By adding another money column to this form, it is possible to have two balance columns—one for a debit balance and one for a credit balance. Note that the explanation space and reference columns are used to provide special information about the transaction.

Technology in Action

Determining what to record is the most critical (and for most businesses the most expensive) point in the accounting process. In computerized systems, it is also the only place where you have to think. After this phase is completed, your input and all further processing just boil down to file merging and report generation. Programmers and management information system types with good accounting backgrounds (such as they should gain from a good principles textbook) are better able to develop effective computerized systems.

Posting

The procedure of transferring journal entries to the ledger accounts is called posting. **This phase of the recording process accumulates the effects of journalized transactions in the individual accounts.**

Posting involves the following steps:

1. In the ledger, enter in the appropriate columns of the account(s) debited the date, journal page, and debit amount shown in the journal.
2. In the reference column of the journal, write the account number to which the debit amount was posted.
3. In the ledger, enter in the appropriate columns of the account(s) credited the date, journal page, and credit amount shown in the journal.
4. In the reference column of the journal, write the account number to which the credit amount was posted.

These steps are diagrammed in Illustration 2-17 using the first journal entry of Softbyte. The boxed numbers indicate the sequence of the steps.

Posting should be performed in chronological order. That is, all the debits and credits of one journal entry should be posted before proceeding to the next journal entry. Under the journalizing procedures described in this chapter, post-

ILLUSTRATION 2-17

Posting a journal entry

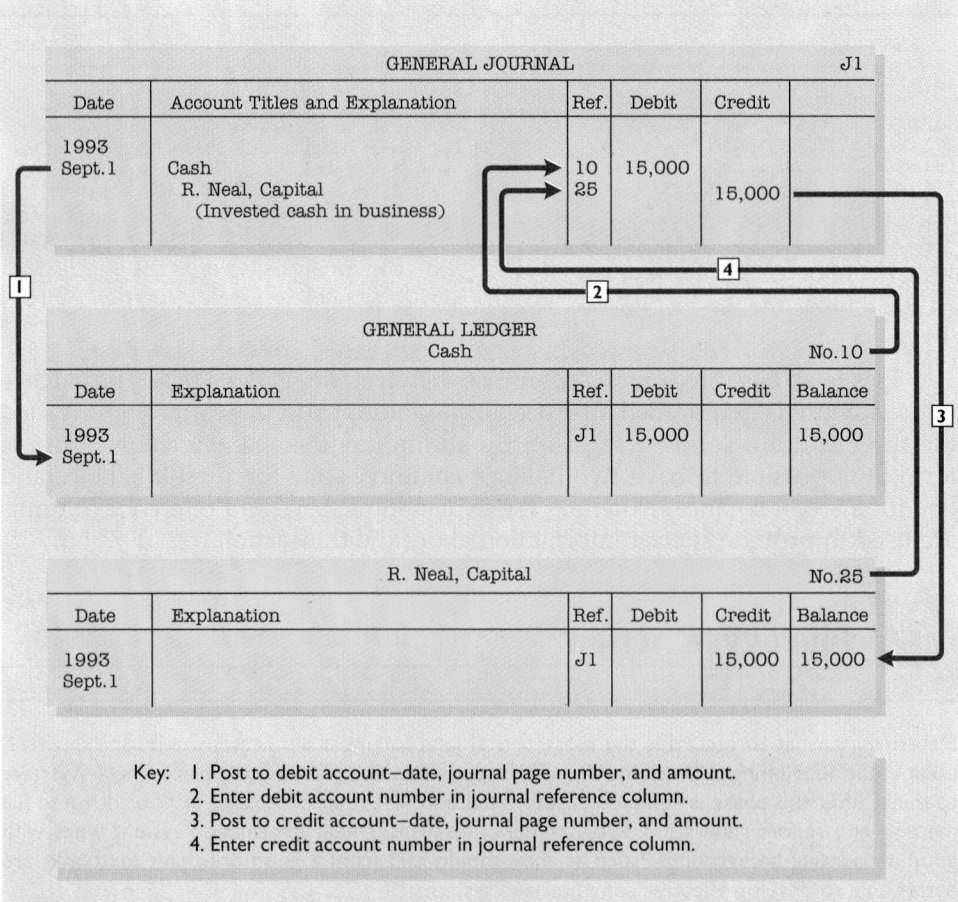

ings should be made on a timely basis to ensure that the ledger is up to date.[3]

The reference column **in the journal** serves several purposes. The numbers in this column indicate the entries that have been posted. After the last entry has been posted, the journal reference column should be scanned to see that all postings have been made.

The reference column **of a ledger** account indicates the journal page from which the transaction has been posted. The explanation space of the ledger account is used infrequently because an explanation already appears in the journal. It generally is used only when detailed analysis of account activity is required.

Chart of Accounts

The number and type of accounts used differ depending on the size, complexity, and type of business involved. For example, the number of accounts depends on the amount of detail desired by management. The management of one company may want one account for all types of utility expense. Another may keep separate expense accounts for each type of utility expenditure, such as gas, electricity, and water. Similarly, a single proprietorship like Softbyte will not have many accounts compared with a corporate giant like Ford Motor Company. Softbyte may be able to manage and report its activities in 20 to 30 accounts, while Ford requires thousands of accounts to keep track of its worldwide activities.

Most companies have a chart of accounts that lists the accounts and the account numbers which identify their location in the ledger. The numbering system used to identify the accounts usually starts with the balance sheet accounts and follows with the income statement accounts.

Accounting in Action · *Business Insight*

The numbering system used to identify the accounts can be quite sophisticated or relatively simple. For example, at Goodyear Tire & Rubber Company an 18-digit system is used. The first three digits identify the division or plant. The second set of three-digit numbers contains the following account classifications:

100–199 Assets	300–399 Revenues
200–299 Liabilities and Owner's Equity	400–599 Expenses

Other digits describe the location of a specific plant, product line, region of the country, and so on.

In this and the next two chapters, we will be explaining the accounting for the proprietorship, Pioneer Advertising Agency (a service enterprise). Accounts 1–19 indicate asset accounts; 20–39 indicate liabilities; 40–49 indicate owner's equity accounts; 50–59, revenues; and 60–69, expenses. The chart of accounts for Pioneer Advertising Agency (C. R. Byrd, owner) is shown in Illustration 2-18. It contains the following accounts, some of which are explained in later chapters:

---

[3]In homework problems, it will be permissible to journalize all transactions before posting any of the journal entries.

ILLUSTRATION 2-18

Chart of accounts

Pioneer Advertising Agency

Assets

1. Cash
6. Fees Receivable
8. Advertising Supplies
10. Prepaid Insurance
15. Office Equipment
16. Accumulated Depreciation—Office Equipment

Liabilities

25. Notes Payable
26. Accounts Payable
27. Interest Payable
28. Unearned Fees
29. Salaries Payable

Owner's Equity

40. C. R. Byrd, Capital
41. C. R. Byrd, Drawing
49. Income Summary

Revenues

50. Fees Earned

Expenses

60. Salaries Expense
61. Advertising Supplies Expense
62. Rent Expense
63. Insurance Expense
64. Interest Expense
65. Depreciation Expense

You will notice that there are gaps in the numbering system of the chart of accounts for Pioneer Advertising. Gaps are left to permit the insertion of new accounts as needed during the life of the business.

Technology in Action

The first step in designing a computerized accounting system is the creation of a chart of accounts. The chart of accounts establishes the framework for the entire data base of accounting information.

From the chart of accounts, the general ledger can be created. Journal entries are simultaneously posted to the ledger accounts when the journal entry is made in most computerized systems. The balances are available at any point in time in such systems.

Obvious errors in the recording process (e.g., unbalanced entries or use of nonexistent accounts) are "flagged" by the system and are not processed until corrected. This correction usually takes place immediately after the error is discovered by the system. Because the initial entry is so important, many systems search for more subtle errors, such as unreasonable dollar amounts for specific accounts.

The Recording Process Illustrated

Helpful hint To correctly record a transaction, you must carefully analyze the event and translate that analysis into debit and credit language.
First: Determine what type of account is involved.
Second: Determine what items increased or decreased and how much.
Third: Translate the increases and decreases into debits and credits.

Illustration 2-19 through Illustration 2-28 show the basic steps in the recording process, using the October transactions of the Pioneer Advertising Agency. Its accounting period is a month. A basic analysis and a debit-credit analysis precede the journalizing and posting of each transaction. Study these transaction analyses carefully. **The purpose of transaction analysis is first to identify the type of account involved, and then to determine whether a debit or a credit to the account is required.** You should always perform this type of analysis before preparing a journal entry. Doing so will help you understand the journal entries discussed in this chapter as well as more complex journal entries to be described in later chapters.

Keep in mind that every journal entry affects one or more of the following items: assets, liabilities, owner's capital, drawings, revenues, or expenses.

ILLUSTRATION 2-19

Investment of cash by owner

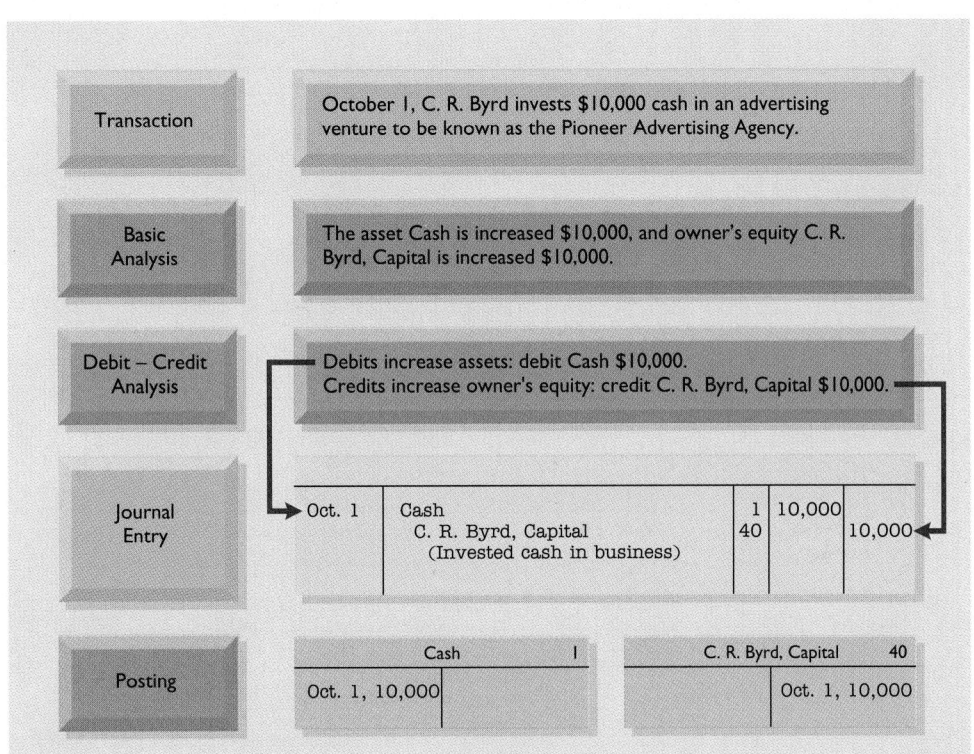

ILLUSTRATION 2-20

Purchase of office equipment

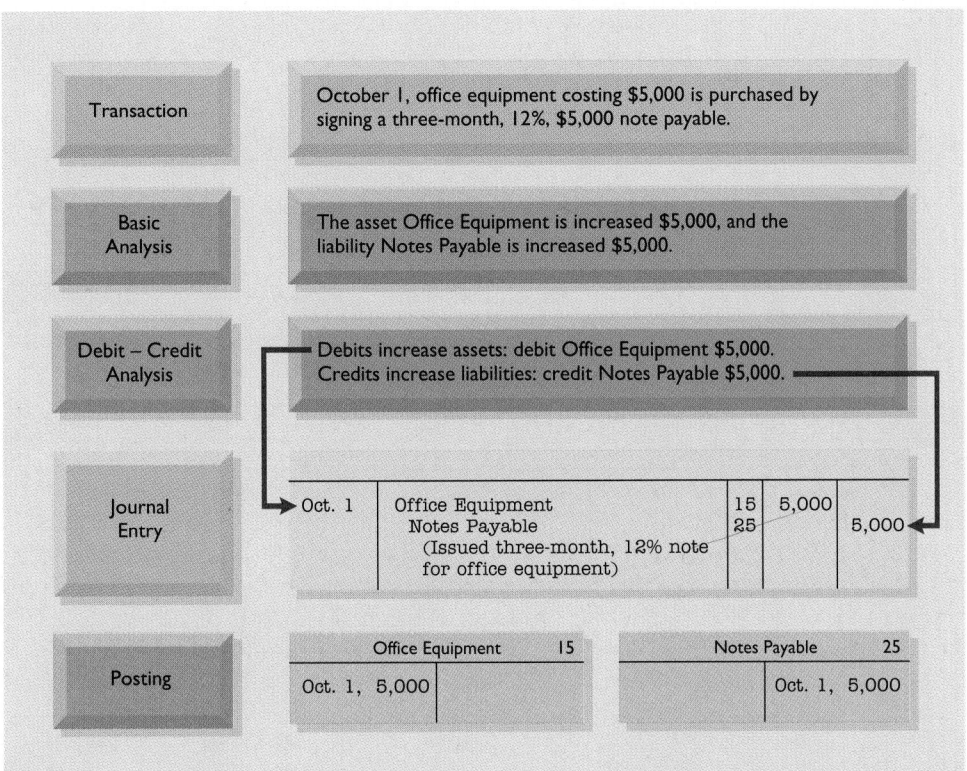

ILLUSTRATION 2-21

Receipt of cash for future service

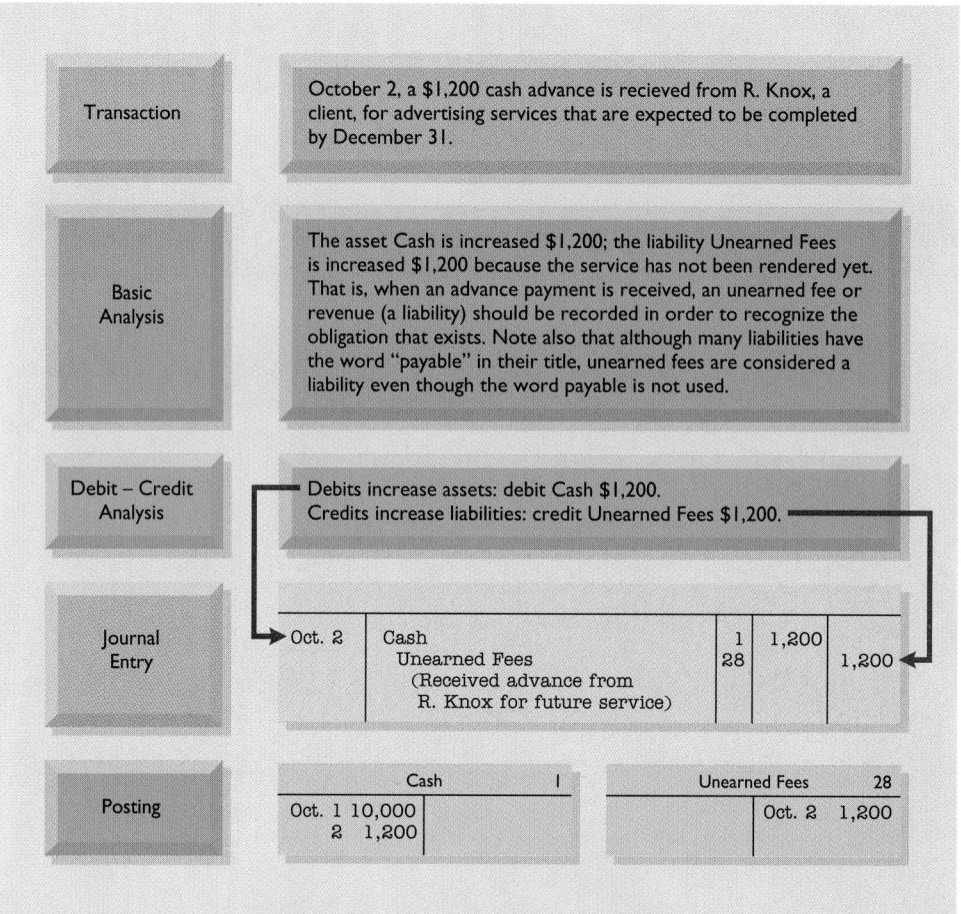

Transaction	October 2, a $1,200 cash advance is recieved from R. Knox, a client, for advertising services that are expected to be completed by December 31.
Basic Analysis	The asset Cash is increased $1,200; the liability Unearned Fees is increased $1,200 because the service has not been rendered yet. That is, when an advance payment is received, an unearned fee or revenue (a liability) should be recorded in order to recognize the obligation that exists. Note also that although many liabilities have the word "payable" in their title, unearned fees are considered a liability even though the word payable is not used.
Debit – Credit Analysis	Debits increase assets: debit Cash $1,200. Credits increase liabilities: credit Unearned Fees $1,200.

Journal Entry

Oct. 2	Cash	1	1,200	
	Unearned Fees	28		1,200
	(Received advance from			
	R. Knox for future service)			

Posting

Cash			1
Oct. 1	10,000		
2	1,200		

Unearned Fees			28
		Oct. 2	1,200

ILLUSTRATION 2-22

Payment of monthly rent

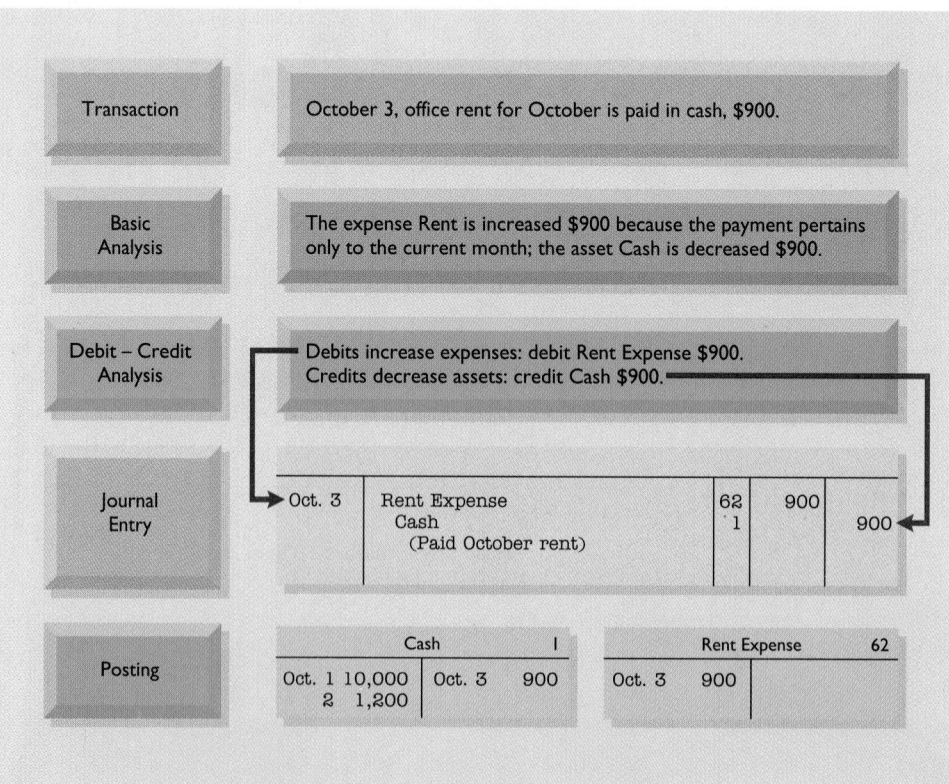

Transaction	October 3, office rent for October is paid in cash, $900.
Basic Analysis	The expense Rent is increased $900 because the payment pertains only to the current month; the asset Cash is decreased $900.
Debit – Credit Analysis	Debits increase expenses: debit Rent Expense $900. Credits decrease assets: credit Cash $900.

Journal Entry

Oct. 3	Rent Expense	62	900	
	Cash	1		900
	(Paid October rent)			

Posting

Cash			1
Oct. 1	10,000	Oct. 3	900
2	1,200		

Rent Expense			62
Oct. 3	900		

ILLUSTRATION 2-23

Payment for insurance

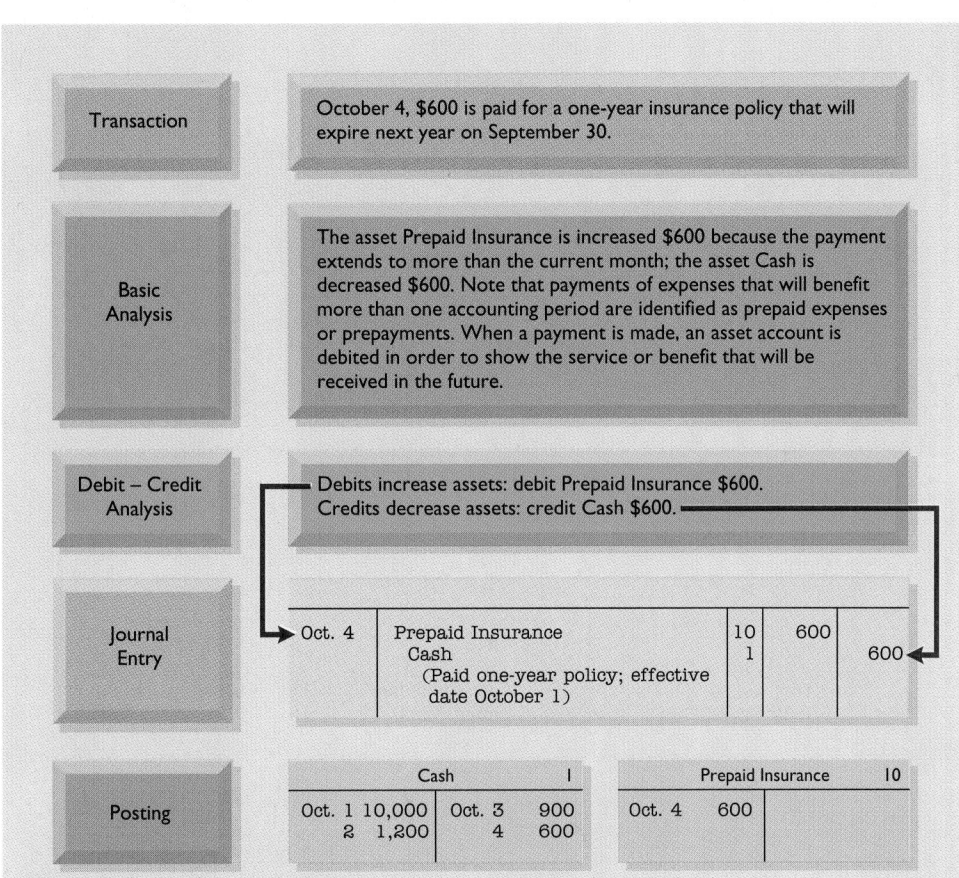

| Transaction | October 4, $600 is paid for a one-year insurance policy that will expire next year on September 30. |

| Basic Analysis | The asset Prepaid Insurance is increased $600 because the payment extends to more than the current month; the asset Cash is decreased $600. Note that payments of expenses that will benefit more than one accounting period are identified as prepaid expenses or prepayments. When a payment is made, an asset account is debited in order to show the service or benefit that will be received in the future. |

Debit – Credit Analysis

Debits increase assets: debit Prepaid Insurance $600.
Credits decrease assets: credit Cash $600.

Journal Entry

Oct. 4	Prepaid Insurance	10	600	
	Cash	1		600
	(Paid one-year policy; effective date October 1)			

Posting

Cash	1
Oct. 1 10,000	Oct. 3 900
2 1,200	4 600

| Prepaid Insurance | 10 |
| Oct. 4 600 | |

ILLUSTRATION 2-24

Purchase of supplies on credit

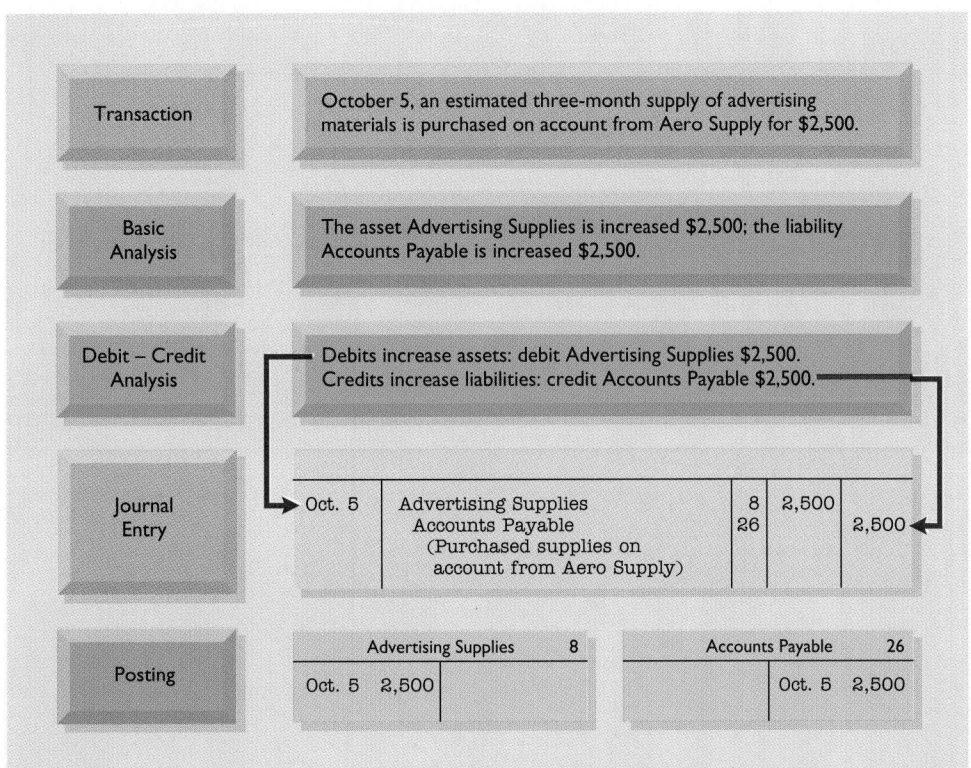

| Transaction | October 5, an estimated three-month supply of advertising materials is purchased on account from Aero Supply for $2,500. |

| Basic Analysis | The asset Advertising Supplies is increased $2,500; the liability Accounts Payable is increased $2,500. |

Debit – Credit Analysis

Debits increase assets: debit Advertising Supplies $2,500.
Credits increase liabilities: credit Accounts Payable $2,500.

Journal Entry

Oct. 5	Advertising Supplies	8	2,500	
	Accounts Payable	26		2,500
	(Purchased supplies on account from Aero Supply)			

Posting

| Advertising Supplies | 8 |
| Oct. 5 2,500 | |

| Accounts Payable | 26 |
| | Oct. 5 2,500 |

ILLUSTRATION 2-25

Hire employees

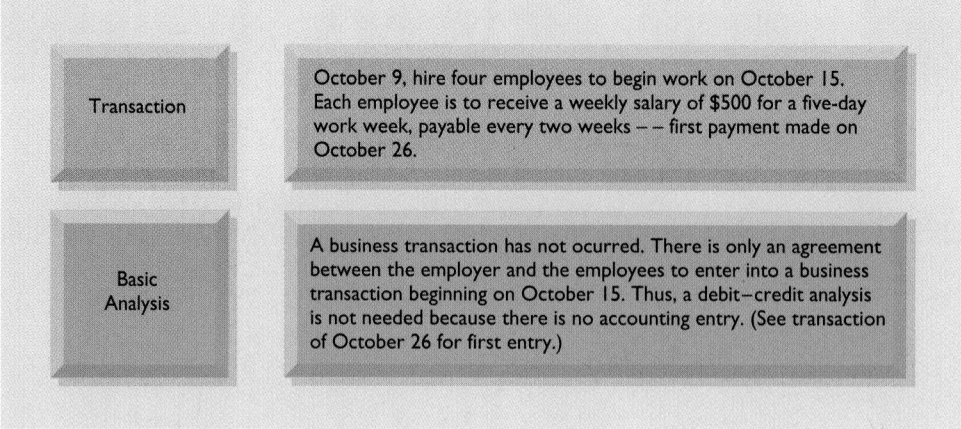

ILLUSTRATION 2-26

Withdrawal of cash by owner

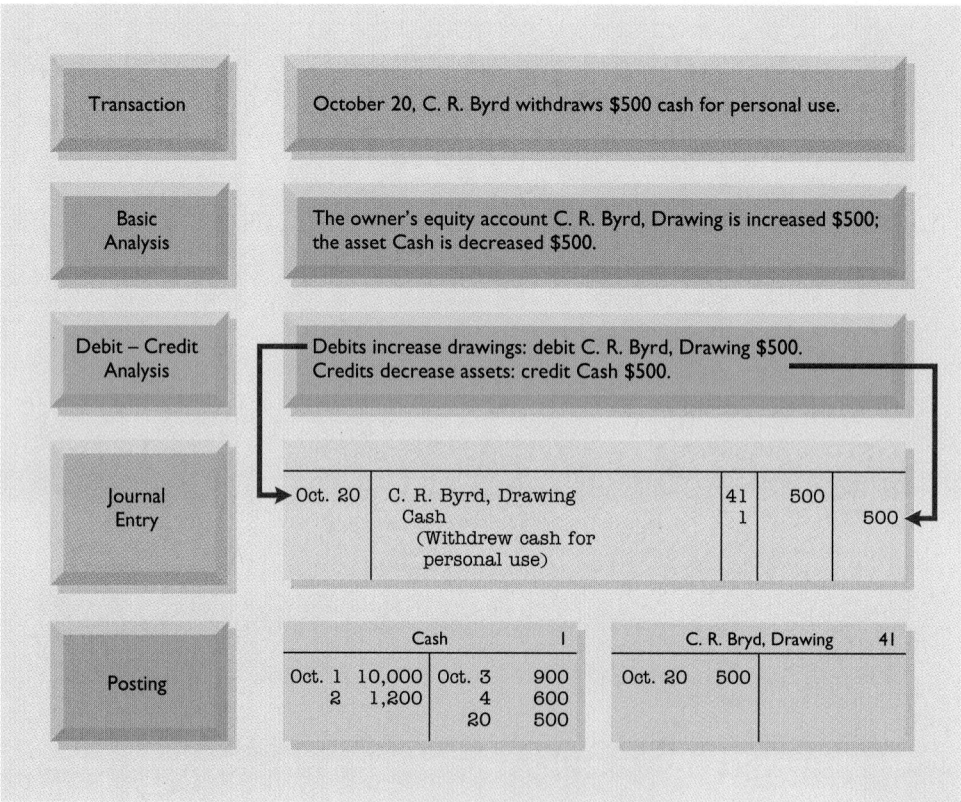

ILLUSTRATION 2-27

Payment of salaries

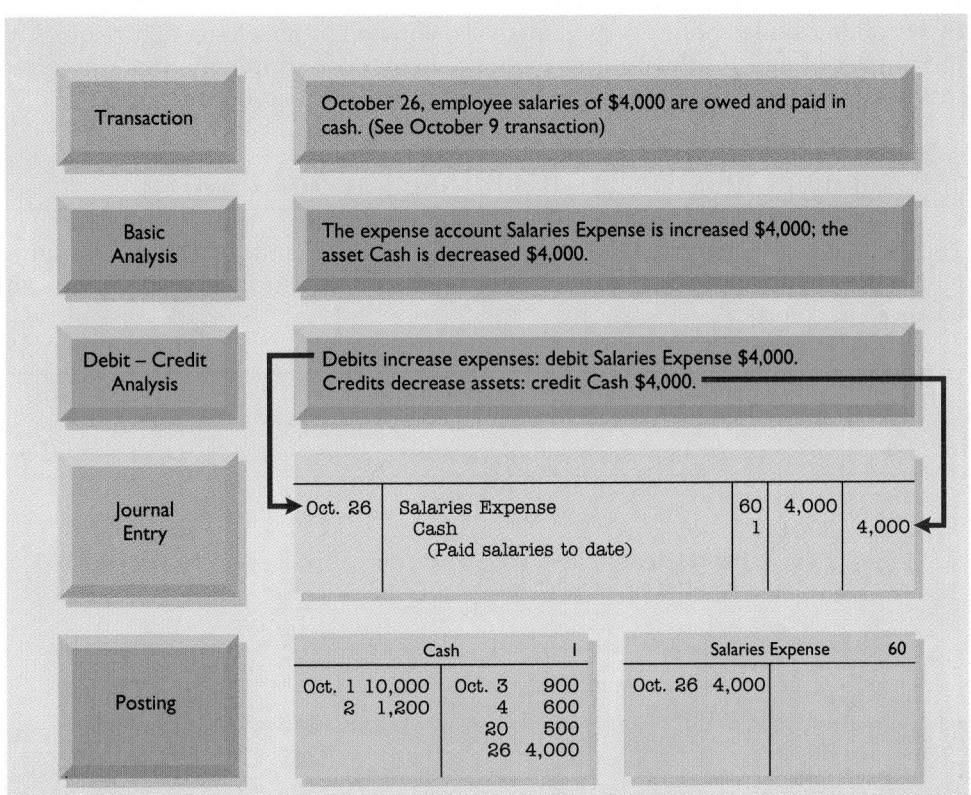

ILLUSTRATION 2-28

Receipt of cash for fees earned

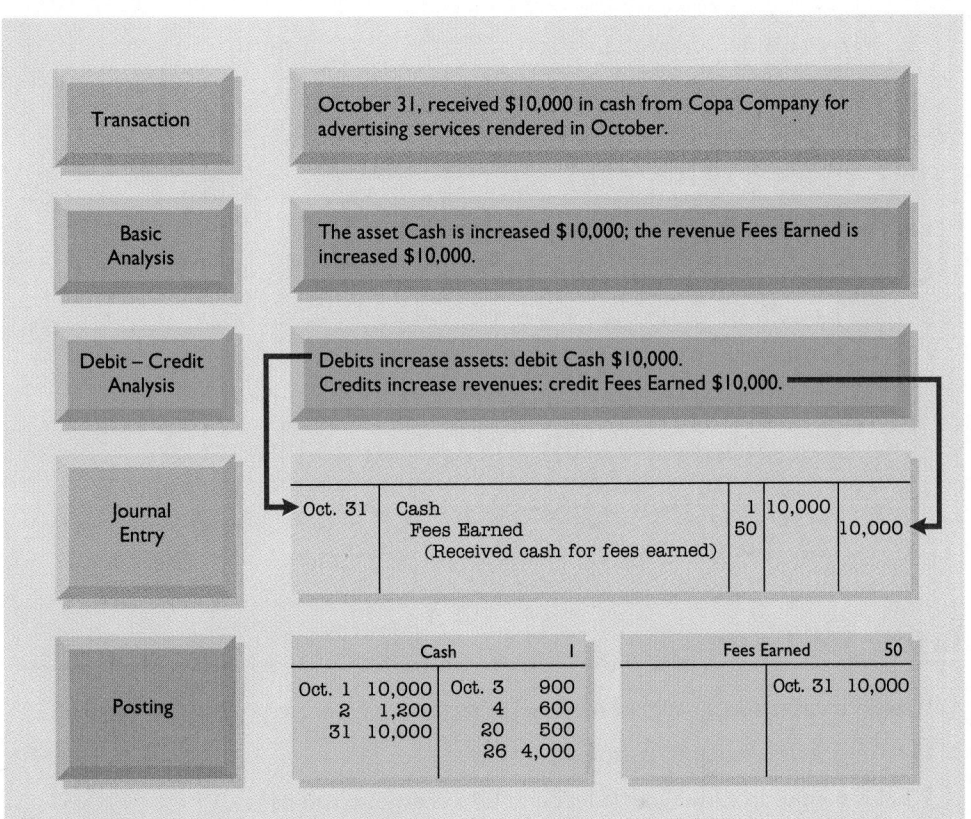

By becoming skilled at transaction analysis, you will be able to recognize quickly the impact of any transaction on these six items. For simplicity, the T-account form is used in the illustrations instead of the standard account form.

Summary Illustration of Journalizing and Posting

The journal for Pioneer Advertising Agency for the month of October is summarized in Illustration 2-29. The ledger is shown in Illustration 2-30 with all balances in color.

ILLUSTRATION 2-29

General journal entries

		GENERAL JOURNAL			Page J1
Date		Account Titles and Explanation	Ref.	Debit	Credit
1993 Oct.	1	Cash	1	10,000	
		C. R. Byrd, Capital	40		10,000
		(Invested cash in business)			
	1	Office Equipment	15	5,000	
		Notes Payable	25		5,000
		(Issued three-month, 12% note for office equipment)			
	2	Cash	1	1,200	
		Unearned Fees	28		1,200
		(Received advance from R. Knox for future services)			
	3	Rent Expense	62	900	
		Cash	1		900
		(Paid October rent)			
	4	Prepaid Insurance	10	600	
		Cash	1		600
		(Paid one-year policy; effective date, October 1)			
	5	Advertising Supplies	8	2,500	
		Accounts Payable	26		2,500
		(Purchased supplies on account from Aero Supply)			
	20	C. R. Byrd, Drawing	41	500	
		Cash	1		500
		(Withdrew cash for personal use)			
	26	Salaries Expense	60	4,000	
		Cash	1		4,000
		(Paid salaries to date)			
	31	Cash	1	10,000	
		Fees Earned	50		10,000
		(Received cash for fees earned)			

Before You Go On . . .

1. What is the correct sequence of the steps in the recording process?

2. How does journalizing differ from posting?

3. What is the purpose of (a) the ledger and (b) a chart of accounts?

ILLUSTRATION 2-30

General ledger

GENERAL LEDGER

Cash					No. 1
Date	Explanation	Ref.	Debit	Credit	Balance
1993					
Oct. 1		J1	10,000		10,000
2		J1	1,200		11,200
3		J1		900	10,300
4		J1		600	9,700
20		J1		500	9,200
26		J1		4,000	5,200
31		J1	10,000		**15,200**

Advertising Supplies					No. 8
Date	Explanation	Ref.	Debit	Credit	Balance
1993					
Oct. 5		J1	2,500		**2,500**

Prepaid Insurance					No. 10
Date	Explanation	Ref.	Debit	Credit	Balance
1993					
Oct. 4		J1	600		**600**

Office Equipment					No. 15
Date	Explanation	Ref.	Debit	Credit	Balance
1993					
Oct. 1		J1	5,000		**5,000**

Notes Payable					No. 25
Date	Explanation	Ref.	Debit	Credit	Balance
1993					
Oct. 1		J1		5,000	**5,000**

Accounts Payable					No. 26
Date	Explanation	Ref.	Debit	Credit	Balance
1993					
Oct. 5		J1		2,500	**2,500**

Unearned Fees					No. 28
Date	Explanation	Ref.	Debit	Credit	Balance
1993					
Oct. 2		J1		1,200	**1,200**

C. R. Byrd, Capital					No. 40
Date	Explanation	Ref.	Debit	Credit	Balance
1993					
Oct. 1		J1		10,000	**10,000**

C. R. Byrd, Drawing					No. 41
Date	Explanation	Ref.	Debit	Credit	Balance
1993					
Oct. 20		J1	500		**500**

Fees Earned					No. 50
Date	Explanation	Ref.	Debit	Credit	Balance
1993					
Oct. 31		J1		10,000	**10,000**

Salaries Expense					No. 60
Date	Explanation	Ref.	Debit	Credit	Balance
1993					
Oct. 26		J1	4,000		**4,000**

Rent Expense					No. 62
Date	Explanation	Ref.	Debit	Credit	Balance
1993					
Oct. 3		J1	900		**900**

Preparing the Trial Balance

A trial balance is a list of accounts and their balances at a given time. Customarily, a trial balance is prepared at the end of an accounting period. The accounts are listed in the order in which they appear in the ledger, with debit balances listed in the left column and credit balances in the right column. The totals of the two columns must be in agreement.

The primary purpose of a trial balance is to prove the mathematical equality of debits and credits after posting. Under the double-entry system this equality will occur when the sum of the debit account balances equals the sum of the

Study Objective 7

Prepare a trial balance and explain its purposes.

Helpful hint A trial balance is so named because it is a test to determine if the sum of the debit balances equals the sum of the credit balances.

credit account balances. **A trial balance also uncovers errors in journalizing and posting. In addition, it is useful in the preparation of financial statements**, as will be explained in the next two chapters. The procedures for preparing a trial balance consist of:

1. Listing the account titles and their balances.
2. Totaling the debit and credit columns.
3. Proving the equality of the two columns.

The trial balance prepared from the ledger of Pioneer Advertising Agency is presented below:

ILLUSTRATION 2-31

A trial balance

PIONEER ADVERTISING AGENCY Trial Balance October 31, 1993		
	Debit	Credit
Cash	$15,200	
Advertising Supplies	2,500	
Prepaid Insurance	600	
Office Equipment	5,000	
Notes Payable		$ 5,000
Accounts Payable		2,500
Unearned Fees		1,200
C. R. Byrd, Capital		10,000
C. R. Byrd, Drawing	500	
Fees Earned		10,000
Salaries Expense	4,000	
Rent Expense	900	
	$28,700	$28,700

Helpful hint If only the debit portion of a journal entry is posted, what procedure should bring this error to light? Answer: Taking a trial balance.

Note that the total debits $28,700 equal the total credits $28,700. Some accountants also show account numbers to the left of the account titles in the trial balance.

Limitations of a Trial Balance

Helpful hint A trial balance is a necessary check point before proceeding to other steps in the accounting process.

A trial balance does not prove that all transactions have been recorded or that the ledger is correct. Numerous errors may exist even though the trial balance columns agree. For example, the trial balance may balance even when (1) a transaction is not journalized, (2) a correct journal entry is not posted, (3) a journal

Accounting in Action · *Business Insight*

According to one large accounting firm, in some audits where a lot of number crunching is done, microcomputers have cut the audit time by 10–20%. For one multinational client with 1,000 sales offices, microcomputers used by Price Waterhouse & Co. auditors analyzed each office's revenues and expenses in *two hours*, pinpointing whether such items as rent and other expense accounts were appropriate—a job that would have taken two days before micros.

entry is posted twice, (4) incorrect accounts are used in journalizing or posting, or (5) offsetting errors are made in recording the amount of a transaction. In other words, as long as equal debits and credits are posted, even to the wrong account or in the wrong amount, the total debits will equal the total credits.

Locating Errors

The procedure for preparing a trial balance is relatively simple. However, in manual systems if the trial balance does not balance, locating an error can be time-consuming, tedious, and frustrating. The error(s) generally results from mathematical mistakes, incorrect postings, or simply transcribing the data incorrectly.

What happens if you are faced with a trial balance that does not balance? First determine the amount of the difference between the two columns of the trial balance. After this amount is known, the following steps are often helpful:

1. If the error is $1, $100, $1,000, re-add the trial balance columns and re-compute the account balances.
2. If the error is divisible by two, scan the trial balance to see whether a balance equal to half the error has been entered in the wrong column.
3. If the error is divisible by nine, retrace the account balances on the trial balance to see whether they are incorrectly copied from the ledger. For example, if a balance was $12 and it was listed as $21, a $9 error has been made. Reversing the order of numbers is called a transposition error.
4. If the error is not divisible by two or nine, as, for example, $365, scan the ledger to see whether an account balance of $365 has been omitted from the trial balance, and scan the journal to see whether a $365 posting has been omitted.

Technology in Action

In a computerized system, the trial balance is often only one column (no debit or credit columns), and the accounts have plus and minus signs associated with them. The final balance therefore is zero. Any errors that develop in a computerized system will undoubtedly involve the initial recording rather than some error in the posting or preparation of a trial balance.

Use of Dollar Signs

Note that dollar signs do not appear in the journals or ledgers. Dollar signs are usually used only in the trial balance and the financial statements. Generally, a dollar sign is shown only for the first item in the column and for the total of that column. A single line is placed under the column of figures to be added or subtracted; the total amount is double underlined to indicate the final sum.

Before You Go On . . .

1. What is a trial balance and how is it prepared?
2. What is the primary purpose of a trial balance?
3. What are the limitations of a trial balance?

Summary of Study Objectives

1. Explain what an account is and how it helps in the recording process. An account is an individual accounting record of increases and decreases in specific asset, liability, and owner's equity items.

2. Define debits and credits and explain how they are used to record business transactions. The terms debit and credit are synonymous with left and right. Assets, drawings, and expenses are increased by debits and decreased by credits. Liabilities, owner's capital, and revenues are increased by credits and decreased by debits.

3. Identify the basic steps in the recording process. The basic steps in the recording process are: (a) analyze each transaction in terms of its effect on the accounts, (b) enter the transaction information in a journal, (c) transfer the journal information to the appropriate accounts in the ledger.

4. Explain what a journal is and how it helps in the recording process. The initial accounting record of a transaction is entered in a journal before the data are entered in the accounts. A journal (a) discloses in one place the complete effect of a transaction, (b) provides a chronological record of transactions, and (c) prevents or locates errors because the debit and credit amounts for each entry can be readily compared.

5. Explain what a ledger is and how it helps in the recording process. The entire group of accounts maintained by a company is referred to collectively as a ledger. The ledger keeps in one place all the information about changes in specific account balances.

6. Explain what posting is and how it helps in the recording process. Posting is the procedure of transferring journal entries to the ledger accounts. This phase of the recording process accumulates the effects of journalized transactions in the individual accounts.

7. Prepare a trial balance and explain its purposes. A trial balance is a list of accounts and their balances at a given time. The primary purpose of the trial balance is to prove the mathematical equality of debits and credits after posting. A trial balance also uncovers errors in journalizing and posting and is useful in preparing financial statements.

GLOSSARY

Account ▪ An individual accounting record of increases and decreases in specific asset, liability, and owner's equity items. (p. 46).

Chart of accounts ▪ A list of accounts and the account numbers which identify their location in the ledger. (p. 57).

Compound entry ▪ An entry that involves three or more accounts. (p. 54).

Credit ▪ The right side of an account. (p. 47).

Debit ▪ The left side of an account. (p. 47).

Double-entry system ▪ A system that records the dual effect of each transaction in appropriate accounts. (p. 48).

General journal ▪ The most basic form of journal. (p. 52).

General ledger ▪ A ledger that contains all asset, liability, and owner's equity accounts. (p. 54).

Journal ▪ An accounting record in which transactions are initially recorded in chronological order. (p. 52).

Journalizing ▪ The procedure of entering transaction data in the journal. (p. 53).

Ledger ▪ The entire group of accounts maintained by a company. (p. 54).

Posting ▪ The procedure of transferring journal entries to the ledger accounts. (p. 56).

Simple entry ▪ An entry that involves only two accounts. (p. 54).

T account ▪ The basic form of an account. (p. 46).

Three-column form of account ▪ A form containing money columns for debit, credit, and balance amounts in an account. (p. 55).

Trial balance ▪ A list of accounts and their balances at a given time. (p. 65).

DEMONSTRATION PROBLEM

Bob Sample opened the Campus Laundromat on September 1. During the first month of operations the following transactions occurred:

Sept. 1 Invested $20,000 cash in the business.
2 Paid $1,000 cash for store rent for the month of September.
3 Purchased washers and dryers for $25,000 paying $10,000 in cash and signing a $15,000 six-month 12% note payable.
4 Paid $1,200 for one-year accident insurance policy.
10 Received bill from the Daily News for advertising the opening of the laundromat, $200.
20 Withdrew $700 cash for personal use.
30 Determined that cash receipts for laundry fees for the month were $6,200.

The chart of accounts for the company is the same as in Pioneer Advertising Agency except for the following: No. 15 Laundry Equipment and No. 61 Advertising Expense.

Instructions
(a) Journalize the September transactions. (Use J1 for the journal page number.)
(b) Open ledger accounts and post the September transactions.
(c) Prepare a trial balance at September 30, 1993.

Solution to Demonstration Problem

(a) **GENERAL JOURNAL**   J1

Date	Account Titles and Explanation	Ref.	Debit	Credit
1993				
Sept. 1	Cash	1	20,000	
	Bob Sample, Capital	40		20,000
	(Invested cash in business)			
2	Rent Expense	62	1,000	
	Cash	1		1,000
	(Paid September rent)			
3	Laundry Equipment	15	25,000	
	Cash	1		10,000
	Notes Payable	25		15,000
	(Purchased laundry equipment for cash and six-month 12% note payable)			
4	Prepaid Insurance	10	1,200	
	Cash	1		1,200
	(Paid one-year insurance policy)			
10	Advertising Expense	61	200	
	Accounts Payable	26		200
	(Received bill from Daily News for advertising)			
20	Bob Sample, Drawing	41	700	
	Cash	1		700
	(Withdrew cash for personal use)			
30	Cash	1	6,200	
	Fees Earned	50		6,200
	(Received cash for laundry fees earned)			

Helpful hints
1. Separate journal entries are made for each transaction.
2. In journalizing, make sure debits equal credits.
3. In journalizing, use specific account titles taken from chart of accounts.
4. Provide appropriate description of journal entry.
5. Arrange ledger in statement order, beginning with the balance sheet accounts.
6. Post in chronological order.
7. Numbers in the reference column indicate the amount has been posted.
8. The trial balance lists accounts in the order in which they appear in the ledger.
9. Debit balances are listed in the left column, and credit balances in the right column.

(b)
GENERAL LEDGER

Cash — No. 1

Date	Explanation	Ref.	Debit	Credit	Balance
1993					
Sept. 1		J1	20,000		20,000
2		J1		1,000	19,000
3		J1		10,000	9,000
4		J1		1,200	7,800
20		J1		700	7,100
30		J1	6,200		13,300

Prepaid Insurance — No. 10

Date	Explanation	Ref.	Debit	Credit	Balance
1993					
Sept. 4		J1	1,200		1,200

Laundry Equipment — No. 15

Date	Explanation	Ref.	Debit	Credit	Balance
1993					
Sept. 3		J1	25,000		25,000

Notes Payable — No. 25

Date	Explanation	Ref.	Debit	Credit	Balance
1993					
Sept. 3		J1		15,000	15,000

Accounts Payable — No. 26

Date	Explanation	Ref.	Debit	Credit	Balance
1993					
Sept. 10		J1		200	200

Bob Sample, Capital — No. 40

Date	Explanation	Ref.	Debit	Credit	Balance
1993					
Sept. 1		J1		20,000	20,000

Bob Sample, Drawing — No. 41

Date	Explanation	Ref.	Debit	Credit	Balance
1993					
Sept. 20		J1	700		700

Fees Earned — No. 50

Date	Explanation	Ref.	Debit	Credit	Balance
1993					
Sept. 30		J1		6,200	6,200

Advertising Expense — No. 61

Date	Explanation	Ref.	Debit	Credit	Balance
1993					
Sept. 10		J1	200		200

Rent Expense — No. 62

Date	Explanation	Ref.	Debit	Credit	Balance
1993					
Sept. 2		J1	1,000		1,000

(c)
CAMPUS LAUNDROMAT
Trial Balance
September 30, 1993

	Debit	Credit
Cash	$13,300	
Prepaid Insurance	1,200	
Laundry Equipment	25,000	
Notes Payable		$15,000
Accounts Payable		200
Bob Sample, Capital		20,000
Bob Sample, Drawing	700	
Fees Earned		6,200
Advertising Expense	200	
Rent Expense	1,000	
	$41,400	$41,400

SELF-STUDY QUESTIONS

Answers are at the end of chapter.

(S.O. 1) 1. Which of the following statements about an account is true?
   a. In its simplest form, an account consists of two parts.
   b. An account is an individual accounting record of increases and decreases in specific asset, liability, and owner's equity items.
   c. There are separate accounts for specific assets and liabilities but only one account for owner's equity items.
   d. The left side of an account is the credit or decrease side.

(S.O. 2) 2. Debits:
   a. increase both assets and liabilities.
   b. decrease both assets and liabilities.
   c. increase assets and decrease liabilities.
   d. decrease assets and increase liabilities.

(S.O. 2) 3. A revenue account:
   a. is increased by debits.
   b. is decreased by credits.
   c. has a normal balance of a debit.
   d. is increased by credits.

(S.O. 2) 4. Accounts that normally have debit balances are:
   a. assets, expenses, and revenues.
   b. assets, expenses, and owner's capital.
   c. assets, liabilities, and owner's drawings.
   d. assets, owner's drawings, and expenses.

(S.O. 3) 5. Which of the following is not part of the recording process?
   a. Analyzing transactions.
   b. Preparing a trial balance.
   c. Entering transactions in a journal.
   d. Posting transactions.

(S.O. 4) 6. Which of the following statements about a journal is false?
   a. It is not a book of original entry.
   b. It provides a chronological record of transactions.

   c. It helps to locate errors because the debit and credit amounts for each entry can be readily compared.
   d. It discloses in one place the complete effect of a transaction.

(S.O. 5) 7. A ledger:
   a. contains only asset and liability accounts.
   b. should show accounts in alphabetical order.
   c. is a collection of the entire group of accounts maintained by a company.
   d. is a book of original entry.

(S.O. 6) 8. Posting:
   a. normally occurs before journalizing.
   b. transfers ledger transaction data to the journal.
   c. is an optional step in the recording process.
   d. transfers journal entries to ledger accounts.

(S.O. 7) 9. A trial balance:
   a. is a list of accounts with their balances at a given time.
   b. proves the mathematical accuracy of journalized transactions.
   c. will not balance if a correct journal entry is posted twice.
   d. proves that all transactions have been recorded.

(S.O. 7) 10. A trial balance will not balance if:
   a. a correct journal entry is posted twice.
   b. the purchase of supplies on account is debited to Supplies and credited to Cash.
   c. a $100 cash drawing by the owner is debited to Owner's Drawing for $1,000 and credited to Cash for $100.
   d. a $450 payment on account is debited to Accounts Payable for $45 and credited to Cash for $45.

QUESTIONS

1. Why is an account referred to as a T account?

2. (a) Distinguish between the terms debit and credit. (b) Give an example of how each term is used in the recording process.

3. Albert Allen, a fellow student, contends that the double-entry system means each transaction must be recorded twice. Is Albert correct? Explain.

4. Lila Lukas, a beginning accounting student, believes debit balances are favorable and credit balances are unfavorable. Is Lila correct? Discuss.

5. State the rules of debit and credit as applied to (a) asset accounts, (b) liability accounts, and (c) owner's capital account.

6. What is the normal balance for each of the following accounts? (a) Fees Receivable. (b) Cash. (c) Owner's Drawing. (d) Accounts Payable. (e) Fees Earned. (f) Wages Expense. (g) Owner's Capital.

7. Indicate whether each of the following accounts is an asset, a liability, or an owner's equity account and whether it would have a debit or credit balance: (a) Accounts Receivable, (b) Accounts Payable, (c) Equipment, (d) Owner's Drawing, (e) Supplies.

8. For the following transactions, indicate the account debited and the account credited:
(a) Supplies are purchased on account.
(b) Cash is received on signing a note payable.
(c) Employees are paid wages in cash.

9. Presented below are a series of accounts. Indicate whether these accounts generally will have (a) debit entries only, (b) credit entries only, (c) both debit and credit entries.
(1) Cash.   (4) Accounts Payable.
(2) Fees Receivable.   (5) Wages Expense.
(3) Owner's Drawing.   (6) Fees Earned.

10. What are the basic steps in the recording process?

11. What are the advantages of using the journal in the recording process?

12. (a) When entering a transaction in the journal, should the debit or credit be written first?
(b) Which should be indented, the debit or credit?

13. Give an example of a compound entry.

14. (a) Can business transaction debits and credits be recorded directly in the ledger accounts?
(b) What are the advantages of first recording transactions in the journal and then posting to the ledger?

15. The account number is entered as the last step in posting the amounts from the journal to the ledger. What is the advantage of this step?

16. Journalize the following business transactions.
(a) C. Strang invests $9,000 in the business.
(b) Insurance of $800 is paid for the year.
(c) Supplies of $1,500 are purchased on account.
(d) Cash of $6,500 is received for services rendered.

17. (a) What is a ledger?   (b) Why is a chart of accounts important?

18. What is a trial balance and what are its purposes?

19. Bart Nickles is confused about how accounting information flows through the accounting system. He believes the flow of information is as follows:
(a) Business transaction occurs.
(b) Debits and credits posted to the ledger.
(c) Information entered in the journal.
(d) Financial statements are prepared.
(e) Trial balance is prepared.
Indicate to Bart the proper flow of the information.

20. Two students are discussing the use of a trial balance. They wonder whether the following errors, each considered separately, would prevent the trial balance from balancing.
(a) The bookkeeper debited Cash for $600 and credited Wages Expense for $600 for payment of wages.
(b) Cash collected on account was debited to Cash for $900 and Fees Earned was credited for $900.
What would you tell them?

BRIEF EXERCISES

BE2–1 For each of the following accounts indicate (a) the effect of a debit or a credit on the account and (b) the normal balance.

1. Accounts Payable.
2. Advertising Expense.
3. Fees Earned.
4. Fees Receivable.
5. R. Ames, Capital.
6. R. Ames, Drawing.

Indicate debit and credit effects and normal balance. (S.O. 2)

BE2–2 Transactions for the H. J. Oates Company for the month of June are presented below. Identify the accounts to be debited and credited for each transaction.

Identify accounts to be debited and credited. (S.O. 2)

June 1 H. J. Oates invests $2,500 cash in a small welding business of which he is the sole proprietor.
  2 Buys equipment on account for $900.
  3 Pays $500 to landlord for June rent.
  12 Bills J. Kronsnoble $300 for welding work done.

BE2–3 Using the data in BE2–2 above, journalize the transactions. (You may omit explanations.)

Journalize transactions. (S.O. 4)

BE2–4 R. A. Sims, a fellow student, is unclear about the basic steps in the recording process. Identify and briefly explain the steps in the order in which they occur.

Identify and explain steps in recording process. (S.O. 3)

BE2–5 J. A. Moore has the following transactions during August of the current year. Indicate (a) the basic analysis and (b) the debit-credit analysis illustrated on pages 59–63 of the text.

Indicate basic and debit-credit analysis. (S.O. 4)

Aug. 1 Opens an office as a financial advisor, investing $5,000 in cash.
  4 Pays insurance in advance for six months, $1,800.
  16 Receives $900 from clients for services rendered.
  27 Pays secretary $500 salary.

BE2–6 Using the data in BE2–5 above, journalize the transactions. (You may omit explanations.)

Journalize transactions. (S.O. 4)

BE2–7 Selected transactions for the Arans Company are presented in journal form below. Post the transactions to T accounts.

Post journal entries to T accounts. (S.O. 6)

J1

Date	Account Titles and Explanation	Ref.	Debit	Credit
May 5	Fees Receivable		3,200	
	Fees Earned			3,200
12	Cash		2,400	
	Fees Receivable			2,400
15	Cash		2,000	
	Fees Earned			2,000

BE2–8 Selected journal entries for the Arans Company are presented in BE2–7. Post the transactions using the standard form of account.

Post journal entries to standard form of account. (S.O. 6)

BE2–9 From the ledger balances given below, prepare a trial balance for the P. J. Carlan Company at June 30, 1993. List the accounts in the order shown on page 66 of the text. All account balances are normal.

Prepare a trial balance. (S.O. 7)

Accounts Payable $3,000, Cash $3,800, P. J. Carlan, Capital $20,000, P. J. Carlan, Drawing $1,200, Equipment $17,000, Fees Earned $6,000, Fees Receivable $2,000, Salaries Expense $4,000, and Rent Expense $1,000.

BE2–10 An inexperienced bookkeeper prepared the following trial balance that does not balance. Prepare a correct trial balance, assuming all account balances are normal.

Prepare a correct trial balance. (S.O. 7)

VEIL COMPANY
Trial Balance
December 31, 1993

	Debit	Credit
Cash	$18,800	
Prepaid Insurance		$ 2,500
Accounts Payable		3,000
Unearned Fees	1,200	
Diane Veil, Capital		17,000
Diane Veil, Drawing		4,500
Fees Earned		25,600
Salaries Expense	18,600	
Rent Expense		2,400
	$38,600	$55,000

EXERCISES

Identify debits, credits, and normal balances.
(S.O. 2)

E2–1   Selected transactions for A. Mont, an interior decorator, in her first month of business, are as follows:

1. Invested $10,000 cash in business.
2. Purchased used car for $4,000 cash for use in business.
3. Purchased supplies on account for $500.
4. Billed customers $1,800 for services performed.
5. Paid $200 cash for advertising start of business.
6. Received $700 cash from customers billed in (4) above.
7. Paid creditor $300 cash on account.
8. Withdrew $500 cash for personal use of owner.

Instructions
For each transaction indicate (a) the basic type of account debited and credited (asset, liability, owner's equity); (b) the specific account debited and credited (cash, fees receivable, fees earned, etc.); (c) whether the specific account is increased or decreased; and (d) the normal balance of the specific account. Use the following format, in which transaction (1) is given as an example:

	Account Debited				Account Credited			
Trans-action	(a) Basic Type	(b) Specific Account	(c) Effect	(d) Normal Balance	(a) Basic Type	(b) Specific Account	(c) Effect	(d) Normal Balance
(1)	Asset	Cash	Increase	Debit	Owner's Equity	A. Mont, Capital	Increase	Credit

Journalize transactions and post using standard account form.
(S.O. 4, 6)

E2–2   Data for A. Mont, interior decorator, are presented in E2–1.

Instructions
Journalize the transactions using journal page J1.

E2–3   Presented below is information related to Lydia's Real Estate Agency:

Analyze transactions and determine their effect on accounts.
(S.O. 2)

Oct. 1 Lydia North begins business as a real estate agent with a cash investment of $13,000.

2 Hires an administrative assistant.

3 Buys office furniture for $1,900, on account.

6 Sells a house and lot for B. Rollins; fees due from Rollins, $3,200 (not paid by Rollins at this time).

10 Receives cash of $140 as fees for renting an apartment for the owner.

27 Pays $700 on the balance indicated in the transaction of October 3.

30 Pays the administrative assistant $960 in salary for October.

Instructions
Prepare the debit-credit analysis for each transaction as illustrated on pages 59–63.

E2–4 Transaction data for Lydia's Real Estate Agency are presented in E2–3.

Journalize transactions.
(S.O. 4)

Instructions
Journalize the transactions.

E2–5 Selected transactions from the journal of T. R Mays, investment broker, are presented below.

Post journal entries and
prepare a trial balance.
(S.O. 6, 7)

Date	Account Titles and Explanation	Ref.	Debit	Credit
Aug. 1	Cash		1,500	
	T. R. Mays, Capital			1,500
10	Cash		2,400	
	Fees Earned			2,400
12	Office Equipment		4,000	
	Cash			1,000
	Notes Payable			3,000
25	Fees Receivable		1,400	
	Fees Earned			1,400
31	Cash		800	
	Fees Receivable			800

Instructions
(a) Post the transactions to T accounts.
(b) Prepare a trial balance at August 31, 1993.

E2–6 The T accounts below summarize the ledger of Hahn Landscaping Company at the end of the first month of operations:

Journalize transactions
from account data and
prepare a trial balance.
(S.O. 4, 7)

	Cash		No. 101
4/1	9,000	4/15	600
4/12	900	4/25	1,500
4/29	400		
4/30	800		

	Unearned Fees		No. 205
		4/30	800

	Fees Receivable		No. 111
4/7	3,200	4/29	400

	R. A. Hahn, Capital		No. 301
		4/1	9,000

	Supplies		No. 126
4/4	1,800		

	Fees Earned		No. 400
		4/7	3,200
		4/12	900

	Accounts Payable		No. 201
4/25	1,500	4/4	1,800

	Salaries Expense		No. 726
4/15	600		

Instructions
(a) Prepare the complete general journal (including explanations) from which the postings to Cash were made.
(b) Prepare a trial balance at April 30, 1993.

Journalize transactions from account data and prepare a trial balance.
(S.O. 4, 7)

E2–7   Presented below is the ledger for Hepworth Co.

Cash			No. 101
10/1	4,000	10/4	400
10/10	650	10/12	1,500
10/10	5,000	10/15	250
10/20	500	10/30	300
10/25	2,000	10/31	500

L. Hepworth, Capital			No. 301
		10/1	4,000
		10/25	2,000

L. Hepworth, Drawing			No. 306
10/30	300		

Accounts Receivable			No. 112
10/6	800	10/20	500
10/20	940		

Service Revenue			No. 407
		10/6	800
		10/10	650
		10/20	940

Supplies			No. 126
10/4	400	10/31	180

Store Wages Expense			No. 628
10/31	500		

Furniture			No. 149
10/3	2,000		

Supplies Expense			No. 631
10/31	180		

Notes Payable			No. 200
		10/10	5,000

Rent Expense			No. 729
10/15	250		

Accounts Payable			No. 201
10/12	1,500	10/3	2,000

Instructions

(a) Reproduce the journal entries for the transactions that occurred on October 1, 10, and 20 and provide explanations for each.

(b) Prepare a trial balance at October 31, 1993.

Prepare journal entries and post using standard account form.
(S.O. 4, 6)

E2–8   Selected transactions for the Elway Company during its first month in business are presented below.

Sept. 1   Invested $15,000 cash in the business.
       5   Purchased equipment for $10,000 paying $5,000 in cash and the balance on account.
      25   Paid $3,000 cash on balance owed for equipment.
      30   Withdrew $1,000 cash for personal use.

Elway's chart of accounts shows: Cash, No. 101; Equipment, No. 157; and Accounts Payable, No. 201; J. Elway, Capital, No. 301; and J. Elway, Drawing, No. 306.

Instructions

(a) Journalize the transactions on page J1 of the journal.

(b) Post the transactions using the standard account form.

Analyze errors and their effects on trial balance.
(S.O. 7)

E2–9   The bookkeeper for Ball's Equipment Repair made a number of errors in journalizing and posting, as described below:

1. A credit posting of $400 to Accounts Receivable was omitted.
2. A debit posting of $750 for Prepaid Insurance was debited to Insurance Expense.
3. A collection on account of $100 was journalized and posted as a debit to Cash $100 and a credit to Fees Earned $100.
4. A credit posting of $300 to Property Taxes Payable was made twice.
5. A cash purchase of supplies for $250 was journalized and posted as a debit to Supplies $25 and a credit to Cash $25.
6. A debit of $456 to Advertising Expense was posted as $465.

Instructions

For each error, indicate (a) whether the trial balance will balance; if the trial balance will not balance, indicate (b) the amount of the difference, and (c) the trial balance column that will have the larger total. Consider each error separately. Use the following form, in which error (1) is given as an example.

	(a)	(b)	(c)
Error	In Balance	Difference	Larger Column
(1)	No	$400	debit

E2–10 The accounts in the ledger of the B & E Delivery Service contain the following balances on July 31, 1993:

Prepare a trial balance. (S.O. 7)

Accounts Receivable	$ 7,642	Prepaid Insurance	$ 1,968
Accounts Payable	7,396	Repair Expense	961
Cash	?	Service Revenue	8,610
Delivery Equipment	49,360	T. Wald, Drawing	700
Gas and Oil Expense	758	T. Wald, Capital	44,636
Insurance Expense	523	Wages Expense	4,428
Notes Payable	18,450	Wages Payable	815

Instructions

Prepare a trial balance with the accounts arranged as illustrated in the chapter and fill in the missing amount for Cash.

PROBLEMS

P2–1 The Parmor Miniature Golf and Driving Range was opened on March 1 by Jack Parr. The following selected events and transactions occurred during March:

Journalize a series of transactions. (S.O. 2, 4)

Mar. 1 Invested $50,000 cash in the business.
      3 Purchased Lee's Golf Land for $38,000 cash. The price consists of land, $23,000, building, $9,000, and equipment, $6,000. (Make one compound entry.)
      5 Advertised the opening of the driving range and miniature golf course, paying advertising expenses of $1,600.
      6 Paid cash $1,480 for a one-year insurance policy.
     10 Purchased golf clubs and other equipment for $1,600 from Palmer Company payable in 30 days.
     18 Received golf fees of $800 in cash.
     19 Sold 100 coupon books for $15.00 each. Each book contains 10 coupons that enable the holder to one round of miniature golf or to hit one bucket of golf balls.
     25 Withdrew $500 cash for personal use.
     30 Paid wages of $700.
     30 Paid Palmer Company in full.
     31 Received $500 of fees in cash.

Jack Parr uses the following accounts: Cash; Prepaid Insurance; Land; Buildings; Equipment; Accounts Payable; Unearned Golf Fees; Jack Parr, Capital; Jack Parr, Drawing; Golf Fees Earned; Advertising Expense; and Wages Expense.

Instructions

Journalize the March transactions.

P2–2 Patricia Bowen is a licensed architect. During the first month of the operation of her business, the following events and transactions occurred.

Journalize transactions, post, and prepare trial balance. (S.O. 2, 4, 6, 7)

April 1 Invested $13,000 cash.
       1 Hired a secretary-receptionist at a salary of $300 per week payable monthly.
       2 Paid office rent for the month, $800.
       3 Purchased architectural supplies on account from Halo Company, $1,500.

10   Completed blueprints on a carport and billed client $900 for services.
11   Received $500 cash advance from R. Weld for the design of a new home.
20   Received $1,500 cash for services completed and delivered to P. Donahue.
30   Paid secretary-receptionist for the month, $1,200.
30   Determined that $400 of supplies had been used.
30   Paid $500 to Halo Company on account.

Patricia uses the following chart of accounts: No. 101 Cash, No. 111 Fees Receivable, No. 126 Supplies, No. 201 Accounts Payable, No. 205 Unearned Fees, No. 301 Patricia Bowen, Capital, No. 400 Fees Earned, No. 631 Supplies Expense, No. 726 Salaries Expense, and No. 729 Rent Expense.

Instructions

(a) Journalize the transactions.

(b) Post to the ledger accounts.

(c) Prepare a trial balance on April 30, 1993.

Journalize transactions, post, and prepare a trial balance.
(S.O. 2, 4, 6, 7)

P2–3   The trial balance of Kent Laundry on September 30 is shown below:

KENT LAUNDRY
Trial Balance
September 30, 1993

Account No.		Debit	Credit
101	Cash	$ 8,500	
112	Accounts Receivable	2,200	
126	Supplies	1,700	
157	Equipment	8,000	
201	Accounts Payable		$ 5,000
206	Unearned Revenue		700
301	Jane Kent, Capital		14,700
		$20,400	$20,400

The October transactions were as follows:

Oct. 5   Received $900 cash from customers on account.
10   Billed customers for services performed $5,500.
15   Paid employee salaries $1,200.
17   Performed $400 of services for customers who paid in advance in August.
20   Paid $1,600 to creditors on account.
29   Withdrew $500 for personal use.
31   Paid utilities $600.
31   Determined that $800 of supplies had been used.

Instructions

(a) Enter the opening balances in the ledger accounts as of October 1. Write "Balance" in the explanation space and insert a check mark (√) in the reference column. Provision should be made for the following additional accounts: No. 306 Jane Kent, Drawing, No. 426 Laundry Revenue, No. 631 Supplies Expense, No. 726 Salaries Expense, and No. 732 Utilities Expense.

(b) Journalize the transactions.

(c) Post to the ledger accounts.

(d) Prepare a trial balance on October 31, 1993.

P2–4 The trial balance of Brian Hayes Co. shown below does not balance.

Prepare a correct trial balance.
(S.O. 7)

BRIAN HAYES CO.
Trial Balance
June 30, 1993

	Debit	Credit
Cash		$ 2,840
Fees Receivable	$ 3,231	
Supplies	800	
Equipment	3,000	
Accounts Payable		2,666
Unearned Fees	1,200·	
B. Hayes, Capital		9,000
B. Hayes, Drawing	800	
Fees Earned		2,380
Wages Expense	3,400	
Office Expense	910	
	$13,341	$16,886

Each of the listed accounts has a normal balance per the general ledger. An examination of the ledger and journal reveals the following errors.

1. Cash received from a customer on account was debited for $570 and Fees Receivable was credited for the same amount. The actual collection was for $750.
2. The purchase of a typewriter on account for $340 was recorded as a debit to Supplies for $340 and a credit to Accounts Payable for $340.
3. Services were performed on account for a client for $890. Fees Receivable was debited for $890 and Fees Earned was credited for $89.
4. A debit posting to Wages Expense of $600 was omitted.
5. A payment on account for $206 was credited to Cash for $206 and credited to Accounts Payable for $260.
6. The withdrawal of $500 cash for Hayes' personal use was debited to Wages Expense for $500 and credited to Cash for $500.

Instructions
Prepare a correct trial balance.

P2–5 The Bay Theater, owned by Leo Anders, will begin operations in March. The Bay will be unique in that it will show only triple features of sequential theme movies. As of February 28, the ledger of Bay showed: No. 101 Cash $16,000, No. 140 Land $42,000, No. 145 Buildings (concession stand, projection room, ticket booth, and screen) $18,000, No. 157 Equipment $16,000, No. 201 Accounts Payable $12,000, and No. 301 L. Anders, Capital $80,000. During the month of March the following events and transactions occurred:

Journalize transactions, post, and prepare a trial balance.
(S.O. 2, 4, 6, 7)

Mar. 2 Acquired the three *Star Wars* movies (*Star Wars*, *The Empire Strikes Back*, and *The Return of the Jedi*) to be shown for the first three weeks of March. The film rental was $12,000; $4,000 was paid in cash and $8,000 will be paid on March 10.

3 Ordered the first three *Star Trek* movies to be shown the last 10 days of March. It will cost $400 per night.

9 Received $6,500 cash from admissions.

10 Paid balance due on *Star Wars* movies rental and $3,000 on February 28 accounts payable.

11 Hired M. Brewer to operate concession stand for 15% of gross receipts payable monthly.

12 Paid advertising expenses $800.

20 Received $7,200 cash from admissions.

20 Received the *Star Trek* movies and paid the rental fee of $4,000.

31 Paid salaries of $3,800.

31 Received statement from M. Brewer showing gross receipts from concessions of

$8,000 and the balance due of $1,200 for March. Brewer paid one-half the balance due and will remit the remainder on April 5.

    31   Received $12,900 cash from admissions.

In addition to the accounts identified above, the chart of accounts includes: No. 112 Accounts Receivable, No. 405 Admission Revenue, No. 406 Concession Revenue, No. 610 Advertising Expense, No. 632 Film Rental Expense, and No. 726 Salaries Expense.

Instructions

(a) Enter the beginning balances to the ledger. Insert a check mark (√) in the reference column of the ledger for the beginning balance.

(b) Journalize the March transactions.

(c) Post the March journal entries to the ledger. Assume that all entries are posted from page 1 of the journal.

(d) Prepare a trial balance on March 31, 1993.

ALTERNATE PROBLEMS

Journalize a series of transactions.
(S.O. 2, 4)

P2–1A The Aerospace Park was started on April 1 by Ed Quint. The following selected events and transactions occurred during April.

Apr. 1 Invested $60,000 cash in the business.

    4 Purchased land costing $30,000 for cash.

    8 Incurred advertising expense of $1,800 on account.

  11 Paid wages to employees $1,500.

  12 Hired park manager at a salary of $4,000 per month, effective May 1.

  13 Paid $1,500 for a one-year insurance policy.

  17 Withdrew $600 cash for personal use.

  20 Received $5,700 in cash for admission fees.

  25 Sold 100 coupon books for $25 each. Each book contains 10 coupons that entitle the holder to one admission to the park.

  30 Received $5,900 in cash admission fees.

  30 Paid $600 on account for advertising incurred on April 8.

Ed Quint uses the following accounts: Cash; Prepaid Insurance; Land; Accounts Payable; Unearned Admissions; Ed Quint, Capital; Ed Quint, Drawing; Admission Revenue; Advertising Expense; and Wages Expense.

Instructions
Journalize the April transactions.

Journalize transactions, post, and prepare a trial balance.
(S.O. 2, 4, 6, 7)

G

P2–2A Iva Holt is a licensed CPA. During the first month of operations of her business, the following events and transactions occurred:

May 1 Invested $42,000 cash.

    2 Hired a secretary-receptionist at a salary of $1,000 per month.

    3 Purchased supplies on account from Read Supply Company, $1,200.

    7 Paid office rent of $900 for the month.

  11 Completed a tax assignment and billed client $1,100 for services rendered.

  12 Received $3,500 advance on a management consulting engagement.

  17 Received cash of $1,200 for services completed for H. Arnold Co.

  31 Paid secretary-receptionist $1,000 salary for the month.

  31 A count of supplies indicated that $840 of supplies are on hand.

  31 Paid 40% of balance due Read Supply Company.

Iva uses the following chart of accounts: No. 101 Cash, No. 111 Fees Receivable, No. 126 Supplies, No. 201 Accounts Payable, No. 205 Unearned Fees, No. 301 Iva Holt, Capital, No. 400 Fees Earned, No. 631 Supplies Expense, No. 726 Salaries Expense, and No. 729 Rent Expense.

Instructions

(a) Journalize the transactions.

(b) Post to the ledger accounts.

(c) Prepare a trial balance on May 31, 1993.

P2–3A The trial balance of Superior Dry Cleaners on June 30 is shown below.

Journalize transactions, post, and prepare a trial balance.
(S.O. 2, 4, 6, 7)

SUPERIOR DRY CLEANERS
Trial Balance
June 30, 1993

Account No.		Debit	Credit
101	Cash	$12,532	
112	Accounts Receivable	10,536	
126	Supplies	4,844	
157	Equipment	25,950	
201	Accounts Payable		$15,878
206	Unearned Revenue		1,730
301	R. Sparrow, Capital		36,254
		$53,862	$53,862

The July transactions were as follows:

July 8 Collected $4,936 in cash on June 30 accounts receivable.
     9 Paid employee salaries $2,100.
    11 Received $4,325 in cash for services rendered.
    14 Paid June 30 creditors $10,750 on account.
    17 Purchased supplies on account $554.
    22 Billed customers for services rendered, $4,700.
    30 Paid employee salaries $3,114, utilities $1,384, and repairs $692.
    31 Determined that $1,038 of supplies had been used.
    31 Withdrew $700 cash for personal use of owner.

Instructions

(a) Enter the opening balances in the ledger accounts as of July 1. Write "Balance" in the explanation space and insert a check mark (√) in the reference column. Provision should be made for the following additional accounts: No. 306 R. Sparrow, Drawing, No. 428 Dry Cleaning Revenue, No. 622 Repair Expense, No. 631 Supplies Expense, No. 726 Salaries Expense, and No. 732 Utilities Expense.

(b) Journalize the transactions.

(c) Post to the ledger accounts.

(d) Prepare a trial balance on July 31, 1993.

P2–4A The trial balance of the Flint Company shown below does not balance.

Prepare a correct trial balance.
(S.O. 7)

FLINT COMPANY
Trial Balance
May 31, 1993

	Debit	Credit
Cash	$ 5,850	
Fees Receivable		$ 2,750
Prepaid Insurance	700	
Equipment	8,000	
Accounts Payable		4,500
Property Taxes Payable	560	
M. A. Flint, Capital		11,700
Fees Earned	6,690	
Salaries Expense	4,200	
Advertising Expense		1,100
Property Tax Expense	800	
	$26,800	$20,050

Your review of the ledger reveals that each account has a normal balance. You also discover the following errors.

1. The totals of the debit sides of Prepaid Insurance, Accounts Payable, and Property Tax Expense were each understated $100.

2. Transposition errors were made in Fees Receivable and Fees Earned. Based on postings made, the correct balances were $2,570 and $6,960, respectively.

3. A debit posting to Salaries Expense of $200 was omitted.

4. A $900 cash drawing by the owner was debited to M. A. Flint, Capital for $900 and credited to Cash for $900.

5. A $420 purchase of Supplies on account was debited to Equipment for $420 and credited to Cash for $420.

6. A cash payment of $250 for advertising was debited to Advertising Expense for $25 and credited to Cash for $25.

7. A collection from a customer for $210 was debited to Cash for $210 and credited to Accounts Payable for $210.

Instructions

Prepare a correct trial balance. (Note: The chart of accounts includes the following: M. A. Flint, Drawing; Supplies; and Supplies Expense.

Journalize transactions, post, and prepare a trial balance.

(S.O. 2, 4, 6, 7)

P2–5A   The Mountain Theater is owned by Frances Hill. All facilities were completed on March 31. At this time, the ledger showed: No. 101 Cash $6,000, No. 140 Land $10,000, No. 145 Buildings (concession stand, projection room, ticket booth, and screen) $8,000, No. 157 Equipment $6,000, No. 201 Accounts Payable $2,000, No. 275 Mortgage Payable $8,000, and No. 301 Frances Hill, Capital $20,000. During April, the following events and transactions occurred.

Apr. 2   Paid film rental of $800 on first movie.
      3   Ordered two additional films at $500 each.
      9   Received $1,800 cash from admissions.
     10   Made $2,000 payment on mortgage and $1,000 on accounts payable.
     11   Hired R. Thoms to operate concession stand for 17% of gross receipts payable monthly.
     12   Paid advertising expenses $300.
     20   Received one of the films ordered on April 3 and was billed $500. The film will be shown in April.
     25   Received $4,200 cash from admissions.
     29   Paid salaries $1,600.
     30   Received statement from R. Thoms showing gross receipts of $1,000 and the balance due of $170 for April. Thoms paid one-half of the balance due and will remit the remainder on May 5.
     30   Prepaid $600 rental on special film to be run in May.

In addition to the accounts identified above, the chart of accounts shows: No. 111 Fees Receivable, No. 136 Prepaid Rentals, No. 405 Admission Revenue, No. 406 Concession Revenue, No. 610 Advertising Expense, No. 632 Film Rental Expense, and No. 726 Salaries Expense.

Instructions

(a) Enter the beginning balances in the ledger as of April 1. Insert a check mark (√) in the reference column of the ledger for the beginning balance.

(b) Journalize the April transactions.

(c) Post the April journal entries to the ledger. Assume that all entries are posted from page 1 of the journal.

(d) Prepare a trial balance on April 30, 1993.

Broadening Your Perspective

FINANCIAL REPORTING PROBLEM

The financial statements of PepsiCo in Appendix L at the back of this textbook and the notes accompanying the statements contain the following selected accounts, and stated in millions of dollars:

Accounts Payable	1,196.6	Income Taxes Payable	492.4
Accounts Receivable	1,481.7	Interest Income	163.3
Interest Expense	615.9	Selling Expenses	7,880.8
Land	880.1	Notes Payable	1,100.0
Cash	186.7	Prepaid Expenses	386.9

Instructions
(a) Answer the following questions:
   1. What is the increase and decrease side for each account?
   2. What is the normal balance for each account?

(b) Identify the probable other account in the transaction and the effect on that account when
   1. Accounts Receivable is decreased.
   2. Notes Payable is increased.
   3. Prepaid Expenses are increased.

(c) Identify the other account(s) that ordinarily would be involved when
   1. Selling Expenses are increased.
   2. Land is increased.

DECISION CASE

Lucy Lars operates the Lars Riding Academy. The Academy's primary sources of revenue are riding fees and lesson fees, which are provided on a cash basis. Lucy also boards horses for owners, who are billed monthly for boarding fees. In a few cases, boarders pay in advance of expected use. For its revenue transactions, the Academy maintains the following accounts: No. 1 Cash, No. 5 Boarding Fees Receivable, No. 27 Unearned Boarding Fees, No. 51 Riding Fees Earned, No. 52 Lesson Fees Earned, and No. 53 Boarding Fees Earned.

The Academy owns 10 horses, a stable, a riding corral, riding equipment, and office equipment. These assets are accounted for in accounts No. 11 Horses, No. 12 Building, No. 13 Riding Corral, No. 14 Riding Equipment, and No. 15 Office Equipment.

The Academy employs stable helpers and an office employee, who receive weekly salaries. At the end of each month, the mail usually brings bills for advertising, utilities, and veterinary service. Other expenses include feed for the horses and insurance. For its expenses, the Academy maintains the following accounts: No. 6 Hay and Feed Supplies, No. 7 Prepaid Insurance, No. 21 Accounts Payable, No. 60 Salaries Expense, No. 61 Advertising Expense, No. 62 Utilities Expense, No. 63 Veterinary Expense, No. 64 Hay and Feed Expense, and No. 65 Insurance Expense.

Lucy Lars' sole source of income is the Academy. Thus, she makes periodic withdrawals of cash for personal living expenses. To record Lucy's equity in the business and her drawings, two accounts are maintained: No. 50 Lucy Lars, Capital, and No. 51 Lucy Lars, Drawing.

During the first month of operations an inexperienced bookkeeper was employed. Lucy Lars asks you to review the following nine entries of the 50 entries made during the month. In each case, the explanation for the entry is correct.

May	1	Cash	15,000	
		Lucy Lars, Capital		15,000
		(Invested $15,000 cash in business)		
	5	Cash	250	
		Riding Fees Earned		250
		(Received $250 cash for lesson fees)		
	7	Cash	300	
		Boarding Fees Earned		300
		(Received $300 for boarding of horses beginning June 1)		
	9	Hay and Feed Expense	1,700	
		Cash		1,700
		(Purchased estimated two months supply of feed and hay for $1,700 on account)		
	14	Riding Equipment	80	
		Cash		800
		(Purchased desk and other office equipment for $800 cash)		
	15	Salaries Expense	400	
		Cash		400
		(Issued check to Lucy Lars for personal use)		
	20	Cash	145	
		Riding Fees Earned		154
		(Received $154 cash for riding fees)		
	31	Veterinary Expense	75	
		Accounts Payable		75
		(Received bill of $75 from veterinarian for services rendered)		
	31	Hay and Feed Expense	960	
		Cash		96
		(Hay and feed used during May of $960)		

Instructions

(a) For each journal entry that is correct, so state. For each journal entry that is incorrect, prepare the entry that should have been made by the bookkeeper.

(b) Which of the incorrect entries would prevent the trial balance from balancing?

(c) What was the correct net income for May, assuming the bookkeeper reported net income of $4,500 after posting all 50 entries?

(d) What was the correct cash balance at May 31, assuming the bookkeeper reported a balance of $12,475 after posting all 50 entries?

CRITICAL THINKING CASE

Now that you have learned the details of the recording process, think back to the beginning of the chapter to Gabriella Torres and her position as office manager at Diabetes & Endocrine Associates.

1. What accounting entries would Gabriella be likely to make to record (a) the rent payment, (b) billing a patient for services rendered, and (c) collecting cash from a patient on account.

2. In what way might Gabriella's day-time job as office manager help in her studies as a night student in accounting and business?

3. How did the first course in accounting help Gabriella in her office manager's job at the medical practice office?

4. What part of Gabriella's work load is performed with the aid of a computer?

5. Prepare a likely list of asset accounts Gabriella has in her general ledger at Diabetes & Endocrine Associates.

ETHICAL CASE

Amy Shalla is the assistant chief accountant at Steeples Company, a manufacturer of computer chips and cellular phones. The company presently has total sales of $20 million. It is the end of the first quarter and Amy is hurriedly trying to prepare a general ledger trial balance so that quarterly financial statements can be prepared and released to management and the regulatory agencies. But the total credits on the trial balance exceed the debits by $1,000. In order to meet the 4 p.m. deadline, Amy decides to force the debits and credits into balance by adding the amount of the difference to the Equipment account. She chose Equipment because it is one of the larger account balances: percentage-wise it will be the least misstated. Amy plugs the difference! She believes that the difference is quite small and will not affect anyone's decisions. She wishes that she had another few days to find the error, but realizes that the financial statements are already late.

Instructions

(a) Who are the stakeholders in this situation?

(b) What are the ethical issues involved in this case?

(c) What are Amy's alternatives?

Answers to Self-Study Questions
1. b   2. c   3. d   4. d   5. b   6. a   7. c   8. d   9. a   10. c

CHAPTER 3

ADJUSTING THE ACCOUNTS

Like many colleges, Arizona State University uses a June 30 fiscal year end. Most schools consider that time the end of their main cycle of activity—the school year. Having an ending date like that might seem neat and tidy. But just like the private sector, colleges must make some adjusting entries to put certain expenses in their proper place.

For example, at ASU, the second summer session begins July 5 but registration takes place the prior February. "We have lots of students who are paying registration fees in February for a session that begins in July," says Carol Balk, ASU's manager of student fee payments. "So we have to make an adjusting entry at fiscal year end to properly account for the revenue collection five months earlier," she says. In other words, the revenue should be counted in the new fiscal year, not the old one. Despite 110 degree heat, ASU, based in Tempe, attracts thousands of students for the summer session. The reason: they don't charge out-of-state tuition rates in the summer to nonresidents.

Another adjusting entry is interest expense. Every June 30 and December 31,

an accrual is made for this item. During the 1980s, Arizona State University had a

substantial building program for which it borrowed over $250 million at an average

interest rate of 7%. It paid these interest costs semiannually on July 1 and January 1.

In the preceding chapter you learned the steps in the accounting cycle that pertain to the recording process. At this point you might think that we are ready to prepare financial statements from the trial balance, but additional steps in the accounting cycle still need to be performed. For example, during the past year, Pioneer Advertising purchased some supplies that are currently reported as an asset. The question is: What amount of the supplies purchased during the period should be reported as an expense? Similarly, office equipment that was purchased by Pioneer during the period is being used now. What portion, if any, of the equipment cost should be recognized as an expense of the current period? Before financial statements are prepared, these and other account balances must be adjusted. The purpose of this chapter is to explain and illustrate the different types of adjustments that accountants prepare. In addition, we illustrate an adjusted trial balance and show its role in preparing financial statements.

Selecting an Accounting Time Period

Study Objective 1

Explain the periodicity assumption.

No adjustments would be necessary if we waited to prepare financial statements until a company such as Pioneer terminated its operations. At the end of Pioneer's existence, we could readily determine its final balance sheet and the amount of lifetime income it earned. The following anecdote illustrates how easy it is to compute lifetime income.

A grocery store owner from the old country kept his accounts payable on a spindle, accounts receivable on a note pad, and cash in a cigar box. His daughter, having just passed the CPA exam, chided the father, "I don't understand how you can run your business this way. How do you know what your profits are?"

"Well," the father replied, "when I got off the boat forty years ago, I had nothing but the pants I was wearing. Today your brother is a doctor, your sister is a college professor, and you are a CPA. Your mother and I have a nice car, a well-furnished house, and a lake home. We have a good business and everything is paid for. So, you add all that together, subtract the pants, and there's your profit."

While the old grocer may be correct in his evaluation, in today's business environment all enterprises find it desirable, and necessary, to report the results of their activities more frequently. For example, management usually wants monthly financial statements and the Internal Revenue Service requires all businesses to file annual tax returns. As a consequence, **accountants make the assumption that the economic life of a business can be divided into artificial time periods**. This assumption is referred to as the periodicity or time period assumption.

Many business transactions affect more than one of these arbitrary time periods. For example, the milking machine bought by Farmer Brown in 1992 and the airplanes purchased by Delta Airlines five years ago are still in use today. Therefore, it is necessary to determine the relevance of each business transaction to specific accounting periods. Doing so may involve subjective judgments and estimates. Generally, the shorter the time period (e.g., a month or a quarter of a year), the more difficult it becomes to determine the proper adjustments to be made.

Fiscal and Calendar Years

Both small and large companies find it necessary to prepare financial statements on a periodic basis to assess their financial condition and results of operations. **Accounting time periods are generally a month, a quarter, or a year.** Monthly and quarterly time periods are often referred to as interim periods. Most large companies are required to prepare both interim (quarterly) and annual financial statements.

   Accounting time periods that are one year in length are referred to as fiscal years. Fiscal years usually begin with the first day of a month and end on the last day of a month, 12 months later. The accounting period most frequently used coincides with the calendar year (January 1 to December 31). However, there are many exceptions. To illustrate, examples of companies with other than a December 31 fiscal year-end are: Delta Air Lines, June 30; Walt Disney Productions, September 30; K-mart Corp., January 31; and Dunkin' Donuts, Inc., October 31.

Recognizing Revenues and Expenses

Determining the amount of revenues and expenses to be reported in a given accounting period can be difficult. Therefore, accountants have developed two principles as part of generally accepted accounting principles (GAAP) that help in this determination.

   One of these principles is the revenue recognition principle. This principle dictates that revenue be recognized in the accounting period in which it is earned. Revenue is considered to be earned in a service enterprise at the time the service is performed. To illustrate, assume that a dry cleaning business cleans clothing on June 30 but customers do not claim and pay for their clothes until the first

> **Study Objective 2**
>
> *Distinguish between the revenue recognition principle and the matching principle.*

Accounting in Action · *Business Insight*

Suppose you are a filmmaker and spend $15 million to produce a film. Over what period should the $15 million be written off? Yes, it should be written off over the economic life of the film. But what is its economic life? The filmmaker must estimate how much revenue will be earned from box office sales, video sales, and television—a period that easily can stretch five years or more. If a filmmaker allocates the cost over five years, and the film produces revenue in the sixth year, proper matching has not occurred. Furthermore, in some cases, films flop, and yet the costs are spread out over five years in the hopes that the films will eventually succeed. For example, in the mid-1980s Orion Pictures (now bankrupt) earned $7.3 million one year, but lost $32 million the next year because it wrote off 40 films that were not producing revenue. It was alleged that the company had overstated its income in earlier years because it did not write these costs off earlier. This case demonstrates the difficulty of properly matching costs to revenues.

week of July. Under the revenue recognition principle, revenue is earned in June when the service is performed and not in July when the cash is received. At June 30, the dry cleaner would report a receivable on its balance sheet and revenue in its income statement for the service performed.

In recognizing expenses, accountants follow the approach of "let the expenses follow the revenues." Thus, expense recognition is tied to revenue recognition. In the preceding example, this means that the salary expense incurred in performing the cleaning service on June 30 should be reported in the income statement for the same period as that in which the service revenue is recognized. The critical issue in expense recognition is when the expense makes its contribution to revenue. This may or may not be the same period in which the expense is paid. If the salary incurred on June 30 is not paid until July, the dry cleaner would report salaries payable on its June 30 balance sheet. The practice of expense recognition is referred to as the matching principle because it dictates that efforts (expenses) be matched with accomplishments (revenues).

Once the assumption is made that the economic life of a business can be divided into artificial time periods, it follows that the revenue recognition and matching principles can be applied. This one assumption and two principles thus provide guidelines as to when revenues and expenses should be reported. These relationships are shown in Illustration 3-1.

ILLUSTRATION 3-1

GAAP relationships in revenue and expense recognition

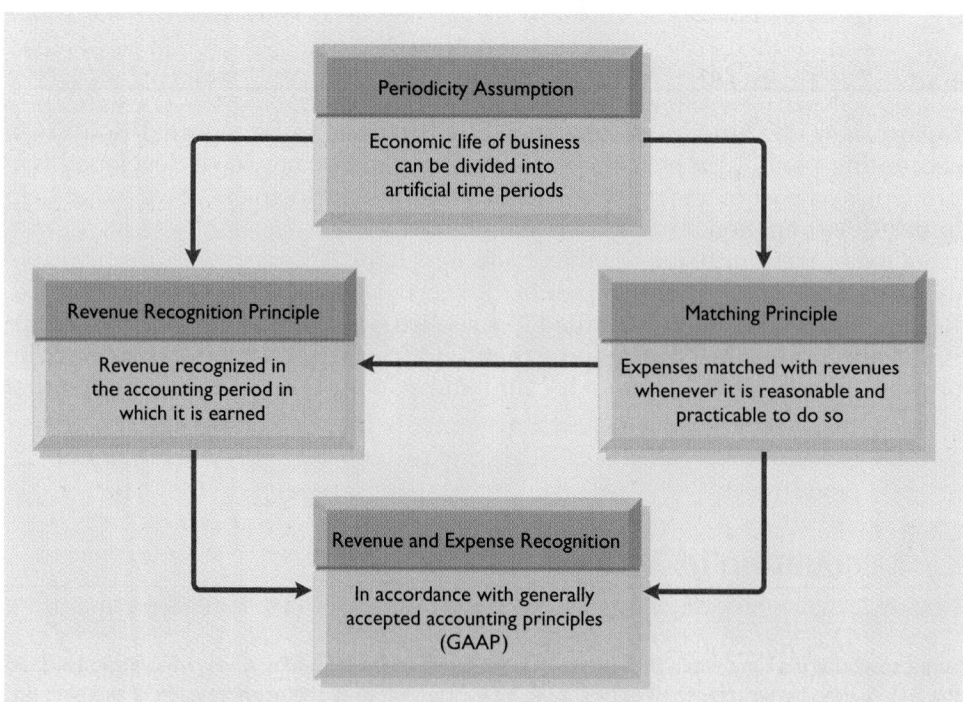

Before You Go On . . .

1. What is the relevance of the periodicity assumption to accounting?

2. What are the revenue recognition and matching principles?

3. What relationships apply under GAAP in recognizing revenues and expenses?

Need for Adjusting Entries

In order for revenues to be recorded in the period in which they are earned, and for expenses to be recognized in the period in which they are incurred, adjusting entries are made at the end of the accounting period. In short, **adjustments are needed to ensure that the revenue recognition and matching principles are followed**. The use of adjusting entries makes it possible to report on the balance sheet the appropriate assets, liabilities, and owner's equity at the statement date and to report on the income statement the proper net income (or loss) for the period. A trial balance may not contain up-to-date and complete financial statement data for the following reasons:

1. Some events, such as the consumption of supplies and the earning of wages by employees, are not journalized daily because it is inexpedient to do so.
2. The expiration of some costs, such as building and equipment deterioration and rent and insurance, is not journalized during the accounting period because these costs expire with the passage of time rather than as a result of recurring daily transactions.
3. Some items, such as the cost of utility service, may be unrecorded because the bill for the service has not been received.

Adjusting entries are required every time financial statements are prepared. An essential starting point is an analysis of each account in the trial balance to determine whether it is complete and up-to-date for financial statement purposes. The analysis requires a thorough understanding of the company's operations and the interrelationship of accounts. The preparation of adjusting entries is often an involved process that requires the services of a skilled professional. In accumulating the adjustment data, the company may need to make inventory counts of supplies and repair parts. Also it may be desirable to prepare supporting schedules of insurance policies, rental agreements, and other contractual commitments. Adjustments are often prepared after the balance sheet date. However, the entries are dated as of the balance sheet date.

Types of Adjusting Entries

Adjusting entries can be classified as either prepayments or accruals. Each of these classes has two subcategories as shown below:

Prepayments

1. Prepaid Expenses. Expenses paid in cash and recorded as assets before they are used or consumed.
2. Unearned Revenues. Revenues received in cash and recorded as liabilities before they are earned.

Accruals

3. Accrued Revenues. Revenues earned but not yet received in cash or recorded.
4. Accrued Expenses. Expenses incurred but not yet paid in cash or recorded.

Specific examples and explanations of each type of adjustment are given in subsequent sections. Each example is based on the October 31 trial balance of Pioneer Advertising Agency, reproduced on the next page from Chapter 2.

ILLUSTRATION 3-2

Trial balance

PIONEER ADVERTISING AGENCY Trial Balance October 31, 1993		
	Debit	Credit
Cash	$15,200	
Advertising Supplies	2,500	
Prepaid Insurance	600	
Office Equipment	5,000	
Notes Payable		$ 5,000
Accounts Payable		2,500
Unearned Fees		1,200
C. R. Byrd, Capital		10,000
C. R. Byrd, Drawing	500	
Fees Earned		10,000
Salaries Expense	4,000	
Rent Expense	900	
	$28,700	$28,700

It will be assumed that Pioneer Advertising uses an accounting period of one month. Thus, monthly adjusting entries will be made. The entries will be dated October 31.

Adjusting Entries for Prepayments

Study Objective 5

Prepare adjusting entries for prepayments.

Helpful hint Remember that credits decrease assets and increase revenues. Debits increase expenses and decrease liabilities.

As indicated earlier, prepayments are either prepaid expenses or unearned revenues. Adjusting entries for prepayments are required at the statement date to record the portion of the prepayment that represents the expense incurred or the revenue earned in the current accounting period. Assuming an adjustment is needed for both types of prepayments, the asset and liability are overstated and the related expense and revenue are understated. For example, in the trial balance, the balance in the asset, Supplies, will show only supplies purchased. This balance is overstated. The related expense account, Supplies Expense, is understated because the cost of supplies used has not been recognized. Thus the adjusting entry for prepayments will decrease a balance sheet account and increase an income statement account. Adjusting entries for prepayments are graphically depicted in Illustration 3-3.

Prepaid Expenses

Payments of expenses that will benefit more than one accounting period are identified as prepaid expenses or prepayments. When a cost is incurred, an asset account is debited to show the service or benefit that will be received in the future. Prepayments often occur in regard to insurance, supplies, advertising, and rent. In addition, prepayments are made when buildings and equipment are purchased.

Prepaid expenses expire either with the passage of time (e.g., rent and insurance) or through use and consumption (e.g., supplies). The expiration of these costs does not require daily recurring entries, which would be unnecessary and impractical. Accordingly, it is customary to postpone the recognition of such cost expirations until financial statements are prepared. At each statement date, adjusting entries are made to record the expenses applicable to the current accounting period and to show the unexpired costs in the asset accounts. **An asset-**

ILLUSTRATION 3-3

Adjusting entries for prepayments

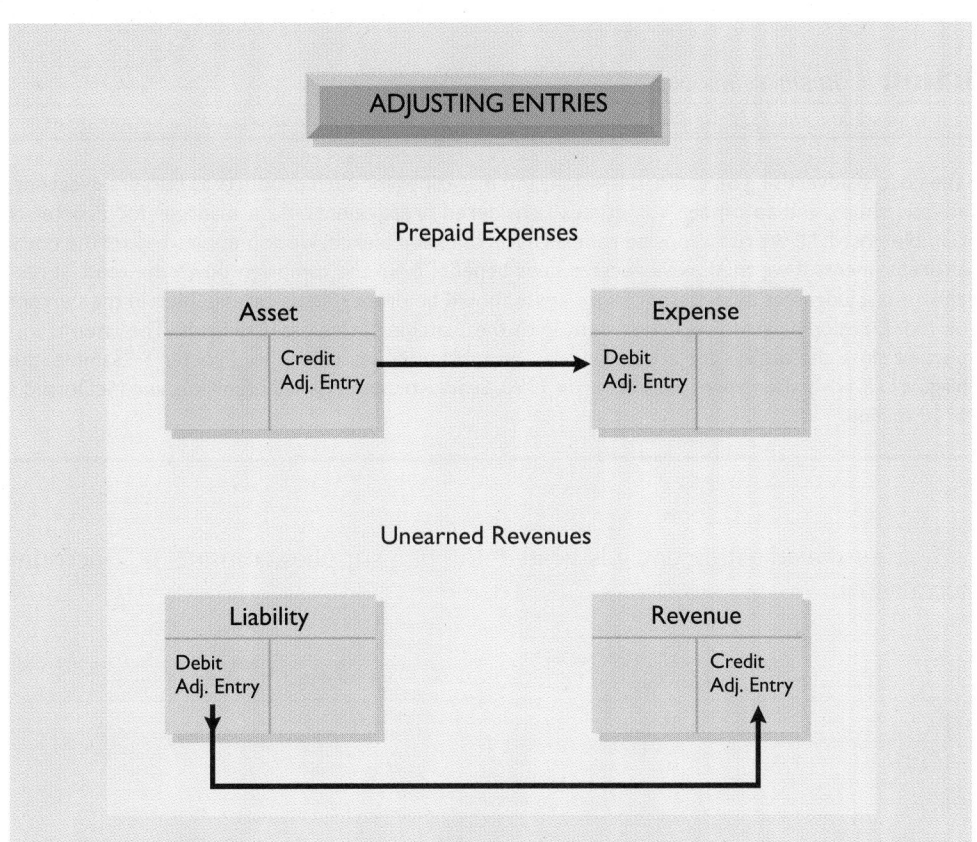

expense relationship exists with prepaid expenses. Prior to adjustment, assets are overstated and expenses are understated. **Thus, the prepaid expense adjusting entry results in a debit to an expense account and a credit to an asset account.**

Supplies

Several different types of supplies are used in a business enterprise. For example, there are **office supplies** such as stationery, paper clips, and pencils, and **advertising supplies** such as graph paper, colored pencils, video film, and poster paper. Supplies are generally debited to an asset account when they are acquired. During the course of operations, supplies are depleted or entirely consumed. However, recognition of supplies used is deferred until the adjustment process when a physical inventory (count) of supplies is taken. The difference between the balance in the Supplies (asset) account and the cost of supplies on hand represents the supplies used (expense) for the period.

Pioneer Advertising Agency purchased advertising supplies costing $2,500 on October 5. The debit was made to the asset Advertising Supplies, and this account shows a balance of $2,500 in the October 31 trial balance. An inventory count at the close of business on October 31 reveals that $1,000 of supplies are still on hand. Thus, the cost of supplies used is $1,500 ($2,500 − $1,000), and the following adjusting entry is made:

Oct. 31	Advertising Supplies Expense	1,500	
	Advertising Supplies		1,500
	(To record supplies used)		

Accounting in Action · *Business Insight*

The cost of advertising on radio, television, and magazines for such products as burgers, bleaches, athletic shoes, and so on are sometimes considered prepayments. As a manager for Procter & Gamble noted, "If we run a long ad campaign for soap and bleach, we sometimes report the costs as prepayments if we think we'll receive sales benefits from the campaign down the road." Presently it is a judgment call whether these costs should be prepayments or expenses in the current period. Developing guidelines consistent with the matching principle is difficult. The issue is important since the outlays for advertising can be substantial. As examples, Procter & Gamble, the biggest U.S. advertiser, spent $2.3 billion in 1990, Sears Roebuck spent $1.5 billion, and McDonald's $760 million.

After the adjusting entry is posted, the two supplies accounts in T-account form show:

ILLUSTRATION 3-4

Supplies accounts after adjustment

Advertising Supplies				Advertising Supplies Expense		
10/5	2,500	10/31 Adj.	1,500	10/31 Adj.	1,500	
10/31 Bal.	1,000					

The asset account Advertising Supplies now shows a balance of $1,000, which is equal to the cost of supplies on hand at the statement date. In addition, Advertising Supplies Expense shows a balance of $1,500, which equals the cost of supplies used in October. If the adjusting entry is not made, October expenses will be understated and net income overstated by $1,500. Moreover, both assets and owner's equity will be overstated by $1,500 on the October 31 balance sheet.

Insurance

Most companies have fire and theft insurance on merchandise and equipment, personal liability insurance for accidents suffered by customers, and automobile insurance on company cars and trucks. The cost of insurance protection is determined by the payment of insurance premiums. The term and coverage are specified in the insurance policy. The minimum term is usually one year, but three- to five-year terms are available and offer lower annual premiums. Insurance premiums normally are charged to the asset account Prepaid Insurance when paid. At the financial statement date it is necessary to debit Insurance Expense and credit Prepaid Insurance for the cost that has expired during the period.

On October 4, Pioneer Advertising Agency paid $600 for a one-year fire insurance policy. The effective date of coverage was October 1. The premium was charged to Prepaid Insurance when it was paid, and this account shows a balance of $600 in the October 31 trial balance. An analysis of the policy reveals that $50 ($600 ÷ 12) of insurance expires each month. Thus, the following adjusting entry is made:

Oct. 31	Insurance Expense	50	
	Prepaid Insurance		50
	(To record insurance expired)		

After the adjusting entry is posted, the accounts show:

ILLUSTRATION 3-5

Insurance accounts after adjustment

Prepaid Insurance				Insurance Expense		
10/4	600	10/31 Adj.	50	10/31 Adj.	50	
10/31 Bal.	550					

The asset Prepaid Insurance shows a balance of $550, which represents the unexpired cost applicable to the remaining 11 months of coverage. At the same time, the balance in Insurance Expense is equal to the insurance cost that has expired in October. If this adjustment is not made, October expenses will be understated by $50 and net income overstated by $50. Moreover, both assets and owner's equity also will be overstated by $50 on the October 31 balance sheet.

Depreciation

A business enterprise typically owns a variety of productive facilities such as buildings, equipment, and motor vehicles. These assets provide a service for a number of years. The term of service is commonly referred to as the useful life of the asset. Because an asset such as a building is expected to provide service for many years, it is recorded as an asset, rather than an expense, in the year it is acquired. As explained in Chapter 1, such assets are recorded at cost, as required by the cost principle. According to the matching principle, a portion of this cost should then be reported as an expense during each period of the asset's useful life. Depreciation is the process of allocating the cost of an asset to expense over its useful life in a rational and systematic manner.

NEED FOR ADJUSTMENT. From an accounting standpoint, the acquisition of productive facilities is viewed essentially as a long-term prepayment for services. The need for making periodic adjusting entries for depreciation is, therefore, the same as described before for other prepaid expenses; that is, to recognize the cost that has expired (expense) during the period and to report the unexpired cost (asset) at the end of the period.

In determining the useful life of a productive facility, consideration must be given to the primary causes of depreciation: actual use, deterioration due to the elements, and obsolescence. At the time an asset is acquired, the effects of these factors cannot be known with certainty, so they must be estimated. Thus, you should recognize that depreciation is an estimate rather than a factual measurement of the cost that has expired. A common procedure in computing depreciation expense is to divide the cost of the asset by its useful life. For example, if cost is $10,000 and useful life is expected to be 10 years, annual depreciation is $1,000.[1]

Helpful hint Depreciation is an estimate—one of many estimates inherent in accounting.

For Pioneer Advertising, depreciation on the office equipment is estimated to be $480 a year, or $40 per month. Accordingly, depreciation for October is recognized by the following adjusting entry:

Oct. 31	Depreciation Expense	40	
	Accumulated Depreciation—Office Equipment		40
	(To record monthly depreciation)		

---

[1]Additional consideration is given to computing depreciation expense in Chapter 10.

After the adjusting entry is posted, the accounts show:

ILLUSTRATION 3-6

*Accounts after adjustment
for depreciation*

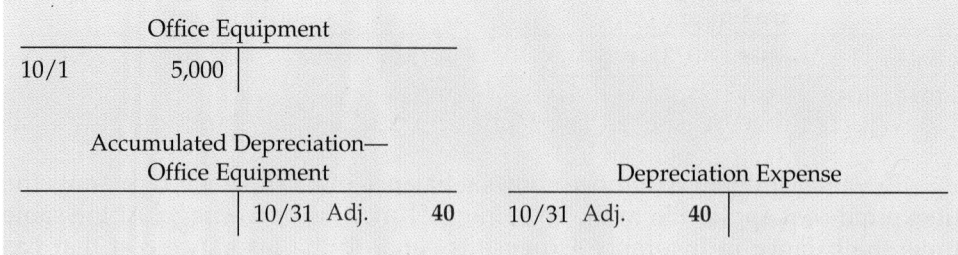

The balance in the accumulated depreciation account will increase $40 each month. Therefore, after journalizing and posting the adjusting entry at November 30, the balance will be $80.

Helpful hint   All contra accounts have increases, decreases, and normal balances opposite to the account to which they relate.

STATEMENT PRESENTATION. Accumulated Depreciation—Office Equipment is a con-tra asset account. This means that it is offset against Office Equipment on the balance sheet and its normal balance is a credit. This account is used instead of crediting Office Equipment in order to permit disclosure of both the original cost of the equipment and the total cost that has expired to date. In the balance sheet, Accumulated Depreciation—Office Equipment is deducted from the related asset account as follows:

ILLUSTRATION 3-7

*Balance sheet presentation of
accumulated depreciation*

Office equipment	$5,000	
Less: Accumulated depreciation—office equipment	40	**$4,960**

The difference between the cost of any depreciable asset and its related accumulated depreciation is referred to as the book value of that asset. In Illustration 3-7, the book value of the equipment at the balance sheet date is $4,960. It is important to realize that the book value and the market value of the asset are generally two different values. The reason is that depreciation is not a matter of valuation, but a means of cost allocation.

Note also that depreciation expense identifies the cost that has expired in October. As in the case of other prepaid adjustments, the omission of this adjusting entry would cause total assets, total owner's equity, and net income to be overstated and depreciation expense to be understated.

If additional equipment is involved, such as delivery or store equipment, or if the company has buildings, depreciation expense is recorded on each of these items. Related accumulated depreciation accounts also are established. These accumulated depreciation accounts would be described in the ledger as follows: Accumulated Depreciation—Delivery Equipment; Accumulated Depreciation—Store Equipment; and Accumulated Depreciation—Buildings.

Unearned Revenues

Revenues received in cash and recorded as liabilities before they are earned are called unearned revenues. Such items as rent, magazine subscriptions, and customer deposits for future service may result in unearned revenues. Airlines such as United, American, and Delta, for instance, treat receipts from the sale of tickets as unearned revenue until the flight service is provided. Unearned revenues are the opposite of prepaid expenses. Indeed, unearned revenue on the books of one company is likely to be a prepayment on the books of the company that has made the advance payment. For example, if identical accounting periods are assumed, a landlord will have unearned rent revenue when a tenant has prepaid rent.

When the payment is received for services to be provided in a future accounting period, an unearned revenue (a liability) account should be credited to recognize the obligation that exists. Unearned revenues are subsequently earned through rendering service to a customer. During the accounting period it may not be practical to make daily recurring entries as the revenue is earned. In such cases, the recognition of earned revenue is delayed until the adjustment process. Then an adjusting entry is made to record the revenue that has been earned and to show the liability that remains. **A liability–revenue account relationship therefore exists with unearned revenues.** In the typical case, liabilities are overstated and revenues are understated prior to adjustment. Thus, **the adjusting entry for unearned revenues results in a debit to a liability account and a credit to a revenue account.**

Pioneer Advertising Agency received $1,200 on October 2 from R. Knox for advertising services expected to be completed by December 31. The payment was credited to Unearned Fees, and this account shows a balance of $1,200 in the October 31 trial balance. When analysis reveals that $400 of those fees has been earned in October, the following adjusting entry is made:

Oct. 31	Unearned Fees	400	
	Fees Earned		400
	(To record fees earned)		

After the adjusting entry is posted, the accounts show:

Unearned Fees				Fees Earned		
10/31 Adj.	400	10/2	1,200		10/31 Bal.	10,000
		10/31 Bal.	800		31 Adj.	400

ILLUSTRATION 3-8

Fees accounts after prepayments adjustment

The liability Unearned Fees now shows a balance of $800, which represents the remaining advertising services expected to be performed in the future. At the same time, Fees Earned shows total revenue earned in October of $10,400. If this adjustment is not made, revenues and net income will be understated by $400 in the income statement. Moreover, liabilities will be overstated and owner's equity will be understated by $400 on the October 31 balance sheet.

Adjusting Entries for Accruals

The second category of adjusting entries is accruals. Adjusting entries for accruals are required to record revenues earned and expenses incurred in the current accounting period that have not been recognized through daily entries. If an accrual adjustment is needed, the revenue account (and the related asset account) and/or the expense account (and the related liability account) is understated. Thus, the adjusting entry for accruals will increase both a balance sheet and an income statement account.

Study Objective 6

Prepare adjusting entries for accruals.

Adjusting entries for accruals are graphically depicted in Illustration 3-9.

ILLUSTRATION 3-9

Adjusting entries for accruals

Helpful hint Remember that debits increase assets and expenses, and credits increase revenues and liabilities.

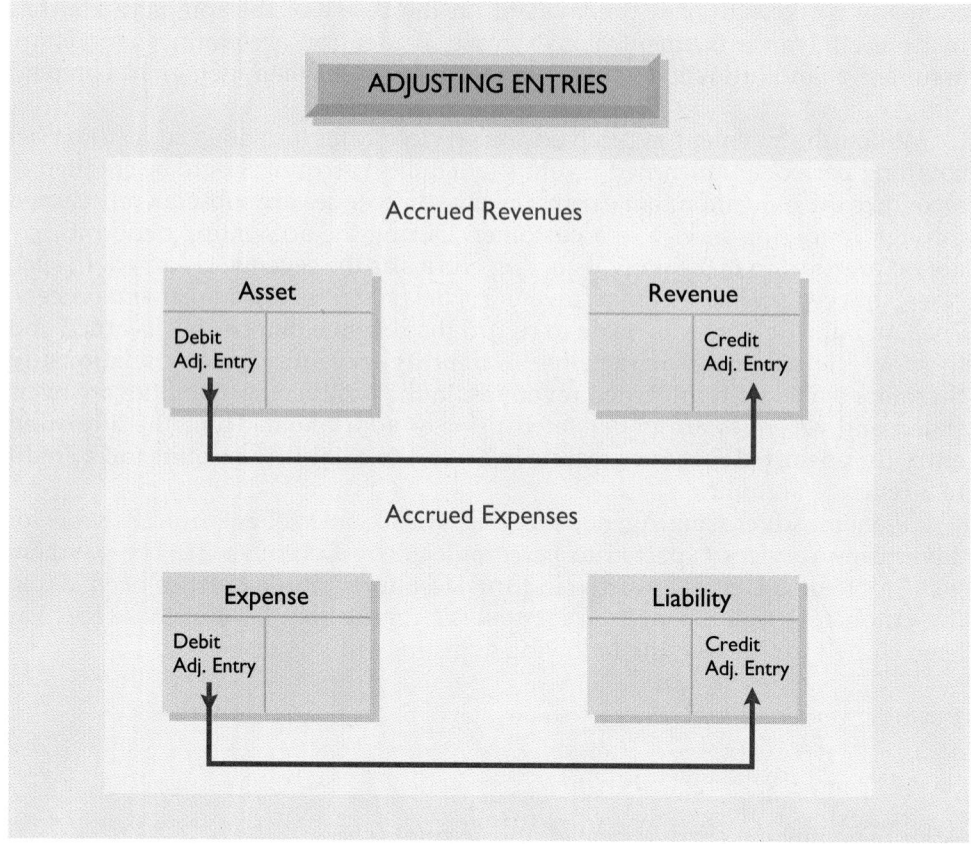

Accrued Revenues

Revenues earned but unrecorded at the statement date are known as accrued revenues or accrued receivables. Accrued revenues may accumulate (accrue) with the passing of time, as in the case of interest and rent. Or they may result from services that have been performed but neither billed nor collected, as in the case of commissions and fees. The former are unrecorded because the earning of interest and rent does not involve daily transactions; the latter may be unrecorded because only a portion of the total service has been provided.

An adjusting entry is required to show the receivable that exists at the balance sheet date and to record the revenue that has been earned during the period. **An asset-revenue account relationship exists with accrued revenues.** Prior to adjustment both assets and revenues are understated. Accordingly, **an adjusting entry for accrued revenues results in a debit to an asset account and a credit to a revenue account.**

In October Pioneer Advertising Agency earned $200 in fees for advertising services that were not billed to clients before October 31. Because these services have not been billed, they have not been recorded. Thus, the following adjusting entry is made:

Oct. 31	Fees Receivable	200	
	Fees Earned		200
	(To accrue fees earned but not billed or collected)		

After the adjusting entry is posted, the accounts show:

ILLUSTRATION 3-10

Fees accounts after accrual adjustment

Fees Receivable			Fees Earned		
10/31 Adj.	200			10/31	10,000
				31	400
				31 Adj.	200
				10/31 Bal.	10,600

The asset Fees Receivable shows that $200 is owed by clients at the balance sheet date. The balance of $10,600 in Fees Earned represents the total fees earned during the month ($10,000 + $400 + $200). If the adjusting entry is not made, assets and owner's equity on the balance sheet, and revenues and net income on the income statement, will all be understated.

In the next accounting period, the clients will be billed. When this occurs, the entry to record the billing should recognize that $200 of fees earned in October have already been recorded in the October 31 adjusting entry. To illustrate, assume that bills totaling $3,000 are mailed to clients on November 10. Of this amount, $200 represents fees earned in October and recorded as Fees Earned in the October 31 adjusting entry. The remaining $2,800 represents fees earned in November. Thus, the following entry is made:

Nov. 10	Fees Receivable	2,800	
	Fees Earned		2,800
	(To record fees billed)		

This entry records the amount of fees earned between November 1 and November 10. The subsequent collection of fees from clients (including the $200 earned in October) will be recorded with a debit to Cash and a credit to Fees Receivable.

Accrued Expenses

Expenses incurred but unrecorded at the statement date are called accrued expenses or accrued liabilities. Interest, rent, taxes, and salaries are examples of accrued expenses. Accrued expenses result from the same causes as accrued revenues. In fact, an accrued expense on the books of one company is an accrued revenue to another company. For example, the $200 accrual of fees by Pioneer is an accrued expense to the client that received the service.

Adjustments for accrued expenses are necessary to record the obligations that exist at the balance sheet date and to recognize the expenses that are applicable to the current accounting period. **A liability–expense relationship exists with accrued expenses.** Prior to adjustment both liabilities and expenses are understated. Therefore, **the adjusting entry for accrued expenses results in a debit to an expense account and a credit to a liability account.**

Accrued Interest

Pioneer Advertising Agency signed a three-month note payable in the amount of $5,000 on October 1. The note requires interest at an annual rate of 12%. The amount of the interest accumulation is determined by three factors: (1) the face value of the note, (2) the interest rate, which is always expressed as an annual rate, and (3) the length of time the note is outstanding. In this instance, the total interest due on the $5,000 note at its due date three months hence is $150 ($5,000 × 12% × 3/12) or $50 for one month. The formula for computing interest

Helpful hint Interest is a cost of borrowing money that accumulates with the passage of time.

and its applicability to Pioneer Advertising Agency for the month of October[2] are shown in Illustration 3-11.

ILLUSTRATION 3-11

Formula for computing interest

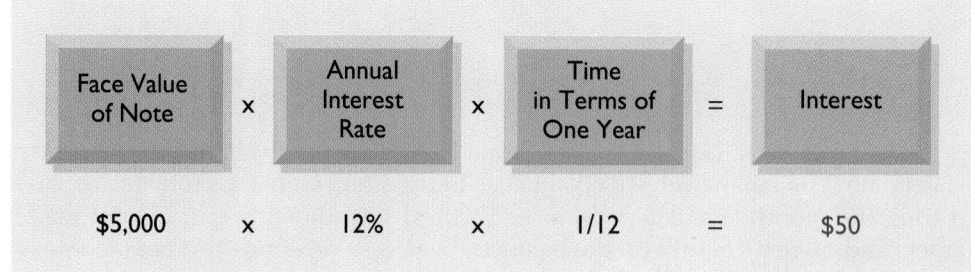

Note that the time period is expressed as a fraction of a year. The accrued expense adjusting entry at October 31 is as follows:

Oct. 31	Interest Expense	50	
	Interest Payable		50
	(To accrue interest on notes payable)		

After this adjusting entry is posted, the accounts show:

ILLUSTRATION 3-12

Interest accounts after adjustment

Interest Expense		Interest Payable	
10/31	50	10/31	50

Interest Expense shows the interest charges applicable to the month of October. The amount of interest owed at the statement date is shown in Interest Payable. It will not be paid until the note comes due at the end of three months. The Interest Payable account is used instead of crediting Notes Payable to disclose the two types of obligations (interest and principal) in the accounts and statements. If this adjusting entry is not made, liabilities and interest expense will be understated, and net income and total owner's equity will be overstated.

Accrued Salaries

Some types of services, such as insurance and rent, are paid for before they are used. Other types of services, such as employee salaries and commissions, are paid for after the services have been performed.

At Pioneer Advertising, salaries were last paid on October 26, and the next payment of salaries will not occur until November 9. As shown in the calendar on page 101, there are three remaining working days in October (October 29–31).

At October 31, the salaries for these days represent an accrued expense and a related liability to Pioneer Advertising. As explained earlier, the employees receive total salaries of $2,000 for a five-day work week, or $400 per day. Thus, accrued salaries at October 31 are $1,200 ($400 × 3), and the adjusting entry is:

Oct. 31	Salaries Expense	1,200	
	Salaries Payable		1,200
	(To record accrued salaries)		

---

[2]The computation of interest will be considered in more depth in later chapters.

After this adjusting entry is posted, the accounts show:

ILLUSTRATION 3-13

Salary accounts after adjustment

Salaries Expense		Salaries Payable	
10/26 4,000			10/31 Adj. **1,200**
31 Adj. **1,200**			
10/31 Bal. **5,200**			

After this adjustment, the balance in Salaries Expense of $5,200 is the actual salary expense for October. The balance in Salaries Payable of $1,200 is the amount of the liability for salaries owed as of October 31. If the $1,200 adjustment for salaries is not recorded, Pioneer's expenses will be understated $1,200, and its liabilities will be understated $1,200.

At Pioneer Advertising, salaries are payable every two weeks. Consequently, the next payday is November 9, when total salaries of $4,000 will again be paid. The payment consists of $1,200 of salaries payable at October 31 plus $2,800 of salaries expense for November (7 working days × $400). Therefore, the following entry is made on November 9:

Nov. 9	Salaries Payable	1,200	
	Salaries Expense	2,800	
	Cash		4,000
	(To record November 9 payroll)		

This entry eliminates the liability for Salaries Payable that was recorded in the October 31 adjusting entry and records the proper amount of Salaries Expense for the period between November 1 and November 9.

Summary of Basic Relationships

Pertinent data on each of the four basic types of adjusting entries are summarized in Illustration 3-14. From an analysis of the adjusting entries shown in the summary, it can be seen that **each adjusting entry affects one balance sheet account and one income statement account.**

ILLUSTRATION 3-14

Summary of adjusting entries

Type of Adjustment	Account Relationship	Accounts Before Adjustment	Adjusting Entry
1. Prepaid Expenses	Assets and Expenses	Assets Overstated Expenses Understated	Dr. Expenses Cr. Assets
2. Unearned Revenues	Liabilities and Revenues	Liabilities Overstated Revenues Understated	Dr. Liabilities Cr. Revenues
3. Accrued Revenues	Assets and Revenues	Assets Understated Revenues Understated	Dr. Assets Cr. Revenues
4. Accrued Expenses	Expenses and Liabilities	Expenses Understated Liabilities Understated	Dr. Expenses Cr. Liabilities

Helpful hint (1) Remember that adjusting entries should not involve debits and credits to cash. (2) Evaluate whether the adjustment makes sense. For example, an adjustment to recognize supplies used should increase supplies expense. (3) Double-check all computations.

Journalizing and Posting Adjusting Entries

The journalizing and posting of adjusting entries for Pioneer Advertising Agency on October 31 are shown in Illustrations 3-15 and 3-16. All adjustments are identified in the ledger by the reference J2 because they are journalized on page 2 of the general journal. A center caption entitled Adjusting Entries may be inserted between the last transaction entry and the first adjusting entry to identify these entries. When reviewing the general ledger in Illustration 3-16, note that the adjustments are highlighted in color.

ILLUSTRATION 3-15

General journal showing adjusting entries

	GENERAL JOURNAL			J2
Date	Account Titles and Explanation	Ref.	Debit	Credit
1993	Adjusting Entries			
Oct. 31	Advertising Supplies Expense	61	1,500	
	Advertising Supplies	8		1,500
	(To record supplies used)			
31	Insurance Expense	63	50	
	Prepaid Insurance	10		50
	(To record insurance expired)			
31	Depreciation Expense	65	40	
	Accumulated Depreciation—Office Equipment	16		40
	(To record monthly depreciation)			
31	Unearned Fees	28	400	
	Fees Earned	50		400
	(To record fees earned)			
31	Fees Receivable	6	200	
	Fees Earned	50		200
	(To accrue fees earned but not billed or collected)			
31	Interest Expense	64	50	
	Interest Payable	27		50
	(To accrue interest on notes payable)			
31	Salaries Expense	60	1,200	
	Salaries Payable	29		1,200
	(To record accrued salaries)			

ILLUSTRATION 3-16

General ledger after adjustment

GENERAL LEDGER

Cash — No. 1

Date	Explanation	Ref.	Debit	Credit	Balance
1993					
Oct. 1		J1	10,000		10,000
2		J1	1,200		11,200
3		J1		900	10,300
4		J1		600	9,700
20		J1		500	9,200
26		J1		4,000	5,200
31		J1	10,000		15,200

Fees Receivable — No. 6

Date	Explanation	Ref.	Debit	Credit	Balance
1993					
Oct. 31	Adj. entry	J2	200		200

Advertising Supplies — No. 8

Date	Explanation	Ref.	Debit	Credit	Balance
1993					
Oct. 5		J1	2,500		2,500
31	Adj. entry	J2		1,500	1,000

Prepaid Insurance — No. 10

Date	Explanation	Ref.	Debit	Credit	Balance
1993					
Oct. 4		J1	600		600
31	Adj. entry	J2		50	550

Office Equipment — No. 15

Date	Explanation	Ref.	Debit	Credit	Balance
1993					
Oct. 1		J1	5,000		5,000

Accumulated Depreciation—Office Equipment — No. 16

Date	Explanation	Ref.	Debit	Credit	Balance
1993					
Oct. 31	Adj. entry	J2		40	40

Notes Payable — No. 25

Date	Explanation	Ref.	Debit	Credit	Balance
1993					
Oct. 1		J1		5,000	5,000

Accounts Payable — No. 26

Date	Explanation	Ref.	Debit	Credit	Balance
1993					
Oct. 5		J1		2,500	2,500

Interest Payable — No. 27

Date	Explanation	Ref.	Debit	Credit	Balance
1993					
Oct. 31	Adj. entry	J2		50	50

Unearned Fees — No. 28

Date	Explanation	Ref.	Debit	Credit	Balance
1993					
Oct. 2		J1		1,200	
31	Adj. entry	J2	400		800

Salaries Payable — No. 29

Date	Explanation	Ref.	Debit	Credit	Balance
1993					
Oct. 31	Adj. entry	J2		1,200	1,200

C. R. Byrd, Capital — No. 40

Date	Explanation	Ref.	Debit	Credit	Balance
1993					
Oct. 1		J1		10,000	10,000

C. R. Byrd, Drawing — No. 41

Date	Explanation	Ref.	Debit	Credit	Balance
1993					
Oct. 20		J1	500		500

Fees Earned — No. 50

Date	Explanation	Ref.	Debit	Credit	Balance
1993					
Oct. 31		J1		10,000	10,000
31	Adj. entry	J2		400	10,400
31	Adj. entry	J2		200	10,600

Salaries Expense — No. 60

Date	Explanation	Ref.	Debit	Credit	Balance
1993					
Oct. 26		J1	4,000		4,000
31	Adj. entry	J2	1,200		5,200

Advertising Supplies Expense — No. 61

Date	Explanation	Ref.	Debit	Credit	Balance
1993					
Oct. 31	Adj. entry	J2	1,500		1,500

Rent Expense — No. 62

Date	Explanation	Ref.	Debit	Credit	Balance
1993					
Oct. 3		J1	900		900

Insurance Expense — No. 63

Date	Explanation	Ref.	Debit	Credit	Balance
1993					
Oct. 31	Adj. entry	J2	50		50

Interest Expense — No. 64

Date	Explanation	Ref.	Debit	Credit	Balance
1993					
Oct. 31	Adj. entry	J2	50		50

Depreciation Expense — No. 65

Date	Explanation	Ref.	Debit	Credit	Balance
1993					
Oct. 31	Adj. entry	J2	40		40

Before You Go On . . .

1. What are the four types of adjusting entries?

2. How do adjusting entries for prepaid expenses differ from those for unearned revenues?

3. How do adjusting entries for accrued revenues differ from those for accrued expenses?

The Adjusted Trial Balance

Study Objective 7

Describe the nature and purpose of an adjusted trial balance.

After all adjusting entries have been journalized and posted, another trial balance is prepared from the ledger accounts. This trial balance is called an adjusted trial balance. An adjusted trial balance shows the balances of all accounts, including those that have been adjusted, at the end of the accounting period. The purpose of an adjusted trial balance is to show the effects of all financial events that have occurred during the accounting period. The procedures for preparing an adjusted trial balance are identical to those described in Chapter 2 for preparing a trial balance.

An adjusted trial balance proves the equality of the total debit balances and the total credit balances in the ledger after all adjustments have been made. The proof provided by an adjusted trial balance, like the proof contained in a trial balance, extends only to the mathematical accuracy of the ledger. Because the accounts contain all data that are needed for financial statements, the

ILLUSTRATION 3-17

Trial balance and adjusted trial balance compared

	Before Adjustment		After Adjustment	
	Dr.	Cr.	Dr.	Cr.
Cash	$15,200		$15,200	
Fees Receivable			200	
Advertising Supplies	2,500		1,000	
Prepaid Insurance	600		550	
Office Equipment	5,000		5,000	
Accumulated Depreciation— Office Equipment				$ 40
Notes Payable		$ 5,000		5,000
Accounts Payable		2,500		2,500
Interest Payable				50
Unearned Fees		1,200		800
Salaries Payable				1,200
C. R. Byrd, Capital		10,000		10,000
C. R. Byrd, Drawing	500		500	
Fees Earned		10,000		10,600
Salaries Expense	4,000		5,200	
Advertising Supplies Expense			1,500	
Rent Expense			900	
	900			
Insurance Expense			50	
Interest Expense			50	
Depreciation Expense			40	
	$28,700	$28,700	$30,190	$30,190

PIONEER ADVERTISING AGENCY
Trial Balances
October 31, 1993

adjusted trial balance provides the primary basis for the preparation of financial statements.

The adjusted trial balance for Pioneer Advertising Agency presented in Illustration 3-17 has been prepared from the ledger accounts shown in Illustration 3-16. To facilitate the comparison of account balances before and after adjustment, the adjusted data are arranged parallel to the trial balance data shown in Illustration 3-2, on page 92, and the amounts affected by the adjusting entries are highlighted in color in the After Adjustment columns.

Financial Statements from an Adjusted Trial Balance

Financial statements can be prepared directly from an adjusted trial balance.
The preparation of financial statements from the adjusted trial balance of Pioneer Advertising Agency and the interrelationship of data are presented in Illustrations 3-18 and 3-19. As shown in Illustration 3-18 the income statement is prepared from the revenue and expense accounts; the owner's equity statement is derived from the owner's capital and drawing accounts and the net income (or net loss) shown in the income statement. As shown in Illustration 3-19 the balance sheet is then prepared from the asset and liability accounts and the ending owner's capital balance as reported in the owner's equity statement.

ILLUSTRATION 3-18

Preparation of the income statement and owner's equity statement from the adjusted trial balance

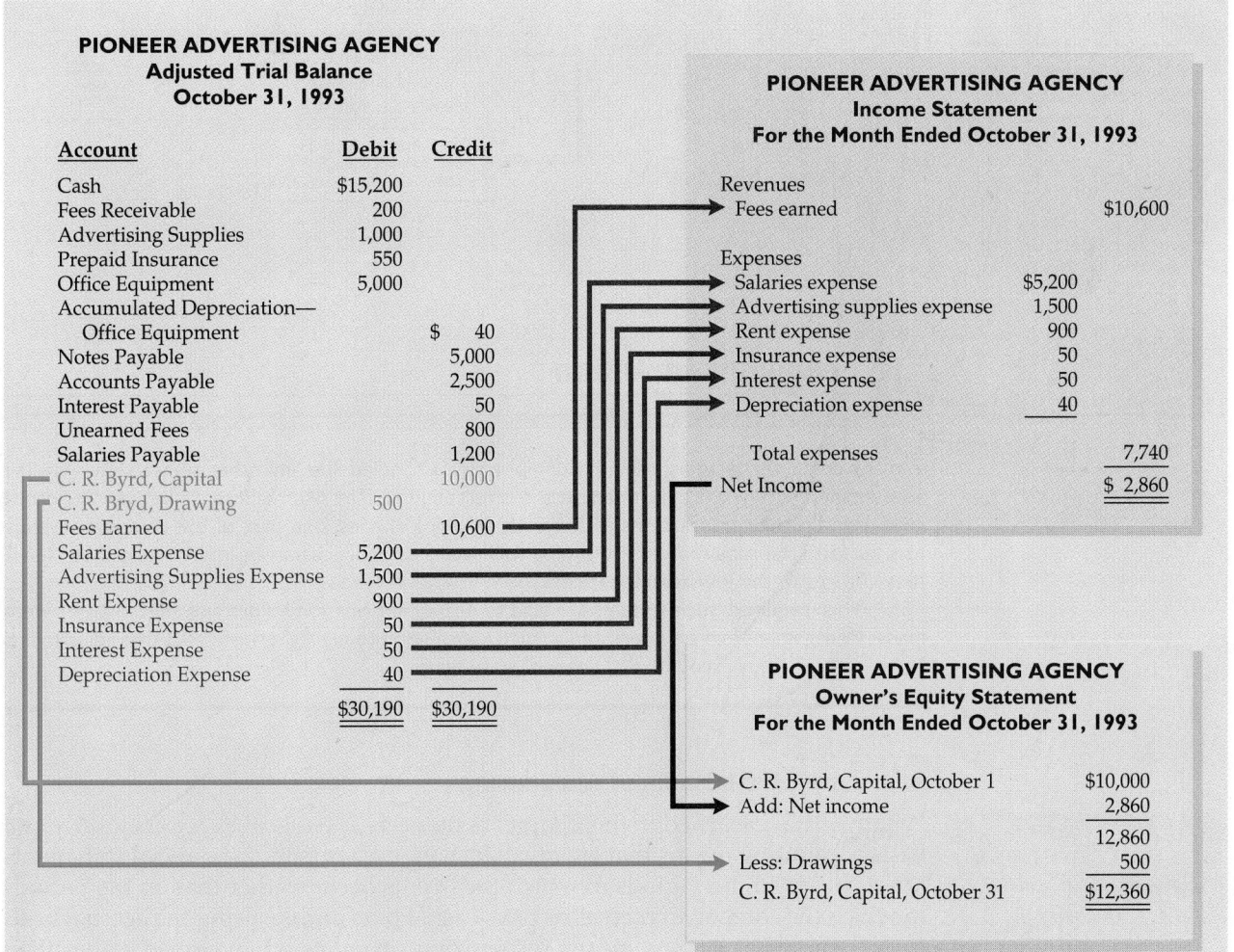

ILLUSTRATION 3-19

*Preparation of the balance
sheet from the adjusted trial
balance*

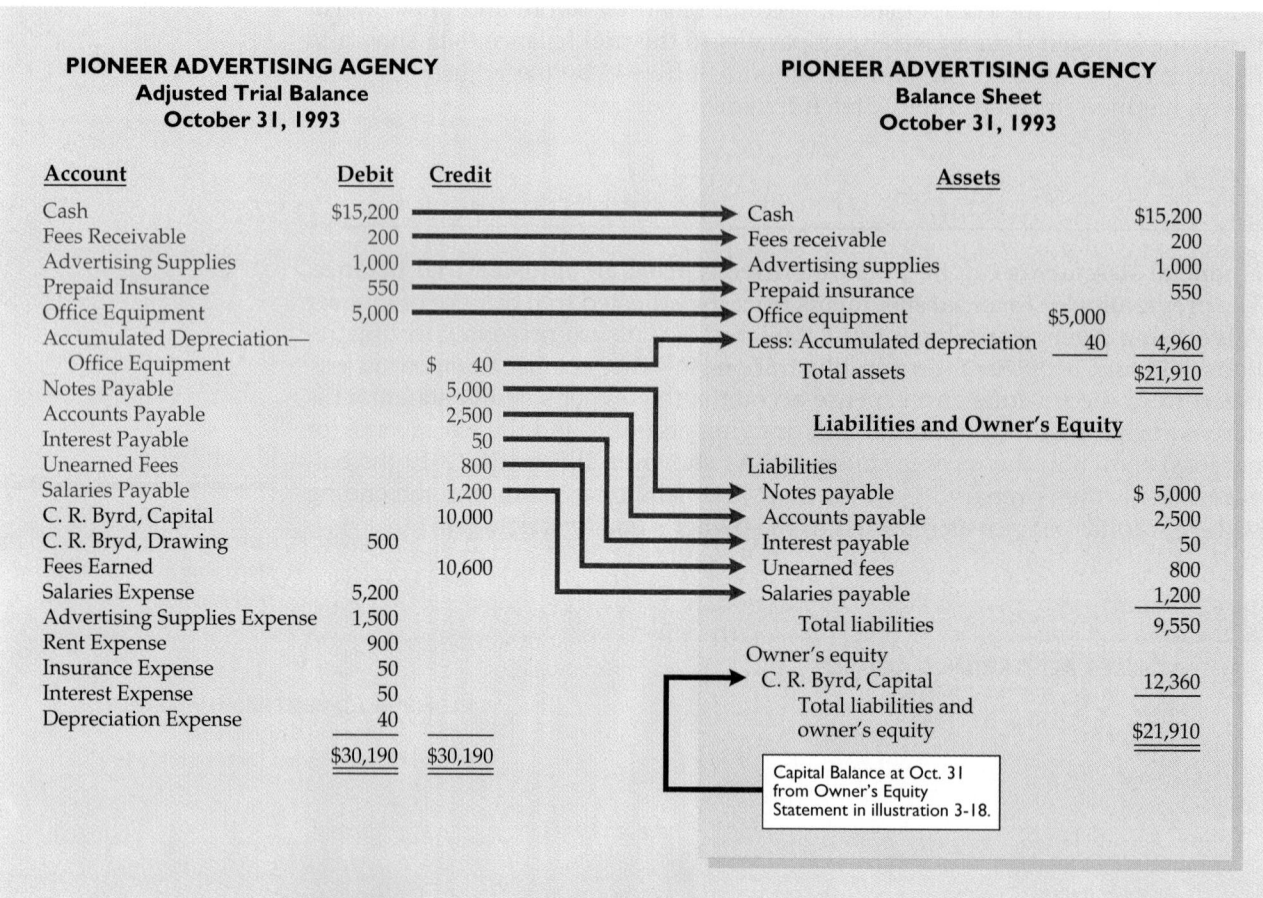

Technology in Action

In many computer systems, the adjusting process is handled like any other transaction, with the accountant inputting the adjustment at the time required. The main difference between adjusting entries and regular transactions is that with adjusting entries, one part of the computer system may perform the required calculation for such items as depreciation or interest and then "feed" these figures to the journalizing process.

When required, such systems are able to display information before and after changes were made. Management may be interested in such information to highlight the impact that adjustments have on the various accounts and financial statements.

Accrual vs. Cash Basis of Accounting

Study Objective 8

*Explain the accrual
basis of accounting.*

What you have learned in this chapter is the accrual basis of accounting. Accrual basis accounting means that events that change a company's financial statements are recorded in the periods in which the events occur, rather than in the periods in which the company receives or pays cash. For example, using the accrual basis to determine net income means recognizing revenues when earned rather than when the cash is received, and recognizing expenses when incurred rather than

Accounting in Action · *Business Insight*

If you are upset about the billions of dollars of taxpayers' money that will be needed to make good on Uncle Sam's guarantees related to the savings and loan bailout, here's one thing you might do: Suggest that your congressional representatives learn accrual accounting.

Presently, the U.S. federal budget measures only cash transactions—how many dollar bills the government pays out and how many it receives in a given year. Let's say that the federal government guarantees loans made by a savings and loan. Since no cash outlay takes place initially, the budget deficit doesn't increase by a cent, even though everyone concerned knows there will be credit losses that Uncle Sam will have to make good. Richard Darman, head of the Office of Management and Budget, notes that "loan guarantees are the budget's invisible Pacmen. You can't see them now, but sooner or later they will gobble up your money." Various loan guarantees are estimated to grow to $838 billion by 1995. Shouldn't the costs related to these guarantees be reported now? One skeptic notes: "This issue doesn't win votes. What's more perfect for a politician than to be able to promise something whose costs won't come due until the future?"

Source: Adapted from "Phony Bookkeeping," *Forbes*, May 1990.

when paid. Information presented on an accrual basis is useful because it reveals relationships that are likely to be important in predicting future results. To illustrate, under accrual accounting, revenues are generally recognized when services are performed so they can be related to the economic environment in which they occur. Trends in revenues are thus more meaningful.

Under cash basis accounting, revenue is recorded only when the cash is received, and an expense is recorded only when cash is paid. As a result, the cash basis of accounting often leads to misleading financial statements. For example, it fails to record revenue which has been earned but for which the cash has not been received, and therefore the revenue recognition principle is violated. In addition, expenses are also not matched with revenues when earned and therefore the matching principle is not followed. **The cash basis of accounting is not in accordance with generally accepted accounting principles.**

Although most companies use the accrual basis of accounting, some small companies use the cash basis of accounting. The cash basis of accounting is justified by these businesses because they often have few receivables and payables. Accountants are sometimes asked to convert cash basis records to the accrual basis. As you might expect, extensive adjusting entries are required for this task.

Before You Go On . . .

1. What is the purpose of an adjusted trial balance?

2. How is an adjusted trial balance prepared?

3. What are the differences between the cash and accrual bases of accounting?

Summary of Study Objectives

1. *Explain the periodicity assumption.* The periodicity or time period assumption assumes that the economic life of a business can be divided into artificial time periods.

2. *Distinguish between the revenue recognition principle and the matching principle.* The revenue recognition principle dictates that revenue be recognized in the accounting period in which it is earned.

The matching principle dictates that expenses be recognized when they make their contribution to revenues.

3. *Explain the need for adjusting entries.* Adjusting entries are made at the end of an accounting period. They ensure that revenues are recorded in the period in which they are earned and that expenses are recognized in the period in which they are incurred.

4. *Identify the major types of adjusting entries.* The major types of adjusting entries are prepaid expenses, unearned revenues, accrued revenues, and accrued expenses.

5. *Prepare adjusting entries for prepayments.* Prepayments are either prepaid expenses or unearned revenues. Adjusting entries for prepayments are required at the statement date to record the portion of the prepayment that represents the expense incurred or the revenue earned in the current accounting period.

6. *Prepare adjusting entries for accruals.* Accruals are either accrued revenues or accrued expenses. Adjusting entries for accruals are required to record revenues earned and expenses incurred in the current accounting period that have not been recognized through daily entries.

7. *Describe the nature and purpose of an adjusted trial balance.* An adjusted trial balance is a trial balance that shows the balances of all accounts, including those that have been adjusted, at the end of an accounting period. The purpose of an adjusted trial balance is to show the effects of all financial events that have occurred during the accounting period.

8. *Explain the accrual basis of accounting.* Accrual basis accounting means that events that change a company's financial statements are recorded in the periods in which the events occur, rather than in the periods in which the company receives or pays cash.

Appendix A   Alternative Treatment of Prepaid Expenses and Unearned Revenues

Study Objective

After studying Appendix A, you should be able to:

9. Prepare adjusting entries for the alternative treatment of prepayments.

In our discussion of adjusting entries for prepaid expenses and unearned revenues, we illustrated transactions for which the initial entries were made to balance sheet accounts. That is, in the case of prepaid expenses, the prepayment was debited to an asset account, and in the case of unearned revenue, the cash received was credited to a liability account. Some businesses use an alternative treatment: At the time an expense is prepaid, it may be debited to an expense account, and at the time of a receipt for future services, it may be credited to a revenue account. The circumstances that justify such entries and the different adjusting entries that may be required are described below. The alternative treatment of prepaid expenses and unearned revenues has the same effect on the financial statements as the procedures described in the chapter.

Prepaid Expenses

Prepaid expenses become expired costs either through the passage of time, as in the case of insurance, or through consumption, as in the case of advertising supplies. If at the time of purchase, the company expects to consume the supplies before the next financial statement date, **it may be more convenient to initially debit an expense account rather than an asset account**. Assume, for example, that Pioneer Advertising expects that all of the supplies purchased on October 5 will be used before October 31. A debit of $2,500 to Advertising Supplies Expense rather than to the asset account, Advertising Supplies, on October 5 will eliminate the need for an adjusting entry on October 31, if all the supplies are used. At October 31, the Advertising Supplies Expense account will show a balance of $2,500, which is equal to the cost of supplies used between October 5 and October 31.

Assume, however, that the company does not use up all the supplies, and an inventory of $1,000 of advertising supplies remains on October 31. In such a case, an adjusting entry is needed. Prior to adjustment:

1. the expense account, Advertising Supplies Expense, is overstated $1,000, and
2. the asset account, Advertising Supplies, is understated $1,000.

Thus the following adjusting entry is made:

Oct. 31	Advertising Supplies	1,000	
	Advertising Supplies Expense		1,000
	(To record supplies inventory)		

After posting the adjusting entry, the accounts show:

ILLUSTRATION A-1

Accounts after adjustment

Advertising Supplies			Advertising Supplies Expense			
10/31 Adj. **1,000**			10/5 2,500	10/31 Adj. **1,000**		
			10/31 Bal. 1,500			

After adjustment, the asset account, Advertising Supplies, shows a balance of $1,000, which is equal to the cost of supplies on hand at October 31. In addition, Advertising Supplies Expense shows a balance of $1,500, which is equal to the cost of supplies used between October 5 and October 31. If the adjusting entry is not made, expenses will be overstated and net income will be understated by $1,000 in the October income statement. Moreover, both assets and owner's equity will be understated by $1,000 on the October 31 balance sheet.

A comparative summary of the entries and accounts for advertising supplies is shown in Illustration A-2.

ILLUSTRATION A-2

Adjustment approaches— a comparison

Prepayment Initially Debited to Asset Account (Per Chapter)			Prepayment Initially Debited to Expense Account (Per Appendix)		
Oct. 5 Advertising Supplies	2,500		Oct. 5 Advertising Supplies		
Accounts Payable	2,500		Expense	2,500	
			Accounts Payable		2,500
Oct. 31 Advertising Supplies			Oct. 31 Advertising Supplies	1,000	
Expense	1,500		Advertising Supplies		
Advertising Supplies	1,500		Expense		1,000

After posting the entries, the accounts appear as follows:

ILLUSTRATION A-3

Comparison of accounts

(Per Chapter) Advertising Supplies			(Per Appendix) Advertising Supplies		
10/5 2,500	10/31 Adj. 1,500		10/31 Adj. **1,000**		
10/31 Bal. **1,000**					

Advertising Supplies Expense			Advertising Supplies Expense		
10/31 Adj. **1,500**			10/5 2,500	10/31 Adj. 1,000	
			10/31 Bal. **1,500**		

Note that the account balances under each alternative are the same at October 31; that is, Advertising Supplies $1,000, and Advertising Supplies Expense $1,500.

Unearned Revenues

Unearned revenues become earned either through the passage of time, as in the case of unearned rent, or through rendering the service, as in the case of unearned fees. Like prepaid expenses, a revenue account may be credited when cash is received for future services and a different adjusting entry may be necessary.

To illustrate, assume when Pioneer Advertising received $1,200 in fees for future services on October 2 that the services were expected to be performed before October 31.[3] In such a case, Fees Earned would be credited. If these fees are in fact earned before October 31, no adjustment is needed. However, if, at the statement date, $800 of the services have not been provided, an adjusting entry is required. Prior to adjustment, the account relationships are:

1. the revenue account, Fees Earned, is overstated $800, and
2. the liability account, Unearned Fees, is understated $800.

Thus, the following adjusting entry is made:

Oct. 31	Fees Earned	800	
	Unearned Fees		800
	(To record unearned fees)		

After posting the adjusting entry, the accounts show:

ILLUSTRATION A-4

Accounts after adjustment

Unearned Fees				Fees Earned				
		10/31 Adj.	800	10/31 Adj.	800	10/2	1,200	
						10/31 Bal.	400	

The liability account, Unearned Fees, shows a balance of $800, which is equal to the services that will be rendered in the future. In addition, the balance in Fees Earned equals the services rendered in October. If the adjusting entry is not made, both revenues and net income will be overstated by $800 in the October income statement. Moreover, liabilities will be understated by $800, and owner's equity will be overstated by $800 on the October 31 balance sheet.

A comparative summary of the entries and accounts for fees earned and unearned is presented in Illustration A-5:

ILLUSTRATION A-5

Adjustment approaches— a comparison

	Unearned Revenue Initially Credited to Liability Account (Per Chapter)			Unearned Revenue Initially Credited to Revenue Account (Per Appendix)		
Oct. 2	Cash	1,200		Oct. 2	Cash	1,200
	Unearned Fees	1,200			Fees Earned	1,200
Oct. 31	Unearned Fees	400		Oct. 31	Fees Earned	800
	Fees Earned	400			Unearned Fees	800

---

[3]This example focuses only on the alternative treatment of unearned revenues. In the interest of simplicity, the entries to Fees Earned pertaining to the immediate earning of fees ($10,000) and the adjusting entry for accrued fees ($200) have been ignored.

After posting the entries, the accounts will show:

ILLUSTRATION A-6

Comparison of accounts

(Per Chapter) Unearned Fees				(Per Appendix) Unearned Fees			
10/31 Adj.	400	10/2	1,200			10/31 Adj.	800
		10/31 Bal.	800				

Fees Earned				Fees Earned			
		10/31 Adj.	400	10/31 Adj.	800	10/2	1,200
						10/31 Bal.	400

Note that the balances in the accounts are the same; that is, Unearned Fees, $800, and Fees Earned, $400.

Summary of Additional Adjustment Relationships

The use of alternative adjusting entries requires additions to the summary of basic relationships presented earlier in Illustration 3-14. The additions are shown in color in Illustration A-7.

ILLUSTRATION A-7

Summary of basic relationships for prepayments

Type of Adjustment	Account Relationship	Reason for Adjustment	Account Balances Before Adjustment	Adjusting Entry
1. Prepaid Expenses	Assets and Expenses	(a) Prepaid expenses initially recorded in asset accounts have been used.	Assets overstated Expenses understated	Dr. Expenses Cr. Assets
		(b) Prepaid expenses initially recorded in expense accounts have not been used.	Assets understated Expenses overstated	Dr. Assets Cr. Expenses
2. Unearned Revenues	Liabilities and Revenues	(a) Unearned revenues initially recorded in liability accounts have been earned.	Liabilities overstated Revenues understated	Dr. Liabilities Cr. Revenues
		(b) Unearned revenues initially recorded in revenue accounts have not been earned.	Liabilities understated Revenues overstated	Dr. Revenues Cr. Liabilities

Alternative adjusting entries are not applicable to accrued revenues and accrued expenses because no entries occur before these types of adjusting entries are made. Hence, the summary data shown in Illustration 3-14 for these two types of adjustments remains unchanged.

Summary of Study Objectives for Appendix A

9. *Prepare adjusting entries for the alternative treatment of prepayments.* When prepayments are initially recorded in expense and revenue accounts, these accounts are overstated prior to adjustment. The adjusting entries for prepaid expenses are a debit to an asset account and a credit to an expense account. Adjusting entries for unearned revenues are a debit to a revenue account and a credit to a liability account.

GLOSSARY

Accrual basis of accounting · Accounting basis in which events that change a company's financial statements are recorded in the periods in which the events occur, rather than in the periods in which the company receives or pays cash. (p. 106).

Accrued expenses (liabilities) · Expenses incurred but not yet paid or recorded. (p. 99).

Accrued revenues (receivables) · Revenues earned but not yet received or recorded. (p. 98).

Adjusted trial balance · A list of accounts and their balances after all adjustments have been made. (p. 104).

Adjusting entries · Entries made at the end of an accounting period to ensure that the revenue recognition and matching principles are followed. (p. 91).

Book value · The difference between the cost of a depreciable asset and its related accumulated depreciation. (p. 96).

Calendar year · An accounting period that extends from January 1 to December 31. (p. 89).

Cash basis of accounting · Revenue is recorded only when cash is received and an expense is recorded only when cash is paid. (p. 107).

Contra asset account · An account that is offset against an asset account on the balance sheet. (p. 96).

Depreciation · The process of allocating the cost of an asset to expense over its useful life in a rational and systematic manner. (p. 95).

Fiscal years · Accounting periods that are one year in length. (p. 89).

Interim periods · Monthly or quarterly accounting time periods. (p. 89).

Matching principle · The principle that efforts (expenses) be matched with accomplishments (revenues). (p. 90).

Periodicity or time period assumption · An assumption that the economic life of a business can be divided into artificial time periods. (p. 88).

Prepaid expenses · Expenses paid in cash and recorded as assets before they are used or consumed. (p. 92).

Revenue recognition principle · The principle that revenue be recognized in the accounting period in which it is earned. (p. 89).

Unearned revenues · A liability created when a business collects cash in advance of performing a service for the customer. (p. 96).

Useful life · The length of service of a productive facility. (p. 95).

DEMONSTRATION PROBLEM

Terry Thomas opens the Green Thumb Lawn Care Company on April 1. At April 30, the trial balance shows the following balances for selected accounts:

Prepaid Insurance	$ 3,600
Equipment	28,000
Notes Payable	20,000
Unearned Fees	4,200
Fees Earned	1,800

Analysis reveals the following additional data pertaining to these accounts:

1. Prepaid insurance is the cost of a two-year insurance policy, effective April 1.
2. Depreciation on the equipment is $500 per month.
3. The note payable is dated April 1. It is a six-month, 12% note.
4. Seven customers paid for the company's six month's lawn service package of $600 beginning in April. These customers were serviced in April.
5. Lawn services rendered other customers but not billed at April 30 totaled $1,500.

Instructions
Prepare the adjusting entries for the month of April. Show computations.

Solution to Demonstration Problem

GENERAL JOURNAL   J2

Date	Account Titles and Explanation	Ref.	Debit	Credit
	Adjusting Entries			
Apr. 30	Insurance Expense		150	
	Prepaid Insurance			150
	(To record insurance expired:			
	$3,600 ÷ 24 = $150 per month)			
30	Depreciation Expense		500	
	Accumulated Depreciation—Equipment			500
	(To record monthly depreciation)			
30	Interest Expense		200	
	Interest Payable			200
	(To accrue interest on notes payable:			
	$20,000 × 12% × 1/12 = $200)			
30	Unearned Fees		700	
	Fees Earned			700
	(To record fees earned: $600 ÷ 6 = $100;			
	$100 per month × 7 = $700)			
30	Fees Receivable		1,500	
	Fees Earned			1,500
	(To accrue fees earned but not billed or			
	collected)			

Helpful hints
1. Note that adjustments are being made for one month.
2. Make computations carefully.
3. Select account titles carefully.
4. Make sure debits are made first and credits are indented.
5. Check that debits equal credits for each entry.

*Note: All **asterisked** Questions, Exercises, and Problems relate to material contained in the Appendix to the chapter.

SELF-STUDY QUESTIONS

Answers are at the end of the chapter.

(S.O. 1) 1. The periodicity assumption states that:
a. revenue should be recognized in the accounting period in which it is earned.
b. the economic life of a business can be divided into artificial time periods.
c. expenses should be matched with revenues.
d. the fiscal year should correspond with the calendar year.

(S.O. 2) 2. The principle which dictates that efforts (expenses) be matched with accomplishments (revenues) is the:
a. revenue recognition principle.
b. cost principle.
c. periodicity principle.
d. matching principle.

(S.O. 3) 3. Adjusting entries are made to ensure that:
a. revenues are recorded in the period in which they are earned.
b. expenses are recognized in the period in which they are incurred.
c. balance sheet and income statement accounts have correct balances at the end of an accounting period.
d. all of the above.

4. Each of the following is a major type (or category) of adjusting entries *except*: (S.O. 4)
a. prepaid expenses.
b. earned revenues.
c. accrued expenses.
d. accrued revenues.

5. The trial balance shows Supplies $1,350 and Supplies Expense $0. If $800 of supplies are on hand at the end of the period, the adjusting entry is: (S.O. 5)
a. Supplies   650
    Supplies Expense   650
b. Supplies   550
    Supplies Expense   550
c. Supplies Expense   750
    Supplies   750
d. Supplies Expense   550
    Supplies   550

6. Adjustments for unearned revenues: (S.O. 5)

a. have an assets and revenues account relationship.
b. decrease liabilities and increase revenues.
c. increase assets and increase revenues.
d. decrease revenues and decrease assets.

(S.O. 6)   7. Adjustments for accrued revenues:
a. have an assets and revenues account relationship.
b. have a liabilities and revenues account relationship.
c. decrease assets and revenues.
d. decrease liabilities and increase revenues.

(S.O. 6)   8. Kathy Kiska earned a salary of $400 for the last week of September. She will be paid on October 1. The adjusting entry for Kathy's employer at September 30 is:
a. Salaries Expense   400
    Salaries Payable   400
b. No entry is required
c. Salaries Expense   400
    Cash   400
d. Salaries Payable   400
    Cash   400

(S.O. 7)   9. Which of the following statements is *incorrect* concerning the adjusted trial balance?
a. An adjusted trial balance proves the equality of the total debit balances and the total credit balances in the ledger after all adjustments are made.
b. The adjusted trial balance provides the primary basis for the preparation of financial statements.
c. The adjusted trial balance is prepared after the adjusting entries have been journalized and posted.
d. The adjusted trial balance lists the account balances segregated by assets and liabilities.

(S.O. 8)   10. One of the following statements about the accrual basis of accounting is *false*. That statement is:
a. Events that change a company's financial statements are recorded in the periods in which the events occur.
b. Revenue is recognized in the period in which it is earned.
c. Revenue is recorded only when cash is received, and expense is recorded only when cash is paid.
d. This basis is in accord with generally accepted accounting principles.

(S.O. 9)   *11. The trial balance shows Supplies $0 and Supplies Expense $1,500. If $700 of supplies are on hand at the end of the period, the adjusting entry is:
a. debit Supplies $800 and credit Supplies Expense $800.
b. debit Supplies Expense $800 and credit Supplies $800.
c. debit Supplies $700 and credit Supplies Expense $700.
d. debit Supplies Expense $700 and credit Supplies $700.

QUESTIONS

1. Explain the periodicity assumption and indicate its importance to accounting.

2. What is meant by (a) a fiscal year? (b) an interim period?

3. Bart Connel, a lawyer, accepts a legal engagement in March, performs the work in April, and is paid in May. If Connel's law firm prepares monthly financial statements, when should it recognize revenue from this engagement? Why?

4. In completing the engagement in (3) above, Connel incurs $2,000 of expenses in March, $3,000 in April, and none in May. How much expense should be deducted from revenues in the month the revenue is recognized? Why?

5. "Adjusting entries are required by the cost principle of accounting." Do you agree? Explain.

6. Why may a trial balance not contain up-to-date and complete financial information?

7. Distinguish between the two categories of adjusting entries and identify the types of adjustments applicable to each category.

8. What account relationship exists with prepaid expenses? What is the debit/credit effect of a prepaid expense adjusting entry?

9. Depreciation is a process of valuation that results in the reporting of the fair market value of the asset." Do you agree? Explain.

10. Explain the differences between depreciation expense and accumulated depreciation.

11. Madonna Company purchased equipment for $12,000. By the current balance sheet date, $8,000 had been depreciated. Indicate the balance sheet presentation of the data.

12. What account relationships exist with unearned revenues? What is the debit/credit effect of an unearned revenue adjusting entry?

13. A company fails to recognize revenue earned but not yet received. Which of the following accounts are involved in the adjusting entry: (a) asset, (b) liability, (c) revenue, or (d) expense? For the accounts selected, indicate whether they would be debited or credited in the entry.

14. A company fails to recognize an expense incurred but not paid. Indicate which of the following accounts is debited and which is credited in the adjusting entry: (a) asset, (b) liability, (c) revenue, or (d) expense.

15. A company makes an accrued revenue adjusting entry for $800 and an accrued expense adjusting entry for $600. How much was net income understated prior to these entries? Explain.

16. On January 9, a company pays $5,000 for salaries of which $1,200 was reported as Salaries Payable on December 31. Give the entry to record the payment.

17. For each of the following items before adjustment, indicate the type of adjusting entry (prepaid expense, unearned revenue, accrued revenue, and accrued expense) that is needed to correct the misstatement. If an item could result in more than one type of adjusting entry, indicate each of the types.
(a) Liabilities are overstated.   (d) Expenses are understated.
(b) Assets are understated.   (e) Assets are overstated.
(c) Liabilities are understated.   (f) Revenue is understated.

18. One half of the adjusting entry is given below. Indicate the account title for the other half of the entry.
(a) Salaries Expense is debited.   (d) Prepaid Advertising is credited.
(b) Depreciation Expense is debited.   (e) Fees Receivable is debited.
(c) Interest Payable is credited.   (f) Unearned Fees is debited.

19. An adjusting entry may affect more than one balance sheet or income statement account. Do you agree? Why or why not?

20. Why is it possible to prepare financial statements directly from an adjusted trial balance?

21. Why do accrual basis financial statements provide more useful information than cash basis statements?

*22. The Adler Company debits Supplies Expense for all purchases of supplies and credits Rent Revenue for all advanced rentals. For each type of adjustment, give the adjusting entry.

BRIEF EXERCISES

BE3–1 The ledger of the Lyons Company includes the following accounts. Explain why each account may require adjustment.
a. Supplies   c. Unearned Fees
b. Depreciation Expense   d. Interest Expense

Explain the need for adjusting entries.
(S.O. 3)

BE3–2 The Rico Company accumulates the following adjustment data at December 31. Indicate (a) the type of adjustment (prepaid expense, accrued revenues and so on), (b) the account relationships (asset/revenue, liability/expense, and so on), and (c) the accounts before adjustment (overstated or understated).

1. Prepaid insurance of $600 has expired.
2. Fees earned but unbilled total $900.
3. Interest of $200 has accumulated on a note payable.
4. Rent collected in advance totaling $800 has been earned.

Identify the major types of adjusting entries.
(S.O. 4)

Prepare adjusting entry for supplies.
(S.O. 5)

BE3–3 The Slade Advertising Company's trial balance at December 31 shows Advertising Supplies $9,500 and Advertising Supplies Expense $0. On December 31, there are $1,500 of supplies on hand. Prepare the adjusting entry at December 31 and, using T accounts, enter the balances in the accounts, post the adjusting entry, and indicate the adjusted balance in each account.

Preparing adjusting entries for depreciation.
(S.O. 5)

BE3–4 At the end of its first year, the trial balance of the Lange Company shows Equipment $25,000 and zero balances in Accumulated Depreciation—Equipment and Depreciation Expense. Depreciation for the year is estimated to be $2,500. Prepare the the adjusting entry for depreciation at December 31, post the adjustments to T accounts, and indicate the balance sheet presentation of the equipment at December 31.

Prepare adjusting entries for prepaid expense.
(S.O. 5)

BE3–5 On July 1, 1993, Bealer Co. pays $18,000 to Mattson Insurance Co. for a three-year insurance contract. Both companies have fiscal years ending December 31. For Bealer Co. journalize and post the entry on July 1 and the adjusting entry on December 31.

Prepare adjusting entry for unearned revenue.
(S.O. 5)

BE3–6 Using the data in BE3–5, journalize and post the entry on July 1 and the adjusting entry on December 31 for Mattson Insurance Co. Mattson uses the accounts Unearned Insurance Revenue and Insurance Revenue.

Prepare adjusting entries for accruals.
(S.O. 6)

BE3–7 The bookkeeper for the Dunes Company asks you to prepare the following accrued adjusting entries at December 31.

1. Interest on notes payable of $400 is accrued.
2. Fees earned but unbilled total $1,200.
3. Salaries earned by employees of $700 have not been recorded.

Use the following account titles: Fees Earned, Fees Receivable, Interest Expense, Interest Payable, Salaries Expense, and Salaries Payable.

Analyze accounts in an adjusted trial balance.
(S.O. 7)

BE3–8 The trial balance of the Luger Company includes the following balance sheet accounts. Identify the accounts that require adjustment. For each account that requires adjustment, indicate (a) the type of adjusting entry (prepaid expenses, unearned revenues, accrued revenues, and accrued expenses) and (b) the related account in the adjusting entry.

Fees Receivable	Notes Payable
Prepaid Insurance	Interest Payable
Equipment	Unearned Fees
Accumulated Depreciation—Equipment	

Prepare an income statement from an adjusted trial balance.
(S.O. 7)

BE3–9 The adjusted trial balance of the Dumars Company at December 31, 1993, includes the following accounts: T. Dumars, Capital $15,600; T. Dumars, Drawing $6,000; Fees Earned $32,400; Salaries Expense $13,000; Insurance Expense $2,000; Rent Expense $4,000; Supplies Expense $1,500; and Depreciation Expense $1,000. Prepare an income statement for the year.

Prepare an owner's equity statement from an adjusted trial balance.
(S.O. 7)

BE3–10 Partial adjusted trial balance data for the Dumars Company is presented in BE3–9. The balance in T. Dumars, Capital is the balance as of January 1. Prepare an owner's equity statement for the year assuming net income is $15,000 for the year.

Prepare adjusting entries under alternative treatment of prepayments.
(S.O. 9)

*BE3–11 The Towne Company records all prepayments in income statement accounts. At April 30, the trial balance shows Supplies Expense $2,800, Fees Earned $9,200, and zero balances in related balance sheet accounts. Prepare the adjusting entries at April 30 assuming (a) $1,200 of supplies on hand and (b) $800 of the fees are unearned.

EXERCISES

Identify types of adjustments and account relationships.
(S.O. 4, 5, 6)

E3–1 The Richards Company accumulates the following adjustment data at December 31.

1. Store supplies of $300 have been used.
2. Fees earned but unbilled total $600.
3. Utility expenses of $225 are unpaid.
4. Fees of $260 collected in advance have been earned.
5. Salaries of $800 are unpaid.
6. Prepaid insurance totaling $350 has expired.

Instructions

For each of the above items indicate:

(a) The type of adjustment (prepaid expense, unearned revenue, accrued revenue, or accrued expense).

(b) The account relationship (asset/revenue, liability/revenue, and so on).

(c) The accounts before adjustment (overstatement or understatement).

E3–2 The ledger of Gail's Rental Agency on March 31 of the current year includes the following selected accounts before adjusting entries have been prepared.

Prepare adjusting entries from selected account data.

(S.O. 5, 6)

	Debit	Credit
Prepaid Insurance	$ 3,600	
Supplies	2,800	
Equipment	25,000	
Accumulated		
Depreciation—Equipment		$ 8,400
Notes Payable		20,000
Unearned Rent Revenue		9,300
Rent Revenue		60,000
Interest Expense	–0–	
Wage Expense	14,000	

An analysis of the accounts shows the following:

1. The equipment depreciates $400 per month.
2. One-third of the unearned rent was earned during the quarter.
3. Interest of $600 is accrued on the notes payable.
4. Supplies on hand total $750.
5. Insurance expires at the rate of $200 per month.

Instructions

Prepare the adjusting entries at March 31, assuming that adjusting entries are made quarterly. Additional accounts are: Depreciation Expense, Insurance Expense, Interest Payable, and Supplies Expense.

E3–3 Jim Caine, D.D.S., opened a dental practice on January 1, 1993. During the first month of operations the following transactions occurred.

Prepare adjusting entries.

(S.O. 5, 6)

1. Performed services for patients who had dental plan insurance. At January 31, $750 of such services was earned but not yet billed to the insurance companies.
2. Utility expenses incurred but not paid prior to January 31 totaled $650.
3. Purchased dental equipment on January 1 for $80,000, paying $20,000 in cash and signing a $60,000, three-year-note payable. The equipment depreciates $400 per month. Interest is $600 per month.
4. Purchased a one-year malpractice insurance policy on January 1 for $12,000.
5. Purchased $1,800 of dental supplies. On January 31, determined that $700 of supplies were on hand.

Instructions

Prepare the adjusting entries on January 31. Account titles are: Accumulated Depreciation—Dental Equipment, Depreciation Expense, Fees Earned, Fees Receivable, Insurance Expense, Interest Expense, Interest Payable, Prepaid Insurance, Supplies, Supplies Expense, Utilities Expense, and Utilities Payable.

E3–4 The trial balance for the Pioneer Advertising Agency is shown in Illustration 3-2, p. 92. In lieu of the adjusting entries shown in the text at October 31, assume the following adjustment data:

Prepare adjusting entries.

(S.O. 5, 6)

1. Advertising supplies on hand at October 31 total $1,200.
2. Expired insurance for the month is $100.
3. Depreciation for the month is $50.
4. Unearned fees earned in October total $500.

5. Fees earned but unbilled at October 31 are $300.

6. Interest accrued at October 31 is $70.

7. Accrued salaries at October 31 are $1,500.

Instructions
Prepare the adjusting entries for the items above.

Prepare correct income statement.
(S.O. 2, 5, 6)

E3–5 The income statement of Weiler Co. for the month of July shows net income of $1,400 based on Fees Earned $5,500, Wages Expense $2,300, Supplies Expense $1,200, and Utilities Expense $600. In reviewing the statement, you discover the following:

1. Insurance expired during July $300 was omitted.

2. Supplies expense includes $200 of supplies that are still on hand at July 31.

3. Depreciation on equipment of $150 was omitted.

4. Accrued but unpaid wages at July 31 of $300 were not included.

5. Fees earned but unrecorded totaled $750.

Instructions
Prepare a correct income statement for July.

Analyze adjusted data
(S.O. 2, 4, 5, 6)

E3–6 A partial adjusted trial balance of the Corbett Company at January 31, 1993 shows the following:

Adjusted Trial Balance

	Debit	Credit
Supplies	$ 800	
Prepaid Insurance	2,400	
Salaries Payable		700
Unearned Fees		750
Supplies Expense	950	
Insurance Expense	400	
Salaries Expense	1,800	
Fees Earned		2,500

Instructions
Answer the following questions, assuming the year begins January 1:

(a) If the amount in Supplies Expense is the January 31 adjusting entry, and $850 of supplies was purchased in January, what was the balance in Supplies on January 1?

(b) If the amount in Insurance Expense is the January 31 adjusting entry, and the original insurance premium was for one year, what was the total premium and when was the policy purchased?

(c) If $2,400 of salaries was paid in January, what was the balance in Salaries Payable at December 31, 1992?

(d) If $1,600 of fees was received in January for services performed in January, what was the balance in Unearned Fees at December 31, 1992?

Journalize basic transactions and adjusting entries.
(S.O. 5, 6)

E3–7 Selected accounts of the Alomas Company are shown below:

Supplies Expense

7/31	400	

Supplies					Salaries Payable		
7/1	Bal.	1,100	7/31	400		7/31	1,200
7/10		300					

Fees Receivable				Unearned Fees			
7/31	400			7/31	800	7/1 Bal.	1,500
						7/20	700

Salaries Expense				Fees Earned	
7/15	1,200		7/14		3,000
7/31	1,200		7/31		800
			7/31		400

Instructions

After analyzing the accounts, journalize (a) the July transactions and (b) the adjusting entries that were made on July 31. (Hint: July transactions were for cash.)

E3–8 The trial balances before and after adjustment for the Roni Company at the end of its fiscal year are presented below.

Prepare adjusting entries from analysis of trial balances.

(S.O. 5, 6, 7)

RONI COMPANY
Trial Balance
August 31, 1993

	Before Adjustment		After Adjustment	
	Dr.	Cr.	Dr.	Cr.
Cash	$10,400		$10,400	
Fees Receivable	8,800		9,500	
Office Supplies	2,300		700	
Prepaid Insurance	4,000		2,200	
Office Equipment	14,000		14,000	
Accumulated Depreciation—Office Equipment		$ 3,600		$ 4,800
Accounts Payable		5,800		5,800
Salaries Payable		–0–		1,000
Unearned Rent Revenue		1,500		700
R. Roni, Capital		15,600		15,600
Fees Earned		34,000		34,700
Rent Revenue		11,000		11,800
Salaries Expense	17,000		18,000	
Office Supplies Expense	–0–		1,600	
Rent Expense	15,000		15,000	
Insurance Expense	–0–		1,800	
Depreciation Expense	–0–		1,200	
	$71,500	$71,500	$74,400	$74,400

Instructions

Prepare the adjusting entries that were made.

E3–9 The adjusted trial balance for the Roni Company is given in E3–8.

Prepare financial statements from adjusted trial balance.

(S.O. 5, 6, 7)

Instructions

Prepare the income and owner's equity statements for the year and the balance sheet at August 31.

E3–10 One proposal that has often surfaced is to put the Federal government on an accrual basis of accounting. This is no small issue because if accrual basis accounting were used, it would mean that billions in government liabilities presently unrecorded would now be shown which would increase the federal deficit substantially.

Furthermore accrual accounting would not permit the following (adopted from an article in the *The Wall Street Journal*, July 6, 1987):

Distinguish between cash and accrual basis of accounting.

(S.O. 8)

The House gave voice approval to an amendment that in its words "would reduce outlays in fiscal year 1988 by shifting into fiscal year 1989 Department of Defense payments to contractors that otherwise would have been made the last 12 days of fiscal year 1988. (Small businesses were exempted out of fear that they would scream bloody murder at writing such deadbeat payment habits into law.)"

Instructions

(a) What is the difference between accrual basis accounting and cash basis accounting?

(b) What role does depreciation play in a cash basis accounting system?

(c) Comment on why politicians might desire a cash basis accounting system over an accrual basis system.

Journalize transactions and adjusting entries using appendix.
(S.O. 5, 6, 9)

*E3–11   At the Kupec Company, prepayments are debited to expense when paid and unearned revenues are credited to revenue when received. During January of the current year, the following transactions occurred:

Jan. 2   Paid $3,600 for fire insurance protection for the year.
      10   Paid $1,700 for supplies.
      15   Received $5,100 in fees for services to be performed in the future.

On January 31, it is determined that $1,200 of the services fees have been earned and that there is $700 of supplies on hand.

Instructions
(a) Journalize and post the January transactions. (Use T accounts.)
(b) Journalize and post the adjusting entries at January 31.
(c) Determine the ending balance in each of the accounts.

PROBLEMS

Prepare adjusting entries, post, and prepare an adjusted trial balance.
(S.O. 5, 6, 7)

P3–1   The trial balance of Kaplan Tours at the end of its first month of operations is presented below:

KAPLAN TOURS
Trial Balance
June 30, 1993

	Debit	Credit
Cash	$ 3,000	
Prepaid Insurance	7,200	
Office Equipment	1,800	
Buses	140,000	
Notes Payable		$ 62,000
Unearned Fees		15,000
Eldon Kaplan, Capital		70,000
Fees Earned		15,900
Salaries Expense	9,000	
Advertising Expense	800	
Gas and Oil Expense	1,100	
	$162,900	$162,900

Other data:

1. The insurance policy has a two-year term beginning June 1, 1993.
2. The monthly depreciation is $50 on office equipment and $2,000 on buses.
3. Interest of $700 accrues on the notes payable each month.
4. Deposits of $1,500 each were received for advanced tour reservations from 10 school groups. At June 30, three of these deposits have been earned.
5. Bus drivers are paid a combined total of $400 per day. At June 30, three days' salaries are unpaid.
6. A senior citizen's organization that had not made an advance deposit took a Canyon tour on June 30 for $1,200. This group was not billed for the services rendered until July 3.

Instructions
(a) Journalize the adjusting entries at June 30, 1993.
(b) Prepare a ledger using the three-column form of account. Enter the trial balance amounts and post the adjusting entries. (Use J2 as the posting reference.)

(c) Prepare an adjusted trial balance at June 30, 1993.

P3–2 The Lake Side Motel opened for business on May 1, 1993. Its trial balance on May 31 is as follows:

Prepare adjusting entries, adjusted trial balance, and financial statements.
(S.O. 5, 6, 7)

LAKE SIDE MOTEL
Trial Balance
May 31, 1993

	Debit	Credit
Cash	$ 2,300	
Prepaid Insurance	1,800	
Supplies	1,900	
Land	15,000	
Lodge	70,000	
Furniture	16,800	
Accounts Payable		$ 4,500
Unearned Rent Revenue		3,600
Mortgage Payable		35,000
Carla Damon, Capital		60,000
Rent Revenue		9,200
Salaries Expense	3,000	
Utilities Expense	1,000	
Advertising Expense	500	
	$112,300	$112,300

Other data:

1. Insurance expires at the rate of $200 per month.
2. An inventory of supplies shows $1,350 of unused supplies on May 31.
3. Annual depreciation is $3,600 on the lodge and $3,000 on furniture.
4. The mortgage interest rate is 12%. (The mortgage was taken out on May 1.)
5. Unearned rent of $1,500 has been earned.
6. Salaries of $300 are accrued and unpaid at May 31.

Instructions

(a) Journalize the adjusting entries on May 31.

(b) Prepare a ledger using the three-column form of account. Enter the trial balance amounts and post the adjusting entries. (Use J1 as the posting reference.)

(c) Prepare an adjusted trial balance on May 31.

(d) Prepare an income statement and an owner's equity statement for the month of May and a balance sheet at May 31.

P3–3 The Kuzman Co. was organized on July 1, 1993. Quarterly financial statements are prepared. The trial balance and adjusted trial balance on September 30 are shown below.

Prepare adjusting entries and financial statements.
(S.O. 5, 6, 7)

	Trial Balance		Adjusted Trial Balance	
	Dr.	Cr.	Dr.	Cr.
Cash	$ 6,700		$ 6,700	
Commissions Receivable	400		800	
Prepaid Rent	1,500		900	
Supplies	1,200		1,000	
Equipment	15,000		15,000	
Accumulated Depreciation—Equipment				$ 350
Notes Payable		$ 5,000		5,000
Accounts Payable		1,510		1,510
Salaries Payable				600
Interest Payable				50
Unearned Rent Revenue		900		600
R. Kuzman, Capital		14,000		14,000
R. Kuzman, Drawing	600		600	

	Trial Balance		Adjusted Trial Balance	
	Dr.	Cr.	Dr.	Cr.
Commission Revenue		14,000		14,400
Rent Revenue		400		700
Salaries Expense	9,000		9,600	
Rent Expense	900		1,500	
Depreciation Expense			350	
Supplies Expense			200	
Utilities Expense	510		510	
Interest Expense			50	
	$35,810	$35,810	$37,210	$37,210

Instructions

(a) Journalize the adjusting entries that were made.

(b) Prepare an income statement and an owner's equity statement for the three months ending September 30 and a balance sheet at September 30.

(c) If the note bears interest at 12%, how many months has it been outstanding?

Prepare adjusting entries.
(S.O. 5, 6)

P3–4 A review of the ledger of the Willow Company at December 31, 1993, produces the following data pertaining to the preparation of annual adjusting entries:

1. Prepaid Insurance $12,800. The company has separate insurance policies on its buildings and its motor vehicles. Policy B4564 on the building was purchased on July 1, 1992, for $9,600. The policy has a term of three years. Policy A2958 on the vehicles was purchased on January 1, 1993, for $4,800. This policy has a term of two years.

2. Unearned Subscription Revenue $49,000. The company began selling magazine subscriptions in 1993 on an annual basis. The selling price of a subscription is $50. A review of subscription contracts reveals the following:

Subscription Date	Number of Subscriptions
October 1	200
November 1	300
December 1	480
	980

3. Notes Payable, $50,000. This balance consists of a note for six months at an annual interest rate of 12%, dated September 1.

4. Salaries Payable $0. There are eight salaried employees. Salaries are paid every Friday for the current week. Five employees receive a salary of $600 each per week, and three employees earn $700 each per week. December 31 is a Wednesday. Employees do not work weekends. All employees worked the last three days of December.

Instructions
Prepare the adjusting entries at December 31, 1993.

Journalize transactions and follow through accounting cycle to preparation of financial statements.
(S.O. 5, 6, 7)

P3–5 On November 1, 1993, the account balances of Fesmore Equipment Repair were as follows:

No.	Debits		No.	Credits	
101	Cash	$ 2,790	154	Accumulated Depreciation	$ 500
112	Accounts Receivable	2,510	201	Accounts Payable	2,100
126	Supplies	1,000	209	Unearned Service Revenue	400
153	Store Equipment	10,000	212	Salaries Payable	500
			301	R. Fesmore, Capital	12,800
		$16,300			$16,300

During November the following summary transactions were completed.

Nov.   8   Paid $1,100 for salaries due employees, of which $600 is for November.

10 Received $1,200 cash from customers on account.

12 Received $1,400 cash for services performed in November.

15 Purchased store equipment on account $3,000.

17 Purchased supplies on account $1,500.

20 Paid creditors on account $2,500.

22 Paid November rent $300.

25 Paid salaries $1,000.

27 Performed services on account and billed customers for services rendered $700.

29 Received $450 from customers for future service.

Adjustment data consist of:

1. Supplies on hand $1,600.
2. Accrued salaries payable $500.
3. Depreciation for the month is $120.
4. Unearned service revenue of $300 is earned.

Instructions

(a) Enter the November 1 balances in the ledger accounts.

(b) Journalize the November transactions.

(c) Post to the ledger accounts. Use J1 for posting reference and No. 407 Service Revenue, No. 615 Depreciation Expense, No. 631 Supplies Expense, No. 726 Salaries Expense, and No. 729 Rent Expense.

(d) Prepare a trial balance at November 30.

(e) Journalize and post adjusting entries.

(f) Prepare an adjusted trial balance.

(g) Prepare an income statement and an owner's equity statement for November and a balance sheet at November 30.

*P3–6 The Glover Graphics Company was organized on January 1, 1993, by Nancy Glover. At the end of the first six months of operations, the trial balance contained the following accounts:

Prepare adjusting entries, adjusted trial balance, and financial statements using appendix.
(S.O. 5, 6, 7, 9)

Debits		Credits	
Cash	$ 9,500	Notes Payable	$ 17,000
Fees Receivable	14,000	Accounts Payable	9,000
Equipment	45,000	Nancy Glover, Capital	25,000
Insurance Expense	1,800	Graphic Fees Earned	52,100
Salaries Expense	30,000	Consulting Fees Earned	5,000
Supplies Expense	2,700		
Advertising Expense	2,000		
Rent Expense	1,500		
Utilities Expense	1,600		
	$108,100		$108,100

Analysis reveals the following additional data:

1. The $2,700 balance in Supplies Expense represents supplies purchased in January. At June 30, there was $1,500 of supplies on hand.
2. The note payable was issued on February 1. It is a 12%, six-month note.
3. The balance in Insurance Expense is the premium on a one-year policy, dated March 1, 1993.
4. Consulting fees are credited to revenue when received. At June 30, consulting fees of $1,000 are unearned.
5. Graphic fees earned but unbilled at June 30 total $2,000.
6. Depreciation is $2,000 per year.

Instructions

(a) Journalize the adjusting entries at June 30 (assume adjustments are recorded every six months).

(b) Prepare an adjusted trial balance.

(c) Prepare an income statement and owner's equity statement for the six months ended June 30 and a balance sheet at June 30.

ALTERNATE PROBLEMS

Prepare adjusting entries, post, and prepare an adjusted trial balance.
(S.O. 5, 6, 7)

P3–1A The Roth Security Service began operations on January 1, 1993. At the end of the first year of operations, the trial balance shows the following:

ROTH SECURITY SERVICE
Trial Balance
December 31, 1993

	Debit	Credit
Cash	$ 12,400	
Fees Receivable	3,200	
Prepaid Insurance	3,600	
Automobiles	58,000	
Notes Payable		$ 45,000
Unearned Fees		2,500
C. Roth, Capital		18,000
Fees Earned		84,000
Salaries Expense	57,000	
Repairs Expense	6,000	
Gas and Oil Expense	9,300	
	$149,500	$149,500

Other data:

1. Fees earned but unbilled $1,800 at December 31.
2. Insurance coverage began on January 1 under a two-year policy.
3. Automobile depreciation is $15,000 for the year.
4. Interest of $5,400 accrued on notes payable for the year.
5. $1,000 of the unearned fees has been earned.
6. Drivers' salaries total $500 per day. At December 31, four days' salaries are unpaid.
7. Repairs to automobiles of $650 have been incurred, but bills have not been received prior to December 31. (Use Accounts Payable.)

Instructions

(a) Journalize the annual adjusting entries at December 31, 1993.

(b) Prepare a ledger using the three-column account form. Enter the trial balance amounts and post the adjusting entries. (Use J15 as the posting reference.)

(c) Prepare an adjusted trial balance at December 31, 1993.

Prepare adjusting entries, adjusted trial balance, and financial statements.
(S.O. 5, 6, 7)

P3–2A The Highland Beach Resort opened for business on June 1 with eight air-conditioned units. Its trial balance on August 31 is as follows:

HIGHLAND BEACH RESORT
Trial Balance
August 31, 1993

	Debit	Credit
Cash	$ 19,600	
Prepaid Insurance	5,400	
Supplies	3,300	
Land	20,000	
Cottages	130,000	
Furniture	26,000	
Accounts Payable		$ 6,500

HIGHLAND BEACH RESORT

	Debit	Credit
Unearned Rent Revenue		6,800
Mortgage Payable		80,000
Tina Lee, Capital		100,000
Tina Lee, Drawing	5,000	
Rent Revenue		80,000
Salaries Expense	51,000	
Utilities Expense	9,400	
Repair Expense	3,600	
	$273,300	$273,300

Other data:

1. Insurance expires at the rate of $300 per month.
2. An inventory count on August 31 shows $700 of supplies on hand.
3. Annual depreciation is $4,800 on cottages and $2,400 on furniture.
4. Unearned rent of $5,000 was earned prior to August 31.
5. Salaries of $400 were unpaid at August 31.
6. Rentals of $800 were due from tenants at August 31. (Use Accounts Receivable.)
7. The mortgage interest rate is 12% per year. (The mortgage was taken out on August 1.)

Instructions

(a) Journalize the adjusting entries on August 31 for the three-month period June 1–August 31.

(b) Prepare a ledger using the three-column form of account. Enter the trial balance amounts and post the adjusting entries. (Use J1 as the posting reference.)

(c) Prepare an adjusted trial balance on August 31.

(d) Prepare an income statement and an owner's equity statement for the three months ending August 31 and a balance sheet as of August 31.

P3–3A The Grand Advertising Agency was founded by Thomas Grand in January of 1989. Presented below are both the adjusted and unadjusted trial balances as of December 31, 1993.

Prepare adjusting entries and financial statements.
(S.O. 5, 6, 7)

GRAND ADVERTISING AGENCY
Trial Balance
December 31, 1993

	Unadjusted		Adjusted	
	Dr.	Cr.	Dr.	Cr.
Cash	$ 12,000		$ 12,000	
Accounts Receivable	19,000		20,000	
Art Supplies	8,400		5,000	
Prepaid Insurance	3,350		2,500	
Printing Equipment	60,000		60,000	
Accumulated Depreciation		$ 28,000		$ 35,000
Accounts Payable		5,000		5,000
Interest Payable		0		150
Notes Payable		5,000		5,000
Unearned Advertising Revenue		7,000		5,600
Salaries Payable		0		1,800
T. Grand, Capital		25,500		25,500
T. Grand, Drawing	12,000		12,000	
Advertising Revenue		58,600		61,000
Salaries Expense	10,000		11,800	
Insurance Expense			850	
Interest Expense	350		500	
Depreciation Expense			7,000	
Art Supplies Expense			3,400	
Rent Expense	4,000		4,000	
	$129,100	$129,100	$139,050	$139,050

Instructions

(a) Journalize the annual adjusting entries that were made.

(b) Prepare an income statement and a statement of owner's equity for the year ending December 31, 1993, and a balance sheet at December 31.

(c) Answer the following questions:
   (1) If the note has been outstanding three months, what is the annual interest rate on that note?
   (2) If the company paid $12,500 in salaries in 1993, what was the balance in Salaries Payable on December 31, 1992?

Prepare adjusting entries.

P3–4A A review of the ledger of Grome Company at December 31, 1993, produces the following data pertaining to the preparation of annual adjusting entries.

1. Salaries Payable $0. There are eight salaried employees. Salaries are paid every Friday for the current week. Five employees receive a salary of $600 each per week, and three employees earn $500 each per week. December 31 is a Tuesday. Employees do not work weekends. All employees worked the last two days of December.

2. Unearned Rent Revenue $369,000. The company began subleasing office space in its new building on November 1. Each tenant is required to make a $5,000 security deposit that is not refundable until occupancy is terminated. At December 31, the company had the following rental contracts that are paid in full for the entire term of the lease.

Date	Term (in months)	Monthly Rent	Number of Leases
Nov. 1	6	$4,000	5
Dec. 1	6	$8,500	4

3. Prepaid Advertising $13,200. This balance consists of payments on two advertising contracts. The contracts provide for monthly advertising in two trade magazines. The terms of the contracts are as follows:

Contract	Date	Amount	Number of Magazine Issues
A650	May 1	$6,000	12
B974	Sept. 1	7,200	24

The first advertisement runs in the month in which the contract is signed.

4. Notes Payable $81,000. This balance consists of a note for one year at an annual interest rate of 12%, dated June 1.

Instructions

Prepare the adjusting entries at December 31, 1993. (Show all computations.)

Journalize transactions and follow through accounting cycle to preparation of financial statements.

P3–5A On September 1, 1993, the account balances of Harden Equipment Repair were as follows:

No.	Debits		No.	Credits	
101	Cash	$ 4,880	154	Accumulated Depreciation	$ 1,500
112	Accounts Receivable	3,520	201	Accounts Payable	3,400
126	Supplies	1,000	209	Unearned Service Revenue	400
153	Store Equipment	15,000	212	Salaries Payable	500
			301	R. Harden, Capital	18,600
		$24,400			$24,400

During September the following summary transactions were completed.

Sept. 8 Paid $1,100 for salaries due employees, of which $600 is for September.
      10 Received $1,200 cash from customers on account.
      12 Received $3,400 cash for services performed in September.
      15 Purchased store equipment on account $3,000.

17 Purchased supplies on account $1,500.

20 Paid creditors $4,500 on account.

22 Paid September rent $500.

25 Paid salaries $1,050.

27 Performed services on account and billed customers for services rendered $900.

29 Received $450 from customers for future service.

Adjustment data consist of:

1. Supplies on hand $1,800.

2. Accrued salaries payable $400.

3. Depreciation is $200 per month.

4. Unearned service revenue of $350 is earned.

Instructions

(a) Enter the September 1 balances in the ledger accounts.

(b) Journalize the September transactions.

(c) Post to the ledger accounts. Use J1 for posting reference and No. 407 Service Revenue, No. 615 Depreciation Expense, No. 631 Supplies Expense, No. 726 Salaries Expense, and No. 729 Rent Expense.

(d) Prepare a trial balance at September 30.

(e) Journalize and post adjusting entries.

(f) Prepare an adjusted trial balance.

(g) Prepare an income statement and an owner's equity statement for September and a balance sheet at September 30.

*B*roadening Your Perspective

FINANCIAL REPORTING PROBLEM

The financial statements of PepsiCo are presented in Appendix L at the end of this textbook.

Instructions

1. Using the consolidated income statement and balance sheet, identify items that may result in adjusting entries for prepayments.

2. Using the consolidated income statement, identify two items that may result in adjusting entries for accruals.

3. Using the Management's Analysis-Financial Condition section, what adjusting entries, if any, increased total liabilities in 1991?

4. Using the Notes to Consolidated Financial Statements section, what was the amount of depreciation expense for 1991 and 1990? How was depreciation expense reported in the income statement? Do you have any suggestions for improving PepsiCo's presentation of accumulated depreciation?

5. Using the Selected Financial Data section, what has been the trend since 1987 for (a) interest expense and (b) interest income?

6. Using the Consolidated Income Statement and the Consolidated Statement of Cash Flows, how much interest was paid in 1991? Where is the remainder presumably reported in the balance sheet?

DECISION CASE

(S.O. 1, 2, 5, 6, 7)   The Vacation Travel Court was organized on April 1, 1992, by Alice Adare. Alice is a good manager but a poor accountant. From the trial balance prepared by a part-time bookkeeper, Alice prepared the following income statement for the quarter that ended March 31, 1993.

VACATION TRAVEL COURT
Income Statement
For the Quarter Ended March 31, 1993

Revenues		
Travel court rental fees		$95,000
Operating expenses		
Advertising	$ 5,200	
Wages	29,800	
Utilities	900	
Depreciation	800	
Repairs	4,000	
Total operating expenses		40,700
Net income		$54,300

Alice knew that something was wrong with the statement because net income had never exceeded $20,000 in any one quarter. Knowing that you are an experienced accountant, she asks you to review the income statement and other data.

Your first look at the trial balance. In addition to the account balances reported above in the income statement, the ledger contains the following additional selected balances at March 31, 1993.

Supplies	$ 5,200
Prepaid Insurance	7,200
Notes Payable	12,000

You then make inquiries and discover the following:

1. Travel court rental fees include advanced rentals for summer month occupancy $28,000.
2. There were $1,400 of supplies on hand at March 31.
3. Prepaid insurance resulted from the payment of a one-year policy on January 1, 1993.
4. The mail on April 1, 1993, brought the following bills: advertising for week of March 24, $110; repairs made March 10, $260; and utilities, $180.
5. There are four employees who receive wages totaling $350 per day. At March 31, two days' wages have been incurred but not paid.
6. The note payable is a three-month 10% note dated January 1, 1993.

Instructions

(a) Prepare a correct income statement for the quarter ended March 31, 1993.

(b) Explain to Alice the accounting principles that she did not recognize in preparing her income statement and their effect on her results.

CRITICAL THINKING CASE

Refer to the opening story about Arizona State University and answer the following questions:

1. What are the purposes of adjusting entries?

2. Why should Arizona State University be concerned about the period in which revenue is recognized?

3. What accounts did Arizona State University probably use to record tuition revenue and interest revenue?

4. What other types of adjusting entries do you believe Arizona State University might make?

ETHICAL CASE

Duemin Company is a pesticide manufacturer. Its sales declined greatly this year due to the passage of legislation outlawing the sale of several of Duemin's chemical pesticides. During the coming year, Duemin will have environmentally safe and competitive replacement chemicals to replace these discontinued products. Sales in the next year are expected to greatly exceed any prior year's. The development in sales and profits appears to be a one-year aberration. But even so, the company president believes that a large dip in current year's profits could cause a significant drop in the market price of Duemin's stock and make it a takeover target. To avoid this possibility, the company president urges Carol Denton, controller, in making this period's year-end adjusting entries to accrue every possible revenue and to defer as many expenses as possible. The president says to Carol, "We need the revenues this year, and next year can easily absorb expenses deferred from this year. We can't let our stock price be hammered down!" Carol didn't get around to recording the adjusting entries until January 17, but she dated the entries December 31 as if they were recorded then. Carol also made every effort to comply with the president's request.

Instructions

(a) Who are the stakeholders in this situation?

(b) What are the ethical considerations of (1) the president's request and (2) Carol's dating the adjusting entries December 31?

(c) Can Carol accrue revenues and defer expenses and still be ethical?

Answers to Self-Study Questions
1. b   2. d   3. d   4. b   5. d   6. b   7. a   8. a   9. d   10. c
11. c

CONCEPTS FOR REVIEW

Before studying this chapter you should know or, if necessary, review:

a. *How to apply the revenue recognition and matching principles. (Ch. 3, pp. 89–90)*

b. *How to make adjusting entries. (Ch. 3, pp. 91–102)*

c. *How to prepare an adjusted trial balance. (Ch. 3, pp. 104–5)*

d. *How to prepare a balance sheet, income statement, and owner's equity statement. (Ch. 3, pp. 105–6)*

CHAPTER 4

COMPLETION OF THE ACCOUNTING CYCLE

Study Objectives

After studying this chapter, you should be able to:

1. **Prepare a work sheet.**

2. **Explain the process of closing the books.**

3. **Describe the content and purpose of a post-closing trial balance.**

4. **State the required steps in the accounting cycle.**

5. **Explain the approaches to preparing correcting entries.**

6. **Identify the sections of a classified balance sheet.**

Stillman College in Tuscaloosa, Alabama is a small private school with 830 students. Because many students come from economically disadvantaged families, the college depends on a disproportionate amount of gifts, private grants, and federal grants for its income. Stillman also tries to keep its costs as low as possible. "Many of our employees are here for love, not for money," says Terre Thompson, comptroller.

Needless to say, monthly financial reports are extremely important in administrating the college. Most of these reports are produced with the aid of a VAX 8350 computer system that is programmed by a software package called Poise. However, one important monthly report is prepared manually by Ms. Thompson with the aid of a work sheet. That report is the monthly and year-to-date revenue and expenditure report. "Management looks at detailed expense reports showing how much they spent this month, how much they spent year-to-date, and what is the remaining budget balance," she says.

"At registration, students are billed for their tuition and fees and room and board. Those transactions come to me. I book the revenue from that and set up the receivable. On the expenditure side, we have payroll and operating costs. Supplies are preauthorized using a purchase-order system. We pay bills twice a month."

Ms. Thompson, who came to Stillman from a background in multinational accounting, also likes to pencil out another monthly statement—one that you will learn about later in this book. "I manually do a statement of cash flows. That's the killer for us, especially with students of limited economic means. We can book all of this wonderful revenue at the beginning of the semester," says Ms. Thompson, "but unless we can collect, we've got cash flow problems." Sometimes students, and even some administrators, have a hard time understanding how you can make money per the books but have no money in the bank."

In Chapter 3 we illustrated different types of adjustments. When the accountant has prepared these adjustments the ledger accounts are accurate and complete. Also in Chapter 3, the adjusting entries for Pioneer Advertising Agency were journalized, posted to the ledger, and an adjusted trial balance was prepared. Financial statements were then prepared directly from the adjusted trial balance. With so many details involved in these end-of-the-period accounting procedures, it is easy to make errors. Locating and correcting errors can cost much time and effort. One way to minimize errors in the records and to simplify the end-of-the-period procedures is to use a work sheet.

Accounting in Action · *Business Insight*

Yes, errors can happen. For example, a flap arose over a clerical error that turned Prudential Insurance Company's $92,885,000 lien on eight container ships into a paltry $92,885 lien. It seems someone failed to notice that three zeros had been dropped on a revision of the lien contract. The case acquired notoriety around the bankruptcy court as the "dot hearing," the "decimal point hearing," and "the three zeros hearing." Prudential eventually settled the case at a cost to it in excess of $8 million.

Source: The Wall Street Journal, March 23, 1988.

In this chapter, we will explain the role of the work sheet in accounting and the remaining steps in the accounting cycle, again using the Pioneer Advertising Agency as an example. Then we will consider (1) correcting entries and (2) classified balance sheets.

Using a Work Sheet

A **work sheet** is a multiple-column form that may be used in the adjustment process and in preparing financial statements. As its name suggests, the work sheet is a working tool or a supplementary device for the accountant. **A work sheet is not a permanent accounting record;** it is neither a journal nor a part of the general ledger. The work sheet is merely a device used to make it easier to prepare adjusting entries and the financial statements. In small companies with relatively few accounts and adjustments, a work sheet may not be needed. In large companies with numerous accounts and many adjustments, it is almost indispensable.

The basic form of a work sheet and the procedure (5 steps) for preparing a work sheet are shown in Illustration 4-1.

Study Objective 1

Prepare a work sheet.

ILLUSTRATION 4-1

Form and procedure for a work sheet

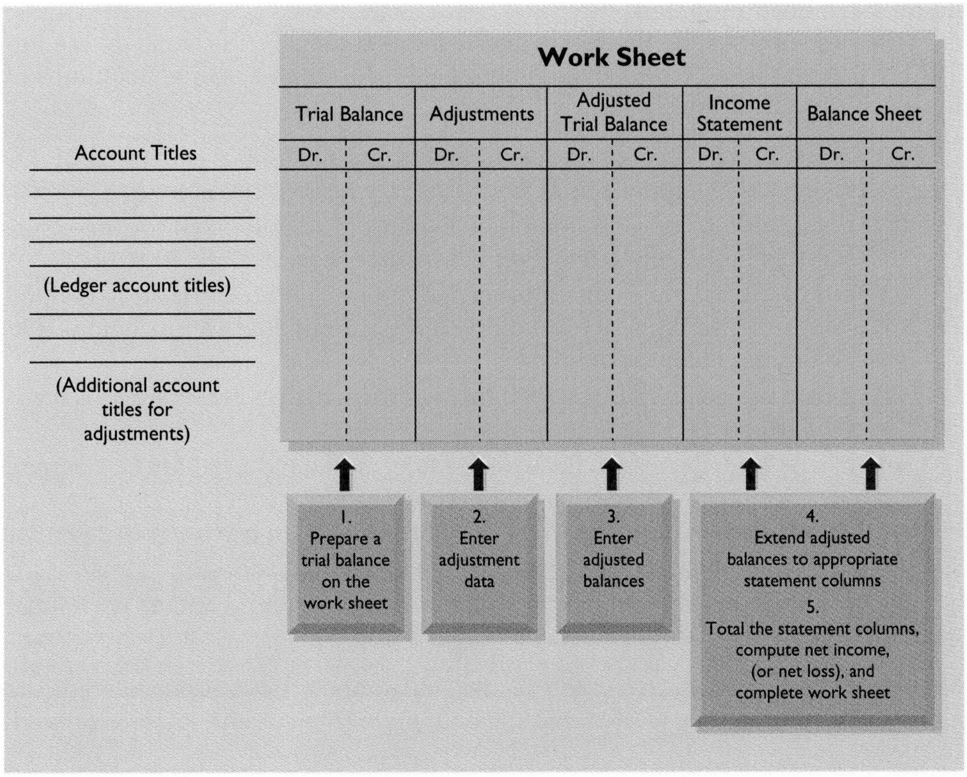

Each of the steps in preparing the work sheet must be performed in the prescribed sequence.

The use of a work sheet is optional. When a work sheet is used, financial statements are prepared from the work sheet. The adjustments are entered in the work sheet columns and are then journalized and posted after the financial statements have been prepared. Thus, management and other interested parties can receive the financial statements at an earlier date.

Preparing a Work Sheet

We will use the October 31 trial balance and adjustment data of Pioneer Advertising in Chapter 3 to illustrate the preparation of a work sheet. Each step of the process is described below and demonstrated in Illustrations 4-2 and 4-3A, B, C, and D.

STEP 1.   PREPARE A TRIAL BALANCE ON THE WORK SHEET. The account title space and trial balance columns are used to prepare a trial balance. The data for the trial balance are taken directly from the ledger accounts. The trial balance for Pioneer Advertising Agency is entered in the trial balance columns of the work sheet as shown in Illustration 4-2.

STEP 2.   ENTER THE ADJUSTMENTS IN THE ADJUSTMENT COLUMNS. Turn over the first transparency, Illustration 4-3A. When a work sheet is used, all adjustments are entered in the adjustment columns. In entering the adjustments, applicable trial balance accounts should be used. If additional accounts are needed, they should be inserted on the lines immediately below the trial balance totals. Each adjustment is indexed and keyed to facilitate the journalizing of the adjusting entry in the general journal. **It is important to recognize that the adjustments are not journalized until after the work sheet is completed and the financial statements have been prepared.**

The adjustments for Pioneer Advertising Agency are the same as the adjustments illustrated on page 102. They are keyed in the adjustment columns of the work sheet as follows:

(a) An additional account, Advertising Supplies Expense, is debited $1,500 for the cost of supplies used, and Advertising Supplies is credited $1,500.

(b) An additional account, Insurance Expense, is debited $50 for the insurance that has expired, and Prepaid Insurance is credited $50.

(c) Two additional accounts are needed. Depreciation Expense is debited $40 for the month's depreciation, and Accumulated Depreciation—Office Equipment is credited $40.

(d) Unearned Fees is debited $400 for fees earned, and Fees Earned is credited $400.

(e) An additional account, Fees Receivable, is debited $200 for fees earned but not billed, and Fees Earned is credited $200.

(f) Two additional accounts are needed. Interest Expense is debited $50 for accrued interest, and Interest Payable is credited $50.

(g) Salaries Expense is debited $1,200 for accrued salaries, and an additional account, Salaries Payable, is credited $1,200.

Note in the Illustration that after all the adjustments have been entered, the adjustment columns are totaled and the equality of the column totals is proved.

STEP 3.   ENTER ADJUSTED BALANCES IN THE ADJUSTED TRIAL BALANCE COLUMNS. Turn over the second transparency, Illustration 4-3B. The adjusted balance of an account is obtained by combining the amounts entered in the first four columns of the work sheet for each account. For example, the Prepaid Insurance account in the trial balance columns has a $600 debit balance. When this is combined with the $50 credit in the adjustment columns, the result is a $550 debit balance recorded in the adjusted trial balance columns. **For each account on the work sheet, the amount in the adjusted trial balance columns is equal to the account balance**

that will appear in the ledger after the adjusting entries have been journalized and posted. The balances in these columns are the same as those in the adjusted trial balance in Illustration 3-17 on page 104.

After the balances of all accounts have been entered in the adjusted trial balance columns, the columns are totaled and their equality is proved. The agreement of the column totals facilitates the completion of the work sheet. If these columns are not in agreement, the statement columns will not balance and the financial statements will be incorrect.

STEP 4. EXTEND ADJUSTED TRIAL BALANCE AMOUNTS TO APPROPRIATE FINANCIAL STATEMENT COLUMNS. Turn over the third transparency, Illustration 4-3C. This step involves the extension of adjusted trial balance amounts to the last four columns of the work sheet. Balance sheet accounts such as Cash and Notes Payable are entered in the balance sheet debit and credit columns, respectively. The balance in accumulated depreciation is extended to the balance sheet credit column. This results because accumulated depreciation is a contra-asset account with a credit balance.

Because the work sheet does not have columns for the owner's equity statement, the balance in owner's capital is extended to the balance sheet credit column. In addition, the balance in owner's drawings is extended to the balance sheet debit column because it is an owner's equity account with a debit balance. The expense and revenue accounts such as Salaries Expense and Fees Earned are entered in the appropriate income statement columns. These extensions are shown in Illustration 4-3C.

STEP 5. TOTAL THE STATEMENT COLUMNS, COMPUTE THE NET INCOME (OR NET LOSS), AND COMPLETE THE WORK SHEET. Turn over the fourth transparency, Illustration 4-3D. Each of the statement columns must be totaled. The net income or loss for the period is then found by computing the difference between the totals of the two income statement columns. If total credits exceed total debits, net income has resulted. In such a case, as shown in Illustration 4-3D, the words "net income" are inserted in the account title space. The amount then is entered in the income statement debit column and the balance sheet credit column. The debit amount balances the income statement columns and the credit amount balances the balance sheet columns. In addition, the credit in the balance sheet column indicates the increase in owner's equity resulting from net income. Conversely, if total debits in the income statement columns exceed total credits, a net loss has occurred. The amount of the net loss is entered in the income statement credit column and the balance sheet debit column.

After the net income or net loss has been entered, new column totals are determined. The totals shown in the debit and credit income statement columns will be identical. The totals shown in the debit and credit balance sheet columns will also be identical. If either the income statement columns or the balance sheet columns are not equal after the net income or net loss has been entered, an error has been made in completing the work sheet. The completed work sheet for Pioneer Advertising Agency is shown in Illustration 4-3D.

Preparing Financial Statements from a Work Sheet

After a work sheet has been completed, the statement columns contain all the data that are required for the preparation of financial statements. The income statement is prepared from the income statement columns, and the balance sheet

Helpful hint Every adjusted trial balance amount must be extended to one of the four statement columns. Debit amounts go to debit columns and credit amounts go to credit columns.

Helpful hint All fives pairs of columns must balance for a work sheet to be complete.

ILLUSTRATION 4-2

Preparing a trial balance

PIONEER ADVERTISING AGENCY
Work Sheet
For the Month Ended October 31, 1993

Account Titles	Trial Balance		Adjustments		Adjusted Trial Balance		Income Statement		Balance Sheet	
	Dr.	Cr.	Dr.	Cr.	Dr.	Cr.	Dr.	Cr.	Dr.	Cr.
Cash	15,200									
Advertising Supplies	2,500									
Prepaid Insurance	600									
Office Equipment	5,000									
Notes Payable		5,000								
Accounts Payable		2,500								
Unearned Fees		1,200								
C. R. Byrd, Capital		10,000								
C. R. Byrd, Drawing	500									
Fees Earned		10,000								
Salaries Expense	4,000									
Rent Expense	900									
Totals	28,700	28,700								

Include all accounts from ledger with balances

Trial balance amounts are taken directly from ledger accounts

ILLUSTRATION 4-4

Financial statements from a work sheet

PIONEER ADVERTISING AGENCY
Income Statement
For the Month Ended October 31, 1993

Revenues		
Fees earned		$10,600
Expenses		
Salaries expense	$5,200	
Advertising supplies expense	1,500	
Rent expense	900	
Insurance expense	50	
Interest expense	50	
Depreciation expense	40	
Total expenses		7,740
Net Income		$ 2,860

PIONEER ADVERTISING AGENCY
Owner's Equity Statement
For the Month Ended October 31, 1993

C. R. Byrd, Capital, October 1	$10,000
Add: Net income	2,860
	12,860
Less: Drawings	500
C. R. Byrd, Capital, October 31	$12,360

PIONEER ADVERTISING AGENCY
Balance Sheet
October 31, 1993

<u>**Assets**</u>

Cash		$15,200
Fees receivable		200
Advertising supplies		1,000
Prepaid insurance		550
Office equipment	$5,000	
Less: Accumulated depreciation	40	4,960
Total assets		$21,910

<u>**Liabilities and Owner's Equity**</u>

Liabilities	
Notes payable	$ 5,000
Accounts payable	2,500
Interest payable	50
Unearned fees	800
Salaries payable	1,200
Total liabilities	9,550
Owner's equity	
C. R. Byrd, Capital	12,360
Total liabilities and owner's equity	$21,910

and owner's equity statement are prepared from the balance sheet columns. The financial statements prepared from the work sheet for Pioneer Advertising Agency are shown in Illustration 4-4. At this point, adjusting entries have not been journalized and posted. Therefore, the ledger does not support all financial statement amounts.

The amount shown for owner's capital on the work sheet is the account balance **before considering drawings and net income (or loss).** When there have been no additional investments of capital by the owner during the period, this amount is the balance at the beginning of the period.

Using a work sheet, accountants can prepare financial statements before adjusting entries are journalized and posted. **However, the completed work sheet is not a substitute for formal financial statements.** Data in the financial statement columns are not properly arranged for statement purposes. Moreover, as noted above, the financial statement presentation for some accounts differs from their statement columns on the work sheet. A work sheet is essentially a working tool of the accountant and is not distributed to management and other parties.

Preparing Adjusting Entries from a Work Sheet

A work sheet is not a journal, and it cannot be used as a basis for posting to ledger accounts. To adjust the accounts, it is necessary to journalize and post the adjustments to the ledger. The adjusting entries are prepared from the adjustment columns of the work sheet. The reference letters in the adjustment columns and the key to the adjustments that appear at the bottom of the work sheet help identify entries. However, writing the key to the adjustments at the bottom of the work sheet is not required. As indicated previously, the journalizing and posting of adjusting entries **follows** the preparation of financial statements when a work sheet is used. The adjusting entries on October 31 for Pioneer Advertising Agency are the same as those shown in Illustration 3-15 (page 102).

Technology in Action

The work sheet can be computerized using an electronic spreadsheet program. The LOTUS 1–2–3 supplement for this textbook is one of the most popular versions of such spreadsheet packages. With a program like LOTUS 1–2–3, you can produce any type of work sheet (accounting or otherwise) that you could produce with paper and pencil on a columnar pad. The tremendous advantage of an electronic work sheet over the paper and pencil version is the ability to change selected data. When data are changed, the computer updates the balance of your computations instantly. More specific applications of electronic spreadsheets will be noted as we proceed.

Before You Go On . . .

1. What are the five steps in preparing a work sheet?

2. How is net income or net loss shown in a work sheet?

3. How does a work sheet relate to preparing financial statements and adjusting entries?

Closing the Books

In Chapter 2, you learned that revenue and expense accounts and the owner's drawing account are subdivisions of owner's capital. Because these accounts relate only to a given accounting period they are considered to be temporary or nominal accounts. In contrast, all balance sheet accounts are considered to be permanent or real accounts because they are carried forward into future accounting periods. Illustration 4-5 identifies the types of accounts in each category.

Study Objective 2

Explain the process of closing the books.

ILLUSTRATION 4-5

Temporary versus permanent accounts

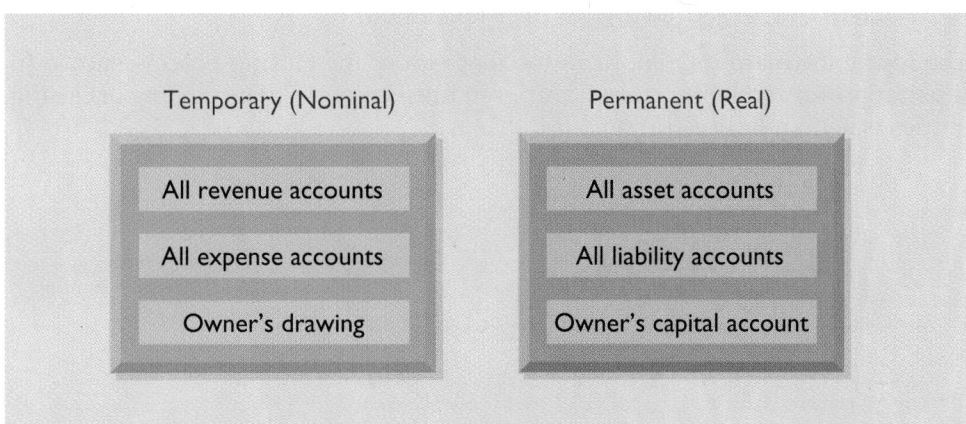

At the end of the accounting period, the temporary account balances are transferred to the permanent owner's equity account, owner's capital, through the preparation of closing entries.[1] Closing entries formally recognize in the ledger the transfer of net income (or loss) and owner's drawings to owner's capital as shown in the owner's equity statement. These entries also produce a zero balance in each temporary account so it can be used to accumulate data in the next accounting period.

Journalizing and posting closing entries is a required step in the accounting cycle. This step is performed after financial statements have been prepared. In contrast to the steps in the cycle that you have already studied, closing entries are generally journalized and posted **only at the end of a company's annual accounting period.** This practice facilitates the preparation of annual financial statements because all temporary accounts will contain data for the entire year. In preparing closing entries, each income statement account could be closed directly to owner's capital. However, to do so would result in excessive detail in the permanent owner's capital account. Accordingly, the revenue and expense accounts are closed to another temporary account, Income Summary, and only the net income (or net loss) is transferred from this account to owner's capital.

Closing Entries

Closing entries are journalized in the general journal. A center caption entitled Closing Entries may be inserted in the journal between the last adjusting entry and the first closing entry to identify these entries. Then the closing entries are posted to the ledger accounts. Closing entries may be prepared directly from the adjusted balances in the ledger, from the income statement and balance sheet columns of the work sheet, or from the income and owner's equity statements.

Helpful hint When the work sheet is used, revenue and expense account data are found in the income statement columns and owner's drawings is in the balance sheet debit column.

---

[1]Closing entries for a partnership and for a corporation are explained in Chapters 14 and 15, respectively.

Separate closing entries could be prepared for each nominal account, but the following four entries accomplish the desired result more efficiently:

1. Debit each revenue account for its balance and credit Income Summary for total revenues.
2. Debit Income Summary for total expenses and credit each expense account for its balance.
3. Debit Income Summary and credit owner's capital for the amount of net income.
4. Debit owner's capital for the balance in the owner's drawing account and credit owner's drawing for the same amount.

The four entries are referenced in the diagram of the closing process shown in Illustration 4-6 and in the journal entries in Illustration 4-7. The posting of closing entries is shown in Illustration 4-8.

ILLUSTRATION 4-6

Diagram of closing process—proprietorship

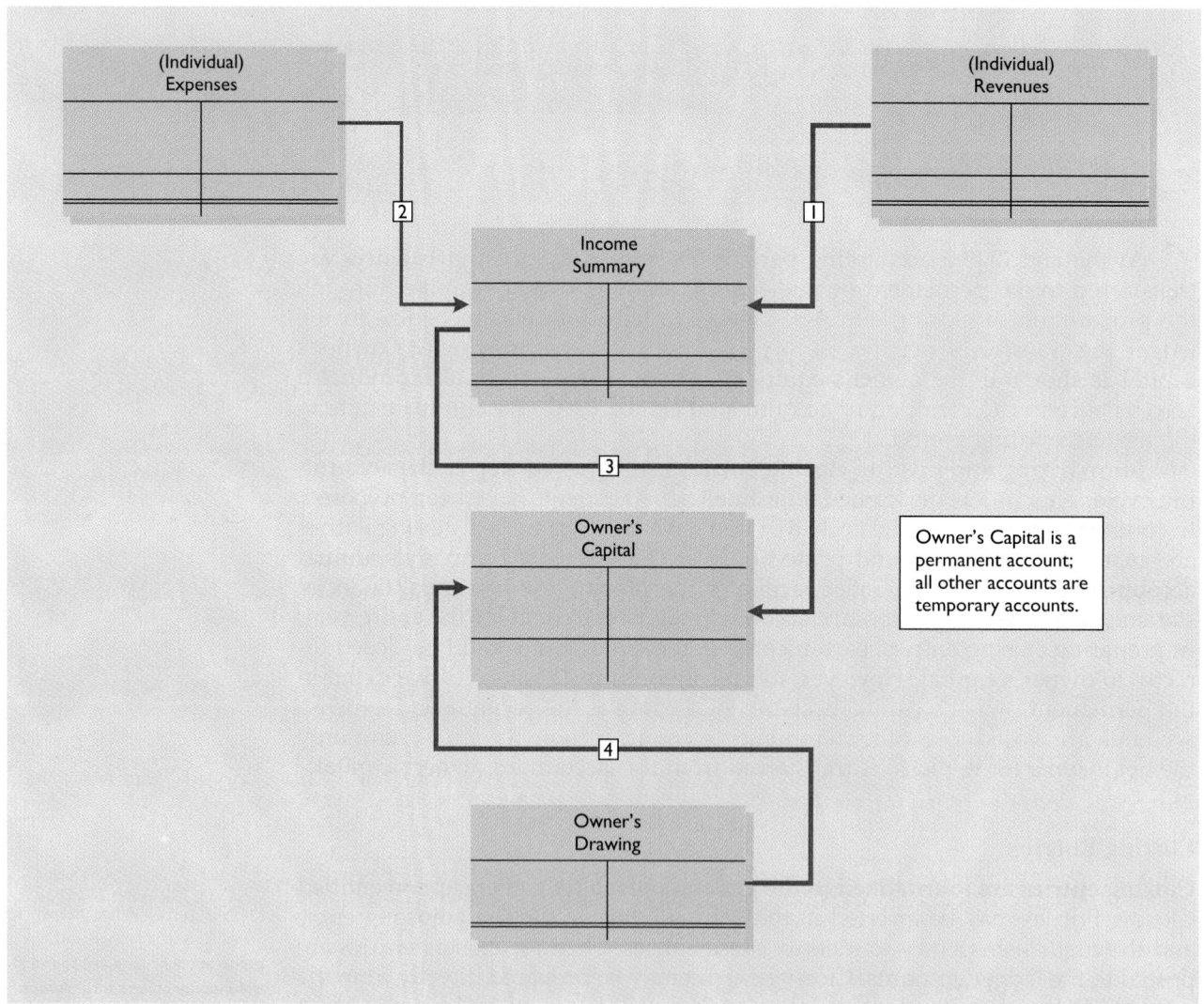

If a net loss has occurred, entry (3) credits Income Summary and debits Owner's Capital.

Closing Entries Illustrated

As explained above, closing entries are generally prepared only at the end of a company's annual accounting period. However, to illustrate the journalizing and posting of closing entries, we will assume that Pioneer Advertising Agency closes its books monthly. The closing entries at October 31 are shown in Illustration 4-7.

ILLUSTRATION 4-7

Closing entries journalized

Date		Account Titles and Explanation	Ref.	Debit	Credit
		GENERAL JOURNAL **J3**			
		Closing Entries			
		(1)			
Oct.	31	Fees Earned	50	10,600	
		Income Summary	49		10,600
		(To close revenue account)			
		(2)			
	31	Income Summary	49	7,740	
		Salaries Expense	60		5,200
		Advertising Supplies Expense	61		1,500
		Rent Expense	62		900
		Insurance Expense	63		50
		Interest Expense	64		50
		Depreciation Expense	65		40
		(To close expense accounts)			
		(3)			
	31	Income Summary	49	2,860	
		C. R. Byrd, Capital	40		2,860
		(To close net income to capital)			
		(4)			
	31	C. R. Byrd, Capital	40	500	
		C. R. Byrd, Drawing	41		500
		(To close drawings to capital)			

Note that the amounts for Income Summary in entries (1) and (2) are the totals of the income statement credit and debit columns, respectively, in the work sheet.

A couple of cautions in preparing closing entries: (1) Avoid unintentionally doubling the revenue and expense balances rather than zeroing them. (2) Do not close owner's drawing through the Income Summary account. Owner's drawings are not expenses, and they are not a factor in determining net income.

Posting of Closing Entries

The posting of the closing entries and the ruling of the accounts are shown in Illustration 4-8. Note that all temporary accounts have zero balances. In addition, you should realize that the balance in Owner's Capital represents the total equity of the owner at the end of the accounting period. This balance is shown on the balance sheet and is the ending capital reported on the owner's equity statement, as shown in Illustration 4-4 on page 137. **The Income Summary account is used only in closing.** No entries are journalized and posted to this account during the year.

As part of the closing process, the **temporary accounts** (revenues and expenses) in T account form are totaled, balanced, and double ruled as shown in Illustration 4-8. The **permanent accounts** (assets, liabilities, and owner's capital) are not closed: A single rule is drawn beneath the current period entries and the

Helpful hint The balance in Income Summary before it is closed must equal the net income or net loss for the period.

ILLUSTRATION 4-8

Posting of closing entries

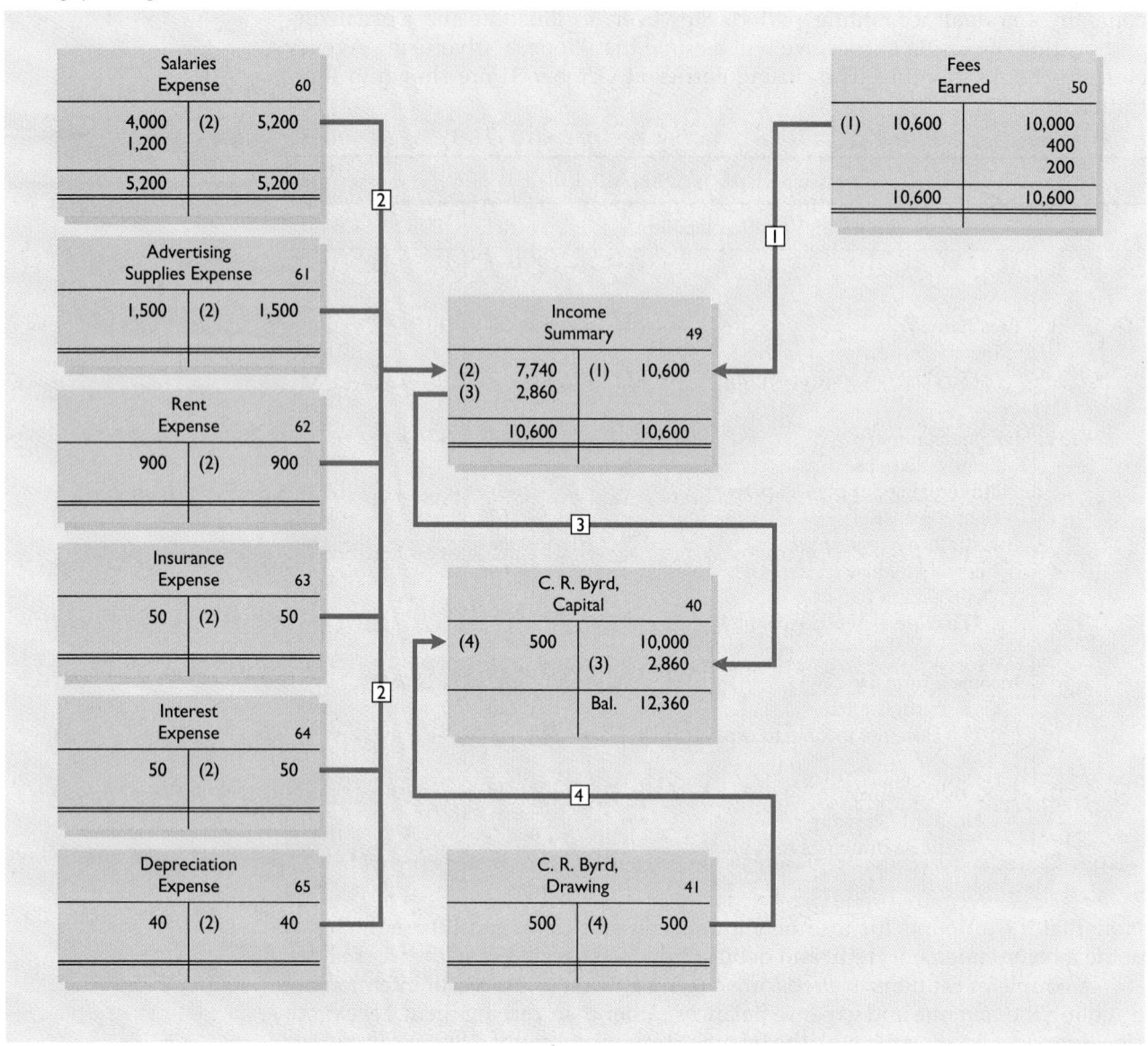

account balance carried forward to the next period is entered below the single rule. (For example, see C. R. Byrd, Capital.)

Preparing a Post-Closing Trial Balance

Study Objective 3

Describe the content and purpose of a post-closing trial balance.

After all closing entries have been journalized and posted, another trial balance, called a post-closing trial balance, is prepared from the ledger. A post-closing trial balance is a list of permanent accounts and their balances after closing entries have been journalized and posted. **The purpose of this trial balance is to prove the equality of the permanent account balances that are carried forward into the next accounting period.** Since all temporary accounts will have zero balances, the post-closing trial balance will contain only permanent—balance sheet—accounts. The procedure for preparing a post-closing trial balance again consists entirely of listing the accounts and their balances. These balances are the same as those reported in the company's balance sheet in Illustration 4-4. The post-closing trial balance for Pioneer Advertising is shown in Illustration 4-9.

ILLUSTRATION 4-9

Post-closing trial balance

PIONEER ADVERTISING AGENCY Post-Closing Trial Balance October 31, 1993		
	Debit	Credit
Cash	$15,200	
Fees Receivable	200	
Advertising Supplies	1,000	
Prepaid Insurance	550	
Office Equipment	5,000	
Accumulated Depreciation—Office Equipment		$ 40
Notes Payable		5,000
Accounts Payable		2,500
Interest Payable		50
Unearned Fees		800
Salaries Payable		1,200
C. R. Byrd, Capital		12,360
	$21,950	$21,950

The post-closing trial balance is prepared from the permanent accounts in the ledger. The permanent accounts of Pioneer Advertising are shown in the general ledger in Illustration 4-10. Because the balance of each account is computed after every posting, no additional work on these accounts is needed as part of the closing process. The remaining accounts in the general ledger are temporary accounts (shown in Illustration 4-11 on page 145). After the closing entries are posted, each temporary account has a zero balance. These accounts are double-ruled to finalize the closing process.

A post-closing trial balance provides evidence that the journalizing and posting of closing entries has been properly completed. In addition, it shows that the accounting equation is in balance at the end of the accounting period. However, as in the case of the trial balance, it does not prove that all transactions have been recorded or that the ledger is correct. For example, the post-closing trial balance will balance if a transaction is not journalized and posted or if a transaction is journalized and posted twice.

ILLUSTRATION 4-10

General ledger: permanent accounts

GENERAL LEDGER

	Cash			No. 1	
Date	Explanation	Ref.	Debit	Credit	Balance
1993					
Oct. 1		J1	10,000		10,000
2		J1	1,200		11,200
3		J1		900	10,300
4		J1		600	9,700
20		J1		500	9,200
26		J1		4,000	5,200
31		J1	10,000		15,200

	Fees Receivable			No. 6	
Date	Explanation	Ref.	Debit	Credit	Balance
1993					
Oct. 31	Adj. entry	J2	200		200

	Advertising Supplies			No. 8	
Date	Explanation	Ref.	Debit	Credit	Balance
1993					
Oct. 5		J1	2,500		2,500
31	Adj. entry	J2		1,500	1,000

	Prepaid Insurance			No. 10	
Date	Explanation	Ref.	Debit	Credit	Balance
1993					
Oct. 4		J1	600		600
31	Adj. entry	J2		50	550

	Office Equipment			No. 15	
Date	Explanation	Ref.	Debit	Credit	Balance
1993					
Oct. 1		J1	5,000		5,000

	Accumulated Depreciation—Office Equipment			No. 15.1	
Date	Explanation	Ref.	Debit	Credit	Balance
1993					
Oct. 31	Adj. entry	J2		40	40

	Notes Payable			No. 25	
Date	Explanation	Ref.	Debit	Credit	Balance
1993					
Oct. 1		J1		5,000	5,000

	Accounts Payable			No. 26	
Date	Explanation	Ref.	Debit	Credit	Balance
1993					
Oct. 5		J1		2,500	2,500

	Interest Payable			No. 27	
Date	Explanation	Ref.	Debit	Credit	Balance
1993					
Oct. 31	Adj. entry	J2		50	50

	Unearned Fees			No. 28	
Date	Explanation	Ref.	Debit	Credit	Balance
1993					
Oct. 2		J1		1,200	1,200
31	Adj. entry	J2	400		800

	Salaries Payable			No. 29	
Date	Explanation	Ref.	Debit	Credit	Balance
1993					
Oct. 31	Adj. entry	J2		1,200	1,200

	C. R. Byrd, Capital			No. 40	
Date	Explanation	Ref.	Debit	Credit	Balance
1993					
Oct. 1		J1		10,000	10,000
31	Closing entry	J3		2,860	12,860
31	Closing entry	J3	500		12,360

Note: The permanent accounts for Pioneer Advertising Agency are shown here; the temporary accounts are shown in Illustration 4-11. Both permanent and temporary accounts are part of the general ledger; they are segregated here to aid in learning.

ILLUSTRATION 4-11

General ledger: temporary accounts

GENERAL LEDGER

C. R. Byrd, Drawing — No. 41

Date	Explanation	Ref.	Debit	Credit	Balance
1993					
Oct. 20		J1	500		500
31	Closing entry	J3		500	–0–

Income Summary — No. 49

Date	Explanation	Ref.	Debit	Credit	Balance
1993					
Oct. 31	Closing entry	J3		10,600	10,600
31	Closing entry	J3	7,740		2,860
31	Closing entry	J3	2,860		–0–

Fees Earned — No. 50

Date	Explanation	Ref.	Debit	Credit	Balance
1993					
Oct. 31		J1		10,000	10,000
31	Adj. entry	J2		400	10,400
31	Adj. entry	J2		200	10,600
31	Closing entry	J3	10,600		–0–

Salaries Expense — No. 60

Date	Explanation	Ref.	Debit	Credit	Balance
1993					
Oct. 26		J1	4,000		4,000
31	Adj. entry	J2	1,200		5,200
31	Closing entry	J3		5,200	–0–

Advertising Supplies Expense — No. 61

Date	Explanation	Ref.	Debit	Credit	Balance
1993					
Oct. 31	Adj. entry	J2	1,500		1,500
31	Closing entry	J3		1,500	–0–

Rent Expense — No. 62

Date	Explanation	Ref.	Debit	Credit	Balance
1993					
Oct. 3		J1	900		900
31	Closing entry	J3		900	–0–

Insurance Expense — No. 63

Date	Explanation	Ref.	Debit	Credit	Balance
1993					
Oct. 31	Adj. entry	J2	50		50
31	Closing entry	J3		50	–0–

Interest Expense — No. 64

Date	Explanation	Ref.	Debit	Credit	Balance
1993					
Oct. 31	Adj. entry	J2	50		50
31	Closing entry	J3		50	–0–

Depreciation Expense — No. 65

Date	Explanation	Ref.	Debit	Credit	Balance
1993					
Oct. 31	Adj. entry	J2	40		40
31	Closing entry	J3		40	–0–

Note: The temporary accounts for Pioneer Advertising Agency are shown here; the permanent accounts are shown in Illustration 4-10. Both permanent and temporary accounts are part of the general ledger; they are segregated here to aid in learning.

Reversing Entries—An Optional Step

Some accountants prefer to reverse certain adjusting entries at the beginning of a new accounting period. A reversing entry is made at the beginning of the next accounting period and is the exact opposite of the adjusting entry made in the previous period. **The preparation of reversing entries is an optional bookkeeping procedure that is not a required step in the accounting cycle.** Accordingly, we have chosen to cover this topic in Appendix B at the end of the chapter.

Before You Go On . . .

1. How do permanent accounts differ from temporary accounts?

2. What four different types of entries are required in closing the books?

3. What is the content and purpose of a post-closing trial balance?

Summary of the Accounting Cycle

Study Objective 4

State the required steps in the accounting cycle.

There are two optional steps in the accounting cycle. A work sheet may be used in the preparation of adjusting entries and financial statements, as explained in this chapter. In addition, reversing entries may be journalized and posted, as explained in the appendix.

The required steps in the accounting cycle are shown graphically in Illustration 4-12. From the graphic you can see that the cycle begins with the analysis of business transactions and ends with the preparation of a post-closing trial balance. The steps in the cycle are performed in sequence and are repeated in each accounting period.

Steps 1–3 may occur daily during the accounting period, as explained in Chapter 2. Steps 4–7 are performed on a periodic basis, such as monthly, quarterly, or annually. Steps 8 and 9, closing entries, and a post-closing trial balance, are usually prepared only at the end of a company's **annual** accounting period.

Correcting Entries

Study Objective 5

Explain the approaches to preparing correcting entries.

Errors that occur in recording transactions should be corrected as soon as they are discovered by journalizing and posting correcting entries. You should recognize several significant differences between correcting entries and adjusting entries. First, adjusting entries are an integral part of the accounting cycle, whereas correcting entries are unnecessary if the records are free of errors. Second, **adjustments are journalized and posted only at the end of an accounting period; in contrast, correcting entries are made whenever an error is discovered**. Finally, adjusting entries always affect at least one balance sheet account and one income statement account. In contrast, correcting entries may involve any combination of accounts in need of correction.

To determine the correcting entry, it is useful to compare the incorrect entry with the correct entry. Doing so helps identify the accounts and amounts that should—and should not—be corrected. After comparison, a correcting entry is made to correct the accounts. This approach is illustrated in the following two cases.

ILLUSTRATION 4-12

Steps in the accounting cycle

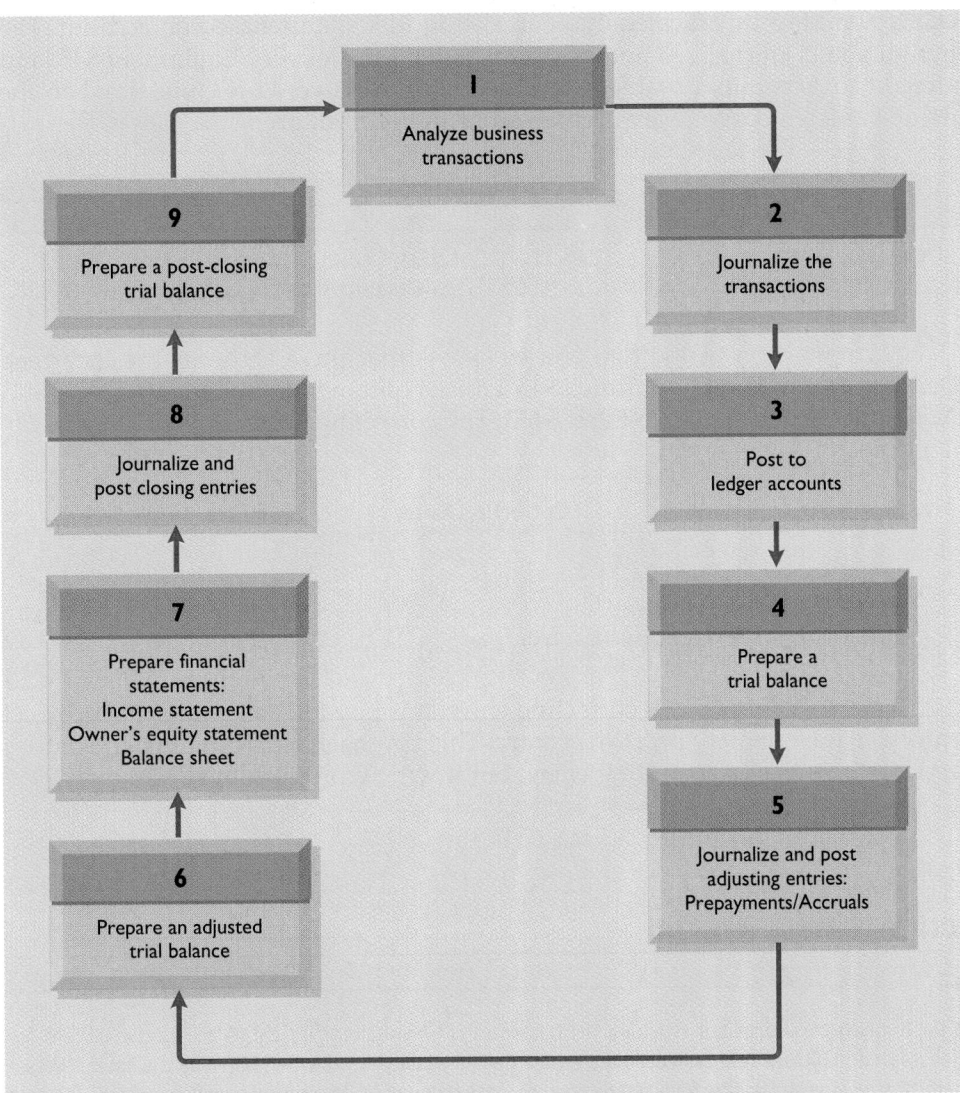

CASE 1. On May 10, a $50 cash collection on account from a customer is journalized and posted as a debit to Cash $50 and a credit to Fees Earned $50. The error is discovered on May 20, when the customer pays the remaining balance in full.

ILLUSTRATION 4-13

Comparison of entries

Incorrect Entry (May 10)			Correct Entry (May 10)		
Cash	50		Cash	50	
Fees Earned		50	Fees Receivable		50

A comparison of the incorrect entry with the correct entry reveals that the debit to Cash $50 is correct. However, the $50 credit to Fees Earned should have been credited to Fees Receivable. As a result, both Fees Earned and Fees Receivable are overstated in the ledger. The following correcting entry is required:

ILLUSTRATION 4-14

Correcting entry

	Correcting Entry		
May 20	Fees Earned	50	
	Fees Receivable		50
	(To correct entry of May 10)		

CASE 2. On May 18, office equipment costing $450 is purchased on account. The transaction is journalized and posted as a debit to Delivery Equipment $45, and a credit to Accounts Payable $45. The error is discovered on June 3, when the monthly statement for May is received from the creditor.

ILLUSTRATION 4-15

Comparison of entries

Incorrect Entry (May 18)			Correct Entry (May 18)		
Delivery Equipment	45		Office Equipment	450	
Accounts Payable		45	Accounts Payable		450

A comparison of the two entries shows that three accounts are incorrect. Delivery Equipment is overstated $45; Office Equipment is understated $450; and Accounts Payable is understated $405. The correcting entry is:

ILLUSTRATION 4-16

Correcting entry

	Correcting Entry		
June 3	Office Equipment	450	
	Delivery Equipment		45
	Accounts Payable		405
	(To correct May 18 entry)		

Instead of preparing a correcting entry, it is possible to reverse the incorrect entry and then prepare the correct entry. This approach will result in more entries and postings than a correcting entry, but it will accomplish the desired result.

Accounting in Action · *Business Insight*

Yale Express, a short-haul trucking firm, turned over much of its cargo to local truckers for delivery completion. Yale collected the entire delivery charge and, when billed by the local trucker, remitted payment for the final phase to the local trucker. Yale used a cutoff period of 20 days into the next accounting period in making its adjusting entries for accrued liabilities. That is, it waited 20 days to receive the local truckers' bills to determine the amount of the unpaid but incurred delivery charges as of the balance sheet date.

On the other hand, Republic Carloading, a nationwide, long-distance freight forwarder, frequently did not receive transportation bills from truckers to whom it passed on cargo until months after the year end. In making its year-end adjusting entries, Republic waited for months in order to include all of these outstanding transportation bills.

When Yale Express merged with Republic Carloading, Yale's vice-president employed the 20 day cutoff procedure for both firms. As a result, millions of dollars of Republic's accrued transportation bills went unrecorded. When the erroneous procedure was detected and correcting entries were made, these and other errors changed a reported profit of $1.14 million into a loss of $1.88 million!

Study Objective 6

Identify the sections of a classified balance sheet.

Classified Financial Statements

The financial statements illustrated up to this point were purposely kept simple. We classified items as assets, liabilities, and owner's equity in the balance sheet, and as revenues and expenses in the income statement. **Financial statements, however, become more useful to management, creditors, and potential investors when the elements are classified into significant subgroups.** In the remainder of this chapter we will introduce you to the primary balance sheet classifications. The classified income statement is presented in Chapter 5.

A **classified balance sheet** generally contains the following standard classifications:

ILLUSTRATION 4-17

Standard balance sheet classifications

Assets	Liabilities and Owner's Equity
Current Assets	Current Liabilities
Long-Term Investments	Long-Term Liabilities
Property, Plant, and Equipment	Owner's (Stockholders') Equity
Intangible Assets	

These sections help the financial statement user to determine such matters as (1) the availability of assets to meet debts as they come due and (2) the claims of short and long-term creditors on total assets. A classified balance sheet also makes it easier to compare companies in the same industry, such as GM, Ford, and Chrysler in the automobile industry. Each of the sections is explained below, except for owners' equity, which has already been discussed.

A complete set of specimen financial statements for PepsiCo, Inc. is shown in Appendix L.

Current Assets

Current assets are cash and other resources that are reasonably expected to be realized in cash or sold or consumed in the business within one year of the balance sheet date or the company's operating cycle, whichever is longer. For example, accounts receivable are included in current assets because they will be realized in cash through collection within one year. In contrast, a prepayment such as supplies is a current asset because of its expected use or consumption in the business within one year.

The **operating cycle** of a company is the average time that is required to go from cash to cash in producing revenues. The term "cycle" suggests a circular flow, which in this case, starts and ends with cash. For example, in municipal transit companies, the operating cycle may be very short since services are rendered entirely on a cash basis. On the other hand, the operating cycle in public utility companies is longer: they bill customers for services rendered and the collection period may extend for several months. Most companies have operating cycles of less than one year. More will be said about operating cycles in later chapters.

In a service enterprise, it is customary to recognize four types of current assets: (1) cash, (2) marketable securities such as U.S. government bonds held as a temporary (short-term) investment, (3) receivables (notes receivable, accounts receivable, and interest receivable), and (4) prepaid expenses (insurance and supplies). **These items are listed in the order of liquidity**, that is, according to their expected realization in cash. This arrangement is illustrated below in the presentation of UAL, Inc. (United Airlines).

ILLUSTRATION 4-18

Current asset section

UAL, INC. (United Airlines)	
Current assets (in thousands)	
Cash	$ 52,368
Marketable securities	389,862
Receivables	721,479
Aircraft fuel, spare parts, and supplies	178,840
Prepaid expenses	83,662
Total current assets	$1,426,211

A company's current assets are important in assessing the company's short-term debt-paying ability, as explained later in the chapter.

Long-Term Investments

Like current assets, long-term investments are resources that can be realized in cash. However, the conversion into cash is not expected within one year or the operating cycle, whichever is longer. In addition, long-term investments are not intended for use or consumption within the business. This category, often just called "investments", normally includes stocks and bonds of other corporations. Deluxe Check Printers Incorporated reported the following in its balance sheet:

ILLUSTRATION 4-19

Long-term investment section

DELUXE CHECK PRINTERS INCORPORATED		
Long-term investments		
Investment in stock of Data Card Corporation	$20,468,000	
Other long-term investments	16,961,000	$37,429,000

Property, Plant, and Equipment

Property, plant, and equipment are tangible resources of a relatively permanent nature that are used in the business and not intended for sale. They are often referred to as plant assets. This category includes land, buildings, machinery and equipment, delivery equipment, and furniture and fixtures. Assets subject to depreciation should be reported at cost less accumulated depreciation. This practice is illustrated in the following presentation of Delta Airlines:

ILLUSTRATION 4-20

Property, plant, and equipment section

DELTA AIRLINES, INC.			
Property, plant, and equipment			
(in thousands)			
Flight equipment	$3,985,796		
Less: Accumulated depreciation	1,713,059	$2,272,737	
Ground equipment	865,628		
Less: Accumulated depreciation	325,618	540,010	$2,812,747

Intangible Assets

Intangible assets are noncurrent resources that do not have physical substance. Intangible assets include patents, copyrights, and trademarks or trade names that give the holder exclusive right of use for a specified period of time. Their value to a company is generally derived from the rights or privileges granted by governmental authority.

In its balance sheet, Brunswick Corporation reported:

ILLUSTRATION 4-21

Intangible assets section

BRUNSWICK CORPORATION	
Intangible assets	
Patents, trademarks, and other intangibles	$10,460,000

Current Liabilities

Current liabilities are obligations that are reasonably expected to be paid from existing current assets or through the creation of other current liabilities. As in the case of current assets, the time period for payment is one year or the operating cycle, whichever is longer. Current liabilities include (1) debts related to the operating cycle, such as accounts payable and wages and salaries payable, and (2) other short-term debts, such as bank loans payable, interest payable, taxes payable, and current maturities of long-term obligations.

The arrangement of items within the current liabilities section has evolved through custom rather than from a prescribed rule. Notes payable is usually listed first, followed by accounts payable. Other items are then listed in any order. The current liability section adapted from the balance sheet of UAL, Inc. (United Airlines) is as follows:

UAL, INC. (United Airlines)	
Current liabilities (in thousands)	
Notes payable	$ 297,518
Accounts payable	382,967
Current maturities of long-term obligations	81,525
Unearned ticket revenue	432,979
Salaries and wages payable	435,622
Taxes payable	80,390
Other current liabilities	240,652
Total current liabilities	$1,951,653

ILLUSTRATION 4-22

Current liabilities section

The relationship between current assets and current liabilities is important in evaluating a company's liquidity—its ability to pay obligations that are expected to become due within the next year or operating cycle. When current assets exceed current liabilities at the balance sheet date, the likelihood for paying the liabilities is favorable. When the reverse is true, short-term creditors may not be paid, and the company may ultimately be forced into bankruptcy.

Accounting in Action · *Business Insight*

On January 27, 1992, R. H. Macy & Co., one of the nation's oldest and largest retailers, filed for bankruptcy after a very weak Christmas sales season worsened its liquidity problems. In the filing, Macy listed assets of $4.95 billion and liabilities of $5.32 billion. On the filing date, it was estimated that Macy had only $200,000 in cash and owed creditors $275 million, including $240 million that was due for payment on January 10, 1992.

Source: The Wall Street Journal, January 28 and January 30, 1992.

Long-Term Liabilities

Obligations expected to be paid after one year are classified as long-term liabilities (or long-term debt). Liabilities in this category include bonds payable, mortgages payable, long-term notes payable, lease liabilities, and obligations under employee pension plans. Many companies report long-term debt maturing after one year as a single amount in the balance sheet and show the details of the debt in the notes that accompany the financial statements. Others list the various sources of long-term liabilities. In its balance sheet, Consolidated Freightways, Inc. reported:

ILLUSTRATION 4-23

Long-term liabilities section

CONSOLIDATED FREIGHTWAYS, INC.	
Long-term liabilities (in thousands)	
Bank notes payable	$10,000
Mortgage payable	2,900
Bonds payable	53,422
Other long-term debt	9,597
Total long-term liabilities	$75,919

Owner's Equity

The content of the owner's equity section varies with the form of business organization. In a proprietorship, there is one capital account. In a partnership, there is a capital account for each partner. For a corporation, owners' equity is divided into two accounts—Capital Stock and Retained Earnings. Investments of capital in the business by the stockholders is recorded in the Capital Stock account. Income retained for use in the business is recorded in the Retained Earnings account. These two accounts are combined and reported as stockholders' equity on the balance sheet. (We'll learn more about these accounts in later chapters.)

In its balance sheet, the Americana Corporation reported its owners' (stockholders') equity section as follows:

ILLUSTRATION 4-24

Stockholders' equity section

AMERICANA CORPORATION		
Stockholders' equity		
Capital stock	$1,000,000	
Retained earnings	200,000	
Total stockholders' equity		$1,200,000

Classified Balance Sheet Illustrated

An unclassified balance sheet of Pioneer Advertising Agency was presented in Illustration 3-19 on page 106. Using the same adjusted trial balance accounts for Pioneer at October 31, 1993, we can prepare the classified balance sheet shown in Illustration 4-25. For illustrative purposes, we have assumed that $1,000 of the notes payable is due currently and $4,000 is long-term.

The balance sheet is most often presented in **report form**, as in Illustration 4-25, with the assets shown above the liabilities and owner's equity. The balance sheet may also be presented in **account form** with the assets section placed on the left and the liabilities and owner's equity section on the right.

ILLUSTRATION 4-25

Classified balance sheet in report form

PIONEER ADVERTISING AGENCY		
Balance Sheet		
October 31, 1993		
Assets		
Current assets		
Cash		$15,200
Fees receivable		200
Advertising supplies		1,000
Prepaid insurance		550
Total current assets		16,950
Property, plant, and equipment		
Office equipment	$5,000	
Less: Accumulated depreciation	40	4,960
Total assets		$21,910
Liabilities and Owner's Equity		
Current liabilities		
Notes payable		$ 1,000
Accounts payable		2,500
Interest payable		50
Unearned fees		800
Salaries payable		1,200
Total current liabilities		5,550
Long-term liabilities		
Notes payable		4,000
Total liabilities		9,550
Owner's equity		
C. R. Byrd, Capital		12,360
Total liabilities and owner's equity		$21,910

Before You Go On . . .

1. What are the required steps in the accounting cycle?

2. What approaches are used in preparing correcting entries?

3. What are the major sections in a classified balance sheet?

*S*ummary of Study Objectives

1. **Prepare a work sheet.** The steps in preparing a work sheet are: (a) prepare a trial balance on the work sheet, (b) enter the adjustments in the adjustment columns, (c) enter adjusted balances in the adjusted trial balance columns, (d) extend adjusted trial balance amounts to appropriate financial statement columns, and (e) total the statement columns, compute net income (or net loss), and complete the work sheet.

2. **Explain the process of closing the books.** Closing

the books occurs at the end of an accounting period. The process is to journalize and post closing entries and then rule and balance all accounts. In closing the books, separate entries are made to close revenues and expenses to Income Summary, Income Summary to owner's capital, and owner's drawings to owner's capital. Only temporary accounts are closed.

3. *Describe the content and purpose of a post-closing trial balance.* A post-closing trial balance contains the balances in permanent accounts that are carried forward to the next accounting period. The purpose of this trial balance is to prove the equality of these balances.

4. *State the required steps in the accounting cycle.* The required steps in the accounting cycle are: (a) analyze business transactions, (b) journalize the transactions, (c) post to ledger accounts, (d) prepare a trial balance, (e) journalize and post adjusting en-

tries, (f) prepare an adjusted trial balance, (g) prepare financial statements, (h) journalize and post closing entries, and (i) prepare a post-closing trial balance.

5. *Explain the approaches to preparing correcting entries.* One approach for determining the correcting entry is to compare the incorrect entry with the correct entry. After comparison, a correcting entry is made to correct the accounts. An alternative to a correcting entry is to reverse the incorrect entry and then prepare the correct entry.

6. *Identify the sections of a classified balance sheet.* In a classified balance sheet, assets are classified as current assets; long-term investments; property, plant, and equipment; or intangibles. Liabilities are classified as either current or long-term. There is also an owner's equity section, which varies with the form of business organization.

APPENDIX B   Reversing Entries

Study Objective

After studying Appendix B, you should be able to:

7. Prepare reversing entries.

After the financial statements are prepared and the books are closed, it is often helpful to reverse some of the adjusting entries before recording the regular transactions of the next period. Such entries are called reversing entries. **A reversing entry is made at the beginning of the next accounting period and is the exact opposite of the adjusting entry made in the previous period.** The recording of reversing entries is an **optional** step in the accounting cycle.

The purpose of reversing entries is to simplify the recording of a subsequent transaction related to an adjusting entry. In Chapter 3, you may recall, the payment of salaries after an adjusting entry resulted in two debits: one to Salaries Payable and the other to Salaries Expense. With reversing entries, the entire subsequent payment can be debited to Salaries Expense. The use of reversing entries does not change the amounts reported in the financial statements. It does, however, simplify the recording of subsequent transactions, because they can be recorded as if the related adjusting entry had never been made.

Illustration of Reversing Entries

Reversing entries are most often used to reverse two types of adjusting entries: accrued revenues and accrued expenses. They are seldom made for prepaid expenses and unearned revenues. To illustrate the optional use of reversing entries for accrued expenses, we will use the salaries expense transactions for Pioneer Advertising Agency. The transaction and adjustment data are as follows:

1. October 26 (initial salary entry): $4,000 of salaries earned between October 15 and October 26 are paid.
2. October 31 (adjusting entry): Salaries earned between October 29 and October 31 are $1,200. These will be paid in the November 9 payroll.

3. November 9 (subsequent salary entry): Salaries paid are $4,000. Of this amount, $1,200 applied to accrued wages payable and $2,800 was earned between November 1 and November 9.

The comparative entries with and without reversing entries are shown in Illustration B-1.

ILLUSTRATION B-1

Comparative entries—not reversing vs. reversing

When Reversing Entries are Not Used (Per Chapter)				When Reversing Entries Are Used (Per Appendix)			
Initial Salary Entry				**Initial Salary Entry**			
Oct. 26	Salaries Expense	4,000		Oct. 26	Salaries Expense	4,000	
	Cash		4,000		Cash		4,000
Adjusting Entry				**Adjusting Entry**			
Oct. 31	Salaries Expense	1,200		Oct. 31	Salaries Expense	1,200	
	Salaries Payable		1,200		Salaries Payable		1,200
Closing Entry				**Closing Entry**			
Oct. 31	Income Summary	5,200		Oct. 31	Income Summary	5,200	
	Salaries Expense		5,200		Salaries Expense		5,200
Reversing Entry				**Reversing Entry**			
Nov. 1	No reversing entry is made.			Nov. 1	Salaries Payable	1,200	
					Salaries Expense		1,200
Subsequent Salary Entry				**Subsequent Salary Entry**			
Nov. 9	Salaries Payable	1,200		Nov. 9	Salaries Expense	4,000	
	Salaries Expense	2,800			Cash		4,000
	Cash		4,000				

The comparative entries show that the first three entries are the same whether or not reversing entries are used. The last two entries, however, are different. The November 1 **reversing entry** eliminates the $1,200 balance in Salaries Payable that was created by the October 31 adjusting entry. The reversing entry also creates a $1,200 credit balance in the Salaries Expense account. As you know, it is unusual for an expense account to have a credit balance. The balance is correct in this instance, though, because it anticipates that the entire amount of the first salary payment in the new accounting period will be debited to Salaries Expense. This debit will eliminate the credit balance, and the resulting debit balance in the expense account will equal the salaries expense incurred in the new accounting period ($2,800 in this example).

When reversing entries are made, all cash payments of expenses can be debited to the expense account. This means that on November 9 (and every payday) Salaries Expense can be debited for the amount paid without regard to the existence of any accrued salaries payable. Being able to make the same entry each time simplifies the recording process.

Technology in Action

Using reversing entries in a computerized accounting system is more efficient than in a manual system. The reversing entry saves writing a program to locate the amount accrued from the preceding period and making the more complicated entry in the current period. That is, the computer does not have to be programmed to determine whether any accrued items exist.

Postings with reversing entries

The posting of the entries with reversing entries is shown in Illustration B-2.

Salaries Expense						Salaries Payable					
10/26 Paid		4,000	10/31 Closing		5,200	11/1	Reversing	1,200	10/31 Adjusting		1,200
31 Adjusting		1,200									
		5,200			5,200						
11/9 Paid		4,000	11/1 Reversing		1,200						

Reversing entries may also be made for accrued revenue adjusting entries. For Pioneer Advertising, the adjusting entry was: Fees Receivable (Dr.) $200 and Fees Earned (Cr.) $200. Thus, the reversing entry on November 1 is:

Nov. 1	Fees Earned		200	
	Fees Receivable			200
	(To reverse October 31 adjusting entry)			

When the accrued fees are collected, Cash is debited and Fees Earned is credited.

Summary of Study Objectives for Appendix B

7. **Prepare reversing entries.** Reversing entries are the direct opposite of the adjusting entry made in the preceding period. They are made at the beginning of a new accounting period to simplify the recording of later transactions related to the adjusting entry. In most cases, only accrued adjusting entries are reversed.

GLOSSARY

Classified balance sheet · A balance sheet that contains a number of standard classifications or sections. (p. 149).

Closing entries · Entries at the end of an accounting period to transfer the balances of temporary accounts to a permanent owner's equity account. (p. 139).

Correcting entries · Entries to correct errors made in recording transactions. (p. 146).

Current assets · Cash and other resources reasonably expected to be realized or sold or consumed in the business within one year or the operating cycle, whichever is longer. (p. 149).

Current liabilities · Obligations reasonably expected to be paid from existing current assets or through the creation of other current liabilities within the next year or operating cycle, whichever is longer. (p. 151).

Income summary · A temporary account used in closing revenue and expense accounts. (p. 139).

Intangible assets · Noncurrent resources that do not have physical substance. (p. 150).

Liquidity · The ability of a company to pay obligations that are expected to become due within the next year or operating cycle. (p. 151).

Long-term investments · Resources not expected to be realized in cash within the next year or operating cycle. (p. 150).

Long-term liabilities · Obligations expected to be paid after one year. (p. 152).

Operating cycle · The average time required to go from cash to cash in producing revenues. (p. 149).

Permanent (real) accounts · Asset, liability, and owner's capital accounts whose balances are carried forward to the next accounting period. (p. 139).

Post-closing trial balance · A list of permanent accounts and their balances after closing entries have been journalized and posted. (p. 142).

Property, plant, and equipment · Assets of a relatively permanent nature that are being used in the business and not intended for resale. (p. 150).

Reversing entry · An entry at the beginning of the next accounting period that is the exact opposite of the adjusting entry made in the previous period. (p. 146).

Stockholders' equity · The ownership claim of shareholders on total assets. It is to a corporation what owner's equity is to a proprietorship. (p. 152).

Temporary (nominal) accounts · Revenue, expense, and drawing accounts whose balances are transferred to owner's capital at the end of an accounting period. (p. 139).

Work sheet · A multiple-column form that may be used in the adjustment process and in preparing financial statements. (p. 133).

DEMONSTRATION PROBLEM

At the end of its first month of operations, the Watson Answering Service has the following unadjusted trial balance:

WATSON ANSWERING SERVICE
August 31, 1993
Trial Balance

	Debit	Credit
Cash	$ 5,400	
Fees Receivable	2,800	
Prepaid Insurance	2,400	
Supplies	1,300	
Equipment	60,000	
Notes Payable		$40,000
Accounts Payable		2,400
Ray Watson, Capital		30,000
Ray Watson, Drawing	1,000	
Fees Earned		4,900
Salaries Expense	3,200	
Utilities Expense	800	
Advertising Expense	400	
	$77,300	$77,300

Helpful hints

1. In completing the work sheet, be sure to (a) key the adjustments, (b) extend adjusted balances to the correct statement columns, and (c) enter net income (or net loss) in the proper columns.

2. In preparing a classified balance sheet, know the contents of each of the sections.

3. In journalizing closing entries, remember that there are only four entries and that owner's drawing is closed to owner's capital.

Other data consist of the following:

1. Insurance expires at the rate of $200 per month.
2. There are $1,000 of supplies on hand at August 31.
3. Monthly depreciation is $900 on the equipment.
4. Interest of $500 has accrued during August on the notes payable.

Instructions

(a) Prepare a work sheet.

(b) Prepare a classified balance sheet assuming $35,000 of the notes payable are long-term.

(c) Journalize the closing entries.

Solution to Demonstration Problem

(a)

WATSON ANSWERING SERVICE
Work Sheet
For the Month Ended August 31, 1993

Account Titles	Trial Balance Dr.	Trial Balance Cr.	Adjustments Dr.	Adjustments Cr.	Adjusted Trial Balance Dr.	Adjusted Trial Balance Cr.	Income Statement Dr.	Income Statement Cr.	Balance Sheet Dr.	Balance Sheet Cr.
Cash	5,400				5,400				5,400	
Fees Receivable	2,800				2,800				2,800	
Prepaid Insurance	2,400			(a) 200	2,200				2,200	
Supplies	1,300			(b) 300	1,000				1,000	
Equipment	60,000				60,000				60,000	
Notes Payable		40,000				40,000				40,000
Accounts Payable		2,400				2,400				2,400
Ray Watson, Capital		30,000				30,000				30,000
Ray Watson, Drawing	1,000				1,000				1,000	
Fees Earned		4,900				4,900		4,900		
Salaries Expense	3,200				3,200		3,200			
Utilities Expense	800				800		800			
Advertising Expense	400				400		400			
Totals	77,300	77,300								
Insurance Expense			(a) 200		200		200			
Supplies Expense			(b) 300		300		300			
Depreciation Expense			(c) 900		900		900			
Accumulated Depreciation— Equipment				(c) 900		900				900
Interest Expense			(d) 500		500		500			
Interest Payable				(d) 500		500				500
Totals			1,900	1,900	78,700	78,700	6,300	4,900	72,400	73,800
Net Loss								1,400	1,400	
Totals							6,300	6,300	73,800	73,800

(b)

WATSON ANSWERING SERVICE
Balance Sheet
August 31, 1993

Assets

Current assets		
Cash		$ 5,400
Fees receivable		2,800
Prepaid insurance		2,200
Supplies		1,000
Total current assets		11,400
Property, plant, and equipment		
Equipment	$60,000	
Less: Accumulated depreciation—equipment	900	59,100
Total assets		$70,500

Liabilities and Owner's Equity

Current liabilities	
Notes payable	$ 5,000
Accounts payable	2,400
Interest payable	500
Total current liabilities	7,900

Long-term liabilities		
Notes payable		35,000
Total liabilities		42,900
Owner's equity		
Ray Watson, Capital		27,600*
Total liabilities and owner's equity		$70,500

*Ray Watson, Capital, $30,000 less drawings $1,000 and net loss $1,400.

(c)

Aug. 31	Fees Earned	4,900	
	Income Summary		4,900
	(To close revenue account)		
31	Income Summary	6,300	
	Salaries Expense		3,200
	Depreciation Expense		900
	Utilities Expense		800
	Interest Expense		500
	Advertising Expense		400
	Supplies Expense		300
	Insurance Expense		200
	(To close expense accounts)		
31	Ray Watson, Capital	1,400	
	Income Summary		1,400
	(To close net loss to capital)		
31	Ray Watson, Capital	1,000	
	Ray Watson, Drawing		1,000
	(To close drawings to capital)		

*Note: All **asterisked** Questions, Exercises, and Problems relate to material contained in the Appendix to each chapter.

SELF-STUDY QUESTIONS

Answers are at the end of the chapter.

(S.O. 1)
1. Which of the following statements is *incorrect* concerning the work sheet?
   a. The work sheet is essentially a working tool of the accountant.
   b. The work sheet cannot be used as a basis for posting to ledger accounts.
   c. The work sheet is distributed to management and other interested parties.
   d. Financial statements can be prepared directly from the work sheet before journalizing and posting the adjusting entries.

(S.O. 1)
2. In a work sheet, net income is entered in the following columns:
   a. income statement (Dr) and balance sheet (Dr).
   b. income statement (Dr) and balance sheet (Cr).
   c. income statement (Cr) and balance sheet (Dr).

   d. income statement (Cr) and balance sheet (Cr).

(S.O. 2)
3. An account that will have a zero balance after closing entries have been journalized and posted is:
   a. Unearned Fees.
   b. Advertising Supplies.
   c. Prepaid Insurance.
   d. Rent Expense.

(S.O. 2)
4. When a net loss has occurred, Income Summary is:
   a. credited and owner's capital is debited.
   b. debited and owner's capital is credited.
   c. debited and owner's drawing is credited.
   d. credited and owner's drawing is debited.

(S.O. 2)
5. The closing process involves separate entries to close (1) expenses, (2) drawings,

(3) revenues and (4) net income (or loss).
The correct sequencing of the entries is:
a. (4), (3), (2), (1)
b. (1), (2), (3), (4)
c. (3), (2), (1), (4)
d. (3), (1), (4), (2)

(S.O. 3)   6. Which types of accounts will appear in
the post-closing trial balance?
a. Temporary (nominal) accounts.
b. Permanent (real) accounts.
c. Accounts shown in the income statement columns of a work sheet.
d. None of the above.

(S.O. 4)   7. All of the following are required steps in
the accounting cycle *except*:
a. preparing a work sheet.
b. journalizing and posting closing
entries.
c. preparing an adjusted trial balance.
d. preparing a post-closing trial balance.

(S.O. 5)   8. Cash of $100 received at the time the
service was rendered was journalized
and posted as a debit to Cash $100 and a
credit to Fees Receivable $100. Assuming
the incorrect entry is not reversed, the
correcting entry is:
a. debit Fees Earned $100 and credit Fees
Receivable $100.
b. debit Cash $100 and credit Fees
Earned $100.
c. debit Fees Receivable $100 and credit
Fees Earned $100.
d. debit Fees Receivable $100 and credit
Cash $100.

9. In a classified balance sheet, assets are   (S.O. 6)
usually classified as:
a. current assets; long-term assets; property, plant, and equipment; and intangible assets.
b. current assets; long-term investments;
property, plant, and equipment; and
other assets.
c. current assets; long-term investments;
property, plant, and equipment; and
intangible assets.
d. current assets; long-term investments;
tangible assets; and intangible assets.

10. Current assets are listed: (S.O. 6)
a. by importance.
b. by liquidity.
c. by longevity.
d. alphabetically.

*11. On December 31, the Scott Company cor-   (S.O. 7)
rectly made an adjusting entry to recog-
nize $2,000 of accrued salaries payable.
On January 8 of the next year, total salaries of $3,500 were paid. Assuming the
correct reversing entry was made on January 1, the entry on January 8 will result
in a credit to Cash $3,500, and the follow-
ing debit(s):
a. Salaries Payable $3,500.
b. Salaries Expense $3,500.
c. Salaries Payable $2,000 and Salaries
Expense $1,500.
d. Salaries Payable $1,500 and Salaries
Expense $2,000.

QUESTIONS

1. "A work sheet is a permanent accounting record and its use is required in the accounting
cycle." Do you agree? Explain.

2. The use of a work sheet affects two steps of the accounting cycle after preparing the trial
balance. What steps are they and how are they affected by the work sheet?

3. What is the relationship, if any, between the amount shown in the adjusted trial balance
column for an account and that account's ledger balance?

4. If a company's revenues are $122,000 and its expenses are $114,000, in which financial
statement columns of the work sheet will the net income of $8,000 appear? When expenses
exceed revenues, in which columns will the difference appear?

5. Why is it necessary to prepare formal financial statements when all of the data are in the
statement columns of the work sheet?

6. Identify the account(s) debited and credited in each of the four closing entries assuming
the company has net income for the year.

7. Describe the nature of the Income Summary account and identify the types of summary data that may be posted to this account.

8. What are the content and purpose of a post-closing trial balance?

9. Which of the following accounts would not appear in the post-closing trial balance? Interest Payable; Equipment; Depreciation Expense; Ben Alschuler, Drawing; Unearned Fees; Accumulated Depreciation—Equipment; and Fees Earned.

10. Distinguish between a reversing entry and an adjusting entry. Are reversing entries required?

11. Indicate, in the sequence in which they are made, the three required steps in the accounting cycle that involve journalizing.

12. Identify, in the sequence in which they are prepared, the three trial balances that are required in the accounting cycle.

13. How do correcting entries differ from adjusting entries?

14. What standard classifications are used in preparing a classified balance sheet?

15. What is meant by the term "operating cycle"?

16. Define current assets. What basis is used for arranging individual items within the current asset section?

17. Distinguish between long-term investments and property, plant, and equipment.

18. How do current liabilities differ from long-term liabilities?

19. (a) What is the term used to describe the owner's equity section of a corporation? (b) Identify the two owner's equity accounts in a corporation and indicate the purpose of each.

20. How does a report form balance sheet differ from an account form balance sheet?

*21. Baum Company prepares reversing entries. If the adjusting entry for interest payable is reversed, what type of an account balance, if any, will there be in Interest Payable and Interest Expense after the reversing entry is posted?

*22. At December 31, accrued salaries payable totaled $2,500. On January 10, total salaries of $7,000 are paid. (a) Assume that reversing entries are made at January 1. Give the January 10 entry and indicate the Salaries Expense account balance after the entry is posted. (b) Repeat part (a) assuming reversing entries are not made.

BRIEF EXERCISES

BE4–1 The steps in using a work sheet are presented in random order below. List the steps in the proper order.

_____ Enter adjustment data.

_____ Total the statement columns, compute net income (loss), and complete the worksheet.

_____ Prepare a trial balance on the work sheet.

_____ Enter adjusted balances.

_____ Extend adjusted balances to appropriate statement columns.

List the steps in preparing a work sheet.
(S.O. 1)

BE4–2 The ledger of Sonders Company includes the following unadjusted balances: Prepaid Insurance $4,200, Fees Earned $58,000, and Salaries Expense $24,000. Adjusting entries are required for (a) expired insurance $1,400, (b) accrued fees receivable $900, and (c) accrued salaries payable $800. Enter the unadjusted balances and adjustments into a work sheet and complete the work sheet for all accounts. Note: You will need to add the following accounts: Fees Receivable, Salaries Payable, and Insurance Expense.

Prepare partial work sheet.
(S.O. 1)

Identify work sheet columns for selected accounts.
(S.O. 1)

BE4–3   The following selected accounts appear in the adjusted trial balance columns of the work sheet for the Farrell Company: Accumulated Depreciation; Depreciation Expense; H. Farrell, Capital; H. Farrell, Drawing; Fees Earned; Supplies; and Unearned Fees. Indicate the financial statement column (income statement Dr., balance sheet Cr., etc.) to which each balance should be extended.

Prepare closing entries from ledger balances.
(S.O. 2)

BE4–4   The ledger of the Ratan Company contains the following balances: T. Ratan, Capital $30,000; T. Ratan, Drawing $2,000; Fees Earned $41,000; Salaries Expense $26,000; and Utilities Expense $3,000. Prepare the closing entries at December 31.

Post closing entries and rule and balance T accounts.
(S.O. 2)

BE4–5   Using the data in BE4–4, enter the balances in T accounts, post the closing entries, and rule and balance the accounts.

Journalize and post closing entries using the three-column form of account.
(S.O. 2)

BE4–6   The income statement for the Edgelake Golf Club for the month ending July 31 shows Green Fees Earned $16,000, Salaries Expense $6,200, Maintenance Expense $2,700, and Net Income $7,100. Prepare the entries to close the revenue and expense accounts. Post the entries to the revenue and expense accounts and complete the closing process for these accounts using the three-column form of account.

Identify post-closing trial balance accounts.
(S.O. 3)

BE4–7   Using the data in BE4–3, identify the accounts that would be included in a post-closing trial balance.

List the required steps in the accounting cycle in sequence.
(S.O. 4)

BE4–8   The required steps in the accounting cycle are listed in random order below. List the steps in proper sequence.

____ Prepare a post-closing trial balance.

____ Prepare an adjusted trial balance.

____ Analyze business transactions.

____ Prepare a trial balance.

____ Journalize the transactions.

____ Journalize and post closing entries.

____ Prepare financial statements.

____ Post to ledger accounts.

____ Journalize and post adjusting entries.

Prepare correcting entries.
(S.O. 5)

BE4–9   In the McKee Company, the following errors were discovered after the transactions had been journalized and posted. Prepare the correcting entries.

1. A collection on account from a customer for $760 was recorded as a debit to Cash $760, and a credit to Fees Earned $760.

2. The purchase of store supplies on account for $1,530 was recorded as a debit to Store Supplies $1,350 and a credit to Accounts Payable $1,350.

Prepare the current asset section of a balance sheet.
(S.O. 6)

BE4–10   The balance sheet debit column of the work sheet for the Livona Company includes the following accounts: Fees Receivable $16,500; Prepaid Insurance $3,600; Cash $18,400; Supplies $5,200, and Marketable Securities $9,200. Prepare the current asset section of the balance sheet listing the accounts in proper sequence.

Prepare reversing entries.
(S.O. 7)

*BE4–11   At October 31, the Diane Company made an accrued expense adjusting entry of $600 for salaries. Prepare the reversing entry on November 1 and indicate the balances in Salaries Payable and Salaries Expense after posting the reversing entry.

EXERCISES

E4–1 The adjusted trial balance columns of the work sheet for Sadie Heber Company are as follows:

Complete work sheet. (S.O. 1)

SADIE HEBER COMPANY
(Partial) Work Sheet
For the Month Ended April 30, 1993

Account Titles	Adjusted Trial Balance Dr.	Adjusted Trial Balance Cr.	Income Statement Dr.	Income Statement Cr.	Balance Sheet Dr.	Balance Sheet Cr.
Cash	19,052					
Fees Receivable	6,840					
Prepaid Rent	2,280					
Equipment	23,050					
Accumulated Depreciation		4,921				
Notes Payable		5,700				
Accounts Payable		5,972				
S. Heber, Capital		33,960				
S. Heber, Drawing	3,650					
Fees Earned		12,590				
Salaries Expense	6,840					
Rent Expense	760					
Depreciation Expense	671					
Interest Expense	57					
Interest Payable		57				
Totals	63,200	63,200				

Instructions

Complete the work sheet.

Prepare financial statements from work sheet. (S.O. 1, 6)

E4–2 Work sheet data for the Sadie Heber Company are presented in E4–1.

Instructions

Prepare an income statement, an owner's equity statement, and a classified balance sheet.

E4–3 Work sheet data for the Sadie Heber Company are presented in E4–1.

Journalize and post closing entries and prepare a post-closing trial balance. (S.O. 2, 3)

Instructions

(a) Journalize the closing entries at April 30.

(b) Post the closing entries to Income Summary and S. Heber, Capital. Use T accounts.

(c) Prepare a post-closing trial balance at April 30.

E4–4 The adjustments columns of the work sheet for the Rogel Company are shown below.

Prepare adjusting entries from a work sheet and extend balances to work sheet columns. (S.O. 1)

Account titles	Adjustments Debit	Adjustments Credit
Fees Receivable	700	
Prepaid Insurance		300
Accumulated Depreciation		1,000
Salaries Payable		600
Fees Earned		700
Salaries Expense	600	
Insurance Expense	300	
Depreciation Expense	1,000	
	2,600	2,600

Instructions

(a) Prepare the adjusting entries.

(b) Assuming the adjusted trial balance amount for each account is normal, indicate the financial statement column to which each balance should be extended.

Derive adjusting entries from work sheet data.
(S.O. 1)

E4–5   Selected work sheet data for the Gordon Company are presented below.

Account Title	Trial Balance Dr.	Trial Balance Cr.	Adjusted Trial Balance Dr.	Adjusted Trial Balance Cr.
Fees Receivable	?		32,000	
Prepaid Insurance	24,000		18,000	
Supplies	9,000		?	
Accumulated Depreciation		12,000		?
Salaries Payable		?		7,000
Fees Earned		90,000		94,000
Insurance Expense			?	
Depreciation Expense			10,000	
Supplies Expense			5,000	
Salaries Expense	?		49,000	

Instructions

(a) Fill in the missing amounts.

(b) Prepare the adjusting entries that were made.

Journalize and post closing entries and prepare a post-closing trial balance.
(S.O. 2, 3)

E4–6   The adjusted trial balance of the Parklane Company at the end of its fiscal year on July 31, 1993, is as follows:

PARKLANE COMPANY
Adjusted Trial Balance
July 31, 1993

No.	Account Title	Debits	Credits
101	Cash	$ 11,940	
112	Accounts Receivable	7,780	
157	Equipment	15,900	
167	Accumulated Depreciation		$ 5,400
201	Accounts Payable		5,220
208	Unearned Rent Revenue		1,800
301	C. Parklane, Capital		45,200
306	C. Parklane, Drawing	14,000	
404	Commission Revenue		63,100
429	Rent Revenue		6,500
711	Depreciation Expense	4,000	
720	Salaries Expense	58,700	
732	Utilities Expense	14,900	
		$127,220	$127,220

Instructions

(a) Prepare the closing entries using page J15.

(b) Post to C. Parklane, Capital and No. 350 Income Summary accounts (use the three-column form).

(c) Prepare a post-closing trial balance at July 31.

Prepare financial statements.
(S.O. 6)

E4–7   The adjusted trial balance for the Parklane Company is presented in E4–6.

Instructions

(a) Prepare an income statement and an owner's equity statement for the year. Parklane did not make any capital investments during the year.

(b) Prepare a classified balance sheet at July 31.

E4–8 Selected accounts for Bart's Barber Shop are presented below. All June 30 postings are from closing entries.

Prepare closing entries and an owner's equity statement.
(S.O. 2)

Salaries Expense			
6/10	3,200	6/30	7,800
6/28	4,600		

Fees Earned			
6/30	15,600	6/15	7,200
		6/24	8,400

E. Bart, Capital			
6/30	2,500	6/1	12,000
		6/30	3,800
		Bal.	13,300

Supplies Expense			
6/12	800	6/30	1,500
6/24	700		

Rent Expense			
6/1	2,500	6/30	2,500

E. Bart, Drawing			
6/13	1,000	6/30	2,500
6/25	1,500		

Instructions

(a) Prepare the closing entries that were made.

(b) Post the closing entries to Income Summary.

E4–9 The Downey Company has an inexperienced accountant. During the first two weeks on the job, the following errors were made in journalizing transactions. All entries were posted as made.

Prepare correcting entries.
(S.O. 5)

1. A payment on account to a creditor of $350 was debited to Accounts Payable $530 and credited to Cash $530.
2. The purchase of supplies on account for $500 was debited to Equipment $50 and credited to Accounts Payable $50.
3. A $400 withdrawal of cash for Downey's personal use was debited to Salaries Expense $400 and credited to Cash $400.

Instructions

Prepare the correcting entries.

E4–10 The adjusted trial balance for Ely's Bowling Alley at December 31, 1993 contains the following accounts.

Prepare a classified balance sheet.
(S.O. 6)

Debits		Credits	
Building	$125,800	T. Ely, Capital	$110,000
Accounts Receivable	13,520	Accumulated Depreciation—Building	45,600
Prepaid Insurance	4,680	Accounts Payable	12,480
Cash	20,840	Mortgage Payable	93,600
Equipment	62,400	Accumulated Depreciation—Equipment	18,720
Land	61,200	Interest Payable	2,600
Insurance Expense	780	Bowling Revenues	14,180
Depreciation Expense	5,360		$297,180
Interest Expense	2,600		
	$297,180		

Instructions

(a) Prepare a classified balance sheet; assume that $13,600 of the mortgage payable will be paid in the next operating cycle of Ely's Bowling Alley.

(b) Comment on Ely's liquidity.

*E4–11 On December 31, the adjusted trial balance of Eber Employment Agency shows the following selected data:

Prepare closing and reversing entries.
(S.O. 2, 4, 7)

Commissions Receivable	$5,000	Commission Revenue	$97,000
Interest Expense	7,800	Interest Payable	2,000

Analysis shows that adjusting entries were made to (a) accrue $5,000 of commission revenue, and (b) accrue $2,000 interest expense.

Instructions

(a) Prepare the closing entries for the temporary accounts at December 31.

(b) Prepare the reversing entries on January 1.

(c) Enter the adjusted trial balance data in the four accounts. Post the entries in (a) and (b) rule and balance the accounts. (Use T accounts.)

(d) Prepare the entries to record (1) the collection of the accrued commissions on January 10, and (2) the payment of all interest due ($2,500) on January 15.

(e) Post the entries in (d) to the temporary accounts.

PROBLEMS

Prepare a work sheet, fi-
nancial statements, and
adjusting and closing
entries.
(S.O. 1, 2, 3, 6)

P4–1   The trial balance columns of the work sheet for Camb Roofing at March 31, 1993, are as follows:

CAMB ROOFING
Work Sheet
For the Month Ended March 31, 1993

Account Titles	Trial Balance	
	Dr.	Cr.
Cash	$ 1,700	
Fees Receivable	2,600	
Roofing Supplies	1,100	
Equipment	6,000	
Accumulated Depreciation—Equipment		$ 1,200
Accounts Payable		1,100
Unearned Fees		300
Janet Camb, Capital		7,000
Janet Camb, Drawing	600	
Fees Earned		3,000
Salaries Expense	500	
Miscellaneous Expense	100	
	$12,600	$12,600

Other data:

1. A physical count reveals only $420 of roofing supplies on hand.
2. Depreciation for March is $200.
3. Unearned fees amounted to $100 on March 31.
4. Accrued salaries are $400.

Instructions

(a) Enter the trial balance on a work sheet and complete the work sheet.

(b) Prepare an income statement and owner's equity statement for the month of March and classified balance sheet at March 31.

(c) Journalize the adjusting entries from the adjustments columns of the work sheet.

(d) Journalize the closing entries from the financial statement column of the work sheet.

Complete work sheet and
prepare financial state-
ments, closing entries, and
post-closing trial balance.
(S.O. 1, 2, 3, 6)

P4–2   The adjusted trial balance columns of the work sheet for the Adams Company is as follows:

ADAMS COMPANY
Work Sheet
For the Year Ended December 31, 1993

Account No.	Account Titles	Adjusted Trial Balance	
		Dr.	Cr.
101	Cash	14,600	
111	Fees Receivable	15,400	
126	Supplies	1,500	
130	Prepaid Insurance	2,800	

Account No.	Account Titles	Adjusted Trial Balance Dr.	Adjusted Trial Balance Cr.
151	Office Equipment	34,000	
152	Accumulated Depreciation—Office Equipment		8,000
200	Notes Payable		15,000
201	Accounts Payable		7,000
212	Salaries Payable		3,000
230	Interest Payable		500
301	H. Adams, Capital		25,000
306	H. Adams, Drawing	10,000	
400	Fees Earned		88,000
610	Advertising Expense	14,000	
631	Supplies Expense	5,700	
711	Depreciation Expense	4,000	
722	Insurance Expense	5,000	
726	Salaries Expense	39,000	
905	Interest Expense	500	
		146,500	146,500

Instructions

(a) Complete the work sheet by extending the balances to the financial statement columns.

(b) Prepare an income statement, owner's equity statement, and a classified balance sheet. $10,000 of the notes payable become due in 1994.

(c) Prepare the closing entries. Use J14 for the journal page.

(d) Post the closing entries and rule and balance the accounts. Use the three-column form of account. Income Summary is No. 350.

(e) Prepare a post-closing trial balance.

P4–3 The completed financial statement columns of the work sheet for Belinda Company are shown below.

Prepare financial statements, closing entries, and post-closing trial balance. (S.O. 1, 2, 3, 6)

BELINDA COMPANY
Work Sheet
For the Year Ended December 31, 1993

Account No.	Account Titles	Income Statement Dr.	Income Statement Cr.	Balance Sheet Dr.	Balance Sheet Cr.
101	Cash			13,600	
111	Fees Receivable			11,500	
130	Prepaid Insurance			3,500	
157	Equipment			26,000	
167	Accumulated Depreciation				5,600
201	Accounts Payable				13,300
212	Salaries Payable				1,000
301	Ann Belinda, Capital				36,000
306	Ann Belinda, Drawing			12,000	
400	Fees Earned		54,000		
622	Repair Expense	1,800			
711	Depreciation Expense	2,600			
722	Insurance Expense	2,200			
726	Salaries Expense	35,000			
732	Utilities Expense	1,700			
	Totals	43,300	54,000	66,600	55,900
	Net Income	10,700			10,700
		54,000	54,000	66,600	66,600

Instructions

(a) Prepare an income statement, owner's equity statement, and a classified balance sheet.

(b) Prepare the closing entries.

(c) Post the closing entries and rule and balance the accounts. Use T-accounts. Income Summary is No. 350.

(d) Prepare a post-closing trial balance.

Complete work sheet and prepare classified balance sheet, entries, and post-closing trial balance. (S.O. 1, 2, 3, 6)

P4–4 Potter Management Services began business on January 1, 1993, with a capital investment of $120,000. The company manages condominiums for owners (Fees Earned) and rents space in its own office building (Rent Revenue). The trial and adjusted trial balance columns of the work sheet at the end of the first year are as follows:

POTTER MANAGEMENT SERVICES
Work Sheet
For the Year Ended December 31, 1993

Account Titles	Trial Balance		Adjusted Trial Balance	
	Dr.	Cr.	Dr.	Cr.
Cash	12,500		12,500	
Accounts Receivable	23,600		23,600	
Prepaid Insurance	3,100		1,600	
Land	55,000		55,000	
Building	107,000		107,000	
Equipment	48,000		48,000	
Accounts Payable		10,400		10,400
Unearned Rent Revenue		4,000		1,800
Mortgage Payable		100,000		100,000
B. Potter, Capital		120,000		120,000
B. Potter, Drawing	20,000		20,000	
Fees Earned		75,600		75,600
Rent Revenue		24,000		26,200
Salaries Expense	32,000		32,000	
Advertising Expense	17,000		17,000	
Utilities Expense	15,800		15,800	
Totals	334,000	334,000		
Insurance Expense			1,500	
Depreciation Expense—Building			2,500	
Accumulated Depreciation—Building				2,500
Depreciation Expense—Equipment			3,900	
Accumulated Depreciation—Equipment				3,900
Interest Expense			12,000	
Interest Payable				12,000
Totals			352,400	352,400

Instructions

(a) Prepare a complete work sheet.

(b) Prepare a classified balance sheet. (Note: $10,000 of the mortgage payable is due for payment next year.)

(c) Journalize the adjusting entries.

(d) Journalize the closing entries.

(e) Prepare a post-closing trial balance.

Complete all steps in accounting cycle. (S.O. 1, 2, 3, 4, 6)

P4–5 Joe Jansen opened Joe's Window Washing on July 1. During July, the following transactions were completed.

July 1 Invested $8,000 cash in the business.

    1 Purchased used truck for $6,000, paying $3,000 cash and the balance on account.

3   Purchased cleaning supplies for $900 on account.

5   Paid $1,200 cash on one-year insurance policy effective July 1.

12 Billed customers $2,500 for cleaning services.

18 Paid $1,000 cash on amount owed on truck and $500 on amount owed on cleaning supplies.

20 Paid $1,200 cash for employee salaries.

21 Collected $1,400 cash from customers billed on July 12.

25 Billed customers $3,000 for cleaning services.

31 Paid gas and oil for month on truck $200.

31 Withdrew $500 cash for personal use.

The chart of accounts for Joe's Window Washing contains the following accounts: No. 101 Cash, No. 111 Fees Receivable, No. 128 Cleaning Supplies, No. 130 Prepaid Insurance, No. 157 Equipment, No. 158 Accumulated Depreciation—Equipment, No. 201 Accounts Payable, No. 212 Salaries Payable, No. 301 Joe Jansen, Capital, No. 306 Joe Jansen, Drawing, No. 350 Income Summary, No. 400 Fees Earned, No. 633 Gas and Oil Expense, No. 634 Cleaning Supplies Expense, No. 711 Depreciation Expense, No. 722 Insurance Expense, No. 726 Salaries Expense.

Instructions

(a) Journalize and post the July transactions. Use page J1 for the journal and the three-column form of account.

(b) Prepare a trial balance at July 31 on a work sheet.

(c) Enter the following adjustments on the work sheet and complete the work sheet.
   (1) Earned but unbilled fees at July 31 were $1,100.
   (2) Depreciation on equipment for the month was $200.
   (3) One-twelfth of the insurance expired.
   (4) An inventory count shows $600 of cleaning supplies on hand at July 31.
   (5) Accrued but unpaid employee salaries were $400.

(d) Prepare the income statement and owner's equity statement for July and a classified balance sheet at July 31.

(e) Journalize and post adjusting entries. Use page J2 for the journal.

(f) Journalize and post closing entries and complete the closing process. Use page J3 for the journal.

(g) Prepare a post-closing trial balance at July 31.

P4–6   Charles Mears, CPA, was retained by Norris TV Repair to prepare financial statements for April 1993. Mears accumulated all the ledger balances per Norris's records and found the following:

Analyze errors and pre- pare correcting entries. (S.O. 5)

NORRIS TV REPAIR
Trial Balance
April 30, 1993

	Debit	Credit
Cash	$ 5,100	
Fees Receivable	3,200	
Supplies	800	
Equipment	10,600	
Accumulated Depreciation		$ 1,350
Accounts Payable		2,100
Salaries Payable		500
Unearned Fees		890
S. Norris, Capital		13,900
Fees Earned		5,450
Salaries Expense	3,300	
Advertising Expense	400	
Miscellaneous Expense	290	
Depreciation Expense	500	
	$24,190	$24,190

Charles Mears reviewed the records and found the following errors:

1. Cash received from a customer on account was recorded as $560 instead of $650.
2. The purchase, on account, of a typewriter costing $340 was recorded as a debit to supplies and a credit to accounts payable for $340.
3. A payment of $30 for advertising expense was entered as a debit to Miscellaneous Expense $30 and a credit to Cash $30.
4. The first salary payment this month was for $1,900, which included $500 of salaries payable on March 31. The payment was recorded as a debit to Salaries Expense $1,900 and a credit to Cash $1,900. (No reversing entries were made on April 1.)
5. A cash payment of repair expense on equipment for $86 was recorded as a debit to Equipment $68 and a credit to Cash $68.

Instructions

(a) Prepare an analysis of each error showing (1) the incorrect entry, (2) the correct entry, and (3) the correcting entry.

(b) Prepare a correct trial balance.

ALTERNATE PROBLEMS

Prepare work sheet, financial statements, and adjusting, and closing entries.
(S.O. 1, 2, 3, 6)

S

P4–1A   Rob Herr began operations as a private investigator on January 1, 1993. The trial balance columns of the work sheet for Herr Company at March 31 are as follows:

HERR COMPANY
Work sheet
For the Quarter Ended March 31, 1993

Account Titles	Trial Balance Dr.	Trial Balance Cr.
Cash	$12,600	
Fees Receivable	5,420	
Supplies	1,050	
Prepaid Insurance	2,400	
Equipment	30,000	
Notes Payable		$10,000
Accounts Payable		12,350
R. Herr, Capital		20,000
R. Herr, Drawing	600	
Fees Earned		13,620
Salaries Expense	1,200	
Travel Expense	1,300	
Rent Expense	1,200	
Miscellaneous Expense	200	
	$55,970	$55,970

Other data:

1. Supplies on hand total $750.
2. Depreciation is $400 per quarter.
3. Interest accrued on six months note payable, issued January 1, $300.
4. Insurance expires at the rate of $150 per month.
5. Fees earned but unbilled at March 31 total $750.

Instructions

(a) Enter the trial balance on a work sheet and complete the work sheet.

(b) Prepare an income statement and owner's equity statement for the quarter and a classified balance sheet at March 31.

(c) Journalize the adjusting entries from the adjustments columns of the work sheet.

(d) Journalize the closing entries from the financial statement columns of the work sheet.

P4–2A The adjusted trial balance columns of the work sheet for the Randi Company is as follows:

Complete worksheet and prepare financial statements, closing entries, and post-closing trial balance. (S.O. 1, 2, 3, 6)

RANDI COMPANY
Work Sheet
For the Year Ended December 31, 1993

Account No.	Account Titles	Adjusted Trial Balance Dr.	Cr.
101	Cash	24,600	
111	Fees Receivable	15,400	
126	Supplies	2,500	
130	Prepaid Insurance	4,800	
151	Office Equipment	44,000	
152	Accumulated Depreciation—Office Equipment		18,000
200	Notes Payable		20,000
201	Accounts Payable		8,000
212	Salaries Payable		3,000
230	Interest Payable		1,000
301	B. Randi, Capital		36,000
306	B. Randi, Drawing	12,000	
400	Fees Earned		79,000
610	Advertising Expense	12,000	
631	Supplies Expense	3,700	
711	Depreciation Expense	6,000	
722	Insurance Expense	4,000	
726	Salaries Expense	35,000	
905	Interest Expense	1,000	
		165,000	165,000

Instructions

(a) Complete the work sheet by extending the balances to the financial statement columns.

(b) Prepare an income statement, owner's equity statement, and a classified balance sheet. $10,000 of the notes payable become due in 1994.

(c) Prepare the closing entries. Use J14 for the journal page.

(d) Post the closing entries and rule and balance the accounts. Use the three-column form of account. Income Summary is No. 350.

(e) Prepare a post-closing trial balance.

P4–3A The completed financial statement columns of the work sheet for Batavia Company are shown below.

Prepare financial statements, closing entries, and post-closing trial balance. (S.O. 1, 2, 3, 6)

BATAVIA COMPANY
Work Sheet
For the Year Ended December 31, 1993

Account No.	Account Titles	Income Statement Dr.	Cr.	Balance Sheet Dr.	Cr.
101	Cash			8,200	
111	Fees Receivable			6,500	
130	Prepaid Insurance			1,800	
157	Equipment			28,000	
167	Accumulated Depreciation				8,600
201	Accounts Payable				12,000
212	Salaries Payable				2,000

BATAVIA COMPANY
Work Sheet
For the Year Ended December 31, 1993

Account No.	Account Titles	Income Statement Dr.	Income Statement Cr.	Balance Sheet Dr.	Balance Sheet Cr.
301	Millie Batavia, Capital				34,000
306	Millie Batavia, Drawing			7,200	
400	Fees Earned		42,000		
622	Repair Expense	3,200			
722	Insurance Expense	1,200			
711	Depreciation Expense	2,800			
726	Salaries Expense	36,000			
732	Utilities Expense	3,700			
	Totals	46,900	42,000	51,700	56,600
	Net Loss		4,900	4,900	
		46,900	46,900	56,600	56,600

Instructions

(a) Prepare an income statement, owner's equity statement, and a classified balance sheet.

(b) Prepare the closing entries.

(c) Post the closing entries and rule and balance the accounts. Use T-accounts. Income Summary is No. 350.

(d) Prepare a post-closing trial balance.

Complete work sheet and prepare classified balance sheet, entries, and post-closing trial balance.
(S.O. 1, 2, 3, 6)

P4–4A   Sparky's Amusement Park Inc. has a fiscal year ending on September 30. Selected data from the September 30 work sheet are presented below:

SPARKY'S AMUSEMENT PARK
Work Sheet
For the Year Ended September 30, 1993

	Trial Balance Dr.	Trial Balance Cr.	Adjusted Trial Balance Dr.	Adjusted Trial Balance Cr.
Cash	37,400		37,400	
Supplies	18,600		1,200	
Prepaid Insurance	31,900		3,900	
Land	80,000		80,000	
Equipment	120,000		120,000	
Accumulated Depreciation		36,200		43,000
Accounts Payable		14,600		14,600
Unearned Admissions		2,700		1,700
Mortgage Payable		50,000		50,000
L. A. Sparks, Capital		109,700		109,700
L. A. Sparks, Drawing	14,000		14,000	
Admission Revenue		278,500		279,500
Salaries Expense	109,000		109,000	
Repair Expense	32,500		32,500	
Advertising Expense	7,400		7,400	
Utilities Expense	16,900		16,900	
Property Taxes Expense	18,000		21,000	
Interest Expense	6,000		12,000	
Totals	491,700	491,700		

	Trial Balance		Adjusted Trial Balance	
	Dr.	Cr.	Dr.	Cr.
Insurance Expense			28,000	
Supplies Expense			17,400	
Interest Payable				6,000
Depreciation Expense			6,800	
Property Taxes Payable				3,000
Totals			507,500	507,500

Instructions

(a) Prepare a complete work sheet.

(b) Prepare a classified balance sheet. (Note: $10,000 of the mortgage payable is due for payment in the next fiscal year.)

(c) Journalize the adjusting entries.

(d) Journalize the closing entries.

(e) Prepare a post-closing trial balance.

P4–5A Jon Jonas opened Jon's Carpet Cleaners on March 1. During March, the following transactions were completed.

Complete all steps in accounting cycle.
(S.O. 1, 2, 3, 4, 6)

Mar. 1 Invested $10,000 cash in the business.
   1 Purchased used truck for $6,000, paying $4,000 cash and the balance on account.
   3 Purchased cleaning supplies for $1,200 on account.
   5 Paid $1,800 cash on one-year insurance policy effective March 1.
  14 Billed customers $2,800 for cleaning services.
  18 Paid $1,500 cash on amount owed on truck and $500 on amount owed on cleaning supplies.
  20 Paid $1,500 cash for employee salaries.
  21 Collected $1,600 cash from customers billed on July 14.
  28 Billed customers $3,200 for cleaning services.
  31 Paid gas and oil for month on truck $200.
  31 Withdrew $800 cash for personal use.

The chart of accounts for Joe's Window Washing contains the following accounts: No. 101 Cash, No. 111 Fees Receivable, No. 128 Cleaning Supplies, No. 130 Prepaid Insurance, No. 157 Equipment, No. 158 Accumulated Depreciation—Equipment, No. 201 Accounts Payable, No. 212 Salaries Payable, No. 301 Jon Jonas, Capital, No. 306 Jon Jonas, Drawing, No. 350 Income Summary, No. 400 Fees Earned, No. 633 Gas and Oil Expense, No. 634 Cleaning Supplies Expense, No. 711 Depreciation Expense, No. 722 Insurance Expense, No. 726 Salaries Expense.

Instructions

(a) Journalize and post the July transactions. Use page J1 for the journal and the three-column form of account.

(b) Prepare a trial balance at March 31 on a work sheet.

(c) Enter the following adjustments on the work sheet and complete the work sheet.
   (1) Earned but unbilled fees at March 31 were $600.
   (2) Depreciation on equipment for the month was $250.
   (3) One-twelfth of the insurance expired.
   (4) An inventory count shows $400 of cleaning supplies on hand at March 31.
   (5) Accrued but unpaid employee salaries were $500.

(d) Prepare the income statement and owner's equity statement for March and a classified balance sheet at March 31.

(e) Journalize and post adjusting entries. Use page J2 for the journal.

(f) Journalize and post closing entries and complete the closing process. Use page J3 for the journal.

(g) Prepare a post-closing trial balance at July 31.

*B*roadening *Your Perspective*

FINANCIAL REPORTING PROBLEM

The financial statements of PepsiCo, Inc. are presented in Appendix L at the end of this text book.

Instructions
Answer the following questions using the Consolidated Balance Sheet and the Notes to Consolidated Financial Statements section.

1. What were PepsiCo's total current assets at December 28, 1991, and December 29, 1990?
2. Are assets included in current assets listed in proper order? Explain.
3. How are PepsiCo's assets classified?
4. What caused "Prepaid expenses and other current assets" to increase in 1991?
5. What were PepsiCo's total current liabilities at December 28, 1991, and December 29, 1990?
6. What was the composition of the company's short-term borrowing balance at December 28, 1991?
7. Why did short-term borrowings decrease so dramatically in 1991?
8. Was PepsiCo's liquidity at December 28, 1991 better or worse than at December 29, 1990? Explain.

DECISION CASE

Moorey Janitorial Service was started two years ago by Pat Moorey. Because business has been exceptionally good, Pat decided on July 1, 1993, to expand operations by acquiring an additional truck and hiring two more assistants. To finance the expansion, Pat obtained on July 1, 1993, a $25,000, 10% bank loan, payable $10,000 on July 1, 1994, and the balance on July 1, 1995. The terms of the loan require the borrower to have $10,000 more current assets then current liabilities at December 31, 1993. If these terms are not met, the bank loan will be refinanced at 15% interest.

At December 31, 1993, the accountant for Moorey Janitorial Service prepared the following balance sheet:

MOOREY JANITORIAL SERVICE
Balance Sheet
December 31, 1993

Assets

Current assets		
Cash		$ 6,500
Accounts receivable		9,000
Janitorial supplies		5,200
Prepaid insurance		4,800
Total current assets		25,500
Property, plant, and equipment		
Cleaning equipment (net)	$22,000	
Delivery trucks (net)	34,000	56,000
Total assets		$81,500

Liabilities and Owner's Equity

Current liabilities		
Notes payable		$10,000
Accounts payable		2,500
Total current liabilities		12,500
Long-term liability		
Notes payable		15,000
Total liabilities		27,500
Owner's equity		
Pat Moorey, Capital		54,000
Total liabilities and owner's equity		$81,500

Pat presented the balance sheet to the bank's loan office on January 2, 1994 confident that the company had met the terms of the loan. The loan officer was not impressed. She said, "We need financial statements audited by a CPA."

A CPA was hired and immediately realized that the balance sheet had been prepared from a trial balance and not from an adjusted trial balance. The adjustment data at the balance sheet date consisted of the following:

1. Earned but unbilled janitorial services were $2,400.
2. Janitorial supplies on hand were $3,500.
3. Prepaid insurance was a three-year policy dated January 1, 1993.
4. December expenses incurred but unpaid at December 31, $250.
5. Interest on the bank loan was not recorded.
6. The amounts for plant assets were net of accumulated depreciation of $4,000 for cleaning equipment and $5,000 for delivery trucks as of January 1, 1993. Depreciation for 1993 was $4,000 for cleaning equipment and $8,000 for delivery trucks.

Instructions

(a) Prepare a correct balance sheet.

(b) Were the terms of the bank loan met? Explain.

CRITICAL THINKING CASE

Refer to the opening story about Stillman College and answer the following questions:

1. What are the steps in the accounting cycle? Where in the accounting cycle does the preparation of a work sheet fit?

2. What monthly financial information should Stillman's president be provided?

3. How might the monthly financial information affect the decision-making at Stillman College?

4. Terre Thompson, comptroller, notes that "students sometimes have a hard time understanding how you can make money on the books but have no money in the bank." Explain how this situation occurs.

ETHICAL CASE

As the controller of Heavenly Perfume Company, you discover a significant misstatement that overstated net income in the prior year's financial statements. The misleading financial statements are contained in the company's annual report which was issued to banks and other creditors less than a month ago. After much thought about the consequences of telling the president, Eddy Kadu, about this misstatement, you gather your courage to embarrassingly inform him. Eddy says, "Hey! What they don't know won't hurt them. But, just so we set the record straight, we'll adjust this year's financial statements for the last year's misstatement. We can absorb that misstatement better in this year than in last year anyway! Just don't make that kind of mistake again."

Instructions
(a) Who are the stakeholders in this situation?
(b) What are the ethical issues in this situation?
(c) What would you do as a controller in this situation?

Answers to Self-Study Questions
1. c   2. b   3. d   4. a   5. d   6. b   7. a   8. c   9. c   10. b
11. b

Concepts for Review

Before studying this chapter, you should know or, if necessary, review:

a. *How to prepare a work sheet. (Ch. 4, p. 133–7)*

b. *How to close revenue, expense, and drawing accounts. (Ch. 4, p. 139–42)*

c. *The steps in the accounting cycle. (Ch. 4, p. 146–7)*

ACCOUNTING FOR MERCHANDISING OPERATIONS

Study Objectives

After studying this chapter, you should be able to:

1. Identify the components in measuring net income in a merchandising company.

2. Explain the entries for sales revenues.

3. State the steps in determining cost of goods sold.

4. Explain the computation and importance of gross profit.

5. Identify the unique features of the income statement for a merchandising company.

6. Explain the steps in the accounting cycle for a merchandising company.

7. Distinguish between a multiple-step and a single-step income statement.

*L*arry Martin is in charge of procuring textbooks for the

Washington State University bookstore in Pullman, Washington. The bookstore sells

about $4 million in textbooks each year. The average inventory at any point in time

is 2,500 titles.

Mr. Martin's big challenge is to order enough books to satisfy demand—but not

too many. For example, say a course historically has sold 75 books. He'll order 85 to

be on the safe side. The reason: if he orders short, he'll have to order additional books

by second-day air express—which is expensive and cuts into profits. If Martin orders

too many, the publisher won't accept for return more than 20% of his original order.

Of course, returns occur all the time, especially when students drop courses

during the first week of class. If the returned books are in "new and resellable"

condition, the publisher will accept return of such books and issue Mr. Martin a

credit memo.

Washington State University starts its fall term before Labor Day. The busy book selling and return period lasts three to four weeks. Therefore, Martin waits until the end of September to take the inventory and determine his returns. That count also tells him his beginning inventory for the next term. At that point, he is ready to order more books.

As you read Chapter 5, think about the journal entry the bookstore would record when returning a textbook to the publisher.

In previous chapters, the accounting cycle was illustrated with service enterprises. Whether it be a professional sports team (Los Angeles Dodgers), a health spa (Vic Tanney), an airline (American Airlines), or a tax return preparation office (H & R Block), these businesses have one thing in common—they charge a fee for the services they perform.

In this chapter, we explain and illustrate another type of enterprise called a **merchandising** or **trading** concern. These enterprises buy and sell goods rather than perform services to earn a profit. Merchandising companies that purchase and sell directly to consumers such as K mart, Sears, Kroger, and Toys R Us are called **retailers**. In contrast, merchandising companies that sell to retailers are known as **wholesalers**. For example, retailer Walgreens might buy goods from wholesaler McKesson & Robbins; Office Depot might buy office supplies from wholesaler United Stationers.

Although the steps in the accounting cycle for a merchandising company are the same as the steps for a service enterprise, you must be sure to understand the additional accounts and entries required in recording merchandising transactions and the proper financial statement presentation of these accounts. The following discussion applies to both retail and wholesale enterprises. Later in the chapter, we also illustrate two income statement forms.

Measuring Income in a Merchandising Company

Study Objective 1

Identify the components in measuring net income in a merchandising company.

Measuring net income for a merchandising company is conceptually the same as for a service enterprise. That is, net income (or loss) results from the matching of expenses with revenues. In a merchandising company, the primary source of revenues is the sale of merchandise, often referred to simply as sales revenue or sales. Expenses are divided into two categories: (1) the cost of goods sold and (2) operating expenses.

The cost of goods sold is the total cost of merchandise sold during the period. This expense is directly related to the revenue recognized from the sale of the goods. You will see later in this chapter exactly how cost of goods sold is calculated.

Sales less cost of goods sold is called the gross profit (or gross margin) on sales. For example, when a pocket calculator costing $15 is sold for $25, the gross profit is $10. Merchandising companies customarily report gross profit on sales in the income statement.

After gross profit is calculated, operating expenses are deducted to determine net income (or loss). Operating expenses are incurred in the process of earning sales revenue. Examples of operating expenses are sales salaries, advertising expense, and insurance expense. The income measurement process for a merchandising company may be diagrammed as shown in Illustration 5-1.

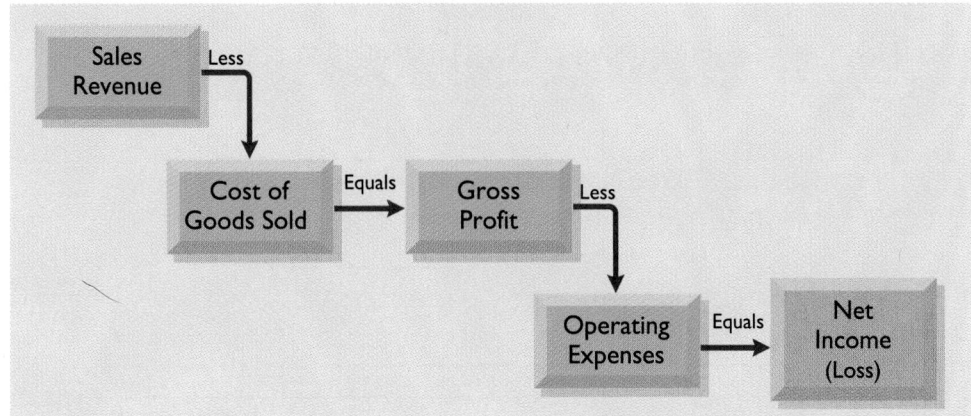

ILLUSTRATION 5-1

Income measurement process for a merchandising company

The operating expenses of a merchandising company include many of the expenses found in a service enterprise. Hence, this chapter focuses primarily on the recording of sales revenues and the related cost of goods sold that produce gross profit.

Sales Revenue

In accordance with the revenue recognition principle, sales revenues, like service revenues, are recorded when earned. Typically, sales revenues are earned when the goods are transferred from the seller to the buyer. At this point, the sales transaction is completed and the sales price is established.

    Sales may be made on credit or for cash. Department stores such as J.C. Penney and Sears have significant amounts of both types of sales. Grocery stores such as Safeway and Kroger normally have cash sales. Wholesalers generally sell most goods on credit. Every sales transaction should be supported by a **business document** that provides written evidence of the sale. **Cash register tapes** provide evidence of cash sales. A sales invoice, like the one shown in Illustration 5-2, provides support for credit sales. The original copy of the invoice goes to the customer, and a copy is kept by the seller for use in recording the sale. The invoice shows the date of sale, customer name, total sales price, and other relevant information.

    To record a sale, an asset account is debited, and the revenue account, Sales, is credited. For cash sales, the Cash account is debited. For credit sales, Accounts Receivable is debited. To illustrate a sale on credit, the following entry is made by Highpoint Electronic Co., for the sales invoice shown in Illustration 5-2.

May 4	Accounts Receivable	3,800	
	Sales		3,800
	(To record credit sale per invoice #731)		

As indicated by this entry, sales revenues can be recorded before cash is actually collected. For credit sales, the amount due may not be collected until the next period. Therefore, the sales revenues earned during a particular period may be significantly different from the cash collected from sales during that same period.

Study Objective 2

Explain the entries for sales revenues.

ILLUSTRATION 5-2

Invoice

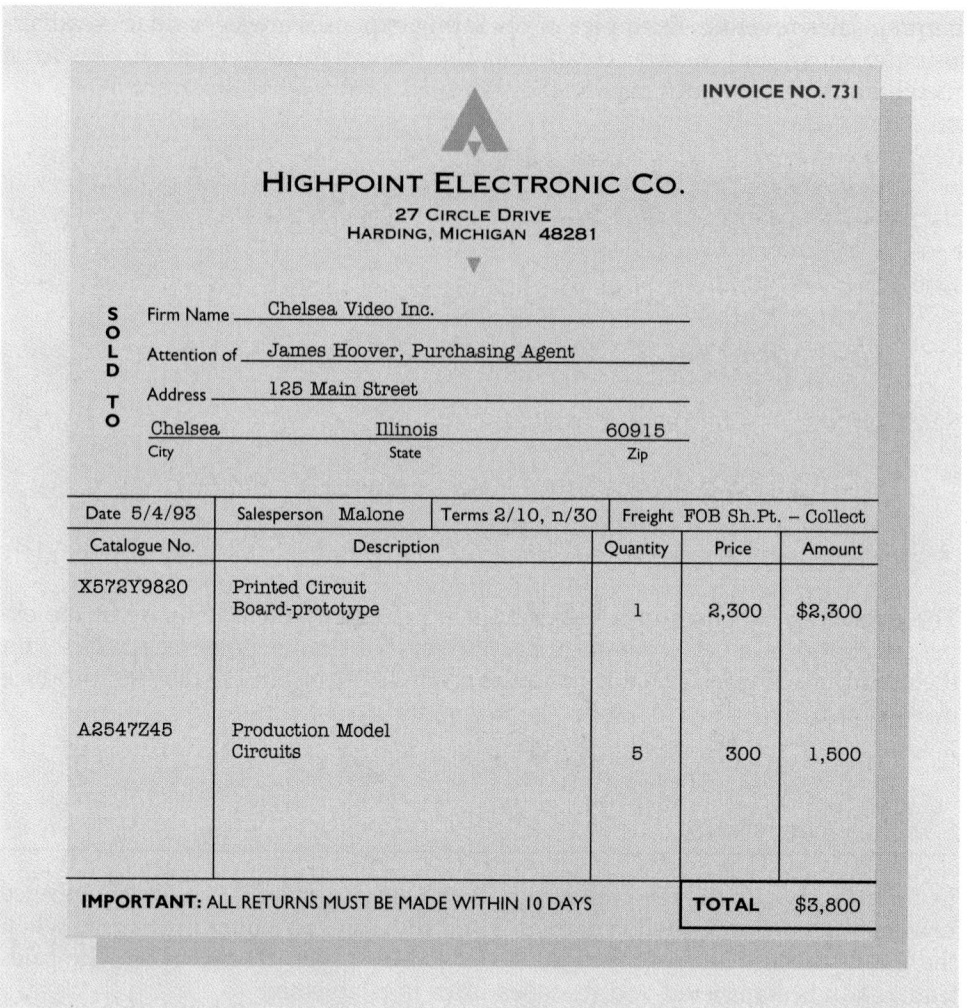

To illustrate a sale for cash, assume that Highpoint's cash register total for cash sales on May 4 is $6,210. The entry, therefore, is:

May 4	Cash	6,210	
	Sales		6,210
	(To record daily cash sales)		

Helpful hint The Sales account is only credited for sales of goods held for resale. Sales of assets not held for resale, such as equipment or land, are credited directly to the asset account.

Merchandising companies may use more than one sales account. For example, Highpoint Electronic Co. may have separate sales accounts for its sales of television sets, video cassette recorders, and microwave ovens. Because sales are the principal source of revenue for a merchandising company, the amount and trend of sales are of critical importance to management, creditors, and other interested parties. An increase in sales from the preceding year or month signifies a growing business and often leads to higher net income. An unfavorable trend may suggest lower future earnings.

Sales Returns and Allowances

A customer may be dissatisfied with the merchandise received because the goods are damaged or defective, of inferior quality, or not in accord with the customer's specifications. In such cases, the customer may return the goods to the seller for credit if the sale was made on credit, or for a cash refund if the sale was originally for cash. This transaction is known as a **sales return**. Alternatively, the customer may choose to keep the merchandise if the seller is willing to grant an allowance (deduction) from the selling price. This transaction is known as a **sales allowance**. For accounting purposes, sales returns and sales allowances are combined into one account, Sales Returns and Allowances.

To give the customer a sales return or allowance, the seller normally prepares a credit memorandum. It is a document issued to inform a customer that a credit has been made to the customer's account receivable for a sales return or allowance. The credit memorandum shown in Illustration 5-3 relates to the sales invoice shown in Illustration 5-2.

ILLUSTRATION 5-3

Credit memorandum

	CREDIT-CM126

HIGHPOINT ELECTRONIC CO.
27 CIRCLE DRIVE
HARDING, MICHIGAN 48281

▼

SOLD TO

Firm Name __Chelsea Video Inc.__

Attention of __James Hoover, Purchasing Agent__

Address __125 Main Street__

Chelsea	Illinois	60915
City	State	Zip

Date 5/8/93	Salesperson Malone	Invoice No. 731	Invoice Date 5/4/93	Approved Reid

Catalogue No.	Description	Quantity	Price	Amount
A2547Z45	Production Model Circuits (Inoperative)	1	300	$300

Cash Refund ☐   Credit Account ☒   Other ☐

The original copy of the credit memorandum is sent to the customer, and a copy is kept by the seller as evidence of the transaction. The seller's entry to record a credit memorandum involves a debit to the Sales Returns and Allowances account and a credit to Accounts Receivable, as shown below:

May 8	Sales Returns and Allowances	300	
	Accounts Receivable		300
	(To record allowance for damaged goods per credit memorandum CM126)		

For a sales return or allowance on a cash sale, a cash refund is normally made. In such case, Sales Returns and Allowances is debited and Cash is credited.

Accounting in Action · *Business Insight*

How high is too high? Returns can become so high that it is questionable whether sales revenue should have been recognized in the first place. An example of high returns is Florafax International Inc., a floral supply company, which was alleged to ship its product without customer authorization on 10 holiday occasions, including 8,562 shipments of its product to customers for Mother's Day and 6,575 for Secretary's Day. The return rate on these shipments went as high as 69% of sales. As one employee noted: "products went out the front door and came in the back door."

An offshoot of high returns is "channel stuffing." In channel stuffing, the seller "sells" its product by providing substantial inducement to buy. Although this helps the sellers' revenue in the short run, the long term can be devastating when the merchandise bought remains on the purchasers' shelves for a long period of time.

Sales Returns and Allowances is a **contra revenue account** to Sales. The normal balance of Sales Returns and Allowances is a debit. A contra account is used, instead of debiting Sales, to disclose the amount of sales returns and allowances in the accounts and in the income statement. Disclosure of this information is important to management: excessive returns and allowances suggest inferior merchandise, inefficiencies in filling orders, errors in billing customers, and mistakes in delivery or shipment of the goods. Moreover, a debit directly to Sales would obscure the relative importance of sales returns and allowances as a percentage of sales. It also could distort comparisons between total sales in different accounting periods.

Sales Discounts

The terms of a credit sale may include an offer of a cash discount, called a sales discount, to the customer for prompt payment of the balance due. This incentive offers advantages to both parties. The purchaser saves money. The seller is able to convert the accounts receivable into cash earlier.

Helpful hint The term "net" in "net 30" means the remaining amount due after subtracting any sales returns and allowances and partial payments.

The credit terms specify the amount and time period for the cash discount. They also indicate the length of time in which the purchaser is expected to pay the full invoice price. In the sales invoice in Illustration 5-2, credit terms are 2/10, n/30, which is read "two-ten, net thirty." This means that a 2% cash discount may be taken on the invoice price (less any returns or allowances) if payment is made within 10 days of the invoice date (the discount period); otherwise, the invoice price less any returns or allowances is due 30 days from the invoice date. Alternatively, the discount period may extend to a specified number of days following the month in which the sale occurs. For example, 1/10 EOM (end-of-month) means that a 1% discount is available if the invoice is paid within the first 10 days of the next month.

When the seller elects not to offer a cash discount for prompt payment, credit terms will specify only the maximum time period for paying the balance due. For example, the time period may be stated as n/30, n/60, or n/10 EOM.

When cash discounts are taken by customers, the seller debits Sales Discounts. To illustrate, assume Chelsea Video Inc. pays the balance due of $3,500 (Sales $3,800 less Sales Returns and Allowances $300) on May 14, the last day of the discount period. The cash discount is $70 ($3,500 × 2%), and the amount of cash paid by Chelsea is $3,430 ($3,500 − $70). Assuming the payment is received by Highpoint Electronic on May 15, the entry is:

May 15	Cash	3,430	
	Sales Discounts	70	
	Accounts Receivable		3,500
	(To record collection within 2/10, n/30 discount period)		

Sales Discounts is a contra revenue account to Sales. Its normal balance is a debit. This account is used, instead of debiting Sales, to disclose the amount of cash discounts taken by customers. If the discount is not taken, Highpoint Electronic debits Cash for $3,500 and credits Accounts Receivable for the same amount at the date of collection.

Statement Presentation

As contra revenue accounts, sales returns and allowances and sales discounts are deducted from sales in the income statement to arrive at net sales. The sales revenues section of the income statement based on assumed data for Highpoint Electronic is as follows:

ILLUSTRATION 5-4

Statement presentation of sales revenues section

HIGHPOINT ELECTRONIC CO. Partial Income Statement		
Sales revenues		
Sales		$480,000
Less: Sales returns and allowances	$12,000	
Sales discounts	8,000	20,000
Net sales		$460,000

This presentation discloses the significant aspects of the company's principal revenue producing activities.

Before You Go On . . .

1. How do the components in measuring net income in a merchandising company differ from those in a service enterprise?

2. What entries are made to record sales, sales returns and allowances, and sales discounts?

3. How are sales and contra revenue accounts reported in the income statement?

Cost of Goods Sold

As you learned earlier in this chapter, the second factor in measuring net income in a merchandising company is the cost of goods sold. The cost of goods sold may be determined each time a sale occurs or at the end of an accounting period. To make the determination when the sale occurs, a company uses a perpetual inventory system. Under this system, detailed records of the cost of each inventory item are maintained and continuously show the inventory that should be on hand. For example, a Ford dealership will have separate inventory records for each Escort, Tempo, Taurus, and Thunderbird. When a car is sold, its cost is

Study Objective 3

State the steps in determining cost of goods sold.

obtained from the inventory records. Perpetual inventory systems have traditionally been used by companies that sell high unit-value items such as automobiles, furniture, television sets, and large home appliances. Much more will be said about perpetual inventory systems in Chapter 9.

When cost of goods sold is determined only at the end of an accounting period, a company is said to be using a periodic inventory system. This system is widely used by companies such as Wal-Mart, True Value hardware stores, and Rexall drugstores that sell thousands of low unit-value items. A periodic inventory system does not require detailed accounting records for each inventory item. Unless there is a specific statement to the contrary, a periodic inventory system will be assumed in this textbook.

To determine the cost of goods sold under a periodic inventory system, it is necessary to (1) record purchases of merchandise, (2) determine the cost of goods purchased, and (3) determine the cost of goods on hand at the beginning and end of the accounting period. These procedures are illustrated in the following sections.

Recording Purchases of Merchandise

When merchandise is purchased for resale to customers, the temporary account, Merchandise Purchases, or simply Purchases, is debited for the cost of the goods. However, not all purchases are debited to Purchases. Purchases of assets acquired for use and not for resale, such as supplies, equipment, and similar items should be debited to specific asset accounts rather than to Purchases.

Like sales, purchases may be made for cash or on account (credit). The purchase is normally recorded by the purchaser when the goods are received from the seller. Every purchase should be supported by business documents that provide written evidence of the transaction. Each cash purchase should be supported by a canceled check or cash register receipt indicating the items purchased. Cash purchases are recorded by a debit to Purchases and a credit to Cash. Each credit purchase should be supported by a purchase invoice indicating the total purchase price and other relevant information. The purchaser does not prepare a separate purchase invoice. Instead, the copy of the sales invoice sent by the seller becomes a purchase invoice to the buyer. The entry by Chelsea Video Inc. for the invoice (Illustration 5-2) shown on page 182 is:

Helpful hint Be careful not to fall into the trap of debiting purchases of equipment or supplies to Purchases.

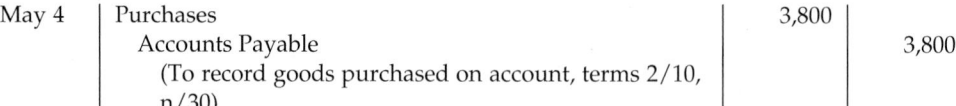

May 4	Purchases	3,800	
	Accounts Payable		3,800
	(To record goods purchased on account, terms 2/10, n/30)		

Purchase Returns and Allowances

A sales return and allowance on the seller's books is recorded as a **purchase return and allowance** on the books of the purchaser. The purchaser initiates the request for a reduction of the balance due through the issuance of a debit memorandum. A debit memorandum is a document issued by a buyer to inform a seller that a debit has been made to the seller's account because of unsatisfactory merchandise. The original copy of the memorandum is sent to the seller and one copy is retained by the purchaser. The information contained in a debit memorandum is similar to the information found in the credit memorandum in Illustration 5-3 (p. 183). The entry by Chelsea Video Inc. for the merchandise returned on May 8 is:

May 8	Accounts Payable	300	
	Purchase Returns and Allowances		300
	(To record allowance for damaged goods)		

Helpful hint Only returns of goods held for resale are credited to Purchase Returns and Allowances. Returns of supplies, for example, should be credited to the Supplies account.

Purchase Returns and Allowances represents a reduction in the cost of goods purchased for resale. It is a **contra account** to Purchases and its normal balance is a credit. The contra account is used instead of crediting Purchases in order to disclose both the dollar amount of returns and allowances and the percentage of gross purchases that have proven to be unsatisfactory. Excessive purchase returns and allowances may indicate inefficiencies in a company's purchasing procedures or the need to find more reliable suppliers.

Credit memorandums and debit memorandums derive their names from the action that the issuer takes on the accounts receivable or payable carried on its books. The purchaser sends a debit memorandum to indicate a **debit** to Accounts Payable and a credit to Purchase Returns and Allowances. Similarly, a seller issues a credit memorandum to indicate a **credit** to Accounts Receivable and a debit to Sales Returns and Allowances.

Purchase Discounts

Credit terms may permit the buyer to claim a cash discount for the prompt payment of a balance due. The buyer calls this discount a purchase discount. Like a sales discount, a purchase discount is based on the invoice cost less returns and allowances, if any. Purchase Discounts is credited for discounts that are taken. The entry to record the May 14 payment by Chelsea Video Inc. to Highpoint Electronic is as follows:

May 14	Accounts Payable	3,500	
	Purchase Discounts		70
	Cash		3,430
	(To record payment within discount period)		

Helpful hint See the same transaction recorded by the seller on page 185.

Purchase Discounts represents a reduction in the cost of goods purchased for resale. As in the case of Purchase Returns and Allowances, Purchase Discounts is a **contra account** to Purchases. Its normal balance is a credit. If Chelsea Video Inc. fails to take the discount,[1] and full payment is made on June 3, Chelsea makes the following entry:

June 3	Accounts Payable	3,500	
	Cash		3,500
	(To record payment with no discount taken)		

A buyer usually should take all available discounts. For example, if Chelsea Video takes the discount, it pays $70 less in cash. Conversely, if it forgoes the discount and invests the $3,500 in a bank savings account for 20 days at 10% interest, it will earn only $19.44 in interest. The savings obtained by taking the discount is computed as follows:

Discount of 2% on $3,500	$70.00
Interest received on $3,500	
(for 20 days at 10%)	19.44
Savings by taking the discount	**$50.56**

ILLUSTRATION 5-5

Savings obtained by taking purchase discount

---

[1]Purchases are sometimes recorded net of the discount. This approach is covered in Chapter 7, page 287.

Alternatively, passing up the discount may be viewed as **paying an interest rate of 2%** for the use of $3,500 for 20 days. This is the equivalent of an annual interest rate of 36% (2% $\times$ 360/20).[2] Obviously, it would be better for Chelsea Video to borrow at prevailing bank interest rates of 8–12% than to lose the discount.

So as not to miss purchase discounts, unpaid invoices should be filed by due dates. For example, Chelsea Video should have a file folder dated May 14 in which all bills to be paid on this date are filed. This procedure helps the purchaser remember the discount date. It also prevents early payment of bills and maximizes the time that available cash can be used for other business purposes.

Technology in Action

In many computer systems, the purchase of goods and the subsequent payment are closely linked. The due date, discount terms, and discount date are entered into the system along with the account names and dollar amounts. When the data have been entered and approved, the system can automatically generate payment checks by the discount date to take advantage of any discounts offered. Such a level of automation may not be necessary for a small firm with only 10 to 20 suppliers. The advantages of such a system quickly surface, though, when hundreds of suppliers are used on a continuous basis, as is the case with many large retailers.

Freight Costs

The sales agreement should indicate whether the seller or the buyer is to pay the cost of transporting the goods to the buyer's place of business. When a common carrier such as a railroad, trucking company, or airline is used, the transportation company prepares a freight bill (often called a bill of lading) in accordance with the sales agreement. Freight terms are expressed as either **FOB shipping point** or **FOB destination**. The letters FOB mean **free on board**. Thus, FOB shipping point means that goods are placed free on board the carrier by the seller, and the buyer pays the freight costs. Conversely, FOB destination means that the goods are placed free on board at the buyer's place of business, and the seller pays the freight. For example, the sales invoice in Illustration 5-2 on page 182 indicates that freight is FOB shipping point. Thus, the buyer (Chelsea Video Inc.) pays the freight charges.

When the purchaser directly incurs the freight costs, the account Freight-in (or Transportation-in) is debited. For example, if upon delivery of the goods on May 6, Chelsea Video Inc. pays Acme Freight Company $150 for freight charges, the entry on Chelsea's books is:

May 6	Freight-in	150	
	Cash		150
	(To record payment of freight, terms FOB shipping point)		

Like Purchases, Freight-in is a temporary account whose normal balance is a debit. **Freight-in is part of cost of goods purchased.** The reason is that cost of goods purchased should include any freight charges necessary to bring the goods

---

[2]For simplicity, we use 360 days rather than 365.

to the purchaser. The use of a Freight-in account enables management to determine the materiality of these costs. If freight costs are significant, management may want to compare the cost of truck, rail, or air freight to find the least expensive alternative. Freight costs are not subject to a purchase discount. Purchase discounts apply on the invoice cost of the merchandise.

In contrast, **freight costs incurred by the seller on outgoing merchandise are an operating expense to the seller**. These costs are debited to Freight-out or Delivery Expense. For example, if the freight terms in Illustration 5-2 had specified FOB destination and Highpoint Electronic paid the $150 freight charges, the entry by Highpoint would be:

May 4	Freight-out	150	
	Cash		150
	(To record payment of freight on goods sold FOB destination)		

When the freight charges are paid by the seller, the seller will usually establish a higher invoice price for the goods.

Determining Cost of Goods Purchased

In explaining the accounting for goods purchased for resale, we discussed the following temporary accounts:

Account	Normal Balance
Purchases	Debit
Purchase Returns and Allowances	Credit
Purchase Discounts	Credit
Freight-in	Debit

ILLUSTRATION 5-6

Normal balances: cost of goods purchased accounts

The procedure for determining the cost of goods purchased is as follows:

1. The accounts with credit balances (Purchase Returns and Allowances and Purchase Discounts) are subtracted from purchases to produce net purchases

2. Freight-in is then added to net purchases to produce cost of goods purchased

To illustrate, assume that Highpoint Electronic shows the following balances for the accounts above: Purchases $325,000; Purchase Returns and Allowances $10,400; Purchase Discounts $6,800; and Freight-in $12,200. Net purchases and cost of goods purchased are $307,800 and $320,000, respectively, as computed in Illustration 5-7:

Purchases			$325,000
(1) Less: Purchase returns and allowances	$10,400		
Purchase discounts	6,800		17,200
Net purchases			**307,800**
(2) Add: Freight-in			12,200
Cost of goods purchased			**$320,000**

ILLUSTRATION 5-7

Computation of net purchases and cost of goods purchased

Determining Cost of Goods on Hand

To **determine the cost of inventory on hand, it is necessary to take a physical inventory**. Taking a physical inventory involves:

1. Counting the units on hand for each item of inventory.
2. Applying unit costs to the total units on hand for each item of inventory.
3. Aggregating the costs for each item of inventory to determine the total cost of goods on hand.

A physical inventory should be taken at or near the balance sheet date. To improve the accuracy of the count, many businesses suspend operations while inventory is being taken.

Technology in Action

Computerized inventory systems greatly simplify inventory taking. Once the item counts have been entered, the computer takes over the chores of applying unit cost data to quantities, determining total inventory, and printing out meaningful inventory summaries. A classic example of this type of system is a typical grocery store. Electronic scanners read bar codes placed on each product. These bar codes enable a computer to identify the product being sold, its sale price, and the cost of the good sold and to update the inventory quantity for this item.

The account Merchandise Inventory is used to record the cost of inventory on hand at the balance sheet date. This amount becomes the beginning inventory for the next accounting period. For Highpoint Electronic, the balance in Merchandise Inventory at December 31, 1992, is $36,000. This amount is also the January 1, 1993, balance in Merchandise Inventory. During 1993, **no entries are made to Merchandise Inventory**. At December 31, 1993, entries will be made to eliminate the beginning inventory and to record the ending inventory, which we will assume is $40,000. These entries are illustrated later in the chapter.

Taking a physical inventory only once a year is a disadvantage because a business is not able to determine the amount of inventory losses during the period. For example, a supermarket chain such as A&P may have inventory losses from spoilage of meats, fruits, and vegetables during the year. A department store like Wal-Mart may have losses from shoplifting. Under a periodic

Accounting in Action · *Ethical Insight*

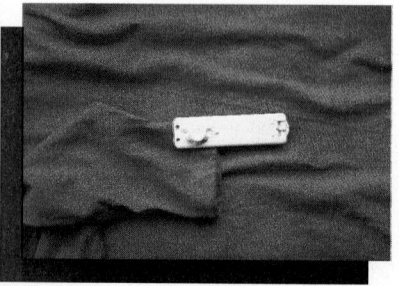

Inventory losses can be substantial. Shoplifting is a big crime in the United States, with a cost of more than $18 billion annually, or 5% of retail sales, not including thefts by store employees. Shoplifting losses have led to the demise of many companies. For example, Dayton-Hudson closed its landmark store in downtown Detroit because of excessive shoplifting losses. Many department stores are trying to reduce shoplifting losses by use of electronic tags on merchandise and by continuous surveillance of customers on closed circuit television.

inventory system, goods not on hand are assumed to have been sold, and are included in the cost of goods sold.

Computing Cost of Goods Sold

Computing the cost of goods sold also involves two steps:

1. The cost of goods purchased is added to the cost of goods on hand at the beginning of the period (beginning inventory) to obtain the cost of goods available for sale.
2. The cost of goods on hand at the end of the period (ending inventory) is subtracted from the cost of goods available for sale to arrive at the **cost of goods sold**.

For Highpoint Electronic the cost of goods available for sale and the cost of goods sold are $356,000 and $316,000, respectively, as shown below.

	Beginning inventory	$ 36,000
(1)	Add: Cost of goods purchased	320,000
	Cost of goods available for sale	356,000
(2)	Less: Ending inventory	40,000
	Cost of goods sold	$316,000

ILLUSTRATION 5-8

Computation of cost of goods available for sale and cost of goods sold

Gross Profit

From Illustration 5-1, you learned that cost of goods sold is deducted from sales revenue to determine **gross profit**. The sales revenue figure used for this computation is net sales. On the basis of the sales data presented in Illustration 5-4 and the cost of goods sold data in Illustration 5-8, the gross profit for Highpoint Electronic is $144,000, computed as follows:

Net sales	$460,000
Cost of goods sold	316,000
Gross profit	$144,000

Study Objective 4

Explain the computation and importance of gross profit.

ILLUSTRATION 5-9

Computation of gross profit

A company's gross profit may also be expressed as a percentage by dividing the amount of gross profit by net sales. For Highpoint Electronic the gross profit rate is 31.3% ($144,000 ÷ $460,000). Gross profit represents the **merchandising profit**

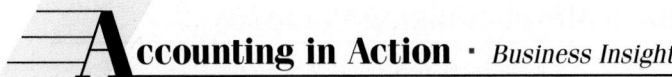

Accounting in Action · *Business Insight*

In a recent year, Woolworth Corporation reported a gross profit rate of 31%; J.C. Penney, 33%; Walgreen Drugs, 28%; and Hartmarx, 36%. Gross profit is critical. "If you don't have someone monitoring it," says one business consultant, "you are asking for instant death." A decline should trigger a search for the cause. The drop could be due to an increase in cost of goods sold or a decrease in sales revenue.

of a company. It is not a measure of the overall profitability of a company, because operating expenses have not been deducted. Nevertheless, the amount and trend of gross profit is closely watched by management and other interested parties.

Operating Expenses

Operating expenses are the third component in measuring net income for a merchandising company. As indicated earlier, these expenses are similar in merchandizing and service enterprises. At Highpoint Electronic, operating expenses were $114,000. Net income is determined by subtracting operating expenses from gross profit. Thus, net income is $30,000 as shown below:

ILLUSTRATION 5-10

Operating expenses in computing net income

Gross profit	$144,000
Operating expenses	114,000
Net income	$ 30,000

Before You Go On . . .

1. Identify the three steps in determining cost of goods sold under a periodic inventory system.

2. What accounts are used in determining the cost of goods purchased?

3. How are cost of goods sold and gross profit computed?

Study Objective 5

Identify the unique features of the income statement for a merchandising company.

Income Statement for a Merchandising Company

The income statement for retailers and wholesalers contains three features not found in the income statement of a service enterprise. These features are: (1) a sales revenue section, (2) a cost of goods sold section, and (3) gross profit. Using assumed data for specific operating expenses, the income statement for Highpoint Electronic is shown in Illustration 5-11.

Accounting Cycle for a Merchandising Company

Study Objective 6

Explain the steps in the accounting cycle for a merchandising company.

Up to this point, we have been primarily concerned with measuring net income in a merchandising company. We have also illustrated the basic entries in recording transactions relating to sales and purchases. Now it is time to consider the remaining steps in the accounting cycle that were identified in Chapter 4.

Each of the required steps in the cycle applies to a merchandising company. Again, a work sheet is an optional step. To illustrate the steps in the cycle, we will assume that Highpoint Electronic uses a work sheet.

HIGHPOINT ELECTRONIC CO.
Income Statement
For the Year Ended December 31, 1993

ILLUSTRATION 5-11

Income statement for a merchandising company

Sales revenues				
Sales				$480,000
Less: Sales returns and allowances			$ 12,000	
Sales discounts			8,000	20,000
Net sales				460,000
Cost of goods sold				
Inventory, January 1			36,000	
Purchases		$325,000		
Less: Purchases returns and allowances	$10,400			
Purchase discounts	6,800	17,200		
Net purchases		307,800		
Add: Freight-in		12,200		
Cost of goods purchased			320,000	
Cost of goods available for sale			356,000	
Inventory, December 31			40,000	
Cost of goods sold				316,000
Gross profit				144,000
Operating expenses				
Store salaries expense			45,000	
Rent expense			19,000	
Utilities expense			17,000	
Advertising expense			16,000	
Depreciation expense—store equipment			8,000	
Freight-out			7,000	
Insurance expense			2,000	
Total operating expenses				114,000
Net income				$ 30,000

Helpful hints The far right column identifies the major subdivisions of the income statement. The next column identifies the primary items comprising cost of goods sold of $316,000 and operating expenses of $114,000; in addition, contra revenue items of $20,000 are reported. The third column explains cost of goods purchased of $320,000. The fourth column reports contra purchase items of $17,200.

Using a Work Sheet

As indicated in Chapter 4, a work sheet enables financial statements to be prepared before the adjusting entries are journalized and posted. The steps in preparing a work sheet for a merchandising company are the same as they are for a service enterprise (see page 133). The work sheet for Highpoint Electronic, shown in Illustration 5-12, contains all the income statement data explained above plus other data. The unique accounts for a merchandising company are shown in capital letters in red.

Trial Balance Columns

Data for the trial balance are obtained from the ledger balances of Highpoint Electronic at December 31. The amount shown for Merchandise Inventory, $36,000, is the beginning inventory.

Adjustments Columns

A merchandising company generally has the same types of adjustments as a service company. As you see in the work sheet, adjustments (a), (b), and (c) are for insurance, depreciation, and salaries. These adjustments were also required for Pioneer Advertising Agency, as illustrated in Chapters 3 and 4.

ILLUSTRATION 5-12

Work sheet for merchandising company

After all adjustment data are entered on the work sheet, the equality of the adjustment column totals is established. The balances in all accounts are then extended to the adjusted trial balance columns.[3]

HIGHPOINT ELECTRONIC CO.
Work Sheet
For the Year Ended December 31, 1993

	Trial Balance Dr.	Trial Balance Cr.	Adjustments Dr.	Adjustments Cr.	Adjusted Trial Balance Dr.	Adjusted Trial Balance Cr.	Income Statement Dr.	Income Statement Cr.	Balance Sheet Dr.	Balance Sheet Cr.
Cash	9,500				9,500				9,500	
Accounts Receivable	16,100				16,100				16,100	
MERCHANDISE INVENTORY	36,000				36,000		36,000	40,000	40,000	
Prepaid Insurance	3,800			(a) 2,000	1,800				1,800	
Store Equipment	80,000				80,000				80,000	
Accumulated Depreciation		16,000		(b) 8,000		24,000				24,000
Accounts Payable		20,400				20,400				20,400
R. A. Lamb, Capital		83,000				83,000				83,000
R. A. Lamb, Drawing	15,000				15,000				15,000	
SALES		480,000				480,000		480,000		
SALES RETURNS AND ALLOWANCES	12,000				12,000		12,000			
SALES DISCOUNTS	8,000				8,000		8,000			
PURCHASES	325,000				325,000		325,000			
PURCHASE RETURNS AND ALLOWANCES		10,400				10,400		10,400		
PURCHASE DISCOUNTS		6,800				6,800		6,800		
FREIGHT-IN	12,200				12,200		12,200			
Freight-out	7,000				7,000		7,000			
Advertising Expense	16,000				16,000		16,000			
Rent Expense	19,000				19,000		19,000			
Store Salaries Expense	40,000		(c) 5,000		45,000		45,000			
Utilities Expense	17,000				17,000		17,000			
Totals	616,600	616,600								
Insurance Expense			(a) 2,000		2,000		2,000			
Depreciation Expense			(b) 8,000		8,000		8,000			
Salaries Payable				(c) 5,000		5,000				5,000
Totals			15,000	15,000	629,600	629,600	507,200	537,200	162,400	132,400
Net Income							30,000			30,000
Totals							537,200	537,200	162,400	162,400

Adjusted Trial Balance

The adjusted trial balance shows the balance of all accounts after adjustment at the end of the accounting period. Note that beginning inventory was not adjusted. Therefore it is extended to the adjusted trial balance in the amount of $36,000.

---

[3]Conceptually, it can be argued that the change between the beginning and ending inventory balances should be shown on the work sheet as an adjustment. We have elected to consider the change in inventory to be part of the closing process. Both approaches are acceptable and accomplish the same objective. The adjusting entry approach is explained and illustrated in Appendix C at the end of the chapter.

Income Statement Columns

The accounts and balances that affect the income statement are transferred from the adjusted trial balance columns to the income statement columns. For Highpoint Electronic, regarding the merchandise accounts in the income statement columns, Sales of $480,000 is shown in the credit column whereas the contra revenue accounts, Sales Returns and Allowances of $12,000 and Sales Discounts of $8,000, are shown in the debit column. Thus, the difference of $460,000 is the net sales shown on the income statement. Similarly, Purchases of $325,000 and Freight-in of $12,200 are extended to the debit column. The contra purchase accounts, Purchase Returns and Allowances of $10,400 and Purchase Discounts of $6,800, are extended to the credit columns.

The work sheet procedures for the account Merchandise Inventory merit specific comment. The procedures are:

1. The beginning balance, $36,000, is extended from the adjusted trial balance column to the **income statement debit column**. From there it can be added in reporting cost of goods available for sale in the income statement.
2. The ending inventory, $40,000, is added to the work sheet by an **income statement credit and a balance sheet debit**. The credit makes it possible to deduct ending inventory from the cost of goods available for sale in the income statement to determine cost of goods sold. The debit means the ending inventory can be reported as an asset on the balance sheet.

These two procedures are specifically illustrated below:

	Income Statement		Balance Sheet	
	Dr.	Cr.	Dr.	Cr.
Merchandise Inventory	(1) 36,000	40,000 ◄——(2)——► 40,000		

ILLUSTRATION 5-13

Work sheet procedures for inventories

The computation for cost of goods sold, taken from the income statement columns in Illustration 5-12, is as follows:

Debit Column		Credit Column	
Beginning inventory	$ 36,000	Ending inventory	$40,000
Purchases	325,000	Purchase returns and allowances	10,400
Freight-in	12,200	Purchase discounts	6,800
Total debits	373,200	Total credits	$57,200
Less: Total credits	57,200		
Cost of goods sold	$316,000		

ILLUSTRATION 5-14

Computation of cost of goods sold from work sheet columns

Finally, all the credits in the income statement column should be totaled and compared to the total of all the debits in the income statement column. If the credits exceed the debits, then the company has net income. In Highpoint Electronic's case there was net income of $30,000. Conversely if the debits exceed the credits, the company would report a net loss.

Helpful hint In a periodic system, cost of goods sold is a computation—it is not a separate account with a balance.

Balance Sheet Columns

The major difference between the balance sheets of a service company and a merchandising company is inventory. For Highpoint Electronic, the ending inventory amount of $40,000 is shown in the balance sheet debit column. Note also that the information to prepare the owner's equity statement is also found in these columns. That is, the capital account of R. A. Lamb is $83,000. The drawings for R. A. Lamb are $15,000. Net income results when the total of the debit column exceeds the total of the credit column in the balance sheet columns of the work sheet. Conversely, a net loss results when the total of the credits exceeds the total of the debit balances.

Preparing Financial Statements

As is true in a service enterprise, financial statements for a merchandising company are prepared from the financial statement columns of the work sheet. The income statement for Highpoint Electronic has already been illustrated.

The owner's equity statement is as follows:

ILLUSTRATION 5-15

Owner's equity statement

HIGHPOINT ELECTRONIC CO. Owner's Equity Statement For the Year Ended December 31, 1993	
R. A. Lamb, Capital January 1	$ 83,000
Add: Net income	30,000
	113,000
Less: Drawings	15,000
R. A. Lamb, Capital December 31	$ 98,000

The classified balance sheet, then, is as follows:

ILLUSTRATION 5-16

Classified balance sheet

HIGHPOINT ELECTRONIC CO. Balance Sheet December 31, 1993		
Assets		
Current assets		
Cash		$ 9,500
Accounts receivable		16,100
Merchandise inventory		40,000
Prepaid insurance		1,800
Total current assets		67,400
Property, plant, and equipment		
Store equipment	$80,000	
Less: Accumulated depreciation—store equipment	24,000	56,000
Total assets		$123,400
Liabilities and Owner's Equity		
Current liabilities		
Accounts payable		$ 20,400
Salaries payable		5,000
Total current liabilities		25,400
Owner's equity		
R. A. Lamb, Capital		98,000
Total liabilities and owner's equity		$123,400

In the balance sheet, merchandise inventory is reported as a current asset immediately below accounts receivable. Recall that items are listed under current assets in the order of liquidity. Merchandise inventory is less liquid than accounts receivable because the goods must first be sold and then collection must be made from the customer.

The normal operating cycle for a merchandising company ordinarily is longer than it is for a service company. Graphically, the cycle can be depicted as shown in Illustration 5-17.

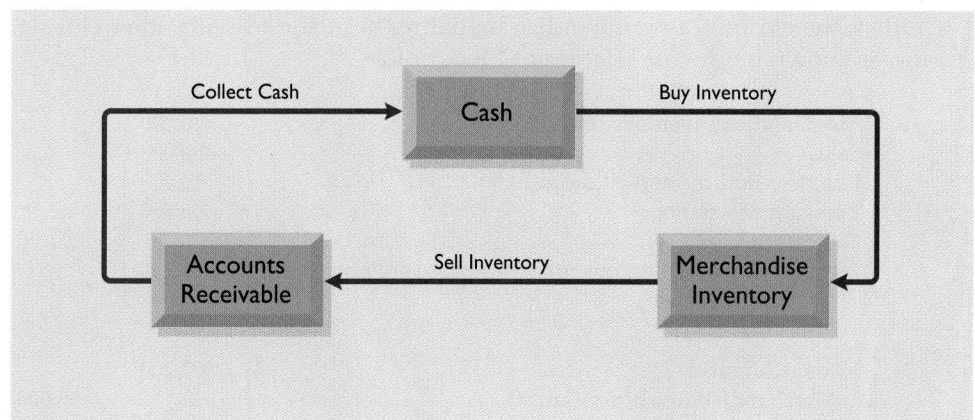

ILLUSTRATION 5-17

Operating cycle for a merchandising company

Journalizing and Posting Adjusting Entries

Adjusting entries are journalized from the adjustment columns of the work sheet. Because the journalizing and posting of the entries are the same as they are for a service enterprise, they are not illustrated here.

Journalizing and Posting Closing Entries

For a merchandising company, like a service enterprise, all accounts that affect the determination of net income are closed to Income Summary. Data for the preparation of closing entries may be obtained from the income statement columns of the work sheet. In journalizing, all debit column amounts are credited, and all credit column amounts are debited. To close the merchandise inventory:

1. The beginning inventory balance is debited to Income Summary and credited to Merchandise Inventory.
2. The ending inventory balance is debited to Merchandise Inventory and credited to Income Summary.

The two entries for Highpoint Electronic are:

			(1)			
Dec. 31	Income Summary				36,000	
	Merchandise Inventory					36,000
	(To close beginning inventory)					
			(2)			
31	Merchandise Inventory				40,000	
	Income Summary					40,000
	(To record ending inventory)					

After posting, the Merchandise Inventory and Income Summary accounts will show the following:

ILLUSTRATION 5-18

Posting closing entries for merchandise inventory

Merchandise Inventory		Income Summary	
1/1 Bal. 36,000	12/31 Close 36,000	12/31 Close 36,000	12/31 Close 40,000
12/31 Close 40,000			
12/31 Bal. 40,000			

Often, the closing of merchandise inventory is included with other closing entries, as shown below for Highpoint Electronic.

Helpful hint Except for merchandise inventory, the easiest way to prepare the first two closing entries is to identify the temporary accounts by their balances and then prepare one entry for the credits and one for the debits.

Helpful hint Close inventory with other accounts in homework problems unless stated otherwise.

Dec. 31	**Merchandise Inventory (Dec. 31)**	**40,000**	
	Sales	480,000	
	Purchase Returns and Allowances	10,400	
	Purchase Discounts	6,800	
	Income Summary		537,200
	(To record ending inventory and close accounts with		
	credit balances)		
31	Income Summary	507,200	
	Merchandise Inventory (Jan. 1)		**36,000**
	Sales Returns and Allowances		12,000
	Sales Discounts		8,000
	Purchases		325,000
	Freight-in		12,200
	Store Salaries Expense		45,000
	Rent Expense		19,000
	Freight-out		7,000
	Advertising Expense		16,000
	Utilities Expense		17,000
	Depreciation Expense		8,000
	Insurance Expense		2,000
	(To close beginning inventory and other income		
	statement accounts with debit balances)		
31	Income Summary	30,000	
	R. A. Lamb, Capital		30,000
	(To transfer net income to capital)		
31	R. A. Lamb, Capital	15,000	
	R. A. Lamb, Drawing		15,000
	(To close drawings to capital)		

After the closing entries are posted, all temporary accounts have zero balances. In addition, R. A. Lamb, Capital has a credit balance of $98,000: beginning balance + net income − drawings ($83,000 + $30,000 − $15,000).

Preparing the Post-Closing Trial Balance

After the closing entries are posted, the post-closing trial balance is prepared. The only new account in the post-closing trial balance is merchandise inventory. The post-closing trial balance for Highpoint Electronic at December 31, 1993, is shown in Illustration 5-19.

ILLUSTRATION 5-19

Post-closing trial balance

HIGHPOINT ELECTRONIC CO.
Post-Closing Trial Balance
December 31, 1993

	Debit	Credit
Cash	$ 9,500	
Accounts receivable	16,100	
Merchandise inventory	40,000	
Prepaid insurance	1,800	
Store equipment	80,000	
Accumulated depreciation		$ 24,000
Accounts payable		20,400
Salaries payable		5,000
R. A. Lamb, Capital		98,000
	$147,400	$147,400

Summary of Merchandising Entries

The entries for the merchandising accounts are summarized in Illustration 5-20.

ILLUSTRATION 5-20

Daily recurring and closing entries

Transactions	Daily Recurring Entries	Dr.	Cr.
Selling merchandise to customers	Cash or Accounts Receivable	XX	
	Sales		XX
Granting sales returns or allowances to customers	Sales Returns and Allowances	XX	
	Cash or Accounts Receivable		XX
Receiving payment from customers within discount period	Cash	XX	
	Sales Discounts	XX	
	Accounts Receivable		XX
Purchasing merchandise for resale	Purchases	XX	
	Cash or Accounts Payable		XX
Paying freight costs on merchandise purchased; FOB shipping point	Freight-in	XX	
	Cash		XX
Paying freight costs on sales; FOB destination	Freight-out	XX	
	Cash		XX
Receiving purchase returns or allowances from suppliers	Cash or Accounts Payable	XX	
	Purchase Returns and Allowances		XX
Paying suppliers within discount period	Accounts Payable	XX	
	Purchase Discounts		XX
	Cash		XX

Events	Closing Entries	Dr.	Cr.
Recording ending inventory and closing accounts with credit balances	Merchandise Inventory	XX	
	Sales	XX	
	Purchase Returns and Allowances	XX	
	Purchase Discounts	XX	
	Income Summary		XX
Closing beginning inventory and accounts with debit balances	Income Summary	XX	
	Merchandise Inventory		XX
	Sales Returns and Allowances		XX
	Sales Discounts		XX
	Purchases		XX
	Freight-in		XX
	Freight-out		XX

Multiple-Step Income Statement

The multiple-step income statement is so named because it shows the numerous steps in determining net income (or net loss). The Highpoint Electronic income statement in Illustration 5-11 is an example. It shows two steps: (1) cost of goods sold was subtracted from net sales, and (2) operating expenses were deducted from gross profit. These steps pertain to the company's principal operating activities. A multiple-step statement provides users with more information about a company's income performance by distinguishing between operating and nonoperating activities. The statement also highlights intermediate components of income and shows subgroupings of expenses.

Nonoperating Activities

Nonoperating activities consist of (1) revenues and expenses that result from secondary or auxiliary operations and (2) gains and losses that are unrelated to the company's operations. The results of nonoperating activities are shown in two sections: Other Revenues and Gains and Other Expenses and Losses. For a merchandising company, these sections will typically include the following items:

ILLUSTRATION 5-21

Items reported in nonoperating sections

Other Revenues and Gains	Other Expenses and Losses
Interest revenue from notes receivable and marketable securities	Interest expense on notes and loans payable
Dividend revenue from investments in capital stock	Casualty losses from recurring causes such as vandalism and accidents
Rent revenue from subleasing a portion of the store	Loss from the sale or abandonment of property, plant, and equipment
Gain from the sale of property, plant, and equipment	Loss from strikes by employees and suppliers

Accounting in Action · *Business Insight*

The distinction between operating and nonoperating activities is crucial to many security analysts. The reason is that operating income is viewed as sustainable and therefore long-term, and nonoperating is viewed as nonrecurring and therefore short-term. For example, it was reported that a large cinema chain in North America was selling some of its assets and counting the gains as part of operating income. As a result, operating losses were being offset by these gains. Because of unfavorable press reaction to this practice, the company revised its financial statements. By not counting its nonrecurring items as part of operating income, its first quarter operating income was changed from $24.9 million to a $22.6 million loss. Although the final net income won't change, hopefully investors will see that income is derived from selling assets rather than from selling movie tickets.

The nonoperating sections are reported in the income statement immediately after the sections that pertain to the company's primary operating activities. These sections are illustrated in Illustration 5-22 using assumed data for Highpoint Electronic.

ILLUSTRATION 5-22

Multiple-step income statement—nonoperating sections and subgrouping of operating expenses

HIGHPOINT ELECTRONIC CO.
Income Statement
For the Year Ended December 31, 1993

Sales revenues			
Sales			$480,000
Less: Sales returns and allowances		$ 12,000	
Sales discounts		8,000	20,000
Net sales			460,000
Cost of goods sold			
Inventory, January 1		36,000	
Purchases	$325,000		
Less: Purchase returns and allowances	$10,400		
Purchase discounts	6,800	17,200	
Net purchases	307,800		
Add: Freight-in	12,200		
Cost of goods purchased		320,000	
Cost of goods available for sale		356,000	
Inventory, December 31		40,000	
Cost of goods sold			316,000
Gross profit			144,000
Operating expenses			
Selling expenses			
Store salaries expense	45,000		
Advertising expense	16,000		
Depreciation expense—store equipment	8,000		
Freight-out	7,000		
Total selling expenses		76,000	
Administrative expenses			
Rent expense	19,000		
Utilities expense	17,000		
Insurance expense	2,000		
Total administrative expenses		38,000	
Total operating expenses			114,000
Income from operations			30,000
Other revenues and gains			
Interest revenue	3,000		
Gain on sale of equipment	600	3,600	
Other expenses and losses			
Interest expense	1,800		
Casualty loss from vandalism	200	2,000	1,600
Net income			$ 31,600

When the two nonoperating sections are included, the label **Income from operations** (or Operating income) precedes them. It clearly identifies the results of operations. Income from operations is determined by subtracting cost of goods sold and operating expenses from net sales. Observe also that the results of the two nonoperating sections are netted. The difference is added to or subtracted from income from operations to determine net income. Finally, within the nonoperating sections, items are generally reported at the net amount. Thus, if a

Helpful hint Operating income relates to the sale of primary goods in the ordinary course of business.

company received a $2,500 insurance settlement on vandalism losses of $2,700, the loss is reported at $200.

Subgrouping of Operating Expenses

In larger companies, operating expenses are often subdivided into selling expenses and administrative expenses, as illustrated in the income statement in Illustration 5-22. Selling expenses are those associated with making sales. They include sales promotional expenses as well as expenses of completing the sale, such as delivery and shipping expenses. Administrative expenses (sometimes called general expenses) relate to general operating activities such as personnel management, accounting, and store security.

When subgroupings are made, some expenses may have to be pro-rated, e.g., 70% to selling and 30% to administrative expenses. For example, if the store building is used for both selling and general functions, building expenses such as depreciation, utilities, and property taxes will need to be allocated.

Any reasonable classification of expenses that serves to inform those who use the statement is satisfactory. For example, the present tendency in statements prepared for management is to present in considerable detail expense data grouped along lines of responsibility.

Single-Step Income Statement

Another format for income statement presentation is the single-step income statement. The statement is so named because only one step, subtracting total expenses from total revenues, is required in determining net income (or net loss).

In a single-step statement, all data are classified under two categories: (1) **Revenues**, which includes both operating revenues and other revenues and gains, or (2) **Expenses**, which includes cost of goods sold, operating expenses, and other expenses and losses. A condensed single-step statement for Highpoint Electronic is illustrated in Illustration 5-23.

ILLUSTRATION 5-23

Single-step income statement

HIGHPOINT ELECTRONIC CO. Income Statement For the Year Ended December 31, 1993		
Revenues		
Net sales		$460,000
Interest revenue		3,000
Gain on sale of equipment		600
Total revenues		463,600
Expenses		
Cost of goods sold	$316,000	
Selling expenses	76,000	
Administrative expenses	38,000	
Interest expense	1,800	
Casualty loss from vandalism	200	
Total expenses		432,000
Net income		$ 31,600

There are two primary reasons for using the single-step form: (1) A company does not realize any type of profit or income until total revenues exceed total expenses, so it makes sense to divide the statement into these two categories.

(2) The form is simpler and easier to read than the multiple-step form. For homework problems, the single-step form of income statement should be used only when it is specifically requested.

Accounting in Action · *Business Insight*

Walgreen Co., Munsingwear, Inc., and Black and Decker are among many companies that use the multiple-step form of income statement. Companies that use the single-step include PepsiCo, General Electric, and Goodyear Tire & Rubber. The PepsiCo income statement is illustrated in the appendix at the end of this textbook. In a recent survey of 600 of the largest companies in the United States, 368 employed the multiple-step form and 232 employed the single-step income statement format.

Before You Go On . . .

1. What features are found in the income statement of a merchandising company that are not in the income statement of a service enterprise?

2. How is the beginning and ending merchandise inventory shown in a work sheet?

3. What are nonoperating activities and how are they reported in the income statement?

4. How does a single-step income statement differ from a multiple-step income statement?

Summary of Study Objectives

1. Identify the components in measuring net income in a merchandising company. The major components in measuring net income in a merchandising company are sales revenue, cost of goods sold, and operating expenses.

2. Explain the entries for sales revenues. In recording sales revenues, entries are required for (a) cash and credit sales, (b) sales returns and allowances, and (c) sales discounts.

3. State the steps in determining cost of goods sold. The steps in determining cost of goods sold are (a) recording the purchase of merchandise, (b) determining the cost of goods purchased, and (c) determining the cost of goods on hand at the beginning and end of the accounting period.

4. Explain the computation and importance of gross profit. Gross profit is computed by subtracting cost of goods sold from net sales. Gross profit represents the merchandising profit of a company, and the amount and trend of gross profit is closely watched by management and other interested parties.

5. Identify the unique features of the income statement for a merchandising company. The income statement for a merchandising company contains three sections: sales revenues, cost of goods sold, and operating expenses.

6. Explain the steps in the acounting cycle for a merchandising company. Each of the required steps in the accounting cycle for a service enterprise applies to a merchandising company. A work sheet is again an optional step.

7. Distinguish between a multiple-step and a single-step income statement. A multiple-step income statement shows numerous steps in determining net income including nonoperating sections. In a single-step income statement all data are classified under two categories, revenues or expenses, and net income is determined by one step.

APPENDIX C Adjusting Entry Method for Merchandise Inventory

Study Objective

After studying Appendix C you should be able to:

8. *Explain how the adjusting entry method is used in the work sheet.*

As stated in this chapter, the change between the beginning and ending inventory balances may be made through adjusting entries rather than through closing entries. Some favor this method because they believe that changes in merchandise inventory should receive the same accounting treatment as changes in the cost of supplies on hand between two points in time. The adjusting entry method is just as acceptable as the closing entry method, and it accomplishes the same objective.

The adjusting entry method affects several steps in the accounting cycle, beginning with the use of a work sheet. Again, these effects are explained and illustrated using Highpoint Electronic as an example.

Using a Work Sheet

In Illustration C-1, you will see a work sheet similar to the work sheet presented in the chapter (Illustration 5-12). The major difference in these two work sheets relates to merchandise inventory. In Illustration C-1, the accounting for merchandise inventory uses the adjusting entry method. In Illustration 5-12, the closing entry method was used. The unique accounts for the adjusting entry method are shown in capital letters in red.

Technology in Action

The adjusting entry method is used in most computerized systems since the programming logic involved is more straightforward. That is, in a computerized system, the command to close the books will close all the temporary accounts to Income Summary. However, if the inventory has not been adjusted, it will not be up-to-date and therefore a misstatement can occur. Some accountants favor the adjusting entry method in manual systems as well.

Trial Balance Columns

The trial balance columns are self-explanatory. The inventory before adjustment is the beginning inventory.

Adjustments Columns

In the adjustments columns of Illustration C-1, you will see two adjusting entries related to inventory. The objective of preparing adjusting entries for merchandise inventory is to adjust the asset balance to the cost of goods on hand at the balance sheet date. To accomplish this objective for merchandise inventory, two adjusting entries are made: (1) the beginning inventory amount is removed from merchandise inventory, and (2) the ending inventory amount is recorded in mer-

ILLUSTRATION C-1

Work sheet—adjusting inventory method

HIGHPOINT ELECTRONIC CO.
Work Sheet
For the Year Ended December 31, 1993

	Trial Balance Dr.	Trial Balance Cr.	Adjustments Dr.	Adjustments Cr.	Adjusted Trial Balance Dr.	Adjusted Trial Balance Cr.	Income Statement Dr.	Income Statement Cr.	Balance Sheet Dr.	Balance Sheet Cr.
Cash	9,500				9,500				9,500	
Accounts Receivable	16,100				16,100				16,100	
MERCHANDISE INVENTORY	36,000		(e) 40,000	(d) 36,000	40,000				40,000	
Prepaid Insurance	3,800			(a) 2,000	1,800				1,800	
Store Equipment	80,000				80,000				80,000	
Accumulated Depreciation		16,000		(b) 8,000		24,000				24,000
Accounts Payable		20,400				20,400				20,400
R. A. Lamb, Capital		83,000				83,000				83,000
R. A. Lamb, Drawing	15,000				15,000				15,000	
SALES		480,000				480,000		480,000		
SALES RETURNS AND ALLOWANCES	12,000				12,000		12,000			
SALES DISCOUNTS	8,000				8,000		8,000			
PURCHASES	325,000				325,000		325,000			
PURCHASE RETURNS AND ALLOWANCES		10,400				10,400		10,400		
PURCHASE DISCOUNTS		6,800				6,800		6,800		
FREIGHT-IN	12,200				12,200		12,200			
Freight-out	7,000				7,000		7,000			
Advertising Expense	16,000				16,000		16,000			
Rent Expense	19,000				19,000		19,000			
Store Salaries Expense	40,000		(c) 5,000		45,000		45,000			
Utilities Expense	17,000				17,000		17,000			
Totals	616,600	616,600								
Insurance Expense			(a) 2,000		2,000		2,000			
Depreciation Expense			(b) 8,000		8,000		8,000			
Salaries Payable				(c) 5,000		5,000				5,000
INCOME SUMMARY			(d) 36,000	(e) 40,000	36,000	40,000	36,000	40,000		
Totals			91,000	91,000	669,600	669,600	507,200	537,200	162,400	132,400
Net Income							30,000			30,000
Totals							537,200	537,200	162,400	162,400

chandise inventory. The entries, using the inventory data for Highpoint Electronic, are as follows:

Dec. 31	Income Summary	36,000	
	Merchandise Inventory		36,000
	(To remove beginning inventory)		
31	Merchandise Inventory	40,000	
	Income Summary		40,000
	(To record ending inventory)		

These entries are identified as adjustments (d) and (e), respectively, in the work sheet.

These entries should be familiar to you. They are exactly the same as the closing entries illustrated on page 197. The only difference is that changes in inventory are reported in the adjustments columns when the adjusting entry approach is used.

After posting, the accounts will show:

ILLUSTRATION C-2

Posting of adjustments for merchandise inventory

Merchandise Inventory		Income Summary	
Jan. 1 Bal. 36,000	Dec. 31 Adj. 36,000	Dec. 31 Adj. 36,000	Dec. 31 Adj. 40,000
Dec. 31 Adj. 40,000			
Dec. 31 Bal. 40,000			

Adjusted Trial Balance Columns

In Illustration C-1, the merchandise inventory amount is extended to the adjusted trial balance debit column. **This amount is the ending inventory for the period.** Both amounts reported in Income Summary are transferred to the adjusted trial balance columns to ensure that these two amounts are reported in the income statement columns. Therefore the net amount, in this case, $4,000 ($40,000 − $36,000), is not reported.

Financial Statement Columns

Complete financial statements are prepared directly from the income statement and balance sheet columns of the work sheet. The use of the financial statement columns should be familiar to you. One difficult subject is the treatment of merchandise inventory and income summary adjustments. A partial work sheet showing just these two items is presented below:

ILLUSTRATION C-3

Partial work sheet

	Trial Balance		Adjustments		Adjusted Trial Balance		Income Statement		Balance Sheet	
	Dr.	Cr.	Dr.	Cr.	Dr.	Cr.	Dr.	Cr.	Dr.	Cr.
Merchandise Inventory	36,000		(e) 40,000	(d) 36,000	40,000				40,000	
Income Summary			(d) 36,000	(e) 40,000	36,000	40,000	36,000	40,000		

In the merchandise inventory line, the $40,000 in the balance sheet debit column is the ending inventory. In the income summary line, the debit in the income statement column indicates the cost of the beginning inventory, and the credit in the income statement column shows the cost of the ending inventory. Complete financial statements are then prepared directly from the income statement and balance sheet columns of the work sheet.

Journalizing and Posting Closing Entries

When the adjusting entry method is followed, merchandise inventory is not part of the closing process. As a result, entries to close the books are as follows:

Dec. 31	Sales	480,000	
	Purchase Returns and Allowances	10,400	
	Purchase Discounts	6,800	
	Income Summary		497,200
	(To close income statement accounts with credit balances)		
31	Income Summary	471,200	
	Sales Returns and Allowances		12,000
	Sales Discounts		8,000
	Purchases		325,000
	Freight-in		12,200
	Store Salaries Expense		45,000
	Rent Expense		19,000
	Freight-out		7,000
	Advertising Expense		16,000
	Utilities Expense		17,000
	Depreciation Expense		8,000
	Insurance Expense		2,000
	(To close income statement accounts with debit balances)		

These entries produce a credit balance in the Income Summary account of $30,000. This amount equals the net income reported for Highpoint Electronic using the closing method. The postings to Income Summary are as follows:

ILLUSTRATION C-4

Postings to Income Summary

```
                       Income Summary
Dec. 31  Adj.       36,000 │ Dec. 31  Adj.       40,000
     31  Close     471,200 │      31  Close     497,200
     31  to Cap.    30,000 │
                   ─────── │                    ───────
                   537,200 │                    537,200
```

Both the closing entry method and the adjusting entry method result in the same accounts and amounts reported in the financial statements. It is a matter of personal preference which method is used.

Summary of Study Objectives for Appendix C

8. *Explain how the adjusting entry method is used in the work sheet.* Under the adjusting entry method, the two adjustments for inventories are entered in the adjustments columns of the work sheet. The balance in Merchandise Inventory is extended to the adjusted trial balance and balance sheet debit columns. The adjustments to Income Summary are extended to the adjusted trial balance and income statement columns. The adjusting entry method is just as acceptable as the closing entry method, and it accomplishes the same objective.

GLOSSARY

Administrative expenses · Expenses relating to general operating activities such as personnel management, accounting, and store security. (p. 202).

Cost of goods available for sale · The sum of the beginning merchandise inventory plus the cost of goods purchased. (p. 191).

Cost of goods purchased · The sum of net purchases plus freight-in. (p. 189).

Cost of goods sold · The total cost of merchandise sold during the period, determined by subtracting ending inventory from the cost of goods available for sale. (p. 180).

Credit memorandum · A document issued by a seller to inform a customer that a credit has been made to the customer's account receivable for a sales return or allowance. (p. 183).

Debit memorandum · A document issued by a buyer to inform a seller that a debit has been made to the seller's account because of unsatisfactory merchandise. (p. 186).

FOB destination · Freight terms indicating that the goods will be placed free on board at the buyer's place of business, and the seller pays the freight costs. (p. 188).

FOB shipping point · Freight terms indicating that goods are placed free on board the carrier by the seller, and the buyer pays the freight costs. (p. 188).

Gross profit · The excess of net sales over the cost of goods sold. (p. 180).

Income from operations · Income from a company's principal operating activity determined by subtracting cost of goods sold and operating expenses from net sales. (p. 201).

Multiple-step income statement · An income statement that shows numerous steps in determining net income (or net loss), including operating and nonoperating sections. (p. 200).

Net purchases · Purchases less purchase returns and allowances and purchase discounts. (p. 189).

Net sales · Sales less sales returns and allowances and sales discounts. (p. 185).

Operating expenses · Expenses incurred in the process of earning sales revenues that are deducted from gross profit in the income statement. (p. 180).

Other expenses and losses · A nonoperating section of the income statement that shows expenses from auxiliary operations and losses unrelated to the company's operations. (p. 200).

Other revenues and gains · A nonoperating section of the income statement that shows revenues from auxiliary operations and gains unrelated to the company's operations. (p. 200).

Periodic inventory system · An inventory system in which detailed records are not maintained and the cost of goods sold is determined only at the end of an accounting period. (p. 186).

Perpetual inventory system · A detailed inventory system in which the cost of each inventory item is maintained and the records continuously show the inventory that should be on hand. (p. 185).

Purchase discount · A cash discount claimed by a buyer for prompt payment of a balance due. (p. 187).

Purchase invoice · A document that supports each credit purchase. (p. 186).

Sales discount · A reduction given by a seller for prompt payment of a credit sale. (p. 184).

Sales invoice · A document that provides support for credit sales. (p. 181).

Sales revenue · Primary source of revenue in a merchandising company. (p. 180).

Selling expenses · Expenses associated with the making of sales. (p. 202).

Single-step income statement · An income statement that shows only one step in determining net income (or net loss). (p. 202).

DEMONSTRATION PROBLEM

The adjusted trial balance columns of the work sheet for the year ended December 31, 1993, for the Dykstra Company are as follows:

Debit		**Credit**	
Cash	$ 14,500	Accumulated Depreciation	$ 18,000
Accounts Receivable	11,100	Notes Payable	25,000
Merchandise Inventory	32,000	Accounts Payable	10,600
Prepaid Insurance	2,500	Gene Dykstra, Capital	81,000
Store Equipment	95,000	Sales	520,000

Gene Dykstra, Drawing	12,000	Purchase Returns and Allowances	9,600
Sales Returns and Allowances	6,700	Purchase Discounts	7,200
Sales Discounts	5,000	Interest Revenue	2,500
Purchases	352,000		$673,900
Freight-in	8,400		
Freight-out	7,600		
Advertising Expense	12,000		
Store Salaries Expense	56,000		
Utilities Expense	18,000		
Rent Expense	24,000		
Depreciation Expense	9,000		
Insurance Expense	4,500		
Interest Expense	3,600		
	$673,900		

Instructions

(a) Enter the adjusted trial balance data on a work sheet. Complete the work sheet assuming that ending merchandise inventory is $29,000.

(b) Prepare an income statement assuming the Dykstra Company does not use subgroupings for operating expenses.

Solution to Demonstration Problem

(a)

DYKSTRA COMPANY
Work Sheet
For the Year Ended December 31, 1993

Account Titles	Adjusted Trial Balance Dr.	Adjusted Trial Balance Cr.	Income Statement Dr.	Income Statement Cr.	Balance Sheet Dr.	Balance Sheet Cr.
Cash	14,500				14,500	
Accounts Receivable	11,100				11,100	
Merchandise Inventory	32,000		32,000	29,000	29,000	
Prepaid Insurance	2,500				2,500	
Store Equipment	95,000				95,000	
Accumulated Depreciation		18,000				18,000
Notes Payable		25,000				25,000
Accounts Payable		10,600				10,600
Gene Dykstra, Capital		81,000				81,000
Gene Dykstra, Drawing	12,000				12,000	
Sales		520,000		520,000		
Sales Returns and Allowances	6,700		6,700			
Sales Discounts	5,000		5,000			
Purchases	352,000		352,000			
Purchase Returns and Allowances		9,600		9,600		
Purchase Discounts		7,200		7,200		
Freight-in	8,400		8,400			
Freight-out	7,600		7,600			
Advertising Expense	12,000		12,000			
Store Salaries Expense	56,000		56,000			
Utilities Expense	18,000		18,000			
Rent Expense	24,000		24,000			
Depreciation Expense	9,000		9,000			
Insurance Expense	4,500		4,500			
Interest Expense	3,600		3,600			
Interest Revenue		2,500		2,500		
Totals	673,900	673,900	538,800	568,300	164,100	134,600
Net Income			29,500			29,500
Totals			568,300	568,300	164,100	164,100

Helpful hint

1. Make sure in the adjusted trial balance that debits and credits are equal before transferring amounts to the income statement and balance sheet columns.
2. Transfer all amounts in the adjusted trial balance to either the income statement or balance sheet columns.
3. The merchandise inventory reported in the adjusted trial balance is the beginning inventory.
4. Record the ending inventory by debiting the balance sheet column and crediting the income statement column.
5. The net income or net loss is the reconciling item in both the income statement and the balance sheet columns.

Helpful hint
1. In preparing the income statement, remember that the key components are net sales, cost of goods sold, gross profit, total operating expenses, and net income (loss). These components are reported in the right-hand column of the income statement.
2. The most difficult computation is cost of goods sold. Think of beginning inventory + cost of goods purchased − ending inventory = cost of goods sold.
3. Nonoperating items follow income from operations.

(b)

DYKSTRA COMPANY
Income Statement
For the Year Ended December 31, 1993

Sales revenues			
Sales			$520,000
Less: Sales returns and allowances		$ 6,700	
Sales discounts		5,000	11,700
Net sales			508,300
Cost of goods sold			
Inventory, January 1		32,000	
Purchases	$352,000		
Less: Purchase returns and allowances	$9,600		
Purchase discounts	7,200	16,800	
Net purchases		335,200	
Add: Freight-in		8,400	
Cost of goods purchased		343,600	
Cost of goods available for sale		375,600	
Inventory, December 31		29,000	
Cost of goods sold			346,600
Gross profit			161,700
Operating expenses			
Store salaries expense		56,000	
Rent expense		24,000	
Utilities expense		18,000	
Advertising expense		12,000	
Depreciation expense		9,000	
Freight-out		7,600	
Insurance expense		4,500	
Total operating expenses			131,100
Income from operations			30,600
Other revenues and gains			
Interest revenue		2,500	
Other expenses and losses			
Interest expense		3,600	1,100
Net income			$ 29,500

*Note: All **asterisked** Questions, Exercises, and Problems relate to material contained in the Appendix to this chapter.

SELF-STUDY QUESTIONS

Answers are at the end of the chapter.

(S.O. 1) 1. Gross profit will result if:
   a. operating expenses are less than net income.
   b. sales revenues are greater than operating expenses.
   c. operating expenses are greater than cost of goods sold.
   d. sales revenues are greater than cost of goods sold.

(S.O. 2) 2. The sales accounts that normally have a debit balance are:
   a. sales.
   b. sales returns and allowances.
   c. sales discounts.
   d. both (b) and (c).

3. A credit sale of $850 is made on June 13, terms 2/10, net/30, on which a return of $50 is granted on June 16. The amount received as payment in full on June 23 is: (S.O. 2)
   a. $833.
   b. $800.
   c. $784.
   d. $850.

4. When goods are purchased for resale by a company: (S.O. 3)
   a. purchases on account are debited to Merchandise Inventory.

b. purchases on account are debited to a Cost of Goods Sold.

c. purchase returns are credited to a Purchase Returns and Allowances account.

d. freight costs are debited to Purchases.

(S.O. 3) 5. In determining cost of goods sold:
   a. freight-in is added to net purchases.
   b. freight-out is added to net purchases.
   c. purchase returns and allowances are deducted from net purchases.
   d. purchase discounts are deducted from net purchases.

(S.O. 3) 6. If beginning inventory is $40,000, cost of goods purchased is $380,000, and ending inventory is $50,000, cost of goods sold is:
   a. $390,000.
   b. $370,000.
   c. $330,000.
   d. $420,000.

(S.O. 4) 7. If sales revenues are $400,000, cost of goods sold is $250,000, and operating expenses are $60,000, the gross profit is:
   a. $90,000.
   b. $150,000.
   c. $340,000.
   d. $400,000.

(S.O. 5) 8. The income statement for a merchandising company shows each of the following features *except*:
   a. gross profit.
   b. cost of goods sold.

c. operating income section.
d. a sales revenue section.

(S.O. 6) 9. In a work sheet, ending merchandise inventory is shown in the following columns (assuming the closing entry method is used):
   a. Adjusted trial balance credit and balance sheet debit.
   b. Income statement debit and balance sheet debit.
   c. Income statement credit and adjusted trial balance debit.
   d. Income statement credit and balance sheet debit.

(S.O. 7) 10. In a single-step income statement:
   a. gross profit is reported.
   b. sales revenues and other revenues and gains are reported in the revenues section of the income statement.
   c. cost of goods sold is not reported.
   d. operating income is separately reported.

(S.O. 8) *11. In using the adjusting entry method to prepare a work sheet:
   a. financial statements can be prepared only after closing entries are made.
   b. changes in merchandise inventory are made in the adjustments columns of the work sheet.
   c. ending inventory appears only in the balance sheet debit column.
   d. beginning inventory is not reported on the trial balance before adjustment.

QUESTIONS

1. How does income measurement differ between a merchandising company and a service company?

2. Cisco Systems has sales revenue of $100,000, cost of goods sold of $60,000, and operating expenses of $20,000. What is its gross profit?

3. Joan Collins believes revenues from credit sales may be earned before they are collected in cash. Do you agree? Explain.

4. (a) What is the primary source document for recording (1) cash sales, (2) credit sales, and (3) sales returns and allowances? (b) Using XXs for amounts, give the journal entry for each of the transactions in part (a).

5. A credit sale is made on July 10 for $700, terms 2/10, n/30. On July 12, $50 of goods are returned for credit. Give the journal entry on July 19 to record the receipt of the balance due within the discount period.

6. Identify the accounts that are added to or deducted from purchases to determine the cost of goods purchased. For each account, indicate (a) whether it is added or deducted and (b) its normal balance.

7. Goods costing $1,500 are purchased on account on July 15 with credit terms of 2/10, n/30. On July 18, a $100 credit memo is received from the supplier for damaged goods. Give the journal entry on July 24 to record payment of the balance due within the discount period.

8. Distinguish between FOB shipping point and FOB destination. Identify the freight terms that will result in a debit to Freight-in by the purchaser and a debit to Freight-out by the seller.

9. In the following separate mini cases, identify the item(s) designated by letter.
(a) Purchases − X − Y = Net purchases.
(b) Cost of goods purchased − Net purchases = X.
(c) Beginning inventory + X = Cost of goods available for sale.
(d) Cost of goods available for sale − Cost of goods sold = X.
(e) Cost of goods sold + Gross profit = X.

10. The Coventry Company reports net sales $800,000, gross profit of $560,000, and net income of $300,000. What are its operating expenses?

11. Identify the distinguishing features of an income statement for a merchandising company.

12. "The accounting cycle for a merchandising company is the same as for a service company." Do you agree? Why or why not?

13. Indicate the columns of the work sheet in which (a) the beginning merchandise inventory, and (b) the ending merchandise inventory will be shown.

14. Why is the normal operating cycle for a merchandising company likely to be longer than for a service company?

15. Prepare the closing entries for the merchandise inventory account, assuming a beginning inventory of $54,000 and an ending inventory of $57,000.

16. What merchandising account, or accounts, will appear in the post-closing trial balance?

17. Identify the sections of a multiple-step income statement that relate to (a) operating activities, and (b) nonoperating activities.

18. Distinguish between the types of functional groupings of operating expenses. What problem is created by these groupings?

19. How does the single-step form of income statement differ from the multiple-step form?

*****20.** Beginning inventory is $72,000 and ending inventory is $79,000. Assuming a work sheet is used with adjusting entries for merchandise inventory:
(a) What amount will appear in the balance sheet debit column for merchandise inventory?
(b) What amounts will appear in the adjustments debit and credit columns for Income Summary?

BRIEF EXERCISES

Compute missing amounts in determining net income.
(S.O. 1)

BE5–1 Presented below are the components in C. Sheen Company's income statement. Determine the missing amounts.

	Sales	Cost of Goods Sold	Gross Profit	Operating Expenses	Net Income
(a)	$75,000	?	$43,500	?	$10,800
(b)	$108,000	$63,000	?	?	29,500
(c)	?	$71,900	$109,600	$39,500	?

Journalize sales transactions.
(S.O. 2)

BE5–2 Prepare the journal entries to record the following transactions on H. Hunter Company's books.

(a) On March 2, H. Hunter Company sold $700,000 of merchandise to B. Streisand Company, terms 2/10, n/30.

(b) On March 6, B. Streisand Company returned $130,000 of the merchandise purchased on March 2 because it was defective.

(c) On March 12, H. Hunter Company received the balance due from B. Streisand Company.

BE5–3 From the information in BE5–2, prepare the journal entries to record these transactions on B. Streisand Company's books.

Journalize purchases transactions.
(S.O. 3)

BE5–4 B. Hope Company provides the following information for the month ended October 31, 1993: Sales on credit $300,000, Cash sales $100,000, Sales discounts $5,000, Sales returns and allowances $25,000. Prepare the sales revenues section of the income statement based on this information.

Prepare sales revenue section of income statement.
(S.O. 2)

BE5–5 Assume that K. Bassinger Company has the following account balances: Purchases $400,000, Purchase Returns and Allowances $11,000, Purchase Discounts $8,000, and Freight-in $17,000. Determine (a) net purchases and (b) cost of goods purchased.

Compute net purchases and cost of goods purchased.
(S.O. 3)

BE5–6 Assume the same information as in BE5–5, and also that K. Bassinger Company has beginning inventory of $60,000, ending inventory of $90,000, and net sales of $630,000. Determine the amounts to be reported for cost of goods sold and gross profit.

Compute cost of goods sold and gross profit.
(S.O. 3, 4)

BE5–7 Presented below is the format of the work sheet presented in the chapter.

Identify work sheet columns for selecting accounts.
(S.O. 6)

Trial Balance		Adjustments		Adjusted Trial Balance		Income Statement		Balance Sheet	
Dr.	Cr.	Dr.	Cr.	Dr.	Cr.	Dr.	Cr.	Dr.	Cr.

Indicate where the following items will appear on the work sheet (a) cash, (b) beginning inventory, (c) accounts payable, (d) ending inventory.

Example

 Cash: Trial balance debit column; Adjusted trial balance debit column; and Balance sheet debit column.

Adjusting entry method.
(S.O. 8)

*BE5–8 Using the information from BE5–7, indicate how these items are presented on the work sheet if the adjusting entry method illustrated in Appendix C is used.

BE5–9 A. Hall Company has the following merchandise account balances: Sales $180,000, Sales Discounts $2,000, Purchases $120,000, Purchase Returns and Allowances $30,000. In addition, it has a beginning inventory of $40,000 and an ending inventory of $30,000. Prepare the entries to record the closing of these items to Income Summary.

Prepare closing entries for merchandise accounts.
(S.O. 6)

BE5–10 Explain where each of the following items would appear on (1) a multiple-step income statement and on (2) a single-step income statement: (a) gain on sale of equipment, (b) casualty loss from vandalism, and (c) cost of goods sold.

Contrast presentation in multiple-step and single-step income statements.
(S.O. 7)

EXERCISES

E5–1 Presented below are the following transactions related to C. Eastwood Company.

Journalize sales transactions.
(S.O. 2)

1. On December 3, C. Eastwood Company sold $400,000 of merchandise to R. Gere Co., terms 2/10, n/30, FOB shipping point.
2. On December 8, R. Gere Co. was granted an allowance of $60,000 for merchandise purchased on December 3.
3. On December 13, C. Eastwood Company received the balance due from R. Gere Co.

Instructions

(a) Prepare the journal entries to record these transactions on the books of C. Eastwood Company.

(b) Assume that C. Eastwood Company received the balance due from R. Gere Co. on January 2 of the following year instead of December 13. Prepare the journal entry to record the receipt of payment on January 2.

Journalize purchases transactions.

(S.O. 3)

E5–2   Presented below is the following information related to N. Nolte Co.

1. On April 5, purchased merchandise from D. DeVito Company for $18,000 terms 2/10, net/30, FOB shipping point.
2. On April 6 paid freight costs of $100 on merchandise purchased from D. DeVito.
3. On April 7, purchased equipment on account for $26,000.
4. On April 8, returned damaged merchandise to D. DeVito Company and was granted a $3,000 allowance.
5. On April 15 paid the amount due to D. DeVito Company in full.

Instructions

(a) Prepare the journal entries to record these transactions on the books of N. Nolte Co.

(b) Assume that N. Nolte Co. paid the balance due to D. DeVito Company on May 4 instead of April 15. Prepare the journal entry to record this payment.

Prepare sales revenues section and closing entries.

(S.O. 2, 5, 6)

E5–3   The adjusted trial balance of the S. Connery Company shows the following data pertaining to sales at the end of its fiscal year October 31: Sales $900,000, Freight-out $12,000, Sales Returns and Allowances $24,000, and Sales Discounts $13,000.

Instructions

(a) Prepare the sales revenues section of the income statement.

(b) Prepare separate closing entries for (1) sales, and (2) the contra accounts to sales.

Prepare purchase entries and closing entries.

(S.O. 3, 6)

E5–4   On June 10, L. Dern Company purchased $5,000 of merchandise from the R. Duvall Company FOB shipping point, terms 2/10, n/30. L. Dern pays the freight costs of $200 on June 11. Damaged goods totaling $300 are returned to R. Duvall for credit on June 12. On June 19, L. Dern pays R. Duvall Company in full, less the purchase discount.

Instructions

(a) Prepare separate entries for each transaction.

(b) Prepare separate closing entries on June 30 for the temporary accounts with (1) debit balances, and (2) credit balances.

Prepare cost of goods sold section and closing entries.

(S.O. 3, 6)

E5–5   The trial balance of the R. Williams Company at the end of its fiscal year, August 31, 1995 includes the following accounts: Merchandise Inventory $17,200, Purchases $142,400, Sales $190,000, Freight-in $4,000, Sales Returns and Allowances $3,000, Freight-out $1,000, and Purchase Returns and Allowances $2,000. The ending merchandise inventory is $28,000.

Instructions

(a) Prepare a cost of goods sold section for the year ending August 31.

(b) Prepare the closing entries for all accounts.

(c) Post the closing entries to Merchandise Inventory.

Prepare an income statement.

(S.O. 6)

E5–6   Presented is information related to K. Douglas Co. for the month of January 1993.

Freight-in	$10,000	Rent expense	20,000
Freight-out	7,000	Salary expense	61,000
Insurance expense	12,000	Sales discounts	8,000
Purchases	200,000	Sales returns and allowances	13,000
Purchase discounts	3,000	Sales revenues	312,000
Purchase returns and allowances	6,000		

Beginning merchandise inventory was $42,000 and ending inventory was $60,000.

Instructions

Prepare an income statement using the format presented on page 193. Operating expenses should not be segregated into selling and administrative expenses.

Compute missing amounts in determining gross profit.

(S.O. 3, 4)

E5–7   Financial information is presented below for three different companies.

	Tate's Cosmetics	Lowe Grocery	Costner Wholesalers
Sales	$90,000	(c)	$144,000
Sales returns	(a)	$ 6,000	12,000
Net sales	74,000	94,000	132,000
Beginning inventory	14,000	(d)	44,000
Purchases	88,000	100,000	(e)
Purchase returns	6,000	10,000	8,000
Ending inventory	(b)	50,000	30,000
Cost of goods sold	64,000	72,000	(f)
Gross profit	10,000	22,000	20,000

Instructions

Determine the missing amounts. Show all computations.

E5–8 Presented below are selected accounts for B. Midler Company as reported in the work sheet at the end of May 1993. Ending merchandise inventory is $75,000.

Complete work sheet and identify accounts for post-closing trial balance. (S.O. 6)

Accounts	Adjusted Trial Balance		Income Statement		Balance Sheet	
	Dr.	Cr.	Dr.	Cr.	Dr.	Cr.
Cash	9,000					
Merchandise Inventory	80,000					
Purchases	240,000					
Purchase Returns and Allowances		30,000				
Sales		450,000				
Sales Returns and Allowances	10,000					
Sales Discounts	5,000					
Rent Expense	42,000					

Instructions

(a) Complete the work sheet by extending amounts reported in the adjusted trial balance to the appropriate columns in the work sheet. The closing entry method is used to account for merchandise inventory. Do not total individual columns.

(b) Identify the merchandising account(s) that will appear in the post-closing trial balance.

E5–9 In its income statement for the year ended December 31, 1993, C. Crawford Company reported the following condensed data.

Prepare multiple-step and single-step income statements. (S.O. 7)

Administrative expenses	$435,000	Selling expenses	$ 690,000
Cost of goods sold	989,000	Loss on sale of equipment	10,000
Interest expense	70,000	Net sales	2,359,000
Interest revenue	46,000		

Instructions

(a) Prepare a multiple-step income statement.

(b) Prepare a single-step income statement.

E5–10 An inexperienced accountant for the G. Davis Company made the following errors in recording merchandising transactions.

Prepare correcting entries for sales and purchases. (S.O. 2, 3)

1. A $150 refund to a customer for faulty merchandise was debited to Sales $150 and credited to Cash $150.
2. A $250 credit purchase of supplies was debited to Purchases $250 and credited to Cash $250.
3. An $80 sales discount was debited to Purchase Discounts.
4. A $50 purchase return was recorded as a debit to Accounts Payable $50 and a credit to Purchase Discounts $50.

5. A cash payment of $30 for freight on merchandise purchases was debited to Purchases $300 and credited to Cash $300.

Instructions

Prepare separate correcting entries for each error, assuming that the incorrect entry is not reversed. (Omit explanations.)

Identify work sheet columns using adjusting entry method.

(S.O. 8)

*E5–11   The J. Candy Company prepares adjusting entries for merchandise inventory at the end of the accounting period. On January 1, the balance in Merchandise Inventory is $27,500 and the inventory on hand at December 31 is $34,700.

Instructions

(a) Determine the amounts and the work sheet columns in which merchandise inventory will appear.

(b) Journalize the adjusting entries for merchandise inventory at December 31.

PROBLEMS

Journalize, post, and prepare partial income statement.

(S.O. 2, 3, 4, 5)

P5–1   The Dorn Hardware Store completed the following merchandising transactions in the month of May. At the beginning of May, the ledger of Dorn showed Cash of $5,000 and S. Dorn, Capital of $5,000.

May 1   Purchased merchandise on account from Depot Wholesale Supply $5,000, terms 2/10, n/30.
2   Sold merchandise on account $4,000, terms 2/10, n/30.
5   Received credit from Depot Wholesale Supply for merchandise returned $200.
9   Received collections in full, less discounts, from customers billed on sales of $4,000 on May 2.
10   Paid Depot Wholesale Supply in full, less discount.
11   Purchased supplies for cash $900.
12   Purchased merchandise for cash $2,400.
15   Received refund for poor quality merchandise from supplier on cash purchase $230.
17   Purchased merchandise from Harlow Distributors $1,900, FOB shipping point, terms 2/10, n/30.
19   Paid freight on May 17 purchase $250.
24   Sold merchandise for cash $6,200.
25   Purchased merchandise from Horicon Inc. $1,000, FOB destination, terms 2/10, n/30.
27   Paid Harlow Distributors in full, less discount.
29   Made refunds to cash customers for defective merchandise $80.
31   Sold merchandise on account $1,600, terms n/30.

Dorn Hardware's chart of accounts includes the following: No. 101 Cash, No. 112 Accounts Receivable, No. 120 Merchandise Inventory, No. 126 Supplies, No. 201 Accounts Payable, No. 301 S. Dorn, Capital, No. 401 Sales, No. 412 Sales Returns and Allowances, No. 414 Sales Discounts, No. 510 Purchases, No. 512 Purchase Returns and Allowances, No. 514 Purchase Discounts, No. 516 Freight-in.

Instructions

(a) Journalize the transactions.

(b) Enter the beginning cash and capital balances and post the transactions. (Use J1 for the journal reference.)

(c) Prepare an income statement through gross profit for the month of May 1993, asssuming ending inventory is $2,400, and no beginning inventory.

Journalize, post, and prepare trial balance and partial income statement.

(S.O. 2, 3, 4, 5)

P5–2   John Clark, a former professional golf star, operates the pro shop at the Pelican Bay Golf Course. At the beginning of the current season on April 1, the ledger of Clark's Pro Shop showed Cash $2,500, Merchandise Inventory $3,500, and J. Clark, Capital $6,000. The following transactions were completed during April.

Apr. 5 Purchased golf bags, clubs, and balls on account from Balata Co. $1,600, FOB shipping point, terms 2/10, n/60.

    7 Paid freight on Balata purchase $80.

    9 Received credit from Balata Co. for merchandise returned $100.

   10 Sold merchandise on account to members $900, terms n/30.

   12 Purchased golf shoes, sweaters, and other accessories on account from Arrow Sportswear $660, terms 1/10, n/30.

   14 Paid Balata Co. in full.

   17 Received credit from Arrow Sportswear for merchandise returned $60.

   20 Made sales on account to members $700, terms n/30.

   21 Paid Arrow Sportswear in full.

   27 Granted credit to members for clothing that did not fit $30.

   30 Made cash sales $600.

   30 Received payments on account from members $1,100.

The chart of accounts for the pro shop includes the following: No. 101 Cash, No. 112 Accounts Receivable, No. 120 Merchandise Inventory, No. 201 Accounts Payable, No. 301 J. Clark, Capital, No. 401 Sales, No. 412 Sales Returns and Allowances, No. 510 Purchases, No. 512 Purchase Returns and Allowances, No. 514 Purchase Discounts, No. 516 Freight-in.

Instructions

(a) Journalize the April transactions.

(b) Enter the beginning balances in the ledger accounts and post the April transactions. (Use J1 for the journal reference.)

(c) Prepare a trial balance on April 30, 1993.

(d) Prepare an income statement through gross profit, assuming merchandise inventory on hand at April 30 is $4,000.

P5–3 The trial balance of the Parton Wholesale Company contained the following accounts at December 31, the end of the company's fiscal year.

Complete accounting cycle beginning with a work sheet.
(S.O. 5, 6, 7)

PARTON WHOLESALE COMPANY
Trial Balance
December 31, 1993

	Debit	Credit
Cash	$ 34,400	
Accounts Receivable	36,600	
Merchandise Inventory	62,400	
Land	92,000	
Buildings	197,000	
Accumulated Depreciation—Buildings		$ 54,000
Equipment	83,500	
Accumulated Depreciation—Equipment		42,400
Notes Payable		50,000
Accounts Payable		37,500
D. Parton, Capital		267,800
D. Parton, Drawing	10,000	
Sales		886,100
Sales Discounts	4,600	
Purchases	725,100	
Purchase Discounts		16,000
Freight-in	12,400	
Salaries Expense	69,800	
Utilities Expense	9,400	
Repair Expense	5,900	
Gas and Oil Expense	7,200	
Insurance Expense	3,500	
	$1,353,800	$1,353,800

Adjustment data:

1. Depreciation is $10,000 on buildings and $9,000 on equipment. (Both are administrative expenses.)
2. Interest of $7,000 is unpaid on notes payable at December 31.

Other data:

1. Merchandise inventory on hand at December 31, 1993, is $90,000.
2. Salaries are 80% selling and 20% administrative.
3. Utilities expense, repair expense, and insurance expense are 100% administrative.
4. $15,000 of the notes payable are payable next year.
5. Gas and oil expense is a selling expense.

Instructions

(a) Enter the trial balance on a work sheet and complete the work sheet.

(b) Prepare a multiple-step income statement and owner's equity statement for the year, and a classified balance sheet at December 31, 1993.

(c) Journalize the adjusting entries.

(d) Journalize the closing entries.

(e) Prepare a post-closing trial balance.

Prepare financial statements and adjusting and closing entries.
(S.O. 5, 6, 7)

P5–4 The Howit Department Store is located in midtown Metro. During the past several years, net income has been declining because of suburban shopping centers. At the end of the company's fiscal year on November 30, 1993, the following accounts appeared in two of its trial balances.

	Trial Balances	
	Unadjusted	Adjusted
Accounts Payable	$ 37,310	$ 37,310
Accounts Receivable	12,770	12,770
Accumulated Depreciation—Delivery Equipment	15,680	19,680
Accumulated Depreciation—Store Equipment	32,300	41,800
Cash	7,000	7,000
Delivery Expense	8,200	8,200
Delivery Equipment	57,000	57,000
Depreciation Expense—Delivery Equipment		4,000
Depreciation Expense—Store Equipment		9,500
Freight-in	5,060	5,060
B. Howit, Capital	84,200	84,200
B. Howit, Drawing	12,000	12,000
Insurance Expense		9,000
Interest Expense	8,000	8,000
Interest Revenue	5,000	5,000
Merchandise Inventory	34,360	34,360
Notes Payable	46,000	46,000
Prepaid Insurance	13,500	4,500
Property Tax Expense		3,500
Purchases	640,000	640,000
Purchase Discounts	7,000	7,000
Purchase Returns and Allowances	3,000	3,000
Rent Expense	19,600	19,600
Salaries Expense	120,000	120,000
Sales	860,000	860,000
Sales Commissions Expense	8,000	14,000
Sales Commissions Payable		6,000
Sales Returns and Allowances	10,000	10,000
Store Equipment	125,000	125,000
Property Taxes Payable		3,500
Utilities Expense	10,000	10,000

Analysis reveals the following additional data:

1. Salaries expense is 70% selling and 30% administrative.
2. Insurance expense is 50% selling and 50% administrative.
3. Merchandise inventory at November 30, 1993 is $36,200.
4. Rent expense, utilities expense, and property tax expense are administrative expenses.
5. Notes payable are due in 1999.

Instructions

(a) Prepare a multiple-step income statement, an owner's equity statement, and a classified balance sheet.

(b) Journalize the adjusting entries that were made.

(c) Journalize the closing entries that are necessary.

P5–5 An inexperienced accountant prepared the following condensed income statement for the Lake Company, a retail firm that has been in business for a number of years.

Prepare correct multiple-step and single-step income statements.
(S.O. 5, 7)

LAKE COMPANY
Income Statement
For Year Ended December 31, 1993

Revenues		
Net sales	$740,000	
Other revenues	24,000	$764,000
Cost of goods sold		
Purchases (net)	540,000	
Inventory increase	15,000	
Cost of goods sold		555,000
Gross profit		209,000
Operating expenses		
Selling expenses	104,000	
Administrative expenses	69,000	173,000
Net earnings		$ 36,000

As an experienced, knowledgeable accountant you review the statement and determine the following facts:

1. Net sales consist of sales $800,000, less delivery expense on merchandise sold $40,000, and sales returns and allowances $20,000.
2. Other revenues consist of purchase discounts $16,000 and rent revenue $8,000.
3. Net purchases include purchases $520,000 and delivery costs on incoming merchandise $20,000.
4. The inventory did increase $15,000, which amounted to 25% of the beginning inventory.
5. Selling expenses consist of salespersons' salaries $80,000, depreciation on accounting equipment $8,000, advertising $10,000, and sales commissions $6,000. The commissions represent commissions paid. At December 31, $4,000 of commissions have been earned by salespersons, but have not been paid.
6. Administrative expenses consist of office salaries $27,000, owner's drawing $4,000, utilities $12,000, interest expense $2,000, and rent $24,000, which includes prepayments totaling $6,000 for the first quarter of 1994.

Instructions

(a) Prepare a correct detailed multiple-step income statement.

(b) Prepare a correct condensed single-step income statement.

Complete a work sheet using the adjusting entry method, prepare adjusting and closing entries and post to some accounts.

*P5–6   The trial balance of Global Enterprises for the year ending December 31, 1993 is shown below.

GLOBAL ENTERPRISES
Trial Balance
December 31, 1993

	Debit	Credit
Cash	$ 14,000	
Accounts Receivable	27,600	
Merchandise Inventory	27,500	
Prepaid Insurance	1,800	
Store Equipment	42,000	
Accumulated Depreciation—Store Equipment		$ 9,000
Accounts Payable		31,200
Rego Roger, Capital		50,300
Sales		238,500
Sales Returns and Allowances	3,600	
Sales Discounts	4,900	
Purchases	172,000	
Freight-in	5,000	
Purchase Returns and Allowances		1,200
Purchase Discounts		2,000
Salaries Expense	27,700	
Utilities Expense	6,100	
	$332,200	$332,200

Other data:

1. Merchandise inventory on hand at December 31, $38,600.
2. Insurance expired $800.
3. Depreciation expense, $3,000.
4. The company uses the adjusting entry method for merchandise inventory.

Instructions

(a) Enter the trial balance on a work sheet and complete the work sheet using the adjusting entry method.

(b) Journalize the adjusting entries.

(c) Prepare the closing entries.

(d) Post the entries in (b) and (c) to Merchandise Inventory, and Income Summary.

ALTERNATE PROBLEMS

Journalize, post, and prepare a partial income statement.

(S.O. 2, 3, 4, 5)

P5–1A   The Midvale Distributing Company completed the following merchandising transactions in the month of April. At the beginning of April, the ledger of Midvale showed cash of $9,000 and S. Midvale capital of $9,000.

Apr. 2   Purchased merchandise on account from Kentucky Supply Co. $4,900, terms 2/10, n/30.

     4   Sold merchandise on account $5,000, FOB destination, terms 2/10, n/30.
     5   Paid $200 freight on April 4 sale.
     6   Received credit from Kentucky Supply Co. for merchandise returned $300.
    11   Paid Kentucky Supply Co. in full, less discount.
    13   Received collections in full, less discounts, from customers billed on April 4.
    14   Purchased merchandise for cash $4,400.
    16   Received refund from supplier on cash purchase of April 14, $500.

18 Purchased merchandise from Pigeon Distributors $4,200, FOB shipping point, terms 2/10, n/30.

20 Paid freight on April 18 purchase $100.

23 Sold merchandise for cash $6,400.

26 Purchased merchandise for cash $2,300.

27 Paid Pigeon Distributors in full, less discount.

29 Made refunds to cash customers for defective merchandise $90.

30 Sold merchandise on account $3,700, terms n/30.

Midvale Company's chart of accounts includes the following: No. 101 Cash, No. 112 Accounts Receivable, No. 120 Merchandise Inventory, No. 201 Accounts Payable, No. 301 S. Midvale, Capital, No. 401 Sales, No. 412 Sales Returns and Allowances, No. 414 Sales Discounts, No. 510 Purchases, No. 512 Purchase Returns and Allowances, No. 514 Purchase Discounts, No. 516 Freight-in, and No. 644 Freight-out.

Instructions

(a) Journalize the transactions.

(b) Enter the beginning cash balances and post the transactions (Use J1 for the journal reference).

(c) Prepare the income statement through gross profit for the month of April, 1993, assuming ending inventory is $8,700, and no beginning inventory.

P5–2A John William, a former professional tennis star, operates the tennis shop at the Jackson Tennis Club. At the beginning of the current season, the ledger of William's Tennis Shop showed Cash $2,500, Merchandise Inventory $1,700, and J. William, Capital $4,200. The following transactions were completed during April.

Journalize, post, and prepare a trial balance and partial income statement. (S.O. 2, 3, 4, 5)

Apr. 4 Purchased racquets and balls from Robert Co. $640 FOB shipping point, terms 3/10, n/30.

6 Paid freight on Robert purchase $40.

8 Sold merchandise to members $900, terms n/30.

10 Received credit of $40 from Robert Co. for a damaged racquet that was returned.

11 Purchased tennis shoes from King Sports, Inc. for cash, $300.

13 Paid Robert Co. in full.

14 Purchased tennis shirts and shorts from Events Sportswear, $700, FOB shipping point, terms 2/10, n/60.

15 Received cash refund of $50 from King Sports, Inc. for damaged merchandise that was returned.

17 Paid freight on Events Sportswear purchase $30.

18 Sold merchandise to members, $800, terms n/30.

20 Received $500 in cash from members in settlement of their accounts.

21 Paid Events Sportswear in full.

27 Granted credit of $30 to members for tennis clothing that did not fit.

30 Sold merchandise to members $900, terms n/30.

30 Received cash payments on account from members, $500.

The chart of accounts for the tennis shop includes the following: No. 101 Cash, No. 112 Accounts Receivable, No. 120 Merchandise Inventory, No. 201 Accounts Payable, No. 301 J. William, Capital, No. 401 Sales, No. 412 Sales Returns and Allowances, No. 510 Purchases, No. 512 Purchase Returns and Allowances, No. 514 Purchase Discounts, No. 516 Freight-in.

Instructions

(a) Journalize the April transactions.

(b) Enter the beginning balances in the ledger accounts and post the April transactions. (Use J1 for the journal reference.)

(c) Prepare a trial balance on April 30.

(d) Prepare an income statement through gross profit, assuming merchandise inventory on hand at April 30 is $1,600.

Complete accounting cycle
beginning with a work
sheet.
(S.O. 5, 6, 7)

P5–3A   The trial balance of the Wall Fashion Center contained the following accounts at November 30, the end of the company's fiscal year.

WALL FASHION CENTER
Trial Balance
November 30, 1993

	Debit	Credit
Cash	$ 16,700	
Accounts Receivable	33,700	
Merchandise Inventory	38,000	
Store Supplies	5,500	
Store Equipment	85,000	
Accumulated Depreciation—Store Equipment		$ 18,000
Delivery Equipment	48,000	
Accumulated Depreciation—Delivery Equipment		6,000
Notes Payable		51,000
Accounts Payable		48,500
N. Wall, Capital		110,000
N. Wall, Drawing	12,000	
Sales		746,600
Sales Returns and Allowances	4,200	
Purchases	503,600	
Purchase Returns and Allowances		6,900
Purchase Discounts		3,700
Freight-in	10,800	
Salaries Expense	140,000	
Advertising Expense	26,400	
Utilities Expense	17,000	
Repair Expense	9,100	
Delivery Expense	16,700	
Rent Expense	24,000	
	$990,700	$990,700

Adjustment data:

1. Store supplies on hand totaled $3,500.
2. Depreciation is $9,000 on the store equipment and $7,000 on the delivery equipment.
3. Interest of $11,000 is accrued on notes payable at November 30.

Other data:

1. Merchandise inventory on hand at November 30, 1993 is $45,000.
2. Salaries expense is 70% selling and 30% administrative.
3. Rent expense and utilities expense are 80% selling and 20% administrative.
4. $30,000 of notes payable are due for payment next year.
5. Repair expense is 100% administrative.

Instructions
(a) Enter the trial balance on a work sheet and complete the work sheet.

(b) Prepare a multiple-step income statement and owner's equity statement for the year and a classified balance sheet as of November 30, 1993.

(c) Journalize the adjusting entries.

(d) Journalize the closing entries.

(e) Prepare a post-closing trial balance.

Prepare financial state-
ments and adjusting and
closing entries.
(S.O. 5, 6, 7)

P5–4A   The Wiley Department Store is located near the Village shopping mall. At the end of the company's fiscal year on December 31, 1993, the following accounts appeared in two of its trial balances.

	Trial Balances	
	Unadjusted	Adjusted
Accounts Payable	$ 89,300	$ 89,300
Accounts Receivable	50,300	50,300
Accumulated Depreciation—Building	42,100	52,500
Accumulated Depreciation—Equipment	29,600	42,900
Building	190,000	190,000
Cash	23,000	23,000
Depreciation Expense—Building		10,400
Depreciation Expense—Equipment		13,300
Equipment	110,000	110,000
Freight-in	3,600	3,600
Insurance Expense		7,200
Interest Expense	3,000	11,000
Interest Payable		8,000
Interest Revenue	4,000	4,000
Merchandise Inventory	40,500	40,500
Mortgage Payable	80,000	80,000
Office Salaries Expense	32,000	32,000
Prepaid Insurance	9,600	2,400
Property Taxes Payable		4,800
Purchases	462,000	462,000
Purchase Discounts	12,000	12,000
Purchase Returns and Allowances	6,400	6,400
Sales Salaries Expense	76,000	76,000
Sales	618,000	618,000
Sales Commissions Expense	11,000	14,500
Sales Commissions Payable		3,500
Sales Returns and Allowances	8,000	8,000
S. Wiley, Capital	176,600	176,600
S. Wiley, Drawing	28,000	28,000
Property Taxes Expense		4,800
Utilities Expense	11,000	11,000

Analysis reveals the following additional data:

1. Merchandise inventory on December 31, 1993 is $70,000.
2. Insurance expense and utilities expense are 60% selling and 40% administrative.
3. $20,000 of the mortgage payable is due for payment next year.
4. Depreciation on the building and property tax expense are administrative expenses; depreciation on the equipment is a selling expense.

Instructions

(a) Prepare a multiple-step income statement, an owner's equity statement, and a classified balance sheet.

(b) Journalize the adjusting entries that were made.

(c) Journalize the closing entries that are necessary.

Prepare correct multiple-step and single-step income statements.
(S.O. 5, 7)

P5–5A A part-time bookkeeper prepared the following income statement for the Porter Company for the year ending December 31, 1993.

PORTER COMPANY
Income Statement
December 31, 1993

Revenues		
Sales		$702,000
Less: Freight-in	$ 17,200	
Discounts	4,100	21,300
Net sales		680,700
Other revenues (net)		300
Total revenues		681,000
Expenses		
Purchases	470,000	
Selling expenses	100,000	
Administrative expenses	50,000	
W. Porter, Drawings	12,000	
Total expenses		632,000
Net income		$ 49,000

As an experienced, knowledgeable accountant you review the statement and determine the following facts:

1. Sales includes $10,000 of deposits from customers for future sales orders.
2. Discounts consist of purchase discounts earned $7,200 and sales discounts granted $11,300.
3. Other revenues contains two items: interest expense $5,000 and interest revenue $5,300.
4. Purchases includes freight-out $14,000 less purchase returns and allowances $9,000.
5. Ending merchandise inventory increased $20,000 from a beginning inventory of $35,000.
6. Selling expenses consist of sales salaries $76,000, advertising $10,000, depreciation on store equipment $7,500, and sales commissions expense $6,500.
7. Administrative expenses consist of office salaries $19,000, utilities expense $8,000, rent expense $16,000, and insurance expense $7,000. Insurance expense includes $1,200 of insurance applicable to 1994.

Instructions
(a) Prepare a correct detailed multiple-step income statement.
(b) Prepare a correct condensed single-step income statement.

Broadening Your Perspective

FINANCIAL REPORTING PROBLEM

Bob Evans Farms, Inc. operates 273 restaurants in 16 states and produces fresh and fully cooked sausage products, fresh salads, and related products distributed to grocery stores in the Midwest, Southwest, and Southeast. For a recent three-year period, Bob Evans Farms reported the following selected income statement data (in millions of dollars):

	1992	1991	1990
Sales	$556.3	$501.3	$454.3
Cost of goods sold	424.3	388.3	357.7
Selling and administrative expenses	72.0	60.3	54.7
Net income	39.3	35.8	27.7

In his letter to the stockholders, the chairman of the board and CEO made the following comments:

"With fiscal year 1992 under our belts and fiscal year 1993 well under way, I am in an enviable position as chairman of our company. Sales are up, profits are up, morale is high, and there has never been a more exciting time to be at Bob Evans Farms."

Instructions

(a) Compute the percentage gains in sales and in net profits from year to year for the three years.

(b) What contribution, if any, did the company's gross profit rate make to the improved earnings?

(c) What was Bob Evans' percentage of net income to net sales in each of the three years? Comment on any trend in this percentage.

DECISION CASE

Three years ago, Kathy Paul and her brother-in-law John Paul opened Paul's Department Store. For the first two years, business was good, but the following condensed income results for 1993 were disappointing.

PAUL'S DEPARTMENT STORE
Income Statement
For the Year Ended December 31, 1993

Net sales		$700,000
Cost of goods sold		546,000
Gross profit		154,000
Operating expenses		
Selling expenses	$100,000	
Administrative expenses	25,000	125,000
Net income		$ 29,000

Kathy believes the problem lies in the relatively low gross profit rate (gross profit divided by net sales) of 22%. John believes the problem is that operating expenses are too high.

Kathy thinks the gross profit rate can be improved by making both of the following changes: (1) increase average selling prices by 17%; this increase is expected to lower sales volume so that total sales will increase only 6%. (2) buy merchandise in larger quantities and take all purchase discounts; these changes are expected to increase the gross profit rate by 3%. Kathy does not anticipate that these changes will have any effect on operating expenses.

John thinks expenses can be cut by making both of the following changes: (1) cut 1993 sales salaries of $60,000 in half and give sales personnel a commission of 2% of net sales. (2) reduce store deliveries to one day per week rather than twice a week; this change will reduce 1993 delivery expenses of $30,000 by 45%. John feels that these changes will not have any effect on net sales.

Kathy and John come to you for help in deciding the best way to improve net income.

Instructions

(a) Prepare a condensed income statement for 1994 assuming (1) Kathy's changes are implemented and (2) John's ideas are adopted.

(b) What is your recommendation to Kathy and John?

(c) Prepare a condensed income statement for 1994 assuming both sets of proposed changes are made.

CRITICAL THINKING CASE

Think back to the vignette about the Washington State University bookstore at the beginning of the chapter and answer the following questions:

1. What kind of inventory system is being used in the bookstore? Why?
2. What entry, if any, would the WSU bookstore make when ordering books? When books are received? When returning books? When allowing the students to return books? When purchasing used books from students?
3. How often is it necessary for Larry Martin to take a physical inventory? Why is it necessary to take an inventory? For the inventory taken in September, does Larry need both quantities and costs? Explain.

ETHICAL CASE

Edna Pelzer was just hired as the assistant treasurer of Yorkshire Stores, a specialty chain store company consisting of nine retail stores concentrated in one metropolitan area. Among other things, the payment of all invoices is centralized in one of the departments Edna will manage. Her primary responsibility is to maintain the company's high credit rating by paying all bills when due and to take advantage of all cash discounts. Jamie Caterino, the former assistant treasurer, who has been promoted to treasurer, is training Edna in her new duties. He instructs Edna that she is to continue the practice of preparing all checks "net of discount" and dating the checks the last day of the discount period. "But," Jamie continues, "we always hold the checks at least four days beyond the discount period before mailing them. That way we get another four days of interest on our money. Most of our creditors need our business and don't complain. And, if they scream about our missing the discount period, we blame it on the mail room or the post office. We've only lost one discount out of every hundred we take that way. I think everybody does it. By the way, welcome to our team!"

Instructions

(a) What are the ethical considerations in this case?

(b) Who are the stakeholders that are harmed or benefitted in this situation?

(c) Should Edna continue the practice started by Jamie? Does she have any choice?

Answers to Self-Study Questions

1. d   2. d   3. c   4. c   5. a   6. b   7. b   8. c   9. d   10. b
11. b

CONCEPTS FOR REVIEW

Before studying this chapter, you should know, or, if necessary, review:

a. *How to perform each of the steps in the accounting cycle. (Ch. 4, pp. 134–46)*

b. *How to record transactions for a merchandising company. (Ch. 5, pp. 181–89)*

c. *How to prepare financial statements for a merchandising company. (Ch. 5, pp. 192–96)*

CHAPTER 6

ACCOUNTING INFORMATION SYSTEMS: MANUAL AND ELECTRONIC DATA PROCESSING

Study Objectives

After studying this chapter, you should be able to:

1. *Identify the basic principles of accounting information system development.*

2. *Explain the major phases involved in the development of an accounting information system.*

3. *Describe the nature and purpose of a subsidiary ledger.*

4. *Explain how special journals are used in journalizing.*

5. *Indicate how a columnar journal is posted.*

6. *Identify the key points in comparing manual and computerized accounting systems.*

*S*ome enterprises still keep track of their finances with paper and pencil. Others are completely computerized. A third group uses a mixture of both.

For Portland Community College (PCC), serving 80,000 Oregon students (mostly part-time) per year, accounting is done by both computer and pencil—but that's about to change. The college is in the process of selecting a new, high-tech accounting system to handle its 80,000 different accounts. "We're taking bids from vendors all over the country," says Jeff Hempe, accounting manager.

Right now, PCC employees must order everything from a pencil sharpener to a $10,000 piece of equipment the old-fashioned way—by filling out a four-part requisition form. When approved, that form turns into a six-part purchase order. To get a purchase paid, the accounts payable department needs a copy of the purchase order, a purchase authorization, a vendor invoice, a receiving document, and a couple of other papers. "When it is done this way, a lot of times you hit snags," says Hempe.

"The vendor can't be paid when accounts payable doesn't have all of the pieces."

With a computer, "each person along the line can find out the status of all the required

approvals simply by looking up the transaction on the computer." Right now, it

takes PCC 60 days to pay a bill because it takes that long to get all of the pieces of

paper processed. Hempe figures the computer will cut the time in half. PCC employees

and the vendors that sell to the university hope he's right.

As we have seen, the accounting system transforms financial **data** into useful **information** that aids investors, creditors, managers, and other interested parties in making financial decisions. This system involves collecting and processing data and disseminating financial information. It is often referred to as the accounting information system.

When an enterprise's operations become too complex or its transactions too numerous to be handled efficiently by a manual accounting system, a computerized accounting system may be installed. But, whether manual or computerized procedures are used to process the transaction data, some basic features and principles apply to both. This chapter will explain some of the features that give an accounting information system, either manual or computerized, the flexibility to accommodate a multitude of transactions.

Principles of an Accounting Information System

Study Objective 1

Identify the basic principles of accounting information system development.

In designing and developing an efficient and effective accounting information system (hereafter referred to simply as the accounting system), it is important that certain basic principles be followed. These principles are:

1. **Cost awareness.** A major consideration in developing an accounting system is cost awareness. The system must be cost effective; the benefits obtained from the information disseminated must outweigh the cost of providing it. For example, the value of each accounting report should be at least equal to the cost of producing it.

2. **Useful output.** To be useful, information must be understandable, relevant, reliable, timely, and accurate. Designers of accounting systems must consider the needs and knowledge of the various users so that the system's output (reports and statements) will be useful. For example, sales managers may need weekly reports of sales and factory supervisors may need daily reports of production. Others with differing responsibilities (such as vice-presidents) may need such reports only monthly or quarterly.

3. **Flexible structure.** The accounting system should be able to accommodate a variety of users and changing information needs. The business environment changes as a result of technological advances, organizational growth, increased competition, government regulation, or changes in accounting principles. When it does, the accounting system should be sufficiently flexible to meet the resulting changes in the demands made upon it.

If the accounting system is cost effective, provides useful output, and has the flexibility to meet future needs, it can provide a valuable service and make a major contribution to both individual and organizational goals.

Developing an Accounting System

Study Objective 2

Explain the major phases involved in the development of an accounting information system.

Good accounting systems do not just happen. They are carefully planned, designed, installed, managed, and refined. Generally, developing an accounting system involves the following four phases:

1. **Analysis.** Analysis involves determining internal and external information needs, identifying sources of information and the need for controls, and studying alternatives. If an existing system is being analyzed, its strengths and weaknesses must be identified.
2. **Design.** For a new system, forms and documents must be designed; methods and procedures selected from alternatives; job descriptions prepared; controls integrated; reports formatted; and equipment selected. Successful systems design depends largely upon the capabilities of the designer. Redesigning an existing system may involve only minor changes, a complete overhaul, or replacement of a manual system by a computerized system.
3. **Implementation.** Whether a new accounting system is created or an existing system is revised, the plan and design must be implemented. New or revised documents, procedures, reports, and processing equipment must be installed and made operational. Personnel must be hired, trained, and closely supervised through a start-up or transition period.
4. **Follow-up.** After the system is up and running, it must be evaluated and monitored for weaknesses and breakdowns. Also, its effectiveness and efficiency must be compared to design and organizational objectives. Corrections in design or changes in implementation may be necessary. Both internal and external audit procedures provide feedback about the soundness of the system.

Illustration 6-1 highlights the relationship of these four phases in the life cycle of the accounting system.

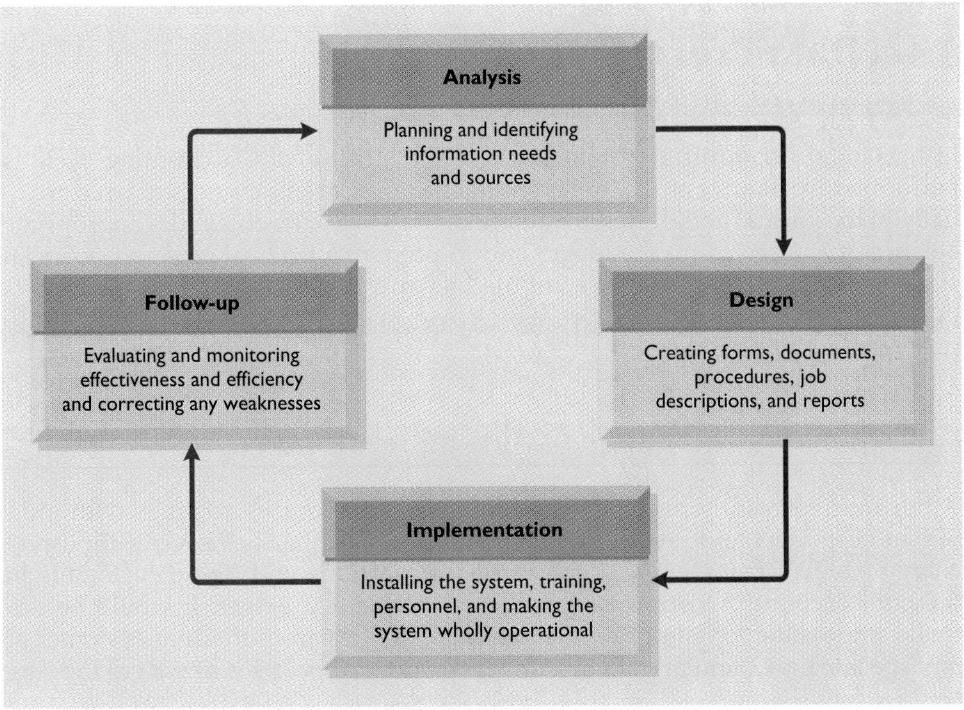

ILLUSTRATION 6-1

Phases in the development of an accounting system

These phases, which represent the life cycle of an accounting system, suggest that few systems remain the same forever. As experience and knowledge are obtained, and as technological and organizational changes occur, the accounting system may also have to grow and change.

In Chapter 2, you were introduced to the general journal/general ledger accounting system. Data processing using only a general journal and a general ledger is orderly and appears to be efficient. However, this type of system is satisfactory only when the volume of transactions is extremely low. To overcome the limitations of this simple system, accountants employ additional journals and ledgers to process large volumes of transactions. The remainder of this chapter describes these additional journals and ledgers. Applications to manual systems are discussed in detail; applications to computerized systems are described briefly.

Technology in Action

At this point you might ask, "Why cover manual accounting systems if the real world uses computerized systems?" Here is the answer:

- The design and structure of manual and computerized systems are essentially the same.
- Small businesses still abound. Most of them begin operations with manual (or even "shoe box") accounting systems. The successful small businesses eventually convert to computerized systems.
- Most students do not (at least not yet) have easy access to electronic data processing (EDP). Even if they did, the vast differences between different EDP hardware and software systems make manual systems much more practical for detailed study in your accounting textbook.

SECTION I   Manual Data Processing

In a **manual accounting system**, each of the steps in the accounting cycle is performed by hand. For example, each accounting transaction is entered manually in the journal and posted manually to the ledger. To obtain the appropriate balance of an account in the ledger and to prepare a trial balance and financial statements, additional manual computations must be made. The following sections discuss how the manual processing system can be more efficiently used to process accounting data.

Expanding the Ledger—Subsidiary Ledgers

Study Objective 3

Describe the nature and purpose of a subsidiary ledger.

A business constantly needs detailed information about its dealings with individual customers and creditors. Imagine a business that has several thousand charge (credit) customers and shows the transactions with these customers in only one account, Accounts Receivable, in the general ledger. It would be virtually impossible to determine the balance owed by an individual customer at any specific time. Similarly, details of transactions affecting a single creditor are needed from time to time, and a single Accounts Payable account in the general ledger cannot make this information available.

To provide this information, companies use a subsidiary ledger to keep track of individual balances. A subsidiary ledger is a group of accounts with a common characteristic (for example, all might be customer accounts, that is, accounts receivable). The subsidiary ledger facilitates the recording process by freeing the general ledger from the details of individual balances. Thus, in addition to the general ledger, a typical merchandising enterprise has subsidiary ledgers containing accounts with customers (accounts receivable or customers' ledger) and creditors (accounts payable or creditors' ledger). The enterprise maintains control accounts in the general ledger that summarize the details in the accounts receivable and accounts payable ledgers. The summary accounts in the general ledger are called control accounts, because the summary accounts control the subsidiary ledgers. **Each general ledger control account balance must equal the composite balance of the individual accounts in the related subsidiary ledger at the end of an accounting period**.

As indicated, two common subsidiary ledgers are: (1) the accounts receivable (or customers') ledger, controlled by the general ledger account, Accounts Receivable; and (2) the accounts payable (or creditors') ledger, controlled by the general ledger account, Accounts Payable. In subsidiary ledgers, the individual accounts are usually arranged in alphabetical order.

An example of a control account and subsidiary ledger for Larson Enterprises is provided in Illustration 6-2. The explanation column in these accounts is not shown in this and subsequent illustrations due to space considerations.

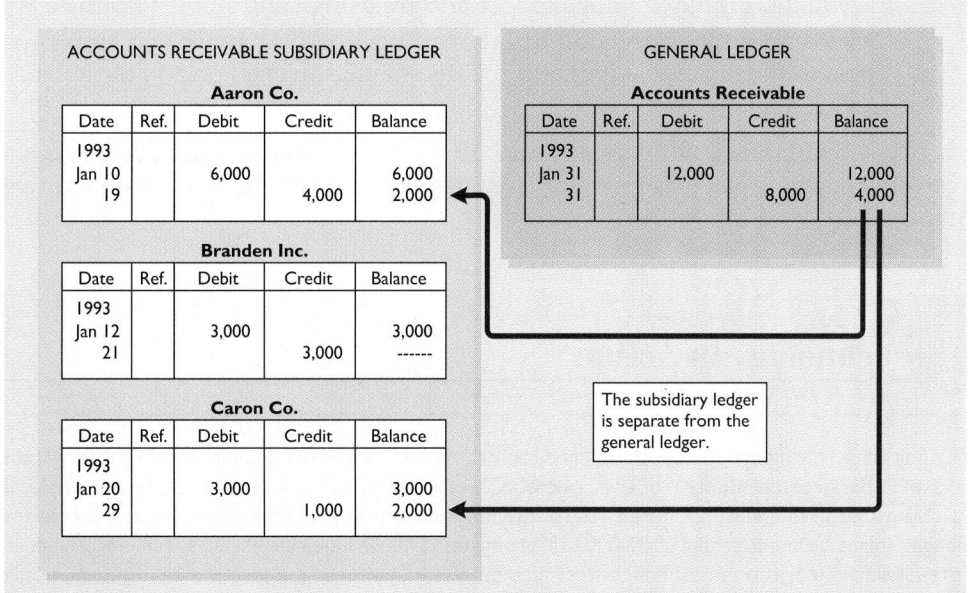

ILLUSTRATION 6-2

Relationship between ledgers

The example is based on the following transactions:

ILLUSTRATION 6-3

Sales and collection transactions

Credit Sales			Collections on Account		
Jan. 10	Aaron Co.	$ 6,000	Jan. 19	Aaron Co.	$ 4,000
12	Branden Inc.	3,000	21	Branden Inc.	3,000
20	Caron Co.	3,000	29	Caron Co.	1,000
		$12,000			$ 8,000

The total debits and credits in Accounts Receivable in the general ledger are reconcilable to the detailed debits and credits in the subsidiary accounts. The balance of $4,000 in the accounts receivable control account agrees with the total of the balances in the individual accounts receivable accounts ($2,000 + $0 + $2,000) in the subsidiary ledger.

Postings are made monthly to the control accounts in the general ledger so that monthly financial statements may be prepared. Postings to the individual accounts in the subsidiary ledger are made daily. The rationale for posting daily is to ensure that current account information can be used as a basis for monitoring credit limits, billing customers, and answering inquiries from customers about their account balances.

Note also in Illustration 6-2 that postings to the control account are made in total at the end of the month, whereas each of the individual transactions is posted daily to the subsidiary ledger. Procedures used for posting entries to the subsidiary ledger and to the general ledger control account generally involve the use of special journals, discussed later in the chapter.

In summary, the advantages of using subsidiary ledgers are that they:

1. **Show transactions affecting one customer or one creditor in a single account**, thus providing necessary up-to-date information on specific account balances.
2. **Free the general ledger of excessive details**. As a result, a trial balance of the general ledger does not contain vast numbers of individual account balances.
3. **Help locate errors in individual accounts** by reducing the number of accounts combined in one ledger and by using controlling accounts.
4. **Make possible a division of labor** in posting by having one employee post to the general ledger and a different employee(s) post to the subsidiary ledgers.

Note that a business may also use control accounts and subsidiary ledgers for other accounts such as inventory, equipment, and selling and administrative expenses.

Technology in Action

Rather than relying on customer or creditor names in a subsidiary ledger, a computer system expands the account number of the control account in a pre-specified manner. For example, if accounts receivable was numbered 10010, the first account in the accounts receivable subsidiary ledger might be numbered 10010-0001. Most systems allow inquiries about specific accounts in the subsidiary ledger or about the control account. With the latter, the system would automatically total all the subsidiary accounts whenever an inquiry to the control account was made.

Before You Go On . . .

1. What are the basic principles to be followed in designing and developing an efficient and effective accounting information system?

2. What are the major phases in the development of an accounting information system?

3. What is a subsidiary ledger, and what purpose does it serve?

Expanding the Journal—Special Journals

So far you have learned to journalize transactions in a two-column general journal and post these entries individually to the general ledger. This procedure is satisfactory in only the very smallest companies. To expedite journalizing and posting transactions, most companies use special journals in addition to the general journal.

A special journal is used to record similar types of transactions, such as all sales of merchandise on account, or all cash receipts. The types of special journals used depend largely on the types of transactions that occur frequently in a business enterprise. Most merchandising enterprises use the following journals to record transactions daily:

> Sales journal—all sales of merchandise on account.
> Cash receipts journal—all cash received (including cash sales).
> Purchases journal—all purchases of merchandise on account.
> Cash payments journal—all cash paid (including cash purchases).

If a transaction cannot be recorded in a special journal, it is recorded in the general journal. For example, if you had special journals only for the four types of transactions listed above, purchase returns and allowances or sales returns and allowances would be reported in the general journal. Similarly, correcting, adjusting, and closing entries are recorded in the general journal. Other types of special journals may be used in some situations. For example, when purchase returns and allowances or sales returns and allowances are frequent, special journals may be used to record these transactions.

Special journals **permit greater division of labor** because several individuals can record entries in different journals at the same time. For example, one employee may be responsible for journalizing all cash receipts, and another for journalizing credit sales. In addition, the use of special journals **reduces the time necessary to complete the posting process**. When special journals are used, monthly postings to some accounts may be substituted for daily postings, as will be illustrated later in the chapter.

Study Objective 4

Explain how special journals are used in journalizing.

Helpful hint Will a special journal or the general journal have the fewest daily entries? Answer: The general journal because all recurring daily entries should be recorded in a special journal in a properly designed system.

Technology in Action

As indicated later in this chapter, computerized accounting systems reduce the processing time even more. Humans are slow, error-prone, and limited in their abilities to process data. A computer can process hundreds of transactions in the time it may take a human to process one transaction.

Sales Journal

The sales journal is used to record sales of merchandise on account. Cash sales of merchandise are entered in the cash receipts journal. Credit sales of assets other than merchandise are entered in the general journal.

Journalizing Credit Sales

All entries in a sales journal are made from sales invoices. Each invoice is pre-numbered to ensure that all invoices are journalized. To illustrate, assume that Karns Wholesale Supply has the following credit sales transactions:

Date	Customer	Invoice No.	Amount	Date	Customer	Invoice No.	Amount
5/3	Abbot Sisters	101	$10,600	5/21	Abbot Sisters	105	$15,400
5/7	Babson Co.	102	11,350	5/24	Deli Co.	106	21,210
5/14	Carson Bros.	103	7,800	5/27	Babson Co.	107	14,570
5/19	Deli Co.	104	9,300				

Each entry in the sales journal used here results in a debit to Accounts Receivable and a credit to Sales. Since each sale on account involves a debit to Accounts Receivable and a credit of equal amount to Sales, only one line is needed in this sales journal to record each transaction.

The sales journal is presented in Illustration 6-5.

KARNS WHOLESALE SUPPLY
Sales Journal   **S1**

Date	Account Debited	Invoice No.	Ref.	Accts. Receivable Dr. Sales Cr.
1993				
May 3	Abbot Sisters	101		10,600
7	Babson Co.	102		11,350
14	Carson Bros.	103		7,800
19	Deli Co.	104		9,300
21	Abbot Sisters	105		15,400
24	Deli Co.	106		21,210
27	Babson Co.	107		14,570
				90,230

The reference (Ref.) column is not used in journalizing. It is used in posting the sales journal as explained below. Also, note that an explanation is not required for each entry.

Posting the Sales Journal

Postings from the sales journal are made **daily to the individual accounts receivable** in the subsidiary ledger and **monthly to the general ledger**, as shown in Illustration 6-6.

A check mark (√) is inserted in the reference posting column to indicate that the daily posting to the customer's account has been made. A check mark (√) is used in this illustration because the subsidiary ledger accounts are not numbered.

ILLUSTRATION 6-6

Posting the sales journal

Karns Wholesale Supply
Sales Journal   S1

Date	Account Debited	Invoice No.	Ref.	Accts. Receivable Dr. Sales Cr.
1993				
May 3	Abbot Sisters	101	√	10,600
7	Babson Co.	102	√	11,350
14	Carson Bros.	103	√	7,800
19	Deli Co.	104	√	9,300
21	Abbot Sisters	105	√	15,400
24	Deli Co.	106	√	21,210
27	Babson Co.	107	√	14,570
				90,230
				(4) / (60)

Totals are posted at the end of the accounting period to the general ledger.

Individual amounts are posted daily to the subsidiary ledger.

ACCOUNTS RECEIVABLE SUBSIDIARY LEDGER

GENERAL LEDGER

Abbot Sisters

Date	Ref.	Debit	Credit	Balance
1993				
May 3	S1	10,600		10,600
21	S1	15,400		26,000

Accounts Receivable   No. 4

Date	Ref.	Debit	Credit	Balance
1993				
May 31	S1	90,230		90,230

Babson Co.

Date	Ref.	Debit	Credit	Balance
1993				
May 7	S1	11,350		11,350
27	S1	14,570		25,920

Sales   No. 60

Date	Ref.	Debit	Credit	Balance
1993				
May 31	S1		90,230	90,230

Carson Bros.

Date	Ref.	Debit	Credit	Balance
1993				
May 14	S1	7,800		7,800

Deli Co.

Date	Ref.	Debit	Credit	Balance
1993				
May 19	S1	9,300		9,300
24	S1	21,210		30,510

The subsidiary ledger is separate from the general ledger.

Technology in Action

In manual systems most files are alphabetical so there is, perhaps, little benefit in numbering accounts. In computerized systems, though, account numbering is essential. In today's information society, we are all numbers in many respects. We have social security numbers, drivers' license numbers, phone numbers, credit card numbers, and so on. At times, this can seem dehumanizing, but the trade-off is in the efficiency of processing files under numerical control. It is far simpler to enter digits than account names. The problem of differentiating accounts with common names (i.e., Jones, Smith) is also greatly reduced with numerical referencing.

At the end of the month, the column total of the sales journal is posted to the general ledger—as a debit to Accounts Receivable (account No. 4) and a credit to Sales (account No. 60). The insertion of the respective account numbers below the column total indicates that the postings have been made. In both the general ledger and subsidiary ledger accounts, the reference S1 indicates that the posting came from page 1 of the sales journal.

Proof of the accuracy of the postings of the sales journal is shown in the following tabulation:

ILLUSTRATION 6-7

Proving the postings of the sales journal

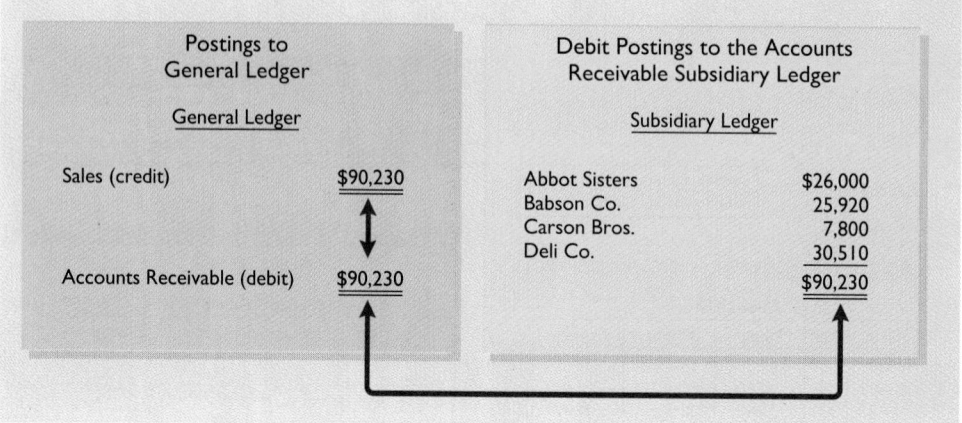

Postings to General Ledger		Debit Postings to the Accounts Receivable Subsidiary Ledger	
General Ledger		**Subsidiary Ledger**	
Sales (credit)	$90,230	Abbot Sisters	$26,000
		Babson Co.	25,920
		Carson Bros.	7,800
		Deli Co.	30,510
Accounts Receivable (debit)	$90,230		$90,230

If management wishes to record its sales by department, additional columns may be provided in the sales journal. For example, a department store may have columns for home furnishings, sporting goods, shoes, etc. In addition, practically all states and cities require a sales tax be charged on items sold, which the company must remit to the state or city. In this case, it is desirable to add an additional credit column to the sales journal for sales tax payable. Sales tax payable is posted in total at the end of the month, similar to sales.

The use of a special journal to record sales on account has a number of advantages. First, the one-line entry for each sales transaction **saves time**, because it is not necessary to write out a debit to accounts receivable and a credit to sales for each transaction. Second, only totals, rather than individual entries, are posted to the general ledger, thus **saving posting time and reducing the possibilities of errors in posting**. Finally, **a division of labor results**, because one individual can take responsibility for the sales journal.

Cash Receipts Journal

All receipts of cash are recorded in the cash receipts journal. The most common types of cash receipts are cash sales of merchandise and collections of accounts receivable. Many other possibilities exist, however, such as receipt of money from bank loans and cash proceeds from disposals of equipment, buildings, or land. A one-column cash receipts journal is not sufficient to accommodate all possible cash receipts transactions. Therefore, a multiple-column cash receipts journal is used. Generally, a cash receipts journal includes debit columns for cash and sales discounts and credit columns for accounts receivable, sales, and "other" accounts. The other accounts category is used when the cash receipt does not involve a cash sale or a collection of accounts receivable. A five-column cash receipts journal is shown in Illustration 6-8. When a special journal has more than one column it is often referred to as a columnar journal.

Additional credit columns may be used if they significantly reduce postings to a specific account. For example, the cash receipts of a loan company, such as Household International, include thousands of collections from customers that are credited to Loans Receivable and Interest Revenue. A significant saving in posting would result from using separate credit columns for Loans Receivable and Interest Revenue, rather than using the other accounts credit column for these amounts. In contrast, a retailer that has only one interest collection a month would not find it useful to have a separate column for interest revenue.

Journalizing Cash Receipts Transactions

To illustrate the journalizing of cash receipts transactions, we will continue with the transactions of Karns Wholesale Supply during the month of May. Collections from customers relate to the entries recorded in the sales journal in Illustration 6-5. The entries in the cash receipts journal are based on the following cash receipts transactions:

May 1 D. A. Karns makes an investment of $5,000 in the business.
   7 Cash sales of merchandise total $1,900.
   10 A check for $10,388 is received from Abbot Sisters in payment of invoice No. 101 for $10,600 less a 2% discount.
   12 Cash sales of merchandise total $2,600.
   17 A check for $11,123 is received from Babson Co. in payment of invoice No. 102 for $11,350 less a 2% discount.
   22 Cash is received by signing a note for $6,000.
   23 A check for $7,644 is received from Carson Bros. in full for invoice No. 103 for $7,800 less a 2% discount.
   28 A check for $9,114 is received from Deli Co. in full for invoice No. 104 for $9,300 less a 2% discount.

Further information about the columns in the cash receipts journal (see Illustration 6-8) is as follows:

Debits:
1. **Cash.** The amount of cash actually received in each transaction is entered in this column; the column total indicates the total cash receipts for the month.
2. **Sales Discounts.** The Sales Discounts column is included so that it is not necessary to enter sales discount items in the general journal. As a result, the collection of an account receivable within the discount period is expressed on one line in the appropriate columns of the cash receipts journal.

Credits:
3. **Accounts Receivable.** The Accounts Receivable column is used to record cash collections on account. The amount entered in this column is the amount to be credited to the individual customer's account.
4. **Sales.** The Sales column records all cash sales of merchandise. Cash sales of plant assets, for example, are not reported in this column.
5. **Other Accounts.** The Other Accounts column, often referred to as the **sundry accounts column**, is used whenever the credit is other than to Accounts Receivable or Sales. For example, in the first entry, $5,000 is entered as a credit to D. A. Karns, Capital.

In a columnar journal, as in a single-column journal, only one line is needed for each entry. There must be equal debit and credit amounts for each line. When the collection from Abbot Sisters on May 10 is journalized, for example, three

Helpful hint When is an account title entered in the "Accounts Credited" column of the cash receipts journal? Answer: A subsidiary ledger title is entered there whenever the entry involves a collection of accounts receivable. A general ledger account title is entered there whenever the entry involves an account that is not the subject of a special column (and an amount must be entered in the "Other Accounts" column). No account title is entered there if neither of the foregoing apply.

ILLUSTRATION 6-8

Journalizing and posting the cash receipts journal

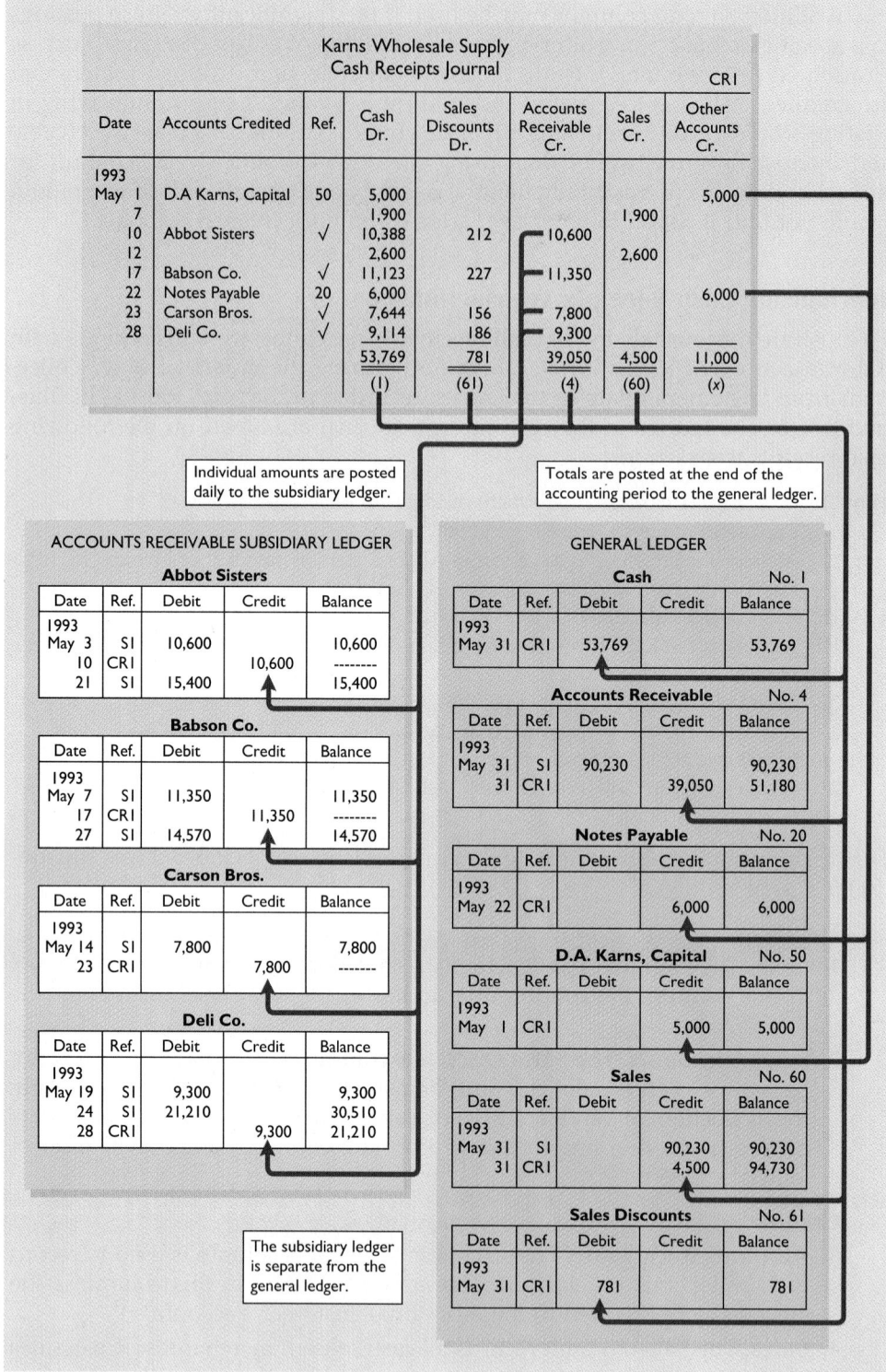

amounts are indicated. Note also that the Accounts Credited column is used to identify both general ledger and subsidiary ledger account titles. The former is illustrated in the May 1 entry for Karns' investment; the latter is illustrated in the May 10 entry for the collection in full from Abbot Sisters.

When the journalizing of a columnar journal has been completed, the amount columns are totaled, and the totals are balanced to prove the equality of debits and credits. The proof for Karns Wholesale Supply is as follows:

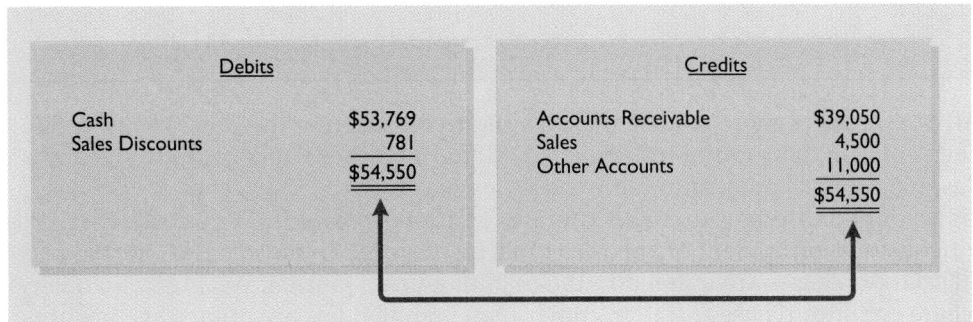

ILLUSTRATION 6-9

Proving the accuracy of the cash receipts journal

Totaling the columns of a journal and proving the equality of the totals is called **footing** and **cross-footing** a journal.

Posting the Cash Receipts Journal

Posting a columnar journal involves the following procedures.

1. All column totals except the total for the Other Accounts column are posted once at the end of the month to the account title specified in the column heading, such as Cash or Accounts Receivable. Account numbers are entered below the column totals to show that they have been posted.
2. The total of the Other Accounts column is not posted. Instead, the individual amounts comprising the total are posted separately to the general ledger accounts specified in the Accounts Credited column. See, for example, the credit posting to D. A. Karns, Capital. The symbol (X) is inserted below the total to this column to indicate that the amount is not posted.
3. The individual amounts in a column, posted in total to a control account (Accounts Receivable, in this case), are posted daily to the subsidiary ledger account specified in the Accounts Credited column. See, for example, the credit posting of $10,600 to Abbot Sisters.

Therefore, cash is posted to account No. 1, accounts receivable to account No. 4, sales to account No. 60, and sales discounts to account No. 61. The symbol CR is used in the ledgers to identify postings from the cash receipts journal.

At the end of the month, the agreement of the balance of the accounts receivable control account with the sum of the customer balances in the subsidiary ledger can be proved as follows:

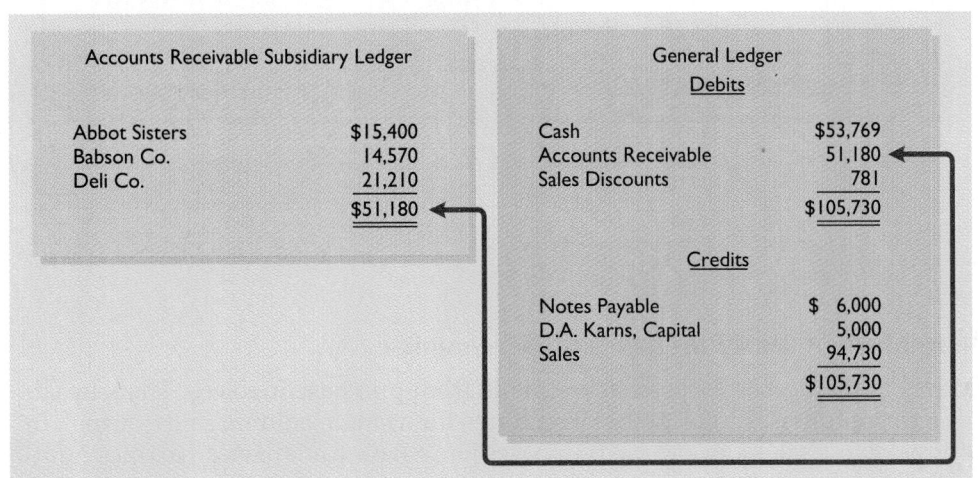

Purchases Journal

Helpful hint   A single column purchases journal only needs to be footed to prove the equality of debits and credits.

All purchases of merchandise on account are recorded in the purchases journal. Each entry in this journal results in a debit to Purchases and a credit to Accounts Payable. When a one-column purchases journal is used, other types of purchases on account and cash purchases cannot be journalized in it. For example, credit purchases of equipment or supplies must be recorded in the general journal, and all cash purchases are entered in the cash payments journal. As illustrated later, where credit purchases for items other than merchandise are numerous, the purchases journal is often expanded to a multi-column format. The single-column purchases journal for Karns Wholesale Supply is shown in Illustration 6-11.

ILLUSTRATION 6-11

Journalizing and posting purchases journal

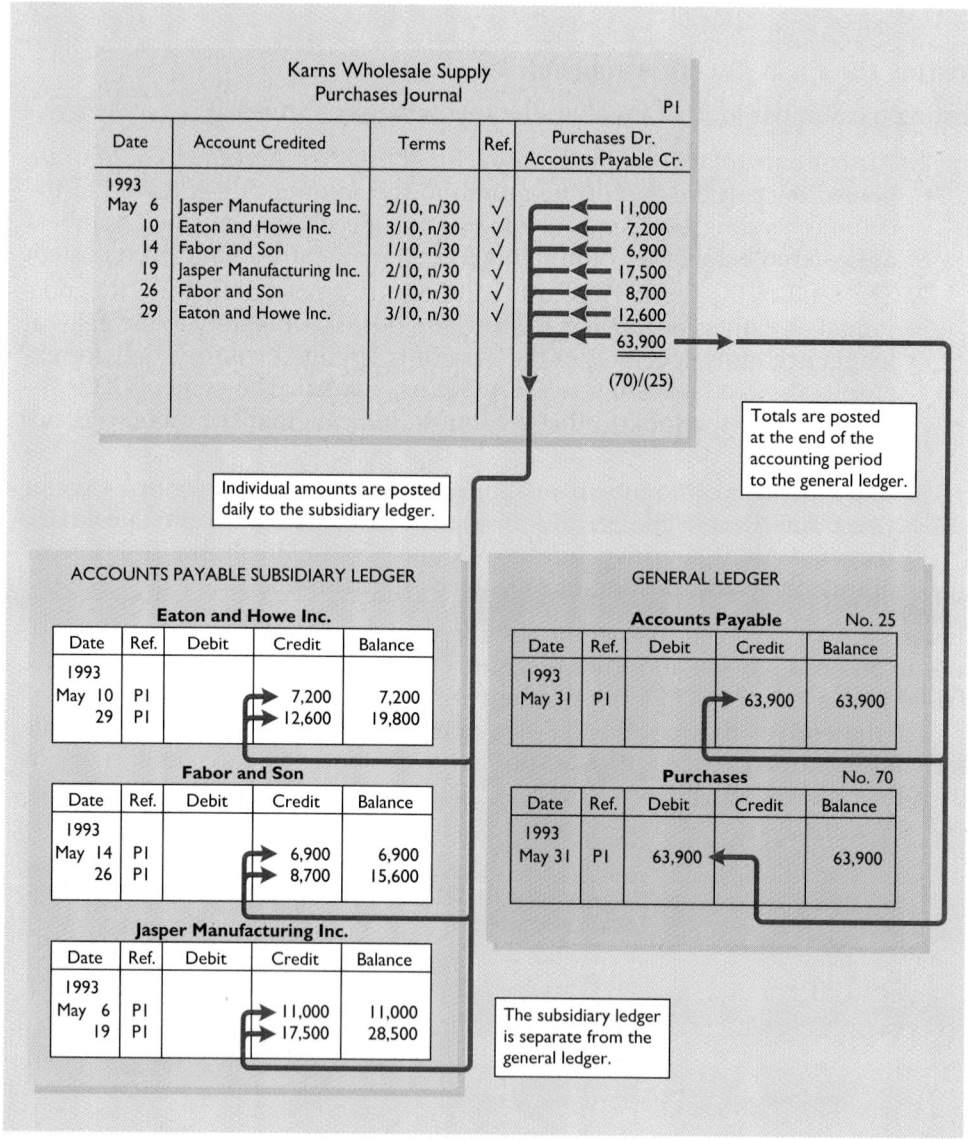

Journalizing Credit Purchases of Merchandise

Entries in the purchases journal are made from purchase invoices. The journalizing procedure is similar to the procedures for a single-column sales journal. In contrast to the sales journal, the purchases journal may not have an invoice number column, because invoices received from different suppliers will not be in numerical sequence. To assure that all purchase invoices are recorded, however, some companies consecutively number each invoice upon receipt and then provide for an internal document number column in the purchases journal.

The entries for Karns Wholesale Supply are based on the following assumed transactions:

Date	Supplier	Amount	Date	Supplier	Amount
5/6	Jasper Manufacturing Inc.	$11,000	5/19	Jasper Manufacturing Inc.	$17,500
5/10	Eaton and Howe, Inc.	7,200	5/26	Fabor and Son	8,700
5/14	Fabor and Son	6,900	5/29	Eaton and Howe, Inc.	12,600

ILLUSTRATION 6-12

Credit purchases transactions

Posting the Purchases Journal

The procedures for posting the purchases journal are similar to those for the sales journal. In this case, postings are made **daily** to the accounts payable ledger and **monthly** to Purchases and Accounts Payable in the general ledger. In both ledgers, the letter P1 is used in the reference column to show that the postings are from page 1 of the purchases journal.

Proof of the accuracy of the postings to both ledgers in this example is shown by the following tabulation:

Helpful hint Postings to subsidiary ledger accounts are done daily because it is often necessary to know a current balance for the subsidiary accounts.

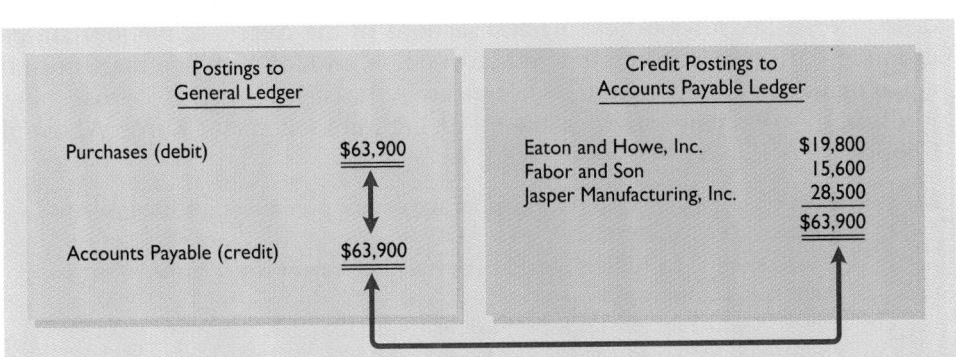

ILLUSTRATION 6-13

Proving the postings of the purchases journal

Expanding the Purchases Journal

Some companies expand the purchases journal to include all types of purchases on account. Instead of one column for purchases and accounts payable, a multiple-column format is used. The multiple-column format usually includes a credit column for accounts payable and debit columns for purchases of merchandise, purchases of office supplies, purchases of store supplies, and other accounts. Illustration 6-14 is an example of a multiple-column purchases journal for Hanover Co. The posting procedures are similar to those used for posting the cash receipts journal illustrated earlier.

Helpful hint A multiple-column purchases journal must be footed and cross-footed to prove the equality of debits and credits.

Cash Payments (Disbursements) Journal

All disbursements of cash are entered in a cash payments or cash disbursements journal. Entries in this journal are made from prenumbered checks. Because cash payments may be made for a variety of purposes, the cash payments journal has multiple columns. A four-column journal is shown in Illustration 6-15.

ILLUSTRATION 6-14

Columnar purchases journal

								Other Accounts Dr.		
Date	Accounts Credited	Ref.	Accounts Payable Cr.	Purchases Dr.	Office Supplies Dr.	Store Supplies Dr.		Account	Ref.	Amount
1993										
June 1	Signe Audio	√	2,000		2,000					
3	Wright Co.	√	1,500	1,500						
5	Orange Tree Co.	√	2,600					Equipment	18	2,600
30	Sue's Business Forms	√	800			800				
			56,600	43,000	7,500	1,200				4,900

HANOVER CO.
Purchases Journal — **P1**

Journalizing Cash Payments Transactions

The procedures for journalizing transactions in this journal are similar to those described earlier for journalizing transactions in the cash receipts journal. For example, each transaction is entered on one line, and for each line there must be equal debit and credit amounts. The entries in the cash payments journal shown in Illustration 6-15 are based on the following transactions for Karns Wholesale Supply:

May 1 Check No. 101 for $1,200 is issued for the annual premium on a fire insurance policy.

3 Check No. 102 for $100 is issued in payment of freight when terms of purchase were FOB shipping point.

8 Check No. 103 for $400 is issued for the purchase of merchandise.

10 Check No. 104 for $10,780 is sent to Jasper Manufacturing Inc. in payment of May 6 invoice for $11,000 less a 2% discount.

19 Check No. 105 for $6,984 is mailed to Eaton and Howe, Inc. in payment of May 10 invoice for $7,200 less a 3% discount.

23 Check No. 106 for $6,831 is sent to Fabor and Son in payment of May 14 invoice for $6,900 less a 1% discount.

28 Check No. 107 for $17,150 is sent to Jasper Manufacturing Inc. in payment of May 19 invoice for $17,500 less a 2% discount.

30 Check No. 108 for $500 is issued to D. A. Karns as a cash withdrawal for personal use.

The symbol CP is used as the posting reference for this journal. Note that whenever an amount is entered in the Other Accounts column, a specific general ledger account must be identified in the Accounts Debited column. The entries for check Nos. 101, 102, and 103 illustrate this situation. Similarly, a subsidiary account must be identified in the Accounts Debited column whenever an amount is entered in the Accounts Payable column, as, for example, the entry for check No. 104.

When the journalizing of the cash payments journal has been completed, the amount columns are totaled. The totals are then balanced to prove the equality of debits and credits.

ILLUSTRATION 6-15

Journalizing and posting the cash payments journal

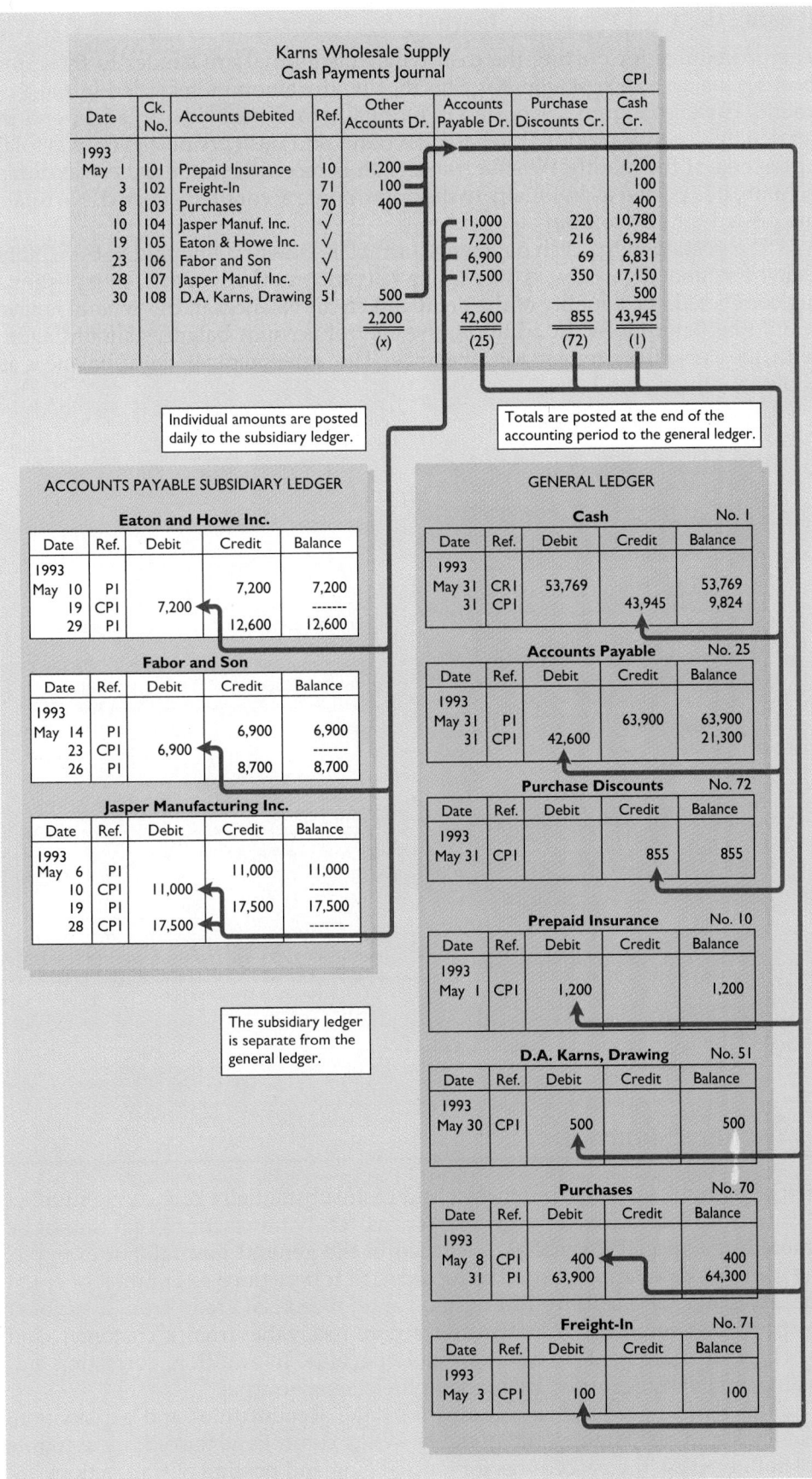

Posting the Cash Payments Journal

The procedures for posting the cash payments journal are similar to those for posting the cash receipts journal. Specifically, the amounts recorded in the Accounts Payable column are posted individually to the subsidiary ledger and in total to the control account. Purchase Discounts and Cash are posted only in total at the end of the month. When a transaction is recorded in the Other Accounts column, it is posted individually to the appropriate account(s) affected. No totals are posted for this column.

The posting of the cash payments journal is shown in Illustration 6-15. Note that the symbol CP is used as the posting reference for this journal. After postings are completed, the equality of the debit and credit balances in the general ledger should be determined. In addition, the control account balances should agree with the subsidiary ledger total balance. The agreement of these balances is shown in Illustration 6-16.

ILLUSTRATION 6-16

*Reconciling accounts payable
subsidiary ledger to control
account*

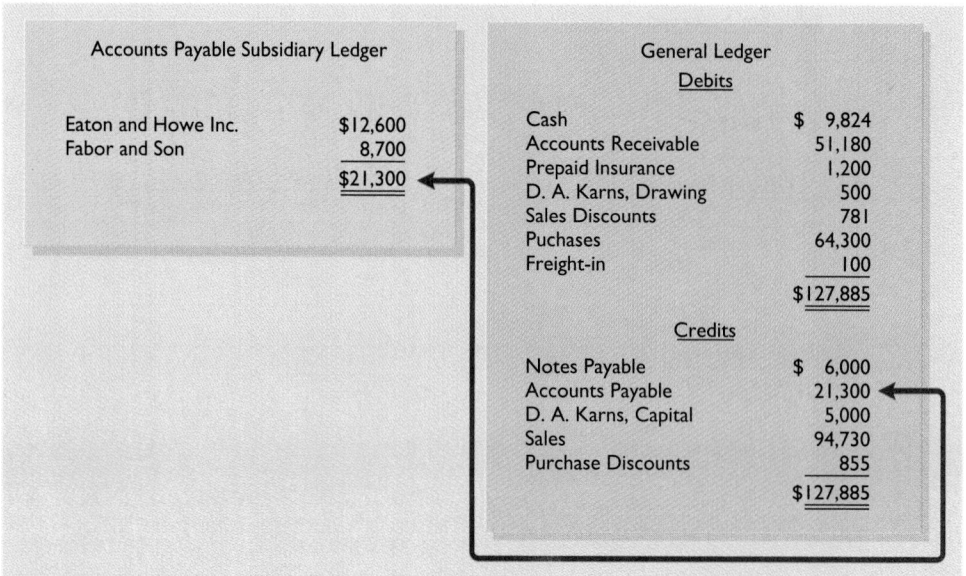

Accounts Payable Subsidiary Ledger	
Eaton and Howe Inc.	$12,600
Fabor and Son	8,700
	$21,300

General Ledger Debits	
Cash	$ 9,824
Accounts Receivable	51,180
Prepaid Insurance	1,200
D. A. Karns, Drawing	500
Sales Discounts	781
Puchases	64,300
Freight-in	100
	$127,885

Credits	
Notes Payable	$ 6,000
Accounts Payable	21,300
D. A. Karns, Capital	5,000
Sales	94,730
Purchase Discounts	855
	$127,885

General Journal

Special journals for sales, purchases, and cash substantially reduce the number of entries that are made in the general journal. **Only transactions that cannot be entered in a special journal are recorded in the general journal.** For example, the general journal may be used to record such transactions as granting of credit to a customer for a sales return or allowance, receipt of credit from a supplier for purchases returned, acceptance of a note receivable from a customer, and purchase of equipment by issuing a note payable. In addition, correcting, adjusting, and closing entries are made in the general journal.

The general journal has columns for date, account titles and explanation, reference, and debit and credit amounts. When control and subsidiary accounts are not involved, the procedures for journalizing and posting of transactions are identical with those described in earlier chapters. However, when control and subsidiary accounts are involved, two modifications of earlier procedures are required:

1. In journalizing, both the control and the subsidiary accounts must be identified.
2. In posting, there must be a dual posting: once to the control account and once to the subsidiary account.

To illustrate, assume that on May 31, Karns Wholesale Supply returns $500 of merchandise for credit to Fabor and Son because of an error in filling its May 26 order. The entry in the general journal and the posting of the entry are shown in Illustration 6-17. Note that if cash is received instead of credit granted on this return, then the transaction is recorded in the cash receipts journal.

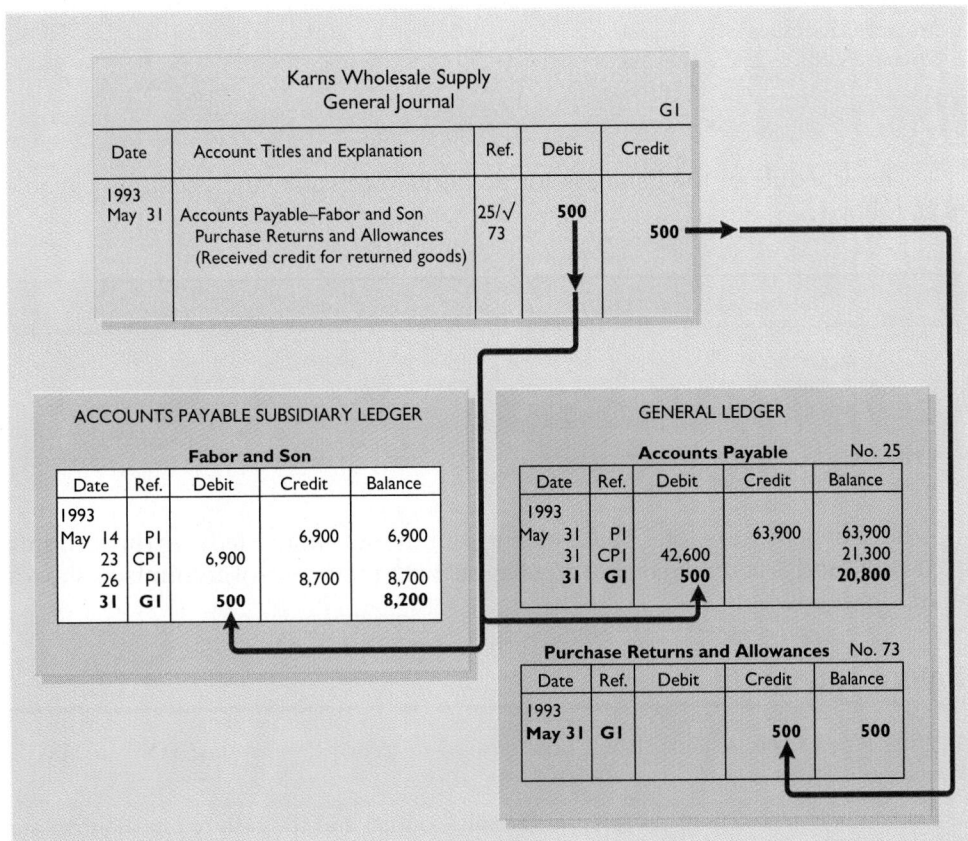

Observe in the journal that two accounts are indicated for the debit and two postings are indicated in the reference column. One amount is posted to the control account and the other to the creditor's account in the subsidiary ledger.

Karns Wholesale Supply—A Recap

Given the transaction information for the month of May, Karns' trial balance based on the general ledger data is shown in Illustration 6-18.

ILLUSTRATION 6-18

Trial balance

KARNS WHOLESALE SUPPLY
Trial Balance
May 31, 1993

	Debit	Credit
Cash	$ 9,824	
Accounts Receivable	51,180	
Prepaid Insurance	1,200	
Notes Payable		$ 6,000
Accounts Payable		20,800
D. A. Karns, Capital		5,000
D. A. Karns, Drawing	500	
Sales		94,730
Sales Discounts	781	
Purchases	64,300	
Freight-in	100	
Purchase Discounts		855
Purchase Returns and Allowances		500
	$127,885	$127,885

The schedule of the balances for accounts receivable and accounts payable is as follows:

ILLUSTRATION 6-19

Proving control accounts in the trial balance

Accounts Receivable	
Abbot Sisters	$15,400
Babson Co.	14,570
Deli Co.	21,210
	$51,180

Accounts Payable	
Eaton and Howe, Inc.	$12,600
Fabor and Son	8,200
	$20,800

It follows that the total of the balances in the subsidiary ledgers for accounts receivable and accounts payable must agree with their control accounts as shown on the trial balance.

Before You Go On . . .

1. What type of special journals are usually used to record transactions? Why are special journals used?

2. Explain how transactions recorded in the sales journal and the cash receipts journal are posted.

3. Identify the special journal used to record the following transactions: sales of merchandise on account, purchases of merchandise on credit, cash withdrawal for personal use, credit received for returned goods, and cash sales.

Direct Posting to Subsidiary Ledgers

Direct posting means posting subsidiary ledger accounts directly from a source document, rather than from a journal. In our earlier explanation of the sales journal, the entries were made from the prenumbered invoices. Postings to the accounts receivable subsidiary ledger were then made from the journal. Under

ILLUSTRATION 6-20

Direct posting illustrated

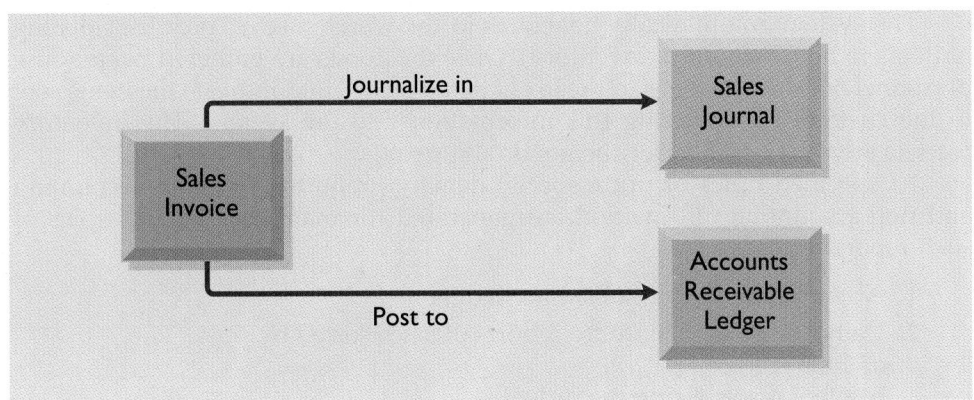

direct posting, the invoice that provides the information for the sales journal entry is sent directly to the employee(s) responsible for maintaining the accounts receivable subsidiary ledger. The invoice is then used to post to the specific accounts receivable account. Direct posting facilitates the updating of subsidiary ledgers because subsidiary ledger clerks do not need access to the journals.

SECTION 2 Electronic Data Processing

Many students ask, "Why study manual systems if the real world uses computerized systems?" The accounting concepts and principles do not change whether the system is manual or computerized. However, the concepts are more easily illustrated in a manual system than in a computerized system. In addition, the exact procedures in a computerized system depend on the computer hardware and software being used. Thus, manual systems have been used up to now in this textbook and will continue to be used in the remainder of the chapters.

Electronic data processing (also called computerized or automated systems) encompasses all processing steps from the initial entry of data into the system to the preparation of financial reports for management. A discussion of a computerized order entry system illustrates many of the common characteristics of a computerized system.

Computerized Order Entry

The system under discussion might be used by a medium-sized mail-order firm, which sells goods using an "800" (toll-free) telephone number. Customers call the number and reach an operator, who enters the sales transaction into the system. The entry screen of the operator resembles an expanded sales journal. Detailed sales information is gathered for each item ordered. In addition, customer information from the accounts receivable data base is also displayed and updated as necessary.

When the final item has been ordered, the operator releases the information into the computer system. The sales transactions are immediately journalized using price information stored in the inventory data base and automatically posted to the general ledger and accounts receivable subsidiary ledger.

The system automatically generates in the warehouse a "pick list" (listing of items to be taken out of inventory). Once the goods are gathered, warehouse personnel note any changes to the list of items picked and indicate the items sent to the customer by entering this information into the system. The inventory records are thus updated for the goods shipped.

At specified times or upon special demand, reports with both accounting and non-accounting information are generated for management. Examples of such reports include:

1. Accounts receivable subsidiary ledger
2. Daily, weekly, or monthly reports of sales sorted by
   a. Item sold
   b. Operator entering the order
   c. Customer
3. Slow-moving or "hot"-selling inventory

Technology in Action

Data processing professionals use the acronym GIGO—garbage-in, garbage-out—to indicate that a computer system is only as good as the data it receives. Data entry is the garbage-in stage of the acronym. Garbage-in is not automated, garbage-out is automated. The real trick (and the expensive part) of both manual and automated systems (either micros, minis, or mainframes) is to get what we might call DIIO, that is, data-in, information-out.

Comparative Advantages of Manual versus Computerized Systems

As previously discussed, there are similarities and differences between manual and computerized systems. One should not conclude that computerized systems are always better. As with any selection, the costs and benefits of each alternative should be weighed before the choice is made. The following key points should be considered when evaluating and comparing manual and computerized systems.

Dollar Costs

The costs of bookkeepers' salaries and manual accounting records must be compared to the costs of computer hardware and software. Computer systems have some hidden costs that must be considered. Such costs include computer training of personnel and salary differences between bookkeepers and competent computer operators to run the system. Another consideration is the possibility that fewer individuals are needed to run a computer system. And, in general, with microcomputers widely available, as well as an abundance of user-friendly software packages, the manual system is losing its comparative advantage in even the smallest businesses.

Processing Speed

When the number of transactions is large, computerized systems offer real advantages. Thousands of transactions can be processed quickly by a computer, and high-speed printers can generate reports. However, delays in computer processing can occur. For example, if transactions are batched (grouped together into like categories and processed at a later time), records and balances may not contain the most up-to-date information. This delay can be avoided by processing transactions using real-time (on-line) processing systems in which data are processed as soon as received. In addition, if back-up hardware and software are not kept, malfunctions and breakdowns may bring the system to a standstill.

Processing Errors

Unless a hardware failure occurs, the computer will not make a processing error. Both hardware and software controls generally ensure accurate processing. Because humans perform the processing in a manual system, the potential for processing errors is greater in the manual system. However, humans may be involved with data entry in a computerized system, so some errors may creep into the system.

Responsiveness

Have you ever tried to call the computer to get your bill corrected? Errors and other problems are generally handled more swiftly and readily in a manual system than in a computerized system. For example, a bookkeeper may be more responsive to customer complaints. Also, an important psychological factor differentiates manual systems from computer systems. In a computerized system, customers become numbers, and customers generally prefer not to be treated as numbers; they like personalized relationships. The computer becomes a mechanical intermediary that neither recognizes individuality nor appreciates the customer's business; it never says "Thank you!"

Report Generation

A definite advantage of computerized systems is the ease with which reports can be prepared. Once the system contains the information, useful manipulations of the information can be performed and printed in a matter of minutes. These "demand" reports are also a result of the computer system's ability to bring together information from different parts of the system, such as sales transactions and the accounts receivable subsidiary ledger.

Although some trade-offs exist between the efficiencies of computers and the personal responsiveness of manual systems, computer systems are gaining so significantly in popularity that manual accounting systems are becoming an endangered species.

A Look into the Future

Initially, computer technology in business was used to automate the accounting system. Much of the clerical work involved in recording and summarizing accounting transaction data was eliminated. However, there was still a problem—a sales transaction was first processed by accountants. Then, this same sales information was reprocessed by production, marketing, and so on for use in their decision making.

Accountants are now beginning to use computer systems to capture all the organizational information and then provide this information to executives in the forms they desire. As one writer noted: Accountants are becoming organization historians by (a) recording complete histories of organizational events and (b) interpreting these histories for decision makers. Thus, an organizational data

Helpful hint An electronic cash register is a good example of computer use in accounting. At the time of each cash receipt, cash, inventory, and sales are updated and posted. In other words, the posting process occurs at the time the transaction takes place.

base of events is developed. This data base is then used to provide information for decision making for both internal and external purposes. These new developments will make accounting even more enjoyable and useful in the future.[1]

Before You Go On . . .

1. Why study a manual system?

2. What are the advantages of using a computerized system to record business transactions?

Summary of Study Objectives

1. Identify the basic principles of accounting information system development. The basic principles in developing an accounting information system are cost awareness, useful output, and flexible structure.

2. Explain the major phases involved in the development of an accounting information system. The major phases in the development of an accounting information system are analysis, design, implementation, and follow-up.

3. Describe the nature and purpose of a subsidiary ledger. A subsidiary ledger is a group of accounts with a common characteristic. It facilitates the recording process by freeing the general ledger from details of individual balances.

4. Explain how special journals are used in journalizing. A special journal is used to group similar types of transactions. In a special journal, only one line is used to record a complete transaction.

5. Indicate how a columnar journal is posted. In posting a columnar journal:
(a) all column totals except for the Other Accounts column are posted once at the end of the month to the account title specified in the column heading.
(b) the total of the Other Accounts column is not posted. Instead, the individual amounts comprising the total are posted separately to the general ledger account specified in the Accounts column.
(c) the individual amounts in a column posted in total to a control account are posted daily to the subsidiary ledger accounts specified in the Accounts column.

6. Identify the key points in comparing manual and computerized accounting systems. The key points in comparing manual and computerized accounting systems are (a) cost considerations, (b) processing speed, (c) processing errors, (d) responsiveness, and (e) generation of reports on demand.

GLOSSARY

Accounting information system · A system that involves collecting and processing data, and disseminating financial information. (p. 230).

Accounts payable (creditors') ledger · A subsidiary ledger that contains accounts with individual creditors. (p. 233).

Accounts receivable (customers') ledger · A subsidiary ledger that contains individual customer accounts. (p. 233).

Batch · Transactions grouped together into like categories and processed at a later time. (p. 251).

Cash payments (disbursements) journal · A special journal used to record all cash paid. (p. 235).

Cash receipts journal · A special journal used to record all cash received. (p. 235).

Columnar journal · A special journal with more than one column. (p. 238).

Control account · An account in the general ledger that controls a subsidiary ledger. (p. 233).

Direct posting · The posting of subsidiary accounts directly from a source document, rather than from a journal. (p. 248).

---

[1]Adapted from an article by Eric L. Denna, ''Real Time Accounting,'' *New Accounting* (December 1990).

Purchases journal · A special journal used to record all purchases of merchandise on account. (p. 235).

Real-time (on-line) · Data processed as soon as received. (p. 251).

Sales journal · A special journal used to record all sales of merchandise on account. (p. 235).

Special journal · A journal that is used to record similar types of transactions such as all credit sales. (p. 235).

Subsidiary ledger · A group of accounts with a common characteristic. (p. 233).

DEMONSTRATION PROBLEM

The Emelia Company uses a five-column cash receipts journal with columns for Cash (Dr.), Sales Discounts (Dr.), Accounts Receivable (Cr.), Sales (Cr.), and Other Accounts (Cr.). Cash receipts transactions for the month of July are as follows:

July 3 Cash sales total $5,800.

5 A check for $6,370 is received from the Jeltz Company in payment of invoice dated June 26 for $6,500 terms 2/10, n/30.

9 An additional investment of $5,000 in cash is made in the business by Betty Emelia, the proprietor.

10 Cash sales total $12,519.

12 A check for $7,275 is received from R. Eliot & Co. in payment of a $7,500 invoice dated July 3, terms 3/10, n/30.

15 A customer advance of $700 cash is received for future sales.

20 Cash sales total $15,472.

22 A check for $5,880 is received from Beck Company in payment of $6,000 invoice dated July 13, terms 2/10, n/30.

29 Cash sales total $17,660.

31 Cash of $200 is received on interest earned for July.

Instructions

(a) Journalize the transactions in the cash receipts journal.

(b) Contrast the posting of the Accounts Receivable and Other Accounts columns.

Solution to Demonstration Problem

(a)

EMELIA COMPANY
Cash Receipts Journal
CR 1

Date	Accounts Credited	Ref.	Cash Dr.	Sales Discounts Dr.	Accounts Receivable Cr.	Sales Cr.	Other Accounts Cr.
7/3			5,800			5,800	
5	Jeltz Company		6,370	130	6,500		
9	Betty Emelia, Capital		5,000				5,000
10			12,519			12,519	
12	R. Eliot & Co.		7,275	225	7,500		
15	Unearned Revenues		700				700
20			15,472			15,472	
22	Beck Company		5,880	120	6,000		
29			17,660			17,660	
31	Interest Revenue		200				200
			76,876	475	20,000	51,451	5,900

Helpful hints

1. All cash receipts are recorded in the cash receipts journal.
2. The "accounts credited" indicate items posted individually to the subsidiary ledger or general ledger.
3. Cash sales are recorded in the cash receipts journal—not in the sales journal.
4. The total debits must equal the total credits.

(b) The Accounts Receivable column is posted as a credit to Accounts Receivable. The individual amounts are credited to the customers' accounts identified in the Accounts Credited column, which are maintained in the accounts receivable subsidiary ledger.

The amounts in the Other Accounts Column are only posted individually. They are credited to the account titles identified in the Accounts Credited column.

SELF-STUDY QUESTIONS

Answers are at the end of the chapter.

(S.O. 1)   1. The basic principles of an accounting information system include all of the following except:
a. cost awareness.
b. flexible structure.
c. periodicity.
d. useful output

(S.O. 2)   2. Which of the following is *not* a major phase in the development of an accounting information system?
a. Responsiveness.
b. Design.
c. Implementation.
d. Follow-up.

(S.O. 3)   3. Which of the following is *incorrect* concerning subsidiary ledgers?
a. A subsidiary ledger is a group of accounts with a common characteristic.
b. The accounts receivable ledger is a subsidiary ledger.
c. The purchases ledger is a common subsidiary ledger for creditor accounts.
d. An advantage of the subsidiary ledger is that it permits a division of labor in posting.

(S.O. 4)   4. A sales journal will be used for:

	Credit sales	Cash sales	Sales discounts
a.	no	yes	yes
b.	yes	no	yes
c.	yes	yes	no
d.	yes	no	no

(S.O. 4)   5. Which of the following statements is correct?
a. The cash receipts journal records sales on account.
b. The purchases journal records all purchases of merchandise whether for cash or on account.
c. The sales discount column is included in the cash receipts journal.
d. Merchandise returned by the buyer is recorded by the seller in the purchases journal.

(S.O. 5)   6. Which of the following is *incorrect* concerning the posting of the cash receipts journal?

a. The total of the Other Accounts column is not posted.
b. All column totals except the total for the Other Accounts column are posted once at the end of the month to the account title specified in the column heading.
c. The individual amounts in a column posted in total to a control account are posted daily to the subsidiary ledger account specified in the Accounts Credited column.
d. The total of all columns are posted daily to the accounts specified in the column heading.

(S.O. 3)   7. Postings from the purchases journal to the subsidiary ledger are generally made:
a. daily.
b. weekly.
c. monthly.
d. yearly.

(S.O. 4)   8. Which statement is *incorrect* regarding the general journal?
a. Only transactions that cannot be entered in a special journal are recorded in the general journal.
b. The general journal may be used to record acceptance of a note receivable for an accounts receivable.
c. Dual postings are always required in the general journal.
d. Correcting, adjusting, and closing entries are made in the general journal.

(S.O. 6)   9. Electronic and manual data processing systems both:
a. begin at the ledger account level.
b. involve human output of data.
c. involve human input of data.
d. process data at approximately the same speed.

(S.O. 6)   10. Which of the following is *not* a key point in evaluating and comparing manual and computerized systems?
a. Cost considerations and processing speed.
b. Processing errors and responsiveness.
c. Generation of "demand" reports.
d. Posting general journals and special journals.

QUESTIONS

1. What are the basic principles of accounting information system development?

2. Roy Scott Company is considering changing its accounting system for its accounts receivable billing procedure. At present, the procedure is performed manually by three clerks. A consultant has recommended that a new computer and related software be purchased for $1,000,000. What basic principle of designing and developing an effective accounting system might be violated by this proposal?

3. Identify the major phases involved in the development of an accounting information system.

4. What are the advantages of using subsidiary ledgers?

5. When are postings normally made to (a) the subsidiary accounts and (b) the general ledger control accounts?

6. Describe the relationship between a control account and a subsidiary account.

7. Identify and explain the four specific journals discussed in the chapter. List an advantage of using each of these journals rather than using only a general journal.

8. A. Morgan Company uses special journals. A sale made on account to K. Hansen for $435 was recorded in a single-column sales journal. A few days later, Hansen returns $70 worth of merchandise for credit. Where should A. Morgan Company record the sales return? Why?

9. A $400 purchase of merchandise on account from Julian Company was properly recorded in the purchases journal. When posted, however, the amount recorded in the subsidiary ledger was $40. How might this error be discovered?

10. Why would special journals used in different businesses not be identical in format? Can you think of a business that would maintain a cash receipts journal but not include a column for accounts receivable?

11. The cash and the accounts receivable columns in the cash receipts journal were mistakenly overadded by $4,000 at the end of the month. (a) Will the customers' ledger agree with the Accounts Receivable control account? (b) Assuming no other errors, will the trial balance totals be equal?

12. The column total of a special journal is posted at month end to only two general ledger accounts. One of these two accounts is Accounts Receivable. What is the name of this special journal? What is the other general ledger account to which the month-end total is posted?

13. In what journal would the following transactions be recorded? (Assume that a single-column sales journal and a single-column purchases journal are used.)
(a) Gave credit to a customer for merchandise purchased on credit and returned.
(b) Recording of depreciation expense for the year.
(c) Sales of merchandise for cash.
(d) Sales of merchandise on account.
(e) Collection of cash on account from a customer.
(f) Purchase of office supplies on account.

14. In what journal would the following transactions be recorded? (Assume that a single-column sales journal and a single-column purchases journal are used.)
(a) Cash received from signing a note payable.
(b) Investment of cash by the owner of the business.
(c) Closing of the expense accounts at the end of the year.
(d) Purchase of merchandise on account.
(e) Payment of cash on account due a supplier.
(f) Received credit for merchandise purchased and returned to supplier.

15. What transactions might be included in a multiple-column purchases journal that would not be included in a single-column purchases journal?

16. Give an example of a transaction in the general journal that causes an entry to be posted twice (i.e., to two accounts), one in the general ledger, the other in the subsidiary ledger. Does this affect the debit/credit equality of the general ledger?

17. Give some examples of appropriate general journal transactions for an organization using special journals.

18. What is direct posting?

19. What are the key points to be considered in evaluating and comparing manual and computerized systems?

BRIEF EXERCISES

Identify basic principles of accounting information system development.
(S.O. 1)

BE6–1 Indicate whether each of the following statements is true or false.

1. In developing an accounting system, cost is relevant. The system must be cost effective; that is, the benefits obtained from the information disseminated must outweigh the cost of providing it.
2. When the environment changes as a result of technological advances, increased competition, or government regulation, an accounting system does not have to be sufficiently flexible to meet the changes in order to save money.
3. When designing an accounting system, we need to think about the needs and knowledge of both the top management and other various users.

Identify major phases in accounting system development.
(S.O. 2)

BE6–2 The development of an accounting system involves four phases: analysis, design, implementation, and follow-up. Identify the statement that best describes each of these four phases.

1. Evaluation and monitoring of effectiveness and efficiency, and correction of weaknesses, implementation, and design.
2. Determining internal and external information needs, identifying information sources and the needs for controls, and studying alternatives.
3. Creation of forms and documents, selection of procedures, and preparation of job descriptions.
4. Implementing new or revised documents, procedures, reports, and processing equipment; hiring and training personnel through a start-up or transition period.

Identify subsidiary ledger balances.
(S.O. 3)

BE6–3 Presented below is information related to Bradley Company for its first month of operations. Identify the balances that appear in the accounts receivable subsidiary ledger and the accounts receivable balance that appears in the general ledger at the end of January.

Credit Sales			Cash Collections		
Jan. 7	Avon Co.	$9,000	Jan. 17	Avon Co.	$7,000
15	Barto Inc.	$6,000	24	Barto Inc.	$5,000
23	Cecil Co.	$8,000	29	Cecil Co.	$8,000

Identify subsidiary ledger accounts.
(S.O. 3)

BE6–4 Identify in what ledger (general or subsidiary) each of the following accounts are shown.

1. Accounts Receivable—Oliva
2. Rent Expense
3. Notes Payable
4. Accounts Payable—Kerns

Identify special journals.
(S.O. 4)

BE6–5 Identify the journal in which each of the following transactions are recorded.

1. Cash sales
2. Owner withdrawal of cash
3. Cash purchase of land
4. Credit sales
5. Receipt of cash for services performed
6. Purchase of merchandise on account

Identify entries to cash receipts journal.
(S.O. 4)

BE6–6 Indicate whether each of the following debits and credits are included in the Cash Receipts journal. (Use "Yes" or "No" to answer this question.)

1. Debit to Sales
2. Credit to Purchase Discounts
3. Debit to Accounts Payable
4. Credit to Accounts Receivable

BE6–7 Stickney Computer Components Inc. uses a columnar Cash Receipts journal. Indicate which column(s) is/are posted only in total, only daily, or both in total and daily.

Indicate postings to cash receipts journal.
(S.O. 5)

1. Sales Discounts   3. Other Accounts
2. Accounts Receivable   4. Cash

BE6–8 The Concord Co. uses special journals and a general journal. Identify the journal in which each of the following transactions is recorded.

Identify transactions for special journals.
(S.O. 4)

1. Purchased merchandise on account.
2. Purchased equipment on account.
3. Sold merchandise on account.
4. Paid utility expense in cash.

BE6–9 Identify the special journal in which the following column headings appear.

Identify transactions for special journals.
(S.O. 4)

1. Sales Discounts Dr.   4. Purchase Dr.
2. Accounts Receivable Cr.   5. Purchase Discount Cr.
3. Cash Dr.   6. Sales Cr.

BE6–10 What are the trade-offs between the efficiencies of computers and the personal responsiveness of manual systems?

Compare manual versus computerized systems.
(S.O. 6)

EXERCISES

E6–1 Trimas Company uses both special journals and a general journal as described in this chapter. On June 30, after all monthly postings had been completed, the Accounts Receivable controlling account in the general ledger had a debit balance of $340,000 and the Accounts Payable controlling account had a credit balance of $97,000.

Determine control account balances and explain posting of special journals.
(S.O. 3, 4)

The July transactions recorded in the special journals are summarized below. No entries affecting accounts receivable and accounts payable were recorded in the general journal for July.

Sales journal   Total sales, $161,400
Purchases journal   Total purchases, $54,360
Cash receipts journal   Accounts receivable column total, $135,000
Cash payments journal   Accounts payable column total, $49,500

Instructions

(a) What is the balance of the Accounts Receivable control account after the monthly postings on July 31?

(b) What is the balance of the Accounts Payable control account after the monthly postings on July 31?

(c) To what accounts is the column total of $161,400 in the sales journal posted?

(d) To what account(s) is the accounts receivable column total of $135,000 in the cash receipts journal posted?

E6–2 Presented below is the subsidiary accounts receivable account of Hector Lopez.

Explain postings to subsidiary ledger.
(S.O. 3)

Date	Ref	Debit	Credit	Balance
1993				
Sept. 2	S31	61,000		61,000
9	G4		12,000	49,000
27	CR8		49,000	—

Instructions
Explain each transaction.

Post various journals to control and subsidiary accounts.
(S.O. 3, 5)

E6–3 On September 1 the balance of the Accounts Receivable controlling account in the general ledger of Columbia Company was $10,960. The customers' subsidiary ledger contained account balances as follows: Bannister, $1,440; Crowley, $2,640; Dotson, $2,060; Seaver, $4,820. At the end of September the various journals contained the following information:

Sales Journal: Sales to Seaver, $800; to Bannister, $1,350; to DeLeon, $1,030; to Dotson, $1,100.

Cash receipts journal: Cash received from Dotson, $1,310; from Seaver, $2,300; from DeLeon, $410; from Crowley, $1,800; from Bannister, $1,240.

General journal: An allowance is granted to Seaver, $110.

Instructions

(a) Set up control and subsidiary accounts and enter the beginning balances. Do not construct the journals.

(b) Post the various journals. Post the items as individual items or as totals, whichever would be the appropriate procedure. (No sales discounts given)

(c) Prepare a list of customers and prove the agreement of the controlling account with the subsidiary ledger.

Record transactions in sales and purchases journal.
(S.O. 3, 4)

E6–4 Harrott Company uses special journals and a general journal. The following transaction occurred during September, 1993.

Sept. 2 Sold merchandise on account to B. Vell, Invoice No. 101, $600, terms n/30.
    10 Purchased merchandise on account from C. Cosgrove $700, terms 2/10, n/30.
    12 Purchased office equipment on account from J. Wells, $6,500.
    20 Paid C. Cosgrove $686 for the merchandise purchased on September 10.
    21 Sold merchandise for L. Scott for $800 cash.
    25 Purchased merchandise on account from P. Lewis $900, terms n/30.

Instructions

(a) Draw a single column sales journal (See Illustration 6-6) and a single column purchase journal (See Illustration 6-11).

(b) Record the transaction(s) for September that should be journalized in the sales journal and the purchases journal.

Record transactions in cash receipts and cash payments journal.
(S.O. 3, 4)

E6–5 Reese Inc. uses special journals and a general journal. The following transactions occurred during May, 1993.

May 1 L. Reese invested $72,000 cash in the business.
    2 Sold merchandise to L. Bean for $6,000 cash.
    3 Purchased merchandise for $8,000 from R. L. Sanchez using Check No. 101.
    14 Paid wages to F. Sparks of $1,000 issuing Check No. 102.
    16 Sold merchandise on account to B. Ready for $900, terms n/30.
    22 A check of $9,000 is received from C. Moody in full for invoice 101; no discount given.

Instructions

(a) Draw a multiple column cash receipts journal (See Illustration 6-8) and a multiple column cash payments journal (See Illustration 6-15).

(b) Record the transaction(s) for May that should be journalized in the cash receipts journal and cash payments journal.

Explain journalizing in cash journals.
(S.O. 4)

E6–6 The Aldus Company uses the columnar cash journals illustrated in the textbook. In April, the following selected cash transactions occurred:

1. Received collection from customer within the 3% discount period.
2. Made a refund to a customer for the return of damaged goods.
3. Purchased merchandise for cash.
4. Paid a creditor within the 3% discount period.
5. Received collection from customer after the 3% discount period had expired.
6. Paid freight on merchandise purchased.
7. Paid cash for office equipment.
8. Received cash refund from supplier for merchandise returned.

9. Made cash sales.

10. Withdrew cash for personal use of owner.

Instructions

Indicate (a) the journal, and (b) the columns in the journal that should be used in recording each transaction.

E6–7 Vencor Company has the following selected transactions during March:

Journalize transactions in general journal and post. (S.O. 3, 4)

Mar. 2 Purchased equipment costing $6,000 from Lifetime Company.

5 Received credit memorandum for $300 from Lynch Company for merchandise damaged in shipment to Vencor.

7 Issued a credit memorandum for $500 to Frey Company for merchandise the customer returned.

Vencor Company uses a one-column purchases journal, the columnar cash journals used in the text, and a general journal.

Instructions

(a) Journalize the transactions in the general journal.

(b) Explain the postings to the control and subsidiary accounts.

E6–8 Below are some typical transactions incurred by the Devine Company.

Indicate journalizing in special journals. (S.O. 4)

1. Return of merchandise sold for credit.
2. Payment of creditors on account.
3. Collection on account from customers.
4. Sold land for cash.
5. Sale of merchandise on account.
6. Sale of merchandise for cash.
7. Received credit for merchandise purchased on credit.
8. Sales discount taken on goods sold.
9. Payment of employee wages.
10. Close income summary to owner's capital.
11. Depreciation on building.
12. Purchase of merchandise on account.
13. Purchase of office supplies for cash.

Instructions

For each transaction, indicate whether it would normally be recorded in a cash receipts journal, cash payments journal, single-column sales journal, single-column purchases journal, or general journal.

E6–9 The general ledger of the Amgen Company contained the following Accounts Payable control account (in T-account form). Also shown is the related subsidiary ledger.

Explain posting to control account and subsidiary ledger. (S.O. 3, 5)

General Ledger

Accounts Payable

Feb. 15	General Journal	1,000	Feb.	1	Balance	26,025
28	?	?		5	General Journal	265
				11	General Journal	550
				28	Purchases	13,700
			Feb. 28		Balance	9,640

Accounts Payable Ledger

Patee

| | Feb. 28 | Bal. | 4,600 |

Wagner

| | Feb. 28 | Bal. | ? |

Gruber

| | Feb. 28 | Bal. | 3,000 |

Instructions

(a) Indicate the missing posting reference and amount in the control account and the missing ending balance in the subsidiary ledger.

(b) Indicate the amounts in the control account that were double-posted (i.e., posted to the control account and the subsidiary accounts).

Prepare purchases and general journals.
(S.O. 3, 4)

E6–10 Selected accounts from the ledgers of the Alpine Company at July 31 showed the following:

GENERAL LEDGER

Store Equipment — No. 153

Date	Explanation	Ref.	Debit	Credit	Balance
July 1		G1	3,600		3,600

Accounts Payable — No. 201

Date	Explanation	Ref.	Debit	Credit	Balance
July 1		G1		3,600	3,600
15		G1		400	4,000
18		G1	100		3,900
25		G1	200		3,700
31		P1		8,400	12,100

Purchases — No. 510

Date	Explanation	Ref.	Debit	Credit	Balance
July 31		P1	8,400		8,400

Freight-in — No. 516

Date	Explanation	Ref.	Debit	Credit	Balance
July 15		G1	400		400

Purchase Returns and Allowances — No. 512

Date	Explanation	Ref.	Debit	Credit	Balance
July 18		G1		100	100
25		G1		200	300

ACCOUNTS PAYABLE LEDGER

Andrew Equipment Co.

Date	Explanation	Ref.	Debit	Credit	Balance
July 1		G1		3,600	3,600

David Co.

Date	Explanation	Ref.	Debit	Credit	Balance
July 14		P1		1,100	1,100
25		G1	200		900

Bradley Co.

Date	Explanation	Ref.	Debit	Credit	Balance
July 3		P1		2,000	2,000
20		P1		700	2,700

Erick Supply Co.

Date	Explanation	Ref.	Debit	Credit	Balance
July 12		P1		500	500
21		P1		400	900

Craig Materials

Date	Explanation	Ref.	Debit	Credit	Balance
July 17		P1		1,400	1,400
18		G1	100		1,300
29		P1		2,300	3,600

Gary Transit

Date	Explanation	Ref.	Debit	Credit	Balance
July 15		G1		400	400

Instructions

From the data prepare:

(a) the single-column purchases journal for July.

(b) the general journal entries for July.

Determine correct posting amount to control account.
(S.O. 5)

E6–11 Olson Products uses both special journals and a general journal as described in this chapter. Olson also posts customers' accounts in the accounts receivable subsidiary ledger directly from duplicate copies of the sales invoices. These postings for the most recent month are included in the subsidiary T accounts below.

	Edmonds		
Bal.	340		250
	180		

	Roemer		
Bal.	150		150
	190		

	Schulz		
Bal.	–0–		145
	145		

	Park		
Bal.	120		120
	190		
	160		

Instructions

Determine the correct amount of the end-of-month posting from the sales journal to the Accounts Receivable controlling account.

PROBLEMS

P6–1 Kimball Company's chart of accounts includes the following selected accounts:

101 Cash	401 Sales
112 Accounts Receivable	414 Sales Discounts
301 A. J. Kimball, Capital	512 Purchase Returns and Allowances

Journalize transactions in cash receipts journal and post to control account and subsidiary ledger.
(S.O. 3, 4, 5)

On June 1 the accounts receivable ledger of the Kimball Company showed the following balances: Block & Son, $2,500; Field Co., $1,900; Green Bros., $1,600; and Mastin Co., $900. The June transactions involving the receipt of cash were as follows:

June 1 The owner, A. J. Kimball, invested additional cash in the business, $9,000.
 3 Received check in full from Mastin Co. less 2% cash discount.
 6 Received check in full from Field Co. less 2% cash discount.
 7 Made cash sales of merchandise totaling $6,135.
 9 Received check in full from Block & Son less 2% cash discount.
 11 Received cash refund from a supplier for damaged merchandise, $200.
 15 Made cash sales of merchandise totaling $4,250.
 20 Received check in full from Green Bros., $1,600.

Instructions

(a) Journalize the transactions above in a five-column cash receipts journal with columns for Cash, Dr.; Sales Discounts, Dr.; Accounts Receivable, Cr.; Sales, Cr.; and Other Accounts, Cr. Foot and crossfoot the journal.

(b) Insert the beginning balances in the Accounts Receivable control and subsidiary accounts and post the June transactions to these accounts.

(c) Prove the agreement of the control account and subsidiary account balances.

P6–2 The Creek Company's chart of accounts includes the following selected accounts:

101 Cash	306 V. Creek, Drawing
130 Prepaid Insurance	510 Purchases
157 Equipment	514 Purchase Discounts
201 Accounts Payable	

Journalize transactions in cash payments journal and post to the general and subsidiary ledger.
(S.O. 3, 4, 5)

On November 1 the accounts payable ledger of the Creek Company showed the following balances: R. Huff & Co., $3,750; G. Paul, $2,350; R. Snyder, $1,000; and Wicks Bros., $1,900. The November transactions involving the payment of cash were as follows:

Nov. 1 Purchased merchandise, check no. 11, $900.
 3 Purchased store equipment, check no. 12, $1,650.
 5 Paid Wicks Bros. balance due of $1,900, less 1% discount, check no. 13, $1,881.
 11 Purchased merchandise, check no. 14, $2,000.
 15 Paid R. Snyder balance due of $1,000, less 3% discount, check no. 15, $970.
 16 V. Creek, the owner, withdraws $500 cash for own use, check no. 16.
 19 Paid G. Paul in full for invoice no. 1245, $1,500 less 2% discount, check no. 17, $1,470.
 25 Paid premium due on one year insurance policy, check no. 18, $3,000.
 30 Paid R. Huff & Co. in full for invoice no. 832, $2,450, check no. 19.

Instructions

(a) Journalize the transctions above in a five-column cash payments journal with columns for Other Accounts, Dr.; Accounts Payable, Dr.; Purchases, Dr.; Purchase Discounts, Cr.; and Cash, Cr. Foot and crossfoot the journal.

(b) Insert the beginning balances in the Accounts Payable control and subsidiary accounts and post the November transactions to these accounts.

(c) Prove the agreement of the control account and the subsidiary account balances.

Journalize transactions in multicolumn purchases journal and post to the general and subsidiary ledgers.

(S.O. 3, 4, 5)

P6–3 The chart of accounts of the Virginia Company includes the following selected accounts:

112 Accounts Receivable	412 Sales Returns and Allowances
126 Supplies	510 Purchases
157 Equipment	512 Purchase Returns and Allowances
201 Accounts Payable	516 Freight-in
401 Sales	610 Advertising Expense

In May the following selected transactions were completed. All purchases and sales were on account except as indicated.

May 2 Purchased merchandise from Vons Company, $8,000.

    3 Received freight bill from Acme Freight on Vons purchase, $400.

    5 Sales were made to Penner Company, $2,600; Hendrix Bros., $2,700; and Nelles Company, $1,500.

    8 Purchased merchandise from Golden Company, $8,000 and Dorn Company, $8,700.

   10 Received credit on merchandise returned to Dorn Company, $500.

   15 Purchased supplies from Engle Supply, $900.

   16 Purchased merchandise from Vons Company, $4,500; and Golden Company, $6,000.

   17 Returned supplies to Engle Supply, receiving credit, $100. (Hint: Credit Supplies.)

   18 Received freight bills on May 16 purchases from Acme Freight, $500.

   20 Returned merchandise to Vons Company receiving credit, $300.

   23 Made sales to Hendrix Bros., $2,400; and Nelles Company, $2,200.

   25 Received bill for advertising from Ball Advertising, $900.

   26 Granted allowance to Nelles Company for merchandise damaged in shipment, $100.

   28 Purchased equipment from Engle Supply, $250.

Instructions

(a) Journalize the transactions above in a purchases journal, a one-column sales journal, and a general journal. The purchases journal should have the following column headings: Date, Accounts Credited (Debited), Ref., Other Accounts Dr., Purchases Dr., Freight-in Dr., and Accounts Payable Cr.

(b) Post to both the general and subsidiary ledger accounts. (Assume that all accounts have zero beginning balances.)

(c) Prove the agreement of the control and subsidiary accounts.

Journalize transactions in special journals.

(S.O. 3, 4, 5)

P6–4 Selected accounts from the chart of accounts of Keller Company are shown below.

101 Cash	401 Sales
112 Accounts Receivable	414 Sales Discounts
126 Supplies	510 Purchases
140 Land	512 Purchase Returns and Allowances
145 Buildings	514 Purchase Discounts
201 Accounts Payable	610 Advertising Expense

During October, Keller completed the following transactions:

Oct. 2 Purchased merchandise on account from Mason Company, $16,500.

4 Sold merchandise on account to Parker Co., $8,100. Invoice no. 204; terms 2/10, n/30.

5 Purchased supplies for cash, $80.

7 Made cash sales for the week totaling $9,160.

9 Paid in full the Mason Company on account less a 2% discount.

10 Purchased merchandise on account from Quinn Corp., $4,200.

12 Received payment from Parker Co. for invoice no. 204.

13 Issued a debit memorandum to Quinn Corp. and returned $250 worth of damaged goods.

14 Made cash sales for the week totaling $8,180.

16 Sold a parcel of land for $27,000 cash, the land's book value.

17 Sold merchandise on account to L. Boyton & Co., $5,350, invoice no. 205, terms 2/10, n/30.

18 Purchased merchandise for cash, $2,125.

21 Made cash sales for the week totaling $8,465.

23 Paid in full the Quinn Corp. on account for the goods kept (no discount).

25 Purchased supplies on account from Frey Co., $260.

25 Sold merchandise on account to Green Corp., $5,220, invoice no. 206, terms 2/10, n/30.

25 Received payment from L. Boyton & Co. for invoice no. 205.

26 Purchased for cash a small parcel of land and a building on the land to use as a storage facility. The total cost of $35,000 was allocated $21,000 to the land and $14,000 to the building.

27 Purchased merchandise on account from Schmid Co., $7,500.

28 Made cash sales for the week totaling $8,540.

30 Purchased merchandise on account from Mason Company, $14,000.

30 Paid advertising bill for the month from the Gazette, $600.

30 Sold merchandise on account to L. Boyton & Co., $4,600. Invoice no. 207; terms 2/10, n/30.

Keller Company uses the following journals:

1. Single-column sales journal.

2. Single-column purchases journal.

3. Cash receipts journal with columns for Cash, Dr.; Sales Discounts, Dr.; Accounts Receivable, Cr.; Sales, Cr.; and Other Accounts, Cr.

4. Cash payments journal with columns for Other Accounts, Dr.; Accounts Payable, Dr.; Supplies, Dr.; Purchase Discounts, Cr.; and Cash, Cr.

5. General journal.

Instructions

Using the selected accounts provided:

(a) Record, in the appropriate journals, the October transactions.

(b) Foot and crossfoot all special journals.

(c) Show how postings would be made by placing ledger account numbers and check marks as needed in the journals. (Actual posting to ledger accounts is not required.)

Journalize in purchase and cash payments journals, post, prepare a trial balance, prove control to subsidiary, prepare adjusting entries, and prepare an adjusted trial balance.

(S.O. 3, 4, 5)

P6–5 Presented below are the sales and cash receipts journals for Tokos Co. for its first month of operations.

SALES JOURNAL   S1

Date	Account Debited	Ref.	Accounts Receivable Debit Sales Credit
Feb. 3	H. Adams		5,000
9	R. Babcock		6,500
12	B. Chambers		7,000
26	L. Dawson		6,000
			24,500

CASH RECEIPTS JOURNAL   CR1

Date	Accounts Credited	Ref.	Cash Debit	Sales Discounts Debit	Accounts Receivable Credit	Sales Credit	Other Accounts Credit
Feb. 1	B. Tokos, Capital		30,000				30,000
2			6,500			6,500	
13	H. Adams		4,950	50	5,000		
18	Purchase Returns and Allowances		150				150
26	R. Babcock		6,500		6,500		
			48,100	50	11,500	6,500	30,150

In addition, the following transactions have not been journalized for February.

Feb. 2 Purchased merchandise on account from S. Healy for $2,000, terms 1/10, n/30.
  7 Purchased merchandise on account from L. Held for $30,000, terms 1/10, n/30.
  9 Paid cash of $1,000 for purchase of supplies.
  12 Paid $1,980 to S. Healy in payment for $2,000 invoice, less 1% discount.
  15 Purchased equipment for $8,000 cash.
  16 Purchased merchandise on account from R. Landly, $2,400, terms 2/10, n/30.
  17 Paid $29,700 to L. Held in payment of $30,000 invoice, less 1% discount.
  20 Withdrew cash of $1,100 from business for personal use.
  21 Purchased merchandise on account from J. Able for $6,500, terms 1/10, n/30.
  28 Paid $2,400 to R. Landly in payment of $2,400 invoice.

Instructions

(a) Open the following accounts in the general ledger.

101 Cash	306 B. Tokos, Drawing
112 Accounts Receivable	401 Sales
126 Supplies	414 Sales Discounts
157 Equipment	510 Purchases
158 Accumulated Depreciation—Equipment	512 Purchase Returns and Allowances
201 Accounts Payable	514 Purchase Discounts
301 B. Tokos, Capital	631 Supplies Expense
	711 Depreciation Expense

(b) Journalize the transactions that have not been journalized in a one-column purchases journal, and the cash payments journal (See Illustration 6-15).

(c) Post to the accounts receivable and accounts payable subsidiary ledgers. Follow the sequence of transactions as shown in the problem.

(d) Post the individual entries and totals to the general ledger.

(e) Prepare a trial balance.

(f) Determine that the subsidiary ledgers agree with the control accounts in the general ledger.

(g) The following adjustments at the end of February are necessary.

1. A count of supplies indicates that $300 is still on hand.
2. Depreciation on equipment for February is $200.

Prepare the adjusting entries and then post the adjusting entries to the general ledger.

(h) Prepare an adjusted trial balance.

P6–6   The post-closing trial balance for Simon Co. is as follows:

Journalize in special journals, post, and prepare a trial balance.
(S.O. 3, 4, 5)

SIMON CO.
Post-Closing Trial Balance
December 31, 1993

	Debit	Credit
Cash	$ 39,500	
Accounts Receivable	15,000	
Notes Receivable	45,000	
Merchandise Inventory	23,000	
Equipment	6,450	
Accumulated Depreciation—Equipment		$ 1,500
Accounts Payable		43,000
S. Simon, Capital		84,450
	$128,950	$128,950

The subsidiary ledgers contain the following information: (1) accounts receivable—R. Barton $2,500; B. Cole $7,500; S. Devine $5,000; (2) accounts payable—S. Field $10,000; R. Gilson $18,000; and D. Harms $15,000.

The transactions for January 1994 are as follows:

Jan.   3   Sell merchandise to B. Senton, $2,000, terms 2/10, n/30.
5   Purchase merchandise from S. Warren, $2,200, terms 2/10, n/30.
7   Receive a check from S. Devine, $3,500.
11   Pay freight on merchandise purchased, $200.
12   Pay rent of $1,000 for January.
13   Receive payment in full from B. Senton.
14   Post all entries to the subsidiary ledgers. Issue a credit memo to acknowledge receipt of damaged merchandise of $700 returned by R. Barton.
15   Send D. Harms a check for $14,850 in full payment of account, discount, $150.
17   Purchase merchandise from D. Lapeska, $1,600, terms 2/10, n/30.
18   Pay sales salaries of $2,800 and office salaries, $1,500.
20   Give R. Gilson a 60-day note for $18,000 in full payment of accounts payable.
23   Total cash sales amount to $8,600.
24   Post all entries to the subsidiary ledgers. Sells merchandise on account to B. Cole, $7,700, terms 1/10, n/30.
27   Send S. Warren a check for $950.
29   Receive payment on a note of $40,000 from S. Lava.
30   Return merchandise of $500 to D. Lapeska for credit. Post all journals to the subsidiary ledger.

Instructions
(a) Open general and subsidiary ledger accounts for the following:

101 Cash	412 Sales Returns and Allowances
112 Accounts Receivable	414 Sales Discounts
115 Notes Receivable	510 Purchases
120 Merchandise Inventory	512 Purchase Returns and Allowances
157 Equipment	514 Purchase Discounts
158 Accumulated Depreciation—Equipment	516 Freight-in
200 Notes Payable	726 Sales Salaries Expense
201 Accounts Payable	727 Office Salaries Expense
301 S. Simon, Capital	729 Rent Expense
401 Sales	

(b) Record the January transactions in a single-column sales journal, a single-column purchases journal, a cash receipts (see Illustration 6-8), a cash payments journal (see Illustration 6-15), and a general journal.

(c) Post the appropriate amounts to the general ledger.

(d) Prepare a trial balance at January 31, 1994.

(e) Determine whether the subsidiary ledgers agree with controlling accounts in the general ledger.

ALTERNATE PROBLEMS

Journalize transactions in cash receipts journal and post to control account and subsidiary ledger.
(S.O. 3, 4, 5)

P6–1A   Lemon Company's chart of accounts includes the following selected accounts:

101 Cash	401 Sales
112 Accounts Receivable	414 Sales Discounts
301 F. Lemon, Capital	512 Purchase Returns and Allowances

On April 1 the accounts receivable ledger of the Lemon Company showed the following balances: Harris, $1,550; Kerl, $1,200; Northeast Co., $2,900; and Smith, $1,600. The April transactions involving the receipt of cash were as follows:

Apr. 1   The owner, F. Lemon, invested additional cash in the business, $6,000.
      4   Received check for payment of account from Smith less 2% cash discount.
      5   Received check for $620 in payment of invoice no. 307 from Northeast Co.
      8   Made cash sales of merchandise totaling $6,245.
     10   Received check for $900 in payment of invoice no. 309 from Harris.
     11   Received cash refund from a supplier for damaged merchandise, $550.
     23   Received check for $1,600 in payment of invoice no. 310 from Northeast Co.
     29   Received check for payment of account in full from Kerl.

Instructions

(a) Journalize the transactions above in a five-column cash receipts journal with columns for Cash, Dr.; Sales Discounts, Dr.; Accounts Receivable, Cr.; Sales, Cr.; and Other Accounts, Cr. Foot and crossfoot the journal.

(b) Insert the beginning balances in the Accounts Receivable control and subsidiary accounts and post the April transactions to these accounts.

(c) Prove the agreement of the control account and subsidiary account balances.

Journalize transactions in cash payments journal and post to control account and subsidiary ledger.
(S.O. 3, 4, 5)

P6–2A   The Simpson Company's chart of accounts includes the following selected accounts:

101 Cash	306 L. Simpson, Drawing
130 Prepaid Insurance	510 Purchases
157 Equipment	514 Purchase Discounts
201 Accounts Payable	

On October 1 the accounts payable ledger of the Simpson Company showed the following balances: Newton Company, $1,600; Martin & Sons, $2,500; Lien, $1,400; and Watson Company, $3,700. The October transactions involving the payment of cash were as follows:

Oct. 1   Purchased merchandise, check no. 63, $700.
      3   Purchased equipment, check no. 64, $800.
      5   Paid Newton Company balance due of $1,600, less 2% discount, check no. 65, $1,568.
     10   Purchased merchandise, check no. 66, $2,250.
     15   Paid Lien balance due of $1,400, check no. 67.
     16   L. Simpson, the owner, pays his personal insurance premium of $400, check no. 68.

19 Paid Martin & Sons in full for invoice no. 610, $1,400 less 2% cash discount, check no. 69, $1,372.

29 Paid Watson Company in full for invoice no. 264, $2,100, check no. 70.

Instructions

(a) Journalize the transactions above in a five-column cash payments journal with columns for Other Accounts, Dr.; Accounts Payable, Dr.; Purchases, Dr.; Purchase Discounts, Cr.; and Cash, Cr. Foot and crossfoot the journal.

(b) Insert the beginning balances in the Accounts Payable control and subsidiary accounts and post the October transactions to these accounts.

(c) Prove the agreement of the control account and the subsidiary account balances.

P6–3A The chart of accounts of the Komag Company includes the following selected accounts:

Journalize transactions in multi-column purchases journal and post to the general and subsidiary ledgers.
(S.O. 3, 4, 5)

112 Accounts Receivable	412 Sales Returns and Allowances
126 Supplies	510 Purchases
157 Equipment	512 Purchase Returns and Allowances
201 Accounts Payable	516 Freight-in
401 Sales	610 Advertising Expense

In July the following selected transactions were completed. All purchases and sales were on account.

July 1 Purchased merchandise from Jansen Company, $8,000.

2 Received freight bill from Johnson Shipping on Jansen purchase, $400.

3 Made sales to Lyons Company, $1,300; and Franklin Bros., $1,900.

5 Purchased merchandise from Maxwell Company, $3,200.

8 Received credit on merchandise returned to Maxwell Company, $300.

13 Purchased store supplies from Apollo Supply, $720.

15 Purchased merchandise from Jansen Company, $3,600; and Sparky Company, $2,800.

16 Made sales to Jackson Company, $3,450; and Franklin Bros., $1,570.

18 Received bill for advertising from Nancy's Advertisements, $600.

21 Sales were made to Lyons Company, $310; and Jeff Company, $2,200.

22 Granted allowance to Lyons Company for merchandise damaged in shipment, $140.

24 Purchased merchandise from Maxwell Company, $3,000.

26 Purchased equipment from Apollo Supply, $600.

28 Received freight bill from Johnson Shipping on Maxwell purchase of July 24, $380.

30 Sales were made to Jackson Company, $3,900.

Instructions

(a) Journalize the transactions above in a purchases journal, a one-column sales journal, and a general journal. The purchases journal should have the following column headings: Date, Accounts Credited (Debited), Ref., Other Accounts Dr., Purchases Dr., Freight-in Dr., and Accounts Payable Cr.

(b) Post to both the general and subsidiary ledger accounts. (Assume that all accounts have zero beginning balances.)

(c) Prove the agreement of the control and subsidiary accounts.

P6–4A Selected accounts from the chart of accounts of Clark Company are shown below.

Journalize transactions in special journals.
(S.O. 3, 4, 5)

101 Cash	412 Sales Returns and Allowances
112 Accounts Receivable	414 Sales Discounts
126 Supplies	510 Purchases
157 Equipment	512 Purchase Returns and Allowances
201 Accounts Payable	514 Purchase Discounts
401 Sales	726 Salaries Expense

During January, Clark completed the following transactions:

Jan. 3   Purchased merchandise on account from Bell Co., $8,900.
      4   Purchased supplies for cash, $80.
      4   Sold merchandise on account to Gilbert, $7,550, invoice no. 371, terms 1/10, n/30.
      5   Issued a debit memorandum to Bell Co. and returned $300 worth of damaged goods.
      6   Made cash sales for the week totaling $3,150.
      8   Purchased merchandise on account from Law Co., $4,500.
      9   Sold merchandise on account to Mays Corp., $5,600, invoice no. 372, terms 1/10, n/30.
     11   Purchased merchandise on account from Hatch Co., $2,700.
     13   Paid in full the Bell Co. on account less a 2% discount.
     13   Made cash sales for the week totaling $5,340.
     15   Received payment from Mays Corp. for invoice no. 372.
     15   Paid semi-monthly salaries of $14,300 to employees.
     17   Received payment from Gilbert for invoice no. 371.
     17   Sold merchandise on account to Amber Co., $1,200, invoice no. 373, terms 1/10, n/30.
     19   Purchased equipment on account from Johnson Corp., $5,500.
     20   Cash sales for the week totaled $3,200.
     20   Paid in full the Law Co. on account less a 2% discount.
     23   Purchased merchandise on account from Bell Co., $7,800.
     24   Purchased merchandise on account from Levine Corp., $4,690.
     27   Made cash sales for the week totaling $3,730.
     30   Received payment from Amber Co. for invoice no. 373.
     31   Paid semi-monthly salaries of $13,200 to employees.
     31   Sold merchandise on account to Gilbert, $7,330, invoice no. 374, terms 1/10, n/30.

Clark Company uses the following journals:

1. Single-column sales journal.
2. Single-column purchases journal.
3. Cash receipts journal with columns for Cash, Dr.; Sales Discounts, Dr.; Accounts Receivable, Cr.; Sales, Cr.; and Other Accounts, Cr.
4. Cash payments journal with columns for Other Accounts, Dr.; Accounts Payable, Dr.; Purchase Discounts, Cr.; and Cash, Cr.
5. General journal.

Instructions
Using the selected accounts provided:

(a) Record, in the appropriate journal noted, the January transactions.

(b) Foot and crossfoot all special journals.

(c) Show how postings would be made by placing ledger account numbers and checkmarks as needed in the journals. (Actual posting to ledger accounts is not required.)

Journalize in sales and cash receipts journals, post, prepare a trial balance, prove control to subsidiary, prepare adjusting entries, and prepare an adjusted trial balance.
(S.O. 3, 4, 5)

P6–5A   Presented below are the purchases and cash payments journal for Collins Co. for its first month of operations.

PURCHASES JOURNAL   P1

Date		Account Credited	Ref.	Purchases Debit Accounts Payable Credit
July	4	J. Dixon		6,800
	5	W. Engel		7,500
	11	R. Gamble		3,720
	13	M. Hill		15,300
	20	D. Jacob		7,800
				41,120

CASH PAYMENTS JOURNAL   CP1

Date	Accounts Debited	Ref.	Other Accounts Debit	Accounts Payable Debit	Purchase Discounts Credit	Cash Credit
July 4	Supplies		600			600
10	W. Engel			7,500	75	7,425
11	Prepaid Rent		6,000			6,000
15	J. Dixon			6,800		6,800
19	Collins, Drawing		2,500			2,500
21	M. Hill			15,300	153	15,147
			9,100	29,600	228	38,472

In addition, the following transactions have not been journalized for July.

July 1 The founder Collins invests $70,000 in cash.

6 Collins ships $6,400 of merchandise to Hardy Co., terms 1/10, n/30.

7 Make cash sales totaling $4,000.

8 Collins sells merchandise on account to D. Washburn, $3,600, terms, 1/10, n/30.

10 Sell merchandise on account to L. Lemansky, $4,900, terms 1/10, n/30.

13 Receive payment in full from D. Washburn.

16 Receive payment in full from L. Lemansky.

20 Receive payment in full from Hardy Co.

21 Sell merchandise on account to S. Kane, $3,000, terms, 1/10, n/30.

29 Return damaged goods to J. Dixon and received cash refund of $450.

Instructions
(a) Open the following accounts in the general ledger.

101 Cash   401 Sales

112 Accounts Receivable   412 Sales Returns and Allowances

127 Store Supplies   414 Sales Discounts

131 Prepaid Rent   510 Purchases

201 Accounts Payable   512 Purchase Returns and Allowances

301 Collins, Capital   514 Purchase Discounts

306 Collins, Drawing   631 Supplies Expense

                             729 Rent Expense

(b) Journalize the transactions that have not been journalized in the single-column sales journal, and the cash receipts journal (see Illustration 6-8), and the general journal.

(c) Post to the accounts receivable and accounts payable subsidiary ledgers. Follow the sequence of transactions as shown in the problem.

(d) Post the individual entries and totals to the general ledger.

(e) Prepare a trial balance.

(f) Determine whether the subsidiary ledgers agree with the controlling accounts in the general ledger.

(g) The following adjustments at the end of July are necessary.
    1. A count of supplies indicates that $140 is still on hand.
    2. Recognize rent expense for July, $500.
    Prepare the necessary entries in the general journal. Post the entries to the general ledger.

(h) Prepare an adjusted trial balance.

*B*roadening Your Perspective

FINANCIAL REPORTING PROBLEM—A MINI-PRACTICE SET

(The working papers that accompany this textbook are needed in order to work this mini-practice set.) Hunt Co. uses both an accounts receivable and an accounts payable subsidiary ledger. Balances related to both the general ledger and the subsidiary ledger for Hunt are indicated in the working papers. Presented below are a series of transactions for Hunt Co. for the month of January. Credit sales terms are 2/10, n/30.

Jan. 3 Sell merchandise on credit to B. Sargent $3,100, invoice No. 510, and to J. Eaton $1,800, invoice No. 511.

5 Purchase merchandise from S. Walden $3,000 and D. Landell $2,200, terms n/30.

7 Receive checks from S. Lowell, $4,000 and B. Jaggar $2,000 after discount period has lapsed.

8 Pay freight on merchandise purchased $180.

9 Send checks to S. Lee for $9,000 less 2% cash discount and D. Nordin for $11,000 less 1% cash discount.

9 Issue credit memo for $300 to J. Eaton for merchandise returned.

10 Summary daily cash sales total $15,500.

11 Sell merchandise on credit to R. Dansig $1,300, invoice No. 512, and to S. Lowell $900, invoice No. 513.

12 Pay rent of $1,000 for January.

13 Receive payment in full from B. Sargent and J. Eaton less cash discounts.

15 Withdraw $800 cash by S. Hunt for personal use.

15 Post all entries to the subsidiary ledgers.

16 Purchase merchandise from D. Nordin $15,000, terms 1/10, n/30; S. Lee $14,200, terms 2/10, n/30; and S. Walden $1,500, terms n/30.

17 Pay $400 cash for office supplies.

18 Return $200 of merchandise to S. Lee and receive credit.

20 Summary daily cash sales total $17,500.

21 Issue $15,000 note to R. Mannon in payment of balance due.

21 Receive payment in full from S. Lowell less cash discount.

22 Sell merchandise on credit to B. Sargent $1,700, invoice No. 514 and to R. Dansig $800, invoice No. 515.

22 Post all entries to the subsidiary ledger.

23 Send checks to D. Nordin and S. Lee in full payment less cash discounts.

25 Sell merchandise on credit to B. Jaggar $3,500, invoice No. 516 and to J. Eaton $6,100, invoice No. 517.

27 Purchase merchandise from D. Nordin $14,500, terms 1/10, n/30; D. Landell $1,200, terms n/30; and S. Walden $2,800, terms n/30.

27 Post all entries to the subsidiary ledger.

28 Pay $200 cash for office supplies.

31 Summary daily cash sales total $21,300.

31 Pay sales salaries $4,300 and office salaries $2,600.

Instructions

(a) Record the January transactions in a single-column sales journal, a single-column purchases journal, a cash receipts journal as shown on page 240, a cash payments journal as shown on page 245, and a two column general journal.

(b) Post the journals to the general ledger.

(c) Prepare a trial balance at January 31, 1994 in the Trial Balance columns of the work sheet. Complete the work sheet using the following additional information.

(1) Office supplies at January 31 total $500.

(2) Insurance coverage expires on October 31, 1994.

(3) Annual depreciation on the equipment is $1,500.

(4) Interest of $60 has accrued on the note payable.

(5) Merchandise inventory at January 31 is $16,000.

(d) Prepare a multiple-step income statement and an owner's equity statement for January and a classified balance sheet at the end of January.

(e) Prepare and post adjusting and closing entries.

(f) Prepare a post-closing trial balance and determine whether the subsidiary ledgers agree with the controlling accounts in the general ledger.

DECISION CASE

Smith & Young is a wholesaler of small appliances and parts. Smith & Young is operated by two owners, Paul Smith and Ann Young. In addition, the company has one employee, a repair specialist, who is on a fixed salary. Revenues are earned through the sale of appliances to retailers (approximately 75% of total revenues), appliance parts to do-it-yourselfers (10%), and the repair of appliances brought to the store (15%). Appliance sales are made on both a credit and cash basis. Customers are billed on prenumbered sales invoices. Credit terms are always net/30 days. All parts sales and repair work are cash only.

Develop design of information systems in both manual and computerized system.

Merchandise is purchased on account from the manufacturers of both the appliances and the parts. Practically all suppliers offer cash discounts for prompt payments, and it is company policy to take all discounts. Most cash payments are made by check. Checks are most frequently issued to suppliers, to trucking companies for freight on merchandise purchases, and to newspapers, radio, and TV stations for advertising. All advertising bills are paid as received. Paul and Ann each make a monthly drawing in cash for personal living expenses. The salaried repairman is paid twice monthly.

Smith & Young currently has a manual accounting system. However, the business is growing and some consideration is being given to an electronic data processing system.

Instructions

(a) Identify the special journals that Smith & Young should have in its manual system. List the column headings appropriate for each of the special journals.

(b) What control and subsidiary accounts should be included in Smith & Young's manual system? Why?

(c) Identify for Paul and Ann the key points they should consider in deciding whether to install a computerized system.

CRITICAL THINKING CASE

Refer to the opening story about Portland Community College in order to answer the following questions.

1. How will the computer for Portland Community College cut in half the time to pay accounts payable?

2. What are some other reasons that Portland Community College might have for switching to a computerized system?

3. Do you see examples of how computerized systems are used on your campus to expedite the information flow?

4. Consider your personal finances. Do you keep track of your expenditures with a computer? If not, why not?

ETHICAL CASE

Triport Products Company operates three divisions, each with its own manufacturing plant and marketing/sales force. The corporate headquarters and central accounting office are in Triport with the plants in Freeport, Rockport, and Bayport, all within 50 miles of Triport. Corporate management treats each division as an independent profit center and encourages competition among them. They each have similar but different product lines. As a competitive incentive, bonuses are awarded each year to the employees of the fastest growing and most profitable division.

Ron Hermann is the manager of Triport's centralized computer accounting operation that keyboards the sales transactions and maintains the accounts receivable for all three divisions. Ron came up in the accounting ranks from the Bayport division where his wife, several relatives, and many friends still work.

As sales documents are keyboarded into the computer, the originating division is identified by code. Most (95%) sales documents are coded while some (5%) are not coded or are coded incorrectly. As the manager, Ron has instructed the keyboard operators to assign the Bayport code to all uncoded and incorrectly coded sales documents. This is done he says, "in order to expedite processing and to keep the computer files current since they are updated daily." All receivables and cash collections for all three divisions are handled by Triport as one subsidiary accounts receivable ledger.

Instructions

(a) Who are the stakeholders in this situation?

(b) What are the ethical issues in this case?

(c) How might the system be improved to prevent this situation?

Answers to Self-Study Questions
1. c   2. a   3. c   4. d   5. c   6. d   7. a   8. c   9. c   10. d

CHAPTER 7

INTERNAL CONTROL AND CASH

Study Objectives

After studying this chapter, you should be able to:

1. *Define internal control.*

2. *Identify the principles of internal control.*

3. *Explain the applications of internal control to cash receipts.*

4. *Describe the applications of internal control to cash disbursements.*

5. *Indicate the control features of a bank account.*

6. *Prepare a bank reconciliation.*

7. *Explain the operation of a petty cash fund.*

At Columbia University, thousands of dollars in cash changes hands between students and dining facility cashiers. Making sure all of the money received by cashiers gets to where it's supposed to go requires a strong internal control system.

For one thing, the register tape that records the sale and the amount of cash received must reconcile with the amount of cash in the drawer at the end of the day. "We see if there are significant overages or shortages at the end of each day for each register," says Susan McLaughlin, director of Columbia's dining facilities. Does that happen very often? "No, because the cashier knows that if there are repeated or significant shortages, disciplinary action will be taken," she says. "There should not be a variance of more than $5, either over or under, at any given time—or else it indicates poor cash handling."

If a student buying a meal at a register sees that a sale isn't rung or if the student doesn't get a receipt, there is a possibility that the cashier is stealing. "We know that taking the receipt is an annoyance," says Ms. McLaughlin, "but it's an absolute mandatory control for us."

Perhaps you know of other cash businesses. As you read this chapter, think about ways in which that business can make sure that all of the cash received is accounted for and gets to where it's supposed to go.

Could there be dishonest employees in the business that you own or manage? Unfortunately, the answer in some cases is Yes. For example, the financial press recently reported the following:

A bookkeeper in a small company diverted $750,000 of bill payments to a personal bank account over a three-year period.

A crackerjack shipping clerk with 28 years of service shipped $125,000 of merchandise to himself.

A computer operator embezzled $21 million from Wells Fargo Bank over a two-year period.

A church treasurer "borrowed" $150,000 of church funds to finance a friend's business dealings.

These situations emphasize the need for a good system of internal control. This chapter explains the essential features of a good internal control system and describes their application to safeguarding of a company's cash. The applications include some cash controls with which you may already be familiar.

What Is Internal Control?

Study Objective 1

Define internal control.

Internal control consists of the plan of organization and all the related methods and measures adopted within a business to:

1. **Safeguard its assets** from employee theft, robbery, and unauthorized use.
2. **Enhance the accuracy and reliability of its accounting records** by reducing the risk of errors (unintentional mistakes) and irregularities (intentional mistakes and misrepresentations) in the accounting process.

The importance of internal control in a company has been recognized by the Congress of the United States. Under the Foreign Corrupt Practices Act of 1977, all major U.S. corporations are required to maintain an adequate system of internal control. Companies that fail to comply are subject to fines, and company officers may be imprisoned. In 1987, the National Commission on Fraudulent Financial Reporting concluded that all companies whose stock is publicly traded should maintain internal controls that can provide reasonable assurance that fraudulent financial reporting will be prevented or subject to early detection.[1]

---

[1]Report of the National Commission on Fraudulent Financial Reporting, October 1987, p. 11.

echnology in Action

Good internal control must be designed into computerized systems. The design starting point is usually the preparation of flow charts that graphically depict each component of a firm's operations. The assembled flow charts serve as the basis for writing detailed programs. Several examples of flow charting are given in this chapter. When attempts to automate or improve accounting systems fail, it is often due to the absence of such well documented procedures.

Principles of Internal Control

To safeguard its assets and enhance the accuracy and reliability of its accounting records, a company follows specific control principles. Of course, internal control measures adopted by a company vary with the size and nature of the business and with management's control philosophy. However, the following principles apply to most enterprises:

Study Objective 2

Identify the principles of internal control.

1. Establishment of responsibility
2. Segregation of duties
3. Documentation procedures
4. Physical, mechanical, and electronic controls
5. Independent internal verification
6. Other controls

Each principle is explained in the following sections.

Establishment of Responsibility

An essential characteristic of internal control is the assignment of responsibility to specific individuals. **Control is most effective when only one person is responsible for a given task.** To illustrate, assume that the cash on hand at the end of the day in a Safeway supermarket is $10 short of the cash rung up on the cash register. If only one person has operated the register, responsibility for the shortage can be assessed quickly. However, if two or more individuals have worked the register, it may be impossible to determine who is responsible for the error unless each person is assigned a separate cash drawer and register key.

Establishing responsibility includes the authorization and approval of transactions. For example, the vice-president of sales should have the authority to establish policies for making credit sales. The policies ordinarily will require written credit department approval of credit sales.

Segregation of Duties

This principle (also identified as separation of functions or division of work) is indispensable in a system of internal control.

There are two common applications of this principle:

1. The responsibility for related activities should be assigned to different individuals.
2. The responsibility for establishing the accountability (keeping the records) for an asset should be separate from the physical custody of that asset.

The rationale for segregation of duties is that the work of one employee should, without a duplication of effort, provide a reliable basis for evaluating the work of another employee.

Related Activities

Related activities that should be assigned to different individuals arise in both the purchasing and selling areas. Related purchasing activities include ordering the merchandise, receiving the goods, and paying (or authorizing payment) for the merchandise. Related selling activities include making a sale, shipping (or delivering) the goods to the customer, and billing the customer. **When one individual is responsible for all of the related activities, the potential for errors and fraud is increased.** In purchasing, for example, orders could be placed with friends or with suppliers who give kickbacks. Similarly, only a cursory count and inspection may be made upon receiving the goods, which can lead to errors and poor-quality merchandise. In addition, payment may be authorized without a careful review of the invoice, or even worse, fictitious invoices may be approved for payment. When the responsibility for ordering, receiving, and paying are assigned to different individuals or departments, the risk of such abuses is minimized. That is, when different individuals perform different duties, their work should provide a basis for evaluating the performance of one or more other employees.

When one person is responsible for related sales transactions, a salesperson could make sales at unauthorized prices to increase sales commissions; a shipping clerk could ship goods to himself, as indicated at the beginning of the chapter; a billing clerk could understate the amount billed for sales made to friends and relatives. These abuses are reduced when salespersons make the sale, shipping department employees ship the goods on the basis of the sales order, and billing department employees prepare the sales invoice after comparing the sales order with the report of goods shipped.

Accounting in Action · *Ethical Insight*

A former EDP employee of Texaco, Inc., and his wife were indicted for stealing thousands of dollars from the company in an accounts payable-type fraud. The employee instructed Texaco's computer to pay his wife rent for land she allegedly leased to Texaco by assigning her an alphanumeric code as a lessor and then ordering that payments be made. The lesson here is simple: "*never* allow the same person to both authorize and pay for goods and services." Doing otherwise violates the segregation-of-duties principle of internal control.

Accountability for Assets

If accounting is to provide a valid basis of accountability for an asset, the accountant should have neither physical custody of the asset nor access to it. Moreover, the custodian of the asset should not maintain or have access to the accounting records. **When one employee maintains the record of the asset that should be on hand, and a different employee has physical custody of the asset, the custodian of the asset is not likely to convert the asset to personal use.** The separation of accounting responsibility from the custody of assets is especially important for cash and inventories because these assets are very vulnerable to unauthorized use or misappropriation.

Documentation Procedures

Documents provide evidence that transactions and events have occurred. For example, the shipping document indicates that the goods have been shipped, and the sales invoice indicates that the customer has been billed for the goods. By adding signatures (or initials) to the documents, the individual(s) responsible for the transaction or event can be identified. Documentation of transactions should be made when the transaction occurs. Documentation of events such as those leading to adjusting entries is generally developed when the adjustments are made.

Several procedures should be established for documents. First, whenever possible, **documents should be prenumbered and all documents should be accounted for**. Prenumbering helps to prevent a transaction from being recorded more than once, or conversely, to prevent the transactions from not being recorded. Second, documents that are **source documents for accounting entries should be promptly forwarded to accounting to help ensure timely recording of the transaction and event**. Thus, this control measure contributes directly to the accuracy and reliability of the accounting records.

Helpful hint An important corollary to prenumbering is that voided documents be kept until all documents are accounted for.

Physical, Mechanical, and Electronic Controls

Use of physical, mechanical, and electronic controls is essential. Physical controls relate primarily to the safeguarding of assets. Such controls include:

1. Safes and vaults to store cash before it is deposited in a bank.
2. Bank safety deposit boxes for important business papers.
3. Locked warehouses for inventories.
4. Fencing of company property.
5. Locked storage cabinets for accounting records.
6. Self-contained computer facilities with pass-key access by authorized personnel.

Physical controls extend to the use of employee identification badges and security guards to prevent unauthorized entry during business hours. In addition, outside security agencies may be engaged to protect company property after business hours.

Electronic controls also contribute to the safeguarding of assets. Many companies (and also homeowners) use electronic burglar alarm systems to prevent break-ins. Moreover, banks and other businesses use television monitors to deter robberies and thefts. In many department stores, including major companies such as Macy's, Baskin's, and Lord & Taylor, sensors are attached to garments in an effort to reduce losses from shoplifting. After a garment is purchased, the salesclerk removes the sensor from the garment. If the sensor is not removed, it will activate an alarm bell when the customer tries to leave the store with the garment.

Mechanical and electronic equipment enhance the accuracy and reliability of the accounting records. For example, in executing transactions

1. Cash registers in stores, gasoline pumps in service stations, and coin machines in metro transportation systems provide locked-in totals of transactions that have occurred.

2. Time clocks "punch" time worked by an employee on time cards and check writing protectors imprint amounts on checks to minimize the risk of altering documents and transaction data.

In recording transactions, electronic data processing systems have

1. Built-in (hardware) controls that promptly detect any malfunctioning of the equipment.

2. Program controls that reject invalid transaction (input) data and produce error and exception reports.

Accounting in Action · *Business Insight*

John Patterson, a young Ohio merchant, couldn't understand why his retail business didn't show a profit. There were lots of customers, but the money just seemed to disappear.

Patterson suspected pilferage and sloppy bookkeeping by store clerks. Frustrated, he placed an order with a Dayton, Ohio, company for two rudimentary cash registers. A year later, Patterson's store was in the black.

"What is a good thing for this little store is a good thing for every retail store in the world," he observed. A few months later, in 1884, John Patterson and his brother, Frank, bought the tiny cash register maker for $6,500. The word around Dayton was that the Patterson boys got stung.

In the following 37 years, John Patterson built National Cash Register Co. into a corporate giant. Patterson died in 1922, the year in which NCR sold its two millionth cash register.

Source: The Wall Street Journal. January 28, 1989.

Independent Internal Verification

Most systems of internal control provide for independent internal verification, (also known as **independent check**). This principle involves the review, comparison, and reconciliation of data prepared by one or several employees. To obtain maximum benefit from the principle:

1. The verification should be made periodically or on a surprise basis.
2. The verification should be done by an employee who is independent of the personnel responsible for the information.
3. Discrepancies and exceptions should be reported to a management level that can take appropriate corrective action.

Independent internal verification is especially useful in comparing recorded accountability with existing assets. The reconciliation by an independent person of the cash balance per books with the cash balance per bank is a common example. The relationship between this principle and the segregation of duties principle is shown graphically in Illustration 7-1.

In large companies, independent internal verification is often assigned to internal auditors. Internal auditors are employees of the company who evaluate on a continuous basis the effectiveness of the company's system of internal control. They periodically review the activities of departments and individuals to determine whether prescribed internal controls are being followed and to make recommendations for improvement. The importance of this function is illustrated by the number of internal auditors employed by companies. In a recent year, AT&T had 350 internal auditors, Exxon had 395, and IBM had 142.

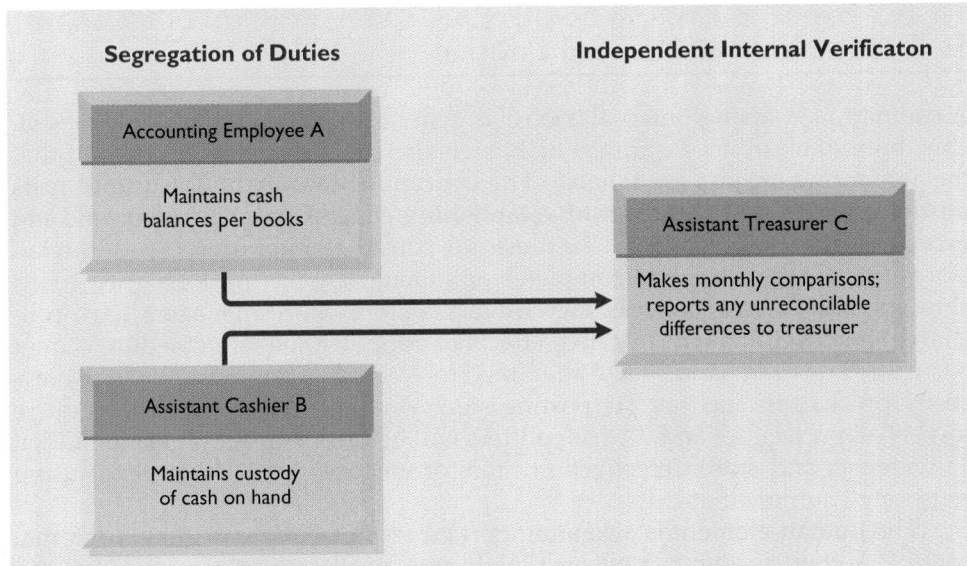

ILLUSTRATION 7-1

Comparison of segregation of duties principle with independent internal verification principle.

Technology in Action

Program controls are those controls built into the computer to prevent intentional or unintentional errors or unauthorized access from occurring. To prevent unauthorized access, the computer system may require that passwords be entered and random personal questions be correctly answered before system access is allowed. Once access has been allowed, other program controls identify data having a value higher or lower than a predetermined amount (limit checks), validate computations (math checks), and detect improper processing order (sequence checks).

A crucial consideration in programming computerized systems is building in controls that limit unauthorized or unintentional tampering. Entire books and movies have been produced with computer system tampering as a major theme. Most programmers would agree that tamper proofing and debugging programs are the most difficult and time-consuming phases of their jobs.

Other Controls

Other control measures include the following:

1. **Bonding of employees who handle cash.** Bonding involves obtaining fidelity insurance protection against misappropriation of assets by dishonest employees. This measure contributes to the safeguarding of cash in two ways: First, the insurance company carefully screens all individuals before adding them to the policy and may reject risky applicants. Second, bonded employees know that the insurance company will vigorously prosecute all offenders.

2. **Rotating employees' duties and requiring employees to take vacations.** These measures are designed to deter employees from attempting any thefts since they will not be able to permanently conceal their improper actions. Many bank embezzlements, for example, have been discovered when the perpetrator has been on vacation or assigned to a new position.

Limitations of Internal Control

A company's system of internal control is generally designed to provide reasonable, but not absolute, assurance that assets are properly safeguarded and that the accounting records are reliable. **The concept of reasonable assurance rests on the premise that the costs of establishing control procedures should not exceed their expected benefit.** To illustrate, consider shoplifting losses in retail stores. Such losses could be completely eliminated by having a security guard stop and search customers as they leave the store. Store managers have concluded, however, that the negative effects of adopting such a procedure cannot be justified. Instead, stores have attempted to "control" shoplifting losses by less costly procedures such as: (1) posting signs saying, "We reserve the right to inspect all packages," and "All shoplifters will be prosecuted," (2) using hidden TV cameras and store detectives to monitor customer activity, and (3) using sensoring equipment at exits.

The **human element** is also an important factor in every system of internal control. A good system can become ineffective as a result of employee fatigue, carelessness, and indifference. For example, a receiving clerk may not bother to count goods received, or may just "fudge" the counts. Moreover, two or more individuals may work together to get around prescribed controls. Such **collusion** can significantly impair the effectiveness of a system, because it eliminates the protection anticipated from segregation of duties. If a supervisor and a cashier collaborate to understate cash receipts, the system of internal control may be negated (at least in the short run). No system of internal control is perfect or infallible.

The size of the business may impose limitations on internal control. In a small company, for example, it may be difficult to apply the principles of segregation of duties and independent internal verification.

Technology in Action

Unfortunately, computer-related frauds have become a major concern. For example, the estimates of direct losses in one of the major computer fraud cases (Equity Funding Insurance Company) ranged from $27 million to $200 million. On the basis of known cases, excluding Equity Funding, the average computer fraud loss is $650,000, compared with an average loss of only $19,000 resulting from other types of white-collar crime.

Computer fraud can be perpetrated almost invisibly and done with electronic speed. Psychologically, stealing with impersonal computer tools can seem far less criminal. Therefore, the moral threshold to commit computer fraud is far lower than in fraud involving person-to-person contact.

Preventing and detecting computer fraud represents a major challenge. One of the best ways for a company to minimize the likelihood of computer fraud is to have a good system of internal control that allows the benefits of computerization to be gained without opening the possibility for rampant fraud.

 # Need for Cash Controls

Just as cash is the beginning of a company's operating cycle, it is usually the starting point for a company's system of internal control. Cash is the one asset that is readily convertible into any other type of asset; it is easily concealed and transported; and it is highly desired. Because of these characteristics, cash is the asset most susceptible to improper diversion and use. Moreover, because of the large volume of cash transactions, numerous errors may occur in executing and recording cash transactions. To safeguard cash and to assure the accuracy of the accounting records for cash, effective internal control over cash is imperative.

Cash consists of coins, currency (paper money), checks, money orders, and money on hand or on deposit in a bank or similar depository. The general rule is that if the bank will accept it for deposit, it is cash. Items such as postage stamps and postdated checks (checks payable in the future) are not cash. Stamps are a prepaid expense; the postdated checks are accounts receivable.

Accounting in Action · *Business Insight*

In 1891, James C. Fargo, president of American Express Co., gave one of his managers a challenge: Devise a piece of paper that will be accepted as money around the world.

Mr. Fargo, back from a long trip in Europe, was frustrated by cumbersome bank letters of credit and confusing exchange rates. He asked Marcellus Fleming Berry, a manager, to come up with a negotiable instrument secure against loss, theft, counterfeit, fraud, and forgery. Mr. Berry created the "Travelers Cheque," using the British spelling. . . .

The checks were a small sideline for American Express: The company's principal business then was forwarding freight. . . . But American Express kept its early lead. In 1891, the company sold checks with a face amount of $9,120, or about $122,000 in today's dollars. In 1988, American Express sold a record $22 billion in checks, giving it more than half of what has become a $40 billion-a-year market.

Source: The Wall Street Journal, January 13, 1989.

Before You Go On . . .

1. What are the primary objectives of internal control?

2. Identify and describe the principles of internal control.

3. What are the limitations of internal control?

Internal Control over Cash Receipts

Cash receipts may result from a variety of sources: cash sales; collections on account from customers; the receipt of interest, rents, and dividends; investments by owners; bank loans; and proceeds from the sale of noncurrent assets. Internal control principles apply to cash receipts transactions as follows:

ILLUSTRATION 7-2

Application of internal control principles to cash receipts

Principle	Application to Cash Receipts
Establishment of responsibility	Only designated personnel such as cashiers and cashier department personnel should be authorized to handle or have access to cash receipts.
Segregation of duties	Different individuals should be assigned the duties of receiving cash, recording cash receipts transactions, and having custody of cash.
Documentation procedures	Documents should include remittance advices for mail receipts, cash register tapes for over-the-counter receipts, and deposit slips for bank deposits.
Physical, mechanical, and electronic controls	Cash should be stored in company safes and bank vaults, and access to storage areas should be limited to authorized personnel; cash registers should be used in executing over-the-counter receipts.
Independent internal verification	Daily cash counts of register receipts should be made by cashier department supervisors; daily comparisons of total receipts and receipts deposited in the bank should be made by the treasurer's office.
Other controls	All personnel who handle cash receipts should be bonded and required to take vacations; cash should be deposited in the bank in total daily.

As might be expected, companies vary considerably in how they apply these principles. Control measures for a retail store that has both over-the-counter and mail receipts are described below.

Over-the-Counter Receipts

Control of over-the-counter receipts is centered on cash registers that are visible to customers. In supermarkets and variety stores such as Kmart, cash registers are placed in check-out lines near the exit(s), whereas in Sears, Roebuck & Co. and J. C. Penney stores each department has its own cash register. When a cash sale occurs, the sale is "rung up" on a cash register **with the amount clearly visible to the customer**. This procedure prevents the cashier from ringing up a lower amount and pocketing the difference. The cashier registers a cash sale manually by punching the appropriate keys on the register or electronically by using electronic scanning equipment. The customer receives an itemized cash register receipt slip and is expected to count the change received. A cash register tape, which is locked into the register until removed by a supervisor or manager, accumulates the daily transactions and totals. When the tape is removed, the supervisor compares the total with the amount of cash in the register. It should show all registered receipts accounted for. The supervisor's findings are reported on a cash count sheet that is signed by both the cashier and supervisor. The cash count sheet used by Alrite Food Mart is shown in Illustration 7-3.

The count sheets, register tapes, and cash are then given to the head cashier. This individual prepares a daily cash summary showing the total cash received

ILLUSTRATION 7-3

Cash count sheet

Store No. ___8___	Date March 8, 1993
1. Opening cash balance	$ 50.00
2. Cash sales per tape (attached)	6,956.20
3. Total cash to be accounted for	7,006.20
4. Cash on hand (see list)	6,996.10
5. Cash (short) or over	$ (10.10)
6. Ending cash balance	$ 50.00
7. Cash for deposit (Line 4 – Line 6)	$6,946.10

Cashier *J. Cruse*   Supervisor *M. Braun*

and the amount from each source, such as cash sales and collections on account. The head cashier sends one copy of the summary to accounting for entry into the cash receipts journal. The other copy goes to the treasurer's office for subsequent comparison with the daily bank deposit. Next, the head cashier prepares a deposit slip (see Illustration 7-6 on page 289) and makes the bank deposit. The total amount deposited should be equal to the total receipts on the daily cash summary. This will assure that all receipts have been placed in the custody of the bank. In accepting the bank deposit, the bank stamps (authenticates) the duplicate deposit slip and sends it to the company treasurer, who makes the comparison with the daily cash summary. The foregoing measures for cash sales are graphically illustrated in Illustration 7-4. The activities of the sales department are shown in a color different from the cashier's department to indicate the segregation of duties in handling cash.

Mail Receipts

Because of your experience as an individual customer, you may be more familiar with over-the-counter receipts than with mail receipts. However, mail receipts resulting from billings and credit sales are by far the most common way cash is received by the greatest variety of businesses. All mail receipts should be received in the presence of two mail clerks. These receipts are generally in the form of checks or money orders and frequently are accompanied by a remittance advice stating the purpose of the check. Each check should be promptly endorsed "For Deposit Only" by use of a company stamp. This restrictive endorsement reduces the likelihood that the check will be diverted to personal use because banks will not give an individual any cash under this type of endorsement.

A list of the checks should be prepared in duplicate showing the name of the issuer of the check, the purpose of the payment, and the amount of the check. Each mail clerk should sign the list to establish responsibility for the data. The original copy of the list, along with the checks and remittance advices, are then sent to the cashier's department, where they are added to over-the-counter receipts in preparing the daily cash summary and in making the daily bank deposit. In addition, a copy of the list is sent to the treasurer's office for comparison with the total mail receipts shown on the daily cash summary to assure that all mail receipts have been included.

ILLUSTRATION 7-4

Executing over-the-counter cash sales

Helpful hint Flowcharts enhance the understanding of the flow of documents, the processing steps, and the internal control procedures.

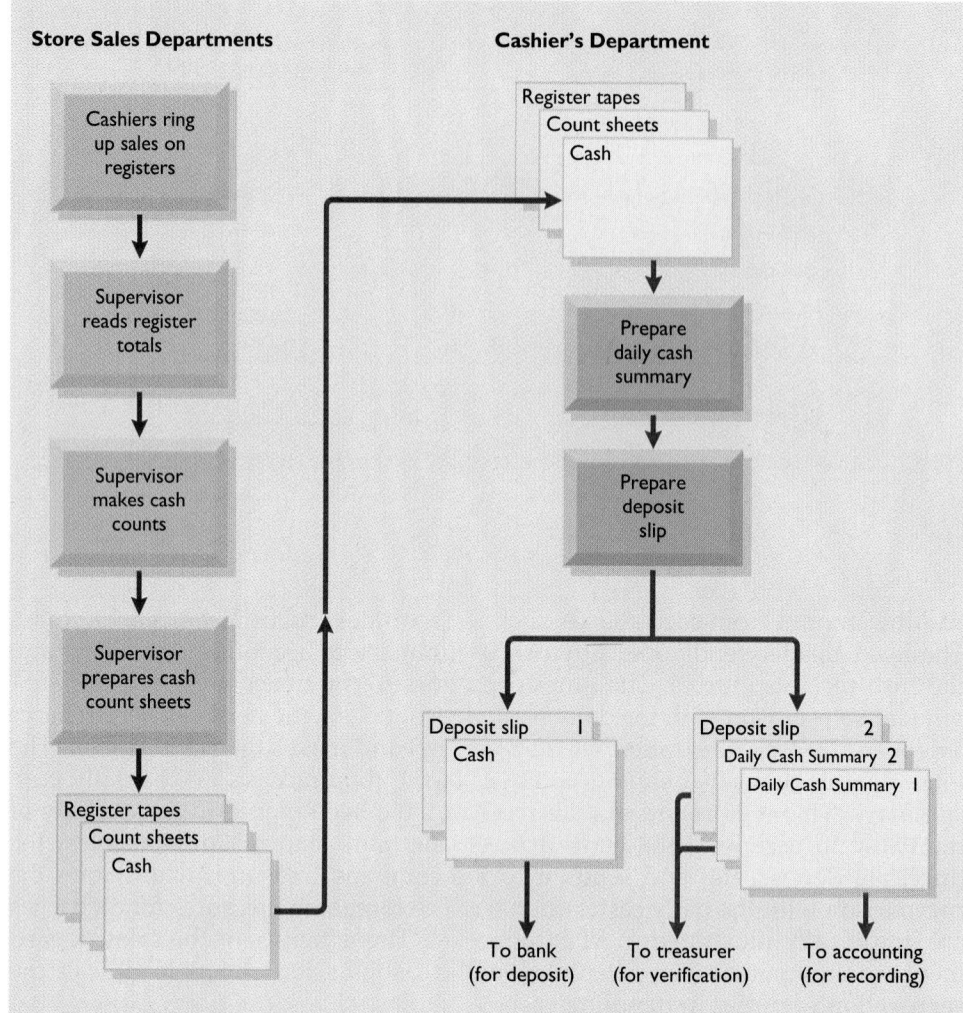

Internal Control over Cash Disbursements

Study Objective 4

Describe the applications of internal control to cash disbursements.

Cash may be disbursed for a variety of reasons, such as to pay expenses and liabilities, or to purchase assets. **Generally more effective internal control over cash disbursements results when payments are made by check, except for incidental amounts that are paid out of petty cash.**[2] Payment by check generally occurs only after specified control procedures have been followed. In addition, the "paid" check provides proof of payment. Principles of internal control apply to cash disbursements as shown in Illustration 7-5:

----

[2]The operation of a petty cash fund is explained on pages 295–7.

Principle	Application to Cash Disbursements
Establishment of responsibility	Only specified individuals such as the treasurer and assistant treasurer should be authorized to sign checks.
Segregation of duties	Different departments or individuals should be assigned the duties of approving an item for payment and paying it; check signers should not record cash disbursement transactions.
Documentation procedures	Prenumbered checks should be used and all checks in a series should be accounted for in recording; each check should be supported by an approved invoice or other documentation.
Physical, mechanical, and electronic controls	Blank checks should be stored in a safe with access restricted to authorized personnel; a checkwriter machine should be used to imprint the amount of the check in indelible ink.
Independent internal verification	Each check should be compared with the approved invoice before it is issued; bank and book balances should be reconciled monthly.
Other controls	After payment, the approved invoice should be stamped PAID.

Voucher System

Most medium and large companies use a voucher system as part of their internal control over cash disbursements. A voucher system is an extensive network of approvals by authorized individuals acting independently to ensure that all disbursements by check are proper. A cash disbursements flow chart and the essential features of a voucher system are explained in Appendix D.

Recording Purchases at Net Amount

Companies know that they can save money by taking advantage of purchase discounts offered on bills and invoices. A control procedure that contributes to taking offered discounts is to use the **net method of recording purchases**. This method initially records all invoices at the net amount. Assume, for example, that an invoice of $2,000 from a supplier allows a discount of 2% ($40) if paid in ten days. The entry, in general journal form, to record the purchase at the net amount is:

Purchases	1,960	
Accounts Payable		1,960

If payment is made within the discount period, the entry to record the payment of $1,960 is:

Accounts Payable	1,960	
Cash		1,960

However, if payment is not made within the discount period, the entry to record the cash payment of $2,000 is:

Accounts Payable	1,960	
Purchase Discounts Lost	40	
Cash		2,000

Purchase Discounts Lost shows the cost to the company of failing to take discounts. It is reported under other expenses and losses in the income statement. From the standpoint of control over cash disbursements, most managers believe it is better to report purchase discounts lost than to report purchase discounts taken as described in Chapter 5. Purchase discounts lost indicates poor bill paying performance that may require corrective measures by management.

Use of a Bank

Study Objective 5

Indicate the control features of a bank account.

The use of a bank contributes significantly to good internal control over cash. A company can safeguard its cash by using a bank as a depository and clearing house for checks received and checks written. Use of a bank minimizes the amount of currency that must be kept on hand. In addition, the use of a bank facilitates the control of cash because a double record is maintained of all bank transactions—one by the business and the other by the bank. The asset account, Cash, maintained by the depositor is the reciprocal of the bank's liability account for each depositor. It should be possible to agree (or reconcile) these accounts at any time.

Opening a bank checking account is a relatively simple procedure. Typically, the bank makes a credit check on the new customer and the depositor is required to sign a **signature card**. The card should contain the signatures of each person authorized to sign checks on the account. The signature card is used by bank employees to validate signatures on the checks.

As soon as possible after an account is opened, the bank will provide the depositor with a book of serially numbered checks and deposit slips imprinted with the depositor's name and address. Each check and deposit slip is imprinted with both a bank and a depositor identification number in magnetic ink to permit computer processing of the transaction.

Many companies have more than one bank account. For efficiency of operations and better control, national retailers like Wal-Mart Stores and Kmart may have regional bank accounts. Similarly, a company such as Exxon with more than 150,000 employees may have a payroll bank account, as well as one or more general bank accounts. In addition, a company may maintain several bank accounts in order to have more than one source for obtaining short-term loans when needed.

Technology in Action

For years, banks have encouraged customers to bank electronically. Overall, the results have been spotty. However, some large banks now provide their customers with software packages for electronic banking using personal computers. The software also allows for electronic bill paying. Thus, you can say good-bye to the monthly ritual of writing out and recording checks and hunting for and licking stamps and envelopes.

Source: "Let Your Fingers Do Your Banking," *Forbes,* August 19, 1991, p. 122.

Making Bank Deposits

Bank deposits should be made by an authorized employee, such as the head cashier. Each deposit must be documented by a deposit slip (ticket), as shown in Illustration 7-6.

ILLUSTRATION 7-6

Deposit slip

CHECKS	LIST SINGLY	DOLLARS	CENTS
1	74 – 331/724	175	40
2	61 – 157/220	292	60
3	19 – 401/710	337	55
4	22 – 815/666	165	72
5	15 – 360/011	145	53
6			
7			
8			
9			
10			
11			
12			
13			
14			
15			
16			
17			
18			
19			
TOTAL		1116	80

ENTER TOTAL ON THE FRONT OF THIS TICKET

DEPOSIT TICKET

W.A. LAIRD COMPANY
77 West Central Avenue,
Midland, Michigan 48654

DATE _____ 19 __ 19 93

National Bank & Trust
Midland, Michigan 48654

CHECKS AND OTHER ITEMS ARE RECEIVED FOR DEPOSIT SUBJECT TO THE PROVISIONS OF THE UNIFORM COMMERCIAL CODE OR ANY APPLICABLE COLLECTION AGREEMENT

CASH	CURRENCY	462	10
	COIN		
LIST CHECKS SINGLY			
TOTAL FROM OTHER SIDE		1116	80
TOTAL		578	90
TOTAL FROM OTHER SIDE			
NET DEPOSIT		1578	90

74—102/724

USE OTHER SIDE FOR ADDITIONAL LISTINGS

BE SURE EACH ITEM IS PROPERLY ENDORSED

Bank code numbers

Front side

Reverse side

Deposit slips are prepared in duplicate. The original is retained by the bank; the duplicate, machine stamped by the bank to establish its authenticity, is retained by the depositor.

Writing Checks

A check is a written order signed by the depositor directing the bank to pay a specified sum of money to a designated recipient. Thus, there are three parties to a check: the **maker** (or drawer) who issues the check, the **bank** (or payer) on which the check is drawn, and the **payee** to whom the check is payable. A check is a negotiable instrument that can be transferred to another party by endorsement. Each check should be accompanied by an explanation of its purposes. In many businesses, this is done by attaching a remittance advice to the check, as shown in Illustration 7-7.

For both individuals and businesses, it is important to know the balance in the checking account at all times. To keep the balance current, each deposit and check should be entered on running balance memorandum forms provided by the bank or on the check stubs contained in the checkbook.

Bank Statements

Each month, the depositor receives a bank statement from the bank. A bank statement shows the depositor's bank transactions and balances. For example, the statement, like the one in Illustration 7-8, shows (1) checks paid and other debits that reduce the balance in the depositor's account, (2) deposits and other credits that increase the balance in the depositor's account, and (3) the account balance after each day's transactions.

Most banks offer depositors the option of receiving "paid" checks with their bank statements. For those who decline, the bank keeps a record of each check on microfilm. Irrespective of the depositor's choice, all "paid" checks are listed in numerical sequence on the bank statement along with the date the check was paid and its amount. Upon paying a check, the bank stamps the check "paid;"

ILLUSTRATION 7-7

Check with remittance advice

Check

Maker → W.A. LAIRD COMPANY
77 West Central Avenue,
Midland, Michigan 48654

No. **448**

April 16 19 93 74—102/724

Payee → Pay to the order of Watkins Wholesale Supply $ 1525.00

Fifteen hundred twenty-five and 00/100 Dollars

Payer → NBT National Bank & Trust
Midland, Michigan 48654

Memo

W.F. Paine

:0624604 97: 457923"02 438

Remittance Advice

Detach this portion before cashing.

Date	Description	Gross Amount	Discount	Net Amount
4-16-93	Invoice No. 27662	1525.00	----	1525.00

W. A. Laird Company, Midland, MI

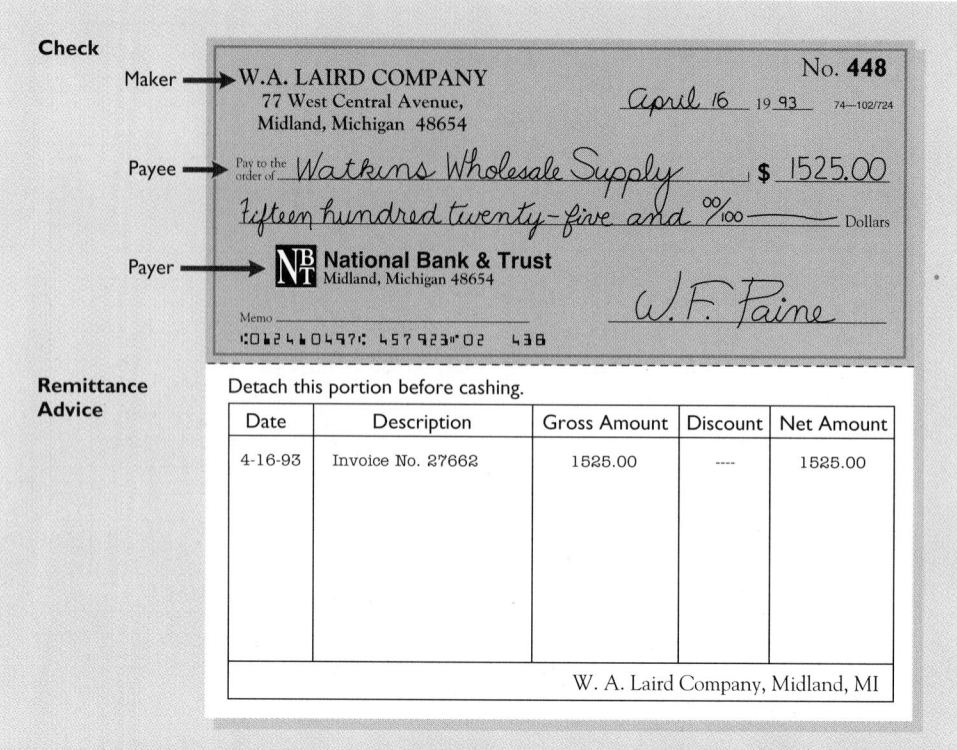

ILLUSTRATION 7-8

Bank statement

National Bank & Trust
Midland, Michigan 48654 Member FDIC

ACCOUNT STATEMENT

W. A. LAIRD COMPANY
77 WEST CENTRAL AVENUE
MIDLAND, MICHIGAN 48654

Statement Date/Credit Line Closing Date: April 30, 1993

457923
ACCOUNT NUMBER

Balance Last Statement	Deposits and Credits		Checks and Debits		Balance This Statement
	No.	Total Amount	No.	Total Amount	
13,256.90	20	34,805.10	26	32,154.55	15,907.45

CHECKS AND DEBITS			DEPOSITS AND CREDITS		DAILY BALANCE	
Date	No.	Amount	Date	Amount	Date	Amount
4–2	435	644.95	4–2	4,276.85	4–2	16,888.80
4–5	436	3,260.00	4–3	2,137.50	4–3	18,249.65
4–4	437	1,185.79	4–5	1,350.47	4–4	17,063.86
4–3	438	776.65	4–7	982.46	4–5	15,154.33
4–8	439	1,781.70	4–8	1,320.28	4–7	14,648.89
4–7	440	1,487.90	4–9 CM	1,035.00	4–8	11,767.47
4–8	441	2,420.00	4–11	2,720.00	4–9	12,802.47
4–11	442	1,585.60	4–12	757.41	4–11	13,936.87
4–12	443	1,226.00	4–13	1,218.56	4–12	13,468.28
4–29	NSF	425.60	4–27	1,545.57	4–27	13,005.45
4–29	459	1,080.30	4–29	2,929.45	4–29	14,429.00
4–30	DM	30.00	4–30	2,128.60	4–30	15,907.45
4–30	461	620.15				

Symbols: **CM** Credit Memo **DM** Debit Memo **EC** Error Correction **INT** Interest Earned **NSF** Not Sufficient Funds **SC** Service Charge

Reconcile Your Account Promptly

Helpful hint Every deposit received by the bank is credited to the customer's account. The reverse occurs when the bank "pays" a check issued by a company on its checking account balance. Payment reduces the bank's liability and is therefore debited to the customer's account with the bank.

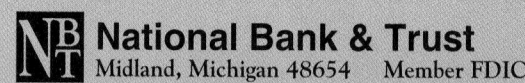

a paid check is sometimes referred to as a **canceled** check. In addition, the bank includes with the bank statement memoranda explaining other debits and credits made by the bank to the depositor's account.

Debit Memorandum

Banks charge a monthly fee for the use of their services. Often the fee is charged only when the average monthly balance in a checking account falls below a specified amount. The fee, called a bank service charge, is often identified on the bank statement by a code symbol such as SC. A debit memorandum explaining the charge is included with the bank statement. Separate debit memoranda may also be issued for other bank services such as the cost of printing checks, issuing traveler's checks, and wiring funds to other locations. The symbol DM is often used for such charges.

A debit memorandum is used by the bank when a previously deposited customer's check "bounces" because of insufficient funds. In such a case, the check is marked NSF (not sufficient funds) by the customer's bank and is returned to the depositor's bank. The bank then debits the depositor's account, as shown by the symbol NSF on the bank statement in Illustration 7-8, and sends the NSF check and debit memorandum to the depositor as notification of the charge. The NSF check creates an accounts receivable for the depositor and reduces cash in the bank account.

Credit Memorandum

A depositor may ask the bank to collect its notes receivable. In such a case, the bank will credit the depositor's account for the cash proceeds of the note, as illustrated on the bank statement by the symbol CM. It will issue a credit memorandum which is sent with the statement to explain the entry. Many banks also offer interest on checking accounts. The interest earned may be indicated on the bank statement by the symbol CM or INT.

Before You Go On . . .

1. How do the principles of internal control apply to cash receipts?
2. How do the principles of internal control apply to cash disbursements?
3. How does the use of a bank contribute to good internal control?

Reconciling the Bank Account

Because the bank and the depositor maintain independent records of the depositor's checking account, it might be presumed that the respective balances will always agree. In fact, the two balances are seldom the same at any given time, and it is necessary to make the balance per books agree with the balance per bank—a process called **reconciling the bank account**. The lack of agreement between the two balances is due to:

Study Objective 6

Prepare a bank reconciliation.

1. **Time lags** that prevent one of the parties from recording the transaction in the same period.
2. **Errors** by either party in recording transactions.

Time lags occur frequently. For example, several days may elapse between the time a check is mailed to a payee and the date the check is paid by the bank.

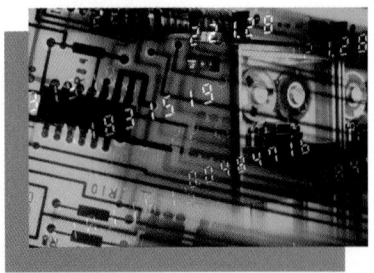

Accounting in Action · *Ethical Insight*

Some firms have used time lags to their advantage. For example, E. F. Hutton managers at one time overdrew their accounts by astronomical amounts—on some days the overdrafts totaled $1 billion—creating interest-free loans they could invest. The loans lasted as long as it took for the covering checks to be collected. Although not technically illegal at the time, Hutton's actions were wrong because it did not have bank permission to do so.

Similarly, when the depositor uses the bank's night depository to make its deposits, there will be a difference of one day between the time the receipts are recorded by the depositor and the time they are recorded by the bank. A time lag also occurs whenever the bank mails a debit or credit memorandum to the depositor.

The incidence of errors depends on the effectiveness of the internal controls maintained by the depositor and the bank. Bank errors are infrequent. However, either party could inadvertently record a $450 check as $45 or $540. In addition, the bank might charge a check drawn by C. D. Berg to the account of C. D. Burg.

Reconciliation Procedure

To obtain maximum benefit from a bank reconciliation, the reconciliation should be prepared by an employee who has no other responsibilities pertaining to cash. When the internal control principle of independent internal verification is not followed in preparing the reconciliation, cash embezzlements may escape unnoticed. For example, a cashier who prepares the reconciliation can embezzle cash and conceal the embezzlement by misstating the reconciliation. Thus, the bank accounts would reconcile and the embezzlement would not be detected.

In reconciling the bank account, it is customary to reconcile the balance per books and balance per bank to their adjusted (correct or true) cash balances. The reconciliation schedule is divided into two sections, as shown in Illustration 7-9. The starting point in preparing the reconciliation is to enter the balance per bank statement and balance per books on the schedule. The following steps should reveal all the reconciling items that cause the difference between the two balances.

Helpful hint Deposits in transit and outstanding checks are reconciling items because of time lags.

1. Compare the individual deposits on the bank statement with deposits in transit from the preceding bank reconciliation and with the deposits per company records or copies of duplicate deposit slips. Deposits not recorded by the bank represent deposits in transit and are added to the balance per bank.

2. Compare the paid checks shown on the bank statement or the paid checks returned with the bank statement with (a) checks outstanding from the preceding bank reconciliation and (b) checks issued by the company as recorded in the cash payments journal. Issued checks that have not been paid by the bank represent outstanding checks that are deducted from the balance per the bank.

3. Note any **errors** discovered in the foregoing steps and list them in the appropriate section of the reconciliation schedule. For example, if a paid check correctly written by the company for $195 was mistakenly recorded by the company for $159, the error of $36 is deducted from the balance

per books. All errors made by the depositor are reconciling items in determining the adjusted cash balance per books. In contrast, all errors made by the bank are reconciling items in determining the adjusted cash balance per the bank.

4. Trace **bank memoranda** to the depositor's records. Any unrecorded memoranda should be listed in the appropriate section of the reconciliation schedule. For example, a $5.00 debit memorandum for bank service charges is deducted from the balance per books, and $32 of interest earned is added to the balance per books.

Bank Reconciliation Illustrated

The bank statement for the Laird Company is shown in Illustration 7-9. It shows a balance per bank of $15,907.45 on April 30, 1993. On this date the balance of cash per books is $11,589.45. From the foregoing steps, the following reconciling items are determined.

1. Deposits in transit: April 30 deposit (received by bank on May 1). $2,201.40

2. Outstanding checks: No. 453 $3,000.00; No. 457 $1,401.30; No. 460 $1,502.70. 5,904.00

3. Errors: Check No. 443 was correctly written by Laird for $1,226.00 and was correctly paid by the bank. However, it was recorded for $1,262.00 by Laird Company. 36.00

4. Bank memoranda.
   a. Debit—NSF check from J. R. Baron for $425.60 425.60
   b. Debit—Printing company checks charge, $30.00 30.00
   c. Credit—Collection of note receivable for $1,000 plus accrued interest $50 less bank collection fee, $15.00 1,035.00

> **Helpful hint** Note in the bank statement that checks No. 459 and 461 have been paid but check No. 460 is not listed. Thus, this check is outstanding. If a complete bank statement were provided, checks No. 453 and 457 would also not be listed. The amounts for these three checks are obtained from the cash payments journal.

The bank reconciliation is as follows:

ILLUSTRATION 7-9

Bank reconciliation

LAIRD COMPANY
Bank Reconciliation
April 30, 1993

Cash balance per bank statement		$15,907.45
Add: Deposits in transit		2,201.40
		18,108.85
Less: Outstanding checks		
No. 453	$3,000.00	
No. 457	1,401.30	
No. 460	1,502.70	5,904.00
Adjusted cash balance per bank		**$12,204.85**
Cash balance per books		$11,589.45
Add: Collection of note receivable, $1,000 plus accrued interest $50, less collection fee $15	$1,035.00	
Error in recording check No. 443	36.00	1,071.00
		12,660.45
Less: NSF check	425.60	
Bank service charge	30.00	455.60
Adjusted cash balance per books		**$12,204.85**

> **Helpful hint** Adjusted balance, true cash balance, correct cash balance, may be used interchangeably.

Accounting in Action · *Business Insight*

Imagine reconciling a bank statement when you have an employee like Billie Hurst. She worked as a librarian at Southwest Missouri State University for 30 years, yet she never got around to cashing paychecks totaling more than $100,000 because she didn't need the money.

The 72-year-old woman got the money anyway when State Treasurer Wendell Bailey presented an $88,100.85 check to Hurst's cousin and guardian, Frances Jane Gleghorn, after a special act of the Legislature made it possible to pay checks more than 5 years old.

Bailey's office said it already had re-issued checks amounting to $20,024.53 for uncashed checks not more than 5 years old, bringing the total reimbursement to $108,125.38.

Hurst occasionally cashed a paycheck, Gleghorn said, but co-workers tried for years to get her to cash the rest of the checks.

Source: Bay City Times, March 24, 1989.

Entries from Bank Reconciliation

Each reconciling item in determining the **adjusted cash balance per books** should be recorded by the depositor. If these items are not journalized and posted, the Cash account will not show the correct balance. The entries for the Laird Company on April 30 are as follows:

Collection of Note Receivable

This entry involves four accounts. Assuming that the interest of $50 has been accrued and the collection fee is charged to Miscellaneous Expense, the entry is:

Helpful hint These entries are classified as adjusting entries. In prior chapters, Cash was an account that did not require adjustment because a bank reconciliation had not been explained.

Apr. 30	Cash	1,035.00	
	Miscellaneous Expense	15.00	
	Notes Receivable		1,000.00
	Interest Receivable		50.00
	(To record collection of notes receivable by bank)		

Book Error

An examination of the cash disbursements journal shows that check No. 443 was a payment on account to Andrea Company, a supplier. The correcting entry is:

Apr. 30	Cash	36.00	
	Accounts Payable—Andrea Company		36.00
	(To correct error in recording check No. 443)		

NSF Check

As indicated earlier, an NSF check becomes an accounts receivable to the depositor. The entry is:

Apr. 30	Accounts Receivable—J. R. Baron	425.60	
	Cash		425.60
	(To record NSF check)		

Bank Service Charges

Check printing charges (DM) and other bank service charges (SC) are debited to Miscellaneous Expense because they are usually nominal in amount. The entry is:

Apr. 30	Miscellaneous Expense	30.00	
	Cash		30.00
	(To record charge for printing company checks)		

The foregoing entries could also be combined into one compound entry. After the entries are posted, the cash account will show the following:

	Cash			
Apr. 30 Bal.	11,589.45	Apr. 30	425.60	
30	1,035.00		30.00	
30	36.00			
Apr. 30 Bal.	12,204.85			

ILLUSTRATION 7-10

Adjusted balance in cash account

The adjusted cash balance in the ledger should agree with the adjusted cash balance per books in the bank reconciliation in Illustration 7-9.

What entries does the bank make? If any bank errors are discovered in preparing the reconciliation, the bank should be notified so it can make the necessary corrections on its records. The bank does not make any entries for deposits in transit or outstanding checks. Only when these items reach the bank will the bank record these items.

Petty Cash Fund

As you learned earlier in the chapter, better internal control over cash disbursements is possible when payments are made by check. However, using checks to pay such small amounts as those for postage due, employee lunches, and taxi fares is both impractical and a nuisance. A common way of handling such payments, while maintaining satisfactory control, is to use a petty cash fund. A petty cash fund is a cash fund used to pay relatively small amounts. The operation of a petty cash fund, often called an **imprest system**, involves (1) establishing the fund, (2) making payments from the fund, and (3) replenishing the fund.[3]

Study Objective 7

Explain the operation of a petty cash fund.

Establishing the Fund

An essential step in establishing a petty cash fund is the appointment of a petty cash custodian who will be responsible for the fund. Also, the size of the fund must be determined. Ordinarily, the amount is expected to cover anticipated disbursements for a three- to four-week period. When the fund is established, a check payable to the petty cash custodian is issued for the stipulated amount. If the Laird Company decides to establish a $100 fund on March 1, the entry in general journal form is:

Mar. 1	Petty Cash	100.00	
	Cash		100.00
	(To establish a petty cash fund)		

---

[3]The term "imprest" means an advance of money for a designated purpose.

The check is then cashed and the proceeds are placed in a locked petty cash box or drawer. Most petty cash funds are established on a fixed amount basis. Moreover, no additional entries will be made to the Petty Cash account unless the stipulated amount of the fund is changed.

Making Payments from the Fund

The custodian of the petty cash fund has the authority to make payments from the fund that conform to prescribed management policies. Usually, management limits the size of expenditures that may be made and does not permit use of the fund for certain types of transactions (such as making short-term loans to employees). Each payment from the fund must be documented on a prenumbered petty cash receipt (or petty cash voucher), as shown in Illustration 7-11. Note that the signatures of both the custodian and the individual receiving payment are required on the receipt. If other supporting documents such as a freight bill or invoice are available, they should be attached to the petty cash receipt.

ILLUSTRATION 7-11

Petty cash receipt

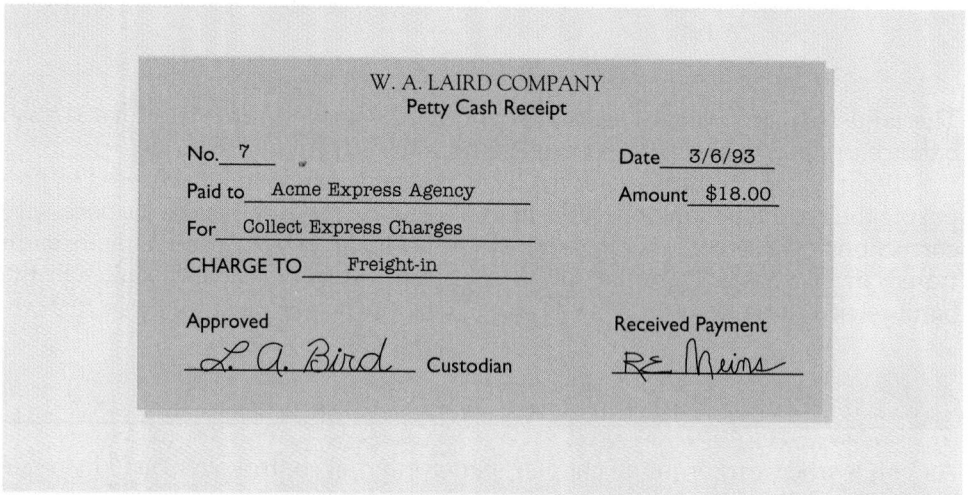

The receipts are kept in the petty cash box until the fund is replenished. As a result, the sum of the petty cash receipts and money in the fund should equal the established total at all times. This means that surprise counts can be made at any time by an independent person, such as an internal auditor, to determine whether the fund is being maintained intact. No accounting entry is made to record a payment at the time it is made from petty cash. It is considered to be both inexpedient and unnecessary to do so. Instead, the accounting effects of each payment are recognized when the fund is replenished.

Replenishing the Fund

When the money in the petty cash fund reaches a minimum level, the fund is replenished. The request for reimbursement is initiated by the petty cash custodian. This individual prepares a schedule (or summary) of the payments that have been made and sends the schedule, supported by petty cash receipts and other documentation, to the treasurer's office. The receipts and supporting documents are examined in the treasurer's office to verify that they were proper payments from the fund. The treasurer then approves the request and a check is prepared to restore the fund to its established amount. At the same time, all supporting documentation is stamped "paid" so that it cannot be submitted again for payment.

To illustrate, assume that on March 15 the petty cash custodian requests a check for $87. The fund contains $13 cash and petty cash receipts for postage $44, freight-in $38, and miscellaneous expenses $5. The entry, in general journal form, to record the check is:

Mar. 15	Postage Expense	44	
	Freight-in	38	
	Miscellaneous Expense	5	
	Cash		87
	(To replenish petty cash fund)		

Note that the Petty Cash account is not affected by the reimbursement entry. Replenishment changes the composition of the fund by replacing the petty cash receipts with cash, but it does not change the balance in the fund.

It may be necessary in replenishing a petty cash fund to recognize a cash shortage or overage. To illustrate, assume in the example above that the custodian had only $12 in cash in the fund plus the receipts as listed. The request for reimbursement would, therefore, have been for $88, and the following entry would be made:

Mar. 15	Postage Expense	44	
	Freight-in	38	
	Miscellaneous Expense	5	
	Cash Over and Short	1	
	Cash		88
	(To replenish petty cash fund)		

Conversely, if the custodian had $14 in cash, the reimbursement request would have been for $86 and Cash Over and Short would have been credited for $1. A debit balance in Cash Over and Short is reported in the income statement as miscellaneous expense; a credit balance is reported as miscellaneous revenue. Cash Over and Short is closed to Income Summary at the end of the year.

A petty cash fund should be replenished at the end of the accounting period regardless of the cash in the fund. Replenishment at this time is necessary in order to recognize the effects of the petty cash payments on the financial statements.

Internal control over a petty cash fund is strengthened by (1) having a supervisor make surprise counts of the fund to ascertain whether the paid vouchers and fund cash equal the imprest amount and (2) canceling or mutilating the paid vouchers so they cannot be resubmitted for reimbursement.

Reporting Cash

Cash on hand, cash in banks, and petty cash are often combined and reported simply as **Cash**. Because it is the most liquid asset owned by a company, cash is listed first in the current asset section of the balance sheet. Some companies use the designation "cash and cash equivalents" in reporting cash as illustrated by the following:

EASTMAN KODAK COMPANY		
	1991	1990
Current assets (in millions)		
Cash and cash equivalents	$783	$735

ILLUSTRATION 7-12

Presentation of cash and cash equivalents

Cash equivalents are highly liquid investments, with maturities of three months or less when purchased, that can be converted into a specific amount of cash. They include money market funds, money market savings certificates, bank certificates of deposit, and treasury bills and notes.

A company may have cash that is restricted for a special purpose. Examples include a payroll bank account for paying salaries and wages, and plant expansion fund cash for financing new construction. If the restricted cash is expected to be used within the next year, the amount should be reported as a current asset. However, when this is not the case, the restricted funds should be reported as a noncurrent asset.

In making loans to depositors, it is common for banks to require the borrowers to maintain minimum cash balances. These minimum balances, called compensating balances, provide the bank with support for the loans. Compensating balances are a restriction on the use of cash that may affect a company's liquidity. Accordingly, compensating balances should be disclosed in the financial statements.

Electronic Funds Transfer (EFT)

To account for and control cash is an expensive and time-consuming process. For example, it was estimated recently that the cost to process a check through a bank system ranges from $0.55 to $1.00 and is increasing. It is not surprising, therefore, that new approaches are being developed to transfer funds among parties without the use of paper (deposit tickets, checks, etc.). Such a procedure is called an Electronic Funds Transfer (EFT). EFT is a disbursement system that uses wire, telephone, telegraph, or computer to transfer cash from one location to another. Use of EFT is quite common. For example, the authors receive no formal payroll checks from their universities, which simply send magnetic tapes to the appropriate banks for deposit. Regular payments such as those for house, car, or insurance are frequently made by EFT.

Technology in Action

The development of EFT will continue. Already it is estimated that 80% of the total volume of bank transactions in the United States are performed using EFT. The computer technology is available to create a "checkless" society. The only major barriers appear to be the individual's concern for privacy and protection and certain legislative constraints. It should be noted that numerous safeguards have been built into EFT systems. However, the possibility of errors and fraud still exists because only a limited number of individuals are involved in the transfers, which may prevent appropriate segregation of duties.

Before You Go On . . .

1. Why is it necessary to reconcile a bank account?

2. What steps are involved in the reconciliation procedure?

3. What information is included in a bank reconciliation?

4. When are entries required in a petty cash system?

Summary of Study Objectives

1. Define internal control. Internal control is the plan of organization and related methods and procedures adopted within a business to safeguard its assets and to enhance the accuracy and reliability of its accounting records.

2. Identify the principles of internal control. The principles of internal control are: establishment of responsibility; segregation of duties; documentation procedures; physical, mechanical, and electronic controls; independent internal verification; and other controls.

3. Explain the applications of internal control to cash receipts. Internal controls over cash receipts include: (a) designating only personnel such as cashiers to handle cash; (b) assigning the duties of receiving cash, recording cash, and custody of cash to different individuals; (c) obtaining remittance advices for mail receipts, cash register tapes for over-the-counter receipts, and deposit slips for bank deposits; (d) using company safes and bank vaults to store cash with access limited to authorized personnel, and using cash registers in executing over-the-counter receipts; (e) making independent daily counts of register receipts and daily comparisons of total receipts with total deposits, and (f) bonding personnel that handle cash and requiring them to take vacations.

4. Describe the applications of internal control to cash disbursements. Internal controls over cash disbursements include: (a) having only specified individuals such as the treasurer authorized to sign checks; (b) assigning the duties of approving items for payment, paying the items, and recording the payment to different individuals; (c) using prenumbered checks and accounting for all checks, with each check supported by an approved invoice; (d) storing blank checks in a safe or vault with access restricted to authorized personnel, and using a checkwriter to imprint amounts on checks; (e) comparing each check with the approved invoice before issuing the check, and making monthly reconciliations of bank and book balances; and (f) after payment, stamping each approved invoice PAID.

5. Indicate the control features of a bank account. A bank account contributes to good internal control by providing physical controls for the storage of cash, minimizing the amount of currency that must be kept on hand, and creating a double record of a depositor's bank transactions.

6. Prepare a bank reconciliation. In reconciling the bank account, it is customary to reconcile the balance per books and balance per bank to their adjusted balances. The steps in determining the reconciling items are to ascertain deposits in transit, outstanding checks, errors by the depositor or the bank, and unrecorded bank memoranda.

7. Explain the operation of a petty cash fund. In operating a petty cash fund, it is necessary to establish the fund, make payments from the fund, and replenish the fund.

APPENDIX D   The Voucher System

The voucher system is an extensive network of approvals by authorized individuals acting independently to ensure that all disbursements by check are proper. The system begins with the authorization to incur the cost or expense. It ends with the issuance of a check for the liability incurred. The internal control principles essential in a voucher system are (1) establishment of responsibility, (2) segregation of duties, (3) documentation procedures, and (4) independent internal verification.

Voucher systems are widely used in medium-sized and large companies. In many of these cases, the system functions within an automated (electronic data processing) accounting system. Voucher systems are rarely found in small companies where the owner/manager can exercise personal surveillance over cash disbursements. The essential features of the voucher system for the Granger Company are explained in the following sections.

Study Objective

After studying Appendix D, you should be able to

8. Explain the essential features of a voucher system.

Preparing the Voucher

At the heart of the voucher system is the prenumbered voucher shown in Illustration D-1. A voucher is an authorization form prepared for each expenditure in a voucher system. The voucher itself may take the form of an envelope, folder, or packet. Vouchers are required for all types of cash disbursements except those made from petty cash. The voucher is prepared in the accounts (vouchers) payable department. Vouchers may be prepared for either the gross amount due as shown in Illustration D-1 or for the net amount due.

The starting point in preparing a voucher is to fill in the appropriate information about the liability on the face of the voucher from the vendor's invoice. Then the vendor's invoice is verified. Verification consists of establishing:

1. The agreement of the invoice with supporting documents, which generally consist of a copy of the purchase order sent to the vendor and a copy of the receiving report when the goods are received.
2. The correctness of prices and terms.
3. The accuracy of extensions and footings.

As each step in the verification is completed, the individual performing the control measure initials the voucher. After these steps are completed, the voucher is approved by a supervisor. The approved voucher, with attached supporting documents, is then sent to accounting for recording.

Recording the Voucher

After the account distribution data on the back of the voucher are completed, the voucher is approved for entry by an accounting supervisor. The voucher is then journalized in the voucher register (or journal). As shown in Illustration

ILLUSTRATION D-2

Voucher register

GRANGER COMPANY
Voucher Register

Date	Voucher No.	Payee	Payment Date	Check No.	Vouchers Payable Cr.	Purchases Dr.	Freight-in Dr.	Other Accounts Dr.	Ref.	Title
1993										
June 1	126	J. B. Plain	June 9	464	600	600				
3	127	Aber Bros.	12	465	1,250	1,250				
5	128	C. R. Olsen	6	463	2,500			2,500	15	Equipment
8	129	A. K. Wilson	25	469	1,400	1,400				
9	130	Acme Frt. Co.	13	466	100		100			
14	131	R. E. Helms			400			400	8	Supplies
17	132	B. D. Hayes	26	470	1,500	1,500				
19	133	N C R. R.	20	467	90		90			
22	134	City Bank	23	468	3,000			3,000	28	Notes Payable
25	135	Daily News			200			200	72	Advertising Expense
27	136	P. T. Marr Co.			900	900				
30	137	E. M. Taylor			1,200	1,200				
					13,140	6,850	190	6,100		
					(26)	(62)	(63)	(X)		

GRANGER COMPANY
Midland, Michigan

To: J.B. Plain Co.

45 State Street

Gary, Indiana

Voucher No: 126

Date: June 1

Due Date: June 10

Attach invoice and supporting documents

Date	Inv. No.	Terms	Description	Amount
5/31	E46953	2/10 n/30	15 Doz. Drills	$600

Supporting Documents Examined	Prices and Terms Correct	Extensions and Footings on Invoice	Voucher Approved Correct
CRB	CRB	CRB	PRS

Account Distribution		Accounting Summary
Debit	**Amount**	
Purchases	600 00	Voucher recorded _____
Freight-in		Check recorded _____
Store Supplies		
Advertising		**Payment Summary**
Delivery Expense		
Wages Payable		Date _____
Repairs		Amount of invoice _____
Sundry		Cash discount _____
		Amount of check _____
		Check number _____
Credit	**Amount**	Approved for payment _____
Vouchers payable	600 00	
Distribution Approved	CRL	

D-2, the voucher register is a columnar journal. The voucher register, which replaces the purchases journal described in Chapter 6, is used to record all types of expenditures. Under a voucher system, every payment by check is preceded by a credit to Vouchers Payable in the voucher register.

Vouchers are entered in numerical sequence, and all vouchers should be accounted for. After the voucher is entered, the accounting employee who journalized the voucher initials the accounting summary on the voucher. Procedures for posting the voucher register are similar to those described for a columnar journal. Although the Vouchers Payable account is used in recording, it is still customary to use the more familiar term, Accounts Payable, in the balance sheet.

Filing the Unpaid Voucher

After the voucher is recorded, it is filed by date of payment in an unpaid voucher file, sometimes called a tickler file. This method of filing facilitates the payment of bills within due dates. At the end of the month, the balance in Vouchers Payable is independently reconciled with the total vouchers in the tickler file. The balance should also equal the total of unpaid vouchers shown in the voucher register. The approving, recording, and filing of the voucher are shown graphically in Illustration D-3.

ILLUSTRATION D-3

Approving, recording, and filing a voucher

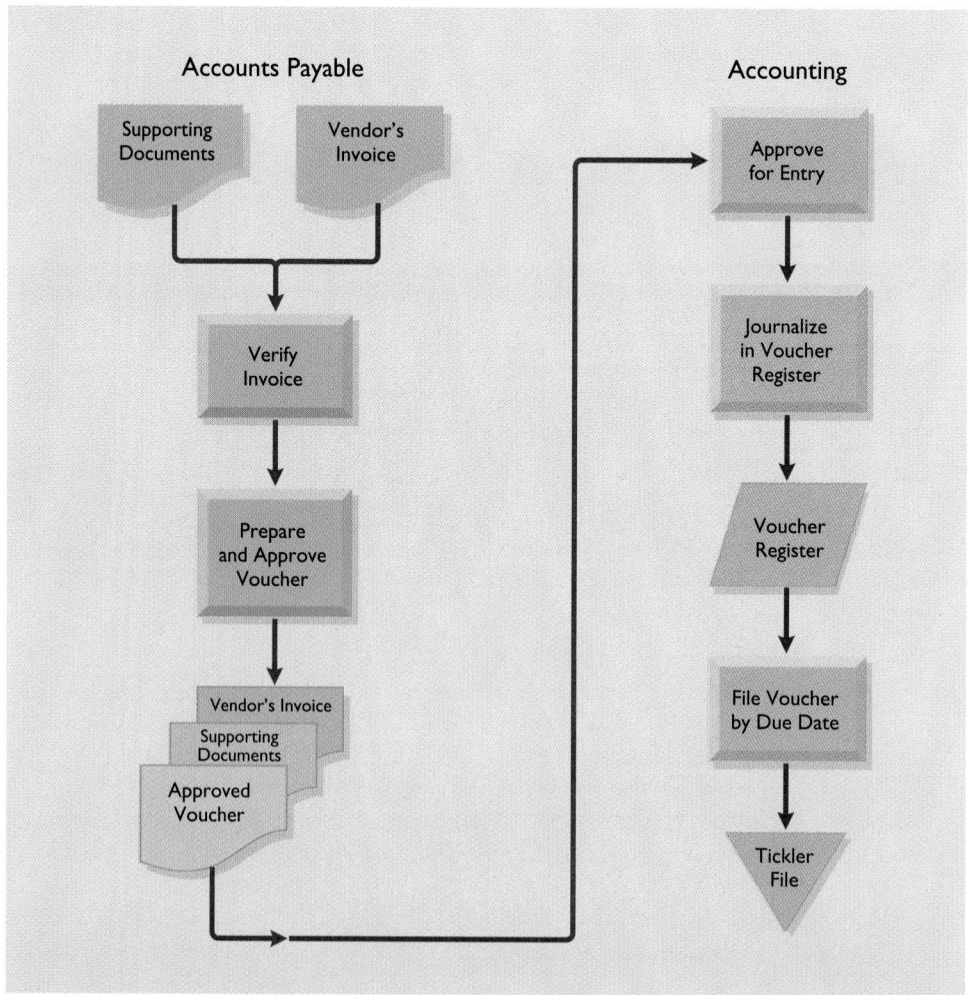

Paying the Voucher

On the due date, the voucher is removed from the tickler file and forwarded to cash disbursements. An authorized employee in cash disbursements reviews the voucher and, assuming everything is in order, approves the voucher for payment. The employee prepares (but does not sign) the check, inserts relevant data in the payment summary of the voucher, and transfers the unsigned check and voucher to the treasurer's office for signature.

In the treasurer's office, the authorized check signer signs the check after determining that proper approval has been given, and that all supporting documents are present. The check signer then:

1. Mails the check to the payee.
2. Stamps (or marks) the voucher and supporting documents PAID to prevent them from being submitted again for payment.
3. Sends the "paid" voucher and a copy of the check to accounting.

Recording Payment of the Voucher

Because all vouchers must be paid by check, the journal for recording checks is called a check register in a voucher system. As illustrated below, the check register contains just three money columns.

ILLUSTRATION D-4

Check register

				GRANGER COMPANY Check Register		
Date	Payee	Voucher No.	Check No.	Vouchers Payable Dr.	Purchase Discounts Cr.	Cash Cr.
1993						
June 6	C. R. Olsen	128	463	2,500		2,500
9	J. B. Plain	126	464	600	12	588
12	Aber Bros.	127	465	1,250	25	1,225
13	Acme Frt. Co.	130	466	100		100
20	N C R. R.	133	467	90		90
23	City Bank	134	468	3,000		3,000
25	A. K. Wilson	129	469	1,400		1,400
26	B. D. Hayes	132	470	1,500	30	1,470
				10,440	67	10,373
				(26)	(64)	(1)

After each check is recorded in numerical sequence, the check number and date of payment are also entered in the payment columns of the voucher register, and the accounting employee completes the accounting summary on the back of the voucher. The "paid" voucher is then filed alphabetically by vendor in a **paid voucher file**. The paying and recording payment of a voucher is graphically shown in Illustration D-5.

The discount column in Illustration D-4 is appropriate when vouchers are prepared for the gross amount due. If vouchers are prepared for the net amount due, the discount column becomes Purchase Discounts Lost—Dr.

ILLUSTRATION D-5

Paying and recording payment of a voucher

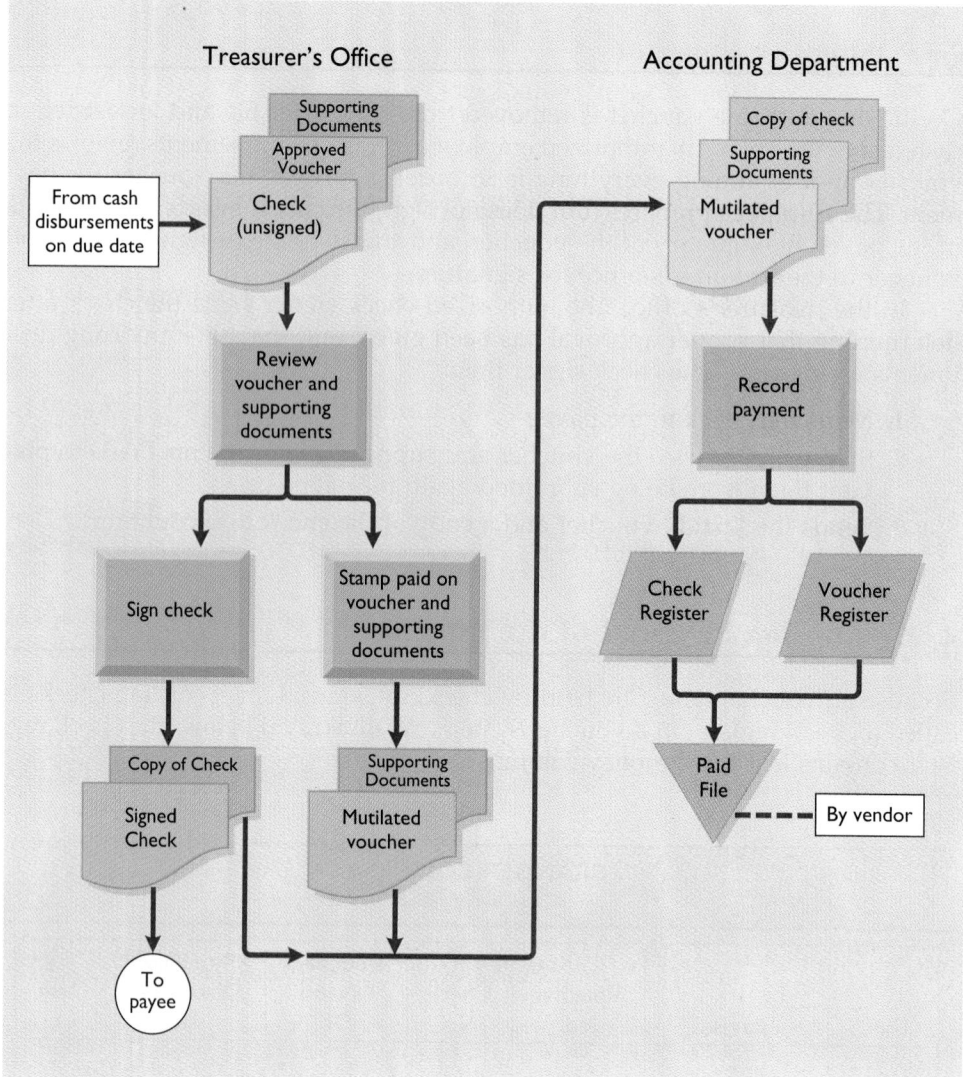

Summary of Study Objectives for Appendix D

8. *Explain the essential features of a voucher system.* A voucher system is an extensive series of prescribed control procedures designed to assure that every disbursement by check is a proper payment. The system begins with the authorization to incur the cost or expense and ends with the issuance of a check for the liability incurred.

GLOSSARY

Bank service charge · A fee charged by a bank for the use of its services. (p. 291).

Bank statement · A statement received monthly from the bank that shows the depositor's bank transactions and balances. (p. 289).

Cash · Resources that consist of coins, currency, checks, money orders, and money on hand or on deposit in a bank. (p. 283).

Cash equivalents · Highly liquid investments, with maturities of three months or less when purchased, that can be converted to a specific amount of cash. (p. 298).

Check · A written order signed by the depositor directing the bank to pay a specified sum of money to a designated recipient. (p. 289).

Check register · The journal used to record payments by check in a voucher system. (p. 303).

Compensating balances · Minimum cash balances required by a bank in support of bank loans. (p. 298).

Deposits in transit · Deposits recorded by the depositor that have not been recorded by the bank. (p. 292).

Electronic funds transfer · A disbursement system that uses wire, telephone, telegraph, or computer to transfer cash from one location to another. (p. 298).

Internal auditors · Company employees who evaluate on a continuous basis the effectiveness of the company's system of internal control. (p. 280).

Internal control · The plan of organization and all the related methods and measures adopted within a business to safeguard its assets and enhance the accuracy and reliability of its accounting records. (p. 276).

NSF check · A check that is not paid by a bank because of insufficient funds in a customer's bank account. (p. 291).

Outstanding checks · Checks issued and recorded by a company that have not been paid by the bank. (p. 292).

Petty cash fund · A cash fund used to pay relatively small amounts. (p. 295).

Tickler file · A file in which unpaid vouchers are filed by date of payment. (p. 302).

Voucher · An authorization form prepared for each expenditure in a voucher system. (p. 300).

Voucher register · A columnar journal used to record all types of expenditures in a voucher system. (p. 300).

Voucher system · An extensive network of approvals by authorized individuals acting independently to ensure that all disbursements by check are proper. (p. 287).

DEMONSTRATION PROBLEM

The Trillo Company's bank statement for May 1993 shows the following data:

Balance 5/1	$12,650	Balance 5/31	$14,280
Debit memorandum:		Credit memorandum:	
NSF check	$ 175	Collection of note receivable	$ 505

The cash balance per books at May 31 is $13,319. Your review of the data reveals the following:

1. The NSF check was from Hup Co., a customer.
2. The note collected by the bank was a $500, three-month, 12% note. The bank charged a $10 collection fee. No interest has been accrued.
3. Outstanding checks at May 31 total $2,410.
4. Deposits in transit at May 31 total $1,752.
5. A Trillo Company check for $352 dated May 10 cleared the bank on May 25. This check, which was a payment on account, was journalized for $325.

Instructions
(a) Prepare a bank reconciliation at May 31.
(b) Journalize the entries required by the reconciliation.

Solution to Demonstration Problem

(a)

TRILLO COMPANY
Bank Reconciliation
May 31, 1993

Cash balance per bank statement	$14,280
Add: Deposits in transit	1,752
	16,032

Helpful hints
1. Follow the four steps used in reconciling items (pp. 292–3).
2. Work carefully to minimize mathematical errors in the reconciliation.
3. All entries are based on reconciling items per books.
4. Make sure the cash ledger balance after posting the reconciling entries agrees with the adjusted cash balance per books.

Less: Outstanding checks		2,410
Adjusted cash balance per bank		$13,622
Cash balance per books		$13,319
Add: Collection of note receivable $500, plus $15 interest less		
collection fee $10		505
		13,824
Less: NSF check	$175	
Error in recording check	27	202
Adjusted cash balance per books		$13,622

(b)

May 31	Cash		505	
	Miscellaneous Expense		10	
	Notes Receivable			500
	Interest Revenue			15
	(To record collection of note by bank)			
	31	Accounts Receivable—Hup Co.	175	
		Cash		175
		(To record NSF check from Hup Co.)		
	31	Accounts Payable	27	
		Cash		27
		(To correct error in recording check)		

*Note: All **asterisked** Questions, Exercises, and Problems relate to material contained in the appendix to each chapter.

SELF-STUDY QUESTIONS

Answers are at the end of the chapter.

(S.O. 1) 1. Internal control is used in a business to safeguard its assets and:
a. prevent fraud.
b. produce correct financial statements.
c. deter employee dishonesty.
d. enhance the accuracy and reliability of its accounting records.

(S.O. 2) 2. The principles of internal control do not include:
a. segregation of duties.
b. management responsibility.
c. documentation procedures.
d. independent internal verification.

(S.O. 2) 3. Physical controls do not include:
a. safes and vaults to store cash.
b. locked warehouses for inventories.
c. independent bank reconciliations.
d. bank safety deposit boxes for important papers.

(S.O. 3) 4. Which of the following items in a cash drawer at November 30 is not cash?
a. Money orders.
b. Coins and currency.
c. A customer check dated November 28.
d. A customer check dated December 1.

(S.O. 3) 5. Permitting only designated personnel such as cashiers to handle cash receipts is an application of the principle of:
a. establishment of responsibility.
b. segregation of duties.
c. independent check.
d. other controls.

(S.O. 4) 6. The use of prenumbered checks in disbursing cash is an application of the principle of:
a. establishment of responsibility.
b. segregation of duties.
c. documentation procedures.
d. physical, mechanical, and electronic controls.

(S.O. 5) 7. The control features of a bank account do not include:
a. minimizing the amount of cash that must be kept on hand.
b. having bank auditors verify the correctness of the bank balance per books.
c. providing a double record of all bank transactions.
d. safeguarding cash by using a bank as a depository.

(S.O. 6) 8. In a bank reconciliation, outstanding checks are:
a. deducted from the book balance.

b. added to the book balance

c. added to the bank balance.

d. deducted from the bank balance.

(S.O. 6) 9. The reconciling item in a bank reconcili- ation that will result in an adjusting entry by the depositor is:

a. outstanding checks.

b. deposit in transit.

c. bank service charges.

d. a bank error.

(S.O. 7) 10. A check is written to replenish a $100 petty cash fund when the fund contains receipts of $94 and $4 in cash. In record-

ing the check,

a. Cash Over and Short should be debited for $2.

b. Petty Cash should be debited for $96.

c. Cash should be credited for $94.

d. Petty Cash should be credited for $2.

*11. Which of the following is *not* unique to a voucher system?   (S.O. 8)

a. A voucher.

b. A tickler file.

c. A check.

d. A paid voucher file.

QUESTIONS

1. Cynthia Bowan believes there is more to internal control than safeguarding company assets. Do you agree? Explain.

2. Identify the principles of internal control.

3. In the corner grocery store, all sales clerks make change out of one cash register. Is this a violation of internal control? Why?

4. J. Dumars is reviewing the principle of segregation of duties. What are the two common applications of this principle?

5. How do documentation procedures contribute to good internal control?

6. What internal control objectives are met by physical, mechanical, and electronic controls?

7. (a) Explain the control principle of independent internal verification. (b) What practices are important in applying this principle?

8. The management of the Glove Company asks you, as the company accountant, to explain (a) the concept of reasonable assurance in internal control and (b) the importance of the human factor in internal control.

9. Midland Inc. owns the following assets at the balance sheet date:

Cash in bank-savings account	$ 4,000
Cash on hand	850
Cash refund due from the IRS	1,000
Checking account balance	15,000
Postdated checks	500

What amount should be reported as cash in the balance sheet?

10. What principle(s) of internal control is (are) involved in making daily cash counts of over-the-counter receipts?

11. Denton Department Stores has just installed new electronic cash registers in its stores. How do cash registers improve internal control over cash receipts?

12. In the Allen Mail Order Company, two mail clerks open all mail receipts. How does this strengthen internal control?

13. To have maximum effective internal control over cash disbursements, all payments should be made by check. Is this true? Explain.

14. The Hardy Company's internal controls over cash disbursements provide for the treasurer to sign checks imprinted by a checkwriter after comparing the check with the approved in- voice. Identify the internal control principles that are present in these controls.

15. How do the principles of physical, mechanical, and electronic controls and other controls apply to cash disbursements?

16. The use of a bank contributes significantly to good internal control over cash. Is this true? Why?

17. Paul Pentz is confused about the lack of agreement between the cash balance per books and the balance per the bank. Explain the causes for the lack of agreement to Paul and give an example of each cause.

18. What are the four steps involved in finding differences between the balance per books and balance per banks?

19. Millie More asks your help concerning an NSF check. Explain to Millie (a) what an NSF check is, (b) how it is treated in a bank reconciliation, and (c) whether it will require an adjusting entry per bank?

20. (a) The operation of a petty cash fund involves three activities. Identify the activities and indicate an internal control principle applicable to each activity.
(b) When are journal entries required in the operation of a petty cash fund?

21. What is the essential feature of an electronic funds transfer (EFT) procedure?

22. What are cash equivalents? How may they be reported in a company's financial statements?

***23.** What principles of internal control are applicable to a voucher system?

***24.** (a) Identify the journals used in recording the issuance and payment of a voucher.
(b) Indicate the files maintained in a voucher system.

BRIEF EXERCISES

Explain the importance of internal control.
(S.O. 1)

BE7–1 Gina Marion is the new owner of Liberty Parking. She has heard about internal control but is not clear about its importance for her business. Explain to Gina the two purposes of internal control and give her one application of each purpose for Liberty Parking.

Identify the internal control principles applicable to cash receipts.
(S.O. 3)

BE7–2 The Rene Company has the following internal control procedures over cash receipts. Identify the internal control principle that is applicable to each procedure.

1. All cashiers are bonded.
2. All over-the-counter receipts are registered on cash registers.
3. Daily cash counts are made by cashier department supervisors.
4. The duties of receiving cash, recording cash, and custody of cash are assigned to different individuals.
5. Only cashiers may operate cash registers.

Identify the internal control principle applicable to cash disbursements.
(S.O. 4)

BE7–3 The Mills Company has the following internal control procedures over cash disbursements. Identify the internal control principle that is applicable to each procedure.

1. Company checks are prenumbered.
2. The bank statement is reconciled monthly by an internal auditor.
3. Only the treasurer or assistant treasurer may sign checks.
4. Blank checks are stored in a safe in the treasurer's office.
5. Check signers are not allowed to record cash disbursement transactions.

Prepare entries for recording invoices at net amount due.
(S.O. 4)

BE7–4 The Pozza Co. records invoices at the net amount due. On May 10, Pozza purchases merchandise on credit at an invoice cost of $700, terms 2/10, n/30. Because of a cash squeeze, Pozza does not pay the invoice until May 29. Prepare the journal entry for the purchase and the payment.

Identify the control features of a bank account.
(S.O. 5)

BE7–5 T. J. Hoad is uncertain about the control features of a bank account. Explain the control benefits of (a) a signature card, (b) a check, and (c) a bank statement.

BE7–6   The following reconciling items are applicable to the bank reconciliation for the Ash Company: (1) deposit in transit, (2) bank debit memorandum for service charge, (3) bank credit memorandum for collecting a note for the depositor, (4) outstanding checks. Indicate how each item should be shown on a bank reconciliation.

Indicate location of reconciling items in a bank reconciliation.
(S.O. 6)

BE7–7   Using the data in BE7–6, indicate (a) the items that will result in an adjustment to the depositor's records and (b) why the other items do not require adjustment.

Identify reconciling items that require adjusting entries.
(S.O. 6)

BE7–8   At July 31, the Lila Company has the following bank information: cash balance per bank, $7,420, outstanding checks $772, deposits in transit $1,700, and a bank service charge $20. Determine the adjusted cash balance per bank at July 31.

Prepare partial bank reconciliation.
(S.O. 6)

BE7–9   At August 31, the Leon Company has a cash balance per books of $9,200 and the following additional data from the bank statement: charge for printing Leon Company checks $25, interest earned on checking account balance $40, and outstanding checks $800. Determine the adjusted cash balance per books at August 31.

Prepare partial bank reconciliation.
(S.O. 6)

BE7–10   On March 20, Grimel's petty cash fund of $100 is replenished when the fund contains $16 in cash and receipts for postage $52, freight-in $22, and travel expense $10. Prepare the journal entry to record the replenishment of the petty cash fund.

Prepare entry to replenish a petty cash fund.
(S.O. 7)

*BE7–11   The Zahn Company begins operations on July 20 and records vouchers at gross amounts. In July, it issues the following vouchers: No. 1 $1,000, No. 2 $2,500, No. 3 $4,000, and No. 4 $3,100. If the July check register shows that voucher Nos. 1 and 3 have been paid in full, what is the balance in vouchers payable at July 31?

Determine vouchers payable balance.
(S.O. 8)

EXERCISES

E7–1   Gino Marino is the owner of Marino's Pizza. Marino's is operated strictly on a carryout basis. Customers pick up their orders at a counter where a clerk exchanges the pizza for cash. While at the counter, the customer can see other employees making the pizzas and the large ovens in which the pizzas are baked.

Identify the principles of internal control.
(S.O. 2)

Instructions
Identify the six principles of internal control and give an example of each principle that you might observe when picking up your pizza. (Note: It may not be possible to observe all the principles.)

E7–2   The following control procedures are used in the Rolen Company for over-the-counter cash receipts.

List internal control weaknesses over cash receipts and suggest improvements.
(S.O. 2, 3)

1. All over-the-counter receipts are registered by three clerks who use a cash register with a single cash drawer.
2. Cashiers are experienced; thus they are not bonded.
3. To minimize the risk of robbery, cash in excess of $100 is stored in an unlocked attache case in the stock room until it is deposited in the bank.
4. At the end of each day, the total receipts are counted by the cashier on duty and reconciled to the cash register total.
5. The company accountant makes the bank deposit and then records the day's receipts.

Instructions
(a) For each procedure, explain the weakness in internal control and identify the control principle that is violated.

(b) For each weakness, suggest a change in procedure that will result in good internal control.

E7–3   As a new staff auditor for the CPA firm of Rawls, King, and Landry you have been assigned to review the internal controls over the cash receipts of the Adirondack Company. Your review reveals the following: Most receipts arrive through the mail. These receipts are promptly endorsed "For Deposit Only," but no list of the checks is prepared by the person

Identify internal control weaknesses over mail receipts and suggest improvements.
(S.O. 3)

opening the mail. Furthermore, you determine that the mail is opened either by the cashier or by the employee who maintains the accounts receivable records. Mail receipts are deposited in the bank weekly.

Instructions

(a) Identify the weaknesses in internal control over mail receipts.

(b) Indicate your recommendations for improvement.

List internal control weaknesses over cash disbursements and suggest improvements.
(S.O. 2, 4)

E7–4 The following control procedures are used in Ann's Linen Shoppe for cash disbursements.

1. Each week, Ann leaves 100 company checks in an unmarked envelope on a shelf behind the cash register.
2. The company checks are unnumbered.
3. The store manager personally approves all payments before signing and issuing checks.
4. After payment, bills are "filed" in a paid invoice folder.
5. The company accountant prepares the bank reconciliation and reports any discrepancies to the owner.

Instructions

(a) For each procedure, explain the weakness in internal control and identify the internal control principle that is violated.

(b) For each weakness, suggest a change in the procedure that will result in good internal control.

Identify internal control weaknesses for cash disbursements and make recommendations for improvement.
(S.O. 4)

E7–5 In the Webber Company, checks are not prenumbered because both the purchasing agent and the treasurer are authorized to issue checks. Each signer has access to unissued checks kept in an unlocked file cabinet. The purchasing agent pays all bills pertaining to goods purchased for resale. Prior to payment, the purchasing agent determines that the goods have been received and verifies the mathematical accuracy of the vendor's invoice. After payment, the invoice is filed by vendor, and the purchasing agent records the payment in the cash disbursements journal. The treasurer pays all other bills following approval by authorized employees. After payment, the treasurer stamps all bills PAID, files them by payment date, and records the checks in the cash disbursements journal. Webber Company maintains one checking account that is reconciled by the treasurer.

Instructions

(a) List the weaknesses in internal control over cash disbursements.

(b) Indicate your recommendations for improvement.

Recording purchases at net.
(S.O. 4)

E7–6 Presented below are transactions related to Ronald Maddell Company.

April 2 Purchase merchandise on account, $1,000, terms 2/10, n/30.
       3 Purchase merchandise on account, $12,000, terms 2/10, n/30.
      12 Paid for merchandise purchased on April 3.
      30 Paid for merchandise purchased on April 2.

Instructions

(a) Prepare journal entries to record these transactions, assuming that the company uses the net method of recording purchases.

(b) What is a primary advantage of using the net method to record purchases?

Determine outstanding checks.
(S.O. 6)

E7–7 On April 30, the bank reconciliation of the Druker Company shows three outstanding checks: No. 254 $650, No. 255 $820, and No. 257 $410. The May bank statement and the May cash payments journal show the following:

Bank Statement			Cash Payments Journal		
Checks Paid			Checks Issued		
Date	Check No.	Amount	Date	Check No.	Amount
5/4	254	650	5/2	258	159
5/2	255	820	5/5	259	275

Date	Check No.	Amount	Date	Check No.	Amount
5/17	258	159	5/10	260	925
5/12	259	275	5/15	261	500
5/20	261	500	5/22	262	750
5/29	263	480	5/24	263	480
			5/29	264	360

Instructions

List the outstanding checks at May 31.

E7–8 The following information pertains to the Leon Company.

1. Cash balance per bank, July 31, $7,463.
2. July bank service charge not recorded by the depositor, $25.
3. Cash balance per books, July 31, $7,200.
4. Deposits in transit, July 31, $1,700.
5. Note for $1,200 collected for Leon in July by the bank, plus interest $36 less fee $20. The collection has not been recorded by Leon but interest has.
6. Outstanding checks, July 31, $772.

Instructions

(a) Prepare a bank reconciliation at July 31.

(b) Journalize the adjusting entries at July 31 on the books of the Leon Company.

Prepare bank reconciliation and adjusting entries.
(S.O. 6)

E7–9 The information below relates to the Cash account in the ledger of the Reston Company.

Balance September 1—$17,150; Cash deposited—$64,000.
Balance September 30—$17,404; Checks written—$63,746.

The September bank statement shows a balance of $16,422 on September 30 and the following memorandum:

Credits		Debits	
Collection of $1,500 note plus interest $30	$1,530	NSF check: J. Hower	$420
Interest earned on checking account	$45	Safety deposit box rent	$20

At September 30, deposits in transit were $4,500 and outstanding checks totaled $2,383.

Instructions

(a) Prepare the bank reconciliation at September 30.

(b) Prepare the adjusting entries at September 30, assuming (1) the NSF check was from a customer on account, and (2) no interest had been accrued on the note.

Prepare bank reconciliation and adjusting entries.
(S.O. 6)

E7–10 The cash records of the Kuritan Company show the following:

1. The June 30 bank reconciliation indicated that deposits in transit total $850. During July the general ledger account Cash shows deposits of $15,750, but the bank statement indicates that only $15,400 in deposits were received during the month.
2. The June 30 bank reconciliation also reported outstanding checks of $920. During the month of July, the Kuritan Company books show that $17,200 of checks were issued, yet the bank statement showed that $16,400 of checks cleared the bank in July.
3. In September, deposits per the bank statement totaled $26,700, deposits per books were $25,400, and deposits in transit at September 30 were $2,400.
4. In September, cash disbursements per books were $23,700, checks clearing the bank were $25,000, and outstanding checks at September 30 were $2,100.

There were no bank debit or credit memoranda and no errors were made by either the bank or the Kuritan Company.

Compute deposits in transit and outstanding checks for two bank reconciliations.
(S.O. 6)

Instructions

Answer the following questions:

(a) In situation (1), what were the deposits in transit at July 31?

(b) In situation (2), what were the outstanding checks at July 31?

(c) In situation (3), what were the deposits in transit at August 31?

(d) In situation (4), what were the outstanding checks at August 31?

Prepare journal entries for a petty cash fund.

E7–11   The Brooks Company uses an imprest petty cash system. The fund was established on March 1 with a balance of $100. During March the following petty cash receipts were found in the petty cash box:

Date	Receipt No.	For	Amount
3/5	1	Stamp Inventory	$38
7	2	Freight-in	19
9	3	Miscellaneous Expense	12
11	4	Travel Expense	24
14	5	Miscellaneous Expense	4

There was no cash over or short. The fund was replenished on March 15. Also on March 15, the amount in the fund was increased to $150.

Instructions

Journalize the entries in March that pertain to the operation of the petty cash fund.

Determine vouchers payable balance and discounts taken.

*E7–12   The Zenko Company uses a voucher system for cash disbursements. During June, the following transactions occurred. All purchases are subject to discount terms of 2/10, n/30. There were no outstanding vouchers at May 31.

Date	Voucher No.	For	Amount
June 1	610	Rent	$ 1,000
5	611	Purchases	8,000
7	612	Wages	2,000
11	613	Purchases	10,000
15	614	Note payable	5,000
19	615	Purchases	4,400
27	616	Purchases	2,600
30	617	Wages	2,000
			$35,000

Date	Check No.	Amount	For Voucher No.
June 2	474	$ 1,000	610
8	475	2,000	612
13	476	7,840	611
16	477	5,000	614
20	478	9,800	613
30	479	2,000	617
		$27,640	

Instructions

Assuming the vouchers are recorded at gross amounts, indicate (1) the balance in Vouchers Payable at June 30 and (2) the purchase discounts taken during the month.

PROBLEMS

Identify internal control weaknesses over cash receipts.

P7–1   Red Fox Theater is located in the Red River Mall. A cashier's booth is located near the entrance to the theater. Two cashiers are employed. One works from 1–5 P.M., the other from 5–9 P.M. Each cashier is bonded. The cashiers receive cash from customers and operate a machine that ejects serially numbered tickets. The rolls of tickets are inserted and locked into the machine by the theater manager at the beginning of each cashier's shift.

After purchasing a ticket, the customer takes the ticket to a doorperson stationed at the entrance of the theater lobby some 60 feet from the cashier's booth. The doorperson tears the ticket in half, admits the customer, and returns the ticket stub to the customer. The other half of the ticket is dropped into a locked box by the doorperson.

At the end of each cashier's shift, the theater manager removes the ticket rolls from the machine and makes a cash count. The cash count sheet is initialed by the cashier. At the end of the day, the manager deposits the receipts in total in a bank night deposit vault located in the mall. In addition, the manager sends copies of the deposit slip and the initialed cash count sheets to the theater company treasurer for verification and to the company's accounting department. Receipts from the first shift are stored in a safe located in the manager's office.

Instructions

(a) Identify the internal control principles and their application to the cash receipts transactions of the Red Fox Theater.

(b) If the doorperson and cashier decide to collaborate to misappropriate cash, what actions might they take?

P7–2 On July 31, 1993, the Rona Company had a cash balance per books of $6,815.30. The statement from the Tri-County Bank on that date showed a balance of $7,075.80. A comparison of the bank statement with the cash account revealed the following facts:

*Prepare a bank reconciliation and adjusting entries.
(S.O. 6)*

    1. The bank service charge for July was $20.

    2. The bank collected a note receivable of $1,200 for Rona Company on July 15, plus $48 of interest. The bank made a $10 charge for the collection. The only entry by Rona Company in July was to accrue interest on the note to July 15.

    3. The July 31 receipts of $1,819.60 were not included in the bank deposits for July. These receipts were deposited by the company in a night deposit vault on July 31.

    4. Company check No. 2480 issued to J. Brokaw, a creditor, for $492 that cleared the bank in July was incorrectly entered in the cash payments journal on July 10 for $429.

    5. Checks outstanding on July 31 totaled $1,475.10.

    6. On July 31, the bank statement showed an NSF charge of $550 for a check received by the company from R. Close, a customer, on account.

Instructions

(a) Prepare the bank reconciliation as of July 31, 1993.

(b) Prepare the necessary adjusting entries at July 31, 1993.

P7–3 The bank portion of the bank reconciliation for the Louda Company at October 31, 1993 was as follows:

*Prepare a bank reconciliation and adjusting entries from detailed data.
(S.O. 6)*

LOUDA COMPANY
Bank Reconciliation
October 31, 1993

Cash balance per bank		$12,367.90
Add: Deposits in transit		1,530.20
		13,898.10

Less: Outstanding checks		
Check Number	Check Amount	
2451	$1,260.40	
2470	720.10	
2471	844.50	
2472	426.80	
2474	1,050.00	4,301.80
Adjusted cash balance per bank		$ 9,596.30

The adjusted cash balance per bank agreed with the cash balance per books at October 31. The November bank statement showed the following checks and deposits.

	Bank Statement			
	Checks		Deposits	
Date	Number	Amount	Date	Amount
11-1	2470	$ 720.10	11-1	$ 1,530.20
11-2	2471	844.50	11-4	1,211.60
11-5	2474	1,050.00	11-8	990.10
11-4	2475	1,640.70	11-13	2,575.00
11-8	2476	2,830.00	11-18	1,472.70

	Bank Statement			
	Checks		Deposits	
Date	Number	Amount	Date	Amount
11-10	2477	$ 600.00	11-21	$ 2,945.00
11-15	2479	1,750.00	11-25	2,567.30
11-18	2480	1,330.00	11-28	1,650.00
11-27	2481	695.40	11-30	1,186.00
11-30	2483	575.50	Total	$16,127.90
11-29	2486	900.00		
	Total	$12,936.20		

The cash records per books for November showed the following:

Cash Payments Journal						Cash Receipts Journal	
Date	Number	Amount	Date	Number	Amount	Date	Amount
11-1	2475	$1,640.70	11-20	2483	$ 575.50	11-3	$ 1,211.60
11-2	2476	2,830.00	11-22	2484	829.50	11-7	990.10
11-2	2477	600.00	11-23	2485	974.80	11-12	2,575.00
11-4	2478	538.20	11-24	2486	900.00	11-17	1,472.70
11-8	2479	1,570.00	11-29	2487	398.00	11-20	2,954.00
11-10	2480	1,330.00	11-30	2488	800.00	11-24	2,567.30
11-15	2481	695.40	Total		$14,294.10	11-27	1,650.00
11-18	2482	612.00				11-29	1,186.00
						11-30	1,225.00
						Total	$15,831.70

The bank statement contained two bank memoranda:

1. A credit of $2,105.00 for the collection of a $2,000 note for Louda Company plus interest of $120 and less a collection fee of $15. Louda Company accrued interest to the maturity of the note.

2. A debit for the printing of additional company checks, $50.00.

At November 30 the cash balance per books was $11,133.90 and the cash balance per the bank statement was $17,614.60. The bank did not make any errors but two errors were made by Louda Company.

Instructions

(a) Prepare a bank reconciliation at November 30.

(b) Prepare the adjusting entries based on the reconciliation. (*Note:* The correction of any errors pertaining to recording checks should be made to Accounts Payable. The correction of any errors relating to recording cash receipts should be made to Accounts Receivable.)

Prepare a bank reconciliation and adjusting entries.
(S.O. 6)

P7–4   The May Company's bank statement from Lane National Bank at August 31, 1993, shows the following information:

Balance, August 1	$17,400	Bank credit memorandum:		
August deposits	73,000	Collection of note		
Checks cleared in August	68,660	receivable plus $90		
Balance, August 31	24,850	interest		$3,090
		Interest earned		40
		Bank debit memorandum		
		Safety deposit box rent		20

A summary of the Cash account in the ledger for August shows: Balance, August 1, $16,900; receipts $77,000; disbursements $73,570; and balance, August 31, $20,330. Analysis reveals that the only reconciling items on the July 31 bank reconciliation were a deposit in transit for $4,000 and outstanding checks of $4,500. The deposit in transit was the first deposit recorded by the bank in August. In addition, you determine that there were two errors involving company checks drawn in August: (1) a check for $400 to a creditor on account that cleared the bank in August was journalized and posted for $420, and (2) a salary check to an employee for $275 was recorded by the bank for $285.

Instructions

(a) Prepare a bank reconciliation at August 31.

(b) Journalize the adjusting entries to be made by May Company at August 31. Assume the interest on the note has been accrued by the company.

P7–5 The MTM Company maintains a petty cash fund for small expenditures. The following transactions occurred over a two-month period:

July 1 Established petty cash fund by writing a check on Metro Bank for $200.

15 Replenished the petty cash fund by writing a check for $194.10. On this date the fund consisted of $5.90 in cash and the following petty cash receipts: Freight-in $94.00, postage expense $42.40, entertainment expense $46.60, and miscellaneous expense $10.70.

31 Replenished the petty cash fund by writing a check for $192.00. At this date, the fund consisted of $8.00 in cash and the following petty cash receipts: Freight-in $82.10, charitable contributions expense $30.00, postage expense $47.80, and miscellaneous expense $32.10.

Aug. 15 Replenished the petty cash fund and increased the amount of the fund to $300 by writing a check for $288.00. On this date, the fund consisted of $12.00 in cash and the following petty cash receipts: Freight-in $74.40, entertainment expense $43.00, postage expense $33.00, and miscellaneous expense $38.00.

31 Replenished petty cash fund by writing a check for $283.00. On this date, the fund consisted of $17 in cash and the following petty cash receipts: Postage expense $145.00, entertainment expense $90.60, and freight-in $45.40.

Journalize and post petty cash fund transactions.
(S.O. 7)

Instructions

(a) Journalize the petty cash transactions.

(b) Post to the Petty Cash account.

(c) What internal control features exist in a petty cash fund?

*P7–6 The Clark Cookie Company uses a voucher system in which all vouchers are recorded at **gross** amounts. The voucher register has debit columns for purchases, freight-in, advertising expense, and other accounts. The following data are obtained from approved vouchers:

Journalize and post transactions in a voucher system.
(S.O. 8)

Cash	Voucher No.	For	Payee	Amount
Sept. 2	201	Merchandise	Sugar Works	$2,700
5	202	Freight-in	Air Freight	150
8	203–5	Baking equipment	Ovens Inc.	9,000
10	206	Advertising	Adams Advertising	200
12	207	Merchandise	Chip Corp.	2,500
13	208	Freight-in	Eastern RR	200
15	209	Petty cash	C. Jackson	100
17	210	Store equipment	Moritz Co.	3,000
21	211	Merchandise	Flour Inc.	2,200
25	212	Advertising	Star Journal	250
26	213–14	Store equipment	Moritz Co.	4,000
27	215	Merchandise	Chip Corp.	2,000
30	216	Salaries payable	Payroll	3,475

Additional Data:

1. Vouchers Nos. 203–5 are for $3,000 each.

2. Voucher No. 209 is for replenishment of the petty cash fund. Petty cash expenditures were freight-in $65, advertising $20, and miscellaneous expenses $15.

3. Voucher No. 213 is for $1,200; voucher No. 214 is for the balance due.

4. All purchases of merchandise are subject to cash discounts of 3/10, n/30. From the check stubs it is learned that the following vouchers were paid in September: Sept. 6, No. 202; Sept. 8, No. 203; Sept. 9, No. 201; Sept. 15, No. 209; Sept. 20, No. 207; Sept. 27, No. 210; Sept. 29, No. 211; and Sept. 30, No. 216. Checks were numbered consecutively beginning with check No. 275.

Instructions

(a) Record the vouchers in the voucher register and the checks in the check register.

(b) Post to the Vouchers Payable account.

(c) Prepare a schedule of unpaid vouchers at September 30 and reconcile the schedule with the balance in Vouchers Payable.

ALTERNATE PROBLEMS

Identify internal control principles over cash disbursements.
(S.O. 2, 4)

P7–1A   Alman Office Supply Company recently changed its system of internal control over cash disbursements. The system includes the following features.

Instead of being unnumbered and manually prepared, all checks must now be pre-numbered and written by using the new checkwriter purchased by the company. Before a check can be issued, each invoice must have the approval of Cindy Morris, the purchasing agent, and Ray Mills, the receiving department supervisor. Checks must be signed by either Frank Malone, the treasurer, or Mary Arno, the assistant treasurer. Before signing a check, the signer is expected to compare the amounts of the check with the amounts on the invoice.

After signing a check, the signer stamps the invoice PAID and inserts within the stamp, the date, check number, and amount of the check. The "paid" invoice is then sent to the accounting department for recording.

Blank checks are stored in a safe in the treasurer's office. The combination to the safe is known only by the treasurer and assistant treasurer. Each month, the bank statement is reconciled with the bank balance per books by the assistant chief accountant.

Instructions

Identify the internal control principles and their application to cash disbursements of Alman Office Supply Company.

Prepare a bank reconciliation and adjusting entries.
(S.O. 6)

P7–2A   On May 31, 1993, the Romell Company had a cash balance per books of $5,781.50. The bank statement from the Community Bank on that date showed a balance of $6,804.60. A comparison of the statement with the cash account revealed the following facts:

1. The statement included a debit memo of $30 for the printing of additional company checks.

2. Cash sales of $836.15 on May 12 were deposited in the bank. The cash receipts journal entry and the deposit slip were incorrectly made for $846.15. The bank credited Romell Company for the correct amount.

3. Outstanding checks at May 31 totaled $1,276.25, and deposits in transit were $936.15.

4. On May 18, the company issued check No. 1181 for $685 to M. Helms, on account. The check, which cleared the bank in May, was incorrectly journalized and posted by Romell Company for $658.

5. A $2,000 note receivable was collected by the bank for Romell Company on May 31 plus $80 interest. The bank charged a collection fee of $20. The only entry made in May by the company for the note was to accrue interest through May 31.

6. Included with the cancelled checks was a check issued by the Teller Company to P. Jonet for $600 that was incorrectly charged to the Romell Company by the bank.

7. On May 31, the bank statement showed an NSF charge of $710 for a check issued by W. Hoad, a customer, to the Romell Company on account.

Instructions

(a) Prepare the bank reconciliation at May 31, 1993.

(b) Prepare the necessary adjusting entries for Romell Company at May 31, 1993.

P7–3A The bank portion of the bank reconciliation for the Bondar Company at November 30, 1993, was as follows:

Prepare a bank reconciliation and adjusting entries from detailed data.
(S.O. 6)

BONDAR COMPANY
Bank Reconciliation
November 30, 1993

Cash balance per bank			$14,367.90
Add: Deposits in transit			2,530.20
			16,898.10

Less: Outstanding checks

Check Number	Check Amount		
3451	$2,260.40		
3470	720.10		
3471	844.50		
3472	1,426.80		
3474	1,050.00		6,301.80
Adjusted cash balance per bank			$10,596.30

The adjusted cash balance per bank agreed with the cash balance per books at November 30. The December bank statement showed the following checks and deposits.

Bank Statement

Checks			Deposits	
Date	Number	Amount	Date	Amount
12-1	3451	$ 2,260.40	12-1	$ 2,530.20
12-2	3471	844.50	12-4	1,211.60
12-7	3472	1,426.80	12-8	2,365.10
12-4	3475	1,640.70	12-16	2,672.70
12-8	3476	1,300.00	12-21	2,945.00
12-10	3477	2,130.00	12-26	2,567.30
12-15	3479	3,080.00	12-29	2,836.00
12-27	3480	600.00	12-30	1,025.00
12-30	3482	475.50	Total	$18,152.90
12-29	3483	1,140.00		
12-31	3485	540.80		
	Total	$15,438.70		

The cash records per books for December showed the following:

Cash Payments Journal

Date	Number	Amount	Date	Number	Amount
12-1	3475	$1,640.70	12-20	3482	$ 475.50
12-2	3476	1,300.00	12-22	3483	1,140.00
12-2	3477	2,130.00	12-23	3484	832.00
12-4	3478	538.20	12-24	3485	450.80
12-8	3479	3,080.00	12-30	3486	1,389.50
12-10	3480	600.00	Total		$14,384.10
12-17	3481	807.40			

Cash Receipts Journal

Date	Amount
12-3	$ 1,211.60
12-7	2,365.10
12-15	2,672.70
12-20	2,954.00
12-25	2,567.30
12-28	2,836.00
12-30	1,025.00
12-31	1,190.40
Total	$16,822.10

The bank statement contained two memoranda:

1. A credit of $2,145 for the collection of a $2,000 note for Bondar Company plus interest of $160 and less a collection fee of $15.00. Bondar Company has not accrued any interest on the note.

2. A debit of $527.10 for an NSF check written by A. Jordan, a customer. At December 31, the check had not been redeposited in the bank.

At December 31 the cash balance per books was $13,034.30 and the cash balance per the bank statement was $18,700.00. The bank did not make any errors but two errors were made by Bondar Company.

Instructions

(a) Prepare a bank reconciliation at December 31.

(b) Prepare the adjusting entries based on the reconciliation. (*Note:* The correction of any errors pertaining to recording checks should be made to Accounts Payable. The correction of any errors relating to recording cash receipts should be made to Accounts Receivable.)

Prepare a bank reconciliation and adjusting entries.
(S.O. 6)

P7–4A   The Coastline Company maintains a checking account at the Marine City Bank. At July 31, selected data from the ledger balance and the bank statement are as follows:

	Cash in Bank	
	Per Books	Per Bank
Balance, July 1	$17,600	$19,200
July receipts	82,000	
July credits		80,070
July disbursements	76,900	
July debits		74,730
Balance, July 31	$22,700	$24,540

Analysis of the bank data reveals that the credits consist of $78,000 of July deposits and a credit memorandum of $2,070 for the collection of a $2,000 note plus interest revenue of $70. The July debits per bank consist of checks cleared, $74,700 and a debit memorandum of $30 for printing additional company checks.

You also discover the following errors involving July checks: (1) a check for $230 to a creditor on account that cleared the bank in July was journalized and posted as $320 and (2) a salary check to an employee for $255 was recorded by the bank for $155.

The June 30 bank reconciliation contained only two reconciling items: deposits in transit $5,000 and outstanding checks of $6,600.

Instructions

(a) Prepare a bank reconciliation at July 31.

(b) Journalize the adjusting entries to be made by Coastline Company at July 31, 1993. Assume that the interest on the note has been accrued.

Journalize and post petty cash fund transactions.
(S.O. 7)

P7–5A   The Levi Company maintains a petty cash fund for small expenditures. The following transactions occurred over a two-month period:

July 1   Established petty cash fund by writing a check on Metro Bank for $200.
  15   Replenished the petty cash fund by writing a check for $194.00. On this date the fund consisted of $6.00 in cash and the following petty cash receipts: Freight-in $94.00, postage expense $42.40, entertainment expense $46.60, and miscellaneous expense $10.90.
  31   Replenished the petty cash fund by writing a check for $192.00. At this date, the fund consisted of $8.00 in cash and the following petty cash receipts: Freight-in $82.10, charitable contributions expense $40.00, postage expense $27.80, and miscellaneous expense $42.10.

Aug. 15   Replenished the petty cash fund and increased the amount of the fund to $300 by writing a check for $287.00. On this date, the fund consisted of $13.00 in cash and the following petty cash receipts: Freight-in $74.40, entertainment expense $43.00, postage expense $33.00, and miscellaneous expense $37.00.
  31   Replenished petty cash fund by writing a check for $283.00. On this date, the fund consisted of $17 in cash and the following petty cash receipts: Postage expense $140.00, travel expense $95.60, and freight-in $46.40.

Instructions

(a) Journalize the petty cash transactions.

(b) Post to the Petty Cash account.

(c) What internal control features exist in a petty cash fund?

P7–6A Mavrick Company is a very profitable small business. It has not, however, given much consideration to internal control. For example, in an attempt to keep clerical and office expenses to a minimum, the company has combined the jobs of cashier and bookkeeper. As a result, Rob Rowe handles all cash receipts, keeps the accounting records, and prepares the monthly bank reconciliations.

Prepare comprehensive bank reconciliation with defalcation and internal control deficiencies.
(S.O. 2, 3, 4, 6)

The balance per the bank statement on October 31, 1993, was $18,400. Outstanding checks were: No. 62 for $126.75, No. 183 for $150, No. 284 for $253.25, No. 862 for $190.71, No. 863 for $226.80, and No. 864 for $165.28. Included with the statement was a credit memorandum of $200 indicating the collection of a note receivable for the Mavrick Company by the bank on October 25. This memorandum has not been recorded by Mavrick Company.

The company's ledger showed one cash account with a balance of $21,912.72. The balance included undeposited cash on hand. Because of the lack of internal controls, Rowe took for personal use all of the undeposited receipts in excess of $3,795.51. He then prepared the following bank reconciliation in an effort to conceal his theft of cash.

Cash balance per books, October 31		$21,912.72
Add: Outstanding checks		
No. 862	$190.71	
No. 863	226.80	
No. 864	165.28	482.79
		22,395.51
Less: Undeposited receipts		3,795.51
Unadjusted balance per bank, October 31		18,600.00
Less: Bank credit memorandum		200.00
Cash balance per bank statement, October 31		$18,400.00

Instructions

(a) Prepare a correct bank reconciliation. (*Hint:* Deduct the amount of the theft from the adjusted balance per books.)

(b) Indicate the three ways that Rowe attempted to conceal the theft and the dollar amount pertaining to each method.

(c) What principles of internal control were violated in this case?

*B*roadening Your Perspective

FINANCIAL REPORTING PROBLEM

The financial statements of PepsiCo, Inc. are presented in Appendix L of this textbook together with two reports: (1) a management report, Management's Responsibility for Financial Statements, and (2) an auditor's report, Report of KPMG Peat Marwick Independent Auditors.

Instructions

Using the financial statements and reports, answer the following questions about PepsiCo's internal controls and cash.

1. What comments, if any, concerning the company's system of internal control are included in each report?

2. What reference, if any, is made to internal auditors in each report?

3. What comments, if any, are made about cash in the report of the certified public accountants?

4. What data about cash and cash equivalents are shown in the consolidated balance sheet (statement of financial condition)?

5. What activities are identified in the consolidated statement of cash flows as being responsible for the changes in cash during 1991?

6. How are cash equivalents defined under the Notes to Consolidated Financial Statements?

DECISION CASE

The board of trustees of a local church is concerned about the internal accounting controls pertaining to the offering collections made at weekly services. They ask you to serve on a three-person audit team with the internal auditor of the university and a CPA who has just joined the church.

At a meeting of the audit team and the board of trustees you learn the following:

1. The church's board of trustees has delegated responsibility for the financial management and audit of the financial records to the finance committee. This group prepares the annual budget and approves major disbursements but is not involved in collections or record keeping. No audit has been made in recent years because the same trusted employee has kept church records and served as financial secretary for 15 years. The church does not carry any fidelity insurance.

2. The collection at the weekly service is taken by a team of ushers who volunteer to serve one month. The ushers take the collection plates to a basement office at the rear of the church. They hand their plates to the head usher and return to the church service. After all plates have been turned in, the head usher counts the cash received. The head usher then places the cash in the church safe along with a notation of the amount counted. The head usher volunteers to serve for three months.

3. The next morning the financial secretary opens the safe and recounts the collection. The secretary withholds $150–$200 in cash, depending on the cash expenditures expected for the week, and deposits the remainder of the collections in the bank. To facilitate the deposit, church members who contribute by check are asked to make their checks payable to "cash."

4. Each month, the financial secretary reconciles the bank statement and submits a copy of the reconciliation to the board of trustees. The reconciliations have rarely contained any bank errors and have never shown any errors per books.

Instructions

(a) Indicate the weaknesses in internal accounting control over the handling of collections.

(b) List the improvements in internal control procedures that you plan to make at the next meeting of the audit team for (1) the ushers, (2) the head usher, (3) the financial secretary, and (4) the finance committee.

(c) What church policies should be changed to improve internal control?

CRITICAL THINKING CASE

Refer to the opening vignette about Columbia University, and answer the following questions:

1. Does Susan have a valid basis for establishing responsibility for overages or shortages? Why or why not?

2. What internal control principles are applicable to reconciling cash register tapes and the amount of cash in the cash drawer at the end of the day?

3. What internal control principle is involved in seeing that a student gets a receipt when buying a meal at a register? How does this requirement contribute to good internal control?

4. Do you think the cashiers are or should be bonded?

ETHICAL CASE

You are the assistant controller in charge of general ledger accounting at Lemon Twist Bottling Company. Your company has a large loan from an insurance company. The loan agreement requires that the company's cash account balance be maintained at $200,000 or more as reported monthly. At June 30 the cash balance is $80,000, which you report to Sam Williams, the financial vice-president. Sam excitedly instructs you to keep the cash receipts book open for one additional day for purposes of the June 30 report to the insurance company. Sam says, "If we don't get that cash balance over $200,000, we'll default on our loan agreement. They could close us down, put us all out of our jobs!" Sam continues, "I talked to Grochum Distributors (one of Lemon Twist's largest customers) this morning and they said they sent us a check for $150,000 yesterday. We should receive it tomorrow. If we include just that one check in our cash balance, we'll be in the clear. It's in the mail!"

Instructions

(a) Who will suffer negative effects if you do not comply with Sam William's instructions? Who will suffer if you do comply?

(b) What are the ethical considerations in this case?

(c) What alternatives do you have?

Answers to Self-Study Questions
1. d   2. b   3. c   4. d   5. a   6. c   7. b   8. d   9. c   10. a
11. c

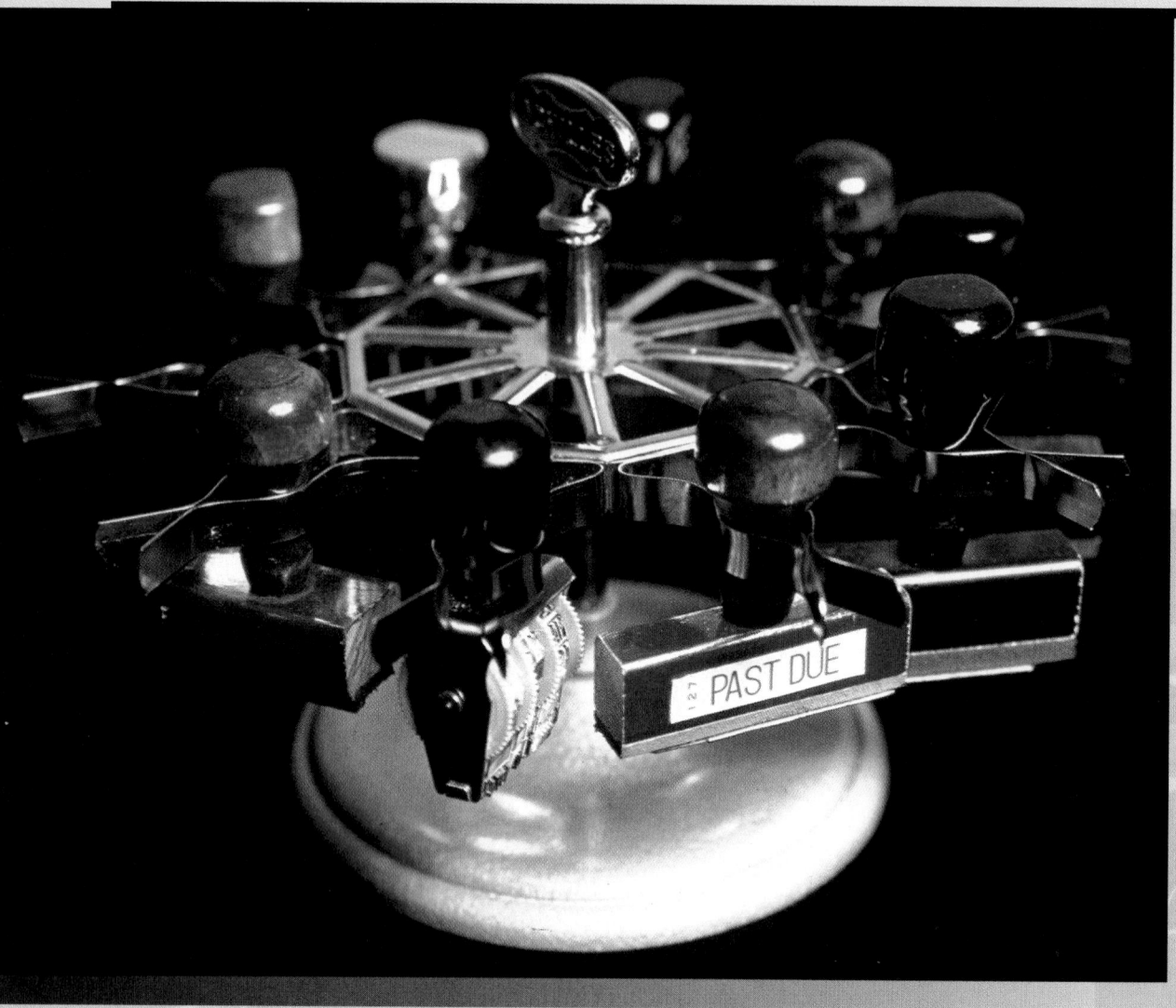

CONCEPTS FOR REVIEW

Before studying this chapter, you should know or, if necessary, review:

a. *How to record sales transactions (Ch. 5, pp. 181–85)*

b. *Why adjusting entries are made (Ch. 3, p. 91)*

c. *How to compute interest (Ch. 3, p. 100)*

CHAPTER 8

ACCOUNTING FOR RECEIVABLES

Study Objectives

After studying this chapter, you should be able to:

1. *Identify the different types of receivables.*

2. *Explain how accounts receivable are recognized in the accounts.*

3. *Distinguish between the methods and bases used to value accounts receivable.*

4. *Describe the entries to record the disposition of accounts receivable.*

5. *Compute the maturity date of, and interest on, notes receivable.*

6. *Explain how notes receivable are recognized in the accounts.*

7. *Describe how notes receivable are valued.*

8. *Describe the entries to record the disposition of notes receivable.*

T*ake a look at your campus newspaper. Read the advertisements—the nearby pizza parlor, a local clothing merchant, maybe a review course for the Law School Admission Test. In many cases these advertisers set up accounts with the campus paper and pay their bills 30 days after the ad runs. The paper keeps track of these accounts and bills them on a timely basis.*

For more than 70 years, the North Carolina State University Technician *has published stories by student writers and run ads by local merchants. "Eighty-five percent of our $400,000 annual operating budget comes from advertising," says Tim Ellington, General Manager—he graduated from NC State in 1987. "The rest comes from student fees."*

Ellington says that the paper requires prepayment from new advertising accounts. After a trial period, the advertiser will be granted a 30-day payment period. From time to time, however, advertisers don't pay on time. "When it comes to bill paying time, our bill often gets put on the bottom of the pile," says Ellington. "If they are going to anger somebody, they'll anger us before they do a supplier."

Once a bill is 30 days past due, the advertiser is sent a letter that says, nicely, "if you haven't sent your payment, please do." At 45 days, the letter isn't as nice: "if we don't receive payment in 30 days, then we could pursue it through small claims court." At 75 days, the newspaper files a small claims suit.

As you read this chapter, think about the journal entries the Technician *would have to make when it sells ad space, when it collects the cash, and when it writes off a bad account.*

This familiar question "Will that be cash or charge?" reminds us that our economy is heavily dependent on the use of credit. Short-term receivables are a major component of current assets and an important factor in the operating cycle of many companies. Recently, for example, at Coca-Cola Company, receivables represented 22% of current assets; at Snap-On-Tools Corporation they totaled 68%. The purpose of this chapter is to discuss the major issues related to the accounting for receivables.

Types of Receivables

Study Objective 1

Identify the different types of receivables.

The term "receivables" refers to amounts due from individuals and other companies. Receivables are claims that are expected to be collected in cash. Receivables are frequently classified as (1) accounts, (2) notes, and (3) other.

Accounts receivable are amounts owed by customers on account. They result from the sale of goods and services. These receivables generally are expected to be collected within 30 to 60 days. They are the most significant type of claim held by a company.

Notes receivable represent claims that are evidenced by formal instruments of credit. The credit instrument normally requires the debtor to pay interest and extends for time periods of 60–90 days or longer. Notes and accounts receivable that result from sales transactions are often called **trade receivables**.

Other receivables include nontrade receivables such as interest receivable, loans to company officers, advances to employees, and income taxes refundable. These are unusual; therefore, they are generally classified and reported as separate items in the balance sheet.

The remainder of this chapter is divided into two sections—accounts receivable and notes receivable. In our coverage of accounts receivable, we emphasize trade accounts receivable because of their importance. Our coverage of notes receivable includes both short-term and long-term notes.

SECTION 1   Accounts Receivable

The three primary accounting problems associated with accounts receivable are:

1. **Recognition** of accounts receivable.
2. **Valuation** of accounts receivable.
3. **Disposition** of accounts receivable.

Study Objective 2

Explain how accounts receivable are recognized in the accounts.

Recognition of Accounts Receivable

The recognition of accounts receivable is relatively straightfoward. In Chapter 5, we saw how accounts receivable are affected by the sale of merchandise. To illustrate, assume that Jordache Co. on July 1, 1993, sells merchandise on account to Polo Company for $1,000 terms 2/10, n/30. On July 5, merchandise worth $100 is returned to Jordache Co. On July 11, payment is received from Polo Company for the balance due. The journal entries to record these transactions on the books of Jordache Co. are as follows:

July 1	Accounts Receivable	1,000	
	Sales		1,000
	(To record sales on account)		
July 5	Sales Returns and Allowances	100	
	Accounts Receivable		100
	(To record merchandise returned)		
July 11	Cash ($900 − $18)	882	
	Sales Discounts ($900 × .02)	18	
	Accounts Receivable		900
	(To record collection of accounts receivable)		

The opportunity to receive a cash discount usually occurs when a manufacturer sells to a wholesaler or a wholesaler sells to a retailer. A discount is given in these situations either to encourage prompt payment or for competitive reasons.

On the other hand, retailers rarely grant cash discounts to customers. For example, we would be surprised if you ever received a cash discount in purchasing goods from any well-known retailer, such as Kmart, Sears, Wal-Mart, and so on. In these situations, most sales are either cash or credit card sales. In fact, when you use a retailer's credit card (J. C. Penney or Sears, for example), instead of giving a discount, the retailer charges interest on the balance due if not paid within a specified period (usually 25–30 days).

To illustrate, assume that you charge on your J. C. Penney credit card a new outfit that costs $300. J. C. Penney will make the following entry at the date of sale:

Accounts Receivable	300	
Sales		300
(To record sale of merchandise)		

J. C. Penney will then send you a monthly statement of this transaction and any others that have occurred during the month. If you fail to pay in full within 30 days, J. C. Penney adds an interest (financing) charge to the balance due.

Although interest rates can vary from state to state, a common rate is 18% per year or 1.5% per month. When financing charges are added, the seller recognizes interest revenue. Assuming that you owe $300 at the end of the month, and J. C. Penney charges 1.5% per month on the balance due, the entry to record interest revenue of $4.50 ($300 × 1.5%) is as follows:

Accounts Receivable	4.50	
Interest Revenue		4.50
(To record interest on amount due)		

Revenue from this source is often substantial for many retailers.

Accounting in Action · *Business Insight*

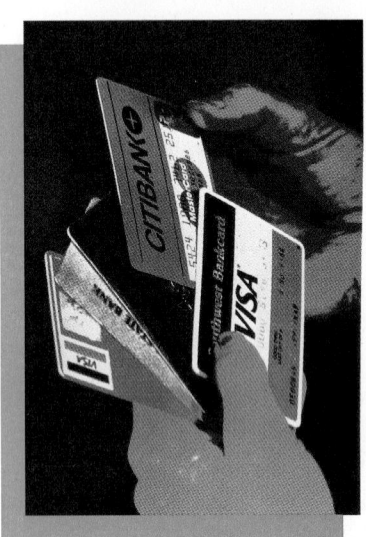

Interest rates on most credit cards are quite high, averaging approximately 18.8%. As a result, consumers are often looking for companies that charge lower rates. But be careful—some companies offer lower interest rates but have eliminated the standard 25-day grace period before finance charges are incurred. Other companies encourage consumers to get more in debt by advertising that only a $1 minimum payment is due on a $1,000 account balance! Then more interest can be earned. Chase Manhattan Corp. markets a credit card that allows credit holders to skip a payment twice a year. However, the outstanding balance continues to incur interest. Other credit card companies calculate finance charges initially on two-month, rather than one-month averages, a practice which often translates into higher interest charges. In short, read the fine print.

Source: "Watching for 'Traps' on Lower Card Rates," *The Wall Street Journal*, February 21, 1992.

Valuation of Accounts Receivable

Study Objective 3

Distinguish between the methods and bases used to value accounts receivable.

Once receivables are recorded in the accounts, the next question is: how should these receivables be reported on the balance sheet? This issue is important because some receivables will become uncollectible. To ensure that receivables are not overstated on the balance sheet, they are stated at their cash (net) realizable value. Cash (net) realizable value is the net amount expected to be received in cash. Receivables are therefore reduced by estimated uncollectible receivables on the balance sheet.

The income statement also is affected by the amount of uncollectibles. An expense for estimated uncollectibles is recorded to make certain that expenses are not understated and are matched with related sales revenue. This expense is reported as bad debt expense on the income statement.

Uncollectible Accounts Receivable

Although each customer must satisfy the credit requirements of the seller before the credit sale is approved, inevitably some accounts receivable become uncollectible. Credit losses may be due to errors in judgment on the part of the seller. On the other hand, they may be due to customer circumstances. For example, a company may experience a decline in sales because of a major downturn in the economy. Similarly, individuals may be laid off from their jobs or be faced with unexpected hospital bills.

In accounting, credit losses are debited to Bad Debts Expense (or Uncollectible Accounts Expense). Such losses are considered a normal and necessary risk of doing business on a credit basis. In fact, from a management point of view, a reasonable amount of uncollectible accounts is evidence of a sound credit policy. When bad debts are abnormally low, the company may be losing profitable business by following a credit policy that is too strict. Of course, abnormally high bad debts indicate a credit policy that is too lenient.

Two methods are used in accounting for uncollectible accounts: (1) the allowance method and (2) the direct write-off method. Each of these methods is explained in the following sections.

Allowance Method

The allowance method is required for financial reporting purposes when bad debts are significant in size. Its essential features are:

Helpful hint In this context, *material* means significant or important.

1. Uncollectible accounts receivable are estimated and matched against sales in the same accounting period in which the sales occurred.
2. Estimated uncollectibles are debited to Bad Debts Expense and credited to Allowance for Doubtful Accounts through an adjusting entry at the end of each period.
3. Actual uncollectibles are debited to Allowance for Doubtful Accounts and credited to Accounts Receivable at the time the specific account is written off.

Recording Estimated Uncollectibles

To illustrate the allowance method, assume that Hampson Furniture has credit sales of $1,200,000 in 1993, of which $200,000 remain uncollected at December 31. The credit manager estimates that $12,000 of these sales will prove uncollectible. The adjusting entry to record the estimated uncollectibles is:

Dec. 31	Bad Debts Expense	12,000	
	Allowance for Doubtful Accounts		12,000
	(To record estimate of uncollectible accounts)		

Bad Debts Expense is reported in the income statement as an operating expense (usually as a selling expense). Thus, the estimated uncollectibles are **matched** with sales in 1993 because the expense is recorded in the same year the sales are made.

Allowance for Doubtful Accounts is a contra asset account that shows the portion of claims on customers that is expected to become uncollectible in the future. A contra account is used instead of a direct credit to the Accounts Receivable account because we do not know which customers will not pay. Although an estimate of the total uncollectible can be made, at this point it is not possible to identify specific accounts receivable that will become uncollectible. Allowance for Doubtful Accounts is not closed at the end of the fiscal year. It is deducted from Accounts Receivable in the current asset section of the balance sheet as follows:

ILLUSTRATION 8-1

Presentation of allowance for doubtful accounts

Current assets		
Cash		$ 14,800
Accounts receivable	$200,000	
Less: Allowance for doubtful accounts	12,000	188,000
Merchandise inventory		310,000
Prepaid expense		25,000
Total current assets		$537,800

The amount of $188,000 represents the expected **cash realizable value** of the accounts receivable at the statement date.

Recording the Write-off of an Uncollectible Account

When all appropriate means of collecting a past-due account have been exhausted and collection appears impossible, the account should be written off. To prevent premature write-offs, each write-off should be formally approved in writing by authorized management personnel. Assume, for example, that the vice-president of finance of Hampson Furniture authorizes the write-off of the $500 balance owed by R. A. Ware on March 1, 1994. The entry to record the write-off is:

Mar. 1	Allowance for Doubtful Accounts	500	
	Accounts Receivable—R. A. Ware		500
	(Write-off of R. A. Ware account)		

Bad Debts Expense is not debited when the write-off occurs. Under the allowance method, every bad debt write-off is debited to the allowance account and not to Bad Debts Expense. (A debit to Bad Debts Expense would be incorrect, because the expense is recognized when the adjusting entry is made for estimated bad debts.) After posting, the general ledger accounts will show:

ILLUSTRATION 8-2

General ledger balances after write-off

Accounts Receivable						Allowance for Doubtful Accounts				
1/1/94 Bal.	200,000	3/1/94	500		3/1/94	500	1/1/94 Bal.	12,000
3/1/94 Bal.	199,500						3/1/94	11,500

A write-off affects only balance sheet accounts. The write-off of the account reduces both Accounts Receivable and the Allowance for Doubtful Accounts. Cash realizable value in the balance sheet, therefore, remains the same, as illustrated below.

ILLUSTRATION 8-3

Cash realizable value comparison

	Before Write-off	**After Write-off**
Accounts receivable	$200,000	$199,500
Allowance for doubtful accounts	12,000	11,500
Cash realizable value	$188,000	$188,000

Recovery of an Uncollectible Account

Occasionally, a company collects from a customer after the account has been written off as uncollectible. Two entries are required to record the recovery of a bad debt: (1) The entry made in writing off the account is reversed to reinstate the customer's account. (2) The collection is journalized in the usual manner. To illustrate, assume that R. A. Ware pays the amount due in full on July 1. The entries are:

		(1)		
July	1	Accounts Receivable—R. A. Ware	500	
		Allowance for Doubtful Accounts		500
		(To reverse write-off of R. A. Ware account)		
		(2)		
	1	Cash	500	
		Accounts Receivable—R. A. Ware		500
		(To record collection from R. A. Ware)		

Note that the recovery of a bad debt, like the write-off of a bad debt, affects only balance sheet accounts. The net effect of the two entries above is a debit to Cash and a credit to Allowance for Doubtful Accounts for $500. Accounts Receivable is debited and the Allowance for Doubtful Accounts is credited for two reasons. First, the company made an error in judgment when it wrote off the accounts receivable. Second, R. A. Ware did pay, and therefore the Accounts Receivable account should show this collection for possible future credit purposes.

Helpful hint Like the write-off, a recovery does not involve the income statement.

Bases Used for Allowance Method

In the preceding explanation, the amount of the expected uncollectibles was given. Two bases are used to determine this amount: **(1) percentage of sales, and (2) percentage of receivables**. Both bases are generally accepted in accounting. The choice is a management decision. It depends on the relative emphasis that management wishes to give to expenses and revenues on the one hand or to cash realizable value of the accounts receivable on the other. The choice is whether to emphasize income statement or balance sheet relationships. Illustration 8-4 compares the two bases.

ILLUSTRATION 8-4

Comparison of bases of estimating uncollectibles

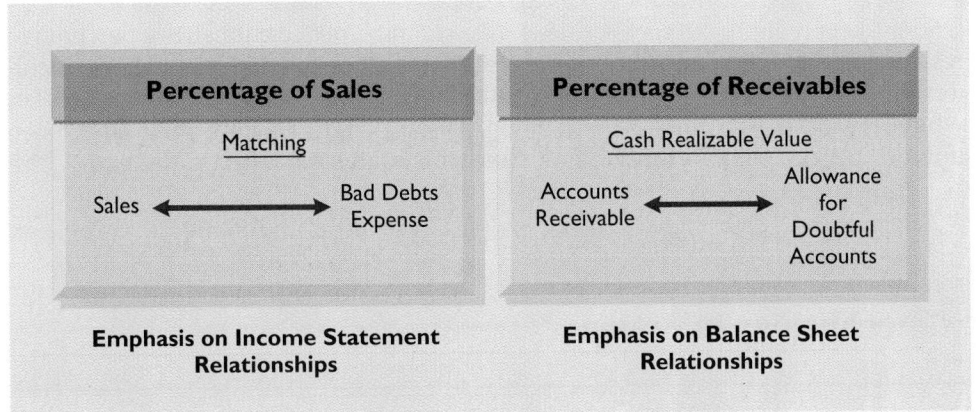

The percentage of sales basis results in the best matching of expenses with revenues—an income statement viewpoint. In contrast, the percentage of receivables basis produces the best estimate of cash realizable value—a balance sheet viewpoint. Under both bases, it is necessary to determine the company's past experience with bad debt losses.

Percentage of Sales

In the percentage of sales basis, management establishes a percentage relationship between the amount of credit sales and expected losses from uncollectible accounts. The percentage is based on past experience and anticipated credit policy.

echnology in Action

In computerized accounts receivable systems, these relationships can be readily obtained from the database of information on customer accounts. Such analysis is often referred to as a history search.

The percentage is usually applied to either total credit sales or net credit sales of the current year. To illustrate, assume that Gonzalez Company elects to use the percentage of sales basis and concludes that 1% of net credit sales will become uncollectible. If net credit sales for 1993 are $800,000, the estimated bad debts expense is $8,000 (1% × $800,000). The adjusting entry is:

Dec. 31	Bad Debts Expense	8,000	
	Allowance for Doubtful Accounts		8,000
	(To record estimated bad debts for year)		

This basis of estimating uncollectibles emphasizes the matching of expenses with revenues. As a result, Bad Debts Expense will show a direct percentage relationship to the sales base on which it is computed. When the adjusting entry is made, the **existing balance in the Allowance for Doubtful Accounts is disregarded**. The adjusted balance in this account should result in a reasonable approximation of the realizable value of the receivables. If actual write-offs differ significantly from the amount estimated, the percentage for future years should be modified.

Percentage of Receivables

Under the percentage of receivables basis, management establishes a percentage relationship between the amount of receivables and expected losses from uncollectible accounts. A schedule (often called an **aging schedule**) is prepared in which customer accounts are classified by the length of time they have been unpaid. Because of its emphasis on time, the analysis is often called aging the accounts receivable.

echnology in Action

The aging schedule is a further example of output that can be obtained from a computerized accounts receivable system. Manually, preparation of this schedule is an onerous and time-consuming task. However, the schedule can be done in minutes on computer systems.

After the accounts are aged, the expected bad debt losses are determined by applying percentages based on past experience to the totals of each category. The longer a receivable is past due, the less likely is it to be collected. As a result, the estimated percentage of uncollectible debts increases as the number of days past due increases. An aging schedule for Dart Company is shown in Illustration 8-5. Total uncollectibles for Dart Company ($2,228) represent the amount of existing customer claims expected to become uncollectible in the future. Thus, this

ILLUSTRATION 8-5

Aging schedule

Customer	Total	Not Yet Due	Number of Days Past Due				
			1–30	31–60	61–90	Over 90	
T. E. Adert	$ 600		$ 300		$ 200	$ 100	
R. C. Bortz	300	$ 300					
B. A. Carl	450		200	$ 250			
O. L. Diker	700	500			200		
T. O. Ebbet	600			300		300	
Others	36,950	26,200	5,200	2,450	1,600	1,500	
	$39,600	$27,000	$5,700	$3,000	$2,000	$1,900	
Estimated Percentage Uncollectible		2%	4%	10%	20%	40%	
Total Estimated Bad Debts	$ 2,228	$ 540	$ 228	$ 300	$ 400	$ 760	

amount represents the **required balance** in Allowance for Doubtful Accounts at the balance sheet date. Accordingly, **the amount of the bad debt adjusting entry is the difference between the required balance and the existing balance in the allowance account**. If the trial balance shows Allowance for Doubtful Accounts with a credit balance of $528, an adjusting entry for $1,700 ($2,228 − $528) is necessary, as shown below:

Dec. 31	Bad Debts Expense	1,700	
	Allowance for Doubtful Accounts		1,700
	(To adjust allowance account to total estimated uncollectibles)		

After the adjusting entry is posted, the accounts of the Dart Company will show:

ILLUSTRATION 8-6

Bad debt accounts after posting

Bad Debts Expense		Allowance for Doubtful Accounts	
12/31 Adj. **1,700**		Bal. 528	
		12/31 Adj. **1,700**	
		Bal. **2,228**	

Occasionally the allowance account will have a **debit balance** prior to adjustment, because write-offs have exceeded previous provisions for bad debts. In such a case the debit balance is **added** to the required balance when the adjusting entry is made. Thus, if there had been a $500 debit balance in the allowance account before adjustment, the adjusting entry would have been for $2,728 ($2,228 + $500) to arrive at a credit balance of $2,228.

The percentage of receivables method will normally result in the better approximation of cash realizable value. This basis, however, will not result in the better matching of expenses with revenues if some customers' accounts are more than one year past due. Under such circumstances, bad debts expense for the current period would include amounts applicable to the sales of a prior period.

A variation in the percentage of receivables approach is to use only a single percentage based on the balance in accounts receivable. At J. C. Penney Company, for example, at one time the Allowance for Doubtful Accounts was 2% of the balance in customers' accounts receivable, regardless of the age of the individual balances.

Direct Write-off Method

Under the direct write-off method, bad debt losses are not estimated and no allowance account is used. When an account is determined to be uncollectible, the loss is charged to Bad Debts Expense. Assume, for example, that Warden Co. writes off M. E. Doran's $200 balance as uncollectible on December 12. The entry is:

Dec. 12	Bad Debts Expense	200	
	Accounts Receivable—M. E. Doran		200
	(To record write-off of M. E. Doran account)		

When this method is used, Bad Debts Expense will show only actual losses from uncollectibles. Accounts receivable will be reported at its gross amount. Moreover, the expense is often recorded in a period different from the period in which the revenue was recorded. Thus, no attempt is made to match bad debt expense to sales revenues in the income statement or to show the cash realizable value of the accounts receivable in the balance sheet. **Consequently, unless bad debt losses are insignificant, the direct write-off method is not acceptable for financial reporting purposes.**

The direct write-off method is, however, used for tax purposes. The Tax Reform Act of 1986 allows a tax deduction for uncollectible accounts only when specific accounts receivable are deemed uncollectible.

Before You Go On . . .

1. What are the different types of receivables?

2. How are accounts receivable recognized in the accounts?

3. What are the essential features of the allowance method?

4. Explain the difference between the percentage of sales and the percentage of receivables methods?

Disposition of Accounts Receivable

Study Objective 4

Describe the entries to record the disposition of accounts receivable.

In the normal course of events, accounts receivable are collected in cash and removed from the books. However, as credit sales and receivables have grown in size and significance, the "normal course of events" has changed. In order to accelerate the receipt of cash from receivables, companies frequently sell the receivables to another company for cash, thereby shortening the cash-to-cash operating cycle.

There are several reasons for the sale of receivables. **First, for competitive reasons, sellers often must provide financing to purchasers of their goods.** For example, in the sale of durable goods, such as automobiles, trucks, industrial

Accounting in Action · *Business Insight*

For example, consider the plight of the local car dealer. Most local dealers simply do not have the financial resources to finance the sale of the car because most loans today are quite large in relationship to the cost of the car. Recently, the percentage of the price financed by the Big Three automobile manufacturers in the United States was 93% of the selling price of the automobile. In addition, the average length of the loan was 53.5 months as compared to 35 months a decade ago. It is no wonder, therefore, that a captive finance subsidiary like General Motors Acceptance Corporation would rank third in total assets behind Citicorp and Chase Manhattan if it were a bank.

and farm equipment, computers, and appliances, a majority of the sales are on a credit basis. Many major companies in these industries have therefore created companies that accept responsibility for accounts receivable financing. General Motors has General Motors Acceptance Corp. (GMAC), Sears has Sears Roebuck Acceptance Corp. (SRAC), Ford has Ford Motor Credit Corp. (FMCC), and Chrysler has Chrysler Finance Corporation (CFC). These companies are referred to as captive finance companies because they are wholly owned by the company making the product. The purpose of captive financing companies is to encourage the sale of their product by assuring financing to buyers.

Second, receivables **may be sold because they may be the only reasonable source of cash.** When money is tight, companies may not be able to borrow money in the usual credit markets. If money is available, the cost of borrowing may be prohibitive. A final reason for selling receivables is that **billing and collection are often time consuming and costly.** As a result, it is often easier for a retailer to sell the receivable to another party with expertise in billing and collection matters. Credit card companies such as MasterCard, VISA, American Express, and Diners Club specialize in billing and collecting accounts receivable.

Illustration One—Sale of Receivables

A common sale of receivables is a sale to a factor. A factor is a finance company or bank that buys receivables from businesses for a fee and then collects the payments directly from the customers. Factoring was traditionally associated with the textiles, apparel, footwear, furniture, and home furnishing industries. It has now spread to many other types of businesses and is a multibillion dollar business. For example, Sears, Roebuck and Co. recently sold $14.8 billion of customer accounts receivable.

Factoring arrangements vary widely, but typically the factor (purchaser of the receivables) charges a commission. It ranges from 1% to 3% of the amount of receivables purchased. To illustrate, assume that Hendredon Furniture factors $600,000 of receivables to Federal Factors, Inc. Federal Factors, Inc. assesses a service charge of 2% of the amount of receivables sold. The journal entry to record the sale by Hendredon Furniture is as follows:

Cash	588,000	
Service Charge Expense (2% × $600,000)	12,000	
Accounts Receivable		600,000
(To record the sale of accounts receivable)		

If the company usually sells its receivables, the service charge expense incurred by Hendredon Furniture is recorded as selling expense. If receivables are sold infrequently, this amount may be reported in the Other Expenses and Losses section of the income statement.

Illustration Two—Credit Card Sales

There were over 900 million credit cards in use recently, more than three credit cards for every man, woman, and child in this country. A common type of credit card is a national credit card such as VISA, MasterCard, and American Express. Three parties are involved when national credit cards are used in making retail sales: (1) the credit card issuer, who is independent of the retailer, (2) the retailer, and (3) the customer. Acceptance of a national credit card is another form of selling the receivable.

The major advantages of these cards to the retailer are:

1. The credit card issuer makes the credit investigation of the customer.
2. The retailer does not have to maintain customer accounts.
3. The retailer is not involved in the collection process, and the credit card issuer absorbs any losses from uncollectible accounts.
4. The retailer receives cash more quickly from the credit card issuer than it would from individual customers.

In exchange for these advantages, the retailer pays the credit card issuer a fee of 2–6% of the invoice price for its services.

VISA and MasterCard Sales

Sales resulting from the use of VISA and MasterCard are considered cash sales by the retailer. These cards are issued by banks. Upon receipt of credit card sales slips from a retailer, the bank immediately adds the amount to the seller's bank balance. These credit card sales slips are therefore recorded in the same manner as checks deposited from a cash sale. Banks generally charge a fee of 2–4% of the credit card sales slips for this service. To illustrate, Trisha Goodyear purchases a number of compact discs for her restaurant from Elton John Co. for $1,000 using her VISA First Bank Card. The service fee that First Bank charges is 3%. The entry to record this transaction by Elton John Co. is as follows:

Cash	970	
Service Charge Expense	30	
Sales		1,000

American Express Sales

Sales using American Express cards are reported as credit sales, not cash sales. Conversion into cash does not occur until American Express remits the net amount to the seller. To illustrate, assume that Four Seasons restaurant accepts an American Express card for a $300 bill. The entry for the sale by Four Seasons (assuming a 5% fee) is:

Accounts Receivable—American Express	285	
Service Charge Expense	15	
Sales		300

Thus American Express will subsequently pay the restaurant $285 which the restaurant will record as follows:

Cash	285	
Accounts Receivable—American Express		285

Service Charge Expense is reported as a selling expense in the income statement by the restaurant.

Before You Go On . . .

1. Why do companies sell their receivables?

2. What is the journal entry when a company sells its receivables to a factor?

3. What are the journal entries when a company records a Visa credit card sale? An American Express credit card sale? Explain the difference.

SECTION 2 Notes Receivable

Credit may also be granted in exchange for a formal credit instrument known as a promissory note. A promissory note is a written promise to pay a specified amount of money on demand or at a definite time. Promissory notes may be used (1) when individuals and companies lend or borrow money, (2) when the amount of the transaction and the credit period exceed normal limits, and (3) in settlement of accounts receivable.

In a promissory note, the party making the promise to pay is called the maker; the party to whom payment is to be made is called the payee. The payee may be specifically identified by name or may be designated simply as the bearer of the note. In the note shown in Illustration 8-7, Brent Company is the maker and Wilma Company is the payee. To the Wilma Company, the promissory note is a note receivable; to the Brent Company, the note is a note payable.

Helpful hint Note the similarities and differences between a note and a check.
Similarities: Both are instruments (documents that are readily transferable by endorsement). Both have a maker and a payee.
Differences: A check is a cash instrument that does not bear interest. A note is a credit instrument that may bear interest.

ILLUSTRATION 8-7

Promissory note

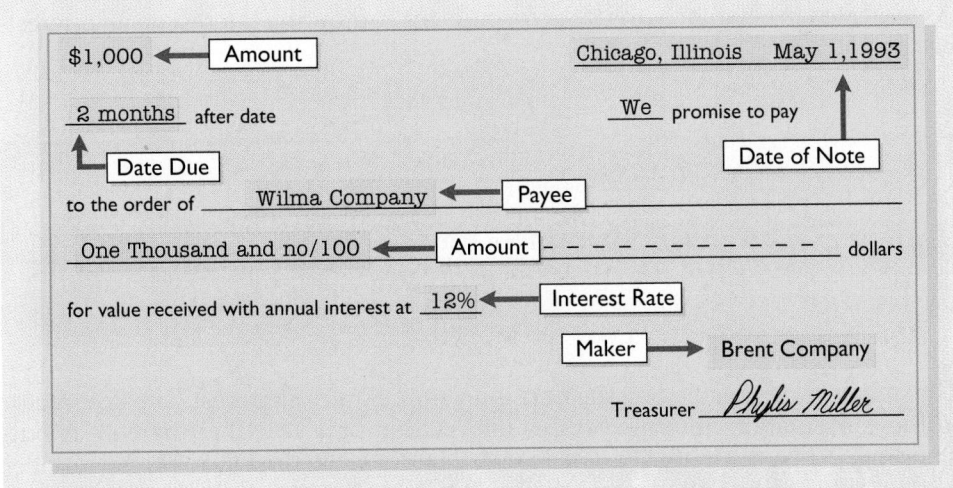

Notes receivable gives the holder a stronger legal claim to assets than accounts receivable. Like accounts receivable, notes receivable can be readily sold to another party. Promissory notes are negotiable instruments (as are checks), which means that, when sold they can be transferred to another party by endorsement.

Determining the Maturity Date

The due date of a promissory note may be stated in one of three ways.

1. On demand, thus: "On demand, I promise to pay. . . ."
2. On a stated date, thus: "On July 23, 1993, I promise to pay. . . ."
3. At the end of a stated period of time, thus:
   a. "One year after date. . . ."
   b. "Two months after date. . . ."
   c. "Ninety days after date. . . ."

When the life of a note is expressed in terms of months, the due date is found by counting the months from the date of issue. For example, the maturity date of a 3-month note dated May 1 is August 1. A note drawn on the last day of a month matures on the last day of a subsequent month; that is, a July 31 note due in 2 months matures on September 30. When the due date is stated in terms of days, it is necessary to count the exact number of days to determine the maturity date. In counting, **the date the note is issued is omitted but the due date is included**. For example, the maturity date of a 60-day note dated July 17 is September 15, computed as follows:

ILLUSTRATION 8-8

Computation of maturity date

Term of note		60
July (31 − 17)	14	
August	31	45
Maturity date, September		15

Computing Interest

As indicated in Chapter 3, the basic formula for computing interest on an interest-bearing note is:

ILLUSTRATION 8-9

Formula for computing interest

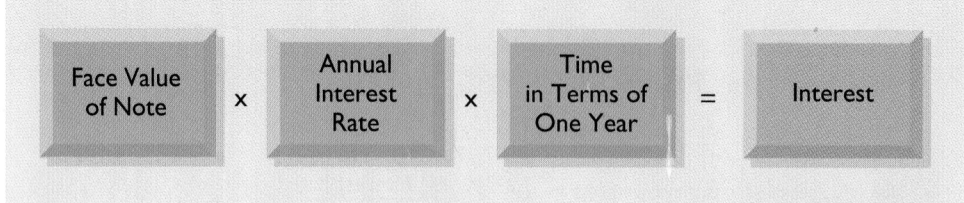

Face Value of Note × Annual Interest Rate × Time in Terms of One Year = Interest

Helpful hint The interest rate specified is the *annual* rate.

The interest rate specified on the note is an annual rate of interest. The time factor in the computation above expresses the fraction of a year that the note is outstanding. When the maturity date is stated in days, the time factor is the number of days divided by 360. When the due date is stated in months, the time factor is the number of months divided by 12. The computation of interest is shown in Illustration 8-10.

ILLUSTRATION 8-10

Computation of interest

Terms of Note	Interest Computation
	Face × Rate × Time = Interest
$ 730, 18%, 120 days	$ 730 × 18% × 120/360 = $ 43.80
$1,000, 15%, 6 months	$1,000 × 15% × 6/12 = $ 75.00
$2,000, 12%, 1 year	$2,000 × 12% × 1/1 = $240.00

There are many different ways to calculate interest. For example, the computation above assumed the total days to be used for the year are 360. Many financial institutions use 365 days to compute interest. It is more profitable to use 360 days because it means that the holder of the note receives more interest than if 365 days are used. For homework problems, assume 360 days.

Accounting for Notes Receivable

Notes receivable are frequently accepted from customers who need to extend the payment of an outstanding account receivable and are often required from high-risk customers. In some industries (e.g., the pleasure and sport boat industry) all credit sales are supported by notes. The majority of notes, however, originate from lending transactions. The basic issues in accounting for notes receivable are the same as those for accounts receivable.

1. **Recognition** of notes receivable.
2. **Valuation** of notes receivable.
3. **Disposition** of notes receivable.

Recognition of Notes Receivable

To illustrate the basic entry for notes receivable, we will use the $1,000, 2-month, 12% promissory note on page 335. Assuming that the note was in settlement of an open account, the entry for the receipt of the note by Wilma Company is:

May 1	Notes Receivable	1,000	
	Accounts Receivable—Brent Company		1,000
	(To record acceptance of Brent Company note)		

> **Study Objective 6**
>
> *Explain how notes receivable are recognized in the accounts.*

Observe that the note receivable is recorded at its **face value**, the value shown on the face of the note. No interest revenue is reported because the revenue recognition principle does not recognize revenue until earned.

Valuation of Notes Receivable

Like accounts receivable, short-term notes receivable are reported at their cash (net) realizable value. The notes receivable allowance account is Allowance for Doubtful Accounts. Valuing short-term notes receivable is the same as valuing accounts receivable. The computations and estimations involved in determining cash realizable value and in recording the proper amount of bad debt expense and related allowance are similar.

> **Study Objective 7**
>
> *Describe how notes receivable are valued.*

Long-term notes receivable, however, pose additional estimation problems. As an example, we need only look at the problems a number of our largest banks are having in collecting their receivables. Loans to less-developed countries are particularly worrisome. The countries need loans for development but often find repayment difficult. U.S. loans (notes) to less-developed countries at one time totaled approximately $135 billion. In Brazil alone, Citibank at one time had loans equivalent to 80% of its stockholders' equity; Chemical Bank had 77% of its equity lent out in Mexico. Determining the proper allowance is understandably difficult for these types of receivables.

Accounting in Action · *International Insight*

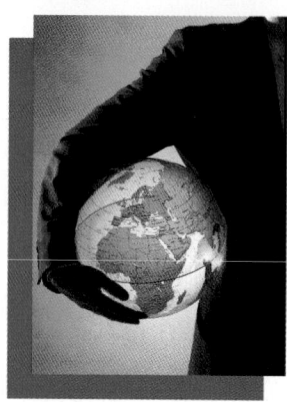

Varied plans are now being proposed to solve the Third World Debt problem. These plans range from encouraging more lending to reducing or forgiving the debt. Presently this debt burden to banks worldwide exceeds $1.3 trillion (as an aside, a trillion is a lot of money—enough money to give every man, woman, and child in the world $250 each [as of mid 1980s]). Why were these loans made? The reasons are numerous, but the three major ones are: (1) to provide stability to these governments and thereby increase trade, (2) the belief that governments would never default on payment, and (3) the desire by banks to increase their income by lending to these countries.

Study Objective 8

Describe the entries to record the disposition of notes receivable.

Disposition of Notes Receivable

Notes may be held to their maturity date, at which time the face value plus accrued interest is collected and the note is removed from the accounts. In some situations, the maker of the note defaults and appropriate adjustment must be made. Finally, in many cases, similar to accounts receivable, the holder of the note speeds up the conversion to cash by selling the receivables. The entries for honoring and dishonoring notes are illustrated below.

Honor of Notes Receivable

A note is **honored** when it is paid in full at its maturity date. For each interest-bearing note, the amount due at maturity is the face value of the note plus interest for the length of time specified on the note.

To illustrate, assume that Wolder Co. lends Higly Inc. $10,000 on June 1, accepting a four-month, 9% interest note. In this situation, interest is $300 ($10,000 × 9% × 4/12); the amount due, the maturity value, is $10,300. To obtain payment, Wolder (the payee) must either present the note to Higly Inc. (the maker) or to the maker's duly appointed agent, such as a bank. Assuming that Wolder presents the note to Higly Inc. on October 1, the maturity date, the entry by Wolder to record the collection is:

Oct. 1	Cash	10,300	
	Notes Receivable		10,000
	Interest Revenue		300
	(To record collection of Higly Inc. note)		

If Wolder Co. prepares financial statements as of September 30, it would be necessary to accrue interest. In this case, the adjusting entry by Wolder would be for four months or $300 as shown on the next page:

Sept. 30	Interest Receivable	300	
	Interest Revenue		300
	(To accrue four months' interest)		

When interest has been accrued, it is necessary to credit Interest Receivable at maturity. The entry by Wolder to record the honoring of the Higly note on October 1 is:

Oct. 1	Cash	10,300	
	Notes Receivable		10,000
	Interest Receivable		300
	(To record collection of note at maturity)		

In this case, Interest Receivable is credited because the receivable was established in the adjusting entry.

Dishonor of Notes Receivable

A **dishonored note** is a note that is not paid in full at maturity. A dishonored note receivable is no longer negotiable. Therefore the Notes Receivable account is usually transferred to an Account Receivable. To illustrate, assume that Higly Inc. on October 1 indicates that it cannot pay at the present time. In this case, Wolder Co. would make the following entry at the time the note is dishonored (assuming no previous accrual of interest):

Oct. 1	Accounts Receivable	10,300	
	Notes Receivable		10,000
	Interest Revenue		300
	(To record the dishonor of the note)		

The amount due (face value and interest) on the note is debited to Accounts Receivable assuming that Wolder Co. expects eventual collection. If there is no hope of collection, the face value of the note should be written off by debiting the Allowance for Doubtful Accounts. No interest revenue would be recorded because collection will not occur.

Sale of Notes Receivable

The accounting for the sale of notes receivable is recorded in a similar manner as the sale of accounts receivable. In some cases, there are additional complications. The sale of notes receivable is not illustrated here but is left for a more advanced course. (See Accounting in Action discussion on next page indicating how notes receivable are sold and resold.)

Financial Statement Presentation of Receivables

Each of the major types of receivables should be identified in the balance sheet or in the notes to the financial statements. Short-term receivables are reported within the current asset section of the balance sheet below temporary investments. Temporary investments appear before short-term receivables, because these investments are more liquid, or nearer to cash. Both the gross amount of receivables and the allowance for doubtful accounts should be reported. Illustration 8-11 shows the current asset presentation of receivables for CPC International Inc.

Accounting in Action · *Business Insight*

How One Receivable Crisscrossed the U.S.

Consider how the following note receivable of $120,000 is sold and resold in different markets in the United States and abroad.

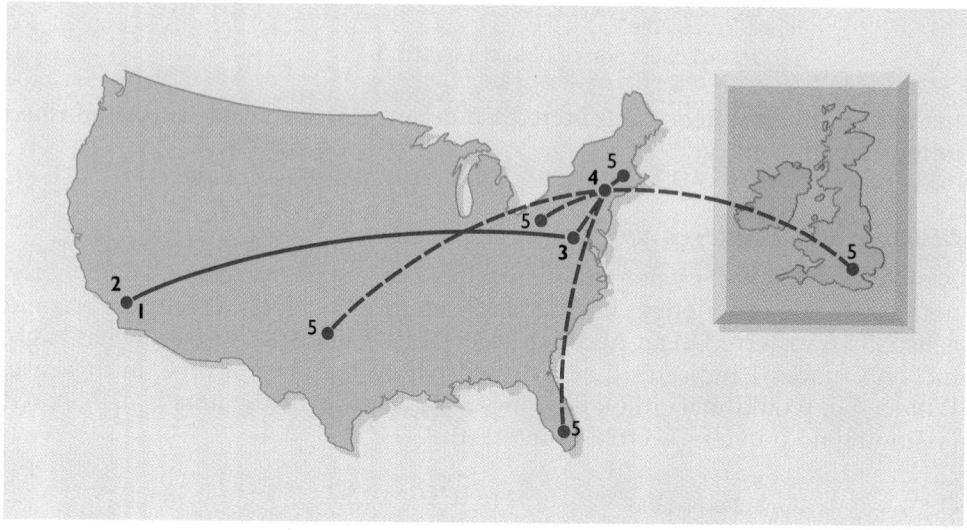

Step 1 *September 1987.* Jim and Erica Vogel buy a four-bedroom home in San Dimas, Calif. They get a $120,000 loan from First Federal S&L of San Gabriel.

Step 2 *December 1987.* First Federal sells the Vogels' receivable to the Federal Home Loan Mortgage Corp., known as Freddie Mac.

Step 3 *December 1987.* In Reston, Va., Freddie Mac puts the Vogels' receivable into a giant pool with more than 6,000 other receivables.

Step 4 *May 1988.* Part of that pool is bought by First Boston Corp. in New York. The pool goes into a $550 million pool.

Step 5 *May/June 1988.* In Hartford, Conn., Cigna Investments Inc. buys $10 million of this pool for its pension accounts.

 May/June 1988. In El Reno, Okla., Globe Savings Bank buys $66 million of the pool to expand its receivable portfolio.

 May/June 1988. In Florida, an S&L buys $40 million of the pool as an interest rate hedge.

 May/June 1988. Other buyers of the pool range from a Pittsburgh S&L to a London commercial bank to a Florida S&L.

Source: The Wall Street Journal, August 17, 1988.

ILLUSTRATION 8-11

Balance sheet presentation of receivables

CPC INTERNATIONAL INC.	
Receivables (in millions)	
Notes receivable	$ 16.6
Accounts receivable	375.1
Other receivables	60.7
Total receivables	452.4
Less: Allowance for doubtful accounts	10.5
Net receivables	$441.9

In the income statement, Bad Debts Expense and Service Charge Expense are reported as selling expenses in the Operating Expense section. Interest Expense is classified under Other Expenses and Losses, and Interest Revenue is shown under Other Revenues and Gains in the nonoperating section of the income statement.

Before You Go On . . .

1. How is interest revenue computed?

2. Give an example of how a note receivable is recorded.

3. Explain the difference between honoring and dishonoring a note receivable.

4. Explain where receivables, allowance for doubtful accounts, bad debts expense, service charge expense, and interest revenue are reported in the financial statements.

Summary of Study Objectives

1. *Identify the different types of receivables.* Receivables are frequently classified as (1) accounts, (2) notes, and (3) other. Accounts receivable are amounts owed by customers on account. Notes receivable represent claims that are evidenced by formal instruments of credit. Other receivables include nontrade receivables such as interest receivable, loans to company officers, advances to employees, and income taxes refundable.

2. *Explain how accounts receivable are recognized in the accounts.* Accounts receivable are recorded at invoice price. They are reduced by Sales Returns and Allowances. Cash discounts reduce the amount received on accounts receivable. When interest is charged on a past due receivable, this interest is added to the accounts receivable balance.

3. *Distinguish between the methods and bases used to value accounts receivable.* There are two methods of accounting for uncollectible accounts: (1) the allowance method and (2) the direct write-off method. Either the percentage of sales or the percentage of receivables basis may be used to estimate uncollectible accounts using the allowance method. The percentage of sales basis emphasizes the matching principle. The percentage of receivables basis emphasizes the cash realizable value of the accounts receivable. An aging schedule is frequently used with this basis.

4. *Describe the entries to record the disposition of accounts receivable.* When an account receivable is collected, accounts receivable is credited. When an account receivable is sold, a service charge expense is charged which reduces the amount collected.

5. *Compute the maturity date of, and interest on, notes receivable.* The maturity date of a note must be computed unless the due date is specified or the note is payable on demand. For a note stated in months, the maturity date is found by counting the months from the date of issue. For a note stated in days, the number of days is counted, omitting the issue date and counting the due date. The formula for computing interest is face value × interest rate × time.

6. *Explain how notes receivable are recognized in the accounts.* Notes receivable are recorded at face value. In some cases, it is necessary to accrue interest prior to maturity. In this case, Interest Receivable is debited and Interest Revenue is credited.

7. *Describe how notes receivable are valued.* Like accounts receivable, notes receivable are reported at their cash (net) realizable value. The notes receivable allowance account is the Allowance for Doubtful Accounts. The computation and estimations involved in valuing notes receivables at cash realizable value, and in recording the proper amount of bad debt expense and related allowance are similar to accounts receivable.

8. *Describe the entries to record the disposition of notes receivable.* Notes can be held to maturity, at which time the face value plus accrued interest is collected and the note is removed from the accounts. However, in many cases, similar to accounts receivable, the holder of the note speeds up the conversion by selling the receivable to another party. In some situations, the maker of the note dishonors the note (defaults), and the note is written off.

GLOSSARY

Aging of accounts receivable · The analysis of customer balances by the length of time they have been unpaid. (p. 330).

Cash (net) realizable value · The net amount expected to be received in cash. (p. 326).

Dishonored note · A note that is not paid in full at maturity. (p. 339).

Maker · The party in a promissory note who is making the promise to pay. (p. 335).

Payee · The party to whom payment of a promissory note is to be made. (p. 335).

Promissory note · A written promise to pay a specified amount of money on demand or at a definite time. (p. 335).

Percentage of receivables basis · Management establishes a percentage relationship between the amount of receivables and the expected losses from uncollectible accounts. (p. 330).

Percentage of sales basis · Management establishes a percentage relationship between the amount of credit sales and expected losses from uncollectible accounts. (p. 329).

DEMONSTRATION PROBLEM

Presented below are selected transactions related to B. Dylan Corp.

Mar. 1 Sold $20,000 of merchandise to Potter Company, terms 2/10, n/30.
      11 Received payment in full from Potter Company for balance due.
      12 Accepted Juno Company's $20,000 6-month, 12% note for balance due.
      13 Made Dylan Corp. credit card sales for $13,200.
      15 Made American Express credit sales totaling $6,700. A 5% service fee is charged by American Express.
      30 Received payment in full from American Express Company less 5% service charge.
Apr. 11 Sold accounts receivable of $8,000 to Harcot Factor. Harcot Factor assesses a service charge of 2% of the amount of receivables sold.
      13 Received collections of $8,200 on Dylan Corp. credit card sales and added finance charges of 1.5% to the remaining balances.
May 10 Wrote off as uncollectible $16,000 of accounts receivable. Dylan uses the percentage of sales basis to estimate bad debts.
June 30 Credit sales for the first six months total $2,000,000 and the bad debt percentage is 1%. At June 30, the balance in the allowance account is $3,500.
July 16 One of the accounts receivable written off in May pays the amount due, $4,000, in full.

Instructions
Prepare the journal entries for the transactions.

Solution to Demonstration Problem

Mar. 1	Accounts Receivable—Potter	20,000	
	Sales		20,000
	(To record sales on account)		
Mar. 11	Cash	19,600	
	Sales Discounts (2% × $20,000)	400	
	Accounts Receivable—Potter		20,000
	(To record collection of accounts receivable)		
Mar. 12	Notes Receivable	20,000	
	Accounts Receivable—Juno		20,000
	(To record acceptance of Juno Company note)		

Helpful hints
1. Accounts receivable are generally recorded at invoice price.
2. Sales returns and allowances and cash discounts reduce the amount received on accounts receivable.
3. When accounts receivable are sold, a service charge expense is incurred by the seller.
4. Bad debts expense is an adjusting entry.
5. Percentage of sales basis ignores any balance in the Allowance account. Percentage of receivables basis does not ignore this balance.
6. Write-offs of accounts receivable affect only balance sheet accounts.

Mar. 13	Accounts Receivable	13,200	
	Sales		13,200
	(To record company credit card sales)		
Mar. 15	Accounts Receivable—American Express	6,365	
	Service Charge Expense (5% × $6,700)	335	
	Sales		6,700
	(To record credit card sales)		
Mar. 30	Cash	6,365	
	Accounts Receivable—American Express		6,365
	(To record redemption of credit card billings)		
Apr. 11	Cash	7,840	
	Service Charge Expense (2% × $8,000)	160	
	Accounts Receivable		8,000
	(To record sale of receivables to factor)		
Apr. 13	Cash	8,200	
	Accounts Receivable		8,200
	(To record collection of accounts receivable)		
	Accounts Receivable [($13,200 − $8,200) × 1.5%]	75	
	Interest Revenue		75
	(To record interest on amount due)		
May 10	Allowance for Doubtful Accounts	16,000	
	Accounts Receivable		16,000
	(To record write-off of accounts receivable)		
June 30	Bad Debts Expense ($2,000,000 × 1%)	20,000	
	Allowance for Doubtful Accounts		20,000
	(To record estimate of uncollectible accounts)		
July 16	Accounts Receivable	4,000	
	Allowance for Doubtful Accounts		4,000
	(To reverse write-off of accounts receivable)		
	Cash	4,000	
	Accounts Receivable		4,000
	(To record collection of accounts receivable)		

SELF-STUDY QUESTIONS

Answers are at the end of the chapter.

(S.O. 2) 1. Jones Company on June 15, 1993 sells merchandise on account to Bullock Co. for $1,000 terms 2/10, n/30. On June 20, Bullock Co. returns merchandise worth $200 to Jones Company. On June 25, payment is received from Bullock Co. for the balance due. What is the amount of cash received?
a. $780
b. $784
c. $800
d. $1,000

2. Which of the following approaches is best described as a balance sheet method? (S.O. 3)
a. Percentage of sales basis
b. Direct write-off method
c. Percentage of receivables basis
d. Both a and b

3. Net sales for the month are $800,000 and bad debt expense for the month is (S.O. 2)

$80,000. The company uses the percentage of sales basis. If the Allowance for Doubtful Accounts has a credit balance of $15,000 before adjustment, what is the balance after adjustment?

a. $15,000
b. $65,000
c. $80,000
d. $95,000

(S.O. 3, 4) 4. In 1993, the D. H. Lawrence Company had credit sales of $750,000 and granted sales discounts of $15,000. On January 1, 1993, Allowance for Doubtful Accounts had a credit balance of $18,000. During 1993, $30,000 of uncollectible accounts receivable were written off. Past experience indicates that 3% of net credit sales become uncollectible. What should be the adjusted balance of Allowance for Doubtful Accounts at December 31, 1993?

a. $10,050
b. $10,500
c. $22,050
d. $34,500

(S.O. 3) 5. An analysis and aging of the accounts receivable of Machiavelli Company at December 31 reveals the following data:

Accounts Receivable	$900,000
Allowance for Doubtful Accounts per books before adjustment	50,000
Amounts expected to become uncollectible	64,000

The cash realizable value of the accounts receivable at December 31, after adjustment, is:

a. $886,000
b. $850,000
c. $836,000
d. $786,000

(S.O. 6) 6. One of the following statements about promissory notes is incorrect. The incorrect statement is:

a. The party making the promise to pay is called the maker.
b. A promissory note is not a negotiable instrument.
c. The party to whom payment is to be made is called the payee.

d. A promissory note is more liquid than an accounts receivable.

7. Which of the following statements about VISA credit card sales is incorrect? (S.O. 4)

a. The credit card issuer makes the credit investigation of the customer.
b. The retailer is not involved in the collection process.
c. The retailer receives cash more quickly than it would from individual customers.
d. Two parties are involved.

8. Morgan Retailers accepted $50,000 of Citibank VISA credit card charges for merchandise sold on July 1, 1993. Citibank charges 3% for its credit card use. The entry to record this transaction by Morgan Retailers will include a credit to sales of $50,000 and a debit(s) to: (S.O. 4)

a. Accounts Receivable $50,000
b. Cash $50,000
c. Accounts Receivable $48,500
    and Service Charge Expense $1,500
d. Cash $48,500
    and Service Charge Expense $1,500

9. Sorenson Co. accepts a $1,000, 2-month, 12% promissory note in settlement of an account with Parton Co. The entry to record this transaction is as follows: (S.O. 6)

a. Notes Receivable   1,000
       Accounts Receivable   1,000
b. Notes Receivable   1,010
       Accounts Receivable   1,010
c. Notes Receivable   1,000
       Sales   1,000
d. Notes Receivable   1,020
       Accounts Receivable   1,020

10. Schlicht Co. holds Osgrove Inc.'s $10,000, 90-day, 10% note. The entry made by Schlicht Co. when the note is collected, assuming no interest has been accrued, is (S.O. 8)

a. Cash   10,250
       Notes Receivable   10,000
       Interest Revenue   250
b. Cash   10,000
       Notes Receivable   10,000
c. Accounts Receivable   10,250
       Notes Receivable   10,000
       Interest Revenue   250
d. Cash   10,250
       Notes Receivable   10,250

QUESTIONS

1. What is the difference between an accounts receivable and a notes receivable?

2. What are some common types of receivables other than accounts receivable or notes receivable?

3. Mobil Oil Company issues its own credit cards. Assume that Mobil Oil charges you $60 on an unpaid balance. Prepare the journal entry that Mobil Oil makes to record this revenue.

4. What are the essential features of the allowance method of accounting for bad debts?

5. Sue Engen cannot understand why cash realizable value does not decrease when an uncollectible account is written off under the allowance method. Clarify this point for Sue Engen.

6. Distinguish between the two bases that may be used in estimating uncollectible accounts.

7. The Carter Company has a credit balance of $3,000 in Allowance for Doubtful Accounts. The estimated bad debts expense under the percentage of sales basis is $4,100, and the total estimated uncollectibles under the percentage of receivables basis is $5,800. Prepare the adjusting entry under each basis.

8. How are bad debts accounted for under the direct write-off method? What are the disadvantages of this method?

9. The Allman Company accepts both its own credit cards and national credit cards. What are the advantages of accepting both types of cards?

10. An article recently appeared in *The Wall Street Journal* that indicated that companies are selling their receivables at a record rate. Why are companies selling their receivables?

11. Reynolds Textiles decides to sell $600,000 of its accounts receivable to First Central Factors Inc. First Central Factors Inc. assesses a service charge of 2% of the amount of receivables sold. Prepare the journal entry that Reynolds Textiles makes to record this sale.

12. Your roommate is uncertain about the advantages of a promissory note. Compare the advantages of a note receivable with those of an accounts receivable.

13. How may the maturity date of a promissory note be stated?

14. Indicate the maturity date of each of the following promissory notes:

Date of Note	Terms
(a) March 11	One year after date of note
(b) May 4	Three months after date
(c) June 10	Thirty days after date
(d) July 1	Sixty days after date

15. Compute the missing amounts for each of the following notes:

	Principal	Annual Interest Rate	Time	Total Interest
(a)	?	12%	90 days	$ 300
(b)	$30,000	10%	3 years	?
(c)	$75,000	?	5 months	$4,375
(d)	$50,000	11%	?	$1,375

16. In determining interest revenue, some financial institutions use 365 days per year whereas others use 360 days. Why might a financial institution use 360 days?

17. The Mayo Company dishonors a note at maturity. What actions by Mayo may occur with the dishonoring of the note?

18. The Petron Company has accounts receivable and notes receivable. How should the receivables be reported on the balance sheet?

BRIEF EXERCISES

Different types of receivables
(S.O. 1)

BE8–1 Presented below are three receivable transactions. Indicate whether these receivables are reported as accounts receivable, notes receivable, or other receivables on a balance sheet.

1. Received a promissory note of $57,000 for services performed.
2. Advanced $10,000 to an employee.
3. Sold merchandise on account for $60,000 to a customer.

Basic accounts receivable transactions
(S.O. 2)

BE8–2 Record the following transactions on the books of Oxford Co.

1. On July 1, Oxford Co. sold merchandise on account to Cambridge Inc. for $15,000, terms 2/10, n/30.
2. On July 8, Cambridge Inc. returned merchandise worth $3,800 to Oxford Co.
3. On July 11, Cambridge Inc. paid for the merchandise.

Entries for allowance method and classifications
(S.O. 3)

BE8–3 During its first year of operations, Cecil Company had credit sales of $3,000,000, of which $600,000 remained uncollected at year-end. The credit manager estimates that $37,000 of these receivables will become uncollectible. (a) Prepare the journal entry to record the estimated uncollectibles. (b) Prepare the current asset section of the balance sheet for Cecil Company, assuming that in addition to the receivables it has cash of $90,000, merchandise inventory of $130,000, and prepaid expenses of $13,000.

Entries for write-off and cash realizable value
(S.O. 3)

BE8–4 At the end of 1993, Searcy Co. has accounts receivable of $700,000 and an allowance for doubtful accounts of $54,000. On January 24, 1994 it is learned that the company's receivable from Hurley Inc. is not collectible and therefore management authorizes a write-off of $9,000. (a) Prepare the journal entry to record the write-off. (b) What is the cash realizable value of the accounts receivable (1) before the write-off and (2) after the write-off?

Entries for collection of bad debt write-off
(S.O. 3)

BE8–5 Assume the same information as BE8–4 and that on March 4, 1994, Searcy Co. receives payment of $9,000 in full from Hurley Co. Prepare the journal entries to record this transaction.

Entry using percentage of sales method
(S.O. 3)

BE8–6 Seles Co. elects to use the percentage of sales basis in 1993 to record bad debt expense and concludes that 2% of net credit sales will become uncollectible. Sales are $700,000 for 1993, Sales Returns and Allowances are $60,000, and the Allowance for Doubtful Accounts has a credit balance of $12,000. Prepare the adjusting entry to record bad debt expense in 1993.

Entry using percentage of receivables method
(S.O. 3)

BE8–7 Marcus Co. uses the percentage of accounts receivable basis to record bad debt expense, and concludes that 1% of accounts receivable will become uncollectible. Accounts receivable are $400,000 at the end of the year, and the allowance for doubtful accounts has a credit balance of $3,000. (a) Prepare the adjusting journal entry to record bad debt expense for 1993. (b) If the allowance for doubtful accounts had a debit balance of $800 instead of credit balance of $3,000, determine the amount to be reported for bad debt expense.

Compute maturity date and interest on note.
(S.O. 5)

BE8–8 Presented below are three promissory notes. Determine the missing amounts.

Date of Note	Terms	Maturity Date	Principal	Annual Interest Rate	Total Interest
(a) April 1	60 days	?	$900,000	15%	?
(b) July 2	30 days	?	79,000	?	$592.50
(c) March 5	6 months	?	56,000	12%	?

Disposition of accounts receivable
(S.O. 4)

BE8–9 Presented below are the following transactions.

1. Stead Restaurant accepted a Visa card in payment of a $100 lunch bill. The bank charges a 3% fee. What entry should Stead make?
2. Mansfield Company sold its accounts receivable of $60,000. What entry should Mansfield make, given a service charge of 3% on the amount of receivables sold.

Notes receivable exchanged for accounts receivable
(S.O. 6)

BE8–10 On January 10, 1992, Nicholas Co. sold merchandise on account to R. Skelly for $10,000, n/30. On February 9, R. Skelly gave Nicholas Co. an 11% promissory note in settlement of this account. Prepare the journal entry to record the sale and the settlement of the accounts receivable.

EXERCISES

E8–1 Presented below are two independent situations that occurred in 1993:

Journalize entries for recognizing accounts receivable.
(S.O. 2)

1. On January 6, Nicklaus Co. sells merchandise on account to Strange Inc. for $4,000, terms 2/10, n/30. On January 16, Strange pays the amount due. Prepare the entries on Nicklaus' books to record the sale and related collection.

2. On January 10, Margaret Trimble uses her Salizar Co. credit card to purchase merchandise from Salizar Co. for $11,000. On February 10, Trimble is billed for the amount due of $11,000. On February 12, Trimble pays $5,000 on the balance due. On March 10, Trimble is billed for the amount due, including interest at 1.5% per month on the unpaid balance as of February 12. Prepare the entries on Salizar Co.'s books related to the transactions that occurred on January 10, February 12, and March 10.

E8–2 The ledger of the Pate Company at the end of the current year shows Accounts Receivable $80,000, Sales $940,000, and Sales Returns and Allowances $40,000.

Journalize entries to record allowance for doubtful accounts using two different bases.
(S.O. 3)

Instructions
(a) If the Allowance for Doubtful Accounts has a credit balance of $800 in the trial balance, journalize the adjusting entry at December 31, assuming bad debts are expected to be (1) 1% of net sales, and (2) 10% of accounts receivable.

(b) If the Allowance for Doubtful Accounts has a debit balance of $600 in the trial balance, journalize the adjusting entry at December 31, assuming bad debts are expected to be (1) .75% of net sales and (2) 8% of accounts receivable.

E8–3 Trevino Company has accounts receivable of $90,500 at March 31. An analysis of the accounts shows the following:

Determine bad debts expense and prepare the adjusting entry for bad debts expense.
(S.O. 3)

Month of Sale	Balance, March 31
March	$65,000
February	12,600
December and January	8,500
November and October	4,400
	$90,500

Credit terms are 2/10, n/30. At March 31, there is a $1,600 credit balance in Allowance for Doubtful Accounts prior to adjustment. The company uses the percentage of receivables basis for estimating uncollectible accounts. The company's estimate of bad debts are as follows:

Age of Accounts	Estimated Percentage Uncollectible
Current	2.0%
1–30 days past due	10.0%
31–90 days past due	30.0%
Over 90 days	50.0%

Instructions
(a) Determine the total estimated uncollectibles.
(b) Prepare the adjusting entry at March 31 to record bad debts expense.

E8–4 On December 31, 1993, Carson Co. estimates that 2% of its net sales of $200,000 will become uncollectible and records this amount as an addition to the Allowance for Doubtful Accounts. On May 11, 1994, Carson Co. determined that Robert Worthy's account was uncollectible and wrote off $900. On June 12, 1994, Worthy paid the amount previously written off.

Percentage of sales basis, write-off, recovery.
(S.O. 3)

Instructions
Prepare the journal entries on December 31, 1993, May 11, 1994, and June 12, 1994.

E8–5 Presented below are two independent situations:

Journalize entries for the sale of accounts receivable.
(S.O. 2, 4)

1. On March 3, Slokar Appliances sells $900,000 of its receivables to Porter Factors Inc. Porter Factors Inc. assesses a finance charge of 3% of the amount of receivables sold. Prepare the entry on Slokar Appliances' books to record the sale of the receivables.

2. On May 10, Montrose Company sold merchandise for $4,000 and accepted the customer's First Business Bank Mastercard. At the end of the day, the First Business Bank Mastercard receipts were deposited in the company's bank account. First Business Bank charges a 4% service charge for credit card sales. Prepare the entry on Montrose Company's books to record the sale of merchandise.

Journalize entries for credit card sales.
(S.O. 4)

E8–6   Presented below are two independent situations that occurred in 1993:

1. On April 2, Paula Zahn uses her J. C. Penney credit card to purchase merchandise from a J. C. Penney store for $1,300. On May 1, Zahn is billed for the $1,300 amount due. Zahn pays $900 on the balance due on May 3. On June 1, Zahn receives a bill for the amount due, including interest at 1.5% per month on the unpaid balance as of May 3. Prepare the entries on J. C. Penney Co.'s books related to the transactions that occurred on April 2, May 3, and June 1.

2. On July 4, Rhodes' Restaurant accepts an American Express card for a $300 dinner bill. American Express charges a 5% service fee. On July 10, American Express pays Rhodes $285. Prepare the entries on Rhodes' books related to the transactions.

Journalize credit card sales and indicate the statement presentation of financing charges and service charge expense.
(S.O. 4)

E8–7   Kohl Stores accepts both its own and national credit cards. During 1993, the following selected summary transactions occurred.

Jan. 15   Made Kohl credit card sales totaling $16,000.
    20   Made American Express credit card sales (service charge fee, 5%) totaling $2,800.
    30   Received payment in full from American Express less a 5% service charge.
Feb. 10   Collected $10,000 on Kohl credit card sales.
    15   Added finance charges of 1.5% to $6,000 of Kohl credit card balances.

Instructions
(a) Journalize the transactions for Kohl Stores.

(b) Indicate the statement presentation of the financing charges and the credit card service expense for Kohl Stores.

Journalize entries for notes receivable transactions.
(S.O. 5, 6)

E8–8   Illinois Supply Co. has the following transactions related to notes receivable during the last two months of 1993.

Nov. 1   Loaned $30,000 cash to A. Gomez on a 1-year, 10% note.
Dec. 11   Sold goods to R. Wright, Inc., receiving a $3,600, 90-day, 12% note.
    16   Received a $4,000, 6-month, 12% note on account from B. Barnes.
    31   Accrued interest revenue on all notes receivable.

Instructions
Journalize the transactions for Illinois Supply Co.

Journalize entries for notes receivable.
(S.O. 5, 6)

E8–9   Record the following transactions for the Brokaw Co. in the general journal:

1993
May 1   Received a $6,000, 1-year, 12% note on account from T. Jones.
Dec. 31   Accrued interest on the Jones' note.
Dec. 31   Closed the interest revenue account.
1994
May 1   Received principal plus interest on the Jones note. (No interest has been accrued in 1994)

Journalize entries for dishonor of notes receivable.
(S.O. 5, 8)

E8–10   On May 2, 1993, Peter Brey Company lends $6,000 to Feingold Inc., issuing a 6-month, 10% note. At the maturity date, November 2, 1993, Feingold indicates that it cannot pay at the present time.

Instructions
(a) Prepare the entry to record the dishonor of the note, assuming that Brey Company expects collection will occur.

(b) Prepare the entry to record the dishonor of the note, assuming that Brey Company does not expect collection in the future.

PROBLEMS

P8–1 At December 31, 1993, Trisha Yearwood Imports reported the following information on its balance sheet:

Accounts receivable	$1,000,000
Less: Allowance for doubtful accounts	60,000

During the first quarter of 1994, the company had the following transactions related to receivables.

1. Sales on account	$2,600,000
2. Sales returns and allowances	40,000
3. Collections of accounts receivable	2,300,000
4. Write-offs of accounts receivable deemed uncollectible	80,000
5. Recovery of bad debts previously written off as uncollectible	25,000

Instructions

(a) Prepare the journal entries to record each of these five transactions. Assume that no cash discounts were taken on the collections of accounts receivable.

(b) Prepare the journal entry to record bad debt expense for the first quarter of 1994, assuming that an aging of accounts receivable indicates that the allowance balance should be $80,000.

Prepare journal entries related to bad debt expense. (S.O. 2, 3)

P8–2 Information related to Ace Company for 1993 is summarized below:

Total credit sales	$1,800,000
Accounts receivable at December 31	$600,000
Bad debts written off	$26,000

Instructions

(a) What amount of bad debt expense will Ace Company report if it uses the direct write-off method of accounting for bad debts?

(b) Assume that Ace Company decides to estimate its bad debt expense to be 2% of credit sales. What amount of bad debt expense will Ace Company record if the Allowance for Doubtful Accounts has a balance of $3,000?

(c) Assume that Ace Company decides to estimate its bad debt expense based on 3% of accounts receivable. What amount of bad debt expense will Ace Company record if the Allowance for Doubtful Accounts balance has a credit balance of $4,000?

(d) What is the weakness of the direct write-off method of reporting bad debt expense?

Computation of bad debts amounts (S.O. 3)

P8–3 Presented below is an aging schedule for Hugable Company.

Journalize entries to record transactions related to bad debts. (S.O. 2, 3)

Customer	Total	Not Yet Due	Number of Days Past Due			
			1–30	31–60	61–90	Over 90
Aber	$ 20,000		$ 9,000	$11,000		
Bohr	30,000	$ 30,000				
Case	50,000	15,000	5,000		$30,000	
Datz	36,000					$36,000
Others	120,000	92,000	15,000	$13,000		
	$256,000	$137,000	$29,000	$24,000	$30,000	$36,000
Estimated Percentage Uncollectible		3%	6%	12%	24%	50%
Total Estimated Bad Debt Expense	$ 33,930	$ 4,110	$ 1,740	$ 2,880	$ 7,200	$18,000

At December 31, 1993, the unadjusted balance in the Allowance for Doubtful Accounts is a credit of $9,000.

Instructions

(a) Journalize and post the adjusting entry for bad debts at December 31, 1993.

(b) Journalize and post to the allowance account the following 1994 events and transactions.
   (1) March 1, a $800 customer balance originating in 1993 is judged uncollectible.
   (2) May 1, a check for $800 is received from the customer whose account was written off as uncollectible on March 1.

(c) Journalize the adjusting entry for bad debts on December 31, 1994, assuming that the unadjusted balance in Allowance for Doubtful Accounts is a debit of $900 and the aging schedule indicates that total estimated bad debts will be $27,100.

Journalize entries to record transactions related to bad debts.

(S.O. 3)

P8–4 Lendl Co. uses 2% of net sales to determine its bad debt expense for the period. At the beginning of the current period, Lendl had an Allowance for Doubtful Accounts of $10,000 (credit). During the period, it had net sales of $900,000 and wrote off as uncollectible accounts receivable of $7,000. However, one of the accounts written off as uncollectible in the amount of $3,000 was recovered before the end of the current period.

Instructions

(a) Prepare the entry to record bad debt expense for the current period.

(b) Prepare the entry to record the write-off of uncollectible accounts during the current period.

(c) Prepare the entries to record the recovery of the uncollectible accounts during the current period.

(d) Determine the ending balance in the Allowance for Doubtful Accounts.

Prepare entries for various note receivable transactions.

(S.O. 2, 4, 5, 6, 7, 8)

G

P8–5 The Bon Jovi Company closes its books monthly. On June 30, selected ledger account balances are

Notes Receivable	$19,400
Interest Receivable	$132.80

Notes Receivable include the following:

Date	Maker	Face	Term	Interest
May 21	Alder Inc.	$6,000	60 days	12%
May 25	Dorn Co.	4,800	60 days	11%
June 30	MJH Corp.	8,600	6 months	12%

During July, the following transactions were completed.

July 5 Made sales of $6,200 on Bon Jovi credit cards.
   14 Made sales of $700 on VISA credit cards. The credit card service charge is 3%.
   16 Added $415 to Bon Jovi charge customer balances for finance charges on unpaid balances.
   20 Received payment in full from Alder Inc. on the amount due.
   25 Received notice that Dorn note has been dishonored. (Assume that Dorn is expected to pay in the future.)

Instructions

(a) Journalize the July transactions and the July 31 adjusting entry for accrued interest receivable. (Interest is computed using 360 days.)

(b) Enter the balances at July 1 in the receivable accounts and post the entries to all of the receivable accounts.

(c) Show the balance sheet presentation of the receivable accounts at July 31.

Prepare entries for various receivables transactions.

(S.O. 2, 4, 5, 6, 7, 8)

P8–6 On January 1, 1993, Coletrain Company had Accounts Receivable $54,200 and Allowance for Doubtful Accounts $4,700. Coletrain Company prepares financial statements annually. During the year the following selected transactions occurred.

Jan. 5 Sold $6,000 of merchandise to Garth Brooks Company, terms n/30.
Feb. 2 Accepted a $6,000, 4-month, 12% promissory note from Garth Brooks Company for balance due.

12 Sold $7,200 of merchandise to Gage Company and accepted Gage's $7,200 two-month, 10% note for the balance due.

26 Sold $5,000 of merchandise to Mathias Co., terms n/10.

Apr. 5 Accepted a $5,000, 3-month, 12% note from Mathias Co. for balance due.

12 Collected Gage Company note in full.

June 2 Collected Garth Brooks Company note in full.

July 5 Mathias Co. dishonors its note of April 5. It is expected that Mathias will eventually pay the amount owed.

15 Sold $3,000 of merchandise to Tritt Inc. and accepted Tritt's $3,000, 3-month, 12% note for the amount due.

Oct. 15 The Tritt Inc. note was dishonored. Tritt Inc. is bankrupt, and there is no hope of future settlement.

Instructions
Journalize the transactions.

ALTERNATE PROBLEMS

P8–1A At December 31, 1993, Bordeaux Inc. reported the following information on its balance sheet.

Accounts Receivable	$960,000
Less: Allowance for doubtful accounts	70,000

Prepare journal entries related to bad debt expense.
(S.O. 2, 3)

During the first quarter of 1994, the company had the following transactions related to receivables.

1. Sales on account	$3,200,000
2. Sales returns and allowances	50,000
3. Collections of accounts receivable	2,800,000
4. Write-offs of accounts receivable deemed uncollectible	90,000
5. Recovery of bad debts previously written off as uncollectible	35,000

Instructions
(a) Prepare the journal entries to record each of these five transactions. Assume that no cash discounts were taken on the collections of accounts receivable.

(b) Prepare the journal entry to record bad debt expense for the first quarter of 1994, assuming that an aging of accounts receivable indicates that the allowance balance should be $110,000.

P8–2A Information related to Duece Company for 1993 is summarized below:

Total credit sales	$2,000,000
Accounts receivable at December 31	$800,000
Bad debts written off	$36,000

Computation of bad debts amounts.
(S.O. 3)

Instructions
(a) What amount of bad debt expense will Duece Company report if it uses the direct write-off method of accounting for bad debts?

(b) Assume that Duece Company decides to estimate its bad debt expense to be 3% of credit sales. What amount of bad debt expense will Duece Company record if it has an Allowance for Doubtful Accounts credit balance of $4,000?

(c) Assume that Duece Company decides to estimate its bad debt expense based on 2% of accounts receivable. What amount of bad debt expense will Duece Company record if it has an Allowance for Doubtful Accounts credit balance of $3,000?

(d) What is the weakness of the direct write-off method of reporting bad debt expense?

Journalize entries to record transactions related to bad debts.
(S.O. 2, 3)

P8–3A   Presented below is an aging schedule for Deep Purple Company.

| Customer | Total | Not Yet Due | Number of Days Past Due | | | |
			1–30	31–60	61–90	Over 90
Anita	$ 22,000		$10,000	$12,000		
Barry	40,000	$ 40,000				
Chagnon	57,000	16,000	6,000		$35,000	
David	37,000					$37,000
Others	126,000	96,000	16,000	14,000		
	$282,000	$152,000	$32,000	$26,000	35,000	$37,000
Estimated Percentage Uncollectible		4%	7%	13%	25%	50%
Total Estimated Bad Debt Expense	$ 38,950	$ 6,080	$ 2,240	$ 3,380	$ 8,750	$18,500

At December 31, 1993 the unadjusted balance in the Allowance for Doubtful Accounts is a credit of $10,000.

Instructions

(a) Journalize and post the adjusting entry for bad debts at December 31, 1993.

(b) Journalize and post to the allowance account the following 1994 events and transactions.
   (1) March 31, an $800 customer balance originating in 1993 is judged uncollectible.
   (2) May 31, a check for $800 is received from the customer whose account was written off as uncollectible on March 31.

(c) Journalize the adjusting entry for bad debts on December 31, 1994, assuming that the unadjusted balance in Allowance for Doubtful Accounts is a debit of $900 and the aging schedule indicates that total estimated bad debts will be $28,300.

Journalize entries to record transactions related to bad debts.
(S.O. 3)

P8–4A   Harmon Co. uses 3% of net sales to determine its bad debt expense for the period. At the beginning of the current period, Harmon had an Allowance for Doubtful Accounts of $9,000 (credit). During the period, it had net sales of $700,000 and wrote off as uncollectible accounts receivable of $7,000. However, one of the accounts written off as uncollectible in the amount of $4,000 was recovered before the end of the current period.

Instructions

(a) Prepare the entry to record bad debt expense for the current period.

(b) Prepare the entry to record the write-off of uncollectible accounts during the current period.

(c) Prepare the entries to record the recovery of the uncollectible accounts during the current period.

(d) Determine the ending balance in the Allowance for Doubtful Accounts.

Prepare entries for various note receivable transactions.
(S.O. 2, 4, 5, 6, 7, 8)

G

P8–5A   The Sallberg Company closes its books monthly. On September 30, selected ledger account balances are:

Notes Receivable	$23,400
Interest Receivable	$182.40

Notes Receivable include the following:

Date	Maker	Face	Term	Interest
Aug. 16	Foran Inc.	$ 8,000	60 days	12%
Aug. 25	Drexler Co.	5,200	2 months	12%
Sept. 30	MGH Corp.	10,200	6 months	19%

Interest is computed using a 360-day year. During October, the following transactions were completed.

Oct. 7   Made sales of $6,900 on Sallberg credit cards.

12   Made sales of $750 on VISA credit cards. The credit card service charge is 4%.

15   Added $485 to Sallberg charge customer balance for finance charges on unpaid balances.

15   Received payment in full from Foran Inc. on the amount due.

25   Received notice that Drexler note has been dishonored. (Assume that Drexler is expected to pay in future.)

Instructions

(a) Journalize the October transactions and the October 31 adjusting entry for accrued interest receivable.

(b) Enter the balances at October 1 in the receivable accounts and post the entries to all of the receivable accounts.

(c) Show the balance sheet presentation of the receivable accounts at October 31.

P8–6A   On January 1, 1993, Uptown Company had Accounts Receivable $146,000, Notes Receivable $15,000, and Allowance for Doubtful Accounts $13,200. The note receivable is from the Annabelle Company. It is a 4-month, 12% note dated December 31, 1992. Uptown Company prepares financial statements annually. During the year the following selected transactions occurred.

Prepare entries for various receivable transactions.
(S.O. 2, 4, 5, 6, 7, 8)

Jan. 5   Sold $12,000 of merchandise to George Company, terms n/15.

20   Accepted George Company's $12,000, 3-month, 13% note for balance due.

Feb. 18   Sold $8,000 of merchandise to Swaim Company and accepted Swaim's $8,000, 6-month, 10% note for the amount due.

Apr. 20   Collected George Company note in full.

30   Received payment in full from Annabelle Company on the amount due.

May 25   Accepted Avery Inc.'s $7,000, 3-month, 12% note in settlement of a past-due balance on account.

Aug. 18   Received payment in full from Swaim Company on note due.

25   The Avery Inc. note was dishonored. Avery Inc. is not bankrupt and future payment is anticipated.

Sept. 1   Sold $10,000 of merchandise to Young Company and accepted a $10,000, 6-month, 10% note for the amount due.

Instructions
Journalize the transactions.

*B*roadening *Your Perspective*

FINANCIAL REPORTING PROBLEM

Moore Company sells office equipment and supplies to many organizations in the city and surrounding area on contract terms of 2/10, n/30. In the past, over 75% of the credit customers have taken advantage of the discount by paying within 10 days of the invoice date.

The number of customers taking the full 30 days to pay has increased within the last year. Current indications are that less than 60% of the customers are now taking the discount. Bad debts as a percentage of gross credit sales have risen from the 1.5% provided in past years to about 4% in the current year.

The controller has responded to a request from the Finance Committee for more information on the collections of accounts receivable with the report reproduced on the next page.

MOORE COMPANY
Accounts Receivable Collections
May 31, 1994

The fact that some credit accounts will prove uncollectible is normal. Annual bad debt write-offs have been 1.5% of gross credit sales over the past five years. During the last fiscal year, this percentage increased to slightly less than 4%. The current Accounts Receivable balance is $1,400,000. The condition of this balance in terms of age and probability of collection is as follows:

Proportion of Total	Age Categories	Probability of Collection
66%	not yet due	99%
16%	less than 30 days past due	96½%
9%	30 to 60 days past due	95%
5%	61 to 120 days past due	91%
2½%	121 to 180 days past due	75%
1½%	over 180 days past due	20%

The Allowance for Doubtful Accounts had a credit balance of $29,500 on June 1, 1993. Moore has provided for a monthly bad debts expense accrual during the current fiscal year based on the assumption that 4% of gross credit sales will be uncollectible. Total gross credit sales for the 1993–94 fiscal year amounted to $2,800,000. Write-offs of bad accounts during the year totaled $106,000.

Instructions

(a) Prepare an accounts receivable aging schedule for the Moore Company using the age categories identified in the controller's report to the Finance Committee showing:
  1. The amount of accounts receivable outstanding for each age category and in total.
  2. The estimated amount that is uncollectible for each category and in total.

(b) Compute the amount of the year-end adjustment necessary to bring Allowance for Doubtful Accounts to the balance indicated by the age analysis. Then prepare the necessary journal entry to adjust the accounting records.

(c) In a recessionary environment with tight credit and high interest rates:
  1. Identify steps Moore Company might consider to improve the accounts receivable situation.
  2. Then evaluate each step identified in terms of the risks and costs involved.

DECISION CASE

James and Jake Berkvom own Casual Fashions. From its inception Casual Fashions has sold merchandise on either a cash or credit basis but no credit cards have been accepted. During the past several months, the Berkvoms have begun to question their sales policies. First, they have lost some sales because of refusing to accept credit cards. Second, representatives of two metropolitan banks have been persuasive in convincing them to accept their national credit cards. One bank, City National Bank, has stated that (1) its credit card fee is 4%, and (2) it pays the retailer 96 cents on each $1 of sales within three days of receiving the credit card billings.

The Berkvoms decide that they should determine the cost of carrying their own credit sales. From the accounting records of the past three years they accumulate the following data:

	1992	1991	1990
Net credit sales	$500,000	$600,000	$400,000
Collection agency fees for slow paying customers	2,450	2,500	2,000
Salary of part-time accounts receivable clerk	3,800	3,800	3,800

Credit and collection expenses as a percentage of net credit sales: uncollectible accounts, 1.6%, billing and mailing costs, 0.5%, and credit investigation fee on new customers, 0.15%.

James and Jake also determine that the average accounts receivable balance outstanding during the year is 5% of net credit sales. The Berkvoms estimate that they could earn an average of 10% annually on cash invested in other business opportunities.

Instructions

(a) Prepare a tabulation showing for each year total credit and collection expenses in dollars and as a percentage of net credit sales.

(b) Determine the net credit and collection expense in dollars and as a percentage of sales after considering the revenue not earned from other investment opportunities. (Note: The income lost on the cash held by the bank for three days is considered to be immaterial.)

(c) Discuss both the financial and nonfinancial factors that are relevant to the decision.

CRITICAL THINKING CASE

Refer back to the story about the North Carolina State University newspaper at the beginning of the chapter.

(a) If you had sold advertising space to a tardy paying client, how would you persuade them to pay?

(b) At what time would you recommend that the newspaper write-off uncollected receivables?

(c) Indicate the accounts to be debited and credited for each of the following transactions of the newspaper: (1) ad space is sold on account; (2) ad space is sold and prepaid; (3) cash is collected on account; (4) the ad is run for the advertiser who prepaid; (5) an uncollectible account is written off.

ETHICAL CASE

Shirt Co. is a subsidiary of Clothes Corp. The controller believes that the yearly allowance for doubtful accounts for Shirt Co. should be 2% of net credit sales. The president of Shirt Co., nervous that the parent company might expect the subsidiary to sustain its 10% growth rate, suggests that the controller increase the allowance for doubtful accounts to 4%. The president thinks that the lower net income, which reflects a 6% growth rate, will be a more sustainable rate for Shirt Co.

Instructions

(a) Who are the stakeholders in this case?

(b) Does the president's request pose an ethical dilemma for the controller?

(c) Should the controller be concerned with Shirt Co.'s growth rate in estimating the allowance? Explain your answer.

Answers to Self-Study Questions
1. b   2. c   3. d   4. a   5. c   6. b   7. d   8. d   9. a   10. a

CHAPTER 9

INVENTORIES

Study Objectives

After studying this chapter, you should be able to:

1. Describe the steps in determining inventory quantities.

2. Explain the basis of accounting for inventories and describe the inventory costing methods.

3. Explain the financial statement effects of each of the inventory costing methods.

4. Identify the factors to consider in selecting an inventory costing method.

5. List the essential accounting features of a perpetual inventory system.

6. Explain the lower of cost or market basis of accounting for inventories.

7. Describe the two methods of estimating inventories.

8. Indicate the effects of inventory errors on the financial statements.

I f you go to a large college or university, chances are that your bookstore or student union has state-of-the-art computer technology for tracking inventories. Instantaneously, the clerk at the check-out stand wooshes your purchases through a scanning machine that automatically rings up the price and deducts the inventory in one instant.

But not all schools have state-of-the-art technology. And some bookstores are small enough that the person managing it can apply a mom-and-pop approach. One such bookstore is at Erie Community College in Buffalo, New York, which produces annual sales of $500,000 per year. Instead of using a ''point-of-sale'' computer, the bookstore uses an old-fashioned cash register. The inventory is counted every month by Joel Damiani, manager. Because the quantity of inventory is relatively small, Damiani, or his two assistants, specifically identify each item when sold. A larger bookstore would have too much inventory to use this approach: a first-in, first-out

(FIFO) or last-in, first-out (LIFO) method would be used—which you'll read about in this chapter.

Damiani is candid, too, about some problems at his store. For one thing, the accounting records were in disarray when he agreed to take the job. "They told me it was going to be a challenge," he says. "And I like challenges." His challenges have included working with the school's accountant to produce a monthly balance sheet and income statement and making sure he has enough inventory of books and supplies on hand for the start of classes. "Sometimes, students say we're not quick enough."

Merchandise inventory is an important factor in determining the cost of goods sold for retailers and wholesalers. In this chapter we will explain the procedures for determining inventory quantities and the methods that may be used in determining the cost of inventory on hand at the balance sheet date. In addition, we will discuss the use of estimates in determining inventory amounts, perpetual inventory systems, and the effects of inventory errors on a company's financial statements.

Importance of Inventories

Inventories affect both the balance sheet and the income statement. In the **balance sheet** of merchandising companies, inventory is frequently the most significant current asset. Of course, its amount and relative importance can vary, even for enterprises in the same industry. For example, J. P. Stevens & Co. at one time reported inventory of $321 million, representing 45% of total current assets, whereas for the same period, J.C. Penney Company reported $1.7 billion of inventory, representing 65% of total current assets. In the **income statement**, inventory is vital in determining the results of operations for a particular period. Moreover, gross profit (net sales less cost of goods sold) is closely watched by management, owners, and other interested parties, as explained in Chapter 5.

Helpful hint An important inventory management concept is inventory turnover. Inventory that turns means sales and profit; inventory that doesn't turn means costs and losses.

Effective inventory management is frequently the key to successful business operations. A delicate balance must be maintained between too little inventory and too much. A merchandiser or manufacturer with too little inventory to meet demand will have dissatisfied customers and sales personnel. One with too much inventory will be burdened with unnecessary costs, as often happens in a recession.

In our economy, inventories are an important barometer of business activity. The U.S. Commerce Department, for example, publishes monthly combined inventory data for retailers, wholesalers, and manufacturers. The amount of inventories and the time required to sell the goods on hand are two indicators that are closely watched. During downturns in the economy, there is an initial build-up of inventories, as the length of time needed to sell existing quantities increases. The reverse effects are generally associated with an upturn in business activity.

Classifying Inventory

In a **merchandising enterprise**, inventory consists of many different items. For example, in a grocery store, canned goods, dairy products, meats, and produce are just a few of the inventory items on hand. These items have two common characteristics: (1) they are owned by the company, and (2) they are in a form ready for sale to customers in the ordinary course of business. Thus, only one inventory classification, **merchandise inventory**, is needed to describe the many different items that make up the total inventory.

In a **manufacturing enterprise**, inventories are also owned by the company, but some goods may not yet be ready for sale. As a result, inventory is usually classified into three categories: finished goods, work in process, and raw materials. For example, General Motors classifies automobiles completed and ready for sale as **finished goods**. The automobiles on the assembly line in various stages of production are classified as **work in process**. The steel, glass, upholstery, and other components that are on hand waiting to be used in the production of automobiles are identified as **raw materials**.

The accounting principles and concepts discussed in this chapter apply to inventory classifications of both merchandising and manufacturing companies. In this chapter we will focus on merchandise inventory. In later chapters we will discuss the accounting for the three inventory classifications used by manufacturers.

Helpful hint Regardless of the classification, all inventories are reported under current assets on the balance sheet.

Determining Inventory Quantities

In order to prepare financial statements, it is necessary to determine the number of units of inventory owned by the company at the statement date. For many companies, this task consists of two steps: (1) taking a physical inventory of goods on hand, and (2) determining the ownership of goods.

Study Objective 1

Describe the steps in determining inventory quantities.

Taking a Physical Inventory

Taking a physical inventory involves actually counting, weighing, or measuring each kind of inventory on hand. In many companies, taking an inventory is a formidable task. Retailers, such as K-mart, True Value Hardware, or your favorite music store have thousands of different inventory items.

An inventory count is generally more accurate when goods are not being sold or received during the counting. Consequently, companies often take the inventory when the business is closed or when business is slow. To minimize errors in taking the inventory, a company should adopt the following **internal control** procedures:

1. The counting should be done by employees who do not have custodial responsibility for the inventory. (Segregation of duties)
2. Each counter should establish the authenticity of each inventory item, e.g., each box does contain a 25-inch television set, and each storage tank does contain gasoline. (Establishment of responsibility)
3. There should be a second count by another employee. (Independent internal verification)
4. Prenumbered inventory tags should be used, and all inventory tags should be accounted for. (Documentation procedures)

5. A designated supervisor should ascertain at the conclusion of the count that all inventory items are tagged and that no items have more than one tag. (Independent internal verification)

After the physical inventory is taken, the quantity of each kind of inventory is listed on inventory summary sheets. To assure the accuracy of the summary sheets, the listing should be verified by a second employee or supervisor. Subsequently, unit costs are applied to the quantities and a total cost of the inventory is determined.

Accounting in Action · *Business Insight*

Failure to observe the foregoing internal control procedures contributed to the Great Salad Oil Swindle. In this case, management intentionally overstated its salad oil inventory, which was stored in large holding tanks. Three procedures contributed to overstating the oil inventory: (1) Water added to the bottom of the holding tanks caused the oil to float to the top. Inventory-taking crews who viewed the holding tanks from the top observed only salad oil, when, in fact, as much as 37 out of 40 feet of many of the holding tanks contained water. (2) The company's inventory records listed more holding tanks than it actually had. The company repainted numbers on the tanks after inventory crews examined them, so the crews counted the same tanks twice. (3) Underground pipes pumped oil from one holding tank to another during the inventory taking; therefore, the same salad oil was counted more than once. Although the salad oil swindle was unusual, it demonstrates the complexities involved in assuring that inventory is properly counted.

Determining Ownership of Goods

Two issues are involved in determining ownership of goods: (1) goods in transit and (2) consigned goods.

Goods in Transit

Goods are considered to be in transit when they are in the hands of a public carrier, such as a railroad, trucking, or airline company at the statement date. Goods in transit should be included in the inventory of the party that has legal title to the goods. Legal title is determined by the terms of sale.

1. When the terms are **FOB (free on board) shipping point**, ownership of the goods passes to the buyer when the public carrier accepts the goods from the seller.
2. When the terms are **FOB destination**, legal title to the goods remains with the seller until the goods reach the buyer.

Significant errors may occur in determining inventory quantities if goods in transit at the statement date are ignored. Assume, for example, that Hargrove Company has 20,000 units of inventory on hand on December 31 and the following goods in transit: (1) **sales** of 1,500 units shipped December 31 FOB destination, and (2) **purchases** of 2,500 units shipped FOB shipping point by the seller on December 31. Hargrove has legal title to both the units sold and the units purchased. Consequently, inventory quantities are understated by 4,000 units (1,500 + 2,500) if units in transit are ignored.

Consigned Goods

In some lines of business, it is customary to acquire merchandise on consignment. Under a consignment arrangement, the holder of the goods (called the *consignee*) does not own the goods. Ownership remains with the shipper of the goods (called the *consignor*) until the goods are actually sold to a customer. Because consigned goods are not owned by the consignee, they should not be included in the consignee's physical inventory count. Conversely, the consignor should include merchandise held by the consignee as part of its inventory.

Accounting in Action · *Business Insight*

Many companies have invested large amounts of time and money in automated inventory systems. One of the most sophisticated is Federal Express' Digitally Assisted Dispatch System (DADS). This system uses hand-held "SuperTrackers" to transmit data about the packages and documents to the firm's computer system. Based on bar codes, the system allows the firm to know where any package is at any time to prevent losses and to fulfill the firm's delivery commitments.

Inventoriable Costs

The cost and matching principles of accounting are essential to an explanation of inventoriable costs.

1. In accordance with the cost principle, the primary basis of accounting for inventories is cost.
2. Under the matching principle, the major objective in accounting for inventories is the matching of appropriate costs with sales revenues.

Study Objective 2

Explain the basis of accounting for inventories and describe the inventory costing methods.

Determining Inventoriable Costs

All expenditures necessary to acquire the goods and to make them ready for sale are included as inventoriable costs. Inventoriable costs may be regarded as a pool of costs that consists of two elements: (1) the cost of the beginning inventory and (2) the cost of goods purchased during the year. As explained in Chapter 5, the sum of these two elements equals the cost of goods available for sale. The individual items included in inventoriable cost are shown in Illustration 9-1.

ILLUSTRATION 9-1

Types of inventoriable costs

Item	Account Title	Effect on Inventoriable Costs
Invoice price	Purchases	Increase
Freight charges paid by purchaser	Freight-in	Increase
Purchase discounts taken by purchaser	Purchase Discounts	Decrease
Purchase returns and allowances granted by the seller	Purchase Returns and Allowances	Decrease

Conceptually, the costs of the purchasing, receiving, and warehousing departments should also be included in inventoriable costs. However, because of the practical difficulties in allocating these costs to individual inventory units, they are generally accounted for as operating expenses in the period in which they are incurred.

Allocating Inventoriable Costs

Inventoriable costs are allocated to ending inventory and to cost of goods sold. Under a periodic inventory system (illustrated in Chapter 5), the allocation is made at the end of the accounting period. First, the costs assignable to the ending inventory are determined. Second, the cost of the ending inventory is subtracted from the cost of goods available for sale to determine the cost of goods sold. Cost of goods sold is then deducted from sales revenues in accordance with the matching principle.

To illustrate, assume that General Suppliers Inc. has a cost of goods available for sale of $120,000, based on a beginning inventory of $20,000 and cost of goods purchased of $100,000. From the physical inventory it is determined that 5,000 units are on hand. The costs applicable to the units are $3.00 per unit. The allocation of the pool of costs is shown in Illustration 9-2. As shown, the $120,000 of goods available for sale are allocated $15,000 to ending inventory and $105,000 to cost of goods sold.

ILLUSTRATION 9-2

Allocation (matching) of pool of costs

Pool of Costs	
Cost of Goods Available for Sale	
Beginning inventory	$ 20,000
Cost of goods purchased	100,000
Cost of goods available for sale	$120,000

Step 1			Step 2	
Ending Inventory			**Cost of Goods Sold**	
Units	Unit Cost	Total Cost	Cost of goods available for sale	$120,000
			Less: Ending inventory	15,000
5,000	$3.00	$15,000	Cost of goods sold	$105,000

Using Actual Physical Flow Costing

Costing of the inventory is complicated because the units on hand for a specific item of inventory may have been purchased at different prices. For example, in a period of rising prices, a company may experience several increases in the cost of identical goods within a given year. Alternatively, unit costs may decline. For example, in the mid-1980s, gasoline dropped 50¢ per gallon. Under such circumstances, how should the different unit costs in the cost of goods available for sale be allocated between the ending inventory and cost of goods sold?

One answer is to use specific identification of the units purchased. This method tracks the **actual physical flow** of the goods. **Each item of inventory is marked, tagged, or coded with its "specific" unit cost.** Items still in inventory at the end of the year are specifically costed to arrive at the total cost of the ending inventory. Assume, for example, that Southland Music Company purchases three 27-inch television sets at costs of $700, $750, and $800, respectively. During the year, two sets are sold at $1,200 each. At December 31, the company determines that the $750 set is still on hand. Accordingly, the ending inventory is $750 and the cost of goods sold is $1,500 ($700 + $800).

Specific identification is possible when a company sells a limited variety of high-unit cost items that can be clearly identified from the time of purchase through the time of sale. Examples of such companies are automobile dealerships (cars, trucks, and vans), music stores (pianos and organs), and antique shops (tables and cabinets).

Ordinarily, however, the identity of goods purchased at a specific cost is lost between the date of purchase and the date of sale. For example, drug, grocery, and hardware stores sell thousands of relatively low unit-cost items of inventory. These items are often indistinguishable from one another, making it impossible or impractical to track each item's cost.

When feasible, specific identification seems to be the ideal method of allocating cost of goods available for sale. Under this method, the ending inventory is reported at actual cost and the actual cost of goods sold is matched against sales revenue. This method, however, may enable management to manipulate net income. For example, assume that a music store has three identical Steinway grand pianos that were purchased at different costs. Management could maximize its net income when selling one piano, by selecting the piano with the lowest cost to match with revenues. Alternatively, it could minimize net income by selecting the highest-cost piano.

Using Assumed Cost Flow Methods

Because specific identification is often impractical, the allocation of inventoriable costs may be made under any of the following cost flow assumptions:

1. First-in, first-out (FIFO).
2. Last-in, first-out (LIFO).
3. Average cost.

There is no accounting requirement that the cost flow assumption be consistent with the physical movement of the goods. The selection of the appropriate cost flow assumption (method) is made by management. The management of companies in the same industry may reach different conclusions as to the most appropriate method.

To illustrate these three inventory costing methods, we will assume that Bow Valley Electronics uses a periodic inventory system and has the information shown below for its Z202 Astro condenser.

ILLUSTRATION 9-3

Inventoriable costs

BOW VALLEY ELECTRONICS
Z202 Astro Condensers

		Units	Unit Cost	Total Cost
1/1	Beginning inventory	100	$10	$ 1,000
4/15	Purchase	200	11	2,200
8/24	Purchase	300	12	3,600
11/27	Purchase	400	13	5,200
		1,000		$12,000

During the year, 550 units were sold and 450 units are on hand at December 31.

First-in, First-out (FIFO)

The FIFO method assumes that the earliest **goods** purchased are the first to be sold. FIFO often parallels the actual physical flow of merchandise because it generally is good business management to sell the oldest units first. Under the FIFO method, therefore, the **costs** of the earliest goods purchased are the first to be recognized as cost of goods sold. The allocation of the cost of goods available for sale at Bow Valley Electronics is shown in Illustration 9-4.

ILLUSTRATION 9-4

Allocation of costs—FIFO method

Pool of Costs
Cost of Goods Available for Sale

Date	Explanation	Units	Unit Cost	Total Cost
1/1	Beginning inventory	100	$10	$ 1,000
4/15	Purchase	200	11	2,200
8/24	Purchase	300	12	3,600
11/27	Purchase	400	13	5,200
	Total	1,000		$12,000

Helpful hint Note the sequencing of the allocation: (1) compute ending inventory and (2) determine cost of goods sold.

Step 1 Ending Inventory				Step 2 Cost of Goods Sold	
Date	Units	Unit Cost	Total Cost		
11/27	400	$13	$5,200	Cost of goods available for sale	$12,000
8/24	50	12	600	Less: Ending inventory	5,800
Total	450		$5,800	Cost of goods sold	$ 6,200

Helpful hint Note that ending inventory of $5,800 and the cost of goods sold of $6,200 equals cost of goods available for sale.

Note that the ending inventory is based on the latest units purchased. That is, **the cost of the ending inventory is obtained by taking the unit cost of the most recent purchase and working backward until all units of inventory have been costed.**

We can verify the accuracy of the cost of goods sold by recognizing that the **first units acquired are the first units sold.** The computations for the 550 units sold are shown in Illustration 9-5.

ILLUSTRATION 9-5

Proof of cost of goods sold

Date	Units		Unit Cost		Total Cost
1/1	100	×	$10	=	$1,000
4/15	200	×	11	=	2,200
8/24	250	×	12	=	3,000
Total	550				$6,200

Last-in, First-out (LIFO)

The LIFO method assumes that the latest goods purchased are the first to be sold. LIFO seldom coincides with the actual physical flow of inventory. Under the LIFO method, therefore, the **costs** of the latest goods purchased are the first to be recognized as cost of goods sold. The allocation of the cost of goods available for sale at Bow Valley Electronics is shown in Illustration 9-6.

ILLUSTRATION 9-6

Allocation of costs—LIFO method

Pool of Costs				
Cost of Goods Available for Sale				
Date	Explanation	Units	Unit Cost	Total Cost
1/1	Beginning inventory	100	$10	$ 1,000
4/15	Purchase	200	11	2,200
8/24	Purchase	300	12	3,600
11/27	Purchase	400	13	5,200
	Total	1,000		$12,000

Step 1				Step 2	
Ending Inventory				Cost of Goods Sold	
Date	Units	Unit Cost	Total Cost		
1/1	100	$10	$1,000	Cost of goods available for sale	$12,000
4/15	200	11	2,200		
8/24	150	12	1,800	Less: Ending inventory	5,000
Total	450		$5,000	Cost of goods sold	$ 7,000

Under the LIFO method, **the cost of the ending inventory is obtained by taking the unit cost of the earliest goods available for sale and working forward until all units of inventory are costed**. As a result, the first costs assigned to ending inventory are the costs of the beginning inventory. Proof of the costs allocated to cost of goods sold is shown in Illustration 9-7.

ILLUSTRATION 9-7

Proof of cost of goods sold

Date	Units		Unit Cost		Total Cost
11/27	400	×	$13	=	$5,200
8/24	150	×	12	=	1,800
Total	550				$7,000

Helpful hint Costs of goods purchased in November therefore can be included in the cost of goods sold of a prior month. Thus, income could be manipulated by purchase of inventory in December.

Note that the cost of the **last** goods in are the **first** to be assigned to cost of goods sold. Under a periodic inventory system, which we are using here, **all goods purchased during the period are assumed to be available for the first sale, regardless of the date of purchase.**

Average Cost

The average cost method assumes that the goods available for sale are homogeneous. Under this method, the allocation of the cost of goods available for sale is made on the basis of the **weighted average unit cost** incurred. The formula and computation of the weighted average unit cost are:

ILLUSTRATION 9-8

Formula for weighted average unit cost

The weighted average unit cost is then applied to the units on hand to determine the cost of the ending inventory. The allocation of the cost of goods available for sale at Bow Valley Electronics is shown in Illustration 9-9.

ILLUSTRATION 9-9

Allocation of costs—average cost method

Pool of Costs
Cost of Goods Available for Sale

Date	Explanation	Units	Unit Cost	Total Cost
1/1	Beginning inventory	100	$10	$ 1,000
4/15	Purchase	200	11	2,200
8/24	Purchase	300	12	3,600
11/27	Purchase	400	13	5,200
	Total	1,000		$12,000

Step 1	Step 2
Ending Inventory	Cost of Goods Sold

$12,000 ÷ 1,000 = $12.00		Cost of goods available for sale	$12,000
Units × Unit Cost = Total Cost		Less: Ending inventory	5,400
450 × $12.00 = $5,400		Cost of goods sold	$ 6,600

We can verify the cost of goods sold under this method by multiplying the units sold by the weighted average unit cost (550 × $12 = $6,600). Note that this method does not use the average of the unit costs. That average is $11.50 ($10 + $11 + $12 + $13 = $46; $46 ÷ 4). The average cost method instead uses the average **weighted** by the quantities purchased at each unit cost.

Financial Statement Effects of Costing Methods

Study Objective 3

Explain the financial statement effects of each of the inventory costing methods.

Each of the three methods discussed is acceptable. For example, Black and Decker Manufacturing Company and Northwest Industries, Inc., currently use the FIFO method of inventory costing. Campbell Soup Company, Krogers, and Walgreen Drugs use LIFO for part or all of their inventory. Bristol-Myers and Motorola use the average cost method. A company may also use more than one costing method concurrently. Del Monte Corporation, for example, uses LIFO for domestic inventories and FIFO for foreign inventories. Illustration 9-10 shows the use of three costing methods in the 600 largest companies in the U.S.

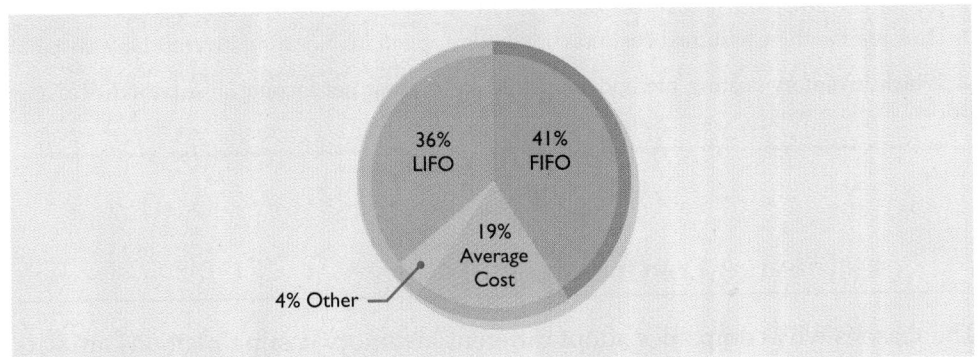

ILLUSTRATION 9-10

Use of costing methods in major U.S. companies

Source: *Accounting Trends and Techniques*, 1991 edition (AICPA, New York, N.Y.).

To understand why these companies might use a particular costing method, let's examine the effects of the different flow assumptions on the financial statements of Bow Valley Electronics. The condensed income statements in Illustration 9-11 assume that Bow Valley sold its 550 units for $11,500, its operating expenses were $2,000, and its income tax rate is 30%.

ILLUSTRATION 9-11

Comparative effects of costing methods

BOW VALLEY ELECTRONICS **Condensed Income Statements**			
	FIFO	LIFO	Average Cost
Sales	$11,500	$11,500	$11,500
Beginning inventory	1,000	1,000	1,000
Purchases	11,000	11,000	11,000
Cost of goods available for sale	12,000	12,000	12,000
Ending inventory	5,800	5,000	5,400
Cost of goods sold	6,200	7,000	6,600
Gross profit	5,300	4,500	4,900
Operating expenses	2,000	2,000	2,000
Income before income taxes[1]	3,300	2,500	2,900
Income tax expense (30%)	990	750	870
Net income	$ 2,310	$ 1,750	$ 2,030

Although the cost of goods available for sale ($12,000) is the same under each of the three inventory costing methods, both the ending inventories and cost of goods sold are different. This difference is due to the unit costs that are allocated to cost of goods sold and to ending inventory. In a period of rising prices (as is the case here), FIFO reports the highest net income ($2,310) and LIFO the lowest ($1,750); average cost falls in the middle ($2,030). If prices are falling, the results from the use of FIFO and LIFO are reversed; that is, FIFO will report the lowest net income and LIFO the highest.

---

[1]It is assumed that Bow Valley is a corporation, and corporations are required to pay income taxes.

Before You Go On . . .

1. What steps are involved in determining inventory quantities?

2. How do the cost and matching principles apply to inventoriable costs?

3. How are the three assumed cost flow methods applied in allocating inventoriable costs?

4. Which inventory costing method produces the highest net income in a period of rising prices? Explain why.

Selecting the Costing Method

Study Objective 4

Identify the factors to consider in selecting an inventory costing method.

The reasons why companies adopt different inventory costing methods are varied, but they usually involve one of the following factors:

1. Balance sheet effects
2. Income statement effects
3. Tax effects

Balance Sheet Effects

A major advantage of the FIFO method is that in a period of inflation, the costs allocated to ending inventory will approximate their current cost. For example, for Bow Valley, 400 of the 450 units in the ending inventory are costed at the November 27 unit cost of $13.

Conversely, a major shortcoming of the LIFO method is that in a period of inflation, the costs allocated to ending inventory may be significantly understated in terms of current cost. This is true for Bow Valley, where the cost of the ending inventory includes the $10 unit cost of the beginning inventory. The understatement becomes greater over prolonged periods of inflation if the inventory includes goods purchased in one or more prior accounting periods.

Income Statement Effects

Each dollar of difference in ending inventory results in a corresponding dollar difference in income before income taxes. For Bow Valley, there is an $800 difference between FIFO and LIFO. In a period of inflation, FIFO produced a higher net income because the lower unit costs of the first units purchased are matched against revenues. To management, higher net income is an advantage: it causes external users to view the company more favorably. In addition, if management bonuses are based on net income, FIFO will provide the basis for higher bonuses.

Some argue that the use of LIFO in a period of inflation enables the company to avoid reporting **paper or phantom profit** as economic gain. To illustrate, assume that Kralik Company buys 200 XR492s at $20 per unit on January 10 and 200 more on December 31 at $24 each. During the year, 200 units are sold at $30 each. The results under FIFO and LIFO are shown in Illustration 9-12.

ILLUSTRATION 9-12

Income statement effects compared

	FIFO		LIFO	
Sales (200 × $30)	$6,000		$6,000	
Cost of goods sold	4,000	(200 × $20)	4,800	(200 × $24)
Gross profit	$2,000		$1,200	

Under LIFO, the company has recovered the current replacement cost ($4,800) of the units sold. Thus, the gross profit in economic terms is real. However, under FIFO, the company has recovered only the January 10 cost ($4,000). To replace the units sold, it must reinvest $800 (200 × $4) of the gross profit. Thus, $800 of the gross profit is said to be phantom or illusory. As a result, reported net income is also overstated in real terms.

Tax Effects

We have seen that both inventory on the balance sheet and net income on the income statement are higher when FIFO is used in a period of inflation. Yet, many companies have switched to LIFO. The reason is that LIFO results in the lowest income taxes (because of lower net income). For example, at Bow Valley Electronics, income taxes are $750 under LIFO, compared to $990 under FIFO. The tax saving of $240 makes more cash available for use in the business.

Accounting in Action · *Business Insight*

Most small firms use the FIFO method. But fears of rising inflation have a growing number shifting to the LIFO method. "With vendor and supplier costs starting to rise again, 20 clients are mulling using LIFO despite its complexities," says James Stephenson of Chicago CPAs Miller, Cooper & Co.

The move to LIFO is just starting. Chicago Heights Steel Co. in Illinois recently boosted cash "by 5% to 10% by lowering income taxes" when it switched to LIFO. Electronic games distributor Atlas Distributing Inc., Chicago, considers a switch "because the costs of our games, made in Japan, are rising 15% a year," says Joseph Serpico, treasurer. If inflation heats up, "the number of companies electing LIFO will rise dramatically," says William Spiro of BDO Seidman, New York.

Source: The Wall Street Journal, April 27, 1989.

Using Inventory Methods Consistently

The method of inventory costing selected by a company should be used consistently from one accounting period to another. Consistent application enhances the comparability of financial statements over successive time periods. In contrast, using the FIFO method in one year and the LIFO method in the next year would make it difficult to compare the net incomes of the two years.

Although consistent application is preferred, it does not mean that a company may *never* change its method of inventory costing. When a different method is adopted, there should be disclosure in the financial statements of the change and its effects on net income. A typical disclosure is shown in Illustration 9-13, using information from recent financial statements of the Quaker Oats Company.

ILLUSTRATION 9-13

Disclosure of change in inventory method

Notes to the Financial Statements:

Note 1 Effective July 1, the Company adopted the LIFO cost flow assumption for valuing the majority of U.S. Grocery Products inventories. The Company believes that the use of the LIFO method better matches current costs with current revenues. The effect of this change on the current year was to decrease net income by $16.0 million.

More will be said about consistency in later chapters.

Perpetual Inventory Systems

Study Objective 5

List the essential accounting features of a perpetual inventory system.

Companies that sell merchandise with high unit values, such as automobiles, furniture, and major home appliances, usually use a perpetual inventory system. The perpetual inventory system is so named because the accounting records continuously (perpetually) show the quantity and cost of the inventory that should be on hand at any time. The accounting features of a perpetual inventory system are:

1. Purchases of merchandise for resale are debited to Inventory rather than to Purchases.
2. Freight-in, purchase returns and allowances, and purchase discounts are recorded in Inventory rather than in separate accounts.
3. Cost of goods sold is recognized for each sale by debiting the account, Cost of Goods Sold, and crediting Inventory.
4. Inventory is a control account that is supported by a subsidiary ledger of individual inventory records. The subsidiary records show the quantity and cost of each type of inventory on hand.

Journalizing Transactions

To illustrate the journalizing of transactions under a perpetual inventory system, we will show how entries are recorded in both a perpetual and a periodic inventory system for Astro Energy, Inc. Transaction and other data pertaining to solar panels, Model A2776 are as follows:

ILLUSTRATION 9-14

*Comparative entries—
periodic vs perpetual*

Periodic System		Perpetual System	
1. There are 4 units in beginning inventory at a cost of $3,000 each.			
The inventory account shows the inventory on hand at $12,000		The inventory account shows the inventory on hand at $12,000	
2. Purchase 12 panels on account at $3,000 each			
Purchases	36,000	Inventory	36,000
Accounts Payable	36,000	Accounts Payable	36,000
3. Return one defective panel for $3,000 credit.			
Accounts Payable	3,000	Accounts Payable	3,000
Purchase Returns and Allowances	3,000	Inventory	3,000
4. Sell 7 panels on account for $5,000 each.			
Accounts Receivable	35,000	Accounts Receivable	35,000
Sales	35,000	Sales	35,000
		Cost of Goods Sold	21,000
		Inventory	21,000
5. End of period entries for inventory accounts (8 units on hand at $3,000 each)			
Closing entries are necessary:		No entries are necessary:	
Income Summary	12,000	The account, Inventory, shows the ending balance, $24,000 ($12,000 + $36,000 − $3,000 − $21,000)	
Merchandise Inventory (Beginning)	12,000		
Merchandise Inventory (Ending)	24,000		
Income Summary	24,000		

Note that in a perpetual system, two entries are required when a sale occurs. Also no closing entries are required for the inventory account at the end of an accounting period. The reason is that the account balance shows the amount of goods that should be on hand. If the physical inventory count confirms this amount, no entries are needed. However, if the physical inventory count does not agree with the balance shown in the control account, an entry will be necessary to make the inventory balance agree with the goods actually on hand. A difference is usually a shortage caused by spoilage or theft. In such a case, an adjusting entry is made in which Cost of Goods Sold is debited and Inventory is credited.

Accounting in Action · *International Insight*

U.S. companies typically choose between LIFO and FIFO. Most choose LIFO because it reduces inventory profits and taxes. However, the international community is considering rules that would ban LIFO entirely and force companies to use FIFO. If this rule were adopted, it would put great pressure on U.S. companies to follow.

The issue is sensitive. As John Wulff, controller for Union Carbide noted, "We were in support of the international effort up until the proposal to eliminate LIFO." Wulff says that if Union Carbide had been suddenly forced to switch from LIFO to FIFO in 1990, its reported $632 million pretax income would have jumped by $300 million. That would have increased Carbide's income tax bill by as much as $120 million.

Do you believe that accounting principles and rules should be the same around the world?

Maintaining the Subsidiary Ledger

As indicated above, the subsidiary ledger consists of individual inventory records for each type of inventory. A typical record is shown in Illustration 9-15, using assumed data. The record shows transaction data for purchases and sales, and the balance on hand. In addition, the record gives the type and model number of the inventory, the location of the goods in the storeroom or warehouse, and suggested minimum and maximum quantities. As in the case of individual customer accounts in the accounts receivable subsidiary ledger, the individual inventory records in the subsidiary ledger are updated after each transaction.

ILLUSTRATION 9-15

Subsidiary ledger inventory record

Item	12" Television Sets						Location: Warehouse 2		Aisle 4	
Model No.	TR65						Maximum Units 30		Minimum Units 5	

	Purchases			Sales			Balance		
Date	Units	Cost	Total	Units	Cost	Total	Units	Cost	Total
1/1							10	$120	$1,200
5				4	$120	$480	6	120	720
8	15	$120	$1,800				21	120	2,520
14				5	120	600	16	120	1,920
20				7	120	840	9	120	1,080
24	10	120	1,200				19	120	2,280
30				8	120	960	11	120	1,320

A perpetual inventory system contributes to better control over inventories than a periodic system. Since the inventory records show the quantities that should be on hand, the goods can be counted at any time to see whether they actually exist. Any shortages uncovered can be investigated immediately. Further, the maximum quantity shown on the inventory record helps prevent over-investment in inventory, and the minimum quantity protects the company from losing sales on "out-of-stock" items.

A major disadvantage of a perpetual inventory system is the additional clerical work and cost involved in maintaining the subsidiary ledger. This difficulty is minimized when a computerized system is used.

Technology in Action

A major benefit of automated accounting systems is that transactions are processed soon after actual occurrence. Large department stores and supermarkets use electronic point-of-sales systems. In these systems, the cash registers are, in effect, computer terminals. Information that can be gathered and processed at the time of an ordinary sale of merchandise includes:

1. Update the perpetual inventory records, indicating if more items need to be ordered from suppliers.
2. Identify the time, date, and place of sale and who sold the item.
3. Verify the selling price of the item, taking any markdowns into account.
4. Check the credit standing of the customer, alerting the checker if the customer is over the credit limit, delinquent in payment, or is using a stolen card.

The use of scanners permits faster, more accurate, and less costly entry of the data into the system.

Applying Costing Methods

The inventory costing methods described earlier for periodic inventory systems also apply to perpetual systems. The specific identification method is the same for either system. However, there are several significant differences in using the cost flow assumption methods. These differences are explained and illustrated in Appendix E.

Valuing Inventory at the Lower of Cost or Market (LCM)

Study Objective 6

Explain the lower of cost or market basis of accounting for inventories.

Suppose you are the owner of a retail store that sells Compaq Desk Pro computers. During a recent 12-month period, the cost of the computers dropped $1,800 (almost 50%). At the end of your fiscal year, you have some of these computers in inventory. Do you think your inventory should be stated at cost, in accordance with the cost principle, or at its lower replacement cost?

In such a case, accountants take the position that (1) a departure from the cost basis of accounting is justified and (2) a writedown to market should be recognized in the period in which the price decline occurs. This is accomplished by valuing the inventory at the lower of cost or market (LCM). LCM is an example of the accounting concept of conservatism. **Conservatism** means that when choosing among accounting alternatives, the best choice is to select the method that is least likely to overstate assets and net income.

Under the LCM basis, market is defined as current replacement cost, not selling price. For a merchandising company, market is the cost of purchasing the same goods at the present time from the usual suppliers in the usual quantities. Current replacement cost is used because a decline in the replacement cost of an item usually leads to a decline in the selling price of the item.

Financial Statement Effects

To illustrate the comparative effects on the income statement, we will use assumed cost of goods available for sales data for the Judson Company. The ending inventory on a cost basis is $75,000; on the LCM basis the ending inventory is $70,000.

ILLUSTRATION 9-16

Comparison of cost basis with LCM basis

Cost		LCM	
Beginning inventory	$ 65,000	Beginning inventory	$ 65,000
Cost of goods purchased	435,000	Cost of goods purchased	435,000
Cost of goods available for sale	500,000	Cost of goods available for sale	500,000
Ending inventory	75,000	Ending inventory	70,000
Cost of goods sold	$425,000	Cost of goods sold	$430,000

The cost of goods sold is higher under LCM than under cost. The difference is the writedown of the inventory from cost to market in the period in which the price decline occurred.

When inventory is valued at market, many companies show the cost of the inventory in parentheses as shown in Illustration 9-17.

ILLUSTRATION 9-17

Balance sheet presentation showing inventory valuation

JUDSON COMPANY	
Partial Balance Sheet	
Current assets	
Cash	$xxxxxx
Accounts receivable	xxxxxx
Inventory at lower of cost ($75,000) or market	70,000
Total current assets	$xxxxxx

Lower of cost or market may also be disclosed in notes to the financial statements, as shown in Illustration 9-27 on page 378.

Methods of Applying LCM

The lower of cost or market basis may be applied to individual items of inventory, major categories of inventory, or total inventory. For example, assume that Len's TV has the following lines of merchandise with costs and market values as indicated. LCM produces the following three results:

ILLUSTRATION 9-18

Alternative lower of cost or market results

			Lower of Cost or Market by:		
	Cost	Market	Individual Items	Major Categories	Total Inventory
Television sets					
Consoles	$ 60,000	$ 55,000	$ 55,000		
Portables	45,000	52,000	45,000		
Total	105,000	107,000		$105,000	
Video equipment					
Recorders	48,000	45,000	45,000		
Movies	15,000	14,000	14,000		
Total	63,000	59,000		59,000	
Total inventory	$168,000	$166,000	$159,000	$164,000	$166,000

The amount entered in the individual items column is the lower of the cost or market amount for **each item**. For the major categories column, the amount is the lower of the total cost or total market for **each category**. Finally, the amount for the total inventory column is the lower of the cost or market for the **entire inventory**. The common practice is to use individual items in determining the LCM valuation. This approach gives the most conservative valuation for balance sheet purposes and also the lowest net income. LCM should be applied consistently from period to period.

Before You Go On . . .

1. What factors should be considered by management in selecting an inventory method?

2. What are the accounting features of a perpetual inventory system?

3. When is it appropriate to value inventories at the lower of cost or market?

Estimating Inventories

Study Objective 7

Describe the two methods of estimating inventories.

Two circumstances explain the reasons for estimating rather than counting inventories. First, management may want monthly or quarterly financial statements but a physical inventory is taken only annually. Second, a fire or other type of casualty may make it impossible to take a physical inventory. The need for estimating inventories is associated primarily with a periodic inventory system because of the absence of detailed inventory records. There are two widely used methods of estimating inventories: (1) the gross profit method and (2) the retail inventory method.

Gross Profit Method

The gross profit method estimates the ending inventory by applying a gross profit rate to net sales. It is widely used in preparing monthly financial statements when physical inventories are not taken. This method is a relatively simple but effective estimation technique. To use this method, a company needs to know its sales revenue, cost of goods available for sale, and gross profit rate. The company then uses the gross profit rate to estimate its gross profit for the accounting period. The formulas for using the gross profit method are given in Illustration 9-19.

ILLUSTRATION 9-19

Gross profit method formulas

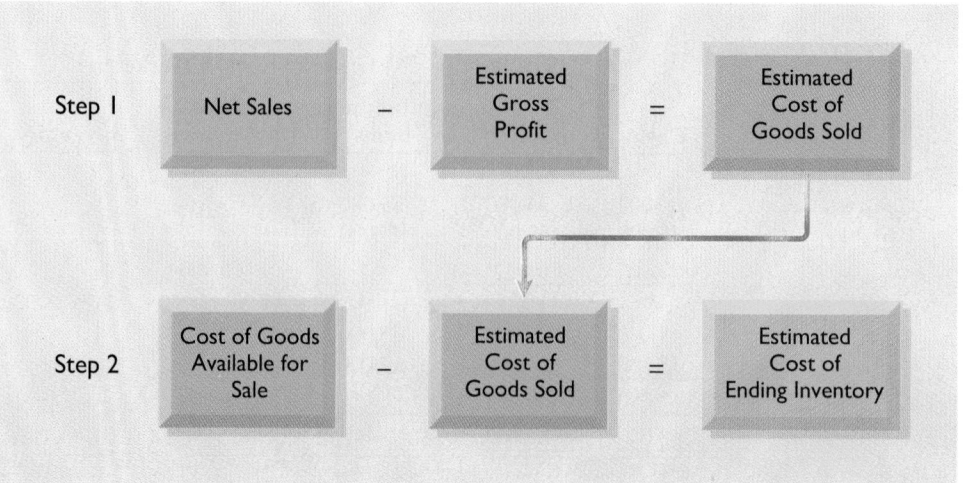

To illustrate, assume that Williams Company wishes to prepare an income statement for the month of January, when its records show net sales, $200,000; beginning inventory, $40,000; and cost of goods purchased, $120,000. In the preceding year, the company realized a 30% gross profit rate, and it expects to earn the same rate this year. Given these facts and assumptions, the estimated cost of the ending inventory at January 31 under the gross profit method is $20,000, computed in Illustration 9-20 as follows:

ILLUSTRATION 9-20

Illustration of gross profit method

	Net sales	$200,000
(1)	Less: Estimated gross profit (30% × $200,000)	60,000
	Estimated cost of goods sold	$140,000
	Beginning inventory	$ 40,000
	Cost of goods purchased	120,000
(2)	Cost of goods available for sale	160,000
	Less: Estimated cost of goods sold	140,000 ←
	Estimated cost of ending inventory	$ 20,000

The gross profit method is based on the assumption that the rate of gross profit will remain constant from one year to the next. It may not remain constant, though, because of a change either in merchandising policies or in market conditions. In such cases, the rate of the prior period should be adjusted to reflect current operating conditions. In some cases, a more accurate estimate may be obtained by applying this method on a department or product-line basis.

The gross profit method should not be used in preparing a company's financial statements at the end of the year. These statements should be based on a physical inventory count.

Retail Inventory Method

A retail store such as K-mart, Ace Hardware, or Wal-Mart has thousands of different types of merchandise at low unit costs. In such cases the application of unit costs to inventory quantities is difficult and time-consuming. An alternative is to use the retail inventory method to estimate the cost of inventory. In most retail concerns, a relationship between cost and sales price can be established. Under the retail inventory method, the cost to retail percentage is then applied to the ending inventory at retail prices to determine inventory at cost.

To use the retail inventory method, a company must maintain records that show both the cost and retail value of the goods available for sale. Under the retail inventory method, the estimated cost of the ending inventory is derived from the formulas presented in Illustration 9-21.

The logic of the retail method can be demonstrated by using unit cost data. Assume that 10 units purchased at $7.00 each are marked to sell for $10 per unit. Thus, the cost to retail ratio is 70% ($70 ÷ $100). If 4 units remain unsold, their retail value is $40 and their cost is $28 ($40 × 70%), which agrees with the total cost of goods on hand on a per unit basis (4 × $7).

The application of the retail method based on the accounting records and supplementary data for Lacy Co. is shown in Illustration 9-22.

Note that it is not necessary to take a physical inventory to determine the estimated cost of goods on hand at any given time.

The retail inventory method also facilitates taking a physical inventory at the end of year. With this method, the goods on hand can be valued at the prices marked on the merchandise. The cost to retail ratio is then applied to the goods actually on hand at retail to determine the ending inventory at cost.

ILLUSTRATION 9-21

*Retail inventory method
formulas*

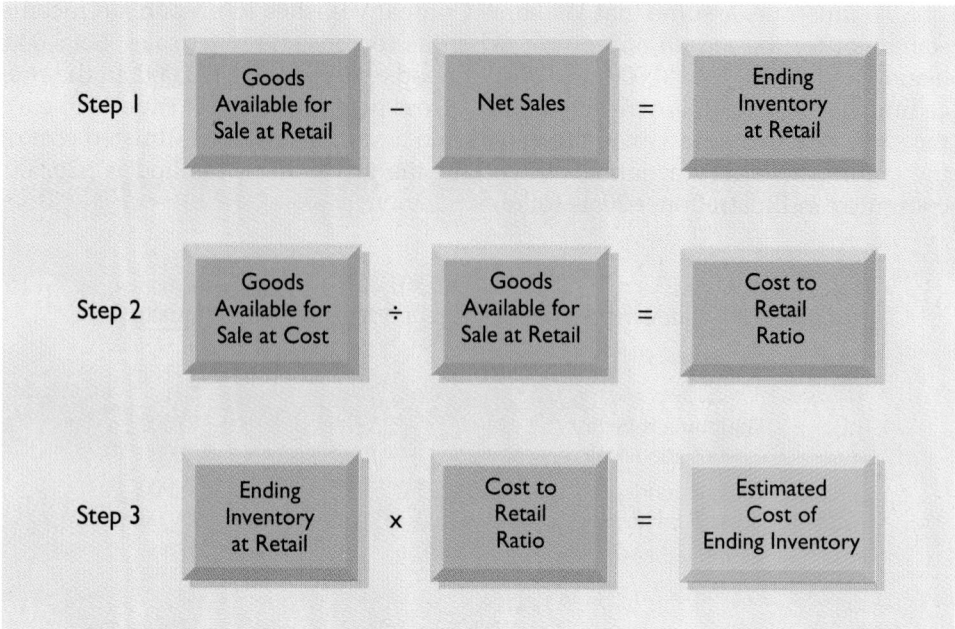

ILLUSTRATION 9-22

*Example of retail inventory
method*

	At Cost	At Retail
Beginning inventory	$14,000	$ 21,500
Goods purchased	61,000	78,500
Goods available for sale	$75,000	100,000
Net sales		70,000
(1) Ending inventory at retail		$ 30,000

(2) Cost to retail ratio = ($75,000 ÷ $100,000) = 75%

(3) Estimated cost of ending inventory = ($30,000 × 75%) $22,500

The major disadvantage of the retail method is that it is an averaging technique. It may produce an incorrect inventory valuation if the mix of the ending inventory is not representative of the mix in the goods available for sale. Assume, for example, that the cost to retail ratio of 75% in the Lacy Co. consists of equal proportions of inventory items that have cost to retail ratios of 70%, 75%, and 80%, respectively. If the ending inventory contains only items with a 70% ratio, an incorrect inventory cost will result. This problem can be minimized by applying the retail method on a departmental or product-line basis.

Inventory Errors

Study Objective 8

*Indicate the effects of
inventory errors on the
financial statements.*

Unfortunately, errors occasionally occur in taking or costing inventory. In some cases, errors are caused by failure to count or price the inventory correctly. In other cases, errors occur because proper recognition is not given to the transfer of legal title to goods that are in transit. When errors occur, they affect both the income statement and the balance sheet.

Income Statement Effects

As you know, both the beginning and ending inventories appear in the income statement. The ending inventory of one period automatically becomes the beginning inventory of the next period. Inventory errors affect the determination of cost of goods sold and net income.

The effects on cost of goods sold can be determined by entering the incorrect data in the following formula and then substituting the correct data.

ILLUSTRATION 9-23

Formula for cost of goods sold

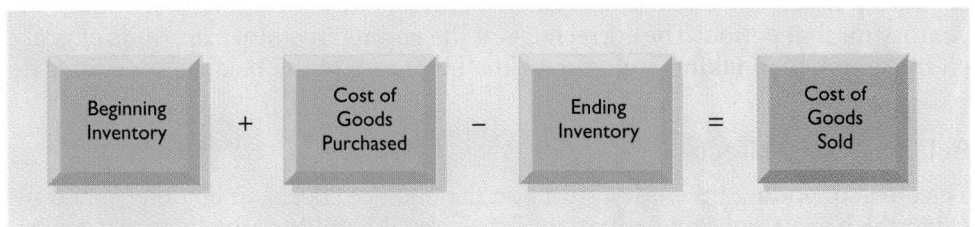

The formula shows that if beginning inventory is understated, cost of goods sold will be understated. On the other hand, an understatement of ending inventory will overstate cost of goods sold. The effects of inventory errors on the current year's income statement are shown in Illustration 9-24.

ILLUSTRATION 9-24

Effects of inventory errors on current year's income statement

Inventory Error	Cost of Goods Sold	Net Income
Understate beginning inventory	Understated	Overstated
Overstate beginning inventory	Overstated	Understated
Understate ending inventory	Overstated	Understated
Overstate ending inventory	Understated	Overstated

An error in ending inventory of the current period will have a reverse effect on net income of the next accounting period. This is shown in Illustration 9-25. Note that the understatement of ending inventory in 1993 results in an understatement of beginning inventory in 1994 and an overstatement of net income in 1994.

ILLUSTRATION 9-25

Effects of inventory errors on two years' income statements

Condensed Income Statement							
	1993				1994		
	Incorrect		Correct		Incorrect		Correct
Sales		$80,000		$80,000		$90,000		$90,000
Beginning inventory	$20,000		$20,000		$12,000		$15,000	
Cost of goods purchased	40,000		40,000		68,000		68,000	
Cost of goods available for sale	60,000		60,000		80,000		83,000	
Ending inventory	12,000		15,000		23,000		23,000	
Cost of goods sold		48,000		45,000		57,000		60,000
Gross profit		32,000		35,000		33,000		30,000
Operating expenses		10,000		10,000		20,000		20,000
Net income		$22,000		$25,000		$13,000		$10,000

($3,000)
Net income understated

$3,000
Net income overstated

Total income for two years correct

Over the two years, total net income is correct because the errors offset one another. Notice that total income using incorrect data is $35,000 ($22,000 + $13,000), which is the same as the total income of $35,000 ($25,000 + $10,000) using correct data. It also should be noted in this example that an error in the beginning inventory does not result in a corresponding error in the ending inventory for that period. The correctness of the ending inventory depends entirely on the accuracy of taking and costing the inventory at the balance sheet date.

Balance Sheet Effects

The effect of ending inventory errors on the balance sheet can be determined by using the basic accounting equation: assets equal liabilities plus owner's equity. Errors in the ending inventory have the following effects on these components:

ILLUSTRATION 9-26

Ending inventory error—balance sheet effects

Ending Inventory Error	Assets	Liabilities	Owner's Equity
Overstated	Overstated	None	Overstated
Understated	Understated	None	Understated

The effect of an error in ending inventory on the subsequent period was shown in Illustration 9-25. Recall that if the error is not corrected, total net income for the two periods would be correct. Thus, total owner's equity reported on the balance sheet at the end of Year two will also be correct.

Financial Statement Presentation

As indicated in an earlier chapter, inventory is classified as a current asset after receivables in the balance sheet, and cost of goods sold is subtracted from sales in the income statement. In addition, there should be disclosure of (1) the major inventory classifications, (2) the basis of accounting (cost or lower of cost or market), and (3) the costing method (FIFO, LIFO, or average).

Colgate-Palmolive Company, for example, reported inventory of $616,067,000 under current assets in a recent balance sheet. The accompanying notes to the financial statements, as shown in Illustration 9-27, disclosed the following information:

ILLUSTRATION 9-27

Inventory disclosures

Colgate-Palmolive Company
Note 1. Inventories Inventories are valued at the lower of cost or market. The last-in, first-out (LIFO) method is used to value substantially all inventories in the U.S. as well as in certain overseas locations. The remaining inventories are valued using the first-in, first-out (FIFO) method.

Before You Go On . . .

1. What formulas are used to estimate the ending inventory under the gross profit method?

2. What formulas are used to estimate the ending inventory under the retail inventory method?

3. How do inventory errors affect financial statements?

Summary of Study Objectives

1. *Describe the steps in determining inventory quantities.* The steps in determining inventory quantities are: (1) taking a physical inventory of goods on hand, and (2) determining the ownership of goods in transit.

2. *Explain the basis of accounting for inventories and describe the inventory costing methods.* The primary basis of accounting for inventories is cost. Cost includes all expenditures necessary to acquire goods and place them in condition ready for sale. Inventoriable costs include the invoice price plus freight-in less purchase discounts and purchase returns and allowances. The inventory costing methods are: specific identification, FIFO, LIFO, and average cost.

3. *Explain the financial statement effects of each of the inventory costing methods.* The cost of goods available for sale may be allocated to cost of goods sold and ending inventory by specific identification or by a method based on an assumed cost flow. These methods have different effects on financial statements during periods of changing prices. When prices are rising, the first-in, first-out method (FIFO) results in lower cost of goods sold and higher net income than the average and the last-in, first-out (LIFO) methods. The reverse is true when prices are falling. In the balance sheet, FIFO results in an ending inventory that is closest to current value, whereas the inventory under LIFO is the farthest from current value.

4. *Identify the factors to consider in selecting an inventory costing method.* The selection of an inventory costing method is a management decision that usually involves one of the following: (a) balance sheet effects, (b) income statement effects, or (c) tax effects.

5. *List the essential accounting features of a perpetual inventory system.* Under a perpetual inventory system, (a) purchases of merchandise for resale are debited to Inventory, (b) all transactions that affect cost of goods purchased are recorded in Inventory, (c) the cost of goods sold is recognized each time a sale occurs by a debit to Cost of Goods Sold and a credit to Inventory, and (d) Inventory is a control account that is supported by a subsidiary ledger of individual inventory records.

6. *Explain the lower of cost or market basis of accounting for inventories.* The lower of cost or market basis (LCM) may be used when the current replacement cost (market) is less than cost. Under LCM, the loss is recognized in the period in which the price decline occurs. LCM may be applied to individual inventory items, major categories of inventory, or to total inventory.

7. *Describe the two methods of estimating inventories.* The two methods of estimating inventories are the gross profit method and the retail inventory method. Under the gross profit method, a gross profit rate is applied to net sales to determine estimated cost of goods sold. Estimated cost of goods sold is then subtracted from cost of goods available for sale to determine the estimated cost of the ending inventory. Under the retail inventory method, a cost to retail ratio is computed by dividing the cost of goods available for sale by the retail value of the goods available for sale. This ratio is then applied to the ending inventory at retail to determine the estimated cost of the ending inventory.

8. *Indicate the effects of inventory errors on the financial statements.* In the income statement of the current year: (a) an error in beginning inventory will have a reverse effect on net income (overstatement of inventory results in understatement of net income) and (b) an error in ending inventory will have a similar effect on net income (overstatement of inventory results in overstatement of net income). If ending inventory errors are not corrected in the following period, their effect on net income for that period is reversed, and total net income for the two years will be correct. In the balance sheet, ending inventory errors will have the same effect on total assets and total owner's equity and no effect on liabilities.

APPENDIX E Inventory Costing in
Perpetual Inventory Systems

Study Objective

After studying Appendix E, you should be able to:

9. Apply the inventory costing methods to perpetual inventory records.

ILLUSTRATION E-1

Purchases and sales data

Each of the inventory costing methods described in the chapter for a periodic inventory system may be used in a perpetual inventory system. To illustrate the application of the three assumed cost flow methods (FIFO, average cost, and LIFO), we will use the data shown in Illustration E-1 for model X268L4 Econo radios in the Home Appliance Mart.

Date	Purchases	Sale	Balance in Units
April 3	4,000 @ $8.00		4,000
April 10	12,000 @ $8.80		16,000
April 26		8,000 units	8,000
April 29	4,000 @ $8.30		12,000

First-In, First-Out (FIFO)

Under FIFO, the cost of the earliest goods on hand prior to each sale is charged to cost of goods sold. Therefore, the cost of goods sold on April 26 consists of the items purchased on April 3 and April 10. The inventory on a FIFO method perpetual system is shown in Illustration E-2:

ILLUSTRATION E-2

Perpetual system—FIFO

Date	Purchases		Sales	Balance	
April 3	(4,000 @ $8.00)	$ 32,000		(4,000 @ $8.00)	$ 32,000
April 10	(12,000 @ $8.80)	$105,600		(4,000 @ $8.00) ⎱ (12,000 @ $8.80) ⎰	$137,600
April 26			(4,000 @ $8.00) (4,000 @ $8.80) ———————— ($67,200)	(8,000 @ $8.80)	$ 70,400
April 29	(4,000 @ $8.30)	$ 33,200		(8,000 @ $8.80) ⎱ (4,000 @ $8.30) ⎰	$103,600

The ending inventory in this situation is $103,600 and the cost of goods sold is $67,200 [(4,000 @ $8.00) + (4,000 @ $8.80)].

The results under FIFO in a perpetual system are the same as in a periodic system. Regardless of the system, the first costs in are the first costs assigned to cost of goods sold.

Average Cost

The average cost method is called the **moving average method** in a perpetual inventory system. Under this method a new average is computed **after each purchase**. The average cost is computed by dividing the cost of goods available for sale by the units on hand. The average cost is then applied to: (1) the units sold, to determine the cost of goods sold, and (2) the remaining units on hand, to determine the ending inventory amount. The application of the average cost method for Home Appliance Mart is shown in Illustration E-3.

Date	Purchases		Sales	Balance	
April 3	(4,000 @ $8.00)	$ 32,000		(4,000 @ $8.00)	$ 32,000
April 10	(12,000 @ $8.80)	$105,600		(16,000 @ $8.60)	$137,600
April 26			8,000 @ $8.60	(8,000 @ $8.60)	$ 68,800
			($68,800)		
April 29	(4,000 @ $8.30)	$ 33,200		(12,000 @ $8.50)	$102,000

ILLUSTRATION E-3

Perpetual system—average cost

As indicated above, a new average is computed each time a purchase is made. On April 10, after 12,000 units are purchased for $105,600, a total of 16,000 units costing $137,600 ($32,000 + $105,600) are on hand. The average unit cost is $137,600 divided by 16,000, or $8.60. This unit cost is used in costing withdrawals until another purchase is made, when a new unit cost is computed. Accordingly, the unit cost of the 8,000 units sold on April 26 is shown at $8.60, and the total cost of goods sold is $68,800. On April 29, following the purchase of 4,000 units for $33,200, there are 12,000 units on hand costing $102,000 ($68,800 + $33,200). The new average cost is $8.50 ($102,000 ÷ 12,000).

Last-In, First-Out (LIFO)

Under the LIFO method using a perpetual system, the cost of the most recent purchase prior to sale is allocated to the units sold. Therefore, the cost of the goods sold on April 26 consists entirely of goods from the April 10 purchase. The ending inventory on a LIFO method is computed in Illustration E-4.

Date	Purchases		Sales	Balance	
April 3	(4,000 @ $8.00)	$ 32,000		(4,000 @ $8.00)	$ 32,000
April 10	(12,000 @ $8.80)	$105,600		(4,000 @ $8.00) (12,000 @ $8.80)	$137,600
April 26			8,000 @ $8.80 ($70,400)	(4,000 @ $8.00) (4,000 @ $8.80)	$ 67,200
April 29	(4,000 @ $8.30)	$ 33,200		(4,000 @ $8.00) (4,000 @ $8.80) (4,000 @ $8.30)	$100,400

ILLUSTRATION E-4

Perpetual system—LIFO

The use of LIFO in a perpetual system will usually produce cost allocations that differ from using LIFO in a periodic system. In a perpetual system, the latest units incurred **prior to each sale** are allocated to cost of goods sold. In contrast, in a periodic system, the latest units incurred during the period are allocated to cost of goods sold.[1] The ending inventory in this example is $100,400 and the cost of goods sold is $70,400.

---

[1]Thus, when a purchase is made after the last sale for the period, the periodic method will apply this purchase to the previous sale. In the example, 4,000 at $8.30 and 4,000 at $8.80, or $68,400 would be allocated to cost of goods sold in April under the LIFO periodic method—leaving an ending inventory of $102,400.

*S*ummary of Study Objectives for Appendix E

9. *Apply the inventory costing methods to perpetual inventory records.* Under FIFO, the cost of the earliest goods on hand prior to each sale is charged to cost of goods sold. Under the average cost method, a new average cost is computed after each purchase. Under LIFO, the cost of the most recent purchase prior to sale is charged to cost of goods sold.

GLOSSARY

Average cost method · An inventory costing method that assumes that the goods available for sale are homogeneous. (p. 366).

Consigned goods · Goods shipped by a consignor who retains ownership to another party called the consignee. (p. 361).

Current replacement cost · The current cost to replace an inventory item. (p. 372).

First-in, first-out method (FIFO) · An inventory costing method that assumes that the costs of the earliest goods acquired are the first to be recognized as cost of goods sold. (p. 364).

Gross profit method · A method for estimating the ending inventory by applying a gross profit rate to net sales. (p. 374).

Inventoriable costs · The pool of costs that consists of two elements: (1) the cost of the beginning inventory and (2) the cost of goods purchased during the period. (p. 361).

Inventory summary sheets · A listing of the quantities and costs of each inventory item as a result of a physical inventory. (p. 360).

Last-in, first-out method (LIFO) · An inventory costing method that assumes that the costs of the latest units purchased are the first to be allocated to cost of goods sold. (p. 365).

Lower of cost or market basis (LCM) (inventories) · A basis whereby inventory is stated at the lower of cost or market (current replacement cost). (p. 372).

Perpetual inventory system · An inventory system in which the quantity and cost of each inventory item is maintained and the records continuously show the inventory that should be on hand at any time. (p. 370).

Retail inventory method · A method used to estimate the cost of the ending inventory by applying a cost to retail ratio to the ending inventory at retail. (p. 375).

Specific identification method · An actual physical flow costing method in which items still in inventory are specifically costed to arrive at the total cost of the ending inventory. (p. 363).

DEMONSTRATION PROBLEM

The Helmers Company has the following inventory, purchases, and sales data for the month of March:

Inventory, March 1		200 units @ $4.00	$ 800
Purchases:			
	March 10	500 units @ $4.50	2,250
	March 20	400 units @ $4.75	1,900
	March 30	300 units @ $5.00	1,500
Sales:			
	March 15	500 units	
	March 25	400 units	

Helmers Company uses a periodic inventory system. The physical inventory count on March 31 shows 500 units on hand.

Instructions

Determine the cost of inventory on hand at March 31 and the cost of goods sold for March under the (a) first-in, first-out (FIFO) method, (b) last-in, first-out (LIFO) method, and (c) average cost method.

Solution to Demonstration Problem

The cost of goods available for sale is $6,450:

Inventory		200 units @ $4.00	$ 800
Purchases:			
	March 10	500 units @ $4.50	2,250
	March 20	400 units @ $4.75	1,900
	March 30	300 units @ $5.00	1,500
	Total cost of goods available for sale		$6,450

The allocation of the pool of costs is as follows:

FIFO Method

Ending Inventory:

Date	Units	Unit Cost	Total Cost	
March 30	300	$5.00	$1,500	
March 20	200	4.75	950	$2,450

Cost of goods sold: $6,450 − $2,450 = $4,000

LIFO Method

Ending Inventory:

Date	Units	Unit Cost	Total Cost	
March 1	200	$4.00	$ 800	
March 10	300	4.50	1,350	$2,150

Cost of goods sold: $6,450 − $2,150 = $4,300

Average Cost Method

Weighted average unit cost: $6,450 ÷ 1,400 = $4.607

Ending inventory: 500 × $4.607 = $2,303.50

Cost of goods sold: $6,450 − $2,303.50 = $4,146.50

Helpful hints
1. For FIFO, the latest costs are allocated to inventory.
2. For LIFO, the earliest costs are allocated to inventory.
3. For average costs, use a weighted average.
4. Remember, the costs allocated to cost of goods sold can be proved.
5. Total purchases are the same under all three costing methods.

*Note: All **asterisked** Questions, Exercises, and Problems relate to material contained in the appendix to each chapter.

SELF-STUDY QUESTIONS

Answers are at the end of the chapter.

(S.O. 1)

1. Which of the following should *not* be included in the physical inventory of a company?
   a. Goods shipped on consignment to another company.
   b. Goods held on consignment from another company.
   c. Goods in transit from another company shipped FOB shipping point.
   d. None of the above.

2. Inventoriable costs consist of two elements: beginning inventory and   (S.O. 2)
   a. cost of goods purchased.
   b. ending inventory.

c. cost of goods sold.

d. cost of goods available for sale.

(S.O. 2) 3. Kam Company has the following:

	Units	Unit Cost
Inventory, Jan. 1	9,000	$11
Purchase, June 19	13,000	12
Purchase, Nov. 8	5,000	13

If 10,000 units are on hand at December 31, the cost of the ending inventory under FIFO is:

a. $130,000.

b. $125,000.

c. $120,000.

d. $100,000.

(S.O. 2) 4. Using the data in (3) above, the cost of the ending inventory under LIFO is:

a. $130,000.

b. $125,000.

c. $111,000.

d. $120,000.

(S.O. 3) 5. In periods of rising prices, LIFO will produce:

a. higher net income than FIFO.

b. lower net income than FIFO.

c. the same net income as FIFO.

d. higher net income than average costing.

(S.O. 4) 6. Factors that affect the selection of an inventory costing method do *not* include:

a. perpetual vs. periodic inventory system.

b. balance sheet effects.

c. income statement effects.

d. tax effects.

(S.O. 5) 7. Which of the following statements is *incorrect* concerning a perpetual inventory system?

a. A perpetual inventory system contributes to better control over inventories.

b. Accounting records continuously show the inventory that should be on hand at any point in time.

c. Purchases are debited to Inventory.

d. The cost of goods sold is recognized when each sale occurs by debiting Cost of Goods Sold and crediting Purchases.

8. The LCM basis may be applied to: (S.O. 6)

a. individual items of inventories.

b. categories of inventories.

c. total inventory.

d. all of the above.

9. Somers Company has sales of $150,000   (S.O. 7) and cost of goods available for sale of $135,000. If the gross profit rate is 40%, the estimated cost of the ending inventory under the gross profit method is:

a. $18,000.

b. $32,000.

c. $45,000.

d. $75,000.

10. In Fran Company, ending inventory is   (S.O. 8) understated $4,000. The effects of this error on the current year's cost of goods sold and net income, respectively, are:

a. overstated, understated.

b. understated, overstated.

c. overstated, overstated.

d. understated, understated.

*11. In a perpetual inventory system,   (S.O. 9)

a. LIFO cost of goods sold will be the same as in a periodic inventory system.

b. average costs are based entirely on unit cost averages.

c. FIFO cost of goods sold will be the same as in a periodic inventory system.

d. a new average is computed under the average cost method after each sale.

QUESTIONS

1. "The key to successful business operations is effective inventory management." Do you agree? Explain.

2. An item must possess two characteristics to be classified as inventory. What are these two characteristics?

3. Your friend Jim has been hired to help take the physical inventory in Casey's Hardware Store. Explain to Jim what this job will entail.

4. (a) Debby Company ships merchandise to Mitchell Corporation on December 30. The merchandise reaches the buyer on January 5. Indicate the terms of sale that will result in the goods being included in (1) Debby's December 31 inventory, and (2) Mitchell's December 31 inventory.

(b) Under what circumstances should Debby Company include consigned goods in its inventory?

5. Joan's Hat Shop received a shipment of hats for which it paid the wholesaler $2,940. The price of the hats was $3,000, but Joan's was given a $60 cash discount and required to pay freight charges of $50. In addition, Joan's paid $100 to cover the travel expenses of an employee who negotiated the purchase of the hats. What amount should Joan's include in inventory? Why?

6. What is the primary basis of accounting for inventories? What is the major objective in accounting for inventories? What accounting principles are involved here?

7. Dave Wies believes that the allocation of inventoriable costs should be based on the actual physical flow of the goods. Explain to Dave why this may be both impractical and inappropriate.

8. What is a major advantage and a major disadvantage of the specific identification method of inventory costing?

9. "The selection of an inventory cost method is an accounting decision." Do you agree? Explain. Once a method has been selected, what accounting requirement applies?

10. Which assumed cost flow inventory costing method:
(a) usually parallels the actual physical flow of merchandise?
(b) assumes that goods available for sale during an accounting period are homogeneous?
(c) assumes that the latest units purchased are the first to be sold?

11. In a period of rising prices, the inventory reported in Plano Company's balance sheet is close to the current cost of the inventory, whereas Yorkville Company's inventory is considerably below its current cost. Identify the inventory costing method being used by each company. Which company has probably been reporting the higher gross profit?

12. Osweg Corporation has been using the FIFO costing method during a prolonged period of inflation. During the same time period, Osweg has been paying out all of its net income as dividends. What adverse effects may result from this policy?

13. Don Lord is uncertain about the accounting features of a perpetual inventory system. Explain these features to Don.

14. Ruth Mullen believes a perpetual inventory system requires a great deal of work for only marginal benefit. Explain to Ruth the advantages of a perpetual inventory system.

15. Lucille Suttor is studying for the next accounting midterm examination. What should Lucille know about (a) departing from the cost basis of accounting for inventories and (b) the meaning of "market" in the lower of cost or market method?

16. Suzy's Music Center has 5 CD players on hand at the balance sheet date that cost $400 each. The current replacement cost is $300 per unit. Under the LCM basis of accounting for inventories, what value should be reported for the CD players on the balance sheet? Why?

17. What methods may be used under the LCM basis of accounting for inventories? Which method will produce the lowest inventory value?

18. Why is it necessary to estimate inventories?

19. Both the gross profit method and the retail inventory method are based on averages. For each method, indicate the average used, how it is determined, and how it is applied.

20. Dan Crest Company has net sales of $360,000 and cost of goods available for sale of $300,000. If the gross profit rate is 30%, what is the estimated cost of the ending inventory? Show computations.

21. Millet Shoe Shop had goods available for sale in 1993 with a retail price of $120,000. The cost of these goods was $84,000. If sales during the period were $100,000, what is the ending inventory at cost using the retail inventory method?

22. Doug Steep Company discovers in 1993 that its ending inventory at December 31, 1992, was $5,000 understated. What effect will this error have on (a) 1992 net income, (b) 1993 net income, and (c) the combined net income for the two years?

23. Richard Gerbe Company's balance sheet shows Inventories $162,800. What additional disclosures should be made?

*24. "When perpetual inventory records are kept, the results under the FIFO and LIFO methods are the same as they would be in a periodic inventory system." Do you agree? Explain.

*25. How does the average method of inventory costing differ between a perpetual inventory system and a periodic inventory system?

BRIEF EXERCISES

Identify items to be included in taking a physical inventory.
(S.O. 1)

BE9–1   The Rosemont Company identifies the following items for possible inclusion in the taking of a physical inventory. Indicate whether each item should be included or excluded from the inventory taking.

    1. Goods held on consignment from another company.
    2. Goods in transit from a supplier shipped FOB destination.
    3. Goods sold but being held for customer pickup.
    4. Goods shipped on consignment by Rosemont to another company.

Identify the components of inventoriable costs.
(S.O. 2)

BE9–2   The ledger of the Wharton Company includes the following items: (1) Freight-in, (2) Purchase Returns and Allowances, (3) Sales Discounts, (4) Purchases, (5) Purchase Discounts. Identify which items are included in inventoriable costs.

Compute ending inventory using FIFO.
(S.O. 2)

BE9–3   In its first month of operations, the Quill Company made three purchases of merchandise in the following sequence: (1) 350 units at $6, (2) 400 units at $7, and (3) 250 units at $8. Compute the cost to be allocated to ending inventory under the FIFO method assuming there are 400 units on hand.

Compute ending inventory using LIFO.
(S.O. 2)

BE9–4   Data for the Quill Company are presented in BE9–3. Compute the cost to be allocated to the ending inventory under the LIFO method assuming there are 400 units on hand.

Compute the ending inventory using average costs.
(S.O. 2)

BE9–5   Data for the Quill Company are presented in BE9–3. Compute the cost to be allocated to the ending inventory under the average cost method assuming there are 400 units on hand.

Journalize transactions in a perpetual inventory system.
(S.O. 5)

BE9–6   The Dyer Company uses a perpetual inventory system. In March, its first month of operations, it has the following transactions: March 3 purchased on account 20 units of Product X at $25 per unit, March 6 returned 2 units for credit, and March 21 sold on account 10 units at $35 per unit. Journalize the three transactions.

Determine the LCM valuation using inventory categories.
(S.O. 6)

BE9–7   The Hawk Appliance Center accumulates the following cost and market data at December 31:

Inventory categories	Cost data	Market data
Cameras	$12,000	$11,200
Camcorders	9,000	9,500
VCRs	14,000	12,800

Compute the lower of cost or market valuation using categories.

Apply the gross profit method.
(S.O. 7)

BE9–8   At May 31, the Jansen Company has net sales of $300,000 and cost of goods available for sale of $220,000. Compute the estimated cost of the ending inventory assuming the gross profit rate is 40%.

Apply the retail inventory method.
(S.O. 7)

BE9–9   On June 30, Hilga's Fabrics has the following data pertaining to the retail inventory method: Goods available for sale: at cost $40,000, at retail $50,000; net sales $30,000, and ending inventory at retail $20,000. Compute the estimated cost of the ending inventory using the retail inventory method.

BE9–10 The Creole Company reports net income of $90,000 in 1993. However, ending inventory was understated $5,000. What is the correct net income for 1993? What effect, if any, will this error have on total assets as reported in the balance sheet at December 31, 1993?

Determine correct income statement amounts.
(S.O. 8)

*****BE9–11** Trumble Department Store uses a perpetual inventory system. Data for Product XX include the following purchases:

Date	Number of units	Unit price
May 5	50	$10
July 29	25	12

Apply FIFO to perpetual records.
(S.O. 9)

On June 1 Trumble sold 30 units, and on August 27, 30 more units. Prepare the perpetual inventory card for the above transactions using the FIFO method of inventory costing.

EXERCISES

E9–1 First Bank and Trust is considering giving Alcorn Company a loan. Before doing so, they decide that further discussions with Alcorn's accountant may be desirable. One area of particular concern is the inventory account, which has a year-end balance of $295,000. Discussions with the accountant reveal the following:

Determine the correct inventory amount.
(S.O. 1, 2)

1. The physical count of the inventory did not include goods costing $95,000 that were shipped to Alcorn FOB destination on December 27, and were still in transit at year-end.

2. Alcorn sold goods costing $35,000 to Peking Company FOB shipping point on December 28. The goods are not expected to arrive in China until January 12. The goods were not included in the physical inventory because they were not in the warehouse.

3. Alcorn received goods costing $25,000 on January 2. The goods were shipped FOB shipping point on December 26 by Cellar Co. The goods were not included in the physical count.

4. Alcorn sold goods costing $40,000 to Sterling of Canada FOB destination on December 30. The goods were received in Canada on January 8. They were not included in Alcorn's physical inventory.

5. Alcorn received goods costing $46,000 on January 2 that were shipped FOB destination on December 29. The shipment was a rush order that was supposed to arrive December 31. This purchase was included in the ending inventory of $295,000.

Instructions
Determine the correct inventory amount on December 31.

E9–2 Mawdey Inc. uses a periodic inventory system. Its records show the following for the month of May, in which 77 units were sold.

Compute inventory and cost of goods sold using FIFO and LIFO.
(S.O. 2)

		Units	Unit Cost	Total Cost
May 1	Inventory	30	$ 8	$240
15	Purchases	25	10	250
24	Purchases	35	12	420
	Totals	90		$910

Instructions
Compute the ending inventory at May 31 using the FIFO and LIFO methods. Prove the amount allocated to cost of goods sold under each method.

E9–3 In June, Durbin Company reports the following for the month of June.

Compute inventory and cost of goods sold using FIFO and LIFO.
(S.O. 2, 3, 4)

		Units	Unit Cost	Total Cost
June 1	Inventory	200	$5	$1,000
12	Purchases	300	6	1,800
23	Purchases	500	7	3,500
30	Inventory	200		

Instructions

(a) Compute the cost of the ending inventory and the cost of goods sold under (1) FIFO and (2) LIFO.

(b) Which costing method gives the higher ending inventory? Why?

(c) Which method results in the higher cost of goods sold? Why?

Compute inventory and cost of goods sold using average costs.
(S.O. 2, 3)

E9–4   Inventory data for the Durbin Company are presented in E9–3.

Instructions

(a) Compute the cost of the ending inventory and the cost of goods sold using the average cost method.

(b) Will the results in (a) be higher or lower than the results under (1) FIFO and (2) LIFO?

(c) Why is the average unit cost not $6?

Journalize and post using a perpetual inventory system.
(S.O. 5)

E9–5   On September 1, College Office Supply had an inventory of 10 high-speed deluxe pocket calculators at a cost of $15 each. The company uses a perpetual inventory system. During September, the following transactions and events occurred.

Sept. 2   Purchased 90 calculators at $15 each from Digital Inc., terms n/30.
        5   Received credit of $60 for the return of four calculators purchased on September 2 that were defective.
        8   Sold 50 calculators for $25 each to University Bookstore, terms 2/10, n/30.
       12   Sold 30 calculators for $25 each to Hilltop Card Shop, terms n/30.
       20   Purchased 20 calculators at $16 each from Sterling Electronics, terms n/30.
       30   Determined that there were 36 calculators on hand.

Instructions
Journalize the September transactions and events.

Determine ending inventory under lower of cost or market inventory method.
(S.O. 6)

E9–6   Cody Camera Shop uses the lower of cost or market basis for its inventory. The following data are available at December 31, 1993.

Item	Units	Unit Cost	Market
Cameras			
Minolta	5	$175	$160
Canon	7	150	152
Light Meters			
Vivitar	12	125	110
Kodak	10	110	135

Instructions
Determine the amount of the ending inventory by applying the lower of cost or market basis to (a) individual items, (b) inventory categories, and (c) the total inventory.

Determine merchandise lost using the gross profit method of estimating inventory.
(S.O. 7)

E9–7   The inventory of Susan Company was destroyed by fire on March 1. From an examination of the accounting records, the following data for the first two months of the year are obtained: Sales $51,000, Sales Returns and Allowances $1,000, Purchases $28,000, Freight-in $1,200, and Purchase Returns and Allowances $1,400.

Instructions
Determine the merchandise lost by fire, assuming

(a) A beginning inventory of $20,000 and a gross profit rate of 30% on net sales.

(b) A beginning inventory of $25,000 and a gross profit rate of 25% on net sales.

Determine ending inventory at cost using retail method.
(S.O. 7)

E9–8   Sharp Shoe Store uses the retail inventory method for its two departments: Women's Shoes and Men's Shoes. The following information for each department is obtained:

Item	Women's Department	Men's Department
Beginning inventory at cost	$ 32,000	$ 46,450
Cost of goods purchased at cost	148,000	137,300
Net sales	188,000	195,000
Beginning inventory at retail	45,000	60,000
Cost of goods purchased at retail	180,000	185,000

Instructions

Compute the estimated cost of the ending inventory for each department under the retail inventory method.

E9–9 Graf Hardware reported cost of goods sold as follows:

	1993	1994
Beginning inventory	$ 20,000	$ 30,000
Cost of goods purchased	150,000	175,000
Cost of goods available for sale	170,000	205,000
Ending inventory	30,000	35,000
Cost of goods sold	$140,000	$170,000

Graf made two errors: (1) 1993 ending inventory was overstated $4,000 and (2) 1994 ending inventory was understated $5,000.

Determine effects of inventory errors.
(S.O. 8)

Instructions

Compute the correct cost of goods sold for each year.

E9–10 Aruba Company reported the following income statement data for a two-year period.

	1993	1994
Sales	$210,000	$250,000
Cost of goods sold		
Beginning inventory	32,000	40,000
Cost of goods purchased	173,000	202,000
Cost of goods available for sale	205,000	242,000
Ending inventory	40,000	52,000
Cost of goods sold	165,000	190,000
Gross profit	$ 45,000	$ 60,000

Aruba uses a periodic inventory system. The inventories at January 1, 1993, and December 31, 1994, are correct. However, the ending inventory at December 31, 1993, was overstated $4,000.

Prepare correct income statements.
(S.O. 8)

Instructions

(a) Prepare correct income statement data for the two years.

(b) What is the cumulative effect of the inventory error on total gross profit for the two years?

*E9–11 Stracka Appliance uses a perpetual inventory system. For its model B47 television sets, the January 1 inventory was four sets at $600 each. During January, the following purchase was made: Jan. 10, 6 units at $640 each. That month, the company had the following sales: Jan. 8, 2 units and Jan. 15, 5 units.

Apply costing methods to perpetual records.
(S.O. 9)

Instructions

Compute the ending inventory under (1) FIFO, (2) LIFO, and (3) average cost.

PROBLEMS

P9–1 Kane Company had a beginning inventory on January 1 of 100 units of Product SXL at a cost of $20 per unit. During the year, the following purchases were made.

Mar. 15	300 units at $24	Sept. 4	300 units at $28
July 20	200 units at 25	Dec. 2	100 units at 30

800 units were sold. Kane Company uses a periodic inventory system.

Determine cost of goods sold and ending inventory, using FIFO, LIFO, and average cost with analysis.
(S.O. 1, 2, 3, 4)

Instructions

(a) Determine the cost of goods available for sale.

(b) Determine (1) the ending inventory, and (2) the cost of goods sold under each of the assumed cost flow methods (FIFO, LIFO, and average). Prove the accuracy of the cost of goods sold under the FIFO and LIFO methods.

(c) Which costing method results in (1) the highest inventory amount for the balance sheet and (2) the highest cost of goods sold for the income statement?

Compute ending inven-
tory, prepare income
statements and answer
questions using FIFO
and LIFO.
(S.O. 1, 2, 3, 4)

P9–2   The management of Tumatoe Inc. asks your help in determining the comparative effects of the FIFO and LIFO cost flow inventory costing methods. For 1993, the accounting records show the following data:

Inventory, January 1 (10,000 units)	$ 35,000
Cost of 110,000 units purchased	460,000
Selling price of 95,000 units sold	665,000
Operating expenses	110,000

Units purchased consisted of 40,000 units at $4.00 on May 10; 50,000 units at $4.20 on August 15; and 20,000 units at $4.50 on November 20. Income taxes are 30%.

Instructions

(a) Prepare comparative condensed income statements for 1993 under FIFO and LIFO. (Show computations of ending inventory.)

(b) Answer the following questions for management:
   (1) Which inventory costing method produces the most meaningful inventory amount for the balance sheet? Why?
   (2) Which inventory costing method produces the most meaningful net income? Why?
   (3) Which inventory costing method is most likely to approximate actual physical flow of the goods? Why?
   (4) How much additional cash will be available for management under LIFO than under FIFO? Why?
   (5) How much of the gross profit under FIFO is illusionary in comparison with the gross profit under LIFO?

Determine LCM valuation
and prepare financial
statements.
(S.O. 6)

P9–3   Banker Appliance Company uses the lower of cost or market (LCM) basis for valuing inventory. Your assistant accountant accumulates the following cost and market data at December 31, 1993.

Item	Quantity	Total Cost	Total Market
Home Freezers			
Y296	20	$ 7,500	$ 7,600
X437	15	6,000	6,300
Total		13,500	13,900
Refrigerators			
T417	12	3,900	3,600
R208	20	7,000	6,400
Total		10,900	10,000
Portable TVs			
A919	5	1,000	1,050
B738	10	2,500	2,300
Total		3,500	3,350
Total inventory		$27,900	$27,250

For the year, net sales for these items were $320,000, beginning inventory was $22,000, and the cost of goods purchased was $260,000.

Instructions

(a) Prepare a schedule showing the inventory valuation under LCM using each of the three methods of application.

(b) Prepare comparative income statements for the year through gross profit using (1) the cost basis and (2) the LCM basis. Use the individual units method for LCM.

(c) In the current asset section of the balance sheet, show the LCM data at December 31. Use the individual units method for LCM.

(d) Which method of applying LCM is most conservative? Why?

Compute gross profit rate
and inventory loss using
gross profit method.
(S.O. 7)

P9–4   Mill Van Company lost all of its inventory in a fire on December 28, 1993. The accounting records showed the following gross profit data for November and December.

	November	December (to 12/28)
Net sales	$400,000	$300,000
Beginning inventory	22,100	29,100
Purchases	314,975	236,000
Purchase returns and allowances	11,800	4,000
Purchase discounts	8,577	6,000
Freight-in	4,402	1,700
Ending inventory	29,100	?

Van is fully insured for fire losses but must prepare a report for the insurance company.

Instructions

(a) Compute the gross profit rate for November.

(b) Using the gross profit rate for November, determine the estimated cost of the inventory lost in the fire.

P9–5 Bucky's Book Store uses the retail inventory method to estimate its monthly ending inventories. The following information is available for two of its departments at October 31, 1993.

Compute ending inventory using retail method. (S.O. 7)

	Hardcovers		Paperbacks	
	Cost	Retail	Cost	Retail
Beginning inventory	$ 260,000	$ 400,000	$ 63,000	$ 90,000
Purchases	1,180,000	1,800,000	268,000	380,000
Freight-in	5,000		2,000	
Purchase discounts	15,000		4,000	
Net sales		1,810,000		363,000

At December 31, Bucky's Book Store takes a physical inventory at retail. The actual retail values of the inventories in each department are: Hardcovers $375,000 and Paperbacks $94,000.

Instructions

(a) Determine the estimated cost of the ending inventory for each department at **October 31,** 1993, using the retail inventory method.

(b) Compute the ending inventory at cost for each department at **December 31,** assuming the cost to retail ratios for the year are 65% for hardcovers and 70% for paperbacks.

P9–6 Superior Auto Sales uses a perpetual inventory system. On April 1, the new car inventory records show total inventory of $140,000 consisting of the following:

Journalize transactions under a perpetual inventory system. (S.O. 5)

G

Model	Units	Unit Cost
Custom Sedans	4	$14,000
Convertibles	3	16,000
Recreational Vans	2	18,000

During April, the following purchases and sales were made on account.

April 5 Purchased three custom sedans for $14,000 each.
   7 Sold two custom sedans for $18,200 each.
  13 Purchased two recreational vans for $18,000 each.
  17 Sold one custom sedan for $18,500.
  20 Purchased two convertibles for $16,000 each.
  22 Returned one convertible purchased on April 20 for $16,000 credit.
  24 Sold three recreational vans for $24,000 each.
  28 Sold two convertibles for $21,000 each.

Instructions

(a) Journalize the transactions using (1) a periodic inventory system and (2) a perpetual inventory system.

(b) Explain the end-of-year entries, if any, for the inventory account under each inventory system.

ALTERNATE PROBLEMS

Determine cost of goods sold and ending inventory, using FIFO, LIFO, and average cost.
(S.O. 1, 2, 3, 4)

P9–1A Steward Company had a beginning inventory of 400 units of Product MLN at a cost of $8.00 per unit. During the year, purchases were:

Feb. 20	700 units at $9.00	Aug. 12	300 units at $11.00
May 5	500 units at $10.00	Dec. 8	100 units at $12.00

Steward Company uses a periodic inventory system. Sales totaled 1,500 units.

Instructions

(a) Determine the cost of goods available for sale.

(b) Determine (1) the ending inventory, and (2) the cost of goods sold under each of the assumed cost flow methods (FIFO, LIFO, and average). Prove the accuracy of the cost of goods sold under the FIFO and LIFO methods.

(c) Which costing method results in (1) the lowest inventory amount for the balance sheet, and (2) the lowest cost of goods sold for the income statement?

Compute ending inventory, prepare income statements and answer questions using FIFO and LIFO.
(S.O. 1, 2, 3, 4)

P9–2A The management of Real Novelty Inc. is reevaluating the appropriateness of using its present inventory costing method, which is average cost. They request your help in determining the results of operations for 1993 if either the FIFO method or the LIFO method had been used. For 1993, the accounting records show the following data:

Inventories		Purchases and Sales	
Beginning (15,000 units)	$34,000	Total net sales (225,000 units)	$865,000
Ending (20,000 units)		Total cost of goods purchased	
		(230,000 units)	578,500

Purchases were made quarterly as follows:

Quarter	Units	Unit Cost	Total Cost
1	60,000	$2.30	$138,000
2	50,000	2.50	125,000
3	50,000	2.60	130,000
4	70,000	2.65	185,500
	230,000		$578,500

Operating expenses were $142,000, and the company's income tax rate is 30%.

Instructions

(a) Prepare comparative condensed income statements for 1993 under FIFO and LIFO. (Show computations of ending inventory.)

(b) Answer the following questions for management:

(1) Which costing method (FIFO or LIFO) produces the more meaningful inventory amount for the balance sheet? Why?

(2) Which costing method (FIFO or LIFO) produces the more meaningful net income? Why?

(3) Which costing method (FIFO or LIFO) is more likely to approximate actual physical flow of the goods? Why?

(4) How much additional cash will be available for management under LIFO than under FIFO? Why?

(5) Will gross profit under the average cost method be higher or lower than (a) FIFO and (b) LIFO? (*Note:* it is not necessary to quantify your answer.)

Determine LCM valuation and prepare financial statements.
(S.O. 6)

P9–3A Bonanza Appliance Company uses the lower of cost or market (LCM) basis for valuing inventory. Your assistant accountant accumulates the following cost and market data at December 31, 1993.

Item	Quantity	Total Cost	Total Market
Washers			
W290	10	$ 3,000	$ 2,800
W430	8	3,200	3,600
Total		6,200	6,400

Dryers			
D330	15	4,800	4,500
D405	5	1,750	1,600
Total		6,550	6,100
Microwaves			
M930	20	7,000	7,400
M940	10	3,000	2,500
Total		10,000	9,900
Total inventory		$22,750	$22,400

For the year, net sales for these items were $300,000, beginning inventory was $25,000 and the cost of goods purchased was $240,000.

Instructions

(a) Prepare a schedule showing the inventory valuation under LCM using each of the three methods of application.

(b) Prepare comparative income statements for the year through gross profit using (1) the cost basis and (2) the LCM basis. Use the individual units method for LCM.

(c) Show the LCM data at December 31 in the current asset section of the balance sheet. Use the individual units method for LCM.

(d) Which method of applying LCM is most conservative? Why?

P9–4A Vanessa Company lost 80% of its inventory in a fire on March 23, 1993. The accounting records showed the following gross profit data for February and March.

Estimate inventory loss using gross profit method. (S.O. 7)

	February	March (to 3/23)
Net sales	$270,000	$260,000
Net purchases	200,800	191,000
Freight-in	2,900	2,500
Beginning inventory	16,500	20,400
Ending inventory	20,400	?

Vanessa Company is fully insured for fire losses but must prepare a report for the insurance company.

Instructions

(a) Compute the gross profit rate for the month of February.

(b) Using the gross profit rate for February, determine both the estimated total inventory and inventory lost in the fire in March.

P9–5A Martill Department Store uses the retail inventory method to estimate its monthly ending inventories. The following information is available for two of its departments at August 31, 1993.

Compute ending inventory and cost of inventory lost using retail method. (S.O. 7)

	Sporting Goods		Jewelry and Cosmetics	
	Cost	Retail	Cost	Retail
Net sales		$1,020,000		$1,160,000
Purchases	$670,000	1,066,000	$731,000	1,158,000
Purchase returns	(26,000)	(40,000)	(12,000)	(20,000)
Purchase discounts	(15,360)	—	(9,440)	—
Freight-in	6,000	—	8,000	—
Beginning inventory	47,360	74,000	38,440	62,000

At December 31, Martill Department Store takes a physical inventory at retail. The actual retail values of the inventories in each department are: Sporting Goods $75,000, and Jewelry and Cosmetics $64,000.

Instructions

(a) Determine the estimated cost of the ending inventory for each department on August 31, 1993 using the retail inventory method.

(b) Compute the ending inventory at cost for each department at December 31, assuming the cost-to-retail ratios are 60% for Sporting Goods and 65% for Jewelry and Cosmetics.

Prepare subsidiary ledger records under a perpetual inventory system.
(S.O. 9)

[G]

*P9–6A   The Family Home Appliance Mart begins operations on May 1. It uses a perpetual inventory system. During May the company had the following purchases and sales for its Model 25 Sureshot camera.

| Date | Purchases | | Sales |
	Units	Unit Cost	Units
May 1	7	$150	
4			5
8	8	$170	
12			5
15	5	$180	
20			4
25			2

Instructions

(a) Determine the inventory under a perpetual inventory system using (1) FIFO, (2) Average Cost, and (3) LIFO. Follow the format shown in the appendix.

(b) Which costing method produces (1) the highest ending inventory valuation and (2) the lowest ending inventory valuation?

Broadening Your Perspective

FINANCIAL REPORTING PROBLEM

The notes that accompany a company's financial statements provide informative details that would clutter the amounts and descriptions presented in the statements. Refer to the financial statements of PepsiCo and the Notes to Consolidated Financial Statements in Appendix L.

Instructions
Answer the following questions. Complete the requirements in millions of dollars, as shown in PepsiCo's annual report.

1. What did PepsiCo report for the amount of inventories in its Consolidated Balance Sheet at December 28, 1991? December 29, 1990?

2. Compute the dollar amount of change and the percentage change in inventories between 1990 and 1991. Compute inventory as a percentage of current assets for 1991.

3. How does PepsiCo value its inventories? Which inventory costing method does PepsiCo use?

4. What two categories of inventories are classified in the note on "Inventories"? Briefly explain what you think is contained in each category.

5. What is the cost of sales (cost of goods sold) reported by PepsiCo for 1991, 1990, and 1989? Compute the percentage of cost of sales to net sales in 1991.

DECISION CASE

On April 10, 1993, fire damaged the office and warehouse of Dibson Company. Most of the accounting records were destroyed but the following account balances were determined as of March 31, 1993: Merchandise Inventory, January 1, 1993, $80,000; Sales (January 1–March 31, 1993), $150,000; Purchases (January 1–March 31, 1993), $84,000.

The company's fiscal year ends on December 31, and it uses a periodic inventory system.

From an analysis of the April bank statement you discover cancelled checks of $4,200 during the period April 1–10 for cash purchases. Deposits during the same period totaled $18,500 of which 60% were collections on accounts receivable and the balance was cash sales.

Correspondence with the company's principal suppliers revealed $12,400 of purchases on account from April 1 to April 10 of which $1,800 was for merchandise in transit on April 10 that was shipped FOB destination.

Correspondence with the company's principal customers produced acknowledgments of credit sales totaling $28,000 from April 1 to April 10. It was estimated that $4,600 of credit sales will never be acknowledged or recovered from customers.

Dibson Company reached an agreement with the insurance company that its fire-loss claim should be based on the average of the gross profit rates for the preceding two years. The financial statements for 1991 and 1992 showed the following data:

	1992	1991
Net sales	$600,000	$480,000
Cost of goods purchased	416,000	356,000
Beginning inventory	60,000	40,000
Ending inventory	80,000	60,000

Inventory with a cost of $18,000 was salvaged from the fire.

Instructions

(a) Determine the balances in (1) Sales and (2) Purchases at April 10.

(b) Determine the average profit rate for the years 1991 and 1992. (*Hint:* Find the gross profit rate for each year and divide the sum by 2.)

(c) Determine the inventory loss as a result of the fire, using the gross profit method.

CRITICAL THINKING CASE

Refer back to the opening story concerning the bookstore at Erie Community College. Answer the following questions.

1. Why might a small bookstore use specific identification to determine inventory but a large bookstore might use FIFO or LIFO?

2. If the inventory is overstated at the end of the month, what effect does this error have on the balance sheet and the income statement?

3. What entry should Damiani make if the ending inventory is overstated?

ETHICAL CASE

Lonergan Wholesale Corp. uses the LIFO method of inventory costing. In the current year, profit at Lonergan is running unusually high. The corporate tax rate is also high this year, but it is scheduled to decline significantly next year. In an effort to lower current year's net income and to take advantage of the changing income tax rate, the president of Lonergan Wholesale instructs the plant accountant to recommend to the purchasing department a large purchase of inventory for delivery three days before the end of the year. The price of the inventory to be purchased has doubled during the year and the purchase will represent a major portion of the ending inventory value.

Instructions

(a) What is the effect of this transaction on this year's and next year's income statement and income tax expense? Why?

(b) If Lonergan Wholesale had been using the FIFO method of inventory costing, would the president give the same directive?

(c) Should the plant accountant order the inventory purchase to lower income? What are the ethical implications of this order?

Answers to Self-Study Questions
1. b   2. a   3. b   4. c   5. b   6. a   7. d   8. d   9. c   10. a
*11. c

CONCEPTS FOR REVIEW

Before studying this chapter, you should know or, if necessary, review, the following concepts:

a. *The periodicity assumption (Ch. 3, p. 88)*

b. *The cost principle (Ch. 1, p. 13) and the matching principle (Ch. 3, p. 90)*

c. *What is depreciation? (Ch. 3, p. 95)*

d. *How to make adjustments for depreciation. (Ch. 3, pp. 95–6)*

PLANT ASSETS: ACQUISITION AND DEPRECIATION

ake a stroll around your campus. Some of those buildings were built before you were born. How much do you think they cost to build? Are they depreciating? Appreciating?

None of these questions is academic. It costs millions of dollars to construct, maintain, and sometimes demolish these campus buildings. Where does the money come from? Partly your tuition, perhaps tax dollars, perhaps contributions. Allocating these dollars can depend upon a reasonable estimate of a building's condition, its remaining life—and of course, its replacement value.

At Westbrook College in Portland, Maine, Ms. Betty-Ann Doucette, the school's controller, recently researched the age of certain buildings on the campus. The reason: a new FASB rule mandates that private colleges report fixed assets and depreciate them. She found that some buildings go back to the nineteenth century. In order to *place an amount on each unrecorded building, she tried to find original construction*

costs and periodic renovations costs, as well as current replacement costs.

"For example, the building I'm in, Goddard Hall, was built in the early part of

this century," says Ms. Doucette. "It's now being depreciated over 40 years and

because it's over eighty years old I show it as fully depreciated." If it is fully depreciated,

does that mean it has a zero value? "On the books it says it does," she says.

Of course, that doesn't mean it's worthless. As you read this chapter, you'll find

out why an asset can have a zero value on the books yet have a substantial market

value.

Plant assets are tangible resources that are used in the operations of the business and are not intended for sale to customers. They are also called **property, plant, and equipment; plant and equipment;** or **fixed assets**. These assets are generally long-lived and are expected to provide services to the company for a number of years. Except for land, plant assets decline in service potential over their useful lives.

In this chapter, we first explain the application of the cost principle of accounting to plant assets. We then describe and compare the depreciation methods that may be used to allocate this cost over the useful life of the asset. The accounting for expenditures incurred during the useful life of an asset is also discussed. The disposal of plant assets and the financial statement presentation of plant assets are explained in Chapter 11.

Importance of Plant Assets

Many companies have substantial investments in plant assets. In public utility companies, for example, net plant assets (plant assets less accumulated depreciation) often represent more than 75% of total assets. Recently net plant assets were 79% of Consolidated Edison's total assets and 92% of Pennsylvania Power & Light Company's. In other types of companies the percentages of plant assets to total assets were:

ILLUSTRATION 10-1

Percentages of plant assets to total assets

McDonald's	86%	Delta Airlines	82%
Marriott Corporation	63%	General Motors Corporation	37%
Dow Chemical Company	43%	Revlon Inc.	26%

In the income statement, the relationship of depreciation expense and maintenance expense to total operating expenses was 10.4% for Consolidated Edison, 9.6% for Delta Airlines, and 6.2% for General Motors.

Classifying Plant Assets

Plant assets are often subdivided into four classes:

1. **Land**, such as a building site.
2. **Land improvements**, such as driveways, parking lots, fences, and underground sprinkler systems.
3. **Buildings**, such as stores, offices, factories, and warehouses.
4. **Equipment**, such as store check-out counters, cash registers, coolers, office furniture, factory machinery, and delivery equipment.

Like the purchase of a home by an individual, the acquisition of plant assets is an important decision for a business enterprise. It is also important for a business enterprise to (1) keep the asset in good operating condition, (2) replace worn-out or outdated facilities, and (3) expand its productive resources as needed. The decline of rail travel in the United States can be traced in part to the failure of railroad companies to meet the first two conditions. Conversely, the growth of air travel in this country can be attributed in part to the general willingness of airline companies to observe these essential conditions.

Determining the Cost of Plant Assets

Plant assets are recorded at cost in accordance with the **cost principle** of accounting. Cost consists of all expenditures necessary to acquire the asset and make it ready for its intended use. For example, the purchase price, freight costs paid by the purchaser, and installation costs are all considered part of the cost of factory machinery.

Cost is measured by the cash paid in a cash transaction or by the cash equivalent price paid when noncash assets are used in payment. **The cash equivalent price is equal to the fair market value of the asset given up or the fair market value of the asset received, whichever is more clearly determinable.** Once cost is established, it becomes the basis of accounting for the plant asset over its useful life. Current market or replacement values are not used. The application of the cost principle to each of the major classes of plant assets is explained in the following sections.

> **Study Objective 1**
>
> *Describe the application of the cost principle to plant assets.*

Land

The cost of land includes (1) the cash purchase price, (2) closing costs such as title and attorney's fees, (3) real estate brokers' commissions, and (4) accrued property taxes and other liens on the land assumed by the purchaser. For example, if the cash price is $50,000 and the purchaser agrees to pay accrued taxes of $5,000, the cost of the land is $55,000.

All necessary costs incurred in making land ready for its intended use are debited to the Land account. When vacant land is acquired, these costs include expenditures for clearing, draining, filling, and grading. Sometimes the land has a building on it that must be removed to make the site suitable for construction of a new building. In this case, all demolition and removal costs less any proceeds from salvaged materials are chargeable to the Land account. To illustrate, assume that Hayes Manufacturing Company acquires real estate at a cash cost of $100,000. The property contains an old warehouse that is razed at a net cost of $6,000 ($7,500 in costs less $1,500 proceeds from salvaged materials). Additional expenditures consist of the attorney's fee, $1,000, and the real estate broker's

> **Helpful hint** Management's intended use is important in applying the cost principle.

commission, $8,000. Given these factors, the cost of the land is $115,000, computed as follows:

Land	
Cash price of property	$100,000
Net removal cost of warehouse	6,000
Attorney's fee	1,000
Real estate broker's commission	8,000
Cost of land	$115,000

In recording the acquisition, Land is debited for $115,000 and Cash is credited for $115,000.

Land Improvements

The cost of land improvements includes all expenditures necessary to make the improvements ready for their intended use. For example, the cost of a new company parking lot will include the amount paid for paving, fencing, and lighting. These improvements have limited useful lives and their maintenance and replacement are the responsibility of the company. Thus, these costs are debited to Land Improvements and are depreciated over the useful lives of the improvements.

Buildings

All necessary expenditures relating to the purchase or construction of a building are charged to the Buildings account. When a building is purchased, such costs include the purchase price, closing costs (attorney's fees, title insurance, etc.), and real estate broker's commission. Costs to make the building ready for its intended use consist of expenditures for remodeling rooms and offices and replacing or repairing the roof, floors, electrical wiring, and plumbing.

When a company constructs a plant, such as the General Motors Saturn automobile facility, cost consists of the contract price plus payments made by the owner for architects' fees, building permits, and excavation costs. In addition, interest costs incurred to finance the project are included in the cost of the asset when a significant period of time is required to get the asset ready for use. In these circumstances, interest costs are considered as necessary a cost as the costs of materials and labor. The inclusion of interest costs in the cost of a constructed building is limited to the construction period. When construction has been completed, subsequent interest payments on funds borrowed to finance the construction are debited to Interest Expense.

Equipment

The cost of equipment consists of the cash purchase price, sales taxes, freight charges, and insurance during transit paid by the purchaser. It also includes expenditures required in assembling, installing, and testing the unit. However, motor vehicle licenses and accident insurance on company trucks and cars are expensed as incurred, because they represent annual recurring expenditures and do not benefit future periods. To illustrate, assume that the Lenard Company purchases a delivery truck at a cash price of $22,000. Related expenditures consist of sales taxes $1,320, painting and lettering $500, motor vehicle license $80, and a three-year accident insurance policy $1,600. The cost of the delivery truck is $23,820 computed as follows:

ILLUSTRATION 10-3

Computation of cost of delivery truck

Delivery Truck	
Cash price	$22,000
Sales taxes	1,320
Painting and lettering	500
Cost of delivery truck	**$23,820**

The motor vehicle license is expensed when incurred and the insurance policy is a prepaid asset. Thus, the summary entry to record the purchase of the truck and related expenditures is:

Delivery Truck	23,820	
License Expense	80	
Prepaid Insurance	1,600	
Cash		25,500
(To record purchase of delivery truck and related expenditures)		

For another example, assume the Merten Company purchases factory machinery at a cash price of $50,000. Related expenditures consist of sales taxes $3,000, insurance during shipping $500, installation and testing $1,000. The cost of the factory machinery is $54,500 computed as follows:

ILLUSTRATION 10-4

Computation of cost of factory machinery

Factory Machinery	
Cash price	$50,000
Sales taxes	3,000
Insurance during shipping	500
Installation and testing	1,000
Cost of factory machinery	**$54,500**

The summary entry to record the purchase and related expenditures is:

Factory Machinery	54,500	
Cash		54,500
(To record purchase of factory machine)		

Lump-Sum Purchase

A lump-sum purchase occurs when more than one type of asset is acquired in a single transaction. The purchase of a furnished condominium and the purchase of a baseball club are examples. In the former, the purchaser acquires an apartment (building), furniture, fixtures, and drapes; in the latter, the purchaser may obtain a ball park, baseball players, uniforms, and equipment.

In a lump-sum purchase, the single lump-sum purchase price must be allocated equitably to the individual components. **The most common method of allocation is based on the relative fair market values of the individual assets.** Assume, for example, that a national hotel chain, such as Hilton or Sheraton, buys a family-owned local motel at a cash cost of $1,200,000 on April 15, 1993. The allocation of the purchase price, using the fair market values of the individual classes of assets, is as follows:

ILLUSTRATION 10-5

Allocation of lump-sum purchase price

Asset Class	Fair Market Value	Percent of Total Fair Market Value		Computation (% × Purchase Price)	Cost Allocation
Land	$ 300,000	20%	($ 300,000 ÷ $1,500,000)	20% × $1,200,000	$ 240,000
Buildings	1,050,000	70	($1,050,000 ÷ $1,500,000)	70% × 1,200,000	840,000
Equipment	150,000	10	($ 150,000 ÷ $1,500,000)	10% × 1,200,000	120,000
	$1,500,000	100%		100%	$1,200,000

The entry to record the lump-sum purchase is

Apr. 15	Land	240,000	
	Buildings	840,000	
	Equipment	120,000	
	Cash		1,200,000
	(To record purchase of motel)		

Normally the book values of the individual assets on the **seller's** books are not used, since they are rarely indicative of fair market values at the date of purchase.

Concept of Depreciation

As explained in Chapter 3, **depreciation is the process of allocating to expense the cost of a plant asset over its useful (service) life in a rational and systematic manner.** Cost allocation is designed to provide for the proper matching of expenses with revenues in accordance with the matching principle.

Depreciation is a process of cost allocation, not a process of asset valuation. Accountants make no attempt to measure the change in an asset's market value during ownership, because plant assets are not held for resale. Thus, the **book value** (cost less accumulated depreciation) of a plant asset may differ significantly from its market value.

During an asset's useful life its revenue-producing ability will decline because of **wear and tear**. A delivery truck that has been driven 100,000 miles will be less useful to a company than one driven only 800 miles. Similarly, trucks and planes exposed to snow and salt will deteriorate faster than equipment that is not exposed to these elements.

A decline in revenue producing ability may also occur because of **obsolescence**. Obsolescence is the process of becoming out of date before the asset phys-

Accounting in Action · *Business Insight*

An asset's useful life can be difficult to determine. Take commercial aircraft as an example. It is generally recognized that neither the aircraft manufacturers, the airlines, or safety experts know how long a modern jet airplane can be flown before its major structural components wear out. One factor affecting life is the extent and frequency of maintenance. But, when the Aloha Airlines Boeing 737 peeled itself open while in flight in the late 1980s, questions about maximum life emerged. It appears that the useful life of an airplane will now be somewhat reduced, not because of economic considerations, but for safety reasons.

ically wears out. The rerouting of major airlines from Chicago's Midway Airport to Chicago-O'Hare International Airport because Midway's runways were too short for jumbo jets is an example. Likewise, diesel train engines made coal-burning locomotives obsolete, and municipal buses sent streetcars to the scrap heap.

Recognition of depreciation does not result in the accumulation of cash for the replacement of the asset. The balance in Accumulated Depreciation represents the total cost that has been charged to expense; it is not a cash fund.

> **Helpful hint** Remember that depreciation is the process of allocating cost over the useful life of an asset. It is not a measure of value.

Factors in Computing Depreciation

Three factors affect the computation of depreciation:

1. **Cost.** Considerations affecting the cost of a depreciable asset have been explained earlier in this chapter. Cost is measured in accordance with the cost principle of accounting. Cost is objective—a fact.

2. **Salvage value.** Salvage value is an estimate of the asset's value at the end of its useful life. The value may be based on the asset's worth as scrap or salvage or on its expected trade-in value. Salvage value is an estimate. In making the estimate, management should consider how it plans to dispose of the asset and its experience with similar assets.

3. **Useful life.** Useful life is an estimate of the expected productive life, also called service life, of the asset. Useful life may be expressed in terms of time, units of activity such as machine hours, or in units of output. Like salvage value, useful life is an estimate. In making the estimate, management should consider such factors as the intended use of the asset, its expected repair and maintenance policies, and the vulnerability of the asset to obsolescence. The company's past experience with similar assets is often helpful in deciding on expected useful life.

Before You Go On . . .

1. What are plant assets? What are the major classes of plant assets? How is the cost principle applied to accounting for plant assets?

2. What is the relationship, if any, of depreciation to (a) cost allocation, (b) asset valuation, and (c) cash accumulation?

3. Explain the factors that affect the computation of depreciation.

Accounting in Action ▪ *Business Insight*

Not all companies use the same useful life for assets. Compare the useful lives used by the Big Three automakers, for example: At one time General Motors wrote off its machinery over 10 years, compared to Ford's 12 years and Chrysler's 11 years. GM also wrote off its buildings over 28 years while Ford used 30 years and Chrysler used 26 years. General Motors also wrote off its dies and equipment used to manufacture car bodies about twice as fast as Ford and three times as fast as Chrysler. Now GM is changing and aligning itself with its principal competitors by applying more liberal depreciation policies that have increased annual income. Should companies in the same industry be required to use the same useful life for the same type of assets?

▰Depreciation Methods

Study Objective 3

Compute periodic depreciation using different methods.

Depreciation is computed using one of the following methods:

1. Straight-line
2. Units of activity
3. Declining-balance
4. Sum-of-the-years'-digits

Like the inventory methods discussed in Chapter 9, each method is acceptable under generally accepted accounting principles. Management selects the method or methods it believes to be appropriate in the circumstances. The objective is to select the method that best measures the asset's contribution to revenue over its useful life. Once a method is chosen, it should be applied consistently over the useful life of the asset. Consistency enhances the comparability of financial statements.

Depreciation affects the balance sheet through accumulated depreciation and the income statement through depreciation expense. Illustration 10-6 shows the use of the different depreciation methods in 600 of the largest companies in the U.S.

ILLUSTRATION 10-6

Use of depreciation methods in major U.S. companies

Source: Accounting Trends & Techniques, 1991 Edition (AICPA, New York, N.Y.)

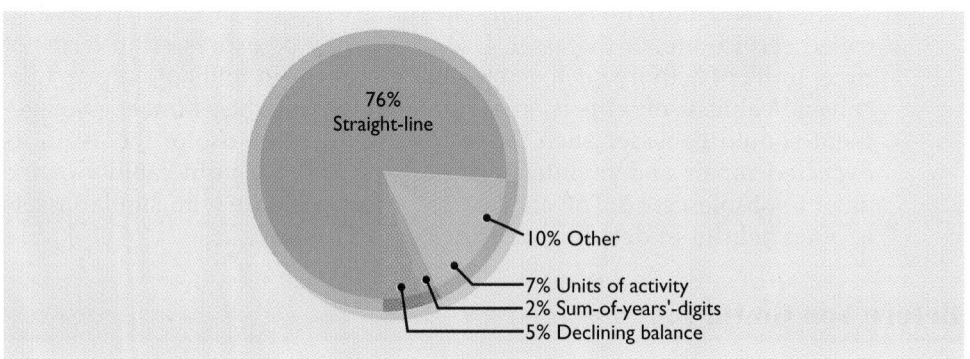

To facilitate the comparison of the four depreciation methods, all computations will be based on the following data applicable to a small delivery truck purchased by Barb's Florists on January 1, 1993.

ILLUSTRATION 10-7

Delivery truck data

Cost	$13,000
Expected salvage value	$ 1,000
Estimated useful life in years	5
Estimated useful life in miles	100,000

Straight Line

Under the straight-line method, depreciation is the same for each year of service life of the asset. It is measured solely by the passage of time. In computing depreciation expense, it is necessary to determine depreciable cost. Depreciable cost is the cost of the asset less its salvage value. It is the total amount subject to depreciation. Depreciable cost is then divided by the asset's useful life to determine depreciation expense. The formulas and computations of depreciation expense in the first year for Barb's Florists are shown in Illustration 10-8.

ILLUSTRATION 10-8

Formula for straight-line method

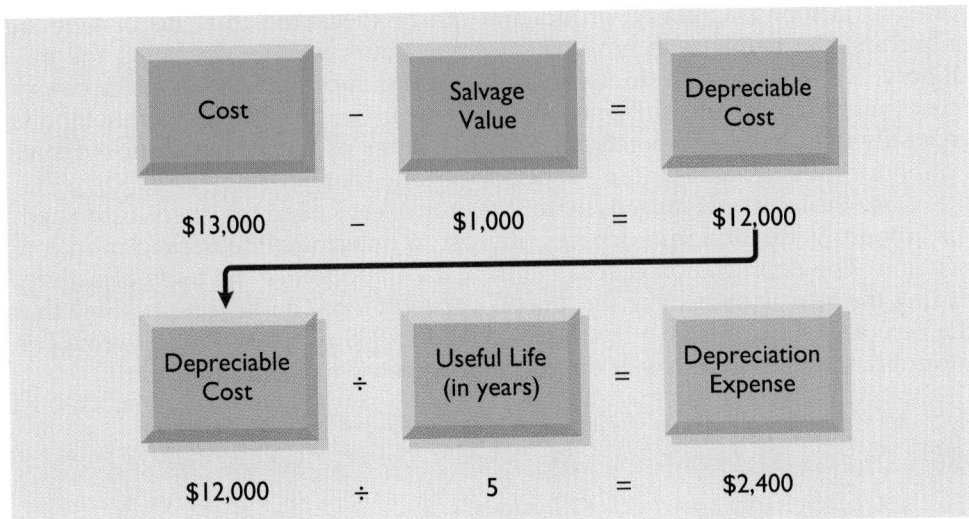

It is also possible to state that the delivery truck is being depreciated at an annual rate. In this case, the rate is 20% (100% ÷ 5 years). When an annual rate is used under the straight-line method, the percentage rate is applied to the depreciable cost of the asset, as follows:

ILLUSTRATION 10-9

Straight-line depreciation schedule

	BARB'S FLORISTS				
	Computation		**Annual**	**End of Year**	
Year	**Depreciable Cost** ×	**Depreciation Rate** =	**Depreciation Expense**	**Accumulated Depreciation**	**Book Value**
1993	$12,000	20%	**$2,400**	$ 2,400	$10,600*
1994	12,000	20	**2,400**	4,800	8,200
1995	12,000	20	**2,400**	7,200	5,800
1996	12,000	20	**2,400**	9,600	3,400
1997	12,000	20	**2,400**	12,000	**1,000**

*($13,000 − $2,400).

Note that the depreciation expense of $2,400 is the same each year, and that the book value at the end of the useful life is equal to the estimated $1,000 salvage value.

What happens when an asset is purchased *during* the year, rather than on January 1, as in our example? In that case, it is necessary to prorate the annual depreciation for the proportion of time used. If Barb's Florists had purchased the delivery truck on April 1, 1993, the depreciation for 1993 would be $1,800 ($12,000 × 20% × 9/12 of a year).

The straight-line method predominates in practice. For example, such large companies as Campbell Soup, Marriott Corporation, and General Mills use the straight-line method. It is simple to apply, and it matches expenses with revenues appropriately when the use of the asset is reasonably uniform throughout the service life.

Units of Activity

Under the units of activity method, instead of expressing the life as a time period, service life is expressed in terms of the total units of production or use expected from the asset, rather than time. The units of activity method is ideally suited to factory machinery: production can be measured in terms of units of output or, alternatively, in terms of machine hours used in operating the machinery. It is also possible to use this method for such items as delivery equipment (miles driven) and airplanes (hours in use). The units of activity method is generally not suitable for such assets as buildings or furniture, because depreciation for these assets is more a function of time than of use.

Once the total units of activity for the entire service life have been estimated, the amount is divided into depreciable cost to determine the depreciation cost per unit. The depreciation cost per unit is then applied to the units of activity during the year to determine the annual depreciation. To illustrate, assume that the delivery truck of Barb's Florists is driven 15,000 miles in the first year. The formulas and computations of depreciation expense in the first year are:

ILLUSTRATION 10-10

Formula for units of activity method

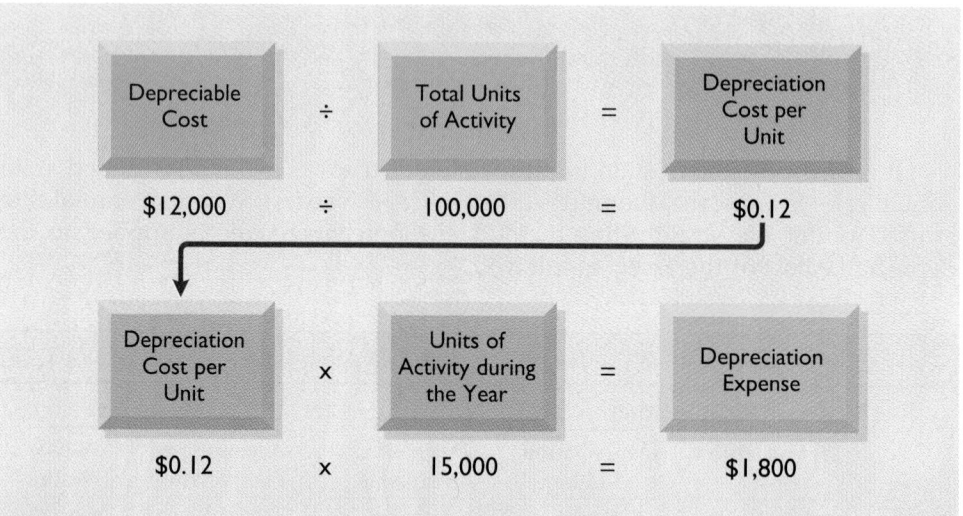

The depreciation schedule, using assumed mileage data, is as follows:

ILLUSTRATION 10-11

Units of activity depreciation schedule

BARB'S FLORISTS					
	Computation		Annual	End of Year	
Year	Units of Activity	× Depreciation Cost/Unit =	Depreciation Expense	Accumulated Depreciation	Book Value
1993	15,000	$.12	**$1,800**	$ 1,800	$11,200*
1994	30,000	.12	**3,600**	5,400	7,600
1995	20,000	.12	**2,400**	7,800	5,200
1996	25,000	.12	**3,000**	10,800	2,200
1997	10,000	.12	**1,200**	12,000	1,000

*($13,000 − $1,800).

The units of activity method is not nearly as popular as the straight-line method (see, for example, Illustration 10-6), primarily because it is often difficult to make a reasonable estimate of total activity. However, this method is used by some very large companies, such as Standard Oil Company of California and Boise Cascade Corporation. When the productivity of the asset varies significantly from one period to another, the units of activity method results in the best matching of expenses with revenues. This method is easy to apply when assets are purchased during the year. In such a case, the productivity of the asset for the partial year is used in computing the depreciation.

Declining-Balance

The declining-balance method produces a decreasing annual depreciation expense over the useful life of the asset. The method is so named because the computation of periodic depreciation is based on a declining book value (cost less accumulated depreciation) of the asset. Annual depreciation expense is computed by multiplying the book value at the beginning of the year by the declining-balance depreciation rate. **The depreciation rate remains constant from year to year, but the book value to which the rate is applied declines each year.** Book value for the first year is the cost of the asset. In subsequent years, book value is the difference between cost and accumulated depreciation at the beginning of the year. **Unlike the other depreciation methods, salvage value is ignored in determining the amount to which the declining balance rate is applied.** Salvage value, however, does limit the total depreciation that can be taken. Depreciation stops when the asset's book value equals expected salvage value.

A common declining-balance rate is double the straight-line rate. As a result, the method is often referred to as the double declining-balance method. If Barb's Florists uses the double declining-balance method, the depreciation rate is 40% (2 × the straight-line rate of 20%). The formula and computation of depreciation for the first year on the delivery truck are:

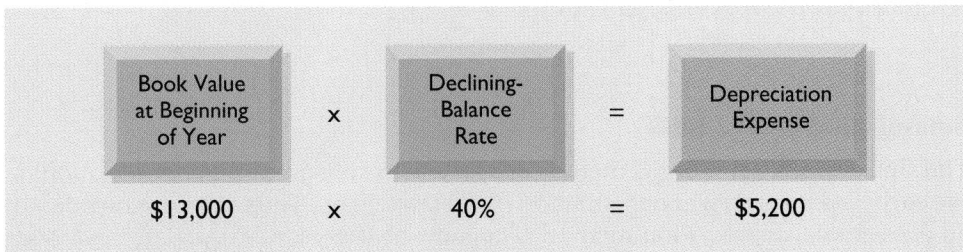

ILLUSTRATION 10-12

Formula for declining-balance method

The depreciation schedule under this method is as follows:

ILLUSTRATION 10-13

Double declining-balance depreciation schedule

	BARB'S FLORISTS				
	Computation		**Annual**	**End of Year**	
Year	**Book Value Beginning of Year** ×	**Depreciation Rate** =	**Depreciation Expense**	**Accumulated Depreciation**	**Book Value**
1993	$13,000	40%	**$5,200**	$ 5,200	$7,800
1994	7,800	40	**3,120**	8,320	4,680
1995	4,680	40	**1,872**	10,192	2,808
1996	2,808	40	**1,123**	11,315	1,685
1997	1,685	40	**685***	12,000	**1,000**

*Computation of $674 ($1,685 × 40%) is adjusted to $685 in order to equal salvage value.)

Helpful hint Book value is variable and the depreciation rate is constant for this method.

You can see that the delivery equipment is 69% depreciated ($8,320 ÷ $12,000) at the end of the second year. Under the straight-line method it would be depreciated 40% ($4,800 ÷ $12,000) at that time. Because the declining-balance method produces higher depreciation expense in the early years than in the later years, it is considered an accelerated depreciation method. The declining-balance method is compatible with the matching principle. The higher depreciation expense in early years is matched with the higher benefits received in these years. Conversely, lower depreciation expense is recognized in later years when the asset's contribution to revenue is less. Also, some assets lose value rapidly

Accounting in Action ▪ *Business Insight*

Why does Gingiss Formal Wear have 70 depreciation accounts and use the units of activity method for its tuxedos? The reason is that Gingiss wants to track wear and tear on each of its 16,000 dinner jackets individually. So now each tuxedo has a bar code, like a supermarket box of cereal. When a tux is rented, a clerk runs it across an electronic scanner. At year-end, the computer adds up the total rentals for each of 15 styles, then divides by expected total use to compute the rate. For instance, on one dolphin-gray tux Gingiss expects a life of 30 rentals. In a recent year the tux was rented 13 times. So depreciation was 43% (13 ÷ 30) of the total cost that period.

because of obsolescence. In these cases, the declining-balance method provides a more appropriate depreciation amount.

When an asset is purchased during the year, it is necessary to prorate the declining-balance depreciation in the first year on a time basis. For example, if Barb's Florists had purchased the delivery equipment on April 1, 1993, depreciation for 1993 would become $3,900 ($13,000 × 40% × 9/12). The book value for computing depreciation in 1994 then becomes $9,100 ($13,000 − $3,900), and the 1994 depreciation is $3,640 ($9,100 × 40%).

Sum-of-the-Years'-Digits

Helpful hint Many view a company that uses accelerated depreciation as being more conservative and thus it is viewed as having a higher quality of earnings.

The sum-of-the-years'-digits method (SYD) also results in higher depreciation in the early years and lower depreciation in the later years. Thus, it too is considered an accelerated depreciation method. The sum-of-the-years'-digits method is so named because the depreciation rate is based on a fraction in which:

1. The numerator is the years of remaining service life from the beginning of the current year.
2. The denominator is **the sum** of the individual years that comprise total service life.

For a useful life of 5 years, the sum-of-the-years'-digits is 15 (1 + 2 + 3 + 4 + 5).[1] Annual depreciation is computed by multiplying depreciable cost by the appropriate SYD fraction. The formula and depreciation in the first year for the delivery truck of Barb's Florists are:

ILLUSTRATION 10-14

Formula for sum-of-the-years'-digits method

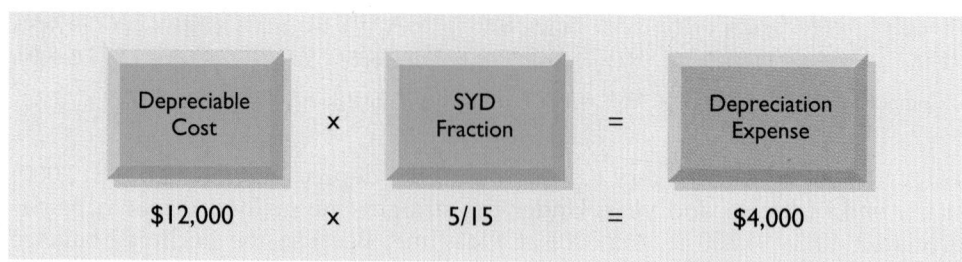

Depreciable Cost	×	SYD Fraction	=	Depreciation Expense
$12,000	×	5/15	=	$4,000

---

[1]A mathematical formula for this computation is **S** = N(N + 1)/2, where N is the number of years of service life, i.e., **S** = 5 (5 + 1)/2 = 15.

For Barb's Florists the depreciation schedule is as follows:

ILLUSTRATION 10-15

*Sum-of-the-years'-digits
depreciation schedule*

BARB'S FLORISTS

Year	Computation Depreciable Cost	×	SYD Fraction	=	Annual Depreciation Expense	End of Year Accumulated Depreciation	Book Value
1993	$12,000	×	5/15	=	**$4,000**	$ 4,000	$9,000*
1994	12,000		4/15		**3,200**	7,200	5,800
1995	12,000		3/15		**2,400**	9,600	3,400
1996	12,000		2/15		**1,600**	11,200	1,800
1997	12,000		1/15		**800**	12,000	**1,000**

*($13,000 − $4,000).

Note that under the sum-of-the-years'-digits method, the denominator (which for Barb's Florists is 15) remains constant, whereas the numerator decreases each year.

Two well-known companies that depreciate their assets using this method are General Electric and Du Pont. The rationale for using this method is the same as for the declining-balance method.

When an asset is acquired during the year, it is necessary to use the full year SYD fraction and then prorate the amount for the time the asset was used during the year and succeeding year. If Barb's Florists had purchased the delivery truck on April 1, the depreciation for 1993 and 1994 would be $3,000 and $3,400, respectively, computed as follows:

ILLUSTRATION 10-16

Fractional year's depreciation

1993	1994
$12,000 × 5/15 × 9/12 = $3,000	$12,000 × 5/15 × 3/12 = $1,000
	$12,000 × 4/15 × 9/12 = 2,400
	$3,400

Note that each SYD fraction must be used for 12 months before moving to the next SYD fraction.

Comparison of Methods

A comparison of annual and total depreciation expense under each of the four methods is shown for Barb's Florists in Illustration 10-17.

ILLUSTRATION 10-17

*Comparison of depreciation
methods*

Year	Straight-Line	Units of Activity	Declining-Balance	Sum-of-the-Years'-Digits
1993	$ 2,400	$ 1,800	$ 5,200	$ 4,000
1994	2,400	3,600	3,120	3,200
1995	2,400	2,400	1,872	2,400
1996	2,400	3,000	1,123	1,600
1997	2,400	1,200	685	800
	$12,000	$12,000	$12,000	$12,000

Accounting in Action · *Business Insight*

Does depreciation make a difference? Consider the ungodly flap that has been raging between churches of all denominations and the FASB because of a proposed accounting rule to force U.S. churches to depreciate, or deduct as an expense, the cost of houses of worship, monuments, and historical treasures. Churches indicate that if they must depreciate their houses of worship, their credit ratings will be downgraded. Feelings are strong. As one church official noted: "The FASB is on the verge of causing more trouble for American churches than all the sinners in their congregations. Our cathedrals last for centuries and often gain in value with age." A retired Treasury Department official says, "Depreciating churches would be like depreciating the Pyramids and the Sphinx of Egypt, and the Sistine Chapel at the Vatican. Figuring such depreciation, the official added, is "the acme of futility." However, as an FASB project manager noted, "But they don't last forever. The Parthenon may still be there, but its roof has fallen in. Physical assets that are exhaustible should be depreciated." What do you think?

Source: The Wall Street Journal, April 16, 1987.

The easiest way to lower depreciation is to switch from accelerated to straight-line. Companies who want to lower their depreciation even further during a recession can switch to units of activity.

Observe that periodic depreciation varies considerably among the methods, but total depreciation is the same for the five-year period. Each method is acceptable in accounting, because each recognizes the decline in service potential of the asset in a rational and systematic manner. The depreciation expense pattern under each method is presented graphically in Illustration 10-18.

Helpful hint The method(s) to be used for an asset that is expected to be more productive in the first half of its useful life is either the declining-balance or sum-of-the-years'-digits methods.

ILLUSTRATION 10-18

Patterns of depreciation

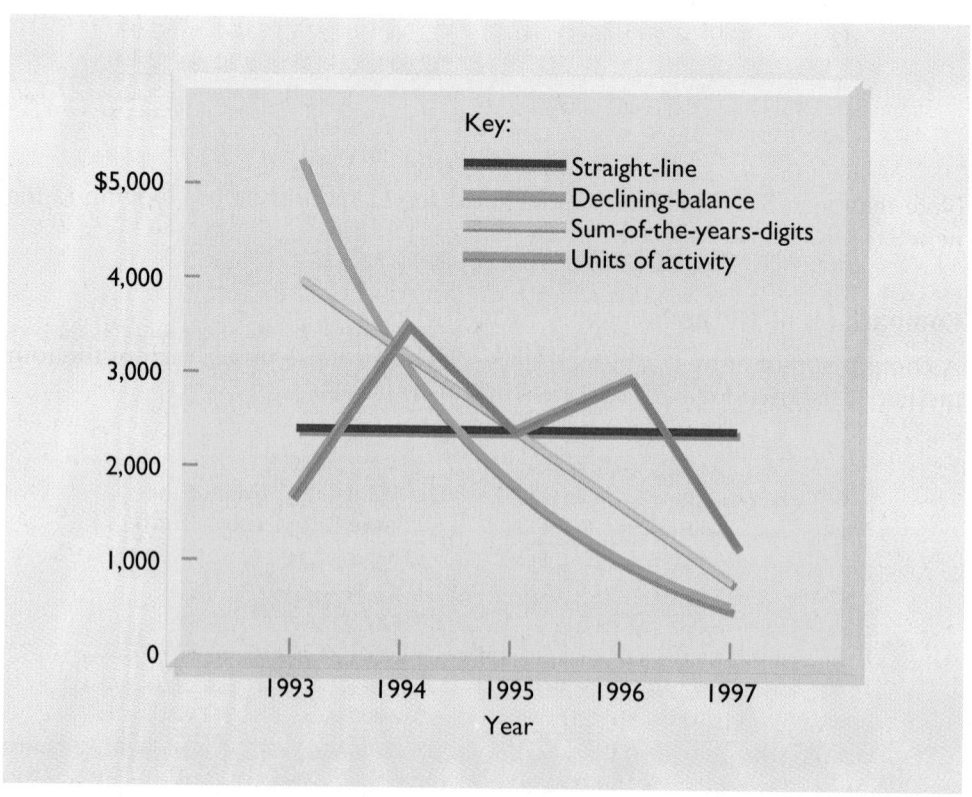

Depreciation and Income Taxes

The tax regulations of the Internal Revenue Service (IRS) do not require the taxpayer to use the same depreciation method on the tax return that is used in preparing financial statements. Consequently, many large corporations use straight-line depreciation in their financial statements to maximize net income. At the same time, a special accelerated depreciation method is used on their tax returns to minimize their income taxes.

For tax purposes, taxpayers must use on their tax returns either the straight-line method or a special accelerated depreciation method called **Modified Accelerated Cost Recovery System** (MACRS). MACRS, which is a result of the Tax Reform Act of 1986, is explained in Appendix F.

Helpful hint Depreciation per GAAP usually will be different than depreciation per IRS rules.

Technology in Action

Software packages to account for plant assets exist for both large and small computer systems. Though varying in complexity, even the smallest packages can maintain a control and subsidiary ledger for plant assets and make the necessary depreciation computations and adjusting entries. Many packages also maintain depreciation schedules for both financial statement and income tax purposes, with reconciliations made for any differences. Even spreadsheet packages contain embedded formulas or functions for calculating depreciation using a variety of methods.

Before You Go On . . .

1. What are the formulas for computing annual depreciation under each of the depreciation methods?

2. How do the methods differ in terms of their effects on annual depreciation over the useful life of the asset?

Revising Periodic Depreciation

Depreciation is one example of the estimation procedures that are part of the accounting process. Annual depreciation expense should be reviewed periodically by management. If wear and tear or obsolescence indicate that annual depreciation is inadequate or excessive, a change in the periodic amount should be made. When a change in an estimate is required, the change is made in **current and future years but not to prior periods**. Thus, when a change is made, (1) there is no correction of previously recorded depreciation expense, and (2) depreciation expense for current and future years is revised. The rationale for this treatment is that continual restatement of prior periods would adversely affect the reader's confidence in financial statements.

To determine the new annual depreciation expense, we compute the depreciable cost at the time of the revision and divide it by remaining useful life. To illustrate, assume that Barb's Florists decides on January 1, 1996, to extend the useful life of the truck one year because of its excellent condition. The company has used the straight-line method to depreciate the asset to date and book value

Study Objective 4

Describe the procedure for revising periodic depreciation.

Helpful hint Use a step-by-step approach: (1) determine new depreciable cost; (2) divide by remaining useful life.

is $5,800 ($13,000 − $7,200). The new annual depreciation is $1,600, computed as follows:

ILLUSTRATION 10-19

Revised depreciation computation

Book value, 1/1/96	$5,800
Less: Salvage value	1,000
Depreciable cost	$4,800
Remaining useful life	3 years (1996–1998)
Revised annual depreciation ($4,800 ÷ 3)	**$1,600**

On January 1, 1996, or at any other time, Barb's Florists makes no entry for the change in estimate. On December 31, 1996, during the preparation of adjusting entries, it would record depreciation expense of $1,600. Significant changes in estimates must be described in the financial statements.

*E*xpenditures During Useful Life

During the useful life of a plant asset a company may incur costs for ordinary repairs, additions, and improvements. Ordinary repairs are expenditures to maintain the operating efficiency and expected productive life of the unit. They usually are fairly small amounts that occur frequently throughout service life. Motor tune-ups and oil changes, the painting of buildings, and the replacing of worn-out gears on factory machinery are examples. These expenditures primarily benefit the current accounting period. Accordingly, they are debited to Repair (or Maintenance) Expense as incurred. Because they are immediately charged against revenues as an expense, these costs are often referred to as revenue expenditures.

Additions and improvements are costs incurred to increase the operating efficiency, productive capacity, or expected useful life of the plant asset. These expenditures are usually material in amount and occur infrequently during the period of ownership. Expenditures for additions and improvements increase the company's investment in productive facilities. Accordingly, they are often referred to as capital expenditures. Most major U.S. corporations disclose the amount of their annual capital expenditures. In a recent year, both IBM and General Motors reported capital expenditures slightly in excess of $6 billion. The accounting for capital expenditures varies depending on the nature of the expenditure.

Additions

An addition generally results in a larger physical unit and increased productive capacity. Additions are debited to the asset account to which the expenditure pertains. Thus, the construction of a new wing to a building is debited to Buildings. Adding paneling to the body of an open pickup truck is debited to Delivery Equipment.

Improvements

Improvements take a variety of forms. In some cases, an improvement results in the replacement of a subunit of a productive asset with a new unit. For example, a factory machine with a 10 h.p. electric motor may be improved by replacing the motor with a 15 h.p. motor. Similarly, a complete overhaul of a truck motor and the sandblasting of a brick building to restore its original appearance are improvements. These improvements are often called extraordinary repairs. The accounting for improvements depends on the effect the capital expenditure has on the asset's useful life.

No Increase in Useful Life

When an improvement does not increase useful life, the cost of the improvement is accounted for as an addition. That is, the cost is debited to the plant asset account. Assume, for example, that Hawkins Company spends $50,000 to sandblast the exterior of its factory building on March 1. If no increase in useful life is expected, the entry to record the improvement is:

Mar. 1	Factory Building	50,000	
	Cash		50,000
	(To record improvement to building)		

Increase in Useful Life

When an improvement increases the useful life of the asset, the cost of the improvement is debited to accumulated depreciation. The reasoning is that the expenditure restores (or makes good) a portion of the depreciation that has been recorded on the asset. In this sense, accumulated depreciation is overstated by the cost of the capital expenditure. To illustrate, assume that on January 1, 1994, Barb's Florists incurs a $2,000 major repair of the motor on its delivery truck. The improvement will increase the useful life of the truck by one year. The entry to record the improvement is:

Jan. 1	Accumulated Depreciation—Delivery Equipment	2,000	
	Cash		2,000
	(To record major overhaul of truck motor)		

Further consideration of improvements is deferred to advanced accounting courses.

Capital Expenditures and Subsequent Depreciation

Every capital expenditure should result in additional depreciation over the asset's remaining useful life. The computation is similar to the procedures described earlier for a revision of periodic depreciation. In this instance, however, it is necessary to determine the revised depreciable cost of the asset **after** recording the capital expenditure. The revised depreciable cost is determined as follows:

Study Objective 6

State the procedure for computing periodic depreciation after a capital expenditure.

ILLUSTRATION 10-20

Computation of revised depreciable cost

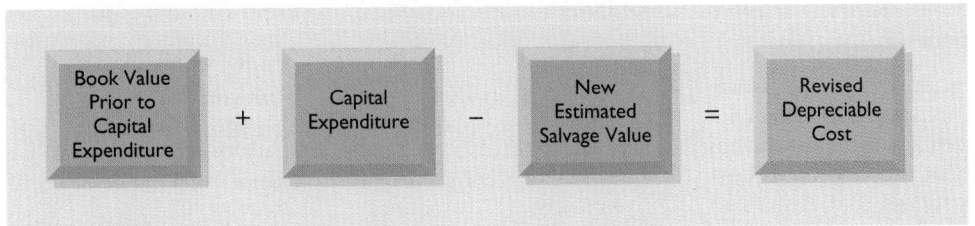

To illustrate, assume that Cisco Company makes a $10,000 major repair to factory machinery. This capital expenditure increases the remaining useful life of the machine to 5 years. In addition, the salvage value is expected to be $4,000. The book value of the factory machine prior to the major repair is $100,000. Under the straight-line method, the new annual depreciation for the remaining five years of useful life is $21,200, computed as shown below:

ILLUSTRATION 10-21

Depreciation after capital expenditure

Book value prior to capital expenditure	$100,000
Add: Cost of capital expenditure	10,000
Book value after capital expenditure	110,000
Less: New estimated salvage value	4,000
Revised depreciable cost	106,000
Remaining useful life	÷ 5
Revised annual depreciation	**$ 21,200**

At the end of the first year after the capital expenditure, Cisco Company will prepare the following entry for depreciation.

Depreciation Expense	21,200	
Accumulated Depreciation—Delivery Equipment		21,200
(To record annual depreciation)		

Before You Go On . . .

1. Are revisions of periodic depreciation made to prior periods? Explain.

2. How does a capital expenditure differ from a revenue expenditure?

3. How is the new annual depreciation computed after a capital expenditure has occurred?

Summary of Study Objectives

1. Describe the application of the cost principle to plant assets. The cost of plant assets includes all expenditures necessary to acquire the asset and make it ready for its intended use. Cost is measured by the cash or cash equivalent price paid. In a lump-sum purchase, cost is allocated on the basis of the relative fair market values of the components.

2. Explain the concept of depreciation. Depreciation is the process of allocating to expense the cost of a plant asset over its useful (service) life in a rational and systematic manner. Depreciation is not a process of valuation, and it is not a process that results in an accumulation of cash. Depreciation is caused by wear and tear and by obsolescence.

3. Compute periodic depreciation using different methods. There are four depreciation methods:

Method	Effect on Annual Depreciation	Formula
Straight-line	Constant amount	Depreciable cost ÷ useful life (in years)
Units of activity	Varying amount	Depreciation cost per unit × units of activity during the year
Declining-balance	Decreasing amount	Book value at beginning of year × declining-balance rate
Sum-of-the-years'-digits	Decreasing amount	Depreciable cost × SYD fraction

4. Describe the procedure for revising periodic depreciation. Revisions of periodic depreciation are made in present and future periods, not retroactively. The new annual depreciation is determined by dividing the depreciable cost at the time of the revision by the remaining useful life.

5. *Distinguish between revenue and capital expenditures and explain the entries for these expenditures.* Revenue expenditures are incurred to maintain the operating efficiency and expected productive life of the asset. These expenditures are debited to Repair Expense as incurred. Capital expenditures increase the operating efficiency, productive capacity, or expected useful life of the asset. Additions are debited to the asset account to which the expenditure per-

tains. Improvements are debited to the principal asset account when useful life remains the same and to accumulated depreciation when useful life is extended.

6. *State the procedure for computing periodic depreciation after a capital expenditure.* After a capital expenditure, it is necessary to compute the book value after the capital expenditure, revised depreciable cost, and remaining useful life. The new annual depreciation is determined by dividing the revised depreciable cost by remaining useful life.

APPENDIX F   Tax Depreciation

The Tax Reform Act of 1986 replaced the Accelerated Cost Recovery System (ACRS) that had been part of tax law since 1981 with the Modified Accelerated Cost Recovery System (MACRS). Under MACRS all depreciable assets are classified according to class life, as determined by their description (i.e., tools, autos, computers, office furniture, aircraft, etc.). All assets fall into one of eight classes, and for each class a specific depreciation method is prescribed. The schedule in Illustration F-1 lists the classes, the type of assets assigned to each class, and the depreciation method prescribed for each class.

Study Objective

After studying Appendix F, you should be able to:

7. Explain the Modified Accelerated Cost Recovery System of depreciaton.

Classes	Illustrative Applicable Assets	Depreciation Method
3-year	Small tools, tractors, horses, and specialized manufacturing devices.	200% declining-balance
5-year	Computers, automobiles and light trucks, small aircraft, construction equipment, and research and development property.	200% declining-balance
7-year	Office furniture, fixtures and equipment, commercial aircraft, and most machinery.	200% declining-balance
10-year	Specialized heavy manufacturing machinery and equipment, and mobile homes.	200% declining-balance
15-year	Billboards, service station buildings, and telephone equipment.	150% declining-balance
20-year	Sewer pipes, most utility property, and land improvements.	150% declining-balance
27½-year	Residential real estate property.	Straight-line
31½-year	Office and other nonresidential real estate property.	Straight-line

ILLUSTRATION F-1

Classes of assets under MACRS

   The depreciation expense is computed based on the tax basis, usually the cost of the asset. When one of the accelerated methods is used, a change is made to the straight-line method in the first year in which straight-line depreciation exceeds the accelerated depreciation. Depreciation computations for income tax purposes are based on the half-year convention; that is, a half year of depreciation is allowable in the year of acquisition and in the year of disposition. For tax purposes, an asset is depreciated to a zero value so that there is no salvage value at the end of its MACRS life.

In order to simplify the application of these depreciation methods, the IRS has published the tables shown in Illustration F-2.

ILLUSTRATION F-2

MACRS depreciation rates by class of property

MACRS DEPRECIATION RATES BY CLASS OF PROPERTY

Recovery Year	3-year (200% DB)	5-year (200% DB)	7-year (200% DB)	10-year (200% DB)	15-year (150% DB)	20-year (150% DB)
1	33.33%	20.00%	14.29%	10.00%	5.00%	3.750%
2	44.45	32.00	24.49	18.00	9.50	7.219
3	14.81*	19.20	17.49	14.40	8.55	6.677
4	7.41	11.52*	12.49	11.52	7.70	6.177
5		11.52	8.93*	9.22	6.93	5.713
6		5.76	8.92	7.37	6.23	5.285
7			8.93	6.55*	5.90*	4.888
8			4.46	6.55	5.90	4.522
9				6.56	5.91	4.462*
10				6.55	5.90	4.461
11				3.28	5.91	4.462
12					5.90	4.461
13					5.91	4.462
14					5.90	4.461
15					5.91	4.462
16					2.95	4.461
17						4.462
18						4.461
19						4.462
20						4.461
21						2.231

*Switchover to straight-line depreciation.

To illustrate the application of MACRS, assume that Nathan Rug Company purchases a computer for $10,000 on January 27, 1994. According to MACRS rules, a computer is a 5-year class asset. Using the rates provided in the MACRS depreciation rate schedule for a 5-year class asset, depreciation is computed as shown in Illustration F-3.

ILLUSTRATION F-3

MACRS depreciation computation

MACRS Depreciation

1994	$10,000 × .20	= $ 2,000
1995	$10,000 × .32	3,200
1996	$10,000 × .192	1,920
1997	$10,000 × .1152	1,152
1998	$10,000 × .1152	1,152
1999	$10,000 × .0576	576
	Total depreciation	$10,000

Note that the date that the asset was purchased in 1994 is not relevant in computing depreciation in the first year. Note also that depreciation on a 5-year class life asset affects the company's tax returns for six years. This results because of the half-year convention.

MACRS is used for income tax purposes only. Annual depreciation under this system generally does not equal the amount of depreciation recorded under generally accepted accounting principles. The effect on net income of this differ-

Accounting in Action · *Business Insight*

Since 1980, taxpayers have labored under five different depreciation regimes. The tax life of certain real property, for instance, has changed from a typical 35 years in 1980 to 15 in 1981, 18 in 1982, 19 in 1984, and 31½ in 1986. It appears that the useful life of a depreciation law is 1.6 years.

And the old rates don't die as each successive law comes into existence. They survive as long as the owner keeps the property. Thus, today's taxpayer has to maintain a working knowledge of five depreciation systems. No deduction is allowed for the wear and tear on taxpayers' brains.

ence between tax depreciation and accounting depreciation is explained in Appendix M.

It should be noted that the straight-line method may be elected in computing depreciation rather than MACRS. The straight-line election is an annual class election, and the method must be applied to all assets within the class acquired in any year.

Summary of Study Objectives for Appendix F

7. Explain the Modified Accelerated Cost Recovery System of depreciation. MACRS is part of the Tax Reform Act of 1986. Under MACRS, all depreciable assets are classified according to class life. All assets fall into one of eight classes, and for each class a specific depreciation method is prescribed.

GLOSSARY

Accelerated depreciation method · A depreciation method that produces higher depreciation expense in the early years than in the later years. (p. 407).

Additions and improvements · Costs incurred to increase the operating efficiency, productive capacity, or expected useful life of the asset. (p. 412).

Capital expenditures · Expenditures that increase the company's investment in productive facilities. (p. 412).

Cash equivalent price · An amount equal to the fair market value of the asset given up or the fair market value of the asset received, whichever is more clearly determinable. (p. 399).

Declining-balance method · A depreciation method that applies a constant rate to the declining book value of the asset and produces a decreasing annual depreciation amount over the useful life of the asset. (p. 407).

Depreciable cost · The cost of the asset less its salvage value. (p. 404).

Lump-sum purchase · A single transaction in which more than one type of asset is acquired. (p. 401).

Modified accelerated cost recovery system (MACRS) · A Tax Reform Act of 1986 system of depreciation in which all depreciable assets are classified according to eight class lives and for most of these classes depreciation is by the declining-balance method until depreciation by the straight-line method exceeds the accelerated depreciation. (p. 415).

Ordinary repairs · Expenditures to maintain the

operating efficiency and expected productive life of the unit. (p. 412).

Plant assets · Tangible resources that are used in the operations of the business and are not intended for sale to customers. (p. 398).

Revenue expenditures · Expenditures charged against revenues as an expense when incurred. (p. 412).

Straight-line method · A method in which periodic

depreciation is the same throughout the service life of the asset. (p. 404).

Sum-of-the-years'-digits method · A depreciation method that produces decreasing periodic depreciation by applying a decreasing fraction to the depreciable cost of the asset. (p. 408).

Units of activity method · A depreciation method in which service life is expressed in terms of the total units of production or use expected from the asset. (p. 405).

DEMONSTRATION PROBLEM

DuPage Company purchases a factory machine at a cost of $18,000 on January 1, 1993. The machine is expected to have a salvage value of $2,000 at the end of its four-year useful life.

During its useful life, the machine is expected to be used 160,000 hours. Actual annual hourly use was: Year 1 40,000, Year 2 60,000, Year 3 35,000, and Year 4 25,000.

Instructions

Prepare depreciation schedules for the following methods: (a) the straight-line, (b) units of activity, (c) declining-balance using double the straight-line rate, and (d) the sum-of-the-years'-digits.

Solution to Demonstration Problem

(a)

Helpful hints

1. Under the straight-line method, the depreciation rate is applied to depreciable cost.

Straight-line Method

Year	Depreciable Cost	×	Depreciation Rate	=	Annual Depreciation Expense	Accumulated Depreciation	Book Value
1993	$16,000		25%		$4,000	$ 4,000	$14,000*
1994	16,000		25%		4,000	8,000	10,000
1995	16,000		25%		4,000	12,000	6,000
1996	16,000		25%		4,000	16,000	2,000

*$18,000 − $4,000.

End of Year columns: Accumulated Depreciation, Book Value

(b)

2. Under the units of activity method, depreciation cost per unit is computed by dividing depreciable cost by total units of activity.

Units of Activity Method

Year	Units of Activity	×	Depreciation Cost/Unit	=	Annual Depreciation Expense	Accumulated Depreciation	Book Value
1993	40,000		$.10		$4,000	$ 4,000	$14,000
1994	60,000		.10		6,000	10,000	8,000
1995	35,000		.10		3,500	13,500	4,500
1996	25,000		.10		2,500	16,000	2,000

Computation columns: Units of Activity, Depreciation Cost/Unit; End of Year columns: Accumulated Depreciation, Book Value

(c)

Declining-Balance Method

Year	Book Value Beginning of Year	×	Depreciation Rate	=	Annual Depreciation Expense	End of Year Accumulated Depreciation	End of Year Book Value
1993	$18,000		50%		$9,000	$ 9,000	$9,000
1994	9,000		50%		4,500	13,500	4,500
1995	4,500		50%		2,250	15,750	2,250
1996	2,250		50%		250*	16,000	2,000

*Adjusted to $250 because ending book value should not be less than expected salvage value.

(d)

Sum-of-the-Years'-Digits' Method

Year	Depreciable Cost	×	SYD Fraction	=	Annual Depreciation Expense	End of Year Accumulated Depreciation	End of Year Book Value
1993	$16,000		4/10		$6,400	$ 6,400	$11,600*
1994	16,000		3/10		4,800	11,200	6,800
1995	16,000		2/10		3,200	14,400	3,600
1996	16,000		1/10		1,600	16,000	2,000

*$18,000 − $6,400.

Helpful hints

3. Under the declining-balance method, the depreciation rate is applied to **book value** at the beginning of the year.

4. Under the sum-of-the-years' digits' method, the SYD fraction is applied to depreciable cost.

***Note:** All **asterisked** Questions, Exercises, and Problems relate to material contained in the appendix to each chapter.

SELF-STUDY QUESTIONS

Answers are at end of chapter.

(S.O. 1)

1. Corrieten Company purchased equipment and the following costs were incurred:

Cash price	$24,000
Sales taxes	1,440
Insurance during transit	200
Installation and testing	500
Total costs	$26,140

What amount should be recorded as the cost of the equipment?
a. $24,000.
b. $25,440.
c. $25,640.
d. $26,140.

(S.O. 1)

2. Zee Company paid $100,000 cash for land, plus attorney's fees $2,000, real estate broker's commissions $4,000, and accrued taxes $3,000. The land should be recorded at:
a. $109,000.
b. $106,000.
c. $102,000.
d. $100,000.

3. In a lump-sum purchase, the allocation of the purchase price should be made on the basis of the individual assets':
a. costs.
b. fair market values.
c. book values.
d. liquidation values.

(S.O. 1)

4. Depreciation is a process of:
a. valuation.
b. cost allocation.
c. cash accumulation.
d. appraisal.

(S.O. 2)

5. The depreciation methods that are most likely to have the highest depreciation in the first year are:
a. straight-line and units of activity.
b. units of activity and declining-balance.
c. declining-balance and sum-of-the-years' digits.
d. sum-of-the-years' digits and straight-line.

(S.O. 3)

6. Cuso Company purchased equipment on January 1, 1993 at a total invoice cost $400,000. The equipment has an estimated salvage value of $10,000 and an es-

(S.O. 3)

timated useful life of five years. The amount of accumulated depreciation at December 31, 1994, if the straight-line method of depreciation is used is:
a. $80,000.
b. $160,000.
c. $78,000.
d. $156,000.

(S.O. 3) 7. Kant Enterprises purchased a truck for $11,000 on January 1, 1993. The truck will have an estimated salvage value of $1,000 at the end of five years. Using the units of activity method, the balance in accumulated depreciation at December 31, 1994, can be computed by the following formula:
a. ($11,000 ÷ Total estimated activity) × Units of activity for 1994.
b. ($10,000 ÷ Total estimated activity) × Units of activity for 1994.
c. ($11,000 ÷ Total estimated activity) × Units of activity for 1993 and 1994.
d. ($10,000 ÷ Total estimated activity) × Units of activity for 1993 and 1994.

(S.O. 4) 8. When there is a change in estimated depreciation:
a. previous depreciation should be corrected.
b. current and future years' depreciation should be revised.
c. only future years' depreciation should be revised.
d. None of the above.

9. Improvements are: (S.O. 5)
a. revenue expenditures.
b. debited to an appropriate asset account when they increase useful life.
c. debited to accumulated depreciation when they do not increase useful life.
d. debited to an appropriate asset account when they do not increase useful life.

10. On January 1 when the book value of a   (S.O. 6) machine is $16,000, Betty Arden Company makes a $3,000 capital expenditure that is expected to increase remaining useful life from six to eight years and increase expected salvage value from $2,000 to $2,400. The revised annual depreciation is:
a. $2,125.
b. $2,075.
c. $2,767.
d. $2,000.

*11. The Modified Accelerated Cost Recovery   (S.O. 7) System:
a. primarily uses the straight-line method of depreciation.
b. classifies assets into life classes.
c. must be elected by a corporation.
d. cannot be used for tax purposes if it is not used for financial reporting purposes.

QUESTIONS

1. Susan Dey is uncertain about the applicability of the cost principle to plant assets. Explain the principle to Susan.

2. Corbin Bernsen claims that there are two classes of plant assets: (a) nondepreciable, and (b) depreciable. Is Corbin correct? What are the principal classes of plant assets?

3. How is cost for a plant asset measured in (a) a cash transaction, and (b) a noncash transaction?

4. Jamie Company acquires the land and building owned by Smitt Company. What types of costs may be incurred to make the asset ready for its intended use if Jamie Company wants to use (a) only the land, and (b) both the land and the building?

5. Your roommate does not understand the difference in accounting for sales taxes and motor vehicle licenses in purchasing a delivery truck. Explain to your roomie the difference and the reasons for it.

6. When can interest costs be added to the construction costs of a building? What limits are imposed on the inclusion of interest costs?

7. In a lump sum purchase it is possible to determine the purchase price and both the book values and fair market values of the acquired assets. Explain the relevance of each amount in allocating cost to the individual assets acquired.

8. In a recent newspaper release, the president of Lawsuit Company asserted that something has to be done about depreciation. The president said, "Depreciation does not come close to accumulating the cash needed to replace the asset at the end of its useful life." What is your response to the president?

9. The decline in usefulness of a plant asset may be due to two principal causes. Identify and explain the two causes.

10. "The selection of a depreciation method is a management decision that may be changed periodically." Do you agree? Explain.

11. Cecile is studying for the next accounting examination. She asks your help on two questions: (a) What is salvage value? (b) Is salvage value used in determining depreciable cost under each depreciation method? Answer Cecile's questions.

12. Contrast the straight-line method and the units of activity method as to (a) useful life, and (b) the pattern of periodic depreciation over useful life.

13. Richard Dysart is having a difficult time with the two accelerated depreciation methods. Explain to Richard the formulas for computing periodic depreciation in (a) the declining-balance method, and (b) the sum-of-the-years'-digits method.

14. Richard says the formulas in Question 13 help. However, he is not sure which of the factors in the two formulas change and which remain constant each year. Clarify these points for Richard.

15. Contrast the effects of the four depreciation methods on annual depreciation expense.

16. In the fourth year of an asset's five-year useful life, the company decides that the asset will have a six-year service life. How should the revision of depreciation be recorded? Why?

17. On January 1, 1993, T. Mason Company concludes that the useful life of equipment purchased for $18,000 on January 1, 1987 will be 12 years, rather than 10 years as originally anticipated. Assuming no salvage value and the straight-line method is applied, compute (a) the book value at January 1, 1993, and (b) 1993 depreciation expense.

18. Distinguish between revenue expenditures and capital expenditures during useful life.

19. Ryan Wood believes that since all additions and improvements are capital expenditures, they should be debited to an accumulated depreciation account. Is Ryan correct? Explain.

20. How is annual depreciation computed following a capital expenditure?

*21. What is the Modified Accelerated Cost Recovery System (MACRS)?

BRIEF EXERCISES

BE10-1   The following expenditures were incurred by the Westrum Company in purchasing land. Cash price $50,000, accrued taxes $3,000, attorneys' fees $2,500, real estate broker's commission, $2,000, and clearing and grading $3,500. What is the cost of the land?

Determine the cost of land.
(S.O. 1)

BE10-2   The Marlene Company incurs the following expenditures in purchasing a truck. Cash price $18,000, accident insurance $2,000, sales taxes $900, motor vehicle license $100, and painting and lettering $400. What is the cost of the truck?

Determine the cost of a truck.
(S.O. 1)

BE10-3   The E-Z Company purchases factory equipment for a cash price of $75,000. Related expenditures consist of insurance during shipping $500, installation $600, and sales taxes $400. What is the cost of the equipment?

Determine the cost of equipment.
(S.O. 1)

BE10-4   The Paxton Company acquires a delivery truck at a cost of $22,000. The truck is expected to have a salvage value of $2,000 at the end of its four-year useful life. Compute annual depreciation for the first and second years using the straight-line method.

Compute straight-line depreciation.
(S.O. 3)

Compute declining-balance depreciation.
(S.O. 3)

BE10–5   Depreciation information for the Paxton Company is given in BE10–4. Assuming the declining-balance depreciation rate is double the straight-line rate, compute annual depreciation for the first and second years under the declining-balance method.

Compute sum-of-the-years'-digits depreciation.
(S.O. 3)

BE10–6   Depreciation information for the Paxton Company is given in BE10–4. Compute annual depreciation for the first two years using the sum-of-the-years'-digits method.

Compute depreciation using the units of activity method.
(S.O. 3)

BE10–7   Deluxe Taxi Service uses the units of activity method in computing depreciation on its taxicabs. Each cab is expected to be driven 120,000 miles. Taxi No. 10 cost $24,500, and it is expected to have a salvage value of $500. Taxi No. 10 is driven 30,000 miles in Year one and 20,000 miles in Year two. Compute the depreciation for each year.

Compute revised depreciation.
(S.O. 4)

BE10–8   On January 1, 1993, the Asler Company ledger shows Equipment $32,000 and Accumulated Depreciation $12,000. The depreciation resulted from using the straight-line method with a useful life of 10 years and salvage value of $2,000. On this date, the company concludes that the equipment has only a remaining useful life of four years with the same salvage value. Compute the revised annual depreciation.

Journalize expenditures during ownership.
(S.O. 5)

BE10–9   In June, the Adams Company had two plant asset expenditures: (1) June 10, paid $2,500 for complete overhaul of delivery truck motor that is expected to extend the useful life of the truck by two years; (2) June 25, paid $30,000 to enclose the receiving dock on the factory building. This expenditure will not extend the useful life of the building. Journalize the transactions.

Compute depreciation after capital expenditure.
(S.O. 6)

BE10–10   On January 1, the Kristi Company has equipment with a book value of $36,000. On this date, a $4,000 capital expenditure is incurred that will result in a remaining useful life of four years and a salvage value of $2,000. Compute the new annual depreciation using the straight-line method.

Compute MACRS depreciation.
(S.O. 7)

*****BE10–11**   Nancy Wall Co. spent $90,000 for a tractor on January 2, 1992. The tractor is in the 3-year MACRS property class. Prepare a schedule showing the MACRS tax depreciation for each year on the tractor using the tax table rates.

EXERCISES

Determine cost of plant acquisitions.
(S.O. 1)

E10–1   The following expenditures relating to plant assets were made by John Somers Company during the first two months of 1993.

1. Paid $250 to have company name and advertising slogan painted on new delivery truck.
2. Paid $75 motor vehicle license fee on the new truck.
3. Paid $850 sales taxes on new delivery truck.
4. Paid $17,500 for parking lots and driveways on new plant site.
5. Paid $5,000 of accrued taxes at time plant site was acquired.
6. Paid $8,000 for installation of new factory machinery.
7. Paid $900 for one-year accident insurance policy on new delivery truck.
8. Paid $200 insurance to cover possible accident loss on new factory machinery while the machinery was in transit.

Instructions

(a) Explain the application of the cost principle in determining the acquisition cost of plant assets.

(b) List the numbers of the foregoing transactions, and opposite each indicate the account title to which each expenditure should be debited.

Determine acquisition costs on land.
(S.O. 1)

E10–2   On March 1, 1993, Roy Orbis Company acquired real estate, on which they planned to construct a small office building, by paying $100,000 in cash. An old warehouse on the property was razed at a cost of $6,600; the salvaged materials were sold for $1,700. Additional expenditures before construction began included $1,100 attorney's fee for work concerning the land purchase, $4,000 real estate broker's fee, $7,800 architect's fee, and $14,000 to put in driveways and a parking lot.

Instructions

(a) Determine the amount to be reported as the cost of the land.

(b) For each cost not used in part (a), indicate the account to be debited.

E10–3 Plant asset acquisitions for selected companies are as follows:

Prepare correct entries for acquisition costs. (S.O. 1)

1. Cress Lithographics purchased a printing press for $50,000 cash. In addition, it paid $3,500 shipping charges, $500 insurance during transit, and $3,000 installation costs. Cress made the following entry for the printing press.

Printing Press	53,000	
Freight-in	3,500	
Insurance Expense	500	
Cash		57,000

2. Estus Company purchased a delivery truck for $18,500 cash. In addition, it paid $1,110 sales taxes, $900 for the first year's insurance, $250 motor vehicle license, and $500 for painting the company name and logo on the truck. The truck was recorded as follows:

Delivery Truck	19,400	
Licenses and Taxes Expense	1,360	
Miscellaneous Expense	500	
Cash		21,260

Instructions

Prepare the entry that should have been made for each acquisition (the correct entry).

E10–4 Rowena Company makes a lump-sum purchase of plant assets at a total cost of $900,000. On the seller's books, land was recorded at cost, $150,000, and the book values of the buildings and equipment were $500,000 and $100,000, respectively. At the time of the purchase, fair market values were: land $160,000, buildings $600,000, and equipment $40,000.

Assign costs in a lump-sum purchase. (S.O. 1)

Instructions

(a) Determine the cost to be assigned to each asset obtained in the lump-sum purchase.

(b) Journalize the purchase assuming the total cost was paid in cash.

E10–5 Armon Company purchased a new machine for $50,000 cash on January 1, 1993. The machine is expected to have a salvage value of $5,000 at the end of its four-year useful life. Paula Armon, the owner, wishes to know the annual depreciation expense over the four-year period under each of the following depreciation methods: (1) straight-line, (2) declining balance using double the straight-line rate, and (3) sum-of-the-years'-digits.

Determine depreciation under a variety of methods. (S.O. 3)

Instructions

(a) Prepare separate depreciation schedules for each of the depreciation methods.

(b) Compare the accumulated depreciation at the end of the second year under each method in dollars and as a percentage of cost.

E10–6 Interstate Bus Lines uses the units-of-activity method in depreciating its buses. One bus was purchased on January 1, 1993 at a cost of $108,000. Over its four year useful life the bus is expected to be driven 100,000 miles. Salvage value is expected to be $8,000.

Compute depreciation under units-of-activity method. (S.O. 3)

Instructions

(a) Compute the depreciation cost per unit.

(b) Prepare a depreciation schedule assuming actual mileage was: Year 1 28,000, Year 2 30,000, Year 3 25,000, and Year 4 17,000.

E10–7 Elvis Costello Company purchased a new machine on October 1, 1993, at a cost of $96,000. The company estimated that the machine will have a salvage value of $12,000. The machine is expected to be used for 84,000 working hours during its six-year life.

Determine depreciation for partial periods. (S.O. 3)

Instructions

Compute the depreciation expense under the following methods for the year indicated: (1) straight-line for 1993, (2) units of activity for 1993, assuming machine usage was 1,700 hours, (3) sum-of-the-years'-digits for 1994, and (4) declining-balance using double the straight-line rate for 1993 and 1994.

Compute revised annual
depreciation.

(S.O. 3, 4)

E10–8   The Wilburys Company acquired two delivery trucks for cash at a cost of $20,000 each on January 1, 1992. It expects each truck to last four years and have a salvage value of $4,000. The straight-line method of depreciation is used and depreciation has been correctly taken during the first three years of useful life. In 1995, the following events and transactions occurred.

Jan. 1   Because truck A is in such good condition, the company decides to extend the useful life of the truck by one year to 12/31/96 with no change in salvage value.

1   Paid cash for a major motor overhaul on truck B at a cost of $3,000. It is expected that this improvement will increase the truck's useful life one year to 12/31/96 with no change in salvage value.

Instructions

(a) Indicate what entry(ies), if any, should be made on January 1, 1995.

(b) Compute the amount of depreciation expense for 1995 on the trucks.

Explain revenue and
capital expenditures.

(S.O. 5)

E10–9   Tim Rubeck and Lila Ripley, presidents of small businesses, were discussing the accounting issue of revenue and capital expenditures. The following is part of their conversation:

Tim: Two good examples of revenue expenditures are the cost of cleaning the exterior of our office building, and the cost of replacing broken windows. All costs of this nature should always be expensed.

Lila: Those are good examples, but on the other hand my company recently had some special situations where the cost of cleaning a building exterior and the cost of replacing windows were capitalized.

Tim: That is definitely incorrect. Those costs are revenue expenditures, not capital expenditures.

Instructions

(a) Discuss what kind of special situations Lila might be referring to.

(b) Evaluate Tim's remarks.

Compute revised annual
depreciation.

(S.O. 3, 4)

E10–10   Lindy Weink, the new controller of the Waterloo Company, has reviewed the expected useful lives and salvage values of selected depreciable assets at the beginning of 1993. Her findings are as follows:

Type of Asset	Date Acquired	Cost	Accumulated Depreciation 1/1/93	Useful Life in Years Old	Useful Life in Years Proposed	Salvage Value Old	Salvage Value Proposed
Building	1/1/87	$800,000	$114,000	40	45	$40,000	$62,000
Warehouse	1/1/90	100,000	11,400	25	20	5,000	3,600

All assets are depreciated by the straight-line method. Waterloo Company uses a calendar year in preparing annual financial statements. After discussion, management has agreed to accept Lindy's proposed changes.

Instructions

(a) Compute the revised annual depreciation on each asset in 1993. (Show computations.)

(b) Prepare the entry (or entries) to record depreciation on the building in 1993.

Journalize capital expenditures and compute revised depreciation.

(S.O. 3, 5, 6)

E10–11   On January 1, 1993, Grody Company had one delivery truck in its Delivery Equipment account as follows:

Cost	$15,000
Accumulated depreciation	8,100
Book value	$ 6,900
Purchase date	1/1/90

The truck has a useful life of five years. Salvage value is 10% of cost. The straight-line method of depreciation is used. On January 1, 1993, the truck was paneled at a cost of $2,600. This addition will increase useful life one year and total salvage value is now estimated to be $2,000.

Instructions

(a) Compute the revised annual depreciation for the truck following the capital expenditure.

(b) Record the 1993 depreciation expense for the truck.

*E10–12   Spencer Co. spent $400,000 on capital expenditures during the year 1993. Included in this total are two machines that cost $80,000 each. The machines are in the three-year class. At the end of their useful lives, the machines are expected to have a $10,000 salvage value each.

Compute MACRS depreciation.
(S.O. 7)

Instructions

Prepare a schedule showing the MACRS depreciation for each year on the machines (use the MACRS tax table rates).

PROBLEMS

P10–1   Soundtrack Company was organized on January 1. During the first year of operations, the following plant asset expenditures and receipts were recorded in random order.

Determine acquisition costs of land and building.
(S.O. 1)

Debits

1. Cost of real estate purchased as a plant site (land $100,000 and building $25,000)	$125,000
2. Installation cost of fences around property	4,000
3. Cost of demolishing building to make land suitable for construction of new building	13,000
4. Excavation costs for new building	20,000
5. Accrued real estate taxes paid at time of purchase of real estate	2,000
6. Cost of parking lots and driveways	12,000
7. Architect's fees on building plans	10,000
8. Real estate taxes paid for the current year on land	3,000
9. Full payment to building contractor	600,000
	$789,000

Credits

10. Proceeds from salvage of demolished building	$ 2,500

Instructions

Analyze the foregoing transactions using the following tabular arrangement. Insert the number of each transaction in the Item space and insert the amounts in the appropriate columns. For amounts entered in the Other Accounts column also indicate the account title.

Item	Land	Building	Other Accounts

P10–2   In recent years, Wind Company has purchased three machines. Because of heavy turnover in the accounting department, a different accountant was in charge of selecting the depreciation method for each machine, and various methods have been selected. Information concerning the machines is summarized below:

Compute depreciation under different methods.
(S.O. 3)

Machine	Acquired	Cost	Salvage Value	Useful Life in Years	Depreciation Method
1	1/1/90	$ 86,000	$ 6,000	10	Straight-line
2	1/1/91	100,000	10,000	8	Declining-balance
3	1/1/92	68,000	5,000	9	Sum-of-the-years'-digits
4	11/1/93	78,000	6,000	6	Units of activity

For the declining balance method, Wind Company uses the double-declining rate. For the units-of-activity method, total machine hours are expected to be 24,000. Actual hours of use in the first three years were: 1993 4,000; 1994 4,500; and 1995 5,000.

Instructions

(a) Compute the amount of accumulated depreciation on each machine at December 31, 1993.

(b) If machine 2 was purchased on April 1 instead of January 1, what is the depreciation expense for this machine in (1) 1991 and (2) 1992?

(c) If machine 3 was purchased on October 1 instead of January 1, what is the depreciation expense for this machine in (1) 1992 and (2) 1993?

Compute depreciation under different methods.
(S.O. 3, 4)
S

P10–3 Keith Whitley Corporation purchased machinery on January 1, 1993, at a cost of $100,000. The estimated useful life of the machinery is four years, with an estimated residual value at the end of that period of $10,000. The company is considering different depreciation methods that could be used for financial reporting purposes.

Instructions

(a) Prepare separate depreciation schedules for the machinery using the following methods: straight-line, declining-balance using double the straight-line rate, and sum-of-the-years'-digits. Round to the nearest dollar.

(b) Which method would result in the highest reported 1993 income? In the highest total reported income over the four-year period?

(c) Which method would result in the lowest reported 1993 income? In the lowest total reported income over the four-year period?

(d) Assume Keith Whitley Corporation decides to use the straight-line method. In 1995, the company decides that the useful life of the machinery will be five years, with a salvage value of $7,000. Prepare the journal entry to record 1995 depreciation.

Compute depreciation and answer questior .
(S.O. 2, 3)

P10–4 The accountant for the Monica Company prepared the following depreciation schedules for a truck with a four-year useful life.

Year	Straight-Line	Declining-Balance	Sum-of-the Years'-Digits
1	$7,000	$15,000	$11,200
2	$7,000	7,500	8,400

Instructions

(a) Answer the following questions:
   1. If Monica is using the double-declining balance rate, what is the cost of the truck?
   2. What is the salvage value, if any, of the truck?
   3. What SYD fraction was used in each year?

(b) Compute the depreciation for Year 3 under each depreciation method.

(c) Which method produces the largest depreciation in Year 3? Which method shows the lowest book value at the end of Year 3? Which method shows the highest book value at the end of Year 3?

(d) Assume the truck cost $50,000 and had an estimated five-year life. If straight-line depreciation in Year 3 is $9,000, what is the salvage value, if any?

(e) Using the assumptions in (d), above, compute depreciation for Years 1 and 2 under both the double-declining balance and SYD methods.

(f) At the end of the asset's useful life, how much of the accumulated depreciation, if any, is in the form of cash?

Record various plant related costs.
(S.O. 3, 5, 6)

P10–5 Murphy Company owns two delivery trucks and uses the straight-line method of depreciation with no salvage value. The company closes its books annually on December 31. The following events and transactions occurred during the first three years.

1993

Jan. 2 Purchased panel truck No. X7654 from Edson Motors for $11,700 cash plus sales taxes $300, and motor vehicle license $75.

Dec. 1 Made minor repairs to truck for cash at cost of $25.
      31 Recorded annual depreciation on basis of a four-year life.

1994

Jan. 2 Purchased panel truck No. Y8379 from Hirt Motor Company for cash, $7,800, plus sales taxes of $200. This was a used 1990 truck, which is expected to last three years from date of purchase.

      2 Installed four new tires to make truck ready for use at a cash cost of $400.

Dec. 31 Recorded depreciation on both trucks.

1995

Jan. 2 Paid $900 for major overhaul of motor on truck No. X7654. This capital expenditure is expected to extend useful life one year with no change in salvage value.

2 Installed two-way CB radio in truck No. Y8379 at a cash cost of $600 to improve efficiency. This capital expenditure will not increase useful life or salvage value.

Dec. 31 Recorded depreciation on both trucks.

Instructions

Journalize the transactions and events.

*P10–6 Nina Inc. reported income before depreciation and income taxes in the first six years of operations as follows:

Determine taxable income under straight-line and MACRS depreciation. (S.O. 7)

Year	Income before depreciation
1	$60,000
2	$70,000
3	$75,000
4	$80,000
5	$82,000
6	$86,000

On January 1 of the first year of operations the company purchased depreciable assets at a cost of $85,000. The assets were expected to have a useful life of 5 years and no salvage value.

Instructions

(a) Determine taxable income for each of the six years, assuming (1) straight-line depreciation, and (2) MACRS depreciation (five-year class life). In using the straight-line method, one-half year's depreciation should be used in Year 1 and Year 6.

(b) Determine the difference in taxable income for each of the six years and in total between the depreciation methods.

ALTERNATE PROBLEMS

P10–1A Vern Goslin Company was organized on January 1. During the first year of operations, the following plant asset expenditures and receipts were recorded in random order.

Determine acquisition costs of land and building. (S.O. 1)

Debits

1. Cost of real estate purchased as a plant site (land $100,000, and building $45,000)	$145,000
2. Accrued real estate taxes paid at time of purchase of real estate	2,000
3. Cost of demolishing building to make land suitable for construction of new building	12,000
4. Cost of filling and grading the land	4,000
5. Excavation costs for new building	20,000
6. Architect's fees on building plans	10,000
7. Full payment to building contractor	700,000
8. Cost of parking lots and driveways	14,000
9. Real estate taxes paid for the current year on land	5,000
	$912,000

Credits

10. Proceeds for salvage of demolished building	$ 3,500

Instructions

Analyze the foregoing transactions using the following tabular arrangement. Insert the number of each transaction in the Item space and insert the amounts in the appropriate columns. For amounts entered in the Other Accounts column, also indicate the account titles.

Item	Land	Building	Other Accounts

Compute depreciation
under different methods.
(S.O. 3)

P10–2A   In recent years, Rapid Transportation purchased three used buses. Because of frequent turnover in the accounting department, a different accountant selected the depreciation method for each bus, and various methods have been selected. Information concerning the buses is summarized below:

Bus	Acquired	Cost	Salvage Value	Useful Life in Years	Depreciation Method
1	1/1/92	$ 96,000	$ 6,000	5	Straight-line
2	1/1/92	120,000	10,000	4	Declining-balance
3	1/1/93	71,360	5,000	6	Sum-of-the-years'-digits
4	1/1/93	80,000	8,000	5	Units-of-activity

For the declining balance method, Rapid Transportation uses the double-declining rate. For the units-of-activity method, total miles are expected to be 120,000. Actual miles of use in the first three years were: 1993 24,000; 1994 34,000; and 1995 30,000.

Instructions

(a) Compute the amount of accumulated depreciation on each bus at December 31, 1994.

(b) If Bus No. 2 was purchased on April 1 instead of January 1, what is the depreciation expense for this bus in (1) 1992 and (2) 1993?

(c) If Bus No. 3 was purchased on July 1 instead of January 1, what is the depreciation expense for this bus in (1) 1993 and (2) 1994.

Compute depreciation
under different methods.
(S.O.3, 4)

P10–3A   Scott Piper Corporation purchased machinery on January 1, 1993 at a cost of $243,000. The estimated useful life of the machinery is five years, with an estimated residual value at the end of that period of $12,000. The company is considering different depreciation methods that could be used for financial reporting purposes.

Instructions

(a) Prepare separate depreciation schedules for the machinery using the following methods: straight-line, declining-balance using double the straight-line rate, and sum-of-the-years'-digits.

(b) Which method would result in the highest reported 1993 income? In the highest total reported income over the five-year period?

(c) Which method would result in the lowest reported 1993 income? In the lowest total reported income over the five-year period?

(d) Assume that Piper decides to use the straight-line method. In 1996, the company decided that the useful life should total seven years, with a salvage value of $22,000. Prepare the journal entry to record 1996 depreciation.

Compute depreciation and
answer questions.
(S.O. 2, 3)

P10–4A   The accountant for the Marion Company prepared the following depreciation schedules for a truck with a five year useful life.

Year	Straight-Line	Declining-Balance	Sum-of-the Years'-Digits
1	$12,000	$26,000	$20,000
2	$12,000	15,600	16,000

Instructions

(a) Answer the following questions:
  1. If Marion is using the double-declining balance rate, what is the cost of the truck?
  2. What is the salvage value, if any, of the truck?
  3. What SYD fraction was used in each year?

(b) Compute the depreciation for Year 3 under each depreciation method.

(c) Which method produces the largest depreciation in Year 3? Which method shows the highest book value at the end of Year 3?

(d) Assume the truck cost $70,000 and had an estimated four-year life. If straight-line depreciation in Year 3 is $16,000, what is the estimated salvage value, if any?

(e) Using the assumptions in (d), above, compute depreciation for Years 1 and 2 under both the double-declining balance and SYD methods.

(f) At the end of the asset's useful life, how much of the accumulated depreciation, if any, is in the form of cash?

P10–5A Bellamy Bros. owns two delivery trucks and uses the straight-line method of depreciation. Salvage value is estimated to be 10% of cost. The company closes its books annually on December 31. The following events and transactions took place during the first three years.

Record various plant related costs.

(S.O. 3, 5, 6)

1993

Jan.	2	Purchased new panel truck No. N4521 from Barr Motors for $17,200 cash plus sales taxes $800, motor vehicle licenses $115, and paid $900 for a one-year accident insurance policy.
Dec.	1	Paid $90 for minor repairs on truck.
	31	Recorded annual depreciation on basis of a four-year life.

1994

Jan.	2	Purchased panel truck No. U2475 from Danny Motor Company for cash $11,000, plus sales taxes of $500. This was a used 1990 truck, which is expected to last three years from date of purchase.
	2	Installed four new tires to make truck ready for use at a cash cost of $400.
Dec.	31	Recorded depreciation on both trucks.

1995

Jan.	2	Paid $1,500 for major overhaul of motor on truck No. N4521. This capital expenditure is expected to extend useful life one year with no change in salvage value.
	2	Installed two-way CB radio in truck No. U2475 at a cash cost of $800 to improve efficiency. This capital expenditure will not increase useful life or salvage value.
Dec.	31	Recorded depreciation on both trucks.

Instructions
Journalize the transactions and events.

*B*roadening *Your Perspective*

FINANCIAL REPORTING PROBLEM

Refer to the financial statements and the Notes to Consolidated Financial Statements of PepsiCo, Inc. in Appendix L, and answer the following questions:

1. How is property, plant, and equipment reported in the Consolidated Balance Sheet? What was the total cost and book value of property, plant, and equipment at December 28, 1991?

2. What method or methods of depreciation are used by PepsiCo for financial reporting purposes?

3. What was the composition of PepsiCo's property, plant, and equipment and the cost of each category at December 28, 1991?

4. What was the amount of depreciation expense for each of the three years 1989–1991?

5. Using Management's Analysis—Financial Condition, what is the amount of property, plant, and equipment purchased in 1991 and 1990? What were the major types of items purchased in 1991?

DECISION CASE

Tammy Company and Hamline Company are two proprietorships that are similar in many respects except that Tammy Company uses the straight-line method and Hamline Company uses the declining-balance method at double the straight-line rate. On January 2, 1991, both companies acquired the following depreciable assets.

Asset	Cost	Salvage Value	Useful Life
Building	$320,000	$20,000	40 years
Equipment	110,000	10,000	10 years

Including the appropriate depreciation charges, annual net income for the companies in the years 1991, 1992, and 1993 and total income for the three years were as follows:

	1991	1992	1993	Total
Tammy Company	$84,000	$88,400	$90,000	$262,400
Hamline Company	68,000	76,000	82,000	226,000

At December 31, 1993, the balance sheets of the two companies are similar except that Hamline Company has more cash than Tammy Company.

Dawna Remmers is interested in buying one of the companies and she comes to you for advice.

Instructions

(a) Determine the annual and total depreciation recorded by each company during the three years.

(b) Assuming that Hamline Company also uses the straight-line method of depreciation instead of the declining-balance method as in (a), prepare comparative income data for the three years.

(c) Which company should Ms. Remmers buy? Why?

CRITICAL THINKING CASE

Refer to the opening story concerning Westbrook College and answer the following questions.

1. What is the purpose of depreciation?

2. How is it possible to have a college building that has a zero value on the books but yet has a substantial market value?

3. What factors are considered in depreciating a college building?

4. If a college building is appreciating in value, why should it be depreciated?

ETHICAL CASE

Tipperary Import Company has purchased a large warehouse at dockside in Seattle where land values are increasing rapidly. Bob Resner, controller, and Anne Seargill, financial vice-president of Tipperary Import are attempting to allocate the $40 million cost of the purchase between the land and the warehouse. The controller, noting that depreciation can only be taken on the warehouse, favors undervaluing the land and placing a very high proportion of the cost on the warehouse, thus reducing taxable income and income taxes. The financial vice-president argues just the opposite, "a very high proportion of the cost should be placed on the land in order to relieve net income of some depreciation charge. We must minimize the negative impact of this purchase on net income in order to keep the company's stock price up."

Instructions

(a) Whose interests are affected by the controller's and the financial vice-president's contrary positions?

(b) What are the ethical issues in this case?

(c) How should the purchase cost be allocated? Why?

Answers to Self-Study Questions
1. d 2. a 3. b 4. b 5. c 6. d 7. d 8. b 9. d 10. b
11. b

CONCEPTS FOR REVIEW

Before studying this chapter you should know or, if necessary, review:

a. *How to determine the cost of a plant asset. (Ch. 10, p. 399–402)*

b. *How to compute depreciation using different depreciation methods. (Ch. 10, p. 403–10)*

c. *How to compute depreciation for partial periods. (Ch. 10, p. 403–10)*

PLANT ASSET DISPOSALS, NATURAL RESOURCES, AND INTANGIBLE ASSETS

Study Objectives

After studying this chapter, you should be able to:

1. *Explain how to account for the disposal of a plant asset through retirement, sale, or exchange.*

2. *Explain the role of subsidiary plant ledgers.*

3. *Identify the basic accounting issues related to natural resources.*

4. *Contrast the accounting for intangible assets with the accounting for plant assets.*

5. *Indicate how plant assets, natural resources, and intangible assets are reported on the balance sheet.*

When you stroll around your campus, chances are you'll see someone wearing a sweater or T-shirt with your school's logo on it. Your sports teams have nicknames. The school's letterhead has a certain design. These trademarks or logos are examples of intangible assets—assets that the school has cultivated very carefully, and will go to great lengths to protect.

At the University of Utah, the university seal has existed for more than a century. The school also has its own logotype, "created several years ago through extensive research," says Michael Jones, director of university publications. "Whenever the university logo or seal is used in a design, it must be approved by my office," he says, noting that occasionally he catches a sample run of some document with the university logo and type in the wrong color or proportions. "We are primarily interested in the misuse of the logo and seal on official stationery or business cards. My primary concern is the image that we portray to the public at large."

How much is such a trademark worth? Jones can't put a dollar figure on it, but he knows it's worth a lot. "We have literally thousands of printed pieces coming off the campus every year. By sending out a consistent image, the public recognizes us in a positive way."

Here's another way to consider a trademark's value. The next time you go into your bookstore, take a look at a sweatshirt with the school logo on it. Then look at the price tag. How much would that sweatshirt be worth, do you think, without the logo?

As the opening story indicates, intangible assets like trademarks and logos are major long-term assets of companies and institutions. Another type of long-term asset is a company's reserves of natural resources such as oil, minerals, or timber. We will look at the accounting for each of these types of assets in this chapter. Before we do so, however, we will first consider another topic, the disposal of plant assets.

SECTION 1   Plant Asset Disposals

The financial press has reported the following business developments:

> "Armco writes off its idle facilities in the depressed oil field business."
> "Times Mirror Co. to sell two television stations."
> "Federal government acquires land from lumber companies for national park system in exchange for other federal land."

As these headlines indicate, plant assets of various types may be disposed of in three ways:

Study Objective 1

Explain how to account for the disposal of a plant asset through retirement, sale, or exchange.

1. Retirement—the plant asset is scrapped or discarded.
2. Sale—the plant asset is sold to another party.
3. Exchange—an existing plant asset is traded in on a new plant asset.

At the time of disposal, it is necessary to determine the book value of the plant asset. The book value is the difference between the cost of the plant asset and the accumulated depreciation to date. If the disposal occurs at any time during the year, depreciation for the fraction of the year to the date of disposal must be recorded. The book value is then eliminated by debiting Accumulated Depreciation for the total depreciation to the date of disposal and crediting the asset account for the cost of the asset.

Accounting in Action · *Business Insight*

When does an asset become impaired (no longer useful)? That is a tough question—one that management has to determine. It is particularly difficult because there are no rules to determine when an asset should be written off. Of course, you can use the following logic—"You know it when you see it"—but that is not very comforting to many accountants. As an example, Squibb Corp. took a write-off of $68 million related to its pharmaceutical operations in South America and Asia because of unstable political and economic conditions. However, the company admitted that there remained a possibility that these assets would be useful in the future.

Retirement of Plant Assets

To illustrate the accounting for a retirement, assume that Hobart Enterprises retires its computer printers, which cost $32,000. The accumulated depreciation on these printers is also $32,000; the equipment, therefore, is fully depreciated (zero book value). The entry to record this retirement is as follows:

Accumulated Depreciation—Printing Equipment	32,000	
Printing Equipment		32,000
(To record retirement of fully depreciated equipment)		

What happens if a fully depreciated plant asset is still useful to the company? In this case, the plant asset and the related accumulated depreciation continue to be reported on the balance sheet without further depreciation or adjustment until the asset is retired. Reporting the asset and related accumulated depreciation on the balance sheet informs the reader of the financial statements that the asset is still being used by the company. However, once an asset is fully depreciated, even if it is still being used, no additional depreciation should be taken. In no situation can the accumulated depreciation on the plant asset exceed its cost.

Helpful hint When a plant asset is disposed of, all amounts related to the asset must be removed from the accounts. This includes the original cost in the asset account and the total depreciation to date in the Accumulated Depreciation account.

If a plant asset is retired before it is fully depreciated, and no scrap or salvage value is received, a loss on disposal occurs. For example, assume that Sunset Company discards delivery equipment that cost $18,000 and has accumulated depreciation of $14,000 at the date of retirement. The entry is as follows:

Accumulated Depreciation—Delivery Equipment	14,000	
Loss on Disposal	4,000	
Delivery Equipment		18,000
(To record retirement of delivery equipment at a loss)		

The loss on disposal is reported in the other expenses and losses section of the income statement.

Sale of Plant Assets

In a disposal by sale, the book value of the asset is compared with the proceeds received from the sale. If the proceeds of the sale exceed the book value of the plant asset, a gain on disposal occurs. If the proceeds of the sale are less than the book value of the plant asset sold, a loss on disposal occurs.

Only by coincidence will the book value and the fair market value of the asset be the same at the time the asset is sold. Gains and losses on sales of plant assets are, therefore, quite common. As an example, Delta Airlines, Inc. reported a $94,343,000 gain on the sale of five Boeing B-727-200 aircraft and five Lockheed L-1011-1 aircraft.

Gain on Disposal

To illustrate a gain, assume that on July 1, 1993, Wright Company sells office furniture for $16,000 cash. The office furniture originally cost $60,000 and as of January 1, 1993, had accumulated depreciation of $41,000. Depreciation for the first six months of 1993 is $8,000. The entry to record depreciation expense and update accumulated depreciation to July 1 is as follows:

July 1	Depreciation Expense	8,000	
	Accumulated Depreciation—Office Furniture		8,000
	(To record depreciation expense for the first six		
	months of 1993)		

After the accumulated depreciation balance is updated, a gain on disposal of $5,000 is computed:

ILLUSTRATION 11-1

Computation of gain on disposal

Cost of office furniture	$60,000
Less: Accumulated depreciation ($41,000 + $8,000)	49,000
Book value at date of disposal	11,000
Proceeds from sale	16,000
Gain on disposal	$ 5,000

The entry to record the sale and the gain on disposal is as follows:

July 1	Cash	16,000	
	Accumulated Depreciation—Office Furniture	49,000	
	Office Furniture		60,000
	Gain on Disposal		5,000
	(To record sale of office furniture at a gain)		

The gain on disposal is reported in the other revenues and gains section of the income statement.

Loss on Disposal

Assume that instead of selling the office furniture for $16,000, Wright sells it for $9,000. In this case, a loss of $2,000 is computed:

ILLUSTRATION 11-2

Computation of loss on disposal

Cost of office furniture	$60,000
Less: Accumulated depreciation	49,000
Book value at date of disposal	11,000
Proceeds from sale	9,000
Loss on disposal	$ 2,000

The entry to record the sale and the loss on disposal is as follows:

July 1	Cash	9,000	
	Accumulated Depreciation—Office Furniture	49,000	
	Loss on Disposal	2,000	
	Office Furniture		60,000
	(To record sale of office furniture at a loss)		

The loss on disposal is reported in the other expenses and losses section of the income statement.

Exchanges of Plant Assets

Plant assets may also be disposed of through exchange. Exchanges can be for either similar or dissimilar assets. Because exchanges of similar assets are more common, they are discussed here.

An exchange of similar assets involves assets of the same type. This occurs, for example, when old delivery equipment is exchanged for new delivery equipment or when old office furniture is exchanged for new office furniture. In an exchange of similar assets, the new asset performs the same function as the old asset.

In exchanges of similar plant assets, **gains on exchanges of plant assets are not recognized: they are deferred and reduce the cost basis of the new asset. Losses are recognized immediately**. This accounting treatment is conservative because it recognizes losses but defers gains.

Gain Treatment

To illustrate the accounting for similar assets, assume that Mark's Express Delivery decides to exchange its old delivery equipment plus cash of $31,000 for new delivery equipment. At this time, the book value of the old delivery equipment is $12,000 (cost $40,000 less accumulated depreciation $28,000). In addition, it is determined that the fair market value of the old delivery equipment is $19,000.

The cost of the new asset received (before deferral of the gain) is equal to the **fair market value of the old asset exchanged plus any cash or other consideration given up**. The cost of the new delivery equipment (before deferral of the gain) is $50,000, computed as follows:

Fair market value of old delivery equipment	$19,000
Cash	31,000
Cost of new delivery equipment (before deferral of gain)	**$50,000**

ILLUSTRATION 11-3

Cost of new equipment (before deferral of gain)

A gain results when the fair market value is greater than the book value of the asset given up. For Mark's Express, there is a gain of $7,000, computed as follows on the disposal:

Fair market value of old delivery equipment	$19,000
Book value of old delivery equipment ($40,000 − $28,000)	12,000
Gain on disposal	**$ 7,000**

ILLUSTRATION 11-4

Computation of gain on disposal

The $7,000 gain on disposal is then offset against the $50,000 cost of the new delivery equipment. The result is a $43,000 cost of the new delivery equipment, after deferral of the gain, as shown in Illustration 11-5.

ILLUSTRATION 11-5

*Cost of new delivery equip-
ment (after deferral of gain)*

Cost of new delivery equipment (before deferral of gain)	$50,000
Less: Gain on disposal	7,000
Cost of new delivery equipment (after deferral of gain)	$43,000

The entry to record the exchange is as follows:

Delivery Equipment (new)	43,000	
Accumulated Depreciation—Delivery Equipment (old)	28,000	
Delivery Equipment (old)		40,000
Cash		31,000
(To record exchange of old delivery equipment for similar new delivery equipment)		

This entry does not eliminate the gain; it just postpones or defers it to future periods. The deferred gain of $7,000 reduces the $50,000 cost to $43,000. As a result, net income in future periods increases because depreciation expense on the newly acquired delivery equipment is less by $7,000.

Loss Treatment

When a loss occurs on the exchange of similar assets, it is recognized immediately—it is not deferred. As indicated earlier, this approach is conservative. To defer the loss would increase the cost of the new asset above its fair market value, which is considered inappropriate.

To illustrate the accounting for a loss, assume that Roland Company exchanged old office equipment for similar new office equipment. The book value of the old office equipment is $26,000 (cost $70,000 less accumulated depreciation $44,000), its fair market value is $10,000, and cash of $81,000 is paid. The cost of the new office equipment, $91,000, is computed as follows:

ILLUSTRATION 11-6

*Computation of cost of new
office equipment*

Fair market value of old office equipment	$10,000
Cash	81,000
Cost of new office equipment	$91,000

Through this exchange, a loss on disposal of $16,000 is determined. A loss results when the book value is greater than the fair market value of the asset given up. The computation is as follows:

ILLUSTRATION 11-7

*Computation of loss on
disposal*

Fair market value of old office equipment	$10,000
Book value of old office equipment ($70,000 − $44,000)	26,000
Loss on disposal	$16,000

The entry to record the exchange is as follows:

Office Equipment (new)	91,000	
Accumulated Depreciation—Office Equipment (old)	44,000	
Loss on Disposal	16,000	
Office Equipment (old)		70,000
Cash		81,000
(To record exchange of old office equipment for similar new equipment)		

If the accepted practice were to defer the loss, the cost of the new office equipment would be $107,000 ($91,000 + $16,000), which is higher than the fair market value of the new asset—an unacceptable result.

Summarizing, the rules for accounting for exchanges of similar assets are as follows:

Type of Event	Recognition
Gain	Defer and reduce cost of new asset
Loss	Recognize immediately

The tax rules for accounting for exchanges and the financial accounting for exchanges of dissimilar assets are recorded differently but are better left for an advanced accounting course.

Subsidiary Plant Ledgers

Strange as it may sound, plant assets—even large buildings—can disappear. Science fiction? No. For example, when one firm started a building program, it demolished an old building on the site. However, by mistake, the contractor demolished an adjacent structure as well. In figuring the loss on demolition, the accounting department failed to consider the smaller adjacent building that was torn down in error. Only after a period of time was it discovered that this $1.2 million asset was still being reported on the company's balance sheet. Although this may be an extreme case, an executive recently estimated that as much as 15% of an industry's plant assets have disappeared but are still listed on company balance sheets.

This example illustrates the need for good internal control of plant assets. **One means of accomplishing this objective is to keep adequate records of each individual asset.** However, to keep such a record in the general ledger is impractical. As a result, most companies have a subsidiary plant ledger for each general ledger account that includes numerous individual assets. The subsidiary plant ledger is a set of records that contains for each plant asset: a description of the individual asset, explanation of transactions, cost, accumulated depreciation, and book value. A company may have separate subsidiary plant ledgers for office equipment, delivery equipment, and factory machinery. An example of a subsidiary plant record for a delivery truck is shown in Illustration 11-8. Note that an account number is provided at the top of each subsidiary plant record. The first three digits of the number indicate the asset account in the general ledger; the latter three digits refer to the account in the subsidiary ledger. This number is often stamped, etched, or affixed to an asset for identification and control purposes.

As indicated, the subsidiary plant ledger is controlled by two general ledger accounts in this case. The control accounts are Delivery Equipment and Accumulated Depreciation—Delivery Equipment. The total of the subsidiary ledger balances should equal the total in the control accounts.

Subsidiary plant ledgers are useful in helping to keep track of periodic depreciation charges and in making entries upon the retirement of individual items. The subsidiary data also help in determining the adequacy of insurance coverage, submitting insurance claims in the event of accidents, and filing income tax returns. The information concerning each plant asset can be expanded to include such items as the cost of repairs, the number of breakdowns on the equipment, and days out of service.

Study Objective 2

Explain the role of subsidiary plant ledgers.

ILLUSTRATION 11-8

Subsidiary plant record

SUBSIDIARY PLANT RECORD

Acct. No. 136-103

Item	1 ton Panel Truck	General Ledger Accounts	Accumulated Depreciation/ Delivery Equipment
Serial No.	X245y102	Description	1990 Ford (new)
Purchased From	Elroy Motor Company	Estimated Life	5 years
Estimated Salvage	$1,000	Annual Depreciation	$2,400
		Depreciation Method	Straight-line

Date	Explanation	Cost Debit	Cost Credit	Cost Bal.	Accumulated Depreciation Debit	Accumulated Depreciation Credit	Accumulated Depreciation Bal.	Book Value
1/1/90	Cash purchase	13,000		13,000				13,000
12/31/90	Annual depreciation					2,400	2,400	10,600
12/31/91	Annual depreciation					2,400	4,800	8,200
12/31/92	Annual depreciation					2,400	7,200	5,800
12/31/93	Annual depreciation					2,400	9,600	3,400
12/31/93	Sold		13,000	-0-	9,600		-0-	-0-

Technology in Action

A typical software program for a computerized system would have each asset on a master file. That file would include information such as date of acquisition, accumulated depreciation, and depreciation methods and lives for both book and tax purposes. The program would automatically compute depreciation for both book and tax purposes and related accumulated depreciation. When an asset is disposed of, the program would figure gain or loss for both book and tax purposes.

Before You Go On . . .

1. What is the proper accounting for the retirement and sale of plant assets?

2. What is the proper accounting for the exchange of similar plant assets?

3. What is the purpose of a subsidiary plant ledger? What type of information does the subsidiary plant ledger contain?

SECTION 2   Natural Resources

Helpful hint   On a balance sheet, natural resources may be described as Timberlands, Mineral Deposits, Oil reserves, and so on.

Natural resources consist of standing timber and underground deposits of oil, gas, and minerals. Such resources include the much-publicized offshore oil deposits of major petroleum companies and the oil deposits for which the Alaskan pipeline was built. These long-lived productive assets have two distinguishing characteristics: (1) they are physically extracted in operations (such as mining, cutting, or pumping), and (2) they are not replaceable. Because of these characteristics, natural resources are frequently called **wasting assets.**

cquisition Cost

The acquisition cost of a natural resource is the cash or cash equivalent price necessary to acquire the resource and prepare it for its intended use. For an already discovered resource, such as an existing coal mine, cost is the price paid for the property.

Determining the cost to capitalize becomes a problem when exploration is involved. For example, some argue that the costs of unsuccessful exploration as well as successful exploration should be capitalized. They believe that, using an oil well as an example, the cost of drilling the dry holes is a cost that is needed to find the commercially profitable wells. As a result, both successful and unsuccessful explorations are capitalized, and the costs are written off to expense over the useful life of the successful wells. This method is often referred to as the full cost approach.

Others disagree, arguing that the costs of only successful projects should be capitalized. They maintain that if only one of 10 exploratory wells becomes commercially viable, it is inappropriate to assign the costs of the 9 unsuccessful wells to the cost of the successful well. This method is referred to as the successful efforts approach. At present, both approaches are used in accounting for natural resources. For example, such companies as American Petrofina, DuPont, Callahan Mining, and Copperweld use full costing, whereas Texaco, Mobil and Gulf use successful efforts.

> ### Study Objective 3
>
> *Identify the basic accounting issues related to natural resources.*

ccounting in Action · *Business Insight*

Should both these alternatives be permitted in accounting? Views are particularly strong on this subject. As one financial expert, commenting on the full cost method, noted: "It lets them call a dry hole an asset, and as far as I am concerned, any company that uses full cost accounting is guilty until proven innocent." On the other hand, companies using the full-cost method argue that "it enables them to undertake risky exploration projects without having sharp swings in their reported earnings." Or as one writer noted: "Forcing companies to use successful efforts accounting would retard domestic oil and gas exploration and imperil national security." The debate raises an interesting question—should accounting be concerned with national security or tell it like it is?

riting Off Acquisition Cost: Depletion

The systematic write-off of the cost of natural resources is called depletion. **The units of activity method is generally used to compute depletion, because periodic depletion generally is a function of the units extracted during the year.** Under this method, the total cost of the natural resource minus salvage value, if any, is divided by the number of units estimated to be in the resource, to obtain a cost per unit of product. The depletion cost per unit is then multiplied by the number of units extracted and sold, to compute the depletion expense. The formula is as follows:

ILLUSTRATION 11-9

*Formula to compute
depletion expense*

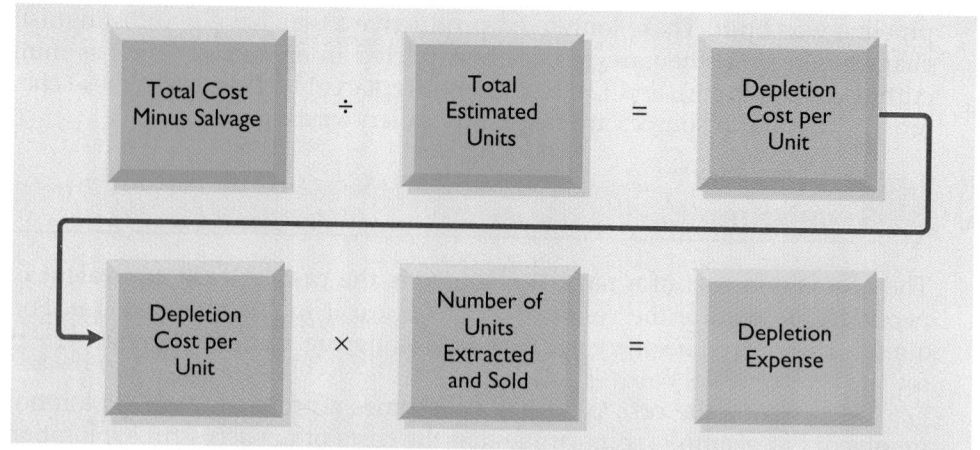

Helpful hint The computation
for depletion is similar to the
computation for depreciation using the units of activity method
of depreciation.

To illustrate, assume that the Lane Coal Company invests $5 million in a
mine estimated to have 10 million tons of coal and no salvage value. In the first
year, 800,000 tons of coal are extracted and sold. Using the formulas above, the
computations are as follows:

$$\$5,000,000 \div 10,000,00 = \$.50 \text{ depletion cost per ton}$$

$$\$.50 \times 800,000 = \$400,000 \text{ depletion expense}$$

The entry to record depletion expense for the first year of operation is as follows:

Dec. 31	Depletion Expense	400,000	
	Accumulated Depletion		400,000
	(To record depletion expense on coal deposits)		

The account Depletion Expense is reported as a part of the cost of producing
the product. Accumulated Depletion, a contra asset account similar to accumulated depreciation, is deducted from the cost of the natural resource in the balance sheet as follows:

ILLUSTRATION 11-10

*Statement presentation of
accumulated depletion*

| Coal mine | $5,000,000 | |
| Less: Accumulated depletion | 400,000 | $4,600,000 |

However, in many companies an Accumulated Depletion account is not used,
and the amount of depletion is credited directly to the natural resource account.
Sometimes, natural resources extracted in one accounting period will not be
sold until a later period. In this case, depletion is not expensed until the resource
is sold. The amount not sold is reported in the current asset section as inventory.

Technology in Action

Firms in the oil and gas industry maintain extensive computerized data bases on their natural
resources. Depletion amounts (in both monetary and physical units) are constantly monitored by
these systems. Revisions in cost projections are automatically updated as new deposits are located
or as estimates on existing deposits are changed. We all see the end result of this accounting at
the gas pump.

Before You Go On . . .

1. What is the difference between the full cost and successful efforts methods in accounting for natural resources?

2. How is depletion expense computed?

3. Explain how information related to natural resources is reported in the financial statements.

SECTION 3 Intangible Assets

Intangible assets are rights, privileges, and competitive advantages that result from the ownership of long-lived assets that do not possess physical substance. Evidence of intangibles may exist in the form of contracts, licenses, and other documents. Intangibles may arise from:

1. Government grants such as patents, copyrights, franchises, trademarks, and trade names.
2. Acquisition of another business in which the purchase price includes a payment for goodwill.
3. Private monopolistic arrangements arising from contractual agreements, such as franchises and leases.

Among the most widely known intangibles are the patents of Polaroid, the franchises of McDonald's, the trade name of Col. Sander's Kentucky Fried Chicken, and the trademark 3M of Minnesota Mining and Manufacturing Company.

Accounting for Intangible Assets

In general, accounting for intangible assets parallels the accounting for plant assets. That is, intangible assets are recorded at cost, and this cost is written off over the useful life of the intangible asset in a rational and systematic manner. At disposal, the book value of the intangible asset is eliminated, and a gain or loss, if any, is recorded.

There are, however, a few differences between accounting for intangible assets and accounting for plant assets. First, the term used to describe the write-off of an intangible asset is amortization, rather than depreciation. To record amortization of an intangible, an amortization expense is debited and the specific intangible asset is credited. An alternative is to credit an accumulated amortization account similar to accumulated depreciation. Most companies, however, choose simply to reduce the cost of the intangible.

A second difference is that **the amortization period of an intangible asset cannot be longer than 40 years**. For example, even if the useful life of an intangible asset is 60 years, it must be written off over 40 years. Conversely, if the useful life is less than 40 years, the useful life is used. This rule ensures that all intangibles, especially those with indeterminable lives, will be written off in a reasonable period of time.

Unlike plant assets, intangible assets are typically amortized on a straight-line basis. The universal use of this method adds comparability in accounting for intangible assets.

Study Objective 4

Contrast the accounting for intangible assets with the accounting for plant assets.

Patents

Helpful hint Emphasize that the cost of a patent is comprised of two items generally. The first is the price paid (if any) and the second is legal fees to defend the patent. Make sure you note that costs incurred initially to develop a patent are not capitalized.

A **patent** is an exclusive right issued by the United States Patent Office that enables the recipient to manufacture, sell, or otherwise control his or her invention for a period of 17 years from the date of the grant. A patent is nonrenewable, but the legal life of a patent may be extended beyond its original term by obtaining new patents for improvements and other changes in the basic design.

The initial cost of a patent is the cash or cash equivalent price paid when the patent is acquired. It should be noted that the saying, "A patent is only as good as the money you're prepared to spend defending it," is very true. Most patents are subject to some type of litigation by competitors. A well-known example is the patent infringement suit won by Polaroid against Eastman Kodak in protecting its patent on instant cameras. If the owner incurs legal costs in successfully defending the patent in an infringement suit, such costs are considered necessary to establish the validity of the patent. Thus, they are added to the Patent account and amortized over the **remaining life** of the patent.

The cost of a patent should be amortized over its legal life or useful life, whichever is shorter. In determining useful life, consideration should be given to obsolescence, inadequacy, and other factors; these may cause a patent to become economically ineffective before the end of its legal life. To illustrate the computation of patent expense, assume that National Labs purchases a patent at a cost of $60,000. If the useful life of the patent is eight years, the annual amortization expense is $7,500 ($60,000 ÷ 8). The entry to record the annual amortization is:

Dec. 31	Patent Expense	7,500	
	Patents		7,500
	(To record patent amortization)		

Patent expense is classified as an operating expense in the income statement.

Copyrights

Copyrights are granted by the federal government, giving the owner the exclusive right to reproduce and sell an artistic or published work. Copyrights extend for the life of the creator plus 50 years. The cost of the copyright consists of the cost of acquiring and defending it. These costs may be only the $10 fee paid to the U.S. Copyright office, or they may amount to a great deal more if a copyright infringement suit is involved.

The useful life of a copyright generally is significantly shorter than its legal life. Similar to other intangible assets, the maximum write-off is 40 years. How-

Accounting in Action • *Business Insight*

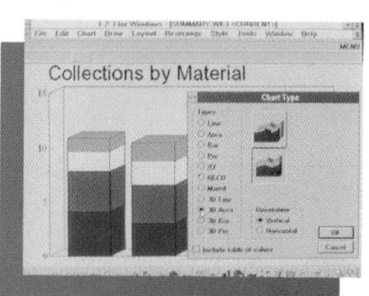

One of the significant new items copyrighted today is computer software. Lotus Development Corporation (Lotus 1-2-3), Microsoft (Windows) and WordPerfect Corporation (WordPerfect) are some examples. These intangible assets—copyrights, in this case—are one of the most valuable assets of these corporations.

ever, because of the difficulties of determining the period over which benefits are to be received, copyrights usually are amortized over a relatively short period of time.

Trademarks and Trade Names

A trademark or trade name is a word, phrase, jingle, or symbol that distinguishes or identifies a particular enterprise or product. Trade names like Wheaties, Trivial Pursuit, Sunkist, Kleenex, Coca-Cola, Big Mac, and Cadillac create immediate product identification in our minds and generally enhance the sale of the product. The creator or original user may obtain exclusive legal right to the trademark or trade name by registering it with the U.S. Patent Office. Such registration provides 20 years' protection and may be renewed indefinitely as long as the trademark or trade name is in use.

If the trademark or trade name is purchased, the cost is the purchase price. If it is developed by the enterprise itself, the cost includes attorney's fees, registration fees, design costs, successful legal defense costs, and other expenditures directly related to securing it.

Accounting in Action · *Business Insight*

Consider the trademarks that Kohlberg, Kravis, Roberts and Company (KKR) received when it purchased RJR Nabisco in 1989. First RJR Nabisco owned 30% of the cigarette market, with such trade names as Camel, Salem, Doral, and Vantage. In the food area, RJR Nabisco owned Oreo, Ritz, Chips Ahoy, Premium Saltines (crackers), Fleischmann's and Blue Bonnet (margarine), Grey Poupon (mustard), Milk Bone, Ortega (Mexican foods), Shredded Wheat, Peek Freans (cookies), Hawaiian Punch, Del Monte, Planters, Life Savers, Baby Ruth, and Butterfinger. It is no wonder that KKR paid approximately $25 billion for the company!

As with other intangibles, the cost of trademarks and trade names must be amortized over the shorter of its useful life or 40 years. Because of the uncertainty involved in estimating the useful life, the cost is frequently amortized over a much shorter period.

Franchises and Licenses

When you drive down the street in your Trans-Am purchased from a General Motors dealer, fill up your tank at the corner Standard Oil station, eat lunch at Wendy's, rent an apartment through Coldwell-Banker realty, or vacation at a Club Med resort, you are dealing with franchises. A franchise is a contractual arrangement under which the franchisor grants the franchisee the right to sell certain products, to render specific services, or to use certain trademarks or trade names, usually within a designated geographical area.

Another type of franchise is that entered into between a governmental body (commonly municipalities) and a business enterprise. This type of franchise permits the enterprise to use public property in performing its services. Examples are the use of city streets for a bus line or taxi service, use of public land for telephone or electric lines, public waterways for a ferry service, or the use of airwaves for radio or TV broadcasting. Such operating rights are referred to as licenses or permits.

Franchises and licenses may be for a definite period of time, an indefinite period, or perpetual. **When costs are identified with the acquisition of the fran-**

Accounting in Action · *Business Insight*

Continual advertising is a key component in maintaining the value of a trademark. In 1989, McDonald's spent $424.8 million on its trademark. Second place went to Kellogg's cereals with $373.3 million. Can you guess some (or all) of the next eight? They are Sears, AT&T, Ford, Budweiser, Chevrolet, Nissan, Burger King, and Toyota.

chise or license, an intangible asset should be recognized. In the case of a limited life, the cost of a franchise (or license) should be amortized as operating expense over the useful life. If the life is indefinite or perpetual, the cost may be amortized over a reasonable period not to exceed 40 years. Annual payments made under a franchise agreement should be entered as operating expenses in the period in which they are incurred.

Goodwill

Usually, the largest intangible asset that appears on a company's balance sheet is goodwill. Goodwill is the value of all favorable attributes that relate to a business enterprise. These include exceptional management, desirable location, good customer relations, skilled employees, high-quality products, fair pricing policies, and harmonious relations with labor unions. Some view goodwill as expected earnings in excess of normal earnings. **Goodwill is, therefore, unusual: unlike other assets such as investments, plant assets, and other intangibles that can be sold individually in the marketplace, goodwill can be identified only with the business as a whole.**

If goodwill can be identified only with the business as a whole, how can it be determined? Certainly, many of the factors above (exceptional management, desirable location, and so on) are present in many business enterprises. However, to determine the amount of goodwill in these types of situations would be too difficult and very subjective. In other words, the recognition of goodwill without any exchange transaction leads to subjective valuations that do not contribute to the reliability of financial statements. **As a result, goodwill is recorded only**

Accounting in Action · *Business Insight*

King World's most valuable asset is the right to license television shows such as "Wheel of Fortune," "Jeopardy," "The Oprah Winfrey Show," and "Inside Edition." Almost 90% of its $396.4 million in a recent year came from the fees associated with the rights to license agreements on these intangible assets.

when there is an exchange transaction that involves the purchase of an entire business.

Determining the Fair Market Value of Assets Acquired

When an entire business is purchased, goodwill is the excess of cost over the fair market value of the net assets (assets less liabilities) acquired. In making the determination, the purchase price (cost) is assigned first to the fair market values of the individual identifiable assets and liabilities acquired. Any remainder of the purchase price is then assigned to goodwill. To illustrate, assume that Hatfield Company has decided to purchase Sausolito Company for $6,100,000 on December 31, 1993. A review of Sausolito's condensed balance sheet indicates the following:

ILLUSTRATION 11-11

Condensed balance sheet

SAUSOLITO COMPANY
Balance Sheet
December 31, 1993

Cash	$ 200,000	Notes payable	$ 950,000
Accounts receivable (net)	640,000	Accounts payable	150,000
Inventories	560,000	L. Sausolito, Capital	3,200,000
Plant assets (net)	2,900,000		
	$4,300,000		$4,300,000

The net assets at cost of Sausolito Company are $3,200,000 as shown by the balance in the capital account and computed as follows:

ILLUSTRATION 11-12

Computation of net assets at historical cost

Total assets	$4,300,000
Total liabilities	1,100,000
Net assets at cost	$3,200,000

If Hatfield is willing to pay $6,100,000 for these net assets, it appears that the amount of goodwill can be easily computed. However, we have to be careful because the assets and liabilities of Sausolito Company are reported at book value, not fair market value. Therefore, **it is necessary to determine the fair market value** of Sausolito's identifiable net assets.

The fair market value of the net assets of Sausolito is $5,250,000, computed as follows:

ILLUSTRATION 11-13

Computation of net assets at fair market value

Assets		
Cash	$ 200,000	
Accounts receivable (net)	640,000	
Inventories	810,000	
Plant assets (net)	4,700,000	
Total assets		$6,350,000
Liabilities		
Notes payable	950,000	
Accounts payable	150,000	
Total liabilities		1,100,000
Net assets at fair market value		$5,250,000

A review of these fair market values indicates that substantial differences between cost and fair market value exist for inventories and plant assets. Inventories on a cost basis are $560,000, but on a fair market value basis they are $810,000. Plant assets are $2,900,000 on a cost basis, but $4,700,000 on a fair market value basis.

Finding differences between cost and fair market values in these two areas is not surprising. For example, Sausolito may have been using a LIFO method to report its inventory cost. If prices have been rising and the company growing, the amount of inventory cost might include costs incurred in much earlier periods at lower price levels. Moreover, as previously explained, depreciation is a process of cost allocation. Consequently, the book value of plant assets may differ significantly from fair market value.

Computing Goodwill

Goodwill is computed as the difference between the purchase price and the fair market value of the net assets acquired. Goodwill for Hatfield's purchase of Sausolito, therefore, is $850,000, computed as follows:

ILLUSTRATION 11-14

Computation of goodwill

Purchase price (cost)	$6,100,000
Less: Fair market value of net assets	5,250,000
Goodwill	**$ 850,000**

In recording the purchase of a business, the net assets are shown at their fair market values, goodwill is recorded at its cost, and cash is credited for the purchase price. Subsequently, goodwill is written off over its useful life, not to exceed 40 years. The amortization entry generally results in a debit to Goodwill Expense and a credit to Goodwill. Goodwill is reported in the balance sheet under Intangible Assets.

Leases

A **lease** is a contractual understanding between a **lessor** (owner of the property) and a **lessee** (renter of the property) that grants the right to use specific property for a period of time in return for cash payments. Lease arrangements are ex-

Accounting in Action · *International Insight*

Does the amortization requirement for goodwill create a disadvantage for U.S. companies? British companies, for example, do not have to amortize goodwill against earnings. Rather, they bypass the income statement completely and charge goodwill directly to stockholders' equity. For example, Pillsbury was purchased by Grand Met, a British firm. Many complained that U.S. companies were reluctant to bid for Pillsbury because it would mean that they would have to record a large amount of goodwill, which would substantially depress income in the future. What should be done when accounting practices are different among countries and perhaps give one country a competitive edge?

tremely popular. Just as you would probably lease a campus apartment rather than buy one, companies also find many advantages to leasing rather than buying. For instance, it is easier to keep up with rapid changes in technology by leasing equipment rather than buying it.

Most lease arrangements grant the lessee the right to use property of the lessor for stipulated periods. In such cases, the rent is included as an expense on the books of the lessee during the period of use. However, special problems develop in the following cases.

Lease Prepayments

If a lump sum payment is made in advance, in addition to periodic rental payments, it is necessary to allocate this prepaid rent to the proper periods. This prepayment, often referred to as a leasehold, gives the lessee the right to use the property for an extended period of time. Leaseholds are reported under intangible assets.

Leasehold Improvements

Lease contracts generally indicate that any improvements made to the property by the lessee revert to the lessor at the end of the lease term. If the lessee, for example, constructs an additional wall in a leased facility, the lessee has the right to benefit from the improvement over the life of the lease, but the improvement becomes the property of the lessor when the lease expires.

The lessee should charge the cost of any improvements to a Leasehold Improvements account. This account should be amortized over the life of the lease or the useful life of the improvement, whichever is shorter. (Note that some accountants classify leasehold improvements as an intangible asset while other accountants classify them as property, plant, and equipment.)

Research and Development Costs

Research and development costs are not intangible costs, but because these expenditures may lead to patents and copyrights, they are discussed in this section. Many companies spend considerable sums of money on research and development in an ongoing effort to develop new products or processes. For example, in a recent year IBM spent over $2.5 billion on research and development, an amount greater than the total expenditure level of many state governments.

Research and development costs present several accounting problems: (1) it is sometimes difficult to assign the costs to specific projects, and (2) there are uncertainties in identifying the extent and timing of future benefits. As a result, research and development costs are usually recorded as an expense when incurred.[1] The expensing of such costs is not contingent on whether the research and development is successful or unsuccessful.

To illustrate, assume that Laser Scanner Company has spent $3,000,000 on research and development. These research and development costs have led to the development of two highly successful patents. The research and development costs, however, cannot be included in the cost of the patent; rather, they are recorded as an expense when incurred.

---

[1]"Accounting for Research and Development Costs," *Statement of Financial Accounting Standards* No. 2 (Stamford, Conn.: FASB, 1974), par. 12.

Accounting in Action · *Business Insight*

Three theologians debate the issue of when life begins. "Three months after conception," states the first. "At the moment of conception," counters the second. "You're both wrong," says the third. "Life begins when the dog dies and the kids leave home."

Accountants, too, argue about when life begins—not human life, but product life. For example, the issue is how to account for the billions spent on software development costs. Should software producers expense development costs as they are incurred? Or capitalize them on the theory that the expense is creating a productive asset? In short, when does product life begin?

The answer matters. Had IBM been forced to expense these costs, its earnings per share would have been cut 72 cents.

Source: Adapted from *Forbes*, June 16, 1986.

Many disagree with this accounting approach. They argue that to expense these costs leads to understated assets and net income. Others, however, argue that capitalizing these costs will lead only to highly speculative assets on the balance sheet. Who is right is difficult to determine. The controversy, however, illustrates how difficult it is to establish proper guidelines for financial reporting.

Financial Statement Presentation

Study Objective 5

Indicate how plant assets, natural resources, and intangible assets are reported on the balance sheet.

Usually plant assets and natural resources are combined under Property, Plant, and Equipment, while intangibles are shown separately under Intangible Assets. Either within the balance sheet or in the notes, there should be disclosure of the balances of the major classes of assets, such as land, buildings, and equipment, and accumulated depreciation by major classes or in total. In addition, the depreciation and amortization methods used should be described and the amount of depreciation and amortization expense for the period disclosed. Illustration 11-15 is an excerpt from Owens-Illinois' balance sheet. The notes to the financial statements of Owens-Illinois identify the major classes of property, plant, and equipment. They also indicate that depreciation is by the straight-line method, depletion is by the units of activity method, and amortization is by the straight-line method.

ILLUSTRATION 11-15

Presentation of property, plant, and equipment and intangible assets

OWENS-ILLINOIS, INC. Partial Balance Sheet (In millions of dollars)			
Property, plant, and equipment			
Timberlands, at cost, less accumulated depletion		$ 95.4	
Buildings and equipment, at cost	$2,207.1		
Less: Accumulated depreciation	1,229.0	978.1	
Total property, plant, and equipment			$1,073.5
Intangibles			
Patents			410.0
Total			$1,483.5

Before You Go On . . .

1. What are the main differences between accounting for intangible assets and plant assets?

2. Identify the major types of intangibles and the proper accounting for them.

3. Explain the accounting for research and development costs.

Summary of Study Objectives

1. *Explain how to account for the disposal of a plant asset through retirement, sale, or exchange.* The accounting for disposal of a plant asset through retirement or sale is as follows:
(a) Eliminate the book value of the plant asset at the date of disposal.
(b) Record cash proceeds, if any.
(c) Account for the difference between the book value and the cash proceeds as a gain or loss on disposal.

In accounting for exchanges of similar assets:
(a) Eliminate the book value of the old asset at the date of the exchange.
(b) Record the acquisition cost of the new asset.
(c) Account for the gain or loss, if any, on the old asset.
1. If a gain, defer and reduce the cost of the new asset.
2. If a loss, recognize it immediately.

2. *Explain the role of subsidiary plant ledgers.* Subsidiary plant ledgers are useful in helping to keep track of periodic depreciation charges and in making entries upon the retirement of individual items. The subsidiary data are also helpful in determining the adequacy of insurance coverage, submitting insurance claims in the event of accidents, and filing income tax returns.

3. *Identify the basic accounting issues related to natural resources.* The basic accounting issues related to natural resources are whether exploration costs on unsuccessful explorations should be capitalized or expensed. Under the full cost approach, both successful and unsuccessful explorations are capitalized and the costs amortized to expense over the useful life of the successful wells. The other approach is to capitalize only the costs of successful explorations. This approach is referred to as the successful efforts approach.

4. *Contrast the accounting for intangible assets with the accounting for plant assets.* The accounting for intangible assets and plant assets is much the same. One difference is that the term used to describe the write-off of an intangible asset is amortization, rather than depreciation. In addition, the amortization of the intangible asset cannot be longer than 40 years. The straight-line method is normally used for amortizing intangible assets.

5. *Indicate how plant assets, natural resources, and intangible assets are reported on the balance sheet.* Usually plant assets and natural resources are combined under Property, Plant, and Equipment, while intangibles are shown separately under Intangible Assets. Either within the balance sheet or in the notes, there should be disclosure of the balances of the major classes of assets, such as land, buildings, and equipment, and accumulated depreciation by major classes or in total. In addition, the depreciation and amortization methods used should be described and the amount of depreciation and amortization expense for the period should be disclosed.

GLOSSARY

Amortization · The periodic write-off of an intangible asset. (p. 443).

Copyright · A right granted by the federal government allowing the owner to reproduce and sell an artistic or published work. (p. 444).

Depletion · The systematic write-off of the cost of natural resources. (p. 441).

Franchise (license) · A contractual arrangement under which the franchisor grants the franchisee the right to sell certain products, or to render specific services, or to use certain trademarks, usually within a designated geographical area. (p. 445)

Full cost approach · Method in which both successful and unsuccessful exploration costs are capitalized and the costs written off to expense over the useful life of the successful wells. (p. 441).

Goodwill · The value of all favorable attributes that relate to a business enterprise. (p. 446).

Intangible assets · Rights, privileges, and competitive advantages that result from the ownership of long-lived assets that do not possess physical substance. (p. 443).

Lease · A contractual understanding between a lessor and a lessee that grants the right to use specific property for a period of time in return for cash payments. (p. 448).

Leasehold · A lease prepayment that gives the lessee the right to use the property for an extended period of time. (p. 449).

Lessee · The renter of leased property. (p. 448).

Lessor · The owner of leased property. (p. 448).

Natural resources (wasting assets) · Assets that consist of standing timber and underground deposits of oil, gas, and minerals. (p. 440).

Patent · An exclusive right issued by the U.S. Patent Office that enables the recipient to manufacture, sell, or otherwise control his or her invention for a period of 17 years from the date of the grant. (p. 444).

Research and development costs · Expenditures that may lead to patents, copyrights, new processes, and products. (p. 449).

Subsidiary plant ledger · A ledger that contains a set of records for each plant asset. (p. 439).

Successful efforts approach · Method in which only the costs of successful exploration are capitalized. (p. 441).

Trademark (trade name) · A word, phrase, jingle, or symbol that distinguishes or identifies a particular enterprise or product. (p. 445).

DEMONSTRATION PROBLEM

On January 1, 1991, the Skyline Limousine Co. purchased a limousine at an acquisition cost of $28,000. The vehicle has been depreciated by the straight-line method using a four-year service life and a $4,000 salvage value. The company's fiscal year ends on December 31.

Instructions
Prepare the journal entry or entries to record the disposal of the limousine assuming that it was:

(1) Retired and scrapped with no salvage value on January 1, 1995.

(2) Sold for $5,000 on July 1, 1994.

(3) Traded in on a new limousine on January 1, 1994. The fair market value of the old vehicle was $9,000 and $22,000 was paid in cash.

(4) Traded in on a new limousine on January 1, 1994. The fair market value of the old vehicle was $11,000 and $22,000 was paid in cash.

Helpful hints
1. At the time of disposal, determine the book value of the asset.
2. Recognize any gain or loss from disposal of the asset.
3. Remove the book value of the asset from the records by debiting accumulated depreciation for the total depreciation to date of disposal and crediting the asset account for the cost of the asset.

Solution to Demonstration Problem

(1)	1/1/95	Accumulated Depreciation—Limousine	24,000	
		Loss on Disposal	4,000	
		Limousine		28,000
		(To record retirement of limousine)		
(2)	7/1/94	Depreciation Expense	3,000	
		Accumulated Depreciation—Limousine		3,000
		(To record depreciation to date of disposal)		
		Cash	5,000	
		Accumulated Depreciation—Limousine	21,000	
		Loss on Disposal	2,000	
		Limousine		28,000
		(To record sale of limousine)		

(3)	1/1/94	Limousine (new)	31,000	
		Accumulated Depreciation—Limousine	18,000	
		Loss on Disposal	1,000	
		Limousine		28,000
		Cash		22,000
		(To record exchange of limousines)		
(4)	1/1/94	Limousine (new)	32,000	
		Accumulated Depreciation—Limousine (old)	18,000	
		Limousine (old)		28,000
		Cash		22,000
		(To record exchange of limousines)		

SELF-STUDY QUESTIONS

Answers are at the end of the chapter.

(S.O.1)   1. A plant asset cost $20,000 when it was purchased on January 1, 1986. It was depreciated by the straight-line method based on an 8-year life with no salvage value. On June 30, 1993, the asset was discarded with no cash proceeds. What gain or loss should be recognized on the retirement?
    a. No gain or loss.
    b. $2,500 loss.
    c. $1,250 loss.
    d. $1,250 gain.

(S.O.1)   2. Schopenhauer Company exchanged an old machine, with a book value of $39,000 and a fair market value of $35,000, and paid $10,000 cash for a similar new machine. At what amount should the machine acquired in the exchange be recorded on the books of Schopenhauer?
    a. $45,000.
    b. $46,000.
    c. $49,000.
    d. $50,000.

(S.O.1)   3. In exchanges of similar assets:
    a. neither gains nor losses are recognized immediately.
    b. gains, but not losses, are recognized immediately.
    c. losses, but not gains, are recognized immediately.
    d. both gains and losses are recognized immediately.

(S.O.2)   4. A subsidiary plant ledger does *not* contain information with respect to an individual asset's:
    a. explanation of transactions.
    b. book value.
    c. fair market value.
    d. salvage value.

(S.O.3)   5. If a company employs the full cost method of accounting for natural resources:
    a. it has higher levels of expense than the successful efforts method in the earlier years.
    b. it reports more natural resource assets on its balance sheet than the successful efforts method.
    c. it capitalizes only the cost of developing successful wells.
    d. it has more dry holes than successful ones or else it would choose the successful efforts method.

(S.O.3)   6. Averroes Company expects to extract 20 million tons of coal from a mine that cost $12 million. If no salvage value is expected, and 2 million tons are mined and sold in the first year, the entry to record depletion will include a:
    a. debit to Accumulated Depletion of $2,000,000.
    b. credit to Depletion Expense of $1,200,000.
    c. debit to Depletion Expense of $1,200,000.
    d. credit to Accumulated Depletion of $2,000,000.

(S.O.4)   7. Indicate which of the following statements is *true*.
    a. Amortization of intangibles is an allocation of cost whereas depreciation of plant assets is a valuation technique.
    b. A contra-asset account must be credited when amortizing an intangible asset.

c. Depreciation describes cost allocation for plant assets, and amortization is the analogous term used for intangible

d. Plant assets are depreciated over their useful lives; intangibles must be amortized over 40 years.

(S.O.4)   8. Dew Company purchased Mallory Co. for $10 million cash. The fair value of Mallory Company's net assets is $7.5 million, and the historical cost of Mallory's net assets is $6 million. On its books, Dew Company should report:

a. $10 million in net assets, of which $4 million is goodwill.

b. $7.5 million in net assets, of which $1.5 million is goodwill.

c. $6 million in net assets and no goodwill.

d. net assets of $10 million of net assets, of which $2.5 million is goodwill.

(S.O.4, 5)   9. Peirce Company incurred $150,000 of research and development costs in its laboratory to develop a patent granted on January 2, 1993. On July 31, 1993, Peirce paid $35,000 for legal fees in a successful defense of the patent. The total amount debited to Patents through July 31, 1993, should be:

a. $150,000.

b. $35,000.

c. $185,000.

d. some other amount.

10. Indicate which of the following statements is *true*.   (S.O.5)

a. Since intangible assets lack physical substance they need only be disclosed in the notes to the financial statements.

b. Goodwill should be reported as a contra-account in the stockholder's equity section.

c. Totals of major classes of assets can be shown in the balance sheet, with asset details disclosed in the notes to the financial statements.

d. Intangible assets are typically combined with plant assets and natural resources and then shown in the property, plant, and equipment section.

QUESTIONS

1. Pat Paulson and Enid Stottrup, two accounting students, are discussing the proper accounting for disposal of plant assets. Pat says, "All you have to do is eliminate the plant asset and related accumulated depreciation and record the gain or loss, where appropriate." How should Enid respond?

2. In what ways may a company dispose of plant assets?

3. How is a gain or loss on the sale of a plant asset computed?

4. Ewing Corporation owns a machine that is fully depreciated but is still being used. How should Ewing account for this asset and report it in the financial statements?

5. Michael Jordon is studying for an accounting test. He is having difficulty with the topic of exchanging similar plant assets. Explain to Michael what steps should be followed when accounting for such an exchange.

6. When similar assets are exchanged, how is the gain or loss on disposal computed?

7. Ice-Master Refrigeration Company trades in an old machine on a new model when the fair market value of the old machine is greater than its book value. Should Ice-Master recognize a gain on disposal? If the fair market value of the old machine is less than its book value, should Ice-Master recognize a loss on disposal?

8. Cisio Company experienced a gain on disposal when exchanging similar machines. In accordance with generally accepted accounting principles, the gain was not recognized. How will Cisio's future financial statements be affected by not recognizing the gain?

9. Why are subsidiary plant ledgers useful?

10. What are natural resources, and what are their distinguishing characteristics?

11. Sandy Shaw and Jo Koehn are arguing about the full cost approach and the successful efforts approach. Shaw says that the full cost approach will provide a greater reported asset value, while Koehn says that the successful efforts approach would. Who is correct?

12. How are intangible assets different from plant assets? How are they the same?

13. What are the similarities and differences between the terms depreciation, depletion, and amortization?

14. Heflin Company hires an accounting intern who says that intangible assets should always be amortized over their legal lives. Is the intern correct? Explain.

15. Define the terms: (a) patent, and (b) franchise.

16. What are the general requirements in accounting for intangible assets?

17. Goodwill has been defined as the value of all favorable attributes that relate to a business enterprise. What types of attributes could result in goodwill?

18. Bob Leno, a business major, is working on a case problem for one of his classes. In this case problem, the company needs to raise cash to market a new product it developed. Saul Cain, an engineering major, takes one look at the company's balance sheet and says, "This company has an awful lot of goodwill. Why don't you recommend that they sell some of it to raise cash?" How should Bob respond to Saul?

19. Under what conditions is goodwill recorded?

20. When an entire business is purchased, how is the amount of goodwill measured?

21. Seattle Company leases a building for 10 years and makes improvements to the building that have a useful life of 15 years. Over what period of years should these improvements be amortized?

22. Often research and development costs provide companies with benefits that last a number of years (for example, these costs can lead to the development of a patent that will increase the company's income for many years). However, generally accepted accounting principles require that such costs be recorded as an expense when incurred. Why?

BRIEF EXERCISES

BE11–1 Prepare journal entries to record the following:

(a) Ruiz Company retires its delivery equipment, which cost $41,000. Accumulated depreciation is also $41,000 on this delivery equipment. No salvage value is received.

(b) Assume the same information as (a), except that accumulated depreciation for Ruiz Company is $35,000, instead of $41,000.

Disposal by retirement
(S.O. 1)

BE11–2 Wiley Company sells office equipment on September 30, 1993, for $21,000 cash. The office equipment originally cost $72,000 and as of January 1, 1993, had accumulated depreciation of $42,000. Depreciation for the first 9 months is $6,250. Prepare the journal entries to (a) update depreciation to September 30, 1993, and (b) record the sale of the equipment.

Disposal by sale
(S.O. 1)

BE11–3 Assume the same facts as BE11–2, except that the office equipment is sold for $38,000 cash. Prepare the journal entries to (a) update depreciation to September 30, 1993, and (b) record the sale of the equipment.

Disposal by sale
(S.O. 1)

BE11–4 Concord Company exchanges old delivery equipment for similar new delivery equipment. The book value of the old delivery equipment is $31,000 (cost $61,000 less accumulated depreciation $30,000), its fair market value is $9,000, and cash of $74,000 is paid. Prepare the entry to record the exchange.

Disposal by exchange
(S.O. 1)

BE11–5 Assume the same information as BE11–4, except that the fair market value of the old delivery equipment is $42,000. Prepare the entry to record the exchange.

Disposal by exchange
(S.O. 1)

BE11–6 Sunshine Mining Co. purchased for $7 million a mine which is estimated to have 28 million tons of ore and no salvage value. In the first year, 4 million tons of ore are extracted and sold. (a) Prepare the journal entry to record depletion expense for the first year. (b) Show how this mine is reported on the balance sheet at the end of the first year.

Accounting for natural resources
(S.O. 3)

Accounting for intangibles—patents
(S.O. 4)

BE11–7 Popper Company purchases a patent for $180,000 on January 2, 1993. Its estimated useful life is 10 years. (a) Prepare the journal entry to record patent expense for the first year. (b) Show how this patent is reported on the balance sheet at the end of the first year.

Accounting for intangibles—goodwill
(S.O. 4)

BE11–8 Hillary Company decides to purchase Clinton Company for $8 million cash. The fair market value of the net assets of Clinton Company is $6 million, and the historical cost of Clinton Company's net assets are $5 million. (a) Compute the amount of goodwill recognized by Hillary Company in this transaction. (b) Prepare the entry to record goodwill amortization for 1993, assuming that goodwill is estimated to have a useful life of 10 years.

Classification of long-lived assets on balance sheet
(S.O. 5)

BE11–9 Presented below is information related to plant assets, natural resources and intangibles at the end of 1993 for Joker Company: buildings $800,000; accumulated depreciation—buildings $650,000; goodwill $410,000; coal mine $200,000; accumulated depletion—coal mine $108,000. Prepare a partial balance sheet of Joker Company for these items.

Classification of plant assets, natural resources, and intangibles
(S.O. 5)

BE11–10 Indicate in what section of the balance sheet the following items are reported. Use the following classifications to identify your answer: property, plant and equipment (PPE), intangibles (I), and other (O).

1. ____ Cash
2. ____ Goodwill
3. ____ Timberlands
4. ____ Delivery equipment

5. ____ Copyrights
6. ____ Inventory
7. ____ Trademarks
8. ____ Accounts receivable

EXERCISES

Journalize entries for disposal of plant assets.
(S.O. 1)

E11–1 Presented below are selected transactions at Beck Company for 1993.

Jan. 1 Retired a piece of machinery that was purchased on January 1, 1983. The machine cost $62,000 on that date, and had a useful life of 10 years with no salvage value.

June 30 Sold a computer that was purchased on January 1, 1990. The computer cost $35,000, and had a useful life of 7 years with no salvage value. The computer was sold for $28,000.

Dec. 31 Discarded a delivery truck that was purchased on January 1, 1987. The truck cost $27,000 and was depreciated based on an 8-year useful life with a $3,000 salvage value.

Instructions
Journalize all entries required on the above dates, including entries to update depreciation, where applicable, on assets disposed of. Beck Company uses straight-line depreciation. (Assume depreciation is up to date as of December 31, 1992.)

Journalize entries for disposal of plant assets.
(S.O. 1)

E11–2 Padgham Corporation sold the following two machines in 1993:

	Cost	Purchase Date	Useful Life	Salvage Value	Depr. Method	Date Sold	Sales Price
Machine A	$47,000	7/1/89	5 years	$2,000	S-L	7/1/93	$18,500
Machine B	$63,000	1/1/90	7 years	$7,000	S-Y-D	10/1/93	$14,000

Instructions
Journalize the entries required to update depreciation and record the sales of the two assets in 1993. Assume that the company has taken depreciation to December 31, 1992 on both machines.

Journalize entries for exchange of similar assets.
(S.O. 1)

E11–3 Presented below are two independent transactions:

1. Noyes Co. exchanged trucks (cost $64,000 less $22,000 accumulated depreciation) plus cash of $17,000 for new trucks. The old trucks had a fair market value of $36,000. Prepare the entry to record the exchange of similar assets by Noyes Co.
2. Greg Inc. trades its used accounting machine (cost $12,000 less $4,000 accumulated depreciation) for a new accounting machine. In addition to exchanging the old ac-

counting machine (which had a fair market value of $9,000), Greg also paid cash of $10,000. Prepare the entry to record the exchange of similar assets by Greg Inc.

E11–4 The Mueller Company exchanges similar equipment with the Logan Company. Also the Evert Company exchanges similar equipment with the Flader Company. The following information pertains to these two exchanges:

	Mueller Co.	Evert Co.
Equipment (cost)	$28,000	$22,000
Accumulated depreciation	20,000	5,000
Fair market value of equipment	12,000	14,000
Cash paid	3,000	–0–

Journalize entries for the exchange of similar plant assets.
(S.O. 1)

Instructions
Prepare the journal entries to record the exchange on the books of Mueller Company and Evert Company.

E11–5 On September 30, 1993, the Neely Company acquired a new machine, exchanging an old machine of similar type that had a fair market value of $13,000. The company paid cash of $15,000 and signed a one-year, 9% note payable for $40,000. At December 31, 1992, the balances in the relevant accounts were:

Machine	$60,000
Accumulated Depreciation—Machine	$25,000

Journalize entries for the exchange of similar plant assets.
(S.O. 1)

The old machine is being depreciated on a straight-line basis using a 9-year useful life, and a $6,000 salvage value.

Instructions
Journalize entries to record 1993 depreciation on the old machine and the acquisition of the new machine.

E11–6 Abner's Delivery Company and Wainwright's Express Delivery exchanged similar delivery trucks on January 1, 1993. Abner's truck cost $18,000, had accumulated depreciation of $13,000, and has a fair market value of $3,000. Wainwright's truck cost $10,000, had accumulated depreciation of $8,000, and has a fair market value of $3,000.

Journalize entries for the exchange of similar plant assets.
(S.O. 1)

Instructions
(a) Journalize the exchange for Abner's Delivery Company.
(b) Journalize the exchange for Wainwright's Express Delivery.

E11–7 On July 1, 1993, Phillips Inc. invested $360,000 in a mine estimated to have 600,000 tons of ore of uniform grade. During the last six months of 1993, 100,000 tons of ore were mined and sold.

Journalize entries for natural resources depletion.
(S.O. 3)

Instructions
(a) Prepare the journal entry to record depletion expense.
(b) Assume that the 100,000 tons of ore were mined, but only 80,000 units were sold. How are the costs applicable to the 20,000 unsold units reported?

E11–8 The following are selected 1993 transactions of Graf Corporation.

Jan. 1 Purchased a small company and recorded goodwill of $120,000. The goodwill has a useful life of 55 years.
May 1 Purchased a patent with an estimated useful life of 5 years and a legal life of 17 years for $15,000.

Prepare adjusting entries for amortization.
(S.O. 4)

Instructions
Prepare all adjusting entries at December 31 to record amortization required by the events above.

E11–9 Chen Corporation will purchase Hall Company for $9,520,000 cash on December 31, 1993. Presented below is Hall Company's balance sheet at that date.

Determine the amount of goodwill and its amortization.
(S.O. 4, 5)

HALL COMPANY
Balance Sheet
December 31, 1993

Cash	$ 140,000	Notes payable	$1,480,000
Temporary investments	350,000	Accounts payable	330,000
Accounts receivable (net)	900,000	J. Hall, Capital	6,530,000
Inventories	950,000		
Plant assets (net)	6,000,000		
Total assets	$8,340,000	Total liabilities and owner's equity	$8,340,000

The fair market values of certain assets exceed their book values, as indicated below.

Assets	Fair market values
Temporary investments	$ 390,000
Inventories	1,200,000
Plant assets (net)	7,100,000

Instructions

(a) What amount should Chen Corporation record as goodwill on December 31, 1993?

(b) Chen chooses to amortize the goodwill over 20 years. What amount should be reported as goodwill on Chen Corporation's balance sheet at December 31, 1994?

Prepare entries to correct errors made in intangible asset account; set up appropriate accounts for different intangibles; amortize intangible assets. (S.O. 4)

E11–10 Collins Company, organized in 1993, has the following transactions related to intangible assets.

1/2/93	Purchased patent (7-year life)	$350,000
4/1/93	Goodwill purchased (indefinite life)	360,000
7/1/93	10-year franchise; expiration date 7/1/2003	450,000
8/1/93	Advance payment on leasehold (4-year lease)	144,000
9/1/93	Research and development costs	185,000

Instructions

Prepare the necessary entries to record these intangibles. All costs incurred were for cash. Make the entries as of December 31, 1993, recording any necessary amortization and reflecting all balances accurately as of that date.

PROBLEMS

Journalize a series of equipment transactions related to purchase, sale, retirement, and depreciation. (S.O. 1, 5)

P11–1 At December 31, 1992, Hamsmith Corporation reported the following as plant assets:

Land		$ 3,000,000
Buildings	$26,500,000	
Less: Accumulated depreciation—buildings	12,100,000	14,400,000
Equipment	40,000,000	
Less: Accumulated depreciation—equipment	5,000,000	35,000,000
Total plant assets		$52,400,000

During 1993, the following selected cash transactions occurred:

April 1 Purchased land for $2,200,000.

May 1 Sold equipment that cost $600,000 when purchased on January 1, 1989. The equipment was sold for $350,000.

June 1 Sold land purchased on June 1, 1983 for $1,800,000. The land cost $500,000.

July 1 Purchased equipment for $1,200,000.

Dec. 31 Retired equipment that cost $500,000 when purchased on December 31, 1983. No salvage value was received.

Instructions

(a) Journalize the above transactions. Hamsmith uses straight-line depreciation for buildings and equipment. The buildings are estimated to have a 40-year useful life and no salvage value; the equipment is estimated to have a 10-year useful life and no salvage value. Update depreciation on assets disposed of at the time of sale or retirement.

(b) Record adjusting entries for depreciation for 1993.

(c) Prepare the plant asset section of Hamsmith's balance sheet at December 31, 1993.

P11–2 Express Co. has delivery equipment that cost $48,000 and that has been depreciated $20,000. Record the disposal under the following assumptions:

Journalize a series of transactions related to disposals of plant assets.
(S.O. 1)

(a) It was scrapped as having no value.

(b) It was sold for $31,000.

(c) It was sold for $18,000.

(d) It was exchanged for similar delivery equipment. The old delivery equipment has a fair market value of $12,000 and $32,000 was paid.

(e) It was exchanged for similar delivery equipment. The old delivery equipment has a fair market value of $35,000 and $19,000 was paid.

P11–3 Carter Company owns the following machinery at January 1, 1993. It uses straight-line (S-L) depreciation for Machine Nos. 1, 2, 3 and sum-of-the-years'-digits (S-Y-D) depreciation for Machine No. 4.

Update depreciation for machines and record sales and exchanges.
(S.O. 1)

Machine No.	Cost	Date Purchased	Useful Life	Salvage	Depreciation Method	Accumulated Depreciation 1/1/93
1	$22,000	1/3/87	8 years	$4,000	S-L	$13,500
2	24,000	1/4/88	8 years	3,600	S-L	?
3	28,000	7/1/88	8 years	4,200	S-L	13,388
4	48,000	1/2/90	6 years	6,000	S-Y-D	?

The following transactions involving machinery occurred during 1993.

Jan. 2 Traded machine No. 1 (fair market value $9,000) for a similar machine (No. 5) and paid a $23,000 cash difference.

July 1 Sold machine No. 2 for $8,325.

1 Traded machine No. 3 (fair market value $11,000) for a similar machine (No. 6) and paid a cash difference of $21,000.

Oct. 1 Sold machine No. 4 for $16,000.

Instructions

(Round all computations to the nearest dollar.)

(a) Complete the last column in the table.

(b) Prepare journal entries for the four transactions. Where necessary, first prepare a journal entry to update depreciation on the machine.

(c) Prepare an adjusting entry at December 31, 1993 to record depreciation expense on machines 5 and 6. Machines 5 and 6 will be depreciated on a straight-line basis over 10 years with no salvage value.

P11–4 The intangible asset section of Roberts Corporation at December 31, 1992, is presented below:

Prepare entries to record transactions related to acquisition and amortization of intangibles; prepare the intangible asset section.
(S.O. 4, 5)

Patent ($60,000 cost less $6,000 amortization)	$54,000
Copyright ($36,000 cost less $14,400 amortization)	21,600
Total	$75,600

The patent was acquired in January of 1992 and has a useful life of 10 years. The copyright was acquired in January of 1989 and also has a useful life of 10 years. The following cash transactions may have affected intangible assets during 1993:

Jan. 2 Paid $9,000 legal costs to successfully defend the patent against infringement by another company.

Jan.–June Developed a new product incurring $140,000 in research and development costs. A patent was granted for the product on July 1, and its useful life is equal to its legal life.

July 1 Acquired Solomon Company for $180,000. The balance sheet of Solomon showed assets of $112,500 and liabilities of $47,500. The fair market value of the recorded assets is $134,000. Solomon also owns a patent, not shown on its balance sheet, that has a fair market value of $8,000. The patent was transferred to Roberts as a part of the $180,000 purchase. The patent will be amortized over 8 years, and any goodwill over 25 years. (Hint: Except for the unrecorded intangible assets, simply debit assets and credit liabilities.)

Sept. 1 Paid $60,000 to a quarterback to appear in commercials advertising the company's products. The commercials will air in September and October.

Oct. 1 Acquired a copyright for $100,000. The copyright has a useful life of 50 years.

Instructions

(a) Prepare journal entries to record the transactions above.

(b) Prepare journal entries to record the 1993 amortization expense for intangible assets.

(c) Prepare the intangible asset section of the balance sheet at December 31, 1993.

Prepare entries to correct errors made in recording and amortizing intangible assets.
(S.O. 4)

P11–5 Due to rapid turnover in the accounting department, a number of transactions involving intangible assets were improperly recorded by Riley Corporation in 1993.

1. Riley developed a new manufacturing process, incurring research and development costs of $102,000. The company also purchased a patent for $37,400. In early January, Riley capitalized $139,400 as the cost of the patents. Patent amortization expense of $8,200 was recorded based on a 17-year useful life.

2. On July 1, 1993, Riley purchased a small company and as a result acquired goodwill of $60,000. Riley recorded a half-year's amortization in 1993, based on a 50-year life ($600 amortization).

3. On September 1, 1993, Riley permanently installed wall partitions, shelving, and counters in a store leased from another company. The cost of $18,000 was debited to Leasehold Improvements. Riley recorded four months' amortization based on the 20-year physical life of the improvements ($300 amortization). The lease extends until December 31, 2001, and is not expected to be renewed.

Instructions

Prepare all journal entries necessary to correct any errors made during 1993. Assume the books have not yet been closed for 1993.

ALTERNATE PROBLEMS

Journalize a series of equipment transactions related to purchase, sale, retirement, and depreciation.
(S.O. 1, 5)

P11–1A At December 31, 1992, Yount Corporation reported the following as plant assets:

Land		$ 4,000,000
Buildings	$28,500,000	
Less: Accumulated depreciation—buildings	12,100,000	16,400,000
Equipment	48,000,000	
Less: Accumulated depreciation—equipment	5,000,000	43,000,000
Total plant assets		$63,400,000

During 1993, the following selected cash transactions occurred:

April 1 Purchased land for $2,630,000.

May 1 Sold equipment that cost $600,000 when purchased on January 1, 1989. The equipment was sold for $370,000.

June 1 Sold land purchased on June 1, 1983, for $1,800,000. The land cost $200,000.

July 1 Purchased equipment for $1,200,000.

Dec. 31 Retired equipment that cost $500,000 when purchased on December 31, 1983. No salvage value was received.

Instructions

(a) Journalize the above transactions. Yount uses straight-line depreciation for buildings and equipment. The buildings are estimated to have a 40-year life and no salvage value; the equipment is estimated to have a 10-year useful life and no salvage value. Update depreciation on assets disposed of at the time of sale or retirement.

(b) Record adjusting entries for depreciation for 1993.

(c) Prepare the plant asset section of Yount's balance sheet at December 31, 1993.

P11–2A Walker Co. has office furniture that cost $80,000 and that has been depreciated $47,000. Record the disposal under the following assumptions:

(a) It was scrapped as having no value.

(b) It was sold for $21,000.

(c) It was sold for $61,000.

(d) It was exchanged for similar office furniture. The old office furniture has a fair market value of $46,000 and $21,000 was paid.

(e) It was exchanged for similar office furniture. The old office furniture has a fair market value of $25,000 and $29,000 was paid.

Journalize a series of transactions related to disposals of plant assets. (S.O. 1)

P11–3A Derzon Corporation owns the following machinery at January 1, 1993. It uses straight-line (S-L) depreciation for Machine Nos. 1, 2, 3 and sum-of-the-years'-digits (S-Y-D) depreciation for Machine No. 4.

Update depreciation for a number of machines and record sales and exchanges. (S.O. 1)

Machine No.	Cost	Date Purchased	Useful Life	Salvage	Depreciation Method	Accumulated Depreciation 1/1/93
1	$32,000	1/3/87	8 years	$4,200	S-L	$20,850
2	36,480	1/4/88	8 years	5,472	S-L	$19,380
3	39,200	7/1/88	8 years	5,760	S-L	?
4	72,000	1/2/90	6 years	9,000	S-Y-D	?

The following transactions involving machinery occurred during 1993.

Jan. 2 Traded machine No. 1 (fair market value $14,000) for a similar machine (No. 5) and paid a $35,000 cash difference.

July 1 Sold machine No. 2 for $11,950.

1 Traded machine No. 3 (fair market value $16,000) for a similar machine (No. 6) and paid a cash difference of $32,000.

Oct. 1 Sold machine No. 4 for $24,300.

Instructions

(Round all computations to the nearest dollar.)

(a) Complete the last column in the table.

(b) Prepare journal entries for the four transactions. Where necessary, first prepare a journal entry to update depreciation on the machine.

(c) Prepare an adjusting entry at December 31, 1993 to record depreciation expense on machines 5 and 6. Machines 5 and 6 will be depreciated on a straight-line basis over 10 years with no salvage value.

P11–4A The intangible asset section of Eikel Company at December 31, 1992, is presented below:

Patent ($70,000 cost less $7,000 amortization)	$63,000
Copyright ($48,000 cost less $19,200 amortization)	28,800
Total	$91,800

Prepare entries to record transactions related to acquisition and amortization of intangibles; prepare the intangible asset section. (S.O. 4, 5)

The patent was acquired in January of 1992 and has a useful life of 10 years. The copyright was acquired in January of 1989 and also has a useful life of 10 years. The following cash transactions may have affected intangible assets during 1993:

Jan. 2 Paid $9,000 legal costs to successfully defend the patent against infringement by another company.

Jan.–June　Developed a new product incurring $140,000 in research and development costs. A patent was granted for the product on July 1, and its useful life is equal to its legal life.

July 1　Acquired Baker Corporation for $238,000. The balance sheet of Baker showed assets of $146,250 and liabilities of $46,750. The fair market value of the recorded assets is $197,200. Baker also owns a patent, not shown on its balance sheet, that has a fair market value of $7,200. The patent was transferred to Eikel as a part of the $238,000 purchase. The patent will be amortized over 6 years, and any goodwill over 25 years. (Hint: Except for the unrecorded intangible assets, simply debit assets and credit liabilities.)

Sept. 1　Paid $80,000 to an extremely large defensive lineman to appear in commercials advertising the company's products. The commercials will air in September and October.

Oct. 1　Acquired a copyright for $80,000. The copyright has a useful life of 50 years.

Instructions

(a) Prepare journal entries to record the transactions above.

(b) Prepare journal entries to record the 1993 amortization expense.

(c) Prepare the intangible asset section of the balance sheet at December 31, 1993.

Prepare entries to correct for errors made in recording and amortizing intangible assets.

(S.O. 4)

P11–5A　Due to rapid turnover in the accounting department, a number of transactions involving intangible assets were improperly recorded by the Glover Company in 1993.

1. Glover developed a new manufacturing process, incurring research and development costs of $136,000. The company also purchased a patent for $39,100. In early January, Glover capitalized $175,100 as the cost of the patents. Patent amortization expense of $10,300 was recorded based on a 17-year useful life.

2. On July 1, 1993, Glover purchased a small company and as a result acquired goodwill of $76,000. Glover recorded a half-year's amortization in 1993, based on a 50-year life ($760 amortization).

3. On September 1, 1993, Glover permanently installed wall partitions, shelving, and counters in a store leased from Schaeffer Realty. The cost of $21,600 was debited to Leasehold Improvements. Glover recorded four months' amortization based on the 20-year physical life of the improvements ($360 amortization). The lease extends until December 31, 2001, and is not expected to be renewed.

Instructions

Prepare all journal entries necessary to correct any errors made during 1993. Assume the books have not yet been closed for 1993.

*B*roadening *Your Perspective*

FINANCIAL REPORTING PROBLEM

Answer the following questions related to PepsiCo, Inc., found in Appendix L to this textbook.

1. Determine the total property, plant and equipment, net of accumulated depreciation and total intangible assets, net of accumulated amortization reported in 1991.

2. Identify the primary reason why PepsiCo has goodwill and other intangibles.

3. What was the amortization for goodwill and other intangibles in 1991, and where was it reported in the income statement? Was it more or less than 1990? What useful life was used to amortize goodwill and other intangibles?

4. What was the amount of research and development expenses PepsiCo incurred in 1991?

5. What is the latest date on which leases expire?

DECISION CASE

Dorn Company is considering the acquisition of two companies whose balance sheets are as follows:

Assets	Roper Metals	Rocket Systems
Cash	$ 70,000	$120,000
Receivables	80,000	90,000
Inventory	120,000	125,000
Plant assets (net)	390,000	440,000
Total Assets	$660,000	$775,000
Liabilities and Owner's Equity		
Current liabilities	$140,000	$180,000
Long-term liabilities	120,000	145,000
Owner's capital	400,000	450,000
Total liabilities and owner's equity	$660,000	$775,000

The current fair market values of the inventories and plant assets are shown below:

	Roper Metals	Rocket Systems
Inventories	$160,000	$185,000
Plant assets	480,000	520,000

The reported book value of the receivables approximate their current fair market value.

The owner of Roper Metals will sell at a price of 170% of the book value of the company's net assets. The owner of Rocket Systems will sell at a price of 180% of the company's net assets.

The management of Dorn has concluded after carefully analyzing the financial position and earnings records of the two companies that it is willing to pay a purchase price of 125% of the fair market value of Roper Metal's net assets and 135% of the fair market value of Rocket System's net assets.

Instructions

(a) Compute the selling price being asked for each company. Show computations.

(b) Compute the purchase price Dorn Company is willing to pay for each company. Show computations.

(c) On the basis of the selling prices being asked and the purchase prices offered, will either purchase occur? Why?

(d) After negotiation, an agreement is reached to purchase Roper Metals for $670,000 and Rocket Systems for $800,000. How much goodwill, if any, should be recognized by Dorn Company in recording the acquisition of each company?

CRITICAL THINKING CASE

Refer to the opening story related to the University of Utah, and answer the following questions.

1. What are intangible assets?

2. Give some examples of intangibles other than a trademark that you might find on your college campus.

3. What would you estimate to be the useful life of your school logo? How might you place a value on the school logo?

4. Give some examples of company or product trademarks or tradenames. Are tradenames and trademarks reported on a company's balance sheet? Explain.

ETHICAL CASE

Imporia Container Company is suffering declining sales of its principal product, nonbiodegradeable plastic cartons. The president, Benny Benson, instructs his controller, John Straight, to lengthen asset lives to reduce depreciation expense. A processing line of automated plastic extruding equipment, purchased for $2.7 million in January 1992 was originally estimated to have a useful life of 8 years and a salvage value of $300,000. Depreciation has been recorded for 2 years on that basis. Benny wants the estimated life changed to 12 years total, the salvage value increased to $500,000, and the straight-line method continued. John is hesitant to make the change, believing it is unethical to increase net income in this manner. Benny says, "Hey, the life is only an estimate and I've heard that our competition uses a 12-year life on their production equipment."

Instructions

(a) Who are the stakeholders in this situation?

(b) Is the change in asset life unethical or simply a good business practice by an astute president?

(c) What is the effect of Benny Benson's proposed change on income before taxes in the year of change?

Answers to Self-Study Questions
1. c   2. a   3. c   4. c   5. b   6. c   7. c   8. d   9. b   10. c

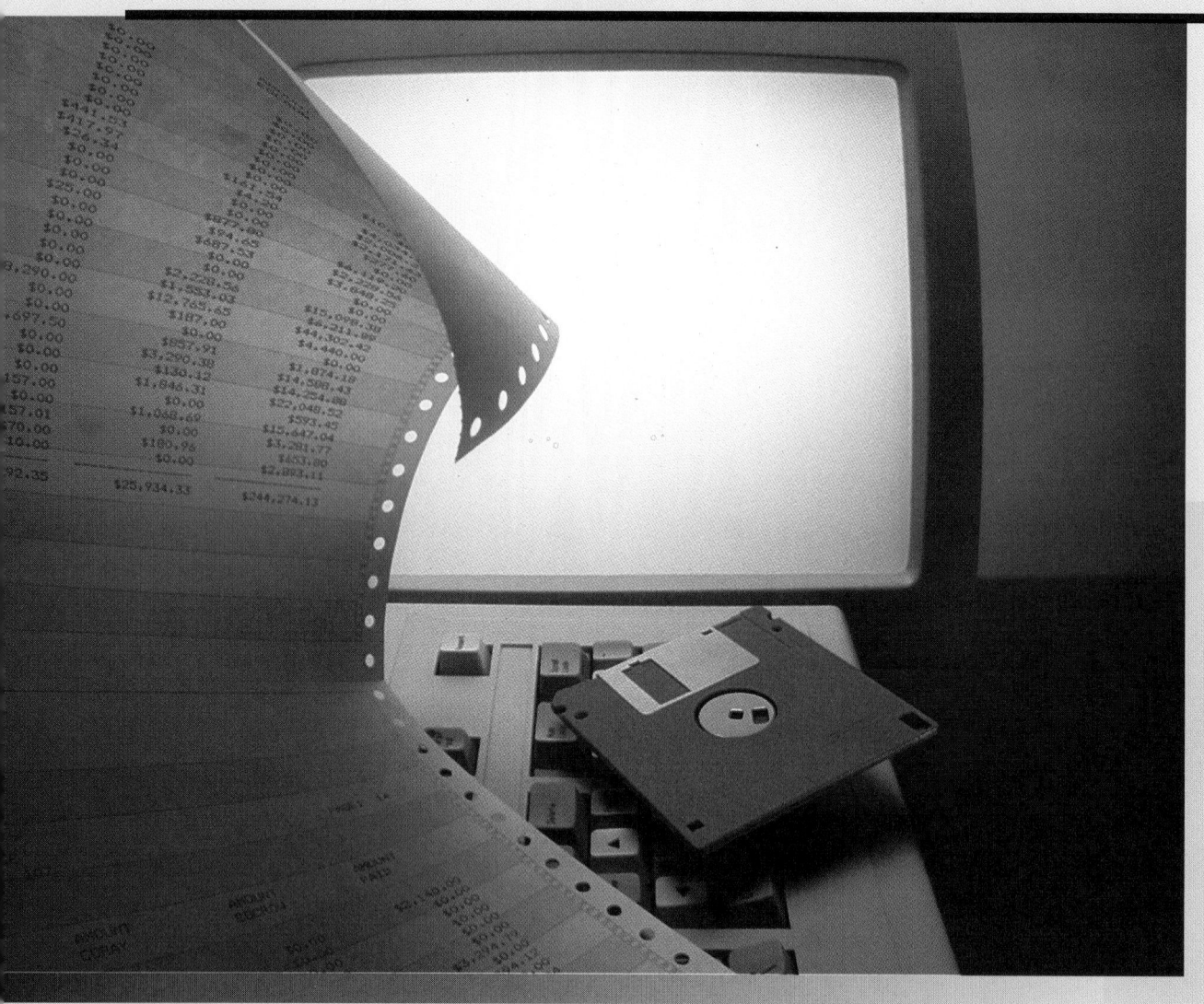

CONCEPTS FOR REVIEW

Before studying this chapter, you should know or, if necessary, review:

a. *The importance of liquidity in evaluating the financial position of a company. (Ch. 4, p. 151)*

b. *How to make adjusting entries related to unearned revenue (Ch. 3, p. 96–7) and accrued expenses (Ch. 3, p. 99–101).*

c. *What are the basic principles of internal control. (Ch. 7, p. 277–282).*

CHAPTER 12

CURRENT LIABILITIES
AND PAYROLL ACCOUNTING

Study Objectives

After studying this chapter, you should be able to:

1. *Explain a current liability and identify the major types of current liabilities.*

2. *Describe the accounting for notes payable.*

3. *Explain the accounting for other current liabilities.*

4. *Describe the accounting and disclosure requirements for contingent liabilities.*

5. *Discuss the objectives of internal control for payroll.*

6. *Compute and record the payroll for a pay period.*

7. *Describe and record employer payroll taxes.*

8. *Identify additional fringe benefits associated with employee compensation.*

W hen it comes to payroll, colleges are very much like the "real world." There's a payroll supervisor, a few clerks, a giant computer, reams of computer printouts—and, of course, paychecks.

Mrs. Dianna Webb is the payroll technician at Casper College in Casper, Wyoming, a school with 6,000 students and 550 people on the payroll. "I take out tax deductions, credit union contributions, tax sheltered annuities, United Way donations, and even court costs or garnishments when an employee has been ordered by a court to pay a debt. Wyoming has no state income tax, so that's one less deduction."

The payroll "staff" consists of just Mrs. Webb and the computer. Their job: process monthly checks for the faculty, administrators, and students and semi-monthly checks for staff. What if she didn't have a computer? "I don't think I'd be able to pay as many people as I do," she laughs.

Just like any other business, she keeps timecards for all hourly employees. The faculty and administrators are on the honor system to work the required number of hours, but even their pay has to be authorized by the Vice-President for Administrative Services.

The computer provides Mrs. Webb with many useful reports: The main report shows the payroll in alphabetical order, listing gross pay, tax deductions, other payroll deductions, and net pay. She also gets a report that lists year-to-date totals. "In May, faculty members get paid the balance on their contracts, so I need to know those year-to-date totals."

Student employees provide one extra wrinkle: they don't have social security taxes withheld during the school year. The reason: federal regulations consider students working for the college and enrolled and attending classes, exempt from social security and medicare taxes. But during the summer months, social security (FICA) is withheld.

Whether it be a college like Casper College, a pizza parlor like Pizza Hut, a public accounting firm like Arthur Andersen & Co., or a large multinational company like IBM, all enterprises have liabilities for payroll. In addition, they also have many other types of liabilities. For example, the purchase of supplies on account, the borrowing of money on a bank loan, or the obligation to pay interest are illustrative.

Liabilities are classified as current or long-term on the balance sheet. We will explain current liabilities in this chapter and long-term liabilities in Chapter 17.

SECTION 1   Current Liabilities

What Is a Current Liability?

Study Objective 1

Explain a current liability and identify the major types of current liabilities.

As explained in Chapter 4, a **current liability** is a debt that can reasonably be expected to be paid (1) from existing current assets or through the creation of other current liabilities, and (2) within one year or the operating cycle, whichever is longer. Debts that do not meet both criteria are classified as long-term liabilities. In most companies, current liabilities are paid within one year out of current assets, rather than through the creation of other liabilities.

Companies must be extremely careful about the relationship of current liabilities to current assets. This relationship is critical in evaluating a company's liquidity, or short-term debt paying ability. A company that has more current liabilities than current assets is usually the subject of some concern because the company may not be able to meet its current obligations when they become due.

Current liabilities include notes payable, accounts payable, unearned revenues, and accrued liabilities such as taxes, salaries and wages, and interest payable. The entries for accounts payable and adjusting entries for some current liabilities have been explained in previous chapters. Other types of current liabilities that are frequently encountered in practice are discussed in the following sections.

Accounting for Notes Payable

Obligations in the form of written promissory notes are recorded as notes payable. Notes payable are often used instead of accounts payable. This gives the lender written documentation of the obligation in case legal remedies are needed to collect the debt. Notes payable usually require the borrower to pay interest and are frequently issued to meet short-term financing needs.

Notes are issued for varying periods. **Those due for payment within one year of the balance sheet date are usually classified as current liabilities.** Notes may be interest bearing or zero-interest bearing. To illustrate these differing interest features, assume that Jeff Sondgeroth Co. needs a four-month $100,000 loan to cover its short-term liquidity needs.

Study Objective 2

Describe the accounting for notes payable.

Interest-Bearing Note Issued

Assume that the First National Bank agrees to lend the $100,000 on March 1, 1993 if Jeff Sondgeroth Co. signs a $100,000, 12%, four-month note. When a promissory note is interest bearing, the amount of assets received upon the issuance of the note is generally equal to the face value of the note. The entry to record the cash received by Jeff Sondgeroth Co. on March 1 is:

Mar. 1	Cash	100,000	
	Notes Payable		100,000
	(To record issuance of 12% four-month note to First National Bank)		

If Jeff Sondgeroth Co. prepares financial statements semiannually, an adjusting entry is required to recognize interest expense and interest payable of $4,000 ($100,000 × 12% × 4/12) at June 30. The adjusting entry is:

June 30	Interest Expense	4,000	
	Interest Payable		4,000
	(To accrue interest for four months on First National Bank note)		

If Sondgeroth prepared financial statements monthly, the adjusting entry at the end of each month would have been $1,000 ($100,000 × 12% × 1/12).

At maturity (July 1), Jeff Sondgeroth Co. must pay the face value of the note ($100,000) plus $4,000 interest ($100,000 × 12% × 4/12).

The entry to record payment of the note and accrued interest is as follows:

July 1	Notes Payable	100,000	
	Interest Payable	4,000	
	Cash		104,000
	(To record payment of First National Bank interest-bearing note and accrued interest at maturity)		

Zero-Interest-Bearing Note Issued

A zero-interest-bearing note may be issued instead of an interest-bearing note. A zero-interest-bearing note does not explicitly state an interest rate on the face of the note. Interest is still charged, however, because the borrower is required at maturity to pay back an amount greater than the cash received at the issuance date. In other words, the borrower receives in cash the present value of the note. The present value equals the face value of the note at maturity minus the interest or discount charged by the lender for the term of the note. In essence, the bank takes its fee "up front" rather than on the date the note matures.

To illustrate, we will assume that Jeff Sondgeroth Co. issues a $104,000 four-month zero-interest-bearing note to the First National Bank. The present value of the note is $100,000.[1] The entry to record this transaction for Jeff Sondgeroth Co. is as follows:

Helpful hint Remember that a zero-interest-bearing note has interest; it is charged through a reduction in the proceeds.	Mar. 1	Cash	100,000	
		Discount on Notes Payable	4,000	
		Notes Payable		104,000
		(To record issuance of four-month, zero-interest-bearing note to First National Bank)		

The Notes Payable account is credited for the face value of the note, which is $4,000 more than the actual cash received. The difference between the cash received and the face value of the note is debited to Discount on Notes Payable. **Discount on Notes Payable is a contra account to Notes Payable and therefore is subtracted from Notes Payable on the balance sheet.** The balance sheet presentation on March 1 is as follows:

ILLUSTRATION 12-1

Statement presentation of discount on notes payable

Current liabilities		
Notes Payable	104,000	
Less: Discount on notes payable	4,000	100,000

The amount of the discount, $4,000 in this case, represents the cost of borrowing $100,000 for four months. Accordingly, the discount is charged to interest expense over the life of the note. That is, the Discount on Notes Payable balance **represents interest expense chargeable to future periods**. Thus, it would be incorrect to debit Interest Expense for $4,000 at the time the loan is obtained.

Assuming that Jeff Sondgeroth Co. prepares financial statements semiannually, an adjusting entry is required to recognize interest expense and to reduce Discount on Notes Payable at June 30. The amount is for four months or $4,000, and the entry is:

June 30	Interest Expense	4,000	
	Discount on Notes Payable		4,000
	(To record interest for four months on First National Bank note)		

If Sondgeroth prepared financial statements monthly, the adjusting entry at the end of each month would have been $1,000 ($4,000 × ¼).

---

[1]The bank rate used in this example to find the present value is slightly less than 12%.

At maturity (July 1) the note is paid. The entry to record payment is:

July 1	Notes Payable	104,000	
	Cash		104,000
	(To record payment of zero-interest-bearing First National Bank note at maturity)		

Interest-Bearing versus Zero-Interest-Bearing Notes

The saying that "there is no such thing as a free lunch" is particularly appropriate for zero-interest-bearing notes. Zero-interest-bearing implies that no interest is charged, which is not true. As you have seen, the accounting results are the same for Jeff Sondgeroth Co. whether an interest-bearing or zero-interest-bearing note is used. These effects are summarized in Illustration 12-2.

Interest-Bearing		**Zero-Interest-Bearing**	
Income Statement		Income Statement	
Interest expense	$ 4,000	Interest expense	$ 4,000
Balance Sheet (at maturity date)		Balance Sheet (at maturity date)	
Notes payable	$100,000	Notes payable	$104,000
Interest payable	4,000	Discount on notes payable	–0–
	$104,000		$104,000

ILLUSTRATION 12-2

Comparison of interest and zero-interest notes

As indicated, interest expense and the liability for notes and interest are the same. Only the accounts employed to report the liability are different.

Accounting for Other Current Liabilities

Three current liabilities have been selected for discussion in the following sections. They are (1) sales taxes payable, (2) unearned revenues, and (3) current maturities of long-term debt.

Study Objective 3

Explain the accounting for other current liabilities.

Sales Taxes Payable

As consumers, we are well aware that many of the products we purchase at retail stores are subject to sales taxes. The tax is expressed as a stated percentage of the sales price. The retailer (or selling company) collects the tax from the customer when the sale occurs, and periodically (usually monthly) remits the collections to the state's department of revenue.

Under most state sales tax laws, the amount of the sale and the amount of the sales tax collected must be rung up separately on the cash register. Gasoline sales are a major exception. The cash register readings are then used to credit Sales and Sales Taxes Payable. Assuming that the cash register readings for March 25 for Cooley Grocery show sales of $10,000 and sales taxes of $600 (sales tax rate of 6%), the entry is:

Helpful hint Watch how sales are rung up at local retailers, to see whether the sales tax is computed separately.

Mar. 25	Cash	10,600	
	Sales		10,000
	Sales Taxes Payable		600
	(To record daily sales and sales taxes)		

When the taxes are remitted to the taxing agency, Sales Taxes Payable is debited and Cash is credited. Thus, Cooley Grocery serves only as a collection agent for

Accounting in Action · *Business Insight*

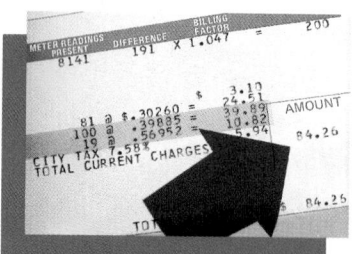

Sales taxes do not apply exclusively to retail companies. They also apply to manufacturing companies, service companies, and public utilities, and the extent of the taxes is increasing. There are now over 9,000 state and local sales taxes, up by more than 1,500 since 1986. "Compliance is becoming much more complex as states expand their sales taxes," says an American Telephone and Telegraph (AT&T) tax attorney. They are also becoming more costly. AT&T employs 76 people to file the company's sales tax returns each year. They also handle the 200 sales tax audits AT&T is presently undergoing, up by more than 30% since the mid-1980s.

Source: Forbes, September 30, 1991.

the taxing authority. The company does not report sales taxes as an expense; it simply forwards the amount paid by the customer to the government.

When sales taxes are not rung up separately on the cash register, total receipts are divided by 100% plus the sales tax percentage to determine sales. To illustrate, assume in the above example that Cooley Grocery "rings up" total receipts, which are $10,600. Because the amount received from the sale is equal to the sales price 100% plus 6% of sales, or 1.06 times the sales total, sales are computed as follows:

$$\$10,600 \div 1.06 = \$10,000.$$

The sales tax amount of $600 is found either by (1) subtracting sales from total receipts ($10,600 − $10,000) or (2) multiplying sales by the sales tax rate ($10,000 × 6%).

Unearned Revenues

A magazine publisher such as Sports Illustrated may receive a customer's check when magazines are ordered, and an airline company, such as American Airlines, often sells tickets for future flights. How do these companies account for unearned revenues that are received before goods are delivered or services are rendered?

1. When the advance is received, Cash is debited, and a current liability account identifying the source of the unearned revenue is credited.
2. When the revenue is earned, the unearned revenue account is debited, and an earned revenue account is credited.

To illustrate, assume that Superior University sells 10,000 season football tickets at $50 each for its five-game home schedule. The entry for the sales of season tickets is:

Aug. 6	Cash	500,000	
	Unearned Football Ticket Revenue		500,000
	(To record sale of 10,000 season tickets)		

As each game is completed, the following entry is made:

Sept. 7	Unearned Football Ticket Revenue	100,000	
	Football Ticket Revenue		100,000
	(To record football ticket revenues earned)		

Unearned Football Ticket Revenue is, therefore, unearned revenue and is reported as a current liability in the balance sheet. As revenue is earned, a transfer from unearned revenue to earned revenue occurs. Unearned revenue is material for some companies: In the airline industry, tickets sold for future flights represent almost 50% of total current liabilities. At United Air Lines, unearned ticket revenue is the largest current liability, recently amounting to over $882 million.

Illustration 12-3 shows specific unearned and earned revenue accounts used in selected types of businesses.

ILLUSTRATION 12-3

Unearned and earned revenue accounts

Type of Business	Account Title	
	Unearned Revenue	**Earned Revenue**
Airline	Unearned Passenger Ticket Revenue	Passenger Revenue
Magazine Publisher	Unearned Subscription Revenue	Subscription Revenue
Hotel	Unearned Rental Revenue	Rental Revenue

Current Maturities of Long-Term Debt

Companies often have a portion of long-term debt that comes due in the current year. For example, assume that Wendy Construction issues a 5-year interest-bearing $25,000 note on January 1, 1993. This note specifies that each January 1, starting January 1, 1994, $5,000 of the note should be paid. When financial statements are prepared on December 31, 1993, $5,000 should be reported as a current liability and $20,000 as a long-term liability. Current maturities of long-term debt are often identified on the balance sheet as **long-term debt due within one year**.

It is not necessary to prepare an adjusting entry to recognize the current maturity of long-term debt. The proper statement classification of each balance sheet account is recognized when the balance sheet is prepared.

Helpful hint. This liability is quite common. PepsiCo, for example, shows current maturities of $619.2 million at December 28, 1991 (See Appendix L).

Contingent Liabilities

Whether it be notes payable, interest payable, accounts payable, sales taxes payable, and so on, we know that an obligation exists to make payment. But suppose that your company is currently involved in a dispute with the Internal Revenue Service (IRS) over the amount of its income tax liability. Do you have to report the disputed amount on the balance sheet as a liability? Or suppose your company is the defendant in a lawsuit in which an adverse decision might result in bankruptcy. How should this major contingency be reported? The answers to these questions are difficult, because these liabilities are dependent—contingent—upon some future event. In other words, a contingent liability is a potential liability that may become an actual liability in the future.

What, then, should be done with contingent liabilities? Fortunately, accountants have adopted guidelines that are helpful in resolving these problems. The guidelines require that:

1. If it is **probable** that the contingency will happen—if it is likely to occur—and the amount can be **reasonably estimated**, the liability should be recorded in the accounts.
2. If it is only **reasonably possible**—if it could happen—then it need be disclosed only in the notes accompanying the financial statements.
3. If the contingency is **remote**—if it is unlikely to occur—it need not be recorded or disclosed.

Study Objective 4

Describe the accounting and disclosure requirements for contingent liabilities.

Accounting in Action · *A Business Insight*

Contingent liabilities abound in the real world. Consider the following: Manville Corp. filed bankruptcy when it was hit by billions of dollars in asbestos product liability claims. A. H. Robins Co. was forced into bankruptcy by claims of women allegedly rendered sterile by its badly designed IUD. Companies having multiple toxic waste sites are faced with cleanup costs that average $10 million to $30 million and can reach as high as $500 million depending on the type of waste. For life and health insurance companies and their stockholders, the cost of AIDS is like an iceberg—everybody wonders how big it really is and what damage it might do in the future; the U.S. Center for Disease Control indicates treatment costs could be $8 billion to $16 billion. And frequent-flyer programs are so popular that airlines at one time owed participants more than 3 million round-trip domestic tickets. That's enough to fly at least 5.4 billion miles, free for the passengers but at what future cost to the airlines?

Recording a Contingent Liability

Helpful hint A good example of a contingency is toxic waste. Corporations have been held increasingly liable for toxic waste cleanup. For example, Shell Oil was held accountable for a $1 billion cleanup of toxic waste near Denver. What about insurance? Insurance companies are arguing that (1) intentional discharges are not covered and (2) general liability policies were never meant to cover this type of situation.

Product warranties are a good example of a contingent liability that should be recorded in the accounts. Warranty contracts result in future costs that may be incurred in replacing defective units or repairing malfunctioning units without charge to the customer for a specified period after the product is sold. Generally, a manufacturer, such as Black & Decker, knows that some warranty costs will be incurred on products sold under warranty. Moreover, on the basis of prior experience with the product (or similar products), the company usually can make a reasonable estimate of the anticipated cost of servicing (honoring) the contract.

The accounting for warranty costs is based on the matching principle. To comply with this principle, **the estimated cost of honoring product warranty contracts should be recognized as an expense in the period in which the sale occurs**. To illustrate, assume that in 1993 Denson Manufacturing Company sells 10,000 washers and dryers at an average price of $600 each. The selling price includes a one-year warranty on parts. It is expected that 500 units (5%) will be defective and that warranty repair costs will average $80 per unit. In the year of sale, warranty contracts are honored on 300 units at a total cost of $24,000.

At December 31, it is necessary to accrue the estimated warranty costs on the 1993 sales. The computation is as follows:

ILLUSTRATION 12-4

Computation of estimated product warranty liability

Number of units sold	10,000
Estimated rate of defective units	× 5%
Total estimated defective units	500
Average warranty repair cost	× $80
Estimated product warranty liability	$40,000

The adjusting entry, therefore, is:

Helpful hint The effects of the adjusting entry are an increase in expenses and increase in liabilities; the effects of the entry to record the honoring of the warranty are a decrease in one liability and either a decrease in assets or an increase in another liability.

Dec. 31	Warranty Expense	40,000	
	Estimated Warranty Liability		40,000
	(To accrue estimated warranty costs)		

The entry to record repair costs incurred in 1993 to honor warranty contracts on 1993 sales is shown in summary form below:

Jan. 1–	Estimated Warranty Liability	24,000	
Dec. 31	Repair Parts/Wages Payable		24,000
	(To record honoring of 300 warranty contracts on 1993 sales)		

Warranty expense of $40,000 is reported under selling expenses in the income statement, and estimated warranty liability of $16,000 ($40,000 − $24,000) is classified as a current liability on the balance sheet.

In the following year, all expenses incurred in honoring warranty contracts on 1993 sales should be debited to Estimated Warranty Liability. To illustrate, assume that 20 defective units are replaced in January, 1994, at an average cost of $80 in parts and labor. The summary entry is:

Jan. 31	Estimated Warranty Liability	1,600	
	Repair Parts/Wages Payable		1,600
	(To record honoring of 20 warranty contracts on 1993 sales)		

Disclosure of Contingent Liabilities

When a contingent liability meets one but not both conditions for recording the contingency described above, or the contingent liability is only reasonably possible, only disclosure of the contingency is required. Examples of contingencies that may require disclosure are pending or threatened lawsuits and assessment of additional income taxes pending an IRS audit of the tax return.

The disclosure should identify the nature of the item, and if known, the amount of the contingency and the expected outcome of the future event. Disclosure is usually accomplished through a note to the financial statements, as illustrated by the following:

USAir

Legal Proceedings

The Company and various subsidiaries have been named as defendants in various suits and proceedings which involve, among other things, environmental concerns about noise and air pollution and employment matters. These suits and proceedings are in various stages of litigation, and the status of the law with respect to several of the issues involved is unsettled. For these reasons the outcome of these suits and proceedings is difficult to predict. In the Company's opinion, however, the disposition of these matters is not likely to have a material adverse effect on its financial condition.

ILLUSTRATION 12-5

Disclosure of contingent liability

Statement Presentation of Current Liabilities

As indicated in Chapter 4, current liabilities are the first category under liabilities on the balance sheet. Each of the principal types of current liabilities is listed separately within the category. In addition, the terms of notes payable and other pertinent information concerning the individual items are disclosed in the notes to the financial statements.

Current liabilities are seldom listed in the order of maturity because of the varying maturity dates that may exist for specific obligations such as notes payable. A more common, and entirely satisfactory, method of presenting current liabilities is to list them by order of magnitude, with the largest obligations first. Many companies, as a matter of custom, show notes payable and accounts pay-

Helpful hint For another example of a current liability section refer to the PepsiCo balance sheet in Appendix L.

able first, regardless of amount. The following adapted excerpt from a recent balance sheet of USX Corp. (formerly U.S. Steel) illustrates this practice.

ILLUSTRATION 12-6

Current liability section

USX CORP.	
Current Liabilities (in millions)	
Notes payable	$ 138
Accounts payable	2,196
Payroll and benefits payable	243
Taxes payable	415
Interest payable	113
Long-term debt due within one year	197
Total current liabilities	3,302

Before You Go On . . .

1. What are the two criteria for classifying a debt as a current liability?

2. How do the entries and statement presentation differ between an interest-bearing and a zero-interest-bearing note payable?

3. How are sales taxes recorded by a retailer? Identify three unearned revenues.

4. What are the accounting guidelines for contingent liabilities?

SECTION 2   Payroll Accounting

As indicated in Illustration 12-6, payroll and related fringe benefits often constitute a substantial percentage of current liabilities. In addition, employee compensation is often the most significant expense that a company incurs. For example, General Motors reported total employees of 691,000 and labor costs of $19.6 billion, or approximately 26% of net sales. Add to labor costs such fringe benefits as health insurance, life insurance, disability insurance, and so on, and you can see why proper accounting and control of payroll are so important.

It should be emphasized that payroll accounting involves more than paying employees' wages. Companies are required by law to maintain payroll records for each employee, file and pay payroll taxes, and comply with numerous state and federal tax laws applicable to employee compensation.[2]

Payroll Defined

The term "payroll" pertains to all salaries and wages paid to employees. Managerial, administrative, and sales personnel are generally paid **salaries**, which are often expressed in terms of a specified amount per month or per year. In

---

[2]Accounting for payroll has become much more complex as a result of these regulations. As one business person commented, "When I started as a college student, there was withholding and there was Social Security. . . . Then all the state programs began, taxes, unemployment, workers' compensation. Payroll became a burden for the small business."

contrast, store clerks, factory employees, and manual laborers are normally paid **wages**, which are based on a rate per hour, or on a piecework basis (such as per unit of product). Frequently, the terms "salaries" and "wages" are used interchangeably.

The term "payroll" does not extend to payments made for personal service by professionals such as certified public accountants, attorneys, and architects. Such professionals are independent contractors, and payments to them are called **fees**, rather than salaries and wages. This distinction is important because government regulations relating to the payment and reporting of payroll taxes apply only to employees.

Importance of Internal Control

Study Objective 5

Discuss the objectives of internal control for payroll.

Internal control was introduced in Chapter 7. As applied to payrolls, the objectives of internal control are (1) to safeguard company assets against unauthorized payments of payrolls and (2) to assure the accuracy and reliability of the accounting records pertaining to payrolls.

Unfortunately, irregularities often result if internal control is lax. For example, one of the largest frauds involved an accountant at a metal fabricating plant who padded the payroll in order to extract funds for his own use. Overstating hours, using unauthorized pay rates, adding fictitious employees to the payroll, continuing terminated employees on the payroll, and distributing duplicate payroll checks are all methods of stealing from a company. Moreover, inaccurate records will result in incorrect paychecks, financial statements, and payroll tax returns.

Technology in Action

In computerized payroll systems, separate programs are often used for internal control purposes. For example, one program generates the actual payroll checks while a second maintains files on personnel currently employed. A third program (perhaps controlled by the internal auditor) can then compare the checks issued by the first program against the active employee records in the second program to detect any fictitious employees.

Payroll activities involve four functions: hiring employees, timekeeping, preparing the payroll, and paying the payroll. For an internal control system to work effectively, these four functions should be assigned to different departments or individuals. To illustrate these functions in more detail, we will examine the case of Academy Company and one of its employees, Michael Jackson.

Hiring Employees

Posting job openings, screening and interviewing applicants, and hiring employees are responsibilities of the personnel department. From a control standpoint, the personnel department provides significant documentation and authorization. When an employee is hired, the personnel department prepares an authorization form like the one used by Academy Company for Michael Jackson shown in Illustration 12-7.

The authorization form is sent to the payroll department, where it is used to place the new employee on the payroll. A chief concern of the personnel

ILLUSTRATION 12-7

Personnel authorization form

ACADEMY COMPANY

Employee Name___Jackson,_____Michael_____   Effective Date____9/01/89_____
                        LAST   FIRST   MI

Classification___Skilled-Level 10_____   Social Security No. ___329-36-9547_____

Branch/Department___Music_____   Division ____Entertainment_____

NEW HIRE	Classification___Clerk_____ Salary Grade__Level 10___ Trans. from Temp. ☐ Rate $_9.00__ per _hour____ Bonus__N/A_____ Non-exempt ☒ Exempt ☐
RATE CHANGE	(Attach Performance Evaluation made within last three (3) months of effective date) New Rate $ __12.00_____ Bonus_____ Non-exempt ☒ Exempt ☐ Present Rate $_9.00_____ Bonus_____ Non-exempt ☒ Exempt ☐ Merit ☒ Promotion ☐ Decrease ☐ Other_____ Previous Increase Date ____None_____ Amount $_____ per_____ Type_____
SEPARATION	Resignation ☐ Discharge ☐ Retirement ☐ Reason_____ _____ Leave of absence ☐ From_____ to_____ Type_____ Last Day Worked_____
APPROVALS	*BEW*_____ *9/1/89*___ *EMW*_____ *9-1-91*___ BRANCH OR DEPT. MANAGER DATE DIVISION V.P. *James E. Speer* DATE PERSONNEL DEPARTMENT

department is ensuring the accuracy of this form. The reason is quite simple: one of the most common types of payroll frauds is adding fictitious employees to the payroll.

The personnel department is also responsible for authorizing (1) changes in pay rates during employment and (2) terminations of employment. In each instance, the authorization should be in writing, and a copy of the change in status should be sent to the payroll department.

Timekeeping

Another area in which internal control is important is timekeeping. Hourly employees are usually required to record time worked by "punching" a time clock. The time of arrival and departure are automatically recorded by the employee when he or she inserts a time card into the clock. The time card for Michael Jackson is shown in Illustration 12-8.

Time clock procedures are often monitored by a supervisor or security guard to make sure an employee punches only one card. At the end of the pay period, the employee's supervisor is generally required to approve the hours shown by signing the time card. When overtime hours are involved, approval by a supervisor should be mandatory to guard against unauthorized overtime. The approved time card is then sent to the payroll department. For salaried employees, a manually prepared weekly or monthly time report kept by a supervisor may be used to record time worked.

ILLUSTRATION 12-8

Time card

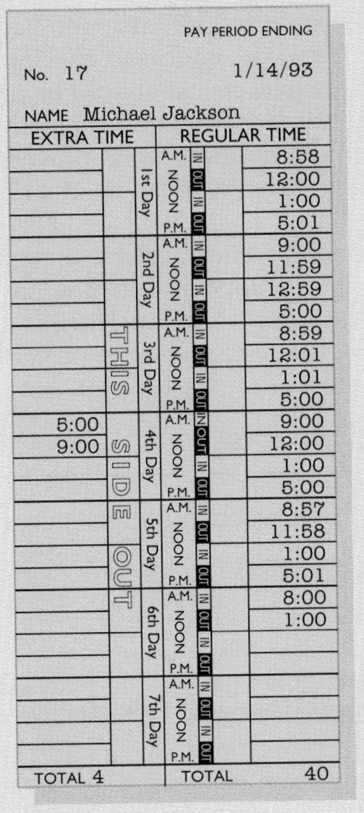

				PAY PERIOD ENDING	

No. 17   **1/14/93**

NAME Michael Jackson

EXTRA TIME		REGULAR TIME		
	1st Day	A.M.	IN	8:58
		NOON	OUT	12:00
			IN	1:00
		P.M.	OUT	5:01
	2nd Day	A.M.	IN	9:00
		NOON	OUT	11:59
			IN	12:59
		P.M.	OUT	5:00
	3rd Day	A.M.	IN	8:59
		NOON	OUT	12:01
			IN	1:01
		P.M.	OUT	5:00
5:00	4th Day	A.M.	IN	9:00
9:00		NOON	OUT	12:00
			IN	1:00
		P.M.	OUT	5:00
	5th Day	A.M.	IN	8:57
		NOON	OUT	11:58
			IN	1:00
		P.M.	OUT	5:01
	6th Day	A.M.	IN	8:00
		NOON	OUT	1:00
			IN	
		P.M.	OUT	
	7th Day	A.M.	IN	
		NOON	OUT	
			IN	
		P.M.	OUT	
TOTAL 4		**TOTAL**		**40**

(THIS SIDE OUT printed vertically in left margin of card)

Preparing the Payroll

The payroll is prepared in the payroll department on the basis of two sources of input: (1) personnel department authorizations and (2) approved time cards. Because of the numerous calculations involved in determining gross wages and payroll deductions, it is customary for a second payroll department employee, working independently, to verify all amounts, and a payroll department supervisor then approves the payroll. The payroll department is also responsible for preparing (but not signing) payroll checks, maintaining payroll records, and preparing payroll tax returns.

Accounting in Action · *Business Insight*

Service bureaus that process payrolls for small businesses are becoming increasingly popular. Payroll processing is considered by many small business owners to be a tedious and painful chore fraught with legal and tax headaches. Small businesses appreciate the advantages service bureaus offer: relatively low cost, simplicity, confidentiality, accuracy, and keeping up to date on changes in rates and the laws.

Paying the Payroll

The payroll is paid by the treasurer's department. **Payment by check minimizes the risk of loss from theft, and the endorsed check provides proof of payment.** For good internal control, payroll checks should be prenumbered, and all checks should be accounted for. All checks must be signed by the treasurer (or a designated agent), and their distribution to employees should be controlled by the treasurer's department. Checks may be distributed by the treasurer or paymaster.[3]

If the payroll is paid in currency, it is customary to have a second person count the cash in each pay envelope and for the paymaster to obtain a signed receipt from the employee upon payment. Thus, if alleged discrepancies arise, adequate safeguards have been established to protect each party involved.

Determining the Payroll

Study Objective 6

Compute and record the payroll for a pay period.

Determining the payroll involves computing (1) gross earnings, (2) payroll deductions, and (3) net pay.

Gross Earnings

Gross earnings, also called gross pay, is the total compensation earned by an employee. There are three major types of gross earnings: wages, salaries, and bonuses.

Total wages for an employee are determined by applying the hourly rate of pay to the number of hours worked. In addition to the hourly pay rate, most companies are required by law to pay a minimum of one and one-half times the regular hourly rate for overtime work in excess of 8 hours per day or 40 hours per week. For example, companies involved in interstate commerce are required by the Fair Labor Standards Act to pay 1½ times the regular wage rate. In addition, many employers pay overtime rates for work done at night, on weekends, and on holidays. The computation of Michael Jackson's gross earnings (total wages) for the 44 hours shown on his time card for the weekly pay period ending January 14 is as follows:

ILLUSTRATION 12-9

Computation of total wages

Type of Pay	Hours	Rate	Gross Earnings
Regular	40	$12.00	$480.00
Overtime	4	18.00	72.00
Total wages			$552.00

This computation assumes that Jackson receives one and one-half times his regular hourly rate ($12.00 × 1.5) for his overtime hours. Union contracts often require that overtime rates be as much as twice the regular rates.

The salary for an employee is generally based on a monthly or yearly rate rather than on an hourly basis. These rates are then applied ratably to the payroll periods used by the company. Most executive and administrative positions are

---

[3]When internal control is weak (such as when authorization forms are lacking), it is imperative that checks be distributed directly to individuals rather than through plant managers. An unscrupulous manager could submit fictitious names and when the checks for these names are received, deposit them to his or her account.

salaried. The Fair Labor Standards Act does not require overtime pay for such positions.

Many companies have **bonus** agreements for management personnel and for some salaried personnel. For example, a recent survey indicated that over 94% of the largest manufacturing companies in the United States provide annual bonuses to their key executives. Bonus arrangements may be based on such factors as increased sales or the amount of net company income. Bonuses may be paid in cash and/or by granting executives the opportunity to acquire shares of stock in the company at favorable prices (called stock option plans). Bonuses have become very lucrative, as companies attempt to retain the services of key executives—so lucrative, in fact, that they have come under intense public scrutiny.

Accounting in Action · *Business Insight*

American Telephone & Telegraph (AT&T) bases its executive pay plan on the performance of the company's stock. The plan gives top executives stock options, but only one-quarter of the options are tied to the current price of the company's stock. The remainder is not available to executives until the price of the stock increases 25% to 50% above the current price. In essence, the compensation plan enables AT&T stockholders to have the benefits of favorable company performance before the executives do.

Source: "Brass at AT&T Get New Carrot, But with String," *The Wall Street Journal,* March 5, 1992.

Payroll Deductions

As anyone who has received a paycheck knows, gross earnings are usually very different from the amount actually received. The difference is attributable to **payroll deductions**. Payroll deductions may be mandatory or voluntary.

Mandatory Deductions

Mandatory deductions consist of FICA taxes and incomes taxes. These deductions do not result in payroll tax expense to the employer because the company only serves as a collection agency for the government.

FICA TAXES. In 1937, Congress enacted the Federal Insurance Contribution Act (FICA). **FICA taxes are designed to provide workers with supplemental retirement, employment disability, and medical benefits.** In 1965, benefits were expanded to include Medicare for individuals over 65 years of age. The benefits are financed by a tax levied on employees' earnings. FICA taxes are commonly referred to as **Social Security taxes**.

The tax rate and the tax base for FICA taxes are set by Congress, and they are changed intermittently. When FICA taxes were first imposed, the rate was 1% on the first $3,000 of gross earnings, or a maximum of $30 per year. The rate and base have changed dramatically since that time! In 1992, the rate was 7.65% on the first $55,500 of gross earnings for each employee, or a maximum of $4,245.75.[4] For purpose of illustration in this chapter, we will assume a rate of

---

[4]The Medicare provision also includes a tax of 1.45% on gross earnings in excess of $55,500, up to $130,200. In our end-of-chapter materials, gross earnings will not exceed $55,500.

8% on the first $50,000 of gross earnings, or a maximum of $4,000. Using the 8% rate, the FICA withholding for Michael Jackson for the weekly pay period ending January 14 is $44.16 ($552 × 8%).

INCOME TAXES. Under the United States pay-as-you-go system of federal income taxes, employers are required to withhold income taxes from employees each pay period. The amount to be withheld is determined by three variables: (1) the employee's gross earnings; (2) the number of allowances claimed by the employee for herself or himself, his or her spouse, and other dependents; and (3) the length of the pay period. **To indicate to the Internal Revenue Service the number of allowances claimed, the employee must complete an** Employee's Withholding Allowance Certificate (Form W-4). As shown in Illustration 12-10, Michael Jackson claims two allowances on his W-4.

ILLUSTRATION 12-10

Form W-4

Form **W-4** (Rev. January 1984)	Department of the Treasury–Internal Revenue Service **Employee's Withholding Allowance Certificate**		OMB No. 1545-0010
1 Type or print your full name Michael Jackson		**2** Your social security number 329-36-9547	
Home address (number and street or rural route) 3413 Mifflin Ave.	**3** Marital Status	☐ Single ☒ Married ☐ Married, but withhold at higher Single rate **Note:** If married, but legally separated, or spouse is a nonresident alien, check the Single box.	

4 Total number of allowances you are claiming (from line F of the worksheet on page 2) **2**
5 Additional amount, if any, you want deducted from each pay . . . . $
6 I claim exemption from withholding because (see instructions and check boxes below that apply):
  a ☐ Last year I did not owe any Federal income tax and had a right to a full refund of ALL income tax withheld, AND
  b ☐ This year I do not expect to owe any Federal income tax and expect to have a right to a full refund of ALL income tax withheld. If both a and b apply, enter the year effective and "EXEMPT" here . . . . . ▶ Year
  c If you entered "EXEMPT" on line 6b, are you a full-time student? . . . . ☐ Yes ☐ No

Under penalties of perjury, I certify that I am entitled to the number of withholding allowances claimed on this certificate, or if claiming exemption from withholding, that I am entitled to claim the exempt status.
Employee's signature ▶ *Michael Jackson*   Date ▶ September 1, 1989

Withholding tables furnished by the Internal Revenue Service indicate the amount of income tax to be withheld from gross wages based on the number of allowances claimed. Separate tables are provided for weekly, biweekly, semimonthly, and monthly pay periods. The portion of the withholding tax table for Michael Jackson (assuming he earns $552 per week) is shown in Illustration 12-11. As indicated in the table, for a weekly salary of $552 with 2 allowances, the income tax to be withheld is $53.00.

Most states and some cities also require employers to withhold income taxes from the earnings of employees. As a general rule, the amounts to be withheld are determined by applying a percentage specified in the state revenue code to the amount withheld for the federal income tax or to the employee's earnings. For the sake of simplicity, we have assumed that Jackson's wages are subject to state income taxes of 2% or $11.04 (2% × $552).

There is no limit on the amount of gross earnings subject to income tax withholdings. In fact, the higher the earnings, the higher the amount of taxes withheld.

Voluntary Deductions

Employees may voluntarily authorize withholdings for charitable, retirement, and other purposes. All voluntary deductions from gross earnings should be authorized in writing by the employee. The authorization(s) may be made individually or as part of a group plan. Deductions for charitable organizations, such as the United Fund, or for financial arrangements, such as U.S. savings

ILLUSTRATION 12-11

Withholding tax table

MARRIED Persons — WEEKLY Payroll Period

(For Wages Paid After February 1992)

And the wages are –		And the number of withholding allowances claimed is –										
At least	But less than	0	1	2	3	4	5	6	7	8	9	10
		The amount of income tax to be withheld shall be –										
480	490	55	49	42	36	29	22	16	9	2	0	0
490	500	57	50	44	37	30	24	17	11	4	0	0
500	510	58	52	45	39	32	25	19	12	5	0	0
510	520	60	53	47	40	33	27	20	14	7	0	0
520	530	61	55	48	42	35	28	22	15	8	2	0
530	540	63	56	50	43	36	30	23	17	10	3	0
540	550	64	58	51	45	38	31	25	18	11	5	0
550	560	66	59	**53**	46	39	33	26	20	13	6	0
560	570	67	61	54	48	41	34	28	21	14	8	1
570	580	69	62	56	49	42	36	29	23	16	9	3
580	590	70	64	57	51	44	37	31	24	17	11	4
590	600	72	65	59	52	45	39	32	26	19	12	6
600	610	73	67	60	54	47	40	34	27	20	14	7
610	620	75	68	62	55	48	42	35	29	22	15	9
620	630	76	70	63	57	50	43	37	30	23	17	10
630	640	78	71	65	58	51	45	38	32	25	18	12
640	650	79	73	66	60	53	46	40	33	26	20	13
650	660	81	74	68	61	54	48	41	35	28	21	15
660	670	82	76	69	63	56	49	43	36	29	23	16
670	680	84	77	71	64	57	51	44	38	31	24	18

bonds and repayment of loans from company credit unions are made individually. In contrast, deductions for union dues, health and life insurance, and pension plans are often made on a group basis. For purpose of illustration, we will assume that Jackson has voluntary deductions of $10 for the United Fund and $5 for union dues.

Technology in Action

With the widespread use of microcomputers, the error-prone task of manually searching tax tables for the proper payroll deductions is becoming extinct even in small businesses. Now computers with entire tax tables stored internally perform this table lookup function without error and calculate accurately all payroll information.

Net Pay

Net (or take-home) pay is determined by subtracting payroll deductions from gross earnings. For Michael Jackson, net pay is $428.80, computed as follows:

ILLUSTRATION 12-12

Computation of net pay

Gross earnings		$552.00
Payroll deductions:		
FICA taxes	$44.16	
Federal income taxes	53.00	
State income taxes	11.04	
United Fund	10.00	
Union dues	5.00	123.20
Net pay		$428.80

Assuming that Michael Jackson's wages for each week during the year are $552, total wages for the year are $28,704 (52 × $552). Thus, all of Jackson's wages are subject to FICA tax during the year. However, if Jackson's wages are $1,000 per week, or $52,000 for the year, only the first $50,000 is subject to FICA taxes. In such case, the maximum FICA withholdings from Michael Jackson would be $4,000 ($50,000 × 8%).

Recording the Payroll

Recording the payroll involves maintaining payroll department records, recognizing payroll expenses and liabilities, and recording payment of the payroll.

Maintaining Payroll Department Records

To comply with state and federal laws, an employer must keep a cumulative record of each employee's gross earnings, deductions, and net pay during the year. The record that provides this information and other essential data is the employee earnings record. Michael Jackson's employee earnings record is shown in Illustration 12-13.

ILLUSTRATION 12-13

Employee earnings record

ACADEMY COMPANY
Employee Earnings Record
For the Year 1993

Name	Michael Jackson	Address	3413 Mifflin Ave.
Social Security Number	329-36-9547		Hampton, Michigan 48292
Date of Birth	December 24, 1959	Telephone	238-9051
Date Employed	September 1, 1989	Date Employment Ended	
Sex	Male	Exemptions	2
Single _____	Married __X__		

1993 Period Ending	Total Hours	Gross Earnings				Deductions						Payment	
		Regular	Overtime	Total	Cumulative	FICA	Fed. Inc. Tax	State Inc. Tax	United Fund	Union Dues	Total	Net Amount	Check No.
1/7	42	480.00	36.00	516.00	516.00	41.28	64.00	10.32	10.00	5.00	130.60	385.40	974
1/14	44	480.00	72.00	552.00	1,068.00	44.16	53.00	11.04	10.00	5.00	123.20	428.80	1028
1/21	43	480.00	54.00	534.00	1,602.00	42.72	68.00	10.68	10.00	5.00	136.40	397.60	1077
1/28	42	480.00	36.00	516.00	2,118.00	41.28	64.00	10.32	10.00	5.00	130.60	385.40	1133
Jan. Total		1,920.00	198.00	2,118.00		169.44	249.00	42.36	40.00	20.00	520.80	1,597.20	

A separate earnings record is kept for each employee; it is updated after each pay period. The cumulative payroll data on the earnings record are used by the employer in (1) determining when an employee has earned the maximum earnings subject to FICA taxes, (2) filing state and federal payroll tax returns (as explained later in the chapter), and (3) providing each employee with a statement of gross earnings and tax withholdings for the year, as shown in Illustration 12-16 on page 489.

In addition to employee earnings records, many companies find it useful to prepare a payroll register to accumulate the gross earnings, deductions, and net pay by employee for each pay period. The payroll register is presented in Illustration 12-14 with the data for Michael Jackson shown in the wages section.

ILLUSTRATION 12-14

Payroll register

ACADEMY COMPANY
Payroll Register
For the Week Ending January 14, 1993

Employee	Total Hours	Earnings			Deductions						Paid		Accounts Debited	
		Regular	Over-time	Gross Pay	FICA	Federal Income Tax	State Income Tax	United Fund	Union Dues	Total Deduc-tions	Net Pay	Check No.	Office Salaries Expense	Wages Expense
Office Salaries														
Arnold, Patricia	40	580.00		580.00	46.40	123.00	11.60	15.00		196.00	384.00	998	580.00	
Canton, Matthew	40	590.00		590.00	47.20	119.00	11.80	20.00		198.00	392.00	999	590.00	
Mueller, William	40	530.00		530.00	42.40	79.00	10.60	11.00		143.00	387.00	1000	530.00	
Subtotal		5,200.00		5,200.00	416.00	1,090.00	104.00	120.00		1,730.00	3,470.00		5,200.00	
Wages														
Bennett, Robin	42	480.00	36.00	516.00	41.28	94.00	10.32	18.00	5.00	168.60	347.40	1025		516.00
Jackson, Michael	44	480.00	72.00	552.00	44.16	53.00	11.04	10.00	5.00	123.20	428.80	1028		552.00
Milroy, Lee	43	480.00	54.00	534.00	42.72	77.00	10.68	10.00	5.00	145.40	388.60	1029		534.00
Subtotal		11,000.00	1,010.00	12,010.00	960.80	2,400.00	240.20	301.50	115.00	4,017.50	7,992.50			12,010.00
Total		16,200.00	1,010.00	17,210.00	1,376.80	3,490.00	344.20	421.50	115.00	5,747.50	11,462.50		5,200.00	12,010.00

Note that this record is a listing of each employee's payroll data for the pay period. In some companies, a payroll register is a journal or book of original entry, and postings are made directly to ledger accounts from the register. In other companies, the payroll register is a memorandum record that provides the data for a general journal entry and subsequent posting to the ledger accounts. In the Academy Company situation, the latter procedure is followed.

Technology in Action

In addition to supplying the entry to record the payroll, the output for a computerized payroll system would include (1) payroll checks, (2) a payroll check register which sorts by check and department, and (3) updated employee earnings records which become the source for monthly, quarterly, and annual reporting of wages to taxing agencies.

Recognizing Payroll Expenses and Liabilities

From the payroll register in Illustration 12-14, the journal entry to record the payroll for the week ending January 14 is:

Jan. 14	Office Salaries Expense	5,200.00	
	Wages Expense	12,010.00	
	FICA Taxes Payable		1,376.80
	Federal Income Taxes Payable		3,490.00
	State Income Taxes Payable		344.20
	United Fund Payable		421.50
	Union Dues Payable		115.00
	Salaries and Wages Payable		11,462.50
	(To record payroll for the week ending January 14)		

Specific liability accounts are credited for the mandatory and voluntary deductions made during the pay period. In the example, debits to Office Salaries and Wages Expense are used for gross earnings. In other cases, there may be additional debits such as Store Salaries and Sales Salaries. The amount credited to Salaries and Wages Payable is the sum of the individual checks the employees will receive.

Recording Payment of the Payroll

Payment by check is made either from the employer's regular bank account or a payroll bank account. Each check is usually accompanied by a detachable **statement of earnings** document that shows the employee's gross earnings, payroll deductions, and net pay. The Academy Company uses its regular bank account for payroll checks. The check and statement of earnings for Michael Jackson are shown in Illustration 12-15.

ILLUSTRATION 12-15

Check and statement of earnings

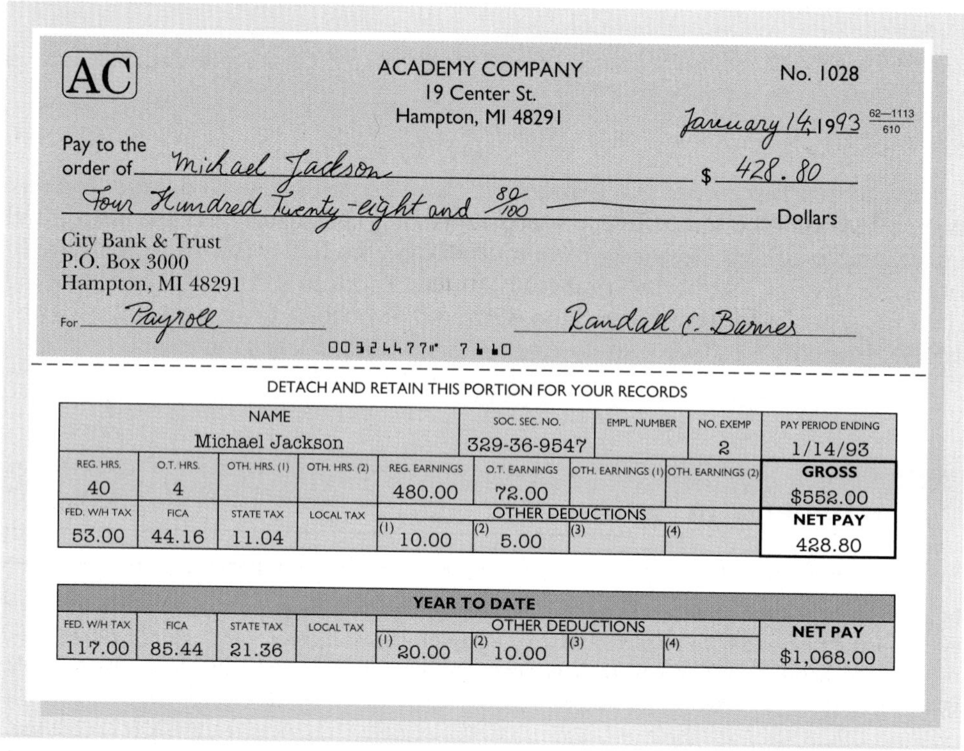

AC

ACADEMY COMPANY
19 Center St.
Hampton, MI 48291

No. 1028

January 14, 1993 62—1113/610

Pay to the order of Michael Jackson $ 428.80

Four Hundred Twenty-eight and 80/100 Dollars

City Bank & Trust
P.O. Box 3000
Hampton, MI 48291

For Payroll

Randall E. Barnes

003244771 7110

DETACH AND RETAIN THIS PORTION FOR YOUR RECORDS

NAME				SOC. SEC. NO.	EMPL. NUMBER	NO. EXEMP	PAY PERIOD ENDING
Michael Jackson				329-36-9547		2	1/14/93
REG. HRS.	O.T. HRS.	OTH. HRS. (1)	OTH. HRS. (2)	REG. EARNINGS	O.T. EARNINGS	OTH. EARNINGS (1)	OTH. EARNINGS (2)	GROSS
40	4			480.00	72.00			$552.00
FED. W/H TAX	FICA	STATE TAX	LOCAL TAX	OTHER DEDUCTIONS (1)	(2)	(3)	(4)	NET PAY
53.00	44.16	11.04		10.00	5.00			428.80

YEAR TO DATE								
FED. W/H TAX	FICA	STATE TAX	LOCAL TAX	OTHER DEDUCTIONS (1)	(2)	(3)	(4)	NET PAY
117.00	85.44	21.36		20.00	10.00			$1,068.00

Following payment of the payroll, the check numbers are entered in the payroll register. The entry to record payment of the payroll for Academy Company is as follows:

Jan. 14	Salaries and Wages Payable	11,462.50	
	Cash		11,462.50
	(To record payment of payroll)		

When currency is used in payment, one check is prepared for the net pay. The check is then cashed, and the coins and currency are inserted in individual pay envelopes for disbursement to individual employees.

Before You Go On . . .

1. Identify two internal control procedures that are applicable to each payroll function.

2. What are the primary sources of gross earnings?

3. What payroll deductions are (a) mandatory and (b) voluntary?

4. What account titles are used in recording a payroll, assuming only mandatory payroll deductions are involved?

Recording and Paying Employer Payroll Taxes

Payroll tax expense results from three taxes levied on **employers** by governmental agencies. These taxes are: FICA, federal unemployment tax, and state unemployment tax. Each of these taxes plus such items as paid vacations and pensions are collectively referred to as "fringe benefits." As indicated earlier, the cost of fringe benefits in many companies is substantial.

Study Objective 7

Describe and record employer payroll taxes.

FICA Taxes

The employer must match each employee's FICA contribution. The matching contribution results in **payroll** tax expense to the employer. Thus, the employer's tax is subject to the same rate and maximum earnings applicable to the employee. The account, FICA Taxes Payable, is used for both the employee's and the employer's FICA contributions. For the January 14 payroll, Academy Company's FICA tax is $1,376.80 ($17,210.00 × 8%).

Federal Unemployment Taxes

The Federal Unemployment Tax Act (FUTA) is another feature of the federal social security program. Federal unemployment taxes provide benefits for a limited period of time to employees who lose their jobs through no fault of their own. Under provisions of the Act, the employer is required to pay a tax of 6.2% on the first $7,000 of gross wages paid to each employee during a calendar year. The law, however, allows the employer a maximum credit of 5.4% on the federal rate for contributions to state unemployment taxes. Because of this provision, state unemployment tax laws generally provide for a 5.4% rate, and the effective federal unemployment tax rate becomes .8% (6.2% − 5.4%). This tax is borne entirely by the employer; there is no deduction or withholding from employees. The account Federal Unemployment Taxes Payable is used to recognize this liability. The federal unemployment tax for Academy Company for the January 14 payroll is $137.68 ($17,210.00 × .8%).

Helpful hint FICA taxes are paid both by the employer and employee. Federal unemployment taxes and (in most states) the state unemployment taxes are borne entirely by the employer.

State Unemployment Taxes

All states have unemployment compensation programs under state unemployment tax acts (SUTA). Like federal unemployment taxes, state unemployment taxes provide benefits to employees who lose their jobs. These taxes are levied on employers. The basic rate is usually 5.4% on the first $7,000 of wages paid to an employee during the year.[5] The basic rate is adjusted according to the em-

---

[5]In a few states, the employee is also required to make a contribution.

ployer's experience rating: Companies with a history of unstable employment may pay more than the basic rate. Regardless of the rate paid, the credit on the federal unemployment tax is still 5.4%. The account State Unemployment Taxes Payable is used for this liability. The state unemployment tax for Academy Company for the January 14 payroll is $929.34 ($17,210.00 × 5.4%).

Recording Employer Payroll Taxes

Employer payroll taxes are usually recorded at the same time the payroll is journalized. The entire amount of gross earnings ($17,210.00) shown in the payroll register in Illustration 12-14 is subject to each of the three taxes mentioned above. Accordingly, the entry to record the payroll tax expense associated with the January 14 payroll is:

Jan. 14	Payroll Tax Expense	2,443.82	
	FICA Taxes Payable		1,376.80
	Federal Unemployment Taxes Payable		137.68
	State Unemployment Taxes Payable		929.34
	(To record employer's payroll taxes on January 14 payroll)		

Separate liability accounts are used instead of a single credit to Payroll Taxes Payable, because these liabilities are payable to different taxing authorities at different dates. The liability accounts are classified as current liabilities since they will be paid within the next year. Payroll Tax Expense is classified on the income statement as an operating expense.

Filing and Remitting Payroll Taxes

Preparation of payroll tax returns is the responsibility of the payroll department; payment of the taxes is made by the treasurer's department. Much of the information for the returns is obtained from employee earnings records.

For purposes of reporting and remitting, FICA taxes and federal income taxes withheld are combined. The taxes must be reported quarterly no later than

Accounting in Action · *Ethics Insight*

The owner of a newly restored Victorian hotel, nestled in a small Massachusetts town, skipped payment of withholding taxes for three quarters. Before long, he received a call from the IRS. After months of haggling, the hotel owner was told that unless he paid the $70,000 owed, the IRS would be forced to liquidate the hotel, the land, and dozens of antiques in the inn, which had taken him and his wife years to acquire.

As this story indicates, cash-hungry small businesses are often tempted to skip or delay paying withholding taxes. Increasingly, federal and state agencies are cracking down on such cheaters. Penalties for late or nonpayment can be devastating: Fines are levied at the rate of 5% of taxes owed for each month a payroll tax isn't filed. And in cases where nothing is paid, penalties of 100% can be applied, with interest added, to the unpaid balance. Under the 100% penalty, the government can padlock the doors, seize assets, and hold the officers or certain other employees personally responsible for the penalties.

What happened to the Massachusetts hotel owner? He's now working on a repayment plan, rather than lose his years of hard work.

one month following the close of each quarter. The remitting requirements depend on the amount of taxes withheld and the length of the pay period. Remittances are made through deposits in either a Federal Reserve Bank or an authorized commercial bank.

Federal unemployment taxes are generally filed and remitted annually on or before January 31 following the preceding year. Earlier payments are required, however, when the tax exceeds a specified amount. State unemployment taxes usually must be filed and paid by the end of the month following each quarter. When payroll taxes are paid, payroll liability accounts are debited and cash is credited.

The employer is also required to provide each employee with a **Wage and Tax Statement (Form W-2)** by January 31 following the end of a calendar year. This statement shows gross earnings, FICA taxes withheld, and income taxes withheld for the year. The required W-2 form for Michael Jackson, using assumed annual data, is shown in Illustration 12-16.

ILLUSTRATION 12-16

W-2 form

Form **W-2 Wage and Tax Statement**

1 Control number	OMB No. 1545-0008		
2 Employer's name, address and ZIP code Academy Company 19 Center St. Hampton, MI 48291		3 Employer's identification number 36-2167852	4 Employer's State number
		5 Stat. employee ☐ Deceased ☐ Legal rep. ☐ 942 emp. ☐ Subtotal ☐ Void ☐	
		6 Allocated tips	7 Advance EIC payment
8 Employee's social security number 329-36-9547	9 Federal income tax withheld $3240.00	10 Wages, tips, other compensation $26,300.00	11 Social security tax withheld $2,104.00
12 Employee's name, address, and ZIP code Michael Jackson 3413 Mifflin Ave. Hampton, MI 48292		13 Social security wages $26,300.00	14 Social security tips
		16	
		17 State income tax $526.00 / 18 State wages, tips, etc.	19 Name of State Michigan
		20 Local income tax / 21 Local wages, tips, etc.	22 Name of locality

The employer must send a copy of each employee's Wage and Tax Statement to the Social Security Administration. This agency subsequently furnishes the Internal Revenue Service with the income data required.

Technology in Action

Large employers, like General Motors, transmit their W-2s to the government on magnetic tape. The taxing agencies copy these tapes directly into their computer system for subsequent comparison against earnings and taxes withheld reported on employee's income tax returns.

Additional Fringe Benefits

Study Objective 8

Identify additional fringe benefits associated with employee compensation.

In addition to the three payroll tax fringe benefits, employers incur other substantial fringe benefit costs. Two of the most important are paid absences and postretirement benefits.

Paid Absences

Employees often have rights to receive compensation for future absences when certain conditions of employment are met. The compensation may pertain to paid vacations, sick pay benefits, and paid holidays. When the payment of such compensation is **probable** and the amount can be **reasonably estimated**, a liability should be accrued for paid future absences. When the amount cannot be reasonably estimated, the potential liability should be disclosed. Ordinarily, vacation pay is the only paid absence that is accrued; the other types of paid absences are only disclosed.[6]

To illustrate, assume that Academy Company employees are entitled to one day's vacation for each month worked. If thirty employees earn an average of $110 per day in a given month, the accrual for vacation benefits in one month is $3,300. The liability is recognized at the end of the month by the following adjusting entry:

Jan. 31	Vacation Benefits Expense	3,300	
	Vacation Benefits Payable		3,300
	(To accrue vacation benefits expense)		

This accrual is required by the matching principle. When vacation benefits are paid, Vacation Benefits Payable is debited and Cash is credited. For example if the above benefits are paid in July, the entry is:

July 31	Vacation Benefits Payable	3,300	
	Cash		3,300
	(To record payment of vacation benefits)		

The magnitude of unpaid absences has gained employers' attention. Take the case of an assistant superintendent of schools who worked for around 20 years and rarely took a vacation or sick day. A month or so before she retired, the city discovered that she was due nearly $30,000 in accrued benefits. Yet that liability was never on the city's books. Or at one time, the city of Dallas had vacation liabilities of $8.6 million and a potential $33 million of sick pay liabilities; yet it had a mere $3.5 million in the general fund for that year.[7]

Postretirement Benefits

The accounting and reporting standards for postretirement benefit payments to employees have been issued under two separate topics: (1) postretirement health care and life insurance benefits and (2) pension plans. For both types of postretirement benefits the employer's costs should be reported as expense during the employee's working years, not during the employee's retirement years.

---

[6]The typical U.S. company provides an average of 12 days of paid vacations for its employees at an average cost of 5% of gross earnings.

[7]Adapted from Alyssa Lappen "Off-the-Book Time Bombs," *Forbes*, May 11, 1981.

Postretirement Health Care and Life Insurance Benefits

Providing medical and related health care benefits for retirees—at one time an inexpensive and highly effective way of generating employee goodwill—has turned into one of corporate America's most worrisome financial problems. Runaway medical cost inflation, earlier retirement, and increased longevity are sending the liability for retiree health plans through the roof for many companies.

Many companies began offering retiree health care coverage in the form of Medicare supplements in the 1960s. Almost all plans operated on a pay-as-you-go basis—the companies simply paid for the bills as they came in, rather than setting aside funds to meet the cost of future benefits. These plans were accounted for on the cash basis rather than the accrual basis. However, the FASB believes shareholders and creditors should know the amount of the employer's obligations. As a result, the FASB now requires accrual accounting for postretirement health care and life insurance benefits.

Pension Plans

A **pension plan** is an agreement whereby an employer provides benefits (payments) to employees after they retire. Over 50 million workers currently participate in pension plans in the United States, and by 1995, assets of private pension plans are expected to reach $3 trillion. The need for proper administration of and

Accounting in Action ▪ *Business Insight*

The battle over fringe benefits has grabbed a starring role in the corporate drama of the 1990s, as benefits continue to outpace wages and salaries. Growing far faster than pay, benefits equaled 38% of wages and salaries in 1990. While vacations and other forms of paid leave take the biggest bite of the benefits pie, medical costs are increasing much more quickly.

Source: Fortune, December 16, 1991.

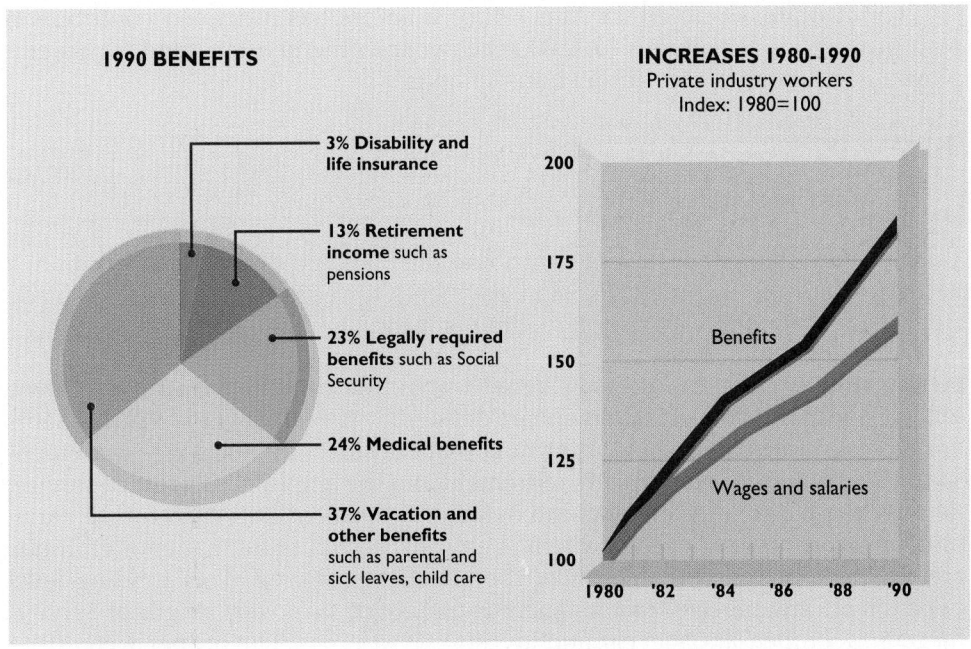

good accounting for pension plans becomes apparent when one appreciates the size of existing pension funds. Most pension plans are subject to the provisions of ERISA (Employee Retirement Income Security Act), a law enacted to curb abuses in the administration and funding of such plans.

Three parties are generally involved in a pension plan. The **employer** (company) sponsors the pension plan. The **plan administrator** receives the contributions from the employer, invests the pension assets, and makes the benefit payments to the **pension recipients** (retired employees). The diagram below shows the three distinct parties involved in a pension plan and indicates the flow of cash among them.

ILLUSTRATION 12-17

Parties in a pension plan

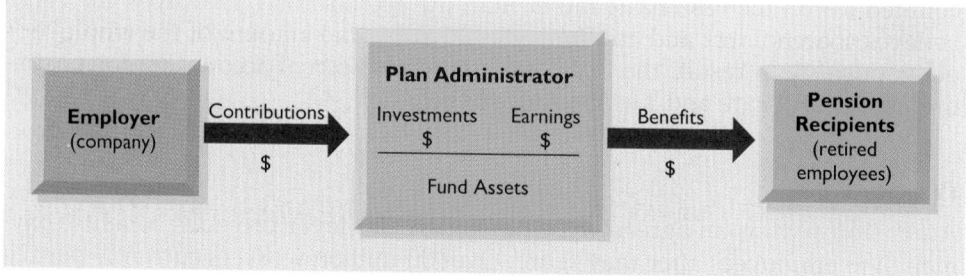

The two most common types of pension arrangements for providing benefits to employees after they retire are defined contribution plans and defined benefit plans.

DEFINED CONTRIBUTION PLAN. In a defined contribution plan, the employer's contribution to the plan is defined by the terms of the plan. That is, the employer agrees to contribute a certain sum each period based on a formula.

The accounting for a defined contribution plan is straightforward: The employer simply makes a contribution each year based on the formula established in the plan. As a result, the employer's obligation is easily determined. It follows that **the amount of the contribution required each period is reported as pension expense. A liability is reported by the employer only if the contribution has not been made in full**.

To illustrate, assume that Alba Office Interiors has a defined contribution plan in which it contributes $200,000 each year to the pension fund for its employees. The entry to record this transaction is:

Pension Expense	200,000	
Cash		200,000
(To record pension expense and contribution to pension fund)		

To the extent that Alba did not contribute the $200,000 defined contribution, a liability would be recorded. Pension payments to retired employees are made from the pension fund by the plan administrator.

DEFINED BENEFIT PLAN. In a defined benefit plan, the benefits that the employee will receive at the time of retirement are defined by the terms of the plan. Benefits are typically calculated using a formula that considers an employee's compensation level when he or she nears retirement and the employee's years of service. Because the benefits in this plan are defined in terms of uncertain future variables, an appropriate funding pattern is established to assure that enough funds are available at retirement to meet the benefits promised. This funding level depends on a number of factors such as employee turnover, length of service, mortality, compensation levels, and investment earnings. **The proper accounting for these plans is complex and is considered in more advanced accounting courses.**

Before You Go On . . .

1. What payroll taxes are levied on employers?

2. What accounts are involved in accruing employer payroll taxes?

3. What accounts are involved in accruing and paying vacation benefits?

4. How does a defined contribution pension plan differ from a defined benefit pension plan?

Summary of Study Objectives

1. *Explain a current liability and identify the major types of current liabilities.* A current liability is a debt that can reasonably be expected to be paid (1) from existing current assets or through the creation of other current liabilities, and (2) within one year or the operating cycle, whichever is longer. The major types of current liabilities are notes payable, accounts payable, unearned revenues, and accrued liabilities such as taxes, salaries and wages, and interest payable.

2. *Describe the accounting for notes payable.* When a promissory note is interest-bearing, the amount of assets received upon the issuance of the note is generally equal to the face value of the note, and interest expense is accrued over the life of the note. When a note is zero-interest-bearing, the borrower receives the discounted or present value of the instrument. A Discount on Notes Payable account is debited for the discount, and this amount is charged to interest expense over the life of the note.

3. *Explain the accounting for other current liabilities.* Sales taxes payable are recorded at the time the related sales occur. The company serves as a collection agent for the taxing authority. Sales taxes are not an expense to the company. Unearned revenues (advances from customers) are initially recorded in an unearned revenue account. As the revenue is earned, a transfer from unearned revenue to earned revenue occurs. The current maturities of long-term debt should be reported as a current liability in the balance sheet.

4. *Describe the accounting and disclosure requirements for contingent liabilities.* If it is probable that (likely to occur) the contingency will happen and the amount is reasonably estimable, the liability should be recorded in the accounts. However, if it is only

reasonably possible (it could occur), then it need be disclosed only in the notes to the financial statements. If the possibility that the contingency will happen is remote (unlikely to occur), it need not be recorded or disclosed.

5. *Discuss the objectives of internal control for payroll.* The objectives of internal control for payroll are (1) to safeguard company assets against unauthorized payments of payrolls, and (2) to assure the accuracy and reliability of the accounting records pertaining to payrolls.

6. *Compute and record the payroll for a pay period.* The computation of the payroll involves gross earnings, payroll deductions, and net pay. In recording the payroll, salaries (or wages) expense is debited for gross earnings, individual tax and other liability accounts are credited for payroll deductions, and salaries (wages) payable is credited for net pay. When the payroll is paid, Salaries and Wages Payable is debited, and Cash is credited.

7. *Describe and record employer payroll taxes.* Employer payroll taxes consist of FICA, federal unemployment taxes, and state unemployment taxes. The taxes are usually accrued at the time the payroll is recorded by debiting Payroll Tax Expense and crediting separate liability accounts for each type of tax.

8. *Identify additional fringe benefits associated with employee compensation.* Additional fringe benefits associated with wages are paid absences (paid vacations, sick pay benefits, and paid holidays), postretirement health care and life insurance, and pensions. The two most common types of pension arrangements are a defined contribution plan and a defined benefit plan.

GLOSSARY

Bonuses · Compensation to management and salaried personnel based on factors such as increased sales or the amount of net income. (p. 481)

Contingent liability · A potential liability that may become an actual liability in the future. (p. 473)

Defined benefit plan · A pension plan in which the benefits that the employee will receive at retirement are defined by the terms of the plan. (p. 492)

Defined contribution plan · A pension plan in which the employer's contribution to the plan is defined by the terms of the plan. (p. 492)

Employee earnings record · A cumulative record of each employee's gross earnings, deductions, and net pay during the year. (p. 484)

Employee's Withholding Allowance Certificate (Form W-4) · An Internal Revenue Service form on which the employee indicates the number of allowances claimed for withholding federal income taxes. (p. 482)

Federal unemployment taxes · Taxes imposed on the employer that provides benefits for a limited time period to employees who lose their jobs through no fault of their own. (p. 487)

FICA taxes · Taxes designed to provide workers with supplemental retirement, employment disability, and medical benefits. (p. 481)

Gross earnings (gross pay) · Total compensation earned by an employee. (p. 480)

Net (or take-home) pay · Gross earnings less payroll deductions. (p. 483)

Payroll deductions. · Deductions from gross earnings to determine an employee's net pay. (p. 481)

Payroll register · A payroll record that shows the gross earnings, deductions, and net pay for each employee for each pay period. (p. 484)

Pension plan · An agreement whereby an employer provides benefits to employees after they retire. (p. 491)

Salaries · Specified amounts per month or per year paid to executive, administrative, and sales personnel. (p. 480)

Statement of earnings · A document attached to a paycheck that indicates the employee's gross earnings, payroll deductions, and net pay. (p. 486)

State unemployment taxes · Taxes imposed on the employer that provide benefits to employees who lose their jobs. (p. 487)

Wage and tax statement (Form W-2) · A form showing gross earnings, FICA taxes withheld, and income taxes withheld which is prepared annually by an employer for each employee. (p. 489)

Wages · Amounts paid to employees based on a rate per hour or on a piece-work basis. (p. 480)

DEMONSTRATION PROBLEM

Indiana Jones Company had the following selected transactions in 1993.

Feb. 1   Signs a $53,000 six-month zero-interest-bearing note payable to CitiBank receiving $50,000 in cash.

10   Cash register sales total $43,200 which includes an 8% sales tax.

28   The payroll for the month consists of Sales Salaries $32,000 and Office Salaries $18,000. All wages are subject to 8% FICA taxes. A total of $8,900 federal income taxes are withheld. The salaries are paid on March 1.

28   The following adjustment data are developed:
1. Interest expense of $500 has been incurred on the note.
2. Employer payroll taxes include 8% FICA taxes, a 5.4% state unemployment tax, and a .8% federal unemployment tax.
3. Some sales were made under warranty. Of the units sold under warranty, 350 are expected to become defective. Repair costs are estimated to be $40 per unit.

Instructions

(a) Journalize the February transactions.

(b) Journalize the adjusting entries at February 28.

Helpful hints
1. Remember that the account Discount on Notes Payable is used with zero-interest notes payable.
2. All payroll taxes are based on gross earnings.
3. Warranty costs are expensed in the period in which the sale occurs.

Solution to Demonstration Problem

(a) Feb. 1 Cash   50,000
      Discount on Notes Payable   3,000
        Notes Payable   53,000
          (Issued six-month zero-interest-bearing note to CitiBank)

     10 Cash   43,200
        Sales   40,000
        Sales Taxes Payable   3,200
          (To record sales and sales taxes payable)

     28 Sales Salaries Expense   32,000
       Office Salaries Expense   18,000
        FICA Taxes Payable (8% × $50,000)   4,000
        Federal Income Taxes Payable   8,900
        Salaries Payable   37,100
          (To record February salaries)

(b) Feb. 28 Interest Expense   500
        Discount on Notes Payable   500
          (To record interest for February on zero-interest-bearing note)

     28 Payroll Tax Expense   7,100
        FICA Taxes Payable   4,000
        Federal Unemployment Taxes Payable   400
         (.8% × $50,000)
        State Unemployment Taxes Payable   2,700
         (5.4% × $50,000)
          (To record employer's payroll taxes on February payroll)

     28 Warranty Expense (350 × $40)   14,000
       Estimated Warranty Liability   14,000
          (To record estimated product warranty liability)

SELF-STUDY QUESTIONS

Answers are at the end of the chapter.

(S.O. 1)

1. The time period for classifying a liability as current is one year or the operating cycle, whichever is:
   a. shorter.
   b. longer.
   c. probable.
   d. possible.

(S.O. 1)

2. To be classified as a current liability, a debt must be expected to be paid:
   a. out of existing current assets.
   b. by creating other current liabilities.
   c. within two years.
   d. both (a) and (b).

(S.O. 2)

3. The difference between the cash proceeds and the face value of a zero-interest-bearing note payable is debited to:
   a. Discount on Notes Payable.
   b. Prepaid Interest.
   c. Interest Expense.
   d. Interest Payable.

(S.O. 3)

4. Reeves Company has total proceeds from sales of $4,410. If the proceeds include sales taxes of 5%, the amount to be credited to Sales is:
   a. $4,000.
   b. $4,189.50.
   c. $4,200.
   d. No correct answer given.

(S.O. 4)

5. A contingency should be recorded in the accounts when:
   a. It is probable the contingency will happen but the amount cannot be reasonably estimated.
   b. It is reasonably possible the contingency will happen and the amount can be reasonably estimated.
   c. It is reasonably possible the contingency will happen but the amount cannot be reasonably estimated.
   d. It is probable the contingency will happen and the amount can be reasonably estimated.

(S.O. 4)   6. At December 31, Hanes Company prepares an adjusting entry for a product
warranty contract. Which of the following
accounts are included in the entry?
   a. Warranty Expense.
   b. Estimated Warranty Liability.
   c. Repair Parts/Wages Payable.
   d. Both (a) and (b).

(S.O. 5)   7. The department that should pay the payroll is the:
   a. timekeeping department.
   b. personnel department.
   c. treasurer's department.
   d. payroll department.

(S.O. 6)   8. J. Barr earns $14 per hour for a 40-hour
week and $21 per hour for any overtime

work. If Barr works 44 hours in a week,
gross earnings are:
   a. $560.
   b. $616.
   c. $644.
   d. $666.

9. Employer payroll taxes do not include: (S.O. 7)
   a. federal unemployment taxes.
   b. state unemployment taxes.
   c. FICA taxes.
   d. federal income taxes.

10. Which of the following is *not* an addi-   (S.O. 8)
tional fringe benefit?
   a. Salaries.
   b. Paid absences.
   c. Paid vacations.
   d. Postretirement pensions.

QUESTIONS

1. What is a current liability?

2. Mayo Co. has a liability that will be paid during the current year, but it is not classified as a current liability. Under what circumstances is this acceptable?

3. What is the principal difference between an interest-bearing note and a zero-interest-bearing note?

4. Aurora University sold 10,000 season football tickets at $70 each for its five-game home schedule. What entries should be made (a) when the tickets were sold and (b) after each game?

5. What is a contingent liability? Give an example of a contingent liability that is usually recorded in the accounts.

6. Under what circumstances is a contingent liability disclosed only in the notes to the financial statements? Under what circumstances is a contingent liability not recorded in the accounts nor disclosed in the notes to the financial statements?

7. You are a newly hired accountant with Steeples Company. On your first day, the controller asks you to identify the main internal control objectives related to payroll accounting. How would you respond?

8. What are the four functions associated with payroll activities?

9. What is the difference between gross pay and net pay? Which amount should a company record as wages or salaries expense?

10. Which payroll tax is levied on both employers and employees?

11. Are the federal and state income taxes withheld from employee paychecks a payroll tax expense for the employer? Explain your answer.

12. What do the following acronyms stand for: FICA, FUTA, and SUTA?

13. What information is shown on a W-4 statement? A W-2 statement?

14. Distinguish between the two types of payroll deductions and give examples of each.

15. What are the primary uses of the employee earnings record?

16. (a) Identify the three types of employer payroll taxes. (b) How are tax liability accounts and payroll tax expense classified in the financial statements?

17. Identify three additional types of fringe benefits associated with employees' compensation.

18. Often during job interviews, the candidate asks the potential employer about the firm's paid absences policy. What are paid absences? How are they accounted for?

19. What are the two types of postretirement benefits? During what years does the FASB advocate expensing the employer's costs of these postretirement benefits?

20. What basis of accounting for the employer's cost of postretirement health care and life insurance benefits has been used by most companies and what basis does the FASB advocate in the future? Explain the basic difference between these methods in recognizing postretirement benefit costs.

21. Identify the three parties in a pension plan. What role does each party have in the plan?

22. Tom Broka and Bryant Gumbs are reviewing pension plans. They ask your help in distinguishing between a defined contribution plan and a defined benefit plan. Explain the principal differences to Tom and Bryant.

BRIEF EXERCISES

BE12–1 Folsom Company has the following obligations at December 31: (a) a note payable for $100,000 due in two years, (b) a ten-year mortgage payable of $200,000 payable in ten $20,000 annual payments, (c) accounts payable of $60,000, and (d) interest payable of $15,000 on the mortgage. For each obligation, indicate whether it should be classified as a current liability.

Identify whether obligations are current liabilities. (S.O. 1)

BE12–2 The Gomez Company borrows $50,000 on July 1 from the bank by signing a $50,000 10% one-year note payable. Prepare the journal entries to record (a) the proceeds of the note and (b) accrued interest at December 31, assuming adjusting entries are made only at the end of the year.

Prepare entries for an interest-bearing note payable. (S.O. 2)

BE12–3 Dufey Company borrows $50,000 from First Bank on June 1 by signing a $52,000 four-month zero-interest-bearing note payable. Prepare the journal entries to record (a) the proceeds of the note and (b) interest expense for the month of June.

Prepare entries for a zero-interest-bearing note payable. (S.O. 2)

BE12–4 Grundy Auto Supply does not segregate sales and sales taxes at the time of sale. The register total for March 16 is $9,450. All sales are subject to a 5% sales tax. Compute sales taxes payable and make the entry to record sales taxes payable and sales.

Compute and record sales taxes payable. (S.O. 3)

BE12–5 On December 1, Filgas Company introduces a new product that includes a one-year warranty on parts. In December 1,000 units are sold. Management believes that 3% of the units will be defective and that the average warranty costs will be $60 per unit. Prepare the adjusting entry at December 31 to accrue the estimated warranty cost.

Prepare adjusting entry for warranty costs. (S.O. 4)

BE12–6 The Lucas Company has the following payroll procedures:

1. The personnel department prepares hiring authorization forms for new hires.
2. Supervisor approves overtime work.
3. The treasurer's department pays employees.
4. A second payroll department employee verifies payroll calculations.

Identify the payroll function to which each procedure pertains.

Identify payroll functions. (S.O. 5)

BE12–7 Pat Forest's regular hourly wage rate is $14, and she receives an hourly rate of $21 for work in excess of 40 hours. During a January pay period, Pat works 43 hours. Pat's federal income tax withholding is $100, and she has no voluntary deductions. Compute Pat Forest's gross earnings and net pay for the pay period.

Compute gross earnings and net pay. (S.O. 6)

BE12–8 Data for Pat Forest are presented in BE12–7. Prepare the journal entries to record (1) Pat's pay for the period and (2) the payment of Pat's wages. Use January 15 for the end of the pay period and the payment date.

Record a payroll and the payment of wages. (S.O. 6)

BE12–9 In January, gross earnings in the Higgins Company totaled $50,000. All earnings are subject to 8% FICA taxes, 5.4% state unemployment taxes, and 0.8% federal unemployment taxes. Prepare the entry to record January payroll tax expense.

Record employer payroll taxes. (S.O. 7)

Record estimated vacation benefits.
(S.O. 8)

BE12–10 In the Reid Company, employees are entitled to one day's vacation for each month worked. In January, 50 employees worked the full month. Record the vacation pay liability for January assuming the average daily pay for each employee is $100.

EXERCISES

Prepare entries for interest-bearing and zero-interest bearing notes.
(S.O. 2)

E12–1 Koch Company is considering two alternative loan arrangements on June 1:

1. Borrow $50,000 from First Bank on a 6-month, $50,000, 12% note.
2. Borrow $50,000 from Second Bank on a 6-month, $53,000, zero-interest-bearing note.

Instructions
For each plan,

(a) Prepare the entry on June 1.

(b) Prepare the adjusting entry on June 30.

(c) Prepare the entry at maturity (December 1), assuming monthly adjusting entries have been made through November 30.

(d) What was the total financing cost (interest expense)?

Journalize sales and related taxes.
(S.O. 3)

E12–2 In providing accounting services to small businesses, you encounter the following situations pertaining to cash sales:

1. Geron Company rings up sales and sales taxes separately on its cash register. On April 10, the register totals are sales, $25,000 and sales taxes, $1,500.
2. Pontiac Company does not segregate sales and sales taxes. Its register total for April 15 is $14,840, which includes a 6% sales tax.

Instructions
Prepare the entry to record the sales transactions and related taxes for each client.

Journalize unearned subscription revenue.
(S.O. 3)

E12–3 Westwood Company publishes a monthly sports magazine, Fishing Preview. Subscriptions to the magazine cost $24 per year. During November 1993, Westwood sells 5,000 subscriptions beginning with the December issue. Westwood prepares financial statements quarterly and recognizes subscription revenue earned at the end of the quarter. The company uses the accounts Unearned Subscription Revenue and Subscription Revenue.

Instructions
(a) Prepare the entry in November for the receipt of the subscriptions.

(b) Prepare the adjusting entry at December 31, 1993, to record subscription revenue earned in December of 1993.

(c) Prepare the adjusting entry at March 31, 1994, to record subscription revenue earned in the first quarter of 1994.

Record estimated liability and expense for warranties.
(S.O. 4)

E12–4 Red Cliff Company sells automatic can openers under a 75-day warranty for defective merchandise. Based on past experience, Red Cliff Company estimates that 3% of the units sold will become defective during the warranty period. Management estimates that the average cost of replacing or repairing a defective unit is $10. The units sold and units defective that occurred during the last two months of 1993 are as follows:

Month	Units Sold	Units Defective Prior to December 31
November	30,000	600
December	32,000	400

Instructions
(a) Determine the estimated warranty liability at December 31 for the units sold in November and December.

(b) Prepare the journal entries to record the estimated liability for warranties and the costs (assume actual costs of $10,000) incurred in honoring 1,000 warranty claims.

(c) Give the entry to record the honoring of 350 warranty contracts in January at an average cost of $10.

E12–5 Murphy Company has the following liability accounts after posting adjusting entries: Accounts Payable $62,000, Unearned Ticket Revenue $24,000, Discount on Notes Payable $5,000, Estimated Warranty Liability $18,000, Interest Payable $12,000, Mortgage Payable $120,000, Notes Payable $80,000, and Sales Taxes Payable $12,000.

Prepare the current liability section of the balance sheet.
(S.O. 1, 2, 3, 4)

Instructions
(a) Prepare the current liability section of the balance sheet, assuming $30,000 of the mortgage is payable next year.

(b) Comment on Murphy Company's liquidity, assuming total current assets are $300,000.

E12–6 Rose Sim's regular hourly wage rate is $15.00, and she receives a wage of 1½ times the regular hourly rate for work in excess of 40 hours. During a March weekly pay period Rose worked 42 hours. Her gross earnings prior to the current week were $19,000. Rose is married and claims two withholding allowances. Her only voluntary deduction is for group hospitalization insurance at $10.00 per week.

Compute net pay and record pay for one employee.
(S.O. 6)

Instructions
(a) Compute the following amounts for Rose's wages for the current week.
  1. Gross earnings.
  2. FICA taxes (assume 8% rate).
  3. Federal income taxes withheld (use wage-bracket table in text).
  4. State income taxes withheld (assume 2.0% rate).
  5. Net pay.
(b) Record Rose's pay, assuming she is an office computer operator.

E12–7 Employee earnings records for the Patrick Company reveal the following gross earnings for four employees through the pay period of December 15.

Compute maximum FICA deductions.
(S.O. 6)

R. Sunberg	$48,500	D. Myers	$49,200
C. Carlsen	$49,600	P. Otto	$50,000

For the pay period ending December 31, each employee's gross earnings is $1,000. The FICA tax rate is 8% on gross earnings of $50,000.

Instructions
Compute the FICA withholdings that should be made for each employee for the December 31 pay period. (Show computations.)

E12–8 Amod Company has the following data for the weekly payroll ending January 31.

Prepare payroll register and record payroll and payroll tax expense.
(S.O. 6, 7)

Employee	\multicolumn{6}{Hours}						Hourly Rate	Federal Income Tax Withholding	Health Insurance
	M	T	W	T	F	S			
A. Hope	8	8	9	8	10	0	$10	$34	$10
B. Innes	8	8	8	8	8	2	12	42	15
C. Stone	9	10	8	8	9	0	12	38	15

Employees are paid 1½ times the regular hourly rate for all hours worked in excess of 40 hours per week. FICA taxes are 8% on the first $50,000 of gross earnings. The Amod Company is subject to 5.4% state unemployment taxes and 0.8% federal unemployment taxes.

Instructions
(a) Prepare the payroll register for the weekly payroll.
(b) Prepare the journal entry to record the payroll and Amod's payroll tax expense.

Compute missing payroll amounts and record payroll.

E12–9 Selected data from a February payroll register for Amanda Company are presented below with some amounts intentionally omitted.

(S.O. 6)

Gross earnings:				
Regular	$8,900	State income taxes	$ (3)
Overtime	(1)	Union dues	100
Total	(2)	Total deductions	(4)
Deductions:		Net Pay	7,310
FICA taxes	$ 760	Accounts debited:	
Federal income taxes	1,140	Warehouse wages	(5)
		Store wages	$5,000

FICA taxes are 8% and state income taxes are 2% of gross earnings.

Instructions

(a) Fill in the missing amounts.

(b) Journalize the February payroll and the payment of the payroll.

Determine employer's
payroll taxes and record
payroll tax expense.
(S.O. 7)

E12–10   According to a payroll register summary of Colson Company, the amount of employee's gross pay in December was $700,000, of which $70,000 was not subject to FICA tax and $680,000 was not subject to state and federal unemployment taxes.

Instructions

(a) Determine the employer's payroll tax expense for the month, using the following rates: FICA, 8%; state unemployment, 5.4%; federal unemployment, 0.8%.

(b) Prepare the journal entry to record December payroll tax expense.

Prepare adjusting entries
for fringe benefits.
(S.O. 8)

E12–11   Mercer Company has two fringe benefit plans for its employees:

1. It grants employees two days' vacation for each month worked. Ten employees worked the entire month of March at an average daily wage of $100 per employee.

2. It has a defined contribution pension plan in which the company contributes 10% of gross earnings. Gross earnings in March were $35,000. The payment to the pension fund has not been made.

Instructions

Prepare the adjusting entries at March 31.

PROBLEMS

Prepare current liability
entries, adjusting entries,
and current liability section.
(S.O. 1, 2, 3, 4)

P12–1   On January 1, 1993, the ledger of Carroll Company contains the following liability accounts.

Accounts Payable	$42,500
Sales Taxes Payable	5,600
Unearned Service Revenue	15,000

During January the following selected transactions occurred:

Jan. 1   Borrowed $30,000 in cash from City Bank on a zero-interest-bearing, six-month note having a face value of $33,000.

1   Borrowed $15,000 in cash from Midland Bank on a four-month, 12%, $15,000 note.

5   Sold merchandise for cash totaling $7,800 which includes 4% sales taxes.

12   Provided services for customers who had made advance payments of $8,000. (Credit Service Revenue.)

14   Paid state treasurer's department for sales taxes collected in December 1992 ($5,600).

20   Sold 500 units of a new product on credit at $52 per unit, plus 4% sales tax. This new product is subject to a 1-year warranty.

25   Sold merchandise for cash totaling $11,440, which includes 4% sales taxes.

Instructions

(a) Journalize the January transactions.

(b) Journalize the adjusting entries at January 31 for (1) the outstanding notes payable, and

(2) estimated warranty liability, assuming warranty costs are expected to equal 8% of sales of the new product.

(c) Prepare the current liability section of the balance sheet at January 31, 1993.

P12–2 Shoppers Drug Store has five employees who are paid on an hourly basis plus time-and-one-half for all hours worked in excess of 40 a week. Payroll data for the week ended February 15, 1993, are presented below:

Prepare payroll register and payroll entries.
(S.O. 6, 7)

Employees	Hours Worked	Hourly Rate	Federal Income Tax Withholdings	United Fund
B. Creek	39	$13.00	$?	$ –0–
C. Crowley	42	12.00	?	5.00
D. Delaware	40	13.00	55	–0–
E. Irvine	44	13.00	52	7.50
G. Klamath	46	12.00	31	5.00

Creek and Crowley are married. They claim 2 and 4 withholding allowances, respectively. The following tax rates are applicable: FICA 8.0%, state income taxes 3%, state unemployment taxes 5.4%, and federal unemployment 0.8%. The first four employees are sales clerks (store wages expense), and the other employee performs administrative duties (office wages expense).

Instructions
(a) Prepare a payroll register for the weekly payroll. (Use the wage-bracket withholding table in the text for federal income tax withholdings.)

(b) Journalize the payroll on February 15, 1993, and the accrual of employer payroll taxes.

(c) Journalize the payment of the payroll on February 16, 1993.

(d) Journalize the deposit in a federal reserve bank on February 28, 1993, of the FICA and federal income taxes payable to the government.

P12–3 The payroll procedures used by three different companies are described below:

Identify internal control weaknesses and make recommendations for improvement.
(S.O. 5)

1. In the Cindy Company each employee is required to mark the hours worked on a clock card. At the end of each pay period, the employee must have this clock card approved by the department manager. The approved card is then given to the payroll department by the employee. Subsequently, the treasurer's department pays the employee by check.

2. In the Selina Company clock cards and time clocks are used. At the end of each pay period, the department manager initials the cards, indicates the rates of pay, and sends them to payroll. A payroll register is prepared from the cards by the payroll department. Cash equal to the total net pay in each department is given to the department manager, who pays the employees in cash.

3. In the Tinker Company employees are required to record hours worked on clock cards by "punching" a time clock. At the end of each pay period, the clock cards are collected by the department manager. The manager prepares a payroll register in duplicate and forwards the original to payroll. In payroll, the summaries are checked for mathematical accuracy and a payroll supervisor pays each employee by check.

Instructions
(a) Indicate the weakness(es) in internal control in each company.

(b) For each weakness, describe the control procedure(s) that will provide effective internal control. Use the following format for your answer.

(a) Weaknesses   (b) Recommended Procedures

P12–4 The following payroll liability accounts are included in the ledger of Sean Dunston Company on January 1, 1993:

Journalize payroll transactions and adjusting entries.
(S.O. 6, 7, 8)

FICA Taxes Payable	$ 662.20
Federal Income Taxes Payable	954.60
State Income Taxes Payable	102.15

Federal Unemployment Taxes Payable	2,400.00
State Unemployment Taxes Payable	1,954.40
Union Dues Payable	150.00
U.S. Savings Bonds Payable	350.00

In January, the following transactions occurred:

Jan. 10 Sent check for $150.00 to union treasurer for union dues.
   12 Deposited check for $1,616.80 in Federal Reserve Bank for FICA taxes and federal income taxes withheld.
   15 Purchased U.S. Savings Bonds for employees by writing check for $350.00.
   17 Paid state income taxes withheld from employees.
   20 Paid federal and state unemployment taxes.
   31 Completed monthly payroll register, which shows office salaries $14,600, store wages $27,400, FICA taxes withheld $3,360, federal income taxes payable $1,654, state income taxes payable $360, union dues payable $400, United Fund contributions payable $1,688 , and net pay $34,538.
   31 Prepared payroll checks for the net pay and distributed checks to employees.

At January 31, the company also makes the following accruals pertaining to employee compensation:

1. Employer payroll taxes: FICA taxes (8%), state unemployment taxes (5.4%), and federal unemployment taxes (0.8%).
2. Vacation pay: 3% of gross earnings.

Instructions
(a) Journalize the January transactions.
(b) Journalize the adjustments pertaining to employee compensation at January 31.

Prepare entries for payroll and payroll taxes, and prepare W-2 data.
(S.O. 6, 7, 8)

P12–5   For the year ended December 31, 1993, McGraw Electrical Repair Company reports the following summary payroll data:

Gross Earnings	
Administrative Salaries	$180,000
Electricians' Wages	370,000
Total	$550,000

Deductions	
FICA taxes	$ 38,000
Federal income taxes withheld	168,000
State income taxes withheld (2.6%)	14,300
United Fund contributions payable	27,500
Hospital insurance premiums	17,200
Total	$265,000

McGraw Company's payroll taxes are: FICA 8%, state unemployment 2.5% (due to a stable employment record), and 0.8% federal unemployment. Gross earnings subject to (1) FICA taxes total $475,000, and (2) unemployment taxes total $400,000.

Instructions
(a) Prepare a summary journal entry at December 31 for the full year's payroll.
(b) Journalize the adjusting entry at December 31 to record the employer's payroll taxes.
(c) The W-2 Wage and Tax Statement requires the following dollar data:

Wages, Tips, Other Compensation	Federal Income Tax Withheld	State Income Tax Withheld	FICA Wages	FICA Tax Withheld

Complete the required data for the following employees:

Employee	Gross Earnings	Federal Income Tax Withheld
A. Osa	$60,000	$27,500
B. Bama	26,000	10,200

P12–6 The following are selected transactions of Newark Company. Newark prepares financial statements *quarterly*.

Journalize and post note transactions and show balance sheet presentation.
(S.O. 2)

Jan. 2   Purchased merchandise on account from McCoy Company, $15,000, terms 2/10, n/30.

Feb. 1   Issued a 12%, 2-month, $15,000 note to McCoy in payment of account.

Mar. 31   Accrued interest for two months on McCoy note.

Apr. 1   Paid face value and interest on McCoy note.

Apr. 1   Borrowed $40,000 from the Federation Bank by issuing a 3-month zero-interest-bearing note with a face value of $41,500.

June 30   Recognized three months interest on Federation Bank note.

July 1   Paid Federation Bank note.

1   Purchased equipment from Scottie Equipment paying $11,000 in cash and signing a 12%, 3-month, $24,000 note.

Sept. 30   Accrued interest for three months on Scottie note.

Oct. 1   Paid face value and interest on Scottie note.

Dec. 1   Borrowed $10,000 from the Federation Bank by issuing a 3-month zero-interest-bearing note with a face value of $10,375.

Dec. 31   Recognized interest expense for one month on Federation Bank note.

Instructions

(a) Prepare journal entries for the above transactions and events.

(b) Post to the accounts, Notes Payable, Interest Payable, Discount on Notes Payable, and Interest Expense.

(c) Show the balance sheet presentation of notes payable at December 31.

(d) What is total interest expense for the year?

ALTERNATE PROBLEMS

P12–1A On January 1, 1993, the ledger of Midler Company contains the following liability accounts:

Prepare current liability entries, adjusting entries, and current liability section.
(S.O. 1, 2, 3, 4)

Accounts Payable	$52,000
Sales Taxes Payable	7,500
Unearned Service Revenue	16,000

During January the following selected transactions occurred:

Jan. 5   Sold merchandise for cash totaling $16,632, which includes 8% sales taxes.

12   Provided services for customers who had made advance payments of $9,000. (Credit Service Revenue)

14   Paid state revenue department for sales taxes collected in December 1992 ($7,500).

16   Borrowed $30,000 in cash from City Bank on a zero-interest-bearing, five-month note having a face value of $32,700.

20   Sold 500 units of a new product on credit at $50 per unit, plus 8% sales tax. This new product is subject to a 1-year warranty.

21   Borrowed $18,000 from Midland Bank on a three-month, 12%, $18,000 note.

25   Sold merchandise for cash totaling $11,340, which includes 8% sales taxes.

Instructions

(a) Journalize the January transactions.

(b) Journalize the adjusting entries at January 31 for (1) the outstanding notes payable, and (2) estimated warranty liability, assuming warranty costs are expected to equal 8% of sales of the new product. (Hint: Use one-half of a month for the City Bank note and one-third of a month for the Midland Bank note.)

(c) Prepare the current liability section of the balance sheet at January 31, 1993.

Prepare payroll register
and payroll entries.
(S.O. 6, 7)

P12–2A   Real-Value Hardware has five employees who are paid on an hourly basis plus time-and-one-half for all hours worked in excess of 40 a week. Payroll data for the week ended March 15, 1993, are presented below:

Employee	Hours Worked	Hourly Rate	Federal Income Tax Withholdings	United Fund
A. Pima	40	$13.00	$?	$5.00
C. Zuni	42	13.00	?	5.00
D. Taos	40	12.75	53	–0–
E. Hopi	44	13.00	52	8.00
G. Mohav	46	13.00	38	5.00

Pima and Zuni are married. They claim zero and four withholding allowances, respectively. The following tax rates are applicable: FICA 8.0%, state income taxes 3%, state unemployment taxes 5.4%, and federal unemployment 0.8%. The first four employees are sales clerks (store wages expense) and the other employee performs administrative duties (office wages expense).

Instructions

(a) Prepare a payroll register for the weekly payroll. (Use the wage-bracket withholding table in the text for federal income tax withholdings.)

(b) Journalize the payroll on March 15, 1993, and the accrual of employer payroll taxes.

(c) Journalize the payment of the payroll on March 16, 1993.

(d) Journalize the deposit in a federal reserve bank on March 31, 1993, of the FICA and federal income taxes payable to the government.

Identify internal control
weaknesses and make
recommendations for
improvement.
(S.O. 5)

P12–3A   Selected payroll procedures of Sortel Company are described below:

1. Department managers interview applicants and on the basis of the interview either hire or reject the applicants. When an applicant is hired, the applicant fills out a W-4 form (Employer's Withholding Exemption Certificate). One copy of the form is sent to the personnel department and one copy is sent to the payroll department as notice that the individual has been hired. On the copy of the W-4 sent to payroll, the managers manually indicate the hourly pay rate for the new hire.

2. The payroll checks are manually signed by the chief accountant and given to the department managers for distribution to employees in their department. The managers are responsible for seeing that any absent employees receive their checks.

3. There are two clerks in the payroll department. The payroll is divided alphabetically with one clerk having employees A to L and the other employees M to Z. Each clerk computes the gross earnings, deductions, and net pay for employees in the section and posts the data to the employee earning records.

Instructions

(a) Indicate the weaknesses in internal control.

(b) For each weakness, describe the control procedures that will provide effective internal control. Use the following format for your answer.

(a) Weaknesses   (b) Recommended Procedures

Journalize payroll trans-
actions and adjusting
entries.
(S.O. 6, 7, 8)

P12–4A   The following payroll liability accounts are included in the ledger of Fisk Company on January 1, 1993:

FICA Taxes Payable	$ 760.00
Federal Income Taxes Payable	954.60
State Income Taxes Payable	108.95
Federal Unemployment Taxes Payable	288.95
State Unemployment Taxes Payable	1,954.40
Union Dues Payable	970.00
U.S. Savings Bonds Payable	360.00

In January, the following transactions occurred:

Jan. 10 Sent check for $970.00 to union treasurer for union dues.

12 Deposited check for $1,714.60 in federal reserve bank for FICA taxes and federal income taxes withheld.

15 Purchased U.S. Savings Bonds for employees by writing check for $360.00.

17 Paid state income taxes withheld from employees.

20 Paid federal and state unemployment taxes.

31 Completed monthly payroll register, which shows office salaries $14,600, store wages $28,400, FICA taxes withheld $3,440, federal income taxes payable $1,684, state income taxes payable $360, union dues payable $400, United Fund contributions payable $1,888, and net pay $35,228.

31 Prepared payroll checks for the net pay and distributed checks to employees.

At January 31, the company also makes the following accrued adjustments pertaining to employee compensation:

1. Employer payroll taxes: FICA taxes (8%), federal unemployment taxes (0.8%), and state unemployment taxes (5.4%).

2. Vacation pay: 3% of gross earnings.

Instructions

(a) Journalize the January transactions.

(b) Journalize the adjustments pertaining to employee compensation at January 31.

P12–5A For the year ended December 31, 1993, Winn Electrical Repair Company reports the following summary payroll data:

Prepare entries for payroll and payroll taxes and prepare W-2 data.
(S.O. 6, 7, 8)

Gross Earnings	
Administrative Salaries	$180,000
Electricians' Wages	470,000
Total	$650,000

Deductions	
FICA taxes	$ 48,000
Federal income taxes withheld	188,000
State income taxes withheld (2.6%)	16,900
United Fund contributions payable	32,500
Hospital insurance premiums	20,300
Total	$305,700

Winn Company's payroll taxes are: FICA 8%, state unemployment 2.5% (due to a stable employment record), and 0.8% federal unemployment. Gross earnings subject to (1) FICA taxes total $600,000; and (2) unemployment taxes total $450,000.

Instructions

(a) Prepare a summary journal entry at December 31 for the full year's payroll.

(b) Journalize the adjusting entry at December 31 to record the employer's payroll taxes.

(c) The W-2 Wage and Tax Statement requires the following dollar data:

Wages, Tips, Other Compensation	Federal Income Tax Withheld	State Income Tax Withheld	FICA Wages	FICA Tax Withheld

Complete the required data for the following employees:

Employee	Gross Earnings	Federal Income Tax Withheld
A. Ute	$62,000	$28,500
B. Yuma	28,000	10,800

*B*roadening Your Perspective

FINANCIAL REPORTING PROBLEM

Refer to the financial statements of PepsiCo, Inc. and the Notes to Consolidated Financial Statements in Appendix L to answer the following questions about current and contingent liabilities and payroll costs.

1. What were PepsiCo's total current liabilities at December 28, 1991? What was the increase/decrease in PepsiCo's total current liabilities from the prior year?
2. How much were the "current maturities of long-term debt" at December 28, 1991?
3. What were the components of total current liabilities on December 28, 1991 (other than "current maturities of long-term debt" already discussed in 2 above)?
4. Where does PepsiCo report its contingent liabilities?
5. What is management's opinion as to the ultimate effect of the "various claims and legal proceedings" pending against the company?
6. What is the amount that PepsiCo is contingently liable under guarantees at December 28, 1991 and December 29, 1990?
7. What type of employee pension plan does PepsiCo have?

DECISION CASE

Speedo Processing Company provides word-processing services for clients and students in a university community. The work for clients is fairly steady throughout the year but the work for students peaks significantly in December and May as a result of term papers, research project reports, and dissertations.

Two years ago, the company attempted to meet the peak demand by hiring part-time help. However, this led to numerous errors and considerable customer dissatisfaction. A year ago, the Company hired four experienced employees on a permanent basis instead of using part-time help. This proved to be much better in terms of productivity and customer satisfaction. However, it has caused an increase in annual payroll costs and a significant decline in annual net income.

Recently, Sue Stone, a sales representative of Hiawatha Services Inc., has made a proposal to the company. Under the plan, Hiawatha Services will provide up to four experienced workers at a daily rate of $100 per person for an 8-hour workday. Hiawatha workers are not available on an hourly basis. Speedo Processing would only have to pay the daily rate for the workers used.

The owner of Speedo Processing, Denise Denby, asks you as the company's accountant, to prepare a report on the expenses that are pertinent to the decision. If the Hiawatha plan is adopted, Denise will terminate the employment of two permanent employees who are each earning an average annual salary of $28,000. The remaining permanent employees each earn an annual income of $28,000. Speedo Processing pays 8% FICA taxes, 0.8% Federal Unemployment Taxes, and 5.4% State Unemployment Taxes. The unemployment taxes only apply to the first $7,000 of gross earnings. In addition, Speedo Processing pays $50 per month for each employee for medical and dental insurance.

Denise indicates that if the Hiawatha Service plan is accepted, her needs for workers will be as follows:

Months	Number	Working Days per Month
January–March	2	20
April–May	3	25
June–October	2	18
November–December	3	23

Instructions

(a) Prepare a report showing the comparative payroll expense of continuing to employ permanent workers compared to adopting the Hiawatha Services Inc. plan.

(b) What other factors should Denise consider before finalizing her decision?

CRITICAL THINKING CASE

Refer back to the story about Dianna Webb at the beginning of the chapter.

1. In addition to withheld employee taxes, what employer taxes would Casper College likely remit?

2. Give some examples of internal control that should be used by Casper College to insure the accuracy and reliability of the payroll records and paychecks.

3. Dianna Webb noted that without a computer "I don't think I'd be able to pay as many people as I do." Explain her statement.

ETHICAL CASE

Jack Sprat owns and manages the Spicy-Saucer Restaurant, a 24-hour restaurant near the city's medical complex. Jack employs nine full-time employees and sixteen part-time employees. He pays all of the full-time employees by check, the amounts of which are determined by Jack's public accountant, Clarence P. Hankes. Jack pays all of his part-time employees in currency that he computes and withdraws directly from his cash register. Clarence has repeatedly urged Jack to pay all employees by check. But as Jack has told his competitor and friend, Bud Juice, who owns the Tasty Diner, "First of all, my part-time employees prefer the currency over a check, and secondly I don't withhold or pay any taxes or workmen's compensation insurance on those wages because they go totally unrecorded and unnoticed."

Instructions

(a) Who are the stakeholders in this situation?

(b) What are the legal and ethical considerations regarding Jack's handling of his payroll?

(c) Clarence P. Hankes is aware of Jack's payment of the part-time payroll in currency. What are his ethical responsibilities in this case?

(d) What internal control principle is violated in this payroll process?

Answers to Self-Study Questions
1. b   2. d   3. a   4. c   5. d   6. d   7. c   8. c   9. d   10. a

CONCEPTS FOR REVIEW

Before studying this chapter, you should know or, if necessary, review:

a. *The two organizations primarily responsible for setting accounting standards. (Ch. 1, p. 12–13)*

b. *The economic entity assumption, the monetary unit assumption, and the periodicity assumption. (Chs. 1 and 3, pp. 13–14, 15, 88–9)*

c. *The cost principle, the revenue recognition principle, and the matching principle. (Chs. 1 and 3, pp. 13, 89–90)*

d. *Some of the ethical issues in accounting practice. (Prologue).*

e. *Some of the international issues in accounting practice. (Prologue).*

CHAPTER 13

ACCOUNTING PRINCIPLES

Study Objectives

After studying this chapter, you should be able to:

1. Explain the meaning of generally accepted accounting principles and identify the key items of the conceptual framework.

2. Describe the basic objectives of financial reporting.

3. Discuss the qualitative characteristics of accounting information and elements of financial statements.

4. Identify and illustrate the basic operating guidelines used by accountants.

5. Understand issues related to ethics and accounting principles.

6. Explain the accounting principles used in international operations.

There are some differences between accounting in the business world and university accounting which you would study in detail if you go on to advanced courses. But there's also one major similarity between the two worlds: both depend heavily on the matching principle.

At Long Beach City College, a 2-year community college with 30,000 students, most of the revenues come from the state of California and the federal government. As a condition of receiving these grants, "we must match expenses against revenues in the right fiscal year," says Catalina Cruz, accounting manager, who has worked in both the corporate and college environment.

For example, the college receives federal funding under the Job Training Partnership Act. "We receive funding from the federal government which allows us to offer classes to students for job preparation. The government specifies the grant periods, for instance, from July 1, 1992 to June 30, 1993. We therefore have to ensure *that all transactions for that project are completed within that fiscal year." As a check, the CPA firm contracted by the college to conduct an annual audit includes a review of this and other similar projects.*

Another project is the amnesty program, the federal government's legalization of foreign nationals. "We get funding to hold classes which would help these people qualify for citizenship. After they pass, we also offer them additional training so that they can get into the workforce quickly." Expenses to offset the grant money are mostly teaching salaries and instructional materials.

By year-end, the goal is to break even. Surpluses, if any, have to be returned. But program managers do not want a deficit either, because these projects are accountable to the college administration, and any overspending will unnecessarily commit the college's general fund.

Up to this point, we have emphasized that enterprises follow certain basic guidelines (such as the cost principle, the matching principle, the economic entity assumption) in reporting financial information. Without these basic guidelines, each enterprise would have to develop its own set of accounting rules and practices. If this happened, we would have to become familiar with every company's peculiar accounting and reporting rules in order to understand their financial statements. Thus, it would be difficult, if not impossible, to compare the financial statements of different companies.

This chapter explores the basic accounting principles in more depth. The chapter is divided into three sections: In Section One we discuss the basic guidelines followed by accountants in developing specific accounting rules. Certain guidelines such as the revenue recognition principle and the matching principle are discussed in detail to indicate the difficult choices that must be made in attempting to present useful financial information. In Section Two we discuss issues related to ethics, accounting principles, and the financial reporting environment. Recently this subject has taken on increasing importance because of fraudulent financial reporting practices that have occurred. In Section Three, we address the issue of accounting principles from an international perspective.

Accounting in Action · *International Insight*

Recognize that different political and cultural influences affect the accounting that occurs in foreign countries. For example, in the Near East, Islamic accounting is presently being considered. If adopted, the changes would introduce religious tenets into accounting practice. In Sweden accounting is considered an instrument to be used to shape fiscal policy. In Europe more emphasis is given to social reporting (more information on employment statistics, health of workers, and so on) because employees and their organizations are strong and demand that type of information.

SECTION I Generally Accepted Accounting Principles

The accounting profession has established a set of rules and practices that are recognized as a general guide for financial reporting purposes. This recognized set of practices is called generally accepted accounting principles (GAAP). "Generally accepted" means that these principles must have "substantial authoritative support." Substantial authoritative support usually comes from two standard-setting bodies: the Financial Accounting Standards Board (FASB) and the Securities and Exchange Commission (SEC).[1]

Accounting principles do not just appear out of thin air—they must be developed or decreed. Since the early 1970s the business and governmental communities have given the FASB the responsibility for developing accounting principles in this country. This job is an ongoing process because accounting principles must change to reflect changes in the business environment and in the needs of users of accounting information.

Prior to the establishment of the FASB, accounting principles were developed on a problem-by-problem basis. Thus, rule-making bodies developed and issued accounting rules and methods to solve specific problems. Critics charged that the problem-by-problem approach led to inconsistent rules and practices over time. Unfortunately, no clearly developed conceptual framework of accounting theory existed for the accounting rule makers to refer to in solving problems.

As a result of these criticisms, the FASB was directed to develop a conceptual framework that would serve as the basis for resolving accounting and reporting problems. The FASB has spent considerable time and effort on this project. The Board views its conceptual framework project as the drafting of "... a constitution, a coherent system of interrelated objectives and fundamentals."[2]

The FASB's conceptual framework consists of the following:

1. Objectives of financial reporting.
2. Qualitative characteristics of accounting information.
3. Elements of financial statements.
4. Operating guidelines (assumptions, principles, and constraints).

Agreement on these four items sets the stage for a coherent set of standards that make accounting practice consistent and uniform. We will discuss each of these four items on the following pages.

Study Objective 1

Explain the meaning of generally accepted accounting principles and identify the key items of the conceptual framework.

---

[1]The SEC is an agency of the U.S. government that was established to administer laws and regulations relating to the exchange of securities and the publication of financial information by U.S. businesses. The agency has the authority to mandate generally accepted accounting principles for companies under its jurisdiction. However, throughout its history, the SEC has been willing to accept the principles set forth by the FASB and similar bodies.

[2]"Conceptual Framework for Financial Accounting and Reporting: Elements of Financial Statements and Their Measurement," *FASB Discussion Memorandum* (Stamford, Conn.: 1976), p. 1.

Objectives of Financial Reporting

Study Objective 2

Describe the basic objectives of financial reporting.

Financial statements are the end product of the accounting process. In small companies, financial statements often are the only means by which financial information is communicated to creditors and other external users. In large companies, however, the communication of financial information is usually made through additional outlets: annual reports that include the financial statements plus financial highlights, five-year financial summaries, and management's discussion and analyses of results of operations and financial condition. Selected portions of the annual report of PepsiCo, Inc. are presented in Appendix L at the end of this textbook.

In developing the conceptual framework, the FASB concluded that the first level of study was to determine the objectives of financial reporting. Determining these objectives required answers to such basic questions as: Who uses financial statements? Why? What information do they need? How knowledgeable about business and accounting are the users of financial statements? How should financial information be reported so that it is best understood?

Answers to these questions may appear obvious. But only if they are answered correctly and completely will it be possible to measure and communicate the most useful information. The FASB's study concluded that the objectives of financial reporting are to provide information that:

1. Is useful to those making investment and credit decisions.
2. Is helpful in assessing future cash flows.
3. Identifies the economic resources (assets), the claims to those resources (liabilities), and the changes in those resources and claims.

The objectives of financial reporting, therefore, begin with a broad concern about providing information that is useful to investors and creditors. The objectives narrow that concern to the investor and creditor interests in the amounts, timing, and uncertainty of future cash flows to the enterprise. Finally, the objectives focus on the financial statements that provide information that help investors and creditors to (1) identify the enterprise's financial strengths and weaknesses, (2) assess the enterprise's liquidity (ability to convert assets to cash) and solvency (ability to pay its debts), and (3) evaluate the enterprise's progress and performance over a period of time.

Before these objectives could be fully implemented in practice, the FASB found it necessary to provide certain fundamental concepts to explain the qualitative characteristics of accounting information and define the elements contained in financial statements.

Qualitative Characteristics of Accounting Information

Study Objective 3

Discuss the qualitative characteristics of accounting information and elements of financial statements.

How does one decide on the amount of information to be disclosed, or the format in which information should be presented, or among alternative methods of measuring assets, liabilities, revenues, and expenses? **The FASB concluded that the overriding criterion by which such accounting choices can be judged is decision usefulness.** The accounting alternative selected or the policy adopted should be the one that generates the most useful financial information for making a decision. To be useful, information should possess the following qualitative characteristics: relevance, reliability, comparability, and consistency.

Relevance

To be **relevant**, accounting information must be capable of making a difference in a decision; that is, it must have a bearing on the decision. Relevant information has either predictive or feedback value. **Predictive value** helps users make predictions about the outcome of past, present, and future events. **Feedback value** confirms or corrects prior expectations. For example, when Exxon issues an annual report, the information in the report is considered relevant because it provides a basis for forecasting future earnings and provides feedback on past performance. In addition, for accounting information to be relevant, it must be **timely**, that is, it must be available to decision makers before it loses its capacity to influence their decisions. Thus, if Exxon reported its financial information only every five years, the information would have limited usefulness for decision-making purposes. Thus, relevant information has predictive or feedback value and it is timely.

Helpful hint What makes accounting information relevant? Answer: Relevant accounting information provides feedback, serves as a basis for predictions, and is timely (current).

Reliability

Reliability is the quality of information that gives assurance that it is free of error and bias; it can be depended on. To be reliable, accounting information must be **verifiable**—we must be able to prove that it is free of error and bias. To be reliable, the information must be a **faithful representation** of what it purports to be—it must be factual. And finally, to be reliable, accounting information must be **neutral**—it cannot be selected, prepared, or presented to favor one set of interested users over another. For the annual report of Exxon to be considered reliable, it must be verifiable by outside parties. To ensure reliability, certified public accountants audit financial statements, just as the Internal Revenue Service audits tax returns for the same purpose.

Helpful hint What makes accounting information reliable? Answer: Reliable accounting information is free from bias, is factual, and is verifiable.

Comparability and Consistency

Accounting information about an enterprise is most useful when it can be compared with accounting information about other enterprises. **Comparability** results when different companies use the same accounting principles. For example, Sears Roebuck, Montgomery Ward, and J.C. Penney all use the cost principle in reporting plant assets on the balance sheet. Moreover, each company uses the revenue recognition and matching principles in determining its net income.

Conceptually, comparability should also extend to the methods used by companies in complying with an accounting principle. Accounting methods include the FIFO and LIFO methods of inventory costing, and the straight-line and sum-of-the-years'-digits methods for depreciation. At this point in the development of a conceptual framework, comparability of methods is not required, even for companies in the same industry. Thus, Ford, General Motors, and Chrysler may use different inventory costing and depreciation methods in their financial statements. The only accounting requirement is that each company must disclose the accounting methods used. From the disclosures, the external user can determine whether the financial information is comparable.

Consistency means using the same accounting principles and methods from year to year within a company. Thus, if a company selects FIFO as the inventory costing method in the first year of operations, it is expected to continue to use FIFO in succeeding years. When financial information has been reported on a consistent basis, the financial statements permit meaningful analysis of trends within a company.

Helpful hint Point out that the consistent use of generally accepted accounting principles is necessary for comparability of financial statements for successive periods for a single entity.

Accounting in Action · *Business Insight*

There is an old story that professors often tell students about a company looking for an account-ant. The company approached the first accountant and asked: "What do you believe our net income will be this year?" The accountant said $4 million dollars. The company asked the second accountant the same question, and the answer was "What would you like it to be?" Guess who got the job? The point is that accounting principles offer flexibility. Therefore it is important that a consistent treatment be provided from period to period. Otherwise it would be very difficult to interpret financial statements. Perhaps no alternative methods should be permitted in account-ing. What do you think?

A company can change to a new method of accounting if management can justify that the new method results in more meaningful financial information. In the year in which the change occurs, there must be disclosure of the change in the notes to the financial statements so that users of the financial statements are aware of the lack of consistency.

The qualitative characteristics of accounting information are highlighted in Illustration 13-1.

ILLUSTRATION 13-1

Qualitative characteristics

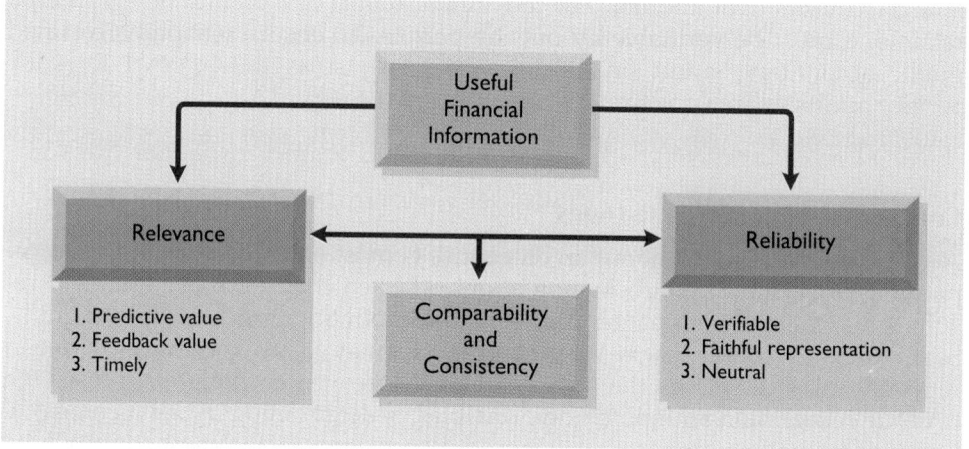

Elements of Financial Statements

An important part of an accounting conceptual framework is a set of definitions that describe the basic terms used in accounting. The FASB has chosen to refer to this set of definitions as the elements of financial statements. They include such terms as assets, liabilities, equity, revenues, and expenses.

Because these elements are so important, it is imperative that they be pre-cisely defined and universally understood and applied. Finding the appropriate definition for many of these elements is not easy. For example, how should an asset be defined? Should the value of a company's employees be reported as an asset on a balance sheet? Should the death of the company's president be re-ported as a loss? A good set of definitions should provide answers to these types of questions. Because you have already encountered most of these definitions in earlier chapters, they are not repeated here.

Before You Go On . . .

1. What are generally accepted accounting principles?

2. What are the basic objectives of financial information?

3. What are the qualitative characteristics that make accounting information useful? Identify two elements of the financial statements.

*O*perating Guidelines

The objectives of financial statements, the qualitative characteristics of accounting information, and the elements of financial statements are very broad. However, because practicing accountants and standard-setting bodies must solve practical problems, more detailed guidelines are needed. In its conceptual framework, the FASB recognizes the need for operating guidelines. We have chosen to classify these guidelines as assumptions, principles, and constraints. These guidelines are well-established and accepted in accounting.

> *Study Objective 4*
>
> *Identify and illustrate the basic operating guidelines used by accountants.*

Assumptions

Assumptions provide a foundation for the accounting process. You have already studied the following major assumptions in preceding chapters:

Economic entity assumption: States that economic events can be identified with a particular unit of accountability. Thus, it is assumed that the activities of IBM can be distinguished from those of other computer companies such as Apple Computer and Unisys Corporation.

Monetary unit assumption: States that only transaction data capable of being expressed in terms of money should be included in the accounting records of the economic entity. For example, one reason why the death of a company president would not be reported as a loss is that it cannot be expressed easily in dollars. An important corollary to the monetary unit assumption is the added assumption that the unit of measure remains sufficiently constant over time. This point will be discussed in more detail later in this chapter.

Periodicity assumption: States that the economic life of a business can be divided into artificial time periods. Thus, it is assumed that the activities of business enterprises such as General Electric, Exxon, or any enterprise can be subdivided into months, quarters, and years for meaningful financial reporting purposes.

Another assumption that accountants use is the going concern assumption. The going concern assumption assumes that the enterprise will continue in operation long enough to carry out its existing objectives and commitments. Experience indicates that, in spite of numerous business failures, companies have a fairly high continuance rate, and it has proved useful to adopt a going concern or continuity assumption for accounting purposes.

The accounting implications of adopting this assumption are critical. If a going concern assumption is not used, then plant assets should be stated at their liquidation value (selling price less cost of disposal)—not at their cost. As a result, depreciation and amortization of these assets is not needed. Each period these assets would simply be reported at their liquidation value. Also, without this assumption, the current–noncurrent classification of assets and liabilities would otherwise lose much of its significance. Labeling anything as fixed or long-term would be difficult to justify.

Acceptance of the going concern assumption gives credibility to the cost principle. If, instead, liquidation were assumed, assets would be better stated at liquidation value than at cost. Only when liquidation appears imminent is the going concern assumption inapplicable.

Principles

On the basis of these fundamental assumptions of accounting, the accounting profession has developed principles that dictate how transactions and other economic events should be recorded and reported. In earlier chapters we discussed the cost principle (Chapter 1) and the revenue recognition and matching principles (Chapter 3). We now examine a number of reporting issues related to these principles. In addition, another principle, the full disclosure principle, is discussed.

Revenue Recognition Principle

Helpful hint Revenue should be recognized in the accounting period in which it is earned, which may not be the period in which the related cash is received. In a retail establishment the point of sale is often the critical point in the process of earning revenue.

The **revenue recognition principle** dictates that revenue should be recognized in the accounting period in which it is earned. Applying this general principle in practice, however, can create difficulties. For example, the financial press often publishes stories questioning the revenue recognition practices of a given company or industry. To illustrate, it was reported that Automatic Inc. was improperly recognizing revenue on goods that had not been shipped and improperly recording revenue at the time of shipment on equipment that was only ordered on approval by customers. Similarly, many questioned the revenue recognition practices of the savings and loan industry, which until recently recorded a large portion of its fees for granting a loan as revenue immediately rather than spreading those fees over the life of the loan.

When a sale is involved, revenue is recognized at the point of sale. The **sales basis** involves an exchange transaction between the seller and buyer, and the sales price provides an objective measure of the amount of revenue realized. There are, however, two exceptions to the sales basis for revenue recognition that have become generally accepted.

Helpful hint In accounting for long-term construction contracts it is appropriate to use the percentage-of-completion method of revenue recognition because the critical event in the earning process is making progress toward completion. The ultimate sale and selling price are assured by the contract.

PERCENTAGE-OF-COMPLETION METHOD. In long-term construction contracts, recognition of revenue is usually required before the contract is completed. For example, assume that Warrior Construction Co. had a contract to build a dam at Windswept Canyon for the U.S. Bureau of the Interior for $400 million. Construction is estimated to take three years (starting in 1991) at a construction cost of $360 million. If Warrior applies the point-of-sale basis, it will report no revenues and no profit in the first two years. But, in 1993 when completion and sale take place, Warrior will report $400 million in revenues, costs of $360 million, and the entire profit of $40 million. Was Warrior really producing no revenues and earning no profit in 1991 and 1992? Obviously not. The dam will be as good as sold when Warrior completes the project according to specifications. Although technically an exchange transaction (transfer of ownership) has not occurred until completion of the dam, the earning process is considered substantially completed at various stages as construction progresses.

To overcome this deficiency, Warrior can apply the percentage-of-completion method. This method recognizes revenue and income over the life of the project on the basis of reasonable estimates of the project's progress toward completion. A project's progress toward completion is measured by comparing the costs incurred in a year to the total estimated costs for the entire project; this is referred to as the **cost-to-cost** approach. That percentage is multiplied by the total revenue for the project; the result is then recognized as revenue for the period. The formulas for this method are as follows:

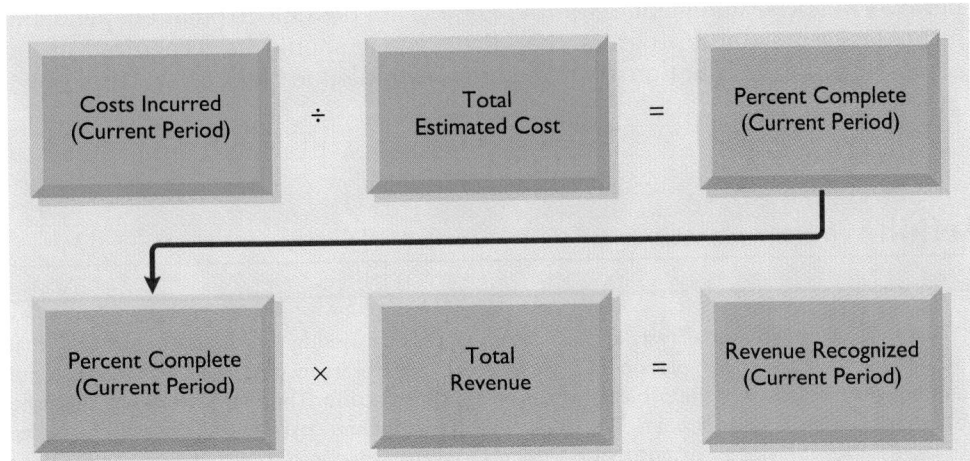

ILLUSTRATION 13-2

Formula to recognize revenue in the percentage-of-completion method

The costs incurred in the current period are then subtracted from the revenue recognized during the current period to arrive at the gross profit.

Let's look at an illustration of the percentage-of-completion method using the cost-to-cost basis to determine the percentage of work completed. Assume that Warrior Construction Co. incurs costs of $54 million in 1991, $180 million in 1992, and $126 million in 1993 on the Windswept Canyon Dam project. The portion of the $400 million of revenue recognized in each of the three years is shown in Illustration 13-3.

ILLUSTRATION 13-3

Revenue recognized—percentage-of-completion method

Year	Costs Incurred (Current Period)	÷	Total Estimated Cost	=	Percent Complete (Current Period)	×	Total Revenue	=	Revenue Recognized (Current Period)
1991	$ 54,000,000		$360,000,000		15%		$400,000,000		$ 60,000,000
1992	180,000,000		360,000,000		50%		400,000,000		200,000,000
1993	126,000,000			Balance required to complete the contract					140,000,000
Totals	$360,000,000								$400,000,000

Note that no estimate is made of the percentage of work completed during the final period. In the final period, all remaining revenue is recognized. In this example, the company's cost estimates have been very accurate; the costs incurred in the third year were 35% of the total estimated cost ($126,000 ÷ $360,000). The gross profit recognized each period is as follows:

Year	Revenue Recognized (Current Period)	−	Actual Cost Incurred (Current Period)	=	Gross Profit Recognized (Current Period)
1991	$ 60,000,000		$ 54,000,000		$ 6,000,000
1992	200,000,000		180,000,000		20,000,000
1993	140,000,000		126,000,000		14,000,000
Totals	$400,000,000		$360,000,000		$40,000,000

ILLUSTRATION 13-4

Gross profit recognized—percentage-of-completion method

Application of the percentage-of-completion method involves some subjectivity. As a result, there is the possibility of error in determining the amount of revenue recognized and net income reported. Yet recognition appears most appropriate here because to wait until completion would seriously distort each period's financial statements. Naturally, if it is not possible to obtain dependable estimates of costs and progress, then the revenue should be recognized at the completion date and not on a percentage-of-completion basis.

Accounting in Action · *Business Insight*

"Hurry up and buy material" was apparently an expression used by Frigitemps, a company that used the percentage-of-completion method. In order to generate income, the company went out and bought materials for the projects it had under construction. The more materials it bought, the more it made—up to a point. The point was reached when cost overruns occurred and led to large losses. It is not surprising that Frigitemps eventually declared bankruptcy because, among other things, it applied percentage of completion too aggressively. In other words, good judgment was not exercised in applying this method.

INSTALLMENT METHOD. Another basis for revenue recognition is the receipt of cash. The cash basis is generally used only when it is difficult to determine the revenue amount at the time of a credit sale because collection is so uncertain. One popular approach to the recognition of revenue using the cash basis is the installment method.

Under the installment method, each cash collection from a customer consists of (1) a partial recovery of the cost of the goods sold, and (2) partial gross profit from the sale. For example, if the gross profit rate at date of sale is 40%, each subsequent receipt consists of 60% recovery of cost of goods sold and 40% gross profit. The formula to recognize gross profit is as follows:

ILLUSTRATION 13-5

Gross profit formula—
installment method

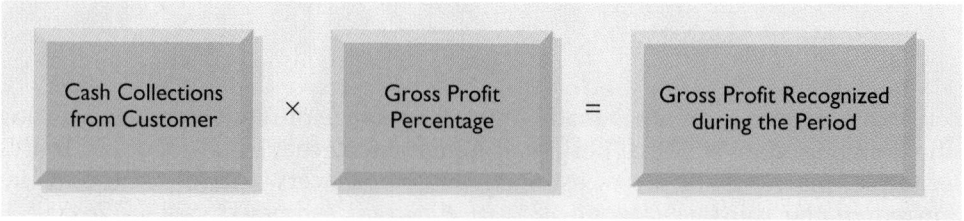

To illustrate, assume that an Iowa farm machinery dealer in the first year of operations had installment sales of $600,000 and a cost of goods sold on installment of $420,000. Total gross profit is, therefore, $180,000 ($600,000 − $420,000), and the gross profit percentage is 30% ($180,000 ÷ $600,000). The collections on the installment sales were as follows: First year, $280,000 (down payment plus monthly payments); second year, $200,000; and, third year, $120,000. The collections of cash and recognition of the gross profit are summarized in Illustration 13-6 (interest charges are ignored in this illustration):

ILLUSTRATION 13-6

Gross profit recognized— installment method

Year	Cash Collected	×	Gross Profit Percentage	=	Gross Profit Recognized
1991	$280,000		30%		$ 84,000
1992	200,000		30%		60,000
1993	120,000		30%		36,000
Total	$600,000				$180,000

Under the installment method of accounting, gross profit is therefore recognized in the period in which the cash is collected.

As indicated earlier, use of the installment method is justified when the risk of not collecting an account receivable may be so great that the sale is not sufficient evidence for revenue to be recognized.

Accounting in Action · *Business Insight*

Datapoint Corp. encouraged its customers to load up with large shipments at the end of the year, allowing Datapoint to report these shipments as revenues, even though payment hadn't been collected. Unfortunately, some of the customers either went broke or quit before paying for the equipment received. As a result, the company had to record substantial bad debts or in some cases reverse previously recorded sales. If Datapoint had used the installment method, this revenue would not have been reported. As a result, revenue recognition practices that are cash-basis oriented, such as the installment method, are becoming more acceptable as it becomes difficult to tell when a sale is a sale.

MATCHING PRINCIPLE (EXPENSE RECOGNITION). Expense recognition is traditionally tied to revenue recognition: "Let the expense follow the revenue." This practice is referred to as the **matching principle** because it dictates that expenses be matched with revenues whenever it is reasonable and practicable to do so. Expenses are not recognized when cash is paid, or when the work is performed, or when the product is produced; they are recognized when the labor (service) or the product actually makes its contribution to revenue.

The problem is that it is sometimes difficult to determine the accounting period in which the expense contributed to the generation of revenues. Several approaches have therefore been devised for matching expenses and revenues on the income statement.

To understand these approaches, it is necessary to examine the nature of expenses. Costs that will generate revenues only in the current accounting period are expensed immediately. They are reported as operating expenses in the income statement. Examples include such costs as advertising, sales salaries, and repairs. These expenses are often called **period costs** (or expenses) because they are expensed in the period in which they are incurred.

Costs that will generate revenues in current and future accounting periods are recognized as assets. Examples include merchandise inventory, prepaid expenses, and plant assets. These costs represent unexpired costs. Unexpired costs associated with merchandise inventory are often referred to as **product costs**. Unexpired costs associated with long-lived assets are sometimes referred to as **capitalized costs**. Unexpired costs become expenses in two ways:

1. **Cost of goods sold.** Costs carried as merchandise inventory are expensed

as cost of goods sold in the period when the sale occurs. Thus, there is a direct matching of expenses with revenues.

2. **Operating expenses.** Unexpired costs become operating expenses through use or consumption (as in the case of store supplies) or through the passage of time (as in the case of prepaid insurance and prepaid rent). The cost of plant assets and other long-lived productive resources is expensed through rational and systematic allocation methods which result in periodic depreciation and amortization. Operating expenses contribute to the revenues of the period but their association with revenues is less direct than for cost of goods sold.

These points about expense recognition are illustrated in Illustration 13-7.

ILLUSTRATION 13-7

Expense recognition pattern

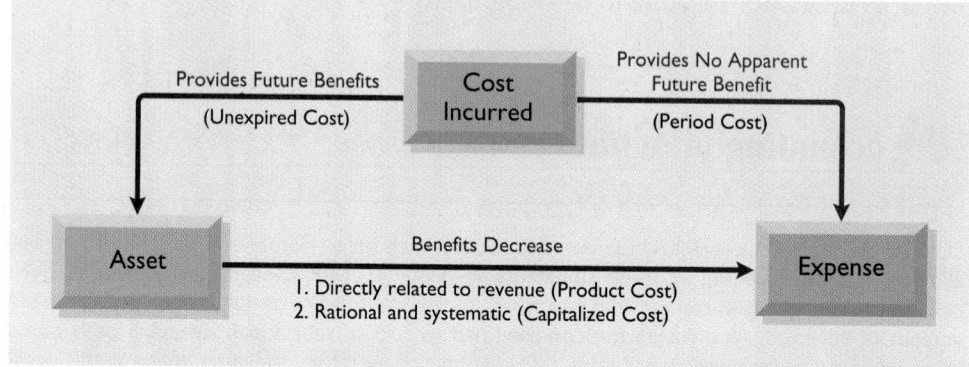

Implementing these guidelines can be difficult. Consider, for example, Harold's Club (a gambling casino) in Reno, Nevada. How should it report expenses related to the payoff of its progressive slot machines? Progressive slot machines, which generally have no ceiling on their jackpots, are capable of providing a lucky winner with all the money that many losers had previously poured into the machines. Payoffs tend to be huge, but infrequent; at Harold's, the progressive slots pay off on average every 4½ months. The basic accounting question is: Can Harold's deduct the millions of dollars sitting in its progressive slot machines from the revenue recognized at the end of the accounting period? One might argue that no, you cannot deduct the money until the "winning handle pull." However, a winning handle pull might not occur for many months or even years.[3]

What would you do in this situation? Although admittedly an estimate would have to be used, the better answer is to match these costs with the revenue recognized, assuming that an average 4½ months' payout is well documented. This example demonstrates the difficulty of applying the matching principle in a practical situation.

Full Disclosure Principle

The full disclosure principle dictates that circumstances and events that make a difference to financial statement users be disclosed. For example, most accountants would agree that Manville Corporation should have disclosed the 52,000 asbestos liability suits (totaling $2 billion) pending against it so that interested parties were made aware of this contingent loss. Similarly, it is generally agreed that companies should disclose the major provisions of employee pension plans and long-term lease contracts.

---

[3]Illustration adapted from *Fortune*, July 7, 1986, p. 100.

Compliance with the full disclosure principle occurs through the data contained in the financial statements and the information in the notes that accompany the statements. The first note in most cases is a **summary of significant accounting policies**. The summary includes, among others, the methods used by the company for inventory costing, depreciation of plant assets, and amortization of intangible assets.

Deciding how much disclosure is enough is difficult. Accountants could disclose every financial event that occurs and every contingency that exists. However, accounting information must be condensed and combined to make it understandable. Providing additional information entails a cost, and the benefits of providing this information in some cases may be less than the costs. Many companies complain of an accounting standards overload. In addition, they object to requirements that force them to disclose confidential information. Determining where to draw the line on disclosure is not easy.

Helpful hint See the specimen financial statements of PepsiCo illustrated in Appendix L for an illustration of a summary of significant accounting policies.

One thing is certain: financial statements were much simpler years ago, when many companies provided little additional information regarding the financial statements. In 1930, General Electric had no notes to the financial statements; today it has over 10 pages of notes! Why this change? A major reason is that the objectives of financial statements have changed. In the past, accountants were interested only in presenting information on what the business had done. Today the objectives of financial reporting are more future-oriented; accounting is trying to provide information that makes it possible to predict the amount, timing, and uncertainty of future cash flows.

Technology in Action

Some accountants are reconsidering the current means of financial reporting. These accountants propose a data base concept of financial reporting. In such a system, all the information from transactions would be stored in a computerized data base to be accessed by various user groups. The main benefit of such a system is the ability to tailor the information requested to the needs of each user.

What makes it controversial? Discussion currently revolves around access and aggregation issues. Questions such as "Who should be allowed to make inquiries of the system?" "What is the lowest/smallest level of information to be provided?" and "Will such a system necessarily improve on the current means of disclosure?" must be answered before such a system can be implemented on a large scale.

Cost Principle

One of the oldest and most basic principles of accounting is the **cost principle**. Cost is used because it is both relevant and reliable. Cost is relevant because it represents the price paid, the assets sacrificed, or the commitment made at date of acquisition. It is the amount for which someone or some entity should be accountable. Cost is reliable because it is objectively measurable, factual, and verifiable. It is the result of an exchange transaction. As a result, cost is the basis used in preparing financial statements.

The cost principle, however, has come under much criticism. It is criticized by some as irrelevant. Subsequent to acquisition, the argument goes, cost is not equivalent to market value or current value. For that matter, as the purchasing power of the dollar changes, so also does the meaning associated with the dollar that is used as the basis of measurement. Consider the classic story about the individual who went to sleep and woke up 10 years later. Hurrying to a telephone, he got through to his broker and asked what his formerly modest stock portfolio was worth. He was told that he was a multi-millionaire—his General Motors stock was worth $5 million and his AT&T stock was up to $10 million. Elated, he was about to inquire about his other holdings, when the telephone operator cut in with "Your time is up. Please deposit $100,000 for the next three minutes."[4]

What this little story demonstrates is that prices can and do change over a period of time, and that one is not necessarily better off when they do. Although the example above is extreme, consider some more realistic data that compare prices in 1980 with what is expected in 1993, assuming prices increase either an average of 6% per year or 12% per year.

ILLUSTRATION 13-8

Example of changing prices

	1980	1993	
Assumed average price increase		6%	12%
Public college, yearly average cost	$ 3,350.00	$ 7,145.00	$ 14,618.00
Average taxi ride, New York City (before tip)	2.95	6.30	12.87
Slice of pizza	.65	1.40	2.84
First-class postage stamp	.15	.32	.65
Run-of-the-mill suburban house, New York City	150,000.00	320,000.00	654,500.00
McDonald's milk shake	.75	1.60	3.27

Helpful hint Are you a winner or loser when you hold cash in a period of inflation? Answer: A loser.

Despite the inevitability of changing prices during a period of inflation, the accounting profession still follows the stable monetary unit assumption in the preparation of a company's primary financial statements. While admitting that some changes in prices do occur, the profession believes the unit of measure (e.g., the dollar) has remained sufficiently constant over time to provide meaningful financial information.

The profession encourages the disclosure of price-level adjusted data in the form of supplemental information presented with financial statements. The two most widely used approaches to show the effects of changing prices on a company's financial statements are (1) constant dollar accounting and (2) current cost accounting.

CONSTANT DOLLAR ACCOUNTING. The real value of the dollar is determined by the goods or services for which it can be exchanged. This real value is commonly called purchasing power. As the economy experiences **inflation** (rising price levels) or **deflation** (falling price levels), the amount of goods or services for which a dollar can be exchanged changes; that is, the purchasing power of the dollar changes from one period to the next. These changes are referred to as **general price level changes**.

Helpful hint With constant dollar accounting, the unit of measure is the purchasing power of a dollar. All items are expressed in terms of units of purchasing power rather than units of money.

Constant dollar accounting restates financial statement items into dollars that have equal purchasing power. As one executive from Shell Oil Company explained, "Constant dollar accounting is a restatement of the traditional financial information into a common unit of measurement." In other words, constant dollar accounting changes the **unit** of measurement; it does not, however, change the underlying accounting principles used to report cost amounts. Constant dollar accounting is cost based.

CURRENT COST ACCOUNTING. The price of a specific item may be affected not only by a change in the general price level, but also by individual market forces. For

---
[4]Adapted from *Barron's*, January 28, 1980, p. 27.

example, during a recent six-year period, certain items changed more or less than the general price level. To illustrate, during this period of time, the cost of a local telephone call increased 150%, guaranteed overnight mail delivery increased 4,575%, a gallon of gasoline decreased over 30%, and a flawless one-carat diamond decreased over 70%. Thus, changes in the specific price of items may be very different from the change in the general price level. These changes are referred to as **specific price level changes**.

A popular means to measure the change in a specific price is current cost. Current cost is the cost of replacing the identical asset owned. Current cost may be approximated by reference to current catalog prices or by applying a specific index to the book value of the asset. Unlike the constant dollar approach, which is simply a restatement of historical dollars into constant purchasing power, the current cost approach changes the **basis** of measurement from cost to current value.

Constraints in Accounting

Constraints permit a company to modify generally accepted accounting principles without reducing the usefulness of the reported information. The constraints are: (1) materiality and (2) conservatism.

Materiality

An item is material when it is likely to influence the decision of a reasonably prudent investor or creditor. It is immaterial if its inclusion or omission has no impact on a decision maker. In short, if the item does not make a difference, GAAP does not have to be followed. To determine the materiality of an amount, that is, to determine its financial significance, the accountant usually compares it with such items as total assets, total liabilities, and net income.

To illustrate how the constraint of materiality is applied, assume that Rodriguez Co. purchases a number of low-cost plant assets, such as wastepaper baskets. Although the proper accounting would appear to be to depreciate these wastepaper baskets over their useful life, they are usually expensed immediately. This practice is justified because these costs are considered immaterial. Establishing depreciation schedules for these assets is costly and time-consuming and will not make a material difference on total assets and net income. Other applications of the materiality constraint are the expensing of small tools or the expensing of any plant assets under a certain dollar amount.

Conservatism

Conservatism means that when in doubt the accountant should choose the solution that will be least likely to overstate assets and income. It does *not* mean *understating* assets or income. Conservatism gives the accountant a guide in difficult situations, and the guide is a reasonable one: do not overstate assets and income.

A common application of the conservatism constraint is the use of the lower of cost or market method for inventories. As indicated in Chapter 9, inventories are reported at market value if market value is below cost. This practice results in a higher cost of goods sold and lower net income. In addition, inventory on the balance sheet is stated at a lower amount when market value is below cost. Other examples of conservatism in accounting are the use of the LIFO method for inventory valuation when prices are rising and the use of accelerated depreciation methods for plant assets. Both these methods result in lower asset carrying values and lower net income than alternative methods.

Before You Go On . . .

1. What are the economic entity assumption, the monetary unit assumption, the periodicity assumption, and the going concern assumption?

2. What are the revenue recognition principle, the matching principle, the full disclosure principle, and the cost principle?

3. What are the materiality constraint and the conservatism constraint?

Summary of Conceptual Framework

The conceptual framework that is followed in developing sound reporting practices starts with a set of objectives for financial reporting and follows with the development of qualities that make information useful. In addition, a set of definitions is developed. Operating guidelines in the form of assumptions and principles are then provided. The conceptual framework also recognizes that important constraints exist on the reporting environment. These points are illustrated graphically below:

ILLUSTRATION 13-9

Conceptual framework

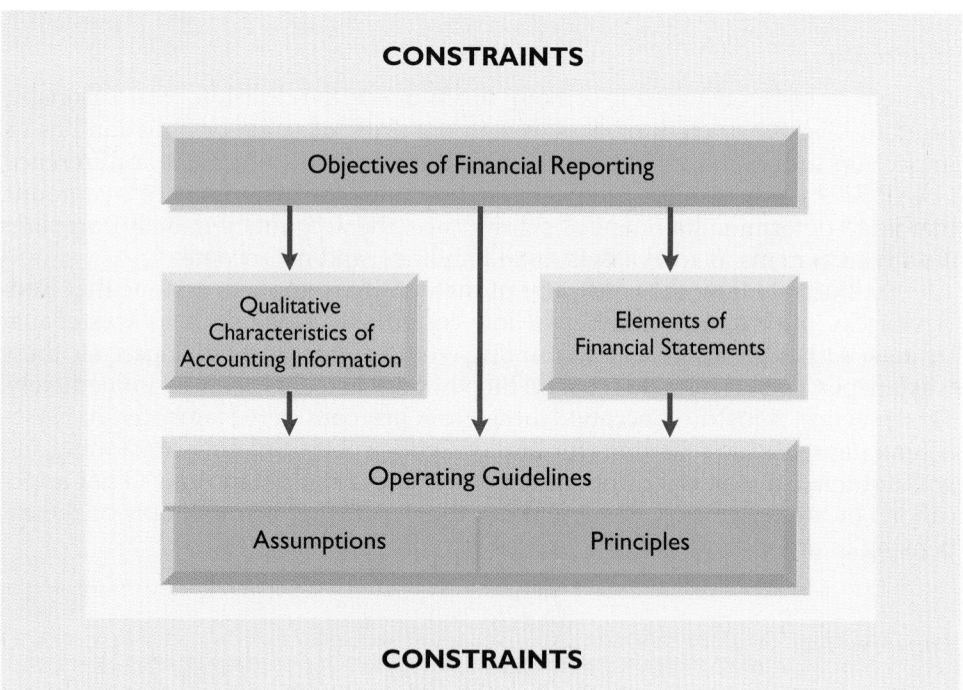

SECTION 2   Accounting Principles and Ethics

As indicated throughout the textbook, one of the most difficult problems facing all segments of society is the question of proper ethical conduct. We are bombarded by exposés of public officials, business executives, and respected leaders

Study Objective 5

Understand issues related to ethics and accounting principles.

who act in a fashion many describe as unethical. Here for example are some of the headlines that have appeared in the financial press recently:

> A consultant admits paying for inside data about arms contracts.
>
> Speaker of the House's downfall reflects ethical lapse.
>
> Auditor violated anti-fraud provisions of federal securities law because he approved false financial statements for E.S.M.
>
> Once hailed as a boy wonder, founder of ZZZZ Best now stands accused of fraud.

Ethics is the process of determining what are and what are not reasonable standards of moral conduct. Simply put, ethics attempts to determine what these reasonable standards of conduct are by systematically addressing at least two basic questions: What is ethically right or wrong? What are my ethical obligations, if any?

The accounting profession has recently focused attention on questions related to ethics because of the number of companies that have engaged in some type of deceptive reporting practice. A number of study groups have, therefore, been formed to examine this problem, often referred to as fraudulent financial reporting.[5] Fraudulent financial reporting is intentional or reckless conduct, whether act or omission, that results in materially misleading financial statements. Such acts can involve the gross and deliberate distortion of corporate records (such as falsifying invoices) or the misapplication of accounting principles (such as failure to disclose material information).

Causes of Fraudulent Financial Reporting

Fraudulent financial reporting usually occurs because of conditions in the internal or external environment.[6] Influences in the **internal environment** relate to poor systems of internal control, management's failure to set an ethical standard, or perhaps a company's poor liquidity or profitability situation. Those in the **external environment** may relate to industry conditions, overall business environment, or legal and regulatory considerations.

General incentives for fraudulent financial reporting are the desire to obtain a higher stock price, to avoid default on a loan agreement, or to make a personal gain of some type (additional compensation, promotion). Situational pressures on the company or an individual manager also may lead to fraudulent financial reporting. Examples of these situational pressures include:

1. Sudden decreases in revenue or market share. A single company or an entire industry can experience these decreases.
2. Unrealistic budget pressures, particularly for short-term results. These pressures may occur when headquarters arbitrarily determines profit objectives and budgets without taking actual conditions into account.
3. Financial pressure resulting from bonus plans that depend on short-term economic performance. This pressure is particularly acute when the bonus is a significant component of the individual's total compensation.

Opportunities for fraudulent financial reporting are present in circumstances when the fraud seems easy to commit and when detection appears difficult.

---

[5]"Report of the National Commission on Fraudulent Financial Reporting" (Washington, D.C., 1987).

[6]The discussion in this section taken from "Report of the National Commission on Fraudulent Financial Reporting," pp. 23–24.

Frequently these opportunities arise from:

1. Lack of vigilance by the board of directors. This situation can occur when the Board is dominated by internal management.

2. Weak or nonexistent internal controls. This situation can occur, for example, when a company's revenue system is overloaded as a result of a rapid expansion of sales, an acquisition of a new division, or the entry into a new, unfamiliar line of business.

3. Unusual or complex transactions. Examples include the consolidation of two companies and the closing of a specific operation.

4. Accounting estimates. These require significant subjective judgment by company management. Examples include contingent liabilities such as product warranties and pending lawsuits.

5. Ineffective internal audit staffs. This situation may result from inadequate staff size and severely limited audit scope.

A weak corporate ethical climate contributes to these situations. Opportunities for fraudulent financial reporting also increase dramatically when the accounting principles followed in reporting transactions are nonexistent, evolving, or subject to varying interpretations.

The financial accounting reporting system in the United States is the envy of the world, yet when human nature is fueled with greed, ego, and deceit even the best system can be undermined. An effective system must be continually maintained and enhanced to counterbalance these weaknesses. Thus, there is need for SEC surveillance and the engagement of independent auditors to perform annual audits.

Before You Go On . . .

1. What is ethics and how does it relate to financial reporting?

2. What is fraudulent financial reporting? What are some conditions that might exist to cause fraudulent financial reporting?

SECTION 3 Accounting Principles
and International Operations

Study Objective 6

Explain the accounting principles used in international operations.

The "world economy" is becoming globalized to the point where the United States is only one in a set of major players. Thus, it is not surprising that a recent important report on business education in the future emphasized that every student must be exposed to the international dimensions of business.

Importance of International Trade

World markets are becoming increasingly intertwined. Foreigners use American computers, eat American breakfast cereals, read American magazines, listen to American rock music, watch American movies and TV shows, and drink American soda. And, Americans drive Japanese cars, wear Italian shoes and Scottish woolens, drink Brazilian coffee and Indian tea, eat Swiss chocolate bars, sit on Danish furniture, and use Arabian oil. The tremendous variety and volume of both exported and imported goods indicates the extensive involvement of U.S. business in international trade. For many U.S. companies, the world is their market.

The following table illustrates the magnitude of foreign sales and type of product sold by U.S. companies.

Company	Foreign Sales as a % of Total	Product
Caterpillar	27.2	Heavy machinery, engines, turbines
Coca-Cola	61.2	Beverages
Eastman Kodak	43.6	Photographic equipment and supplies
E.I. duPont de Nemours	43.5	Specialty chemicals
Exxon	74.9	Petroleum, chemicals
Ford Motor	36.7	Motor vehicles and parts
General Motors	30.3	Motor vehicles and parts
Hewlett-Packard	54.5	Computers, electronics
IBM	60.7	Computers and related equipment
Philip Morris Cos.	23.6	Tobacco, beverages, food products

ILLUSTRATION 13-10

Foreign sales and type of product

Firms that conduct their operations in more than one country through subsidiaries, divisions, or branches in foreign countries are referred to as **multinational corporations**. The accounting for multinational corporations is complicated because foreign currencies are involved. These international transactions and operations must be translated into U.S. dollars.

Accounting in Action · *International Insight*

In 1991, for the first time, McDonald's opened more restaurants overseas than in the United States: 427 abroad compared with just 188 in the United States. The top 10 McDonald's restaurants in sales and profits are on foreign soil. The busiest McDonald's are in Moscow, on the Champs-Elysees in Paris, and in central Rome. In 1992 McDonald's opened its first store in Beijing, China. In 1991, 37% of McDonald's sales and 40% of the company's operating income came from outside the United States.

Source: The New York Times, April 17, 1992.

Foreign Exchange Rates

An **exchange rate** is the value of one currency expressed in terms of another currency. Exchange rates are used to convert one currency into a different currency. For example, in Illustration 13-11, the British pound was quoted recently as equivalent to $1.8560, while the French franc was quoted as equivalent to $0.1887. These rates mean that it would take $1.8560 to buy 1 British pound and 18.87 cents to buy 1 French franc. This form of exchange rate (in terms of the number of domestic units—U.S. dollars) is referred to as a **direct exchange quotation**. It is also possible for the exchange rate to be quoted in terms of the number of foreign units that are equal to one U.S. dollar. This form is referred to as an **indirect exchange quotation**. For example, recently the Japanese yen was quoted at a rate of 127 yen to the U.S. dollar. This means that it would take 127 yen to buy 1 dollar. To avoid confusion, we will quote exchange rates only in terms of the number of U.S. dollars it takes to buy 1 unit of the foreign currency (a direct exchange quotation). Thus, for the yen we will use an exchange rate of $0.00786. The following table illustrates some selected direct exchange rates.

ILLUSTRATION 13-11

Selected foreign exchange rates

Helpful hint (1) How many Italian lira are required to buy one U.S. dollar? (2) How many German marks are equivalent to one U.S. dollar? Answers: (1) $1 divided by .00084 = 1,190.48 = 1,191 Italian lira. (2) $1 divided by .63460 = 1.5758 German marks.

Country	Currency	Price in U.S. dollars
Brazil	Cruzado	$0.00033
Britain	Pound	1.85600
Canada	Dollar	.83630
France	Franc	.18866
Germany	Mark	.63460
Italy	Lira	.00084
Japan	Yen	.00786
Mexico	Peso	.00032
Saudi Arabia	Riyal	.26738
Spain	Peseta	.01007

Source: The Wall Street Journal, June 19, 1992.

Exchange rates change continually to reflect changes in the demand for and supply of different currencies.

Translating Foreign Currency Transactions

Many U.S. companies conduct transactions with customers, suppliers, and banks in foreign countries. Some transactions, such as the purchase and sale of crude oil, are expressed and settled in terms of the U.S. dollar. These transactions present no accounting problem for the U.S. firm because it has no need to use an exchange rate. When transactions are expressed in U.S. dollars, the foreign company accepts, and the U.S. company avoids, the risks and rewards related to changes in currency exchange rates. However, when a U.S. company agrees to transact business expressed in terms of foreign currencies, it accepts the risks and rewards related to changes in currency exchange rates.

When transactions are expressed in terms of the foreign currency, the accounting entries must nevertheless be recorded by the U.S. company in U.S. dollars. That requires translating the foreign currency into U.S. dollars at the exchange rates in effect on the days foreign exchange transactions occur. The following paragraphs illustrate the accounting for foreign purchases.

An Illustration

When a U.S. company purchases from a foreign firm, it may be billed either in U.S. currency or in foreign currency. For example, assume that American Oil Company purchases oil from Saudi Arabia Inc. for $300,000, which is **billed and payable in U.S. currency**. The entries to record the purchase on December 10 and the subsequent payment on December 27 are similar to any transaction expressed in terms of U.S. dollars, as shown below.

Dec. 10	Purchases	300,000	
	Accounts Payable—Saudi Arabia Inc.		300,000
	(To record the purchase of merchandise on account)		
Dec. 27	Accounts Payable—Saudi Arabia Inc.	300,000	
	Cash		300,000
	(To record payment on account)		

However, if Saudi Arabia Inc. **bills American Oil Company in Saudi Arabia riyals and requires payment in riyals, an exchange gain or loss may be incurred by American Oil**. An exchange gain or loss occurs if the exchange rate of dollars to riyals changes between the date of purchase and the date of payment. For example, assume that the purchase of oil for $300,000 above was billed and payable in 1,200,000 riyals, reflecting an exchange rate of $.25 on December 10. And, assume that the exchange rate on December 27, the date of payment, had risen to $.28. On December 10, $300,000 was equivalent to 1,200,000 riyals, but on December 27, $336,000 was equivalent to 1,200,000 riyals. The entries to record the purchase and the payment are as follows:

Dec. 10	Purchases (1,200,000 riyals @ $.25)	300,000	
	Accounts Payable—Saudi Arabia Inc.		300,000
	(To record the purchase of merchandise on account)		
Dec. 27	Accounts Payable—Saudi Arabia Inc.	300,000	
	Foreign Exchange Loss	36,000	
	Cash (1,200,000 riyals @ $.28)		336,000
	(To record payment on account and exchange loss)		

American Oil Co. incurred a foreign exchange loss of $36,000 because it agreed to pay a fixed number of Saudi Arabia riyals, and by the time payment was made the riyal increased in value relative to the U.S. dollar. If the exchange rate of the riyal decreased, say to $.20, American Oil would have realized a foreign exchange gain of $60,000 [1,200,000 riyals $\times$ ($.25 - $.20)].

Financial Statement Presentation

For financial reporting purposes, a Foreign Exchange Gain is reported under other revenues and gains and a Foreign Exchange Loss is reported under other expenses and losses in the income statement. For example, American Oil Co.'s exchange loss of $36,000, would be reported on its income statement for the period ended December 31, as shown in Illustration 13-12.

AMERICAN OIL CO. Partial Income Statement For the Period Ended December 31	
Income from operations	XXXXXX
Other expenses and losses	
Foreign exchange loss	36,000
Income before income taxes	XXXXXX

ILLUSTRATION 13-12

Presentation of exchange loss on income statement

Uniform International Accounting Standards

Many investment and credit decisions require the analysis and interpretation of foreign financial statements. Unfortunately, there is little uniformity in accounting standards from country to country, and there are few recognized worldwide accounting standards. This lack of uniformity is the result of different legal systems, different processes for developing accounting standards, differences in governmental requirements, and differences in economic environments.

Accounting in Action · *International Insight*

Here is how four countries account for research and development costs:

COUNTRY	ACCOUNTING TREATMENT
United States	Expenditures are expensed.
United Kingdom	Certain expenditures may be capitalized.
Germany	Expenditures are expensed.
Japan	Expenditures may be capitalized and amortized over five years.

Thus, a research and development expenditure of $100 million is totally charged to expense in the current period in the United States and Germany. This expense could range from zero to $100 million in the United Kingdom and from $20 million to $100 million in Japan! Do you believe that accounting principles should be comparable across countries?

Source: Adapted from *1991 International Accounting Summaries,* John Wiley & Sons, Inc.

Some efforts have been made to obtain uniformity in international accounting practices. In 1973 the International Accounting Standards Committee (IASC) was formed by agreement of accounting organizations in the United States, United Kingdom, Canada, Australia, France, Germany, Japan, Mexico, and the Netherlands. The IASC now has more than 80 accounting organizations representing more than 60 countries participating in the development of international accounting standards. To date, over 30 International Accounting Standards have been issued for IASC members to introduce to their respective countries. But, because the IASC has no enforcement powers, these standards are by no means universally applied. They are, however, generally followed by the large multinational companies that are audited by international public accounting firms. Thus, the foundation has been laid for considerable progress toward greater uniformity in international accounting.

Before You Go On . . .

1. What is a foreign exchange rate? What is a direct exchange quotation? What is an indirect exchange quotation?

2. How are foreign exchange gains and losses computed?

3. What is the purpose of the International Accounting Standards Committee?

Summary of Study Objectives

1. *Explain the meaning of generally accepted accounting principles and identify the key items of the conceptual framework.* Generally accepted accounting principles are a set of rules and practices that are recognized as a general guide for financial reporting purposes. Generally accepted means that these principles must have "substantial authoritative support." The key items of the conceptual framework are: (1) objectives of financial reporting; (2) qualitative characteristics of accounting information; (3) elements of financial statements; and (4) operating guidelines (assumptions, principles, and constraints).

2. *Describe the basic objectives of financial reporting.* The basic objectives of financial reporting are to provide information that is (1) useful to those making investment and credit decisions; (2) helpful in assessing future cash flows; and (3) helpful in identifying economic resources (assets), the claims to those resources (liabilities), and the changes in those resources and claims.

3. *Discuss the qualitative characteristics of accounting information and elements of financial statements.* To judge usefulness, information should possess the following qualitative characteristics: relevance, reliability, comparability, and consistency. The elements of financial statements are a set of definitions that can be used to describe the basic terms used in accounting.

4. *Identify and illustrate the basic operating guidelines used by accountants.* The operating guidelines followed by accountants are assumptions, principles, and constraints. The major assumptions are: economic entity, monetary unit, periodicity, and going concern. The major principles are: revenue recognition, matching, full disclosure, and cost. The major constraints are materiality and conservatism.

5. *Understand issues related to ethics and account-*

ing principles. The accounting profession has recently become concerned about questions related to ethics— standards of ethical conduct—because of the number of companies that have engaged in some type of deceptive reporting practice. Fraudulent financial reporting usually occurs because of conditions in the internal or external environment. Influences in the internal environment relate to poor systems of internal control, management's attitude toward ethics, or perhaps a company's liquidity or profitability situation. Those in the external environment may relate to industry conditions, overall business environment, or legal and regulatory considerations.

6. *Explain the accounting principles used in international operations.* When transactions are expressed in terms of a foreign currency, the accounting entries must be recorded by the U.S. company in U.S. dollars. That requires translating the foreign currency into U.S. dollars at the exchange rates in effect on the days foreign exchange transactions occur. This often gives rise to foreign exchange gains or losses.

GLOSSARY

Comparability · Ability to compare accounting information of different companies because they use the same accounting principles. (p. 513).

Conceptual framework · A coherent system of interrelated objectives and fundamentals that can lead to consistent standards. (p. 511).

Conservatism · The approach of choosing an accounting method when in doubt that will least likely overstate assets and net income. (p. 523).

Consistency · Use of the same accounting principles and methods from year to year within a company. (p. 513).

Constant dollar accounting · A type of accounting that restates financial statement items into dollars that have equal purchasing power. (p. 522).

Current cost · The cost of replacing the identical asset owned; a measure of the change in a specific price. (p. 523).

Elements of financial statements · Definitions of basic terms used in accounting. (p. 514).

Exchange rate · Value of one currency expressed in terms of another currency. (p. 527).

Fraudulent financial reporting · Intentional or reckless conduct, whether act or omission, that results in materially misleading financial statements. (p. 525).

Full disclosure principle · Dictates that circumstances and events that make a difference to financial statement users should be disclosed. (p. 520).

Generally accepted accounting principles (GAAP) · A set of rules and practices, having substantial authoritative support, that are recognized as a general guide for financial reporting purposes. (p. 511).

Going concern assumption · The assumption that the enterprise will continue in operation long enough to carry out its existing objectives and commitments. (p. 515).

Installment method · A method of recognizing revenue using the cash basis; each cash collection consists of a partial recovery of cost of goods sold and partial gross profit from the sale. (p. 518).

Materiality · The constraint of determining if an item is important enough to likely influence the decision of a reasonably prudent investor or creditor. (p. 523).

Percentage-of-completion method · Recognizes revenue and income on a construction project on the basis of costs incurred during the period to the total estimated costs for the project. (p. 516).

Purchasing power · The amount of goods and services for which a dollar can be exchanged. (p. 522).

Relevance · Information capable of making a difference in a decision. (p. 513).

Reliability · The quality of information that gives assurance that it is free of error and bias. (p. 513).

DEMONSTRATION PROBLEM 1

Carver Construction Company is under contract to build a high-rise condominium at a contract price of $2,000,000. The building will take 18 months to complete at an estimated cost of $1,400,000. Construction began in November, 1992, and was finished in April, 1994. Actual construction costs incurred in each year were: 1992, $140,000; 1993; $910,000; and 1994, $350,000.

Instructions

Compute the gross profit to be recognized in each year.

Helpful hint

(1) Percent complete is determined by dividing costs incurred by total estimated costs.

(2) Percent complete is multiplied by contract price to find revenue recognized.

(3) Gross profit equals revenue recognized less actual costs incurred.

(4) Percentage of completion method recognizes revenue as the construction occurs—it is viewed as a series of sales.

Solution to Demonstration Problem

Year	Costs Incurred (Current Period)	÷ Total Estimated Cost =	Percent Complete (Current Period)	×	Total Revenue	=	Revenue Recognized (Current Period)
1992	$ 140,000	$1,400,000	10%		$2,000,000		$ 200,000
1993	910,000	1,400,000	65%		2,000,000		1,300,000
1994	350,000	Balance to complete contract					500,000
	$1,400,000						$2,000,000

Year	Revenue Recognized (Current Period)	−	Actual Costs Incurred (Current Period)	=	Gross Profit Recognized (Current Period)
1992	$ 200,000		$ 140,000		$ 60,000
1993	1,300,000		910,000		390,000
1994	500,000		350,000		150,000
	$2,000,000		$1,400,000		$600,000

DEMONSTRATION PROBLEM 2

Valdes Inc. uses the installment method in accounting for its sales. During its first year of operations, it had installment sales of $900,000 and a cost of goods sold on installments of $600,000. The collections on installment sales were as follows: First year, $330,000; second year, $420,000; and third year, $150,000.

Instructions

Compute the amount of gross profit to be recognized each year.

Helpful hint

(1) Installment method used when receipt of cash is uncertain.

(2) Must always find gross profit percentage.

(3) Gross profit recognized each period results from cash collected times gross profit percentage.

Solution to Demonstration Problem

Year	Cash Collected	×	Gross Profit Percentage*	=	Gross Profit Recognized
One	$330,000		33⅓%		$110,000
Two	420,000		33⅓%		140,000
Three	150,000		33⅓%		50,000
	$900,000				$300,000

*$900,000 − $600,000 = $300,000; $300,000 ÷ $900,000 = 33⅓%

SELF-STUDY QUESTIONS

Answers are at the end of the chapter.

(S.O. 1) 1. Generally accepted accounting principles are:
a. usually established by the Internal Revenue Service.
b. a set of rules and practices that are recognized as a general guide for financial reporting.
c. the guidelines used to resolve ethical dilemmas.
d. fundamental truths that can be derived from the laws of nature.

(S.O. 2) 2. Which of the following is *not* an objective of financial reporting?
a. Provide information that is useful in investment and credit decisions.
b. Provide information about economic resources, claims to those resources, and changes in them.
c. Provide information on the liquidation value of a business.
d. Provide information that is useful in assessing future cash flows.

(S.O. 3) 3. The primary criterion by which accounting information can be judged is:
a. consistency.
b. decision-usefulness.
c. predictive value.
d. comparability.

(S.O. 3) 4. Verifiability is an ingredient of:

	Reliability	Relevance
a.	Yes	Yes
b.	No	Yes
c.	Yes	No
d.	No	No

(S.O. 4) 5. Valuing assets at their liquidation value rather than their cost is *inconsistent* with the:
a. periodicity assumption.
b. matching principle.
c. materiality constraint.
d. going concern assumption.

(S.O. 4) 6. Gonzalez's Construction Company began a long-term construction contract on January 1, 1993. The contract is expected to be completed in 1994 at a total cost of $20,000,000. Gonzalez's revenue for the project is $24,000,000. Gonzalez incurred contract costs of $5,000,000 in 1993. What gross profit should be recognized in 1993?
a. $6,000,000.
b. $1,000,000.
c. $4,000,000.
d. $2,000,000.

(S.O. 4) 7. Glackin Company had installment sales of $1,000,000 in their first year of operations. The cost of goods sold on installment was $650,000, and Glackin collected a total of $400,000 on the installment sales. Using the installment method, how much gross profit should be recognized in the first year?
a. $140,000.
b. $250,000.
c. $260,000.
d. $350,000.

(S.O. 4) 8. The accounting concept that refers to the tendency of accountants to resolve uncertainty in favor of understating assets and revenues is known as (the):
a. conservatism.
b. materiality.
c. matching principle.
d. monetary unit assumption.

(S.O. 5) 9. Which of the following statements is *incorrect*?
a. Opportunities for fraudulent financial reporting are decreased when internal controls are strong.
b. Ineffective internal audit staffs can lead to fraudulent financial reporting.
c. Companies that have bonus plans based on short-term economic performance are less likely to have fraudulent financial reporting.
d. Fraudulent financial reporting is the intentional or reckless conduct, whether act or omission, that results in materially misleading financial statements.

(S.O. 6) 10. Which of the following statements is *incorrect*?
a. An exchange rate is the value of one currency expressed in terms of another currency.
b. When a U.S. company makes a purchase that is billable and payable in a foreign currency, it may recognize a foreign exchange loss or gain.
c. In the income statement, foreign exchange gains and losses are reported as part of income from operations.
d. When the purchase is billable in a foreign currency, accounts payable is credited by the U.S. company for U.S. dollars using the exchange rate at the billing date.

QUESTIONS

1. Prior to the establishment of the Financial Accounting Standards Board, accounting principles had been developed on a problem-by-problem basis. Has the Financial Accounting Standards Board attempted to change this approach to problem solving? How?

2. What are the major objectives of financial reporting?

3. Define relevance and reliability. What characteristics are needed for information to be relevant? Reliable?

4. Ray Aldag, the president of Maynard Company, is pleased. Maynard substantially increased its net income in 1992 while keeping its unit inventory relatively the same. Tom Erhardt, chief accountant, cautions Aldag, however. Erhardt says that since Maynard changed from the LIFO to the FIFO method of inventory valuation, there is a consistency problem and it would be difficult to determine if Maynard is better off. Is Erhardt correct? Why?

5. What is the distinction between comparability and consistency?

6. Why is it necessary for accountants to assume that an economic entity will remain a going concern?

7. When should revenue be recognized? Why has the date of sale been chosen as the point at which to recognize the revenue resulting from the entire producing and selling process?

8. Richter Construction Company has a $200 million contract to build a bridge. Its total estimated cost for the project is $170 million. Costs incurred in the first year of the project were $17 million. Richter appropriately uses the percentage-of-completion method. How much revenue and gross profit should Richter recognize in the first year of the project?

9. Merchandise with a cost of $80,000 was sold during the year for $100,000. Cash collected for the year amounted to $60,000. How much gross profit should be recognized during the year if the company uses the installment method?

10. Distinguish between product costs and period costs.

11. (a) Where does the accountant disclose information about an entity's financial position, operations, and cash flows? (b) The full disclosure principle recognizes that the nature and amount of information included in financial reports reflects a series of judgmental trade-offs. What are the objectives of these trade-offs?

12. Sue Leonard is the president of Borders Books. She has no accounting background. Leonard cannot understand why current cost is not used as the basis for accounting measurement and reporting. Explain what basis is used and why.

13. (a) What is meant by constant dollar accounting? (b) What is purchasing power?

14. What is current cost accounting? How does it differ from constant dollar accounting?

15. What is the accounting profession's position on reporting changing price information?

16. Describe the two constraints inherent in the presentation of accounting information.

17. What is fraudulent financial reporting?

18. What are the incentives for individuals to become involved in fraudulent financial reporting?

19. What is the difference between a **direct exchange quotation** and an **indirect exchange quotation**?

20. If an American firm does business with a Japanese firm and all their transactions take place in Japanese yen, which firm may incur an exchange gain or loss and why?

BRIEF EXERCISES

BE13–1 Indicate whether each of the following statements is true or false.

Generally accepted accounting principles.
(S.O. 1)

   1. ____ GAAP is a set of rules and practices established by the accounting profession to serve as a general guide for financial reporting purposes.

   2. ____ "*Generally accepted*" means that these principles must have "substantial authoritative support."

   3. ____ Substantial authoritative support for GAAP usually comes from two standard-setting bodies: the FASB and the IRS.

BE13–2 Indicate which of the following items is(are) included in the FASB's conceptual framework. (Use "Yes" or "No" to answer this question.)

Items included in conceptual framework.
(S.O. 1)

   1. ____ Objectives of financial reporting.

   2. ____ Analysis of financial statement ratios.

   3. ____ Qualitative characteristics of accounting information.

BE13–3 According to the FASB's conceptual framework, which of the following are objectives of financial reporting? (Use "Yes" or "No" to answer this question.)

Objectives of financial reporting.
(S.O. 2)

   1. ____ Provide information that is useful to those making investment and credit decisions.

   2. ____ Provide information that identifies the economic resources (assets), the claims to those resources (liabilities), and the changes in those resources and claims.

   3. ____ Provide information that is helpful in assessing past cash flows and stock prices.

BE13–4 Presented below is a chart of the qualitative characteristics of accounting information. Fill in the blanks from (a) to (e).

Qualitative characteristics.
(S.O. 3)

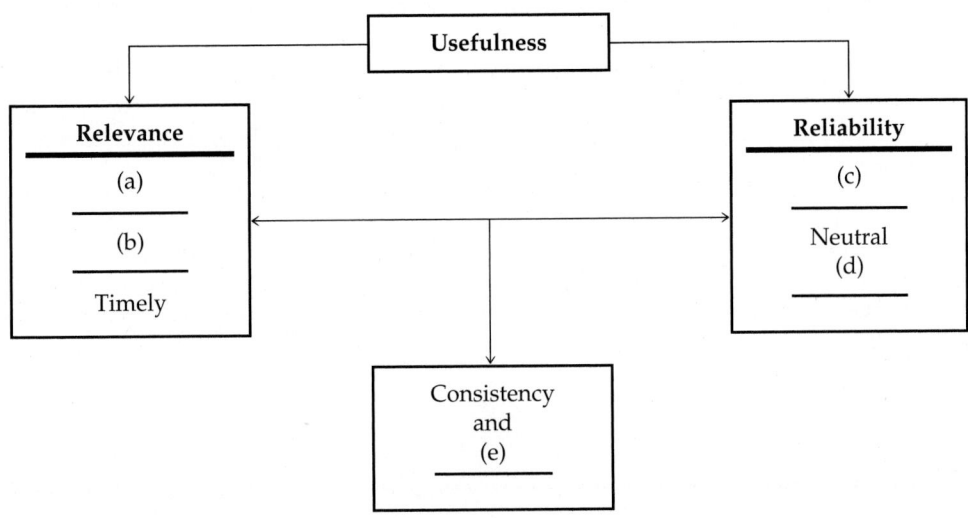

BE13–5 Given the *qualitative characteristics* of accounting established by the FASB's conceptual framework, complete each of the following statements:

Qualitative characteristics.
(S.O. 3)

   1. ____ is the quality of information that gives assurance that it is free of error and bias; it can be depended on.

   2. ____ For information to be ____, it should have predictive or feedback value, and it must be presented on a timely basis.

   3. ____ means using the same accounting principles and methods from year to year within a company.

BE13–6 Presented below is a set of qualitative characteristics of accounting information.

Qualitative characteristics.
(S.O. 3)

(a) Predictive value   (c) Verifiable

(b) Neutral   (d) Timely

Match these qualitative characteristics to the following statements, using letters a through d.

1. ____ Accounting information cannot be selected, prepared, or presented to favor one set of interested users over another.

2. ____ Accounting information should help users make predictions about the outcome of past, present, and future events.

3. ____ Accounting information must be available to decision makers before it loses its capacity to influence their decisions.

4. ____ Accounting information must be proved to be free of error and bias.

Operating guidelines.
(S.O. 4)

BE13–7   Presented below are four concepts discussed in this chapter.

(a) Periodicity assumption   (c) Full disclosure principle
(b) Cost principle   (d) Conservatism

Match these concepts to the following accounting practices. Each letter can be used only once.

1. ____ Recording inventory at its purchase price.
2. ____ Preparing financial statements on an annual basis.
3. ____ Using notes and supplementary schedules in the financial statements.
4. ____ Using the lower of cost or market method for inventory valuation.

Revenue recognition principle—percentage of completion.
(S.O. 4)

BE13–8   Emerson Construction Company is under contract to build a commercial building at a price of $4,000,000. Construction began in January 1993 and was finished in December 1995. Total estimated construction costs are $2,800,000. Actual construction costs incurred in each year were: 1993, $280,000; 1994, $1,820,000; 1995, $700,000. Compute the revenue to be recognized in each year using the *percentage-of-completion* method.

Revenue recognition method—installment method.
(S.O. 4)

BE13–9   Walder Co. uses the installment method to determine its net income. During its first year of operations, it had installment sales of $800,000 and a cost of goods sold of $600,000. The collections on installment sales were as follows: first year $350,000; second year $450,000. Determine the gross profit recognized for the first and second year.

Accounting principles in international operations.
(S.O. 6)

BE13–10   Presented below is information related to Harcroft Inc. Prepare entries to record these transactions.

Dec. 10 Purchased merchandise on account from London Co., a British Co., for 90,000 pounds. The exchange rate is $1.85 per pound.

Dec. 20 Paid London Co. the full amount due from the Dec. 10 transaction. The exchange rate for the British pound is now $1.87.

EXERCISES

Identify the assumption, principle, or constraint that has been violated.
(S.O. 4)

E13–1   A number of accounting reporting situations are described below.

1. In preparing its financial statements, Seco Company omitted information concerning its method of accounting for inventories.

2. Tercek Company recognizes revenue at the end of the production cycle, but before sale. The price of the product, as well as the amount that can be sold, is not certain.

3. Shea Company uses the direct write-off method of accounting for uncollectible accounts.

4. Revsine Hospital Supply Corporation reports only current assets and current liabilities on its balance sheet. Property, plant, and equipment and bonds payable are reported as current assets and current liabilities, respectively. Liquidation of the company is unlikely.

5. Barton Inc. is carrying inventory at its current market value of $100,000. Inventory had an original cost of $110,000.

6. Bonilla Company is in its fifth year of operation and has yet to issue financial statements. (Do not use full disclosure principle.)

7. Steph Wolfson, president of the Classic Music Company, bought a computer for her personal use. She paid for the computer by using company funds and debited the "computers" account.

8. Watts Company has inventory on hand that cost $400,000. Watts reports inventory on its balance sheet at its current market value of $425,000.

Instructions
For each of the above, list the assumption, principle, or constraint that has been violated, if any. List only one term for each case.

Identify the assumption, principle, or constraint that has been violated and prepare correct entries. (S.O. 4)

E13-2 Presented below are some business transactions that occurred during 1993 for Mallot Co.

(a) Equipment worth $90,000 was acquired at a cost of $72,000 from a company that had water damage in a flood. The following entry was made:

Equipment	90,000	
Cash		72,000
Gain		18,000

(b) Merchandise inventory with a cost of $208,000 is reported at its market value of $260,000. The following entry was made:

Merchandise Inventory	52,000	
Gain		52,000

(c) An account receivable has been deemed to be a bad debt. The following entry was made:

Allowance for Doubtful Accounts	7,000	
Accounts Receivable		7,000

(d) The president of Mallot Co., George Winston, purchased a truck for personal use and charged it to his expense account. The following entry was made:

Travel Expense	18,000	
Cash		18,000

(e) An electric pencil sharpener costing $66 is being depreciated over 6 years. The following entry was made:

Depreciation Expense—Pencil Sharpener	11	
Accumulated Depreciation—Pencil Sharpener		11

Instructions
In each of the situations above, identify the assumption, principle, or constraint that has been violated, if any, and discuss the appropriateness of the journal entries. Give the correct journal entry, if necessary.

Identify accounting assumptions, principles, and constraints to different situations. (S.O. 4)

E13-3 Presented below are the assumptions, principles, and constraints discussed in this chapter:

(a) Economic entity assumption
(b) Going concern assumption
(c) Monetary unit assumption
(d) Periodicity assumption

(e) Cost principle
(f) Matching principle
(g) Full disclosure principle
(h) Materiality

Instructions
Identify by letter the accounting assumption, principle, or constraint that describes each situation below. Do not use a letter more than once.

1. Is the rationale for why plant assets are not reported at liquidation value. (Do not use historical cost principle.)

2. Ensures that all relevant financial information is reported.

3. Indicates that personal and business record-keeping should be separately maintained.

4. Assumes that the dollar is the "measuring stick" used to report on financial performance.

5. Separates financial information into time periods for reporting purpose.

6. Requires that the operational guidelines be followed for all significant items.

7. Requires recognition of expenses in the same period as related revenues.

8. Indicates that market value changes subsequent to purchase are not recorded in the accounts.

Determine the amount of revenue to be recognized.
(S.O. 4)

E13–4   Consider the following transactions of Mucklow Company for 1993.

1. Sold a 6-month insurance policy to Taylor Corporation for $6,000 on March 1.

2. Leased office space to Excel Supplies for a 1-year period beginning October 1. The rent of $36,000 was paid in advance.

3. A sales order for merchandise costing $9,000 that had a sales price of $12,000 was received on December 28 from Warfield Company. The goods were shipped FOB shipping point on December 31 and Warfield received them on January 3.

4. Signed a long-term contract to construct a building at a total price of $1,800,000. Total estimated cost of construction is $1,200,000. During 1993, the company incurred $200,000 of costs and collected $330,000 in cash. The percentage of completion method is used to recognize revenue.

5. Merchandise inventory on hand at year-end amounted to $160,000. Mucklow expects to sell the inventory in 1994 for $180,000.

Instructions

For each item above, indicate the amount of revenue Mucklow should recognize in calendar year 1993. Explain.

Determine gross profit for construction projects.
(S.O. 4)

S

E13–5   Prinz Construction Company currently has one long-term construction project. The project has a contract price of $150,000,000 with total estimated costs of $100,000,000. Prinz appropriately uses the percentage-of-completion method. After two years of construction, the following costs have been accumulated.

Actual cost incurred, Year 1	$30,000,000
Total estimated cost remaining after Year 1	70,000,000
Actual cost incurred, Year 2	40,000,000
Total estimated cost remaining after Year 2	30,000,000

Instructions

Determine the gross profit for each of the first two years of the construction contract.

Determine gross profit using installment sales and point-of-sale bases.
(S.O. 4)

E13–6   Wiley Company sold equipment for $300,000 in 1992. Collections on the sale were as follows: 1992, $50,000; 1993, $190,000; 1994, $60,000. Wiley's cost of goods sold is typically 75% of sales.

Instructions

(a) Determine Wiley's gross profit for 1992, 1993, and 1994, assuming that Wiley recognizes income under the installment method.

(b) Determine Wiley's gross profit for 1992, 1993, and 1994, assuming that Wiley recognizes income under the point-of-sale basis.

Discuss fraudulent financial reporting and ethical issues.
(S.O. 5)

E13–7   Sue Marshall was the assistant to the Vice President of Finance at Parsons, Inc. Parsons, Inc. manufactures IBM-compatible PCs. In June, Sue was asked to develop an earnings forecast for this year. She was excited about the assignment because Parsons, Inc. was planning a stock offering in the near future and this forecast would be crucial to the offering's success.

During fiscal year 1993 (which ended May 31), the company posted a small profit. Net sales increased 10%, and the cost of sales had climbed by only 4.5% over 1992. The company had managed to cut its operating expenses by 4%, and by the end of the year, it had after-tax income of $.5 million.

By late June, Sue thought she had finished her forecast. It looked like a good year with anticipated increases in net sales of 20% to $70.3 million and operating expenses of 16% to $39.6 million. She estimated year-end net income would be between $1.8 million and $2.2 million. To celebrate completing the forecast, Sue had dinner with her friend, Tom, who was Sue's counterpart at Parsons' major computer chip supplier. It wasn't much of a celebration, however, as Sue learned that Tom was 100% certain Parsons' chip supply would be cut by 15% in the near future due to heavy demand. Sue knew this would significantly hurt Parsons' manufacturing capability, as the chips were not readily available from other sources. The forecast would have to be revised.

The next morning, Sue raised this point with the VP of Finance, Paul. Surprisingly, Paul told Sue to issue the forecast as is. The stock offering would be made in two weeks. Should the rumor turn out to be true, they could issue a revised forecast after the offering.

Sue was confident her friend's information was accurate. She felt caught between her various responsibilities. If the price of Parsons stock dropped sharply, Parsons would not be able to raise sufficient cash to finance the product development the company badly needed. Yet, Sue also felt responsible to those who would trust and/or be impacted by her forecast.

Instructions

(a) What is fraudulent financial reporting?

(b) What are incentives for fraudulent financial reporting?

(c) What are the facts of this case?

(d) What are Sue's alternatives?

(e) What would you do in Sue's situation?

E13–8 Presented below are selected transactions of Atkins, Inc., a U.S. company.

Prepare journal entries for foreign purchases.
(S.O. 6)

Dec. 18 Purchased merchandise on account from Delon Company, a French firm, for 90,000 francs. The exchange rate is $.19 per franc.

Dec. 18 Purchased merchandise on account from Paris Corporation, a French firm. $30,000 U.S. dollars are due in one month.

Dec. 29 Paid 90,000 francs to Delon. The exchange rate is $.17 per franc.

Dec. 30 Paid $30,000 to Paris. The exchange rate is $.16 per franc.

Instructions
Prepare journal entries for Atkins for the above transactions.

PROBLEMS

P13–1 Garner and Simon are accountants for Bryant Computers. They are having disagreements concerning the following transactions that occurred during the calendar year 1993.

Analyze transactions to identify accounting principle or assumption violated and preparation of correct entries.
(S.O. 1, 4)

1. Bryant purchased equipment for $35,000 at a going-out-of-business sale. The equipment was worth $45,000. Garner believes that the following entry should be made:

Equipment	45,000	
Cash		35,000
Gain		10,000

2. A 1-year insurance policy was purchased by Bryant on September 1, 1993 for $12,000. Garner believes that the following entry should be made on September 1:

Insurance Expense	12,000	
Cash		12,000

3. Land costing $60,000 was appraised at $90,000. Garner suggests the following journal entry:

Land	30,000	
Gain on Appreciation of Land		30,000

4. Depreciation for the year was $18,000. Since net income is expected to be lower this year, Garner suggests deferring depreciation to a year when there is more net income.

5. Bryant bought a custom-made piece of equipment for $18,000. This equipment has a useful life of 6 years. Bryant depreciates equipment using the straight-line method. "Since the equipment is custom made, it will have no resale value and, therefore,

shouldn't be depreciated but instead expensed immediately," argues Garner. "Besides, it provides for lower net income."

6. Garner suggests that equipment should be reported on the balance sheet at its liquidation value, which is $15,000 less than its cost.

Simon disagrees with Garner on each of the above situations.

Instructions

For each transaction, indicate why Simon disagrees. Identify the accounting principle or assumption that Garner would be violating if his suggestions were used. Prepare the correct journal entry for each transaction, if any.

Determine the appropriateness of journal entries in terms of generally accepted accounting principles.
(S.O. 4)

P13–2 Presented below are a number of business transactions that occurred during the current year for Keller, Inc.

1. Because the general level of prices increased during the current year, Keller, Inc. determined that there was a $20,000 understatement of depreciation expense on its equipment and decided to record it in its accounts. The following entry was made:

Depreciation Expense	20,000	
Accumulated Depreciation		20,000

2. Materials were purchased on March 31 for $65,000 and this amount was entered in the Materials account. On December 31, the materials would have cost $85,000, so the following entry was made:

Inventory	20,000	
Gain on Inventories		20,000

3. An order for $30,000 has been received from a customer for products on hand. This order is to be shipped on January 9 next year. The following entry was made:

Accounts Receivable	30,000	
Sales		30,000

4. Because of a "flood sale," equipment obviously worth $230,000 was acquired at a cost of $150,000. The following entry was made:

Equipment	230,000	
Cash		150,000
Gain on Purchase of Equipment		80,000

5. The president of Keller, Inc. used his expense account to purchase a new Saab 9000 solely for personal use. The following entry was made:

Miscellaneous Expense	34,000	
Cash		34,000

Instructions

In each of the situations above, discuss the appropriateness of the journal entries in terms of generally accepted accounting principles.

Recognize gross profit using the percentage-of-completion method.
(S.O. 4)

P13–3 Grainger Construction Company is involved in a long-term construction contract to build an office building at a total estimated cost of $30 million. Additional information follows:

	Office Building	
	Cash Collections	Actual Costs Incurred
1992	$ 9,000,000	$ 4,500,000
1993	9,000,000	6,000,000
1994	12,500,000	10,500,000
1995	9,500,000	9,000,000

The project is completed in 1995 and all cash to be received from the contract has been received.

Instructions

Prepare a schedule to determine the gross profit for 1992, 1993, 1994, and 1995 for the long-term construction contract using the percentage-of-completion method.

P13–4 Grainger sold apartments it had constructed to Mattson Management Company for $2.5 million. Grainger's cost to construct the apartments was $2 million. Grainger appropriately uses the installment method. Additional information follows:

	Cash Collected
1992	$ 800,000
1993	1,100,000
1994	600,000

Prepare a schedule to determine the gross profit for 1992, 1993, and 1994 from the installment sale.

P13–5 Presented below are the assumptions, principles, and constraints used in this chapter.

(a) Economic entity assumption

(b) Going concern assumption

(c) Monetary unit assumption

(d) Periodicity assumption

(e) Full disclosure principle

(f) Revenue recognition principle

(g) Matching principle

(h) Cost principle

(i) Materiality

(j) Conservatism

Identify by letter the accounting assumption, principle, or constraint that describes each situation below. Do not use a letter more than once.

1. Assumes that the dollar is the measuring stick used to report financial information.
2. Allocates expenses to revenues in proper period.
3. Repair tools are expensed when purchased. (Do not use conservatism)
4. Separates financial information into time periods for reporting purposes.
5. Market value changes subsequent to purchase are not recorded in the accounts. (Do not use revenue recognition principle).
6. Lower of cost or market is used to value inventories.
7. Ensures that all relevant financial information is reported.
8. Indicates that personal and business record keeping should be separately maintained.

P13–6 Kiwi Company purchases merchandise from various foreign companies that require payment in local currencies. Listed below are selected transactions for Kiwi in 1992.

Oct. 10 Purchased merchandise on account from Danthur Company, a Swiss firm. The merchandise cost 80,000 Swiss francs and payment is due within 30 days. The exchange rate for the Swiss franc is $0.70.

Nov. 9 Paid Swiss francs to Danthur Company for the purchase made on October 10 at an exchange rate of $0.72.

Instructions

(a) Prepare journal entries to record the transactions for the Kiwi Company.

(b) Indicate how the foreign exchange gain or loss should be reported in the financial statements.

ALTERNATE PROBLEMS

P13–1A Molitor and Yount are accountants for Brewer Printers. They are having disagreements concerning the following transactions that occurred during the year.

1. Depreciation for the year was $26,000. Since net income is expected to be lower this year, Molitor suggests deferring depreciation to a year when there is more net income.
2. Brewer bought equipment for $30,000, including installation costs. The equipment has a useful life of 5 years. Brewer depreciates equipment using the straight-line method. "Since the equipment as installed into our system cannot be removed without considerable damage, it will have no resale value, and therefore should not be depreciated but instead expensed immediately," argues Molitor. "Besides, it lowers net income."

3. Molitor suggests that Brewer should carry equipment on the balance sheet at its liquidation value, which is $20,000 less than its cost.

4. Brewer purchased equipment at a fire sale for $21,000. The equipment was worth $26,000. Molitor believes that the following entry should be made:

Equipment	26,000	
Cash		21,000
Gain		5,000

5. Brewer rented office space for 1 year starting October 1, 1992. The total amount of $24,000 was paid in advance. Molitor believes that the following entry should be made on October 1:

Rent Expense	24,000	
Cash		24,000

6. Land costing $41,000 was appraised at $49,000. Molitor suggests the following journal entry:

Land	8,000	
Gain on Appreciation of Land		8,000

Yount disagrees with Molitor on each of the situations above.

Instructions

For each transaction, indicate why Yount disagrees. Identify the accounting principle or assumption that Molitor would be violating if his suggestions were used. Prepare the correct journal entry for each transaction, if any.

Determine the appropriateness of journal entries in terms of generally accepted accounting principles. (S.O. 4)

P13–2A   Presented below are a number of business transactions that occurred during the current year for Chen, Inc.

1. An order for $70,000 has been received from a customer for products on hand. This order is to be shipped on January 9 next year. The following entry was made:

Accounts Receivable	70,000	
Sales		70,000

2. Because of a "flood sale," equipment obviously worth $300,000 was acquired at a cost of $250,000. The following entry was made:

Equipment	300,000	
Cash		250,000
Gain on Purchase of Equipment		50,000

3. The president of Chen, Inc. used his expense account to purchase a Mercedes-Benz 190 solely for personal use. The following entry was made:

Miscellaneous Expense	28,000	
Cash		28,000

4. Because the general level of prices increased during the current year, Chen, Inc. determined that there was a $40,000 understatement of depreciation expense on its equipment and decided to record it in its accounts. The following entry was made:

Depreciation Expense	40,000	
Accumulated Depreciation		40,000

5. Land was purchased on April 30 for $200,000 and this amount was entered in the Land account. On December 31, the land would have cost $230,000, so the following entry was made:

Land	30,000	
Gain on Land		30,000

Instructions

In each of the situations above, discuss the appropriateness of the journal entries in terms of generally accepted accounting principles.

P13–3A   Bradley Construction Company is involved in a long-term construction contract. Bradley contracted to build a health club with a total estimated cost of $20 million. Additional information follows:

Recognize gross profit using the percentage-of-completion. (S.O. 4)

	Health Club	
	Cash Collections	Actual Costs Incurred
1992	$ 4,500,000	$3,000,000
1993	10,000,000	8,000,000
1994	8,000,000	5,000,000
1995	2,500,000	4,000,000

The project was completed in 1995 and all cash collections related to the contract have been received.

Instructions

Prepare a schedule to determine the gross profit for 1992, 1993, 1994, and 1995 for the long-term construction contract, using the percentage-of-completion method.

P13–4A   Cecil Inc. sold condominiums it had constructed to Parker Management Company for $6 million. Cecil's cost to construct the condominiums was $4.5 million. Cecil appropriately uses the installment method. Additional information follows:

Recognize gross profit using the installment method. (S.O. 4)

	Cash Collected
1992	$ 900,000
1993	3,600,000
1994	1,500,000

Instructions

Prepare a schedule to determine the gross profit for 1992, 1993, and 1994 from the installment sale.

P13–5A   Presented below are the assumptions, principles, and constraints used in this chapter.

Identify accounting assumptions, principles, and constraints. (S.O. 4)

(a) Economic entity assumption
(b) Going concern assumption
(c) Monetary unit assumption
(d) Periodicity assumption
(e) Full disclosure principle

(f) Revenue recognition principle
(g) Matching principle
(h) Cost principle
(i) Materiality
(j) Conservatism

Identify by letter the accounting assumption, principle, or constraint that describes each situation below. Do not use a letter more than once.

1. All important information related to inventories is presented in the footnotes or in the financial statements.
2. When in doubt, it is better to understate rather than overstate net income.
3. Revenue is recorded at the point of sale.
4. Reporting must be done at defined intervals.
5. Each entity is kept as a unit distinct from its owner or owners.
6. An allowance for doubtful accounts is established. (Do not use conservatism.)
7. Pencil sharpeners are expensed when purchased.
8. The death of the president is not recorded in the accounts.
9. Assets are not stated at their liquidation value. (Do not use cost principle.)

P13–6A   Digital Company purchases merchandise from various foreign companies that require payment in local currencies. Listed below are selected transactions for Digital in 1992.

Prepare journal entries to record transactions involving foreign currency translation, and indicate how to report the foreign exchange gain or loss in the financial statements. (S.O. 6)

Oct. 12   Purchased merchandise on account from Hocht Company, a German firm. The merchandise cost 90,000 German marks and payment is due within 30 days. The exchange rate for the German mark is $0.63.

Nov. 10   Paid German marks to Hocht Company for the purchase made on October 12 at an exchange rate of $0.68.

Instructions

(a) Prepare journal entries to record the transactions for the Digital Company.

(b) Indicate how the foreign exchange gain or loss should be reported in the financial statements.

*B*roadening Your Perspective

FINANCIAL REPORTING PROBLEM

Sue Farino has successfully completed her first accounting course during the spring semester and is now working as a management trainee for First Arizona Bank during the summer. One of her fellow management trainees, Bill Harlow, is taking the same accounting course this summer and has been having a "lot of trouble." On the second examination, for example, Bill Harlow became confused about inventory valuation methods and completely missed all the points on a problem involving LIFO and FIFO.

Bill's instructor recently indicated that the third examination will probably have a number of essay questions dealing with accounting principle issues. Bill is quite concerned about the third examination for two reasons. First, he has never taken an accounting examination where essay answers were required. Second, Bill feels he has to do well on this examination to get an acceptable grade in the course.

Bill has therefore asked Sue to help him prepare for the next examination. Sue agrees, and suggests that Bill develop a set of possible questions on the accounting principles material that they might discuss.

Instructions

Answer the following questions that were developed by Bill.

1. What is a conceptual framework?
2. Why is there a need for a conceptual framework?
3. What are the objectives of financial reporting?
4. If you had to explain generally accepted accounting principles to a nonaccountant, what essential characteristics would you include in your explanation?
5. What are the qualitative characteristics of accounting? Explain each one.
6. Identify the basic assumptions used in accounting.
7. What are two major constraints involved in financial reporting? Explain both of them.

DECISION CASE

Hauck Industries has two operating divisions—Devany Construction Division and German Securities Division. Both divisions maintain their own accounting system and method of revenue recognition.

Devany Construction Division

During the fiscal year ended November 30, 1993, Devany Construction Division had one construction project in process. A $30,000,000 contract for construction of a civic center was granted on June 19, 1993, and construction began on August 1, 1993. Estimated costs of completion at the contract date were $26,000,000 over a two-year time period from the date of the contract. On November 30, 1993, construction costs of $8,000,000 had been incurred. The construction costs to complete the remainder of the project were reviewed on November 30, 1993, and were estimated to amount to only $16,000,000 because of an expected decline in raw materials costs. Revenue recognition is based upon a percentage-of-completion method.

German Securities Division

German Securities Division works through manufacturers' agents in various cities. Orders for alarm systems and down payments are forwarded from agents, and the Division ships the goods f.o.b. factory directly to customers (usually police departments and security guard companies). Customers are billed directly for the balance due plus actual shipping costs. The firm received orders for $6,000,000 of goods during the fiscal year ended November 30, 1993. Down payments of $600,000 were received and goods with a selling price of $5,000,000 were billed and shipped. Actual freight costs of $100,000 were also billed. Commissions of 10% on product price are paid manufacturing agents after goods are shipped to customers. Such goods are warranted for 90 days after shipment, and warranty returns have been about 1% of sales. Revenue is recognized at the point of sale by this division.

Instructions

(a) There are a variety of methods of revenue recognition. Define and describe each of the following methods of revenue recognition and indicate whether each is in accordance with generally accepted accounting principles.
1. Point of sale.
2. Percentage-of-completion.
3. Installment contract.

(b) Compute the revenue to be recognized in fiscal year 1993 for both operating divisions of Hauck Industries in accordance with generally accepted accounting principles.

CRITICAL THINKING CASE

Review the opening story about Catalina Cruz, accounting manager at Long Beach City College, and answer the following questions:

1. Why is the matching principle important in accounting for government grants?

2. Give some examples of grant or special programs that the matching principle might be applied to at your college or university.

3. What are some examples of costs that Long Beach Community College might properly charge to its grant or special programs?

ETHICAL CASE

When the Financial Accounting Standards Board issues new standards, the required implementation date is usually 12 months or more from date of issuance, with early implementation encouraged. Kathy Johnston, accountant at Redondo Corporation, discusses with her financial vice-president the need for early implementation of a recently issued standard that would result in a much fairer presentation of the company's financial condition and earnings. When the financial vice-president determines that early implementation of the standard will adversely affect reported net income for the year, he strongly discourages Kathy from implementing the standard until it is required.

Instructions

(a) Who are the stakeholders in this situation?

(b) What, if any, are the ethical considerations in this situation?

(c) What does Kathy have to gain by advocating early implementation? Who might be affected by the decision against early implementation?

Answers to Self-Study Questions
1. b   2. c   3. b   4. c   5. d   6. b   7. a   8. a   9. c   10. c

Concepts for Review

*Before studying this chapter,
you should know or, if necessary, review:*

a. *The cost principle of accounting. (Ch. 1, p. 13)*

b. *The owner's equity statement. (Ch. 1, p. 24)*

c. *How to make closing entries
and prepare the post-closing
trial balance. (Ch. 4,
p. 139–45)*

d. *The steps in the accounting
cycle. (Ch. 4, p. 146–7)*

e. *The format of classified
financial statements.
(Ch. 4, p. 148–52)*

CHAPTER 14

ACCOUNTING FOR PARTNERSHIPS

Study Objectives

After studying this chapter, you should be able to:

1. Identify the characteristics of the partnership form of business organization.

2. Explain the accounting entries for the formation of a partnership.

3. Identify the bases for dividing net income or net loss.

4. Describe the form and content of partnership financial statements.

5. Explain the effects of the entries when a new partner is admitted.

6. Describe the effects of the entries when a partner withdraws from the firm.

7. Prepare the entries to record the liquidation of a partnership.

T here's a very good chance that you'll become a partner with someone in business or a profession. Doctors, dentists, lawyers, entrepreneurs, and accountants often become partners to share the work, share the profits, and share the risk.

Kenneth Williams has been a partner in the international accounting firm of Coopers & Lybrand for some 20 years. Williams heads up the firm's education audit practice. Why audit a university? "I don't know a university that doesn't have debt outstanding to build buildings or buy equipment," he says. "Also, the trustees have a responsibility to make sure the endowment is handled properly."

CPA firms can help universities cut costs. "A faculty member wanted to change his address because he had moved," he recalls. "It took four approval signoffs and five pieces of paper to get that done." Needless to say, the CPAs suggested a more efficient approach. He notes that schools shouldn't make academic decisions based on *financial considerations—but dollars shouldn't be ignored either. "I made a suggestion to one of my clients, a very small college, to 'direct cost' some of their courses. In the language department, they found that French cost $850 per student, German cost $975 per student and Russian cost $2,300 per student. Only 8 students on campus wanted to take Russian."*

Accounting courses usually have plenty of students—many of whom go on to major in the subject and then apply for work at a big accounting firm. From there, it takes 10–12 years to become a partner. "As a partner, you share in the profits and the losses," says Williams. "By law, I am liable for the actions of my partners."

Partnerships are common in retail establishments and in small manufacturing companies. Similarly, if you enter a profession such as accounting, law, or medicine, you may find it desirable to form a partnership with other professionals in your field. Professional partnerships vary in size from a medical partnership of 3 to 5 doctors to 150 to 200 partners in a large law firm and more than 2,000 partners in a Big Six international accounting firm.

It is not surprising, therefore, that the partnership form of business organization is growing at a fast rate in the United States. In a recent 25-year period, partnerships increased 60% to more than 1.5 million.[1] In this chapter we will discuss the essential features of the partnership form of business organization and explain the major issues in accounting for partnerships.

Characteristics of a Partnership

Study Objective 1

Identify the characteristics of the partnership form of business organization.

The Uniform Partnership Act provides the basic rules for the formation and operation of partnerships in more than 90% of the states. This act defines a **partnership** as "an association of two or more persons to carry on as co-owners of a business for profit." The partnership form of business organization is not restricted to any particular type of business, but it is most often used in relatively small companies and in professional fields, as mentioned above.

The principal characteristics of the partnership form of business organization are pictured in Illustration 14-1.

ILLUSTRATION 14-1

Characteristics of a partnership

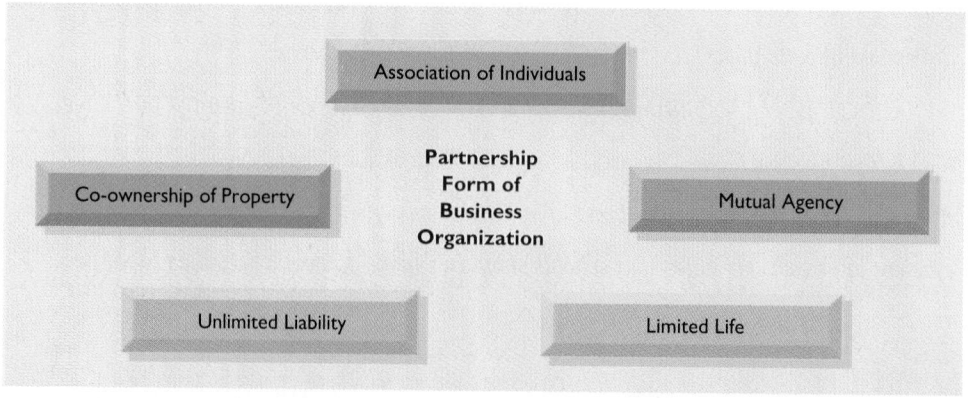

[1]Internal Revenue Service Publication No. 1289, *Source Book: Partnership Returns.*

Association of Individuals

A partnership is a voluntary association of two or more individuals based on a legally binding contract. The contract may be written, oral, or implied. Under the Uniform Partnership Act, a partnership is considered a legal entity for certain purposes. For instance, property (land, buildings, equipment) can be owned in the name of the partnership, and the firm can sue or be sued. **A partnership also represents an accounting entity for financial reporting purposes.** Thus, the purely personal assets, liabilities, and transactions of the partners are excluded from the accounting records of the partnership, just as they are in a proprietorship.

The net income of a partnership is not taxed as a separate entity. However, a partnership is required to file an information tax return showing partnership net income and each partner's share of net income. Each partner's share is taxable at personal tax rates, regardless of the amount of net income withdrawn from the business during the year.

Mutual Agency

Mutual agency means that each partner acts on behalf of the partnership when engaging in partnership business. The act of any partner is binding on all other partners, even when partners act beyond the scope of their authority, so long as the act appears to be appropriate for the partnership. For example, a partner of a grocery store who purchases a delivery truck creates a binding contract in the name of the partnership, even if the partnership agreement denies this authority. On the other hand, if a partner in a law firm purchased a snowmobile for the partnership, such an act would not be binding on the partnership, because it is clearly outside the scope of partnership business.

Helpful hint Because of mutual agency, an individual should be extremely cautious in selecting partners.

Limited Life

A partnership does not have unlimited life. Its continuance as a going concern rests in the partnership contract. A partnership may be ended voluntarily at any time through the acceptance of a new partner into the firm or the withdrawal of a partner. A partnership may be ended involuntarily by the death or incapacity of a partner. Thus the life of a partnership is indefinite. In short, any change in the number of partners, regardless of the cause, effects the dissolution of the partnership. Dissolution does not necessarily mean that the business ends. If the continuing partners agree, operations can continue without interruption by forming a new partnership.

Unlimited Liability

Each partner is personally and individually liable for all partnership liabilities. Creditors' claims attach first to partnership assets and then to the personal resources of any partner, irrespective of that partner's equity in the company. To illustrate, assume that: (1) the Rowe-Sanchez partnership is terminated when the claims of company creditors exceed partnership assets by $30,000, and (2) L. Rowe's personal assets total $40,000 but B. Sanchez has no personal assets. Creditors can collect their total claims from Rowe regardless of Rowe's equity in the firm, even though Sanchez and Rowe may be equal partners. Rowe, in turn, has a legal claim on Sanchez, but this would be worthless under the conditions described. Some states allow **limited partnerships** in which the liability of a partner is limited to the partner's equity. However, there must always be at least one partner with unlimited liability, often referred to as the **general partner.**

Accounting in Action · *Business Insight*

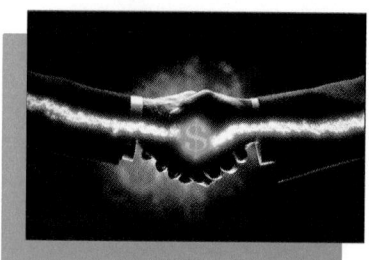

Although limited partnerships limit a partner's liability, they provide no guarantee that a partner will receive a return or for that matter even get back his or her original investment. Thousands of limited partnerships were marketed in the 1980s, involving over $100 billion in investment in just about everything from apartment buildings and office complexes to airliners, oil and gas wells, and cable television systems. Unfortunately the Tax Reform Acts of the 1980s have made these types of investments less attractive and therefore prices have dropped. The problem is further compounded because limited partners who might want to sell have been finding it difficult to find anyone to buy. Those who do buy want low prices and high yields, which means the seller receives substantially less than his or her original investment.

Co-Ownership of Property

Partnership assets are co-owned by the partners. Once assets have been invested in the partnership, they are owned jointly by all the partners. Moreover, if the partnership is terminated, the assets do not legally revert to the original contributor. Each partner has a claim on total assets equal to the balance in his or her respective capital account. This claim does not attach to specific assets that an individual partner may have contributed to the firm.

Similarly, if a partner invests a building valued at $100,000 in the partnership, and the building is sold later at a gain of $20,000, that partner does not personally receive the entire gain. Partnership net income (or net loss) is also co-owned. **If the partnership agreement does not specify to the contrary, all net income or net loss is shared equally by the partners.** As you will see later, however, the partnership agreement may provide for unequal sharing of net income or net loss.

Advantages and Disadvantages of a Partnership

What are the major advantages and disadvantages of a partnership? One major advantage is that the **skills and resources of two or more individuals can be combined**. For example, a large public accounting firm such as Price Waterhouse must have combined expertise in auditing, taxation, and management consulting, not to mention specialists within each of these areas. In addition, a partnership does not have to contend with the "red tape" that a corporation must face. That is, a partnership is **easily formed and is relatively free from governmental regulations and restrictions**. Decisions can be made quickly on substantive matters affecting the firm, whereas in a corporation, formal meetings with the board of directors are often needed.

On the other hand, the major disadvantages of a partnership are **mutual agency**, **limited life**, and **unlimited liability**. Unlimited liability is particularly troublesome to many individuals, because they may lose not only their initial investment but also their personal assets, if they are needed to pay partnership creditors. As a result, it is often difficult to obtain large amounts of investment capital in a partnership. That is one reason why the largest business enterprises in the United States are corporations, not partnerships.

The advantages and disadvantages of the partnership form of business organization are summarized in Illustration 14-2.

ILLUSTRATION 14-2

Advantages and disadvantages of a partnership

Advantages	Disadvantages
Combining skills and resources of two or more individuals	Mutual agency
Ease of formation	Limited life
Freedom from governmental regulations and restrictions	Unlimited liability
Ease of decision making	

The Partnership Agreement

A partnership is created by a contract expressing the voluntary agreement of two or more individuals. The written agreement, often referred to as the partnership agreement or **articles of co-partnership**, contains such basic information as the name and principal location of the firm, the purpose of the business, and date of inception. In addition, different relationships that will exist among the partners, such as the following, should be specified:

1. Names and capital contributions of partners.
2. Rights and duties of partners.
3. Basis for sharing net income or net loss.
4. Provision for withdrawals of assets.
5. Procedures for submitting disputes to arbitration.
6. Procedures for the withdrawal or addition of a partner.
7. Rights and duties of surviving partners in the event of a partner's death.

The importance of a written contract cannot be overemphasized. The agreement should be drawn with care and should attempt to anticipate all possible situations, contingencies, and disagreements. The help of a lawyer is highly desirable in preparing the agreement. A poorly drawn contract may create friction among the partners and eventually cause the termination of the partnership.

Forming a Partnership

Each partner's initial investment in a partnership should be recorded at the **fair market value of the assets at the date of their transfer to the partnership.** The values assigned must be agreed to by all of the partners.

To illustrate, assume that A. Rolfe and T. Shea combine their proprietorships to start a partnership named U.S. Software. The firm will specialize in developing financial modeling software packages. Rolfe and Shea invest in the partnership as follows:

Study Objective 2

Explain the accounting entries for the formation of a partnership.

ILLUSTRATION 14-3

Book and market value of assets invested

	Book Value		Market Value	
	A. Rolfe	T. Shea	A. Rolfe	T. Shea
Cash	$ 8,000	$ 9,000	$ 8,000	$ 9,000
Office equipment	5,000		4,000	
Accumulated depreciation	(2,000)			
Accounts receivable		4,000		4,000
Allowance for doubtful accounts		(700)		(1,000)
	$11,000	$12,300	$12,000	$12,000

Helpful hint The cost principle applies—cash and the fair-market value of non-cash assets.

The entries to record the investments are:

Investment of A. Rolfe

Cash	8,000	
Office Equipment	4,000	
A. Rolfe, Capital		12,000
(To record investment of Rolfe)		

Investment of T. Shea

Cash	9,000	
Accounts Receivable	4,000	
Allowance for Doubtful Accounts		1,000
T. Shea, Capital		12,000
(To record investment of Shea)		

Note that neither the original cost of the equipment ($5,000) nor its book value ($5,000 − $2,000) is recorded by the partnership. The equipment is recorded at its fair market value, $4,000. Since the equipment has not been used by the partnership, there can be no accumulated depreciation. In contrast, the gross claims on customers ($4,000) are carried forward to the partnership, and the allowance for doubtful accounts is adjusted to $1,000 to arrive at a cash (net) realizable value of $3,000. A partnership may start with an Allowance for Doubtful Accounts account, because this balance pertains to existing accounts receivable that are expected to be uncollectible in the future. In addition, this procedure maintains the control and subsidiary relationship between accounts receivable and the customers' ledger.

After the partnership has been formed, the accounting for its transactions is similar to accounting for transactions of any other type of business organization. For example, all transactions with outside parties, such as the purchase or sale of merchandise inventory and the payment or receipt of cash, should be recorded in the same manner for a partnership as for a proprietorship.

The steps in the accounting cycle described in Chapter 4 for a proprietorship also apply to a partnership. For example, it is necessary to prepare a trial balance and to journalize and post adjusting entries. In addition, a work sheet may be used. There are minor differences in journalizing and posting closing entries and in preparing financial statements, as explained in the following sections. The differences occur because there is more than one owner in a partnership.

Before You Go On . . .

1. What are the distinguishing characteristics of a partnership?

2. What are the principal advantages and disadvantages of a partnership?

3. How should a partner's initial investment of assets be valued?

Study Objective 3

Identify the bases for dividing net income or net loss.

Dividing Net Income or Net Loss

Partnership net income or net loss is shared equally unless the partnership contract specifically indicates otherwise. The same basis of division usually applies to both net income and net loss. As a result, it is customary to refer to the basis as the income ratio, the **income and loss ratio**, or the **profit and loss ratio**. Because of its wide acceptance, we will use the term **income ratio** to identify the basis for dividing both net income and net loss. A partner's share of net income or net loss is recognized in the accounts through closing entries.

Closing Entries

As in the case of a proprietorship, four entries are required in preparing closing entries for a partnership. The entries are:

1. Debit each revenue account for its balance and credit Income Summary for total revenues.
2. Debit Income Summary for total expenses and credit each expense account for its balance.
3. Debit Income Summary for its balance and credit each partner's capital account for his or her share of net income. Conversely, credit Income Summary and debit each partner's capital account for his or her share of net loss.
4. Debit each partner's capital account for the balance in that partner's drawing account, and credit each partner's drawing account for the same amount.

The first two entries are the same as in a proprietorship. The last two entries are different because (1) there are two or more owners' capital and drawing accounts and (2) it is necessary to divide net income (or net loss) among the partners.

To illustrate the last two closing entries, we will assume that the AB Company has net income of $32,000 for 1993. The partners, L. Arbor and D. Barnett, share net income and net loss equally, and drawings for the year were Arbor $8,000 and Barnett $6,000. The closing entries are:

Dec. 31	Income Summary	32,000	
	L. Arbor, Capital ($32,000 × 50%)		16,000
	D. Barnett, Capital ($32,000 × 50%)		16,000
	(To transfer net income to owners' capital accounts)		
31	L. Arbor, Capital	8,000	
	D. Barnett, Capital	6,000	
	L. Arbor, Drawing		8,000
	D. Barnett, Drawing		6,000
	(To close drawing accounts to capital accounts)		

ILLUSTRATION 14-4

Closing net income and drawing accounts

Assuming the beginning capital balance is $47,000 for Arbor and $36,000 for Barnett, the capital and drawing accounts will show the following after posting the closing entries:

ILLUSTRATION 14-5

Partners' capital and drawing accounts after closing

L. Arbor, Capital			D. Barnett, Capital		
12/31 Clos. 8,000	1/1 Bal. 47,000		12/31 Clos. 6,000	1/1 Bal. 36,000	
	12/31 Clos. 16,000			12/31 Clos. 16,000	
	12/31 Bal. 55,000			12/31 Bal. 46,000	

L. Arbor, Drawing			D. Barnett, Drawing		
12/31 Bal. 8,000	12/31 Clos. 8,000		12/31 Bal. 6,000	12/31 Clos. 6,000	

As in a proprietorship, the partners' capital accounts are permanent accounts; the partners' drawing accounts are temporary accounts. Normally, the capital accounts will have credit balances and the drawing accounts will have debit balances. Drawing accounts are debited when partners withdraw cash or other assets from the partnership for personal use. For example, the partnership agreement may permit each partner to withdraw cash monthly for personal living expenses.

Income Ratios

As indicated earlier, the partnership agreement should specify the basis for sharing net income or net loss. The following are typical of the ratios that may be used.

1. A fixed ratio, expressed as a proportion (6:4), a percentage (70% and 30%), or a fraction (2/3 and 1/3).
2. A ratio based either on capital balances at the beginning of the year or on average capital balances during the year.
3. Salaries to partners and the remainder on a fixed ratio.
4. Interest on partners' capitals and the remainder on a fixed ratio.
5. Salaries to partners, interest on partners' capitals, and the remainder on a fixed ratio.

The objective is to reach agreement on a basis that will equitably reflect the differences among partners in terms of their capital investment and service to the partnership.

A fixed ratio is easy to apply, and it may be an equitable basis in some circumstances. Assume, for example, that Hughes and Lane are partners. Each contributes the same amount of capital, but Hughes expects to work full-time in the partnership and Lane expects to work only half-time. Accordingly, the partners agree to a fixed ratio of 2/3 to Hughes and 1/3 to Lane.

A ratio based on capital balances may be appropriate when the funds invested in the partnership are considered the critical factor. Capital balances may also be equitable when a manager is hired to run the business and the partners do not plan to take an active role in daily operations.

The three remaining ratios (3, 4, and 5) give specific recognition to differences that may exist among partners. These ratios provide salary allowances for time worked and interest allowances for capital invested. Then, any remaining net income or net loss is allocated on a fixed ratio. Some caution needs to be exercised in working with these types of income ratios. These ratios pertain exclusively to the computations that are required in dividing net income or net loss.

Accounting in Action · *Business Insight*

Partners in professional firms can and do make substantial incomes. For example, take public accounting. In one large international public accounting firm, the average earnings of all partners in a recent year was $175,000 and the individual earnings of the five most highly compensated partners ranged from $400,000 to $800,000. Note, however, that the compensation of partners in most large partnerships differs in both form and substance from the compensation of a corporate executive. Partners are not guaranteed an annual salary. Compensation is entirely dependent upon each year's operating results. Substantial investment is required of each partner. This capital is at risk for the partner's entire career—often 25–30 years—without an established return and is repayable on leaving without adjustment for inflation or appreciation in value.

Salaries to partners and interest on partners' capitals are not expenses of the partnership. Therefore, these items do not enter into the matching of expenses with revenues and the determination of net income or net loss. For a partnership, as well as for other entities, salaries expense pertains to the cost of services performed by employees, and interest expense relates to the cost of borrowing money from creditors. Partners in their ownership capacity are not considered either **employees** or **creditors**. Thus, when the income ratio includes a salary allowance for partners, some partnership agreements permit the partner to make monthly withdrawals of cash based on their "salary." In such cases, the withdrawals are debited to the partner's drawing account.

Salaries, Interest, and Remainder on a Fixed Ratio

Under this income ratio the provisions for salaries and interest must be applied **before** the remainder is allocated on the specified fixed ratio. **This is true even if the provisions exceed net income or the partnership has suffered a net loss for the year.** Detailed information concerning the division of net income or net loss should be shown at the bottom of the income statement.

To illustrate this income ratio, assume that Sara King and Ray Lee are co-partners in the Kingslee Company. The partnership agreement provides for (1) salary allowances of $8,400 to King and $6,000 to Lee, (2) interest allowances of 10% on capital balances at the beginning of the year, and (3) the remainder equally. Capital balances on January 1 were King, $28,000, and Lee, $24,000. In 1993, partnership net income is $22,000. The division of net income is as follows:

ILLUSTRATION 14-6

Income statement with division of net income

KINGSLEE COMPANY
Income Statement
For the Year Ended December 31, 1993

	Sales	$200,000
	Net income	$ 22,000

Division of Net Income

	Sara King	Ray Lee	Total
Salary allowance	$ 8,400	$6,000	$14,400
Interest allowance			
Sara King ($28,000 × 10%)	2,800		
Ray Lee ($24,000 × 10%)		2,400	
Total interest			5,200
Total salaries and interest	11,200	8,400	19,600
Remaining income, $2,400			
($22,000 − $19,600)			
Sara King ($2,400 × 50%)	1,200		
Ray Lee ($2,400 × 50%)		1,200	
Total remainder			2,400
Total division	$12,400	$9,600	$22,000

The entry to record the division of net income is:

Dec. 31	Income Summary	22,000	
	Sara King, Capital		12,400
	Ray Lee, Capital		9,600
	(To close net income to partners' capitals)		

To illustrate a situation in which the salary and interest allowances exceed net income, assume that net income in the Kingslee Company is only $18,000. In this case, the salary and interest allowances will create a deficiency of $1,600 ($19,600 − $18,000). Since the computations of the allowances are the same as those in the preceding example, we will begin the division of net income with total salaries and interest as follows:

ILLUSTRATION 14-7

Division of net income—income deficiency

	Sara King	Ray Lee	Total
Total salaries and interest	$11,200	$8,400	$19,600
Remaining deficiency ($1,600)			
($18,000 − $19,600)			
Sara King ($1,600 × 50%)	(800)		
Ray Lee ($1,600 × 50%)		(800)	
Total remainder			(1,600)
Total division	$10,400	$7,600	$18,000

Partnership Financial Statements

Study Objective 4

Describe the form and content of partnership financial statements.

The financial statements of a partnership are similar to those of a proprietorship. The differences are related to the fact that a number of owners are involved in a partnership. The income statement for a partnership is identical to the income statement for a proprietorship except for the division of net income, as shown earlier.

The owners' equity statement for a partnership is called the **partners' capital statement**. Its function is to explain the changes in each partner's capital account and in total partnership capital during the year. As in a proprietorship, changes in capital may result from three causes: additional capital investment, drawings, and net income or net loss.

The partners' capital statement for the Kingslee Company shown below is based on the division of $22,000 of net income in Illustration 14-6. The statement includes assumed data for the additional investment and drawings.

ILLUSTRATION 14-8

Partners' capital statement

KINGSLEE COMPANY
Partners' Capital Statement
For the Year Ended December 31, 1993

	Sara King	Ray Lee	Total
Capital, January 1	$28,000	$24,000	$52,000
Add: Additional investment	2,000		2,000
Net income	12,400	9,600	22,000
	42,400	33,600	76,000
Less: Drawings	7,000	5,000	12,000
Capital, December 31	$35,400	$28,600	$64,000

Helpful hint As in a proprietorship, owner's capital may change from (1) additional investment, (2) drawings, and (3) net income or loss.

The partners' capital statement is prepared from the income statement and the partners' capital and drawing accounts.

The balance sheet for a partnership is the same as for a proprietorship except in the owner's equity section. In a partnership, the capital balances of each partner are shown in the balance sheet. The owners' equity section for Kingslee Company would show the following:

KINGSLEE COMPANY Partial Balance Sheet December 31, 1993		
Total liabilities (assumed amount)		$115,000
Owners' equity		
Sara King, Capital	$35,400	
Ray Lee, Capital	28,600	
Total owners' equity		64,000
Total liabilities and owners' equity		$179,000

ILLUSTRATION 14-9

Owners' equity section of a partnership balance sheet

Before You Go On . . .

1. What are the closing entries for a partnership?

2. What income ratios may be used in a partnership?

3. How do partnership financial statements differ from proprietorship financial statements?

Admission of a Partner

The admission of a new partner results in the legal dissolution of the existing partnership and the beginning of a new partnership. From an economic standpoint, however, the admission of a new partner (or partners) may be of minor significance in the continuity of the business. For example, in large public accounting or law firms, partners are admitted annually without any change in operating policies established by the continuing partners. **To recognize the economic effects, it is necessary only to open a capital account for each new partner.** The entries described and illustrated below are based on the assumption that the accounting records of the predecessor firm will continue to be used by the new partnership.

A new partner may be admitted either by (1) purchasing the interest of one or more existing partners, or (2) investing assets in the partnership. The former affects only the capital accounts of the partners who are parties to the transaction. The latter increases both net assets (total assets less total liabilities) and total capital of the partnership.

Study Objective 5

Explain the effects of the entries when a new partner is admitted.

Purchase of a Partner's Interest

The admission of a partner by purchase of an interest in the firm is a personal transaction between one or more existing partners and the new partner. Each party is acting as an individual separate from the partnership entity. The price paid is negotiated and determined by the individuals involved. It may be equal to or different from the capital equity acquired. The amount of the purchase price passes directly from the new partner to the partners who are giving up part or all of their ownership claims. Any money or other consideration exchanged is the personal property of the participants and *not* the property of the partnership. Upon purchase of an interest, the new partner acquires each selling partner's capital interest and income ratio. A partner does not have to obtain the approval of the other partners to sell his or her interest. However, the Uniform Partnership Act provides that the purchaser does not become a partner until he or she is accepted into the firm by the continuing partners.

Helpful hint In a purchase of an interest, the partnership is **not** a participant in the transaction. For example, no cash is distributed from the partnership.

Accounting for the purchase of an interest is straightforward. As far as the partnership is concerned, only the realignment of partners' capital is recorded. **Each partner's capital account is debited for the ownership claims that have been relinquished, and the new partner's capital account is credited with the capital equity purchased.** Total assets, total liabilities, and total capital remain unchanged, as do all individual asset and liability accounts.

To illustrate, assume that L. Carson agrees to pay $10,000 each to C. Ames and D. Barker for one-third of their interest in the Ames–Barker partnership. At the time of the admission of Carson, each partner has a $30,000 capital balance. Both partners, therefore, give up $10,000 of their capital equity. The entry to record the admission of Carson is:

C. Ames, Capital	10,000	
D. Barker, Capital	10,000	
L. Carson, Capital		20,000
(To record admission of Carson by purchase)		

ILLUSTRATION 14-10

Ledger balances after purchase of a partner's interest

The effect of this entry on net assets and partners' capital is shown below:

Net Assets		C. Ames, Capital		D. Barker, Capital		L. Carson, Capital	
60,000		10,000	30,000	10,000	30,000		20,000
			Bal. 20,000		Bal. 20,000		

Note that net assets remain unchanged at $60,000 and each partner has a $20,000 capital balance. Note also that Ames and Barker continue as partners in the firm but each has a different capital interest.

Regardless of the amount paid by Carson for the one-third interest, the entry above would be exactly the same. For example, if Carson pays $12,000 each to Ames and Barker for a one-third interest in the partnership, the foregoing entry is still made. The cash paid by Carson goes directly to the individual partners and not to the partnership.

Investment of Assets in a Partnership

The admission of a partner by an investment of assets is a transaction between the new partner and the partnership. Often referred to simply as admission by investment, the transaction increases both the net assets and total capital of the partnership. To illustrate, assume that instead of purchasing an interest, Carson invests $30,000 in cash in the Ames–Barker partnership for a 1/3 capital interest. In such a case, the entry is:

Cash	30,000	
L. Carson, Capital		30,000
(To record admission of new partner)		

ILLUSTRATION 14-11

Ledger balances after investment of assets

The effects of this transaction on the partnership accounts may be shown as follows:

Net Assets		C. Ames, Capital		D. Barker, Capital		L. Carson, Capital	
60,000			30,000		30,000		30,000
30,000							
Bal. 90,000							

Note that both assets and total capital have increased by $30,000.

Remember that Carson's 1/3 capital interest might not result in a 1/3 income ratio. Carson's income ratio should be specified in the new partnership agreement, and it may or may not be equal to the 1/3 capital interest.

The different effects between the purchase of an interest and admission by investment are shown in the comparison of the net assets and capital balances in Illustration 14-12.

ILLUSTRATION 14-12

Comparison of purchase of an interest and admission by investment

Purchase of an Interest		Admission by Investment	
Net Assets	$60,000	Net Assets	$90,000
Capital		Capital	
C. Ames	$20,000	C. Ames	$30,000
D. Barker	20,000	D. Barker	30,000
L. Carson	20,000	L. Carson	30,000
Total capital	$60,000	Total capital	$90,000

When an interest is purchased, the total net assets and total capital of the partnership do not change. However, when a partner is admitted by investment, both the total net assets and the total capital change.

In the case of admission by investment, further complications occur when the new partner's investment differs from the capital equity acquired. When those amounts are not the same, the difference is considered a bonus either to (1) the existing (old) partners or (2) the new partner.

Bonus to Old Partners

The existing partners may be unwilling to admit a new partner without receiving a bonus for both personal and business reasons. In an established firm, existing partners may insist on a bonus as compensation for the personal sacrifices they have made for the company over the years. Two accounting-related factors underlie the business reason. First, total partners' capital equals the **book value** of the recorded net assets of the partnership. At the time the new partner is admitted, the fair market values of assets such as land and buildings may be higher than their book values. Second, when the partnership has been profitable, goodwill may exist. However, the goodwill will not be recorded or included in total partners' capital. In such cases the new partner is usually willing to pay the bonus to become a partner.

A bonus to old partners results when the new partner's capital credit on the date of admittance is less than his or her investment in the firm. The bonus results in **an increase in the capital balances of the old partners that is allocated to them on the basis of their income ratios before the admission of the new partner.**

To illustrate, assume that the Bart–Cohen partnership owned by Sam Bart and Tom Cohen has a total capital of $120,000 when Lea Eden is admitted to the partnership. Lea acquires a 25% ownership (capital) interest by making a cash investment of $80,000 in the partnership. The procedure for determining Eden's capital credit and the bonus to the old partners is as follows:

1. **Determine the total capital of the new partnership** by adding the new partner's investment to the total capital of the old partnership. In this case the total capital of the new firm is $200,000, computed as follows:

Total capital of existing partnership	$120,000
Investment by new partner, Eden	80,000
Total capital of new partnership	$200,000

Helpful hint (1) The debit to Cash is greater than the new partner's capital credit. (2) Credits to old partner's capitals are needed for equal debits and credits.

2. **Determine the new partner's capital credit** by multiplying the total capital of the new partnership by the new partner's ownership interest. Eden's capital credit is $50,000 ($200,000 × 25%).

3. **Determine the amount of bonus** by subtracting the new partner's capital credit from the new partner's investment. The bonus in this case is $30,000 ($80,000 − $50,000).

4. **Allocate the bonus to the old partners on the basis of their income ratios.** Assuming the ratios are Bart, 60%, and Cohen, 40%, the allocation is: Bart, $18,000 ($30,000 × 60%) and Cohen, $12,000 ($30,000 × 40%).

The entry to record the admission of Eden is:

Cash	80,000	
Sam Bart, Capital		18,000
Tom Cohen, Capital		12,000
Lea Eden, Capital		50,000
(To record admission of Eden and bonus to old partners)		

Bonus to New Partner

A bonus to a new partner results when the new partner's capital credit is greater than his or her investment of assets in the firm. This may occur when the new partner possesses resources or special attributes that are desired by the partnership. For example, when bank interest rates are high, the new partner may be able to supply cash that is urgently needed for expansion or to meet maturing debts. Alternatively, the new partner may be a recognized expert or authority in a relevant field. Thus, an engineering firm may be willing to give a world-renowned engineer a bonus to join the firm. Similarly, the partners of a sporting goods store may offer a bonus to a sports celebrity in order to add the athlete's name to the partnership name. A bonus to a new partner may also result when recorded book values on the partnership books are higher than their market values.

A bonus to a new partner results in a **decrease in the capital balances of the old partners based on their income ratios before the admission of the new partner**. To illustrate, assume that Lea Eden invests $20,000 in cash for a 25% ownership interest in the Bart–Cohen partnership. Using the procedures described in the preceding section, the computations for Eden's capital credit and the bonus are as follows:

ILLUSTRATION 14-13

Computation of capital credit and bonus to new partner

1.	Total capital of Bart–Cohen partnership		$120,000
	Investment by new partner, Eden		20,000
	Total capital of new partnership		$140,000
2.	Eden's capital credit (25% × $140,000)		$ 35,000
3.	Bonus to Eden ($35,000 − $20,000)		$ 15,000
4.	Allocation of bonus:		
	Bart ($15,000 × 60%)	$9,000	
	Cohen ($15,000 × 40%)	6,000	$ 15,000

The entry to record the admission of Eden is as follows:

Cash	20,000	
Sam Bart, Capital	9,000	
Tom Cohen, Capital	6,000	
Lea Eden, Capital		35,000
(To record Eden's admission and bonus)		

Withdrawal of a Partner

A partner may withdraw from a partnership **voluntarily** by selling his or her equity in the firm or **involuntarily** by reaching mandatory retirement age or dying. The withdrawal of a partner, like the admission of a partner, legally dissolves the partnership. The legal effects may be recognized in accounting for a withdrawal by dissolving the firm. However, it is customary to record only the economic effects. As indicated earlier, the partnership agreement should specify the terms of withdrawal. The withdrawal of a partner may be accomplished by (1) payment from partners' personal assets or (2) payment from partnership assets. The former affects only the partners' capital accounts. The latter decreases total net assets and total capital of the partnership.

> **Study Objective 6**
>
> *Describe the effects of the entries when a partner withdraws from the firm.*

Payment from Partners' Personal Assets

The withdrawal of a partner when payment is made from partners' personal assets is the direct opposite of admitting a new partner who purchases a partner's interest. Payment from partners' personal assets is a personal transaction between the partners. Payment to the retiring partner is made directly from the remaining partners' personal assets. Partnership assets are not involved in any way, and total capital does not change. Thus, the effect on the partnership is limited to a realignment of the partners' capital balances.

To illustrate, assume that Anne Morz, Mary Nead, and Jill Odom have capital balances of $25,000, $15,000, and $10,000, respectively, when Morz and Nead agree to buy out Odom's interest. Each of them agrees to pay Odom $8,000 in exchange for one-half of Odom's total interest of $10,000. The entry to record the withdrawal is:

Jill Odom, Capital	10,000	
Anne Morz, Capital		5,000
Mary Nead, Capital		5,000
(To record purchase of Odom's interest)		

Helpful hint If each purchaser acquires one-fourth of Odom's total interest, the debit becomes $5,000 and the credits $2,500.

ILLUSTRATION 14-14

Ledger balances after payment from partners' personal assets

The effect of this entry on the partnership accounts is shown below:

Net Assets		Anne Morz, Capital		Mary Nead, Capital		Jill Odom, Capital	
50,000			25,000		15,000	10,000	10,000
			5,000		5,000		Bal. –0–
		Bal. 30,000		Bal. 20,000			

Note that net assets and total capital remain the same at $50,000. Note also that the $16,000 paid to Odom is not recorded. Odom's capital is debited only for $10,000, not for the $16,000 that she received. Similarly, both Morz and Nead credit their capital accounts for only $5,000, not the $8,000 they each paid. Morz and Nead will share net income or net loss equally unless they specifically indicate another income ratio in the partnership agreement.

Payment from Partnership Assets

Using partnership assets to pay for a withdrawing partner's interest is the reverse of admitting a partner through the investment of assets in the partnership. Payment from partnership assets is a transaction that involves the partnership. Both partnership net assets and total capital are decreased.

Many partnership agreements provide that the amount paid should be based on the fair market value of the assets at the time of the partner's withdrawal. When this basis is required, some accountants maintain that any differences between recorded asset balances and their fair market values should be (1) recorded by an adjusting entry and (2) allocated to all partners on the basis of their income ratios. There are serious flaws in this position. Recording the revaluations violates the cost principle, which requires that assets be stated at original cost. It also is a departure from the going-concern assumption, which assumes the entity will continue indefinitely. The terms of the partnership contract should not dictate the accounting for the event.

In accounting for a withdrawal by payment from partnership assets:

1. Asset revaluations should not be recorded.
2. Any difference between the amount paid and the withdrawing partner's capital balance should be considered a bonus to the retiring partner or a bonus to the remaining partners.

Bonus to Retiring Partner

A bonus may be paid to a retiring partner when (1) the fair market value of partnership assets is more than their book value; (2) there is unrecorded goodwill resulting from the partnership's superior earnings record; or (3) the remaining partners are anxious to remove the partner from the firm. **The bonus is deducted from the remaining partners' capital balances on the basis of their income ratios at the time of the withdrawal.**

To illustrate, assume that the following capital balances exist in the RST partnership: Fred Roman $50,000, Dee Sand $30,000, and Betty Terk $20,000. The partners share income in the ratio of 3:2:1, respectively. Terk retires from the partnership and receives a cash payment of $25,000 from the firm. The procedure for determining the bonus to the retiring partner and the allocation of the bonus to the remaining partners is as follows:

1. **Determine the amount of the bonus** by subtracting the retiring partner's capital balance from the cash paid by the partnership. The bonus in this case is $5,000 ($25,000 − $20,000).
2. **Allocate the bonus to the remaining partners on the basis of their income ratios.** The ratios of Roman and Sand are 3:2. Thus, the allocation of the $5,000 bonus is: Roman $3,000 ($5,000 × 3/5) and Sand $2,000 ($5,000 × 2/5).

The entry to record the withdrawal of Terk is:

Betty Terk, Capital	20,000	
Fred Roman, Capital	3,000	
Dee Sand, Capital	2,000	
Cash		25,000
(To record withdrawal of and bonus to Terk)		

The remaining partners, Roman and Sand, will recover the bonus given to Terk as the undervalued assets are sold or used in the partnership.

Bonus to Remaining Partners

The retiring partner may give a bonus to the remaining partners when (1) recorded assets are overvalued, (2) the partnership has a poor earnings record, or (3) the partner is anxious to leave the partnership. In such cases, the cash paid to the retiring partner will be less than the retiring partner's capital balance. The bonus will be allocated (credited) to the capital accounts of the remaining partners on the basis of their income ratios.

To illustrate, assume that, instead of the example above, Terk is paid only $16,000 for her $20,000 equity upon withdrawing from the RST partnership. In such case:

1. The bonus to remaining partners is $4,000 ($20,000 − $16,000).
2. The allocation of the $4,000 bonus is: Roman $2,400 ($4,000 × 3/5) and Sand $1,600 ($4,000 × 2/5).

The entry to record the withdrawal is:

Betty Terk, Capital	20,000	
Fred Roman, Capital		2,400
Dee Sand, Capital		1,600
Cash		16,000
(To record withdrawal of Terk and bonus to remaining partners)		

It is important to note that if Sand had withdrawn from the partnership, any bonus would be divided between Roman and Terk on the basis of their income ratio which is 3:1 or 75% and 25%.

Death of a Partner

The death of a partner dissolves the partnership, but provision generally is made for the surviving partners to continue operations. When a partner dies, it usually is necessary to determine the partner's equity at the date of death. This is done by (1) determining the net income or loss for the year to date, (2) closing the books, and (3) preparing financial statements. The partnership agreement may also require an audit of the financial statements by independent auditors and a revaluation of assets by an independent appraisal firm.

The surviving partners may agree either to (1) purchase the deceased partner's equity from their personal assets or (2) use partnership assets to settle with the deceased partner's estate. In both instances, the entries to record the withdrawal of the partner are similar to those presented in previous illustrations.

To facilitate the payment from partnership assets, some companies obtain life insurance policies on each partner with the partnership as the beneficiary. The proceeds from the insurance policy on the deceased partner are then used to settle with the estate.

Liquidation of a Partnership

The liquidation of a partnership terminates the business. It entails selling the assets of the firm, paying liabilities, and distributing any remaining assets to the partners. Liquidation may result from the sale of the business by mutual agreement of the partners, from the death of a partner, or from bankruptcy. In contrast to the dissolution of a partnership, liquidation ends both the legal and economic life of the entity.

From an accounting standpoint, liquidation should be preceded by completing the accounting cycle for the partnership for the final operating period. This includes preparing adjusting entries and financial statements. It also involves preparing closing entries and a post-closing trial balance. Thus, only balance sheet accounts should be open as the liquidation process begins.

Study Objective 7

Prepare the entries to record the liquidation of a partnership.

The liquidation process may occur at a specific point in time or it may occur over a period of time. In liquidation, the sale of noncash assets for cash is called **realization**, and the difference between book value and the cash proceeds is called the **gain or loss on realization**. To liquidate a partnership, it is necessary to:

Helpful hint These steps are indispensable to correct homework and examination results.

1. Sell noncash assets for cash and recognize a gain or loss on realization.
2. Allocate the gain or loss on realization to the partners on their income ratios.
3. Pay partnership liabilities in cash.
4. Distribute remaining cash to partners on the basis of their capital balances.

Each of the steps must be performed in sequence because creditors must be paid before partners receive any cash distributions. Each step also must be recorded by an accounting entry.

When a partnership is liquidated, all partners may have credit balances in their capital accounts (no capital deficiency) or at least one partner's capital account may have a debit balance (a capital deficiency). To illustrate each of these conditions, assume that the Ace Company is liquidated when its ledger shows the following assets, liabilities, and owners' equity accounts.

ILLUSTRATION 14-15

Account balances prior to liquidation

Assets		Liabilities and Owners' Equity	
Cash	$ 5,000	Notes payable	$15,000
Accounts receivable	15,000	Accounts payable	16,000
Inventory	18,000	R. Arnet, Capital	15,000
Equipment	35,000	P. Carey, Capital	17,800
Accum. depr.—equipment	(8,000)	W. Eaton, Capital	1,200
	$65,000		$65,000

No Capital Deficiency

By mutual agreement of the partners, the company is liquidated. The agreement provides for (1) a cash sale of the noncash assets of the partnership to Jackson Enterprises for $75,000, and (2) payment of partnership liabilities by the partnership. The income ratios of the partners are 3:2:1, respectively. The steps in the liquidation process are as follows:

1. The noncash assets (accounts receivable, inventory, and equipment) are sold for $75,000. Since the book value of these assets is $60,000 ($15,000 + $18,000 + $35,000 − $8,000), a gain of $15,000 is realized on the sale. The entry is:

(1)

Cash	75,000	
Accumulated Depreciation—Equipment	8,000	
Accounts Receivable		15,000
Inventory		18,000
Equipment		35,000
Gain on Realization		15,000
(To record realization of noncash assets)		

2. The gain on realization of $15,000 is allocated to the partners on their income ratios, which are 3:2:1. The entry is:

(2)

Gain on Realization	15,000	
R. Arnet, Capital ($15,000 × 3/6)		7,500
P. Carey, Capital ($15,000 × 2/6)		5,000
W. Eaton, Capital ($15,000 × 1/6)		2,500
(To allocate gain to partners' capitals)		

Helpful hint Unless the partnership agreement states to the contrary, the income ratio also applies to realization gains and losses.

3. Partnership liabilities consist of Notes Payable $15,000 and Accounts Payable $16,000. Creditors are paid in full by a cash payment of $31,000. The entry is:

(3)

Notes Payable	15,000	
Accounts Payable	16,000	
Cash		31,000
(To record payment of partnership liabilities)		

4. The remaining cash is distributed to the partners on the basis of **their capital balances**. After the entries in the first three steps are posted, all partnership accounts, including Gain on Realization, will have zero balances except for four accounts: Cash $49,000; R. Arnet, Capital $22,500; P. Carey, Capital $22,800; and W. Eaton, Capital $3,700, as shown below:

ILLUSTRATION 14-16

Ledger accounts before distribution of cash

Cash					R. Arnet, Capital				P. Carey, Capital				W. Eaton, Capital		
Bal.	5,000	(3)	31,000			Bal.	15,000			Bal.	17,800			Bal.	1,200
(1)	75,000					(2)	7,500			(2)	5,000			(2)	2,500
Bal.	**49,000**					**Bal.**	**22,500**			**Bal.**	**22,800**			**Bal.**	**3,700**

The entry to record the distribution of cash is as follows:

(4)

R. Arnet, Capital	22,500	
P. Carey, Capital	22,800	
W. Eaton, Capital	3,700	
Cash		49,000
(To record distribution of cash to partners)		

After this entry is posted, all partnership accounts will have zero balances, as shown in Illustration 14-17.

ILLUSTRATION 14-17

Partnership accounts after distribution of cash

Cash				R. Arnet, Capital				P. Carey, Capital				W. Eaton, Capital			
Bal.	5,000	(3)	31,000	(4)	22,500	Bal.	15,000	(4)	22,800	Bal.	17,800	(4)	3,700	Bal.	1,200
(1)	75,000	(4)	49,000			(2)	7,500			(2)	5,000			(2)	2,500
Bal.	**–0–**					**Bal.**	**–0–**			**Bal.**	**–0–**			**Bal.**	**–0–**

A word of caution: **Cash should not be distributed to partners on the basis of their income-sharing ratios.** On this basis, for example, Arnet would receive three-sixths, or $24,500, which would produce an erroneous debit balance of $2,000. The income ratio is a proper basis for allocating net income or loss, but it is not a proper basis for making the final distribution of cash to the partners.

Helpful hint Zero balances after posting is a quick proof of the accuracy of the cash distribution entry.

Schedule of Cash Payments

Some accountants prepare a cash payments schedule to determine the distribution of cash to the partners in the liquidation of a partnership. The schedule of cash payments, sometimes called a **safe cash payments schedule**, is organized around the basic accounting equation. The schedule for the Ace Company is shown in Illustration 14-18. The numbers in parentheses refer to the four required steps in the liquidation of a partnership. They also identify the accounting entries that must be made. The cash payments schedule is especially useful when the liquidation process extends over a period of time.

ILLUSTRATION 14-18

Schedule of cash payments, no capital deficiency

ACE COMPANY Schedule of Cash Payments													
Item		Cash	+	Noncash Assets	=	Liabilities	+	R. Arnet Capital	+	P. Carey Capital	+	W. Eaton Capital	
Balances before liquidation		5,000	+	60,000	=	31,000	+	15,000	+	17,800	+	1,200	
Sales of noncash assets and allocation of gain	(1)&(2)	75,000	+	(60,000)	=			7,500	+	5,000	+	2,500	
New balances		80,000	+	-0-	=	31,000	+	22,500	+	22,800	+	3,700	
Pay liabilities	(3)	(31,000)			=	(31,000)							
New balances		49,000	+	-0-	=	-0-	+	22,500	+	22,800	+	3,700	
Cash distribution to partners	(4)	(49,000)			=			(22,500)	+	(22,800)	+	(3,700)	
Final balances		-0-		-0-		-0-		-0-		-0-		-0-	

Capital Deficiency

A capital deficiency may be caused by net losses or excessive drawings before liquidation or by losses suffered during liquidation. To illustrate, assume that Ace Company is on the brink of bankruptcy. The partners decide to liquidate and proceed to have a "going-out-of-business" sale in which merchandise is sold at substantial discounts, and the equipment is sold at auction. Cash proceeds from these sales and collections from customers total only $42,000. Accordingly, the loss from liquidation is $18,000 ($60,000 − $42,000).

1. The entry for the realization of noncash assets is:

(1)		
Cash	42,000	
Accumulated Depreciation—Equipment	8,000	
Loss on Realization	18,000	
Accounts Receivable		15,000
Inventory		18,000
Equipment		35,000
(To record realization of noncash assets)		

2. The loss on realization is allocated to the partners on the basis of their income ratios. The entry is:

(2)		
R. Arnet, Capital ($18,000 × 3/6)	9,000	
P. Carey, Capital ($18,000 × 2/6)	6,000	
W. Eaton, Capital ($18,000 × 1/6)	3,000	
Loss on Realization		18,000
(To allocate loss on realization to partners)		

3. Partnership liabilities are paid. This entry is the same as in the previous example.

(3)

Notes Payable	15,000	
Accounts Payable	16,000	
Cash		31,000
(To record payment of partnership liabilities)		

4. After posting the three entries, two accounts will have debit balances—Cash, $16,000, and W. Eaton, Capital, $1,800—and two accounts will have credit balances—R. Arnet, Capital, $6,000, and P. Carey, Capital, $11,800, as shown below:

ILLUSTRATION 14-19

Ledger accounts before distribution of cash

Cash				R. Arnet, Capital				P. Carey, Capital				W. Eaton, Capital			
Bal.	5,000	(3)	31,000	(2)	9,000	Bal.	15,000	(2)	6,000	Bal.	17,800	(2)	3,000	Bal.	1,200
(1)	42,000					Bal.	6,000			Bal.	11,800	Bal.	1,800		
Bal.	16,000														

Eaton has a capital deficiency of $1,800. Eaton, therefore, owes the partnership $1,800, and Arnet and Carey have a legally enforceable claim against Eaton's personal assets. The distribution of cash is still made on the basis of capital balances. However, the amount will vary depending on the manner in which the deficiency is settled.

Payment of Deficiency

If the partner with the capital deficiency pays the amount owed the partnership, the deficiency is eliminated. To illustrate, assume that Eaton pays $1,800 to the partnership. The entry is:

(a)

Cash	1,800	
W. Eaton, Capital		1,800
(Payment of capital deficiency by Eaton)		

ILLUSTRATION 14-20

Ledger balances after paying capital deficiency

After posting this entry, account balances are as follows:

Cash				R. Arnet, Capital				P. Carey, Capital				W. Eaton, Capital			
Bal.	5,000	(3)	31,000	(2)	9,000	Bal.	15,000	(2)	6,000	Bal.	17,800	(2)	3,000	Bal.	1,200
(1)	42,000					Bal.	6,000			Bal.	11,800			(a)	1,800
(a)	1,800													Bal.	-0-
Bal.	17,800														

The cash balance of $17,800 is now equal to the credit balances in the capital accounts (Arnet $6,000 + Carey $11,800), and cash is distributed on the basis of these balances. The entry is:

R. Arnet, Capital	6,000	
P. Carey, Capital	11,800	
Cash		17,800
(To record distribution of cash to the partners)		

After this entry is posted, all accounts will have zero balances.

Nonpayment of Deficiency

If a partner with a capital deficiency is unable to pay the amount owed to the partnership, the partners with credit balances must absorb the loss. The loss is allocated on the basis of the income ratios that exist between the partners with credit balances. The income ratios of Arnet and Carey are 3:2 or 3/5 and 2/5, respectively. Thus, the following entry is made to remove Eaton's capital deficiency:

(a)

R. Arnet, Capital ($1,800 × 3/5)	1,080	
P. Carey, Capital ($1,800 × 2/5)	720	
W. Eaton, Capital		1,800
(To record write-off of capital deficiency)		

ILLUSTRATION 14-21

Ledger balances after non-payment of capital deficiency

After posting this entry, the cash and capital accounts will have the following balances:

Cash				R. Arnet, Capital				P. Carey, Capital				W. Eaton, Capital			
Bal.	5,000	(3)	31,000	(2)	9,000	Bal.	15,000	(2)	6,000	Bal.	17,800	(2)	3,000	Bal.	1,200
(1)	42,000			(a)	1,080			(a)	720					(a)	1,800
Bal.	16,000					Bal.	4,920			Bal.	11,080			Bal.	–0–

The cash balance of $16,000 now equals the sum of the credit balances in the capital accounts (Arnet $4,920 + Carey $11,080). The entry to record the distribution of cash is:

R. Arnet, Capital	4,920	
P. Carey, Capital	11,080	
Cash		16,000
(To record distribution of cash to partners)		

After this entry is posted, all accounts will have zero balances.

Before You Go On . . .

1. How does the accounting for admission by purchase of an interest differ from investing assets in the partnership?

2. Contrast the accounting effects of the withdrawal of a partner by payment from (a) personal assets and (b) partnership assets.

3. What basis is used in the liquidation of a partnership in (a) allocating gain or loss on realization and (b) distributing cash to partners?

Summary of Study Objectives

1. *Identify the characteristics of the partnership form of business organization.* The principal characteristics of a partnership are: (a) association of individuals, (b) mutual agency, (c) limited life, (d) unlimited liability, and (e) co-ownership of property.

2. *Explain the accounting entries for the formation of a partnership.* When a partnership is formed, each partner's initial investment should be recorded at the fair market value of the assets at the date of their transfer to the partnership.

3. *Identify the bases for dividing net income or net loss.* Net income or net loss is divided on the basis of the income ratio, which may be (a) a fixed ratio, (b) a ratio based on beginning or average capital balances, (c) salaries to partners and the remainder on a fixed ratio, (d) interest on partners' capitals and the remainder on a fixed ratio, and (e) salaries to partners, interest on partners' capitals, and the remainder on a fixed ratio.

4. *Describe the form and content of partnership financial statements.* The financial statements of a partnership are similar to those of a proprietorship. The principal differences are: (a) the division of net income is shown on the income statement, (b) the owner's equity statement is called a partners' capital statement, and (c) each partner's capital is reported on the balance sheet.

5. *Explain the effects of the entries when a new partner is admitted.* The entry to record the admittance of a new partner by purchase of a partner's interest affects only partners' capital accounts. The entries to record the admittance by investment of assets in the partnership (a) increases both net assets and total capital and (b) may result in recognition of a bonus to either the old partners or the new partner.

6. *Describe the effects of the entries when a partner withdraws from the firm.* The entry to record a withdrawal from the firm when payment is made from partners' personal assets only affects partners' capital accounts. The entry to record a withdrawal when payment is made from partnership assets (a) decreases net assets and total capital and (b) may result in recognizing a bonus either to the retiring partner or the remaining partners.

7. *Prepare the entries to record the liquidation of a partnership.* When a partnership is liquidated, it is necessary to record the (a) sale of noncash assets, (b) allocation of the gain or loss on realization, (c) payment of partnership liabilities, and (d) distribution of cash to the partners.

GLOSSARY

Admission by investment · Admission of a partner by investing assets in the partnership, in which both partnership net assets and total capital increase. (p. 558).

Admission by purchase of an interest · Admission of a partner in a personal transaction between an existing partner and the new partner, which does not change total partnership assets or total capital. (p. 557).

Capital deficiency · A debit balance in a partner's capital account after allocation of gain or loss. (p. 564).

Income ratio · The basis for dividing both net income and net loss in a partnership. (p. 552).

No capital deficiency · All partners have credit balances after allocation of gain or loss. (p. 564).

Partners' capital statement · The owners' equity statement for a partnership which shows the changes in each partner's capital balance and in total partnership capital during the year. (p. 556).

Partnership · An association of two or more persons to carry on as co-owners of a business for profit. (p. 548).

Partnership agreement · A contract expressing the voluntary agreement of two or more individuals in a partnership. (p. 551).

Partnership dissolution · A change in the number of partners which does not necessarily terminate the business. (p. 549).

Partnership liquidation · Termination of both the legal and economic life of the entity. (p. 563).

Schedule of cash payments · A schedule showing the distribution of cash to the partners in the liquidation of a partnership. (p. 566).

Withdrawal from partners' personal assets · Withdrawal of a partner in a personal transaction between partners, which does not change total partnership assets or total capital. (p. 561).

Withdrawal from partnership assets · Withdrawal of a partner in a transaction involving the partnership which decreases both partnership net assets and total capital. (p. 561).

DEMONSTRATION PROBLEM

On January 1, 1993, the capital balances in the Hollingsworth Company are Lois Holly $26,000, and Jim Worth $24,000. In 1993, the company reports net income of $30,000. The income ratio provides for salary allowances of $12,000 for Holly and $10,000 to Worth and the remainder equally. Neither partner had any drawings in 1993.

In 1994, assume that the following independent transactions occur on January 1:

1. Donna Reichenbacher purchases one-half of Holly's capital interest for $25,000.
2. Marsha Mears is admitted with a 25% capital interest by a cash investment of $40,000.
3. Stan Wells is admitted with a 35% capital interest by a cash investment of $40,000.

Instructions

(a) Prepare a schedule showing the distribution of net income in 1993.

(b) Journalize the division of 1993 net income to the partners.

(c) Journalize each of the independent transactions that occurred on January 1, 1994.

Helpful hints

1. Journalizing the division of net income is a closing entry.
2. The entry for purchase of an interest involves only capital accounts.
3. The entry for admission by investment must have a debit to cash.
4. Allocation of a bonus occurs only in admission by investment.

Solution to Demonstration Problem

(a) Net income $30,000

Division of Net Income

	Lois Holly	Jim Worth	Total
Salary allowance	$12,000	$10,000	$22,000
Remaining income $8,000 ($30,000 − $22,000)			
Lois Holly ($8,000 × 50%)	4,000		
Jim Worth ($8,000 × 50%)		4,000	
Total remainder			8,000
Total division	$16,000	$14,000	$30,000

(b) 12/31/93   Income Summary   30,000
        Lois Holly, Capital ($12,000 + $4,000)   16,000
        Jim Worth, Capital ($10,000 + $4,000)   14,000
          (To close net income to partners' capitals)

(1)

(c) 1/1/94   Lois Holly, Capital ($26,000 + $16,000) × ½)   21,000
        Donna Reichenbacher, Capital   21,000
          (To record purchase of one-half of Holly's interest)

(2)

1/1/94	Cash	40,000	
	Lois Holly, Capital		5,000
	Jim Worth, Capital		5,000
	Marsha Mears, Capital		30,000
	(To record admission of Mears and bonus to old partners)		

Total capital after investment: $120,000
(Holly, $42,000, Worth $38,000, Mears investment $40,000)

Mears' capital credit (25% × $120,000)	$30,000
Bonus to old partners ($40,000 − $30,000)	$10,000

Allocation of bonus:

Holly ($10,000 × 50%)	$ 5,000	
Worth ($10,000 × 50%)	5,000	$10,000

(3)

1/1/94	Cash	40,000	
	Lois Holly, Capital	1,000	
	Jim Worth, Capital	1,000	
	Stan Wells, Capital		42,000
	(To record Wells' admission and bonus)		

Wells' capital credit (35% × $120,000)	$42,000
Bonus to Wells ($42,000 − $40,000)	$ 2,000

Allocation of bonus:

Holly ($2,000 × 50%)	$1,000	
Worth ($2,000 × 50%)	1,000	$ 2,000

SELF-STUDY QUESTIONS

Answers are at the end of the chapter.

(S.O. 1) 1. Which of the following is *not* a characteristic of a partnership?
a. Unlimited liability.
b. Taxable entity.
c. Mutual agency.
d. Limited life.

(S.O. 1) 2. The advantages of a partnership do *not* include:
a. unlimited liability.
b. ease of formation.
c. freedom from government regulation.
d. ease of decision making.

(S.O. 2) 3. Upon formation of a partnership, each partner's initial investment of assets should be recorded at their:
a. book values.
b. market values.
c. cost.
d. appraised values.

(S.O. 3) 4. The ABC Company reports net income of $60,000. If partners A, B, and C have an income ratio of 50%, 30%, and 20%, respectively, B's share of the net income is:
a. $30,000.
b. $12,000.
c. $18,000.
d. No correct answer given.

(S.O. 3) 5. Using the data in (4) above, what is C's share of net income if the percentages are applicable after each partner receives a $10,000 salary allowance?
a. $12,000.
b. $20,000.
c. $22,000.
d. $16,000.

(S.O. 4) 6. Which of the following statements about partnership financial statements is true?
a. The owners' equity statement is called the partners' capital statement.

b. The distribution of net income is shown on the balance sheet.

c. Only the total of all partner capital balances is shown in the balance sheet.

d. Details of the distribution of net income are shown in the owners' equity statement.

(S.O. 5)   7. R. Ranken purchases one-half of K. Kim's capital interest in the K & L partnership for $22,000. If the capital balances of Kim and L. Lars are $40,000 and $30,000, respectively, Ranken's capital balance following the purchase is:

a. $22,000.

b. $35,000.

c. $20,000.

d. $15,000.

(S.O. 5)   8. Capital balances in the DEA partnership are D Capital $60,000, E Capital $50,000, and A Capital $40,000, and income ratios are 5:3:2, respectively. The DEAR partnership is formed by admitting R to the firm with a cash investment of $60,000 for a 25% capital interest. The bonus to be credited to E Capital in admitting R is:

a. $10,000.

b. $7,500.

c. $3,750.

d. $2,250.

9. Capital balances in the TERM partnership   (S.O. 6) are T Capital $50,000, E Capital $40,000, R Capital $30,000, and M Capital $20,000, and income ratios are 4:3:2:1, respectively. M withdraws from the firm following payment of $29,000 in cash from the partnership. R's capital balance after recording the withdrawal of M is:

a. $28,000.

b. $27,300.

c. $27,000.

d. $21,000.

10. In the liquidation of a partnership it is   (S.O. 7) necessary to (1) distribute cash to the partners, (2) sell noncash assets, (3) allocate any gain or loss on realization to the partners, and (4) pay liabilities. These steps should be performed in the following order:

a. (3), (2), (1), (4)

b. (2), (3), (1), (4)

c. (2), (3), (4), (1)

d. (3), (2), (4), (1)

QUESTIONS

1. In discussing with his tax attorney the possibility of forming a partnership, Bill Kant becomes confused about two terms used by his attorney, "mutual agency" and "unlimited liability." Explain the meaning of these two terms as they apply to a partnership.

2. Lois Gilger and Lynn Scott are considering opening a fashion agency called Personna, but they cannot decide the form of organization to use. Explain to them the possible advantages and disadvantages of the partnership form of organization.

3. Ray Darling has been listening to a discussion about new tax reform proposals in which limited partnerships in real estate will be hit hard. Explain the terms (a) "limited partnership" and (b) "general partner."

4. S. Brown and D. Clarke form a partnership. Brown contributes land with a book value of $50,000 and a fair market value of $65,000. Brown also contributes equipment with a book value of $52,000 and a fair market value of $55,000. The partnership assumes a $20,000 mortgage on the land. What should be the balance in Brown's capital account upon formation of the partnership?

5. R. Hay, S. Ines, and L. Joyne have a partnership called Express Wings. A dispute has arisen among the partners because Hay has invested twice as much in assets as the other two partners and believes net income and net losses should be shared in accordance with the capital ratios. The partnership agreement does not specify the division of profits and losses. How will net income and net loss be divided?

6. S. Hark and R. Green are discussing how income and losses should be divided in a partnership they plan to form. What factors should be considered in determining the division of net income or net loss?

7. R. Lowrey and S. Montoy have capital balances of $40,000 and $60,000, respectively, in a partnership. The partnership agreement indicates that net income or net loss should be shared

partnership. The partnership agreement indicates that net income or net loss should be shared equally. If the net income for the partnership is $20,000, how should the net income be divided?

8. H. Asto and S. Sunde share net income and net loss equally. (a) Which account(s) is (are) debited and credited to record the division of net income between the partners? (b) If H. Asto withdraws $30,000 in cash for personal use in lieu of salary, which account is debited and which is credited?

9. Partners R. Rowen and B. Sander are provided salary allowances of $29,000 and $27,000, respectively. They divide the remainder of the partnership income in a ratio of 60:40. If partnership net income was $51,000, how much is allocated to Rowen and Sander?

10. Are the financial statements of a partnership similar to those of a proprietorship? Discuss.

11. Holly Carter decides to pay Mark Waller $30,000 for a one-third interest in the partnership of Waller and Rose. What effect does this transaction have on partnership net assets?

12. R. Minor decides to invest $18,000 in a partnership for a 1/6 capital interest. How much do the partnership's net assets increase? Does Minor also acquire a 1/6 income ratio through this investment?

13. Santo purchases Ramos' interest in the Morgan–Ramos partnership for $72,000. Assuming that Ramos has a $68,000 capital balance in the partnership, what journal entry is made by the partnership to record this transaction?

14. Jan Jackson has a $38,000 capital balance in a partnership. She sells her interest to Karen Crest for $42,000 cash. What entry is made by the partnership for this transaction?

15. Randi Rolf retires from the partnership of Swan, Tanks, and Rolf. She receives $91,000 of partnership assets in settlement of her capital balance of $75,000. Assuming that the income-sharing ratios are 5:3:2, respectively, how much of Rolf's bonus is debited to Tanks' capital account?

16. Your roommate argues that partnership assets should be revalued in situations like those in question 15. Why is this generally not done?

17. How is a deceased partner's equity determined?

18. Ray Riley claims that the steps in liquidating a partnership may be performed in any order. Do you agree? Explain.

19. Joe and Joan are discussing the liquidation of a partnership. Joe maintains that all cash should be distributed to partners on the basis of their income ratios. Is Joe correct? Explain.

20. In continuing their discussion, Joan says that even in the case of a capital deficiency, all cash should still be distributed on the basis of capital balances. Is Joan correct? Explain.

21. Mike, Larry, and Jean have income ratios of 5:3:2 and capital balances of $34,000, $29,000, and $28,000, respectively. Noncash assets are sold at a gain. After creditors are paid, $109,000 of cash is available for distribution to the partners. How much cash should be paid to Larry?

22. Before the final distribution of cash, account balances are: Cash $24,000; R. Kahn, Capital $18,000 (cr); M. Moss, Capital $10,000 (cr); and T. Zaret, Capital $4,000 (dr). Zaret is unable to pay any of the capital deficiency. If the income-sharing ratios are 5:3:2, respectively, how much cash should be paid to M. Moss?

BRIEF EXERCISES

BE14–1 R. Alford and B. Starr decide to organize the ALL-Star partnership. Alford invests $15,000 cash, and Starr contributes $10,000 and equipment having a book value of $3,000. Prepare the entry to record Starr's investment in the partnership, assuming the equipment has a fair market value of $4,500.

Journalize entries in forming a partnership.
(S.O. 2)

Prepare portion of opening balance sheet for partnership.
(S.O. 2)

BE14–2   C. Weld and G. Kamp decide to merge their proprietorships into a partnership called WeldKamp Company. The balance sheet of Kamp Co. shows:

Accounts Receivable	$15,000	
Less: Allowance for Doubtful Accounts	1,200	$13,800
Equipment	20,000	
Less: Accumulated Depreciation	8,000	12,000

The partners agree that the net realizable value of the receivables is $13,000 and that the fair market value of the equipment is $10,000. Indicate how the four accounts should appear in the opening balance sheet of the partnership.

Journalize the division of net income using fixed income ratios.
(S.O. 3)

BE14–3   B&R Co. reports net income of $70,000. The income ratios are: B 60% and R 40%. Indicate the division of net income to each partner and prepare the entry to distribute the net income.

Compute division of net income with a salary allowance and fixed ratios.
(S.O. 3)

BE14–4   Mel Co. reports net income of $50,000. Partner salary allowances are M $10,000, E $5,000, and L $5,000. Indicate the division of net income to each partner, assuming the fixed ratio is 40:40:20, respectively.

Show division of net income when allowances exceed net income.
(S.O. 3)

BE14–5   S&T Co. reports net income of $20,000. Interest allowances are S $5,000 and T $4,000; salary allowances are S $15,000 and T $10,000; the remainder is shared equally. Show the distribution of income on the income statement.

Journalize admission by purchase of an interest.
(S.O. 5)

BE14–6   In the ABC Co. capital balances are: Ali $30,000, Babson $25,000, and Carter $20,000. The partners share income equally. Daniel is admitted to the firm by purchasing one-half of Ali's interest for $20,000. Journalize the admission of Daniel to the partnership.

Journalize admission by investment.
(S.O. 5)

BE14–7   In the EZ Co., capital balances are Edie $40,000 and Zane $30,000. The partners share income equally. Kerns is admitted to the firm with a 40% interest by an investment of cash of $40,000. Journalize the admission of Kerns.

Journalize withdrawal paid by personal assets.
(S.O. 6)

BE14–8   Capital balances in DEB Co. are Drake $40,000, Embs $30,000, and Boyd $20,000. Drake and Embs each agree to pay Boyd $12,000 from their personal assets. Drake and Embs each receive 50% of Boyd's equity. The partners share income equally. Journalize the withdrawal of Boyd.

Journalize withdrawal paid by partnership assets.
(S.O. 6)

BE14–9   Data pertaining to DEB Co. are presented in BE14–8. Instead of payment from personal assets, assume that Boyd receives $24,000 from partnership assets in withdrawing from the firm. Journalize the withdrawal of Boyd.

Journalize final cash distribution in liquidation.
(S.O. 7)

BE14–10   After liquidating noncash assets and paying creditors, account balances in the ARB Co. are Cash $18,000, A Capital (Cr.) $9,000, R Capital (Cr.) $5,000, and B Capital (Cr.) $4,000. The partners share income equally. Journalize the final distribution of cash to the partners.

EXERCISES

Journalize entry for formation of a partnership.
(S.O. 2)

E14–1   Thad Karl has owned and operated a proprietorship for several years. On January 1, he decides to terminate this business and become a partner in the firm of Payne and Karl. Karl's investment in the partnership consists of $15,000 in cash, and the following assets of the proprietorship: accounts receivable $14,000 less allowance for doubtful accounts of $2,000, and equipment $20,000 less accumulated depreciation of $4,000. It is agreed that the allowance for doubtful accounts should be $1,000 for the partnership, and the fair market value of the equipment is $17,000.

Instructions

Prepare schedule showing distribution of net income and closing entry.
(S.O. 3)

Journalize Karl's admission to the firm of Payne and Karl.

E14–2   R. Huma and W. Kahl have capital balances on January 1 of $50,000 and $40,000, respectively. The partnership income sharing agreement provides for (1) annual salaries of $14,000 for Huma and $12,000 for Kahl, (2) interest at 10% on beginning capital balances, and (3) remaining income or loss to be shared 70% by Huma and 30% by Kahl.

Instructions

(a) Prepare a schedule showing the distribution of net income, assuming net income is (1) $45,000 and (2) $18,000.

(b) Journalize the allocation of net income in each of the situations above.

E14–3 In the Salton Co., beginning capital balances on January 1, 1993, are M. Salz $20,000 and C. Toni $18,000. During the year, drawings were Salz $6,000 and Toni $5,000. Net income was $30,000, and the partners share income equally.

Prepare partners' capital statement and partial balance sheet.
(S.O. 4)

Instructions

(a) Prepare the partners' capital statement for the year.

(b) Prepare the owners' equity section of the balance sheet at December 31, 1993.

E14–4 T. Haft, K. Rose, and J. Lamp share income on a 5:3:2 basis. They have capital balances of $32,000, $24,000, and $21,000, respectively, when R. Zahn is admitted to the partnership.

Journalize admission of a new partner by purchase of an interest.
(S.O. 5)

Instructions

Prepare the journal entry to record the admission of Zahn under each of the following assumptions:

(a) Purchase of one-half of Haft's equity for $18,000.

(b) Purchase of one-half of Rose's equity for $10,000.

(c) Purchase of one-third of Lamp's equity for $9,000.

E14–5 Joe Keho and Mike McClore share income on a 6:4 basis. They have capital balances of $90,000 and $70,000, respectively, when Ed Kehler is admitted to the partnership.

Journalize admission of a new partner by investment.
(S.O. 5)

Instructions

Prepare the journal entry to record the admission of Ed Kehler under each of the following assumptions:

(a) Investment of $80,000 cash for a one-fourth ownership interest with bonuses to the existing partners.

(b) Investment of $40,000 cash for a one-fourth ownership interest with a bonus to the new partner.

E14–6 Mary Lohr, Vera Miles, and Debra Noll have capital balances of $50,000, $30,000, and $24,000, respectively, and their income ratios are 5:3:2. Noll withdraws from the partnership under each of the following independent conditions:

Journalize withdrawal of a partner with payment from partners' personal assets.
(S.O. 6)

1. Lohr and Miles agree to purchase Noll's equity by paying $15,000 each from their personal assets. Each purchaser receives 50% of Noll's equity.

2. Miles agrees to purchase all of Noll's equity by paying $20,000 cash from her personal assets.

3. Lohr agrees to purchase all of Noll's equity by paying $23,000 cash from her personal assets.

Instructions

Journalize the withdrawal of Noll under each of the assumptions above.

E14–7 Dale Phillips, Keith White, and Dan Maran have capital balances of $95,000, $75,000, and $60,000, respectively. They share income or loss on a 5:3:2 basis. White withdraws from the partnership under each of the following conditions:

Journalize withdrawal of a partner with payment from partnership assets.
(S.O. 6)

1. White is paid $82,000 in cash from partnership assets, and a bonus is granted to the retiring partner.

2. White is paid $61,000 in cash from partnership assets, and bonuses are granted to the remaining partners.

Instructions

Journalize the withdrawal of White under each of the assumptions above.

E14–8 The Baylee Company at December 31 has cash $20,000, noncash assets $100,000, liabilities $55,000, and the following capital balances: Bayer $40,000 and Leech $25,000. The firm is liquidated, and $110,000 in cash is received for the noncash assets. Bayer and Leech income ratios are 60% and 40%, respectively.

Prepare cash distribution schedule.
(S.O. 7)

Instructions
Prepare a cash distribution schedule.

Journalize transactions in a liquidation.
(S.O. 7)

E14–9   Data for the Baylee partnership are presented in E14–8.

Instructions
Prepare the entries to record (1) the sale of noncash assets, (2) the allocation of the gain or loss on liquidation to the partners, (3) payment of creditors, and (4) distribution of cash to the partners.

Journalize transactions with a capital deficiency.
(S.O. 7)

E14–10   Prior to the distribution of cash to the partners, the accounts in the MEL Company are: Cash $30,000, M Capital (Cr.) $18,000, E Capital (Cr.) $16,000, and L Capital (Dr.) $4,000. The income ratios are 5:3:2, respectively.

Instructions
(a) Prepare the entry to record (1) L's payment of $4,000 in cash to the partnership and (2) the distribution of cash to the partners with credit balances.

(b) Prepare the entry to record (1) the absorption of L's capital deficiency by the other partners and (2) the distribution of cash to the partners with credit balances.

PROBLEMS

Prepare entries for formation of a partnership and a balance sheet.
(S.O. 2, 4)

P14–1   The post-closing trial balances of two proprietorships on January 1, 1993, are presented below.

	Creal Company		Donal Company	
	Dr.	Cr.	Dr.	Cr.
Cash	$ 6,500		$ 8,000	
Accounts receivable	15,000		23,000	
Allowance for doubtful accounts		$ 2,500		$ 4,000
Merchandise inventory	28,000		17,000	
Equipment	52,000		30,000	
Accumulated depreciation—equipment		24,000		13,000
Notes payable		20,000		
Accounts payable		25,000		37,000
R. T. Creal, Capital		30,000		
A. C. Donal, Capital				24,000
	$101,500	$101,500	$78,000	$78,000

Creal and Donal decide to form the Donal Creal Company with the following agreed upon valuations for noncash assets:

	Creal Company	Donal Company
Accounts receivable	$15,000	$23,000
Allowance for doubtful accounts	4,500	5,000
Merchandise inventory	30,000	20,000
Equipment	31,000	18,000

All cash will be transferred to the partnership, and the partnership will assume all the liabilities of the two proprietorships. Further, it is agreed that Creal will invest $15,000 in cash, and Donal will invest $5,000 in cash.

Instructions
(a) Prepare separate journal entries to record the transfer of each proprietorship's assets and liabilities to the partnership.

(b) Journalize the additional cash investment by each partner.

(c) Prepare a balance sheet for the partnership on January 1, 1993.

P14-2 At the end of its first year of operations on December 31, 1993, the LMN Company's accounts show the following:

Journalize divisions of net income and prepare a partners' capital statement.
(S.O. 3, 4)

Partner	Drawings	Capital
Lois Lang	$12,000	$30,000
Mary Moor	9,000	20,000
Sue Norton	6,000	10,000

The capital balance represents each partner's initial capital investment. Therefore, net income or net loss for 1993 has not been closed to the partners' capital accounts.

Instructions
(a) Journalize the entry to record the division of net income for 1993 under each of the following assumptions:
  (1) Net income is $25,000, and income is shared 5:3:2.
  (2) Net income is $30,000; Lang and Moor are given salary allowances of $10,000 and $8,000, respectively, and the remainder is shared equally.
  (3) Net income is $25,200; each partner is allowed interest of 10% on beginning capital balances; Lang is given a $15,000 salary allowance; and the remainder is shared equally.

(b) Prepare a schedule showing the division of net income under assumption (3) above.

(c) Prepare a partner's capital statement for the year under assumption (3) above.

P14-3 At April 30, partners' capital balances in the ELM Company are: A. Ellis $50,000, C. Leon $24,000, and W. Matt $16,000. The income sharing ratios are 3:2:1, respectively. On May 1, the ELMO Company is formed by admitting N. Ortiz to the firm as a partner.

Journalize admission of a partner under different assumptions.
(S.O. 5)

Instructions
(a) Journalize the admission of Ortiz under each of the following assumptions:
  (1) Ortiz purchases one-half of Matt's ownership interest by paying Matt $9,000 in cash.
  (2) Ortiz purchases one-half of Leon's ownership interest by paying Leon $15,000 in cash.
  (3) Ortiz invests $35,000 cash in the partnership for a 40% ownership interest that includes a bonus to the new partner.
  (4) Ortiz invests $30,000 in the partnership for a 20% ownership interest and bonuses are given to the old partners.

(b) Matt's capital balance is $18,000 after admitting Ortiz to the partnership by investment. If Matt's ownership interest is 12% of total partnership capital, what was Ortiz's cash investment and the total bonus to the old partners?

P14-4 On December 31, the capital balances and income ratios in the ART Company are as follows:

Journalize withdrawal of a partner under different assumptions.
(S.O. 6)

Partner	Capital Balance	Income Ratio
E. Attle	$70,000	60%
P. Ross	30,000	30
L. Tower	20,000	10

Instructions
(a) Journalize the withdrawal of Tower under each of the following assumptions:
  (1) Each of the remaining partners agrees to pay $12,000 in cash from personal funds to purchase Tower's ownership equity. Each receives 50% of Tower's equity.
  (2) Ross agrees to purchase Tower's ownership interest for $18,000 in cash.
  (3) From partnership assets, Tower is paid $26,000, which includes a bonus to the retiring partner.
  (4) Tower is paid $17,000 from partnership assets, and bonuses to the remaining partners are recognized.

(b) If Ross' capital balance after Tower's withdrawal is $33,000, what was the total bonus to the remaining partners and the cash paid by the partnership to Tower?

P14-5 The partners in the Great Lakes Company decide to liquidate the firm when the balance sheet shows the following:

Prepare entries and schedule of cash payments in liquidation of a partnership.
(S.O. 7)

GREAT LAKES COMPANY
Balance Sheet
April 30, 1993

Assets		Liabilities and Owners' Equity	
Cash	$24,000	Notes payable	$12,000
Accounts receivable	18,000	Accounts payable	26,000
Allowance for doubtful accounts	(1,000)	Wages payable	2,000
Merchandise inventory	30,000	T. E. Huron, Capital	24,000
Equipment	17,000	P. A. Erie, Capital	12,800
Accumulated depreciation—equip.	(8,000)	C. R. Lake, Capital	3,200
Total	$80,000	Total	$80,000

The partners share income and loss 5:3:2. During the process of liquidation, the transactions below were completed in the following sequence:

1. A total of $48,000 was received from converting noncash assets into cash.
2. Liabilities were paid in full.
3. Cash was paid to the partners with credit balances.

Instructions

(a) Prepare a cash distribution schedule.

(b) Prepare general journal entries to record the transactions.

(c) Post to the cash and capital accounts.

ALTERNATE PROBLEMS

Prepare entries for formation of a partnership and a balance sheet.
(S.O. 2, 4)

G

P14–1A The post-closing trial balances of two proprietorships on January 1, 1993 are presented below.

	Hamp Company		Mill Company	
	Dr.	Cr.	Dr.	Cr.
Cash	$ 13,000		$16,000	
Accounts receivable	17,500		26,000	
Allowance for doubtful accounts		$ 3,000		$ 4,400
Merchandise inventory	26,500		18,400	
Equipment	45,000		28,000	
Accumulated depreciation—equipment		24,000		12,000
Notes payable		20,000		15,000
Accounts payable		20,000		31,000
L. Hamp, Capital		35,000		
P. Mill, Capital				26,000
	$102,000	$102,000	$88,400	$88,400

Hamp and Mill decide to form the Hamp Mill Company with the following agreed upon valuations for noncash assets:

	Hamp Company	Mill Company
Accounts receivable	$17,500	$26,000
Allowance for doubtful accounts	3,500	4,000
Merchandise inventory	28,000	21,000
Equipment	25,000	18,000

All cash will be transferred to the partnership, and the partnership will assume all the liabilities of the two proprietorships. Further, it is agreed that Hamp will invest $20,000 in cash and Mill will invest $9,000 in cash.

Instructions

(a) Prepare separate journal entries to record the transfer of each proprietorship's assets and liabilities to the partnership.

(b) Journalize the additional cash investment by each partner.

(c) Prepare a balance sheet for the partnership on January 1, 1993.

P14-2A At the end of its first year of operations on December 31, 1993, HRT Company's accounts show the following:

Journalize divisions of net income and prepare a partners' capital statement.
(S.O. 3, 4)

Partner	Drawings	Capital
Sue Horton	$23,000	$45,000
Tracey Rugen	14,000	30,000
Eileen Thors	10,000	25,000

The capital balance represents each partner's initial capital investment; therefore, net income or net loss for 1993 has not been closed to the partners' capital accounts.

Instructions

(a) Journalize the entry to record the division of net income for the year 1993 under each of the following assumptions:
   (1) Net income is $30,000, and income is shared 6:3:1.
   (2) Net income is $34,000; Horton and Rugen are given salary allowances of $15,000 and $10,000, respectively; and the remainder is shared equally.
   (3) Net income is $22,000; each partner is allowed interest of 10% on beginning capital balances; Horton is given a $15,000 salary allowance; and the remainder is shared equally.

(b) Prepare a schedule showing the division of net income under assumption (3) above.

(c) Prepare a partners' capital statement for the year under assumption (3) above.

P14-3A At April 30, partners' capital balances in NSZ Company are: A. Nolan $60,000, D. Spoda $36,000, and T. Zale $14,000. The income sharing ratios are 5:4:1, respectively. On May 1, the NSZO Company is formed by admitting M. Otton to the firm as a partner.

Journalize admission of a partner under different assumptions.
(S.O. 5)

Instructions

(a) Journalize the admission of Otton under each of the following assumptions:
   (1) Otton purchases one-half of Zale's ownership interest by paying Zale $16,000 in cash.
   (2) Otton purchases one-half of Spoda's ownership interest by paying Spoda $20,000 in cash.
   (3) Otton invests $60,000 for a 30% ownership interest, and bonuses are given to the old partners.
   (4) Otton invests $40,000 for a 30% ownership interest, which includes a bonus to the new partner.

(b) Spoda's capital balance is $32,000 after admitting Otton to the partnership by investment. If Spoda's ownership interest is 20% of total partnership capital, what was Otton's cash investment and the bonus to the new partner?

P14-4A On December 31, the capital balances and income ratios in the BAG Company are as follows:

Journalize withdrawal of a partner under different assumptions.
(S.O. 6)

Partner	Capital Balance	Income Ratio
R. Bird	$60,000	50%
D. Alman	40,000	30%
P. Garth	32,000	20%

Instructions

(a) Journalize the withdrawal of Garth under each of the following assumptions:
   (1) Each of the continuing partners agrees to pay $18,000 in cash from personal funds to purchase Garth's ownership equity. Each receives 50% of Garth's equity.
   (2) Alman agrees to purchase Garth's ownership interest for $30,000 cash.
   (3) Garth is paid $40,000 from partnership assets, which includes a bonus to the retiring partner.

(4) Garth is paid $28,000 from partnership assets and bonuses to the remaining partners are recognized.

(b) If Alman's capital balance after Garth's withdrawal is $42,250, what was the total bonus to the remaining partners and the cash paid by the partnership to Garth?

Prepare entries and schedules of cash payments with a capital deficiency in liquidation of a partnership.

(S.O. 7)

P14–5A The partners in the JRW Company decide to liquidate the firm when the balance sheet shows the following:

JRW COMPANY
Balance Sheet
May 31, 1993

Assets		Liabilities and Owners' Equity	
Cash	$ 27,500	Notes payable	$ 13,500
Accounts receivable	24,000	Accounts payable	28,000
Allowance for doubtful accounts	(1,000)	Wages payable	2,800
Merchandise inventory	34,500	M. Jagger, Capital	35,000
Equipment	21,000	K. Richards, Capital	20,000
Accumulated depreciation—equipment	(5,500)	R. Wood, Capital	1,200
Total	$100,500	Total	$100,500

The partners share income and loss 5:3:2. During the process of liquidation, the following transactions were completed in the following sequence:

1. A total of $53,000 was received from converting noncash assets into cash.
2. Liabilities were paid in full.
3. Wood paid his capital deficiency.
4. Cash was paid to the partners with credit balances.

Instructions

(a) Prepare general journal entries to record the transactions.

(b) Post to the cash and capital accounts.

(c) Assume that Wood is unable to pay the capital deficiency.
   (1) Prepare the entry to allocate Wood's debit balance to Jagger and Richards.
   (2) Prepare the entry to record the final distribution of cash.

*B*roadening *Your Perspective*

FINANCIAL REPORTING PROBLEM

The RAM Company was owned by Jane Root, Pat Aker, and Paula Munn. On May 31, Paula retired and the partnership was liquidated. After closing the partnership books, the balance sheet showed the following:

RAM COMPANY
Balance Sheet
May 31, 1993

Assets		Liabilities and Owners' Equity	
Cash	$ 9,000	Notes Payable	$12,000
Accounts receivable	14,000	Accounts payable	9,000
Inventory	30,000	Root, Capital	30,000
Equipment	40,000	Aker, Capital	20,000
Accumulated depr.	(12,000)	Munn, Capital	10,000
Total	$81,000	Total	$81,000

The income ratios are Root 30%, Aker 50%, and Munn 20%. In June, $87,000 in cash was realized from noncash assets and partnership liabilities were paid in full. The three partners disagree on the basis for allocating the $15,000 gain on realization and distributing the remaining cash of $75,000.

Munn argues that the allocation of the gain and the distribution of cash should both be made equally since the partnership was terminated by mutual consent of each of the partners.

Root contends that the allocation of the gain and the distribution of the cash should both be made on the basis of capital balances because the income ratio is not applicable to liquidation.

Aker believes that the gain should be allocated on the basis of income ratios since these ratios apply to both net income or net loss and to realization gains and losses, and that the cash should be allocated on the basis of capital balances.

The partners agree to settle their dispute on the basis of your recommendation as an expert accountant.

Instructions

(a) Prepare separate cash payment schedules based on the positions of each partner. (Use one column for noncash assets and one column for liabilities).

(b) Compare the difference in cash received by each partner under each basis.

(c) Explain the proper basis for allocating the gain and distributing the cash.

DECISION CASE

Bart Holman and Sally Izo, as two professionals in the finance area, have worked for Advanced Leasing for a number of years. Advanced Leasing is a company that leases high-tech medical equipment to hospitals. Bart and Sally have decided that, with their financial expertise, they might start their own company to provide consulting services to individuals interested in leasing equipment. One form of organization they are considering is a partnership.

If they start a partnership, each individual plans to contribute $15,000 in cash. In addition, Bart has a used IBM microcomputer that originally cost $3,800, which he intends to invest in the partnership. The computer has a present market value of $1,800.

Although both Bart and Sally are financial wizards, they do not know a great deal about how a partnership operates. As a result, they have come to you for advice.

Instructions
Answer the following questions:

(a) What are the major disadvantages of starting a partnership?

(b) What type of document is needed for a partnership and what should this document contain?

(c) Both Bart and Sally plan to work full-time in the new partnership. Therefore they believe that net income or net loss should be shared equally. However, they are wondering how they can provide compensation to Bart Holman for his additional investment of the microcomputer. What would you tell them?

(d) Bart is not sure how the computer equipment should be reported on his tax return. What would you tell him?

(e) As indicated above, Bart and Sally have worked together for a number of years. Bart's skills complement Sally's and vice versa. If one of them dies, it will be very difficult for the other to maintain the business, not to mention the difficulty of paying the deceased partner's estate for his or her partnership interest. What would you tell them to do?

CRITICAL THINKING CASE

Refer back to the opening story about the public accounting firm of Coopers & Lybrand. Answer the following questions.

1. Why are partners in one part of the country worried about liability issues related to the partnership that occur in another part of the country?

2. What are the advantages and disadvantages of the partnership form of organization?

3. Why might it cost less to offer a French class than a Russian class on a college campus?

4. In what way do you think financial considerations affect course offerings at your school?

ETHICAL CASE

Susan and Karen operate a beauty salon as partners who share profits and losses equally. The success of their business has exceeded their expectations and is operating quite profitably. Karen is anxious to maximize profits and schedules appointments from 8 a.m. to 6 p.m. daily, even sacrificing some lunch hours to accommodate regular customers. Susan schedules her appointments from 9 a.m. to 5 p.m. and takes long lunch hours. Susan regularly makes significantly larger withdrawals of cash than Karen does. But, she says, "Karen, you needn't worry, I never make a withdrawal without you knowing about it, so it is properly recorded in my Drawing account and charged against my capital at the end of the year." Susan's withdrawals to date are double Karen's.

Instructions

(a) Who are the stakeholders in this situation?

(b) Identify the problems with Susan's actions and discuss the ethical considerations of her actions.

(c) How might the partnership agreement be revised to accommodate the differences in Susan's and Karen's work and withdrawal habits?

Answers to Self-Study Questions
1. b   2. a   3. b   4. c   5. d   6. a   7. c   8. d   9. a   10. c

CHAPTER 15

CORPORATIONS: ORGANIZATION AND CAPITAL STOCK TRANSACTIONS

Study Objectives

After studying this chapter, you should be able to:

1. Identify and discuss the major characteristics of a corporation.

2. Differentiate between paid-in capital and retained earnings.

3. Record the issuance of common stock.

4. Explain the accounting for treasury stock.

5. Differentiate preferred stock from common stock.

6. Prepare a stockholders' equity section.

7. Compute book value per share.

I f you were to drive around the loop at the University of California at Irvine (UCI), you would see many examples of the work of a huge local corporation known as The Irvine Company. Indeed, UCI—more than most college campuses—was created by a corporation.

The Irvine Company is a real estate developer and builder of communities, shopping centers, and hotels. About 30 years ago, the company decided that it was important to have a major university be part of its master plan for the new community of Irvine. And so the company donated 1,000 prime acres to the University of California, which was looking to add campuses beyond such giants as UC Berkeley and UCLA.

Today, The Irvine Company is responsible for the student basketball arena (through a major personal donation by its chairman, Donald Bren), a new Executive MBA program, and the "Marketplace," a shopping complex that connects to the *school by a pedestrian bridge. The "Marketplace" has a six-screen movie theatre, a comedy club, nine restaurants, and many specialty stores. Also on campus is the Irvine Barclay Theatre. "The students shop in our shopping centers and many live in our apartment buildings," says a company spokesman. "The City of Irvine, the Irvine Company, and all of Orange County benefit from having a strong university."*

In 1992, UC Irvine celebrated its twenty-fifth anniversary. Indeed, Irvine and much of the entire county were largely undeveloped when UCI was conceived. Today, UCI is a bustling campus with 15,000 students and distinguished departments in the arts and sciences. Many ideas generated in UCI laboratories have become the basis for brand new corporations creating new markets in science and medicine.

As indicated above, corporations have substantial resources. In fact, the dominant form of business organization in the United States in terms of dollar volume of sales, earnings, and employees is the corporation. All of the 500 largest industrial companies in the U.S. are corporations. One of the biggest, Exxon, reported sales of $103 billion, net income of $5.6 billion, and total employees of 180,000. Exxon's sales figure is larger than the gross domestic product of such countries as Thailand ($92 billion), Greece ($70 billion), Israel ($58 billion), and Venezuela ($53 billion). It is important, therefore, that you have a basic understanding of the corporate form of business organization and the accounting for a corporation. In this chapter we will explain the essential features of a corporation and the accounting for a corporation's capital stock transactions.

What Is a Corporation?

In 1819, Chief Justice John Marshall defined a corporation as "an artificial being, invisible, intangible, and existing only in contemplation of law." This definition has become the foundation for the prevailing legal interpretation that a corporation is an **entity separate and distinct from its owners**.

A corporation is created by law, and its continued existence is dependent upon the corporate statutes of the state in which it is incorporated. As a legal entity, a corporation has most of the rights and privileges of a person. The major exceptions relate to privileges that can be exercised only by a living person, such as the right to vote or to hold public office. At the same time, a corporation is subject to the same duties and responsibilities as a person.

Corporations may be classified in a variety of ways. Two of the more common bases are by purpose and by ownership. A corporation may be organized for the purpose of making a **profit**, or it may be **nonprofit**. Corporations for profit include such well-known companies as McDonald's, General Motors, and Apple Computer. Nonprofit corporations are organized for charitable, medical, and educational purposes and include the Salvation Army, American Cancer Society, and the Ford Foundation.

Classification by **ownership** distinguishes between publicly held and privately held corporations. A publicly held corporation has thousands of stockholders, and its stock is regularly traded on a national securities market such as the New York Stock Exchange. Most of the largest U.S. corporations are publicly held. Examples of publicly held corporations are International Business Machines, Caterpillar Inc., and General Electric. In contrast, a privately held corporation, often referred to as a closely held corporation, has only a few stockholders, and does not offer its stock for sale to the general public. Privately held companies are generally much smaller than publicly held companies.

Characteristics of a Corporation

A number of characteristics distinguish a corporation from proprietorships and partnerships. The most important of these characteristics are explained below.

Study Objective 1

Identify and discuss the major characteristics of a corporation.

Separate Legal Existence

As an entity separate and distinct from its owners, the corporation acts under its own name rather than in the name of its stockholders. A corporation may buy, own, and sell property, borrow money, and enter into legally binding contracts in its own name. It may also sue or be sued, and it pays its own taxes.

In contrast to a partnership, in which the acts of the owners (partners) bind the partnership, the acts of the owners (stockholders) do not bind the corporation unless such owners are duly appointed agents of the corporation. For example, if you owned shares of Ford Motor Company stock, you would not have the right to purchase automobile parts for the company unless you were appointed as an agent of the corporation.

Helpful hint Stockholders are also called shareholders because they own shares of stock.

Limited Liability of Stockholders

Since a corporation is a separate legal entity, creditors ordinarily have recourse only to corporate assets to satisfy their claims. The liability of stockholders is normally limited to their investment in the corporation, and creditors have no legal claim on the personal assets of the owners unless fraud has occurred. Thus, even in the event of bankruptcy of the corporation, stockholders' losses are generally limited to their capital investment in the corporation.

Transferable Ownership Rights

Ownership of a corporation is shown in shares of capital stock, which are transferable units. Stockholders may dispose of part or all of their interest in a corporation simply by selling their stock. In contrast to the transfer of an ownership interest in a partnership, which requires the consent of each owner, the transfer of stock is entirely at the discretion of the stockholder. It does not require the approval of either the corporation or other stockholders. The transfer of ownership rights between stockholders normally has no effect on the operating activities of the corporation or on a corporation's assets, liabilities, and total ownership equity. That is, the enterprise does not participate in the transfer of these ownership rights after it issues the capital stock.

Ability to Acquire Capital

It generally is relatively easy for a corporation to obtain capital through the issuance of stock. Buying stock in a corporation is often more attractive to an investor than investing in a partnership. A stockholder has limited liability, and shares of stock are readily transferable. Moreover, many individuals can become stockholders by investing small amounts of money. In sum, the ability of a successful corporation to obtain capital is virtually unlimited.

Continuous Life

The life of a corporation is stated in its charter; it may be perpetual or it may be limited to a specific number of years. If it is limited, the period of existence can be extended through renewal of the charter. Since a corporation is a separate legal entity, the life of a corporation and its continuance as a going concern are not affected by the withdrawal, death, or incapacity of a stockholder, employee, or officer. As a result, a successful enterprise can have a continuous and perpetual life.

Corporation Management

Although stockholders legally own the corporation, they manage the corporation indirectly through a board of directors they elect. The board, in turn, formulates the operating policies for the company and selects officers, such as a president and one or more vice-presidents, to execute policy and to perform daily management functions.

A typical organization chart showing the delegation of responsibility is shown in Illustration 15-1. The **president** is the chief executive officer with direct responsibility for managing the business. As the organization chart shows, the president delegates responsibility to other officers. The chief accounting officer is the **controller**. The controller's responsibilities include (1) maintaining the accounting records, (2) maintaining an adequate system of internal control, and (3) preparing financial statements, tax returns, and internal reports. The **treasurer**

ILLUSTRATION 15-1
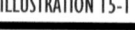

Corporation organization chart

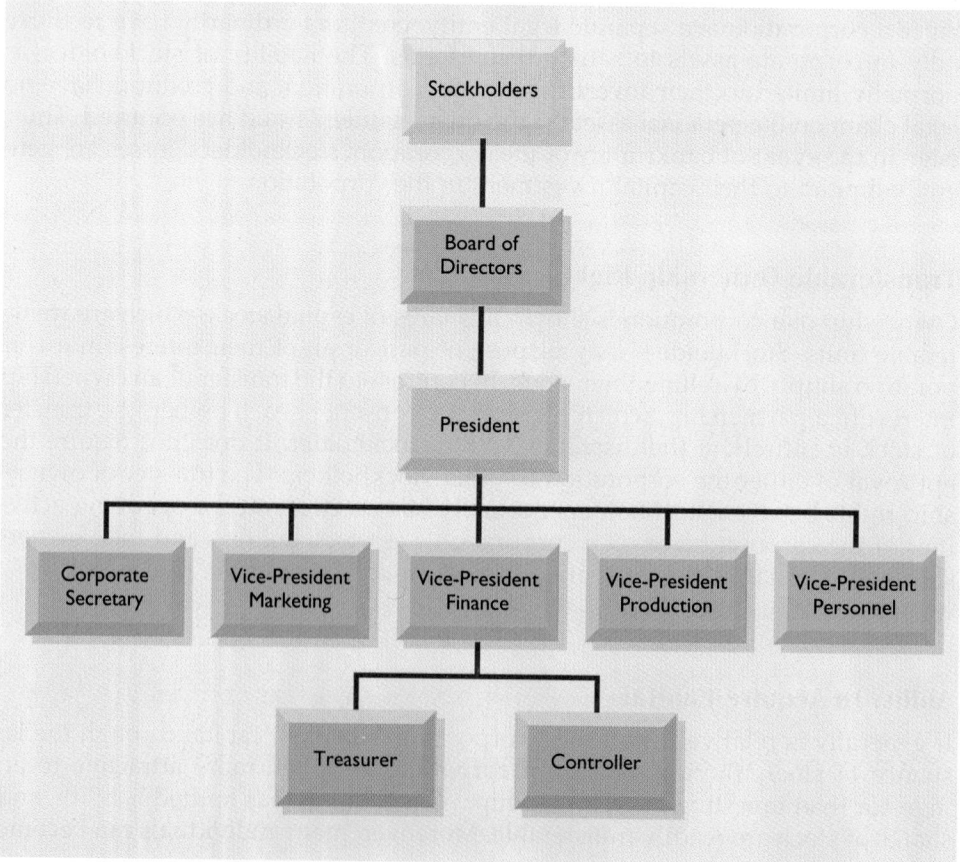

has custody of the corporation's funds and is responsible for maintaining the company's cash position.

The organizational structure of a corporation enables a company to hire professional managers to run the business. On the other hand, the separation of ownership and management prevents owners from having an active role in managing the company, which some owners like to have.

Accounting in Action · *Business Insight*

An interesting question is: Who runs a corporation—the stockholders or the board of directors? This issue has taken on increased importance because stockholders and boards of directors are often on the opposite side of the fence these days when potential takeovers occur.

A classic example is the unfriendly takeover bid made by Paramount Communication Inc. for Time Inc. Paramount bid up Time's stock price substantially; many stockholders said sell—but Time's board of directors had other plans. They were in the process of trying to make a friendly deal with Warner Communications. Some stockholders said, "Let's vote on what we should do." But Time decided to proceed without a stockholders' vote, even though the board of directors knew the Warner deal would depress Time's stock price in the short term. They figured that many stockholders would prefer to accept the Paramount bid. The stockholders sued to overturn the deal with Warner Communications but lost. The judge wrote: "Corporation law does not operate on the theory that directors, in exercising their powers to manage the firm, are obligated to follow the wishes of a majority of stockholders. In fact, the directors, not the stockholders, are charged with the duty to manage the firm."

Government Regulations

A corporation is subject to numerous state and federal regulations. For example, state laws usually prescribe the requirements for issuing stock, the distributions permitted to stockholders, and the effects of retiring stock, as well as other procedures and restrictions. Similarly, federal securities laws govern the sale of capital stock to the general public, and most publicly held corporations are required to make extensive disclosure of their financial affairs to the Securities and Exchange Commission through quarterly and annual reports. In addition, when a corporate stock is listed and traded on organized securities markets, the corporation must comply with the reporting requirements of these exchanges.

Government regulations are designed to protect the owners of the corporation. Unlike the owners of unincorporated entities, most stockholders do not participate in the day-to-day management of the company.

Additional Taxes

Neither proprietorships nor partnerships pay income taxes. The owner's share of these organizations' earnings is reported on his or her personal income tax return. Taxes are then paid by the individual on this amount. Corporations, on the other hand, must pay federal and state income taxes. These taxes are substantial: they can amount to as much as 40% of taxable income. In addition, stockholders are required to pay taxes on cash dividends, which are pro rata distributions of net income. Thus, many argue that corporate income is **taxed twice (double taxation)**, once at the corporate level, and again at the individual level.

From the foregoing, we can identify the following advantages and disadvantages of a corporation compared to a proprietorship and partnership.

ILLUSTRATION 15-2

Advantages and disadvantages of a corporation

Advantages	Disadvantages
Separate legal existence	Corporation management—separation of
Limited liability of stockholders	ownership and management
Transferable ownership rights	Government regulations
Ability to acquire capital	Additional taxes
Continuous life	
Corporation management—professional	
managers	

Forming a Corporation

The initial step in the formation of a corporation is to file an application with the Secretary of State in the state in which incorporation is desired. The application contains the following types of information: (1) the name, purpose, and duration of the proposed corporation; (2) amounts, kinds, and number of shares of capital stock to be authorized; and (3) the address of the corporation's principal office, (4) the names and addresses of the incorporators, and (5) the shares of stock to which each has subscribed.

After the incorporation fee is paid and the application approved, a charter is granted. The charter may be an approved copy of the application form or it may be a separate document containing the same basic data. The issuance of the charter, often referred to as the **articles of incorporation**, creates the corporation. Upon receipt of the charter, by-laws are developed. The by-laws[1] establish the internal rules and procedures for conducting the affairs of the corporation and indicate the powers and relationships of the stockholders, directors, and officers of the enterprise.

Accounting in Action · *Business Insight*

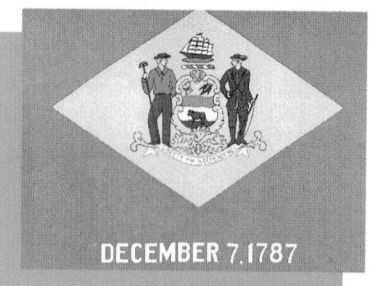

DECEMBER 7, 1787

More than 50% of the Fortune 500 corporations are incorporated in Delaware. A primary reason is the state courts' long-standing "business judgment rule." The rule provides that as long as directors exercise "due care" in the interests of stockholders, their actions will not be second-guessed by the courts. The rule has enabled directors to reject hostile takeover offers, even with hefty premiums, or spurn takeovers simply because they did not want to sell the company. However, new interpretations of the rule appear to be emerging. In a recent case, the state court ruled for the attacker. On appeal, the Delaware supreme court ruled for the directors but gave the following guideline to the state courts: "Was the board's response reasonable in the light of the threat posed?"

Source: Fortune, July 17, 1989.

---

[1]Following approval by two-thirds of the stockholders, the by-laws become binding upon all stockholders, directors, and officers. Legally, a corporation is regulated first by the laws of the state, second by its charter, and third by its by-laws. Care must be exercised to ensure that the provisions of the by-laws are not in conflict with either state laws or the charter.

Regardless of the number of states in which a corporation has operating divisions, it is incorporated in only one state. It is to the company's advantage to incorporate in a state whose laws are favorable to the corporate form of business organization. General Motors, for example, is incorporated in Delaware, whereas USX Corp. is a New Jersey corporation. In fact, some corporations have increasingly been incorporating in states with rules favorable to existing management. For example, Gulf Oil changed its state of incorporation to Delaware to thwart possible unfriendly takeovers. There, certain defensive tactics against takeovers can be approved by the board of directors alone, without a vote by shareholders.

Corporations engaged in interstate commerce must obtain a license from each state in which they do business. The license subjects the corporation's operating activities to the general corporation laws of the state. Costs incurred in the formation of a corporation are called organization costs. These costs include fees to underwriters for handling stock and bond issues, legal fees, state incorporation fees, and promotional expenditures involved in the organization of the business. These organization costs are capitalized as an intangible asset entitled Organization Costs. It may be argued that organization costs have an asset life equal to the life of the corporation. Many companies, however, amortize these costs over an arbitrary period of time, up to a maximum of 40 years. Because income tax regulations require the amortization of organization costs over a period of at least five years, some companies prefer to use the same period of amortization for accounting purposes. Determining the amount to be recorded when capital stock is used to pay for organization costs is explained later in the chapter.

Corporate Capital

Owners' equity in a corporation is identified as **stockholders' equity, shareholder's equity**, or **corporate capital**. The stockholders' equity section of a corporation's balance sheet consists of: (1) paid-in (contributed) capital, and (2) retained earnings (earned capital). The distinction between paid-in capital and retained earnings is important from both a legal and an economic point of view. Legally, dividends can be declared out of retained earnings in all states but in many states dividends cannot be declared out of paid-in capital. Economically, management, stockholders, and others look to earnings for the continued existence and growth of the corporation.

Study Objective 2

Differentiate between paid-in capital and retained earnings.

Paid-in Capital

Paid-in capital is the term used to describe the total amount paid in on capital stock. The principal source of **paid-in capital** is the investment of cash and other assets in the corporation by stockholders in exchange for capital stock. When a corporation has only one class of capital stock, the stock is identified as **common stock**.

Retained Earnings

Retained earnings is net income retained in a corporation. Net income is recorded in Retained Earnings by a closing entry in which Income Summary is debited and Retained Earnings is credited. For example, assuming that net income for Delta Robotics in its first year of operations is $130,000, the closing entry is:

Income Summary	130,000	
Retained Earnings		130,000
(To close income summary and transfer net income to retained earnings)		

If Delta Robotics has a balance of $800,000 in Common Stock at the end of its first year, its stockholders' equity section is as follows:

ILLUSTRATION 15-3

Stockholders' equity section

Stockholders' equity		
Paid-in capital		
Common stock	$800,000	
Retained earnings	130,000	
Total stockholders' equity		$930,000

The following illustration compares the owners' equity (stockholders' equity) accounts reported on a balance sheet for a proprietorship, a partnership, and a corporation.

ILLUSTRATION 15-4

Comparison of owners' equity accounts

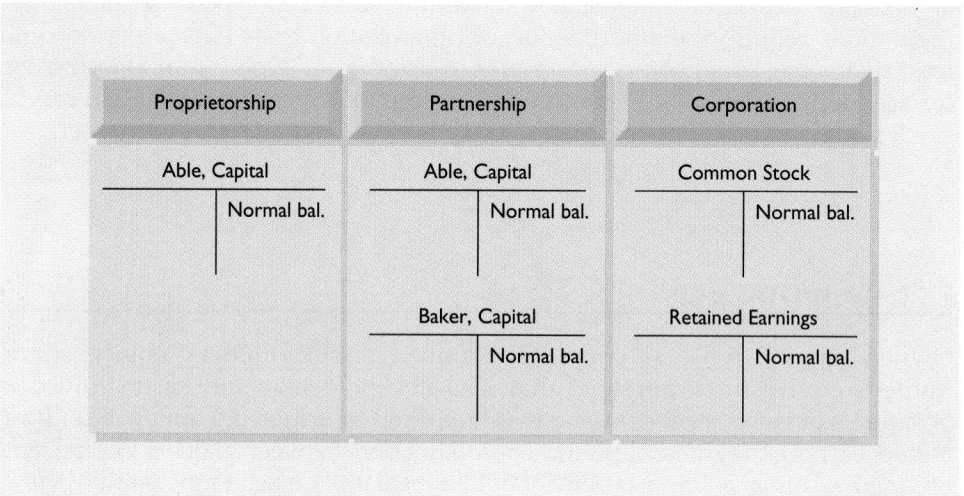

Ownership Rights of Stockholders

Each share of common stock gives the stockholder the following ownership rights.

1. **To vote.** Each share of stock entitles the owner to one vote in the election of the board of directors and in corporate actions that require stockholder approval. Stockholders who cannot attend stockholders' meetings usually can delegate their voting rights to an agent. This is done by signing a legal document called a **proxy** which instructs the agent how to vote the shares of stock.

2. **To share in corporate earnings.** Through the receipt of dividends, a stockholder participates in corporate earnings.

3. **To maintain the same percentage ownership when additional shares of common stock are issued.** In most states, common stockholders are granted the right to purchase, in proportion to their present holdings, any additional shares of stock. Because this right applies before the additional

Accounting in Action · *International Insight*

In Japan, stockholders are considered to be far less important to a corporation than employees, customers, and suppliers. Stockholders are rarely asked to vote on an issue, and the notion of bending corporate policy to favor stockholders borders on the heretical in Japan. This attitude toward stockholders appears to be slowly changing, however, as influential Japanese are advocating listening to investors, raising the extremely low dividends paid by Japanese corporations, and improving disclosure of financial information.

Source: The Wall Street Journal, June 27, 1989.

shares can be sold to the general public, it is referred to as the **preemptive right.**[2]

4. **To share in assets upon liquidation.** Common stockholders have a claim on corporate assets in proportion to their holdings if the corporation is terminated. This claim is often referred to as a **residual claim,** because the claims of owners are paid last from whatever assets remain after other claims have been paid.

The ownership rights of a share of stock are stated in the articles of incorporation or in the by-laws.

Proof of stock ownership is evidenced by a printed or engraved form known as a stock certificate. As shown in Illustration 15-5, the face of the certificate

ILLUSTRATION 15-5

A stock certificate

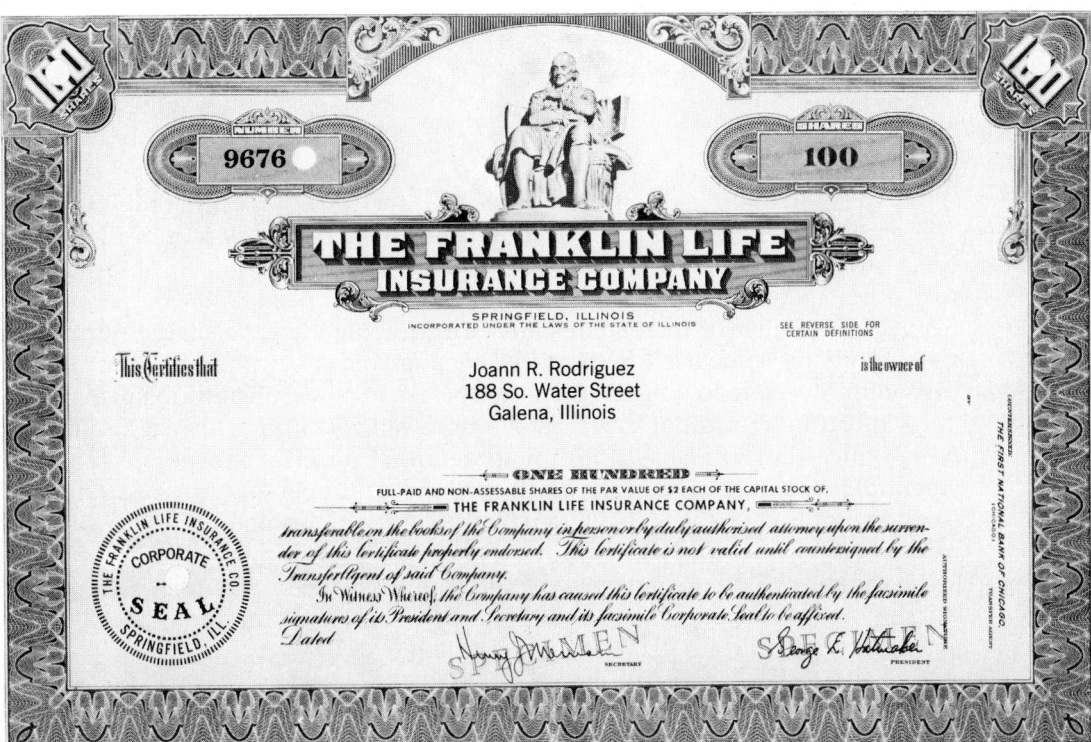

---

[2]A number of companies have eliminated the preemptive right, because they believe it makes an unnecessary and cumbersome demand on management. For example, IBM, by stockholder approval, has dropped its preemptive right for stockholders.

shows the name of the corporation, the stockholder's name, the class and special features of the stock, the number of shares owned, and the signatures of duly authorized corporate officials. Certificates are prenumbered to facilitate their accountability; they may be issued for any quantity of shares.

Before You Go On . . .

1. What are the advantages and disadvantages of a corporation compared to a proprietorship and a partnership?

2. Identify the principal steps in forming a corporation.

3. What is paid-in capital? What is retained earnings? What is the difference in the owners' equity (stockholders' equity) section of a balance sheet between a proprietorship and a corporation?

4. What rights are inherent in owning a share of stock in a corporation?

Characteristics of Stock Issuance

Study Objective 3

Record the issuance of common stock.

In considering the issuance (or sale) of stock, a corporation must resolve a number of basic questions: How many shares should be authorized for sale? How should the stock be issued? At what price should the shares be issued? Should a par value or no-par value be assigned the stock? For purposes of discussion, these questions are considered under the following headings:

1. Authorized stock.
2. Issuance of stock.
3. Market value of stock.
4. Par and no-par value stocks.

Authorized Stock

The amount of stock that a corporation is **authorized** to sell is indicated in its charter. The total amount of authorized stock at the time of incorporation normally anticipates both initial and subsequent capital needs of a company. As a result, the number of total shares authorized generally exceeds the number of shares initially sold. If all authorized stock is sold, a corporation must obtain consent of the state to amend its charter before it can issue additional shares.

The authorization of capital stock does not result in a formal accounting entry, since the event has no immediate effect on either corporate assets or stockholders' equity. However, disclosure of the number of shares of authorized stock is required in the stockholders' equity section. To determine the number of unissued shares that can be issued without amending the charter, the total shares issued are subtracted from the total authorized. For example, if Advanced Micro was authorized to sell 100,000 shares of common stock and issued 80,000 shares, there would be 20,000 unissued shares.

Issuance of Stock

A corporation may issue common stock directly to investors or indirectly through an investment banking firm (brokerage house) that specializes in bringing securities to the attention of prospective investors. Direct issue is typical in closely held companies, whereas indirect issue is customary for a publicly held corporation.

In an indirect issue, the investment banking firm may agree to **underwrite** the entire stock issue. Under this arrangement, the investment banker buys the stock from the corporation at a stipulated price and resells the shares to investors. The corporation avoids any risk of being unable to sell the shares, and it obtains immediate use of the cash received from the underwriter. The investment banking firm, in turn, assumes the risk of reselling the shares in return for an underwriting fee—the profits expected to be realized from a sales price to the public higher than the price paid to the corporation.[3] For example, Kolff Medical, maker of the Jarvik artificial heart, used an underwriter to help it issue common stock to the public. The underwriter charged a 6.6% underwriting fee on Kolff Medical's approximate $20 million public offering.

Market Value of Stock

How does a corporation set the market price for a new issue of stock? Among the factors to be considered are (1) the company's anticipated future earnings, (2) its expected dividend rate per share, (3) its current financial position, (4) the current state of the economy, and (5) the current state of the securities market.

The stock of publicly held companies is traded on organized exchanges at dollar prices per share established by the interaction between buyers and sellers. In general, the prices set by the marketplace tend to follow the trend of a company's earnings and dividends. However, factors beyond a company's control, such as the imposition of an oil embargo, new estimates on the size of the national debt, changes in interest rates, and the outcome of a presidential election, may cause day-to-day fluctuations in market prices.

The volume of trading is heavy. Shares in excess of 150 million are often traded daily on the New York Stock Exchange alone. For each listed security the financial press reports the highs and lows of the stock during the year, the total volume of stock traded for a given day, the high and low price for the day, and the closing market price, with the net change for the day. The listing for Boeing Aircraft is shown below:

ILLUSTRATION 15-6

Stock market price information

| | 52 Weeks | | Sales | | | | Net |
Stock	High	Low	3/26	High	Low	Close	Change
Boeing	54⅝	41¼	12378	44¼	43½	43⅝	+⅛

These numbers indicate that the high and low market prices for the last 52 weeks have been 54⅝ and 41¼; the trading volume for March 26 was 1,237,800 shares; the high and low and the close for that date were 44¼, 43½, and 43⅝, respectively; and the net change for the day is an increase of ⅛ or $0.125 per share.

---

[3]Alternatively, the investment banking firm may agree only to enter into a **best efforts** contract with the corporation. In such cases, the banker agrees to sell as many shares as possible at a specified price, and the corporation bears the risk of unsold stock. Under a best efforts arrangement, the banking firm is paid a fee or commission for its services.

Technology in Action

The giant, publicly held corporation could not exist without the organized stock markets, and the stock markets could not exist without massive computerization. Not too many years ago, the NYSE "ticker" would run behind, or trading would even be halted, when sales exceeded 30 million shares or so. Now, with sales sometimes in excess of 200 million shares, the NYSE and its companion exchanges throughout the country operate efficiently with computer technology.

The trading of capital stock on securities exchanges involves the transfer of issued shares from an existing stockholder to another investor. Consequently, these transactions have no impact on a corporation's stockholders' equity section.

Par and No-Par Value Stocks

Par value stock is capital stock that has been assigned a value per share in the corporate charter. The par value may be any amount selected by the corporation. Generally, the amount of par value is quite low, because states often levy a tax on the corporation based on par value. For example, International Business Machines has a par of $1.25, Ford Motor Company, $1 par, General Motors Corporation, $1.67, and PepsiCo has 1⅔ cents.

Par value is not indicative of the worth or market value of the stock. As indicated above, IBM has a par value of $1.25, but its recent market price was $85 per share. **The significance of par value is a legal matter.** Par value represents the legal capital per share that must be retained in the business for the protection of corporate creditors. That is, it is not available for withdrawal by stockholders. Thus, most states require the corporation to sell its shares at par or above.

No-par value stock is capital stock that has not been assigned a value in the corporate charter. No-par value is often issued because some confusion still exists concerning par value and fair market value. If shares have no par value, the questionable treatment of using par value as a basis for fair market value never arises. The major disadvantage of no-par stock is that some states levy a high tax on the shares issued. No-par value stock is quite common today. For example, Procter & Gamble and North American Van Lines both have no-par stock. In many states the board of directors is permitted to assign a stated value to the no-par shares, which becomes the legal capital per share. The stated value of no-par stock may be changed at any time by action of the directors. Stated value, like par value, is not indicative of the market value of the stock. When there is no assigned stated value, the entire proceeds received upon issuance of the stock is considered to be legal capital.

The relationship of par and no-par value to legal capital is graphically shown below.

ILLUSTRATION 15-7

Relationship of par and no-par value stock to legal capital

Stock	Legal Capital per Share
Par value ──────────────────→	Par value
No-par value with stated value ──────→	Stated value
No-par value without stated value ─────→	Entire proceeds

As will be explained, a common stock account is credited for the legal capital per share each time stock is issued.

Accounting for Common Stock Issues

The primary objectives in accounting for the issuance of common stock are to (1) identify the specific sources of paid-in capital and (2) maintain the distinction between paid-in capital and retained earnings. As shown below, the sale and issue of common stock affects only paid-in capital accounts.

Issuing Par Value Common Stock for Cash

Because par value does not indicate a stock's market value, the cash proceeds from issuing par value stock may be equal to, greater than, or less than par value. When the issuance of common stock for cash is recorded, the par value of the shares is credited to Common Stock, and the portion of the proceeds that is above or below par value is recorded in a separate paid-in capital account.

To illustrate, assume that Hydro-Slide, Inc. issues 1,000 shares of $1 par value common stock at par for cash. The entry to record this transaction is:

Cash	1,000	
Common Stock		1,000
(To record issuance of 1,000 shares of $1 par common stock at par)		

If Hydro-Slide, Inc. issues an additional 1,000 shares of the $1 par value common stock for cash at $5 per share, the entry is:

Cash	5,000	
Common Stock		1,000
Paid-in Capital in Excess of Par Value		4,000
(To record issuance of 1,000 shares of common stock in excess of par)		

The total paid-in capital from these two transactions is $6,000, and the legal capital is $2,000. If Hydro-Slide, Inc. has retained earnings of $27,000, the stockholders' equity section is as follows:

Stockholders' equity	
Paid-in capital	
Common stock	$ 2,000
Paid-in capital in excess of par value	4,000
Total paid-in capital	6,000
Retained earnings	27,000
Total stockholders' equity	$33,000

ILLUSTRATION 15-8

Stockholders' equity—paid-in capital in excess of par value

When stock is issued for less than par value, the account Paid-in Capital in Excess of Par Value is debited, if a credit balance exists in this account. If a credit balance does not exist, then the amount less than par is debited to Retained Earnings. This situation occurs only rarely: The sale of common stock below par value is not permitted in most states, because stockholders may be held personally liable for the difference between the price paid upon original sale and par value.

Issuing No-Par Common Stock for Cash

When no-par common stock has a stated value, the entries are similar to those illustrated for par value stock. The stated value represents legal capital and therefore is credited to Common Stock. In addition, when the selling price of no-par stock exceeds stated value, the excess is credited to Paid-in Capital in Excess of Stated Value. As an example, assume that instead of $1 par value stock, Hydro-Slide, Inc. has $5 stated value no-par stock and that it issues 5,000 shares at $8 per share for cash. The entry is:

Cash	40,000	
Common Stock		25,000
Paid-in Capital in Excess of Stated Value		15,000
(To record issue of 5,000 shares of $5 stated value no-par stock)		

Paid-in Capital in Excess of Stated Value is reported as part of paid-in capital in the stockholders' equity section.

When no-par stock does not have a stated value, the entire proceeds from the issue become legal capital and are credited to Common Stock. Thus, if Hydro-Slide does not assign a stated value to its no-par stock, the issuance of the 5,000 shares at $8 per share for cash is recorded as follows:

Cash	40,000	
Common Stock		40,000
(To record issue of 5,000 shares of no-par stock)		

The amount of legal capital for Hydro-Slide with a $5 stated value is $25,000; without a stated value, it is $40,000.

Issuing Common Stock for Services or Noncash Assets

Stock may be issued for services (compensation to attorneys, consultants, and others) or for noncash assets (land, buildings, and equipment). In such cases, a question arises as to the cost that should be recognized in the exchange transaction. **To comply with the cost principle in a non-cash transaction, cost is the cash equivalent price. Thus, cost is either the fair market value of the consideration given up or the fair market value of the consideration received, whichever is more clearly determinable.**

To illustrate, assume that the attorneys for Advanced Design Inc., agree to accept 4,000 shares of $1 par value common stock in payment of their bill of $5,000 for services performed in helping the company to incorporate. At the time of the exchange, there is no established market price for the stock. In this case, the market value of the consideration received, $5,000, is more clearly evident. Accordingly, the entry is:

Organization Costs	5,000	
Common Stock		4,000
Paid-in Capital in Excess of Par Value		1,000
(To record issuance of 4,000 shares of $1 par value stock to attorneys)		

As explained earlier, organization costs are classified as an intangible asset in the balance sheet.

In contrast, assume that Athletic Research Inc. is a publicly held corporation whose $5 par value stock is actively traded at $8 per share. The company issues 10,000 shares of stock to acquire land recently advertised for sale at $90,000. On the basis of these facts the most clearly evident value is the market price of the consideration given, $80,000. Thus, the transaction is recorded as follows:

Land	80,000	
Common Stock		50,000
Paid-in Capital in Excess of Par Value		30,000
(To record issuance of 10,000 shares of $5 par value stock for land)		

As illustrated in these examples, **the par value of the stock is never a factor in determining the cost of the assets received**. This is also true of the stated value of no-par stock.

Sale of Common Stock on a Subscription Basis

Instead of selling stock for cash, a corporation may sell stock on a subscription basis. The **subscription agreement** usually requires the investor to pay the contract price over a series of installment payments. The corporation does not issue the shares until the contract price is paid in full. Stock may be sold on a subscription basis when a corporation offers stock to its employees to encourage them to acquire an ownership interest in the company. In addition, small businesses may use stock subscriptions because they do not want to incur the cost of underwriting the sale of their stock.

Stock subscriptions occur infrequently in practice. Consequently, the accounting and reporting of stock subscriptions are deferred to advanced accounting courses.

Donated Capital

Donated capital results when a corporation receives assets as a result of a gift or donation from municipalities, charitable foundations, or other sources. If the donation is received in cash, Cash is debited and Donated Capital is credited for the amount received.

A problem of valuation arises when the donation involves a noncash asset. Assume, for example, that Southern Corporation receives land having a fair market value of $195,000 from a municipality as a donation. Should the plant site be valued at cost to Southern, which is zero, or should it be recorded at fair market value? The use of cost in this case is inappropriate, because no basis of accountability for the asset received would exist. Fair market value should be used, because it provides a more realistic basis of accountability for the resources received through the donation. Thus, the entry is:

Land	195,000	
Donated Capital		195,000
(To record donation of land from city)		

Donated Capital is classified as part of paid-in capital in the stockholders' equity section of the balance sheet.

Accounting for Treasury Stock

Helpful hint Treasury stock is so named because the company often holds the shares in its treasury for safekeeping.

Treasury stock is a corporation's own stock that has been issued, fully paid for, and reacquired by the corporation but not retired. A corporation may acquire treasury stock to:

1. Reissue the shares to officers and employees under bonus and stock compensation plans.
2. Increase trading of the company's stock in the securities market in the hopes of enhancing its market value.
3. Have additional shares available for use in the acquisition of other companies.
4. Reduce the number of shares outstanding and thereby increase earnings per share.

Many corporations have treasury stock. For example, one survey of 600 companies in the United States indicated that 65% have treasury stock.[4] Specifically, in a recent year, Monsanto reported 41.5 million treasury shares, PepsiCo 74 million, and Gillette 57.7 million.

Purchase of Treasury Stock

The cost method is generally used in accounting for treasury stock. This method derives its name from the fact that the Treasury Stock account is maintained at the cost of shares purchased. Under the cost method, Treasury Stock is debited at the price paid to reacquire the shares, and the same amount is credited to Treasury Stock when the shares are sold. To illustrate, assume that on January 1, 1993, the stockholders' equity section of Mead, Inc. has 100,000 shares of $5 par value common stock outstanding (all issued at par value) and Retained Earnings of $200,000.

The stockholders' equity section before purchase of treasury stock is as follows:

ILLUSTRATION 15-9

Stockholders' equity with no treasury stock

Stockholders' equity	
Paid-in capital	
Common stock, $5 par value, 100,000 shares issued and outstanding	$500,000
Retained earnings	200,000
Total stockholders' equity	$700,000

On February 1, 1993, Mead acquires 4,000 shares of its stock at $8 per share. The entry is:

Feb. 1	Treasury Stock	32,000	
	Cash		32,000
	(To record purchase of 4,000 shares of treasury stock at $8 per share)		

Note that Treasury Stock is debited for the cost of the shares purchased. The original paid-in capital account, Common Stock, is not affected because the number of issued shares does not change. Treasury Stock is a contra stockholders'

---

[4]*Accounting Trends & Techniques 1991* (New York: American Institute of Certified Public Accountants).

equity account. **Thus, the acquisition of treasury stock reduces both paid-in capital and retained earnings.**

The stockholders' equity section of Mead, Inc., after purchase of treasury stock is as follows:

ILLUSTRATION 15-10

Stockholders' equity with treasury stock

Stockholders' equity	
Paid-in capital	
Common stock, $5 par value, 100,000 shares issued and 96,000 shares outstanding	$500,000
Retained earnings	200,000
Total paid-in capital and retained earnings	700,000
Less: Treasury stock (4,000 shares)	32,000
Total stockholders' equity	$668,000

Both the number of shares issued (100,000) and the number in the treasury (4,000) are disclosed. The difference is the number of shares of stock outstanding (96,000). The term outstanding stock means the number of shares of issued stock that are being held by stockholders.

Some maintain that treasury stock should be reported as an asset because it can be sold for cash. Under this reasoning, unissued stock should also be shown as an asset, clearly an erroneous conclusion. Rather than being an asset, treasury stock reduces stockholder claims on corporate assets. This effect is correctly shown by reporting treasury stock as a deduction from total paid-in capital and retained earnings.

Disposal of Treasury Stock

Treasury stock is usually sold or retired. The accounting for its sale is different when treasury stock is sold above cost than when it is sold below cost.

Sale of Treasury Stock above Cost

Treasury stock is often sold. If the selling price of the treasury shares is equal to cost, the sale of the shares is recorded by a debit to Cash and a credit to Treasury Stock. When the selling price of the shares is greater than cost, the difference is credited to Paid-in Capital from Treasury Stock. To illustrate, assume that 1,000 shares of treasury stock of Mead, Inc., previously acquired at $8 per share, are sold at $10 per share on July 1. The entry is as follows:

Helpful hint Treasury stock transactions are classified as capital stock transactions. As in the case of issuing stock, the income statement is not involved.

July 1	Cash	10,000	
	Treasury Stock		8,000
	Paid-in Capital from Treasury Stock		2,000
	(To record sale of 1,000 shares of treasury stock above cost)		

The $2,000 credit in the entry is *not* made to Gain on Sale of Treasury Stock for two reasons: (1) Gains on sales occur when assets are sold and treasury stock is not an asset. (2) A corporation does not realize a gain or suffer a loss from stock transactions with its own stockholders. Thus, paid-in capital arising from the sale of treasury stock should not be included in the measurement of net income. Paid-in capital from Treasury Stock is listed separately on the balance sheet as a part of paid-in capital.

Sale of Treasury Stock below Cost

When treasury stock is sold below its cost, the excess of cost over selling price is usually debited to Paid-in Capital from Treasury Stock. Thus, if Mead, Inc. sells an additional 800 shares of treasury stock on October 1 at $7 per share, the entry is as follows:

Oct. 1	Cash	5,600	
	Paid-in Capital from Treasury Stock	800	
	Treasury Stock		6,400
	(To record sale of 800 shares of treasury stock below cost)		

Observe from the two sales entries that (1) Treasury Stock is credited at cost in each entry, (2) Paid-in Capital from Treasury Stock is used for the difference between the cost and resale price of the shares, and (3) the original paid-in capital account, Common Stock, again is not affected. **The sale of treasury stock increases both total assets and total stockholders' equity.**

After posting the foregoing entries, the treasury stock accounts will show the following balances on October 1:

ILLUSTRATION 15-11

Treasury stock accounts

Treasury Stock				Paid-in Capital from Treasury Stock			
Feb. 1	32,000	July 1	8,000	Oct. 1	800	July 1	2,000
		Oct. 1	6,400				
Oct. 1 Bal.	17,600					Oct. 1 Bal.	1,200

When the credit balance in Paid-in Capital from Treasury Stock is eliminated, any additional excess of cost over selling price is debited to Retained Earnings. To illustrate, assume that Mead, Inc., sells its remaining 2,200 shares at $7 per share on December 1. The excess of cost over selling price is $2,200 [2,200 × ($8 − $7)]. In this case, $1,200 of the excess is debited to Paid-in Capital from Treasury Stock, and the remainder is debited to Retained Earnings. The entry is:

Dec. 1	Cash	15,400	
	Paid-in Capital from Treasury Stock	1,200	
	Retained Earnings	1,000	
	Treasury Stock		17,600
	(To record sale of 2,200 shares of treasury stock at $7 per share)		

Retiring Treasury Stock

The board of directors may approve the retiring of treasury shares. This decision results in cancellation of the treasury stock and a reduction in the number of shares of issued stock. The accounting effects are similar to the sale of treasury stock except that debits are made to the paid-in capital accounts applicable to the retired shares instead of to cash. For example, if the shares are originally sold at par, Common Stock is debited for the par value per share. If the shares are originally sold at $3 above par value, a debit to Paid-in Capital in Excess of Par Value for $3 per share is also required.

To illustrate, assume that Ottman Company originally issued 10,000 shares of $10 par common stock for $120,000 ($12 per share) on January 2, 1993. Ottman then purchased 1,000 shares of treasury stock for $11,000 ($11 per share) on

November 5, 1993. Ottman decides to retire the treasury stock on December 10, 1993. The paid-in capital accounts applicable to the treasury stock are: Common Stock $10,000 (1,000 shares × $10) and Paid-in Capital in Excess of Par Value 2,000 (1,000 shares × $2). Thus, the entry to record the retirement is as follows:

Dec. 10	Common Stock	10,000	
	Paid-in Capital in Excess of Par Value	2,000	
	Treasury Stock		11,000
	Paid-in Capital from Treasury Stock		1,000
	(To record retirement of 1,000 shares of treasury		
	stock)		

In this case, the cost of the treasury stock ($11,000) is less than the applicable paid-in capital ($12,000). Accordingly, the difference is credited to Paid-in Capital from Treasury Stock. If the reverse was true, the excess of applicable paid-in capital over the cost of treasury stock is debited to Paid-in Capital from Treasury Stock until this account has a zero balance. Any additional amount is then debited to Retained Earnings.

Before You Go On . . .

1. Explain the accounting for par and no-par common stock issued for cash. Explain the accounting for the issuance of stock for services or noncash assets.

2. What is treasury stock, and why may companies acquire it?

3. How is treasury stock recorded? Where is treasury stock reported in the financial statements? Does a company record gains and losses on treasury stock transactions? Explain.

Preferred Stock

To appeal to a larger segment of potential investors, a corporation may issue both common and preferred stock. Preferred stock has contractual provisions that give it a preference or priority over common stock in certain areas. Typically, preferred stockholders have a preference as to (1) dividends and (2) assets in the event of liquidation. However, they generally do not have voting rights.

    Like common stock, preferred stock may be issued for cash, or for noncash assets. The entries for these transactions are similar to the entries for common stock. When a corporation has more than one class of stock, each paid-in capital account title should identify the stock to which it relates (e.g., Preferred Stock, Common Stock, Paid-in Capital in Excess of Par Value—Preferred Stock, and Paid-in Capital in Excess of Par Value—Common Stock). Assume that Stine Corporation issues 10,000 shares of $10 par value preferred stock for $12 cash per share. The entry to record the issuance is:

Study Objective 5

Differentiate preferred stock from common stock.

Cash		120,000	
Preferred Stock			100,000
Paid-in Capital in Excess of Par Value—Preferred Stock			20,000
(To record the issuance of 10,000 shares of $10 par value			
preferred stock)			

    Preferred stock may have either a par value or no-par value. For example, Walgreen Drug Co. has $.50 par value preferred and General Motors has three classes of no-par preferred stock, each with a stated value of $100. In the stockholders' equity section, preferred stock is shown first because of its dividend and liquidation preferences over common stock.

Dividend Preferences

As indicated before, preferred stockholders have the right to share in the distribution of corporate income before common stockholders. For example, if the dividend rate on preferred stock is $5 per share, common shareholders will not receive any dividends in the current year until preferred stockholders have received $5 per share. The first claim to dividends does not, however, guarantee dividends. Dividends depend on many factors, such as adequate retained earnings and availability of cash.

The per share dividend amount is stated as a percentage of the par value of preferred stock or as a specified amount. For example, the Crane Company specifies 3 3/4% dividend on its $100 par value preferred ($100 × 3 3/4% = $3.75 per share), whereas DuPont has both a $4.50 and a $3.50 series of no-par preferred stock.

Cumulative Dividend

Preferred stock contracts often contain a cumulative dividend feature. This right means that preferred stockholders must be paid both current-year dividends and unpaid prior-year dividends before common stockholders receive any dividends. When preferred stock is cumulative, preferred dividends not declared in a given period are called **dividends in arrears**. To illustrate, assume that Scientific-Leasing has 5,000 shares of 7%, $100 par value cumulative preferred stock outstanding. The annual dividend is $35,000 (5,000 × $7 per share). If dividends are two years in arrears, preferred stockholders are entitled to receive the following dividends in the current year before any distribution is made to common stockholders:

ILLUSTRATION 15-12

Computation of total dividends to preferred stock

Dividends in arrears ($35,000 × 2)	$ 70,000
Current year dividends	35,000
Total preferred dividends	**$105,000**

Dividends in arrears are not considered a liability, because no obligation exists until the dividend is declared by the board of directors. However, the amount of dividends in arrears should be disclosed in the notes to the financial

Accounting in Action ▪ *Business Insight*

Dividends in arrears can extend for fairly long periods of time. Long Island Lighting Company's directors voted recently to make up some $390 million in preferred dividends that had been in arrears since 1984 and to resume normal quarterly preferred payments. The announcement resulted from an agreement between the company and New York state to abandon a nuclear power plant in exchange for sizable rate increases over the next ten years.

statements, so that investors can assess the potential impact of this commitment on the corporation's financial position.

No dividends may be paid on common stock while any dividend on preferred stock is in arrears. The cumulative feature is often critical in investor acceptance of a preferred stock issue. When preferred stock is noncumulative, a dividend passed in any year is lost forever. Companies that are unable to meet their dividend obligations are not looked upon favorably by the investment community. As one financial officer noted in discussing one company's failure to pay its cumulative preferred dividend for a period of time, "Not meeting your obligations on something like that is a major black mark on your record." The accounting entries for preferred stock dividends are explained in Chapter 16.

Participating Dividend

Preferred stock may also have a participating dividend feature. This right enables the preferred stockholder to share ratably (proportionately) with common stockholders in any dividends beyond the rate specified on the preferred stock. The participating feature does not apply until common stockholders receive a percentage rate of return on their shares equal to the specified dividend rate on preferred stock. The issuance of participating preferred stock is rare.

Liquidation Preference

Most preferred stocks have a preference on corporate assets if the corporation fails. This feature provides security for the preferred stockholder. The preference to assets may be for the par value of the shares or for a specified liquidating value. For example, Commonwealth Edison issued preferred stock that entitles the holders to receive $31.80 per share, plus accrued and unpaid dividends, in the event of involuntary liquidation. The liquidation preference is used in litigation pertaining to bankruptcy lawsuits involving the respective claims of creditors and preferred stockholders.

Convertible Preferred Stock

The attractiveness of preferred stock as an investment is enhanced by adding a conversion privilege. Convertible preferred stock provides for the exchange of preferred stock into common stock at a specified ratio.

Convertible preferreds are purchased by investors who want the greater security of a preferred stock, but who also desire the added option of conversion if the market value of the common stock increases significantly. To illustrate, assume that Ross Industries issues at par value 1,000 shares of $100 par value convertible preferred stock. One share of preferred is convertible into 10 shares of $5 par value common (current price $9 per share). At this point, it would not be advantageous for the holders of the preferred to convert, because they would exchange preferred stock worth $100,000 (1,000 × $100) for common stock worth $90,000 (10,000 × $9). However, if the price of the common stock were to increase above $10 per share, it often would be advantageous for the preferred holders to convert.

In recording the conversion, it is customary to transfer the amount paid in on the preferred stock to appropriate common stock accounts. To illustrate, assume that the 1,000 shares of Ross Industries preferred issued at $100 par value are converted into 10,000 shares of common stock ($5 par) when the market value per share of the two classes of stock are $101 and $12 respectively. The entry to record the conversion is:

Preferred Stock	100,000	
Common Stock		50,000
Paid-in Capital in Excess of Par Value—Common Stock		50,000
(To record conversion of 1,000 shares of preferred stock into		
10,000 shares of $5 par value common stock)		

The conversion of preferred stock does not result in either gain or loss to the corporation. If the preferred stock was issued for more than its par value, the paid-in capital in excess of the par value on the preferred stock should be eliminated. **Note that the market values of the shares at the time of the transaction are not considered in recording the transaction.** The reason is that the exchange of shares is made directly through the corporation and the corporation has not received any assets equal to fair market value.

Callable Preferred Stock

Many preferred stocks are callable. A callable preferred stock grants the issuing corporation the right to purchase the stock from stockholders at specified future dates and prices. The **call (or redemption) price** is frequently slightly above the par or stated value of the shares. The callable feature offers some flexibility to a corporation by enabling it to eliminate this type of equity security when it is advantageous to do so. When preferred stock is callable, the call price tends to set a ceiling on the market price of the shares.

Statement Presentation of Stockholders' Equity

Study Objective 6

Prepare a stockholders' equity section.

In the stockholders' equity section, paid-in capital and retained earnings are reported and the specific sources of paid-in capital are identified.

Within paid-in capital, two classifications are recognized:

1. **Capital stock**, which consists of preferred and common stock. Preferred stock is shown before common stock because of its preferential rights. Information as to the par value, shares authorized, shares issued, and shares outstanding is also reported for each class of stock.
2. **Additional paid-in capital**, which includes the excess of amounts paid in over par or stated value, paid-in capital from treasury stock, and donated capital.

The stockholders' equity section of Connally Inc. shown in Illustration 15-13 includes most of the accounts discussed in this chapter. The disclosures pertaining to Connally's common stock indicate that 400,000 shares are issued, 100,000 shares are unissued (500,000 authorized less 400,000 issued), and 390,000 shares are outstanding (400,000 issued less 10,000 shares in treasury).

In published annual reports, subclassifications within the stockholders' equity section are seldom presented. Moreover, the individual sources of additional paid-in capital are often combined and reported as a single amount as shown in Illustration 15-14.

In practice, the term "capital surplus" is sometimes used in place of additional paid-in capital and "earned surplus" in place of retained earnings. The use of the term "surplus" suggests that an excess amount of funds is available. Such is not necessarily the case, and that is why **the term surplus should not be employed in accounting**. Unfortunately, a number of financial statements still include these terms.

ILLUSTRATION 15-13

Stockholders' equity section

CONNALLY INC. Partial Balance Sheet		
Stockholders' equity		
Paid-in capital		
Capital stock		
9% preferred stock, $100 par value, callable at $120, cumulative, 10,000 shares authorized, 6,000 shares issued and outstanding		$ 600,000
Common stock, no par, $5 stated value, 500,000 shares authorized, 400,000 shares issued, and 390,000 outstanding		2,000,000
Total capital stock		2,600,000
Additional paid-in capital		
In excess of par value—preferred stock	$ 30,000	
In excess of stated value—common stock	860,000	
From treasury stock	40,000	
Donated capital	100,000	
Total additional paid-in capital		1,030,000
Total paid-in capital		3,630,000
Retained earnings		1,058,000
Total paid-in capital and retained earnings		4,688,000
Less: Treasury stock—common (10,000 shares)		(80,000)
Total stockholders' equity		$4,608,000

ILLUSTRATION 15-14

Published stockholders' equity section

MARTIN MARIETTA CORPORATION		
Stockholders' equity		
Common stock	$ 49,530,000	
Additional paid-in capital	211,751,000	
Retained earnings	1,542,622,000	
Total stockholders' equity		$1,803,903,000

Book Value—Another Per Share Amount

You have learned about a number of per share amounts in this chapter. Another per share amount of some importance is book value per share. This per share amount represents **the equity a common stockholder has in the net assets of the corporation** from owning one share of stock. Since the net assets of a corporation must be equal to total stockholders' equity, the formula for computing book value per share when a company has only one class of stock outstanding is:

ILLUSTRATION 15-15

Book value per share formula

Thus, if the Marlo Corporation has total stockholders' equity of $1,500,000 (Common Stock $1,000,000 and Retained Earnings $500,000) and 50,000 shares of common stock outstanding, book value per share is $30 ($1,500,000 ÷ 50,000).

When a company has both preferred and common stock, the computation of book value is more complex. Since preferred stockholders have a prior claim on net assets over common stockholders, their equity must be deducted from total stockholders' equity to determine the stockholders' equity applicable to the common stock. The preferred stock equity consists of the call (or redemption) price of the stock plus any dividends in arrears. If the preferred stock does not have a call price, par value is used. Preferred stockholders ordinarily do not have a right to amounts paid-in in excess of par value. Accordingly, such amounts are assigned to the common stock equity in computing book value.

To illustrate, we will use the stockholders' equity section of Connally Inc. shown in Illustration 15-13. Connally's preferred stock is callable at $120 per share and cumulative. Assume that dividends on Connally's preferred stock were in arrears for the current year, $54,000 (6,000 × $9). The computation of book value is as follows:

ILLUSTRATION 15-16

Computation of book value per share with preferred stock

Total stockholders' equity		$4,608,000
Less: Preferred stock equity		
Call price (6,000 × $120)	$720,000	
Dividends in arrears (6,000 × $9)	54,000	774,000
Common stock equity		$3,834,000
Shares of common stock outstanding		390,000
Book value per share ($3,834,000 ÷ 390,000)		$9.83

Note that the paid-in capital in excess of par value of preferred stock, $30,000, **is not assigned to the preferred stock equity**.

Book value per share is not synonymous with the value of the stock in liquidation ("break-up value"). If the corporation is liquidated, it is unlikely that noncash assets can be converted into cash without gain or loss to the company.

Moreover, like the book value of a plant asset, **book value per share may not equal fair market value**. Book value is based on recorded costs; market value reflects the subjective judgment of thousands of stockholders and prospective investors about a company's potential for future earnings and dividends. Market value per share may exceed book value per share, but that fact does not necessarily mean that the stock is overpriced. The correlation between book value and the annual range of a company's market value per share is often remote, as indicated by the following recent data:

ILLUSTRATION 15-17

Book and market values compared

Company	Book Value (year-end)	Market Range (for year)
Delta Airlines, Inc.	$50	$53–79
Boise Cascade Corporation	$37	$18–29
Sears Roebuck and Co.	$40	$24–44

Book value per share *is* useful in determining the trend of a stockholder's per share equity in a corporation. It is also significant in many contracts and in court cases where the rights of individual parties are based on cost information.

Supporting Stock Records and Procedures

To maintain a complete record of its stock transactions with individual stockholders, a corporation must maintain subsidiary stockholders' ledgers for each class of stock issued. A corporation also keeps a stock transfer book, which is a log of transfers of stock among investors. The stock transfer book facilitates the updating of the stockholders' ledger.

Instead of maintaining its own supporting stock records and transfer book, a corporation may engage a bank or trust company to serve as a transfer agent and registrar. Periodically, this outside agency provides the corporation with a current list of registered stockholders.

An important source of accounting information in a corporation is the **minutes book**, which contains a record of decisions made at the annual stockholders' meeting and at meetings of the board of directors. For example, the minutes book will reveal the board of directors' authorizations for dividends, compensation of officers, and commitments to purchase major plant assets. The minutes book is usually kept by the corporate secretary.

Technology in Action

Computer technology is needed to keep track of the stock transactions for most large corporations. The task of keeping track of 2 million shareholders of General Motors would be virtually impossible without such computer systems. Many firms specialize in keeping track of shareholder transactions for other firms. Using large computerized systems, such companies take on duties involving distribution of corporate financial data and dividend distributions.

Before You Go On . . .

1. What features differentiate preferred stock from common stock?

2. What are the similarities and differences between accounting for preferred stock and common stock issues?

3. Identify the classifications within the paid-in capital section and the totals that are stated in the stockholders' equity section of a balance sheet.

4. What is the formula for computing book value per share when there is (a) only one class of stock and (b) both preferred and common stock?

Summary of Study Objectives

1. *Identify and discuss the major characteristics of a corporation.* The major characteristics of a corporation are separate legal existence, limited liability of stockholders, transferable ownership rights, ability to acquire capital, continuous life, corporation management, government regulations, and additional taxes.

2. *Differentiate between paid-in capital and retained earnings.* Paid-in capital is the total amount paid in on capital stock. It is often referred to as contributed capital. Retained earnings is net income retained in a corporation. It is often referred to as earned capital.

3. Record the issuance of common stock. When the issuance of common stock for cash is recorded, the par value of the shares is credited to Common Stock and the portion of the proceeds that is above or below par value is recorded in a separate paid-in capital account. When no-par common stock has a stated value, the entries are similar to those for par value stock. When no-par does not have a stated value, the entire proceeds from the issue become legal capital and are credited to Common Stock.

4. Explain the accounting for treasury stock. The cost method is generally used in accounting for treasury stock. Under this approach, Treasury Stock is debited at the price paid to reacquire the shares, and the same amount is credited to Treasury Stock when the shares are sold. The difference between the sales price and cost is recorded in stockholders' equity accounts, not in income statement accounts. When treasury stock is retired, applicable paid-in capital accounts are debited.

5. Differentiate preferred stock from common stock. Preferred stock has contractual provisions that give it priority over common stock in certain areas. Typically, preferred stockholders have a preference as to (1) dividends and (2) assets in the event of liquida-

tion. However, they usually do not have voting rights. In addition, preferred stock may be convertible and/or callable. A convertible preferred stock entitles the holder of the preferred stock to convert those shares to common stock in a specified ratio. The callable feature grants to the issuing corporation the right to purchase the stock from stockholders at specified future dates and prices.

6. Prepare a stockholders' equity section. In the stockholders' equity section, paid-in capital and retained earnings are reported and specific sources of paid-in capital are identified. Within paid-in capital, two classifications are shown: capital stock and additional paid-in capital. If a corporation has treasury stock, the cost of treasury stock is deducted from total paid-in capital and retained earnings to obtain total stockholders' equity.

7. Compute book value per share. Book value per share represents the equity a common stockholder has in the net assets of a corporation from owning one share of stock. When there is only common stock outstanding, the formula for computing book value is: Total Stockholders' Equity ÷ Number of Common Shares Outstanding = Book Value per Share.

GLOSSARY

Authorized stock · The amount of stock that a corporation is authorized to sell as indicated in its charter. (p. 594).

Book value per share · The equity a common stockholder has in the net assets of the corporation from owning one share of stock. (p. 607).

By-laws · The internal rules and procedures for conducting the affairs of a corporation. (p. 590).

Callable preferred stock · Preferred stock that grants the issuer the right to purchase the stock from stockholders at specified future dates and prices. (p. 606).

Charter · A document that creates a corporation. (p. 590).

Convertible preferred stock · Preferred stock that provides for the exchange of preferred stock into common stock at a specified ratio. (p. 605).

Corporation · A business organized as a legal entity separate and distinct from its owners under state corporation law. (p. 586).

Cumulative dividend · A feature of preferred stock entitling the stockholder to receive current and unpaid prior-year dividends before common stockholders receive any dividends. (p. 604).

Donated capital · Paid-in capital that results from the gift or donation of assets to a corporation. (p. 599).

Legal capital · The amount per share of stock that must be retained in the business for the protection of corporate creditors. (p. 596).

Minutes book · A record of decisions made at the annual stockholders' meeting and at meetings of the board of directors. (p. 609).

No-par value stock · Capital stock that has not been assigned a value in the corporate charter. (p. 596).

Organization costs · Costs incurred in the formation of a corporation. (p. 591).

Outstanding stock · Capital stock that has been issued and is being held by stockholders. (p. 601).

Paid-in capital · Total amount paid in on capital stock. (p. 591).

Par value stock · Capital stock that has been assigned a value per share in the corporate charter. (p. 596).

Participating dividend · A feature of preferred stock enabling the stockholder to share ratably with common stockholders in any dividends beyond the rate specified on the preferred stock. (p. 605).

Preferred stock · Capital stock that has contractual preferences over common stock in certain areas. (p. 603).

Privately held corporation · A corporation that has only a few stockholders and whose stock is not available for sale to the general public. (p. 587).

Publicly held corporation · A corporation that has thousands of stockholders and whose stock is regularly traded on a national securities market. (p. 586).

Retained earnings · Net income retained in the corporation. (p. 591).

Stated value · The amount per share assigned by the board of directors to no-par stock that becomes legal capital per share. (p. 596).

Treasury stock · A corporation's own stock that has been issued, fully paid for, and reacquired by the corporation but not retired. (p. 600).

DEMONSTRATION PROBLEM

The Rolman Corporation is authorized to issue 1,000,000 shares of $5 par value common stock. During 1993, its first year, the company has the following stock transactions.

Jan. 10 Issued 400,000 shares of stock at $8 per share.

July 1 Issued 100,000 shares of stock for land. The land had an asking price of $900,000. The stock is currently selling on a national exchange at $8.25 per share.

Sept. 1 Purchased 10,000 shares of common stock for the treasury at $9.00 per share.

Dec. 1 Sold 4,000 shares of the treasury stock at $10 per share.

Instructions

(a) Journalize the transactions.

(b) Prepare the stockholders' equity section assuming the company had retained earnings of $200,000 at December 31, 1993.

Solution to Demonstration Problem

(a) Jan. 10	Cash	3,200,000	
	Common Stock		2,000,000
	Paid-in Capital in Excess of Par Value		1,200,000
	(To record issuance of 400,000 shares of $5 par value stock)		
July 1	Land	825,000	
	Common Stock		500,000
	Paid-in Capital in Excess of Par Value		325,000
	(To record issuance of 100,000 shares of $5 par value stock for land)		
Sept. 1	Treasury Stock	90,000	
	Cash		90,000
	(To record purchase of 10,000 shares of treasury stock at cost)		
Dec. 1	Cash	40,000	
	Treasury Stock		36,000
	Paid-in Capital from Treasury Stock		4,000
	(To record sale of 4,000 shares of treasury stock above cost)		

Helpful hints

1. When common stock has a par value, Common Stock is always credited for par value.
2. In a noncash transaction, fair market value should be used.
3. The Treasury Stock account is debited and credited at cost.
4. Differences between the cost and selling price of treasury stock are recorded in stockholders' equity accounts, not as gains or losses.

(b) Stockholders' equity
    Paid-in capital
        Capital Stock
            Common stock, $5 par, 1,000,000 shares authorized,
            500,000 shares issued, 494,000 shares outstanding $2,500,000
        Additional paid-in capital
            In excess of par value $1,525,000
            From treasury stock   4,000
                Total additional paid-in capital   1,529,000
                Total paid-in capital   4,029,000
        Retained earnings   200,000
                Total paid-in capital and retained earnings   4,229,000
        Less: Treasury stock (6,000 shares)   54,000
                Total stockholders' equity $4,175,000

SELF-STUDY QUESTIONS

Answers are at the end of the chapter.

(S.O. 1)   1. Which of the following is *not* a major ad-
            vantage of a corporation?
            a. Separate legal existence.
            b. Additional taxes.
            c. Continuous life.
            d. Transferable ownership rights.

(S.O. 1)   2. A major disadvantage of a corporation is:
            a. government regulation.
            b. limited liability of stockholders.
            c. transferable ownership rights.
            d. None of the above.

(S.O. 2)   3. Which of the following statements is *false*?
            a. Ownership of common stock gives the
               owner a voting right.
            b. The stockholders' equity section be-
               gins with paid-in capital.
            c. Legal capital per share applies to par
               value stock but not to no-par value
               stock.
            d. The authorization of capital stock does
               not result in a formal accounting entry.

(S.O. 2)   4. The account, Retained Earnings, is:
            a. net income retained in the corporation.
            b. a subdivision of paid-in capital.
            c. reported as an expense in the income
               statement.
            d. closed to capital stock.

(S.O. 3)   5. ABC Corporation issues 1,000 shares of
            $10 par value common stock at $12 per
            share. In recording the transaction, cred-
            its are made to:
            a. Common Stock $10,000 and Paid-in
               Capital in Excess of Par $2,000.
            b. Common Stock $12,000.
            c. Common Stock $10,000 and Paid-in

Capital in Excess of Stated Value,
$2,000.
            d. Common Stock $10,000 and Retained
               Earnings $2,000.

(S.O. 4)   6. XYZ, Inc., sells 100 shares of $5 par value
            treasury stock at $14 per share. If the cost
            of acquiring the shares was $10 per share,
            the entry for the sale should include cred-
            its to:
            a. Treasury Stock $500 and Paid-in Cap-
               ital from Treasury Stock $900.
            b. Treasury Stock $1,000 and Paid-in
               Capital from Treasury Stock $400.
            c. Treasury Stock $1,000 and Retained
               Earnings $400.
            d. Treasury Stock $1,000 and Paid-in
               Capital in Excess of Par $400.

(S.O. 4)   7. In the stockholders' equity section, the
            cost of treasury stock is deducted from:
            a. Common stock in paid-in capital.
            b. Retained earnings.
            c. Total stockholders' equity.
            d. Total paid-in capital and retained
               earnings.

(S.O. 5)   8. Preferred stock may have priority over
            common stock *except* in:
            a. dividends.
            b. assets in the event of liquidation.
            c. voting.
            d. conversion.

(S.O. 6)   9. Which of the following is *not* reported un-
            der additional paid-in capital?
            a. Common stock.
            b. Paid-in capital in excess of par value.
            c. Donated capital.
            d. Paid-in capital from treasury stock.

(S.O. 7) 10. The ledger of JFK, Inc., shows common stock, common treasury stock, and no preferred stock. For this company, the formula for computing book value per share is:
  a. Total paid-in capital and retained earnings divided by the number of shares of common stock issued.
  b. Common stock divided by the number of shares of common stock issued.
  c. Total stockholders' equity divided by the number of shares of common stock issued.
  d. Total stockholders' equity divided by the number of shares of common stock outstanding.

QUESTIONS

1. Distinguish between a publicly held and a privately held corporation.

2. Mark Koner and Sally Sharp are discussing the advantages and disadvantages of a corporation. Mark indicates one major advantage is that a stockholder's liability to the creditors of a corporation is less than a partner's liability to the creditors of a partnership. Do you agree? Why?

3. A corporation has been defined as an entity separate and distinct from its owners. In what ways is a corporation a separate legal entity?

4. On the Senate floor recently, one senator stated that taxes should be eliminated on dividends of common and preferred stock. He said that to tax these dividends amounts to "double taxation." What is "double taxation"?

5. What are the basic ownership rights of common stockholders in the absence of restrictive provisions?

6. What are the two principal components of stockholders' equity?

7. What is paid-in capital? Give three examples.

8. How do the financial statements for a corporation differ from the statements for a proprietorship?

9. The corporate charter of Betterman Corporation allows the issuance of a maximum of 100,000 shares of common stock. During its first two years of operations, Betterman sold 65,000 shares to shareholders and reacquired 7,000 of these shares. After these transactions, how many shares are authorized, issued, and outstanding?

10. Which is the better investment, common stock with a par value of $5 per share or common stock with a par value of $20 per share?

11. What factors help determine the market value of stock?

12. What effect does the issuance of stock at a price above par value have on the issuer's net income? Explain.

13. Why is common stock usually not issued at a price that is less than par value?

14. Land appraised at $80,000 is purchased by issuing 1,000 shares of $20 par value common stock. The market price of the shares at the time of the exchange, based on active trading in the securities market, is $85 per share. Should the land be recorded at $20,000, $80,000, or $85,000? Explain.

15. Seabron, Inc., has donated capital. (a) What are the sources of donated capital? (b) How should this capital be reported?

16. How should the receipt of land as a donation be recorded by the corporation that received the donation?

17. For what reasons might IBM repurchase some of its stock (treasury stock)?

18. Gilmore, Inc., purchases 1,000 shares of its own previously issued $5 par common stock for $12,000. Assuming the shares are held in the treasury, what effect does this transaction have on (a) net income, (b) total assets, (c) total paid-in capital, and (d) total stockholders' equity?

19. The treasury stock purchased in question 18 above is resold by Gilmore, Inc., for $13,500. What effect does this transaction have on (a) net income, (b) total assets, (c) total paid-in capital, and (d) total stockholders' equity?

20. (a) What are the principal differences between common stock and preferred stock?
(b) Preferred stock may be cumulative or participating or both. Discuss these features.

21. A preferred stockholder exercises her right to convert her convertible preferred stock into common stock. What effect does this have on (a) the corporation's total assets, (b) its total liabilities, and (c) total stockholders' equity?

22. What is the formula for computing book value when a corporation only has common stock?

23. WAT, Inc.'s common stock has a par value of $1, a book value of $29, and a current market value of $15. Explain why these amounts are all different.

24. Indicate how each of the following accounts should be classified in the stockholders' equity section.
(a) Common stock
(b) Retained earnings
(c) Paid-in capital in excess of par value
(d) Treasury stock
(e) Paid-in capital from treasury stock
(f) Paid-in capital in excess of stated value
(g) Donated capital
(h) Preferred stock

BRIEF EXERCISES

Advantages and disadvantages of a corporation. (S.O. 1)

BE15–1 Tracy Thomas is studying for her accounting midterm examination. Identify for Tracy, the advantages and disadvantages of the corporate form of business organization.

Closing entries for a corporation. (S.O. 2)

BE15–2 At December 31, Mile High Corporation reports net income of $500,000. Prepare the entry to close net income.

Issuance of par value common stock. (S.O. 3)

BE15–3 On May 10, Arvada Corporation issues 1,000 shares of $10 par value common stock for cash at $15 per share. Journalize the issuance of the stock.

Issuance of no-par value common stock. (S.O. 3)

BE15–4 On June 1, Eagle Inc. issues 2,000 shares of no-par common stock at a cash price of $8 per share. Journalize the issuance of the shares assuming the stock has a stated value of $1 per share.

Issuance of stock in a non-cash transaction. (S.O. 3)

BE15–5 Spiro Inc's $10 par value common stock is actively traded at a market value of $15 per share. Spiro issues 5,000 shares to purchase land advertised for sale at $80,000. Journalize the issuance of the stock in acquiring the land.

Donation of land. (S.O. 3)

BE15–6 Eastern Corporation receives land having a fair market value of $200,000 from a municipality as a donation. Journalize the donation.

Treasury stock transactions. (S.O. 4)

BE15–7 On July 1, ARB Corporation purchases 500 shares of its $5 par value common stock for the treasury at a cash price of $8 per share. On September 1, it sells 300 shares of the treasury stock for cash at $10 per share. Journalize the two treasury stock transactions.

Issuance of preferred stock. (S.O. 5)

BE15–8 Ozark Inc. issues 5,000 shares of $100 par value preferred stock for cash at $110 per share. Journalize the issuance of the preferred stock.

Stockholders' equity section. (S.O. 6)

BE15–9 Anita Corporation has the following accounts at December 31: Common Stock, $10 par, 5,000 shares issued, $50,000; Paid-in Capital in Excess of Par Value $10,000; Retained Earnings $19,000; and Treasury Stock—Common, 500 shares, $7,000. Prepare the stockholders' equity section of the balance sheet.

Book value per share. (S.O. 7)

BE15–10 The balance sheet for Myrna Inc. shows the following: total paid-in capital and retained earnings $860,000, total stockholders' equity $840,000, common stock issued 44,000 shares, and common stock outstanding 42,000 shares. Compute the book value per share.

EXERCISES

E15–1 During its first year of operations, the Beamer Corporation had the following trans-actions pertaining to its common stock.

Jan. 10   Issued 80,000 shares for cash at $5 per share.
July 1   Issued 30,000 shares for cash at $6 per share.

Instructions

(a) Journalize the transactions, assuming that the common stock has a par value of $5 per share.

(b) Journalize the transactions, assuming that the common stock is no-par with a stated value of $1 per share.

Journalize issuance of common stock.
(S.O. 3)

E15–2 Santiago Co. had the following transactions during the current period:

Mar. 2   Issued 5,000 shares of $1 par value common stock to attorneys in payment of a bill for $27,000 for services rendered in helping the company to incorporate.
June 12   Issued 60,000 shares of $1 par value common stock for cash of $375,000.
July 11   Issued 1,000 shares of $100 par value preferred stock for cash at $105 per share.
Nov. 28   Purchased 2,000 shares of treasury stock for $78,000.

Instructions
Journalize the transactions.

Entries for issuance of common and preferred stock and purchase of treasury stock.
(S.O. 3, 4, 5)

E15–3 As an auditor for the CPA firm of Ball and Haft, you encounter the following situa-tions in auditing different clients.

1. The Ruth Corporation is a closely held corporation whose stock is not publicly traded. On December 5, the corporation acquired land by issuing 5,000 shares of its $20 par value common stock. The owners' asking price for the land was $120,000, and the fair market value of the land was $115,000.

2. The Hand Corporation is a publicly held corporation whose common stock is traded on the securities markets. On June 1, it acquired land by issuing 20,000 shares of its $10 par value stock. At the time of the exchange, the land was advertised for sale at $250,000, and the stock was selling at $12 per share.

3. The Vital Corporation received land having a fair market value of $300,000 as a do-nation from the city of Greenview. The gift was made when Vital Corporation agreed to build its new plant on the land.

Instructions
Prepare the journal entries for each of the situations above.

Journalize noncash com-mon stock and donated capital transactions.
(S.O. 3)

E15–4 On January 1, 1993, the stockholders' equity section of the Marto Corporation shows: Common stock ($5 par value) $1,500,000; Paid-in capital in excess of par value $1,000,000; and Retained earnings $1,200,000. During the year, the following treasury stock transactions occurred:

Mar. 1   Purchased 50,000 shares for cash at $14 per share.
July 1   Sold 10,000 treasury shares for cash at $16 per share.
Sept. 1   Sold 8,000 treasury shares for cash at $12 per share.

Instructions

(a) Journalize the treasury stock transactions.

(b) Restate the entry for September 1, assuming the treasury shares were sold at $10 per share.

Journalize treasury stock transactions.
(S.O. 4)

E15–5 Talley Corporation is authorized to issue both preferred and common stock. The par value of the preferred is $50. During the first year of operations, the company had the following events and transactions pertaining to its preferred stock:

Feb. 1   Issued 30,000 shares for cash at $52 per share.
July 1   Issued 10,000 shares for cash at $57 per share.

Instructions

(a) Journalize the transactions.

Journalize preferred stock transactions and indicate statement presentation.
(S.O. 5, 6)

(b) Post to the stockholders' equity accounts.

(c) Indicate the statement presentation of the accounts.

Journalize conversion of preferred stock.
(S.O. 5)

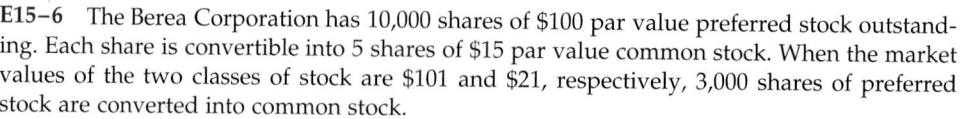

E15–6   The Berea Corporation has 10,000 shares of $100 par value preferred stock outstanding. Each share is convertible into 5 shares of $15 par value common stock. When the market values of the two classes of stock are $101 and $21, respectively, 3,000 shares of preferred stock are converted into common stock.

Instructions

(a) Journalize the conversion of the 3,000 shares.

(b) Repeat (a) assuming that market values at conversion are $105 and $25, respectively.

(c) Repeat (a) assuming each share is convertible into 8 shares of $10 par value common stock.

Prepare correct entries for capital stock transactions.
(S.O. 3, 4, 5)

E15–7   The Beal Corporation recently hired a new accountant with extensive experience in accounting for partnerships. Because of the pressure of the new job, the accountant was unable to review what he had learned earlier about corporation accounting. During the first month, he made the following entries for the corporation's capital stock:

May 2	Cash	168,000	
	Capital Stock		168,000
	(Issued 12,000 shares of $5 par value common stock at $14 per share)		
10	Cash	600,000	
	Capital Stock		600,000
	(Issued 10,000 shares of $50 par value preferred stock at $60 per share)		
15	Capital Stock	14,000	
	Cash		14,000
	(Purchased 1,000 shares of common stock for the treasury at $14 per share)		
31	Cash	7,500	
	Capital Stock		2,500
	Gain on Sale of Stock		5,000
	(Sold 500 shares of treasury stock at $15 per share)		

Instructions

On the basis of the explanation for each entry, prepare the entry that should have been made for the capital stock transactions.

Answer questions about stockholders' equity section.
(S.O. 3, 4, 5, 6)

E15–8   The stockholders' equity section of the Dooley Corporation at December 31 is as follows:

Paid-in capital

Preferred stock, cumulative, 10,000 shares authorized, 6,000 shares issued and outstanding	$ 600,000
Common stock, no par, 750,000 shares authorized, 600,000 shares issued	1,800,000
Total paid-in capital	2,400,000
Retained earnings	1,158,000
Total paid-in capital and retained earnings	3,558,000
Less: Treasury stock (16,000 common shares)	(64,000)
Total stockholders' equity	$3,494,000

Instructions

From a review of the stockholders' equity section, answer the following questions.

(a) How many shares of common stock are outstanding?

(b) What is the stated value of the common stock?

(c) What is the par value of the preferred stock?

(d) If the annual dividend on preferred stock is $48,000, what is the dividend rate on preferred stock?

(e) If dividends of $96,000 were in arrears on preferred stock, what would be the balance reported for Retained Earnings?

E15–9 In a recent year, the stockholders' equity section of the Aluminum Company of America (Alcoa) showed the following (in alphabetical order): Additional (paid-in) Capital $680.5, Common stock $88.3, Preferred stock $66.0, and Retained earnings $3,750.2. All dollar data are in millions.

Prepare a stockholders' equity section and compute book value.
(S.O. 6, 7)

The preferred stock has 660,000 shares authorized with a par value of $100 and an annual $3.75 per share cumulative dividend preference. At December 31, all authorized preferred stock is issued and outstanding. There are 300 million shares of $1 par value common stock authorized of which 88.3 million are outstanding at December 31.

Instructions
(a) Prepare the stockholders' equity section, including disclosure of all relevant data.

(b) Compute the book value per share of common stock, assuming there are no preferred dividends in arrears. (Round to two decimals.)

E15–10 The ledger of Minturn Corporation contains the following accounts: Common Stock, Preferred Stock, Treasury Stock—Common, Donated Capital, Paid-in Capital in Excess of Par Value—Preferred Stock, Paid-in Capital in Excess of Stated Value—Common Stock, Paid-in Capital from Treasury Stock, and Retained Earnings.

Classify stockholders' equity accounts.
(S.O. 6)

Instructions
Classify each account using the following tabular alignment:

| | Paid-in Capital | | | |
| | Capital | | Retained | |
Account	Stock	Additional	Earnings	Other

E15–11 At December 31, Kilgore Corporation has total stockholders' equity of $3,000,000. Included in this total are Preferred stock $500,000 and Paid-in capital in excess of par value—Preferred stock $50,000. There are 10,000 shares of $50 par value 10% cumulative preferred stock outstanding. At December 31, 200,000 shares of common stock are outstanding.

Compute book value per share with preferred stock.
(S.O. 7)

Instructions
Compute the book value per share of common stock, under each of the following assumptions:

(a) There are no preferred dividends in arrears, and the preferred stock does not have a call price.

(b) Preferred dividends are two years in arrears, and the preferred stock has a call price of $60 per share.

PROBLEMS

P15–1 The Mopar Corporation was organized on January 1, 1993. It is authorized to issue 20,000 shares of 6%, $50 par value preferred stock, and 500,000 shares of no-par common stock with a stated value of $1 per share. The following stock transactions were completed during the first year:

Journalize stock transactions, post, and prepare paid-in capital section.
(S.O. 3, 5, 6)

Jan. 10 Issued 100,000 shares of common stock for cash at $3 per share.
Mar. 1 Issued 10,000 shares of preferred stock for cash at $51 per share.
Apr. 1 Issued 25,000 shares of common stock for land. The asking price of the land was $90,000; the fair market value of the land was $85,000.
May 1 Issued 75,000 shares of common stock for cash at $4 per share.
Aug. 1 Issued 10,000 shares of common stock to attorneys in payment of their bill for $50,000 pertaining to services rendered in helping the company organize.
Sept. 1 Issued 5,000 shares of common stock for cash at $6 per share.
Nov. 1 Issued 2,000 shares of preferred stock for cash at $54 per share.

Instructions

(a) Journalize the transactions.

(b) Post to the stockholders' equity accounts. (Use J1 as the posting reference.)

(c) Prepare the paid-in capital section of stockholders' equity at December 31, 1993.

Journalize treasury stock transactions, post, and prepare stockholders' equity section.
(S.O. 4, 6)

P15–2   The Lory Corporation had the following stockholders' equity accounts on January 1, 1993: Common Stock ($1 par) $400,000, Paid-in Capital in Excess of Par Value $500,000, and Retained Earnings $100,000. In 1993, the company had the following treasury stock transactions:

Mar. 1   Purchased 5,000 shares at $8 per share.
June 1   Sold 1,000 shares at $10 per share.
Sept. 1   Sold 2,000 shares at $9 per share.
Dec. 1   Sold 1,000 shares at $6 per share.

Lory Corporation uses the cost method of accounting for treasury stock. In 1993, the company reported net income of $50,000.

Instructions

(a) Journalize the treasury stock transactions, and prepare the closing entry at December 31, 1993 for net income.

(b) Open accounts for (1) Paid-in Capital from Treasury Stock, (2) Treasury Stock, and (3) Retained Earnings. Post to these accounts using J12 as the posting reference.

(c) Prepare the stockholders' equity section for Lory Corporation at December 31, 1993.

(d) On May 1, 1994, Lory Corporation retires the remaining 1,000 treasury shares. Paid-in capital applicable to the shares was $7 per share. Prepare the entry to record the retirement.

Journalize and post trans-actions, prepare stock-holders' equity section, and compute book value.
(S.O. 2, 3, 4, 5, 6, 7)

P15–3   The stockholders' equity accounts of the Rutlan Corporation on January 1, 1993, were as follows:

Preferred Stock (10%, $100 par noncumulative, 5,000 shares authorized)	$ 300,000
Common Stock ($5 stated value, 300,000 shares authorized)	1,000,000
Paid-in Capital in Excess of Par Value—Preferred Stock	15,000
Paid-in Capital in Excess of Stated Value—Common Stock	400,000
Retained Earnings	488,000
Treasury Stock—Common (5,000 shares)	40,000

During 1993, the corporation had the following transactions and events pertaining to its stock-holders' equity:

Feb.   1   Issued 4,000 shares of common stock for $25,000.
Mar. 20   Purchased 1,000 additional shares of common treasury stock at $8 per share.
June 14   Sold 4,000 shares of treasury stock—common for $34,000.
Sept.   3   Issued 2,000 shares of common stock for a patent valued at $13,000.
Dec. 31   Determined that net income for the year was $113,000.

Instructions

(a) Journalize the transactions and the closing entry for net income.

(b) Enter the beginning balances in the accounts and post the journal entries to the stockhold-ers' equity accounts. (Use J1 as the posting reference.)

(c) Prepare a stockholders' equity section at December 31, 1993.

(d) Compute the book value per share of common stock at December 31, 1993, assuming the preferred stock does not have a call price.

Journalize and post pre-ferred stock transactions and prepare stockholders' equity section.
(S.O. 2, 5, 6)

P15–4   Landen Corporation is authorized to issue 10,000 shares of $100 par value, 10% con-vertible preferred stock and 200,000 shares of $10 par value common stock. On January 1, 1993, the ledger contained the following stockholders' equity balances:

Preferred Stock (4,000 shares)	$400,000
Paid-in Capital in Excess of Par Value—Preferred	40,000
Common Stock (70,000 shares)	700,000
Paid-in Capital in Excess of Par Value—Common	350,000
Retained Earnings	300,000

During 1993, the following transactions occurred:

Feb. 1 Issued 1,000 shares of preferred stock for land having a fair market value of $125,000.

Mar. 1 Issued 1,000 shares of preferred stock for cash at $120 per share.

July 1 Holders of 2,000 shares of preferred stock purchased at $110 per share converted the shares into common stock. Each share of preferred was convertible into 10 shares of common stock. Market values were: preferred stock $122 and common stock $15.

Sept. 1 Issued 400 shares of preferred stock for a patent. The asking price of the patent was $60,000. Market values were: preferred stock $125 and patent, indeterminable.

Dec. 1 Holders of 1,000 shares of preferred stock purchased at $115 per share converted the shares into common stock. Each share of preferred was convertible into 10 shares of common stock. Market values were: preferred stock $125 and common stock $16.

Dec. 31 Net income for the year was $200,000. No dividends were declared.

Instructions

(a) Journalize the transactions and the closing entry for net income.

(b) Post to the stockholders' equity accounts. (Use J2 as the posting reference.)

(c) Prepare a stockholders' equity section at December 31, 1993.

P15–5 The following stockholders' equity accounts arranged alphabetically are in the ledger of Durbin Corporation at December 31, 1993:

Prepare stockholders' equity section and compute book value.
(S.O. 6, 7)

Common Stock ($10 stated value)	$1,500,000
Donated Capital	200,000
Paid-in Capital from Treasury Stock	6,000
Paid-in Capital in Excess of Stated Value—Common Stock	900,000
Paid-in Capital in Excess of Par Value—Preferred Stock	80,000
Preferred Stock (8%, $100 par, noncumulative)	400,000
Retained Earnings	992,000
Treasury Stock—Common (8,000 shares)	88,000

Instructions

(a) Prepare a stockholders' equity section at December 31, 1993.

(b) Compute the book value per share of the common stock, assuming the preferred stock has a call price of $110 per share.

P15–6 Sargent Corporation has been authorized to issue 20,000 shares of $100 par value, 10%, noncumulative preferred stock and 1,000,000 shares of no-par common stock. The corporation assigned a $2.50 stated value to the common stock. At December 31, 1993, the ledger contained the following balances pertaining to stockholders' equity:

Prepare entries for stock transactions and stockholders' equity section.
(S.O. 3, 4, 5, 6)

Preferred Stock	$ 120,000
Paid-in Capital in Excess of Par Value—Preferred	4,000
Common Stock	1,000,000
Paid-in Capital in Excess of Stated Value—Common	2,850,000
Treasury Stock—Common (1,000 shares)	12,000
Paid-in Capital from Treasury Stock	1,000
Retained earnings	82,000

The preferred stock was issued for land having a fair market value of $124,000. All common stock issued was for cash. In November, 1,500 shares of common stock were purchased for the treasury at a per share cost of $12. In December, 500 shares of treasury stock were sold for $14 per share. No dividends were declared in 1993.

Instructions

(a) Prepare the journal entries for the:
   (1) Issuance of preferred stock for land.
   (2) Issuance of common stock for cash.
   (3) Purchase of common treasury stock for cash.
   (4) Sale of treasury stock for cash.

(b) Prepare the stockholders' equity section at December 31, 1993.

ALTERNATE PROBLEMS

Journalize stock transactions, post, and prepare paid-in capital section.
(S.O. 3, 5, 6)

P15–1A The Dryland Corporation was organized on January 1, 1993. It is authorized to issue 10,000 shares of 8%, $100 par value preferred stock, and 500,000 shares of no-par common stock with a stated value of $2 per share. The following stock transactions were completed during the first year:

Jan. 10 Issued 80,000 shares of common stock for cash at $3 per share.
Mar. 1 Issued 5,000 shares of preferred stock for cash at $104 per share.
Apr. 1 Issued 24,000 shares of common stock for land. The asking price of the land was $90,000; the fair market value of the land was $80,000.
May 1 Issued 80,000 shares of common stock for cash at $4 per share.
Aug. 1 Issued 10,000 shares of common stock to attorneys in payment of their bill of $50,000 for services rendered in helping the company organize.
Sept. 1 Issued 10,000 shares of common stock for cash at $5 per share.
Nov. 1 Issued 1,000 shares of preferred stock for cash at $107 per share.

Instructions

(a) Journalize the transactions.

(b) Post to the stockholders' equity accounts. (Use J5 as the posting reference.)

(c) Prepare the paid-in capital section of stockholders' equity at December 31, 1993.

Journalize treasury stock transactions, post, and prepare stockholders' equity section.
(S.O. 4, 6)

P15–2A The Rena Corporation had the following stockholders' equity accounts on January 1, 1993: Common Stock ($5 par) $500,000, Paid-in Capital in Excess of Par Value $200,000, and Retained Earnings $100,000. In 1993, the company had the following treasury stock transactions:

Mar. 1 Purchased 5,000 shares at $9 per share.
June 1 Sold 1,000 shares at $12 per share.
Sept. 1 Sold 2,000 shares at $10 per share.
Dec. 1 Sold 1,000 shares at $8 per share.

Rena Corporation uses the cost method of accounting for treasury stock. In 1993, the company reported net income of $40,000.

Instructions

(a) Journalize the treasury stock transactions and prepare the closing entry at December 31, 1993 for net income.

(b) Open accounts for (1) Paid-in Capital from Treasury Stock, (2) Treasury Stock, and (3) Retained Earnings. Post to these accounts using J10 as the posting reference.

(c) Prepare the stockholders' equity section for Rena Corporation at December 31, 1993.

(d) On May 1, 1994, Rena Corporation retires the remaining 1,000 treasury shares. Paid-in capital applicable to the shares was $7 per share. Prepare the entry to record the retirement.

Journalize and post transactions, prepare stockholders' equity section, and compute book value.
(S.O. 2, 3, 4, 5, 6, 7)

P15–3A The stockholders' equity accounts of the Clinton Corporation on January 1, 1993, were as follows:

Preferred Stock (12%, $50 par cumulative, 10,000 shares authorized)	$ 400,000
Common Stock ($1 stated value, 2,000,000 shares authorized)	1,000,000
Paid-in Capital in Excess of Par Value—Preferred Stock	80,000
Paid-in Capital in Excess of Stated Value—Common Stock	1,400,000
Retained Earnings	1,816,000
Treasury Stock—Common (10,000 shares)	40,000

During 1993, the corporation had the following transactions and events pertaining to its stockholders' equity:

Feb. 1 Issued 20,000 shares of common stock for $100,000.
Apr. 14 Sold 6,000 shares of treasury stock—common for $28,000.
Sept. 3 Issued 5,000 shares of common stock for a patent valued at $25,000.
Nov. 10 Purchased 1,000 shares of common stock for the treasury at a cost of $6,000.
Dec. 31 Determined that net income for the year was $275,000.

The preferred stock has a call price of $55 per share and no dividends were declared during the year.

Instructions

(a) Journalize the transactions and the closing entry for net income.

(b) Enter the beginning balances in the accounts and post the journal entries to the stockholders' equity accounts. (Use J5 for the posting reference.)

(c) Prepare a stockholders' equity section at December 31, 1993, including the disclosure of the preferred dividends in arrears.

(d) Compute the book value per share of common stock at December 31, 1993. (Round to two decimals.)

P15–4A   Denison Corporation is authorized to issue 10,000 shares of $100 par value, 10% convertible preferred stock and 125,000 shares of $10 par value common stock. On January 1, 1993, the ledger contained the following stockholders' equity balances:

Preferred Stock (5,000 shares)	$500,000
Paid-in Capital in Excess of Par Value—Preferred	50,000
Common Stock (70,000 shares)	700,000
Paid-in Capital in Excess of Par Value—Common	350,000
Retained Earnings	300,000

Journalize and post preferred stock transactions and prepare stockholders' equity section.
(S.O. 2, 5, 6)

G

During 1993, the following transactions occurred:

Feb. 1   Issued 1,000 shares of preferred stock for land having a fair market value of $125,000.

Mar. 1   Issued 1,000 shares of preferred stock for cash at $120 per share.

July 1   Holders of 2,000 shares of preferred stock purchased at $110 per share converted the shares into common stock. Each share of preferred was convertible into 8 shares of common stock. Market values were: preferred stock $122 and common stock $17.

Sept. 1   Issued 400 shares of preferred stock for a patent. The asking price of the patent was $60,000. Market values were: preferred stock $125 and patent indeterminable.

Dec. 1   Holders of 1,000 shares of preferred stock purchased at $120 per share converted the shares into common stock. Each share of preferred was convertible into 8 shares of common stock. Market values were: preferred stock $125 and common stock $16.

Dec. 31   Net income for the year was $240,000. No dividends were declared.

Instructions

(a) Journalize the transactions and the closing entry for net income.

(b) Post to the stockholders' equity accounts. (Use J2 for the posting reference.)

(c) Prepare a stockholders' equity section at December 31, 1993.

P15–5A   The following stockholders' equity accounts arranged alphabetically are in the ledger of Jordan Corporation at December 31, 1993:

Common Stock ($5 stated value)	$2,500,000
Donated Capital	500,000
Paid-in Capital from Treasury Stock	10,000
Paid-in Capital in Excess of Stated Value—Common Stock	1,500,000
Paid-in Capital in Excess of Par Value—Preferred Stock	192,000
Preferred Stock (8%, $50 par, noncumulative)	800,000
Retained Earnings	1,713,000
Treasury Stock—Common (10,000 shares)	130,000

Prepare stockholders' equity section and compute book value.
(S.O. 6, 7)

Instructions

(a) Prepare a stockholders' equity section at December 31, 1993.

(b) Compute the book value per share of the common stock, assuming the preferred stock has a call price of $60 per share and two years dividends are in arrears.

*B*roadening Your Perspective

FINANCIAL REPORTING PROBLEM

The stockholders' equity section for PepsiCo, Inc. is shown in the Consolidated Balance Sheet in Appendix L. You will also find data relative to this problem on other pages of the Appendix.

Instructions
Answer the following questions.

1. What is the par or stated value per share of PepsiCo's common stock?
2. What percentage of PepsiCo's authorized common stock was issued at December 28, 1991? (Round to nearest full percentage.)
3. How many shares of common stock were outstanding at December 28, 1991, and at December 29, 1990?
4. What was book value per share at December 28, 1991, and at December 29, 1990? (Note: The cumulative translation adjustment is part of stockholders' equity.) Compare your answers with the amounts reported in the Financial Summary.
5. What were the growth rates for book value per share for one, five, and ten years as shown in Selected Financial Data?
6. What was the closing market price per share at December 28, 1991, and at December 29, 1990, as reported under Capital Stock Information?
7. How did PepsiCo's stock performance compare with the performance of a leading financial index, Standard & Poor's 400 companies?
8. What was the low and high quarterly cash dividend during 1991 and 1990? What significant historical facts are stated concerning PepsiCo's dividend policy?

DECISION CASE

The stockholders' meeting for Mandel Corporation has been in progress for some time. The chief financial officer for Mandel is presently reviewing the company's financial statements and is explaining the items that comprise the stockholders' equity section of the balance sheet for the current year. The stockholders' equity section of Mandel Corporation at December 31, 1993, is as follows:

Paid-in capital		
Capital stock		
Preferred stock, authorized 1,000,000 shares cumulative, $100 par value, $8 per share, 6,000 shares issued and outstanding		$ 600,000
Common stock, authorized 5,000,000 shares, $1 par value, 3,000,000 shares issued, and 2,700,000 outstanding		3,000,000
Total capital stock		3,600,000
Additional paid-in capital		
In excess of par value-preferred stock	$ 50,000	
In excess of par value-common stock	25,000,000	
Total additional paid-in capital		25,050,000
Total paid-in capital		28,650,000
Retained earnings		900,000
Total paid-in capital and retained earnings		29,550,000
Less: Common treasury stock (300,000 shares)		9,300,000
Total stockholders' equity		$20,250,000

A number of questions regarding the stockholders' equity section of the Mandel Corporation's balance sheet have been raised at the meeting.

Instructions

Answer the following questions as if you were the chief financial officer for Mandel Corporation.

(a) "What does the cumulative provision related to the preferred stock mean?"

(b) "I thought the common stock was presently selling at $29.75, and yet the company has the stock stated at $1 per share. How can that be?"

(c) "Why is the company buying back its common stock? Furthermore, the treasury stock has a debit balance because it is subtracted from stockholders' equity. Why is treasury stock not reported as an asset if it has a debit balance?"

(d) "Why is it necessary to show additional paid-in capital? Why not just show common stock at the total amount paid in?"

CRITICAL THINKING CASE

Refer back to the opening story concerning the University of California–Irvine. Use what you've learned in the chapter to answer the following questions.

1. Why is it easier for a corporation to provide support for a new campus than it would be for a proprietorship or partnership to do so?

2. To what extent do corporations finance your campus? To what extent has research developed by your school been used to form new companies off campus?

3. Speculate as to why The Irvine Company made such a generous contribution.

4. What journal entry would the University of California make to record the donation of the land it received?

ETHICAL CASE

The R & D division of Simplex Chemical Corp. has just developed a chemical for sterilizing the vicious Brazilian "killer bees" which are invading Mexico and the extreme southern states of the U.S. The president of Simplex is anxious to get the chemical on the market because Simplex's profits need a boost—his job is in jeopardy because of decreasing sales and profits. Simplex has an opportunity to sell this chemical in foreign Central American countries where the laws are much more relaxed than in the U.S. The director of Simplex's R & D division strongly recommends further testing in the laboratory for side-effects of this chemical on other insects, birds, animals, plants, and even humans. He cautions the president, "We could be sued from all sides if the chemical has tragic side effects that we didn't even test for in the labs." The president answers, "We can't wait an additional year for your lab tests. We can avoid losses from such lawsuits by establishing a separate wholly owned corporation to shield Simplex Corp. from such law suits. We can't lose any more than our investment in the new corporation, and we'll invest just the patent covering this chemical. We'll reap the benefits if the chemical works and is safe and avoid the losses from lawsuits if its a disaster."

The next week Simplex creates a new wholly owned corporation called Zoebee Inc., sells the chemical patent to it for $10, and watches the spraying begin.

Instructions

(a) Who are the stakeholders in this situation?

(b) Are the president's motives and actions ethical?

(c) Can Simplex shield itself against losses of Zoebee Inc.?

Answers to Self-Study Questions
1. b   2. a   3. c   4. a   5. a   6. b   7. d   8. c   9. a   10. d

CONCEPTS FOR REVIEW

Before studying this chapter, you should know or, if necessary, review:

a. *Why it is important to distinguish between paid-in capital and retained earnings. (Ch. 15, p. 591–2)*

b. *The significance of legal capital in accounting for capital stock transactions. (Ch. 15, p. 596)*

c. *The form and content of the stockholders' equity section of the balance sheet. (Ch. 15, p. 606–7)*

d. *The rights of cumulative preferred stockholders to dividends. (Ch. 15, p. 604–5)*

CHAPTER 16

CORPORATIONS: DIVIDENDS, RETAINED EARNINGS, AND INCOME REPORTING

Study Objectives

After studying this chapter, you should be able to:

1. *Prepare the entries for cash dividends and stock dividends.*

2. *Identify the items that are reported in a retained earnings statement.*

3. *Prepare a comprehensive stockholders' equity section.*

4. *Describe the form and content of corporation income statements.*

5. *Explain the concept of intraperiod tax allocation.*

6. *Indicate the statement presentation of material items not typical of regular operations.*

7. *Compute earnings per share.*

I n these days of escalating educational costs, colleges and universities rely heavily on dividend income. Many schools invest their funds in a diversified portfolio of stocks—and rely on dividend income to pay operating costs.

At Emory University in Atlanta, "the dividends we earn are used for operating the university," says Wayne Coon, who oversees the $1.6 billion endowment fund, made up of bequests or gifts of stocks, bonds, real estate partnerships, and venture capital.

Many years ago, the university received a sizable gift of Coca-Cola stock. Indeed, half of the school's endowment is made up of this one issue. The university holds over 20 million shares of the Atlanta-based soft drink company. In 1992, Coke was paying a dividend of $0.56 per share. The market price of Coke's stock was as high as $45 per share in 1992. "Our goal for the endowment is total return". "If we sold our Coke stock and bought, for example, telephone stock, we would increase our *dividend income but our endowment probably wouldn't grow as fast," says Coon, who says Coke has returned about 25% per year (dividends plus price appreciation) for the past decade.*

One advantage for universities is that, as nonprofit entities, they don't pay income taxes on the dividends they receive on their endowment funds. If they did, they'd receive roughly a third less income. Another good thing about dividend income: it rarely drops, like interest income.

"Our long-range investment goal is to beat inflation by 6 percentage points," says Coon. That means that if inflation is 4%, then the school wants to achieve a total return—dividends plus capital appreciation—of 10%.

In order to continue in business, corporations must be profitable. Some of the net income earned is distributed to stockholders in the form of dividends. The remainder is retained and reinvested in the business. This chapter begins with a discussion of dividends. Consideration is then given to retained earnings and finally to corporation income statements.

Dividends

Study Objective 1

Prepare the entries for cash dividends and stock dividends.

A dividend **is a distribution by a corporation to its stockholders on a pro rata (equal) basis.** Potential buyers and sellers of a corporation's stock are very interested in a company's dividend policies and practices. Dividends may take four forms: cash, property, scrip (promissory note to pay cash), or (capital) stock. Cash dividends, which predominate in practice, and stock dividends, which are declared with some frequency, will be the focus of discussion in this chapter.

Dividends may be expressed as a percentage of the par or stated value of the stock or as a dollar amount per share. In the financial press, **dividends are generally reported quarterly as a dollar amount per share**. For example, the Dow Chemical Company at one time raised its quarterly dividend to 80 cents a share, up 10 cents per share from the previous quarter and 33% from the past year.

Cash Dividends

A cash dividend is a pro rata distribution of cash to stockholders. For a cash dividend to occur, a corporation must have:

1. **Retained earnings.** The legality of a cash dividend depends on state corporation laws. In general, cash dividends based on retained earnings are legal, and distributions based on common stock (legal capital) are illegal. Statutory provisions vary considerably with respect to cash dividends based on paid-in capital in excess of par or stated value. Many states permit such dividends. A dividend based on paid-in capital is termed a liquidating dividend, because the amount originally paid in by stockholders is being reduced or "liquidated."

2. **Adequate cash.** The legality of a dividend does not indicate a company's ability to pay a dividend. For example, a company such as PepsiCo, with a cash balance of $187 million and retained earnings of $5,470 million, could legally declare a dividend of $5,470 million. However, if it attempted to pay the dividend, it would need to raise additional cash through the sale of other assets or through additional financing. It follows that before declaring a cash dividend, the board of directors must carefully consider both current and future demands on the company's cash resources. In some cases, current liabilities may make a cash dividend inappropriate; in other cases, a major plant expansion program may warrant only a relatively small dividend.

3. **Declared dividends.** The board of directors has full authority to determine the amount of income to be distributed in the form of a dividend and the amount to be retained in the business. Dividends do not accrue like interest on a note payable, and they are not a liability until declared.

The amount and timing of a dividend are important issues for management to consider. Many companies declare and pay cash dividends quarterly. The payment of a large cash dividend could lead to liquidity problems for the enterprise. Conversely, a small dividend may cause unhappiness among stockholders who expect to receive a reasonable cash payment from the company on a periodic basis.

Entries for Cash Dividends

Three dates are important in connection with dividends: (1) the declaration date, (2) the record date, and (3) the payment date. Normally, there is a time span of two to four weeks between each date. Accounting entries are required on two of the dates—the declaration date and the payment date.

On the declaration date, the board of directors formally declares (authorizes) the cash dividend and announces it to stockholders. The declaration of a cash dividend **commits the corporation to a binding legal obligation** that cannot be rescinded. Thus, an entry is required to recognize the decrease in retained earnings and the increase in the liability, Dividends Payable. To illustrate, assume that on December 1, 1993, the directors of Media General declare a 50¢ per share

---

Accounting in Action · *Business Insight*

In order to remain in business, companies must honor their interest payments to creditors, bankers, and bondholders. But the payment of dividends to stockholders is another matter. Good, solid companies can survive, even thrive, without such payouts. In fact, managements might consider dividend payments unnecessary, even harmful to the company. Pay your creditors, by all means. But, fork over perfectly good cash to stockholders as dividends? "Why give money to those strangers?" is the response of one company president.

Investors must keep an eye on the company's dividend policy. For most companies, regular boosts in the face of irregular earnings can be a warning signal. So can the refusal of management to lower dividends when earnings fall or capital requirements rise. Companies with high dividends and rising debt may be borrowing money to pay shareholders. For investors who are seeking high returns on their stock investments, low dividends may mean high returns.

Adapted from Thornton O'Glove, The Quality of Earnings, 1987.

cash dividend on 100,000 shares of $10 par value common stock. The dividend is $50,000 (100,000 × 50¢), and the entry to record the declaration is:

Declaration Date

Dec. 1	Retained Earnings	50,000	
	Dividends Payable		50,000
	(To record declaration of cash dividend)		

Dividends Payable is a current liability because it will normally be paid within the next several months. Instead of debiting Retained Earnings, the account Dividends may be debited. This account provides additional information in the ledger. For example, a company may have separate dividend accounts for each class of stock. When a dividend account is used, its balance is transferred to Retained Earnings at the end of the year by a closing entry. Consequently, the effect of the declaration is the same; retained earnings is decreased and a current liability is increased. For homework problems, you should use the Retained Earnings account for recording dividend declarations.

The record date marks the time when ownership of the outstanding shares is determined for dividend purposes from the stockholders' records maintained by the corporation. The time interval between the declaration date and the record date enables the corporation to update its stock ownership records. Between the declaration date and record date, the number of shares outstanding should remain the same. Thus, the purpose of the record date is to identify the persons or entities that will receive the dividend, not to determine the amount of the dividend liability. For Media General, the record date is December 22. No entry is required on this date because the corporation's liability recognized on the declaration date is unchanged:

Record Date

Dec. 22			
	No entry necessary		

On the payment date, dividend checks are mailed to the stockholders and the payment of the dividend is recorded. Assuming that the payment date is January 20 for Media General, the entry on that date is:

Payment Date

Jan. 20	Dividends Payable	50,000	
	Cash		50,000
	(To record payment of cash dividend)		

Note that payment of the dividend reduces both current assets and current liabilities but has no effect on stockholders' equity. The cumulative effect of the declaration and payment of a cash dividend on a company's financial statements is to **decrease both stockholders' equity and total assets**.

Technology in Action

A casual glance at *The Wall Street Journal* reveals the vast amount of stock traded on the national and regional stock exchanges. Thousands of shares of a single company's stock may change hands each day. Companies must rely on computers to keep track of the volume of transactions for both ownership and dividend purposes. With dividends, a review of the computer records on the date of record would reveal which parties should receive dividend distributions in a timely fashion.

Allocating Cash Dividends between Preferred and Common Stock

As explained in Chapter 15, preferred stock has priority over common stock in regard to dividends. That is, cash dividends must be paid to preferred stockholders before common stockholders are paid any dividends.

To illustrate, we will assume that IBR Inc. has 1,000 shares of 8% $100 par value cumulative preferred stock and 50,000 shares of $10 par value common stock outstanding at December 31, 1993. The required annual dividend for preferred stock is $8,000 (1,000 × $8). At December 31, 1993, the directors declare a $6,000 cash dividend. The entire amount goes to preferred stockholders because of their dividend preference. The entry to record the declaration of the dividend is:

Dec. 31	Retained Earnings	6,000	
	Dividends Payable		6,000
	(To record $6 per share cash dividend to preferred		
	stockholders)		

Because of the cumulative feature, dividends of $2 per share are in arrears on preferred stock for 1993. These dividends must be paid to preferred stockholders before any dividends are paid to common stockholders. As explained in Chapter 15, dividends in arrears should be disclosed in the financial statements.

At December 31, 1994, IBR declares a $50,000 cash dividend. The allocation of the dividend to the two classes of stock is as follows:

Total dividend		$50,000
Allocated to preferred stock		
Dividends in arrears, 1993 (1,000 × $2)	$2,000	
1994 dividend (1,000 × $8)	8,000	10,000
Remainder allocated to common stock		$40,000

ILLUSTRATION 16-1

Allocating dividends to preferred and common stock

The entry to record the declaration of the dividend is:

Dec. 31	Retained Earnings	50,000	
	Dividends Payable		50,000
	(To record declaration of cash dividends of $10,000		
	to preferred stock and $40,000 to common stock)		

If the preferred stock were not cumulative, preferred stockholders would have received only $8,000 in dividends in 1994 and common stockholders would have received $42,000.

Stock Dividends

A stock dividend is a pro rata distribution of the corporation's own stock to stockholders. Whereas a cash dividend is paid in cash, a stock dividend is paid in stock. **A stock dividend results in a decrease in retained earnings and an increase in paid-in capital.** Unlike a cash dividend, a stock dividend does not decrease total stockholders' equity or total assets.

To illustrate a stock dividend, assume that you have a 2% ownership interest in Cetus Inc. by virtue of owning 20 of its 1,000 shares of common stock. In a 10% stock dividend (100 shares), you would receive two shares (10% × 20 shares) but your ownership interest would remain at 2% (22 ÷ 1,100). You now own more shares of stock but your ownership interest has not changed. Moreover, no cash is disbursed and no liabilities have been assumed by the corporation.

What then are the purposes and benefits of a stock dividend? Corporations issue stock dividends generally for one or more of the following reasons:

1. To satisfy stockholders' dividend expectations without spending cash.
2. To increase the marketability of its stock by increasing the number of shares outstanding and thereby decreasing the market price per share. Decreasing the market price of the stock makes it easier for smaller investors to purchase the shares.
3. To emphasize that a portion of stockholders' equity has been permanently reinvested in the business and therefore is unavailable for cash dividends.

The size of the stock dividend and the value to be assigned to each dividend share are determined by the board of directors when the dividend is declared. The per share amount must be at least equal to the par or stated value in order to meet legal requirements.

The accounting profession distinguishes between a small stock dividend (less than 20–25% of the corporation's issued stock) and a large stock dividend (greater than 20–25%). It recommends that the directors assign the fair market value per share for small stock dividends. The recommendation is based on the assumption that a small stock dividend will have little effect on the market price of the shares previously outstanding. Thus, many stockholders consider small stock dividends to be distributions of earnings equal to the fair market value of the shares distributed. The amount to be assigned for a large stock dividend is not specified by the accounting profession. However, par or stated value per share is normally assigned. Small stock dividends predominate in practice. Thus, we will illustrate only the entries for small stock dividends.

Entries for Stock Dividends

To illustrate the accounting for stock dividends, assume that Medland Corporation has a balance of $300,000 in retained earnings and declares a 10% stock dividend on its 50,000 shares of $10 par value common stock. The current fair market value of its stock is $15 per share. The number of shares to be issued is 5,000 (10% × 50,000) and the total amount to be debited to Retained Earnings is $75,000 (5,000 × $15). The entry to record this transaction at the declaration date is as follows:

Retained Earnings	75,000	
Common Stock Dividends Distributable		50,000
Paid-in Capital in Excess of Par Value		25,000
(To record declaration of 10% stock dividend)		

Note that Retained Earnings is debited for the fair market value of the stock issued; Common Stock Dividends Distributable is credited for the par value of the dividend shares (5,000 × $10); and the excess over par (5,000 × $5) is credited to an additional paid-in capital account. Common Stock Dividends Distributable is a stockholders' equity account; it is not a liability because assets will not be used to pay the dividend. If a balance sheet is prepared before the dividend shares are issued, the distributable account is reported in paid-in capital as an addition to common stock issued, as shown below:

ILLUSTRATION 16-2

Statement presentation of common stock dividends distributable

Paid-in capital		
Common stock	$500,000	
Common stock dividends distributable	50,000	$550,000

When the dividend shares are issued, Common Stock Dividends Distributable is debited and Common Stock is credited as follows:

Common Stock Dividends Distributable	50,000	
Common Stock		50,000
(To record issuance of 5,000 shares in a stock dividend)		

Effects of Stock Dividends

Stock dividends change the composition of stockholders' equity because a portion of retained earnings is transferred to paid-in capital. However, total stockholders' equity remains the same. Stock dividends also have no effect on the par or stated value per share, but the number of shares outstanding increases and the book value per share decreases. These effects are shown below for the Medland Corporation.

ILLUSTRATION 16-3

Stock dividend effects

Stockholders' equity	Before Dividend	After Dividend
Paid-in capital		
Common stock, $10 par	$500,000	$550,000
Paid-in capital in excess of par value	—	25,000
Total paid-in capital	500,000	575,000
Retained earnings	300,000	225,000
Total stockholders' equity	$800,000	$800,000
Outstanding shares	50,000	55,000
Book value per share	$ 16.00	$ 14.55

In this example, total paid-in capital is increased by $75,000 and retained earnings is decreased by the same amount. Note also that total stockholders' equity remains unchanged at $800,000.

Stock Splits

A stock split, like a stock dividend, involves the issuance of additional shares of stock to stockholders according to their percentage ownership. However, a stock split results in a reduction in the par or stated value per share. The purpose of a stock split is to increase the marketability of the stock by lowering its market value per share. This, in turn, makes it easier for the corporation to issue additional stock. The effect of a split on market value is generally inversely proportional to the size of the split. For example, after a 4-for-1 stock split, the market value of IBM stock fell from $284 to approximately $71. In announcing the split, the chief executive of IBM said, "We want to make our stock more attractive to the small investor."

    In a stock split, the number of shares is increased in the same proportion that par or stated value per share is decreased. For example, in a 2 for 1 split, one share of $10 par value stock is exchanged for two shares of $5 par value stock. A stock split does not have any effect on total paid-in capital, retained earnings, and total stockholders' equity. However, the number of shares outstanding increases and book value per share decreases. These effects are shown in Illustration 16-4 for the Medland Corporation, assuming that instead of a 10% stock dividend, Medland splits its 50,000 shares of common stock on a 2 for 1 basis.

Helpful hint A stock split changes the par value per share but does not affect any balances in stockholders' equity.

ILLUSTRATION 16-4

Stock split effects

Stockholders' equity	Before Stock Split	After Stock Split
Paid-in capital		
Common stock	$500,000	$500,000
Paid-in capital in excess of par value	–0–	–0–
Total paid-in capital	500,000	500,000
Retained earnings	300,000	300,000
Total stockholders' equity	$800,000	$800,000
Outstanding shares	50,000	100,000
Book value per share	$16.00	$8.00

Because a stock split does not affect the balances in any stockholders' equity accounts, **it is not necessary to journalize a stock split**. Significant differences between stock splits and stock dividends are shown in Illustration 16-5:

ILLUSTRATION 16-5

Effects of stock splits and stock dividends differentiated

Item	Stock Split	Stock Dividend
Total paid-in capital	No change	Increase
Total retained earnings	No change	Decrease
Total par value (common stock)	No change	Increase
Par value per share	Decrease	No change

Before You Go On . . .

1. What entries are made for cash dividends on (a) the declaration date, (b) the record date, and (c) the payment date?

2. Distinguish between a small and large stock dividend and indicate the basis for valuing each kind of dividend.

3. Contrast the effects of a small stock dividend and a 2 for 1 stock split on (a) stockholders' equity, (b) outstanding shares, and (c) book value per share.

Retained Earnings

Study Objective 2

Identify the items that are reported in a retained earnings statement.

Retained earnings is net income that is retained in the business. The balance in retained earnings is part of the stockholders' claim on the total assets of the corporation. It does not, however, represent a claim on any specific asset. Nor can the amount of retained earnings be associated with the balance of any asset account. For example, a $100,000 balance in retained earnings does not mean that there should be $100,000 in cash. The reason is that the cash resulting from the excess of revenues over expenses may have been used to purchase buildings, equipment, and other assets. Illustration 16-6 shows the relationship of cash to

ILLUSTRATION 16-6

Retained earnings and cash balances

Company	Retained Earnings	Cash
Sears, Roebuck and Co.	$13,514	$4,650
Caterpillar Inc.	3,138	104
Monsanto	4,459	189
USX Corporation	2,451	263

retained earnings in selected companies. (All data are in millions of dollars.)

When expenses exceed revenues, a **net loss** results. In contrast to net income, a net loss is debited to Retained Earnings in preparing closing entries. This is done even if a debit balance results in Retained Earnings. **Net losses are not debited to paid-in capital accounts.** This would destroy the distinction between paid-in and earned capital. A debit balance in retained earnings is identified as a deficit and is reported as a deduction in the stockholders' equity section, as shown below:

ILLUSTRATION 16-7

Stockholders' equity with deficit

Stockholders' equity	
Paid-in capital	
Common stock	$800,000
Retained earnings (deficit)	(50,000)
Total stockholders' equity	$750,000

Prior Period Adjustments

Suppose that after the books have been closed and the financial statements have been issued, a corporation discovers that a material error has been made in reporting net income of a prior year. How should this situation be recorded in the accounts and reported in the financial statements? The correction of this error is known as a prior period adjustment. The correction is made directly to Retained Earnings because the effect of the error is now in this account; the net income for the prior period has been recorded in retained earnings through the journalizing and posting of closing entries.

To illustrate, assume that General Microwave discovers in 1993 that it understated depreciation expense in 1991 by $300,000 as a result of computational errors. These errors overstated net income for 1991, and the current balance in retained earnings is also overstated. The entry for the prior period adjustment, assuming all tax effects are ignored, is as follows:

Retained Earnings	300,000	
Accumulated Depreciation		300,000
(To adjust for understatement of depreciation in a prior period)		

A debit to an income statement account in 1993 would be incorrect because the error pertains to a prior year.

Prior period adjustments are reported in the retained earnings statement.[1] They are added (or deducted) from the beginning retained earnings balance to show the adjusted beginning balance. Assuming General Microwave has a beginning balance of $800,000 in retained earnings, the prior period adjustment is reported as follows:

ILLUSTRATION 16-8

Statement presentation of prior period adjustments

(Partial) Retained Earnings Statement	
Balance, January 1, as reported	$800,000
Correction for understatement of depreciation in prior period	300,000
Balance, January 1, as adjusted	$500,000

---

[1]A complete retained earnings statement is shown in Illustration 16-11 on page 635.

Reporting the correction in the current year's income statement would be incorrect because it applies to a prior year's income statement.

Normally, any errors made in a given year are discovered and corrected before the financial statements for that year are issued. Thus, prior period adjustments occur infrequently. Nevertheless, they are required at times. For example, Saxon Industries, Inc., upon discovering that the inventory it reported in the previous period was overstated by $24 million, recorded a prior period adjustment to its retained earnings balance in the current year.

Retained Earnings Restrictions

The balance in retained earnings is generally available for dividend declarations. Some companies state this fact. For example, in the notes to its financial statements, Martin Marietta Corporation states:

> At December 31, retained earnings were unrestricted and available for dividend payments.

In some cases, however, there may be retained earnings restrictions that make a portion of the balance currently unavailable for dividends. Restrictions result from one or more of the following causes: legal, contractual, or voluntary.

Legal restrictions. Many states require a corporation to restrict retained earnings for the cost of treasury stock purchased. The restriction serves to keep intact the corporation's legal capital that is temporarily being held as treasury stock. When the treasury stock is sold, the restriction is lifted.

Contractual restrictions. Long-term debt contracts may impose a restriction on retained earnings as a condition for the loan. The restriction limits the use of corporate assets for the payment of dividends. Thus, it reduces the possibility that the corporation will be unable to meet required loan payments.

Voluntary restrictions. The board of directors of a corporation may voluntarily create retained earnings restrictions for specific purposes. For example, the board may authorize a restriction for the purpose of future plant expansion. By reducing the amount of retained earnings available for dividends, more cash may be available for the planned expansion.

Retained earnings restrictions are generally disclosed in the notes to the financial statements. For example, Pratt & Lambert, a leading producer of architectural finishes (paint) has the following note in a recent financial statement.

ILLUSTRATION 16-9

Disclosure of restriction

Pratt & Lambert
Note D Long-term Debt and Retained Earnings
Loan agreements contain, among other covenants, a restriction on the payment of dividends, which at December 31, 1991, limits future dividend payments to $20,565,000 plus 75% of future net income.

Retained Earnings Statement

The retained earnings statement shows the changes in retained earnings during the year. The statement is prepared from the Retained Earnings account. Transactions and events that affect retained earnings are tabulated in account form as shown in Illustration 16-10.

ILLUSTRATION 16-10

Debits and credits to retained earnings

Retained Earnings	
1. Net loss	1. Net income
2. Prior period adjustments for overstatement of net income	2. Prior period adjustments for understatement of net income
3. Cash and stock dividends	
4. Some disposals of treasury stock	

As indicated, net income increases retained earnings and a net loss decreases retained earnings. Prior period adjustments may either increase or decrease retained earnings, whereas both cash and stock dividends decrease retained earnings. The circumstances when treasury stock transactions decrease retained earnings are explained in Chapter 15. The retained earnings statement for Graber Inc., based on assumed data, is as follows:

ILLUSTRATION 16-11

Retained earnings statement

GRABER INC. **Retained Earnings Statement** **For the Year Ended December 31, 1993**		
Balance, January 1, as reported		$1,050,000
Correction for understatement of net income in prior period (inventory error)		50,000
Balance, January 1, as adjusted		1,100,000
Add: Net income		360,000
		1,460,000
Less: Cash dividends	$100,000	
Stock dividends	200,000	300,000
Balance, December 31		$1,160,000

Stockholders' Equity Section

The stockholders' equity section of the balance sheet of Graber Inc. is presented in Illustration 16-12. Note that (1) Common Stock Dividends Distributable is shown under capital stock in paid-in capital and (2) a retained earnings restriction is disclosed in the notes.

    Instead of presenting a detailed stockholders' equity section in the balance sheet and a retained earnings statement, many companies prepare a stockholders' equity statement. This statement shows the changes in each stockholders' equity account and in total stockholders' equity that have occurred during the year. An example of a stockholders' equity statement is illustrated in Appendix G to this chapter and in PepsiCo's financial statements in Appendix L.

> **Study Objective 3**
>
> *Prepare a comprehensive stockholders' equity section.*

Before You Go On . . .

1. What is a prior period adjustment and how is it reported?

2. How are retained earnings restrictions generally reported?

3. What are the principal sources of debits and credits to Retained Earnings?

4. How are stock dividends distributable reported in the stockholders' equity section?

ILLUSTRATION 16-12

Comprehensive stockholders' equity section

GRABER INC. Partial Balance Sheet			
Stockholders' equity			
Paid-in capital			
Capital stock			
9% Preferred stock, $100 par value, cumulative, callable at $120, 10,000 shares authorized, 6,000 shares issued and outstanding			$ 600,000
Common stock, no par, $5 stated value, 500,000 shares authorized, 400,000 shares issued and 390,000 outstanding		$2,000,000	
Common stock dividends distributable		50,000	2,050,000
Total capital stock			2,650,000
Additional paid-in capital			
In excess of par value—preferred stock		30,000	
In excess of stated value—common stock		950,000	
Donated capital		100,000	
Total additional paid-in capital			1,080,000
Total paid-in capital			3,730,000
Retained earnings (see Note R)			1,160,000
Total paid-in capital and retained earnings			4,890,000
Less: Treasury stock—common (10,000 shares)			80,000
Total stockholders' equity			$4,810,000

Note R: Retained earnings is restricted for the cost of treasury stock, $80,000.

Corporation Income Statements

Study Objective 4

Describe the form and content of corporation income statements.

Income statements for corporations are the same as the statements for proprietorships or partnerships except for the reporting of income taxes. For income tax purposes, corporations are considered to be a separate legal entity. As a result, **income taxes (or income tax expense)** are reported in a separate section of the corporation income statement before net income. The condensed income statement for Leads Inc. in Illustration 16-13 shows a typical presentation. Note that income before income taxes is reported before income tax expense.

ILLUSTRATION 16-13

Income statement with income taxes

Helpful hint Corporations may also use the single-step form of income statement discussed in Chapter 5.

LEADS INC. Income Statement For the Year Ended December 31, 1993	
Sales	$800,000
Cost of goods sold	600,000
Gross profit	200,000
Operating expenses	50,000
Income from operations	150,000
Other revenues and gains	10,000
Other expenses and losses	4,000
Income before income taxes	156,000
Income tax expense	46,800
Net income	$109,200

Income tax expense and the related liability for income taxes payable are recorded as part of the adjusting process preceding financial statement preparation. Using the data above for Leads Inc., the adjusting entry for income tax expense at December 31, 1993, would be as follows:

Income Tax Expense	46,800	
Income Taxes Payable		46,800
(To record income taxes for 1993)		

Another illustration of income tax is presented in the income statement of PepsiCo in Appendix L.

Expansion of the Income Statement

The income statements that you studied in earlier chapters provide considerable insight into a company's income-related activities. In studying such statements, the user may ask: (1) Are the results typical for this company? (2) Are the results a reasonable indicator of the company's future earnings?

To provide answers to these questions, accountants have concluded that additional sections should be added to the income statement to **report material items not typical of regular operations**. These items are reported in the income statement immediately before net income. The nontypical items include (1) discontinued operations, (2) extraordinary items, and (3) changes in accounting principle. Each item reported in the income statement should be carefully explained in the notes to the financial statements. The income statement should also report the income tax expense or savings applicable to each item, as explained in the following section.

Accounting in Action ▪ *Business Insight*

Net income and its components reported in the income statement measure a company's performance. The amount and trend of net income (earnings) are, therefore, of vital importance to management, stockholders, and creditors. Net income provides an indication of the amount of dividends that a company may distribute, and it results in an increase in retained earnings.

Reported net income has a major effect on the market price of a company's stock at a given point in time. For example, when IBM announced that its net income would be 7.7% lower, the price of its stock dropped $3.875 per share in one day. Conversely, when St. Regis Paper reported that its net income was 20% greater than expected, its market price per share increased $3 per share in one day.

Intraperiod Tax Allocation

Intraperiod tax allocation refers to the procedure of associating income taxes with the specific item that directly affects the income taxes for the period. Under intraperiod tax allocation, the applicable income tax expense or tax saving is shown for income before income taxes and each of the three nontypical items identified above. Intraperiod tax allocation provides statement users with informative disclosure as to the income tax effects on these components. The general concept is "let the tax follow the income or loss."

Study Objective 5

Explain the concept of intraperiod tax allocation.

To illustrate the importance of intraperiod tax allocation, we will first show the misleading results that may occur when intraperiod tax allocation is not followed. Assume that Dale Realty Corporation has income before income tax of $250,000, an extraordinary loss from a flood of $80,000, and, therefore, taxable income of $170,000. Both the extraordinary loss and taxable income are subject to a 30% tax rate. Without intraperiod tax allocation, the income statement will show:

ILLUSTRATION 16-14

Income statement without tax allocation

Partial Income Statement	
	Without Tax Allocation
Income before income taxes	$250,000
Income tax expense ($170,000 × 30%)	51,000
Income before extraordinary item	199,000
Extraordinary loss from flood	80,000
Net income	$119,000

This presentation is misleading because the income taxes do not follow the income or loss. The tax effects of income before income taxes and the extraordinary loss have been combined in reporting income tax expense of $51,000. Thus, income tax expense is understated $24,000 (30% × $80,000), and the effect of the extraordinary loss on net income is overstated by the same amount.

Under intraperiod tax allocation, the tax rate of 30% is applied to income before income taxes of $250,000 to show income taxes of $75,000, and the extraordinary item of $80,000 is reported net of the $24,000 tax saving, as shown below.

ILLUSTRATION 16-15

Income statement with tax allocation

Partial Income Statement	
	With Tax Allocation
Income before income taxes	$250,000
Income tax expense ($250,000 × 30%)	75,000
Income before extraordinary item	175,000
Extraordinary loss from flood, net of $24,000 income tax saving	56,000
Net income	$119,000

Note that net income remains unchanged at $119,000 when intraperiod tax allocation is applied. However, intraperiod tax allocation matches the tax to the items that affect the tax and corrects the deficiencies of the first presentation.

Study Objective 6

Indicate the statement presentation of material items not typical of regular operations.

Discontinued Operations

To downsize its operations, General Dynamics Corp. sold its missile business to Hughes Aircraft Co. for $450 million. In its income statement, General Dynamics was required to report the sale in a separate section entitled "discontinued operations."

Discontinued operations refers to the disposal of a significant segment of a business, such as the cessation of an entire activity or the elimination of a major class of customers. Thus, the decision by the Singer Co. to end its manufacture and sale of computers and the decision to close all overseas offices and terminate all foreign sales were both reported as discontinued operations. On the other hand, the phasing out of a model or part of a line of business is not considered to be a disposal of a segment.

When the disposal of a significant segment occurs, the income statement should report both income from continuing operations and income (or loss) from discontinued operations. **The income (loss) from discontinued operations consists of the income (loss) from operations and the gain (loss) on disposal of the segment.** To illustrate, assume that Acro Energy Inc. has revenues of $2.5 million and expenses of $1.7 million from continuing operations in 1993. The company, therefore, has income before income taxes of $800,000. During 1993 the company discontinued and sold its unprofitable chemical division. The loss in 1993 from chemical operations (net of $60,000 taxes) was $140,000 and the loss on disposal of the chemical division (net of $30,000 taxes) was $70,000. Assuming a 30% tax rate on income before income taxes, the income statement presentation is shown below.

ILLUSTRATION 16-16

Statement presentation of discontinued operations

ACRO ENERGY INC. Partial Income Statement For the Year Ended December 31, 1993		
Income before income taxes		$800,000
Income tax expense		240,000
Income from continuing operations		560,000
Discontinued operations		
Loss from operations of chemical division, net of $60,000 income tax saving	$140,000	
Loss from disposal of chemical division, net of $30,000 income tax saving	70,000	210,000
Net income		$350,000

Helpful hint Observe the dual disclosures: (1) the results of operations of the discontinued division must be eliminated from the results of continuing operations and (2) the disposal of the operation.

Note that the caption "Income from continuing operations" is used and that a section "Discontinued operations" is added. **Within the new section, both the operating loss and the loss on disposal are reported net of applicable income taxes.** This presentation clearly indicates the separate effects of continuing operations and discontinued operations on net income.

Extraordinary Items

Extraordinary items are events and transactions that meet two conditions: (1) **unusual in nature, and** (2) **infrequent in occurrence.** To be considered unusual, the item should be abnormal and be only incidentally related to the customary activities of the entity. To be regarded as infrequent, the event or transaction should not be reasonably expected to recur in the foreseeable future. Both criteria must be evaluated in terms of the environment in which the entity operates. Thus, Weyerhaeuser Co. reported the $36 million in damages to its timberland caused by the eruption of Mount St. Helens as an extraordinary item because the event was both unusual and infrequent. In contrast, Florida Citrus Company does not report frost damage to its citrus crop as an extraordinary item because frost damage is not viewed as infrequent. Illustration 16-17 shows the appropriate classification of extraordinary and ordinary items.

ILLUSTRATION 16-17

Examples of extraordinary and ordinary items

Extraordinary	Ordinary
1. Effects of major casualties (acts of God), if rare in the area	1. Effects of major casualties (acts of God), frequent in the area.
2. Expropriation (takeover) of property by a foreign government.	2. Write-down of inventories or write-off of receivables.
3. Effects of a newly enacted law or regulation such as a condemnation action on company property by a governmental agency.	3. Losses attributable to labor strikes.
	4. Gains or losses from sales of property, plant, or equipment.

Extraordinary items are reported net of taxes in a separate section of the income statement immediately below discontinued operations. To illustrate, assume that in 1993 a revolutionary foreign government expropriated property held as an investment by Acro Energy Inc. If the loss is $70,000, before applicable income taxes of $21,000, the income statement presentation will show a deduction of $49,000 as follows:

ILLUSTRATION 16-18

Statement presentation of extraordinary items

ACRO ENERGY INC.
Partial Income Statement
For the Year Ended December 31, 1993

Income before income taxes		$800,000
Income tax expense		240,000
Income from continuing operations		560,000
Discontinued operations		
Loss from operations of chemical division, net of $60,000 income tax saving	$140,000	
Loss from disposal of chemical division, net of $30,000 income tax saving	70,000	210,000
Income before extraordinary item		350,000
Extraordinary item		
Expropriation of investment, net of $21,000 income tax saving		49,000
Net income		$301,000

Accounting in Action · *Business Insight*

In the recession of the early 1990s, many companies closed some of their plants and reduced the size of their work force. The costs incurred in these activities, called plant restructuring costs, are reported as other expenses and losses in the income statement. These costs are not considered to be an extraordinary item because plant closings are neither unusual nor infrequent in many industries. Plant restructuring costs often have a significant effect on net income as illustrated by the following:

Union Pacific Corp. $585 million after-tax charge, of which $492 million applies to the disposal of 7,100 miles of the Union Pacific Railroad.

Borden, Inc. $71.6 million before-tax charge for business reorganization costs as well as severance, relocation, and other employee-related expenses.

As illustrated, the caption "Income before extraordinary item" is added immediately before the section for the extraordinary item. This presentation clearly indicates the effect of the extraordinary item on net income. If there are no discontinued operations, the third line of the income statement in Illustration 16-18 would be labeled "Income before extraordinary item."

If a transaction or event meets one (but not both) of the criteria for an extraordinary item, it is reported under either "Other revenues and gains" or "Other expenses and losses" at its gross amount (not net of tax). This is true, for example, of gains (losses) resulting from the sale of property, plant, and equipment, as explained in Chapter 11.

Change in Accounting Principle

For ease of comparison, financial statements are expected to be prepared on a basis **consistent** with that used for the preceding period. That is, where a choice of accounting principles is available, the principle initially chosen should be consistently applied from period to period. A change in an accounting principle occurs when the principle used in the current year is different from the one used in the preceding year. A change is permitted, when (1) management can show that the new principle is preferable to the old principle, and (2) the effects of the change are clearly disclosed in the income statement. Examples of a change in accounting principle include a change in depreciation methods (e.g., declining-balance to straight-line) and a change in inventory costing methods (e.g., FIFO to average cost). The effect of a change in an accounting principle on net income may be significant.

Accounting in Action · *Business Insight*

Sometimes a change in accounting principle is mandated by the Financial Accounting Standards Board. An example is the change in accounting for postretirement benefits other than pensions required by Statement of Financial Accounting Standards 106. In its 1991 income statement, Owens-Corning Fiberglas Corporation reported a charge of $227 million net of income taxes of $117 million under Cumulative Effect of Accounting Change. An accompanying note explained that the charge resulted from adopting the new standard for its domestic postretirement plans.

When a change in an accounting principle has occurred,

1. The new principle should be used in reporting the results of operations of the current year.
2. The cumulative effect of the change on all prior year income statements should be disclosed net of applicable taxes in a special section immediately preceding net income.

To illustrate, we will assume that at the beginning of 1993, Acro Energy Inc. changes from the straight-line method to the declining-balance method for equipment purchased on January 1, 1990. The cumulative effect on prior year income statements (statements for 1990–1992) is to increase depreciation expense and decrease income before income taxes by $24,000. Assuming a 30% tax rate, the net of tax effect of the change is $16,800 ($24,000 × 70%). The income statement presentation is shown in Illustration 16-19.

ILLUSTRATION 16-19

Statement presentation of cumulative effect of change in accounting principle

ACRO ENERGY INC. Partial Income Statement For the Year Ended December 31, 1993		
Income before income taxes		$800,000
Income tax expense		240,000
Income from continuing operations		560,000
Discontinued operations		
Loss from operations of chemical division, net of $60,000 income tax saving	$140,000	
Loss from disposal of chemical division, net of $30,000 income tax saving	70,000	210,000
Income before extraordinary item and cumulative effect of change in accounting principle		350,000
Extraordinary item		
Expropriation of investment, net of $21,000 income tax saving		49,000
Cumulative effect of change in accounting principle		
Effect on prior years of change in depreciation method, net of $7,200 income tax saving		16,800
Net income		$284,200

The income statement for Acro Energy will also show depreciation expense for the current year. The amount is based on the new depreciation method. In this case the caption "Income before extraordinary item and cumulative effect of change in accounting principle" is inserted immediately following the effects of discontinued operations. This presentation clearly indicates the cumulative effect of the change on prior years' income. If a company does not have either discontinued operations or extraordinary items, the label, "Income Before Cumulative Effect of Change in Accounting Principle" is used in place of "Income from Continuing Operations." A complete income statement showing all material items not typical of regular operations is illustrated in the demonstration problem (p. 648–9)

Before You Go On . . .

1. What is the unique feature of a corporation income statement?

2. What is the primary objective of intraperiod tax allocation?

3. What are the similarities and differences in reporting material items not typical of regular operations?

Study Objective 7

Compute earnings per share.

 **E**arnings Per Share

Earnings per share data are frequently reported in the financial press and are widely used by stockholders and potential investors in evaluating the profitability of a company. Investors, especially, attempt to link earnings per share to the market price per share.[2] Earnings per share (EPS) indicates the net income

---

[2]The ratio of the market price per share to the earnings per share is referred to as the *price-earnings ratio.* This ratio is reported in *The Wall Street Journal* and other newspapers for common stocks listed on major stock exchanges.

earned by each share of outstanding common stock. Thus, **earnings per share is reported only for common stock**. The formula for computing earnings per share when there has been no change in outstanding shares during the year is as follows:

ILLUSTRATION 16-20

Earnings per share formula—no change in outstanding shares

For example, if Modem Inc. has net income of $200,000 and 50,000 shares of common stock outstanding for the year, earnings per share is $4 ($200,000 ÷ 50,000).

Because of the importance of earnings per share (EPS), most companies are required to report it on the face of the income statement. Generally this amount is simply reported below net income on the statement. For Modem Inc. the presentation would be:

Net income	$200,000
Earnings per share	$ 4.00

ILLUSTRATION 16-21

Basic earnings per share disclosure

When the income statement contains any of the three additional sections described earlier in the chapter, EPS should be disclosed for each component. Assuming that Acro Energy had 100,000 shares of common stock outstanding during the year, the additional EPS disclosures for the income statement shown in Illustration 16-19 would be as shown below.

ILLUSTRATION 16-22

Additional earnings per share disclosures

Net income	$284,200
Earnings per share	
Income from continuing operations	$5.60
Loss from discontinued operations	(2.10)
Income before extraordinary item and cumulative effect of change	
in accounting principle	3.50
Extraordinary loss	(.49)
Cumulative effect of change in accounting principle	(.17)
Net income	$2.84

These disclosures enable the decision maker to recognize the effects on EPS of income from continuing operations, as distinguished from income or loss from material items not typical of regular operations. **Earnings per share from continuing operations is generally the most useful per share amount**, because it represents the results of continuing and ordinary business activity. Thus, it provides the best basis for predicting future operating results.

Additional Considerations

The computation of earnings per share may involve one or all of the following: (1) weighted average shares outstanding, (2) preferred stock dividends, and (3) complex capital structures.

Weighted Average Shares Outstanding

If there has been any change in the number of shares of common stock outstanding during the year, the weighted average shares outstanding should be used in computing EPS. The weighted average shares are computed by determining the time a given number of shares is outstanding during the period. To illustrate, assume that Rally Inc. had 100,000 shares of common stock outstanding on January 1 and issued an additional 10,000 shares of stock on October 1. The weighted average number of shares of stock for the year is computed as follows:[3]

ILLUSTRATION 16-23

Computation of weighted average shares outstanding

100,000 shares × 9/12 of a year	75,000
110,000 shares × 3/12 of a year	27,500
Weighted average shares outstanding	**102,500**

The weighted average is used because the issuance or purchase of stock changes the amount of net assets that is available during the period on which to earn revenues.

Preferred Stock Dividends

Earnings per share relates to earnings per share of **common stock**. When a corporation has both preferred and common stock outstanding, the current year's dividend declared on preferred stock is subtracted from net income to arrive at **income available to common stockholders**. Assuming weighted average common stock is involved, the formula for computing EPS is:

ILLUSTRATION 16-24

Expanded earnings per share formula

To illustrate, assume that Rally Inc. reports net income of $211,000 on its 102,500 weighted average common shares. During the year it also declares a $6,000 dividend on its preferred stock. Therefore, Rally has $205,000 ($211,000 − $6,000) available for common stock dividends. Earnings per share is $2 ($205,000 ÷ 102,500). If the preferred stock is cumulative, the dividend for the current year is deducted whether or not it is declared.

Complex Capital Structure

When a corporation has securities that may be converted into common stock, which, if converted, would reduce or dilute earnings per share, the corporation is said to have a complex capital structure. Two examples of such securities are

---

[3]An alternative acceptable computation of weighted average shares outstanding is:

100,000 × 12/12 =	100,000	shares outstanding for a full year.
10,000 × 3/12 =	2,500	shares outstanding for three months annualized.
	102,500	Total weighted average shares outstanding.

convertible bonds (discussed in Chapter 17) and convertible preferred stock. The adverse effect that these securities can have on EPS is significant and, more important, unexpected unless financial statements in some manner call attention to the potential dilutive effect.

Two earnings per share figures are computed and reported when convertible securities have a material effect on EPS.[4] The first EPS figure, referred to as primary earnings per share is based on the weighted average common shares outstanding plus shares referred to as common stock equivalents. Common stock equivalents are securities that will probably be converted into common shares. For example, convertible preferred stock might be classified as a common stock equivalent if it is likely to be converted into common stock. Special tests are used to determine whether the convertible security is in substance equivalent to common stock.

The second EPS figure, referred to as fully diluted earnings per share, assumes the maximum dilution possible. It reflects the dilution in earnings per share that would occur if *all* dilutive securities were converted into common shares. Potentially dilutive securities that are not considered a common stock equivalent for computing primary earnings per share are included for computing fully diluted earnings per share. Thus, **fully diluted earnings per share is lower than or equal to primary earnings per share**. The following excerpt from the income statement of the J.C. Penney Company illustrates the statement presentation of primary and fully diluted earnings per share.

J.C. PENNEY COMPANY	
Net income (in millions)	$577
Earnings per share	
Primary	$4.59
Fully diluted	$4.33

The computations for computing primary and fully diluted earnings per share are complex; they are discussed extensively in advanced accounting courses.

Before You Go On . . .

1. Explain the components of the formula for computing earnings per share when there is only common stock and outstanding shares are unchanged during the year.

2. How are weighted average shares outstanding computed?

3. What effects may preferred stock have on the formula for computing earnings per share?

4. What is the difference between primary and fully diluted earnings per share?

---

[4]The profession in *APB Opinion No. 15*, ''Earnings Per Share'' (New York: AICPA, 1969), considers material dilutive effect to exist when the potential dilution to earnings per share is 3% or more.

Summary of Study Objectives

1. Prepare the entries for cash dividends and stock dividends. Entries for both cash and stock dividends are required at the declaration date and the payment date. At the declaration date the entries are: Cash dividend—debit Retained Earnings and credit Dividends Payable; small stock dividend—debit Retained Earnings, credit Paid-in Capital in Excess of Par (or Stated) Value and credit Common Stock Dividends Distributable. At the payment date, the entries for cash and stock dividends, respectively, are debit Dividends Payable and credit Cash, and debit Common Stock Dividends Distributable and credit Common Stock.

2. Identify the items that are reported in a retained earnings statement. Each of the individual debits and credits to retained earnings should be reported in the retained earnings statement. Additions consist of net income and prior period adjustments to correct understatements of prior years' net income. Deductions consist of net loss, adjustments to correct overstatements of prior years' net income, cash and stock dividends, and some disposals of treasury stock.

3. Prepare a comprehensive stockholders' equity section. A comprehensive stockholders' equity section includes all stockholders' equity accounts. It consists of two sections: paid-in capital and retained earnings. It should also include notes to the financial statements that explain any restrictions on retained earnings and any dividends in arrears.

4. Describe the form and content of corporation income statements. The form and content of corporation income statements is similar to the statements of proprietorships and partnerships with one exception. Income taxes or income tax expense must be reported in a separate section before net income in the corporation's income statement.

5. Explain the concept of intraperiod tax allocation. Intraperiod tax allocation refers to the procedure of associating income taxes with the specific item that directly affects the income taxes for the period.

6. Indicate the statement presentation of material items not typical of regular operations. Material items not typical of regular operations are reported net of taxes in sections on the income statement immediately before net income. These items include (a) discontinued operations, (b) extraordinary items, and (c) changes in accounting principle.

7. Compute earnings per share. Earnings per share is computed by dividing net income by the number of common shares outstanding during the period. Additional problems arise when shares outstanding must be weighted and when preferred stock dividends and complex capital structures are involved.

APPENDIX G   Stockholders' Equity Statement

Study Objective

After studying Appendix G, you should be able to:

8. Describe the use and content of the stockholders' equity statement.

When balance sheets and income statements are presented by a corporation, there should also be disclosure of changes in the separate accounts comprising stockholders' equity. Disclosure of such changes is necessary to make the financial statements sufficiently informative for users. The disclosures may be made in an additional statement or in the notes to the financial statements.

Many corporations make the disclosures in a stockholders' equity statement. The statement shows the changes in **each** stockholders' equity account and in **total** stockholders' equity during the year. As shown in Illustration G-1 the stockholders' equity statement is prepared in columnar form with columns for each account and for total stockholders' equity. The transactions are then identified and their effects are shown in the appropriate columns.

In practice, additional columns are usually provided to show the number of shares of issued stock and treasury stock. The stockholders' equity statement for PepsiCo, Inc., for a three-year period is shown in Appendix L at the back of this textbook. When this statement is presented, a retained earnings statement is not necessary because the retained earnings column explains the changes in this account.

	Common Stock ($5 Par)	Paid-in Capital in Excess of Par	Retained Earnings	Treasury Stock	Total
HAMPTON CORPORATION Stockholders' Equity Statement For the Year Ended December 31, 1993					
Balance January 1	300,000	$200,000	$650,000	$(34,000)	$1,116,000
Issued 5,000 shares of common stock at $15	25,000	50,000			75,000
Declared a $40,000 cash dividend			(40,000)		(40,000)
Purchased 2,000 shares for treasury at $16				(32,000)	(32,000)
Net income for year			240,000		240,000
Balance December 31	$325,000	$250,000	$850,000	$(66,000)	$1,359,000

Summary of Study Objectives for Appendix G

8. *Describe the use and content of the stockholders' equity statement.* Corporations must disclose changes in stockholders' equity accounts and may choose to do so by issuing a separate stockholders' equity statement. This statement, prepared in columnar form, shows changes in each stockholders' equity account and in total stockholders' equity during the accounting period. When this statement is presented, a statement of retained earnings is not necessary.

GLOSSARY

Cash dividend · A pro rata distribution of cash to stockholders. (p. 626).

Change in accounting principle · The use of a principle in the current year that is different from the one used in the preceding year. (p. 641).

Complex capital structure · A situation in which a corporation has securities outstanding that may be converted into common stock, which, if converted, would reduce or dilute earnings per share. (p. 644).

Declaration date · The date the board of directors formally declares the dividend and announces it to stockholders. (p. 627).

Deficit · A debit balance in retained earnings. (p. 633).

Discontinued operations · The disposal of a significant segment of a business. (p. 638).

Dividend · A distribution by a corporation to its stockholders on a pro rata (equal) basis. (p. 626).

Earnings per share · The net income earned by each share of outstanding common stock. (p. 642).

Extraordinary items · Events and transactions that are unusual in nature and infrequent in occurrence. (p. 639).

Fully diluted earnings per share · An amount that shows the maximum dilution possible in earnings per share. (p. 645).

Intraperiod tax allocation · The procedure of associating income taxes with the specific item that directly affects the income taxes for the period. (p. 637).

Liquidating dividend · A dividend declared out of paid-in capital. (p. 626).

Payment date · The date dividend checks are mailed to stockholders. (p. 628).

Primary earnings per share · The amount of earnings per share based on the weighted average common shares outstanding plus common stock equivalents. (p. 645).

Prior period adjustment · The correction of an error in previously issued financial statements. (p. 633).

Record date · The date when ownership of outstanding shares is determined for dividend purposes. (p. 628).

Retained earnings restrictions · Circumstances that make a portion of retained earnings currently unavailable for dividends. (p. 634).

Retained earnings statement · A financial statement that shows the changes in retained earnings during the year. (p. 634).

Stock dividend · A pro rata distribution of the corporation's own stock to stockholders. (p. 629).

Stockholders' equity statement · A statement that shows the changes in each stockholders' equity account and in total stockholders' equity during the year. (p. 635).

Stock split · The issuance of additional shares of stock to stockholders accompanied by a reduction in the par or stated value per share. (p. 631).

DEMONSTRATION PROBLEM

The events and transactions of the Dever Corporation for the year ending December 31, 1993, resulted in the following data:

Cost of goods sold	$2,600,000
Net sales	4,400,000
Other expenses and losses	9,600
Other revenues and gains	5,600
Selling and administrative expenses	1,100,000
Income from operations of plastics division	70,000
Gain on sale of plastics division	500,000
Loss from tornado disaster (extraordinary loss)	600,000
Cumulative effect of changing from the straight line depreciation to double-declining-balance (increase in depreciation expense)	300,000

Analysis reveals that

1. All items are before the applicable income tax rate of 30%.
2. The plastics division was sold on July 1.
3. All operating data for the plastics division have been segregated.
4. There were 100,000 shares of common stock outstanding during the year.

Instructions

Prepare an income statement for the year, including the presentation of earnings per share data.

Solution to Demonstration Problem

Helpful hints

1. Remember that material items not typical of operations are reported in separate sections net of taxes.
2. Income taxes should be associated with the item that affects the taxes.
3. A corporation income statement will have income tax expense when there is income before income tax.
4. All data presented in determining income before income taxes is the same as for unincorporated companies.

DEVER CORPORATION
Income Statement
For the Year Ended December 31, 1993

Net sales		$4,400,000
Cost of goods sold		2,600,000
Gross profit		1,800,000
Selling and administrative expenses		1,100,000
Income from operations		700,000
Other revenues and gains	$ 5,600	
Other expenses and losses	9,600	4,000
Income before income taxes		696,000
Income tax expense ($696,000 × 30%)		208,800
Income from continuing operations		487,200

Discontinued operations		
Income from operations of plastics division, net of $21,000 income taxes ($70,000 × 30%)	49,000	
Gain on sale of plastics division, net of $150,000 income taxes ($500,000 × 30%)	350,000	399,000
Income before extraordinary item and cumulative effect of change in accounting principle		886,200
Extraordinary item		
Tornado loss, net of income tax saving $180,000 ($600,000 × 30%)		420,000
Cumulative effect of change in accounting principle		
Effect on prior years of change in depreciation method, net of $90,000 income tax saving ($300,000 × 30%)		210,000
Net income		$ 256,200
Earnings per share		
Income from continuing operations		$4.87
Gain from discontinued operations		3.99
Income before extraordinary item and cumulative effect of change in accounting principle		8.86
Extraordinary loss		(4.20)
Cumulative effect of change in accounting principle		(2.10)
Net income		$2.56

*Note: All **asterisked** Questions, Exercises, and Problems relate to material contained in the Appendix to the chapter.

SELF-STUDY QUESTIONS

Answers are at the end of the chapter.

(S.O. 1) 1. Entries for cash dividends are required on the:
   a. declaration date and the record date.
   b. record date and the payment date
   c. declaration date, record date, and payment date.
   d. declaration date and the payment date.

(S.O. 1) 2. Which of the following statements about small stock dividends is true?
   a. A debit to Retained Earnings for the par value of the shares issued should be made.
   b. Market value per share should be assigned to the dividend shares.
   c. A stock dividend decreases total stockholders' equity.
   d. A stock dividend ordinarily will have no effect on book value per share of stock.

(S.O. 2) 3. All but one of the following is reported in a retained earnings statement. The exception is:

   a. cash and stock dividends.
   b. net income and net loss.
   c. sales of treasury stock above cost.
   d. some disposals of treasury stock below cost.

4. A prior period adjustment is: (S.O. 2)
   a. a correction of an error that is made directly to retained earnings.
   b. reported in the income statement as a nontypical item.
   c. reported directly in the stockholders' equity section.
   d. reported in the retained earnings statement as an adjustment of the ending balance of retained earnings.

5. In the stockholders' equity section, Stock (S.O. 3) Dividends Distributable is reported as a(an):
   a. deduction from total paid-in capital and retained earnings.
   b. addition in additional paid-in capital.
   c. addition in capital stock.
   d. deduction from retained earnings.

(S.O. 4)   6. Corporation income statements may be the same as the income statements for unincorporated companies *except* for:
    a. income tax expense.
    b. gross profit.
    c. operating income.
    d. net sales.

(S.O. 5)   7. Intraperiod tax allocation refers to the:
    a. allocation of income taxes to different accounting periods.
    b. association of income taxes with the items that directly affect the income taxes for the period.
    c. system of deferring income taxes to later accounting periods.
    d. reporting of income taxes by interim accounting periods.

(S.O. 6)   8. In reporting discontinued operations, the income statement should show in a special section:
    a. gains and losses on the disposal of the discontinued segment.
    b. gains and losses from operations of the discontinued segment.
    c. Neither (a) nor (b).
    d. Both (a) and (b).

(S.O. 6)   9. The Rand Corporation has income before taxes of $400,000 and an extraordinary loss of $100,000. If the income tax rate is 25% on all items, the income statement should show income before extraordinary items and extraordinary items, respectively, of:
    a. $325,000 and $100,000.
    b. $325,000 and $75,000.
    c. $300,000 and $75,000.
    d. $300,000 and $100,000.

(S.O. 7)   10. The income statement for Nadeen, Inc. shows income before income taxes $700,000, income tax expense $210,000, and net income $490,000. If Nadeen has 100,000 shares of common stock outstanding throughout the year, earnings per share is:
    a. $7.00.
    b. $2.10.
    c. $4.90.
    d. no correct answer given.

(S.O. 8)   *11. When a stockholders' equity statement is presented it is not necessary to prepare a(an)
    a. balance sheet.
    b. retained earnings statement.
    c. income statement.
    d. none of the above.

QUESTIONS

1. What are the three conditions that must exist before a cash dividend is paid?

2. Three dates associated with Galena Company's cash dividend are May 1, May 15, and May 31. Discuss the significance of each date and give the entry at each date.

3. Contrast the effects of a cash dividend and a stock dividend on a corporation's balance sheet.

4. Jill Sims asks, "Since stock dividends don't change anything, why declare them?" What is your answer to Jill?

5. The Bella Corporation has 10,000 shares of $15 par value common stock outstanding when they announce a 2 for 1 split. Before the split, the stock had a market price of $140 per share. After the split, how many shares of stock will be outstanding, and what will be the approximate market price per share?

6. The board of directors is considering a stock split or a stock dividend. They understand that total stockholders' equity will remain the same under either action. However, they are not sure of the different effects of the two types of actions on other aspects of stockholders' equity. Explain the differences to the directors.

7. What is a prior period adjustment and how is it reported in the financial statements?

8. The ABC Corporation has a retained earnings balance of $240,000 on January 1. During the year, a prior period adjustment of $90,000 is recorded because of the overstatement of depreciation in the prior period. Show the retained earnings statement presentation of these data.

9. What is the purpose of a retained earnings restriction? Identify the possible causes of retained earnings restrictions.

10. How are retained earnings restrictions generally reported in the financial statements?

11. Identify the events which result in credits and debits to retained earnings.

12. Omar Radha believes that both the beginning and ending balances in retained earnings are shown in the stockholders' equity section. Is Omar correct? Discuss.

13. Doria Nelson, who owns many investments in common stock, says, "I don't care what a company's net income is. The balance sheet tells me everything I need to know!" How do you respond to Doria?

14. What is the unique feature of a corporation income statement? Illustrate this feature, using assumed data.

15. Define the term "intraperiod tax allocation." Why is this type of allocation important?

16. Why is it important to report discontinued operations separately from income from continuing operations?

17. You are considering investing in Percy Transportation, which reports 1993 earnings per share of $6.50 on income before extraordinary items and $4.75 on net income. Which EPS figure would you consider more relevant to your investment decision? Why?

18. Iron Inc. reported 1992 earnings per share of $3.26 and had no extraordinary items. In 1993, EPS on income before extraordinary items was $2.99, and EPS on net income was $3.49. Is this a favorable trend?

19. Indicate which of the following items would be reported as an extraordinary item in Larus Corporation's income statement.
(a) Loss from damages caused by volcano eruption.
(b) Loss from sale of temporary investments.
(c) Loss attributable to a labor strike.
(d) Loss caused when manufacture of a product was prohibited by the Food and Drug Administration.
(e) Loss from flood damage (the Black River floods every two to three years).
(f) Write-down of obsolete inventory.
(g) Expropriation of a factory by a foreign government.

20. When studying for an accounting test, a fellow student says, "Changes in accounting principle are reported in the retained earnings statement." Is your friend correct, or should he study harder?

21. Why must preferred stock dividends be subtracted from net income in computing earnings per share?

22. Jean Maris owns 100 shares of Yellow Corporation. She tells you, "The corporation earned net income of $1,000,000 and had 200,000 shares of common stock outstanding. That should be earnings per share of $5.00. But they reported primary earnings per share of $4.10 and fully diluted earnings per share of $3.69." Explain the meaning of these EPS figures to Jean Maris.

*23. What is the purpose of a stockholders' equity statement?

BRIEF EXERCISES

BE16–1 The Seabee Corporation has 10,000 shares of common stock outstanding. It declares a $1 per share cash dividend on November 1 to stockholders of record on December 1. The dividend is paid on December 31. Prepare the entries on the appropriate dates to record the declaration and payment of the cash dividend.

Prepare entries for a cash dividend.
(S.O. 1)

BE16–2 Satina Corporation has 100,000 shares of $10 par value common stock outstanding. It declares a 10% stock dividend on December 1 when the market value per share is $12. The dividend shares are issued on December 31. Prepare the entries for the declaration and payment of the stock dividend.

Prepare entries for a stock dividend.
(S.O. 1)

BE16–3 The stockholders' equity section of the Desi Corporation consists of common stock ($10 par) $1,000,000 and retained earnings $400,000. A 10% stock dividend (10,000 shares) is declared when the market value per share is $12. Show the before and after effects of the

Show before and after effects of a stock dividend.
(S.O. 1)

dividend on (a) the components of stockholders' equity, (b) shares outstanding, and (c) book value per share.

Prepare a retained earnings statement. (S.O. 3)	**BE16–4** For the year ending December 31, 1993, Maddy Inc. reports net income $182,000 and dividends $75,000. Prepare the retained earnings statement for the year assuming the balance in retained earnings on January 1, 1993, was $220,000.
Show correct intraperiod tax allocation. (S.O. 4, 5)	**BE16–5** An inexperienced accountant for the Lima Corporation showed the following in the income statement: Income before income taxes $300,000, Income tax expense $72,000, Extraordinary loss from flood (before taxes) $60,000, and Net income $168,000. The extraordinary loss and taxable income are both subject to a 30% tax rate. Prepare a correct income statement using intraperiod tax allocation.
Prepare discontinued operations section of income statement. (S.O. 5, 6)	**BE16–6** On June 30, the Osbern Corporation discontinued its operations in Mexico. During the year, the operating loss was $400,000 before taxes. On September 1, Osbern disposed of the Mexico facility at a pretax loss of $150,000. The applicable tax rate is 30%. Show the discontinued operations section of the income statement.
Prepare change in accounting principle section of income statement. (S.O. 6)	**BE16–7** On January 1, 1993, Shirli, Inc. changed from the straight-line method of depreciation to the declining-balance method. The cumulative effect of the change was to increase prior years' depreciation by $40,000 and 1993 depreciation by $8,000. Show the change in accounting principle section of the 1993 income statement, assuming the tax rate is 30%.
Show earnings per share data in income statement. (S.O. 7)	**BE16–8** Geneva Corporation's income statement shows: Income from continuing operations $580,000, Loss from discontinued operations $200,000, Extraordinary loss $80,000, and Cumulative effect of a change in accounting principle that increases net income $40,000. Show the earnings per share data in the income statement, assuming there are 100,000 shares of common stock outstanding at December 31.
Compute earnings per share. (S.O. 7)	**BE16–9** The Darlin Corporation reports net income of $360,000 and a weighted average of 200,000 shares of common stock outstanding for the year. Compute the earnings per share of common stock.
Compute earnings per share with cumulative preferred stock. (S.O. 7)	**BE16–10** Income and common stock data for the Darlin Corporation are presented in BE16–9. Assume also that Darlin has cumulative preferred stock dividends for the current year of $20,000 that were declared and paid. Compute the earnings per share of common stock.
Prepare stockholders' equity statement. (S.O. 8)	***BE16–11** On January 1, 1993, the Ritz Corporation had the following stockholders' equity balances: Common Stock $200,000, Paid-in Capital in Excess of Stated Value $300,000, and Retained Earnings $250,000. During 1993, it earned net income of $80,000 and declared a cash dividend of $20,000. Prepare a stockholders' equity statement for the year.

EXERCISES

Journalize cash dividends and indicate statement presentation. (S.O. 1)	**E16–1** On January 1, Tarow Corporation had 75,000 shares of no-par common stock issued and outstanding. The stock has a stated value of $5 per share. During the year, the following occurred:

Apr.   1   Issued 5,000 additional shares of common stock.
June 15   Declared a cash dividend of $1 per share to stockholders of record on June 30.
July 10   Paid the $1 cash dividend.
Dec.   1   Issued 2,000 additional shares of common stock.
         15   Declared a cash dividend on outstanding shares of $1.20 per share to stockholders of record on December 31.

Instructions
(a) Prepare the entries, if any, on each of the three dividend dates.

(b) How are dividends and dividends payable reported in the financial statements prepared at December 31?

E16–2 The Omaha Corporation was organized on January 1, 1991. During its first year, the corporation issued 2,000 shares of $50 par value preferred stock and 100,000 shares of $10 par value common stock. At December 31, the company declared the following cash dividends: 1991 $5,000, 1992 $12,000, and 1993 $30,000.

Allocate cash dividends to preferred and common stock.
(S.O. 1)

Instructions

(a) Show the allocation of dividends to each class of stock, assuming the preferred stock dividend is 9% and not cumulative.

(b) Show the allocation of dividends to each class of stock assuming the preferred stock dividend is 10% and cumulative.

(c) Journalize the declaration of the cash dividend at December 31, 1993, under part (b).

E16–3 On January 1, 1993, the Keyes Corporation had $1,500,000 of common stock outstanding that was issued at par and retained earnings of $750,000. The company issued 50,000 shares of common stock at par on July 1 and earned net income of $400,000 for the year.

Journalize stock dividends.
(S.O. 1)

Instructions

Journalize the declaration of a 10% stock dividend on December 10, 1993, for the following independent assumptions:
(1) Par value is $10 and market value is $15.
(2) Par value is $5 and market value is $20.

E16–4 On October 31, the stockholders' equity section of the Sarah Lane Company consists of Common stock $800,000 and Retained earnings $400,000. Sarah is considering the following two courses of action: (1) declaring a 10% stock dividend on the 80,000 $10 par value shares outstanding or (2) effecting a 2-for-1 stock split that will reduce par value to $5 per share. The current market price is $15 per share.

Compare effects of a stock dividend and a stock split.
(S.O. 1)

Instructions

Prepare a tabular summary of the effects of the alternative actions on the components of stockholders' equity, outstanding shares, and book value per share. Use the following column headings: Before Action, After Stock Dividend, and After Stock Split.

E16–5 On October 1, 1993, Valentine Corporation's stockholders' equity is as follows:

Compute book value per share and indicate account balances after a stock dividend.
(S.O. 1, 3)

Common stock $10 par value	$200,000
Paid-in capital in excess of par value	25,000
Retained earnings	175,000
Total stockholders' equity	$400,000

On October 1, Valentine declares and distributes a 10% stock dividend when the market value of the stock is $15 per share.

Instructions

(a) Compute the book value per share (1) before the stock dividend and (2) after the stock dividend. (Round to two decimals.)

(b) Indicate the balances in the three stockholders' equity accounts after the stock dividend shares have been distributed.

E16–6 During 1993, the Kittle Corporation had the following transactions and events:

Indicate the effects on stockholders' equity components.
(S.O. 1, 2, 3)

1. Issued par value common stock for cash at par value.
2. Declared a cash dividend.
3. Completed a 3-for-1 stock split in which $15 par value stock was changed to $5 par value stock.
4. Declared a stock dividend when the market value was higher than par value.
5. Made a prior period adjustment for overstatement of net income.
6. Issued the shares of common stock required by the stock dividend declaration in no. 4 above.
7. Paid the cash dividend in no. 2 above.
8. Issued par value common stock for cash above par value.

Instructions

Indicate the effect(s) of each of the foregoing items on the subdivisions of stockholders' equity. Present your answer in tabular form with the following columns. Use (I) for increase, (D) for decrease, and (NE) for no effect. Item 1 is given as an example.

	Paid-in Capital		
Item	Capital Stock	Additional	Retained Earnings
1.	I	NE	NE

Prepare correcting entries for dividends and a stock split.
(S.O. 1)

E16–7   Before preparing financial statements for the current year, the chief accountant for the Downey Company discovered the following errors in the accounts:

1. The declaration and payment of $25,000 cash dividend was recorded as a debit to Interest Expense $25,000 and a credit to Cash $25,000.

2. A 10% stock dividend (1,000 shares) was declared on the $10 par value stock when the market value per share was $17. The only entry made was: Retained Earnings (Dr.) $10,000 and Dividend Payable (Cr.) $10,000. The shares have not been issued.

3. A 4-for-1 stock split involving the issue of 400,000 shares of $5 par value common stock for 100,000 shares of $20 par value common stock was recorded as a debit to Retained Earnings $2,000,000 and a credit to Common Stock $2,000,000.

Instructions

Prepare the correcting entries at December 31.

Prepare a retained earnings statement.
(S.O. 2, 3)

E16–8   On January 1, 1993, Valdez Corporation had Retained Earnings of $580,000. During the year, Valdez had the following selected transactions:

1. Declared cash dividends $120,000.

2. Corrected overstatement of 1992 net income because of depreciation error $30,000.

3. Earned net income $310,000.

4. Declared stock dividends $60,000.

Instructions

Prepare a retained earnings statement for the year.

Prepare a stockholders' equity section.
(S.O. 3)

E16–9   The following accounts appear in the ledger of Odom Inc. after the books are closed at December 31.

Common Stock, no par, $1 stated value, 400,000 shares authorized; 300,000 shares issued	$ 300,000
Common Stock Dividends Distributable	75,000
Paid-in Capital in Excess of Stated Value—Common Stock	1,200,000
Preferred Stock, $5 par value, 8%, 40,000 shares authorized; 30,000 shares issued	150,000
Retained Earnings	700,000
Treasury Stock (10,000 common shares)	60,000
Paid-in Capital in Excess of Par Value—Preferred Stock	124,000
Donated Capital	120,000

Instructions

Prepare stockholders' equity section at December 31, assuming retained earnings is restricted for plant expansion in the amount of $100,000.

Prepare a correct income statement.
(S.O. 4, 5, 6)

E16–10   For its fiscal year ending October 31, 1993, the Packer Corporation reports the following partial data:

Income before income taxes	$640,000
Income tax expense (30% × $500,000)	150,000
Income before extraordinary items	490,000
Extraordinary loss from fire	140,000
Net income	$350,000

The fire loss is considered an extraordinary item. The income tax rate is 30% on all items.

Instructions

(a) Prepare a correct income statement, beginning with income before income taxes.

(b) Why is the company prepared income statement misleading?

E16–11 The Davis Company has income from continuing operations of $240,000 for the year ended December 31, 1993. It also has the following items (before considering income taxes): (1) an extraordinary fire loss of $60,000, (2) a gain of $40,000 on the discontinuance of a division, (3) a cumulative change in an accounting principle that resulted in an increase in prior year's depreciation of $30,000, and (4) a correction of an error in last year's financial statements that resulted in a $20,000 understatement of 1992 net income. Assume all items are subject to income taxes at a 30% tax rate.

Prepare income statement. (S.O. 4, 5, 6)

Instructions

(a) Prepare an income statement, beginning with income from continuing operations.

(b) Indicate the statement presentation of any item not included in (a) above.

E16–12 The Morse Corporation has a simple capital structure. At December 31, 1993, the company has $200,000 of $100 par value, 8%, preferred stock outstanding and $1,000,000 of $10 par value common stock issued. Morse's net income for the year is $600,000.

Compute earnings per share under different assumptions. (S.O. 7)

Instructions

Compute the earnings per share of common stock under the following independent situations. (Round to two decimals.)

(a) The dividend to preferred stockholders was declared, and there has been no change in the number of shares of common stock outstanding during the year.

(b) The dividend to preferred stockholders was declared, and 20,000 shares of common stock were issued on April 1, 1993.

(c) The dividend to preferred stockholders was not declared, and 10,000 shares of common treasury stock were held throughout the year. The preferred stock is cumulative.

*E16–13 Harcastle, Inc. has the following stockholders' equity balances at January 1, 1993: Common Stock ($5 par) $600,000, Paid-in Capital in Excess of Par Value $230,000, and Retained Earnings $160,000. In 1993, the following transactions and events occurred:

Prepare stockholders' equity statement. (S.O. 8)

1. Issued 10,000 additional shares of common stock for $75,000.
2. Declared and paid a cash dividend of $30,000.
3. Net income was $100,000.

Instructions

Prepare a stockholders' equity statement for the year ended December 31, 1993.

PROBLEMS

P16–1 On January 1, 1993, Wirth Corporation had the following stockholders' equity accounts:

Prepare dividend entries and stockholders' equity section. (S.O. 1, 3)

Common Stock ($10 par value, 80,000 shares issued and outstanding)	$800,000
Paid-in Capital in Excess of Par Value	200,000
Retained Earnings	540,000

During the year, the following transactions occurred:

Jan. 15 Declared a $1 cash dividend per share to stockholders of record on January 31, payable February 15.

Feb. 15 Paid the dividend declared in January.

Apr. 15 Declared a 10% stock dividend to stockholders of record on April 30, distributable May 15. On April 15, the market price of the stock was $13 per share.

May 15 Issued the shares for the stock dividend.

July 1 Announced a 2-for-1 stock split. The market price per share prior to the announcement was $15. (The new par value is $5.)

Dec. 1 Declared a $.50 per share cash dividend to stockholders of record on December 15, payable January 10, 1994.

  31 Determined that net income for the year was $220,000.

Instructions

(a) Journalize the transactions and the closing entry for net income.

(b) Enter the beginning balances and post the entries to the stockholders' equity accounts. (*Note:* Open additional stockholders' equity accounts as needed.)

(c) Prepare a stockholders' equity section at December 31.

Journalize and post transactions, and prepare retained earnings statement and stockholders' equity section.

(S.O. 1, 2, 3)

P16–2 The stockholders' equity accounts of Ortmar, Inc. at January 1, 1993, are as follows:

Preferred Stock, $100 par, 8%	$400,000
Common Stock, $5 par	900,000
Paid-in Capital in Excess of Par Value—Preferred Stock	100,000
Paid-in Capital in Excess of Par Value—Common Stock	200,000
Retained Earnings	500,000

During 1993, the company had the following transactions and events:

July 1 Declared a $.50 cash dividend on common stock.

Aug. 1 Discovered a $72,000 overstatement of 1992 depreciation. Ignore income taxes.

Sept. 1 Paid the cash dividend declared on July 1.

Dec. 1 Declared 10% stock dividend on common stock when the market value of the stock was $12 per share.

  15 Declared an 8% cash dividend on preferred stock payable January 31, 1994.

  31 Determined that net income for the year was $350,000.

Instructions

(a) Journalize the transactions and the closing entry for net income.

(b) Enter the beginning balances in the accounts and post to the stockholders' equity accounts. (*Note:* Open additional stockholders' equity accounts as needed.)

(c) Prepare a retained earnings statement for the year.

(d) Prepare a stockholders' equity section at December 31, 1993.

Prepare retained earnings statement and stockholders' equity section and compute earnings per share.

(S.O. 1, 2, 3, 7)

P16–3 The ledger of Rene Corporation at December 31, 1993, after the books have been closed, contains the following stockholders' equity accounts:

Preferred Stock (10,000 shares issued)	$1,000,000
Common Stock (400,000 shares issued)	2,000,000
Paid-in Capital in Excess of Par Value—Preferred	200,000
Paid-in Capital in Excess of Par Value—Common	1,200,000
Common Stock Dividends Distributable	100,000
Retained Earnings	2,460,000

A review of the accounting records reveals the following:

1. No errors have been made in recording 1993 transactions or in preparing the closing entry for net income.

2. Preferred stock is 10% $100 par value, non-cumulative, and callable at $125. Since January 1, 1992, 10,000 shares have been outstanding; 20,000 shares are authorized.

3. Common stock is no-par with a stated value of $5 per share; 600,000 shares are authorized.

4. The January 1 balance in Retained Earnings was $2,200,000.

5. On July 1, 100,000 shares of common stock were sold for cash at $8 per share.

6. A cash dividend of $400,000 was declared and properly allocated to preferred and common stock on November 1. No dividends were paid to preferred stockholders in 1992.

7. On December 31, a 5% stock dividend was declared out of retained earnings when the market price per share was $7.

8. Net income for the year was $800,000.

9. On December 31, 1993, the directors authorized disclosure of a $100,000 restriction of retained earnings for plant expansion. (Use Note A.)

Instructions

(a) Reproduce the retained earnings account (T account) for the year.

(b) Prepare a retained earnings statement for the year.

(c) Prepare a stockholders' equity section at December 31.

(d) Compute the earnings per share of common stock using the weighted average shares outstanding for the year.

(e) Compute the allocation of the cash dividend to preferred and common stock.

P16–4 The Trailblazer Corporation owns a number of travel agencies and a chain of motels in the Northwest. Its condensed operating results for 1993 show the following:

Prepare income statement with discontinued operations and an extraordinary loss, and compute earnings per share.
(S.O. 4, 5, 6, 7)

Operating revenues	$14,580,000
Operating expenses	10,600,000
Income from operations	$ 3,980,000

An additional analysis of the data indicate that the travel agencies are very profitable but the motel chain has been unprofitable. Through September 30, the motels lost $500,000 from operating revenues of $4,200,000 and operating expenses of $4,700,000. On October 1, the motel operation was discontinued and sold at a loss of $1,200,000 before taxes. The motel operating results are included in income from operations, but the loss on disposal is not included in the operating results shown above. During the year, the corporation had other expenses and losses of $80,000, which is not included in the operating results. In November, a condemnation action was taken against the company to obtain property for a new national park. As a result, the corporation suffered an extraordinary loss of $900,000 before taxes which is not included in the operating results. The corporation is in a 30% tax bracket.

At December 31, Trailblazer has 480,000 shares of $1 par value common stock outstanding, of which 120,000 were issued on November 1.

Instructions

(a) Prepare a condensed income statement for the year.

(b) Compute all of the earnings per share amounts that should appear on the income statement. (Round to two decimals.)

P16–5 The ledger of the Hecket Corporation at December 31, 1993, contains the following summary data:

Prepare expanded income statement and compute earnings per share data.
(S.O. 4, 5, 6, 7)

Net sales	$1,500,000	Cost of goods sold	$800,000
Selling expenses	110,000	Administrative expenses	140,000
Other revenues and gains	40,000	Other expenses and losses	30,000

Your analysis reveals the following additional information that is not included in the above data.

1. The entire ceramics division was discontinued on August 31. The loss from operations for this division before income taxes was $150,000. The ceramics division was sold at a gain of $60,000 before income taxes.

2. On July 12, a fire occurred in one plant that resulted in an extraordinary loss of $80,000 before income taxes.

3. During the year, Hecket changed its depreciation method from straight-line to declining balance. The cumulative effect of the change on prior years' net income was a decrease of $30,000 before taxes. (Assume that depreciation under the new method is correctly included in the ledger data.)

4. The income tax rate on all items is 30%.

Instructions

(a) Prepare an income statement for the year ended December 31, 1993, using the format illustrated in the demonstration problem.

(b) Prepare the earnings per share data that should appear in the income statement, assuming there were 100,000 shares of common stock outstanding throughout the year.

*P16–6 On January 1, 1993, Simpson Inc. had the following stockholders' equity balances:

Prepare stockholders' equity statement.
(S.O. 8)

Common Stock (500,000 shares issued)	$1,000,000
Paid-in Capital in Excess of Par Value	500,000

Stock Dividends Distributable		100,000
Retained Earnings		600,000

During 1993, the following transactions and events occurred:

1. Issued 50,000 shares of $2 par value common stock as a result of 10% stock dividend declared on December 15, 1992.
2. Issued 30,000 shares of common stock for cash at $5 per share.
3. Purchased 20,000 shares of common stock for the treasury at $6 per share.
4. Declared and paid a cash dividend of $150,000.
5. Sold 5,000 shares of treasury stock for cash at $6 per share.
6. Earned net income of $300,000.

Instructions
Prepare a stockholders' equity statement for the year.

ALTERNATE PROBLEMS

Prepare dividend entries and stockholders' equity section.
(S.O. 1, 3)

P16–1A   On January 1, 1993, the Stengel Corporation had the following stockholders' equity accounts:

Common Stock ($20 par value, 60,000 shares issued and outstanding)	$1,200,000
Paid-in Capital in Excess of Par Value	200,000
Retained Earnings	500,000

During the year, the following transactions occurred:

Feb. 1   Declared a $1 cash dividend per share to stockholders of record on February 15, payable March 1.
Mar. 1   Paid the dividend declared in February.
Apr. 1   Announced a 4 for 1 stock split. Prior to the split, the market price per share was $36.
July 1   Declared a 5% stock dividend to stockholders of record on July 15, distributable July 31. On July 1, the market price of the stock was $10 per share.
     31   Issued the shares for the stock dividend.
Dec. 1   Declared a $.50 per share dividend to stockholders of record on December 15, payable January 5, 1994.
     31   Determined that net income for the year was $325,000.

Instructions
(a) Journalize the transactions and closing entries.
(b) Enter the beginning balances and post the entries to the stockholders' equity accounts. (*Note:* Open additional stockholders' equity accounts as needed.)
(c) Prepare a stockholders' equity section at December 31.

Journalize and post transactions, and prepare retained earnings statement and stockholders' equity section.
(S.O. 1, 2, 3)

P16–2A   The stockholders' equity accounts of the Fryman Company at January 1, 1993, are as follows:

Preferred Stock, 9%, $50 par	$300,000
Common Stock, $2 par	500,000
Paid-in Capital in Excess of Par Value—Preferred Stock	200,000
Paid-in Capital in Excess of Par Value—Common Stock	300,000
Retained Earnings	600,000

During 1993, the company had the following transactions and events:

July 1   Declared a $.50 cash dividend on common stock.
Aug. 1   Discovered $45,000 understatement of 1992 depreciation. Ignore income taxes.
Sept. 1   Paid the cash dividend declared on July 1.

Dec. 1 Declared 10% stock dividend on common stock when the market value of the stock was $18 per share.

15 Declared a 9% cash dividend on preferred stock payable January 15, 1994.

31 Determined that net income for the year was $380,000.

31 Recognized a $200,000 restriction of retained earnings for plant expansion.

Instructions

(a) Journalize the transactions, events, and closing entries.

(b) Enter the beginning balances in the accounts and post to the stockholders' equity accounts. (*Note:* Open additional stockholders' equity accounts as needed.)

(c) Prepare a retained earnings statement for the year.

(d) Prepare a stockholders' equity section at December 31, 1993.

P16–3A The post-closing trial balance of the Currier Corporation at December 31, 1993, contains the following stockholders' equity accounts:

Prepare retained earnings statement and stockholders' equity section and compute earnings per share.

(S.O. 1, 2, 3, 7)

Preferred Stock (15,000 shares issued)	$ 750,000
Common Stock (250,000 shares issued)	2,500,000
Paid-in Capital in Excess of Par Value—Preferred	250,000
Paid-in Capital in Excess of Par Value—Common	500,000
Common Stock Dividends Distributable	200,000
Retained Earnings	763,000

A review of the accounting records reveals the following:

1. No errors have been made in recording 1993 transactions or in preparing the closing entry for net income.

2. Preferred stock is $50 par, 10%, and cumulative. 15,000 shares have been outstanding since January 1, 1992.

3. Authorized stock is 20,000 shares of preferred, 500,000 shares of common with a $10 par value.

4. The January 1 balance in Retained Earnings was $920,000.

5. On July 1, 25,000 shares of common stock were sold for cash at $16 per share.

6. On September 1, the company discovered an understatement error of $60,000 in computing depreciation in 1992. The net of tax effect of $42,000 was properly debited directly to Retained Earnings.

7. A cash dividend of $250,000 was declared and properly allocated to preferred and common stock on October 1. No dividends were paid to preferred stockholders in 1992.

8. On December 31, an 8% stock dividend was declared out of retained earnings when the market price per share was $16.

9. Net income for the year was $455,000.

10. On December 31, 1993, the directors authorized disclosure of a $200,000 restriction of retained earnings for plant expansion. (Use Note X.)

Instructions

(a) Reproduce the retained earnings account for the year.

(b) Prepare a retained earnings statement for the year.

(c) Prepare a stockholders' equity section at December 31.

(d) Compute the earnings per share of common stock using the weighted average shares outstanding for the year.

(e) Compute the allocation of the cash dividend to preferred and common stock.

P16–4A The Resort Corporation owns a number of cruise ships and a chain of hotels. The hotels, which have not been profitable, were discontinued on September 1, 1993. The 1993 operating results for the company were as follows:

Prepare income statement with discontinued operations and extraordinary loss, and compute earnings per share.

(S.O. 4, 5, 6, 7)

Operating revenues	$12,600,000
Operating expenses	8,600,000
Operating income	$ 4,000,000

Analysis discloses that these data include the operating results of the hotel chain, which were: operating revenues $3,000,000 and operating expenses $4,000,000. The hotels were sold at a gain of $500,000 before taxes. This gain is not included in the operating results. During the year, Resort suffered an extraordinary fire loss of $700,000 before taxes which is not included in the operating results. In 1993, the company had other revenues and gains of $100,000, which are not included in the operating results. The corporation is in the 30% income tax bracket.

Resort Corporation had 360,000 shares of common stock outstanding on January 1, 1993 and issued an additional 120,000 shares on August 1, 1993.

Instructions

(a) Prepare a condensed income statement.

(b) Compute the earnings per share data that should appear in the income statement.

Prepare expanded income statement and compute earnings per share data.

(S.O. 4, 5, 6, 7)

P16–5A The ledger of the Genoa Corporation at December 31, 1993, contains the following summary data:

Net sales	$1,800,000	Cost of goods sold	$1,000,000
Selling expenses	120,000	Administrative expenses	130,000
Other revenues and gains	20,000	Other expenses and losses	28,000

Your analysis reveals the following additional information that is not included in the above data.

1. The entire puzzles division was discontinued on August 31. The gain from operations for this division before income taxes was $50,000. The puzzles division was sold at a loss of $70,000 before income taxes.

2. On May 15, company property was expropriated for an interstate highway. The settlement resulted in an extraordinary gain of $100,000 before income taxes.

3. During the year, Genoa changed its depreciation method from sum-of-the-years' digits to straight-line. The cumulative effect of the change on prior years' net income was an increase of $40,000 before taxes. (Assume that depreciation under the new method is correctly included in the ledger data.)

4. The income tax rate on all items is 30%.

Instructions

(a) Prepare an income statement for the year ended December 31, 1993, using the format illustrated in the demonstration problem.

(b) Prepare the earnings per share data that should appear in the income statement, assuming there were 100,000 shares of common stock outstanding throughout the year.

*B*roadening Your Perspective

FINANCIAL REPORTING PROBLEM

The BFGoodrich Company is a diversified manufacturer of tires, vinyl products, speciality chemicals, and aerospace products. Selected financial data, in millions of dollars, for a recent two-year period were as follows.

	Current Year	Prior Year
Sales	$2,416.7	$2,023.5
Total operating income	298.0	200.7
Income from continuing operations	209.9	83.6
Income (loss) from discontinued operations (net of taxes)	(16.9)	(4.4)
Extraordinary items (net of taxes)		25.8
Cumulative effect of change in method of accounting for taxes	2.7	

Net income	195.7	105.0
Dividends on preferred stock	8.8	9.8
Dividends on common stock	43.3	37.0
Income retained in the business at end of year	548.9	405.3

The notes to the company's financial statements indicate that the weighted average number of common shares outstanding (in 000 of shares) were 25,179 for the current year and 23,651 for the prior year. In addition, the stockholders' equity section of the balance sheet shows that at December 31, of the current year, there were 25,554,627 shares of common stock issued and 352,396 shares of common stock held in the treasury.

Instructions

(a) Present the earnings per share data for the company for each year.

(b) Comment on the relative importance of material nontypical items in each year.

(c) Prepare a retained earning statement for the current year.

(d) What was the total dividend per share of common stock for the current year?

DECISION CASE

General Dynamics develops, produces, and supports innovative, reliable, and highly sophisticated military and commercial products. In July of a recent year, the corporation announced that its Quincy Shipbuilding Division (Quincy) will be closed following the completion of the Maritime Prepositioning Ship construction program.

Prior to discontinuance, the operating results of Quincy were net sales $246.8 million, income from operations before income taxes $28.3 million, and income taxes $12.5 million. The corporation's loss on disposition of Quincy was $5.0 million, net of $4.3 million income tax benefits.

From its other operating activities, General Dynamics' financial results were net sales $8,163.8 million, cost of goods sold $6,958.8 million, and selling and administrative expenses $537.0 million. In addition, the corporation had interest expense of $17.2 million and interest revenue of $3.6 million. Income taxes were $282.9 million.

General Dynamics had an average of 42.3 million shares of common stock outstanding during the year.

Instructions

(a) Prepare the income statement for the year, assuming that the year ended on December 31, 1993. Show earnings per share data on the income statement. All dollars should be stated in millions, except for per share amounts. For example, $8 million would be shown as $8.0.

(b) In the preceding year, Quincy's earnings were $51.6 million before income taxes of $22.8 million. For comparative purposes, General Dynamics reported earnings per share of $.61 from discontinued operations for Quincy in the preceding year.

    (1) What was the average number of common shares outstanding during the preceding year?

    (2) If earnings per share from continuing operations was $7.47, what was income from continuing operations during the preceding year? (Round to two decimals.)

CRITICAL THINKING CASE

To answer the following questions, refer to the opening Emory University story.

1. What kind of investments make up the $1.6 billion endowment fund of Emory University? Of what significance to Emory's endowment fund are the Coca-Cola shares of stock?

2. What is the dividend yield (using market value) on each share of Coca-Cola stock? Prepare the quarterly journal entry (accounts and amount) recorded by Emory University when it receives a dividend from Coca-Cola.

3. What is the "total return" on an investment? What total return does Emory University attempt to achieve on its endowment funds? What average annual total return has Emory earned on its Coca-Cola stock over the past decade?

ETHICAL CASE

Flambeau Corporation has paid 60 consecutive quarterly cash dividends (15 years). The last six months, however, have been a real cash drain on the company as profit margins have been greatly narrowed by increasing competition. With a cash balance only sufficient to meet day-to-day operating needs, the president, Vince Ramsey, has decided that a stock dividend instead of a cash dividend should be declared. He tells Flambeau's financial vice-president, Janice Rahn, to issue a press release stating that the company is extending its consecutive dividend record with the issuance of a 5% stock dividend. "Write the press release convincing the stockholders that the stock dividend is just as good as a cash dividend," he orders. "Just watch our stock rise when we announce the stock dividend; it must be a good thing if that happens."

Instructions

(a) Who are the stakeholders in this situation?

(b) Is there anything unethical about President Ramsey's intentions or actions?

(c) What is the effect of a stock dividend on a corporation's stockholders' equity accounts? Which would you rather receive as a stockholder, a cash dividend or a stock dividend? Why?

Answers to Self-Study Questions
1. d   2. b   3. c   4. a   5. c   6. a   7. b   8. d   9. c   10. c
11. b

CONCEPTS FOR REVIEW

Before studying this chapter, you should know or, if necessary, review:

a. *What is a long-term liability? a current liability? (Ch. 4, p. 151–2).*

b. *How to record adjusting entries for interest expense and payable. (Ch. 3, p. 99–100).*

c. *How to record entries for the issuance of notes payable and related interest expense. (Ch. 12, p. 469–71).*

d. *What are leases? (Ch. 11, p. 448–9).*

LONG-TERM LIABILITIES

Every year, hundreds of college campuses around the country build new buildings. As you can imagine, these buildings are very expensive. Where do most schools get the money for these projects? From long-term bonds.

At the University of Kentucky (UK), "revenue" bonds are being issued to build buildings on the Lexington campus, where 23,000 students study, and on 14 community colleges throughout the state, where another 46,000 students go to school. A revenue bond is secured by student fees—in other words, the school's revenues are pledged as collateral to guarantee payment of the bond. Currently the outstanding debt on the Lexington campus buildings totals $137 million. The total debt on the community college buildings equals $121 million. The interest rates on the bonds range from 3% (issued in 1970 and guaranteed by a federal program) to 9% (issued in 1983). The bonds generally have maturities ranging from 10 to 20 years.

Additional "guarantees" for bond purchasers are the ratings given the bonds by professional rating agencies. "Our bonds are rated AA — by Standard & Poor's Corp. and A1 by Moody's Investor Service," says Henry Clay Owen, UK's treasurer. "That's well above investment grade," he says. "We always have a very good market for our bonds. People in Kentucky identify very closely with the university. Even though the bonds are rated AA —, they trade at AAA because they're so easy to sell."

One advantage for investors: the bonds are tax exempt. So, a recent issue offering 6.5% is the equivalent of 10% to those individuals in the top tax bracket. "I would feel very comfortable buying UK bonds because it's inconceivable to me that there would ever be a default," says Owen.

As you read this chapter, think about the entries the University of Kentucky would make for the bonds that it issues.

Imagine that you had to finance construction of Byron, a nuclear power plant servicing much of Northern Illinois, which cost in excess of $4 billion. Long-term financing is desirable because refinancing the project on a year-by-year basis would be time consuming, if not risky, if financing suddenly became difficult to obtain. For long-term financing, enterprises may use either equity financing (usually common stock) or debt financing. Equity financing is available, but common stockholders might not favor this source because of the decrease in earnings per

Accounting in Action · *Business Insight*

Our liability discussion in this chapter is relatively traditional. However, it is important to understand that we saw in the late 1980s the leveraging of corporate America. A spectacular group of characters invented ways to take over some of the largest and most prestigious companies in America through the use of debt. Names such as Boone Pickens, Ivan Boesky, Michael Milken, and Carl Icahn became familiar to all those involved in high finance. An obscure firm at one time, Kohlberg Kravis Roberts & Co. (KKR) learned the intricacies of leveraged buyouts (in which management or a third party takes over a company, financing it with debt) so well that it now routinely is involved in takeovers of some of the country's largest corporations.

Why the use of debt? The approach is relatively simple—buy a company using debt, sell off assets to pay off the debt, and then after this procedure sell stock, and, hopefully, reap a bonanza. Consider the example of Beatrice Cos. KKR bought Beatrice for a premium of approximately 50% over its initial stock price. What KKR saw in Beatrice was a group of well-known brand names—Playtex undergarments, Samsonite luggage, Tropicana orange juice, La Choy Chinese food, and Hunt's catsup. It then sold off some of these companies and then resold the restructured company to the public at a handsome profit. Although this strategy sometimes works, in other cases what has happened is that the acquired company is saddled with an enormous debt load that has been difficult to pay off. As a result, the 1990s have found many companies conserving cash in order to pay these interest costs. Unfortunately conserving cash has led to layoffs, dividend reductions, and in some cases massive restructurings.

share that would result. Instead, long-term debt, with its accompanying interest cost, is an attractive alternative. Such debt is used by many large corporations. For example, United Air Lines has had more than one and a half dollars of long-term debt ($2.9 billion) to every dollar of stockholders' equity ($1.8 billion). Potomac Electric Power Company has had a one-to-one ratio of long-term debt to stockholders' equity.

Long-term liabilities are obligations that are expected to be paid after one year. In this chapter we will explain the accounting for the principal types of obligations reported in the long-term liability section of the balance sheet. These obligations may be in the form of bonds, long-term notes, and lease liabilities.

Why Issue Bonds?

Bonds are a form of interest bearing notes payable used by corporations. Bonds, like common stock, are sold in small denominations (usually a thousand dollars or multiples of a thousand dollars). As a result, bonds attract many investors.

In contrast, the two other principal types of long-term debt financing, notes payable and leasing, usually involve one individual, a company, or a financial institution. Notes payable and leasing are therefore seldom sufficient to furnish the funds needed for plant expansion and major projects like the Byron nuclear plant or new buildings at the University of Kentucky. To obtain large amounts of long-term capital, corporate management usually must decide whether to issue bonds or to use equity financing.

From the standpoint of the corporation seeking long-term financing, bonds offer the following advantages over common stock:

> ### Study Objective 1
>
> *Explain why bonds are issued and their major characteristics.*

1. **Stockholder control is not affected.** Bondholders do not have voting rights, so current stockholders retain full control of the company.
2. **Tax savings result.** Bond interest is deductible for tax purposes; dividends on stock are not. For example, if a bond pays 10% interest and the corporation is in the 30% tax bracket, the net cash cost to the corporation is only 7%. If a corporation pays a 10% cash dividend, the cash resources of the company are reduced by the full 10%.
3. **Income to common stockholders may increase.** If a company can earn more on borrowed funds (bonds) than the interest cost on these funds, the income to common stockholders will increase. For example, if a company can earn 15% on money obtained from issuing $1,000,000 bonds at 12%, income before taxes will increase $30,000 (3% × $1,000,000). This phenomenon, known as **leveraging or trading on the equity**, is discussed further in Chapter 20.
4. **Earnings per share of common stock may be higher.** Although bond interest expense will reduce net income, earnings per share of common stock will often be higher under bond financing because no additional shares of common stock are issued.

To illustrate the potential effect on earnings per share, assume that Microsystems, Inc. is considering two plans for financing the construction of a new $5 million plant. Plan A involves issuance of 200,000 shares of common stock at the current market price of $25 per share. Plan B involves issuance of $5 million, 12% bonds at face value. Income before interest and taxes on the new plant will be $1.5 million; income taxes are expected to be 30%. Microsystems currently has 100,000 shares of common stock outstanding. The alternative effects on earnings per share are shown in Illustration 17-1.

ILLUSTRATION 17-1

Effects on earnings per share—stocks vs. bonds

	Plan A Issue stock	Plan B Issue bonds
Income before interest and taxes	$1,500,000	$1,500,000
Interest (12% × $5,000,000)	—	600,000
Income before income taxes	1,500,000	900,000
Income tax expense (30%)	450,000	270,000
Net income	$1,050,000	$ 630,000
Outstanding shares	300,000	100,000
Earnings per share	$ 3.50	$ 6.30

Note that net income is $420,000 ($1,050,000 − $630,000) less with long-term debt financing (bonds). However, earnings per share is higher because there are 200,000 fewer shares of common stock outstanding.

The major disadvantages resulting from the use of bonds are that interest must be paid on a periodic basis and the principal (face value) of the bonds must be paid at maturity. A company with fluctuating earnings and a relatively weak cash position may experience great difficulty in meeting interest requirements in periods of low earnings. In addition, if the earnings on the borrowed funds fall below the cost of debt during the term of the bonds, trading on the equity will result in a net loss to stockholders. During a recession, many corporations find that trading on the equity (leveraging) magnifies their losses and contributes significantly to their financial problems.

Characteristics of Bond Issuance

As in the case of issuing capital stock, a number of basic questions need to be resolved in issuing bonds: What type of bond should be sold? How should the bond be sold? At what price should the bonds be issued? For purposes of discussion these questions are considered in the following sections:

1. Types of bonds.
2. Issuing procedures.
3. Trading of bonds.
4. Determining the market value of bonds.

Types of Bonds

Bonds may have many different features. Some types of bonds commonly issued are:

SECURED AND UNSECURED BONDS. Secured bonds have specific assets of the issuer pledged as collateral for the bonds. A bond secured by real estate, for example, is called a mortgage bond. A bond secured by specific assets set aside to retire the bonds is called a sinking fund bond. (This type of bond is discussed later in the chapter.) Unsecured bonds are issued against the general credit of the borrower. These bonds, called debenture bonds, are used extensively by large corporations with good credit ratings. For example, in a recent annual report, DuPont reported over $2 billion of debenture bonds outstanding.

TERM AND SERIAL BONDS. Bonds that are due for payment (mature) at a single specified future date are called term bonds. In contrast, bonds that mature in installments are called serial bonds. For example, Caterpillar Inc. debentures due in

Accounting in Action ▪ *Business Insight*

Although bonds are generally secured by solid substantial assets like land, buildings, and equipment, exceptions occur. For example Trans World Airlines Inc. (TWA) at one time decided to issue $300 million of high-yielding five-year bonds. TWA's bonds would be secured by a grab bag of assets, including some durable spare parts, but also a lot of disposable items that TWA has in its warehouses, such as light bulbs and gaskets. Some are calling the planned TWA bonds "light bulb bonds." As one financial expert noted: "You've got to admit that some security is better than none." However, another noted, "They're digging pretty far down the barrel."

Source: The Wall Street Journal, June 2, 1989.

2007 are term bonds, and their debentures due between 1993 and 2007 are serial bonds.

REGISTERED AND BEARER BONDS. Bonds issued in the name of the owner are called registered bonds; interest payments are made by check to bondholders of record. Bonds not registered are called bearer (or coupon) bonds; bondholders are required to send in coupons to receive interest payments. Coupon bonds may be transferred directly to another party. In contrast, the transfer of registered bonds requires cancellation of the bonds by the corporation and the issuance of new bonds. With minor exceptions, most bonds issued today are registered bonds.

CONVERTIBLE AND CALLABLE BONDS. Bonds that permit bondholders to convert them into common stock at their option are called convertible bonds. Bonds subject to retirement at a stated dollar amount prior to maturity at the option of the issuer are known as callable bonds

> **Helpful hint** It is the bond-holder's option to convert a convertible bond but it is the issuer's option to call and redeem the bond.

Issuing Procedures

State laws grant corporations the power to issue bonds. Within the corporation, formal approval by both the board of directors and stockholders is usually required before bonds can be issued. **In authorizing the bond issue, the board of directors must stipulate the total number of bonds to be authorized, total face (par) value, and the contractual interest rate.**

The total bond authorization often exceeds the number of bonds originally issued. This is done intentionally to help ensure that the corporation will have the flexibility it needs to meet future cash requirements. Face value or par value is the amount due at the maturity date. The contractual interest rate, often referred to as the **stated rate**, is used to determine the amount of cash interest the borrower pays and the investor receives. Usually the contractual rate is stated as an annual rate, and interest is generally paid semiannually.

The terms of the bond issue are set forth in a formal legal document called a bond indenture. In addition to the terms, the indenture summarizes the respective rights and privileges of the bondholders and their trustees, as well as the obligations and commitments of the issuing company. The **trustee** keeps records of each bondholder, maintains custody of unissued bonds, and holds conditional title to pledged property.

After the bond indenture is prepared, **bond certificates** are printed. The indenture and the certificate are separate documents. A bond certificate is shown in Illustration 17-2. Bonds are generally sold through an investment company that specializes in selling securities. In most cases, the issue is underwritten by the investment company. Under an underwriting arrangement, the company

> **Helpful hint** Do not confuse the terms indenture and debenture. Indenture refers to the formal bond document (contract). Debenture bonds are unsecured bonds.

ILLUSTRATION 17-2

Bond certificate

sells the bonds to the investment company, which, in turn, sells the bonds to individual investors.

Trading of Bonds

Corporate bonds, like capital stock, are traded on national securities markets. Thus, bondholders have the opportunity to convert their holdings into cash at any time by selling the bonds at the current market price. **Bond prices are quoted as a percentage of the face value of the bond, which is usually $1,000.** Thus, a $1,000 bond with a quoted price of 97 means that the selling price of the bond is 97% of face value, or $970 in this case. Bond prices and trading activity are published daily in newspapers and the financial press, as illustrated by the following:

ILLUSTRATION 17-3

Market information for bonds

Bonds	Current Yield	Volume	Close	Net Change
K mart 8⅜ 17	8.4	35	100¼	+ ⅞

The information in Illustration 17-3 indicates that K mart Corporation has outstanding 8⅜%, $1,000 bonds maturing in 2017 and currently yielding a 8.4% return. In addition, 35 bonds were traded on this day; and at the close of trading, the price was 100¼. The net change column indicates the difference between the day's closing price and the previous day's closing price.

Transactions between a bondholder and other investors are not journalized by the issuing corporation. If Tom Smith sells bonds that are bought by Faith Jones, the issuing corporation does not journalize the transaction (although it does keep records of the names of bondholders in the case of registered bonds). A corporation makes journal entries only when it issues or buys back bonds.

Helpful hint (1) What is the price of a $1,000 bond trading at 95¼? (2) What is the price of a $1,000 bond trading at 101⅞? Answers: (1) $952.50 and (2) $1,018.75.

Determining the Market Value of Bonds

If you were an investor interested in purchasing bonds, how would you determine how much to pay for a bond? To be more specific, assume that Coronet, Inc., issues a zero-interest bond with a face value of $1,000,000 due in 20 years. For these bonds, the only cash you receive is a million dollars at the end of 20 years. Would you pay a million dollars for this bond? We hope not, because a million dollars received 20 years from now is not the same as a million dollars received today. The reason you would not pay a million dollars relates to what is called the **time value of money**. If you had a million dollars today, you would invest it and earn interest such that at the end of 20 years, your investment would be worth much more than a million dollars. Thus, if someone is going to pay you a million dollars 20 years from now, you would want to find its equivalent today, or its **present value**. In other words, you would want to determine how much must be invested today at current interest rates to have a million dollars in 20 years.

The market value (present value) of a bond is, therefore, a function of three factors: (1) the dollar amounts to be received, (2) the length of time until the amounts are received, and (3) the market rate of interest. The market rate of interest is the rate investors demand for loaning funds to the corporation. The process of finding the present value is referred to as **discounting** the future amounts. To illustrate, assume that Laughlin Steel issues $10,000,000 of 12% bonds, due in 10 years with interest payable semiannually. The purchaser of the bonds would receive the following two cash payments: (1) **principal** $10,000,000 to be paid at maturity, and (2) twenty $600,000 **interest payments** ($10,000,000 × 12% × ½) over the term of the bonds. The present values of these amounts are approximately as shown in Illustration 17-4.

Accounting in Action · *Business Insight*

Present value computations are not limited to bonds. Any obligation due in the future should be discounted to find its present value. For example, what is the present value of liabilities for future health benefits to yet-to-be-retired workers or the liabilities of companies to be paid 10 years in the future? In most cases, liabilities are discounted, although there are exceptions such as warranties and income taxes. The FASB has undertaken a comprehensive examination to determine under what conditions obligations should be discounted and what interest rate should be used in discounting. To date, the issue remains unresolved.

ILLUSTRATION 17-4

Computing the market price of bonds

Present value of $10,000,000 received in 20 periods	$ 3,118,000
Present value of $600,000 received semiannually for 20 periods	6,882,000
Market price of bonds	**$10,000,000**

Tables are available to provide the present value numbers to be used, or they can be determined mathematically.[1] Further discussion of the concepts and the mechanics of these computations is provided in Appendix N.

Before You Go On . . .

1. What are the advantages of bond versus stock financing?

2. What are secured versus unsecured bonds, term versus serial bonds, registered versus bearer bonds, and callable versus convertible bonds?

3. Explain the terms face value, contractual interest rate, and bond indenture.

4. Explain why you would prefer to receive $1 million today rather than five years from now.

*I*ssuing Bonds at Face Value

Study Objective 2

Prepare the entries for the issuance of bonds and interest expense.

To illustrate the accounting for bonds, assume that Devor Corporation issues 1,000, 10-year, 9%, $1,000 bonds dated January 1, 1993 at 100 (100% of face value). The entry to record the sale is:

Jan. 1	Cash	1,000,000	
	Bonds Payable		1,000,000
	(To record sale of bonds at face value)		

Bonds payable are reported in the long-term liability section of the balance sheet because the maturity date is January 1, 2003.

Over the term (life) of the bonds, entries are required for bond interest. Interest on bonds payable is computed in the same manner as interest on notes payable. Assuming that interest is payable semiannually on January 1 and July 1 on the bonds described above, interest of $45,000 ($1,000,000 × 9% × 6/12) must be paid on July 1, 1993. The entry for the payment, assuming no previous accrual of interest, is:

July 1	Bond Interest Expense	45,000	
	Cash		45,000
	(To record payment of bond interest)		

At December 31, an adjusting entry is required to recognize the $45,000 of interest expense incurred since July 1. The entry is:

Dec. 31	Bond Interest Expense	45,000	
	Bond Interest Payable		45,000
	(To accrue bond interest)		

Bond interest payable is classified as a current liability, because it is scheduled

---

[1]For those knowledgeable in the use of present value tables, the computations in this example are: $10,000,000 × .31180 = $3,118,000 and $600,000 × 11.46992 = $6,882,000 (rounded).

for payment within the next year. When the interest is paid on January 1, 1994, Bond Interest Payable is debited and Cash is credited for $45,000.

At the maturity date (January 1, 2003), Devor Corporation is required to make the final payment of interest and to pay the face value of the bonds. The entry is:

Jan. 1	Bonds Payable	1,000,000	
	Bond Interest Payable	45,000	
	Cash		1,045,000
	(To record final payment of bond interest and		
	payment of bonds at maturity)		

*I*ssuing Bonds Below or Above Face Value

The previous illustrations assumed that the interest rate paid on bonds, often referred to as the contractual (stated) interest rate and the market (effective) interest rate were the same. The contractual interest rate is the rate applied to the face (par) value to arrive at the interest paid in a year. The market interest rate is the rate investors demand for loaning funds to the corporation. When the contractual interest rate and the market interest rate are the same, bonds sell at face value.

However, market interest rates change daily. They are influenced by the type of bond issued, the state of the economy, current industry conditions and the company's individual performance. As a result, the contractual and market interest rates often differ and therefore bonds sell below or above face value.

To illustrate, suppose that investors have one of two options: purchase bonds that have a market rate of interest of 10% or purchase bonds that have a contractual rate of interest of 8%. Assuming that the bonds are of equal risk, investors will select the 10% investment. To make the investments equal, investors will demand a rate of interest higher than the contractual interest rate on the 8% bonds. Because investors cannot change the contractual interest rate, they will pay less than the face value for the bond. By paying less for the bond, they can obtain the market rate of interest. In these cases, **bonds sell at a discount**.

Conversely, if the market rate of interest is **lower** than the contractual interest rate, investors will have to pay more than face value for the bonds. That is, if the market rate of interest is 8%, but the contractual interest rate is 9%, the issuer will require more funds from the investor. In these cases, **bonds are sold at a premium**. These relationships are shown graphically in Illustration 17-5.

Issuance of bonds at an amount different from face value is quite common. By the time a company prints the bond certificates and markets the bonds, it will

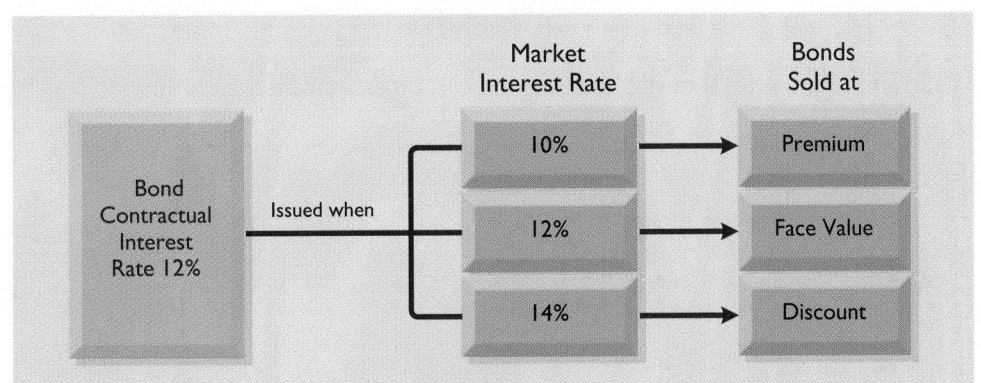

ILLUSTRATION 17-5

Interest rates and bond prices

be a coincidence if the market rate and the contractual rate are the same. Thus, the issuance of bonds at a discount does not mean that the financial strength of the issuer is suspect. Conversely, the sale of bonds at a premium does not indicate that the financial strength of the issuer is exceptional.

Bonds Issued at a Discount

To illustrate the issuance of bonds at a discount, assume that on January 1, 1993, Candlestick, Inc. sells $1 million, 5-year, 13% bonds at 98 (98% of par) with interest payable on July 1 and January 1. The entry to record the issuance is:

Jan. 1	Cash	980,000	
	Discount on Bonds Payable	20,000	
	Bonds Payable		1,000,000
	(To record sale of bonds at a discount)		

Although Discount on Bonds Payable has a debit balance, it is not an asset. **Rather it is a contra account, which is deducted from bonds payable,** as illustrated below.

ILLUSTRATION 17-6

Statement presentation of discount on bonds payable

Long-term liabilities		
Bonds payable	$1,000,000	
Less: Discount on bonds payable	20,000	$980,000

Helpful hint Carrying value (book value) of bonds issued at a discount is determined by subtracting the balance of the discount account from the balance of the Bonds Payable account.

The $980,000 represents the **carrying (or book) value** of the bonds. On the date of issue this amount equals the market price.

The issuance of bonds below face value causes the total cost of borrowing to differ from the bond interest paid. That is, the issuing corporation must pay not only the stated rate of interest over the term of the bonds, but also the face value (rather than the issuance price) at maturity. Therefore, the difference between the issuance price and face value of the bonds—the discount—is an **additional cost of borrowing that should be recorded as bond interest expense over the life of the bonds.** The total cost of borrowing $980,000 for Candlestick, Inc. is $670,000, computed as follows:

ILLUSTRATION 17-7

Total cost of borrowing— bonds issued at discount

Bonds Issued at a Discount	
Semiannual interest payments	
$(1,000,000 \times 13\% \times \frac{1}{2} = \$65,000; \$65,000 \times 10)$	$650,000
Add: Bond discount ($1,000,000 − $980,000)	20,000
Total cost of borrowing	$670,000

Alternatively, the total cost of borrowing can be determined as follows:

ILLUSTRATION 17-8

Alternative computation of total cost of borrowing— bonds issued at discount

Bonds Issued at a Discount	
Principal at maturity	$1,000,000
Semiannual interest payments ($65,000 × 10)	650,000
Cash to be paid to bondholders	1,650,000
Cash received from bondholders	980,000
Total cost of borrowing	$ 670,000

Amortization of Bond Discount

To comply with the matching principle, it follows that bond discount should be allocated systematically to each accounting period benefiting from the use of the cash proceeds.

One method, the straight-line method of amortization, allocates the same amount each interest period.[2] The amount is determined as follows:

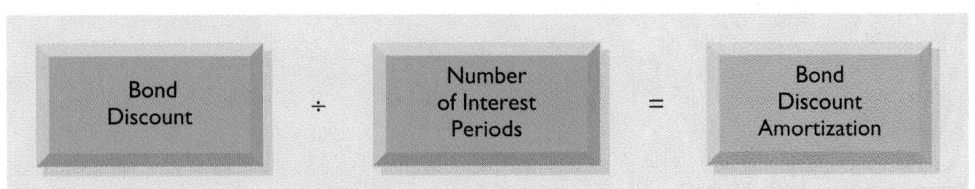

ILLUSTRATION 17-9

Formula for straight-line method of bond discount amortization

In this example, the bond discount amortization is $2,000 ($20,000 ÷ 10). The entry to record the payment of bond interest and the amortization of bond discount on the first interest date (July 1, 1993) is:

July 1	Bond Interest Expense	67,000	
	Discount on Bonds Payable		2,000
	Cash		65,000
	(To record payment of bond interest and amortization of bond discount)		

At December 31, the adjusting entry is:

Dec. 31	Bond Interest Expense	67,000	
	Discount on Bonds Payable		2,000
	Bond Interest Payable		65,000
	(To record accrued bond interest and amortization of bond discount)		

Over the term of the bonds, the balance in Discount on Bonds Payable will decrease annually by the same amount until it has a zero balance at the maturity date of the bonds. Thus, the carrying value of the bonds at maturity will be equal to the face value of the bonds.

Preparing a bond discount amortization schedule as shown in Illustration 17-10 is useful to determine interest expense, discount amortization and the carrying value of the bond. As indicated, the interest expense recorded each period is $67,000. Also note that the carrying value of the bond increases $2,000 each period until it reaches its face value $1,000,000 at the end of period 10.

Bonds Issued at a Premium

The issuance of bonds at a premium can be illustrated by assuming the Candlestick, Inc. bonds described above are sold at 102 (102% of par) rather than at 98.

---

[2]Another method, the effective interest method, is discussed in Appendix H at the end of this chapter.

ILLUSTRATION 17-10

*Bond discount amortization
schedule*

Semiannual Interest Periods	(A) Interest to be Paid (6.5% × $1,000,000)	(B) Interest Expense to Be Recorded (A) + (C)	(C) Discount Amortization ($20,000 ÷ 10)	(D) Unamortized Discount (D) − (C)	(E) Bond Carrying Value ($1,000,000 − D)
Issue date				$20,000	$ 980,000
1	$ 65,000	$ 67,000	$ 2,000	18,000	982,000
2	65,000	67,000	2,000	16,000	984,000
3	65,000	67,000	2,000	14,000	986,000
4	65,000	67,000	2,000	12,000	988,000
5	65,000	67,000	2,000	10,000	990,000
6	65,000	67,000	2,000	8,000	992,000
7	65,000	67,000	2,000	6,000	994,000
8	65,000	67,000	2,000	4,000	996,000
9	65,000	67,000	2,000	2,000	998,000
10	65,000	67,000	2,000	–0–	1,000,000
	$650,000	$670,000	$20,000		

Column (A) remains constant because the face value of the bonds ($1,000,000) is multiplied by the semiannual contractual interest rate (6.5%) each period.

Column (B) is computed as the interest paid (Column A) plus the discount amortization (Column C).

Column (C) indicates the discount amortization each period.

Column (D) decreases each period by the same amount until it reaches zero at maturity.

Column (E) increases each period by the amount of discount amortization until it equals the face value at maturity.

The entry to record the sale is:

Jan. 1	Cash	1,020,000	
	Bonds Payable		1,000,000
	Premium on Bonds Payable		20,000
	(To record sale of bonds at a premium)		

Premium on Bonds Payable is an account that is added to bonds payable as shown below:

ILLUSTRATION 17-11

*Statement presentation of
bond premium*

Long-term liabilities
Bonds payable	$1,000,000	
Add: Premium on bonds payable	20,000	$1,020,000

The sale of bonds above face value causes the total cost of borrowing to be less than the bond interest paid, because the borrower is not required to pay the bond premium at the maturity date of the bonds. Thus, the premium is considered to be a reduction in the cost of borrowing that should be credited to Bond Interest Expense over the life of the bonds. The total cost of borrowing $1,020,000 for Candlestick, Inc. is $630,000, computed as follows:

ILLUSTRATION 17-12

Total cost of borrowing—bonds issued at a premium

Bonds Issued at a Premium	
Semiannual interest payments	
($1,000,000 × 13% × ½ = $65,000; $65,000 × 10)	$650,000
Less: Bond premium ($1,020,000 − $1,000,000)	20,000
Total cost of borrowing	**$630,000**

Alternatively, the cost of borrowing can be computed as follows:

ILLUSTRATION 17-13

Alternative computation of total cost of borrowing—bonds issued at a premium

Bonds Issued at a Premium	
Principal at maturity	$1,000,000
Semiannual interest payments ($65,000 × 10)	650,000
Cash to be paid to bondholders	1,650,000
Cash received from bondholders	1,020,000
Total cost of borrowing	**$ 630,000**

Amortization of Bond Premium

The premium amortization for each interest period is $2,000 ($20,000 ÷ 10). The entry to record the first payment of interest on July 1 is:

July 1	Bond Interest Expense	63,000	
	Premium on Bonds Payable	2,000	
	Cash		65,000
	(To record payment of bond interest and amortization of bond premium)		

At December 31, the adjusting entry is:

Dec. 31	Bond Interest Expense	63,000	
	Premium on Bonds Payable	2,000	
	Bond Interest Payable		65,000
	(To record accrued bond interest and amortization of bond premium)		

Over the term of the bonds, the balance in Premium on Bonds Payable will decrease annually by the same amount until it has a zero balance at maturity. Preparing a bond premium amortization schedule as shown in Illustration 17-14 is useful to determine interest expense, discount amortized, and the carrying value of the bond. As indicated, the interest expense recorded each period is $63,000. Also note that the carrying value of the bond decreases $2,000 each period until it reaches its face value $1,000,000 at the end of period 10.

ILLUSTRATION 17-14

*Bond premium amortization
schedule*

Semiannual Interest Periods	(A) Interest to be Paid (6.5% × $1,000,000)	(B) Interest Expense to Be Recorded (A) − (C)	(C) Premium Amortization ($20,000 ÷ 10)	(D) Unamortized Premium (D) − (C)	(E) Bond Carrying Value ($1,000,000 + D)
Issue date				$20,000	$1,020,000
1	$ 65,000	$ 63,000	$ 2,000	18,000	1,018,000
2	65,000	63,000	2,000	16,000	1,016,000
3	65,000	63,000	2,000	14,000	1,014,000
4	65,000	63,000	2,000	12,000	1,012,000
5	65,000	63,000	2,000	10,000	1,010,000
6	65,000	63,000	2,000	8,000	1,008,000
7	65,000	63,000	2,000	6,000	1,006,000
8	65,000	63,000	2,000	4,000	1,004,000
9	65,000	63,000	2,000	2,000	1,002,000
10	65,000	63,000	2,000	–0–	1,000,000
	$650,000	$630,000	$20,000		

Column (A) remains constant because the face value of the bonds ($1,000,000) is multiplied by the semiannual contractual interest rate (6.5%) each period.

Column (B) is computed as the interest paid (Column A) less the premium amortization (Column C).

Column (C) indicates the premium amortization each period.

Column (D) decreases each period by the same amount until it reaches zero at maturity.

Column (E) decreases each period by the amount of premium amortization until it equals the face value at maturity.

Issuing Bonds Between Interest Dates

Bonds are often issued between interest payment dates. **When this occurs, the issuer requires the investor to pay the market price for the bonds plus accrued interest since the last interest date.** At the next interest date, the corporation will return the accrued interest to the investor by paying the full amount of interest due on outstanding bonds.

To illustrate, assume that Deer Corporation sells $1,000,000, 9% bonds at face value plus accrued interest on March 1. Interest is payable semiannually on July 1 and January 1. The accrued interest is $15,000 ($1,000,000 × 9% × 2/12). The total proceeds on the sale of the bonds, therefore, are $1,015,000, and the entry to record the sale is:

Mar. 1	Cash	1,015,000	
	Bonds Payable		1,000,000
	Bond Interest Payable		15,000
	(To record sale of bonds at face value plus accrued interest)		

At the first interest date, it is necessary to eliminate the bond interest payable balance and to recognize interest expense for the four months (March 1–June 30) the bonds have been outstanding. Interest expense in this example is, therefore, $30,000 ($1,000,000 × 9% × 4/12). The entry on July 1 for the $45,000 interest payment is:

July 1	Bond Interest Payable	15,000	
	Bond Interest Expense	30,000	
	Cash		45,000
	(To record payment of bond interest)		

Why does Deer Corporation collect interest at the time of issuance and then return this interest at the time of payment? The rationale: Collection of accrued interest at the issuance date allows the company to pay a full period's interest to all bondholders at the next interest payment date. This procedure therefore saves bookkeeping costs. Deer Corporation does not have to determine the individual amount of interest due each holder based on the time each bond has been outstanding during the interest period.

In other words, if bonds are not sold "with accrued interest," Deer Corporation would have to keep track of the purchaser and the dates that the bonds were purchased. This procedure would be necessary to ensure that each bondholder received the correct amount of interest. By selling the bonds "with accrued interest," Deer does not have to maintain detailed records and cost savings occur.

Before You Go On . . .

1. What entry is made to record the issuance of bonds payable of $1 million at 100? at 96? at 102?

2. Why do bonds sell at a discount? at a premium? at face value?

3. Explain the accounting for bonds sold between interest dates.

Redemption of Bonds Before Maturity

Bonds may be redeemed before maturity. The decision to retire bonds before maturity is made by a company's financial managers. They may decide to do so because of sufficient present and anticipated cash resources or for the saving in interest that may be realized. When bonds are retired before maturity, it is necessary to (1) eliminate the carrying value of the bonds at the redemption date, (2) record the cash paid, and (3) recognize the gain or loss on redemption. The carrying value of the bonds is the face value of the bonds less unamortized bond discount or plus unamortized bond premium at the redemption date.

To illustrate, assume at the end of the eighth period Candlestick, Inc. (which sold its bonds at a premium per Illustration 17-14) retires its bonds at 103 after paying the semiannual interest. The carrying value of the bonds at the redemption date, as shown in the bond premium amortization schedule, is $1,004,000. The entry to record the redemption at the end of the eighth interest period (January 1, 1997) is:

Jan. 1	Bonds Payable	1,000,000	
	Premium on Bonds Payable	4,000	
	Loss on Bond Redemption	26,000	
	Cash		1,030,000
	(To record redemption of bonds at 103)		

Note that the loss of $26,000 is the difference between the cash paid of $1,030,000 and the carrying value of the bonds of $1,004,000. Losses (gains) on bond re-

Study Objective 3

Describe the entries when bonds are redeemed or converted prior to maturity.

Helpful hint If a bond is redeemed prior to its maturity date and its carrying value exceeds its redemption price, will the retirement result in a gain or a loss on redemption? Answer: Gain.

demption are reported in the income statement as extraordinary items as required by the accounting profession.

Conversion of Bonds

Convertible bonds have features that are attractive both to bondholders and to the issuer. The conversion often gives bondholders an opportunity to benefit if the market price of the common stock increases substantially. Furthermore, until conversion, the bondholder receives interest on the bond. For the issuer, the bonds sell at a higher price and pay a lower rate of interest than comparable debt securities that do not have a conversion option. Many corporations, such as USAir, USX Corp., and Chrysler Corporation, have convertible bonds outstanding.

When the conversion of bonds into common stock is recorded, the current market prices of the bonds and the stock are ignored. Instead, the **carrying value** of the bonds is transferred to paid-in capital accounts, and no gain or loss is recognized. To illustrate, assume that on July 1 Saunders Associates converts $100,000 bonds sold at face value into 2,000 shares of $10 par value common stock. Both the bonds and the common stock have a market value of $130,000. The entry to record the conversion is:

July 1	Bonds Payable	100,000	
	Common Stock		20,000
	Paid-in Capital in Excess of Par		80,000
	(To record bond conversion)		

Helpful hint The method of recording this conversion of bonds to stock is called the book value method because the amount of the book value of the bonds is removed from the liability accounts and recorded as common stock and related paid-in capital.

Note that the current market price of the bonds and stocks ($130,000) is not considered in making the entry. This method of recording the bond conversion is often referred to as the book (or carrying) value method.

Bond Sinking Funds

Study Objective 4

Indicate the entries required for a bond sinking fund.

Many bond issues require the borrower to make periodic cash contributions to a sinking (redemption) fund over the life of the bonds. A sinking fund is cash or other assets set aside to retire debt. In other words, it is like a savings account that is used to pay back bondholders. **A sinking fund makes the bonds more attractive to investors, because the fund enhances the likelihood that the bonds will be redeemed at maturity.** For example, Texaco and Alcoa have sinking funds for their debenture bonds. These bonds are often referred to as sinking fund bonds.

Sinking funds are usually under the control of a trustee, such as a bank or a trust company. The trustee may be permitted to invest the periodic deposits in high-quality income-producing securities. It is expected that the deposits plus the earnings from the investments will equal the face value of the bonds at maturity. Shortly before the maturity date, the trustee sells the securities and uses the total cash in the fund to redeem the bonds. Any excess cash in the fund is returned to the issuer.

To illustrate, assume that Bountiful Corporation issues $1 million par value, 5-year bonds on January 1. The terms of the bond indenture indicate that Bountiful must make annual deposits with a sinking fund trustee, starting at the end of the first year. The amount of the annual cash contribution is $215,000. The entry to record this contribution by Bountiful Corporation at the end of the first year is as follows:

| Dec. 31 | Bond Sinking Fund | 215,000 | |
| | Cash | | 215,000 |

At the end of the second year, Bountiful Corporation records actual earnings on the assets in the sinking fund of $16,500. The entry to record this revenue is as follows:

| Dec. 31 | Bond Sinking Fund | 16,500 | |
| | Bond Sinking Fund Revenue | | 16,500 |

At the maturity date, sinking fund assets are used to redeem the bonds. The entry to record the redemption, assuming that the sinking fund has $985,000 in cash, is as follows:

Jan. 1	Bonds Payable	1,000,000	
	Bond Sinking Fund		985,000
	Cash		15,000
	(To redeem bonds at maturity)		

In this case, Bountiful Corporation had to make up for the deficiency by paying an additional $15,000. If the sinking fund had excess cash, it would be returned to Bountiful.

The bond sinking fund is reported as a single amount in the investment section of the balance sheet. Bond sinking fund revenue is classified as other revenues and gains in the income statement.

The bond contract may also require the corporation to establish a restriction on its retained earnings. As explained in Chapter 16, this restriction is reported as a note in the financial statements.

Accounting for Long-Term Notes Payable

The use of notes payable in long-term debt financing is quite common. Long-term notes payable are similar to short-term interest-bearing notes payable except that the term of the note exceeds one year. In periods of unstable interest rates, long-term notes may tie the interest rate to changes in the market rate for comparable loans. Examples are the 8.03% adjustable rate notes issued by General Motors and the floating rate notes issued by American Express Company.

A long-term note may be secured by a document called a **mortgage** that pledges title to specific units of property as security for a loan. Mortgage notes payable are widely used in the purchase of homes by individuals and in the acquisition of plant assets by many small and some large companies. For example, approximately 18% of McDonald's (the fast-food restaurant) long-term debt relates to mortgage notes on land, buildings, and improvements. Like other long-term notes payable, the mortgage loan terms may stipulate either a fixed or an adjustable interest rate. Typically, the terms require the borrower to make installment payments over the term of the loan. Each payment consists of (1) interest on the unpaid balance of the loan, and (2) a reduction of loan principal. The interest decreases each period, while the portion applied to the loan principal increases.

Mortgage notes payable are recorded initially at face value, and entries are required subsequently for each installment payment. To illustrate, assume that Porter Technology Inc. issues a $500,000, 12%, 20-year mortgage note on December 31, 1993 to obtain needed financing for the construction of a new research laboratory. The terms provide for semiannual installment payments, exclusive

Study Objective 5

Describe the accounting for long-term notes payable.

of real estate taxes and insurance, of $33,231. The installment payment schedule for the first two years is as follows:

ILLUSTRATION 17-15

Mortgage installment payment schedule

Semiannual Interest Period	(A) Cash Payment	(B) Interest Expense (D) × 6%	(C) Reduction of Principal (A) − (B)	(D) Principal Balance (D) − (C)
Issue date				$500,000
1	$33,231	$30,000	$3,231	496,769
2	33,231	29,806	3,425	493,344
3	33,231	29,601	3,630	489,714
4	33,231	29,383	3,848	485,866

The entries to record the mortgage loan and first installment payment are as follows:

Dec. 31	Cash	500,000	
	Mortgage Notes Payable		500,000
	(To record mortgage loan)		

June 30	Interest Expense	30,000	
	Mortgage Notes Payable	3,231	
	Cash		33,231
	(To record semiannual payment on mortgage)		

In the balance sheet, the reduction in principal for the next year is reported as a current liability, and the remaining unpaid principal balance is classified as a long-term liability. At December 31, 1994, the total liability is $493,344 of which $7,478 ($3,630 + $3,848) is current, and $485,866 ($493,344 − $7,478) is long-term.

Technology in Action

Many electronic spreadsheet programs can create a schedule of installment loan payments. One reason that this is so practical is that you can put in the data for your own mortgage loan and get an illustration that really hits home.

Lease Liability

Study Objective 6

Contrast the accounting for operating and capital leases.

As indicated in Chapter 11, a lease is a contractual arrangement between the lessor (owner of the property) and a lessee (renter of the property) that grants the right to use specific property for a period of time in return for cash payments. Leasing is big business. For example, an estimated $140 billion of capital equipment was leased in a recent year. This amount equals approximately one-third of equipment financed that year. The two most common types of leases are operating leases and capital leases.

Accounting in Action ▪ *Business Insight*

As an excellent example of the magnitude of leasing, leased planes account for nearly 40% of the U.S. fleet, The reasons for leasing are many but involve favorable tax treatment, increased flexibility, and low airline income. As passenger volume is expected to double in the next 20 years, some industry analysts estimate that approximately $400 billion in airplanes will be needed, and it is anticipated that much of the financing will be done through leasing. Leasing is particularly attractive to lessors because airplanes have relatively long lives, have a ready secondhand market, and have a significant resale value. Or take the commercial truck fleet—over one third of heavy-duty trucks are presently leased.

Operating Leases

The renting of an apartment and the rental of a car at an airport are examples of **operating leases**. In an operating lease **the intent is temporary use of the property by the lessee with continued ownership of the property by the lessor.** The lease (or rental) payments are recorded as an expense by the lessee and as revenue by the lessor. For example, assuming that a sales representative for Western Inc. leases a car from Hertz Car Rental at the Los Angeles airport and that Hertz charges a total of $275, the entry by the lessee, Western Inc., is:

Car Rental Expense	275	
Cash		275
(To record payment of lease rental charge)		

In addition, the lessee may incur other costs during the lease period. For example, in the case above, the lessee may be required to pay for gas and oil. These costs are also reported as an expense.

Capital Leases

In most lease contracts, a periodic payment is made by the lessee and is recorded as rent expense in the income statement. However, in some cases, the lease contract transfers substantially all the benefits and risks of ownership to the lessee, so that the lease is in effect a purchase of the property. This type of lease is called a capital lease because the present value of the cash payments for the lease are capitalized and recorded as an asset. The lessee must record the lease **as an asset** if any **one** of the following conditions exists:

Helpful hint A capital lease situation is one in which although it is legally a rental case, it is in substance an installment purchase by the lessee. Accounting standards require that we account for substance over form in such a situation.

1. **The lease transfers ownership of the property to the lessee.** *Rationale:* If during the lease term, the lessee receives ownership of the asset, the leased asset should be reported as an asset on the lessee's books.
2. **The lease contains a bargain purchase option.** *Rationale:* If during the term of the lease, the lessee can purchase the asset at a price substantially below its fair market value, the lessee will obviously exercise this option. Thus, the lease should be reported as a leased asset on the lessee's books.
3. **The lease term is equal to 75% or more of the economic life of the leased property.** *Rationale:* If the lease term is for much of the asset's useful life, the asset should be recorded by the lessee.
4. **The present value of the lease payments equals or exceeds 90% of the fair market value of the leased property.** *Rationale:* If the present value of the lease payments is equal to or almost equal to the fair market value

of the asset, the lessee has essentially purchased the asset. As a result, the leased asset should be recorded on the books of the lessee.

To illustrate, assume the Gonzalez Company decides to lease new equipment. Gonzalez leases the equipment for four years; its economic life is estimated to be five years. The present value of the lease payments is $190,000 which is equal to the fair market value of the equipment. There is no transfer of ownership during the lease term nor is there any bargain purchase option.

In this example, Gonzalez has essentially purchased the equipment. Conditions 3 and 4 have been met: First, the lease term is 75% or more of the economic life of the asset, and second, the present value of cash payments is equal to the equipment's fair market value. The entry to record the transaction is as follows:

Leased Asset—Equipment	190,000	
Lease Liability		190,000
(To record leased asset and lease liability)		

The leased asset is reported on the balance sheet under plant assets. The lease liability is reported as a liability on the balance sheet. **The portion of the lease liability expected to be paid in the next year is reported as a current liability. The remainder is classified as a long-term liability.** For example, in a recent year, Uniroyal, Inc. reported $5.3 million as the current portion of a lease liability and $86.5 million as a long-term liability.

Most lessees do not like to report leases on their balance sheets. The reason is that the lease liability increases the company's total liabilities. This, in turn, may make it more difficult for the company to obtain needed funds from lenders. As a result, companies attempt to keep leased assets and lease liabilities off the balance sheet by not meeting any one of the four conditions mentioned above. This procedure of keeping liabilities off the balance sheet is often referred to as **off-balance sheet financing**.

Study Objective 7

Identify the requirements for the financial statement presentation of long-term liabilities.

Statement Presentation of Long-Term Liabilities

Long-term liabilities are reported in a separate section of the balance sheet immediately following current liabilities, as shown below.

ILLUSTRATION 17-16

Balance sheet presentation of long-term liabilities

Long-term liabilities		
Bonds payable 10% due in 2009	$1,000,000	
Less: Discount on Bonds Payable	80,000	$ 920,000
Mortgage notes payable, 11%, due in 2015		
and secured by plant assets		500,000
Lease liability		540,000
Total long-term liabilities		$1,960,000

Alternatively, summary data may be presented in the balance sheet with detailed data (such as interest rates, maturity dates, conversion privileges and assets pledged as collateral) being shown in a supporting schedule. The current maturities of long-term debt should be reported under current liabilities if they are to be paid from current assets.

Before You Go On . . .

1. Explain the accounting for redemption of bonds before maturity by payment in cash; by conversion into common stock.

2. What is the purpose of the bond sinking fund? Where is a bond sinking fund reported in the financial statements? Explain the accounting for long-term mortgage notes payable.

3. What is the difference in accounting for an operating lease versus a capital lease? Explain the four conditions used to determine whether the lease contract transfers substantially all the benefits and risks of ownership.

Summary of Study Objectives

1. *Explain why bonds are issued and their major characteristics.* Bonds may be sold to many investors, and they offer the following advantages over common stock: (a) stockholder control is not affected, (b) tax savings result, (c) income to common stockholders may increase, (d) earnings per share of common stock may be higher. Corporations issue many different types of bonds generally through an investment company. Bonds trade on national securities markets. The market value of a bond is a function of three factors: the dollar amounts to be received, the length of time until the amounts are received, and the market rate of interest.

2. *Prepare the entries for the issuance of bonds and interest expense.* When bonds are issued, Cash is debited for the cash proceeds and Bonds Payable is credited for the face value of the bonds. In addition, Bond Interest Payable is credited if there is accrued interest, and the accounts Premium on Bonds Payable and Discount on Bonds Payable are used to show the bond premium and bond discount.

3. *Describe the entries when bonds are redeemed or converted prior to maturity.* When bonds are redeemed before maturity, it is necessary to (a) eliminate the carrying value of the bonds at the redemption date, (b) record the cash paid, and (c) recognize the gain or loss on redemption. When bonds are con-

verted to common stock, the book (or carrying) value of the bonds is transferred to appropriate paid-in capital accounts, and no gain or loss is recognized.

4. *Indicate the entries required for a bond sinking fund.* Entries are required for a bond sinking fund to record (a) periodic contributions, (b) annual revenue, and (c) redemption of the bonds.

5. *Describe the accounting for long-term notes payable.* Each payment consists of (1) interest on the unpaid balance of the loan, and (2) a reduction of loan principal. The interest decreases each period, while the portion applied to the loan principal increases each period.

6. *Contrast the accounting for operating and capital leases.* For an operating lease, lease (or rental) payments are recorded as an expense by the lessee (renter). For a capital lease, the lessee records the asset and related obligation at the present value of the future lease payments.

7. *Identify the requirements for the financial statement presentation of long-term liabilities.* The nature and amount of each long-term debt should be reported in the balance sheet or in schedules in the notes accompanying the statements.

APPENDIX H　Effective Interest Amortization

Study Objective

After studying Appendix H, you should be able to:

8. Contrast the effects of the straight-line and effective interest methods of amortizing bond discount and bond premium.

The straight-line method of amortization that you studied in the chapter has a conceptual deficiency. It does not completely satisfy the matching principle. Under this method, interest expense as a percentage of the carrying value of the bonds varies each interest period. This can be seen by using data from the first three interest periods of the bond amortization schedule shown in Illustration 17-10.

ILLUSTRATION H-1

Interest percentage rates under straight-line method

Semiannual Interest Period	Interest Expense to Be Recorded (A)	Bond Carrying Value (B)	Interest Expense as a Percentage of Carrying Value (A) ÷ (B)
1	$67,000	$980,000	6.84%
2	67,000	982,000	6.82%
3	67,000	984,000	6.81%

Note that interest expense as a percentage of carrying value is declining in each interest period. However, to completely comply with the matching principle, interest expense as a percentage of carrying value should not change over the life of the bonds. This percentage, referred to as the effective rate of interest, is established when the bonds are issued and remains constant in each interest period. The effective interest method of amortization accomplishes this result.

Under the effective interest method, the amortization of bond discount or bond premium results in periodic interest expense equal to a constant percentage of the carrying value of the bonds. The effective interest method results in varying amounts of amortization and interest expense per period but a constant percentage rate; the straight-line method results in constant amounts of amortization and interest expense per period but a varying percentage rate. The following steps are required under the effective interest method:

1. Bond interest expense is computed first by multiplying the carrying value of the bonds at the beginning of the interest period by the effective interest rate.
2. The credit to cash (or bond interest payable) is computed by multiplying the face value of the bonds by the contractual rate of interest.
3. The bond discount or bond premium amortization is then determined by the difference between the amounts computed in steps (1) and (2).

These steps are graphically depicted in Illustration H-2.

ILLUSTRATION H-2

Computation of amortization—effective interest method

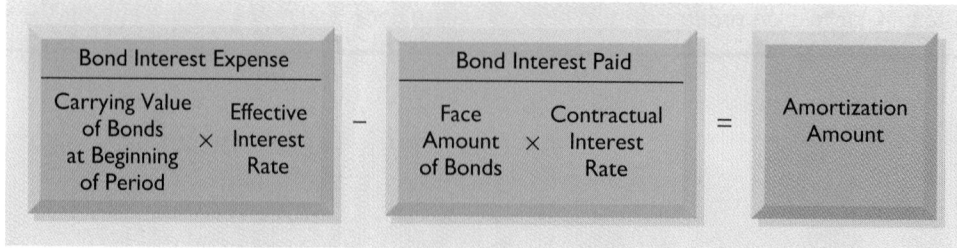

Both the straight-line and effective interest methods of amortization result in the same total amount of interest expense over the term of the bonds. Furthermore, interest expense each interest period is generally comparable in amount. However, **when the amounts are materially different, the effective interest method is required under generally accepted accounting principles (GAAP).**

Bonds Issued at a Discount

To illustrate the effective interest method of bond discount amortization, assume that Wrightway Corporation issues $100,000 of 10%, 5-year bonds on January 1, 1993, with interest payable each July 1 and January 1. The bonds sell for $92,639 (92.639% of par), which results in bond discount of $7,361 ($100,000 − $92,639) and an effective interest rate of 12%. (Note that the $92,639 can be proven as shown in Appendix N). Preparing a bond discount amortization schedule in Illustration H-3 facilitates the recording of interest expense and the discount amortization.

ILLUSTRATION H-3

Bond discount amortization schedule

WRIGHTWAY CORPORATION
Bond Discount Amortization
Effective Interest Method—Semiannual Interest Payments
10% Bonds Issued at 12%

Semiannual Interest Periods	(A) Interest to be Paid (5% × $100,000)	(B) Interest Expense to be Recorded (6% × Preceding Bond Carrying Value)	(C) Discount Amortization (B) − (A)	(D) Unamortized Discount (D) − (C)	(E) Bond Carrying Value ($100,000 − D)
Issue date				$7,361	$ 92,639
1	$ 5,000	$ 5,558 (6% × $92,639)	$ 558	6,803	93,197
2	5,000	5,592 (6% × $93,197)	592	6,211	93,789
3	5,000	5,627 (6% × $93,789)	627	5,584	94,416
4	5,000	5,665 (6% × $94,416)	665	4,919	95,081
5	5,000	5,705 (6% × $95,081)	705	4,214	95,786
6	5,000	5,747 (6% × $95,786)	747	3,467	96,533
7	5,000	5,792 (6% × $96,533)	792	2,675	97,325
8	5,000	5,840 (6% × $97,325)	840	1,835	98,165
9	5,000	5,890 (6% × $98,165)	890	945	99,055
10	5,000	5,945* (6% × $99,055)	945	–0–	100,000
	$50,000	$57,361	$7,361		

Column (A) remains constant because the face value of the bonds ($100,000) is multiplied by the semiannual contractual interest rate (5%) each period.

Column (B) is computed as the preceding bond carrying value times the semiannual effective interest rate (6%).

Column (C) indicates the discount amortization each period.

Column (D) decreases each period until it reaches zero at maturity.

Column (E) increases each period until it equals face value at maturity.

*$2 difference due to rounding.

Note that interest expense as a percentage of carrying value remains constant at 6%.

For the first interest period, the computations of bond interest expense and the bond discount amortization are as follows:

Bond interest expense ($92,639 × 6%)	$5,558
Contractual interest ($100,000 × 5%)	5,000
Bond discount amortization	$ 558

ILLUSTRATION H-4

Computation of bond discount amortization

As a result, the entry to record the payment of interest and amortization of bond discount by Wrightway Corporation on July 1, 1993 is:

July 1	Bond Interest Expense	5,558	
	Discount on Bonds Payable		558
	Cash		5,000
	(To record payment of bond interest and amortization of bond discount)		

For the second interest period, bond interest expense will be $5,592 ($93,197 × 6%), and the discount amortization will be $592. At December 31, the following adjusting entry is made:

Dec. 31	Bond Interest Expense	5,592	
	Discount on Bonds Payable		592
	Bond Interest Payable		5,000
	(To record accrued interest and amortization of bond discount)		

Total bond interest expense for 1993 is $11,150 ($5,558 + $5,592). On January 1, payment of the interest is recorded by a debit to Bond Interest Payable and a credit to Cash.

Technology in Action

The amortization schedule is an excellent example of an accounting computation efficiently and effectively performed by an electronic spreadsheet. Once the selling price, face amount, contractual rate of interest, effective rate of interest, and number of interest periods are determined and entered into the spreadsheet, all of the computations until maturity can be performed by the computer. Note that the amortization and adjusting entries can be taken directly from the amortization schedule.

Bonds Issued at a Premium

The amortization of bond premium by the effective interest method is similar to the procedures described for bond discount. As an example, assume that Wrightway Corporation issues its $100,000, 10%, 5-year bonds on January 1, 1993, with interest payable on July 1 and January 1. The bonds sell for $108,111, which results in bond premium of $8,111 and an effective interest rate of 8%. (Note that $108,111 can be proven as shown in Appendix N). The bond premium amortization schedule is shown in Illustration H-5.

		(B)			
		Interest Expense	**(C)**	**(D)**	**(E)**
		to be Recorded	**Premium**	**Unamortized**	**Bond**
Semiannual	**(A)**	**(4% × Preceding Bond**	**Amortization**	**Premium**	**Carrying Value**
Interest	**Interest to be Paid**	**Carry Value)**	**(A) − (B)**	**(D) − (C)**	**($100,000 + D)**
Periods	**(5% × $100,000)**				
Issue date				$8,111	$108,111
1	$ 5,000	$ 4,324 (4% × $108,111)	$ 676	7,435	107,435
2	5,000	4,297 (4% × $107,435)	703	6,732	106,732
3	5,000	4,269 (4% × $106,732)	731	6,001	106,001
4	5,000	4,240 (4% × $106,001)	760	5,241	105,241
5	5,000	4,210 (4% × $105,241)	790	4,451	104,451
6	5,000	4,178 (4% × $104,451)	822	3,629	103,629
7	5,000	4,145 (4% × $103,629)	855	2,774	102,774
8	5,000	4,111 (4% × $102,774)	889	1,885	101,885
9	5,000	4,075 (4% × $101,885)	925	960	100,960
10	5,000	4,040* (4% × $100,960)	960	–0–	100,000
	$50,000	$41,889	$8,111		

WRIGHTWAY CORPORATION
Bond Premium Amortization
Effective Interest Method—Semiannual Interest Payments
10% Bonds Issued at 8%

Column (A) remains constant because the face value of the bonds ($100,000) is multiplied by the semiannual contractual interest rate (5%) each period.

Column (B) is computed as the carrying value of the bonds times the semiannual effective interest rate (4%).

Column (C) indicates the premium amortization each period.

Column (D) decreases each period until it reaches zero at maturity.

Column (E) decreases each period until it equals face value at maturity.

*$2 difference due to rounding.

For the first interest period, the computations of bond interest expense and the bond premium amortization are:

Bond interest expense ($108,111 × 4%)	$4,324
Contractual interest ($100,000 × 5%)	5,000
Bond premium amortization	$ 676

The entry on the first interest date is:

July 1	Bond Interest Expense	4,324	
	Premium on Bonds Payable	676	
	Cash		5,000
	(To record payment of bond interest and amortization of bond premium)		

For the second interest period, interest expense will be $4,297, and the premium amortization will be $703. Total bond interest expense for 1993 is $8,621 ($4,324 + $4,297).

Summary of Study Objectives for Appendix H

8. Contrast the effects of the straight-line and effective interest methods of amortizing bond discount and bond premium. The straight-line method of amortization results in a constant amount of amortization and interest expense per period but a varying percentage rate. In contrast, the effective interest method results in varying amounts of amortization and interest expense per period but a constant percentage rate of interest. The effective interest method generally results in a better matching of expenses with revenues. When the difference between the straight-line and effective interest method is material, the use of the effective interest method is required under GAAP.

GLOSSARY

Bearer (coupon) bonds · Bonds issued to bearer that are unregistered and holders must send in coupons to receive interest payments. (p. 669).

Bond indenture · A legal document that sets forth the terms of the bond issue. (p. 669).

Bonds · A form of interest bearing notes payable used by corporations. (p. 667).

Callable bonds · Bonds that are subject to call and retirement at a stated dollar amount prior to maturity at the option of the issuer. (p. 669).

Capital lease · A contractual arrangement that transfers substantially all the benefits and risks of ownership to the lessee so that the lease is in effect a purchase of the property. (p. 683).

Convertible bonds · Bonds that permit bondholders to convert them into common stock at their option. (p. 669).

Contractual (stated) interest rate · Rate used to determine the amount of cash interest the borrower pays—and the investor receives. (p. 669).

Debenture bonds · Unsecured bonds issued against the credit of the borrower. (p. 668).

Effective interest method of amortization · A method of writing off bond discount or bond premium that results in a periodic interest expense equal to a constant percentage of the carrying value of the bonds. (p. 686).

Effective rate of interest · Rate established when the bonds are issued and remains constant in each interest period. (p. 686).

Face (or par) value · Amount due at the maturity date of the bond. (p. 669).

Long-term liabilities · Obligations expected to be paid after one year. (p. 667).

Market interest rate · The rate investors demand for loaning funds to the corporation. (p. 671).

Mortgage bond · A bond secured by real estate. (p. 668).

Operating lease · A contractual arrangement giving the lessee temporary use of the property with continued ownership of the property by the lessor. (p. 683).

Registered bonds · Bonds issued in the name of the owner. (p. 669).

Secured bonds · Bonds that have specific assets of the issuer pledged as collateral. (p. 668).

Serial bonds · Bonds that mature in installments. (p. 668).

Sinking fund · Cash or other assets segregated to retire debt. (p. 680).

Straight-line method of amortization · A method of writing off bond discount or bond premium that results in a periodic interest expense that is the same amount each interest period. (p. 675).

Term bonds · Bonds that mature at a single specified future date. (p. 668).

Unsecured bonds · Bonds issued against the general credit of the borrower. Also called debenture bonds. (p. 668).

DEMONSTRATION PROBLEM 1

Snyder Software Inc. has successfully developed a new spreadsheet program. However, to produce and market the program, the company needed $2.0 million of additional financing. On December 31, 1993, Snyder borrowed money as follows:

1. Snyder issued $500,000, 11%, 10-year convertible bonds. The bonds sold at face value and pay semiannual interest on January 1 and July 1. Each $1,000 bond is convertible into 30 shares of Snyder's $20 par value common stock.

2. Snyder issued $1.0 million, 10%, 10-year bonds for $885,301. Interest is payable semiannually on January 1 and July 1. Snyder uses the straight-line method of amortization.

3. Snyder also issued a $500,000, 12%, 15-year mortgage note payable. The terms provide for semiannual installment payments of $36,324 on June 30 and December 31.

Instructions

1. For the convertible bonds, prepare journal entries for:
   (a) the issuance of the bonds on January 1, 1994.
   (b) interest expense on July 1 and December 31, 1994.
   (c) the payment of interest on January 1, 1995.
   (d) the conversion of all bonds into common stock on January 1, 1995 when the market value of the common stock was $67 per share.

2. For the 10 year, 10% bonds:
   (a) journalize the issuance of the bonds on January 1, 1994.
   (b) prepare a bond discount amortization schedule for the first six interest periods.
   (c) prepare the journal entries for interest expense and amortization of bond discount in 1994.
   (d) prepare the entry for the redemption of the bonds at 101 on January 1, 1997 after paying the interest due on this date.

3. For the mortgage note payable, prepare
   (a) The entry for the issuance of the note on December 31, 1993.
   (b) A payment schedule for the first four installment payments.
   (c) Indicate the current and noncurrent amounts for the mortgage note payable at December 31, 1994.

Solution to Demonstration Problem 1

1. (a) 1994

Jan. 1	Cash	500,000	
	Bonds Payable		500,000
	(To record issue of 11%, 10-year		
	convertible bonds at face value)		

(b) 1994

July 1	Bond Interest Expense	27,500	
	Cash ($500,000 × .055)		27,500
	(To record payment of semiannual		
	interest)		
Dec. 31	Bond Interest Expense	27,500	
	Bond Interest Payable		27,500
	(To record accrual of semiannual		
	bond interest)		

(c) 1995

Jan. 1	Bond Interest Payable	27,500	
	Cash		27,500
	(To record payment of accrued interest)		

Helpful hints

1. Interest is usually paid semi-annually. Be careful to use only six months' interest in your computations.
2. Upon conversion, the book value of the bonds is removed from the liability accounts and recorded as common stock and related paid-in capital.

(d)

Jan. 1	Bonds Payable	500,000	
	Common Stock		300,000*
	Paid-in Capital in Excess of Par Value		
	(To record conversion of bonds into common stock)		200,000
	*($500,000 ÷ $1,000 = 500 bonds; 500 × 30 = 15,000 shares; 15,000 × $20 = $300,000		

2. (a) 1994

Jan. 1	Cash	885,301	
	Discount on Bonds Payable	114,699	
	Bonds Payable		1,000,000
	(To record issuance of bonds at a discount)		

(b)

Semiannual Interest Period	Interest to Be Paid	Interest Expense to Be Recorded	Discount Amortization	Unamortized Discount	Bond Carrying Value
Issue date				$114,699	$885,301
1	$50,000	$55,735	$5,735	108,964	891,036
2	50,000	55,735	5,735	103,229	896,771
3	50,000	55,735	5,735	97,494	902,506
4	50,000	55,735	5,735	91,759	908,241
5	50,000	55,735	5,735	86,024	913,976
6	50,000	55,735	5,735	80,289	919,711

(c) 1994

July 1	Bond Interest Expense	55,735	
	Discount on Bonds Payable		5,735
	Cash		50,000
	(To record payment of semiannual interest and amortization of bond discount)		
Dec. 31	Bond Interest Expense	55,735	
	Discount on Bonds Payable		5,735
	Bond Interest Payable		50,000
	(To record accrual of semiannual interest and amortization of bond discount)		

Helpful hints

1. Discount on bonds payable is a contra liability account.
2. Amortization of bond discount increases bond interest expense.
3. Bond interest expense is the same each period when the straight-line method is used.
4. Loss on bond redemption occurs when the cash paid is greater than the bond carrying value.

(d) 1997

Jan. 1	Bonds Payable	1,000,000	
	Loss on Bond Redemption	90,289*	
	Discount on Bonds Payable		80,289
	Cash		1,010,000
	(To record redemption of bonds at 101)		
	*($1,010,000 − $919,711)		

3. (a) 1993

Dec. 31	Cash	500,000	
	Mortgage Notes Payable		500,000
	(To record issuance of mortgage note payable)		

Helpful hints
1. Interest expense decreases each period because the principal is decreasing each period.
2. Each payment consists of (1) interest on the unpaid loan balance and (2) a reduction of the loan principal.

(b)

Semiannual Interest Period	Cash Payment	Interest Expense	Reduction of Principal	Principal Balance
Issue date				$500,000
1	$36,324	$30,000	$6,324	493,676
2	36,324	29,621	6,703	486,973
3	36,324	29,218	7,106	479,867
4	36,324	28,792	7,532	472,335

(c) Current liability $14,638 ($7,106 + $7,532)
    Long-term liability $472,335.

DEMONSTRATION PROBLEM 2 (Appendix Problem)

Gardner Corporation issues $1,750,000, 10-year, 12% bonds on December 31, 1993 at $1,820,000 to yield 10%. The bonds pay semiannual interest June 30 and December 31. Gardner uses the effective interest method of amortization.

Instructions
(a) Prepare the journal entry to record the issuance of the bonds.
(b) Prepare the journal entry to record the payment of interest on June 30, 1994.

Solution to Demonstration Problem 2

(a) 1993

Dec. 31	Cash	1,820,000	
	Premium on Bonds Payable		70,000
	Bonds Payable		1,750,000
	(To record issuance of bonds at a premium)		

1994			
June 30	Bond Interest Expense	91,000*	
	Premium on Bonds Payable	14,000**	
	Cash		105,000
	(To record payment of semiannual interest and amortization of bond premium)		
	*($1,820,000 × 5%)		
	**($105,000 − $91,000)		

Helpful hints
1. Bond carrying value at beginning of period times effective interest rate equals interest expense.
2. Credit to cash (or bond interest payable) is computed by multiplying the face value of the bonds by the contractual interest rate.
3. Bond premium or discount amortization is the difference between (1) and (2).
4. Interest expense increases when the effective interest method is used for bonds issued at a discount. The reason is that a constant percentage is applied to an increasing book value to compute interest expense.

***Note:** All **asterisked** Questions, Exercises, and Problems relate to material contained in the Appendix to each chapter.

SELF-STUDY QUESTIONS

Answers are at the end of the chapter.

(S.O. 1)
1. The term used for bonds that are unsecured is:
  a. callable bonds.
  b. debenture bonds.
  c. indenture bonds.
  d. bearer bonds.

2. Carson Inc. issues 10-year bonds with a maturity value of $200,000. If the bonds are issued at a premium, this indicates that:
  a. the market interest rate exceeds the contractual interest rate.

(S.O. 2)

b. the contractual interest rate exceeds the market interest rate.

c. the contractual interest rate and the market interest rate are the same.

d. no relationship exists between the two rates.

(S.O. 2) 3. On January 1, the Shirley Corporation issues $500,000, 5-year, 12% bonds at 96 with interest payable on July 1 and January 1. The entry on July 1 to record payment of bond interest and the amortization of bond discount using the straight-line method will include a:

a. debit to Interest Expense, $30,000.

b. debit to Interest Expense, $60,000.

c. credit to Discount on Bonds Payable, $2,000.

d. credit to Discount on Bonds Payable, $4,000.

(S.O. 2) 4. For the bonds issued in question 3, above, what is the carrying value of the bonds at the end of the fourth interest period?

a. $496,000.

b. $488,000.

c. $472,000.

d. $464,000.

(S.O. 2) 5. When the interest payment dates of a bond are May 1 and November 1, and a bond issue is sold on June 1, the amount of cash received by the issuer will be:

a. decreased by accrued interest from June 1 to November 1

b. decreased by accrued interest from May 1 to June 1

c. increased by accrued interest from June 1 to November 1

d. increased by accrued interest from May 1 to June 1

(S.O. 3) 6. Gesner Corporation retires its $100,000 face value bonds at 105 on January 1, following the payment of semiannual interest. The carrying value of the bonds at the redemption date is $103,745. The entry to record the redemption will include a:

a. credit of $3,745 to Loss on Bond Redemption.

b. debit of $5,000 to Premium on Bonds Payable.

c. credit of $1,255 to Gain on Bond Redemption.

d. debit of $3,745 to Premium on Bonds Payable.

(S.O. 3) 7. Carlson Inc. converts $600,000 of bonds sold at face value into 10,000 shares of common stock, par value $1. Both the bonds and the stock have a market value of $760,000. What amount should be credited to Paid-in Capital in Excess of Par as a result of the conversion?

a. $10,000

b. $160,000

c. $590,000

d. $600,000

8. Sauger Company has a bond sinking (S.O. 4) fund in the amount of $400,000. Where should this amount be reported on the balance sheet?

a. current asset section

b. investments section

c. current liability section

d. long-term liability section

9. Anderson Inc. issues a $497,000, 10% (S.O. 5) 3-year mortgage note on January 1, 1993. The note will be paid in three annual installments of $200,000, each payable at the end of the year. What is the amount of interest expense that should be recognized by Anderson Inc. in the second year?

a. $16,567

b. $34,670

c. $49,740

d. $347,600

10. Lease A does not contain a bargain pur- (S.O. 6) chase option, but the lease term is equal to 90 percent of the estimated economic life of the leased property. Lease B does not transfer ownership of the property to the lessee by the end of the lease term, but the lease term is equal to 75 percent of the estimated economic life of the leased property. How should the lessee classify these leases?

	Lease A	Lease B
a.	Operating lease	Capital lease
b.	Operating lease	Operating lease
c.	Capital lease	Capital lease
d.	Capital lease	Operating lease

*11. On January 1, Vesalius, Inc. issued (S.O. 8) $1,000,000, 9% bonds for $939,000. The market rate of interest for these bonds is 10%. Interest is payable annually on December 31. Vesalius uses the effective interest method of amortizing bond discount. At the end of the first year, Vesalius should report unamortized bond discount of:

a. $57,100.

b. $54,900.

c. $51,610.

d. $51,000.

*12. On January 1, Dios Corporation issued (S.O. 8) $1,000,000, 14%, 5-year bonds with interest payable on July 1 and January 1. The bonds sold for $1,098,540. The market rate of interest for these bonds was 12%. On the first interest date, using the effec-

tive interest method, the debit entry to
Bond Interest Expense is for:
a. $60,000.

b. $65,912.
c. $76,898.
d. $131,825.

QUESTIONS

1. Reno Company is considering financing the purchase of a new office building through bond financing. What are the possible advantages of bond financing over common stock financing? Explain.

2. What is a long-term liability? Give some examples.

3. Explain each of the following terms as they relate to a bond issue: (a) debenture; (b) secured; (c) serial; (d) registered; and (e) callable.

4. Describe the two major obligations incurred by a company when bonds are issued.

5. Assume that Stone Inc. sold bonds with a par value of $100,000 for $104,000. Was the market rate of interest equal to, less than, or greater than the bonds' contractual rate of interest? Explain.

6. Barbara Secord and Jack Chopin are discussing how the market price of a bond is determined. Barbara believes that the market price of a bond is solely a function of the amount of the principal payment at the end of the term of a bond. Is she right? Discuss.

7. If a 10%, 10-year, $500,000 bond is issued at par and interest is paid semiannually, what is the amount of the interest payment at the end of the first semiannual period?

8. If the Bonds Payable account has a balance of $900,000 and the Discount on Bonds Payable account has a balance of $30,000, what is the carrying value of the bonds?

9. Explain the straight-line method of amortizing discount and premium on bonds payable.

10. Mohs Corporation issues $200,000 of 8%, 5-year bonds on January 1, 1993, at 104. Assuming that the straight-line method is used to amortize the premium, what is the total amount of interest expense for 1993?

11. Which accounts are debited and which are credited if a bond issue originally sold at a premium is redeemed at 97 immediately following the payment of interest?

12. Dryden Corporation is considering issuing a convertible bond. What is a convertible bond? Discuss the advantages of a convertible bond from the standpoint of (a) the bondholders and (b) the issuing corporation.

13. The financial statements of Kenora Inc. disclose that it has a bond sinking fund. What is a bond sinking fund? What is its purpose?

14. Doug Barwick, a friend of yours, has recently purchased a home for $125,000, paying $25,000 down and the remainder financed by a 10½% mortgage, payable at $483.18 per month. At the end of the first year, Doug receives a statement from the bank indicating that only $350 of principal was paid during the year. At this rate, he calculates that it will take over 285 years to pay off the mortgage. Is he right? Discuss.

15. (a) What is a lease agreement? (b) What are the two most common types of leases? (c) Distinguish between the two types of leases.

16. Mitchell Company rents a warehouse on a month-to-month basis for the storage of its excess inventory. The company periodically must rent space when its production greatly exceeds actual sales. What is the nature of this type of lease agreement, and what accounting treatment should be accorded it?

17. Rodriguez Company entered into an agreement to lease 12 computers from Rochester Electronics Inc. The present value of the lease payments is $186,300. Assuming that this is a capital lease, what entry would Rodriguez Company make on the date of the lease agreement?

18. In general, what are the requirements for the financial statement presentation of long-term liabilities?

*19. Terry Ament is discussing the advantages of the effective interest method of bond amortization with his accounting staff. What do you think Terry is saying?

*20. Sunset Corporation issues $400,000 of 9% 5-year bonds on January 1, 1993 at 104. If Sunset uses the effective interest method in amortizing the premium, will the annual interest expense increase or decrease over the life of the bonds? Explain.

BRIEF EXERCISES

Comparison of bond versus stock financing.
(S.O. 1)

BE17–1 Ogden Company is considering two alternatives to finance its construction of a new $2 million plant:

(a) Issuance of 200,000 shares of common stock at the market price of $10 per share.

(b) Issuance of $2 million, 10% bonds at par.

Complete the following table.

	Issue Stock	Issue Bond
Income before interest and taxes	$1,000,000	$1,000,000
Interest expense from bonds		
Income before income taxes	$	$
Income tax expense (30%)		
Net income	$	$
Outstanding shares		700,000
Earnings per share		

Journal entries for bonds issued at face value.
(S.O. 2)

BE17–2 Sharp Corporation issued 1,000, 10%, 5-year, $1,000 bonds dated January 1, 1993 at 100. (a) Prepare the journal entry to record the sale of these bonds on January 1, 1993. (b) Prepare the journal entry to record the first interest payment on July 1, 1993 (interest payable semiannually), assuming no previous accrual of interest. (c) Prepare the adjusting journal entry on December 31, 1993 to record interest expense.

Journal entries for bonds issued at a discount.
(S.O. 2)

BE17–3 Simpson Company issues $2 million, 10 year, 8% bonds with interest payable on July 1 and January 1 at 98. The straight-line method is used to amortize bond discount. (a) Prepare the journal entry to record the sale of these bonds on January 1, 1993. (b) Prepare the journal entry to record interest expense and bond discount amortization on July 1, 1993, assuming no previous accrual of interest.

Journal entries for bonds issued at a premium.
(S.O. 2)

BE17–4 Hercules Inc. issues $5 million, 5-year, 10% bonds with interest payable on July 1 and January 1 at 104. The straight-line method is used to amortize bond premium. (a) Prepare the journal entry to record the sale of these bonds on January 1, 1993. (b) Prepare the journal entry to record interest expense and bond premium amortization on July 1, 1993, assuming no previous accrual of interest.

Journal entries for bonds issued between interest dates.
(S.O. 2)

BE17–5 Gooding Inc. has outstanding $1 million, 10-year, 9% bonds with interest payable on July 1 and January 1. The bonds were dated January 1, 1993, but were issued on May 1, 1993 at face value plus accrued interest. (a) Prepare the journal entry to record the sale of the bonds on May 1, 1993. (b) Prepare the journal entry to record the interest payment on July 1, 1993.

Redemption of bonds.
(S.O. 3)

BE17–6 The balance sheet for Hathaway Company reports the following information on July 1, 1993:

Long-term liabilities		
Bonds payable	$1,000,000	
Less: Discount on bonds payable	60,000	$940,000

Hathaway decides to redeem these bonds at 101 after paying semiannual interest. Prepare the journal entry to record the redemption on July 1, 1993.

Accounting for bond sinking fund.
(S.O. 4)

BE17–7 Findorf Company establishes a sinking fund for its $1 million, 5-year bonds. On January 1, 1993 it makes a contribution of $160,000. At the end of 1993, the sinking fund had earned $12,000. (a) Prepare the journal entry to record the contribution made into the sinking fund on January 1, 1993. (b) Prepare the journal entry to record the revenue earned in the sinking fund in 1993. (c) Assume that on January 1, 1998, the sinking fund assets were used to redeem the bonds. Prepare the journal entry to record this redemption, assuming that the sinking fund had a cash balance of $1 million.

BE17–8 Edmonds Inc. issues a $300,000, 10% 10-year mortgage note on December 31, 1993 to obtain financing for a new building. The terms provide for semiannual installment payments of $24,073. Prepare the entry to record the mortgage loan on December 31, 1993 and the first installment payment.

Accounting for long-term notes payable.
(S.O. 5)

BE17–9 Prepare the journal entries that the lessee should make to record the following transactions:

1. The lessee makes a lease payment of $100,000 to the lessor in an operating lease transaction.
2. Goldberg Company leases a new building from Brace Construction, Inc. The present value of the lease payments is $600,000. The lease qualifies as a capital lease.

Contrast accounting for operating and capital lease.
(S.O. 6)

BE17–10 Presented below are long-term liability items for Warren Company at December 31, 1993. Prepare the long-term liabilities section of the balance sheet for Warren Company.

Bonds payable, due 1998	$900,000
Lease liability	50,000
Notes payable, due 2000	80,000
Discount on bonds payable	35,000

Financial statement presentation of long-term liabilities.
(S.O. 7)

*BE17–11 Presented below is the partial bond discount amortization schedule for Morales Corp. Morales uses the effective interest method of amortization.

Effective interest method of bond amortization.
(S.O. 8)

Semiannual Interest Periods	Interest to be Paid	Interest Expense to be Recorded	Discount Amortization	Unamortized Discount	Bond Carrying Value
Issue date				$62,311	$937,689
1	$45,000	$46,884	$1,884	60,427	939,573
2	45,000	46,979	1,979	58,448	941,552

Instructions

(a) Prepare the journal entry to record the payment of interest and the discount amortization at the end of period 1.

(b) Explain why interest expense is greater than interest paid.

(c) Explain why interest expense will increase each period.

EXERCISES

E17–1 Sundown Airlines is considering two alternatives for the financing of a purchase of a fleet of airplanes. These two alternatives are:

Compare two alternatives of financing—issuance of common stock vs. issuance of bonds.
(S.O. 1)

1. Issue 60,000 shares of common stock at $45 per share. (Cash dividends have not been paid nor is the payment of any contemplated.)
2. Issue 13%, 10-year bonds at par for $2,700,000.

It is estimated that the company will earn $900,000 before interest and taxes as a result of this purchase. The company has an estimated tax rate of 30% and has 90,000 shares of common stock outstanding prior to the new financing.

Instructions

Determine the effect on net income and earnings per share for these two methods of financing.

E17–2 On January 1, the Founder Company issued $90,000 of 12%, 10-year bonds at par. Interest is payable semiannually on July 1 and January 1. Interest is not accrued on June 30.

Journal entries for issuance of bonds and payment and accrual of bond interest.
(S.O. 2)

Instructions

Present journal entries to record:

(a) The issuance of the bonds.

(b) The payment of interest on July 1.

(c) The accrual of interest on December 31.

Journal entries to record issuance of bonds, payment of interest, and amortization of premium. (S.O. 2)

E17–3 Provo Company issued $240,000 of 9%, 20-year bonds on January 1, 1993, at 102. Interest is payable semiannually on July 1 and January 1. Provo uses straight-line amortization for bond premium or discount. Interest is not accrued on June 30.

Instructions

Prepare the journal entries to record:

(a) The issuance of the bonds.

(b) The payment of interest and the premium amortization on July 1, 1993.

(c) The accrual of interest and the premium amortization on December 31, 1993.

Journal entries to record issuance of bonds, payment of interest, and amortization of discount. (S.O. 2)

E17–4 Colter Company issued $180,000 of 11%, 10-year bonds on December 31, 1992 for $170,000. Interest is payable semiannually on June 30 and December 31. Colter uses the straight-line method to amortize bond premium or discount.

Instructions

Prepare the journal entries to record:

(a) The issuance of the bonds.

(b) The payment of interest and the discount amortization on June 30, 1993.

(c) The payment of interest and the discount amortization on December 31, 1993.

Journal entries to record issuance of bonds between interest dates, and payment and accrual of interest. (S.O. 2)

E17–5 On March 1, the Stettler Company issued $72,000 of 10%, 10-year bonds dated January 1 at par plus accrued interest. Interest is payable semiannually on July 1 and January 1.

Instructions

Present journal entries to record:

(a) The issuance of the bonds.

(b) The payment of interest on July 1. Interest is not accrued on June 30.

(c) The accrual of interest on December 31.

Journal entries for redemption of bonds and conversion of bonds into common stock. (S.O. 3)

E17–6 Presented below are three independent situations:

(a) Price Corporation retired $120,000 par value of 12% bonds on June 30, 1993, at 103. The carrying value of the bonds at the redemption date was $107,500. The bonds pay semiannual interest and the interest payment due on June 30, 1993, has been made and recorded.

(b) Young, Inc. retired $150,000 par value of 12.5% bonds on June 30, 1993, at 98. The carrying value of the bonds at the redemption date was $151,000. The bonds pay semiannual interest and the interest payment due on June 30, 1993, has been made and recorded.

(c) Waterhouse Company has $80,000 of 8%, 12-year convertible bonds outstanding. These bonds were sold at par and pay semiannual interest on June 30 and December 31 of each year. The bonds are convertible into 30 shares of Jefferson $2 par common stock for each $1,000 worth of bonds. On December 31, 1993, after the bond interest has been paid, $20,000 par value of bonds was converted. The market value of Jefferson common stock was $44 per share on December 31, 1993.

Instructions

For each independent situation above, prepare the appropriate journal entry for the redemption or conversion of the bonds.

Journal entries to record sinking fund deposit, revenue earned on fund assets, and redemption of bonds. (S.O. 4)

E17–7 Chung Co. decides to establish a sinking fund for its $6,000,000, 20-year bonds that are outstanding. The trustee indicates that an annual contribution of $163,000 should be made at the end of each year. The sinking fund earned $9,900 in the second year. At the maturity date, the sinking fund had a balance of $5,960,000.

Instructions

Prepare the journal entries to record:

(a) The first contribution by Chung Co.

(b) The actual earnings in the second year.

(c) The redemption of the bonds at maturity.

E17–8 The Peron Co. receives $110,000 when it issues a $110,000, 10%, mortgage note payable to finance the construction of a building at December 31, 1993. The terms provide for semiannual installment payments of $7,000 on June 30 and December 31.

Journal entries to record mortgage note and installment payments.
(S.O. 5)

Instructions

Prepare the journal entries to record the mortgage loan and the first two installment payments.

E17–9 Presented below are two independent situations.

1. Plante Car Rental leased a car to Rockefeller Company for one year. Terms of the operating lease agreement call for monthly payments of $600.
2. On January 1, 1993, Wizard Inc. entered into an agreement to lease 20 computers from Kilgust Electronics. The terms of the lease agreement require three annual rental payments of $120,000 (including 10% interest) beginning December 31, 1993. The present value of the three rental payments is $298,422. Wizard considers this a capital lease.

Journal entries for operating lease and capital lease.
(S.O. 6)

Instructions

(a) Prepare the appropriate journal entry to be made by Rockefeller Company for the first lease payment.

(b) Prepare the journal entry to record the lease agreement on the books of Wizard Inc. on January 1, 1993.

E17–10 The adjusted trial balance for Viola Corporation at the end of the current year contained the following accounts:

Statement presentation of long-term liabilities.
(S.O. 7)

Bond interest payable	$ 9,000
Lease liability	59,500
Bonds payable, due 1997	120,000
Premium on bonds payable	42,000
Bond sinking fund	241,600

Instructions

(a) Prepare the long-term liabilities section of the balance sheet.

(b) Indicate the proper balance sheet classification for the account(s) listed above that do not belong in the long-term liabilities section.

*E17–11 Paris Corporation issued $260,000 of 9%, 10-year bonds on January 1, 1993, for $243,799. This price resulted in an effective interest rate of 10% on the bonds. Interest is payable semiannually on July 1 and January 1. Paris uses the effective interest method to amortize bond premium or discount. Interest is not accrued on June 30.

Journal entries for issuance of bonds payment of interest, and amortization of discount using effective interest method.
(S.O. 8)

Instructions

Prepare the journal entries to record (round to the nearest dollar):

(a) The issuance of the bonds.

(b) The payment of interest and the discount amortization on July 1, 1993.

(c) The accrual of interest and the discount amortization on December 31, 1993.

*E17–12 Colter Company issued $180,000 of 11%, 10-year bonds on January 1, 1993 for $191,216. This price resulted in an effective interest rate of 10% on the bonds. Interest is payable semiannually on July 1 and January 1. Colter uses the effective interest method to amortize bond premium or discount. Interest is not accrued on June 30.

Journal entries for issuance of bonds, payment of interest, and amortization of premium using effective interest method.
(S.O. 8)

Instructions

Prepare the journal entries to record (round to the nearest dollar):

(a) The issuance of the bonds.

(b) The payment of interest and the discount amortization on July 1, 1993.

(c) The accrual of interest and the premium amortization on December 31, 1993.

PROBLEMS

Prepare journal entries to record issuance of bonds, interest accrual, and amortization for two years.
(S.O. 2, 7)

P17–1   McDuff Company sold $4,000,000 of 9%, 20-year bonds on January 1, 1993. The bonds were dated January 1, 1993, and pay interest on January 1 and July 1. McDuff Company uses the straight-line method to amortize bond premium or discount. The bonds were sold at 94. Assume no interest is accrued on June 30.

Instructions

(a) Prepare the journal entry to record the issuance of the bonds on January 1, 1993.

(b) Prepare a bond discount amortization schedule for the first four interest periods.

(c) Prepare the journal entries for interest and the amortization of the discount in 1993 and 1994.

(d) Show the balance sheet presentation of the bond liability at December 31, 1994.

Prepare journal entries to record issuance of bonds, interest, and amortization of bond premium and discount.
(S.O. 2, 7)

P17–2   Bush Corporation sold $1,500,000 of 8%, 10-year bonds on January 1, 1993. The bonds were dated January 1, 1993 and pay interest on July 1 and January 1. Bush Corporation uses the straight-line method to amortize bond premium or discount. Assume no interest is accrued on June 30.

Instructions

(a) Prepare all the necessary journal entries to record the issuance of the bonds and bond interest expense for 1993, assuming that the bonds sold at 104.

(b) Prepare journal entries as in part (a) assuming that the bonds sold at 97.

(c) Show balance sheet presentation for each bond issue at December 31, 1993.

Prepare journal entries to record interest payments, discount amortization, and redemption of bonds.
(S.O. 2, 3)

P17–3   The following is taken from the Birk Corp. balance sheet at December 31, 1993:

Current liabilities		
Bond interest payable (for six months		
from July 1 to December 31)		$132,000
Long-term liabilities		
Bonds payable, 11%, due		
January 1, 2004	$2,400,000	
Less: Discount on bonds payable	84,000	$2,316,000

Interest is payable semiannually on January 1 and July 1. The bonds are callable on any semi-annual interest date. Birk uses straight-line amortization for any bond premium or discount. From December 31, 1993 the bonds will be outstanding for an additional 10 years or 120 months. Assume no interest is accrued on June 30.

Instructions

(Round all computations to the nearest dollar.)

(a) Journalize the payment of bond interest on January 1, 1994.

(b) Prepare the entry to amortize bond discount and to pay the interest due on July 1, 1994.

(c) Assume on July 1, 1994, after paying interest that Birk Corp. calls bonds having a face value of $800,000. The call price is 101. Record the redemption of the bonds.

(d) Prepare the adjusting entry at December 31, 1994 to amortize bond discount and to accrue interest on the remaining bonds.

Prepare installment payments schedule and journal entries for a mortgage note payable.
(S.O. 5)

P17–4   Rankin Electronics issues a $900,000 10% 10-year mortgage note on December 31, 1992 to help finance a plant expansion program. The terms provide for semiannual installment payments, exclusive of real estate taxes and insurance of $72,218. Payments are due June 30 and December 31.

Instructions

(a) Prepare an installment payments schedule for the first two years.

(b) Prepare the entries for (1) the mortgage loan and (2) the first two installment payments.

(c) Show how the total mortgage liability should be reported on the balance sheet at December 31, 1993.

P17-5 Presented below are three different lease transactions in which Casper Enterprises engaged in 1993. Assume that all lease transactions start on January 1, 1993. In no case does Casper receive title to the properties leased during or at the end of the lease term.

Analyze three different lease situations and prepare journal entries. (S.O. 7)

	Lessor		
	Lornegren Associates	Potter Co.	Haskell Inc.
Type of property	Bulldozer	Truck	Furniture
Bargain purchase option	None	None	None
Lease term	4 years	6 years	3 years
Estimated economic life	8 years	7 years	5 years
Yearly rental	$13,000	$ 6,000	$ 5,000
Fair market value of leased asset	$80,000	$29,000	$27,500
Present value of the lease rental payments	$48,000	$27,000	$12,000

Instructions

(a) Identify the leases above as operating or capital leases. Explain.

(b) How should the lease transaction for Potter Co. be recorded on January 1, 1993?

(c) How should the lease transactions for Haskell Inc. be recorded in 1993?

*P17-6 On June 30, 1993, Globe Satellites issued $1,500,000 face value of 9%, 10-year bonds at $1,406,534. This price resulted in an effective interest rate of 10% on the bonds. Globe uses the effective interest method to amortize bond premium or discount. The bonds pay semi-annual interest June 30 and December 31.

Prepare journal entries to record issuance of bonds, payment of interest, and amortization of bond discount using effective interest method. (S.O. 8)   S

Instructions

(Round all computations to the nearest dollar.)

(a) Prepare the journal entry to record the issuance of the bonds on June 30, 1993.

(b) Prepare the journal entry to record the payment of interest and the amortization of the discount on December 31, 1993.

(c) Prepare the journal entry to record the payment of interest and the amortization of the discount on June 30, 1994.

(d) Prepare the journal entry to record the payment of interest and the amortization of the discount on December 31, 1994.

(e) Prepare an amortization table through December 31, 1994 (three interest periods) for this bond issue.

*P17-7 On June 30, 1993, Peal Chemical Company issued $2,200,000 face value of 13%, 10-year bonds at $2,326,159. This price resulted in a 12% effective interest rate on the bonds. Peal uses the effective interest method to amortize bond premium or discount. The bonds pay semiannual interest on each June 30 and December 31.

Prepare journal entries to record issuance of bonds, payment of interest, and amortization of premium using effective interest method. In addition, answer questions. (S.O. 8)

Instructions

(a) Prepare the journal entries to record the following transactions.
 (1) The issuance of the bonds on June 30, 1993.
 (2) The payment of interest and the amortization of the premium on December 31, 1993.
 (3) The payment of interest and the amortization of the premium on June 30, 1994.
 (4) The payment of interest and the amortization of the premium on December 31, 1994.

(b) Show the proper balance sheet presentation for the liability for bonds payable on the December 31, 1994, balance sheet.

(c) Provide the answers to the following questions.
 (1) What amount of interest expense is reported for 1994?
 (2) Will the bond interest expense reported in 1994 be the same as, greater than, or less than the amount that would be reported if the straight-line method of amortization were used?
 (3) Determine the total cost of borrowing over the life of the bond.
 (4) Will the total bond interest expense be greater than, the same as, or less than the total interest expense if the straight-line method of amortization were used?

ALTERNATE PROBLEMS

Prepare journal entries to record issuance of bonds, interest accrual, and amortization for two years.
(S.O. 2,7)

P17–1A Gore Electric sold $3,000,000 of 10%, 10-year bonds on January 1, 1993. The bonds were dated January 1 and pay interest July 1 and January 1. Gore Electric uses the straight-line method to amortize bond premium or discount. The bonds were sold at 102. Assume no interest is accrued on June 30.

Instructions

(a) Prepare the journal entry to record the issuance of the bonds on January 1, 1993.

(b) Prepare a bond premium amortization schedule for the first four interest periods.

(c) Prepare the journal entries for interest and the amortization of the premium in 1993 and 1994.

(d) Show the balance sheet presentation of the bond liability at December 31, 1994.

Prepare journal entries to record issuance of bonds, interest, and amortization of bond premium and discount.
(S.O. 2,7)

P17–2A Abbott Company sold $1,500,000 of 12%, 10-year bonds on July 1, 1993. The bonds were dated July 1, 1993 and pay interest July 1 and January 1. Abbott Company uses the straight-line method to amortize bond premium or discount. Assume no interest is accrued on June 30.

Instructions

(a) Prepare all the necessary journal entries to record the issuance of the bonds and bond interest expense for 1993, assuming that the bonds sold at 102.

(b) Prepare journal entries as in part (a) assuming that the bonds sold at 96 plus accrued interest.

(c) Show balance sheet presentation for each bond issue at December 31, 1993.

Prepare journal entries to record interest payments, premium amortization, and redemption of bonds.
(S.O. 2, 3)

P17–3A The following is taken from the Powell Oil Company balance sheet at December 31, 1993:

Current liabilities		
Bond interest payable (for six months from July 1 to December 31)		$ 216,000
Long-term liabilities		
Bonds payable, 12% due January 1, 2004	$3,600,000	
Add: Premium on Bonds Payable	300,000	$3,900,000

Interest is payable semiannually on January 1 and July 1. The bonds are callable on any semiannual interest date. Powell uses straight-line amortization for any bond premium or discount. From December 31, 1993, the bonds will be outstanding for an additional 10 years or 120 months. Assume no interest is accrued on June 30.

Instructions

(a) Journalize the payment of bond interest on January 1, 1994.

(b) Prepare the entry to amortize bond premium and to pay the interest due on July 1, 1994.

(c) Assume on July 1, 1994, after paying interest, that Powell Company calls bonds having a face value of $1,800,000. The call price is 103. Record the redemption of the bonds.

(d) Prepare the adjusting entry at December 31, 1994 to amortize bond premium and to accrue interest on the remaining bonds.

Prepare installment schedule and journal entries for a mortgage note payable.
(S.O. 5)

P17–4A Astro Electronics issues an $800,000 12%, 10-year mortgage note on December 31, 1992. The proceeds from the note are to be used in financing a new research laboratory. The terms of the note provide for semiannual installment payments, exclusive of real estate taxes and insurance, of $69,748. Payments are due June 30 and December 31.

Instructions

(a) Prepare an installment payments schedule for the first two years.

(b) Prepare the entries for (1) the loan and (2) the first two installment payments.

(c) Show how the total mortgage liability should be reported on the balance sheet at December 31, 1993.

P17–5A Presented below are three different lease transactions that occurred for Brett Inc. in 1993. Assume that all lease contracts start on January 1, 1993. In no case does Brett receive title to the properties leased during or at the end of the lease term.

Analyze three different lease situations and prepare journal entries. (S.O. 7)

	Lessor		
	Hung Delivery	Williams Co.	Cecil Auto
Type of property	Computer	Delivery equipment	Automobile
Yearly rental	$ 8,000	$ 4,000	$ 3,700
Lease term	6 years	4 years	2 years
Estimated economic life	7 years	7 years	5 years
Fair market value of lease asset	$44,000	$19,000	$11,000
Present value of the lease rental payments	$43,000	$13,000	$ 6,400
Bargain purchase option	None	None	None

Instructions

(a) Which of the leases above are operating leases and which are capital leases? Explain.

(b) How should the lease transaction for Williams Co. be recorded in 1993?

(c) How should the lease transaction for Hung Delivery be recorded on January 1, 1993?

*P17–6A On June 30, 1993, Maddox Corporation issued $1,500,000 face value of 12%, 10-year bonds at $1,686,934. This price resulted in an effective interest rate of 10% on the bonds. Maddox uses the effective interest method to amortize bond premium or discount. The bonds pay semiannual interest June 30 and December 31.

Prepare journal entries to record issuance of bonds, payment of interest, and amortization of bond premium using effective interest method. (S.O. 2)

Instructions

(Round all computations to the nearest dollar.)

(a) Prepare the journal entry to record the issuance of the bonds on June 30, 1993.

(b) Prepare the journal entry to record the payment of interest and the amortization of the premium on December 31, 1993.

(c) Prepare the journal entry to record the payment of interest and the amortization of the premium on June 30, 1994.

(d) Prepare the journal entry to record the payment of interest and the amortization of the premium on December 31, 1994.

(e) Prepare an amortization table through December 31, 1994 (three interest periods), for this bond issue.

*P17–7A On June 30, 1993, the Clemens Company issued $2,200,000 face value of 14%, 10-year bonds at $1,984,005. This price resulted in an effective interest rate of 16% on the bonds. Clemens uses the effective interest method to amortize bond premium or discount. The bonds pay semiannual interest June 30 and December 31.

Prepare journal entries to record issuance of bonds, payment of interest, and amortization of discount using effective interest method. In addition, answer questions. (S.O. 2, 8)

Instructions

(a) Prepare the journal entries to record the following transactions.
  (1) The issuance of the bonds on June 30, 1993.
  (2) The payment of interest and the amortization of the discount on December 31, 1993.
  (3) The payment of interest and the amortization of the discount on June 30, 1994.
  (4) The payment of interest and the amortization of the discount on December 31, 1994.

(b) Show the proper balance sheet presentation for the liability for bonds payable on the December 31, 1994, balance sheet.

(c) Provide the answers to the following questions.
  (1) What amount of interest expense is reported for 1994?
  (2) Will the bond interest expense reported in 1994 be the same as, greater than, or less than the amount that would be reported if the straight-line method of amortization were used?
  (3) Determine the total cost of borrowing over the life of the bond.
  (4) Will the total bond interest expense be greater than, the same as, or less than the total interest expense that would be reported if the straight-line method of amortization were used?

*B*roadening Your Perspective

FINANCIAL REPORTING PROBLEM

Presented below are selected portions of the notes to the financial statements of CF Industries, Inc.

Long-Term Debt

Long-term debt is summarized as follows (000s omitted):

	December 31, 1991
Unsecured variable interest rate note (weighted average interest rate of 9.3% and 9.6% at December 31, 1991 and 1990, respectively) due in quarterly installments through 1993	$ 3,000
9.75% first mortgage bonds secured by a lien on phosphate rock reserves, due $7.0 million annually through 1996	35,000
8.625% to 9.875% mortgage notes secured by various distribution facilities, due monthly through 2003	13,023
Capital lease obligations	36,877
Total long-term debt	87,900
Less current portion	15,574
	$72,326

Certain borrowings are collateralized by property, plant and equipment. Maintenance of specified minimum working capital (current assets less current liabilities) and stockholders' equity levels, specified maximum debt ratios and investments are also required.

Long-term debt maturities for the four years succeeding December 31, 1992 are $8.7 million in 1993, $8.0 million in 1994, $8.0 million in 1995 and $8.2 million in 1996.

Leases

The present value of future minimum capital lease payments and the future minimum lease payments under noncancelable operating leases at December 31, 1991 are:

	Capital Lease Payments	Operating Lease Payments
1992	$ 7,733	$3,067
1993	6,791	2,052
1994	6,730	1,056
1995	6,788	918
1996	6,785	86
Thereafter	13,441	6
Future minimum lease payments	48,268	$7,185
Less equivalent interest	11,391	
Present value	36,877	
Less current portion	5,570	
	$31,307	

Rent expense for operating leases was $7.0 million for the year ended December 31, 1991, $5.3 million for 1990 and $5.6 million for 1989.

Instructions

(a) Indicate how much long-term debt is outstanding and what are the different types of debt CF Industries reports.

(b) Why do you think the loan agreement contains debt covenants requiring minimum working capital and stockholders' equity levels, and specified maximum debt ratios and investments?

(c) What type of leases does CF Industries, Inc. use? What is the amount of the current portion of the lease obligation?

DECISION CASE

Presented below is the condensed balance sheet for Express, Inc. as of December 31, 1993:

EXPRESS, INC.
Balance Sheet
December 31, 1993

Current assets	$ 800,000	Current liabilities	$1,200,000
Plant assets	1,600,000	Long-term liabilities	700,000
		Common stock	400,000
		Retained earnings	100,000
Total	$2,400,000	Total	$2,400,000

Express has decided that it needs to purchase a new crane for its operations. The new crane costs $900,000 and has a useful life of 15 years. However, Express' bank has refused to provide any help in financing the purchase of the new equipment, even though Express is willing to pay an above market interest rate for the financing.

The chief financial officer for Express, Lisa Colder, has discussed with the manufacturer of the crane the possibility of a lease arrangement. After some negotiation, the manufacturer of the equipment agrees to lease the crane to Express under the following terms: length of the lease, 7 years; payments, $100,000 per year. The present value of the lease payments is $548,732.

The board of directors at Express is delighted with this new lease. They reason they have the use of the crane for the next seven years. In addition, Lisa Colder notes that this type of financing is a good deal because it will keep debt off the balance sheet.

Instructions
(a) Why do you think the bank decided not to lend money to Express, Inc.?
(b) How should this lease transaction be reported in the financial statements?
(c) What did Lisa Colder mean when she said "leasing will keep debt off the balance sheet"?

CRITICAL THINKING CASE

Refer to the opening vignette concerning the long-term bonds issued by the University of Kentucky. Answer the following questions:

1. The University of Kentucky's bonds are rated AA- by Standard & Poors and A1 by Moody's Investor Service. Why is it important to the University of Kentucky that its bonds have a high bond rating?

2. Explain the meaning of the tax exempt status of the University of Kentucky bonds. What does it mean to say that "a recent issue offering 6.5% is the equivalent of 10% to those individuals in the top tax bracket."

3. Why does the state use bonds to finance the buildings rather than taking the funds out of general revenues?

ETHICAL CASE

Andy Vicksic is the president, founder, and majority owner of Consulier Medical Corporation, an emerging medical technology products company. Consulier is in dire need of additional capital to keep operating and to bring several promising products to final development, testing, and production. Andy as owner of 51% of the outstanding stock, manages the company's operations. He places heavy emphasis on research and development and long-term growth. The other principal stockholder is Jim Caterino who, as a nonemployee investor, owns 40% of the stock. Jim would like to deemphasize the R & D functions and emphasize the marketing function to maximize short-run sales and profits from existing products. He believes this strategy would raise the market price of Consulier's stock.

All of Andy's personal capital and borrowing power is tied up in his 51% stock ownership. He knows that any offering of additional shares of stock will dilute his controlling interest because he won't be able to participate in such an issuance. But, Jim has money and would likely buy enough shares to gain control of Consulier. He then would dictate the company's future direction, even if it meant replacing Andy as president and CEO.

The company already has considerable debt. Raising additional debt will be costly, will adversely affect Consulier's credit rating, and increase the company's reported losses due to the growth in interest expense. Jim and the other minority stockholders express opposition to the assumption of additional debt, fearing the company will be pushed to the brink of bankruptcy. Wanting to maintain his control and to preserve the direction of "his" company, Andy is doing everything to avoid a stock issuance and is contemplating a large issuance of bonds, even if it means the bonds are issued at a large discount and high effective interest rate.

Instructions

(a) Who are the stakeholders in this situation?

(b) What are the ethical issues in this case?

(c) What would you do if you were Andy?

Answers to Self-Study Questions
1. b   2. b   3. c   4. b   5. d   6. d   7. c   8. b   9. b   10. c
*11. a   *12. b

CHAPTER 18

INVESTMENTS

Study Objectives

After studying this chapter, you should be able to:

1. Explain the accounting for temporary investments.

2. Indicate the effects of reporting temporary investments at the lower of cost or market value.

3. Explain the accounting for long-term investments in bonds.

4. Identify the accounting guidelines for long-term investments in stock.

5. Describe the content of a work sheet for a consolidated balance sheet.

6. Explain the form and content of consolidated financial statements.

*O*ne of the biggest jobs on any campus is managing money: the endowment fund, the operating cash fund, and the many funds that are reserved for special programs and grants. At the University of Colorado, Boulder, that big job falls on the shoulders of Glen Stine, who oversees some $1 billion in investable funds.

The endowment fund, a relatively small $85 million of bequests and gifts to the university, is mostly invested in the stock market. The rest is in long-term bonds. Because the endowment fund is not being used for short-term purposes, Mr. Stine says he feels comfortable investing about 70% in the stock market. The market is a relatively volatile place to put money—but a place that has outperformed most other investments over the past thirty years.

When it comes to the cash for day-to-day operations, the stock market is just too risky. "The cash funds of the university are invested overnight in money market instruments or high-grade commercial paper," he says. Both are safe and liquid, but *both offer a low rate of return. "The return isn't nearly as high as we would like to get," he concedes. That's not his fault: In the spring of 1992, interest rates are extremely low. The operating budget is hurt as a result. "Next year, I'm expecting to have $2 million less of interest revenue because of the low interest rates," he says.*

Do those low interest rates make it tempting to go for more return at more risk? "We have had an explicit policy on our cash funds that we are looking for safety first," says Stine. "We don't feel that going into the stock market allows us to pick the time that we can get our money out," he says.

Many corporations have substantial temporary (short-term) and long-term investments. For example, in a recent balance sheet, the Aluminum Company of America (Alcoa) reported $575.3 million of short-term investments and $240.0 million of long-term investments. The proportion of investments to total assets is also significant for some companies. In a recent year, investments were 44% of total assets in Sears Roebuck and Co. and 36% in American Express Company.

This chapter is divided into three sections: First, accounting for temporary investments is explained. Second, consideration is given to the accounting for long-term investments in bonds and stock. Third, we discuss the principles of preparing consolidated financial statements for large companies such as PepsiCo, Philip Morris, and Alcoa, that partially or wholly own other companies.

SECTION 1　Temporary Investments

Many companies experience seasonal fluctuations in sales. A Cape Cod marina will have higher sales in the spring and summer than in the fall and winter, whereas the reverse will be true for an Aspen ski shop. Thus, at the end of their operating cycles, many companies may have cash on hand that is temporarily idle pending the start of another operating cycle. Until the cash is needed in operations, many companies invest the excess funds to earn interest and dividends. The relationship of temporary investments to the operating cycle is graphically depicted in Illustration 18-1.

ILLUSTRATION 18-1

Temporary investments and the operating cycle

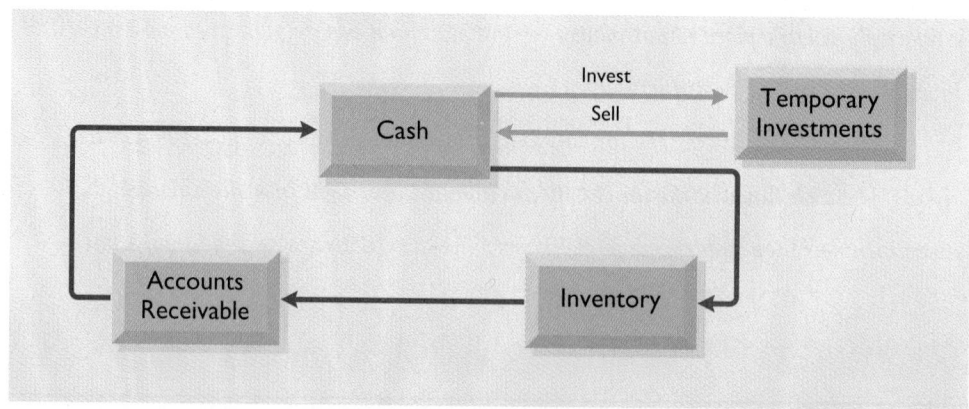

What Are Temporary Investments

Temporary investments are securities, held by a company, that are readily marketable and intended to be converted into cash within the next year or operating cycle, whichever is longer. Investments that do not meet both criteria are classified as long-term investments. Temporary investments consist of (1) short-term paper,[1] (2) marketable equity securities (capital stock), and (3) marketable debt securities (notes and bonds).

Readily Marketable

An investment is readily marketable when it can be sold easily whenever the need for cash arises. Short-term paper meets this criterion because it can be sold readily to other investors. Stocks and bonds traded on organized securities markets, such as the New York Stock Exchange, are readily marketable because they can be bought and sold daily. In contrast, there may be only a limited market for the securities issued by small corporations and no market for the securities of a privately held company.

Intent to Convert

Intent to convert means that management intends to sell the investment within the next year or operating cycle, whichever is longer. Generally, this criterion is satisfied when the investment is considered a resource that will be used whenever the need for cash arises. For example, an Aspen ski resort may invest idle cash during the summer months with the intent to sell the securities to buy supplies and equipment shortly before the next winter season. This investment is considered temporary even if lack of snow cancels the next ski season and eliminates the need to convert the securities into cash as intended.

Accounting for Temporary Investments

In accounting for temporary investments, entries are required to record (1) the acquisition, (2) interest and dividend revenue, and (3) the sale. **At acquisition, the cost principle applies.** Cost includes all expenditures necessary to acquire these investments, such as the price paid plus brokerage fees (commissions), if any. The entries for marketable equity securities and marketable debt securities are illustrated below.

Study Objective 1

Explain the accounting for temporary investments.

Marketable Equity Securities

Marketable equity securities are investments in the capital stock of corporations that are currently traded in the securities market. When a company holds marketable securities of several different corporations, the group of securities is identified as an investment portfolio.

---

[1]Short-term paper includes (1) certificates of deposits (CDs) issued by banks, (2) money market certificates issued by banks and savings and loan associations, (3) treasury bills issued by the U.S. government, and (4) commercial paper issued by corporations with good credit ratings.

ENTRIES AT ACQUISITION. The starting point in accounting for marketable equity securities is cost. Assume, for example, that on July 1, 1993, Kuhl Corporation acquires 1,000 shares of Beal Corporation common stock at $40 per share plus brokerage fees of $500. The entry for the purchase is:

July 1	Marketable Equity Securities	40,500	
	Cash		40,500
	(To record purchase of 1,000 shares of Beal Corporation common stock)		

Marketable Equity Securities is a general ledger control account. It is supported by a subsidiary ledger that contains separate accounts for each type of security purchased.

ENTRIES FOR DIVIDENDS. During the time the stock is held, entries are required for any cash dividends received. Thus, if a $2.00 per share dividend is received by Kuhl Corporation on December 31, the entry is:

Dec. 31	Cash	2,000	
	Dividend Revenue		2,000
	(To record receipt of a cash dividend)		

Dividend Revenue is reported under other revenues and gains in the income statement. Unlike interest on notes and bonds, dividends do not accrue.

ENTRIES FOR SALE OF SECURITIES. When the securities are sold, the difference between the net proceeds (sales price less brokerage fees) from the sale and the cost of the securities is recognized as a gain or a loss. Assume, for instance, that Kuhl Corporation receives net proceeds of $39,500 on the sale of its Beal stock on February 10, 1994. Since the securities cost $40,500, a loss of $1,000 has been incurred. The entry to record the sale is:

Feb. 10	Cash	39,500	
	Loss on Sale of Marketable Equity Securities	1,000	
	Marketable Equity Securities		40,500
	(To record sale of Beal common stock)		

The loss account is reported under other expenses and losses in the income statement, whereas a gain on sale is shown under other revenues and gains.

Marketable Debt Securities

Marketable debt securities are investments in government and corporation bonds that are currently traded in the securities market. Bonds usually pay interest semiannually. The accounting entries for marketable debt securities are basically the same as those for marketable equity securities. For example, marketable debt securities should be recorded at cost, which includes the market price of the bonds plus brokerage fees, but excludes any accrued interest. The principal differences are: (1) the account Marketable Debt Securities is used, and (2) both the receipt of interest and the accrual of interest revenue must be recorded. These differences are illustrated below.

ENTRIES AT ACQUISITION. Assume that Kuhl Corporation acquires 50 Doan Inc. 12%, 10-year, $1,000 bonds on January 1, 1993 for $54,000 including brokerage fees.

The entry to record the investment is:

Jan. 1	Marketable Debt Securities	54,000	
	Cash		54,000
	(To record purchase of 50 Doan Inc. bonds)		

ENTRIES FOR BOND INTEREST. The bonds pay interest of $3,000 semiannually on July 1 and January 1 ($50,000 $\times$ 12% $\times$ ½). The entry for the receipt of interest on July 1 is:

July 1	Cash	3,000	
	Bond Interest Revenue		3,000
	(To record receipt of interest on Doan Inc. bonds)		

If Kuhl Corporation's fiscal year ends on December 31, it is necessary to accrue the interest of $3,000 earned since July 1. The adjusting entry is:

Dec. 31	Bond Interest Receivable	3,000	
	Bond Interest Revenue		3,000
	(To accrue interest on Doan Inc. bonds)		

Bond Interest Receivable is reported as a current asset in the balance sheet; Bond Interest Revenue is reported under other revenues and gains in the income statement. When the interest is received on January 1, the entry is:

Jan. 1	Cash	3,000	
	Bond Interest Receivable		3,000
	(To record receipt of accrued interest)		

A credit to Bond Interest Revenue at this time is incorrect because the interest revenue was earned in the preceding accounting period.

ENTRIES FOR SALE OF BONDS. When the bonds are sold, it is necessary to credit the investment account for the cost of the bonds. Any difference between the proceeds from sale and the cost of the bonds is recorded as a gain or loss. Assume, for example, that Kuhl Corporation sells the Doan Inc. bonds on January 1, 1994, for $58,000 after receiving the interest due.

    The entry to record the sale is:

Jan. 1	Cash	58,000	
	Marketable Debt Securities		54,000
	Gain on Sale of Marketable Debt Securities		4,000
	(To record sale of Doan Inc. bonds)		

The gain on sale of marketable debt securities is reported under other revenues and gains in the income statement.

Valuation at Lower of Cost or Market

Study Objective 2

Indicate the effects of reporting temporary investments at the lower of cost or market value.

During the time marketable equity securities are held, there may be significant fluctuations in the market value of the stock. The Dow-Jones Industrial Average of common stocks illustrates the volatile nature of stock prices. This average, which is based on the market prices of 30 large corporations, drops drastically during downturns in the economy and jumps dramatically during upturns. In light of such fluctuations, how should marketable equity securities be valued at the balance sheet date? Valuation could be at cost, at market value, or at the lower of cost or market value. Market value would seem to be the best approach because it represents the expected cash realizable value of the securities.

The accounting profession, however, has adopted the lower of cost or market method for valuing marketable securities. This method requires that a *marketable equity securities portfolio* be reported at the **lower of aggregate cost or market value determined at the balance sheet date**. This approach is conservative because all losses are recognized, but gains are not. However, companies are not required to use the lower of cost or market method for *marketable debt securities* because debt securities have a fixed value at maturity.

Recognizing Decline in Value

In recognizing a decline in value below cost, a **contra asset account** is used in the balance sheet, and an **unrealized loss account** is reported in the income statement. To illustrate, assume that Kuhl Corporation has the following portfolio of marketable equity securities at December 31, 1993:

ILLUSTRATION 18-2

Portfolio of marketable equity securities

Security	Cost	Market Value
Beal common	$40,500	$39,200
Conwey common	18,000	20,000
Doram preferred	32,500	28,800
	$91,000	$88,000

Aggregate cost exceeds market value by $3,000 ($91,000 − $88,000). This decline in value is recorded by Kuhl Corporation through the following adjusting entry:

Dec. 31	Unrealized Loss on Valuation of Short-term Marketable Equity Securities	3,000	
	Allowance for Excess of Cost Over Market Value		3,000
	(To record excess of aggregate cost over market value of marketable equity securities)		

Accounting in Action · *Business Insight*

What do Treasury Secretary Nicholas Brady and Federal Reserve Board Chairman Alan Greenspan have in common? They both oppose recent efforts by the SEC and the FASB to require investment securities to be reported at market value. The issue is emotional: If market value were adopted, many financial institutions would have large write-offs to net income which would directly affect stockholders' equity, and many financial institutions would appear insolvent or close to it. As a result, this change might undermine investors' and depositors' confidence in these financial institutions. In addition, financial institutions would be less likely to take on longer term loans because the value of such securities would fluctuate more.

The SEC and the FASB appear to disagree. They advise a look at the lessons provided by the savings and loan industry: In 1981, the savings and loan industry reported total stockholders' equity of $28 billion on a cost basis. On a market value basis, stockholders' equity was a negative $178 billion! Perhaps if regulators and legislators had recognized this situation they would have forced these "sick" savings and loans to raise more capital or be closed. Then the American taxpayer would not be saddled with bailing out these institutions in the 1990s. What do you think?

The loss is considered to be **unrealized**, because none of the securities have actually been sold. In the income statement, the loss is reported under other expenses and losses. The allowance account is deducted from marketable equity securities in the current asset section of the balance sheet as shown in Illustration 18-3:

ILLUSTRATION 18-3

Marketable equity securities	$91,000	
Less: Allowance for excess of cost over market value	3,000	$88,000

Presentation of aggregate cost in excess of market value

The balance in the allowance account relates to the **entire portfolio** of securities. Separate allowances are not kept for each security. At each subsequent balance sheet date, the allowance account is adjusted to show the excess of aggregate cost over market value. These entries are complex and are left for more advanced courses.

Subsequent Sale of Securities

When securities in the portfolio are sold, the securities account is credited for the cost of the shares and the balance in the allowance account is ignored. For example, if the Doram preferred stock is sold on March 1, 1994, for $34,000, the entry for the sale is:

Mar. 1	Cash	34,000	
	Marketable Equity Securities		32,500
	Gain on Sale of Marketable Equity Securities		1,500
	(To record sale of Doram preferred stock)		

Similarly, if the Conwey common stock is sold, the basis for computing gain or loss is cost. Thus, if the Conwey stock is sold for $21,000, net of brokerage fees, the gain on sale is $3,000 ($21,000 − $18,000).

Financial Statement Presentation

Because of their high liquidity, temporary investments are listed immediately below cash in the current asset section of the balance sheet. The basis of valuation (cost or lower of cost or market) should be disclosed either in the body of the statement or in the accompanying notes. When aggregate cost is greater than market value, an allowance account is presented as shown earlier. If market value exceeds aggregate cost, the disclosure may be made in a parenthetical note. Many companies make disclosures like the following:

ILLUSTRATION 18-4

WALGREEN CO.	
Marketable securities, at cost which approximates market	$63,126,000

Presentation of cost and market data

The income statement effects of temporary investments are reported in the non-operating section as follows:

ILLUSTRATION 18-5

Other Revenues and Gains	**Other Expenses and Losses**
Interest revenue	Loss on sale of marketable equity (debt) securities
Dividend revenue	
Gain on sale of marketable equity (debt) securities	Unrealized loss on valuation of short-term marketable equity securities

Income statement presentation

Before You Go On . . .

1. What criteria must be met to classify an investment as temporary?

2. What entries are required in accounting for marketable equity securities?

3. What entries are required in accounting for marketable debt securities?

4. What accounts are used in preparing the adjusting entry under the lower of cost or market method?

SECTION 2   Long-Term Investments

As indicated earlier, investments are considered to be long-term when they do not meet the criteria for a temporary investment. **Long-term investments** include (1) investments in bonds and capital stock as explained below, (2) bond sinking funds that were explained in Chapter 17, and (3) long-term receivables and advances (loans) to other companies.

Investments in Bonds

Study Objective 3

Explain the accounting for long-term investments in bonds.

Long-term investments in bonds consist of a wide variety of city, state, and federal bonds as well as bonds issued by corporations. Recall from Chapter 17, that bonds are rated on the basis of their quality. Thus, an investor can minimize risk by buying only highly rated bonds. An investment in high-quality U.S. government bonds, for example, is virtually risk free. Long-term investments in bonds are generally made for the purpose of earning periodic interest rather than for market appreciation.

Accounting for long-term investments in bonds is similar to the accounting for marketable debt securities. For example, **the investment is recorded at cost, which consists of the market price of the bonds plus brokerage fees but excludes any accrued interest**. Entries are made periodically for the receipt and accrual of bond interest. Additional entries, however, are required when the cost of the bonds differs from the face value of the bonds.

A bond sells at a discount (below face value) when the prevailing market (effective) rate of interest for the security is higher than the stated (contractual) interest rate. Conversely, a bond sells at a premium (above face value) when the foregoing relationship between the market and stated interest rate is reversed. **For a long-term investment in bonds, any bond discount or premium is amortized to interest revenue over the remaining term of the bonds.** Like the issuer of the bonds, the investor uses either the straight-line or the effective interest method of amortization. The effective interest method is required under generally accepted accounting principles when the annual amounts between the two amortization methods are materially different.

To illustrate the entries, we will repeat the transactions given earlier for marketable debt securities. In this case, however, it will be assumed that the bonds will be held as a long-term investment.

ENTRY AT ACQUISITION. Recall that Kuhl Corporation paid $54,000 for bonds having a face value of $50,000. The entry to record the investment is:

Jan. 1	Investment in Doan Inc. Bonds	54,000	
	Cash		54,000
	(To record purchase of 50 Doan Inc. bonds)		

Note that the cost of the bonds is debited to an asset account, as are all purchases of assets under the cost principle of accounting. Unlike the issuer of the bonds, who is responsible for paying the face value at maturity, the investor often will not hold the bond investment to maturity. Therefore, **the investor does not use separate accounts for bond premium and bond discount**.

ENTRIES FOR BOND INTEREST. The Doan Inc. bonds were purchased at a premium because the cost was greater than the face value of the bonds. **At the first interest date, it is necessary to amortize the bond premium.** Kuhl Corporation elects to use the straight-line method. Under this method, the amortization amount will be the same for each interest period. The amount for the 10-year Doan bonds is $200 ($4,000 ÷ 20). Thus, the entry for the receipt of interest on July 1 is:

July 1	Cash	3,000	
	Investment in Doan Inc. Bonds		200
	Bond Interest Revenue		2,800
	(To record receipt of semiannual bond interest)		

When bonds are purchased at a discount, the investment account is debited when the discount is amortized.

Kuhl Corporation prepares financial statements annually on December 31. At this date, it is necessary to accrue the interest earned and to amortize the bond premium for the second interest period. The entry is the same as on July 1 except that Bond Interest Receivable is debited.

Dec. 31	Bond Interest Receivable	3,000	
	Investment in Doan Inc. Bonds		200
	Bond Interest Revenue		2,800
	(To accrue interest earned and amortize bond premium)		

After posting the two 1993 interest entries, the investment account will have a balance of $53,600 at December 31 as shown below:

Investment in Doan Inc. Bonds			
Jan. 1	54,000	July 1	200
		Dec. 31	200
Dec. 31 Bal	53,600		

The receipt of interest on January 1 is recorded by a debit to Cash for $3,000 and a credit to Bond Interest Receivable for $3,000.

ENTRY FOR SALE OF BONDS. To record the sale of long-term bonds **the investment account is credited for the book value of the bonds at the sale date**. To illustrate, assume that the Doan Inc. bonds are sold for $58,000 in cash on January 1, 1994. At this date, the book value of the bonds is $53,600. Thus, the entry to record the sale is:

Jan. 1	Cash	58,000	
	Investment in Doan Inc. Bonds		53,600
	Gain on Sale of Bonds		4,400
	(To record sale of bonds)		

The account, Gain on Sale of Bonds, is reported in the income statement under other revenues and gains. A loss on the sale of bonds is reported under other expenses and losses.

Investments in Stocks

Study Objective 4

Identify the accounting guidelines for long-term investments in stock.

A corporation may have a variety of motives in purchasing the capital stock of another corporation. Usually, however, the primary reason is to increase its own net income. This may be achieved through (1) the receipt of dividends, (2) appreciation in the market value of the stock, or (3) use of the investment for expanding or diversifying its own operations. For example, at one time Gulf & Western Industries, Inc., had the following investments in common stock that affected its operations:

ILLUSTRATION 18-6

Diversified investments of Gulf & Western Industries, Inc.

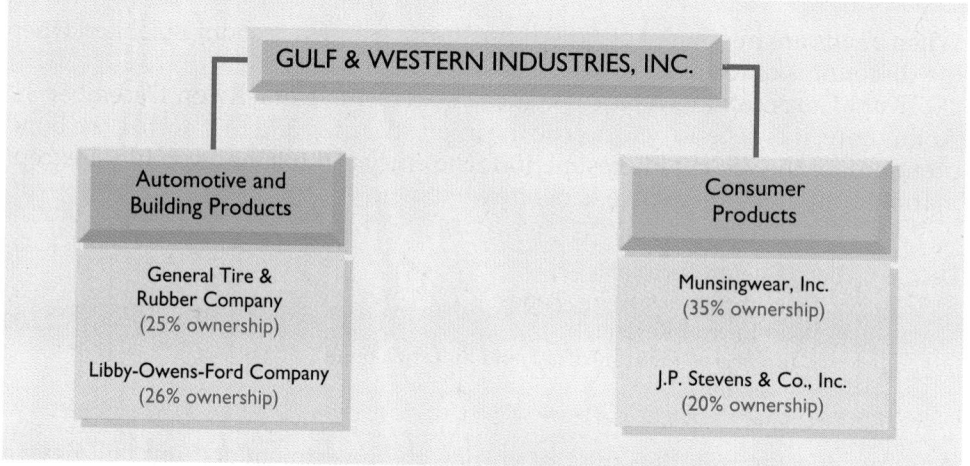

The accounting for long-term investments in common stock is based on the extent of the investor's influence on the operating and financial affairs of the issuing corporation (commonly called the investee) as shown in Illustration 18-7. In some cases, depending on the degree of investor influence, net income of the investee is considered to be income to the investor.

ILLUSTRATION 18-7

Accounting guidelines for stock investments

Investor's Ownership Interest in Investee's Common Stock	Presumed Influence on Investee	Accounting Guidelines
Less than 20%	Insignificant	Lower of cost or market method
Between 20% and 50%	Significant	Equity method
More than 50%	Controlling	Consolidated financial statements

The presumed influence may be negated by extenuating circumstances. For example, a company that acquires a 25% interest in another company in a "hostile" takeover may not have any significant influence over the investee.[2] In other words, companies are required to use judgment instead of blindly following the guidelines. On the following pages we will explain and illustrate the application of each guideline.

Lower of Cost or Market Method

As indicated above, when an investor owns less than 20% of the common stock of another corporation, it is presumed that the investor has relatively little influence on the investee. **As a result, net income earned by the investee is not considered a proper basis for recognizing income from the investment by the investor**. The reason is that the investee may choose to retain for use in the business increased net assets resulting from profitable operations. **Therefore, net income is not considered earned by the investor until cash dividends are declared by the investee.**

Under the **lower of cost or market method**, the investment in common stock is initially recorded at cost. The investor (1) makes no entry for net income or net loss reported by the investee and (2) credits cash dividends received to Dividend Revenue.

To illustrate, assume that Saxon Company acquires 10% of Nolex Inc.'s 100,000 shares of common stock at a cost of $15 per share on March 4, 1993. The entry is as follows:

Mar. 4	Investment in Nolex Common Stock	150,000	
	Cash		150,000
	(To record purchase of 10,000 shares)		

At the end of 1993, Nolex reports $80,000 of net income and declares and pays a $50,000 ($.50 per share) cash dividend. The only entry required by Saxon is for the dividends received of $5,000 (10,000 shares × $.50) as shown below:

Dec. 31	Cash	5,000	
	Dividend Revenue		5,000
	(To record receipt of $.50 per share dividend)		

Note that no entry is made to record Saxon Company's 10% share of Nolex Inc.'s net income.

When the stock is sold, the Investment account is credited for the cost of the shares sold. Thus, if 5,000 shares of Nolex common stock are sold on February 3, 1994 at $18 per share, a gain of $3 per share is realized, and the following entry results:

Feb. 3	Cash	90,000	
	Investment in Nolex Common Stock		75,000
	Gain on Sale of Nolex Common Stock		15,000
	(To record sale of 5,000 shares of Nolex Stock)		

The gain is reported in the other revenues and gains section of the income statement.

---

[2]Among the factors that should be considered in determining an investor's influence are whether (1) the investor has representation on the investee's board of directors, (2) the investor participates in the investee's policy-making process, (3) there are material transactions between the investor and investee, and (4) the common stock held by other stockholders is concentrated or dispersed.

The lower of cost or market method also applies to long-term investments in preferred stocks. Because preferred stock is usually nonvoting, ownership of preferred stock gives the investor no opportunity to exert significant influence over the affairs of the investee.

Reporting at Lower of Cost or Market

The application of the lower of cost or market method to long-term marketable equity securities is similar to the procedures followed for short-term marketable equity securities.[3] The major difference is that the unrealized loss account that results when market value is less than cost **is reported as a deduction from total stockholders' equity and not as a loss on the income statement**. The reason is that long-term marketable securities have a greater likelihood of recovery from a decline in market value before they are sold than do short-term marketable equity securities.

To illustrate, assume that on December 31, 1993, the aggregate cost of the long-term marketable equity securities portfolio held by Dawson, Inc., exceeds aggregate market value by $100,000. The entry to recognize the unrealized loss is:

Dec. 31	Unrealized Loss on Valuation of Long-Term Marketable Equity Securities	100,000	
	Allowance for Excess of Cost over Market Value		100,000
	(To value long-term investments at lower of cost or market)		

The allowance account is a contra asset account that is deducted from the investment account in the balance sheet. The unrealized loss account is reported under stockholders' equity. Assuming that Dawson, Inc., has common stock of $3,000,000 and retained earnings of $1,500,000, the statement presentation of the unrealized loss is as follows:

ILLUSTRATION 18-8

Statement presentation of unrealized loss

Stockholders' equity	
Common stock	$3,000,000
Retained earnings	1,500,000
Total paid-in capital and retained earnings	4,500,000
Less: Unrealized loss on long-term marketable equity securities	(100,000)
Total stockholders' equity	$4,400,000

Note that the presentation of the unrealized loss is similar to the statement presentation of treasury stock within the stockholders' equity section. This presentation informs the statement user of the potential loss that may be suffered from its investment in long-term marketable equity securities.

Equity Method

When an investor owns between 20% and 50% of the common stock of a corporation, it is generally presumed that the investor has significant influence over the financial and operating activities of the investee. **As a result, the investor should record its share of the net income of the investee in the year when it**

---

[3]Throughout this discussion we have assumed that the securities are marketable. If the securities are nonmarketable, they are carried at cost and lower of cost or market is not applied to them.

is earned. In this case, the investor can ensure that any net asset increases resulting from net income will be paid in dividends if desired. To delay recognizing the investor's share of net income until a cash dividend is declared ignores the fact that the investor is better off by the investee's earned income.

Using dividends as a basis for recognizing income poses an additional problem. For example, assume that the investee reports a net loss, but the investor exerts influence to force a dividend payment from the investee. In this case, the investor reports income, even though the investee is experiencing a loss. **In other words, if dividends are used as a basis for recognizing income, the economics of the situation are not properly reported.**

Under the equity method, the investment in common stock is initially recorded at cost, and the investment account is adjusted annually to show the investor's equity in the investee. Each year, the investor (1) debits the investment account and credits revenue for its share of the investee's net income[4] and (2) credits dividends received to the investment account. The investment account is reduced for dividends received, because the net assets of the investee are decreased when a dividend is paid.

To illustrate, assume that Milar Corporation acquires a 30% equity in the common stock of Beck Company for $120,000 on January 1, 1993. The entry to record this transaction is:

Jan. 1	Investment in Beck Common Stock	120,000	
	Cash		120,000
	(To record purchase of Beck common stock)		

For 1993, Beck reports net income of $100,000 and declares and pays a $40,000 cash dividend. Milar is required to record (1) its share of Beck's income, $30,000 (30% × $100,000) and (2) the reduction in the investment account for the dividends received, $12,000 ($40,000 × 30%). The entries are:

(1)

Dec. 31	Investment in Beck Common Stock	30,000	
	Revenue from Investment in Beck Company		30,000
	(To record 30% equity in Beck's 1993 net income)		

(2)

Dec. 31	Cash	12,000	
	Investment in Beck Common Stock		12,000
	(To record dividends received)		

After posting the transactions for the year, the investment accounts will show the following:

Investment in Beck Common Stock				Revenue from Investment in Beck Company	
Jan. 1	120,000	Dec. 31	12,000		
Dec. 31	30,000			Dec. 31	30,000
Dec. 31 Bal.	138,000				

During the year, the investment account has increased by $18,000. This $18,000 is Milar's 30% equity in the $60,000 increase in Beck's retained earnings ($100,000

---

[4]Conversely, the investor debits a loss account and credits the investment account for its share of the investee's net loss.

Accounting in Action · *Business Insight*

Applying the equity method of accounting may have a significant effect on the investor's operating results. During the recent recession, the following effects were reported in millions of dollars:

COMPANY	EARNINGS (LOSS) FROM EQUITY METHOD	NET INCOME
Dow Chemical	$118	$942
Phillips Petroleum	43	258
Clark Equipment	(23)	(337)
Union Carbide	(21)	(9)
Borden	(24)	295
Dana	41	13

— $40,000). In addition, Milar will report $30,000 of revenue from its investment, which is 30% of Beck's net income of $100,000. Note that the difference between reported income under the cost method and reported revenue under the equity method can be significant. For example, Milar would report only $12,000 of dividend revenue (30% × $40,000) under the cost method, with no change in the investment account.

Receipt of Stock Dividends or Stock Splits

While holding stock as an investment, the investor may receive additional shares of stock as a result of a stock dividend or a stock split. Both events result in an increase in the number of shares held. However, neither event results in revenue to the investor, because (1) no assets are received, and (2) the investor's percentage ownership interest in the issuing corporation remains the same.

The investor, therefore, does not make a formal accounting entry for a stock dividend or a stock split under either the lower of cost or market or equity method. Instead, a notation is made in the investment account indicating the additional shares that have been received. The carrying value of the investment at the time of the event is then divided by the total shares currently being held to determine a new cost per share basis for the stock.

To illustrate, assume that the Landon Corporation holds 10,000 shares (15%) of the common stock of Jones, Inc. acquired at a cost of $132,000 ($13.20 per share). The issuer effects a 2-for-1 stock split on May 1 and declares a 10% stock dividend on December 1. The revised cost after each event is $6.60 and $6.00 per share, as shown in Illustration 18-9.

ILLUSTRATION 18-9

Stock split and stock dividend effects on cost per share

Transaction	Shares Acquired	Total Cost	Cost per Share
Purchase	10,000	$132,000	$13.20
Stock split (2-for-1)	10,000	–0–	–0–
Total shares	20,000	132,000	6.60
Stock dividend (10%)	2,000	–0–	–0–
Total shares	22,000	$132,000	$ 6.00

If Landon Company sells 1,000 shares of Jones Inc. on December 20 (after the stock split and stock dividend) at $8.00 per share, the following entry is made:

Dec. 20	Cash	8,000	
	Investment in Jones Common Stock		6,000
	Gain on Sale of Investment		2,000
	(To record sale of 1,000 shares of common stock)		

Note that the investment account is credited for the adjusted cost per share ($6.00) rather than the original cost per share ($13.20).

Statement Presentation of Long-term Investments

Long-term investments are generally reported in a separate section of the balance sheet, immediately below current assets. Investments in bonds are stated at their book value, which is cost plus or minus amortization to the balance sheet date. Investments in stock may be reported at cost, at the lower of cost or market value, or at equity. The basis of valuation should be stated.

In the income statement, revenue recognized under the equity method is reported under other revenues and gains. Losses recognized under the equity method are shown under other expenses and losses. Interest and dividend revenue and gains and losses from the sale of long-term investments are also reported in the nonoperating sections of the income statement.

Before You Go On . . .

1. How does the accounting for long-term investments in bonds differ from the accounting for marketable debt securities?

2. What are the accounting guidelines in accounting for long-term investments in stock?

3. Where is the unrealized loss on long-term marketable equity securities shown in financial statements?

4. What entries are made under the equity method when (a) the investor receives a cash dividend from the investee and (b) the investee reports net income for the year?

SECTION 3 Consolidated Financial Statements

When a company owns more than 50% of the common stock of another company, **consolidated financial statements** are usually prepared; that is, the investor and the investee report their assets, liabilities, revenues, and expenses as one company. Provided below are examples of two companies that prepare consolidated statements and some of the companies they have owned.

ILLUSTRATION 18-10

Examples of investor and investee relationships

Beatrice Foods	American Brands, Inc.
Tropicana Frozen Juices	American Tobacco Company
Switzer Candy Company	Master Lock Company
Samsonite Corporation	Pinkerton's Security Service
Dannon Yogurt Company	Titleist Golf Company

Companies under common control are referred to as **affiliated companies**.

Parent and Subsidiary Company Relationships

A company that owns more than 50% of the common stock of another entity is known as the parent company. The entity whose stock is owned by the parent company is called the subsidiary company. Because of its stock ownership, the parent company has a controlling interest in the subsidiary company.

Philip Morris, Inc., for example, owns 100% of the common stock of Kraft General Foods Corporation. The common stockholders of Philip Morris elect the board of directors of the company, who, in turn, select the officers and managers of the company. The board of directors will control the property owned by the corporation, which includes the common stock of Kraft General Foods. Thus, they are in a position to elect the board of directors of Kraft General Foods and, in effect, control its operations. These relationships are graphically illustrated below.

ILLUSTRATION 18-11

Philip Morris Inc.'s control of Kraft General Foods Corporation

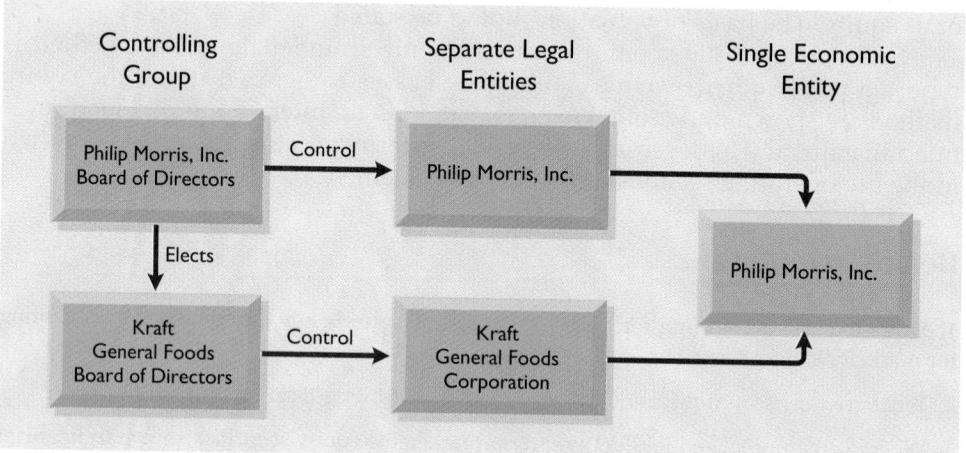

If the parent company acquires 100% of the stock of the subsidiary, that subsidiary is said to be **wholly owned**. When the parent company's controlling interest in a subsidiary is less than 100%, the subsidiary is only **partially owned**. Under this arrangement, the ownership of the subsidiary is divided into two classes: (1) the majority interest represented by the stockholders who own the controlling interest, and (2) the minority interest represented by the stockholders who are not part of the controlling group.

Purpose of Consolidated Financial Statements

Helpful hint If parent (A) has three wholly owned subsidiaries (B, C, & D), there are four separate legal entities, but only one economic entity from the viewpoint of the shareholders of the parent company.

Consolidated financial statements present the assets and liabilities controlled by the parent company and the aggregate profitability of the affiliated companies. They are prepared in addition to the financial statements for each of the individual parent and subsidiary companies. **Consolidated statements are especially useful to the stockholders, board of directors, and management of the parent company.** Moreover, consolidated statements inform creditors, prospective investors, and regulatory agencies as to the magnitude and scope of operations of the companies operating under common control. For example, regulators and the courts undoubtedly used the consolidated statements of American Telephone & Telegraph (AT&T) to determine whether a breakup of AT&T was in the public interest.

Conversely, consolidated financial statements are of limited value to mi-

nority stockholders and creditors of the subsidiary companies, because they do not report separate financial position or earning power of any of the individual entities. For this information, interested parties should use the financial statements of the separate subsidiary companies.

Preparing a Consolidated Balance Sheet

Consolidated balance sheets are prepared from the individual balance sheets of the affiliated companies. They are not prepared from ledger accounts kept by the consolidated entity because only the separate legal entities maintain accounting records.

All items in the individual balance sheets are included in the consolidated balance sheet except amounts that pertain to transactions between the affiliated companies. Transactions between the affiliated companies are identified as intercompany transactions. The process of excluding these transactions in preparing consolidated statements is referred to as intercompany eliminations. These eliminations are necessary to avoid overstating assets, liabilities, and stockholders' equity in the consolidated balance sheet. For example, amounts owed by a subsidiary to a parent company and the related receivable reported by the parent company would be eliminated. The objective in a consolidated balance sheet is to show only obligations to and receivables from parties who are not part of the affiliated group of companies.

Helpful hint Eliminations are aptly named because they eliminate duplicate data. They are not adjustments.

To illustrate, assume that on January 1, 1993, Powers Construction Company pays $150,000 in cash for 100% of Serto Brick Company's common stock. Powers Company records the investment at cost, as required by the cost principle. The separate balance sheets of the two companies immediately after the purchase, together with combined and consolidated data, are presented in Illustration 18-12.[5] The balances in the "combined" column are obtained by adding the items in the separate balance sheets of the affiliated companies. The combined totals do not represent a consolidated balance sheet, because there has been a double counting of assets and owners' equity in the amount of $150,000.

ILLUSTRATION 18-12

Combined and consolidated information

POWERS COMPANY AND SERTO COMPANY
Balance Sheets
January 1, 1993

Assets	Powers Company	Serto Company	Combined Data	Consolidated Data
Current assets	$ 50,000	$ 80,000	$130,000	$130,000
Investment in Serto Company common stock	150,000		150,000	–0–
Plant and equipment (net)	325,000	145,000	470,000	470,000
Total assets	$525,000	$225,000	$750,000	$600,000
Liabilities and stockholders' equity				
Current liabilities	$ 50,000	$ 75,000	$125,000	$125,000
Common stock	300,000	100,000	400,000	300,000
Retained earnings	175,000	50,000	225,000	175,000
Total liabilities and stockholders' equity	$525,000	$225,000	$750,000	$600,000

---

[5]Condensed data will be used throughout this material to keep details at a minimum.

The Investment in Serto Company common stock that appears on the balance sheet of Powers Company represents an interest in the net assets of Serto. As a result, there has been a double counting of assets. Similarly, there has been a double counting in stockholders' equity, because the common stock of Serto Company is completely owned by the stockholders of Powers Company.

The balances in the consolidated data column are the amounts that should appear in the consolidated balance sheet. The double counting has been eliminated by showing Investment in Serto Company at zero and by reporting only the common stock and retained earnings of Powers Company as stockholders' equity.

Use of a Work Sheet—Cost Equal to Book Value

Study Objective 5

Describe the content of a work sheet for a consolidated balance sheet.

The preparation of consolidated balance sheets is usually facilitated by the use of a work sheet. As shown in Illustration 18-13, the work sheet for a consolidated balance sheet contains columns for (1) the balance sheet data for the separate legal entities, (2) intercompany eliminations, and (3) consolidated data. All data in the work sheet relate to the preceding example in which Powers Company acquires 100% ownership of Serto Company for $150,000. In this case, the cost of the investment, $150,000, is equal to the book value $150,000 ($225,000 − $75,000) of the subsidiary's net assets. The intercompany elimination results in a credit to the Investment account maintained by Powers Company for its balance, $150,000, and debits to the Common Stock and Retained Earnings accounts of Serto Company for their respective balances, $100,000 and $50,000.

Helpful hint As in the case of the work sheets explained earlier in this textbook, consolidated work sheets are also optional.

It is important to recognize that intercompany eliminations are made solely on the work sheet to present correct consolidated data. They are not journalized or posted by either of the affiliated companies and therefore do not affect the ledger accounts. Powers Company's investment account and Serto Company's common stock and retained earnings accounts are reported by the separate entities in preparing their own financial statements.

ILLUSTRATION 18-13

Work sheet—Cost equals book value

POWERS COMPANY AND SUBSIDIARY
Work Sheet—Consolidated Balance Sheet
January 1, 1993 (Acquisition Date)

Assets	Powers Company	Serto Company	Eliminations Dr.	Eliminations Cr.	Consolidated Data
Current assets	50,000	80,000			130,000
Investment in Serto Company common stock	150,000			150,000	–0–
Plant and equipment (net)	325,000	145,000			470,000
Totals	525,000	225,000			600,000
Liabilities and stockholders' equity					
Current liabilities	50,000	75,000			125,000
Common stock—Powers Company	300,000				300,000
Common stock—Serto Company		100,000	100,000		–0–
Retained earnings—Powers Company	175,000				175,000
Retained earnings—Serto Company		50,000	50,000		–0–
Totals	525,000	225,000	150,000	150,000	600,000

Technology in Action

The consolidated work sheet is another good spreadsheet application. At this stage in the course, we hope you have familiarized yourself enough with electronic spreadsheets to be able to create your own templates. If not, this is a good work sheet to attempt since the required instructions are very straightforward.

However, computer programs are available that can merge multiple general ledgers for consolidated entities. All you need to do is supply the eliminating information, enter a few command keystrokes, and the consolidated financial statements will come off the printer, ready for distribution.

Use of a Work Sheet—Cost Above Book Value

The cost of acquiring the common stock of another company may be above or below its book value. The management of the parent company may pay more than book value because it believes (1) the fair market values of identifiable assets such as land, buildings, and equipment are higher than their recorded book values or (2) the subsidiary's future earnings prospects warrant a payment for goodwill.

To illustrate, assume the same data used above, except that Powers Company pays $165,000 in cash for 100% of Serto's common stock. The excess of cost over book value is $15,000 ($165,000 − $150,000). This amount is separately recognized in eliminating the parent company's investment account, as shown in Illustration 18-14.

ILLUSTRATION 18-14

Work sheet—Cost above book value

POWERS COMPANY AND SUBSIDIARY **Work Sheet—Consolidated Balance Sheet** **January 1, 1993 (Acquisition Date)**					
Assets	Powers Company	Serto Company	Eliminations Dr.	Eliminations Cr.	Consolidated Data
Current assets	35,000	80,000			115,000
Investment in Serto Company common stock	165,000			165,000	-0-
Plant and equipment (net)	325,000	145,000			470,000
EXCESS OF COST OVER BOOK VALUE OF SUBSIDIARY			15,000		15,000
Totals	525,000	225,000			600,000
Liabilities and stockholders' equity					
Current liabilities	50,000	75,000			125,000
Common stock—Powers Company	300,000				300,000
Common stock—Serto Company		100,000	100,000		-0-
Retained earnings—Powers Company	175,000				175,000
Retained earnings—Serto Company		50,000	50,000		-0-
Totals	525,000	225,000	165,000	165,000	600,000

Note that a separate line is added to the work sheet for the excess of cost over book value of subsidiary.

Total assets and total liabilities and stockholders' equity are the same as in the preceding example ($600,000). However, in this case, total assets include $15,000 of Excess of Cost Over Book Value of Subsidiary. The disposition of the excess is explained in the next section.

Content of a Consolidated Balance Sheet

Study Objective 6

Explain the form and content of consolidated financial statements.

To illustrate a consolidated balance sheet, we will use the work sheet shown in Illustration 18-14. This work sheet shows an excess of cost over book value of $15,000. In the consolidated balance sheet, this amount is first allocated to specific assets, such as inventory and plant equipment, if their fair market values on the acquisition date exceed their book values. Any remainder is considered to be goodwill. For Powers Company, assume that the fair market value of property and equipment is $155,000. Thus, $10,000 of the excess of cost over book value is allocated to property and equipment, and the remainder, $5,000, is allocated to goodwill.

The condensed consolidated balance sheet of Powers Company is shown in Illustration 18-15. As explained in Chapter 11, goodwill would be amortized by the straight-line method over the period benefited, but not in excess of 40 years.

ILLUSTRATION 18-15

Consolidated balance sheet

POWERS COMPANY
Consolidated Balance Sheet
January 1, 1993

Assets

Current assets		$115,000
Plant and equipment (net)		480,000
Goodwill		5,000
Total assets		$600,000

Liabilities and Stockholders' Equity

Current liabilities		$125,000
Stockholders' equity		
Common stock	$300,000	
Retained earnings	175,000	475,000
Total liabilities and stockholders' equity		$600,000

Numerous examples of sections of classified balance sheets have been presented in this and the preceding three corporation chapters. The consolidated balance sheet shown in Illustration 18-16 includes such topics from previous chapters as the issuance of par value common stock and organization costs (Chapter 15), restrictions of retained earnings (Chapter 16), and issuance of long-term bonds and bond sinking funds (Chapter 17). From this chapter, the statement includes investments in short-term marketable equity securities, long-term investments in stocks using the cost and equity methods, and goodwill arising from the preparation of a consolidated balance sheet. Illustration 18-16 also includes descriptive notations within the statement such as the basis for valuing merchandise and two notes to the statement.

PACE CORPORATION
Consolidated Balance Sheet
December 31, 1993

Assets

Current assets			
Cash			$ 21,000
Marketable equity securities		$ 62,000	
Less: Allowance for excess of cost over market value		2,000	60,000
Accounts receivable		84,000	
Less: Allowance for doubtful accounts		4,000	80,000
Merchandise inventory, at FIFO cost			130,000
Prepaid insurance			13,000
Total current assets			304,000
Investments			
Bond sinking fund		100,000	
Investment in stock of less than 20% owned companies, at cost which approximates market value		50,000	
Investment in stock of 20-50% owned companies, at equity		150,000	
Total investments			300,000
Property, plant, and equipment			
Land		200,000	
Buildings	$800,000		
Less: Accumulated depreciation	200,000	600,000	
Equipment	180,000		
Less: Accumulated depreciation	54,000	126,000	
Total property, plant, and equipment			926,000
Intangible assets			
Goodwill (Note 1)		100,000	
Organization costs		70,000	
Total intangible assets			170,000
Total assets			$1,700,000

Liabilities and Stockholders' Equity

Current liabilities			
Notes payable			$ 100,000
Accounts payable			85,000
Bond interest payable			10,000
Federal income taxes payable			60,000
Total current liabilities			255,000
Long-term liabilities			
Bonds payable, 10%, due 2010		$300,000	
Less: Discount on bonds		10,000	
Total long-term liabilities			290,000
Total liabilities			545,000

ILLUSTRATION 18-16 (*Continued*)

Stockholders' equity		
Paid-in capital		
Common stock, $10 par value, 200,000 shares authorized, 80,000 shares issued and outstanding	800,000	
Paid-in capital in excess of par value	100,000	
Total paid-in capital	900,000	
Retained earnings (Note 2)	255,000	
Total stockholders' equity		1,155,000
Total liabilities and stockholders' equity		$1,700,000

Note 1. Goodwill from acquisition of wholly owned subsidiaries is amortized by the straight-line method over 40 years.

Note 2. Retained earnings of $100,000 is restricted for plant expansion.

Consolidated Income Statement

A consolidated income statement is also prepared for affiliated companies. This statement shows the results of operations of affiliated companies as though they are one economic unit. This means that the statement shows only revenue and expense transactions between the consolidated entity and companies and individuals who are outside the affiliated group. Consequently, all intercompany revenue and expense transactions must be eliminated. Intercompany transactions such as sales between affiliates and interest on loans charged by one affiliate to another must be eliminated. A work sheet facilitates the preparation of consolidated income statements in the same manner as it does for the balance sheet.

Before You Go On . . .

1. Why are eliminations needed in preparing consolidated financial statements?

2. What eliminations are made for the parent company's investment in the common stock of a subsidiary company?

3. How may the excess of cost over book value be reported in a consolidated balance sheet?

Accounting in Action · *Business Insight*

Through innovative financial restructuring, the Coca-Cola Company at one time eliminated a substantial amount of non-intercompany debt. It sold to the public 51% of two bottling companies. The "49% solution," as insiders call the strategy, enabled Coca-Cola to keep effective control over the businesses and it swept $3 billion of debt from its consolidated balance sheet. (It no longer consolidated the two bottling companies). At the same time the new companies obtained independent access to equity markets to satisfy their own voracious appetites for capital.

Source: *The Wall Street Journal*, October 8, 1987.

Summary of Study Objectives

1. Explain the accounting for temporary investments. Entries for investments in marketable equity securities are required when the stocks are acquired, dividends are received, and the securities are sold. Entries for investments in marketable debt securities are required when the bonds are purchased, interest is received and accrued, and the bonds are sold.

2. Indicate the effects of reporting temporary investments at the lower of cost or market value. Under this method of valuation, marketable equity securities are reported at the lower of aggregate cost or market value of the investment portfolio determined at the balance sheet date. The balance sheet will show a contra asset account for the excess of cost over market value, and the income statement will show an unrealized loss account.

3. Explain the accounting for long-term investments in bonds. The accounting for long-term investments in bonds is the same as for temporary investments in bonds, except that bond premium and bond discount must be amortized by either the straight-line or effective interest method. When long-term bonds are sold, it is necessary to credit the investment account for the book value of the bonds at the sale date.

4. Identify the accounting guidelines for long-term investments in stock. The guidelines are based on the investor's ownership interest and presumed influence on the investee. When ownership is less than 20%, the lower of cost or market should be used. When ownership is between 20% and 50%, the equity method should be used. When ownership is more than 50%, consolidated financial statements should be prepared.

5. Describe the content of a work sheet and a consolidated balance sheet. The work sheet for a consolidated balance sheet contains columns for (a) the balance sheet data for the separate entities, (b) intercompany eliminations, and (c) consolidated data.

6. Explain the form and content of consolidated financial statements. Consolidated financial statements are similar in form and content to the financial statements of an individual corporation. A consolidated balance sheet shows the assets and liabilities controlled by the parent company. A consolidated income statement shows the results of operations of affiliated companies as though they are one economic unit.

APPENDIX I Business Combinations—
Purchase vs. Pooling of Interests

A business combination occurs when one entity acquires part or all of another entity for the purpose of combining resources. In a business combination, (1) one or more of the acquired enterprises may become a subsidiary of the acquiring company, (2) the acquired enterprise may transfer its net assets to the acquiring company, or (3) each of the entities may transfer its net assets to a newly formed enterprise. The purchase method and the pooling-of-interests method are both acceptable in accounting for business combinations, but both cannot be used for the same business combination. Both methods are used in practice, as illustrated below.

Study Objective 7

After studying Appendix I, you should be able to:

7. Distinguish between the methods of accounting for a business combination.

General Electric Company

The company acquired 100% of the outstanding common stock of RCA for $6.4 billion in cash. This acquisition was accounted for as a **purchase**.

American Express Company

The company exchanged 21.3 million of its common stock for all the outstanding stock of Shearson Loeb Rhoades Inc. This acquisition was accounted for as a **pooling of interests**.

ILLUSTRATION I-I

Examples of purchase and pooling of interests

From an accounting standpoint, the critical difference between these business combinations (acquisitions) is the manner of payment. General Electric used cash whereas American Express used only common stock. When the acquiring company obtains 90% or more of another company's common stock by issuing its own common stock, the acquisition is usually deemed a pooling of interests. When this condition is not met, the business combination is considered a purchase.

Balance Sheet Effects

Under the purchase method,

1. The assets of the acquired company are recorded by the acquiring company at their fair market values.
2. The excess of cost (i.e., the purchase price) over the sum of the fair market values of the assets less liabilities assumed is recognized as goodwill.
3. No part of the stockholders' equity of the acquired company is recorded on the books of the purchaser.

The rationale underlying the purchase method is that when cash (or other assets) is the primary means of payment, the ownership interests in the acquired company are eliminated and a purchase has taken place. As a result, the assets of the acquired company should be recorded at cost. Recall that cost and fair market value are the same at the date of acquisition. The purchase method has been assumed in preparing consolidated financial statements in this chapter.

In contrast, under the pooling-of-interests method,

1. The assets of the acquired company are recorded by the acquiring company at their book values.
2. No goodwill is recognized.
3. The retained earnings of the acquired company are added to the retained earnings of the purchaser.

The rationale underlying the pooling-of-interests method is that when the business combination is accomplished primarily by the issuance of the common stock of the acquiring company, the ownership interests in the acquired company are continued. As a result, no revaluation of assets is necessary, since the ownership interest of the acquired company is not eliminated. In a pooling of interests, it is assumed that two companies have combined their stockholders, resources, and operations. As one writer has noted, "It is like two rivers flowing into one, each now unidentifiable."

Income Statement Effects

There are also significant differences between the two methods in reporting net income in the year of acquisition. **Under the purchase method, only the acquired company's net income earned after the date of acquisition is included in the purchaser's net income.** Net income that preceded the acquisition date is excluded. This treatment is based on the view that the benefits (net income) from any purchase do not begin until after the date of acquisition.

In contrast, under the pooling-of-interests method, the acquired company's entire net income in the year of acquisition is included in the purchaser's net income. This treatment is based on the view that since the companies have

Accounting in Action · *Business Insight*

In some cases future earnings can be higher under the purchase method than the pooling-of-interests method. A good example is the merger of Capital Cities, Inc. with ABC. When Capital Cities, Inc. merged with ABC, it drastically reduced the cost basis of several ABC television flops, such as "Amerika", to fair market value. This reduction amounted to $290 million and was added to goodwill recognized in purchase accounting. As a result, Capital Cities will not have to report operating losses on the "turkey" programs over their remaining useful lives, which are short. Instead, the losses are spread by a goodwill amortization over forty years. As a result, purchase accounting improved earnings in the year of acquisition by almost 50 percent.

Source: Forbes, December 28, 1987 adapted.

combined their operations, the income statement should report the net income earned from the beginning of the year. For example, American Express Company acquired Shearson Loeb Rhoades on June 29, and Shearson's net income of $56 million for the first six months of the year was added to American Express' net income of $185 million for the same period in reporting the net income of the combined companies. However, under the purchase method, American Express could report only $185 million of net income. As a result, in the year of acquisition, net income will be higher under a pooling of interests than under a purchase.

In addition, the prospects for future earnings are generally higher under the pooling-of-interests method than under the purchase method, because of the following factors:

Pooling-of-Interests Method	Purchase Method
• Depreciation on book values of acquired depreciable assets is continued. • Goodwill amortization cannot occur.	• Depreciation on fair market values of acquired depreciable assets. • Goodwill amortization may occur.

ILLUSTRATION I-2

Effects on future earnings

However, if the assets of the acquired company are overvalued, the purchase method will result in higher earnings than the pooling-of-interests method. The notes to the financial statements should indicate that a business combination occurred and the method of accounting that was used.

Summary of Study Objectives for Appendix I

7. *Distinguish between the methods of accounting for a business combination.* Under the purchase method, (a) the assets of the acquired company are recorded at their fair market values and goodwill may be recognized, (b) no part of the stockholders' equity of the acquired company is recorded by the purchaser, and (c) only the acquired company's net income after the date of acquisition is included in the purchaser's net income. Under the pooling-of-interests method, the assets of the acquired company are recorded by the acquiring company at their book values, and no goodwill is recognized. The retained earnings of the acquired company are added to the retained earnings of the purchaser. In a pooling, the acquired company's entire net income in the year of acquisition is included in the purchaser's net income.

GLOSSARY

Business combination · The acquisition by one entity of part or all of another entity for the purpose of combining resources. (p. 731)

Consolidated financial statements · Financial statements that present the assets and liabilities controlled by the parent company and the aggregate profitability of the affiliated companies. (p. 724)

Controlling interest · Ownership of more than 50% of the common stock of another entity. (p. 724)

Equity method · An accounting method in which the investment in common stock is initially recorded at cost, and the investment account is then adjusted annually to show the investor's equity in the investee. (p. 721)

Intercompany eliminations · Eliminations made to exclude the effects of intercompany transactions in preparing consolidated statements. (p. 725)

Intercompany transactions · Transactions between affiliated companies. (p. 725)

Investment portfolio · The holding of a group of securities of different corporations. (p. 711)

Long-term investments · Investments that are not readily marketable or that management does not intend to convert into cash within the next year or operating cycle, whichever is longer. (p. 711)

Lower of cost or market method · An accounting method in which marketable equity securities are reported at aggregate cost or market value, whichever is lower. (p. 714)

Majority interest · The stockholders who own the controlling interest in a subsidiary company. (p. 724)

Marketable debt securities · Government and corporation bonds that are currently traded in the securities markets. (p. 712)

Marketable equity securities · Capital stock of corporations that are currently traded in the securities markets. (p. 711)

Minority interest · The stockholders who are not part of the controlling group in a subsidiary company. (p. 724)

Parent company · A company that owns more than 50% of the common stock of another entity. (p. 724)

Pooling-of-interests method · A method of accounting for a business combination in which the assets of the acquired company are recorded by the acquiring company at their book values and no goodwill is recognized. (p. 732)

Purchase method · A method of accounting for a business combination in which the assets of the acquired company are recorded by the acquiring company at their fair market values, and the excess of cost over the sum of the fair market values of the assets less liabilities assumed is recognized as goodwill. (p. 732)

Subsidiary company · A company in which more than 50% of its stock is owned by another company. (p. 724)

Temporary investments · Investments that are readily marketable and intended to be converted into cash within the next year or operating cycle, whichever is longer. (p. 711)

DEMONSTRATION PROBLEM

In its first year of operations, the DeMarco Company had the following selected transactions in short-term marketable equity securities:

June	1	Purchased for cash 600 shares of Sanburg common stock at $24 per share plus $300 brokerage fees.
July	1	Purchased for cash 800 shares of Cey common stock at $33 per share plus $600 brokerage fees.
Sept.	1	Received a $1 per share cash dividend from Cey Corporation.
Nov.	1	Sold 200 shares of Sanburg common stock for cash at $27 per share less $150 brokerage fees.
Dec.	15	Received a $.50 per share cash dividend on Sanburg common stock.

At December 31, the market values per share were: Sanburg $25 and Cey $30.

Instructions

(a) Journalize the transactions.

(b) Prepare the adjusting entry at December 31 to report the securities at the lower of cost or market value.

Solution to Demonstration Problem

(a) June	1	Marketable Equity Securities		14,700	
		Cash			14,700
		(Purchased 600 shares of Sanburg common stock)			
July	1	Marketable Equity Securities		27,000	
		Cash			27,000
		(Purchased 800 shares of Cey common stock)			
Sept.	1	Cash		800	
		Dividend Revenue			800
		(Received $1 per share cash dividend from Cey Corporation)			
Nov.	1	Cash		5,250	
		Marketable Equity Securities			4,900
		Gain on Sale of Marketable Equity Securities			350
		(Sold 200 shares of Sanburg common stock)			
Dec.	15	Cash		200	
		Dividend Revenue			200
		(Received $.50 per share dividend from Sanburg Corporation)			
(b) Dec.	31	Unrealized Loss on Valuation of Short-term Marketable Equity Securities		2,800	
		Allowance for Excess of Cost over Market Value			2,800
		(To record excess of aggregate cost over market value):			

Security	Cost	Market
Sanburg common stock	$ 9,800	$10,000
Cey common stock	27,000	24,000
	$36,800	$34,000

*Note: All **asterisked** glossary entries, Questions, Exercises, and Problems relate to material contained in the Appendix to the chapter.

SELF-STUDY QUESTIONS

Answers are at the end of the chapter.

(S.O. 1) 1. Temporary investments must be readily marketable and be expected to be sold within:
   a. three months from the date of purchase.
   b. the next year or operating cycle, whichever is shorter.
   c. the next year or operating cycle, whichever is longer.
   d. the operating cycle.

(S.O. 1) 2. Pryor Company receives net proceeds of $42,000 on the sale of marketable equity securities that cost $39,500. This transaction will result in reporting in the income statement a:
   a. loss of $2,500 under other expenses and losses.
   b. loss of $2,500 under operating expenses.
   c. gain of $2,500 under other revenues and gains.
   d. gain of $2,500 under operating revenues.

(S.O. 1)   3. Hanes Company sells marketable debt securities costing $26,000 for $28,000 plus accrued interest that has been recorded. In journalizing the sale, credits are:
a. Marketable Debt Securities and Loss on Sale of Marketable Debt Securities.
b. Marketable Debt Securities and Gain on Sale of Marketable Debt Securities.
c. Marketable Equity Securities and Bond Interest Receivable.
d. No correct answer given.

(S.O. 2)   4. At the end of the first year of operations, the aggregate cost of the short-term marketable equity securities portfolio is $120,000 and aggregate market value is $115,000. The financial statements should show:
a. a contra asset of $5,000 and a realized loss of $5,000.
b. a contra asset of $5,000 and an unrealized loss of $5,000 in the stockholders' equity section.
c. a contra asset of $5,000 in the current asset section and an unrealized loss in other expenses and losses of $5,000.
d. a contra asset of $5,000 in the current asset section and a realized loss of $5,000 in other expenses and losses.

(S.O. 2)   5. In the next accounting period, the securities in Question 4 are sold for $116,000. The entry for the sale should include a:
a. debit for $4,000 to a realized loss account.
b. debit for $4,000 to a contra asset valuation account.
c. debit for $4,000 to an unrealized loss account.
d. credit for $1,000 to a realized gain account.

(S.O. 3)   6. The discount amortized on long-term bonds held as an investment:
a. decreases the investment account.
b. decreases bond interest receivable.
c. increases bond interest revenue.
d. increases bond interest receivable.

(S.O. 4)   7. The equity method of accounting for long-term investments in stock should be used when the investor has significant influence over an investee and owns:
a. between 20% and 50% of the investee's common stock.
b. 20% or more of the investee's common stock.

c. more than 50% of the investee's common stock.
d. less than 20% of the investee's common stock.

8. In the balance sheet, Unrealized Loss on Long-term Marketable Equity securities is reported as a: (S.O. 4)
a. contra asset account.
b. contra stockholders' equity account.
c. loss in the income statement.
d. loss in the retained earnings statement.

9. Pate Company pays $175,000 for 100% of Sinko's common stock when Sinko's stockholders' equity consists of Common Stock $100,000 and Retained Earnings $60,000. In the work sheet for the consolidated balance sheet, the eliminations will include a: (S.O. 5)
a. credit to Investment in Sinko Common Stock, $160,000.
b. credit to Excess of Book Value over Cost of Subsidiary, $15,000.
c. debit to Retained Earnings, $75,000.
d. debit to Excess of Cost over Book Value of Subsidiary, $15,000.

10. Which one of the following statements about consolidated income statements is *false*?   (S.O. 6)
a. A work sheet facilitates the preparation of the statement.
b. The consolidated income statement shows the results of operations of affiliated companies as a single economic unit.
c. All revenue and expense transactions between parent and subsidiary companies are eliminated.
d. When a subsidiary is wholly owned, the form and content of the statement will differ from the income statement of an individual corporation.

*11. Under the purchase method of accounting for a business combination: (S.O. 7)
a. goodwill is not recognized.
b. stockholders' equity of the acquired company is recorded on the books of the purchaser.
c. acquired assets are recorded at their fair market values.
d. the acquired company's entire net income in the year of acquisition is included in the purchaser's net income.

QUESTIONS

1. Kirk Wholesale Supply owns stock in Xerox Corporation, which it intends to hold indefinitely because of some negative tax consequences if sold. Should the investment in Xerox be classified as a temporary investment? Why?

2. To acquire Mega Corporation stock, R. L. Duran pays $65,000 in cash plus $1,500 broker's fees. What entry should be made for this investment, assuming the stock is readily marketable?

3. Ann Adler is confused about losses and gains on the sale of marketable equity securities. Explain to Ann (a) how the gain or loss is computed, and (b) the statement presentation of the gains and losses.

4. Art Arno is studying for his next accounting examination. What should Art know about the similarities and differences between accounting for short-term marketable debt securities and marketable equity securities?

5. Clio Company sells Cross's bonds costing $40,000 for $45,000, including $3,000 of accrued interest. In recording the sale, Clio books a $5,000 gain. Is this correct? Explain.

6. Wendy Walner is the controller of G-Products, Inc. At December 31, the company's portfolio of short-term marketable equity securities shows cost $74,000 and market $70,000. Indicate how Wendy would report these data in the financial statements prepared on December 31.

7. In the following year, one-half of the securities in Question 6 are sold for $36,000. What gain or loss was realized from the sale?

8. How does the accounting for marketable debt securities differ from the accounting for marketable equity securities?

9. CinCo pays $27,000 for 10-year, 12% ABC bonds having a face value of $25,000. The bonds will be held as a long-term investment. What is the amount of the premium amortization and the credit to bond interest revenue for the first semiannual interest period using the straight-line method?

10. Assume that the bonds in question 9 are sold for $29,000 after receiving interest for the second interest period. What is the gain or loss on sale of bonds?

11. (a) What are the guidelines for using the lower of cost or market method of accounting for investments in stock?
(b) When is revenue recognized under this method?

12. (a) When should a long-term investment in common stock be accounted for by the equity method?
(b) When is revenue recognized under this method?

13. Malon Corporation uses the equity method to account for its ownership of 35% of the common stock of Flynn Packing. During 1993 Flynn reported a net income of $80,000 and declares and pays cash dividends of $10,000. What recognition should Malon Corporation give to these events?

14. Reo Company's portfolio of long-term marketable equity securities at December 31 shows total cost of $192,000 and total market value of $185,000. Prepare the adjusting entry under the lower of cost or market method.

15. What is the proper statement presentation of the account Unrealized Loss on Valuation of Long-term Marketable Equity Securities?

16. Jane Myer, a business major, received notice that she was to receive a 10% stock dividend on her 100-share Old Second Bank common stock investment. She has come to you to ask advice about what to do with her windfall. Explain to Jane what a stock dividend is and is not.

17. What are consolidated financial statements?

18. (a) What asset and owners' equity balances are eliminated in preparing a consolidated balance sheet for a parent and a wholly owned subsidiary? (b) Why are they eliminated?

19. Weller Company pays $320,000 to purchase all the outstanding common stock of Wood Corporation. At the date of purchase the net assets of Wood have a book value of $290,000. Weller's management allocates $20,000 of the excess cost to undervalued land on the books of Wood. What should be done with the rest of the excess?

*20. Bymor Corporation acquired all of Frienda Mine common stock by issuing its own common shares in a 1-for-1 stock exchange. Is this business combination accounted for as a purchase or a pooling of interests? Why?

BRIEF EXERCISES

Journalize entries for marketable equity securities. (S.O. 1)

BE18–1   On August 1, the McLain Company buys 1,000 shares of ABC common stock for $35,000 cash plus brokerage fees of $600. On December 1, the marketable equity securities are sold for $38,000 in cash. Journalize the purchase and sale of the common stock.

Journalize entries for marketable debt securities. (S.O. 1)

BE18–2   The Phelps Corporation purchased marketable debt securities for $41,500 on January 1, 1993. On July 1, 1993, Phelps received cash interest of $2,075. Journalize the purchase and receipt of interest. Assume that no interest has been accrued.

Prepare an adjusting entry under lower of cost or market method. (S.O. 2)

BE18–3   Cost and market value data for the marketable securities portfolio of the Michele Company at December 31 are $62,000 and $59,000, respectively. Prepare the adjusting entry to record the securities at the lower of cost or market.

Indicate statement presentation of accounts. (S.O. 2)

BE18–4   For the data presented in BE18–3, show the financial statement of the securities and related accounts.

Amortize premium for long-term investment. (S.O. 3)

BE18–5   The Swan Corporation owns $100,000 of 10-year XYZ bonds that were purchased as a long-term investment at a cost of $110,000 on January 1, 1993. The interest rate of the bonds is 10% payable semiannually on July 1 and January 1. Prepare the entries to amortize bond premium and accrue interest at June 30, 1993 using the straight-line method.

Apply lower of cost or market method. (S.O.4)

BE18–6   The Duggen Corporation holds marketable equity securities costing $72,000 as a long-term investment. At December 31, the market value of the portfolio is $65,000. Prepare the adjusting entry to record the securities at the lower of cost or market. Indicate the statement presentation of the account credited in your entry.

Record transactions under the equity method of accounting. (S.O. 4)

BE18–7   The Harmon Company owns 20% of the Hook Company. For the current year Hook reports net income of $150,000 and declares and pays a $50,000 cash dividend. Record Harmon's equity in Hook's net income and the receipt of dividends from Hook.

Record sale of common stock after a stock split. (S.O. 4)

BE18–8   Hepp, Inc. acquires 2,000 shares of ABC Corporation common stock at a cost of $15 per share. During the year the stock is split on a 3-for-1 basis. Following the stock split, 500 shares are sold for cash at $7 per share. Journalize the stock sale.

Prepare partial consolidated work sheet when cost equals book value. (S.O. 5)

BE18–9   Provo Company acquires 100% of the common stock of Stanton Company for $180,000 cash. On the acquisition date, Stanton's ledger shows Common Stock $120,000 and Retained Earnings $60,000. Complete the work sheet for the following accounts: Provo—Investment in Stanton Common Stock, Stanton—Common Stock, and Stanton—Retained Earnings.

Prepare partial consolidated work sheet when cost exceeds book value. (S.O. 5)

BE18–10   Data for the Provo and Stanton companies are given in BE18–9. Instead of paying $180,000, assume that Provo pays $200,000 to acquire the 100% interest in Stanton Company. Complete the work sheet for the accounts identified in BE18–9 and for the excess of cost over book value.

Effects on net income of purchase and pooling of interests. (S.O. 7)

*BE18–11   Pomey Corporation purchased 100% of Sund Company on August 10, 1993, by issuing common stock worth $900,000. The book value of the net assets of Sund Company were $800,000 at that time. Explain why the consolidated earnings of the two companies will probably be higher if the pooling-of-interests method is used to record the business combination as opposed to the purchase method.

EXERCISES

E18–1 The Malea Company had the following transactions pertaining to short-term marketable equity securities:

Journalize marketable equity securities transactions.
(S.O. 1)

Feb. 1 Purchased 800 shares of ABC common stock for $8,200 cash plus brokerage fees of $200.

July 1 Received cash dividends of $1 per share on ABC common stock.

Sept. 1 Sold 300 shares of ABC common stock for $4,000 less brokerage fees of $100.

Dec. 1 Received cash dividends of $1 per share on ABC common stock.

Instructions

(a) Journalize the transactions.

(b) Explain how dividend revenue and the gain (loss) on sale should be reported in the income statement.

E18–2 The Piper Corporation had the following transactions pertaining to marketable debt securities held as a temporary investment:

Journalize marketable debt securities transactions and accrue interest.
(S.O. 1)

Jan. 1 Purchased 60 10%, $1,000 Harris Co. bonds for $60,000 cash plus brokerage fees of $900. Interest is payable semiannually on July 1 and January 1.

July 1 Received semiannual interest on Harris Co. bonds.

July 1 Sold 30 Harris Co. bonds for $32,000 less $400 brokerage fees.

Instructions

(a) Journalize the transactions.

(b) Prepare the adjusting entry for the accrual of interest at December 31.

E18–3 At December 31, 1993, the short-term marketable equity securities portfolio for Nielson, Inc., is as follows:

Prepare adjusting entry for lower of cost or market valuation.
(S.O. 1, 2)

Security	Cost	Market
A	$17,500	$15,000
B	12,500	14,000
C	23,000	21,000
	$53,000	$50,000

On January 20, 1994, Nielson, Inc., sold security A for $14,900. The sale proceeds are net of brokerage fees.

Instructions

(a) Prepare the adjusting entry at December 31, 1993, to report the portfolio at the lower of cost or market value.

(b) Show the balance sheet and income statement presentation of the lower of cost or market data at December 31, 1993.

(c) Prepare the journal entry for the 1994 sale.

E18–4 The Levon Corporation had the following transactions pertaining to long-term investments in bonds in 1993:

Journalize long-term bond transactions for bonds purchased at a premium.
(S.O. 3)

Jan. 1 Purchased 70 DCR $1,000, 10%, 10-year bonds for $76,000 cash. The bonds pay interest semiannually on January 1 and July 1.

July 1 Received semiannual interest on bonds and amortized bond premium for the first interest period.

Dec. 31 Accrued bond interest and amortized bond premium for the second interest period.

Instructions

(a) Journalize the 1993 transactions, assuming the straight-line method of amortization is used.

(b) Journalize the receipt of interest on January 1, 1994.

(c) Record the sale of the bonds on January 1, 1994, for $74,000 cash.

Journalize long-term bond transactions for bonds purchased at a discount.
(S.O. 3)

E18–5   The Kerr Company had the following transactions pertaining to long-term investments in bonds in 1993:

Jan. 1   Purchased 50 UPS $1,000, 10% 10-year bonds for $46,000 cash. The bonds pay interest semiannually on January 1 and July 1.

July 1   Received semiannual interest on bonds and amortized bond discount for the first interest period.

Dec. 31   Accrued interest and amortized bond discount for the second interest period.

Instructions

(a) Journalize the 1993 transactions, assuming the straight-line method is used.

(b) Journalize the receipt of interest on January 1, 1994.

(c) Record the sale of the bonds on January 1, 1994, for $47,500 cash.

Journalize transactions for long-term investments in stocks.
(S.O. 4)

E18–6   McCormick Inc. had the following transactions pertaining to long-term investments in common stock:

Jan. 1   Purchased 1,000 shares of Starr Corporation common stock (5%) for $70,000 cash plus $1,400 broker's commission.

July 1   Received a cash dividend of $9 per share.

Dec. 1   Sold 500 shares of Starr Corporation common stock for $37,000 cash less $800 broker's commission.

Dec. 31   Received a cash dividend of $9 per share.

Instructions
Journalize the transactions.

Record long-term marketable equity securities at the lower of cost or market value.
(S.O. 4)

E18–7   On July 1, 1993, the portfolio of long-term marketable equity securities held by the Berryhill Corporation consisted of the following purchases:

1. 1,000 shares of Hobart common stock purchased at a cost of $44 per share.
2. 2,000 shares of Monroe common stock purchased at a cost of $51 per share.

Subsequent to the purchases, Hobart declared and completed a 10% stock dividend, and Monroe executed a 3-for-1 stock split. At December 31, 1993 market values per share were Hobart $38 and Monroe $16.

Instructions

(a) Determine the number of shares, cost per share, and total cost for each security at December 31, 1993.

(b) Prepare a schedule showing the cost and market value of the portfolio at December 31, 1993.

(c) Prepare the adjusting entry to report the portfolio at the lower of cost or market value at December 31, 1993.

(d) Explain the statement presentation of the accounts used in part (c).

Journalize entries under cost or market and equity methods.
(S.O. 4)

E18–8   Presented below are two independent situations:

1. Karen Cosmetics acquired 10% of the 200,000 shares of common stock of Bell Fashion at a total cost of $12 per share on March 18, 1993. On June 30, Bell declared and paid a $75,000 dividend. On December 31, Bell reported net income of $122,000 for the year. At December 31, the market price of Bell Fashion was $15 per share.

2. Barb, Inc., obtained significant influence over Diner Corporation by buying 30% of Diner's 30,000 outstanding shares of common stock at a total cost of $9 per share on January 1, 1993. On June 15, Diner declared and paid a cash dividend of $35,000. On December 31, Diner reported a net income of $80,000 for the year.

Instructions
Prepare all the necessary journal entries for 1993 for (a) Karen Cosmetics and (b) Barb, Inc.

Prepare consolidated work sheet when cost equals book value.
(S.O. 5)

E18–9   On January 1, Swiss Corporation acquires 100% of Arco Inc. for $200,000 in cash. The condensed balance sheets of the two corporations immediately following the acquisition are as follows:

	Swiss Corporation	Arco Inc.
Current assets	$ 60,000	$ 40,000
Investment in Arco Inc. common stock	200,000	
Plant and equipment (net)	300,000	210,000
	$560,000	$250,000
Current liabilities	$180,000	$ 50,000
Common stock	225,000	75,000
Retained earnings	155,000	125,000
	$560,000	$250,000

Instructions
Prepare a work sheet for a consolidated balance sheet.

E18–10 Data for the Swiss and Arco corporations are presented in E18–9. Assume that instead of paying $200,000 in cash for Arco Inc., Swiss Corporation pays $215,000 in cash. Thus, at the acquisition date, the assets of Swiss Corporation are: Current assets $45,000, Investment in Arco Inc. Common Stock $215,000, and Plant and Equipment (net) $300,000.

Prepare consolidated work sheet when cost exceeds book value.
(S.O. 5)

Instructions
Prepare a work sheet for a consolidated balance sheet.

*E18–11 Bulla has been negotiating several months to purchase Salis, Inc. The book value of the net assets of Salis, Inc., is $9,000,000. At current market prices, Bulla Co. would issue $12,000,000 in common stock in exchange for all the common stock of Salis. The difference of $3,000,000 between cost and book value is attributable one-half to undervalued assets (inventory and property, plant and equipment) and the other half to a favorable earning capacity for Salis. Bulla and Salis reported $500,000 and $350,000 of net income for 1993, respectively. The business combination occurs on December 31, 1993.

Compute goodwill and net income in a business combination.
(S.O. 7)

Instructions
Compute (1) the amount of goodwill to be recognized and (2) net income to be reported under each of the following assumptions:

(a) Bulla Co. accounts for the combination as a pooling-of-interests.

(b) Bulla Co. accounts for the combination as a purchase.

PROBLEMS

P18–1 In January 1993, the management of the Reed Company concludes that it has sufficient cash to permit some temporary investments in marketable securities. During the year, the following transactions occurred:

Journalize temporary investment transactions, prepare adjusting entry, and show statement presentation.
(S.O. 1, 2)

Feb. 1 Purchased 800 shares of IBF common stock for $32,000 plus brokerage fees of $800.
Mar. 1 Purchased 500 shares of RST common stock for $15,000 plus brokerage fees of $500.
Apr. 1 Purchased 60 $1,000, 12% CRT bonds for $60,000 plus $1,200 brokerage fees. Interest is payable semiannually on April 1 and October 1.
July 1 Received a cash dividend of $.60 per share on the IBF common stock.
Aug. 1 Sold 200 shares of IBF common stock at $42 per share less brokerage fees of $350.
Sept. 1 Received a $1 per share cash dividend on the RST common stock.
Oct. 1 Received the semiannual interest on the CRT bonds.
Oct. 1 Sold the CRT bonds for $63,000 less $1,000 brokerage fees.

At December 31, the market value of the IBF and RST common stocks were $39 and $30 per share, respectively.

Instructions
(a) Journalize the transactions and post to the accounts, Marketable Equity Securities and Marketable Debt Securities. (Use the T-account form.)

(b) Prepare the adjusting entry at December 31, 1993, to report the marketable equity securities at the lower of cost or market value.

(c) Show the balance sheet presentation of marketable equity securities at December 31, 1993.

(d) Identify the income statement accounts and give the statement classification of each account.

Journalize long-term bond transactions and show balance sheet presentation.
(S.O. 3)

P18–2 The Lund Corporation has decided to change its investment strategy from short-term securities to long-term bonds. Lund Corporation uses the straight-line method of amortization. Its fiscal year ends on December 31. All bonds are acquired on their issue date. All bonds mature in 10 years, and interest is payable semiannually on January 1 and July 1. Lund Corporation does not keep separate accounts for bond discount or bond premium. The following transactions and events occurred over a two-year period:

1993

Jan.	1	Purchased $50,000 RAM Corporation 12% bonds for $52,000, including brokerage fees.
July	1	Received interest on RAM bonds.
Dec.	31	Accrued interest and amortized bond premium on RAM bonds.

1994

Jan.	1	Received interest on RAM bonds.
Jan.	1	Sold $25,000 RAM bonds for $27,500, net of brokerage fees.
July	1	Received interest on RAM bonds.
July	1	Purchased $70,000 CAL Corporation 10% bonds for $64,000 including brokerage fees.
Dec.	31	Accrued interest and amortized bond premium and bond discount on bonds held. (Make separate entries for each bond.)

Instructions

(a) Journalize the transactions using separate investment accounts for each bond.

(b) Show the balance sheet presentation of the bonds and bond interest receivable at December 31, 1994.

Journalize transactions and adjusting entry for long-term marketable equity securities.
(S.O. 4)

P18–3 On December 31, 1992, Harmon Associates owned the following portfolio of long-term marketable equity securities:

Common Stock	Shares	Cost
A Co.	1,000	$50,000
B Co.	6,000	36,000
C Co.	1,200	24,000

On this date, the market value of the portfolio was higher than cost. The securities are not held for influence or control over the investees. In 1993, the following transactions occurred:

July	1	Received $1 per share semiannual cash dividend on B Co. common stock.
Aug.	1	Received $.50 per share cash dividend on A Co. common stock.
Sept.	1	Sold 500 shares of B Co. common stock for cash at $8 per share less brokerage fees of $100.
Oct.	1	Sold 400 shares of A Co. common stock for cash at $54 per share less brokerage fees of $600.
Nov.	1	Received $1 per share cash dividend on C Co. common stock.
Dec.	15	Received $.50 per share cash dividend on A Co. common stock.
	31	Received $1 per share semiannual cash dividend on B Co. common stock.

At December 31, the market values per share of the common stocks were: A Co. $47, B Co. $6, and C Co. $18.

Instructions

(a) Journalize the 1993 transactions and post to the account, Marketable Equity Securities. (Use the T-account form.)

(b) Prepare the adjusting entry at December 31, 1993, to show the portfolio at the lower of cost or market value. (Show computations.)

(c) Show the balance sheet presentation of the investments at December 31, 1993. At this date, Harmon Associates has common stock $2,000,000 and retained earnings $1,200,000.

P18–4 Cardinal Concrete acquired 20% of the outstanding common stock of Edra, Inc., on January 1, 1993, by paying $1,200,000 for 50,000 shares. Edra declared and paid an $.80 per share cash dividend on June 30 and again on December 31, 1993. Edra reported net income of $700,000 for the year.

Prepare entries under lower of cost or market and equity methods and tabulate differences.
(S.O. 4)

Instructions

(a) Prepare the journal entries for Cardinal Concrete for 1993 assuming Cardinal cannot exercise significant influence over Edra(i.e., use the lower of cost or market method).

(b) Repeat (a) assuming Cardinal can exercise significant influence over Edra (i.e., use the equity method of accounting).

(c) In tabular form, indicate the investment and income statement account balances at December 31, 1993, under each method of accounting.

P18–5 Neal Company purchased all the outstanding common stock of Wheaton Company on December 31, 1993. Just before the purchase, the condensed balance sheets of the two companies were as follows:

Prepare consolidated work sheet and balance sheet when cost exceeds book value.
(S.O. 5, 6)

	Neal Company	Wheaton Company
Current assets	$1,476,000	$379,000
Plant and equipment (net)	1,882,000	353,000
	$3,358,000	$732,000
Current liabilities	$ 868,000	$ 92,000
Common stock	1,947,000	360,000
Retained earnings	543,000	280,000
	$3,358,000	$732,000

Neal used current assets of $726,000 to acquire the stock of Wheaton. The excess of this purchase price over the book value of Wheaton's net assets is determined to be attributable $30,000 to Wheaton's plant and equipment and the remainder to goodwill.

Instructions

(a) Prepare the entry for Neal Company's acquisition of Wheaton Company stock.

(b) Prepare a consolidated work sheet at December 31, 1993.

(c) Prepare a consolidated balance sheet at December 31, 1993.

P18–6 The following are in Hi-Tech Company's long-term investment portfolio of marketable securities at December 31, 1992.

Journalize long-term stock transactions and show statement presentation.
(S.O. 4)

	Cost
500 shares of Awixa Corporation common stock.	$26,000
700 shares of HAL Corporation common stock.	42,000
400 shares of Renda Corporation preferred stock.	16,800

On December 31, the cost of the portfolio exceeded market value by $2,000. Hi-Tech had the following transactions related to the securities during 1993:

Jan. 7 Sold 500 shares of Awixa Corporation common stock at $56 per share less brokerage fees of $700.

Jan. 10 Purchased 200 shares, $70 par value common stock of Mintor Corporation at $78 per share, plus brokerage fees of $240.

26 Received a cash dividend of $1.15 per share on HAL Corporation common stock.

Feb. 2 Received cash dividends of $.40 per share on Renda Corporation preferred stock.

10 Sold all 400 shares of Renda Corporation preferred stock at $28.00 per share less brokerage fees of $180.

April 30 Received 700 shares of HAL Corporation common stock as a result of a 2-for-1 stock split.

July 1 Received a cash dividend of $1.00 per share on HAL Corporation common stock.

Aug. 3 Received 20 shares of Mintor Corporation common stock as the result of a 10% stock dividend.

Sept. 1 Purchased an additional 400 shares of the $70 par value common stock of Mintor Corporation at $82 per share, plus brokerage fees of $400.

Dec. 15 Received a cash dividend of $1.50 per share on Mintor Corporation common stock.

At December 31, 1993, the prevailing market prices for the investments held by Hi-Tech were:

HAL Corporation common stock	$32 per share
Mintor Corporation common stock	$70 per share

Hi-Tech uses separate account titles for each investment, such as Investment in HAL Corporation Common Stock.

Instructions

(a) Prepare journal entries to record the transactions.

(b) Post to the investment accounts. (Use T accounts.)

(c) Prepare the adjusting entry to recognize the unrealized loss (if any) on the marketable equity securities portfolio at December 31, 1993.

(d) Show the balance sheet presentation at December 31, 1993, assuming only aggregate data are reported.

Prepare a consolidated balance sheet.
(S.O. 6)

P18–7 The following data, presented in alphabetical order, are taken from the consolidated work sheet for the Oklahoma Corporation and its wholly owned subsidiary, Tulsa, Inc., after all eliminations have been made.

Accounts payable	$ 240,000
Accounts receivable	110,000
Accumulated depreciation—building	180,000
Accumulated depreciation—equipment	52,000
Allowance for doubtful accounts	6,000
Allowance for excess of cost over market value of short-term marketable equity securities	5,000
Bonds payable, 10% due 2010	400,000
Bond sinking fund	100,000
Buildings	900,000
Cash	92,000
Common stock, $5 par value, 500,000 shares authorized, 300,000 shares issued	1,500,000
Discount on Bonds Payable	20,000
Dividends Payable	50,000
Equipment	275,000
Goodwill	200,000
Income taxes payable	120,000
Investment in Dallas Inc. bonds (long-term)	260,000
Investment in Houston Inc, stock (30% ownership), at equity	240,000
Land	500,000
Marketable equity securities (short-term), cost	190,000
Merchandise inventory	170,000
Notes payable	70,000
Organization costs	50,000
Paid-in capital in excess of par value	200,000
Prepaid insurance	16,000
Retained earnings	300,000

Instructions

Prepare a consolidated balance sheet at December 31, 1993.

*P18–8 The following information related to the separate balance sheets of Burns, Inc. and Sutter Company:

Assets	Burns, Inc.	Sutter Company
Cash	$160,000	$ 60,000
Notes receivable	50,000	25,000
Accounts receivable	25,000	7,500
Merchandise inventory	93,000	75,000
Marketable equity securities (current)	–0–	10,000
Investment in Sutter common stock	120,000	–0–
Total assets	$448,000	$177,500
Liabilities and Stockholders' Equity		
Notes payable (short term)	$ 50,000	$ 50,000
Accounts payable	110,000	22,500
Accrued liabilities	25,000	5,000
Common stock	90,000	40,000
Retained earnings	173,000	60,000
Total liabilities and stockholders' equity	$448,000	$177,500

These balance sheets were prepared immediately after Burns paid cash to acquire all the common stock of Sutter Company.

Instructions

(a) Should the business combination be recorded under the purchase or pooling-of-interests method? Explain.

(b) How much goodwill, if any, would be shown on the consolidated balance sheet? Assume that book value and market value are the same for the net assets of Sutter Company.

(c) What is the amount of consolidated retained earnings?

(d) What amount is reported for total assets on the consolidated balance sheet?

(e) Why might a company choose pooling of interests accounting instead of purchase accounting in a business combination?

Identify the type of business combination and answer questions about consolidated financial statements.
(S.O. 5, 6, 7)

ALTERNATE PROBLEMS

P18–1A In January, 1993, the management of the Mead Company concludes that it has sufficient cash to permit some temporary investments in marketable securities. During the year, the following transactions occurred:

Feb. 1 Purchased 600 shares of CBF common stock for $31,800 plus brokerage fees of $600.

Mar. 1 Purchased 800 shares of RSD common stock for $20,000 plus brokerage fees of $400.

Apr. 1 Purchased 50 $1,000, 12% MRT bonds for $50,000 plus $1,000 brokerage fees. Interest is payable semiannually on April 1 and October 1.

July 1 Received a cash dividend of $.60 per share on the CBF common stock.

Aug. 1 Sold 200 shares of CBF common stock at $56 per share less brokerage fees of $200.

Sept. 1 Received a $1 per share cash dividend on the RSD common stock.

Oct. 1 Received the semiannual interest on the MRT bonds.

Oct. 1 Sold the MRT bonds for $51,000 less $1,000 brokerage fees.

At December 31, the market value of the CBF and RSD common stocks were $55 and $24 per share, respectively.

Journalize temporary investment transactions, prepare adjusting entry, and show statement presentation.
(S.O. 1, 2)

Instructions

(a) Journalize the transactions and post to the accounts Marketable Equity Securities and Marketable Debt Securities. (Use the T-account form.)

(b) Prepare the adjusting entry at December 31, 1993, to report the marketable equity securities at the lower of cost or market value.

(c) Show the balance sheet presentation of marketable equity securities at December 31, 1993.

(d) Identify the income statement accounts and give the statement classification of each account.

Journalize long-term bond transactions and show balance sheet presentation. (S.O. 3)

P18–2A   The Fremont Corporation has decided to change its investment strategy from short-term securities to long-term bonds. Fremont Corporation uses the straight-line method of amortization. Its fiscal year ends on December 31. All bonds are acquired on their issue date. All bonds mature in 10 years, and interest is payable semiannually on January 1 and July 1. Fremont Corporation does not keep separate accounts for bond discount or bond premium. The following transactions and events occurred over a two-year period:

<u>1993</u>

Jan. 1   Purchased $60,000 DOT Corporation 12% bonds for $63,000, including brokerage fees.
July 1   Received interest on DOT bonds.
Dec. 31   Accrued interest and amortized bond premium on DOT bonds.

<u>1994</u>

Jan. 1   Received interest on DOT bonds.
Jan. 1   Sold $30,000 DOT bonds for $31,200 net of brokerage fees.
July 1   Received interest on DOT bonds.
July 1   Purchased $50,000 PAT Corporation 10% bonds for $46,000, including brokerage fees.
Dec. 31   Accrued interest and amortized bond premium and bond discount on bonds held. (Make separate entries for each bond.)

Instructions

(a) Journalize the transactions using separate investment accounts for each bond.

(b) Show the balance sheet presentation of the bonds and bond interest receivable at December 31, 1994.

Journalize transactions and adjusting entry for long-term marketable equity securities. (S.O. 4)

P18–3A   On December 31, 1993, Karen Associates owned the following portfolio of long-term marketable equity securities. The securities are not held for influence or control of the investee.

Common Stock	Shares	Cost
X Co.	2,000	$90,000
Y Co.	5,000	45,000
Z Co.	1,500	30,000

On this date, the market value of the portfolio was higher than cost. In 1994, the following transactions occurred.

July 1   Received $1 per share semiannual cash dividend on Y Co. common stock.
     8   Received 4,000 shares of X Co. common stock in a 3 for 1 stock split.
Aug. 1   Received $.50 per share cash dividend on X Co. common stock.
Sept. 1   Sold 700 shares of Y Co. common stock for cash at $8 per share less brokerage fees of $200.
Oct. 1   Sold 600 shares of X Co. common stock for cash at $18 per share less brokerage fees of $500.
Nov. 1   Received $1 per share cash dividend on Z Co. common stock.
Dec. 15   Received $.50 per share cash dividend on X Co. common stock.
     31   Received $1 per share semiannual cash dividend on Y Co. common stock.

At December 31, the market values per share of the common stocks were: X Co. $16, Y Co. $8, and Z Co. $17.

Instructions

(a) Journalize the 1994 transactions and post to the account Marketable Equity Securities. (Use the T-account form.)

(b) Prepare the adjusting entry at December 31, 1994, to show the portfolio at the lower of cost or market value. (Show computations.)

(c) Show the balance sheet presentation of the investments at December 31, 1994. At this date, Karen Associates has common stock $1,500,000 and retained earnings $1,000,000.

P18–4A DFM Services acquired 30% of the outstanding common stock of BNA Company on January 1, 1993, by paying $800,000 for the 40,000 shares. BNA declared and paid $.20 per share cash dividends on March 15, June 15, September 15, and December 15, 1993. BNA reported net income of $350,000 for the year.

Prepare entries under the lower of cost or market and equity methods and tabulate differences. (S.O. 4)

Instructions

(a) Prepare the journal entries for DFM Services for 1993 assuming DFM cannot exercise significant influence over BNA (i.e., use the lower of cost or market method of accounting).

(b) Repeat (a) assuming DFM can exercise significant influence over BNA (i.e., use the equity method of accounting).

(c) In tabular form, indicate the investment and income statement account balances at December 31, 1993, under each method of accounting.

P18–5A Linger Corporation purchased all the outstanding common stock of Chrissy Foods, Inc. on December 31, 1993. Just before the purchase, the condensed balance sheets of the two companies appeared as follows:

Prepare consolidated work sheet and balance sheet when cost exceeds book value. (S.O. 6)

	Linger Corporation	Chrissy Foods, Inc.
Current assets	$1,480,000	$ 439,500
Plant and equipment (net)	2,100,000	672,000
	$3,580,000	$1,111,500
Current liabilities	$ 578,000	$ 92,500
Common stock	1,950,000	525,000
Retained earnings	1,052,000	494,000
	$3,580,000	$1,111,500

Linger used current assets of $1,200,000 to acquire the stock of Chrissy Foods. The excess of this purchase price over the book value of Chrissy Foods' net assets is determined to be attributable $81,000 to Chrissy Foods' plant and equipment and the remainder to goodwill.

Instructions

(a) Prepare the entry for Linger's acquisition of Chrissy Foods, Inc. stock.

(b) Prepare a consolidated work sheet at December 31, 1993.

(c) Prepare a consolidated balance sheet at December 31, 1993.

*B*roadening Your Perspective

FINANCIAL REPORTING PROBLEM

The annual report of PepsiCo, Inc. is presented in Appendix L.

Instructions

Answer the following questions.

1. What information about investments is reported in the consolidated balance sheet?

2. Based on the information under Assets in Management's Analysis of Financial Condition, what is the nature of PepsiCo, Inc.'s short-term investments?

3. Using the information under Interest Income in Management's Analysis of the Results of Operations, what effect did investments have on Income from Continuing Operations Before Income Taxes in 1991?

4. Using the Statement of Cash Flows, did cash flows from investment activities increase or decrease in 1991 and by how much?

5. Based on the information under Investment Activities in Management's Analysis of Cash Flows, what types of investments have been made in (a) recent years and (b) 1991? Does management expect investing activity to increase in 1992?

6. From the Notes to Consolidated Financial Statements:
    (a) What principles of consolidation were followed by PepsiCo, Inc?
    (b) How were PepsiCo's acquisitions and investments in affiliates financed in 1991?
    (c) How were the acquisitions accounted for?
    (d) Did any goodwill or other intangibles result from the 1991 acquisitions? Explain.
    (e) How are goodwill and other intangibles amortized?

DECISION CASE

At the beginning of the question and answer portion of the annual stockholders' meeting of Revell Corporation, stockholder Carol Finstrom asks, "Why did management sell the holdings in AHM Company at a loss when this company has been very profitable during the period its stock was held by Revell?"

Since president Larry Wisdom has just concluded his speech on the recent success and bright future of Revell, he is taken aback by this question and responds, "I remember we paid $1,100,000 for that stock some years ago, and I am sure we sold that stock at a much higher price. You must be mistaken."

Finstrom retorts, "Well, right here in footnote number 7 to the annual report it shows that 240,000 shares, a 30% interest in AHM, was sold on the last day of the year. Also, it states that AHM earned $550,000 this year and paid out $150,000 in cash dividends. Further, a summary statement indicates that in past years, while Revell held AHM stock, AHM earned $1,240,000 and paid out $440,000 in dividends. Finally, the income statement for this year shows a loss on the sale of AHM stock of $180,000. So, I doubt that I am mistaken."

Red-faced, president Wisdom turns to you.

Instructions
What dollar amount did Revell receive upon the sale of the AHM stock? Explain why both stockholder Finstrom and president Wisdom are correct.

CRITICAL THINKING CASE

Refer to the University of Colorado-Boulder funds management story at the beginning of this chapter and use what you learned in this chapter to answer the following questions:

1. The stock market is depicted as "a relatively volatile place to put money" and "is just too risky." Glen Stine concluded by saying, "We don't feel that going into the stock market allows us to pick the time that we can get our money out." Why then did Mr. Stine feel comfortable investing about 70% of the endowment fund in the stock market?

2. Where does the University of Colorado invest the cash used in day-to-day operations? What is one drawback to these investments?

3. How might Mr. Stine protect the University's various funds from interest rate volatility?

4. If Mr. Stine invests in 20-year blue chip (high-grade, AA+) corporate bonds today, what rate of interest would they pay? What are the names of three corporations that have high-grade bonds outstanding?

ETHICAL CASE

Denson Fashions Corporation holds a portfolio of stock as a short-term marketable security. The market value of the portfolio is greater than its original cost, even though some holdings have decreased in value. Shirley Denson, the financial vice-president, and Jo Niceley, the controller, are considering the sale of a part of this stock portfolio. Shirley wants to sell only those holdings which have increased in value, in order to increase net income this year. Jo disagrees and wants to sell securities that have recently declined in value. Jo contends that the company is having a good earnings year and therefore the losses will help to smooth the income this year. As a result, the company will have built-in gains for future periods when the company may not be as profitable.

Instructions
Is there an ethical issue in this discussion? Can either of their recommendations be implemented?

Answers to Self-Study Questions
1. c   2. c   3. b   4. c   5. a   6. c   7. a   8. b   9. d   10. d
11. c

CONCEPTS FOR REVIEW

Before studying this chapter you should know or, if necessary, review:

a. *The difference between the accrual basis and the cash basis of accounting. (Ch. 3, p. 106–7)*
b. *The major items included in a corporation's balance sheet. (Ch. 18, p. 728–9)*
c. *The major items included in a corporation's income statement. (Ch. 16, p. 636)*

STATEMENT OF CASH FLOWS

For Gerald Biby, vice president and chief financial officer of Kilian Community College in Sioux Falls, South Dakota, the statement of cash flows was the difference between being able to refinance a mortgage and being turned down by six local banks. "We recently wanted to refinance a $125,000 mortgage on a piece of property that we own," he says. "It was the statement of cash flows that finally showed our lender that we had the cash flow to service the debt."

As he explains, the traditional financial statement for a not-for-profit, educational institution shows revenues and all expenditures, even the capital expenditures. According to this format, which the banks focused on initially, Kilian Community College was just breaking even. "In the business world, if we had spent $250,000 on a computer system, then we would have put that on a depreciation schedule. But in the non-profit arena, it's typical that the entire $250,000 is written off as an expense against the general fund." The statement of cash flows showed the bankers that one of *the uses of funds was really the purchase of computer equipment that had several years of life.*

The statement of cash flows has over 30 different classifications including tuition, fees, bookstore revenues, and so on. The school has 250 students, charges $70 a credit hour (12 hours is a full-time schedule), and has five terms each year.

The bankers granted the refinancing when they saw that the college's source of funds exceeded the loan repayments, including principal and interest, by a ratio of 3-to-1. Not only did the school get the loan, but it did so at a favorable rate. "We were able to cut the mortgage rate to prime plus 1% from prime plus 3%."

As the preceding story indicates, the balance sheet, income statement, and retained earnings statement do not always show the whole picture of the financial condition of a company or institution. In fact, looking at the three traditional financial statements of some well-known companies, a thoughtful investor might have questions like the following: How did Eastman Kodak finance cash dividends of $649 million in 1991 when it earned only $17 million? How was IBM able to absorb a $2.3 billion charge for postretirement benefits in 1991 when it reported its first-ever loss of $2.8 billion? How could Delta Airlines purchase new planes costing $900 million in a year in which it reported a net loss of $86 million? How did Kohlberg Kravis Roberts finance its record-shattering $25 billion purchase of RJR Nabisco? Answers to these and similar questions can be found in a fourth basic financial statement, the **statement of cash flows**. As you will see in studying this chapter, a company's reported earnings may in fact, have little resemblance to the firm's actual cash flow generated as a result of doing business.

Purpose of the Statement of Cash Flows

Study Objective 1

Indicate the primary purpose of the statement of cash flows.

The primary purpose of the statement of cash flows is to provide information about the cash receipts and cash payments of an entity during a period. A secondary objective is to provide information about the operating, investing, and financing activities of the entity during the period.[1] The statement of cash flows reports the cash receipts, cash payments, and net change in cash resulting from the operating, investing, and financing activities of an enterprise during a period in a format that reconciles the beginning and ending cash balances.

A statement of cash flows is needed because the other three basic financial statements present only limited and fragmentary information about a company's cash flows (cash receipts and cash payments). For example, comparative balance sheets show the increase in property, plant, and equipment during the year, but they do not show how the additions were financed or paid for. The income statement shows net income, but it does not indicate the amount of cash generated by operating activities. Similarly, the retained earnings statement shows cash dividends declared but not the cash dividends paid during the year. None

---

[1]"Statement of Cash Flows," *Statement of Financial Accounting Standards No. 95* (Stamford, Conn.: FASB, 1987).

of these statements presents a detailed summary of the net change in cash as a result of operating, investing, and financing activities during the period.

Reporting the causes of changes in cash is considered useful because investors, creditors, and other interested parties want to know what is happening to a company's most liquid resource—its cash. A statement of cash flows helps us know what is happening. It provides answers to the following simple, but important, questions about the enterprise:

1. Where did the cash come from during the period?
2. What was the cash used for during the period?
3. What was the change in the cash balance during the period?

Meaning of Cash Flows

The statement of cash flows is generally prepared using "**cash and cash equivalents**" as its basis. Cash equivalents are short-term, highly liquid investments that are both:

1. Readily convertible to known amounts of cash, and
2. So near their maturity that their market value is relatively insensitive to changes in interest rates.

Generally, only investments with original maturities of three months or less qualify under this definition. Examples of cash equivalents are Treasury bills, commercial paper (short-term corporate notes), and money market funds. All typically are purchased with cash that is in excess of immediate needs. Note that since cash and cash equivalents are viewed as the same, transfers between cash and cash equivalents are not treated as cash receipts and cash payments—i.e., they are not reported in the statement of cash flows. The term cash when used in this chapter includes cash and cash equivalents.

Classification of Cash Flows

The statement of cash flows classifies cash receipts and cash payments by operating, investing, and financing activities. Transactions and other events characteristic of each kind of activity are as follows:

1. Operating activities include the cash effects of transactions that create revenues and expenses and thus enter into the determination of net income.
2. Investing activities include (a) acquiring and disposing of investments and productive long-lived assets and (b) lending money and collecting the loans.

3. Financing activities include (a) obtaining cash from issuing debt and repaying the amounts borrowed, and (b) obtaining cash from stockholders and providing them with a return on their investment.

The category of operating activities is the most important because it shows the cash provided by company operations. This source of cash is generally considered to be the best measure of a company's ability to generate sufficient cash to continue as a going concern. Illustration 19-1 lists typical cash receipts and cash payments within each of the three classifications. Study the list carefully. It will prove very useful in solving homework exercises and problems.

ILLUSTRATION 19-1

Typical receipts and payments classified by activity.

Helpful hint Operating activities generally relate to changes in current assets and current liabilities. Investing activities generally relate to changes in noncurrent assets, and financing activities relate to changes in noncurrent liabilities and stockholders' equity accounts.

Types of Cash Inflows and Outflows

Operating activities
Cash inflows
  From sale of goods or services.
  From returns on loans (interest received) and on equity securities (dividends received).
Cash outflows
  To suppliers for inventory.
  To employees for services.
  To government for taxes.
  To lenders for interest.
  To others for expenses.
Investing activities
Cash inflows
  From sale of property, plant, and equipment.
  From sale of debt or equity securities of other entities.
  From collection of principal on loans to other entities.
Cash outflows
  To purchase property, plant, and equipment.
  To purchase debt or equity securities of other entities.
  To make loans to other entities.
Financing activities
Cash inflows
  From sale of equity securities (company's own stock).
  From issuance of debt (bonds and notes).
Cash outflows
  To stockholders as dividends.
  To redeem long-term debt or reacquire capital stock.

As you can see, some cash flows relating to investing or financing activities are classified as operating activities. For example, receipts of investment revenue (interest and dividends) and payments of interest to lenders are classified as operating activities because these items are reported in the income statement.

Note that, generally, (1) operating activities involve income determination (income statement) items, (2) investing activities involve cash flows resulting from changes in investments and long-term asset items, and (3) financing activities involve cash flows resulting from changes in long-term liability and stockholders' equity items.

Significant Noncash Activities

If the statement of cash flows reports only the effects of cash transactions, some significant noncash investing and financing activities may be omitted. Examples of significant noncash activities are:

1. Issuance of common stock to purchase assets.
2. Conversion of bonds into common stock.
3. Issuance of debt to purchase assets.
4. Exchanges of plant assets.

Significant financing and investing activities not affecting cash are not reported in the body of the statement of cash flows. However, these activities are reported in either a separate schedule at the bottom of the statement of cash flows or in a separate note or supplementary schedule to the financial statements.

The reporting of these activities in a separate note or supplementary schedule satisfies the full disclosure principle because it identifies significant noncash investing and financing activities of the enterprise. In solving homework assignments you should present significant noncash investing and financing activities in a separate schedule at the bottom of the statement of cash flows (see lower section of Illustration 19-2).

Helpful hint Do not include noncash investing and financing activities in the body of the statement of cash flows. Report this information in a separate schedule at the bottom of the statement.

Accounting in Action · *Business Insight*

The differences between companies' net income and net cash provided by operating activities is illustrated by the following net income per share and cash flow per share data for six different computer software companies:

	PER SHARE	
COMPANY/SOFTWARE	NET INCOME	CASH FLOW
Borland/PC languages, applications	$0.03	$ – 0.25
Computer Associates/mainframe utilities	1.25	0.43
Lotus Development/PC spreadsheets	1.58	1.30
Microsoft/MS-DOS, applications	2.22	0.61
Oracle/relational database program	0.65	0.13
Systematics/banking systems	1.39	1.69

Except for Systematics, the cash flow per share is lower than earnings per share for all of these software companies. Why?

Format of Statement of Cash Flows

The three activities discussed above—operating, investing, and financing—plus the significant noncash investing and financing activities constitute the general format of the statement of cash flows. A widely used form of the statement of cash flows is shown in Illustration 19-2.

As illustrated, the cash flows from operating activities section always appears first, followed by the investing activities and the financing activities sections. Also, **the individual inflows and outflows from investing and financing activities are reported separately**. Thus, cash outflow for the purchase of property, plant, and equipment is reported separately from the cash inflow from the

ILLUSTRATION 19-2

Format of statement of cash flows

COMPANY NAME Statement of Cash Flows Period Covered		
Cash flows from operating activities		
(List of individual items)	XX	
Net cash provided (used) by operating activities		XXX
Cash flows from investing activities		
(List of individual inflows and outflows)	XX	
Net cash provided (used) by investing activities		XXX
Cash flows from financing activities		
(List of individual inflows and outflows)	XX	
Net cash provided (used) by financing activities		XXX
Net increase (decrease) in cash		XXX
Cash at beginning of period		XXX
Cash at end of period		XXX
Noncash investing and financing activities		
(List of individual noncash transactions)		XXX

sale of property, plant, and equipment. Similarly, the cash inflow from the issuance of debt securities is reported separately from the cash outflow for the retirement of debt. Not reporting the inflows and outflows separately obscures the investing and financing activities of the enterprise and thus makes it more difficult to assess future cash flows.

The operating, investing, and financing activities as reported result in either net cash provided or used by each activity. The net cash provided or used by each activity is totaled to show the net increase (decrease) in cash for the period. The beginning-of-the-period cash balance is then increased or decreased by the net change in cash for the period to reconcile to the end of the period cash balance. Finally, if the company has any significant noncash investing and financing activities, they are reported in a separate schedule at the bottom of the statement.

Preparing the Statement of Cash Flows

The statement of cash flows is prepared differently than the three other basic financial statements. First, it is not prepared from an adjusted trial balance. Because the statement requires detailed information concerning the changes in account balances that occurred between two periods of time, an adjusted trial balance will not provide the necessary data for the statement. Second, the statement of cash flows deals with cash receipts and payments. As a result, **the accrual concept is not used in the preparation of a statement of cash flows**.

The information to prepare this statement usually comes from three sources:

Comparative balance sheet. Information in this statement indicates the amount of the changes in assets, liabilities, and stockholders' equities from the beginning to the end of the period.

Current income statement. Information in this statement helps the reader determine the amount of cash provided by or used by operations during the period.

Additional information. Additional information includes transaction data that are needed to determine how cash was provided or used during the period.

Preparing the statement of cash flows from these data sources involves three major steps:

1. **Determine the net increase/decrease in cash.** The difference between the beginning and ending cash balances can be easily computed from comparative balance sheets.
2. **Determine net cash provided/used by operating activities.** This step involves analyzing not only the current year's income statement but also comparative balance sheets and selected additional data.
3. **Determine net cash provided/used by investing and financing activities.** This step involves analyzing comparative balance sheet data and selected additional information for their effects on cash.

Indirect and Direct Methods

In order to perform Step 2, the operating activities section of the statement of cash flows must be converted from an accrual basis to a cash basis. This may be done by either of two methods: (1) the indirect method or (2) the direct method. Both methods arrive at the same total amount for "Net cash provided by operating activities," but they differ in disclosing the items that comprise the total amount. The indirect method is used extensively in practice. The following pie chart indicates its high usage.[2]

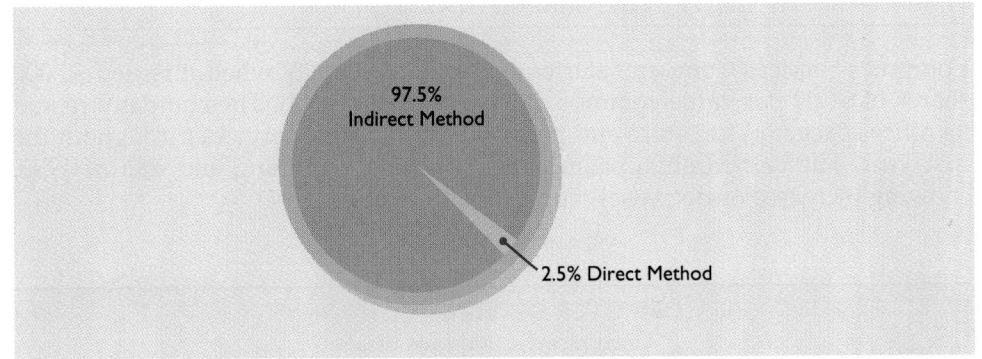

97.5%
Indirect Method

2.5% Direct Method

ILLUSTRATION 19-3

Usage of indirect and direct methods

Companies favor the use of the indirect method for two reasons: (1) it is easier to prepare, and (2) it focuses on the differences between net income and net cash flow from operating activities.

Others, however, favor the direct method. The direct method shows operating cash receipts and payments. Thus, it is more consistent with the objective of a statement of cash flows. The FASB has expressed a preference for the direct method. But when the direct method is used, the net cash flow from operating activities as computed using the indirect method must also be reported in a separate schedule.

Section 1 of this chapter illustrates the indirect method; Section 2 illustrates the direct method. These sections are independent of each other; only one or the other need be covered in order to understand and prepare the statement of cash flows.

---

[2]*Accounting Trends and Techniques–1991* (New York: American Institute of Certified Public Accountants, 1992), page 420.

Before You Go On . . .

1. What is the primary purpose of a statement of cash flows?

2. What are the major classifications of cash flows on the statement of cash flows?

3. What are the three major steps in the preparation of a statement of cash flows?

SECTION 1 Statement of Cash Flows—Indirect Method

Study Objective 3

Prepare a statement of cash flows using the indirect method.

To explain and illustrate the indirect method, we will use the transactions of the Computer Services Company for two years—1993 and 1994. Annual statements of cash flows will be prepared. Basic transactions will be used in the first year with additional transactions added in the second year.

First Year of Operations—1993

Computer Services Company started on January 1, 1993, when it issued 50,000 shares of $1.00 par value common stock for $50,000 cash. The company rented its office space and furniture and performed consulting services throughout the first year. The comparative balance sheets at the beginning and end of 1993, showing increases or decreases, appear in Illustration 19-4.

ILLUSTRATION 19-4

Comparative balance sheet, 1993, with increases and decreases

Helpful hint Note that although each of the balance sheet items of Computer Services increased, their individual effects are not the same. Some of these increases are cash inflows, and some are cash outflows.

COMPUTER SERVICES COMPANY
Comparative Balance Sheet

Assets	Dec. 31, 1993	Jan. 1, 1993	Change Increase/Decrease
Cash	$34,000	$ –0–	$34,000 Increase
Accounts receivable	30,000	–0–	30,000 Increase
Equipment	10,000	–0–	10,000 Increase
Total	$74,000	$ –0–	
Liabilities and Stockholders' Equity			
Accounts payable	$ 4,000	$ –0–	$ 4,000 Increase
Common stock	50,000	–0–	50,000 Increase
Retained earnings	20,000	–0–	20,000 Increase
Total	$74,000	$ –0–	

The income statement and additional information for Computer Services Company are shown in Illustration 19-5.

ILLUSTRATION 19-5

Income statement and additional information, 1993

COMPUTER SERVICES COMPANY
Income Statement
For the Year Ended December 31, 1993

Revenues	$85,000
Operating expenses	40,000
Income before income taxes	45,000
Income tax expense	10,000
Net income	$35,000

Additional information:
(a) Examination of selected data indicates that a dividend of $15,000 was paid during the year.
(b) The equipment was purchased at the end of 1993. No depreciation is taken in 1993.

Determining the Net Increase/Decrease in Cash (Step 1)

To prepare a statement of cash flows, the first step is **determining the net increase or decrease in cash**. This is a simple computation. For example, Computer Services Company had no cash on hand at the beginning of 1993, but $34,000 was on hand at the end of 1993. Thus, the change in cash for 1993 was an increase of $34,000.

Determining Net Cash Provided/Used by Operating Activities (Step 2)

To determine net cash provided by operating activities under the indirect method, net income is adjusted for items that did not affect cash. A useful starting point in **determining net cash provided by operating activities** is to understand why net income must be converted. Under generally accepted accounting principles, most companies use the accrual basis of accounting. This basis requires that revenue be recorded when earned and that expenses be recorded when incurred. Earned revenues may include credit sales that have not been collected in cash and expenses incurred that may not have been paid in cash. Thus, under the accrual basis of accounting, net income will not indicate the net cash provided by operating activities.

The indirect method (or reconciliation method) starts with net income and converts it to net cash provided by operating activities. In other words, **the indirect method adjusts net income for items that affected reported net income but did not affect cash** as shown in Illustration 19-6. That is, noncash charges in the income statement are added back to net income and noncash credits are

Helpful hint You may wish to insert the beginning and ending cash balances and the increase/decrease in cash necessitated by these balances immediately into the statement of cash flows. The net increase/decrease is the target amount. The net cash flows from the three classes of activity must equal the target amount.

ILLUSTRATION 19-6

Net income versus net cash provided by operating activities

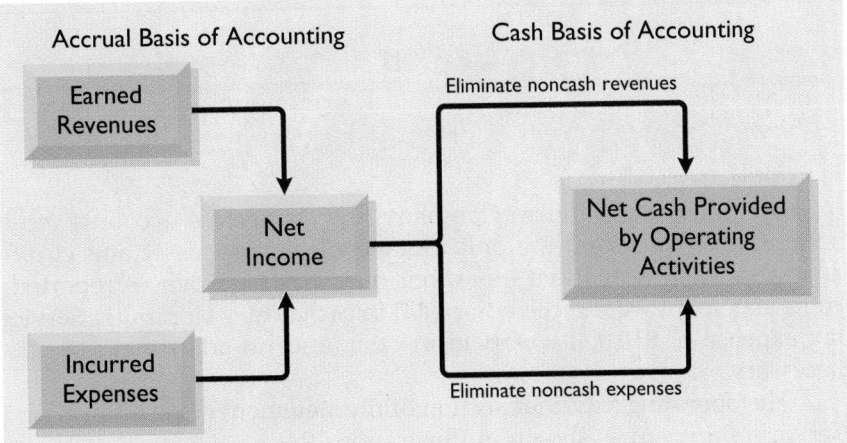

deducted to compute net cash provided by operating activities. A useful starting point to identify the adjustments to net income is to analyze the current asset and current liability accounts other than cash (receivables, payables, prepayments, and inventories) for their effects on cash. Explanations for the adjustments to net income for Computer Services Company under the indirect method are as follows.

INCREASE IN ACCOUNTS RECEIVABLE. When accounts receivable increase during the year, revenues on an accrual basis are higher than revenues on a cash basis. In other words, operations of the period led to increased revenues, **but not all of these revenues resulted in an increase in cash**. Some of the increase in revenues resulted in an increase in accounts receivable. To convert net income to net cash provided by operating activities, the increase of $30,000 in accounts receivable must be deducted from net income.

A T-account analysis shows why the cash receipts from customers are less than revenues on an accrual basis.

ILLUSTRATION 19-7

Analysis of accounts receivable

ACCOUNTS RECEIVABLE				
1/1/93 Balance	–0–	Receipts from customers	55,000
Revenues	85,000		
12/31/93 Balance	30,000		

INCREASE IN ACCOUNTS PAYABLE. In the first year, operating expenses incurred on account were credited to Accounts Payable. When accounts payable increase during the year, operating expenses on an accural basis are higher than they are on a cash basis. For Computer Services, operating expenses reported in the income statement were $40,000. However, since Accounts Payable increased $4,000, only $36,000 ($40,000 − $4,000) of the expenses were paid in cash. To adjust net income to net cash provided by operating activities, the increase of $4,000 in accounts payable must be added to net income.

A T-account analysis also indicates that payments to creditors are less than operating expenses.

ILLUSTRATION 19-8

Analysis of accounts payable

ACCOUNTS PAYABLE				
Payments to creditors	36,000	1/1/93 Balances	–0–
		Operating expenses	40,000
		12/31/93 Balance	4,000

For Computer Services Company, the changes in accounts receivable and accounts payable were the only changes in current asset and current liability accounts. This means that any other revenues or expenses reported in the income statement were received or paid in cash. Thus, Computer Services' income tax expense of $10,000 was paid in cash, and no adjustment of net income is necessary.

The operating activities section of the statement of cash flows for Computer Services Company is shown in Illustration 19-9.

Cash flows from operating activities		
Net income		$35,000
Adjustments to reconcile net income to net cash provided by operating activities:		
Increase in accounts receivable	$(30,000)	
Increase in accounts payable	4,000	(26,000)
Net cash provided by operating activities		**$ 9,000**

Determining Net Cash Provided/Used by Investing and Financing Activities (Step 3)

The third and final step in preparing the statement of cash flows begins with a study of the balance sheet to determine changes in noncurrent accounts. The changes in each noncurrent account are then analyzed using selected transaction data to determine the effect, if any, the changes had on cash.

In Computer Services Company, the three noncurrent accounts are Equipment, Common Stock, and Retained Earnings, and all three have increased during the year. What caused these increases? No transaction data are given for the increases in Equipment of $10,000 and Common Stock of $50,000. In solving your homework, you can conclude that any unexplained differences in noncurrent accounts involve cash. Thus, the increase in equipment is assumed to be a purchase of equipment for $10,000 cash. This purchase is reported as a cash outflow in the investing activities section. The increase in common stock is assumed to result from the issuance of common stock for $50,000 cash. It is reported as an inflow of cash in the financing activities section of the statement of cash flows.

The reasons for the net increase of $20,000 in the Retained Earnings account are determined by analysis. First, net income increased retained earnings by $35,000. Second, the additional information provided below the income statement in Illustration 19-5 indicates that a cash dividend of $15,000 was paid. The $35,000 increase due to net income is reported in the operating activities section. The cash dividend paid is reported in the financing activities section.

This analysis can also be made directly from the Retained Earnings account in the ledger of Computer Services Company as shown in Illustration 19-10:

ILLUSTRATION 19-10

Analysis of retained earnings

RETAINED EARNINGS				
12/31/93 Cash dividend	15,000	1/1/93 Balance		–0–
		12/31/93 Net income		35,000
		12/31/93 Balance		20,000

The $20,000 increase in Retained Earnings in 1993 is a **net** change. When a net change in a noncurrent balance sheet account has occurred during the year, it generally is necessary to report the causes of the net change separately in the statement of cash flows.

Statement of Cash Flows—1993

Having completed the three steps above, the statement of cash flows is prepared now. The statement starts with the operating activities section, followed by the investing activities section, and then the financing activities section. The statement of cash flows for Computer Services Company is shown in Illustration 19-11.

ILLUSTRATION 19-11

Statement of cash flows,
1993—indirect method

COMPUTER SERVICES COMPANY Statement of Cash Flows For the Year Ended December 31, 1993			
Cash flows from operating activities			
Net income			$35,000
Adjustments to reconcile net income to net cash provided by operating activities:			
Increase in accounts receivable		$(30,000)	
Increase in accounts payable		4,000	(26,000)
Net cash provided by operating activities			9,000
Cash flows from investing activities			
Purchase of equipment		(10,000)	
Net cash used by investing activities			(10,000)
Cash flows from financing activities			
Issuance of common stock		50,000	
Payment of cash dividends		(15,000)	
Net cash provided by financing activities			35,000
Net increase in cash			34,000
Cash at beginning of period			–0–
Cash at end of period			$34,000

Computer Services' statement of cash flows for 1993 shows that operating activities **provided** $9,000 cash, investing activities **used** $10,000 cash, and financing activities **provided** $35,000 cash. The increase in cash of $34,000 reported in the statement of cash flows agrees with the increase of $34,000 shown as the change in the cash account in the comparative balance sheet.

Second Year of Operations—1994

Presented in Illustrations 19-12 and 19-13 is information related to the second year of operations for Computer Services Company.

ILLUSTRATION 19-12

Comparative balance sheet,
1994, with increases and
decreases

COMPUTER SERVICES COMPANY Comparative Balance Sheet December 31			
Assets	1994	1993	Change Increase/Decrease
Cash	$ 56,000	$34,000	$ 22,000 Increase
Accounts receivable	20,000	30,000	10,000 Decrease
Prepaid expenses	4,000	–0–	4,000 Increase
Land	130,000	–0–	130,000 Increase
Building	160,000	–0–	160,000 Increase
Accumulated depreciation—building	(11,000)	–0–	11,000 Increase
Equipment	27,000	10,000	17,000 Increase
Accumulated depreciation—equipment	(3,000)	–0–	3,000 Increase
Total	$383,000	$74,000	
Liabilities and Stockholders' Equity			
Accounts payable	$ 59,000	$ 4,000	$ 55,000 Increase
Bonds payable	130,000	–0–	130,000 Increase
Common stock	50,000	50,000	–0–
Retained earnings	144,000	20,000	124,000 Increase
Total	$383,000	$74,000	

ILLUSTRATION 19-13

Income statement and additional information, 1994

COMPUTER SERVICES COMPANY
Income Statement
For the Year Ended December 31, 1994

Revenues		$507,000
Operating expenses (excluding depreciation)	$261,000	
Depreciation expense	15,000	
Loss on sale of equipment	3,000	279,000
Income from operations		228,000
Income tax expense		89,000
Net income		$139,000

Additional information:
(a) In 1994, the company paid a $15,000 cash dividend.
(b) The company obtained land through the issuance of $130,000 of long-term bonds.
(c) A building costing $160,000 was purchased for cash; equipment costing $25,000 was also purchased for cash.
(d) During 1994, the company sold equipment with a book value of $7,000 (cost $8,000, less accumulated depreciation $1,000) for $4,000 cash.

Determining the Net Increase/Decrease in Cash (Step 1)

To prepare a statement of cash flows from this information, the first step is to **determine the net increase or decrease in cash**. As indicated from the information presented, cash increased $22,000 ($56,000 − $34,000). The second and third steps are discussed below.

Determining Net Cash Provided/Used by Operating Activities (Step 2)

Net income on an accrual basis must be adjusted to arrive at net cash provided/used by operating activities. Explanations for the adjustments to net income for Computer Services in 1994 are as follows:

DECREASE IN ACCOUNTS RECEIVABLE. Accounts receivable decreases during the period because cash receipts are higher than revenues reported on an accrual basis. To adjust net income to net cash provided by operating activities, the decrease of $10,000 in accounts receivable must be added to net income.

Helpful hint Decrease in accounts receivable: Indicates that cash collections were greater than sales. Increase in accounts receivable: Indicates that sales were greater than cash collections. Increase in prepaid expenses: Indicates that the amount paid for the prepayments exceeded the amount that was recorded as an expense. Decrease in prepaid expenses: Indicates that the amount recorded as an expense exceeded the amount of cash paid for the prepayments.

INCREASE IN PREPAID EXPENSES. When prepaid expenses increase during a period, expenses in an accrual basis income statement are lower than cash paid for expenses. Cash payments have been made in the current period, but expenses (as charges to the income statement) have been deferred to future periods. To convert net income to net cash provided by operating activities, the increase of $4,000 in prepaid expenses must be deducted from net income. An increase in prepaid expenses results in a decrease in cash during the period.

Helpful hint An increase in accounts payable indicates that expenses incurred exceed the cash paid for expenses that period.

INCREASE IN ACCOUNTS PAYABLE. Like the increase in 1993, the 1994 increase of $55,000 in accounts payable must be added to net income to convert to net cash provided by operating activities.

DEPRECIATION EXPENSE. During 1994, Computer Services Company reported depreciation expense of $15,000. Of this amount, $11,000 related to the building and

$4,000 to the equipment. These two amounts were determined by analyzing the accumulated depreciation accounts.

INCREASE IN ACCUMULATED DEPRECIATION—BUILDING. As shown in Illustration 19-12, accumulated depreciation increased $11,000. This change represents the depreciation expense on the building for the year. Because depreciation expense is a noncash charge, it is added back to net income in order to arrive at net cash provided by operating activities.

INCREASE IN ACCUMULATED DEPRECIATION—EQUIPMENT. The increase in the Accumulated Depreciation—Equipment account was $3,000. This amount does not represent depreciation expense for the year because the additional information indicates that this account was decreased (debited $1,000) as a result of the sale of the equipment. Thus depreciation expense for 1994 was $4,000 ($3,000 + $1,000). This amount is added to net income to determine net cash provided by operating activities. The T-account below provides information about the changes that occurred in this account in 1994.

ILLUSTRATION 19-14

Analysis of accumulated depreciation—equipment

ACCUMULATED DEPRECIATION—EQUIPMENT			
Accumulated depreciation on equipment sold	1,000	1/1/94 Balance	–0–
		Depreciation expense	4,000
		12/31/94 Balance	3,000

Depreciation expense on the building of $11,000 plus depreciation expense on the equipment of $4,000 equals the depreciation expense of $15,000 reported on the income statement.

Other charges to expense that do not require the use of cash, such as the amortization of intangible assets and depletion expense, are treated in the same manner as depreciation. Depreciation and similar noncash charges are frequently listed in the statement of cash flows as the first adjustments to net income.

LOSS ON SALE OF EQUIPMENT. On the income statement, Computer Services Company reported a $3,000 loss on the sale of equipment (book value $7,000, less cash proceeds $4,000). The loss reduced net income but did not reduce cash. Thus the loss is added to net income in determining net cash provided by operating activities.[3]

As a result of the foregoing, net cash provided by operating activities is $218,000 as computed in Illustration 19-15.

Determining Net Cash Provided/Used by Investing and Financing Activities (Step 3)

After the items affecting the net cash provided by operating activities are determined, the next step involves analyzing the remaining changes in balance sheet accounts.

---

[3]If a gain on sale occurs, a different situation results. To allow a gain to flow through to net cash provided by operating activities would be double-counting the gain—once in net income and again in the investing activities section as part of the cash proceeds from sale. As a result, a gain is deducted from net income in reporting net cash provided by operating activities.

ILLUSTRATION 19-15

Computation of net cash provided by operating activities, 1994

Net income		$139,000
Adjustments to reconcile net income to net cash provided by operating activities:		
Depreciation expense	$15,000	
Loss on sale of equipment	3,000	
Decrease in accounts receivable	10,000	
Increase in prepaid expenses	(4,000)	
Increase in accounts payable	55,000	79,000
Net cash provided by operating activities		$218,000

INCREASE IN LAND. As indicated from the change in the land account, land of $130,000 was purchased through the issuance of long-term bonds. Although the issuance of bonds payable for land has no effect on cash, it is a significant noncash investing and financing activity that merits disclosure. As indicated earlier, these activities are disclosed in a separate schedule at the bottom of the statement of cash flows.

INCREASE IN BUILDING. As indicated in the additional data, an office building was acquired using cash of $160,000. This transaction is a cash outflow reported in the investing section.

INCREASE IN EQUIPMENT. The equipment account increased $17,000. Based on the additional information, this was a net increase that resulted from two transactions: (1) a purchase of equipment of $25,000 and (2) the sale of equipment costing $8,000 for $4,000. These transactions are classified as investing activities, and each transaction should be reported separately. Thus the purchase of equipment should be reported as an outflow of cash for $25,000 and the sale should be reported as an inflow of cash for $4,000. The T-account below shows the reasons for the change in this account during the year.

ILLUSTRATION 19-16

Analysis of equipment

EQUIPMENT				
1/1/94	Balance	10,000	Cost of equipment sold	8,000
	Purchase of equipment	25,000		
12/31/94	Balance	27,000		

INCREASE IN BONDS PAYABLE. The bonds payable account increased $130,000. As shown in the additional information, land was acquired from the issuance of these bonds. As indicated earlier, this transaction is reported in a separate schedule at the bottom of the statement.

INCREASE IN RETAINED EARNINGS. Retained earnings increased $124,000 during the year. This increase can be explained by two factors: (1) net income of $139,000 increased retained earnings and (2) dividends of $15,000 decreased retained earnings. Net income is adjusted to net cash provided by operating activities in the operating activities section. Payment of the dividends is a cash outflow that is reported as a financing activity.

Helpful hint When stocks or bonds are issued for cash, it is the amount of the issuance price (proceeds) that will appear on the statement of cash flows as a financing inflow (rather than the amount of par value of the stocks or bonds).

Helpful hint It is the **payment** of dividends, not the declaration, that appears on the cash flow statement.

Statement of Cash Flows—1994

Combining the foregoing items, a statement of cash flows for 1994 for Computer Services Company, is presented in Illustration 19-17.

ILLUSTRATION 19-17

Statement of cash flows, 1994

COMPUTER SERVICES COMPANY Statement of Cash Flows For the Year Ended December 31, 1994		
Cash flows from operating activities		
Net income		$139,000
Adjustments to reconcile net income to net cash		
provided by operating activities:		
Depreciation expense	$ 15,000	
Loss on sale of equipment	3,000	
Decrease in accounts receivable	10,000	
Increase in prepaid expenses	(4,000)	
Increase in accounts payable	55,000	79,000
Net cash provided by operating activities		218,000
Cash flows from investing activities		
Purchase of building	$(160,000)	
Purchase of equipment	(25,000)	
Sale of equipment	4,000	
Net cash used by investing activities		(181,000)
Cash flows from financing activities		
Payment of cash dividends	(15,000)	
Net cash used by financing activities		(15,000)
Net increase in cash		22,000
Cash at beginning of period		34,000
Cash at end of period		$ 56,000
Noncash investing and financing activities		
Issuance of bonds payable to purchase land		$130,000

Helpful hint Note that in the investing activities and financing activities sections, positive numbers indicate cash inflows (receipts) and negative numbers indicate cash outflows (payments).

Summary of Conversion to Net Cash Provided by Operating Activities—Indirect Method

As shown in the previous illustrations, the statement of cash flows starts with net income and adds (or deducts) items not affecting cash to arrive at net cash provided by operating activities. The additions and deductions consist of (1) changes in specific current assets and current liabilities and (2) noncash charges reported in the income statement. A summary of the current assets and current liabilities is provided first.

ILLUSTRATION 19-18

Adjustments for current assets and current liabilities

Helpful hints

1. Increase in a current asset is deducted from net income.
2. Decrease in a current asset is added to net income.
3. Increase in a current liability is added to net income.
4. Decrease in a current liability is deducted from net income.

	Adjustments to Convert Net Income to Net Cash Provided by Operating Activities	
Current assets and current liabilities	Add to Net Income	Deduct from Net Income
Accounts receivable	Decrease	Increase
Inventory	Decrease	Increase
Prepaid expenses	Decrease	Increase
Accounts payable	Increase	Decrease
Accrued expenses payable	Increase	Decrease

The noncash charges reported in the income statement are reported as follows:

ILLUSTRATION 19-19

Adjustments for noncash charges

Noncash charges	Adjustments to Convert Net Income to Net Cash Provided by Operating Activities
Depreciation expense	Add
Patent amortization expense	Add
Depletion expense	Add
Loss on sale of asset	Add

Usefulness of the Statement of Cash Flows

The information in a statement of cash flows should help investors, creditors, and others assess various aspects of the firm's financial position:

1. **The entity's ability to generate future cash flows.** A primary objective of financial reporting is to provide information that makes it possible to predict the amounts, timing, and uncertainty of future cash flows. By examining relationships between such items as sales and net cash provided by operating activities, or cash provided by operations and increases or decreases in cash, investors and others can make predictions of the amount, timing, and uncertainty of future cash flows better than from accrual basis data.

2. **The entity's ability to pay dividends and meet obligations.** Simply put, if a company does not have adequate cash, employees cannot be paid, debts settled, dividends paid, or equipment acquired. A statement of cash flows indicates how cash is used and its sources. Employees, creditors, stockholders, and customers should be particularly interested in this statement, because it alone shows the flows of cash in a business.

3. **The reasons for the difference between net income and net cash flow from operating activities.** The net income number is important, because it provides information on the success or failure of a business enterprise from one period to another. However, some are critical of accrual basis net income because estimates must be made to arrive at it. As a result, the reliability of the number is often challenged. Such is not the case with cash. Thus, many readers of the financial statement want to know the reasons for the difference between net income and net cash provided by operating activities. Then they can assess for themselves the reliability of the income number.

4. **The cash investing and financing transactions during the period.** By examining a company's investing activities (purchase and sales of assets other than its products) and its financing transactions (borrowings and repayments of borrowings, investments by owners and distributions to owners), a financial statement reader can better understand why assets and liabilities increased or decreased during the period. For example, the following questions might be answered with such information:

   How did cash increase when there was a net loss for the period?
   How were the proceeds of the bond issue used?
   How was the expansion in the plant and equipment financed?

Why were dividends not increased?
How was the retirement of debt accomplished?
How much money was borrowed during the year?
Is cash flow greater or less than net income?

Accounting in Action · *Business Insights*

Cash flow has taken on increasing importance, since the period in the 1980s when merger mania spread across this country. Raiders want companies that generate strong, steady cash flow. When raiders borrow heavily to buy a company, they can use the cash flow to pay the interest on the acquisition loan. A good illustration of the importance of cash flow data was the merger negotiations that occurred among Time, Warner Communications, and Paramount Communications Inc. Time decided to take over Warner Communications, at the same time Paramount Communications was interested in taking over Time, Inc. In the skirmish that took place, it became clear that all the companies were looking at cash flow because of the large debt needed to finance the merger. As indicated in the financial press, "Paramount, Time, and Warner, all traditional earnings-oriented companies, are now saying earnings aren't nearly as important as combining and building assets that will generate cash in the future."

Source: The Wall Street Journal, June 27, 1989.

Before You Go On . . .

1. What is the format of the operating activities section of the statement of cash flows using the indirect method?

2. Where is depreciation expense shown on a statement of cash flows using the indirect method?

3. Where are significant noncash investing and financing activities shown in a statement of cash flows? Give some examples.

4. Why is the statement of cash flows useful? What key information does it convey?

DEMONSTRATION PROBLEM (INDIRECT METHOD)

Presented below is information related to Reynolds Company.

REYNOLDS COMPANY
Comparative Balance Sheet
December 31

Assets	1994	1993	Change Increase/Decrease
Cash	$ 54,000	$ 37,000	$ 17,000 Increase
Accounts receivable	68,000	26,000	42,000 Increase
Inventories	54,000	–0–	54,000 Increase
Prepaid expenses	4,000	6,000	2,000 Decrease
Land	45,000	70,000	25,000 Decrease
Buildings	200,000	200,000	–0–

Assets	1994	1993	Change Increase/Decrease
Accumulated depreciation—buildings	(21,000)	(11,000)	10,000 Increase
Equipment	193,000	68,000	125,000 Increase
Accumulated depreciation—equipment	(28,000)	(10,000)	18,000 Increase
Totals	$569,000	$386,000	
Liabilities and Stockholders' Equity			
Accounts payable	$ 23,000	$ 40,000	$ 17,000 Decrease
Accrued expenses payable	10,000	–0–	10,000 Increase
Bonds payable	110,000	150,000	40,000 Decrease
Common stock ($1 par)	220,000	60,000	160,000 Increase
Retained earnings	206,000	136,000	70,000 Increase
Totals	$569,000	$386,000	

REYNOLDS COMPANY
Income Statement
For the Year Ended December 31, 1994

Revenues		$890,000
Cost of goods sold	$465,000	
Operating expenses	221,000	
Interest expense	12,000	
Loss on sale of equipment	2,000	700,000
Income from operations		190,000
Income tax expense		65,000
Net income		$125,000

Additional information:
(a) Operating expenses include depreciation expense of $33,000 and charges from prepaid expenses of $2,000.
(b) Land was sold at its book value for cash.
(c) Cash dividends of $55,000 were declared and paid in 1994.
(d) Interest expense of $12,000 was paid in cash.
(e) Equipment with a cost of $166,000 was purchased for cash. Equipment with a cost of $41,000 and a book value of $36,000 was sold for $34,000 cash.
(f) Bonds of $10,000 were redeemed at their book value for cash; bonds of $30,000 were converted into common stock.
(g) Common stock ($1 par) of $130,000 was issued for cash.
(h) Accounts payable pertain to merchandise suppliers.

Instructions
Prepare a statement of cash flows using the indirect method.

Solution to Demonstration Problem

REYNOLDS COMPANY
Statement of Cash Flows
For the Year Ended December 31, 1994

Cash flows from operating activities		
Net income		$125,000
Adjustments to reconcile net income to net cash provided by operating activities:		
Depreciation expense	$ 33,000	
Increase in accounts receivable	(42,000)	
Increase in inventories	(54,000)	
Decrease in prepaid expenses	2,000	
Decrease in accounts payable	(17,000)	
Increase in accrued expenses payable	10,000	
Loss on sale of equipment	2,000	(66,000)
Net cash provided by operating activities		59,000

Helpful hints To prepare the statement of cash flows:
1. Determine the net increase/decrease in cash.
2. Determine net cash provided/used by operating activities.
3. Determine net cash provided/used by investing and financing activities.
4. Operating activities generally relate to changes in current assets and current liabilities.
5. Investing activities generally relate to changes in non-current assets.
6. Financing activities generally relate to changes in non-current liabilities and stockholders' equity accounts.

Helpful hint   You may wish to insert the beginning and ending cash balances and the increase/decrease in cash necessitated by these balances immediately into the statement of cash flows. The net increase/decrease is the target amount. The net cash flows from the three classes of activities must equal the target amount.

Cash flows from investing activities		
Sale of land	25,000	
Sale of equipment	34,000	
Purchase of equipment	(166,000)	
Net cash used by investing activities		(107,000)
Cash flows from financing activities		
Redemption of bonds	(10,000)	
Sale of common stock	130,000	
Payment of dividends	(55,000)	
Net cash provided by financing activities		65,000
Net increase in cash		17,000
Cash at beginning of period		37,000
Cash at end of period		$ 54,000
Noncash investing and financing activities		
Conversion of bonds into common stock		$ 30,000

SECTION 2   Statement of Cash Flows—Direct Method

To explain and illustrate the direct method, we will use the transactions of Juarez Company for two years, 1993 and 1994. Annual statements of cash flow will be prepared. Basic transactions will be used in the first year with additional transactions added in the second year.

First Year of Operations—1993

Study Objective 4

Prepare a statement of cash flows using the direct method.

Juarez Company began business on January 1, 1993, when it issued 300,000 shares of $1 par value common stock for $300,000 cash. The company rented office and sales space along with equipment. The comparative balance sheet at the beginning and end of 1993 and the changes in each account are shown in Illustration 19-20. The income statement and additional information for Juarez Company are shown in Illustration 19-21.

Determining the Net Increase/Decrease in Cash (Step 1)

The comparative balance sheet for Juarez Company shows a zero cash balance at January 1, 1993, and a cash balance of $159,000 at December 31, 1993. Thus, the change in cash for 1993 was a net increase of $159,000.

Determining the Net Cash Provided/Used by Operating Activities (Step 2)

Under the direct method, net cash provided by operating activities is computed by **adjusting each item in the income statement** from the accrual basis to the

JUAREZ COMPANY
Comparative Balance Sheet

Assets	Dec. 31, 1993	Jan. 1, 1993	Change Increase/Decrease
Cash	$159,000	$-0-	$159,000 Increase
Accounts receivable	15,000	-0-	15,000 Increase
Inventory	160,000	-0-	160,000 Increase
Prepaid expenses	8,000	-0-	8,000 Increase
Land	80,000	-0-	80,000 Increase
Total	$422,000	$-0-	
Liabilities and Stockholders' Equity			
Accounts payable	$ 60,000	$-0-	$ 60,000 Increase
Accrued expenses payable	20,000	-0-	20,000 Increase
Common stock	300,000	-0-	300,000 Increase
Retained earnings	42,000	-0-	42,000 Increase
Total	$422,000	$-0-	

ILLUSTRATION 19-21

Income statement and additional information, 1993

JUAREZ COMPANY
Income Statement
For the Year Ended December 31, 1993

Revenues from sales	$780,000
Cost of goods sold	450,000
Gross profit	330,000
Operating expenses	170,000
Income before income taxes	160,000
Income tax expense	48,000
Net income	$112,000

Additional information:
(a) Dividends of $70,000 were declared and paid in cash.
(b) The accounts payable increase resulted from the purchase of merchandise.

cash basis. To simplify and condense the operating activities section, only major classes of operating cash receipts and cash payments are reported. The difference between these major classes of cash receipts and cash payments is the net cash provided by operating activities as shown in Illustration 19-22.

An efficient way to apply the direct method is to analyze the revenues and expenses reported in the income statement in the order in which they are listed. Cash receipts and cash payments related to these revenues and expenses should then be determined. The direct method adjustments for Juarez Company in 1993 to determine net cash provided by operating activities are presented in the following sections.

CASH RECEIPTS FROM CUSTOMERS. The income statement for Juarez Company reported revenues from customers of $780,000. To determine cash receipts from customers, it is necessary to consider the change in accounts receivable during the year. When accounts receivable increase during the year, revenues on an accrual basis are higher than cash receipts from customers. In other words, operations led to increased revenues, but not all of these revenues resulted in cash receipts. To

ILLUSTRATION 19-22

Major classes of cash receipts and payments

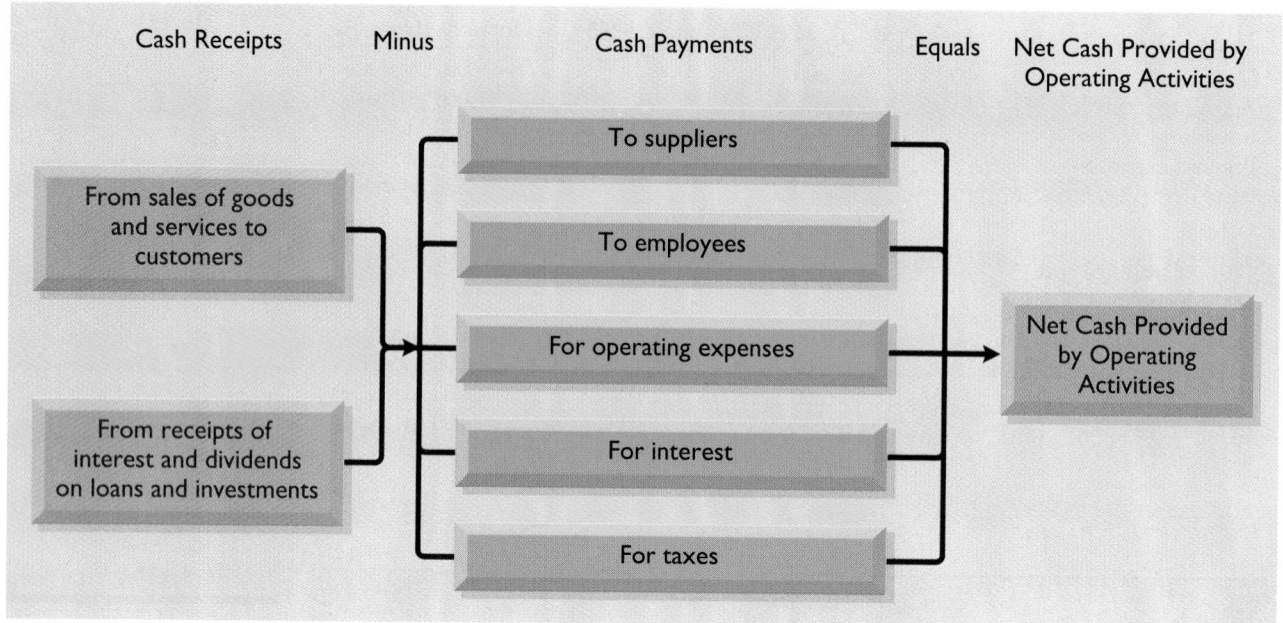

determine the amount of increase in cash receipts, deduct the amount of the increase in accounts receivable from the total sales revenues. Conversely, a decrease in accounts receivable is added to sales revenues, because cash receipts from customers then exceed sales revenues.

For Juarez Company, accounts receivable increased $15,000. Thus, cash receipts from customers were $765,000, computed as follows:

ILLUSTRATION 19-23

Computation of cash receipts from customers

Revenues from sales	$780,000
Deduct: Increase in accounts receivable	15,000
Cash receipts from customers	**$765,000**

Cash receipts from customers may also be determined from an analysis of the Accounts Receivable account as shown in Illustration 19-24.

ILLUSTRATION 19-24

Analysis of accounts receivable

ACCOUNTS RECEIVABLE				
1/1/93	Balance	-0-	Receipts from customers	765,000
	Revenues from sales	780,000		
12/31/93	Balance	15,000		

Helpful hint The T-account shows that revenue less increase in receivables equals cash receipts.

The relationships between cash receipts from customers, revenues from sales, and changes in accounts receivable are shown in Illustration 19-25.

CASH PAYMENTS TO SUPPLIERS. Juarez Company reported cost of goods sold on its income statement of $450,000. To determine cash payments to suppliers, it is first necessary to find purchases for the year. To find purchases, cost of goods sold is adjusted for the change in inventory. When inventory increases during the

ILLUSTRATION 19-25

Formula to compute cash receipts from customers

Cash receipts from customers	=	Revenues from sales	+ Decrease in accounts receivable or – Increase in accounts receivable

year, it means that purchases this year exceed cost of goods sold. As a result, the increase in inventory is added to cost of goods sold to arrive at purchases.

In 1993, Juarez Company's inventory increased $160,000. Purchases, therefore, are computed as follows:

ILLUSTRATION 19-26

Computation of purchases

Cost of goods sold	$450,000
Add: Increase in inventory	160,000
Purchases	$610,000

After purchases are computed, cash payments to suppliers are determined by adjusting purchases for the change in accounts payable. When accounts payable increase during the year, purchases on an accrual basis are higher than they are on a cash basis. As a result, an increase in accounts payable is deducted from purchases to arrive at cash payments to suppliers. Conversely, a decrease in accounts payable is added to purchases because cash payments to suppliers exceed purchases. Cash payments to suppliers were $550,000, computed as follows:

ILLUSTRATION 19-27

Computation of cash payments to suppliers

Purchases	$610,000
Deduct: Increase in accounts payable	60,000
Cash payments to suppliers	$550,000

Cash payments to suppliers may also be determined from an analysis of the Accounts Payable account as shown in Illustration 19-28.

ILLUSTRATION 19-28

Analysis of accounts payable

ACCOUNTS PAYABLE				
Payments to suppliers	550,000	1/1/93	Balance	–0–
			Purchases	610,000
		12/31/93	Balance	60,000

The relationship between cash payments to customers, cost of goods sold, changes in inventory, and changes in account payable are shown in the following formula.

Helpful hint The T-account shows that purchases less increase in accounts payable equals payments to suppliers.

ILLUSTRATION 19-29

Formula to compute cash payments to suppliers

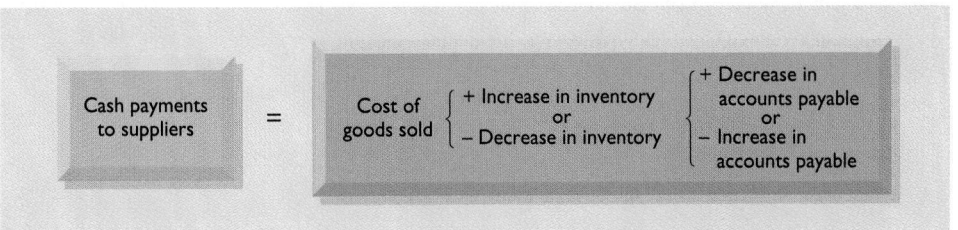

Cash payments to suppliers	=	Cost of goods sold	+ Increase in inventory or – Decrease in inventory	+ Decrease in accounts payable or – Increase in accounts payable

CASH PAYMENTS FOR OPERATING EXPENSES. Operating expenses of $170,000 were reported on Juarez's income statement. To determine the cash paid for operating expenses, this amount must be adjusted for any changes in prepaid expenses and accrued expenses payable. For example, when prepaid expenses increased $8,000 during the year, cash paid for operating expenses was $8,000 higher than operating expenses reported on the income statement. To convert operating expenses to cash payments for operating expenses, the increase of $8,000 must be added to operating expenses. Conversely, if prepaid expenses decrease during the year, the decrease must be deducted from operating expenses.

Operating expenses must also be adjusted for changes in accrued expenses payable. When accrued expenses payable increase during the year, operating expenses on an accrual basis are higher than they are in a cash basis. As a result, an increase in accrued expenses payable is deducted from operating expenses to arrive at cash payments for operating expenses. Conversely, a decrease in accrued expenses payable is added to operating expenses because cash payments exceed operating expenses.

Juarez Company's cash payments for operating expenses were $158,000, computed as follows:

ILLUSTRATION 19-30

Computation of cash payments for operating expenses

Operating expenses	$170,000
Add: Increase in prepaid expenses	8,000
Deduct: Increase in accrued expenses payable	(20,000)
Cash payments for operating expenses	$158,000

The relationships among cash payments for operating expenses, changes in prepaid expenses, and changes in accrued expenses payable are shown in the following formula.

ILLUSTRATION 19-31

Formula to compute cash payments for operating expenses

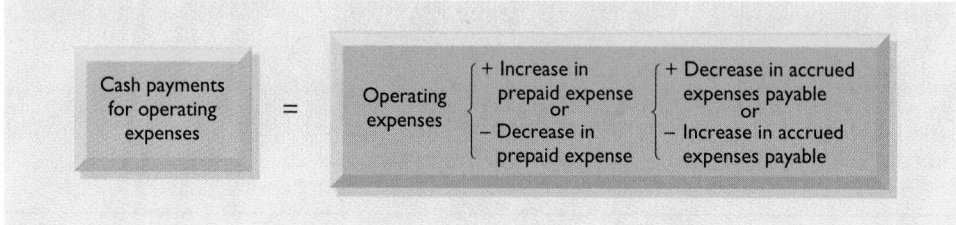

CASH PAYMENTS FOR INCOME TAXES. The income statement for Juarez shows income tax expense of $48,000. This amount equals the cash paid because the comparative balance sheet indicated no income taxes payable at either the beginning or end of the year.

All of the revenues and expenses in the 1993 income statement have now been adjusted to a cash basis. The operating activities section of the statement of cash flows is as follows:

ILLUSTRATION 19-32

Operating activities section—direct method

Cash flows from operating activities		
Cash receipts from customers		$765,000
Cash payments:		
To suppliers	$550,000	
For operating expenses	158,000	
For income taxes	48,000	756,000
Net cash provided by operating activities		$ 9,000

Determining Net Cash Provided/Used by Investing and Financing Activities (Step 3)

Preparing the investing and financing activities sections of the statement of cash flows begins with a determination of the changes in noncurrent accounts reported in the comparative balance sheet. The change in each account is then analyzed using the additional information to determine the effect, if any, the change had on cash.

INCREASE IN LAND. No additional information is given for the increase in land. In such case, you are to assume that the increase affected cash. You should also make the same type of assumption in solving homework problems when the cause of a change in a noncurrent account is not explained. The purchase of land is an investing activity. Thus, an outflow of cash of $80,000 for the purchase of land should be reported in the investing activities section.

INCREASE IN COMMON STOCK. As indicated earlier, 300,000 shares of $1 par value stock were sold for $300,000 cash. The issuance of common stock is a financing activity. Thus, a cash inflow of $300,000 from the issuance of common stock is reported in the financing activities section.

INCREASE IN RETAINED EARNINGS. For the Retained Earnings account, the reasons for the net increase of $42,000 are determined by analysis. First, net income increased retained earnings by $112,000. Second, the additional information section indicates that a cash dividend of $70,000 was paid. The adjustment of revenues and expenses to arrive at net cash provided by operations was done in Step 2 above. The cash dividend paid is reported as an outflow of cash in the financing activities section.

> **Helpful hint** It is the payment of dividends, not the declaration, that appears on the cash flow statement.

This analysis can also be made directly from the Retained Earnings account in the ledger of Juarez Company as shown in Illustration 19-33.

ILLUSTRATION 19-33

Analysis of retained earnings

RETAINED EARNINGS			
12/31/93 Cash dividend	70,000	1/1/93 Balance	–0–
		12/31/93 Net income	112,000
		12/31/93 Balance	42,000

The $42,000 increase in Retained Earnings in 1993 is a net change. When a net change in a noncurrent balance sheet account has occurred during the year, it generally is necessary to report the individual items that cause the net change.

Statement of Cash Flows—1993

The statement of cash flows can now be prepared. The operating activities section is reported first, followed by the investing and financing activities sections. The statement of cash flows for Juarez Company for 1993 is shown in Illustration 19-34.

The statement of cash flows shows that operating activities provided $9,000 of the net increase in cash of $159,000. Financing activities provided $230,000 of cash, and investing activities used $80,000 of cash. The net increase in cash for the year of $159,000 agrees with the increase in cash of $159,000 reported in the comparative balance sheet.

ILLUSTRATION 19-34

Statement of cash flows,
1993

Helpful hint Note that in the investing activities and financing activities sections, positive numbers indicate cash inflows (receipts) and negative numbers indicate cash outflows (payments).

JUAREZ COMPANY Statement of Cash Flows For the Year Ended December 31, 1993		
Cash flows from operating activities		
Cash receipts from customers		$765,000
Cash payments:		
To suppliers	$550,000	
For operating expenses	158,000	
For income taxes	48,000	756,000
Net cash provided by operating activities		9,000
Cash flows from investing activities		
Purchase of land	(80,000)	
Net cash used by investing activities		(80,000)
Cash flows from financing activities		
Issuance of common stock	300,000	
Payment of cash dividend	(70,000)	
Net cash provided by financing activities		230,000
Net increase in cash		159,000
Cash at beginning of period		–0–
Cash at end of period		$159,000

Second Year of Operations—1994

Illustration 19-35 and 19-36 present the comparative balance sheet, the income statement, and additional information pertaining to the second year of operations for Juarez Company.

ILLUSTRATION 19-35

Comparative balance sheet,
1994 with increases and
decreases

JUAREZ COMPANY Comparative Balance Sheet December 31			
Assets	1994	1993	Change Increase/Decrease
Cash	$191,000	$159,000	$ 32,000 Increase
Accounts receivable	12,000	15,000	3,000 Decrease
Inventory	130,000	160,000	30,000 Decrease
Prepaid expenses	6,000	8,000	2,000 Decrease
Land	180,000	80,000	100,000 Increase
Equipment	160,000	–0–	160,000 Increase
Accumulated depreciation—equipment	(16,000)	–0–	16,000 Increase
Total	$663,000	$422,000	
Liabilities and Stockholders' equity			
Accounts payable	$ 52,000	$ 60,000	$ 8,000 Decrease
Accrued expenses payable	15,000	20,000	5,000 Decrease
Income taxes payable	12,000	–0–	12,000 Increase
Bonds payable	90,000	–0–	90,000 Increase
Common stock	400,000	300,000	100,000 Increase
Retained earnings	94,000	42,000	52,000 Increase
Total	$663,000	$422,000	

ILLUSTRATION 19-36

Income statement and additional information, 1994

JUAREZ COMPANY
Income Statement
For the Year Ended December 31, 1994

Revenues from sales		$975,000
Cost of goods sold	$660,000	
Operating expenses (excluding depreciation)	176,000	
Depreciation expense	18,000	
Loss on sale of store equipment	1,000	855,000
Income before income taxes		120,000
Income tax expense		36,000
Net income		$ 84,000

Additional information:
(a) In 1994, the company declared and paid a $32,000 cash dividend.
(b) Bonds were issued at face value for $90,000 in cash.
(c) Equipment costing $180,000 was purchased for cash.
(d) Equipment costing $20,000 was sold for $17,000 cash when the book value of the equipment was $18,000.
(e) Common stock of $100,000 was issued to acquire land.

Determining the Net Increase/Decrease in Cash (Step 1)

The comparative balance sheet shows a beginning cash balance of $159,000 and an ending cash balance of $191,000. Thus, there was a net increase in cash in 1994 of $32,000.

Determining Net Cash Provided/Used in Operating Activities (Step 2)

CASH RECEIPTS FROM CUSTOMERS. Revenues from sales were $975,000. Since accounts receivable decreased $3,000, cash receipts from customers were greater than sales revenues. Cash receipts from customers were $978,000, computed as follows:

ILLUSTRATION 19-37

Computation of cash receipts from customers

Revenues from sales	$975,000
Add: Decrease in accounts receivable	3,000
Cash receipts from customers	$978,000

CASH PAYMENTS TO SUPPLIERS. The conversion of cost of goods sold to purchases and purchases to cash payments to suppliers is similar to the computations made in 1993. For 1994, purchases are computed using cost of goods sold of $660,000 from the income statement and the decrease in inventory of $30,000 from the comparative balance sheet. Purchases are then adjusted by the decrease in accounts payable of $8,000. Cash payments to suppliers were $638,000, computed as follows:

ILLUSTRATION 19-38

Computation of cash payments to suppliers

Cost of goods sold	$660,000
Deduct: Decrease in inventory	30,000
Purchases	630,000
Add: Decrease in accounts payable	8,000
Cash payments to suppliers	$638,000

CASH PAYMENTS FOR OPERATING EXPENSES. Operating expenses (exclusive of depreciation expense) for 1994 were reported at $176,000. This amount is then adjusted for changes in prepaid expenses and accrued expenses payable to arrive at cash payments for operating expenses.

As indicated from the comparative balance sheet, prepaid expenses decreased $2,000 during the year. This means that $2,000 was allocated to operating expenses (thereby increasing operating expenses), but cash payments did not increase by that $2,000. To arrive at cash payments for operating expenses, the decrease in prepaid expenses is deducted from operating expenses.

Accrued operating expenses decreased $5,000 during the period. As a result, cash payments were higher by $5,000 than the amount reported for operating expenses. The decrease in accrued expenses payable is added to operating expenses. Cash payments for operating expenses were $179,000, computed as follows:

ILLUSTRATION 19-39

Computation of cash payments for operating expenses

Operating expenses, exclusive of depreciation	$176,000
Deduct: Decrease in prepaid expenses	(2,000)
Add: Decrease in accrued expenses payable	5,000
Cash payments for operating expenses	**$179,000**

DEPRECIATION EXPENSE AND LOSS ON SALE OF EQUIPMENT. Operating expenses are shown exclusive of depreciation. Depreciation expense in 1994 was $18,000. Depreciation expense is not shown on a statement of cash flows because it is a noncash charge. If the amount for operating expenses includes depreciation expense, operating expenses must be reduced by the amount of depreciation in arriving at cash payments for operating expenses.

The loss on sale of equipment of $1,000 is also a noncash charge. The loss on sale of equipment reduces net income, but it does not reduce cash. Thus, the loss on sale of equipment is not reported on a statement of cash flows.

Other charges to expense that do not require the use of cash, such as the amortization of intangible assets and depletion expense, are treated in the same manner as depreciation.

CASH PAYMENTS FOR INCOME TAXES. Income tax expense reported on the income statement was $36,000. Income taxes payable, however, increased $12,000 which means that $12,000 of the income taxes have not been paid. As a result, income taxes paid were less than income taxes reported on the income statement. Cash payments for income taxes were, therefore, $24,000 as shown below.

ILLUSTRATION 19-40

Computation of cash payments for income taxes

Income tax expense	$36,000
Deduct: Increase in income taxes payable	12,000
Cash payments for income taxes	**$24,000**

The relationships of cash payments for income taxes, income tax expense, and changes in income taxes payable are shown in the following formula.

ILLUSTRATION 19-41

Formula to compute cash payments for income taxes

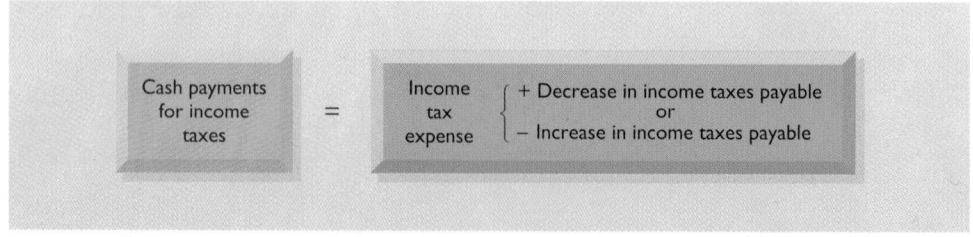

INCREASE IN LAND. Land increased $100,000. The additional information section indicates that common stock was issued to purchase the land. Although the issuance of common stock for land has no effect on cash, it is a significant noncash investing and financing transaction that requires disclosure. As indicated earlier, these activities are disclosed in a separate schedule at the bottom of the statement of cash flows.

INCREASE IN EQUIPMENT. The comparative balance sheet shows that equipment increased $160,000 in 1994. The additional information in Illustration 19-36 indicates that the increase resulted from two investing transactions: (1) equipment costing $180,000 was purchased for cash, and (2) equipment costing $20,000 was sold for $17,000 cash when its book value was $18,000. The relevant data for the statement of cash flows is the cash paid for the purchase and the cash proceeds from the sale. For Juarez Company, the investing activities section will show: Purchase of equipment $180,000, as an outflow of cash; and sale of equipment $17,000, as an inflow of cash. The two amounts should not be netted because one is an outflow of cash and the other is an inflow of cash; both flows should be shown.

The analysis of the changes in Equipment should include the related Accumulated Depreciation account. These two accounts for Juarez Company are shown in Illustration 19-42.

EQUIPMENT				
1/1/94	Balance	–0–	Cost of equipment sold	20,000
	Cash purchase	180,000		
12/31/94	Balance	160,000		

ACCUMULATED DEPRECIATION—EQUIPMENT				
Sale of equipment	2,000	1/1/94	Balance	–0–
			Depreciation expense	18,000
		12/31/94	Balance	16,000

ILLUSTRATION 19-42

Analysis of equipment and related accumulated depreciation

INCREASE IN BONDS PAYABLE. Bonds Payable increased $90,000. The additional information in Illustration 19-36 indicates that bonds with a face value of $90,000 were issued for $90,000 cash. The issuance of bonds is a financing activity. For Juarez Company, there is an inflow of cash of $90,000 from the issuance of bonds.

INCREASE IN COMMON STOCK. The Common Stock account increased $100,000. As indicated from the additional information, land was acquired from the issuance of common stock. This transaction is a significant noncash investing and financing transaction that should be reported in a separate schedule at the bottom of the statement.

INCREASE IN RETAINED EARNINGS. The net increase in Retained Earnings of $52,000 resulted from net income of $84,000 and the declaration and payment of a cash dividend of $32,000. Net income is not reported in the statement of cash flows under the direct method. Cash dividends paid of $32,000 are reported in the financing activities section as an outflow of cash.

Statement of Cash Flows—1994

The statement of cash flows for Juarez Company is shown in Illustration 19-43.

ILLUSTRATION 19-43

Statement of cash flows, 1994

JUAREZ COMPANY Statement of Cash Flows For the Year Ended December 31, 1994		
Cash flows from operating activities		
Cash receipts from customers		$978,000
Cash payments:		
To suppliers	$638,000	
For operating expenses	179,000	
For income taxes	24,000	841,000
Net cash provided by operating activities		137,000
Cash flows from investing activities		
Purchase of equipment	(180,000)	
Sale of equipment	17,000	
Net cash used by investing activities		(163,000)
Cash flows from financing activities		
Issuance of bonds payable	90,000	
Payment of cash dividends	(32,000)	
Net cash provided by financing activities		58,000
Net increase in cash		32,000
Cash at beginning of period		159,000
Cash at end of period		$191,000
Noncash investing and financing activities		
Issuance of common stock to purchase land		$100,000

*U*sefulness of the Statement of Cash Flows

The information in a statement of cash flows should help investors, creditors, and others assess various aspects of the firm's financial position:

1. **The entity's ability to generate future cash flows.** A primary objective of financial reporting is to provide information that makes it possible to predict the amounts, timing, and uncertainty of future cash flows. By examining relationships between such items as sales and net cash provided by operating activities, or cash provided by operations and increases or decreases in cash, investors and others can make predictions of the amount, timing, and uncertainty of future cash flows better than from accrual basis data.

2. **The entity's ability to pay dividends and meet obligations.** Simply put, if a company does not have adequate cash, employees cannot be paid, debts settled, dividends paid, or equipment acquired. A statement of cash flows indicates how cash is used and its sources. Employees, creditors, stockholders, and customers should be particularly interested in this statement, because it alone shows the flows of cash in a business.

3. **The reasons for the difference between net income and net cash flow from operating activities.** The net income number is important, because

it provides information on the success or failure of a business enterprise from one period to another. However, some are critical of accrual basis net income because estimates must be made to arrive at it. As a result, the reliability of the number is often challenged. Such is not the case with cash. Thus, many readers of the financial statement want to know the reasons for the difference between net income and net cash provided by operating activities. Then they can assess for themselves the reliability of the income number.

4. **The cash investing and financing transactions during the period.** By examining a company's investing activities (purchase and sales of assets other than its products) and its financing transactions (borrowings and repayments of borrowings, investments by owners and distributions to owners), a financial statement reader can better understand why assets and liabilities increased or decreased during the period. For example, the following questions might be answered with such information:

How did cash increase when there was a net loss for the period?
How were the proceeds of the bond issue used?
How was the expansion in the plant and equipment financed?
Why were dividends not increased?
How was the retirement of debt accomplished?
How much money was borrowed during the year?
Is cash flow greater or less than net income?

Accounting in Action · *Business Insights*

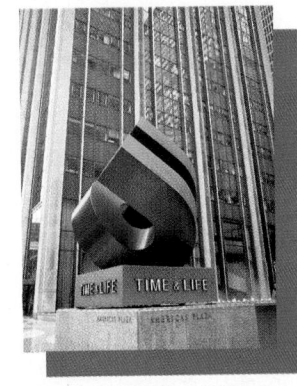

Cash flow has taken on increasing importance, since the period in the 1980s when merger mania spread across this country. Raiders want companies that generate strong, steady cash flow. When raiders borrow heavily to buy a company, they can use the cash flow to pay the interest on the acquisition loan. A good illustration of the importance of cash flow data was the merger negotiations that occurred among Time, Warner Communications, and Paramount Communications Inc. Time decided to take over Warner Communications, at the same time Paramount Communications was interested in taking over Time, Inc. In the skirmish that took place, it became clear that all the companies were looking at cash flow because of the large debt needed to finance the merger. As indicated in the financial press, "Paramount, Time, and Warner, all traditional earnings-oriented companies, are now saying earnings aren't nearly as important as combining and building assets that will generate cash in the future."

Source: The Wall Street Journal, June 27, 1989.

Before You Go On

1. What is the format of the operating activities section of the statement of cash flows using the direct method?

2. Where is depreciation expense shown on a statement of cash flows using the direct method?

3. Where are significant noncash investing and financing activities shown on a statement of cash flows? Give some examples.

DEMONSTRATION PROBLEM (DIRECT METHOD)

Presented below is information related to Reynolds Company.

REYNOLDS COMPANY
Comparative Balance Sheet
December 31

Assets	1994	1993	Change Increase/Decrease
Cash	$ 54,000	$ 37,000	$ 17,000 Increase
Accounts receivable	68,000	26,000	42,000 Increase
Inventories	54,000	–0–	54,000 Increase
Prepaid expenses	4,000	6,000	2,000 Decrease
Land	45,000	70,000	25,000 Decrease
Buildings	200,000	200,000	–0–
Accumulated depreciation—buildings	(21,000)	(11,000)	10,000 Increase
Equipment	193,000	68,000	125,000 Increase
Accumulated depreciation—equipment	(28,000)	(10,000)	18,000 Increase
Totals	$569,000	$386,000	

Liabilities and Stockholders' Equity			
Accounts payable	$ 23,000	$ 40,000	$ 17,000 Decrease
Accrued expenses payable	10,000	–0–	10,000 Increase
Bonds payable	110,000	150,000	40,000 Decrease
Common stock ($1 par)	220,000	60,000	160,000 Increase
Retained earnings	206,000	136,000	70,000 Increase
Totals	$569,000	$386,000	

REYNOLDS COMPANY
Income Statement
For the Year Ended December 31, 1994

Revenues		$890,000
Cost of goods sold	$465,000	
Operating expenses	221,000	
Interest expense	12,000	
Loss on sale of equipment	2,000	700,000
Income from operations		190,000
Income tax expense		65,000
Net income		$125,000

Additional information:

(a) Operating expenses include depreciation expense of $33,000 and charges from prepaid expenses of $2,000.

(b) Land was sold at its book value for cash.

(c) Cash dividends of $55,000 were declared and paid in 1994.

(d) Interest expense of $12,000 was paid in cash.

(e) Equipment with a cost of $166,000 was purchased for cash. Equipment with a cost of $41,000 and a book value of $36,000 was sold for $34,000 cash.

(f) Bonds of $10,000 were redeemed at their book value for cash; bonds of $30,000 were converted into common stock.

(g) Common stock ($1 par) of $130,000 was issued for cash.

(h) Accounts payable pertain to merchandise suppliers.

Instructions

Prepare a statement of cash flows using the direct method.

Solution to Demonstration Problem

REYNOLDS COMPANY
Statement of Cash Flows
For the Year Ended December 31, 1994

Cash flows from operating activities			
Cash receipts from customers			$848,000[a]
Cash payments:			
To suppliers		$536,000[b]	
For operating expenses		176,000[c]	
For interest expense		12,000	
For income taxes		65,000	789,000
Net cash provided by operating activities			59,000
Cash flows from investing activities			
Sale of land		25,000	
Sale of equipment		34,000	
Purchase of equipment		(166,000)	
Net cash used by investing activities			(107,000)
Cash flows from financing activities			
Redemption of bonds		(10,000)	
Sale of common stock		130,000	
Payment of dividends		(55,000)	
Net cash provided by financing activities			65,000
Net increase in cash			17,000
Cash at beginning of period			37,000
Cash at end of period			$ 54,000
Noncash investing and financing activities			
Conversion of bonds into common stock			$ 30,000

Computations:
[a]$848,000 = $890,000 − $42,000
[b]$536,000 = $465,000 + $54,000 + $17,000
[c]$176,000 = $221,000 − $33,000 − $2,000 − $10,000
Technically, an additional schedule reconciling net income to net cash provided by operating activities should be presented as part of the statement of cash flows when using the direct method.

Helpful hints To prepare the statement of cash flows:
1. Determine the net increase/decrease in cash.
2. Determine net cash provided/used by operating activities.
3. Determine net cash provided/used by investing and financing activities.
4. Operating activities generally relate to changes in current assets and current liabilities.
5. Investing activities generally relate to changes in non-current assets.
6. Financing activities generally relate to changes in non-current liabilities and stockholders' equity accounts.

Summary of Study Objectives

1. Indicate the primary purpose of the statement of cash flows. The primary purpose of the statement of cash flows is to provide information about the cash receipts and cash payments of an entity during a period. A secondary objective is to provide information about the operating, investing, and financing activities of the entity during the period.

2. Distinguish between operating, investing, and financing activities. Operating activities include the cash effects of transactions that enter into the determination of net income. Investing activities involve cash flows resulting from changes in investments and long-term asset items. Financing activities involve cash flows resulting from changes in long-term liability and stockholders' equity items.

3. Prepare a statement of cash flows using the indirect method. The preparation of a statement of cash flows involves three major steps: (1) determine the net increase or decrease in cash; (2) determine net cash provided (used) by operating activities; and (3) determine net cash flows provided (used) by investing and financing activities. Under the indirect

method, accrual basis net income is adjusted to net cash provided by operating activities.

4. *Prepare a statement of cash flows using the direct method.* The preparation of the statement of cash flows involves three major steps: (1) determine the net increase or decrease in cash; (2) determine net cash provided (used) by operating activities; and (3) determine net cash flows provided (used) by investing and financing activities. The direct method reports cash receipts less cash payments to arrive at net cash provided by operating activities.

APPENDIX J Using a Work Sheet for Preparing the Statement of Cash Flows—Indirect Method

Study Objective 5

Explain the guidelines and procedural steps in using a work sheet to prepare the statement of cash flows.

When numerous adjustments of net income are necessary, **many accountants prefer to use a work sheet to assemble and classify the data that will appear on the statement of cash flows.** The work sheet is merely a device that aids in the preparation of the statement; its use is optional. The skeleton format of the work sheet for preparation of the statement of cash flows is shown in Illustration J-1.

ILLUSTRATION J-I

Format of work sheet

XYZ COMPANY
Work Sheet
Statement of Cash Flows
For the Year Ended . . .

Balance Sheet Accounts	End of Last Year Balances	Reconciling Items Debits	Reconciling Items Credits	End of Current Year Balances
Debit balance accounts	XX	XX	XX	XX
	XX	XX	XX	XX
Totals	XXX			XXX
Credit balance accounts	XX	XX	XX	XX
	XX	XX	XX	XX
Totals	XXX			XXX
Statement of Cash Flows Effects				
Operating activities				
Net income		XX		
Adjustments		XX	XX	
Investing activities				
Receipts and payments		XX	XX	
Financing activities				
Receipts and payments		XX	XX	
Totals		XXX	XXX	
Increase (decrease) in cash		(XX)	XX	
Totals		XXX	XXX	

The following guidelines are important in using a work sheet:

1. In the balance sheet accounts section, **accounts with debit balances are listed separately from those with credit balances**. This means, for example, that Accumulated Depreciation is listed under credit balances and not as a contra account under debit balances. The beginning and ending balances of each account are entered in the appropriate columns. The transactions that caused the change in the account balance during the year are entered as reconciling items in the two middle columns. After all reconciling items have been entered, each line pertaining to a balance sheet account should "foot across." That is, the beginning balance plus or minus the reconciling item(s) must equal the ending balance. When this agreement exists for all balance sheet accounts, all changes in account balances have been reconciled.

2. The bottom portion of the work sheet consists of the operating, investing, and financing activities sections. Accordingly, it provides the information necessary to prepare the formal statement of cash flows. **Inflows of cash are entered as debits in the reconciling columns and outflows of cash are entered as credits in the reconciling columns.** Thus, in this section, the sale of equipment for cash at book value is entered as a debit under inflows of cash from investing activities. Similarly, the purchase of land for cash is entered as a credit under outflows of cash for investing activities.

3. **The reconciling items shown in the work sheet are not entered in any journal or posted to any account.** They do not represent either adjustments or corrections of the balance sheet accounts. They are used only to facilitate the preparation of the statement of cash flows.

Preparing the Work Sheet

As in the case of work sheets illustrated in earlier chapters, the preparation of a work sheet involves a series of prescribed steps. The steps in this case are:

1. Enter the balance sheet accounts and their beginning and ending balances in the balance sheet accounts section.

2. Enter the data that explains the changes in the balance sheet accounts (other than cash) and their effects on the statement of cash flows in the reconciling columns of the work sheet.

3. Enter the increase or decrease in cash on the cash line and at the bottom of the work sheet. This entry should enable the totals of the reconciling columns to be in agreement.

To illustrate the preparation of a work sheet, we will use the 1994 data for Computer Services Company. Your familiarity with these data should help you understand the use of a work sheet. For ease of reference, the comparative balance sheets, income statement, and selected data for 1994 are presented in Illustrations J-2 and J-3.

Determining the Reconciling Items

Several approaches may be used to determine the reconciling items. For example, the changes affecting net cash provided by operating activities could be completed first and then the effects of financing and investing transactions could be determined. Alternatively, the balance sheet accounts can be analyzed in the

ILLUSTRATION J-2

Comparative balance sheet 1994, with increases and decreases

COMPUTER SERVICES COMPANY
Comparative Balance Sheet
December 31

Assets	1994	1993	Change Increase/Decrease
Cash	$ 56,000	$34,000	$ 22,000 Increase
Accounts receivable	20,000	30,000	10,000 Decrease
Prepaid expenses	4,000	-0-	4,000 Increase
Land	130,000	-0-	130,000 Increase
Building	160,000	-0-	160,000 Increase
Accumulated depreciation—building	(11,000)	-0-	11,000 Increase
Equipment	27,000	10,000	17,000 Increase
Accumulated depreciation—equipment	(3,000)	-0-	3,000 Increase
Total	$383,000	$74,000	
Liabilities and Stockholders' Equity			
Accounts payable	$ 59,000	$ 4,000	$ 55,000 Increase
Bonds payable	130,000	-0-	130,000 Increase
Common stock	50,000	50,000	-0-
Retained earnings	144,000	20,000	124,000 Increase
Total	$383,000	$74,000	

ILLUSTRATION J-3

Income statement and additional information, 1994

COMPUTER SERVICES COMPANY
Income Statement
For the Year Ended December 31, 1994

Revenues		$507,000
Operating expenses (excluding depreciation)	$261,000	
Depreciation expense	15,000	
Loss on sale of equipment	3,000	279,000
Income from operations		228,000
Income tax expense		89,000
Net income		$139,000

Additional information:
(a) In 1994, the company paid a $15,000 cash dividend.
(b) The company obtained land through the issuance of $130,000 of long-term bonds.
(c) A building costing $160,000 was purchased for cash; equipment costing $25,000 was also purchased for cash.
(d) During 1994, the company sold equipment with a book value of $7,000 (cost $8,000, less accumulated depreciation $1,000) for $4,000 cash.

order in which they are listed on the work sheet. We will follow this latter approach for Computer Services, except for cash. As indicated above, cash is handled last.

ACCOUNTS RECEIVABLE. The decrease of $10,000 in accounts receivable means that cash collections from revenues are higher than the revenues reported in the income statement. To convert net income to net cash provided by operating activities, the decrease of $10,000 must be added to net income. The entry in the reconciling columns of the work sheet is:

(a)   Operating—Decrease in Accounts Receivable   10,000
                Accounts Receivable   10,000

PREPAID EXPENSES. An increase of $4,000 in prepaid expenses means that expenses deducted in determining net income are less than expenses that were paid in cash. Thus, the increase of $4,000 must be deducted from net income in deter-

mining net cash provided by operating activities. The work sheet entry is:

(b)   Prepaid Expenses   4,000
           Operating—Increase in Prepaid Expenses   4,000

LAND. The increase in land of $130,000 resulted from a purchase through the issuance of long-term bonds. This transaction should be reported as a significant noncash investing and financing activity. The work sheet entry is:

(c)   Land   130,000
           Bonds Payable   130,000

BUILDING. The cash purchase of a building for $160,000 is an investing activity cash outflow. The entry in the reconciling columns of the work sheet is:

(d)   Building   160,000
           Investing—Purchase of Building   160,000

EQUIPMENT. The increase in equipment of $17,000 resulted from a cash purchase of $25,000 and the sale of equipment costing $8,000. The book value of the equipment was $7,000, the cash proceeds were $4,000, and a loss of $3,000 was recorded. The work sheet entries are:

(e)   Equipment   25,000
           Investing—Purchase of Equipment   25,000

(f)   Investing—Sale of Equipment   4,000
           Operating—Loss on Sale of Equipment   3,000
           Accumulated Depreciation—Equipment   1,000
           Equipment   8,000

ACCOUNTS PAYABLE. The increase of $55,000 in accounts payable must be added to net income to obtain net cash provided by operating activities. The following work sheet entry is made:

(g)   Operating—Increase in Accounts Payable   55,000
           Accounts Payable   55,000

BONDS PAYABLE. The increase of $130,000 in this account resulted from the issuance of bonds for land. This is a significant noncash investing and financing activity. Work sheet entry (c) above is the only entry necessary.

ACCUMULATED DEPRECIATION—BUILDING AND ACCUMULATED DEPRECIATION—EQUIPMENT. The increases in these accounts of $11,000 and $4,000, respectively, resulted from depreciation expense. Depreciation expense is a noncash charge that must be added to net income in determining net cash provided by operating activities. The work sheet entries are:

(h)   Operating—Depreciation Expense—Building   11,000
           Accumulated Depreciation—Building   11,000

(i)   Operating—Depreciation Expense—Equipment   4,000
           Accumulated Depreciation—Equipment   4,000

RETAINED EARNINGS. The $124,000 increase in retained earnings resulted from net income of $139,000 and the declaration of a $15,000 cash dividend that was paid in 1994. Net income is included in net cash provided by operating activities and the dividends are a financing activity cash outflow. The entries in the reconciling columns of the work sheet are:

(j)   Operating—Net Income   139,000
           Retained Earnings   139,000

(k)   Retained Earnings   15,000
           Financing—Payment of Dividends   15,000

DISPOSITION OF CHANGE IN CASH. The firm's cash increased $22,000 in 1994. The final entry on the work sheet, therefore, is:

(l)   Cash   22,000
                 Increase in cash   22,000

As shown in the work sheet, the increase in cash is entered in the reconciling credit column as a **balancing** amount. This entry should complete the reconciliation of the changes in the balance sheet accounts. In addition, it should permit the totals of the reconciling columns to be in agreement. When all changes have been explained and the reconciling columns are in agreement, the reconciling columns are ruled to complete the work sheet. The completed work sheet for Computer Services Company is shown in Illustration J-4.

ILLUSTRATION J-4

Completed work sheet

COMPUTER SERVICES COMPANY
Work Sheet
Statement of Cash Flows
For the Year Ended December 31, 1994

Balance Sheet Accounts	Balance 12/31/93	Reconciling Items Debit		Reconciling Items Credit		Balance 12/31/94
Debits						
Cash	34,000	(l)	22,000			56,000
Accounts receivable	30,000			(a)	10,000	20,000
Prepaid expenses	–0–	(b)	4,000			4,000
Land	–0–	(c)	130,000*			130,000
Building	–0–	(d)	160,000			160,000
Equipment	10,000	(e)	25,000	(f)	8,000	27,000
Total	74,000					397,000
Credits						
Accounts payable	4,000			(g)	55,000	59,000
Bonds payable	–0–			(c)	130,000*	130,000
Accumulated depreciation—building	–0–			(h)	11,000	11,000
Accumulated depreciation—equipment	–0–	(f)	1,000	(i)	4,000	3,000
Common stock	50,000					50,000
Retained earnings	20,000	(k)	15,000	(j)	139,000	144,000
Total	74,000					397,000
Statement of Cash Flows Effects						
Operating activities						
Net income		(j)	139,000			
Decrease in accounts receivable		(a)	10,000			
Increase in prepaid expenses				(b)	4,000	
Increase in accounts payable		(g)	55,000			
Depreciation expense—building		(h)	11,000			
Depreciation expense—equipment		(i)	4,000			
Loss on sale of equipment		(f)	3,000			
Investing activities						
Purchase of building				(d)	160,000	
Purchase of equipment				(e)	25,000	
Sale of equipment		(f)	4,000			
Financing activities						
Payment of dividends				(k)	15,000	
Totals			583,000		561,000	
Increase in cash				(l)	22,000	
Totals			583,000		583,000	

*Significant noncash investing and financing activity.

Preparing the Statement

The statement of cash flows is prepared primarily from the data that appears in the work sheet under Statement of Cash Flows Effects. The reconciling columns should also be scanned for any asterisked items that designate significant non-cash activities. The formal statement was shown in Illustration 19-17.

Summary of Study Objectives for Appendix J

5. Explain the guidelines and procedural steps in using a work sheet to prepare the statement of cash flows. When there are numerous adjustments, a work sheet can be a helpful tool in preparing the statement of cash flows. Key guidelines for using a work sheet are: (1) list accounts with debit balances separately from those with credit balances; (2) in the reconciling columns in the bottom portion of the work sheet, show cash inflows as debits and cash outflows as credits; (3) do not enter reconciling items in any journal or account but use them only to help prepare the statement of cash flows.

The steps in preparing the work sheet are: (1) enter beginning and ending balances of balance sheet accounts; (2) enter debits and credits in reconciling columns; (3) enter the increase or decrease in cash in two places as a balancing amount.

GLOSSARY

Direct method · A method of determining the "net cash provided by operating activities" in which cash receipts from revenues are compared item by item with cash payments for expenses. (p. 770)

Financing activities · Cash flow activities that include (a) obtaining cash from issuing debt and repaying the amounts borrowed and (b) obtaining cash from stockholders and providing them with a return on their investment. (p. 754)

Indirect method · A method of preparing a statement of cash flows in which net income is adjusted for items that did not affect cash to determine net cash provided by operating activities. (p. 759)

Investing activities · Cash flow activities that include (a) lending money and collecting on those loans and (b) acquiring and disposing of investments and productive long-lived assets. (p. 753)

Operating activities · Cash flow activities that include the cash effects of transactions that create revenues and expenses and thus enter into the determination of net income. (p. 753)

Statement of cash flows · A basic financial statement that provides information about the cash receipts and cash payments of an entity during a period, classified as operating, investing, and financing activities, in a format that reconciles the beginning and ending cash balances. (p. 752)

DEMONSTRATION PROBLEM

The income statement for the year ended December 31, 1993, for John Kosinski Manufacturing Company contains the following condensed information:

Revenues		$6,583,000
Operating expenses (excluding depreciation)	$4,920,000	
Depreciation expense	880,000	5,800,000
Income before income taxes		783,000
Income tax expense		353,000
Net income		$ 430,000

Included in operating expenses is a $24,000 loss resulting from the sale of machinery for $270,000 cash. Machinery was purchased at a cost of $750,000. The following balances are reported on Kosinski's comparative balance sheet at December 31:

	1993	1992
Cash	$672,000	$130,000
Accounts receivable	775,000	610,000
Inventories	834,000	867,000
Accounts payable	521,000	501,000

Income tax expense of $353,000 represents the amount paid in 1993. Dividends declared and paid in 1993 totaled $200,000.

Instructions
(a) Prepare the statement of cash flows using the indirect method.
(b) Prepare the statement of cash flows using the direct method.

Helpful hint This demonstration problem illustrates both the direct and indirect methods using the same basic data. Note the similarities and the differences between the two methods. Both methods report the same information in the investing and financing activities sections. The cash flow from operating activities section reports different information, but the amount, net cash provided by operating activities, is the same for both methods.

Solution to Demonstration Problem

JOHN KOSINSKI MANUFACTURING COMPANY
Statement of Cash Flows
For the Year Ended December 31, 1993

(a)   (Indirect Method)

Cash flows from operating activities		
Net income		$ 430,000
Adjustments to reconcile net income to net cash provided by operating activities:		
Depreciation expense	$880,000	
Loss on sale of machinery	24,000	
Increase in accounts receivable	(165,000)	
Decrease in inventories	33,000	
Increase in accounts payable	20,000	792,000
Net cash provided by operating activities		1,222,000
Cash flows from investing activities		
Sale of machinery	270,000	
Purchase of machinery	(750,000)	
Net cash used by investing activities		(480,000)
Cash flows from financing activities		
Payment of cash dividends		(200,000)
Net increase in cash		542,000
Cash at beginning of period		130,000
Cash at end of period		$672,000

(b)   (Direct Method)

Cash flows from operating activities		
Cash collections from customers		$6,418,000 *
Cash payments for operating expenses		4,843,000 **
Income before income taxes		1,575,000
Cash payment for income taxes		353,000
Net cash provided by operating activities		1,222,000
Cash flows from investing activities		
Sale of machinery	$270,000	
Purchase of machinery	(750,000)	
Net cash used by investing activities		(480,000)
Cash flows from financing activities		
Payment of cash dividends		(200,000)
Net increase in cash		542,000
Cash at beginning of period		130,000
Cash at end of period		$ 672,000

Direct Method Computations

* Computation of cash collections from customers:	
Revenues per the income statement	$6,583,000
Less increase in accounts receivable	165,000
Cash collections from customers	$6,418,000
** Computation of cash payments for operating expenses:	
Operating expenses per the income statement	$4,920,000
Deduct loss from sale of machinery	(24,000)
Deduct decrease in inventories	(33,000)
Deduct increase in accounts payable	(20,000)
Cash payments for operating expenses	$4,843,000

*Note: All **asterisked** Questions, Exercises, and Problems relate to material contained in the Appendix to each chapter.

SELF-STUDY QUESTIONS

Answers are at the end of the chapter.

(S.O. 1)   1. Which of the following is **incorrect** about the statement of cash flows?
   a. It is a fourth basic financial statement.
   b. It provides information about cash receipts and cash payments of an entity during a period.
   c. It provides information about the operating, investing, and financing activities of the business.
   d. It reconciles the ending cash account balance to the balance per the bank statement.

(S.O. 2)   2. The statement of cash flows classifies cash receipts and cash payments by the following activities:
   a. investing, financing, and operating.
   b. operating and nonoperating.
   c. financing, operating, and nonoperating.
   d. investing, financing, and nonoperating.

(S.O. 2)   3. An example of a cash flow from an operating activity is:
   a. payment of cash for redemption of bonds.
   b. receipt of cash from the sale of capital stock.
   c. payment of cash dividends to the company's stockholders.
   d. none of the above.

(S.O. 2)   4. An example of a cash flow from an investing activity is:
   a. receipt of cash from the issuance of bonds payable.
   b. receipt of cash from the sale of equipment.
   c. payment of cash to repurchase outstanding capital stock.
   d. payment of cash dividends to stockholders.

(S.O. 2)   5. Cash dividends paid to stockholders are classified on the statement of cash flows as:
   a. operating activities.
   b. investing activities.
   c. financing activities.
   d. a combination of the above.

(S.O. 2)   6. An example of a cash flow from a financing activity is:
   a. receipt of cash from sale of land.
   b. purchase of equipment for cash.
   c. issuance of common stock for cash.
   d. none of the above.

(S.O. 2)   7. Which of the following about the statement of cash flows is **incorrect**?
   a. The direct method may be used to report cash provided by operations.
   b. The statement shows the cash provided (used) for three categories of activity.
   c. The indirect method may be used to report cash provided by operations.
   d. The operating section is the last section of the statement.

Questions 8 and 9 apply only to the indirect method.

(S.O. 3)   8. Net income is $108,000, accounts payable increased $10,000 during the year, inven-

tory decreased $6,000 during the year, and accounts receivable increased $12,000 during the year. Under the indirect method, net cash provided by operations is:

a. $102,000.
b. $112,000.
c. $124,000.
d. $136,000.

(S.O. 3) 9. Noncash charges that are added back to net income in determining cash provided by operations under the indirect method do **not** include:

a. depreciation expense.
b. amortization expense.
c. an increase in inventory.
d. loss on sale of equipment.

Questions 10 and 11 apply only to the direct method.

(S.O. 4) 10. The beginning balance in accounts receivable is $54,000, and the ending balance is $42,000. Sales during the period are $129,000. Cash receipts from customers is:

a. $117,000.
b. $129,000.

c. $135,000.
d. $141,000.

11. Which of the following items is reported on a cash flow statement prepared by the direct method? (S.O. 4)

a. loss on sale of building.
b. increase in accounts receivable.
c. cash payments to suppliers.
d. depreciation expense.

12. The statement of cash flows should **not** be used to evaluate an entity's ability to: (S.O. 3)

a. generate future cash flows.
b. earn net income.
c. pay dividends.
d. meet obligations.

*13. In a work sheet for the statement of cash flows, a decrease in accounts receivable is entered in the reconciling columns as a credit to Accounts Receivable and a debit in the: (S.O. 5)

a. operating activities section.
b. investing activities section.
c. financing activities section.
d. none of the above.

QUESTIONS

1. What is the purpose of the statement of cash flows? What information does it provide?

2. Why are businesses now using the statement of cash flows?

3. What are "cash equivalents"? How do cash equivalents affect the statement of cash flows?

4. Differentiate between investing activities and financing activities.

5. What are the major sources (inflows) of cash in a statement of cash flows? What are the major uses (outflows) of cash?

6. Why is it important to disclose certain noncash transactions? How should they be disclosed?

7. Wilma Flintstone and Barny Kublestone were discussing the presentation format of the statement of cash flows of Rock Candy Co. At the bottom of Rock Candy's statement of cash flows was a separate section entitled "Noncash investing and financing activities." Give three examples of significant noncash transactions that would be reported in this section.

8. Why is it necessary to use comparative balance sheets, a current income statement, and certain transaction data in preparing a statement of cash flows?

9. Contrast the advantages and disadvantages of the direct and indirect methods. Are both methods acceptable? Which method is preferred by the FASB? Which method is more popular?

10. When the total cash inflows exceed the total cash outflows in the statement of cash flows, how and where is this excess identified?

11. Describe the indirect method for determining net cash provided by operating activities.

12. Why is it necessary to convert accrual based net income to cash basis income when preparing a statement of cash flows?

13. The president of Aerosmith Company is puzzled. During the last year, the company experienced a net loss of $900,000, yet its cash increased $300,000 during the same period of time. Explain to the president how this situation could occur.

14. Identify five items that are adjustments to reconcile net income to net cash provided by operating activities under the indirect method.

15. Why and how is depreciation expense reported in a statement prepared using the indirect method?

16. Why is the statement of cash flows useful?

17. During 1993, Johnny Carson Company converted $1,500,000 of its total $2,000,000 of bonds payable into common stock. Indicate how the transaction would be reported on a statement of cash flows, if at all.

18. Describe the direct method for determining net cash provided by operating activities.

19. Give the formulas under the direct method for computing (a) cash receipts from customers and (b) cash payments to suppliers.

20. Cindy Crawford Inc. reported sales of $2 million for 1993. Accounts receivable decreased $200,000 and accounts payable increased $300,000. Compute cash receipts from customers, assuming that the receivable and payable transactions related to operations.

21. Why is depreciation expense not reported in the direct-method cash flow from operating activities section?

*22. Why is it advantageous to use a work sheet when preparing a statement of cash flows? Is a work sheet required to prepare a statement of cash flows?

BRIEF EXERCISES

BE19–1 Cisco, Inc., reported net income of $2.5 million in 1993. Depreciation for the year was $260,000, accounts receivable increased $350,000, and accounts payable increased $310,000. Compute net cash provided by operating activities using the indirect approach.

Compute cash provided by operating activities— indirect method. (S.O. 3)

BE19–2 The net income for Cheers Engineering Co. for 1993 was $280,000. For 1993, depreciation on plant assets was $60,000, and the company incurred a loss on sale of plant assets of $8,000. Compute net cash provided by operating activities under the indirect method.

Compute cash provided by operating activities— indirect method. (S.O. 3)

BE19–3 Each of the following items must be considered in preparing a statement of cash flows for Murphy Brown Co. for the year ended December 31, 1993. For each item, state how it should be shown in the statement of cash flows for 1993.

Indicate statement presentation of selected transactions. (S.O. 2)

(a) Issued bonds for $200,000 cash.

(b) Purchased equipment for $150,000 cash.

(c) Declared and paid a $50,000 cash dividend.

(d) Sold land costing $20,000 for $20,000 cash.

B19–4 The comparative balance sheet for the Rolen Company shows the following changes in noncash current asset accounts: accounts receivable decrease $80,000, prepaid expenses increase $12,000, and inventories increase $20,000. Compute net cash provided by operating activities using the indirect method assuming that net income is $200,000.

Compute net cash provided by operating activities using indirect method. (S.O. 3)

BE19–5 Classify the following items as an operating, investing, or financing activity. Assume all items involve cash unless there is information to the contrary.

Classify items by activities. (S.O. 2)

(a) Purchase of equipment.
(d) Depreciation.

(b) Redemption of bonds.
(e) Issuance of capital stock.

(c) Sale of building.
(f) Payment of dividends.

BE19–6 Billy Idol Corporation has accounts receivable of $14,000 at 1/1/93 and $26,000 at 12/31/93. Sales revenues were $480,000 for the year 1993. What is the amount of cash receipts from customers in 1993?

Compute receipts from customers using direct method. (S.O. 4)

BE19–7 Depeche Mode Corporation reported income taxes of $70,000 on its 1993 income statement and income taxes payable of $12,000 at December 31, 1992, and $10,000 at December 31, 1993. What amount of cash payments were made for income taxes during 1993?

Compute cash payments for income taxes using direct method. (S.O. 4)

Compute cash payments for operating expenses using direct method. (S.O. 4)

BE19–8   Excile Corporation reports operating expenses of $90,000 excluding depreciation expense of $15,000 for 1993. During the year prepaid expenses decreased $6,600 and accrued expenses payable increased $2,400. Compute the cash payments for operating expenses in 1993.

Determine cash received in sale of equipment. (S.O. 3, 4)

BE19–9   The T-accounts for Equipment and the related Accumulated Depreciation for Randy Travis Company at the end of 1993 are as follows:

Equipment					Accumulated Depreciation			
Beg. bal.	80,000	Disposals	22,000		Disposals	5,500	Beg. bal.	44,500
Acquisitions	41,600						Depr.	12,000
End. bal.	99,600						End. bal.	51,000

In addition, Randy Travis Company's income statement reported a loss on the sale of equipment of $4,700. What amount was reported on the statement of cash flows as "cash flow from sale of equipment"?

Identify financing activity transactions. (S.O. 2)

BE19–10   The following T-account is a summary of the cash account of Anita Baker Company.

Cash (Summary Form)			
Balance, 1/1/93	8,000		
Receipts from customers	364,000	Payments for goods	200,000
Dividends on stock investments	6,000	Payments for operating expenses	140,000
Proceeds from sale of equipment	36,000	Interest paid	10,000
Proceeds from issuance of bonds		Taxes paid	8,000
payable	100,000	Dividends paid	30,000
Balance, 12/31/93	126,000		

For Anita Baker Company what amount of net cash provided (used) by financing activities should be reported in the statement of cash flows?

Indicate entries in work sheet. (S.O. 5)

*__*BE19–11__   Using the data in BE19–8, indicate how the changes in prepaid expenses and accrued expenses payable should be entered in the reconciling columns of a work sheet. Assume that beginning balances were: prepaid expenses, $18,600 and accrued expenses payable, $8,200.

EXERCISES

Classify transactions by type of activity. (S.O. 2)

E19–1   John Goodman Company had the following transactions during 1993:

1. Issued $50,000 par value common stock for cash.
2. Purchased a machine for $30,000, giving a long-term note in exchange.
3. Collected $16,000 of accounts receivable.
4. Declared and paid a cash dividend of $25,000.
5. Sold a long-term investment with a cost of $15,000 for $15,000 cash.
6. Issued $200,000 par value common stock upon conversion of bonds having a face value of $200,000.
7. Paid $18,000 on accounts payable.

Instructions
Analyze the transactions above and indicate whether each transaction resulted in a cash flow from (a) operating activities, (b) investing activities, (c) financing activities, or (d) noncash investing and financing activities.

Prepare the operating activities section—indirect method. (S.O. 3)

E19–2   Joe Pesci Company reported net income of $195,000 for 1993. Pesci also reported depreciation expense of $35,000, and a loss of $5,000 on the sale of equipment. The comparative balance sheet shows an increase in accounts receivable of $15,000 for the year, a $7,000 increase in accounts payable, and a decrease in prepaid expenses $4,000.

Instructions

Prepare the operating activities section of the statement of cash flows for 1993. Use the indirect method.

E19–3   The current sections of Dolly Barton Company's balance sheets at December 31, 1992 and 1993, are presented below.

Prepare the operating activities section—indirect method.
(S.O. 3)

	1993	1992
Current assets		
Cash	$105,000	$ 99,000
Accounts receivable	110,000	89,000
Inventory	171,000	186,000
Prepaid expenses	27,000	32,000
Total current assets	$413,000	$406,000
Current liabilities		
Accrued expenses payable	$ 15,000	$ 5,000
Accounts payable	$ 85,000	$ 92,000
Total current liabilities	$100,000	$ 97,000

Barton's net income for 1993 was $122,000. Depreciation expense was $25,000.

Instructions

Prepare the net cash provided by operating activities section of Dolly Barton Company's statement of cash flows for the year ended December 31, 1993 using the indirect method.

E19–4   Presented below are three accounts that appear in the general ledger of Robert Duvall Corp.:

Prepare partial statement of cash flows—indirect method.
(S.O. 3)

Equipment

Date		Debit	Credit	Balance
Jan. 1, 1993	Balance			160,000
July 31	Purchase of equipment	70,000		230,000
Sept. 2	Cost of equipment constructed	53,000		283,000
Nov. 10	Cost of equipment sold		45,000	238,000

Accumulated Depreciation—Equipment

Date		Debit	Credit	Balance
Jan. 1, 1993	Balance			71,000
Nov. 10	Accumulated depreciation on equipment sold	30,000		41,000
Dec. 31	Depreciation for 1993		24,000	65,000

Retained Earnings

Date		Debit	Credit	Balance
Jan. 1, 1993	Balance			105,000
Aug. 23	Dividends (cash)	14,000		91,000
Dec. 31	Net income		47,000	138,000

Instructions

From the postings in the accounts above, indicate how the information is reported on a statement of cash flows by preparing a partial statement of cash flows using the indirect method. The loss on sale of equipment was $8,000.

E19–5   A comparative balance sheet for Oprah Winfrey Company is presented below.

Prepare a statement of cash flows—indirect method.
(S.O. 3)

	December 31	
Assets	1993	1992
Cash	$ 63,000	$ 22,000
Accounts receivable	85,000	66,000
Inventories	180,000	189,000
Land	75,000	110,000
Equipment	260,000	200,000
Accumulated depreciation	(66,000)	(42,000)
Total	$597,000	$545,000

Liabilities and Stockholders' Equity

Accounts payable	$ 34,000	$ 47,000
Bonds payable	150,000	200,000
Common stock ($1 par)	214,000	164,000
Retained earnings	199,000	134,000
Total	$597,000	$545,000

Additional information:

1. Net income for 1993 was $105,000.
2. Cash dividends of $40,000 were declared and paid.
3. Bonds payable amounting to $50,000 were redeemed for cash $50,000.
4. Common stock was issued for $50,000 cash.

Instructions

Prepare a statement of cash flows for 1993 using the indirect method.

E19–6   An analysis of comparative balance sheets, the current year's income statement and the general ledger accounts of Pierce Brosnan Corp. uncovered the following items. Assume all items involve cash unless there is information to the contrary.

(a) Payment of dividends.
(b) Purchase of land.
(c) Sale of building at book value.
(d) Exchange of land for patent.
(e) Depreciation.
(f) Redemption of bonds.
(g) Receipt of interest on notes receivable.

(h) Issuance of capital stock.
(i) Amortization of patent.
(j) Issuance of bonds for land.
(k) Payment of interest on notes payable.
(l) Conversion of bonds into common stock.
(m) Receipt of dividends on investment in stock.
(n) Loss on sale of land.

Instructions

Indicate how the above items should be classified in the statement of cash flows using the following four major classifications: operating activity (indirect method), investing activity, financing activity, and significant noncash investing and financing activity.

E19–7   Kelly McGillis Company has just completed its first year of operations on December 31, 1993. Its initial income statement showed that Kelly McGillis had revenues of $157,000 and operating expenses of $78,000. Accounts receivable and accounts payable at year end were $45,000 and $33,000, respectively. Assume that accounts payable related to operating expenses. Ignore income taxes.

Instructions

Compute net cash provided by operating activities using the direct method.

E19–8   The income statement for the Garcia Company shows cost of goods sold $355,000 and operating expenses (exclusive of depreciation) $230,000. The comparative balance sheet for the year shows that inventory increased $5,000, prepaid expenses decreased $6,000, accounts payable (merchandise supplies) decreased $8,000, and accrued expenses payable increased $9,000.

Instructions

Using the direct method, compute (a) cash payments to suppliers and (b) cash payments for operating expenses.

E19–9   The 1994 accounting records of Flyproper Airlines reveal the following transactions and events.

Payment of interest	$ 6,000	Collection of accounts receivable	$178,000
Cash sales	48,000	Payment of salaries and wages	68,000
Receipt of dividend revenue	14,000	Depreciation expense	16,000
Payment of income taxes	16,000	Proceeds from sale of aircraft	812,000
Net income	38,000	Purchase of equipment for cash	22,000
Payment of accounts payable for		Loss on sale of aircraft	3,000
merchandise	90,000	Payment of dividends	14,000
Payment for land	74,000	Payment of operating expenses	20,000

Margin notes:

Classify transactions by type of activity.
(S.O. 2)

Compute cash provided by operating activities—direct method.
(S.O. 4)

Compute cash payments—direct method.
(S.O. 4)

Compute cash flow from operating activities—direct method
(S.O. 2, 4)

Instructions

Prepare the cash flows from operating activities section using the direct method. (Not all of the above items will be used.)

E19–10 The following information is taken from the 1994 general ledger of Joan Robinson Company:

Calculate cash flows—
direct method
(S.O. 4)

Rent	Rent expense	$ 31,000
	Prepaid rent, January 1	4,900
	Prepaid rent, December 31	3,000
Salaries	Salaries expense	$ 54,000
	Salaries payable, January 1	5,000
	Salaries payable, December 31	8,000
Sales	Revenue from sales	$180,000
	Accounts receivable, January 1	12,000
	Accounts receivable, December 31	9,000

Instructions

In each of above cases, compute the amount that should be reported in the operating activities section of the statement of cash flows applying the direct method.

*E19–11

Prepare a work sheet.
(S.O. 5)

Instructions

Refer to Exercise E19–5 (Oprah Winfrey Company) and use these data to prepare a work sheet for a statement of cash flows for 1993. Enter the reconciling items directly on the work sheet, identifying the entries alphabetically.

PROBLEMS

P19–1 The income statement of Beethoven Company is shown below:

Prepare the operating ac-
tivities section—indirect
method.
(S.O. 3)
S

BEETHOVEN COMPANY
Income Statement
For the Year Ended November 30, 1993

Sales		$6,900,000
Cost of goods sold		
Beginning inventory	$1,900,000	
Purchases	4,400,000	
Goods available for sale	6,300,000	
Ending inventory	1,600,000	
Cost of goods sold		4,700,000
Gross profit		2,200,000
Operating expenses		
Selling expenses	450,000	
Administrative expenses	700,000	1,150,000
Net income		$1,050,000

Additional information:

1. Accounts receivable decreased $350,000 during the year.
2. Prepaid expenses increased $150,000 during the year.
3. Accounts payable to suppliers of merchandise decreased $300,000 during the year.
4. Accrued expenses payable decreased $100,000 during the year.
5. Administrative expenses include depreciation expense of $60,000.

Instructions

Prepare the operating activities section of the statement of cash flows for the year ended November 30, 1993, for Beethoven Company, using the indirect method.

P19–2 Data for the Beethoven Company are presented in P19–1.

Prepare operating activi-
ties section—direct
method. (S.O. 4)

Instructions

Prepare the operating activities section of the statement of cash flows using the direct method.

Prepare the operating ac-
tivities section—direct
method.
(S.O. 4)

P19–3   Bach Company's income statement for the year ended December 31, 1993, contained the following condensed information:

Revenue from fees		$840,000
Operating expenses (excluding depreciation)	$624,000	
Depreciation expense	60,000	
Loss on sale of equipment	26,000	710,000
Income before income taxes		130,000
Income tax expense		40,000
Net income		$ 90,000

Bach's balance sheet contained the following comparative data at December 31:

	1993	1992
Accounts receivable	$37,000	$55,000
Accounts payable	41,000	33,000
Income taxes payable	4,000	9,000

(Accounts payable pertains to operating expenses.)

Instructions

Prepare the operating activities section of the statement of cash flows using the direct method.

Prepare the operating ac-
tivities section—indirect
method
(S.O. 4)

P19–4

Instructions

Using the data from Problem 19-3, prepare the operating activities section of the statement of cash flows using the indirect method.

Prepare a statement of
cash flows—indirect
method.
(S.O. 3)

P19–5   The financial statements of Patrick Swayze Company appear below:

PATRICK SWAYZE COMPANY
Comparative Balance Sheet
December 31

Assets	1993	1992
Cash	$ 29,000	$ 13,000
Accounts receivable	26,000	14,000
Merchandise inventory	25,000	35,000
Property, plant, and equipment	60,000	78,000
Accumulated depreciation	(20,000)	(24,000)
Total	$120,000	$116,000

Liabilities and Stockholders' Equity		
Accounts payable	$ 29,000	$ 23,000
Income taxes payable	3,000	8,000
Bonds payable	27,000	33,000
Common stock	18,000	14,000
Retained earnings	43,000	38,000
Total	$120,000	$116,000

PATRICK SWAYZE COMPANY
Income Statement
For the Year Ended December 31, 1993

Sales		$220,000
Cost of goods sold		180,000
Gross profit		40,000
Selling expenses	$18,000	
Administrative expenses	6,000	24,000
Income from operations		16,000
Interest expense		2,000

Income before income taxes	14,000	
Income tax expense	4,000	
Net income	$ 10,000	

The following additional data were provided:

1. Dividends declared and paid were $5,000.

2. During the year equipment was sold for $8,500 cash. This equipment cost $18,000 originally and had a book value of $8,500 at the time of sale.

3. All depreciation expense is in the selling expense category.

4. All sales and purchases are on account.

Instructions
Prepare a statement of cash flows using the indirect method.

P19–6 Data for the Patrick Swayze Company are presented in P19–5. Further analysis reveals the following:

1. Accounts payable pertain to merchandise suppliers.

2. All operating expenses except for depreciation were paid in cash.

Prepare a statement of cash flows—direct method. (S.O. 4)

Instructions
Prepare a statement of cash flows for Patrick Swayze Company using the direct method.

P19–7 Condensed financial data of Fern Gully Company appear below.

Prepare a statement of cash flows—indirect method. (S.O. 3)

FERN GULLY COMPANY
Comparative Balance Sheet
December 31

Assets	1993	1992
Cash	$ 97,800	$ 38,400
Accounts receivable	90,800	33,000
Inventories	112,500	102,850
Prepaid expenses	18,400	16,000
Investments	108,000	94,000
Plant assets	270,000	242,500
Accumulated depreciation	(50,000)	(52,000)
	$647,500	$474,750

Liabilities and Stockholders' Equity		
Accounts payable	$ 92,000	$ 67,300
Accrued expenses payable	16,500	17,000
Bonds payable	85,000	110,000
Common stock	220,000	175,000
Retained earnings	234,000	105,450
	$647,500	$474,750

FERN GULLY COMPANY
Income Statement Data
For the Year Ended December 31, 1993

Sales		$342,780
Less:		
Cost of goods sold	$115,460	
Operating expenses (excluding depreciation)	12,410	
Depreciation expense	46,500	
Income taxes	7,275	
Interest expense	2,730	
Loss on sale of plant assets	7,500	191,875
Net income		$150,905

Additional information:

1. New plant assets costing $85,000 were purchased for cash during the year.
2. Old plant assets having an original cost of $57,500 were sold for $1,500 cash.
3. Bonds were redeemed at face value for cash.
4. A cash dividend of $22,355 was declared and paid during the year.

Instructions

Prepare a statement of cash flows using the indirect method.

Prepare a statement of cash flows—direct method. (S.O. 4)

P19–8   Data for the Fern Gully Company are presented in P19–7. Further analysis reveals that accounts payable pertains to merchandise creditors.

Instructions

Prepare a statement of cash flows for Fern Gully Company using the direct method.

P19–9   Presented below is the comparative balance sheet for Cousin Vinny's Toy Company as of December 31:

Prepare a statement of cash flows—indirect method.
(S.O. 3)

COUSIN VINNY'S TOY COMPANY
Comparative Balance Sheet
December 31

	1993	1992
Assets		
Cash	$ 41,000	$ 45,000
Accounts receivable	47,500	52,000
Inventory	151,450	142,000
Prepaid expenses	16,780	21,000
Land	100,000	130,000
Equipment	228,000	155,000
Accumulated depreciation—equipment	(45,000)	(35,000)
Building	200,000	200,000
Accumulated depreciation—building	(60,000)	(40,000)
	$679,730	$670,000
Liabilities and Stockholders' Equity		
Accounts payable	$ 43,670	$ 40,000
Bonds payable	250,000	300,000
Common stock, $1 par	200,000	100,000
Retained earnings	186,060	230,000
	$679,730	$670,000

Additional information:

1. Operating expenses include depreciation expense of $42,000 and charges from prepaid expenses of $4,220.
2. Land was sold for cash at book value.
3. Cash dividends of $82,990 were paid.
4. Net income for 1993 was $39,050.
5. Equipment was purchased for $95,000 cash. In addition, equipment costing $22,000 with a book value of $10,000 was sold for $8,100 cash.
6. Bonds were converted at face value by issuing 50,000 shares of $1 par value common stock.

Instructions

Prepare a statement of cash flows for the year ended December 31, 1993, using the indirect method.

Prepare a work sheet.
(S.O. 5)

*P19–10

Instructions

Refer to Problem 19–7 (Fern Gully Company) and use these data to prepare a work sheet for a statement of cash flows for 1993. Enter the reconciling entries directly on the work sheet, identifying the entries alphabetically.

ALTERNATE PROBLEMS

P19–1A The income statement of Charlie Brown Company is shown below:

Prepare the operating activities section—indirect method.
(S.O. 3)

CHARLIE BROWN COMPANY
Income Statement
For the Year Ended December 31, 1993

Sales		$7,100,000
Cost of goods sold		
Beginning inventory	$1,700,000	
Purchases	5,430,000	
Goods available for sale	7,130,000	
Ending inventory	1,920,000	
Cost of goods sold		5,210,000
Gross profit		1,890,000
Operating expenses		
Selling expenses	400,000	
Administrative expense	525,000	
Depreciation expense	75,000	
Amortization expense	30,000	1,030,000
Net income		$ 860,000

Additional information:

1. Accounts receivable increased $510,000 during the year.
2. Prepaid expenses increased $170,000 during the year.
3. Accounts payable to merchandise suppliers increased $45,000 during the year.
4. Accrued expenses payable decreased $180,000 during the year.

Instructions
Prepare the operating activities section of the statement of cash flows for the year ended December 31, 1993, for Charlie Brown Company, using the indirect method.

P19–2A Data for the Charlie Brown Company are presented in P19–1A.

Prepare the operating activities section—direct method. (S.O. 4)

Instructions
Prepare the operating activities section of the statement of cash flows using the direct method.

P19–3A The income statement of Comet International Inc. for the year ended December 31, 1993, reported the following condensed information:

Prepare the operating activities section—direct method.
(S.O. 4)

Revenue from fees	$430,000
Operating expenses	280,000
Income from operations	150,000
Income tax expense	47,000
Net income	$103,000

Comet's balance sheet contained the following comparative data at December 31:

	1993	1992
Accounts receivable	$50,000	$40,000
Accounts payable	32,000	41,000
Income taxes payable	6,000	4,000

Comet has no depreciable assets. Accounts payable pertains to operating expenses.

Instructions
Prepare the operating activities section of the statement of cash flows using the direct method.

P19–4A

Instructions
Using the data from Problem 19-3A, prepare the operating activities section of the statement of cash flows using the indirect method.

Prepare the operating activities section—indirect method. (S.O. 3)

Prepare a statement of
cash flows—indirect
method.
(S.O. 2, 3)

P19–5A   The financial statements of Sean Semor Company appear below:

SEAN SEMOR COMPANY
Comparative Balance Sheet
December 31

Assets		1993		1992
Cash		$ 26,000		$ 13,000
Accounts receivable		16,000		14,000
Merchandise inventory		38,000		35,000
Property, plant, and equipment	$70,000		$78,000	
Less accumulated depreciation	(30,000)	40,000	(24,000)	54,000
Total		$120,000		$116,000

Liabilities and Stockholders' Equity	1993	1992
Accounts payable	$ 27,000	$ 33,000
Income taxes payable	15,000	20,000
Bonds payable	20,000	10,000
Common stock	25,000	25,000
Retained earnings	33,000	28,000
Total	$120,000	$116,000

SEAN SEMOR COMPANY
Income Statement
For the Year Ended December 31, 1993

Sales		$240,000
Cost of goods sold		180,000
Gross profit		60,000
Selling expenses	$28,000	
Administrative expenses	6,000	34,000
Income from operations		26,000
Interest expense		2,000
Income before income taxes		24,000
Income tax expense		7,000
Net income		$ 17,000

The following additional data were provided:

1. Dividends of $12,000 were declared and paid.
2. During the year equipment was sold for $10,000 cash. This equipment cost $15,000 originally and had a book value of $10,000 at the time of sale.
3. All depreciation expense, $11,000, is in the selling expense category.
4. All sales and purchases are on account.
5. Additional equipment was purchased for $7,000 cash.

Instructions
Prepare a statement of cash flows using the indirect method.

Prepare a statement of
cash flows—direct
method.
(S.O. 4)

P19–6A   Data for the Sean Semor Company are presented in P19–5A. Further analysis reveals the following:

1. Accounts payable pertains to merchandise creditors.
2. All operating expenses except for depreciation are paid in cash.

Instructions
Prepare a statement of cash flows using the direct method.

P19–7A Condensed financial data of Norumbega Company appear below:

Prepare statement of cash flows—indirect method.
(S.O. 3)

NORUMBEGA COMPANY
Comparative Balance Sheet
December 31

	1993	1992
Assets		
Cash	$ 96,700	$ 47,250
Accounts receivable	86,800	57,000
Inventories	121,900	102,650
Investments	84,500	87,000
Plant assets	250,000	205,000
Accumulated depreciation	(49,500)	(40,000)
	$590,400	$458,900
Liabilities and Stockholders' Equity		
Accounts payable	$ 52,700	$ 48,280
Accrued expenses payable	12,100	18,830
Bonds payable	100,000	70,000
Common stock	250,000	200,000
Retained earnings	175,600	121,790
	$590,400	$458,900

NORUMBEGA COMPANY
Income Statement Data
For the Year Ended December 31, 1993

Sales		$297,500
Gain on sale of plant assets		8,750
		306,250
Less:		
Cost of goods sold	$99,460	
Operating expenses (excluding depreciation expense)	14,670	
Depreciation expense	49,700	
Income taxes	7,275	
Interest expense	2,940	174,045
Net income		$132,205

Additional information:

1. New plant assets costing $92,000 were purchased for cash during the year.
2. Investments were sold at cost.
3. Plant assets costing $47,000 were sold at a gain of $8,750.
4. A cash dividend of $78,395 was declared and paid during the year.

Instructions
Prepare a statement of cash flows using the indirect method.

P19–8A Data for Norumbega Company are presented in P19–7A. Further analysis reveals that accounts payable pertains to merchandise creditors.

Prepare a statement of cash flows—direct method. (S.O. 4)

Instructions
Prepare a statement of cash flows for Norumbega Company using the direct method.

Prepare a statement of
cash flows—indirect
method.
(S.O. 3)

P19–9A Presented below is the comparative balance sheet for Camden Maine Company at December 31:

CAMDEN MAINE COMPANY
Comparative Balance Sheet
December 31

	1993	1992
Cash	$ 40,000	$ 57,000
Accounts receivable	77,000	64,000
Inventory	132,000	140,000
Prepaid expenses	12,140	16,540
Land	125,000	150,000
Equipment	200,000	175,000
Accumulated depreciation—equipment	(60,000)	(42,000)
Building	250,000	250,000
Accumulated depreciation—building	(75,000)	(50,000)
	$701,140	$760,540
Accounts payable	$ 33,000	$ 45,000
Bonds payable	235,000	265,000
Common stock, $1 par	280,000	250,000
Retained earnings	153,140	200,540
	$701,140	$760,540

Additional information:

1. Operating expenses include depreciation expense $70,000 and charges from prepaid expenses of $4,400.

2. Land was sold for cash at cost.

3. Cash dividends of $74,290 were paid.

4. Net income for 1993 was $26,890.

5. Equipment was purchased for $65,000 cash. In addition, equipment costing $40,000 with a book value of $13,000 was sold for $15,000 cash.

6. Bonds were converted at face value by issuing 30,000 shares of $1 par value common stock.

Instructions

Prepare a statement of cash flows for 1993 using the indirect method.

Prepare a work sheet
(S.O. 5)

*P19–10A

Instructions
Refer to Problem 19–7A (Norumbega Company) and use this data to prepare a work sheet for a statement of cash flows. Enter the reconciling items directly in the work sheet columns, identifying the debit and credit amounts alphabetically.

Broadening Your Perspective

FINANCIAL REPORTING PROBLEM

Refer to the financial statements of PepsiCo, Inc. presented in Appendix L and answer the following questions:

1. What was the amount of net cash provided by operating activities (continuing operations) for the year ended December 28, 1991? For the year ended December 29, 1990?

2. What was the amount of increase or decrease in cash and cash equivalents for the year ended December 28, 1991? For the year ended December 29, 1990?

3. Which method of computing net cash provided by operating activities does PepsiCo use?

4. From your analysis of the 1991 statement of cash flows, was the change in notes and accounts receivable a decrease or an increase? Was the change in inventories a decrease or an increase? Was the change in accounts payable a decrease or an increase?

5. What was the total (gross) outflow of cash for investing activities for 1991?

6. What was the amount of interest paid in 1991? What was the amount of income taxes paid in 1991?

7. What four significant noncash investing and financing activities did PepsiCo complete in 1991?

DECISION CASE

Greg Rhoda and Debra Sondgeroth are examining the following statement of cash flows for L.L. Bean Trading Company for the year ended January 31, 1994.

L.L. BEAN TRADING COMPANY
Statement of Cash Flows
For the Year Ended January 31, 1994

Sources of cash	
From sales of merchandise	$370,000
From sale of capital stock	420,000
From sale of investment (purchased below)	80,000
From depreciation	55,000
From issuance of note for truck	20,000
From interest on investments	8,000
Total sources of cash	953,000
Uses of cash	
For purchase of fixtures and equipment	340,000
For merchandise purchased for resale	260,000
For operating expenses (including depreciation)	160,000
For purchase of investment	75,000
For purchase of truck by issuance of note	20,000
For purchase of treasury stock	10,000
For interest on note payable	3,000
Total uses of cash	868,000
Net increase in cash	$ 85,000

Greg claims that L.L. Bean's statement of cash flows is an excellent portrayal of a superb first year with cash increasing $85,000. Debra replies that it was not a superb first year, that the year was an operating failure, that the statement was incorrectly presented, and that $85,000 is not the actual increase in cash. The cash balance at the beginning of the year was $140,000.

Instructions

(a) With whom do you agree, Greg or Debra? Explain your position.

(b) Using the data provided, prepare a statement of cash flows in proper form using the indirect method. The only noncash items in the income statement are depreciation and the gain from the sale of the investment.

CRITICAL THINKING CASE

Refer to the opening story of Gerald Biby's attempt to refinance Kilian Community College's mortgage. Answer the following questions:

1. How was the purchase of the $250,000 computer system presented on the "traditional educational institution financial statement" so that it negatively affected Biby's ability to refinance the mortgage?

2. How was the purchase of the $250,000 computer system presented on the statement of cash flows? How did the preparation of the statement of cash flows aid Biby in securing the refinancing of the mortgage?

3. Compute an estimate of Kilian Community College's annual tuition revenue.

ETHICAL CASE

Puebla Corporation is a medium-sized wholesaler of automotive parts. It has ten stockholders that have been paid a total of $1 million in cash dividends for eight consecutive years. The Board of Director's policy requires that in order for this dividend to be declared, net cash provided by operating activities as reported in Puebla's current year's statement of cash flows must be in excess of $1 million. President and CEO Phil Monat's job is secure so long as he produces annual operating cash flows to support the usual dividend.

At the end of the current year, controller Rick Rodgers presents President Monat with some disappointing news—the net cash provided by operating activities is calculated by the indirect method to be only $970,000. The president says to Rick, "We must get that amount above $1 million. Isn't there some way to increase operating cash flow by another $30,000?" Rick answers, "These figures were prepared by my assistant. I'll go back to my office and see what I can do." The president replies, "I know you won't let me down, Rick."

Upon close scrutiny of the statement of cash flows, Rick concludes that he can get the operating cash flows above $1 million by reclassifying a $60,000 two-year note payable listed in the financing activities section as "Proceeds from bank loan—$60,000." He will report the note instead as "Increase in payables—$60,000" and treat it as an adjustment of net income in the operating activities section. He returns to the president saying, "You can tell the Board to declare their usual dividend. Our net cash flow provided by operating activities is $1,030,000." "Good boy, Rick! I knew I could count on you," exalts the president.

Instructions

(a) Who are the stakeholders in this situation?

(b) Was there anything unethical about the president's actions? Was there anything unethical about the controller's actions?

(c) Are the Board members or anyone else likely to discover the misclassification?

Answers to Self-Study Questions
1. d   2. a   3. d   4. b   5. c   6. c   7. d   8. b   9. c   10. d
11. c   12. b   13. a

CONCEPTS FOR REVIEW

Before studying this chapter, you should know or, if necessary, review:

a. *The contents and classification of a corporate balance sheet (Ch. 18, p. 728–30)*

b. *The contents and classification of a corporate income statement (Ch. 16, p. 637–42)*

c. *Who are the various users of financial statement information (Ch. 1, p. 4–6)*

d. *How to compute earnings per share (EPS) (Ch. 16, p. 642–5)*

e. *How the liquidity of a company is determined (Ch. 4, p. 151)*

CHAPTER 20

FINANCIAL STATEMENT ANALYSIS

Study Objectives

After studying this chapter, you should be able to:

1. Discuss the need for comparative analysis.

2. Identify the tools of financial statement analysis.

3. Explain and apply horizontal (trend) analysis.

4. Describe and apply vertical analysis.

5. Identify and compute ratios and describe their purpose and use in analyzing a firm's liquidity, profitability, and solvency.

6. Recognize the limitations of financial statement analysis.

W hen big banks and insurance companies lend millions of dollars to colleges and universities, the lenders understandably want to know that their money is secure. That's why they demand that the schools provide certain financial statement ratios.

At the University of Chicago, John R. Kroll is responsible for putting together some 40 different ratios—ranging from measures of liquidity to qualitative factors such as student SAT scores.

One balance sheet ratio measures the relationship of equity to debt. "A ratio of 1-to-1 says that if a calamity strikes, you could liquidate your net assets and pay off your debt. Your 'A'-rated institutions, as measured by Standard & Poor's, a New York rating agency, have a ratio of 2-to-1. 'AAA' institutions—the highest ranking, have a 4-to-1 ratio. We have a 5.5-to-1 ratio."

Kroll says the good equity-to-debt ratio helped the university borrow $100

million recently in order to build two new buildings. "Buildings are financed in one

of two ways," he says. "Either people give money to build the building, or you have

to go out and borrow cash and pay it off over a long period of time."

Another key ratio is the endowment ratio—the ratio of endowment gifts the

university has received to the number of students. The more endowment a school has,

the less pressure it has to find money from other sources.

Lenders are even interested in SAT scores. The reason: "The stronger the

student, the more demand there is to attend your institution," says Kroll.

If you had excess cash which you wanted to invest, what would you do with it? One of the most popular forms of investments is in stocks or bonds. If stocks are your choice, should your investment be in conservative utility stocks such as Pacific Gas & Electric Company or in speculative research or high-tech stocks such as Genetic Inc. or Satellite Communications Corp.? If you choose to buy bonds, should you invest in General Electric's quality bonds, which generally have greater stability, less risk (AAA rated), and lower yields, or in Sunshine Mining bonds that offer higher rates of return but are less stable and of greater risk (BCC rated)? To answer these types of questions, it is helpful for you to understand how to analyze and interpret financial statement information.

In analyzing and interpreting financial statement information, three major characteristics are generally evaluated: **liquidity**, **profitability**, and **solvency**. For example, a **short-term creditor**, such as a bank, is primarily interested in the ability of the borrower to pay obligations when they come due. The liquidity of the borrower in such a case is extremely important in evaluating the safety of a loan. A **long-term creditor**, such as a bondholder, however, looks to indicators such as profitability and solvency that indicate the firm's ability to survive over a long period of time. Long-term creditors analyze earnings per share, the relationship of income to total assets invested, the amount of debt in the company's existing capital structure, and the ability to meet interest payments when due to determine whether money should be lent and at what interest rate. Similarly, **stockholders** are interested in the profitability and solvency of the enterprise when assessing the likelihood of dividends and the growth potential of the stock.

Need for Comparative Analysis

Study Objective 1

Discuss the need for comparative analysis.

Any item reported in a financial statement has significance: its inclusion indicates that the item exists at a given time and in a certain quantity. For example, when Xerox Corporation reports $326,200,000 on its balance sheet as cash, we know that Xerox Corporation did have cash and that the quantity was $326,200,000. But whether it represents an increase over prior years, much less whether it is adequate in relation to the company's needs, cannot be determined from the amount alone. This amount must be compared with other financial data to obtain this information.

Comparisons can be made on a number of different bases. The following three are illustrated in this chapter.

1. **Intracompany basis**—Comparisons within a company are often useful to detect changes in financial relationships and significant trends. For ex-

ample, a comparison of Xerox's current year's cash amount with the prior year's cash amount shows either an increase or a decrease. Likewise, a comparison of Xerox's year-end cash amount with the amount of its total assets at year-end shows the proportion of total assets in the form of cash.

2. **Intercompany basis**—Comparisons with other companies provide insight into a company's competitive position. For example, Xerox's total sales for the year can be compared with the total sales of its competitors in the copying equipment area such as Canon or Savin.

3. **Industry averages**—Comparisons with industry averages provide information as to a company's relative position within the industry. For example, Xerox's financial data can be compared with the averages for the copying equipment industry compiled by financial ratings organizations such as Dun & Bradstreet, Moody's, and Standard & Poor's.

*T*ools of Financial Statement Analysis

Various tools are used in financial statement analysis to highlight the significance of financial statement data. Three basic tools are:

1. Horizontal analysis.
2. Vertical analysis.
3. Ratio analysis.

Study Objective 2

Identify the tools of financial statement analysis.

Horizontal Analysis

Horizontal analysis, also called **trend analysis**, is a technique for evaluating a series of financial statement data over a period of time. Its purpose is to determine the increase or decrease that has taken place, expressed as either an amount or a percentage. For example, the recent net sales figures of Kellogg Company are as follows:

Study Objective 3

Explain and apply horizontal (trend) analysis.

ILLUSTRATION 20-1

Kellogg's net sales

KELLOGG COMPANY (Net Sales Stated in Millions)				
1991	1990	1989	1988	1987
$5,786.6	$5,181.4	$4,651.7	$4,348.8	$3,793.0

If we assume that 1987 is the base year, we can measure all percentage increases or decreases from this base period amount as follows:

$$\frac{\text{Current year amount} - \text{Base year amount}}{\text{Base year amount}}$$

For example, we can determine that net sales for Kellogg Company increased approximately 14.7% [($4,348.8 − $3,793.0) ÷ $3,793.0] from 1987 to 1988. Similarly, we can determine that net sales increased over 52.6% [($5,786.6 − $3,793.0) ÷ $3,793.0] from 1987 to 1991. The percentage of the base period for each of the five years, assuming 1987 as the base period, is shown in Illustration 20-2.[1]

---

[1]While comparative balance sheets are generally prepared for two consecutive years and comparative income statements are prepared for three consecutive years, many companies publish selected comparative financial data for a 5- or 10-year period to facilitate further trend analysis.

ILLUSTRATION 20-2

*Horizontal analysis of
Kellogg's net sales*

KELLOGG COMPANY				
(Net Sales Stated in Millions)				
Base Period 1987				
1991	1990	1989	1988	1987
$5,786.6	$5,181.4	$4,651.7	$4,348.8	$3,793.0
153%	137%	123%	115%	100%

To further illustrate horizontal analysis, we will use the financial statements of Quality Department Store Inc., a downtown full-line department store in a southeastern city of 55,000 population. Its two-year condensed balance sheets for 1993 and 1992 showing dollar and percentage changes are presented below.

ILLUSTRATION 20-3

*Horizontal analysis of a
balance sheet*

QUALITY DEPARTMENT STORE INC.				
Condensed Balance Sheet				
December 31				
			Increase or (Decrease) during 1993	
	1993	1992	Amount	Percentage
Assets				
Current assets	$1,020,000	$ 945,000	$ 75,000	7.9%
Plant assets (net)	800,000	632,500	167,500	26.5%
Intangible assets	15,000	17,500	(2,500)	(14.3%)
Total assets	$1,835,000	$1,595,000	$240,000	15.0%
Liabilities				
Current liabilities	$ 344,500	$ 303,000	$ 41,500	13.7%
Long-term liabilities	487,500	497,000	(9,500)	(1.9%)
Total liabilities	832,000	800,000	32,000	4.0%
Stockholders' Equity				
Common stock, $1 par	275,400	270,000	5,400	2.0%
Retained earnings	727,600	525,000	202,600	38.6%
Total stockholders' equity	1,003,000	795,000	208,000	26.2%
Total liabilities and stockholders' equity	$1,835,000	$1,595,000	$240,000	15.0%

Helpful hint It is difficult to comprehend the significance of a change when only the dollar amount of change is examined. When the change is expressed in percentage form, it is easier to grasp the true magnitude of the change.

The comparative balance sheet in Illustration 20-3 shows that a number of changes have occurred in Quality Department Store's financial structure from 1992 to 1993. In the asset section, current assets increased $75,000, or 7.9% ($75,000 ÷ $945,000), and plant assets (net) increased $167,500, or 26.5%. In the liabilities section, current liabilities increased $41,500, or 13.7%, while long-term liabilities decreased $9,500, or 1.9%. In the stockholders' equity section, we find that retained earnings increased $202,600, or 38.6%. This suggests that the company expanded its asset base during 1993 and financed this expansion primarily by retaining income in the business rather than assuming additional long-term debt.

Presented in Illustration 20-4 is a two-year comparative income statement of Quality Department Store Inc. for the years 1993 and 1992 in a condensed format.

ILLUSTRATION 20-4

Horizontal analysis of an income statement

QUALITY DEPARTMENT STORE INC.
Condensed Income Statement
For the Years Ended December 31

	1993	1992	Increase or (Decrease) during 1993 Amount	Percentage
Sales	$2,195,000	$1,960,000	$235,000	12.0%
Sales returns and allowances	98,000	123,000	(25,000)	(20.3%)
Net sales	2,097,000	1,837,000	260,000	14.2%
Cost of goods sold	1,281,000	1,140,000	141,000	12.4%
Gross profit	816,000	697,000	119,000	17.1%
Selling expenses	253,000	211,500	41,500	19.6%
Administrative expenses	104,000	108,500	(4,500)	(4.1%)
Total operating expenses	357,000	320,000	37,000	11.6%
Income from operations	459,000	377,000	82,000	21.8%
Other revenues and gains				
Interest and dividends	9,000	11,000	(2,000)	(18.2%)
Other expenses and losses				
Interest expense	36,000	40,500	(4,500)	(11.1%)
Income before income taxes	432,000	347,500	84,500	24.3%
Income tax expense	168,200	139,000	29,200	21.0%
Net income	$ 263,800	$ 208,500	$ 55,300	26.5%

Helpful hint Note that while the amount column is additive (the total is $55,300), the percentage column is not additive (the total is not 26.5%). A separate percentage has been calculated for each item.

Horizontal analysis of the income statements shows the following changes:

1. Net sales increased $260,000, or 14.2% ($260,000 ÷ $1,837,000).
2. Cost of goods sold increased $141,000, or 12.4% ($141,000 ÷ $1,140,000).
3. Total operating expenses increased $37,000, or 11.6% ($37,000 ÷ $320,000).

Overall, gross profit and net income were up substantially. Gross profit, for example, increased 17.1% and net income 26.5%. It appears, therefore, that Quality's profit trend is favorable.

Presented in Illustration 20-5 is Quality Department Store's comparative retained earnings statement for the years 1993 and 1992 analyzed horizontally. Net income increased $55,300, or 26.5%, whereas dividends on the common stock increased only $1,200, or 2%. Ending retained earnings, as shown in the horizontal analysis of the balance sheet, increased 38.6%. As indicated earlier, Quality

ILLUSTRATION 20-5

Horizontal analysis of a retained earnings statement

QUALITY DEPARTMENT STORE INC.
Retained Earnings Statement
For the Years Ended December 31

	1993	1992	Increase or (Decrease) during 1993 Amount	Percentage
Retained earnings, Jan. 1	$525,000	$376,500	$148,500	39.4%
Add: Net income	263,800	208,500	55,300	26.5%
	788,800	585,000	203,800	
Deduct: Dividends	61,200	60,000	1,200	2.0%
Retained earnings, Dec. 31	$727,600	$525,000	$202,600	38.6%

Department Store Inc. retained a significant portion of its net income to finance expenditures for additional plant facilities.

The measurement of changes from period to period in terms of percentages is relatively straightforward and is quite useful. However, complications can result in making the computations. If an item has no value in a base year or preceding year and a value in the next year, no percentage change can be computed. And if a negative amount appears in the base or preceding period and a positive amount exists the following year, or vice versa, no percentage change can be computed.

Vertical Analysis

Study Objective 4

Describe and apply vertical analysis.

Vertical analysis, sometimes referred to as **common size analysis**, is a technique for evaluating financial statement data that expresses each item within a financial statement in terms of a percent of a base amount. For example, on a balance sheet we might say that current assets are 22% of total assets (total assets being the base amount). Or on an income statement, we might say that selling expenses are 16% of net sales (net sales being the base amount).

Presented in Illustration 20-6 is the comparative balance sheet of Quality Department Store Inc. for 1993 and 1992 analyzed vertically. The base for the asset items is total assets, and the base for the liability and stockholders' equity items is total liabilities and stockholders' equity.

ILLUSTRATION 20-6

Vertical analysis of a balance sheet

QUALITY DEPARTMENT STORE INC.
Condensed Balance Sheet
December 31

	1993 Amount	1993 Percent	1992 Amount	1992 Percent
Assets				
Current assets	$1,020,000	55.6%	$ 945,000	59.2%
Plant assets (net)	800,000	43.6%	632,500	39.7%
Intangible assets	15,000	.8%	17,500	1.1%
Total assets	$1,835,000	100.0%	$1,595,000	100.0%
Liabilities				
Current liabilities	$ 344,500	18.8%	$ 303,000	19.0%
Long-term liabilities	487,500	26.5%	497,000	31.2%
Total liabilities	832,000	45.3%	800,000	50.2%
Stockholders' Equity				
Common stock, $1 par	275,400	15.0%	270,000	16.9%
Retained earnings	727,600	39.7%	525,000	32.9%
Total stockholders' equity	1,003,000	54.7%	795,000	49.8%
Total liabilities and stockholders' equity	$1,835,000	100.0%	$1,595,000	100.0%

Helpful hint The formulas for calculating these percentages are:

$$\frac{\text{Each item on B/S}}{\text{Total Assets}} = \%$$

$$\frac{\text{Each item on Inc. St.}}{\text{Net Sales}} = \%$$

In addition to showing the relative size of each category on the balance sheet, vertical analysis may show the percentage change in the individual asset, liability, and stockholders' equity items. In this case, even though current assets increased $75,000 from 1992 to 1993, they decreased from 59.2% to 55.6% of total assets. Plant assets (net) have increased from 39.7% to 43.6% of total assets, while retained earnings have increased from 32.9% to 39.7% of total liabilities and stockholders' equity. These results reinforce the earlier observations that Quality is choosing to finance its growth through retention of earnings rather than through the issuance of additional debt.

Vertical analysis of the comparative income statements of Quality, shown in Illustration 20-7, reveals that cost of goods sold as a percentage of net sales declined 1% (62.1% vs. 61.1%) and total operating expenses declined 0.4% (17.4% vs. 17.0%). As a result, it is not surprising to see net income as a percent of net sales increase from 11.4% to 12.6%. As indicated from the horizontal analysis, Quality appears to be a profitable enterprise that is becoming even more successful.

ILLUSTRATION 20-7

Vertical analysis of an income statement

QUALITY DEPARTMENT STORE INC.
Condensed Income Statement
For the Years Ended December 31

	1993 Amount	1993 Percent	1992 Amount	1992 Percent
Sales	$2,195,000	104.7%	$1,960,000	106.7%
Sales returns and allowances	98,000	4.7%	123,000	6.7%
Net sales	2,097,000	100.0%	1,837,000	100.0%
Cost of goods sold	1,281,000	61.1%	1,140,000	62.1%
Gross profit	816,000	38.9%	697,000	37.9%
Selling expenses	253,000	12.0%	211,500	11.5%
Administrative expenses	104,000	5.0%	108,500	5.9%
Total operating expenses	357,000	17.0%	320,000	17.4%
Income from operations	459,000	21.9%	377,000	20.5%
Other revenues and gains Interest and dividends	9,000	0.4%	11,000	0.6%
Other expenses and losses Interest expense	36,000	1.7%	40,500	2.2%
Income before income taxes	432,000	20.6%	347,500	18.9%
Income tax expense	168,200	8.0%	139,000	7.5%
Net income	$ 263,800	12.6%	$ 208,500	11.4%

An associated benefit of vertical analysis is that it enables you to compare companies of different sizes. For example, Quality's main competitor is a J.C. Penney store in a nearby town. Using vertical analysis, the condensed income statements of the small local retail enterprise, Quality Department Store Inc., can be more meaningfully compared with the income statement of a giant international retailer, J.C. Penney Company, as shown in Illustration 20-8.

Although J.C. Penney's net sales are 6,556 times greater than the net sales of relatively tiny Quality Department Store, vertical analysis eliminates this difference in size. The percentages show that Quality's and Penney's gross profit rates were somewhat comparable at 38.9% and 32.8%, while the percentages related to income from operations were significantly different at 21.9% and 7.7%. This disparity can be attributed to Quality's selling and administrative expense percentage (17%) which is much lower than Penney's (25.1%). Although Penney earned net income more than 1,500 times larger than Quality's, Penney's net income as a **percent of each sales dollar** (2.9%) is less than one quarter of Quality's (12.6%).

ILLUSTRATION 20-8

*Intercompany income state-
ment comparison*

CONDENSED INCOME STATEMENTS

(in thousands)	Quality Department Store Inc. Dollars	Quality Department Store Inc. Percent	J.C. Penney Company Dollars	J.C. Penney Company Percent
Net sales	$2,097	100.0%	$13,747,000	100.0%
Cost of goods sold	1,281	61.1%	9,240,000	67.2%
Gross profit	816	38.9%	4,507,000	32.8%
Selling and administrative expenses	357	17.0%	3,454,000	25.1%
Income from operations	459	21.9%	1,053,000	7.7%
Other expenses and revenues (including income taxes)	195	9.3%	656,000	4.8%
Net income	$ 264	12.6%	$ 397,000	2.9%

Before You Go On . . .

1. What are the different bases that might be used to compare financial information?

2. What is horizontal analysis?

3. What is vertical analysis?

Ratio Analysis

A ratio expresses the mathematical relationship between one quantity and another. The relationship is expressed in terms of either a percentage, a rate, or a simple proportion. To illustrate, recently IBM Corporation had current assets of $40,969,000,000 and current liabilities of $33,624,000,000. Because the cash to pay current liabilities is included within the current assets or will flow from other current assets such as receivables and inventories, a ratio of current assets to current liabilities can be computed. This relationship could be expressed as a **percentage** by stating that current assets are 122% of current liabilities, as a **rate** by stating that current assets are 1.22 times as great as current liabilities, or as a **proportion** by stating that the relationship of current assets to current liabilities is 1.22:1.

Technology in Action

Many general ledger accounting programs include the generation of financial ratios as routine output. All the ratio computations presented in this chapter can be done with electronic spreadsheets as well. There are also many programs available written specifically for financial statement analysis. These packages are written for both general purpose use and use in specific industries. For example, financial institutions routinely use over 60 ratios geared specifically to the banking industry.

Key Financial Ratios

For analysis of the primary financial statements, ratios can be classified as follows:

Study Objective 5

Identify and compute ratios and describe their purpose and use in analyzing a firm's liquidity, profitability, and solvency.

1. Liquidity ratios—measures of the short-term ability of the enterprise to pay its maturing obligations and to meet unexpected needs for cash.
2. Profitability ratios—measures of the income or operating success of an enterprise for a given period of time.
3. Solvency ratios—measures of the ability of the enterprise to survive over a long period of time.

As a tool of analysis, ratios can provide clues to underlying conditions that may not be apparent from an inspection of the individual components of a particular ratio. But a single ratio by itself is not very meaningful. Accordingly, in the following discussion we will use:

1. **Intracompany comparisons** covering two years for the Quality Department Store.
2. **Industry average comparisons** based on Dun & Bradstreet's median ratios for department stores and *Forbes'* and *Business Week's* nonfood retailing industry averages.
3. **Intercompany comparisons** based on the J.C. Penney Company, Inc. as Quality Department Store's principal competitor.

Liquidity Ratios

Liquidity ratios measure the short-term ability of the enterprise to pay its maturing obligations and to meet unexpected needs for cash. Short-term creditors such as bankers and suppliers are particularly interested in assessing **liquidity**. The ratios that can be used to determine the enterprise's short-term debt-paying ability are the current ratio, the acid-test ratio, receivables turnover, and inventory turnover.

1. CURRENT RATIO. The current ratio expresses the relationship of current assets to current liabilities, computed by dividing current assets by current liabilities. It is a widely used measure for evaluating a company's liquidity and short-term debt-paying ability. It is sometimes referred to as the working capital ratio because **working capital** is the excess of current assets over current liabilities. The current ratio is a more dependable indicator of liquidity than working capital. Two companies with the same amount of working capital may have significantly different current ratios. The 1993 and 1992 current ratios for Quality Department Store and comparative data are shown in Illustration 20-9.

What do the measures actually mean? The 1993 ratio of 2.96:1 means that for every dollar of current liabilities, Quality has $2.96 of current assets. Quality's current ratio has decreased in the current year. However, compared to the industry average of 1.5:1, and J.C. Penney Company's 2.4:1 current ratio, Quality appears to be reasonably liquid.

The current ratio is only one measure of determining liquidity. It does not take into account the composition of the current assets. For example, a satisfactory current ratio does not disclose the fact that a portion of the current assets may be tied up in slow-moving inventory. A dollar of cash is more readily available to pay the bills than is a dollar of slow-moving inventory.

ILLUSTRATION 20-9

Current ratio

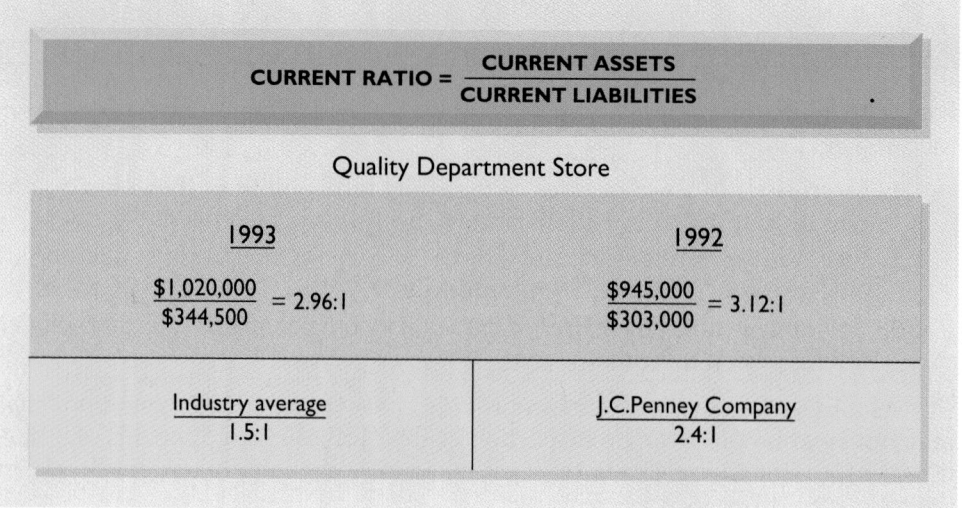

2. **ACID-TEST RATIO.** The acid-test or quick ratio is a measure of a company's immediate short-term liquidity, computed by dividing the sum of cash, marketable securities, and net receivables by current liabilities. Thus, it is an important complement to the current ratio. For example, assume that the current assets of Quality Department Store for 1993 and 1992 consist of the following items:

ILLUSTRATION 20-10

Current assets of Quality Department Store

	1993	1992
Current assets		
Cash	$ 100,000	$155,000
Marketable securities	20,000	70,000
Receivables (net)	230,000	180,000
Inventory	620,000	500,000
Prepaid expenses	50,000	40,000
Total current assets	$1,020,000	$945,000

Accounting in Action · *Business Insight*

The apparent simplicity of the current ratio can have real world limitations because an addition of equal amounts to both the numerator and the denominator causes the ratio to decrease. Assume for example, that a company has $2,000,000 of current assets and $1,000,000 of current liabilities; its current ratio is 2:1. If it purchases $1,000,000 of inventory on account, it will have $3,000,000 of current assets and $2,000,000 of current liabilities; its current ratio will decrease to 1.5:1. If, instead, the company pays off $500,000 of its current liabilities, it will have $1,500,000 of current assets and $500,000 of current liabilities, and its current ratio will increase to 3:1. Thus, any trend analysis should be done with care, since the ratio is susceptible to quick changes and is easily influenced by management.

Cash, marketable securities (short-term), and receivables (net) are highly liquid as compared with the inventory and prepaid expenses. The inventory may not be readily saleable and the prepaid expenses may not be transferable to others. The 1993 and 1992 acid-test ratios for Quality Department Store and comparative data are as follows:

ILLUSTRATION 20-11

Acid-test ratio

$$\text{ACID-TEST RATIO} = \frac{\text{CASH} + \text{MARKETABLE SECURITIES} + \text{RECEIVABLES (NET)}}{\text{CURRENT LIABILITIES}}$$

Quality Department Store

1993	1992
$\dfrac{\$100,000 + \$20,000 + \$230,000}{\$344,500} = 1.02{:}1$	$\dfrac{\$155,000 + \$70,000 + \$180,000}{\$303,000} = 1.34{:}1$
Industry average 1:1	J.C.Penney Company 1.03:1

Is an acid-test ratio of 1.02:1 adequate? The ratio has declined in 1993. However, when compared with the industry median of 1:1 and J.C. Penney's 1.03:1, Quality's acid-test ratio seems adequate.

3. RECEIVABLES TURNOVER. Liquidity may be measured by how quickly certain assets can be converted to cash. How liquid, for example, are the receivables? The ratio used to assess the liquidity of the receivables is the receivables turnover ratio. This ratio measures the number of times, on average, receivables are collected during the period. The receivables turnover ratio is computed by dividing net credit sales (net sales less cash sales) by the average net receivables during the year. Unless seasonal factors are significant, average net receivables outstanding can be computed from the beginning and ending balance of the net receivables.[3]

Assuming that all sales are credit sales and the balance of accounts receivable (net) at the beginning of 1992 is $200,000, the receivables turnover ratio for Quality Department Store and comparative data are shown in Illustration 20-12. Quality's receivables turnover improved in 1993. The turnover of 10.23 times compares quite favorably with J.C. Penney's 3.23 times, but it is slightly below the department store industry's median of 13.4 times.

A popular variant of the receivables turnover ratio is to convert it into an **average collection period** in terms of days. This is done by dividing the turnover ratio into 365 days. For example, the receivable turnover in 1993 of 10.23 times is divided into 365 days to obtain approximately 35.7 days. This means that the average collection period for receivables is 36 days, or approximately every five weeks. The average collection period is frequently used to assess the effectiveness

---

[3]If seasonal factors are significant, the average receivables balance might be determined by using monthly amounts.

ILLUSTRATION 20-12

Receivables turnover

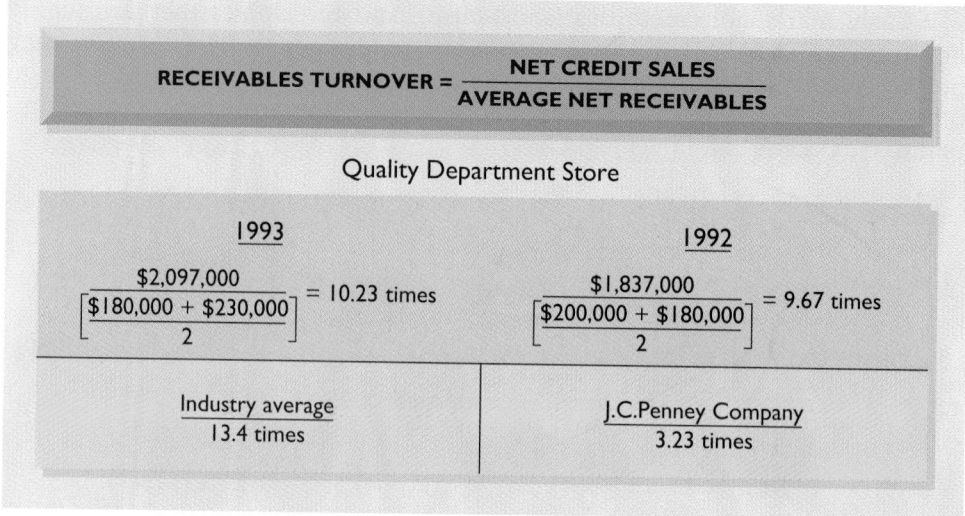

$$\text{RECEIVABLES TURNOVER} = \frac{\text{NET CREDIT SALES}}{\text{AVERAGE NET RECEIVABLES}}$$

Quality Department Store

1993	1992
$\dfrac{\$2,097,000}{\left[\dfrac{\$180,000 + \$230,000}{2}\right]} = 10.23$ times	$\dfrac{\$1,837,000}{\left[\dfrac{\$200,000 + \$180,000}{2}\right]} = 9.67$ times
Industry average 13.4 times	J.C. Penney Company 3.23 times

of a company's credit and collection policies. The general rule is that the collection period should not greatly exceed the credit term period (i.e., the time allowed for payment).

Accounting in Action · *Business Insight*

In some cases, receivable turnover may be misleading. Some companies, especially large retail chains, encourage credit and revolving charge sales, and they slow collections in order to earn a healthy return on the outstanding receivables in the form of interest at rates of 18% to 22%. This may explain why J.C. Penney's turnover is only 3.23 times. In general, however, the faster the turnover, the greater the reliance that can be placed on the current and acid-test ratios for assessing liquidity.

4. INVENTORY TURNOVER. The inventory turnover ratio measures the number of times on average the inventory is sold during the period. Its purpose is to measure the liquidity of the inventory. The inventory turnover is computed by dividing cost of goods sold by the average inventory during the period. Unless seasonal factors are significant, average inventory can be computed from the beginning and ending inventory balances. Assuming that the inventory balance for Quality Department Store at the beginning of 1992 was $450,000, its inventory turnover and comparative data are as shown in Illustration 20-13. Quality's inventory turnover declined slightly in 1993. The turnover ratio of 2.29 times is relatively low compared with the industry average of 3.2 and J.C. Penney's 3.63. Generally, the faster the inventory turnover, the less cash that is tied up in inventory and the less the chance of inventory obsolescence.

A variant of the inventory turnover ratio is to compute the **average days to sell the inventory**. For example, the inventory turnover in 1993 of 2.29 times

ILLUSTRATION 20-13

Inventory turnover

$$\textbf{INVENTORY TURNOVER} = \frac{\textbf{COST OF GOODS SOLD}}{\textbf{AVERAGE INVENTORY}}$$

Quality Department Store

1993	1992
$\dfrac{\$1,281,000}{\left[\dfrac{\$500,000 + \$620,000}{2}\right]}$ = 2.29 times	$\dfrac{\$1,140,000}{\left[\dfrac{\$450,000 + \$500,000}{2}\right]}$ = 2.4 times
Industry average 3.2 times	J.C. Penney Company 3.63 times

divided into 365 is approximately 159 days. An average selling time of 159 days is also relatively high compared with the industry average of 114 days (365 ÷ 3.2) and J.C. Penney Company's 101 days (365 ÷ 3.63).

 **ccounting in Action** ▪ *Business Insight*

Inventory turnover ratios vary considerably among industries. For example, grocery store chains have a turnover of 10 times and an average selling period of 37 days. In contrast, jewelry stores have an average turnover of 1.3 times and an average selling period of 281 days. Within a company there may be significant differences in inventory turnover among different types of products. Thus, in a grocery store the turnover of perishable items such as produce, meats, and dairy products will be faster than the turnover of soaps and detergents.

Profitability Ratios

Profitability ratios measure the income or operating success of an enterprise for a given period of time. Income, or the lack of it, affects the company's ability to obtain debt and equity financing, the company's liquidity position, and the company's ability to grow. As a consequence, creditors and investors alike are interested in evaluating earning power (profitability). Profitability is frequently used as the ultimate test of management's operating effectiveness.

5. PROFIT MARGIN. The profit margin ratio (rate of return on sales) is a measure of the percentage of each dollar of sales that results in net income. It is computed by dividing net income by net sales for the period. Quality Department Store's profit margin ratios and comparative data are shown in Illustration 20-14.

Quality experienced an increase in its profit margin from 1992 to 1993. Its profit margin is unusually high in comparison with the industry average of 4.1% and J.C. Penney Company's 3.9%.

ILLUSTRATION 20-14

Profit margin ratio

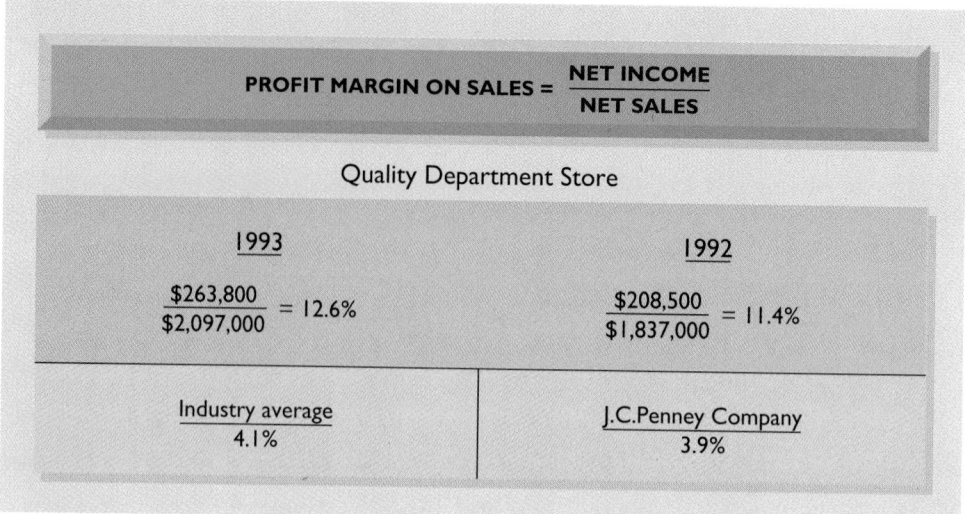

High-volume (high inventory turnover) enterprises such as grocery stores (Safeway or Kroger) and discount stores (Kmart or Wal-Mart) generally experience low profit margins, whereas low-volume enterprises such as jewelry stores (Tiffany & Co.) or airplane manufacturers (Boeing Aircraft) have high profit margins.

6. ASSET TURNOVER. The asset turnover ratio measures how efficiently a company uses its assets to generate sales. It is determined by dividing net sales by average assets for the period. The resulting number shows the dollars of sales produced by each dollar invested in assets. Unless seasonal factors are significant, average total assets can be computed from the beginning and ending balance of total assets. Assuming that the total assets at the beginning of 1992 were $1,446,000, the 1993 and 1992 asset turnover ratios for Quality Department Store and comparative data are as follows:

ILLUSTRATION 20-15

Asset turnover

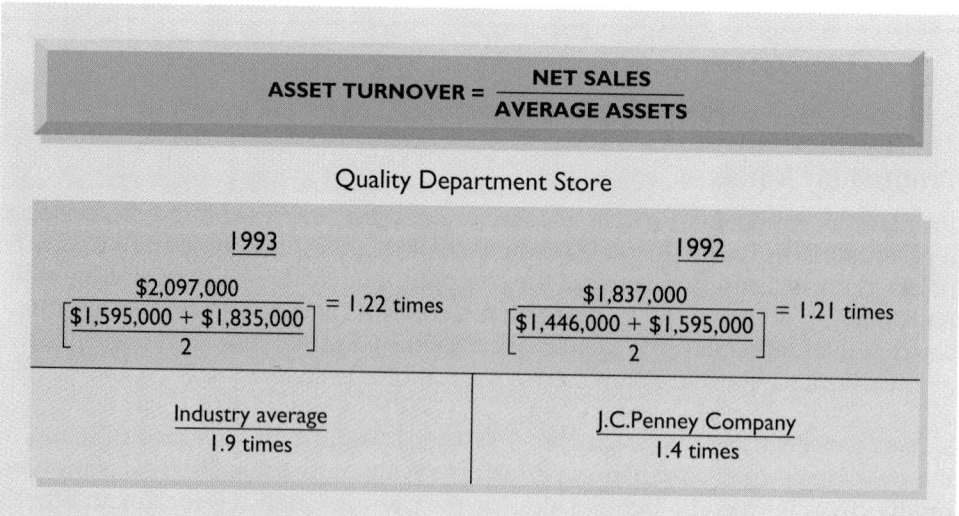

The asset turnover ratio shows that Quality generated sales of $1.22 in 1993 for each dollar it had invested in assets. The ratio changed little from 1992 to 1993.

Quality's asset turnover ratio is below the industry median of 1.9 times and J.C. Penney's ratio of 1.4 times.

Asset turnover ratios vary considerably among industries. For example, a large utility company like Union Electric Company (St. Louis) has a ratio of 0.36 times, and the large grocery chain Great Atlantic and Pacific Tea (A&P) has a ratio of 3.6 times.

7. RETURN ON ASSETS. An overall measure of profitability is the return on assets ratio. This ratio measures the rate earned on each dollar invested in assets. It is computed by dividing net income by average assets. The 1993 and 1992 return on assets for Quality Department Store and comparative data are shown below.

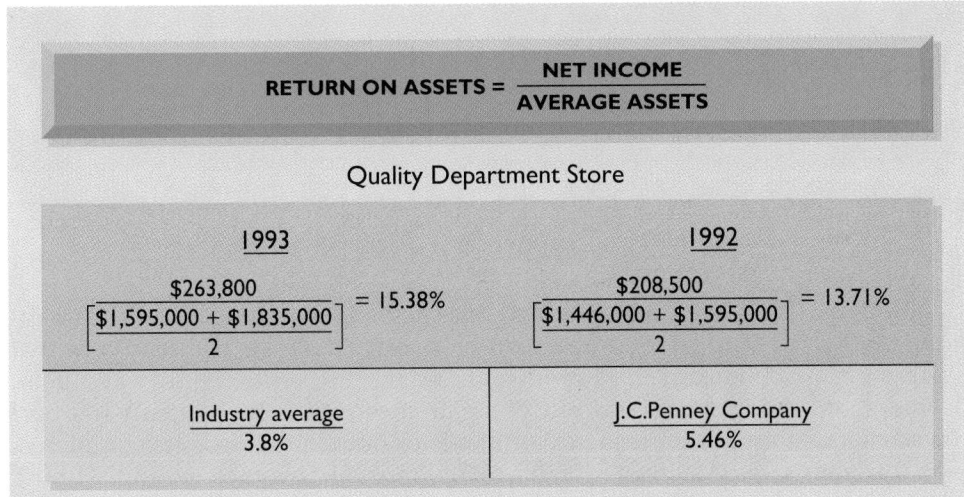

ILLUSTRATION 20-16

Return on assets

Quality's return on assets improved from 1992 to 1993. Its return of 15.38% is very high, compared with the department store industry median of 3.8% and J.C. Penney Company's 5.46%.

8. RETURN ON COMMON STOCKHOLDERS' EQUITY. Another widely used ratio that measures profitability from the common stockholder's viewpoint is return on common stockholders' equity. This ratio shows how many dollars of net income were earned for each dollar invested by the owners. It is computed by dividing net income by average common stockholders' equity. Assuming that common stockholders' equity at the beginning of 1992 was $667,000, the 1993 and 1992 ratios for Quality Department Store and comparative data are shown in Illustration 20-17.

Quality's rate of return on common stockholders' equity is unusually high at 29.3%, considering an industry average of 15.3% and a rate of 13.1% for J.C. Penney Company. Quality's return on equity compares favorably with industry leaders, such as Wal-Mart Stores (23%), May Department Stores (17.9%), and Kmart (14.5%).

When preferred stock is present, **preferred dividend** requirements are deducted from net income to compute income available to common stockholders. Similarly, the par value of preferred stock (or call price, if applicable) must be deducted from total stockholders' equity to arrive at the amount of common

ILLUSTRATION 20-17

*Return on common stock-
holders' equity*

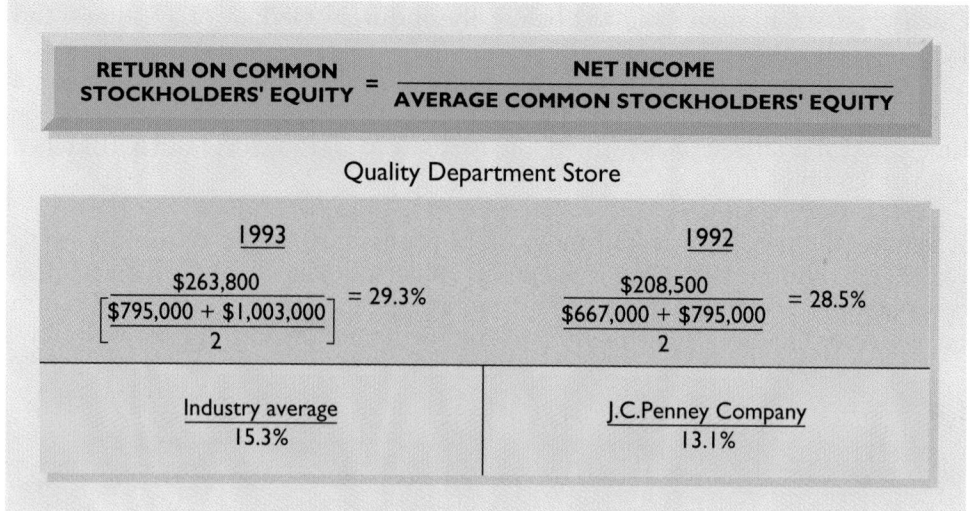

stock equity used in this ratio. The ratio then appears as follows:

ILLUSTRATION 20-18

*Return on common stock-
holders' equity with pre-
ferred stock*

$$\text{Rate of return on common stockholders' equity} = \frac{\text{Net income} - \text{preferred dividends}}{\text{Average common stockholders' equity}}$$

Note that Quality's rate of return on stockholders' equity (29.3%) is substantially higher than its rate of return on assets (15.38%). The reason is that Quality has made effective use of leverage or trading on the equity at a gain. Leveraging or trading on the equity at a gain means that the company has borrowed money through the issuance of bonds or notes at a lower rate of interest than it is able to earn by using the borrowed money. Leverage is simply trying to use money supplied by nonowners to increase the return to the owners. A comparison of the rate of return on total assets with the rate of interest paid for borrowed money indicates the profitability of trading on the equity. Note that trading on the equity is a two-way street: for example, if you borrow money at 11% and earn only 8% on it, you are trading on the equity at a loss. Quality Department Store earns more on its borrowed funds than it has to pay in the form of interest. Thus the return to stockholders exceeds the return on the assets, benefiting from the positive leveraging.

9. EARNINGS PER SHARE (EPS). Earnings per share of stock is a measure of the net income earned on each share of common stock. As explained in Chapter 16, it is computed by dividing net income by the number of weighted average common shares outstanding during the year. Stockholders usually think in terms of the number of shares they own or plan to buy or sell. Reducing net income earned to a per share basis provides a useful perspective for determining profitability. Assuming that there is no change in the number of outstanding shares during 1992 and that the 1993 increase occurred midyear, the net income per share for Quality Department Store for 1993 and 1992 is computed as shown in Illustration 20-19.

Note that no industry or J.C. Penney data are presented. Such comparisons are not meaningful because of the wide variations in the number of shares of outstanding stock among companies. Quality's earnings per share increased 20 cents per share in 1993. This represents a 26% increase over the 1992 earnings per share of 77 cents.

When the term "net income per share" or "earnings per share" is used, it refers to the amount of net income applicable to each share of **common stock**.

ILLUSTRATION 20-19

Earnings per share

$$\text{EARNINGS PER SHARE} = \frac{\text{NET INCOME}}{\text{WEIGHTED AVERAGE COMMON SHARES OUTSTANDING}}$$

Quality Department Store

1993	1992
$\dfrac{\$263,800}{\left[\dfrac{270,000 + 275,400}{2}\right]} = \$.97$	$\dfrac{\$208,500}{270,000} = \$.77$

Therefore, in computing net income per share, if there are preferred dividends declared for the period, they must be deducted from net income to arrive at income available to the common stockholders.

10. PRICE-EARNINGS RATIO. The price-earnings ratio is an oft-quoted statistic that measures the ratio of the market price of each share of common stock to the earnings per share. The price-earnings (PE) ratio is a reflection of investors' assessments of a company's future earnings. It is computed by dividing the market price per share of the stock by earnings per share. Assuming that the market price of Quality Department Store Inc. stock is $8 in 1992 and $12 in 1993, the price-earnings ratio is computed as follows:

ILLUSTRATION 20-20

Price-earnings ratio

$$\text{PRICE-EARNINGS RATIO} = \frac{\text{MARKET PRICE PER SHARE OF STOCK}}{\text{EARNINGS PER SHARE}}$$

Quality Department Store

1993	1992
$\dfrac{\$12.00}{\$ .97} = 12.4 \text{ times}$	$\dfrac{\$8.00}{\$ .77} = 10.4 \text{ times}$
Industry average 15 times	J.C.Penney Company 8 times

In 1993 each share of Quality's stock sold for 12.4 times the amount that was earned on each share. Quality's price-earnings ratio is less than the industry average of 15 times but is significantly higher than the ratio of 8 for J.C. Penney Company. The average price-earnings ratio for the stocks that constitute the Dow-Jones industrial average on the New York Stock Exchange in mid-1992 was an unusually high 18 times.

11. PAYOUT RATIO. The payout ratio measures the percentage of earnings distributed in the form of cash dividends. It is computed by dividing cash dividends by net income. Companies that have high growth rates are characterized by low

Accounting in Action · *Business Insight*

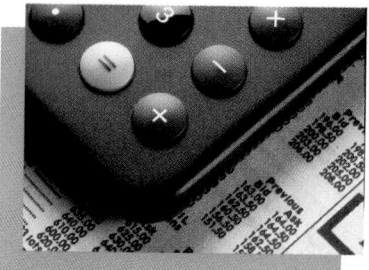

For the stock of some companies, investors are willing to pay over 20 times the current per-share earnings because they feel the future growth in earnings will provide an adequate return on the investment. Examples of companies with price-earnings ratios over 20 are Coca-Cola (33), Toys 'R' Us (30), and Wal-Mart (38). Examples of companies with low price-earnings ratios are Boeing (9), Travelers Insurance (7), and Chase Manhattan Bank (8).

payout ratios because they reinvest most of their net income into the business. The 1993 and 1992 payout ratios for Quality Department Store are computed as follows:

ILLUSTRATION 20-21

Payout ratio

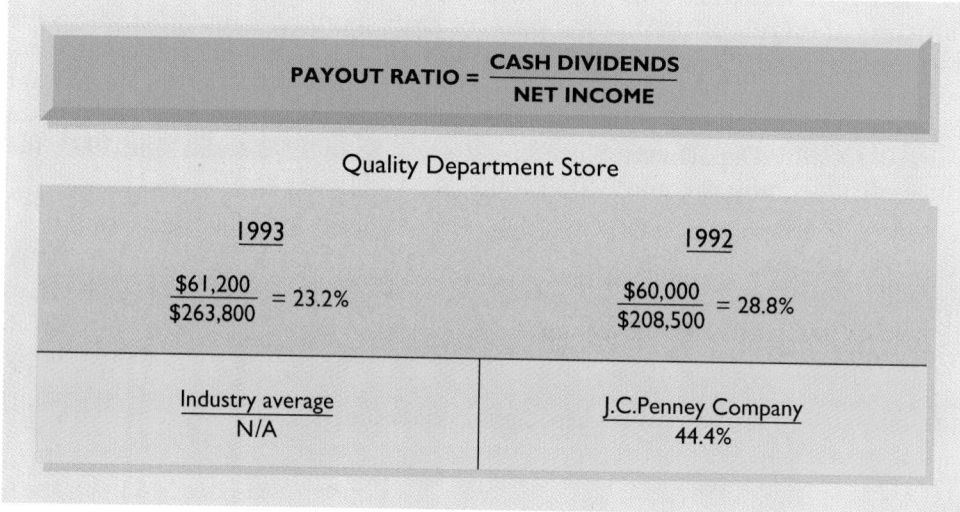

$$\text{PAYOUT RATIO} = \frac{\text{CASH DIVIDENDS}}{\text{NET INCOME}}$$

Quality Department Store

1993	1992
$\dfrac{\$61,200}{\$263,800} = 23.2\%$	$\dfrac{\$60,000}{\$208,500} = 28.8\%$
Industry average N/A	J.C.Penney Company 44.4%

Quality's payout ratio is comparatively low when compared with J.C. Penney's payout ratio of 44.4%. As indicated earlier, the company has apparently decided to fund its purchase of plant assets through retention of earnings.

Accounting in Action · *Business Insight*

Generally, companies with stable earnings have high payout ratios. For example, a utility such as Potomac Electric Company has had an 86% payout ratio over the last five years, and Amoco Corporation has had a 63% payout over the same period. Conversely, companies that are expanding rapidly, such as Toys 'R' Us and Quest Medical, have never paid a cash dividend.

Solvency Ratios

Solvency ratios measure the ability of the enterprise to survive over a long period of time. Long-term creditors and stockholders are interested in a company's long-run solvency, particularly its ability to pay interest as it comes due and to repay the face value of the debt at maturity. Debt to total assets and times interest earned are two ratios that provide information about debt paying ability.

12. DEBT TO TOTAL ASSETS. The debt to total assets ratio measures the percentage of the total assets provided by creditors (this ratio indicates the degree of leveraging). It is computed by dividing total debt (both current and long-term liabilities) by total assets. This ratio provides some indication of the company's ability to withstand losses without impairing the interests of creditors. The higher the percentage of debt to total assets, the greater the risk that the company may be unable to meet its maturing obligations. The 1993 and 1992 ratios for Quality Department Store and comparative data are as follows:

ILLUSTRATION 20-22

Debt to total assets

$$\text{DEBT TO TOTAL ASSETS} = \frac{\text{TOTAL DEBT}}{\text{TOTAL ASSETS}}$$

Quality Department Store

1993	1992
$\dfrac{\$832,000}{\$1,835,000} = 45.3\%$	$\dfrac{\$800,000}{\$1,595,000} = 50.2\%$
Industry average 30%	J.C. Penney Company 60%

A ratio of 45.3% means that creditors have provided 45.3% of Quality Department Store's total assets. Quality's 45.3% is above the industry average of 30%, but it is considerably below the 60% ratio of J.C. Penney Company. The lower the ratio, the more equity "buffer" there is available to the creditors if the company becomes insolvent. Thus, from the creditors' point of view, a low ratio of debt to total assets is usually desirable.

The adequacy of this ratio is often judged in the light of the company's earnings. Generally, companies with relatively stable earnings, such as public utilities, have higher debt to total assets ratios than cyclical companies with widely fluctuating earnings, such as many high-tech companies. (See Accounting in Action on the next page for examples of debt to total assets ratios for selected companies.)

13. TIMES INTEREST EARNED. The times interest earned ratio (also called interest coverage) provides an indication of the company's ability to meet interest payments as they come due. It is computed by dividing income before interest ex-

ILLUSTRATION 20-23

Times interest earned

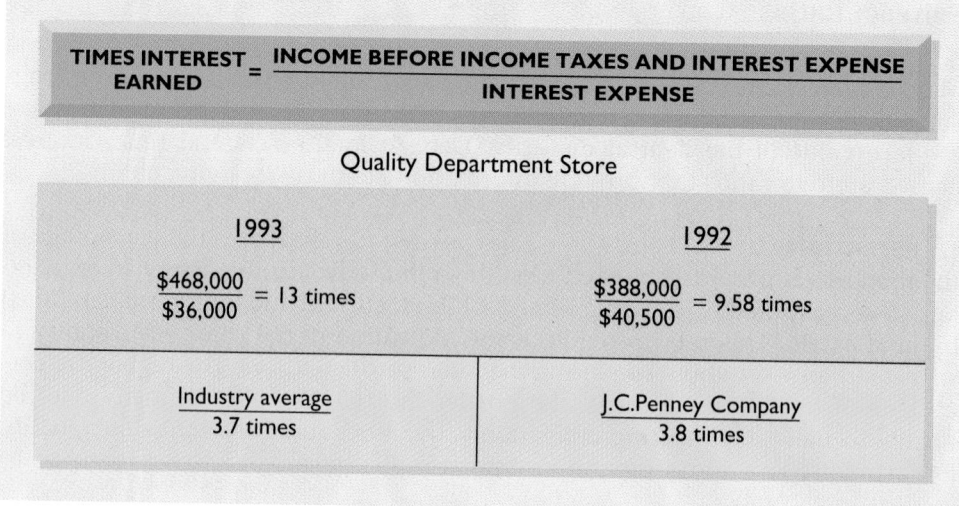

$$\text{TIMES INTEREST EARNED} = \frac{\text{INCOME BEFORE INCOME TAXES AND INTEREST EXPENSE}}{\text{INTEREST EXPENSE}}$$

Quality Department Store

1993	1992
$\dfrac{\$468,000}{\$36,000} = 13$ times	$\dfrac{\$388,000}{\$40,500} = 9.58$ times
Industry average 3.7 times	J.C. Penney Company 3.8 times

pense and income taxes by interest expense. The 1993 and 1992 ratios for Quality Department Store and comparative data are shown in Illustration 20-23. Note that the times interest earned ratio uses income before income taxes and interest expense, because this amount represents the amount available to cover interest. For Quality Department Store the 1993 amount of $468,000 is computed by taking the income before income taxes of $432,000 and adding back the $36,000 of interest expense. The interest expense of Quality is well covered at 13 times relative to the industry average of 3.7 times and J.C. Penney Company's 3.8 times.

Accounting in Action ▪ *Business Insight*

Examples of debt to total assets ratios for selected companies are:

	TOTAL DEBT TO TOTAL ASSETS AS A PERCENT
Union Electric Company	59%
Quest Medical, Inc.	3%
Itel Corporation	78%
General Electric Company	16%
Glamis Gold Ltd.	28%
Eastman Kodak Company	75%

Another means used in practice to measure this same leverage phenomenon is the "debt to equity ratio." It shows the relative use of borrowed funds (total liabilities) as compared to resources invested by the owners. Because this ratio may be computed in several ways, care should be taken when making internal comparisons. Debt may be defined to include only the noncurrent portion of the liabilities, and intangible assets may be excluded from owner's equity (resulting in tangible net worth).

Technology in Action

In terms of the types of financial information that are available and the ratios used by various industries, you should be aware that what can be practically covered in this textbook only gives you the "Titanic approach." That is, you are seeing only the tip of the iceberg compared to the vast data bases and different types of ratio analysis that are available on computers. The availability of information is not a problem. The real trick is to be discriminating enough to perform relevant analysis and to select pertinent comparative data.

Before You Go On . . .

1. What are liquidity ratios? Explain the current ratio, acid-test ratio, receivables turnover ratio, and inventory turnover ratio.

2. What are profitability ratios? Explain the profit margin ratio, asset turnover ratio, return on assets ratio, return on common stockholders' equity ratio, earnings per share, price-earnings ratio, and payout ratio.

3. What are solvency ratios? Explain the debt to total assets ratio and times interest earned ratio.

Limitations of Financial Analysis

Significant business decisions are frequently made using one or more of the three analytical tools illustrated in this chapter. You should be aware of some of the limitations of these tools and of the financial statements on which they are based.

> **Study Objective 6**
>
> *Recognize the limitations of financial statement analysis.*

Estimates

Financial statements contain numerous estimates. Estimates, for example, are used in determining the allowance for uncollectible receivables, periodic depreciation, the costs of warranties, and contingent losses. To the extent that these estimates are inaccurate, the financial ratios and percentages are inaccurate.

Cost

Traditional financial statements are based on cost and are not adjusted for price-level changes. Comparisons of unadjusted financial data from different periods may be rendered invalid by significant inflation or deflation. For example, a five-year comparison of J.C. Penney's revenues shows a growth of 21%. But this growth trend is invalidated to the extent that the general price-level increased more than 30% during the same five-year period.

Alternative Accounting Methods

Variations among companies in the application of generally accepted accounting principles may hamper comparability. For example, one company may use the FIFO method of inventory costing, while another company in the same industry may use LIFO. If inventory is a significant asset to both companies, it is unlikely that their current ratios are comparable. For example, if General Motors Corporation had used FIFO instead of LIFO in valuing its inventories, its inventories would have been 26% higher, significantly affecting the current ratio (and other ratios as well). In addition to differences in inventory costing methods, differences also exist in reporting such items as depreciation, depletion, and amortization. While these differences in accounting methods might be detectable from reading the notes to the financial statements, adjusting the financial data to compensate for the different methods is difficult, if not impossible in some cases.

Atypical Data

Fiscal year-end data may not be typical of the financial condition during the year. Firms frequently establish a fiscal year-end that coincides with the low point in operating activity or in inventory levels. Therefore, certain account balances (cash, receivables, payables, and inventories) may not be representative of the balances in the accounts during the year.

Diversification of Firms

Diversification in American industry also limits the usefulness of financial analysis. Many firms today are so diversified that they cannot be classified by industry. Others appear to be comparable but are not. You might think that PepsiCo, Inc., and Coca-Cola Company would be comparable as soft drink industry competitors. But are they comparable when PepsiCo, in addition to producing Pepsi-Cola, owns Pizza Hut, Kentucky Fried Chicken, Taco Bell, and Frito-Lay; and Coca-Cola, in addition to producing Coke, owns Hi-C (fruit drinks), Minute Maid (frozen concentrate), and Columbia Pictures (motion pictures, TV shows, and commercials)?

Summary of Study Objectives

1. Discuss the need for comparative analysis. Comparative analysis is performed to evaluate a firm's short-term liquidity, profitability, and long-term solvency. Comparisons can detect change in financial relationships and significant trends and provide insight into a company's competitive position and relative position in its industry.

2. Identify the tools of financial statement analysis. Financial statements may be analyzed horizontally, vertically, and with ratios.

3. Explain and apply horizontal (trend) analysis. Horizontal analysis is a technique for evaluating a

series of data over a period of time to determine the increase or decrease that has taken place, expressed as either an amount or a percentage.

4. Describe and apply vertical analysis. Vertical analysis is a technique that expresses each item within a financial statement in terms of a percentage of a relevant total or a base amount.

5. Identify and compute ratios and describe their purpose and use in analyzing a firm's liquidity, profitability, and solvency. A summary of financial ratios is as follows:

Ratio	Formula	Purpose or Use
Liquidity Ratios		
1. Current ratio	$\dfrac{\text{Current assets}}{\text{Current liabilities}}$	Measures short-term debt-paying ability.
2. Acid-test or quick ratio	$\dfrac{\text{Cash + marketable securities + receivables (net)}}{\text{Current liabilities}}$	Measures immediate short-term liquidity.
3. Receivables turnover	$\dfrac{\text{Net credit sales}}{\text{Average net receivables}}$	Measures liquidity of receivables.

Ratio	Formula	Purpose or Use
Liquidity Ratios		
4. Inventory turnover	$\dfrac{\text{Cost of goods sold}}{\text{Average inventory}}$	Measures liquidity of inventory.
Profitability Ratios		
5. Profit margin	$\dfrac{\text{Net income}}{\text{Net sales}}$	Measures net income generated by each dollar of sales.
6. Asset turnover	$\dfrac{\text{Net sales}}{\text{Average assets}}$	Measures how efficiently assets are used to generate sales.
7. Return on assets	$\dfrac{\text{Net income}}{\text{Average assets}}$	Measures overall profitability of assets used.
8. Return on common stockholders' equity	$\dfrac{\text{Net income}}{\text{Average common stockholders' equity}}$	Measures profitability of owner's investment.
9. Earnings per share	$\dfrac{\text{Net income}}{\text{Weighted average common shares outstanding}}$	Measures net income earned on each share of common stock.
10. Price-earnings ratio	$\dfrac{\text{Market price per share of stock}}{\text{Earnings per share}}$	Measures the ratio of the market price per share to earnings per share.
11. Payout ratio	$\dfrac{\text{Cash dividends}}{\text{Net income}}$	Measures percentage of earnings distributed in the form of cash dividends.
Solvency Ratios		
12. Debt to total assets	$\dfrac{\text{Total debt}}{\text{Total assets}}$	Measures the percentage of total assets provided by creditors.
13. Times interest earned	$\dfrac{\text{Income before income taxes and interest expense}}{\text{Interest expense}}$	Measures ability to meet interest payments as they come due.

6. Recognize the limitations of financial statement analysis. The usefulness of analytical tools is limited by the use of estimates, the cost basis, the application of alternative accounting methods, atypical data at year-end, and the diversification of firms.

GLOSSARY

Acid-test ratio · A measure of a company's immediate short-term liquidity, computed by dividing the sum of cash, marketable securities, and (net) receivables by current liabilities. (p. 818)

Asset turnover ratio · A measure of how efficiently a company uses its assets to generate sales, computed by dividing net sales by average assets. (p. 822)

Current ratio · A measure that expresses the relationship of current assets to current liabilities, computed by dividing current assets by current liabilities. (p. 817)

Debt to total assets ratio · Measures the percentage of total assets provided by creditors computed by dividing total debt by total assets. (p. 827)

Earnings per share · The net income earned by each share of common stock, computed by dividing net income by the weighted average common shares outstanding. (p. 824)

Horizontal analysis · A technique for evaluating a series of financial statement data over a period of time to determine the increase (decrease) that has taken place, expressed as either an amount or a percentage. (p. 811)

Inventory turnover ratio · A measure of the liquidity of inventory, computed by dividing cost of goods sold by average inventory. (p. 820)

Leveraging · Borrowing money at a lower rate of interest than can be earned by using the borrowed money (also referred to as trading on the equity). (p. 824)

Liquidity ratios · Measures of the short-term ability

of the enterprise to pay its maturing obligations and to meet unexpected needs for cash. (p. 817)

Payout ratio · Measures the percentage of earnings distributed in the form of cash dividends, computed by dividing cash dividends by net income. (p. 825)

Price-earnings ratio · Measures the ratio of the market price of each share of common stock to the earnings per share, computed by dividing the market price of the stock by earnings per share. (p. 825)

Profitability ratios · Measures of the income or operating success of an enterprise for a given period of time. (p. 817)

Profit margin ratio · Measures net income generated by each dollar of sales, computed by dividing net income by net sales. (p. 821)

Quick ratio · Another name for acid-test ratio; see acid-test ratio. (p. 818)

Ratio · An expression of the mathematical relationship between one quantity and another. The relationship may be expressed either as a percentage, a rate, or a simple proportion. (p. 816)

Receivables turnover ratio · A measure of the liquidity of receivables, computed by dividing net credit sales by average net receivables. (p. 819)

Return on assets ratio · An overall measure of profitability, computed by dividing net income by average assets. (p. 823)

Return on common stockholders' equity · Measures the dollars of net income earned for each dollar invested by the owners, computed by dividing net income by average common stockholders' equity. (p. 823)

Solvency ratios · Measures of the ability of the enterprise to survive over a long period of time. (p. 817)

Times interest earned ratio · Measures a company's ability to meet interest payments as they come due computed by dividing income before interest expense and income taxes by interest expense. (p. 827)

Trading on the equity · Same as leveraging. (p. 824)

Vertical analysis · A technique for evaluating financial statement data that expresses each item within a financial statement in terms of a percent of a base amount. (p. 814)

DEMONSTRATION PROBLEM

The condensed financial statements of Kellogg Company for the years 1991 and 1990 are presented below:

KELLOGG COMPANY
Balance Sheet
December 31

Assets

	(In millions)	
	1991	1990
Current assets		
Cash and short-term investments	$ 178.0	$ 100.5
Accounts receivable (net)	420.0	430.2
Inventories	401.1	359.7
Prepaid expenses	173.9	151.0
Total current assets	1,173.0	1,041.4
Property, plant, and equipment (net)	2,646.5	2,595.4
Intangibles and other assets	106.3	112.6
Total assets	3,925.8	3,749.4

Liabilities and Stockholders' Equity

Current liabilities	$1,324.4	$1,109.6
Long-term liabilities	441.6	738.0
Stockholders' equity—common	2,159.8	1,901.8
Total liabilities and stockholders' equity	3,925.8	$3,749.4

KELLOGG COMPANY
Income Statement
For the Year Ended December 31

	(In millions)	
	1991	1990
Revenues	5,801.2	$5,176.3
Cost and expenses		
Cost of goods sold	2,828.7	2,676.6
Selling and administrative expenses	1,930.0	1,618.8
Interest expense	58.3	66.2
Total costs and expenses	4,817.0	4,361.6
Income before income taxes	984.2	814.7
Income tax expense	378.2	311.9
Net income	$ 606.0	$ 502.8

Instructions

Compute the following ratios for Kellogg for 1991 and 1990.

(a) Current ratio.

(b) Inventory turnover (Inventory 12/31/89, $349.0).

(c) Profit margin ratio.

(d) Return on assets (Assets 12/31/89, $3,390.4).

(e) Return on common stockholders' equity (Equity 12/31/89, $1,634.4).

(f) Debt to total assets.

(g) Times interest earned.

Solution to Demonstration Problem

	1991	1990
(a) Current ratio:		
$1,173.0 ÷ $1,324.4 =	.89:1	
$1,041.4 ÷ $1,109.6 =		.94:1
(b) Inventory turnover:		
$2,828.7 ÷ [($401.1 + $359.7) ÷ 2] =	7.4 times	
$2,676.6 ÷ [($359.7 + $349.0) ÷ 2] =		7.6 times
(c) Profit margin:		
$606.0 ÷ $5,801.2 =	10.4%	
$502.8 ÷ $5,176.3 =		9.7%
(d) Return on assets:		
$606.0 ÷ [($3,925.8 + $3,749.4) ÷ 2] =	15.8%	
$502.8 ÷ [($3,749.4 + $3,390.4) ÷ 2] =		14.1%
(e) Return on common stockholders' equity:		
$606.0 ÷ [($2,159.8 + $1,901.8) ÷ 2] =	29.8%	
$502.8 ÷ [($1,901.8 + $1,634.4) ÷ 2] =		28.4%
(f) Debt to total assets:		
$1,766.0 ÷ $3,925.8 =	45.0%	
$1,847.6 ÷ $3,749.4 =		49.3%
(g) Times interest earned:		
($606.0 + $378.2 + $58.3) ÷ $58.3 =	17.9 times	
($502.8 + $311.9 + $66.2) ÷ $66.2 =		13.3 times

Helpful hints

1. Remember that the current ratio includes all current assets; acid-test ratio uses only cash, marketable securities, and net receivables.

2. Use average balances for turnover ratios like inventory, receivables, and assets.

3. Return on assets is greater or smaller than return on common stockholders' equity depending on cost of debt.

SELF-STUDY QUESTIONS

Answers are at the end of the chapter.

(S.O. 1)   1. Comparisons of data within a company are an example of the following comparative basis:
  a. Industry averages.
  b. Intercompany.
  c. Intracompany.
  d. None of the above.

(S.O. 3)   2. In trend (horizontal) analysis, each item is expressed as a percentage of the:
  a. net income amount.
  b. stockholders' equity amount.
  c. base year amount.
  d. total assets amount.

(S.O. 4)   3. In vertical analysis, the base amount for depreciation expense is generally:
  a. depreciation expense in a previous year.
  b. net sales.
  c. gross profit.
  d. fixed assets.

(S.O. 4)   4. The following schedule is a display of what type of analysis?

	Amount	Percent
Current assets	$200,000	25%
Property, plant, and equipment	600,000	75%
Total assets	$800,000	

  a. Horizontal analysis.
  b. Vertical analysis.
  c. Differential analysis.
  d. Ratio analysis.

(S.O. 3)   5. Leland Corporation reported net sales of $300,000, $360,000, and $390,000 in the years 1991, 1992, and 1993 respectively. If 1991 is the base year, what is the trend percentage for 1993?
  a. 77%.
  b. 108%.
  c. 120%.
  d. 130%.

(S.O. 4)   6. Which of the following measures is an evaluation of a firm's ability to pay current liabilities?
  a. Acid-test ratio.
  b. Current ratio.
  c. Working capital.
  d. All of the above.

(S.O. 4)   7. A measure useful in evaluating the efficiency in managing inventories is:
  a. inventory turnover ratio.
  b. average days to sell inventory.
  c. both A and B.
  d. none of the above.

(S.O. 5)   8. Which of the following is *not* a liquidity ratio?
  a. Current ratio.
  b. Inventory turnover.
  c. Asset turnover.
  d. Receivables turnover.

(S.O. 5)   9. Plano Corporation reported net income $24,000, net sales $200,000, and average assets $400,000 for 1993. The 1993 profit margin was:
  a. 6%.
  b. 12%.
  c. 50%.
  d. 200%.

(S.O. 6)   10. Which of the following is generally not considered to be a limitation of financial analysis?
  a. Use of ratio analysis.
  b. Use of estimates.
  c. Use of cost.
  d. Use of alternative accounting methods.

QUESTIONS

1. What are the characteristics of a business enterprise that can be evaluated when analyzing and interpreting financial statement data? Who is interested in these characteristics?

2. By comparing reported financial data, valuable insights can be provided. Name and describe three different bases of comparing financial information.

3. Two popular methods of financial statement analysis are horizontal analysis and vertical analysis. Explain the difference between these two methods.

4. (a) If Howat Company had net income of $540,000 in 1993 and it experienced a 24.5%

increase in net income for 1994, what is its net income for 1994? (b) If six cents of every dollar of Howat's revenue is net income in 1993, what is the dollar amount of 1993 revenue?

5. What is a ratio? What are the different ways of expressing the relationship of two amounts? What information does a ratio provide?

6. Name the major ratios useful in assessing (a) liquidity and (b) solvency.

7. Tom Robinson is puzzled. His company had a profit margin of 10% in 1993. He feels that this is an indication that the company is doing well. Joan Graham, his accountant, says that more information is needed to determine Tom's financial well-being. Who is correct? Why?

8. What do the following classes of ratios measure? (a) Liquidity ratios. (b) Profitability ratios. (c) Solvency ratios.

9. What is the difference between the current ratio and the acid-test ratio?

10. Terry Bullock Company, a retail store, has a receivables turnover ratio of 4.5 times. The industry average is 12.5 times. Does Bullock have a collection problem with its receivables?

11. Which ratios should be used to help answer the following questions?
(a) How near to sale is the inventory on hand?
(b) How efficient is a company in using its assets to produce sales?
(c) How many dollars of net income were earned for each dollar invested by the owners?
(d) How able is a company to meet interest charges as they fall due?

12. The price-earnings ratio of McDonnell Douglas (aircraft builder) was 5, and the price-earnings ratio of Microsoft (computer software) was 43. Which company did the stock market favor? Explain.

13. What is the formula for computing the payout ratio? Would you expect this ratio to be high or low for a growth company?

14. Holding all other factors constant, indicate whether each of the following changes generally signals good or bad news about a company:
(a) Increase in the current ratio.
(b) Decrease in inventory turnover.
(c) Increase in profit margin.
(d) Decrease in earnings per share.
(e) Increase in price-earnings ratio.
(f) Increase in debt to total assets ratio.
(g) Increase in book value per share.
(h) Decrease in times interest earned.

15. The return on total assets for Windsong Corporation is 8.6%. During the same year Windsong's return on common stockholders' equity is 12.8%. What is the explanation for the difference in the two rates?

16. Which two ratios do you think should be of greatest interest to:
(a) A bank contemplating a short-term loan?
(b) A pension fund considering the purchase of 20-year bonds?
(c) A common stockholder?

17. (a) What is meant by leveraging? (b) How would you determine the profitability of leveraging?

18. Chris Inc. has net income of $260,000, weighted average shares of common stock outstanding of 50,000, and preferred dividends for the period of $40,000. What is Chris's earnings per share of common stock? Phil Remmers, the president of Chris Inc., believes the computed EPS of the company is high. Comment.

19. Identify and briefly explain four limitations of financial analysis.

20. Explain how the choice of one of the following accounting methods over the other raises or lowers a company's net income during a period of continuing inflation:
(a) Use of a 6-year life for machinery instead of a 9-year life.
(b) Use of FIFO instead of LIFO for inventory costing.
(c) Use of straight-line depreciation instead of accelerated declining-balance depreciation.

BRIEF EXERCISES

Prepare horizontal analysis.
(S.O. 3)

BE20-1   Using the following data from the comparative balance sheet of All-Brand Company, illustrate horizontal analysis:

	December 31, 1994	December 31, 1993
Accounts receivable	$ 600,000	$ 400,000
Inventory	$ 800,000	$ 600,000
Total assets	$3,200,000	$2,800,000

Prepare vertical analysis.
(S.O. 4)

BE20-2   Using the same data presented above in BE20-1 for All-Brand Company, illustrate vertical analysis.

Calculate percentage of change.
(S.O. 3)

BE20-3   Net income was $480,000 in 1992, $420,000 in 1993, and $504,000 in 1994. What is the percentage of change from (1) 1992 to 1993 and (2) 1993 to 1994? Is the change an increase or a decrease?

Calculate percentage of change.
(S.O. 3)

BE20-4   If the Cavaliers Company had net income of $672,300 in 1994 and it experienced a 24.5% increase in net income over 1993, what was its 1993 net income?

Calculate change in net income.
(S.O. 4)

BE20-5   Vertical analysis (common size) percentages for Waubonsee Company's sales, cost of goods sold, and expenses are shown below:

Vertical Analysis	1994	1993	1992
Sales	100.0	100.0	100.0
Cost of goods sold	58.2	62.4	64.5
Expenses	25.0	26.6	29.5

Did Waubonsee's net income as a percent of sales increase, decrease, or remain unchanged over the 3-year period presented above? Provide numerical support for your answer.

Calculate change in net income.
(S.O. 3)

BE20-6   Horizontal analysis (trend analysis) percentages for DuPage & Triton Company's sales, cost of goods sold, and expenses are shown below:

Horizontal Analysis	1994	1993	1992
Sales	96.2	106.8	100.0
Cost of goods sold	102.0	97.0	100.0
Expenses	110.6	95.4	100.0

Did DuPage & Triton's net income increase, decrease, or remain unchanged over the 3-year period presented above?

Calculate liquidity ratios.
(S.O. 5)

BE20-7   Selected condensed data taken from the balance sheet of Bob Evans Farms at December 31, 1993, are as follows:

Cash	$ 5,200,000
Accounts receivable	17,840,000
Inventory	30,500,000
Other current assets	6,080,000
Total current assets	$59,620,000
Total current liabilities	$23,770,000

At December 31, 1993, what are the (1) working capital, (2) current ratio, and (3) the acid-test ratio?

Calculate profitability ratios.
(S.O. 5)

BE20-8   Chicago Bulls Corporation has net income of $15 million and net revenue of $100 million in 1993. Its assets were $11.5 million at the beginning of the year and $14 million at the end of the year. What are (a) the Bulls' asset turnover ratio and (b) profit margin ratio? (Round to two decimals.)

Evaluate collection of accounts receivable.
(S.O. 5)

BE20-9   The following data are taken from the financial statements of Diet-Rite Company:

	1994	1993
Accounts receivable (net), end of year	$ 560,000	$ 510,000
Net sales on account	5,500,000	4,100,000
Terms for all sales are 1/10, n/45.		

Compute for each year (1) the receivables turnover and (2) the average collection period. What conclusions about the management of accounts receivable can be drawn from these data? At the end of 1992, accounts receivable (net) was $490,000.

BE20–10 The following data were taken from the income statements of Otis S. Company:

Evaluate management of inventory.
(S.O. 5)

	1994	1993
Sales	$6,420,000	$6,240,000
Beginning inventory	980,000	837,000
Purchases	4,540,000	4,661,000
Ending inventory	1,020,000	980,000

Compute for each year (1) the inventory turnover ratio and (2) the average days to sell the inventory. What conclusions concerning the management of the inventory can be drawn from these data?

BE20–11 Hayworth Products Company has owners' equity of $400,000 and net income of $50,000. It has a payout ratio of 25% and a rate of return on assets of 16%. How much did Hayworth Products Company pay in cash dividends, and what were its average assets?

Calculate profitability ratios.
(S.O. 5)

EXERCISES

E20–1 Financial information for Merchandiser Company is presented below:

Prepare horizontal analysis.
(S.O. 3)

	December 31, 1993	December 31, 1992
Current assets	$120,000	$100,000
Plant assets (net)	400,000	330,000
Current liabilities	90,000	70,000
Long-term liabilities	145,000	95,000
Common stock, $1 par	150,000	115,000
Retained earnings	135,000	150,000

Instructions
Prepare a schedule showing a horizontal analysis for 1993 using 1992 as the base year.

E20–2 Operating data for Fleetwood Mac Corporation are presented below:

Prepare vertical analysis.
(S.O. 4)

	1994	1993
Sales	$800,000	$600,000
Cost of goods sold	472,000	390,000
Selling expenses	120,000	72,000
Administrative expenses	80,000	54,000
Income tax expense	49,000	33,000
Net income	79,000	51,000

Instructions
Prepare a schedule showing a vertical analysis for 1994 and 1993.

E20–3 The comparative balance sheets of Olympia Corporation are presented below:

Prepare horizontal and vertical analyses.
(S.O. 4, 5)

OLYMPIA CORPORATION
Comparative Balance Sheets
As of December 31

	1994	1993
Assets		
Current assets	$ 76,000	$ 80,000
Property, plant, & equipment (net)	99,000	90,000
Intangibles	20,000	40,000
Total assets	$195,000	$210,000

OLYMPIA CORPORATION *(continued)*

	1994	1993
Liabilities & stockholders' equity		
Current liabilities	$ 40,800	$ 48,000
Long-term liabilities	138,000	150,000
Stockholders' equity	16,200	12,000
Total liabilities & stockholders' equity	$195,000	$210,000

Instructions

Prepare a horizontal analysis of the balance sheet data for Olympia Corporation using 1993 as a base. (Show the amount of increase or decrease as well.)

Prepare vertical analysis.
(S.O. 3, 4)

E20–4 Using the data presented above in E20–3, prepare a vertical analysis of the balance sheet data for Olympia Corporation in columnar form for both years.

Prepare horizontal and vertical analyses.
(S.O. 3, 4)

E20–5 The comparative income statements of Olympia Corporation are shown below:

OLYMPIA CORPORATION
Comparative Income Statements
For the Years Ended December 31

	1994	1993
Net sales	$550,000	$550,000
Cost of goods sold	440,000	450,000
Gross profit	$110,000	$100,000
Operating expenses	57,200	52,000
Net income	$ 52,800	$ 48,000

Instructions

(a) Prepare a horizontal analysis of the income statement data for Olympia Corporation using 1993 as a base. (Show the amounts of increase or decrease.)

(b) Prepare a vertical analysis of the income statement data for Olympia Corporation in columnar form for both years.

Perform current and acid-test ratio analysis.
(S.O. 5)

E20–6 Flaum Incorporated had the following transactions occur involving current assets and current liabilities during February 1993:

Feb. 3 Accounts receivable of $15,000 are collected.
    7 Equipment is purchased for $25,000 cash.
    11 Paid $3,000 for a 3-year insurance policy.
    14 Accounts payable of $12,000 are paid.
    18 Dividends are declared, $6,000.

Additional information:

1. As of February 1, 1993, current assets were $140,000 and current liabilities were $50,000.

2. As of February 1, 1993, current assets included $15,000 of inventory and $5,000 of prepaid expenses.

Instructions

(Follow the rounding procedures used in the chapter.)

(a) Compute the current ratio as of the beginning of the month and after each transaction.

(b) Compute the acid-test ratio as of the beginning of the month and after each transaction.

Compute selected ratios.
(S.O. 5)

E20–7 Georgetti Company has the following comparative balance sheet data:

	December 31, 1993	December 31, 1992
Cash	$ 20,000	$ 30,000
Receivables (net)	65,000	60,000
Inventories	60,000	50,000
Plant assets (net)	200,000	180,000
	$345,000	$320,000

	December 31, 1993	December 31, 1992
Accounts payable	$ 50,000	$ 60,000
Mortgage payable (15%)	100,000	100,000
Common stock, $10 par	140,000	120,000
Retained earnings	55,000	40,000
	$345,000	$320,000

Additional information for 1993:

1. The net income was $25,000.
2. Sales on account were $420,000. Sales returns and allowances amounted to $20,000.
3. Cost of goods sold was $180,000.

Instructions
(Follow the rounding procedures used in the chapter.) Compute the following ratios at December 31, 1993:

(a) Current.

(b) Acid-test.

(c) Receivables turnover.

(d) Inventory turnover.

E20–8 Selected comparative statement data for Wacker Products Company are presented below. All balance sheet data are as of December 31.

Compute selected ratios.
(S.O. 5)

	1993	1992
Net sales	$800,000	$720,000
Cost of goods sold	480,000	40,000
Interest expense	7,000	5,000
Net income	56,000	42,000
Accounts receivable	120,000	100,000
Inventory	85,000	75,000
Total assets	600,000	500,000
Total common stockholders' equity	450,000	325,000

Instructions
(Follow the rounding procedures used in the chapter.) Compute the following ratios for 1993:

(a) Profit margin.

(b) Asset turnover.

(c) Return on assets.

(d) Return on common stockholders' equity.

E20–9 The income statement for the year ended December 31, 1993, of Jean Pfeifer, Inc. appears below.

Compute selected ratios.
(S.O. 5)

Sales	$400,000
Cost of goods sold	230,000
Gross profit	170,000
Expenses (including $20,000 interest and $24,000 income taxes)	100,000
Net income	$ 70,000

Additional information:

1. Common stock outstanding January 1, 1993, was 30,000 shares. On July 1, 1993, 10,000 more shares were issued.
2. The market price of Jean Pfeifer, Inc. stock was $15 in 1993.
3. Cash dividends of $25,000 were paid, $5,000 of which were to preferred stockholders.

Instructions

(Follow the rounding procedures used in the chapter.) Compute the following ratios for 1993.

(a) Earnings per share.

(b) Price-earnings.

(c) Payout.

(d) Times interest earned.

Compute amounts from ratios.
(S.O. 5)

E20–10 Barbara Schrader Corporation experienced a fire on December 31, 1993, in which its financial records were partially destroyed. It has been able to salvage some of the records and has ascertained the following balances:

	December 31, 1993	December 31, 1992
Cash	$ 30,000	$ 10,000
Receivables (net)	72,500	126,000
Inventory	200,000	180,000
Accounts payable	50,000	90,000
Notes payable	30,000	60,000
Common stock, $100 par	400,000	400,000
Retained earnings	113,500	101,000

Additional information:

1. The inventory turnover is 3.6 times.
2. The return on common stockholders' equity is 22%. The company had no additional paid-in capital.
3. The receivables turnover is 9.4 times.
4. The return on assets is 20%.
5. Total assets at December 31, 1992, were $605,225.

Instructions

(Follow the rounding procedures used in the chapter.) Compute the following for Barbara Schrader Corporation:

(a) Cost of goods sold for 1993.

(b) Net sales for 1993.

(c) Net income for 1993.

(d) Total assets at December 31, 1993.

PROBLEMS

Prepare vertical analysis and comment on profitability.
(S.O. 4, 5)

P20–1 Comparative statement data for Brokaw Company and News Company, two competitors, appear below. All balance sheet data are as of December 31, 1993, and December 31, 1992.

	Brokaw Company		News Company	
	1993	1992	1993	1992
Net sales	$1,549,035		$339,038	
Cost of goods sold	1,080,490		238,006	
Operating expenses	302,275		79,000	
Interest expense	6,800		1,252	
Income tax expense	83,710		10,600	
Current assets	325,975	$312,410	83,336	$ 79,467
Plant assets (net)	521,310	500,000	139,728	125,812
Current liabilities	66,325	75,815	35,348	30,281
Long-term liabilities	108,500	90,000	29,620	25,000
Common stock, $10 par	500,000	500,000	120,000	120,000
Retained earnings	172,460	146,595	38,096	29,998

Instructions

(a) Prepare a vertical analysis of the 1993 income statement data for Brokaw Company and News Company in columnar form.

(b) Comment on the relative profitability of the companies by computing the return on assets and the return on common stockholders' equity ratios for both companies.

Compute ratios from balance sheet and income statement.
(S.O. 5)

P20–2 The comparative statements of Michael Jordan Company are presented below:

MICHAEL JORDAN COMPANY
Income Statement
For the Year Ended December 31

	1993	1992
Net sales	$1,818,500	$1,750,500
Cost of goods sold	1,005,500	996,000
Gross profit	813,000	754,500
Selling and administrative expense	506,000	479,000
Income from operations	307,000	275,500
Other expenses and losses		
Interest expense	18,000	19,000
Income before income taxes	289,000	256,500
Income tax expense	86,700	77,000
Net income	$ 202,300	$ 179,500

MICHAEL JORDAN COMPANY
Balance Sheet
December 31

	1993	1992
Assets		
Current assets		
Cash	$ 60,100	$ 64,200
Marketable securities	54,000	50,000
Accounts receivable (net)	107,800	102,800
Inventory	123,000	115,500
Total current assets	344,900	332,500
Plant assets (net)	625,300	520,300
Total assets	$970,200	$852,800
Liabilities and stockholders' equity		
Current liabilities		
Accounts payable	$150,000	$145,400
Income taxes payable	43,500	42,000
Total current liabilities	193,500	187,400
Bonds payable	210,000	200,000
Total liabilities	403,500	387,400
Stockholders' equity		
Common stock ($5 par)	280,000	300,000
Retained earnings	286,700	165,400
Total stockholders' equity	566,700	465,400
Total liabilities and stockholders' equity	$970,200	$852,800

On July 1, 1993, 4,000 shares were repurchased and canceled. All sales were on account.

Instructions

(Follow the rounding procedures used in the chapter.) Compute the following ratios for 1993:

(a) Earnings per share.

(b) Return on common stockholders' equity.

(c) Return on assets.

(d) Current.

(e) Acid-test.
(f) Receivables turnover.
(g) Inventory turnover.

(h) Times interest earned.
(i) Asset turnover.
(j) Debt to total assets.

P20–3 Condensed balance sheet and income statement data for Ditkavich Corporation appear below:

Perform ratio analysis.
(S.O. 5)

DITKAVICH CORPORATION
Balance Sheet
December 31

	1993	1992	1991
Cash	$ 25,000	$ 20,000	$ 18,000
Receivables (net)	50,000	45,000	48,000
Other current assets	90,000	85,000	64,000
Investments	75,000	70,000	45,000
Plant and equipment (net)	400,000	370,000	358,000
	$640,000	$590,000	$533,000
Current liabilities	$ 75,000	$ 80,000	$ 70,000
Long-term debt	80,000	85,000	50,000
Common stock, $10 par	340,000	300,000	300,000
Retained earnings	145,000	125,000	113,000
	$640,000	$590,000	$533,000

DITKAVICH CORPORATION
Income Statement
For the Years Ended December 31

	1993	1992
Sales	$740,000	$700,000
Less: Sales returns and allowances	40,000	50,000
Net sales	700,000	650,000
Cost of goods sold	420,000	400,000
Gross profit	280,000	250,000
Operating expenses (including income taxes)	236,000	218,000
Net income	$ 44,000	$ 32,000

Additional information:

1. The market price of Ditkavich's common stock was $4.00, $5.00, and $7.25 for 1991, 1992, and 1993, respectively.

2. All dividends were paid in cash.

3. On July 1, 1993, 4,000 shares of common stock were issued.

Instructions
(Follow the rounding procedures used in the chapter.)

(a) Compute the following ratios for 1992 and 1993:
    (1) Profit margin.
    (2) Asset turnover.
    (3) Earnings per share.
    (4) Price-earnings.
    (5) Payout.
    (6) Debt to total assets.

(b) Based on the ratios calculated, discuss briefly the improvement or lack thereof in financial position and operating results from 1992 to 1993 of the Ditkavich Corporation.

P20–4 Financial information for Carolina Company is presented below:

Compute ratios, commenting on overall liquidity and profitability. (S.O. 5)

CAROLINA COMPANY
Balance Sheet
December 31

Assets	1993	1992
Cash	$ 70,000	$ 65,000
Short-term investments	45,000	40,000
Receivables (net)	94,000	90,000
Inventories	130,000	125,000
Prepaid expenses	25,000	23,000
Land	130,000	130,000
Building and equipment (net)	190,000	175,000
	$684,000	$648,000

Liabilities and stockholders' equity	1993	1992
Notes payable	$100,000	$100,000
Accounts payable	45,000	42,000
Accrued liabilities	40,000	40,000
Bonds payable, due 1995	150,000	150,000
Common stock, $10 par	200,000	200,000
Retained earnings	149,000	116,000
	$684,000	$648,000

CAROLINA COMPANY
Income Statement
For the Years Ended December 31

	1993	1992
Sales	$850,000	$790,000
Cost of goods sold	620,000	575,000
Gross profit	230,000	215,000
Operating expenses	194,000	180,000
Net income	$ 36,000	$ 35,000

Additional information:

1. Inventory at the beginning of 1992 was $115,000.
2. Receivables at the beginning of 1992 were $88,000.
3. Total assets at the beginning of 1992 were $630,000.
4. No common stock transactions occurred during 1992 or 1993.
5. All sales were on account.

Instructions
(Follow the rounding procedures used in the chapter.)

(a) Indicate by using ratios, the change in liquidity and profitability of Carolina Company from 1992 to 1993. (Note: Not all profitability ratios can be computed.)

(b) Given below are three independent situations and a ratio that may be affected. For each situation, compute the affected ratio (1) as of December 31, 1993, and (2) as of December 31, 1994, after giving effect to the situation. Net income for 1994 was $40,000. Total assets on December 31, 1994, were $700,000.

Situation	Ratio
1. 18,000 shares of common stock were sold at par on July 1, 1994.	Return on common stockholders' equity
2. All of the notes payable were paid in 1994.	Debt to total assets
3. Market price of common stock was $11 and $12.80 on December 31, 1993 and 1994, respectively.	Price-earnings ratio

Compute ratios, perform analysis, and identify limitations.
(S.O. 5, 6)

P20–5 Comparative data for three competing microphone companies for the year 1993 appear below:

	Chicago Company	Milwaukee Company	Cleveland Company
Net sales (all on account)	$1,347,510	$1,094,340	$610,400
Cost of goods sold	624,000	497,710	302,250
Operating expenses	359,140	330,050	189,140
Interest expense	27,830	19,100	12,810
Income tax expense	100,080	67,390	32,030
Net income	$ 236,460	$ 180,090	$ 74,170
Current assets	$ 315,800	$ 294,100	$257,500
Plant assets (net)	800,000	718,000	640,900
Other assets	90,100	77,400	87,400
Total assets	$1,205,900	$1,089,500	$985,800
Current liabilities	$ 194,600	$ 187,700	$147,900
Long-term liabilities	479,000	500,000	275,000
Stockholders' equity	532,300	401,800	562,900
Total liabilities and stockholders' equity	$1,205,900	$1,089,500	$985,800
Additional information:			
Average receivables	$ 105,700	$ 92,700	$ 74,300
Average inventory	192,300	175,600	151,000
Average assets	1,160,200	1,070,200	952,500
Common stockholders' equity (January 1)	500,100	498,200	500,000
Par value of common stock	4	5	10
Weighted average shares outstanding	70,000	50,000	28,000
Market price per share of stock	46	50	33
Cash dividends paid	70,000	42,000	12,000

Instructions
(Follow the rounding procedures used in the chapter.)

(a) Compute the following ratios for the three companies above:

(1) Current.	(7) Return on common stockholders' equity
(2) Receivables turnover.	(8) Earnings per share.
(3) Inventory turnover.	(9) Price-earnings.
(4) Profit margin.	(10) Payout.
(5) Asset turnover.	(11) Debt to total assets.
(6) Return on assets.	(12) Times interest earned.

Rank the companies numerically (1 is the best) using the following format:

	Chicago	Milwaukee	Cleveland
Ratio Name	Ratio Rank	Ratio Rank	Ratio Rank

(b) Comment on the relative liquidity, profitability, and solvency of each company.

(c) What limitations are there in the analysis above?

P20–6 The comparative statements of Spectra Vision Company are presented below:

Compute numerous ratios.
(S.O. 5)

SPECTRA VISION COMPANY
Income Statement
For Year Ended December 31

	1993	1992
Net sales (all on account)	$600,000	$520,000
Expenses		
Cost of goods sold	415,000	354,000
Selling and administrative	120,800	114,800
Interest expense	7,200	6,000
Income tax expense	18,000	14,000
Total expenses	561,000	488,800
Net income	$ 39,000	$ 31,200

SPECTRA VISION COMPANY
Balance Sheet
December 31

	1993	1992
Assets		
Current assets		
Cash	$ 21,000	$ 18,000
Marketable securities	18,000	15,000
Accounts receivable (net)	92,000	74,000
Inventory	84,000	70,000
Total current assets	215,000	177,000
Plant assets (net)	423,000	383,000
Total assets	$638,000	$560,000
Liabilities and stockholders' equity		
Current liabilities		
Accounts payable	$112,000	$110,000
Income taxes payable	23,000	20,000
Total current liabilities	135,000	130,000
Long-term liabilities		
Bonds payable	130,000	80,000
Total liabilities	265,000	210,000
Stockholders' equity		
Common stock ($5 par)	150,000	150,000
Retained earnings	223,000	200,000
Total stockholders' equity	373,000	350,000
Total liabilities and stockholders' equity	$638,000	$560,000

Additional data:
The common stock recently sold at $22.50 per share.

Instructions
(Follow the rounding procedures used in the chapter.) Compute the following ratios for 1993:

(a) Current.
(b) Acid-test.
(c) Receivables turnover.
(d) Inventory turnover.
(e) Profit margin.
(f) Asset turnover.
(g) Return on assets.

(h) Return on common stockholders' equity.
(i) Earnings per share.
(j) Price-earnings.
(k) Payout.
(l) Debt to total assets.
(m) Times interest earned.

Compute missing
information given a set
of ratios.
(S.O. 5)

P20–7 Presented below is an incomplete income statement and an incomplete comparative balance sheet of Vermont Corporation:

VERMONT CORPORATION
Income Statement
For the Year Ended December 31, 1993

Sales	$11,000,000
Cost of goods sold	?
Gross profit	?
Operating expenses	1,665,000
Income from operations	?
Other expenses and losses	
Interest expense	?
Incomed before income taxes	?
Income tax expense	560,000
Net income	$?

VERMONT CORPORATION
Balance Sheet
December 31

	1993	1992
Assets		
Current assets		
Cash	$ 450,000	$ 375,000
Accounts receivable (net)	?	950,000
Inventory	?	1,720,000
Total current assets	?	3,045,000
Plant assets (net)	4,620,000	3,955,000
Total assets	$?	$7,000,000
Liabilities and stockholders' equity		
Current liabilities	$?	$ 825,000
Long-term notes payable	?	2,800,000
Total liabilities	?	3,625,000
Common stock, $1 par	3,000,000	3,000,000
Retained earnings	400,000	375,000
Total stockholders' equity	3,400,000	3,375,000
Total liabilities and stockholders' equity	$?	$7,000,000

Additional information:

1. The receivables turnover for 1993 is 10 times.
2. All sales are on account.
3. The profit margin for 1993 is 14.5%.
4. Return on assets is 22% for 1993.
5. The current ratio on December 31, 1993, is 3.2:1.
6. The inventory turnover for 1993 is 4.8 times.

Instructions

Compute the missing information given the ratios above. Show computations. (Note: Start with one ratio and derive as much information as possible from it before trying another ratio. List all missing amounts under the ratio used to find the information.)

ALTERNATIVE PROBLEMS

P20–1A Comparative statement data for Garth Company and Brooks Company, two competitors, appear below. All balance sheet data are as of December 31, 1993, and December 31, 1992.

Prepare vertical analysis and comment on profitability.
(S.O. 4, 5)

	Garth Company		Brooks Company	
	1993	1992	1993	1992
Net sales	$250,000		$1,200,000	
Cost of goods sold	160,000		720,000	
Operating expenses	51,000		252,000	
Interest expense	3,000		10,000	
Income tax expense	14,000		90,000	
Current assets	130,000	$110,000	700,000	$650,000
Plant assets (net)	305,000	270,000	800,000	750,000
Current liabilities	60,000	52,000	250,000	275,000
Long-term liabilities	50,000	68,000	200,000	150,000
Common stock	260,000	210,000	750,000	700,000
Retained earnings	65,000	50,000	300,000	275,000

Instructions

(a) Prepare a vertical analysis of the 1993 income statement data for Garth Company and Brooks Company in columnar form.

(b) Comment on the relative profitability of the companies by computing the return on assets and the return on common stockholders' equity ratios for both companies.

P20–2A The comparative statements of the Marty Rosenberg Company are presented below:

Compute ratios from balance sheet and income statement.
(S.O. 5)

MARTY ROSENBERG COMPANY
Income Statement
For the Year Ended December 31

	1993	1992
Net sales	$660,000	$624,000
Cost of goods sold	440,000	405,600
Gross profit	220,000	218,400
Selling and administrative expense	143,880	149,760
Income from operations	76,120	68,640
Other expenses and losses		
Interest expense	7,920	7,200
Income before income taxes	68,200	61,440
Income tax expense	25,300	24,000
Net income	$ 42,900	$ 37,440

MARTY ROSENBERG COMPANY
Balance Sheet
December 31

	1993	1992
Assets		
Current assets		
Cash	$ 23,100	$ 21,600
Marketable securities	34,800	33,000
Accounts receivable (net)	106,200	93,800
Inventory	72,400	64,000
Total current assets	236,500	212,400
Plant assets (net)	465,300	459,600
Total assets	$701,800	$672,000

MARTY ROSENBERG COMPANY *(continued)*

	1993	1992
Liabilities and stockholders' equity		
Current liabilities		
Accounts payable	$134,200	$132,000
Income taxes payable	25,300	24,000
Total current liabilities	159,500	156,000
Bonds payable	132,000	120,000
Total liabilities	291,500	276,000
Stockholders' equity		
Common stock ($10 par)	137,500	150,000
Retained earnings	272,800	246,000
Total stockholders' equity	410,300	396,000
Total liabilities and stockholders' equity	$701,800	$672,000

On July 1, 1993, 1,250 shares were repurchased and canceled. All sales were on account.

Instructions

(Follow the rounding procedures used in the chapter.) Compute the following ratios for 1993:

(a) Earnings per share.
(b) Return on common stockholders' equity.
(c) Return on assets.
(d) Current.
(e) Acid-test.

(f) Receivables turnover.
(g) Inventory turnover.
(h) Times interest earned.
(i) Asset turnover.
(j) Debt to total assets.

Perform ratio analysis.
(S.O. 5)

P20–3A Condensed balance sheet and income statement data for Maddox Corporation appear below:

MADDOX CORPORATION
Balance Sheet
December 31

	1993	1992	1991
Cash	$ 40,000	$ 24,000	$ 20,000
Receivables (net)	70,000	45,000	48,000
Other current assets	80,000	75,000	62,000
Investments	90,000	70,000	50,000
Plant and equipment (net)	450,000	400,000	360,000
	$730,000	$614,000	$540,000
Current liabilities	$ 98,000	$ 75,000	$ 70,000
Long-term debt	97,000	75,000	65,000
Common stock, $10 par	400,000	340,000	300,000
Retained earnings	135,000	124,000	105,000
	$730,000	$614,000	$540,000

MADDOX CORPORATION
Income Statement
For the Years Ended December 31

	1993	1992
Sales	$700,000	$750,000
Less: Sales returns and allowances	40,000	50,000
Net sales	660,000	700,000
Cost of goods sold	420,000	400,000
Gross profit	240,000	300,000
Operating expenses (including income taxes)	194,000	237,000
Net income	$ 46,000	$ 63,000

Additional information:

1. The market price of Maddox's common stock was $5.00, $4.50, and $2.50 for 1991, 1992, and 1993, respectively.
2. All dividends were paid in cash.
3. On July 1, 1992, 4,000 shares of common stock were issued and on July 1, 1993 6,000 shares were issued.

Instructions
(Follow the rounding procedures used in the chapter.)

(a) Compute the following ratios for 1992 and 1993:
   (1) Profit margin.
   (2) Asset turnover.
   (3) Earnings per share.
   (4) Price-earnings.
   (5) Payout.
   (6) Debt to total assets.

(b) Based on the ratios calculated, discuss briefly the improvement or lack thereof in financial position and operating results from 1992 to 1993 of the Maddox Corporation.

P20–4A Financial information for Star Trek Company is presented below:

Compute ratios, commenting on overall liquidity and profitability.
(S.O. 5)

STAR TREK COMPANY
Balance Sheet
December 31

	1993	1992
Assets		
Cash	$ 50,000	$ 42,000
Short-term investments	80,000	100,000
Receivables (net)	100,000	87,000
Inventories	440,000	400,000
Prepaid expenses	25,000	31,000
Land	75,000	75,000
Building and equipment (net)	570,000	500,000
	$1,340,000	$1,235,000
Liabilities and stockholders' equity		
Notes payable	$ 125,000	$ 125,000
Accounts payable	160,000	140,000
Accrued liabilities	50,000	50,000
Bonds payable, due 1995	200,000	200,000
Common stock, $5 par	500,000	500,000
Retained earnings	305,000	220,000
	$1,340,000	$1,235,000

STAR TREK COMPANY
Income Statement
For the Years Ended December 31

	1993	1992
Sales	$1,000,000	$ 940,000
Cost of goods sold	650,000	635,000
Gross profit	350,000	305,000
Operating expenses	235,000	215,000
Net income	$ 115,000	$ 90,000

Additional information:

1. Inventory at the beginning of 1992 was $350,000.

2. Receivables at the beginning of 1992 were $80,000.

3. Total assets at the beginning of 1992 were $1,175,000.

4. No common stock transactions occurred during 1992 or 1993.

5. All sales were on account.

Instructions

(Follow the rounding procedure used in the chapter.)

(a) Indicate by using ratios, the change in liquidity and profitability of Star Trek Company from 1992 to 1993. (Note: Not all profitability ratios can be computed.)

(b) Given below are three independent situations and a ratio that may be affected. For each situation, compute the affected ratio (1) as of December 31, 1993, and (2) as of December 31, 1994, after giving effect to the situation. Net income for 1994 was $125,000. Total assets on December 31, 1994, were $1,500,000.

Situation	Ratio
(1) 65,000 shares of common stock were sold at par on July 1, 1994.	Return on common stockholders' equity
(2) All of the notes payable were paid in 1994.	Debt to total assets
(3) Market price of common stock on December 31, 1994, was $6. Market price on December 31, 1993 was $5.	Price-earnings ratio

Compute ratios, perform analysis, and identify limitations.
(S.O. 5, 6)

P20–5A Comparative data for three competing guitar companies for the year 1993 appears below:

	Tinkers Company	Evers Company	Chance Company
Net sales (all on account)	$340,787	$203,423	$201,858
Cost of goods sold	209,708	129,804	122,835
Operating expenses	105,500	64,400	66,499
Interest expense	1,537	751	1,084
Income tax expense	7,416	2,360	3,459
Net income	$ 16,626	$ 6,108	$ 7,981
Current assets	$ 78,234	$ 54,168	$106,459
Plant assets (net)	125,114	71,323	112,800
Other assets	26,795	18,325	12,011
Total assets	$230,143	$143,816	$231,270
Current liabilities	$ 16,878	$ 50,002	$ 33,100
Long-term liabilities	25,080	19,253	104,744
Common stockholders' equity	188,185	74,561	93,426
Total liabilities and stockholders' equity	$230,143	$143,816	$231,270
Additional information:			
Average receivables	$ 15,000	$ 9,200	$ 12,400
Average inventory	30,000	20,000	28,500
Average assets	235,400	128,600	225,000
Stockholders' equity (January 1)	150,015	70,039	87,324
Par value of common stock	10	5	2
Weighted average shares outstanding	5,000	8,000	20,000
Market price per share of stock	22	7	3
Cash dividends paid	6,000	2,400	2,800

Instructions

(Follow the rounding procedures used in the chapter.)

(a) Compute the following ratios for the three companies above:
  (1) Current
  (2) Receivables turnover.
  (3) Inventory turnover.
  (4) Profit margin.
  (5) Asset turnover.
  (6) Return on assets.

(7) Return on common stockholders' equity.
(8) Earnings per share.
(9) Price-earnings.

(10) Payout.
(11) Debt to total assets.
(12) Times interest earned.

Rank the companies numerically (1 is the best) using the following format:

	Tinkers	Evers	Chance
Ratio Name	Ratio Rank	Ratio Rank	Ratio Rank

(b) Comment on the relative liquidity, profitability, and solvency of each company.

(c) What limitations are there in the analysis above?

Broadening Your Perspective

FINANCIAL REPORTING PROBLEM

Your parents are considering investing in PepsiCo, Inc. common stock. They ask you, as an accounting expert, to make an analysis of the company for them. Fortunately, excerpts from a current annual report of PepsiCo are presented in Appendix L of this textbook. Note that all amounts omit 000,000's (i.e., all dollar amounts are in millions).

Instructions
(Follow the approach in the chapter for rounding numbers.)

(a) Make a five-year trend analysis, using 1987 as the base year, of (1) net sales, and (2) income from continuing operations. Comment on the significance of the trend results.

(b) Compute for 1991 and 1990 the (1) current ratio, (2) acid-test ratio, (3) receivables turnover (assuming that notes and accounts receivable less allowance for doubtful accounts was $1,197 at December 30, 1989), and (4) inventory turnover. Assume that inventory as of December 30, 1989, was $514.1 and that all sales are credit sales. What conclusions can you reach about PepsiCo's short-term liquidity from these data?

(c) Compute for 1991 and 1990, the (1) profit margin, (2) asset turnover, (3) return on assets, and (4) return on common stockholders' equity. How would you evaluate PepsiCo's profitability? Assume that total assets at December 30, 1989, were $14,139.4 and the total stockholders' equity at December 30, 1989, was $4,032.6.

(d) Compute for 1991 and 1990, the (1) debt to total assets, and (2) times interest earned. How would you evaluate PepsiCo's long-term solvency?

(e) What information outside the annual report may also be useful to your parents in making a decision about PepsiCo., Inc.?

DECISION CASE

As the CPA for J. Martinez Manufacturing Inc., you have been requested to develop some key ratios from the comparative financial statements. This information is to be used to convince creditors that J. Martinez Manufacturing Inc. is solvent and to support the use of going-concern valuation procedures in the financial statements.

The data requested and the computations developed from the financial statements follow:

	1994	1993
Current ratio	3.1 times	2.1 times
Acid-test ratio	.8 times	1.4 times
Property, plant, and equipment to stockholders' equity	2.8 times	2.2 times
Sales to stockholders' equity	2.3 times	2.7 times

	1994	1993
Net income	Up 32%	Down 8%
Earnings per share	$3.30	$2.50
Book value per share	Up 8%	Up 11%

Instructions

(a) J. Martinez Manufacturing Inc. asks you to prepare a list of brief comments stating how each of these items supports the solvency and going concern potential of the business. The company wishes to use these comments to support its presentation of data to its creditors. You are to prepare the comments as requested, giving the implications and the limitations of each item separately, and then the collective inference that may be drawn from them about J. Martinez's solvency and going-concern potential.

(b) Having done as the client requested in part (a), prepare a brief listing of additional ratio-analysis-type data for this client which you think its creditors are going to ask for to supplement the data provided in part (a). Explain why you think the additional data will be helpful to these creditors in evaluating the client's solvency.

(c) What warnings should you offer these creditors about the limitations of ratio analysis for the purpose stated here?

CRITICAL THINKING CASE

Refer to the University of Chicago story at the opening of the chapter to answer the following questions:

1. What financial ratio(s) helped John R. Kroll of the university receive financing for the school? What other ratios or data are provided by a university when borrowing funds? What relevant information is provided by these ratios or data?

2. What are the sources of funds for a private university?

3. How are educational institutions rated and what equity to debt ratio applies to these ratings? What is the University of Chicago's equity to debt ratio?

ETHICAL CASE

Vern Fairly, president of Fairly Industries, wishes to issue a press release to bolster his company's image and maybe even its stock price, which has been gradually falling. You have been asked as controller to provide a list of twenty financial ratios along with some other operating statistics relative to Fairly Industries' first quarter financials and operations. Two days after you provide the ratios and data requested, you are asked by Roberto Sanchez, the public relations director of Fairly, to proof the accuracy of the financial and operating data contained in the press release written by the president and edited by Roberto. In the news release, the president highlights the sales increase of 25% over last year's first quarter and the positive change in the current ratio from 1.5:1 last year to 3:1 this year. He also emphasizes that production was up 50% over the prior year's first quarter. You note that the release contains only positive or improved ratios and none of the negative or deteriorated ratios. For instance, no mention is made that the debt to total assets ratio has increased from 35% to 55%, that inventories are up 89%, and that while the current ratio improved, the acid-test ratio fell from 1:1 to .5:1. Nor is there any mention that the reported profit for the quarter would have been a loss had not the estimated lives of Fairly's plant and machinery been increased by 30%. Roberto emphasized, "The Pres wants this release by early this afternoon."

Instructions

(a) Who are the stakeholders in this situation?

(b) Is there anything unethical in President Fairly's actions?

(c) Should you as controller remain silent? Does Roberto have any responsibility?

Answers to Self-Study Questions
1. c   2. c   3. b   4. b   5. d   6. d   7. c   8. c   9. b   10. a

CHAPTER 21

MANAGERIAL ACCOUNTING

You've heard of the Big Three Automakers—that's shorthand for General Motors, Ford, and Chrysler, the three big domestic car companies. Well, there's also the Big Three U.S. Bicycle makers—Huffy, Murray, and Roadmaster. Like their automotive counterparts, the bike makers have a big challenge: produce domestically a bicycle at a reasonable sticker price when there's a lot of foreign competition.

Murray (short for Murray Ohio Manufacturing Co.) has found a way to keep costs and prices down—and to make a profit. The company manufactures 15,000 bicycles per day at its plant in southern Tennessee. Instead of marketing the bikes to independent bicycle stores, they sell their products to mass merchants such as Sears.

A bicycle's direct materials include steel, tires, spokes, hubs, and brakes. "We take steel and turn it into tubing which in turn becomes the bike frame," says Tom Appleton, product manager. "You do have some planned scrap," he says, because *you might want to stamp out a round sprocket out of a square piece of steel. ''By*

taking a round part out of a square piece, you've automatically got around 25%

scrap,'' he says, ''which we sell to scrap dealers at five percent of its original cost.

Then, there's unplanned scrap which occurs when one of the workers—to put it

bluntly—makes a mistake. We also sell this scrap but we lose the labor cost.''

The direct labor time to make a Murray bike is only about 30 minutes. And

that's one good reason why an American manufacturer can do well with global

competition. ''The key is to manage your costs better than the next guy,'' says

Appleton. The most expensive Murray bicycle retails for $250 and they sold approxi-

mately 3 million units to the U.S. market in 1991.

Beginning with this chapter, we will turn our attention to issues illustrated in the preceding story—internal issues of the firm, such as costs of materials, the cost of labor, and the relationships among costs, volume, and profits. Up to this point, we have described the preparation of annual financial statements. These financial statements represent the principal end product of financial accounting. The remaining chapters of this textbook focus on managerial accounting, which includes the preparation of reports for **internal users** within an enterprise.

In this chapter, we first highlight the major differences between managerial accounting and financial accounting. Then we explain the functions that management should perform in the organization. Finally, cost concepts and manufacturing financial statements are explained and illustrated.

Managerial Accounting

Managerial accounting, also called management accounting, is a field of accounting that provides economic and financial information for managers and other internal users. The activities that are part of managerial accounting (and the chapters in which they are discussed) are as follows:

1. Explaining manufacturing and nonmanufacturing costs and how they are reported in the financial statements (Chapter 21).
2. Computing the cost to an entity of rendering a service or manufacturing a product (Chapters 22 and 23).
3. Determining the behavior of costs and expenses as activity levels change and analyzing cost–volume–profit relationships within a company (Chapter 24).
4. Assisting management in profit planning and formalizing the plans in the form of budgets (Chapter 25).
5. Providing a basis for controlling costs and expenses by comparing actual results with planned objectives and standard costs (Chapters 26 and 27).
6. Accumulating and presenting relevant data for management decision making (Chapter 28).

Managerial accounting applies to all types of businesses—service, merchandising, and manufacturing—and to all forms of business organizations—proprietorships, partnerships, and corporations. Moreover, managerial accounting is needed in not-for-profit entities as well as in profit-oriented enterprises.

Comparing Managerial and Financial Accounting

There are both similarities and differences between managerial and financial accounting. An important similarity is that each field of accounting deals with the economic events of an enterprise. Thus, their interests overlap. For example, determining the unit cost of manufacturing a product is part of managerial accounting. In contrast, reporting the total cost of goods manufactured and sold is part of financial accounting. In addition, both managerial and financial accounting require that the results of an entity's economic events be quantified and be communicated to interested parties. The diverse needs for economic data among parties interested in an enterprise are responsible for many of the differences between the two fields of accounting. The principal differences are as follows:

Study Objective 1

Explain the distinguishing features of managerial accounting.

Primary Users

Financial accounting is primarily concerned with **external users**, such as stockholders, creditors, and regulatory agencies. In contrast, managerial accounting relates primarily to **internal users** who are officers (top management), department heads, managers, and supervisors in the company.

Type and Frequency of Reports

Classified financial statements are the end product of financial accounting. They are prepared quarterly and annually. In managerial accounting, data are communicated through **internal reports**. These reports may be prepared daily, weekly, monthly, quarterly, annually, or as needed. Internal reports satisfy management's need for timely information.

Purpose of Reports

The financial statements produced by financial accounting are considered to be **general-purpose reports** for all users. These reports must be adapted by the user to the decision that is to be made. Conversely, in managerial accounting, reports can be designed for use by a particular user for a specific decision. To a large degree, internal reports are **special-purpose reports**.

Content of Reports

Information in financial statements generally pertains to the enterprise as a whole and usually is highly aggregated (condensed). The data are normally limited to information developed within the double-entry accounting system. Therefore, the reports are based on completed transactions and include only cost data. The reporting standard is **generally accepted accounting principles**.

Information in internal reports usually pertains to subunits of the entity such as divisions, departments, and branches. Accordingly, the data are often very detailed. The content of internal reports often extends beyond the double-entry accounting system. Thus, the reports may show all amounts at market values or the effects of prospective events. Managerial reports need not be prepared in dollars—units and labor or machine hours may be used—and the data often are less objective than financial reports. **Moreover, the data do not have to be reported in accordance with generally accepted accounting principles. The reporting standard for internal reports is relevance to the decision to be made.**

Helpful hint Financial accounting information is heavily regulated. These regulations cannot help but impact cost accounting reporting practices. As a result, many companies find it difficult to change their cost accounting practices if they deviate from what is presently required for external reporting.

ILLUSTRATION 21-1

*Differences between financial
and managerial accounting*

The principal differences between financial accounting and managerial accounting are summarized below.

	Financial Accounting	**Managerial Accounting**
Primary Users of Reports	• External users, who are stockholders, creditors, and regulatory agencies.	• Internal users, who are officers, department heads, managers, and supervisors in the company.
Types and Frequency of Reports	• Classified financial statements. • Issued quarterly and annually.	• Internal reports. • Issued as frequently as the need arises.
Purpose of Reports	• To provide general-purpose information for all users.	• To provide special-purpose information for a particular user for a specific decision.
Content of Reports	• Pertains to entity as a whole and is highly aggregated (condensed). • Limited to double-entry accounting system and cost data. • Reporting standard is generally accepted accounting principles.	• Pertains to subunits of the entity and may be very detailed. • May extend beyond double-entry accounting system to any type of relevant data. • Reporting standard is relevance to the decision to be made.

Management Functions

Study Objective 2

*Identify the three
broad functions of
management.*

The management of an organization performs three broad functions. They are:

1. Planning.
2. Organizing and directing.
3. Controlling.

In performing these functions, management must make decisions that have a significant impact on the organization.

Planning requires management to look ahead and to establish objectives. These objectives are often as diverse as maximizing short-term profits and market share, maintaining a commitment to environmental protection, and contributing to social programs. Today, a key objective of management appears to be to add value to the business under its control. As one CEO noted, "An individual who doesn't make the company more valuable may well have control taken away." Or as the president of Union Carbide recently stated, "You have to keep looking at the boundary conditions, thinking the unthinkable. Should I sell one of the businesses? Should I buy another?" Or as the CEO of Marriot indicated, "It took the company over a decade to figure out that it had special expertise in running hospitality and food-service operations, building lodgings, and financial packaging the real estate involved for sale to investors. Coming to this realization entailed getting out of the cruise ship business, travel agencies, and theme parks."

Organizing and directing involves coordinating a company's diverse activities and human resources to produce a smooth-running operation. This function relates to the implementation of planned objectives. For example, in companies such as Campbell Soup Company, IBM, General Motors, and Oscar Mayer, purchasing, manufacturing, warehousing, and selling must be coordinated. Similarly, it is necessary to select executives, appoint managers and supervisors, and

ccounting in Action · *Business Insight*

Business researchers have identified different organization types, or "corporate cultures." The ways in which organizing and directing are carried out differ from one organization type to another:

1. Academies—For the steady climber who must thoroughly master each new job and make one company his or her career home. A classic academy is IBM because as one expert noted: "You don't move ahead until you perform where you are."

2. Clubs—For the individual who strives to fit in. What counts isn't individual achievement, but sincerity, commitment, and doing things for the good of the group. An example is United Parcel of America where one executive noted: "When decisions have to be made we get everyone's opinion, and the company feels like a family to a lot of us."

3. Baseball teams—For those who like to consider themselves free agents. In these situations, companies seek out talent of all ages and experience and reward them by what they produce. They don't care how committed you'll be tomorrow—they want cutting-edge results today. Examples are accounting firms like Price Waterhouse and consulting firms like First Boston Corp.

4. Fortresses—For those who like crisis situations. Many fortresses are companies concerned with survival. Many fortresses are academies, clubs, or baseball teams that have failed in the market place and are struggling to reverse their fortunes. Others are in a perpetual boom-and-bust cycle, such as natural resources companies.

Note that companies do change. Apple Computer started out as a baseball team but is now becoming an academy. And with deregulation, banks—once clubs—are fast evolving into baseball teams.

Source: Adapted from an article by Carol Hymowitz, "Which Corporate Culture Fits You," *The Wall Street Journal*, July 17, 1989.

hire and train employees. Most companies prepare **organization charts** to show the interrelationship of activities and the delegation of authority and responsibility within the company.

The third management function, **controlling,** is the process of keeping the firm's activities on track. In controlling operations, management determines whether planned goals are being met and what changes are necessary when there are deviations from targeted objectives.

How do managers achieve control? In small organizations, a manager might use personal observation. A smart manager in a small operation should know the right questions to ask and how to evaluate the answers. But such a system in a large organization would be chaotic. Imagine the president of Ford Motor Company attempting to determine whether planned objectives are being met without some record of what has happened and what is expected to occur. Thus, a formal system of evaluation that includes such items as budgets, responsibility centers, and performance evaluation reports is typically used in large businesses.

As pictured in Illustration 21-2, the three functions of management may be depicted as the spokes of a wheel that move around the axle or hub of decision making. Decision making is not a separate management function. Rather, it is the outcome of the exercise of good judgment in planning, organizing and directing, and controlling.

As indicated earlier, management is faced with many difficult decisions in planning. Should they sell off unprofitable divisions and allocate resources in

ILLUSTRATION 21-2

Three functions of management

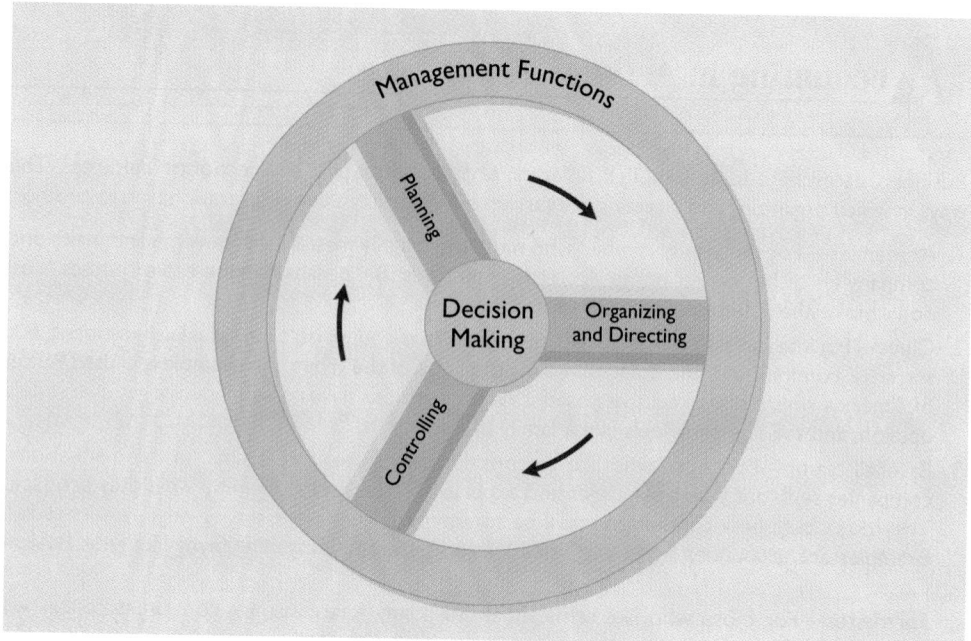

other areas? Should the company commit itself to total quality rather than the bottom line? Should management take a short-term viewpoint or a long-term viewpoint? In organizing and directing, should management adopt the Japanese form of management, which is more participative, or is a more dictatorial style more efficient? And in controlling an organization, should the methods of controls be stringent or relaxed? These are the types of decisions that management must make.

You are now ready to study specific applications of managerial accounting. As you study the managerial chapters, you will encounter many new terms, concepts, and reports. At the same time, you will find some new uses and interpretations of a number of familiar financial accounting terms.

Technology in Action

The use of computers is as important in managerial accounting as in financial accounting. As one expert on manufacturing recently noted "I am convinced that the manufacturers that survive in the 1990s will be those with an unbelievable amount of automation and computerization. The winners will have true computer-integrated manufacturing (CIM). In such a scenario, computers will do everything. They will design the parts, tell you if they can be built, set up the machines on the line, inspect the products, and pop them out on the loading dock with a computerized bill of lading."

Source: Grant Thornton Manufacturing Climates Survey, June 1989, p. 18.

Before You Go On . . .

1. Compare financial accounting and managerial accounting, identifying the principal differences.

2. Identify and discuss the three broad functions of management.

Managerial Cost Concepts

To perform the three management functions effectively, management needs information. One very important type of information is related to costs. For example, questions such as the following need answering:

1. What costs are involved in making a product?
2. If production volume is decreased, will costs decrease?
3. What impact will automation have on total costs?
4. How can costs best be controlled in the organization?

To answer these questions, management needs reliable and relevant cost information. We now explain and illustrate the costs that management uses.

Manufacturing Costs

Manufacturing consists of activities and processes that convert raw materials into finished goods. Contrast this type of operation with merchandising, which sells merchandise in the form in which it is purchased. Manufacturing costs are typically classified as follows:

1. Direct materials.
2. Direct labor.
3. Manufacturing overhead.

Study Objective 3

Define the three classes of manufacturing costs.

Direct Materials

To obtain the materials that will be converted into the finished product, the manufacturer purchases raw materials. **Raw materials** represent the basic materials and parts that are to be used in the manufacturing process. For example, steel, plastics, and tires are raw materials in making automobiles.

Raw materials that can be physically and conveniently associated with the finished product during the manufacturing process are called direct materials. Examples include flour in the baking of bread, syrup in the bottling of soft drinks, and steel in the making of automobiles.

Conversely, some raw materials cannot be easily associated with the finished product; these are considered indirect materials. Indirect materials (1) do not physically become part of the finished product, such as lubricants, rosin, and polishing compounds used in the manufacturing process, or (2) cannot be traced because their physical association with the finished product is too small in terms of cost, such as cotter pins, lock washers, and the like. Indirect materials are accounted for as part of manufacturing overhead.

Helpful hint The manufacturer of a product uses masking tape to protect certain sections of the product while other sections are painted. The tape is removed and thrown away when the paint is dry. Should the cost of tape be accounted for as direct or indirect materials? Answer: Indirect

Direct Labor

The work of factory employees that can be physically and conveniently associated with converting raw materials into finished goods is considered direct labor. Bottlers in a soft drink plant, bakers in a bakery, and typesetters in a print shop are examples of employees whose activities are usually classified as direct labor. In contrast, the wages of maintenance people, timekeepers, and supervisors are usually identified as indirect labor because their efforts have no physical association with the finished product, or it is impractical to trace the costs to the goods produced. Like indirect materials, indirect labor is classified as manufacturing overhead.

Helpful hint Machine operator No. 1 operates a machine that polishes a product as a part of the manufacturing process. Machine operator No. 2 operates an automobile elevator that is used in parking the cars of employees of the factory. Should either of these wages be classified as direct labor? Answer: Only the wages of machine operator No. 1.

Accounting in Action · *Business Insight*

The trend toward more automated and computerized factories will change the way managers and employees interact. For one thing, managers will have fewer direct labor employees to supervise because fewer will be needed on the line. Instead of standing in one spot all day, employees and managers will become more mobile, monitoring the computers that handle the production, and involving themselves in a variety of jobs.

Jobs will be more varied. As machines do more of the repetitive work, employees and managers will need to be more problem-solvers than "cogs in a machine." They will need to be more analytical, to receive more technical training, and to be more highly educated. As a result, they also will be more highly paid.

Source: Grant Thornton Manufacturing Climates Survey, June, 1989, p. 19.

Manufacturing Overhead

Manufacturing overhead consists of costs that are indirectly associated with the manufacture of the finished product. These costs may also be defined as manufacturing costs that cannot be classified as either direct materials or direct labor. Manufacturing overhead includes indirect materials, indirect labor, depreciation on factory buildings and machinery, and insurance, taxes, and maintenance on factory facilities. Terms such as **factory overhead**, **indirect manufacturing costs**, and **burden** are sometimes used instead of manufacturing overhead.

The magnitude of the three different product costs in terms of the total product cost is provided in the following chart, which covers seven industries:[1]

ILLUSTRATION 21-3

Product cost components by industry

	PRODUCT COST BY INDUSTRY (Percentage of Total Manufacturing Cost)		
Industry	Direct Materials	Direct Labor	Manufacturing Overhead
Aerospace	51.7%	19.3%	29.0%
Computers	69.9	7.5	22.5
Electronics	48.6	15.1	36.3
Industrial and farm equipment	46.0	12.8	41.2
Metal products	52.0	15.7	32.3
Motor vehicles and parts	63.8	7.8	28.4
Scientific and photographic equipment	52.3	11.3	36.5
Average for seven industries	54.4%	12.9%	32.6%

Note that the direct labor component is the smallest. This component of product cost is dropping substantially because of automation. In some companies, direct labor has become as little as 5% of the total cost.

---

[1]James A. Hendricks, "Applying Cost Accounting to Factory Automation," *Management Accounting*, December 1988, p. 26.

Accounting in Action · *Business Insight*

In valuing inventories, accountants include three types of costs: materials, overhead, and labor. Allocating materials and labor costs to specific products is fairly straightforward. But accountants have big trouble dealing with overhead, a black hole that swallows up everything from the equipment used to fashion a product to the security guard who watches over the plant at night. How much of the purchasing agent's salary is attributable to the semiconductor chip, how much to the typewriter, how much to the hundred other products made in the same plant? What about the grease that keeps the machines humming, or the computers that make sure paychecks come out on time? Boiled down to its simplest form, the question becomes: Which products cause which costs?

Source: Fortune, October 12, 1987.

Product and Period Costs

Each of the manufacturing cost elements (direct materials, direct labor, and manufacturing overhead) are product costs. As the term suggests, product costs are costs that are a necessary and integral part of producing the finished product. Product costs are also called **inventoriable costs**. These costs do not become expenses under the matching principle until the inventory to which they attach is sold. The expense is cost of goods sold. Direct materials and direct labor are often referred to as prime costs because of their direct association with the manufacturing of the finished product. In addition, because direct labor and manufacturing overhead are incurred in converting raw materials into finished goods, these two cost elements are often referred to as conversion costs.

Period costs are costs that are identified with a specific time period rather than with a salable product. These costs relate to nonmanufacturing costs and therefore are not inventoriable costs. Period costs include selling and administrative expenses that are deducted from revenues in the period in which they are incurred.

The foregoing relationships and cost terms are summarized in Illustration 21-4. Our main concern in this chapter is with product costs.

> **Study Objective 4**
>
> *Determine the difference between product and period costs.*

Before You Go On . . .

1. What are the major cost classifications involved in manufacturing a product?

2. What are product and period costs and their relationship to the manufacturing process?

Manufacturing Costs in the Financial Statements

The financial statements of a manufacturing company are very similar to those of a merchandising company. The principal differences pertain to the cost of goods sold section of the income statement and the current assets section of the balance sheet.

> **Study Objective 5**
>
> *Explain the difference between a merchandising and a manufacturing income statement.*

ILLUSTRATION 21-4

Product versus period costs

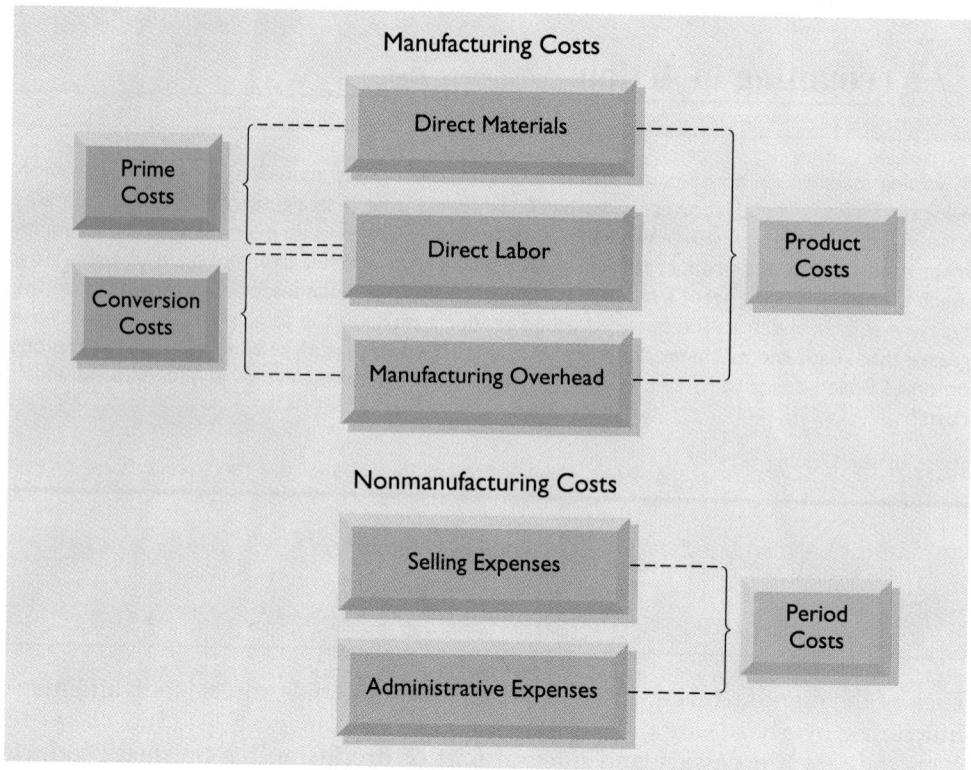

Income Statement

The income statements of a merchandising company and a manufacturing company differ in the cost of goods sold section. For a merchandising company, cost of goods sold is computed by adding the beginning merchandise inventory and the **cost of goods purchased** and subtracting the ending merchandise inventory. For a manufacturing company, cost of goods sold is computed by adding the beginning finished goods inventory and **cost of goods manufactured** and subtracting the ending finished goods inventory. The different components are shown graphically below:

Helpful hint Cost of goods manufactured in a manufacturing company is like cost of goods purchased in a merchandising company.

ILLUSTRATION 21-5

Cost of goods sold components

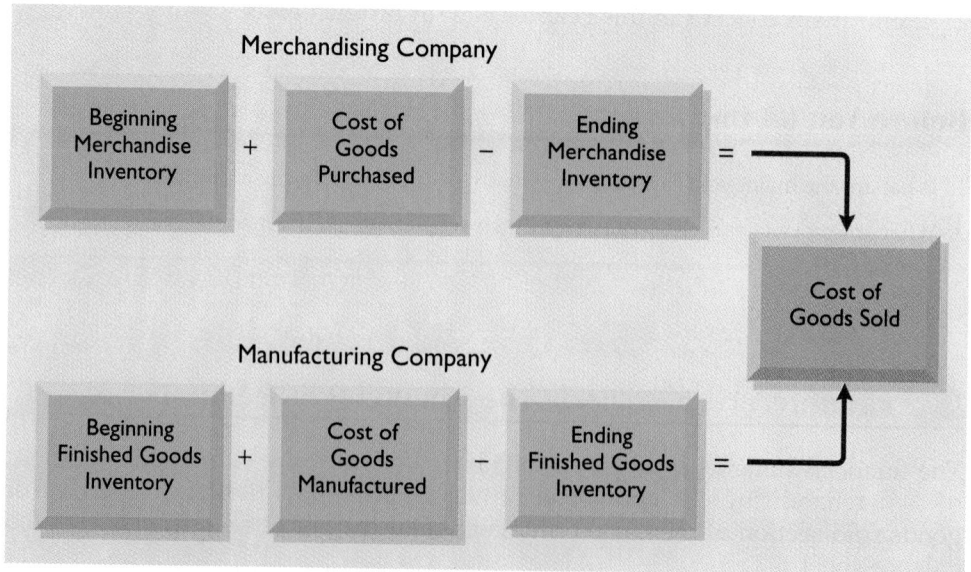

The cost of goods sold sections for merchandising and manufacturing enterprises presented below illustrate the different presentations:

Merchandise Company Partial Income Statement For the Year Ended December 31, 1993		Manufacturing Company Partial Income Statement For the Year Ended December 31, 1993	
Cost of goods sold		Cost of goods sold	
Merchandise inventory, January 1	$ 70,000	Finished goods inventory, January 1	$ 90,000
Cost of goods purchased	650,000	Cost of goods manufactured (see schedule)	370,000
Cost of Goods Available for Sale	720,000	Cost of Goods Available for Sale	460,000
Merchandise inventory, December 31	400,000	Finished goods inventory, December 31	80,000
Cost of goods sold	$320,000	Cost of goods sold	$380,000

The other sections of an income statement are similar for both a merchandising and a manufacturing company.

A number of accounts are involved in determining the cost of goods manufactured. To eliminate excessive detail in the income statement, it is customary to show in the income statement only the total cost of goods manufactured and to present the details in a Cost of Goods Manufactured Schedule. This schedule is shown in Illustration 21-8.

Determining the Cost of Goods Manufactured

An example may be helpful in showing how the cost of goods manufactured for a period is determined. Assume that the Ford Motor Company has a number of automobiles in various stages of production on January 1. In total, these partially completed units are called **work in process inventory**. The vehicles that are partially completed when the accounting period begins are considered **beginning work in process inventory**. The costs assigned to beginning work in process inventory are based on the **manufacturing costs incurred in the prior period**. In the current year, Ford Motor continues the production of automobiles. The manufacturing costs incurred in the current year are used first to complete the work in process on January 1 and then to start the production of other vehicles. The sum of the direct materials costs, direct labor costs, and manufacturing overhead incurred in the current year is the total manufacturing costs **for the current year**.

We now have two cost amounts: (1) the cost of the beginning work in process and (2) the total manufacturing costs for the current period. The sum of these costs is the total cost of work in process for the year.

At the end of the year, some vehicles may be only partially completed. The costs of these units become the cost of the **ending work in process inventory**. To find the cost of goods manufactured, we subtract this cost from the total cost of work in process.

The determination of the cost of goods manufactured is shown graphically in Illustration 21-7.

Cost of Goods Manufactured Schedule

An internal financial schedule called the **the cost of goods manufactured schedule** shows each of the cost elements explained in Illustration 21-7. The schedule for Olsen Manufacturing Company using assumed data is shown in Illustration 21-8. Note that detailed data are presented for direct materials and manufacturing overhead.

Study Objective 6

Indicate how cost of goods manufactured is determined.

Helpful hint Does the amount of "total manufacturing costs for the current year" include the amount of "beginning work in process inventory?" Answer: No

ILLUSTRATION 21-7

Cost of goods manufactured formula

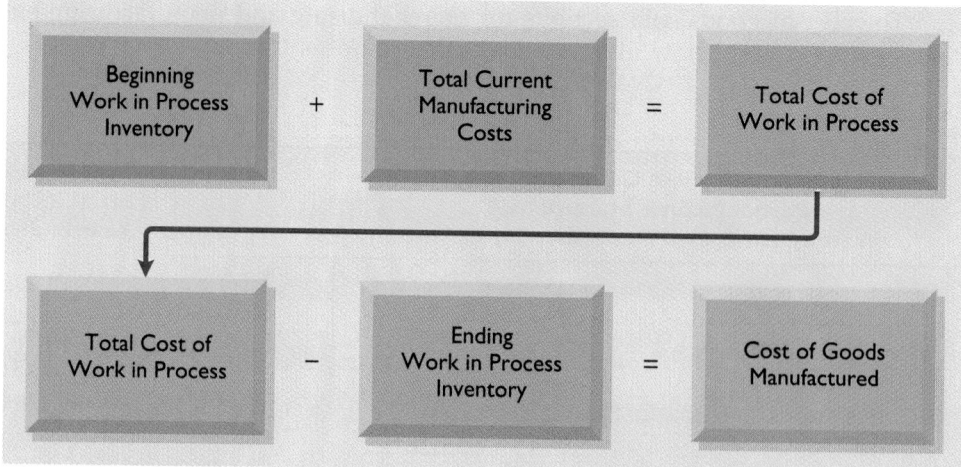

A review of Illustration 21-7 along with an examination of the cost of goods manufactured schedule, Illustration 21-8, should help you distinguish between "total manufacturing costs" and "cost of goods manufactured." The difference is the effect of the change in work in process during the period.

ILLUSTRATION 21-8

Cost of goods manufactured schedule

OLSEN MANUFACTURING COMPANY			
Cost of Goods Manufactured Schedule			
For the Year Ended December 31, 1993			
Work in process, January 1			$ 18,400
Direct materials			
Raw materials inventory, January 1	$ 16,700		
Raw materials purchases	152,500		
Total raw materials available for use	169,200		
Less: Raw materials inventory, December 31	22,800		
Direct materials used		$146,400	
Direct labor		175,600	
Manufacturing overhead			
Indirect labor	14,300		
Factory repairs	12,600		
Factory utilities	10,100		
Factory depreciation	9,440		
Factory insurance	8,360		
Total manufacturing overhead		54,800	
Total manufacturing costs			376,800
Total cost of work in process			395,200
Less: Work in process, December 31			25,200
Cost of goods manufactured			$370,000

Balance Sheet

Study Objective 7

Explain the difference between a merchandising and a manufacturing balance sheet.

Unlike the balance sheet for a merchandising company, which shows just one category of inventory, the balance sheet for a manufacturing company may have three inventory accounts. They are:

Finished Goods Inventory, which shows the cost of completed goods on hand.

Work in Process Inventory, which shows the cost applicable to units that have been started into production but are only partially completed.

ILLUSTRATION 21-9

Current assets sections of merchandising and manufacturing balance sheets

Merchandising Company Balance Sheet December 31, 1993		Manufacturing Company Balance Sheet December 31, 1993		
Current assets		Current assets		
Cash	$100,000	Cash		$180,000
Receivables (net)	210,000	Receivables (net)		210,000
Merchandise inventory	400,000	Inventories:		
Prepaid expenses	22,000	Finished goods	$80,000	
Total current assets	$732,000	Work in process	25,200	
		Raw materials	22,800	128,000
		Prepaid expenses		18,000
		Total current assets		$536,000

Raw Materials Inventory, which shows the cost of raw materials on hand. Finished Goods Inventory is to a manufacturing enterprise what Merchandise Inventory is to a merchandising firm because it represents the goods available for sale.

The current assets sections presented in Illustration 21-9 contrast the presentation of inventories of a merchandising company and those of a manufacturing company. Manufacturing inventories are generally listed in the order of their expected realization in cash. Thus, finished goods inventory is listed first. The remainder of the balance sheet is similar for the two types of companies.

Each step in the accounting cycle for a merchandising company is applicable to a manufacturing company. For example, prior to preparing financial statements, adjusting entries are required. The adjusting entries are essentially the same as those of a merchandising company.

The closing entries for a manufacturing company are also similar to those of a merchandising company. The use of a work sheet in the accounting cycle and the journalizing of closing entries for a manufacturing company are illustrated in Appendix K.

Before You Go On . . .

1. How does the content of an income statement differ between a merchandising company and a manufacturing company?

2. What items appear on a cost of goods manufactured schedule?

3. How does the content of the balance sheet differ between a merchandising company and a manufacturing company?

Cost Concepts—A Review

You have learned a number of cost concepts in this chapter. Because many of these concepts are new, we believe an extended example illustrating how these various cost concepts are used will be helpful. To illustrate, assume that Northridge Company manufactures and sells pre-hung metal doors. Recently, it has decided to start selling pre-hung wood doors as well. An old warehouse that the company presently owns will be used to manufacture these doors. To manufacture and sell these pre-hung wood doors, Northridge has the following costs:

1. The material cost (wood) for each door is $10.
2. Labor costs involved in constructing a wood door are $8 per door.
3. Depreciation on the new equipment used to make the wood door using the straight-line method is $25,000 per year.
4. Property taxes on the old warehouse used to make the wood doors are $6,000 per year.
5. Advertising costs for the pre-hung wood doors total $2,500 per month or $30,000 per year.
6. Sales commissions related to pre-hung wood doors sold are $4 per door.
7. Maintenance salaries for the old warehouse are $28,000.
8. Salary of plant manager in charge of pre-hung wood doors is $70,000.
9. Cost of shipping pre-hung wood doors is $12 per door sold.

ILLUSTRATION 21-10

Assignment of costs to cost categories

These manufacturing and sales costs can be assigned to the various categories shown in Illustration 21-10.

	Product Costs					
Cost Item	**Direct Materials**	**Direct Labor**	**Manufacturing Overhead**	**Period Costs**	**Prime Costs**	**Conversion Costs**
1. Material cost ($10) per door	X				X	
2. Labor costs ($8) per door		X			X	X
3. Depreciation on new equipment ($25,000 per year)			X			X
4. Property taxes ($6,000 per year)			X			X
5. Advertising costs ($30,000 per year)				X		
6. Sales commissions ($4 per door)				X		
7. Maintenance salaries ($28,000 per year)			X			X
8. Salary of plant manager ($70,000)			X			X
9. Cost of shipping pre-hung doors ($12 per door)				X		

Total manufacturing costs are the sum of the direct materials, direct labor, and manufacturing overhead costs. For example, assume that Northridge Company produced 10,000 pre-hung wood doors the first year. The total manufacturing costs are:

ILLUSTRATION 21-11

Computation of total production cost

Cost Item	Manufacturing Cost
Material cost ($10 × 10,000)	$100,000
Labor cost ($8 × 10,000)	80,000
Depreciation on new equipment	25,000
Property taxes	6,000
Maintenance salaries	28,000
Salary of plant manager	70,000
Total manufacturing costs	$309,000

If total manufacturing cost are $309,000, then the manufacturing cost per unit (cost to produce one pre-hung wood door) is $30.90 ($309,000 ÷ 10,000).

The cost concepts above will be used extensively in subsequent chapters. Study Illustration 21-10 carefully. If you do not understand any of these classifications, go back and reread the appropriate section in this chapter.

Summary of Study Objectives

1. Explain the distinguishing features of managerial accounting. The distinguishing features of managerial accounting are:

Primary users of reports—internal users, who are officers, department heads, managers, and supervisors in the company.

Type and frequency of reports—internal reports that are issued as frequently as the need arises.

Purpose of reports—to provide special-purpose information for a particular user for a specific decision.

Content of reports—pertains to subunits of the entity and may be very detailed; may extend beyond double-entry accounting systems; the reporting standard is relevance to the decision being made.

2. Identify the three broad functions of management. The three functions are planning, organizing and directing, and controlling. Planning requires management to look ahead and to establish objectives. Organizing and directing involves coordinating the diverse activities and human resources of a company to produce a smooth-running operation. Controlling is the process of keeping the activities on track.

3. Define the three classes of manufacturing costs. Manufacturing costs are typically classified as either (1) direct materials, (2) direct labor, or (3) manufacturing overhead. Raw materials that can be physically and conveniently associated with the finished product during the manufacturing process are called direct materials. The work of factory employees that can be physically and conveniently associated with converting raw materials into finished goods is considered direct labor. Manufacturing overhead con-

sists of costs that are indirectly associated with the manufacture of the finished product.

4. Determine the difference between product and period costs. Product costs are costs that are a necessary and integral part of producing the finished product. Product costs are also called inventoriable costs. These costs do not become expenses under the matching principle until the inventory to which they attach is sold. Period costs are costs that are identified with a specific time period rather than with a salable product. These costs relate to nonmanufacturing costs and therefore are not inventoriable costs.

5. Explain the difference between a merchandising and a manufacturing income statement. The difference between a merchandising and a manufacturing income statement is in the cost of goods sold section. A manufacturing cost of goods sold section shows beginning and ending finished goods inventories and the cost of goods manufactured.

6. Indicate how cost of goods manufactured is determined. The cost of the beginning work in process is added to the total manufacturing costs for the current year to arrive at the total cost of work in process for the year. The ending work in process is then subtracted from the total cost of work in process to arrive at the cost of goods manufactured.

7. Explain the difference between a merchandising and a manufacturing balance sheet. The difference between a manufacturing and a merchandising balance sheet is in the current asset section. In the current asset section of a manufacturing company's balance sheet, three inventory accounts are presented: finished goods inventory, work in process inventory, and raw materials inventory.

APPENDIX K Accounting Cycle for a Manufacturing Company

Study Objectives

After studying Appendix K, you should be able to:

8. Prepare a work sheet as well as closing entries for a manufacturing company.

The accounting cycle for a manufacturing company is the same as for a merchandising company when a periodic inventory system is used. Except for the additional manufacturing inventories and manufacturing cost accounts, the journalizing and posting of transactions is the same. Similarly, the preparation of a trial balance and the journalizing and posting of adjusting entries are the same. Some changes, however, occur in the use of a work sheet and in preparing closing entries.

To illustrate the changes in the work sheet, we will use the cost of goods manufactured schedule for Olsen Manufacturing presented in Illustration 21-8 of the chapter and other assumed data. For convenience, the cost of goods manufactured schedule is reproduced below:

ILLUSTRATION K-1

Cost of goods manufactured schedule

OLSEN MANUFACTURING COMPANY **Cost of Goods Manufactured Schedule** **For the Year Ended December 31, 1993**			
Work in process, January 1			$ 18,400
Direct materials			
Raw materials inventory, January 1	$ 16,700		
Raw materials purchases	152,500		
Total raw materials available for use	169,200		
Less: Raw materials inventory, December 31	22,800		
Direct materials used		$146,400	
Direct labor		175,600	
Manufacturing overhead			
Indirect labor	14,300		
Factory repairs	12,600		
Factory utilities	10,100		
Factory depreciation	9,440		
Factory insurance	8,360		
Total manufacturing overhead		54,800	
Total manufacturing costs			376,800
Total cost of work in process			395,200
Less: Work in process, December 31			25,200
Cost of goods manufactured			$370,000

Work Sheet

When a work sheet is used in the preparation of financial statements, two additional columns are needed for the cost of goods manufactured schedule. As illustrated in the work sheet in Illustration K-2, debit and credit columns for this schedule have been inserted before the income statement columns.

In the cost of goods manufactured columns, the beginning inventories of raw materials and work in process are entered as debits. In addition, all the manufacturing costs are entered as debits. The reason is that each of these

OLSEN MANUFACTURING COMPANY
(Partial) Work Sheet
For the Year Ended December 31, 1993

	Adjusted Trial Balance		Cost of Goods Manufactured		Income Statement		Balance Sheet	
	Dr.	Cr.	Dr.	Cr.	Dr.	Cr.	Dr.	Cr.
Cash	42,500						42,500	
Accounts Receivable (Net)	71,900						71,900	
Finished Goods Inv.	24,600				24,600	19,500	19,500	
Work in Process Inv.	18,400		18,400	25,200			25,200	
Raw Materials Inv.	16,700		16,700	22,800			22,800	
Plant Assets	724,000						724,000	
Accumulated Depr.		278,400						278,400
Notes Payable		100,000						100,000
Accounts Payable		40,000						40,000
Income Taxes Payable		5,000						5,000
Common Stock		200,000						200,000
Retained Earnings		205,100						205,100
Sales		680,000				680,000		
Raw Materials Purchases	152,500		152,500					
Direct Labor	175,600		175,600					
Indirect Labor	14,300		14,300					
Factory Repairs	12,600		12,600					
Factory Utilities	10,100		10,100					
Factory Depreciation	9,440		9,440					
Factory Insurance	8,360		8,360					
Selling Expenses	114,900				114,900			
Administrative Exp.	92,600				92,600			
Income Tax Exp.	20,000				20,000			
Totals	1,508,500	1,508,500	418,000	48,000				
Cost of Goods Manufactured				370,000	370,000			
Totals			418,000	418,000	622,100	699,500	905,900	828,500
Net Income					77,400			77,400
Totals					699,500	699,500	905,900	905,900

amounts increase cost of goods manufactured. Ending inventories for raw materials and work in process are entered as credits in the cost of goods manufactured columns because they have the opposite effect—they decrease cost of goods manufactured. The balancing amount for these columns is the cost of goods manufactured. Note that the amount, $370,000, agrees with the amount reported for cost of goods manufactured in Illustration 21-8. This amount is also entered in the income statement debit column.

The income statement and balance sheet columns for a manufacturing company are basically the same as for a merchandising company. For example, the treatment of the finished goods inventories is identical with the treatment of merchandise inventory. That is, the beginning inventory is entered in the debit column, and the ending finished goods inventory is entered in the income statement credit column and the balance sheet debit column.

As in the case of a merchandising company, financial statements can be prepared from the statement columns of the work sheet. In addition, the cost of goods manufactured schedule can also be prepared directly from the work sheet.

Closing Entries

The closing entries for a manufacturing company are different than for a merchandising company. **A Manufacturing Summary account is used to close all accounts that appear in the cost of goods manufactured schedule.** The balance of the Manufacturing Summary account is the Cost of Goods Manufactured for the period. The closing entries can be prepared from the cost of goods manufactured and income statement columns of the work sheet. As illustrated below, the closing entries for the manufacturing accounts are prepared first. The closing entries for Olsen Manufacturing are as follows:

Date	Account	Debit	Credit
Dec. 31	Work in Process Inventory (Dec. 31)	25,200	
	Raw Materials Inventory (Dec. 31)	22,800	
	Manufacturing Summary		48,000
	(To record ending raw materials and work in process inventories)		
31	**Manufacturing Summary**	418,000	
	Work in Process Inventory (Jan. 1)		18,400
	Raw Materials Inventory (Jan. 1)		16,700
	Raw Materials Purchases		152,500
	Direct Labor		175,600
	Indirect Labor		14,300
	Factory Repairs		12,600
	Factory Utilities		10,100
	Factory Depreciation		9,440
	Factory Insurance		8,360
	(To close beginning raw materials and work in process inventories and manufacturing cost accounts)		
31	Finished Goods Inventory (Dec. 31)	19,500	
	Sales	680,000	
	Income Summary		699,500
	(To record ending finished goods inventory and close sales account)		
31	Income Summary	622,100	
	Finished Goods Inventory (Jan. 1)		24,600
	Manufacturing Summary		370,000
	Selling Expenses		114,900
	Administrative Expenses		92,600
	Income Tax Expense		20,000
	(To close beginning finished goods inventory, manufacturing summary, and expense accounts)		
31	Income Summary	77,400	
	Retained Earnings		77,400
	(To close net income to retained earnings)		

After posting, the summary accounts will show the following:

Manufacturing Summary

Dec. 31	Close	418,000	Dec. 31	Close	48,000
			31	Close	370,000

Income Summary

Dec. 31	Close	622,100	Dec. 31	Close	699,500
31	Close	77,400			

These data precisely track the closing entries. It also would be possible to post each account balance to the Manufacturing Summary account.

Summary of Study Objectives for Appendix K

8. Prepare a work sheet as well as closing entries for a manufacturing company. Two additional columns are needed in the work sheet for the cost of goods manufactured. In these columns, the beginning inventories of direct materials and work in process are entered as debits and the ending inventories are entered as credits; all manufacturing costs are entered as debits. To close all of the accounts that appear in the cost of goods manufactured schedule, a Manufacturing Summary account is used.

GLOSSARY

Conversion costs · Direct labor and manufacturing overhead costs incurred in converting raw materials into finished goods. (p. 863).

Cost of goods manufactured · Total cost of work in process less the cost of the ending work in process inventory. (p. 865).

Direct labor · The work of factory employees that can be physically and conveniently associated with converting raw materials into finished goods. (p. 861).

Direct materials · Raw materials that can be physically and conveniently associated with manufacturing the finished product. (p. 861).

Indirect labor · Work of factory employees that has no physical association with the finished product, or it is impractical to trace the costs to the goods produced. (p. 861).

Indirect materials · Raw materials that do not physically become part of the finished product or cannot be traced because their physical association with the finished product is too small. (p. 861).

Managerial accounting · A field of accounting that provides economic and financial information for managers and other internal users. Also called management accounting. (p. 856).

Manufacturing overhead · Manufacturing costs that are indirectly associated with the manufacture of the finished product. (p. 862).

Period costs · Costs that are identified with a specific time period and charged to expense as incurred. (p. 863).

Prime costs · Direct materials and direct labor. (p. 863).

Product costs · Costs that are a necessary and integral part of producing the finished product. Also called inventoriable costs. (p. 863).

Total cost of work in process · Cost of the beginning work in process plus total manufacturing costs for the current period. (p. 865).

Total manufacturing costs · The sum of direct materials, direct labor, and manufacturing overhead incurred in the current period. (p. 865).

DEMONSTRATION PROBLEM 1

The Superior Manufacturing Company has the following cost and expense data for the year ending December 31, 1993.

Raw materials, 1/1/93	$ 30,000	Insurance, factory	$ 14,000
Raw materials, 12/31/93	20,000	Property taxes, factory building	6,000
Raw materials purchased	205,000	Sales (net)	1,500,000
Indirect materials	15,000	Delivery expenses	100,000
Work in process, 1/1/93	80,000	Sales commissions	150,000
Work in process, 12/31/93	50,000	Indirect labor	90,000
Finished goods, 1/1/93	110,000	Factory machinery rent	40,000
Finished goods, 12/31/93	120,000	Factory utilities	65,000
Direct labor	350,000	Depreciation, factory building	24,000
Factory manager's salary	35,000	Administrative expenses	300,000

Instructions

(a) Prepare a cost of goods manufactured schedule for Superior Company for 1993.

(b) Prepare an income statement for Superior Company for 1993.

(c) Assume that Superior Company's ledgers show the balances of the following current asset accounts: Cash, $17,000, Accounts Receivable (net), $120,000, Prepaid Expenses, $13,000, and Short-term Investments, $26,000. Prepare the current assets section of the balance sheet for Superior Company as of December 31, 1993.

Helpful hints

1. Beginning work in process is the first item in the cost of goods manufactured schedule.
2. Total manufacturing costs are the sum of direct materials used, direct labor and total manufacturing overhead.
3. Total cost of work in process is the sum of beginning work in process and total manufacturing costs.
4. Cos. of goods manufactured is total cost of work in process less ending work in process.
5. The cost of goods sold section of the income statement shows beginning and ending finished goods inventory and cost of goods manufactured.
6. In the balance sheet, manufacturing inventories are listed in the order of their expected realization in cash, with finished goods first.

Solution to Demonstration Problem 1

(a)

SUPERIOR MANUFACTURING COMPANY
Cost of Goods Manufactured Schedule
For the Year Ended December 31, 1993

Work in process, 1/1			$ 80,000
Direct materials			
Raw materials inventory, 1/1	$ 30,000		
Raw materials purchased	205,000		
Total raw materials available for use	235,000		
Less: Raw materials inventory, 12/31	20,000		
Direct materials used		$215,000	
Direct labor		350,000	
Manufacturing overhead			
Indirect labor	90,000		
Factory utilities	65,000		
Factory machinery rent	40,000		
Factory manager's salary	35,000		
Depreciation on building	24,000		
Indirect materials	15,000		
Factory insurance	14,000		
Property taxes	6,000		
Total manufacturing overhead		289,000	

Total manufacturing costs	854,000
Total cost of work in process	934,000
Less: Work in process, 12/31	50,000
Cost of goods manufactured	$884,000

(b)

SUPERIOR MANUFACTURING COMPANY
Income Statement
For the Year Ended December 31, 1993

Sales (net)		$1,500,000
Cost of goods sold		
Finished goods inventory, January 1	$110,000	
Cost of goods manufactured	884,000	
Cost of goods available for sale	994,000	
Less: Finished goods inventory, December 31	120,000	
Cost of goods sold		874,000
Gross profit		626,000
Operating expenses		
Administrative expenses	300,000	
Sales commissions	150,000	
Delivery expenses	100,000	
Total operating expenses		550,000
Net income		$ 76,000

(c)

SUPERIOR MANUFACTURING COMPANY
(Partial) Balance Sheet
December 31, 1993

Current assets		
Cash		$ 17,000
Short-term investments		26,000
Accounts receivable (net)		120,000
Inventories:		
Finished goods	$120,000	
Work in process	50,000	
Raw materials	20,000	190,000
Prepaid expenses		13,000
Total current assets		$366,000

DEMONSTRATION PROBLEM 2

The Giant Company specializes in manufacturing different models of racing bicycles. A new model, the Jaquar, has been well accepted. As a result, the company has established a separate manufacturing facility to produce these bicycles. The company produces 1,000 bicycles per month. Giant's monthly manufacturing cost and other expenses data related to these bicycles are as follows:

1. Rent on manufacturing equipment (lease cost)	$2,000/month	3. Raw materials (frames, tires, etc.)	$80/bicycle
2. Insurance on manufacturing building	$750/month	4. Utility costs for manufacturing facility	$1,000/month

5. Supplies for general office	$800/month			10. Manufacturing supervisor's salary	$3,000/month	
6. Wages for assembly line workers in manufacturing facility	$30/bicycle			11. Advertising for bicycles	$30,000/year	
7. Depreciation on office equipment	$650/month			12. Sales commissions	$10/bicycle	
8. Miscellaneous materials (lubricants, solders, etc.)	$1.20/bicycle			13. Depreciation on manufacturing building	$1,500/month	
9. Property taxes on manufacturing building	$2,400/year					

Instructions

(a) Prepare an answer sheet with the following column headings:

	Product Costs					
Cost Item	Direct Materials	Direct Labor	Manufacturing Overhead	Period Costs	Prime Costs	Conversion Costs

Enter each cost item on your answer sheet, placing an "X" mark under the appropriate headings.

(b) Compute total manufacturing costs for the month.

Helpful hints

1. Remember the definitions of: Prime costs = direct materials and direct labor. Conversion costs = Direct labor and manufacturing overhead costs incurred in converting raw materials into finished goods.
2. Make sure you are doing the computations for the appropriate period: month, year, unit, etc.
3. Period costs are not manufacturing costs and, therefore, are not inventoriable.
4. Product costs are manufacturing costs and are inventoriable.

Solution to Demonstration Problem 2

	Product Costs					
Cost Item	Direct Materials	Direct Labor	Manufacturing Overhead	Period Costs	Prime Costs	Conversion Costs
1. Rent on equipment ($2,000/month)			X			X
2. Insurance on manufacturing building ($750/month)			X			X
3. Raw materials ($80/bicycle)	X				X	
4. Manufacturing utilities ($1,000/month)			X			X
5. Office supplies ($800/month)				X		
6. Wages for workers ($30/bicycle)		X			X	X
7. Depreciation on office equipment ($650/month)				X		
8. Miscellaneous materials ($1.20/bicycle)			X			X
9. Property taxes on building ($2,400/year)			X			X
10. Manufacturing supervisor's salary ($3,000/month)			X			X
11. Advertising cost ($30,000/year)				X		

| 12. Sales commissions ($10/bicycle) | | X | |
| 13. Depreciation on manufacturing building ($1,500/month) | X | | X |

(b)	Cost Item	Manufacturing Cost
	Rent on equipment	$ 2,000
	Insurance	750
	Raw materials ($80 × 1,000)	80,000
	Manufacturing utilities	1,000
	Labor ($30 × 1,000)	30,000
	Miscellaneous materials ($1.20 × 1,000)	1,200
	Property taxes ($2,400 ÷ 12)	200
	Manufacturing supervisor's salary	3,000
	Depreciation on building	1,500
	Total manufacturing costs	$119,650

*Note: All **asterisked** Questions, Exercises, and Problems relate to material contained in the Appendix to the chapter.

SELF-STUDY QUESTIONS

Answers are at the end of chapter.

(S.O. 1) 1. Managerial accounting:
a. places emphasis on special-purpose information.
b. is governed by generally accepted accounting principles.
c. pertains to the entity as a whole and is highly aggregated.
d. is limited to cost data.

(S.O. 2) 2. The management of an organization performs three broad functions. They are:
a. planning, organizing and directing, and selling.
b. planning, manufacturing, and controlling.
c. planning, organizing and directing, and controlling.
d. organizing and directing, manufacturing, and controlling.

(S.O. 3) 3. Direct materials are a:

	Conversion Cost	Manufacturing Cost	Prime Cost
a.	Yes	Yes	No
b.	Yes	Yes	Yes
c.	No	Yes	Yes
d.	No	No	No

(S.O. 3) 4. Indirect labor is a:
a. nonmanufacturing cost.
b. prime cost.
c. period cost.
d. conversion cost.

(S.O. 3) 5. Which of the following costs would be included in manufacturing overhead of a computer manufacturer?
a. the cost of the 3½ inch disk drives.
b. the wages earned by computer assemblers.
c. depreciation on testing equipment.
d. the cost of the memory chips.

(S.O. 3) 6. Which of the following is *not* an element of manufacturing overhead?
a. product inspector's salary.
b. plant manager's salary.
c. factory repairman's wages.
d. president's salary.

(S.O. 4) 7. Which of the following costs is *not* considered a cost of manufacturing a product?
a. factory utilities.
b. direct labor.
c. sales salaries.
d. direct materials.

(S.O. 5)

8. For the year, Redden Company has cost of goods manufactured of $550,000, beginning finished goods inventory of $200,000, and ending finished goods inventory of $250,000. The cost of goods sold is:
   a. $450,000.
   b. $500,000.
   c. $550,000.
   d. $600,000.

(S.O. 6)

9. A cost of goods manufactured schedule shows beginning and ending inventories for:
   a. work in process only.
   b. raw materials and work in process only.
   c. raw materials only.
   d. raw materials, work in process, and finished goods.

10. In a manufacturing company balance sheet, three inventories may be reported: (1) raw materials, (2) work in process, and (3) finished goods. Indicate in what sequence these inventories generally appear on a balance sheet.
    a. (1), (2), (3)
    b. (2), (3), (1)
    c. (3), (2), (1)
    d. (3), (1), (2)

(S.O. 7)

*11. Which of the following is extended to the Income Statement columns on a manufacturing work sheet?
    a. beginning raw materials inventory.
    b. beginning work in process inventory.
    c. beginning finished goods inventory.
    d. dividends declared and paid.

(S.O. 8)

QUESTIONS

1. Managerial accounting provides accounting information for managers of manufacturing corporations. Is this an accurate description of managerial accounting? Explain.

2. Linda Moran believes that the only similarity between managerial accounting and financial accounting is that they both deal with economic events of an enterprise. Is Linda correct? Discuss.

3. Contrast the type and frequency of reports prepared by managerial accountants and financial accountants.

4. How do reports prepared in managerial accounting differ as to purpose and content from reports prepared in financial accounting?

5. Tammy Weiland is studying for the next accounting midterm examination. Summarize for Tammy what she should know about management functions.

6. Decision making is management's most important function. Do you agree? Why or why not?

7. Pat Redden is studying for her next accounting examination. Explain to Pat what she should know about the differences between the income statements for a manufacturing company and a merchandising company.

8. Lul Batten is unclear as to the difference between the balance sheets of a merchandising company and a manufacturing company. Explain the difference to Lul.

9. How are manufacturing costs classified?

10. Richard Way claims that the distinction between direct and indirect materials is based entirely on physical association with the product. Is Richard correct? Why?

11. Alma Jean Elbert is confused about the differences between a product cost and a period cost. Explain the differences to Alma Jean.

12. Carol King also asks your help with the terms (a) "prime costs" and (b) "conversion costs." Distinguish between the terms.

13. In Plano Molding Company, direct materials are $12,000, direct labor is $18,000, and manufacturing overhead is $9,000. What is the amount of (a) prime costs and (b) conversion costs?

14. Identify the differences in the cost of goods sold section of an income statement between a merchandising company and a manufacturing company.

15. The determination of the cost of goods manufactured involves the following factors: (A) beginning work in process inventory, (B) total manufacturing costs, and (C) ending work in process inventory. Identify the meaning of x in the following formulas:
(a) A + B = x
(b) A + B − C = x

16. Artis Manufacturing has beginning raw materials inventory $22,000, ending raw materials inventory $18,000, and raw materials purchases $180,000. What is the cost of direct materials used?

17. Elite Manufacturing Inc. has beginning work in process $27,200, direct materials used $210,000, direct labor $200,000, total manufacturing overhead $120,000, and ending work in process $32,000. What are total manufacturing costs?

18. Using the data in Q17, what are (a) the total cost of work in process and (b) the cost of goods manufactured?

19. In what order should manufacturing inventories be listed in a balance sheet?

*20. How, if at all, does the accounting cycle differ between a manufacturing company and a merchandising company?

*21. What typical account balances are carried into the cost of goods manufactured columns of the manufacturing work sheet?

*22. Prepare the closing entries for (a) ending work in process and raw materials inventories and (b) manufacturing summary. Use XXXs for amounts.

BRIEF EXERCISES

BE21–1 Complete the following comparison table between managerial and financial accounting.

Distinguish between managerial and financial accounting. (S.O. 1)

	Primary users	Type of reports	Frequency of reports	Purpose of reports	Reporting standards
Financial accounting					
Managerial accounting					

BE21–2 Listed below are three functions of the management of an organization:

(a) Planning (b) Organizing and directing (c) Controlling

Identify the three management functions. (S.O. 2)

Identify each of the following statements which best describes each of the above functions.

1. ____ is the process of keeping the activities on track. Management must determine whether goals are being met and what changes are necessary when there are deviations.
2. ____ require(s) management to look ahead and to establish objectives. A key objective of management appears to be to add value to the business.
3. ____ involve(s) coordinating the diverse activities and human resources of a company to produce a smooth-running operation. This function relates to the implementation of planned objectives.

BE21–3 Determine whether each of the following costs should be classified as "direct materials" (DM), "direct labor" (DL), or "manufacturing overhead" (MO):

Classify manufacturing costs. (S.O. 3)

1. ____ Insurance on factory equipment and machinery.
2. ____ Depreciation on factory equipment.
3. ____ Wages paid to production workers.
4. ____ Frames and tires used in manufacturing bicycles.

BE21–4 Identify whether each of the following costs should be classified as product costs or period costs:

Identify product and period costs. (S.O. 4)

1. ____ Direct labor. 4. ____ Selling expenses.
2. ____ Advertising expenses. 5. ____ Manufacturing overhead.
3. ____ Direct material. 6. ____ Administrative expenses.

Classify manufacturing costs.
(S.O. 3)

BE21–5 Indicate whether each of the following costs of an automobile manufacturer would be classified as direct materials, direct labor, or manufacturing overhead:

1. Windshield. 5. Factory machinery lubricants.
2. Wages of assembly line worker. 6. Tires.
3. Engine. 7. Salary of painting supervisor.
4. Depreciation of factory machinery. 8. Steering wheel.

Compute total manufacturing costs and total cost of work in process.
(S.O. 6)

BE21–6 Decal Manufacturing Company has the following data: direct labor $260,000, direct materials used $180,000, total manufacturing overhead $200,000, and beginning work in process $25,000. Compute (a) total manufacturing costs and (b) total cost of work in process.

Prepare current asset section.
(S.O. 7)

BE21–7 In alphabetical order below are current asset items for Widget Company's balance sheet at December 31, 1993. Prepare the current asset section (including a complete heading).

Accounts receivable	$300,000
Cash	60,000
Finished goods	75,000
Prepaid expenses	38,000
Raw materials	68,000
Work in process	91,000

Determine missing amounts in computing total manufacturing costs.
(S.O. 6)

BE21–8 Presented below are incomplete 1993 manufacturing cost data for the Continental Corporation. Determine the missing amounts.

	Direct Material Used	Direct Labor Used	Factory Overhead	Total Manufacturing Costs
1.	$39,000	$41,000	$ 50,000	?
2.	?	$88,000	$110,000	$296,000
3.	$55,000	?	$ 95,000	$300,000

Determine missing amounts in computing cost of goods manufactured.
(S.O. 6)

BE21–9 Use the same data from BE21–8 above. Compute the cost of goods manufactured for Continental Corporation in 1993.

	Total Manufacturing Costs	Work in Process (1/1)	Work in Process (12/31)	Cost of Goods Manufactured
1.	?	$120,000	$86,000	?
2.	$296,000	?	$98,000	$308,000
3.	$300,000	$480,000	?	$705,000

Classify manufacturing costs.
(S.O. 3, 4)

BE21–10 Presented below are Green Company's monthly manufacturing cost data related to its personal computer product:

(a) Raw material (CPU, chips, etc.)	$ 85,000
(b) Utilities for manufacturing equipment	$116,000
(c) Depreciation on manufacturing building	$880,000
(d) Wages for production workers	$191,000

Enter each cost item on the following table, placing an "X" under the appropriate headings.

	Product Costs				
	Direct Material	Direct Labor	Factory Overhead	Prime Costs	Conversion Costs
(a)					
(b)					
(c)					
(d)					

*BE21–11   A work sheet is used in preparing financial statements for Sunbird Manufacturing Company. The following accounts are included in the adjusted trial balance: Finished Goods Inventory $28,000, Work in Process Inventory $21,600, Raw Materials Purchases, $175,000 and Direct Labor $140,000. Indicate the work sheet column(s) to which each account should be extended.

Identify work sheet columns for selected accounts.

(S.O. 8)

EXERCISES

E21–1   Presented below is a list of costs and expenses usually incurred by Galway Corporation, a manufacturer of furniture, in its factory:

1. Factory machinery depreciation.
2. Glue, nails, paint, and other small parts used in production.
3. Wages paid to assembly line workers.
4. Factory supervisors' salaries.
5. Insurance on machines.
6. Salaries for night security guards.
7. Wood used in manufacturing furniture.
8. Property taxes on the factory building.
9. Factory repairs.
10. Factory utilities.

Classify costs into three classes of manufacturing costs.

(S.O. 3)

Instructions
Classify the above items into the following categories: direct materials, direct labor, and manufacturing overhead.

E21–2   The Limerick Company reports the following costs and expenses in May:

Determine the total amount of various types of costs.

(S.O. 3, 4)

Factory utilities	$ 9,500	Direct labor	$79,100
Depreciation on factory		Sales salaries	49,400
equipment	12,650	Property taxes on factory	
Depreciation on delivery trucks	3,500	building	2,500
Indirect factory labor	48,900	Repairs to office equipment	1,300
Indirect materials	96,200	Factory repairs	2,000
Direct materials used	137,800	Advertising	18,000
Factory manager's salary	8,000	Office supplies used	3,000

Instructions
From the information, determine the total amount of:

(a) Prime costs.

(b) Manufacturing overhead.

(c) Conversion costs.

(d) Product costs.

(e) Period costs.

E21–3   The Killarney Manufacturing Company produces blankets. From its accounting records it prepares the following schedule and financial statements on a yearly basis:

Indicate in which schedule or financial statement(s) different cost items will appear.

(S.O. 5, 6, 7)

(a) Cost of goods manufactured schedule

(b) Income statement

(c) Balance sheet

The following items are found in its ledger and accompanying data:

1. Cost of goods manufactured
2. Factory maintenance salaries
3. Depreciation on delivery equipment
4. Cost of goods available for sale
5. Direct materials used

6. Heat and electricity for factory
7. Repairs to roof of factory building
8. Cost of raw materials purchases
9. Direct labor
10. Raw materials inventory, 1/1

11. Work in process inventory, 12/31
12. Finished goods inventory, 1/1
13. Indirect labor

14. Depreciation on factory machinery
15. Finished goods inventory, 12/31
16. Work in process, 1/1

Instructions
List the items (1)–(16). For each item, indicate by using the appropriate letter or letters, the schedule and/or financial statement(s) in which the item will appear.

Determine the missing amount of different cost items.
(S.O. 6)

E21–4   Manufacturing cost data for Tralee Company are presented below:

	Case A	Case B	Case C
Direct materials used	(a)	$75,000	$130,000
Direct labor	$ 60,000	86,000	(g)
Manufacturing overhead	42,500	81,600	102,000
Total manufacturing costs	190,650	(d)	260,000
Work in process 1/1/94	(b)	16,500	(h)
Total cost of work in process	221,500	(e)	307,000
Work in process 12/31/94	(c)	9,000	70,000
Cost of goods manufactured	185,275	(f)	(i)

Instructions
Indicate the missing amount for each letter.

Determine the missing amount of different cost items and prepare a condensed cost of goods manufactured schedule.
(S.O. 5, 6)

E21–5   Incomplete manufacturing cost data for the Clonakilty Company for 1994 are presented as follows:

	Direct Materials Used	Direct Labor Used	Manufacturing Overhead	Total Manufacturing Costs	Work in Process 1/1	Work in Process 12/31	Cost of Goods Manufactured
(1)	$130,000	$140,000	$ 70,000	(a)	$30,000	(b)	$360,000
(2)	(c)	200,000	130,000	$450,000	(d)	$40,000	470,000
(3)	80,000	100,000	(e)	260,000	60,000	80,000	(f)
(4)	70,000	(g)	75,000	290,000	45,000	(h)	270,000

Instructions
(a) Indicate the missing amount for each letter.

(b) Prepare a condensed cost of goods manufactured schedule for situation (1) for the year ended December 31, 1994.

Prepare a cost of goods manufactured schedule and a partial income statement.
(S.O. 5, 6)

E21–6   Tipperary Corporation has the following cost records for June, 1994:

Factory utilities	$ 400	Indirect factory labor	$ 4,000
Depreciation, factory equipment	1,700	Direct materials used	20,000
Direct labor	25,000	Work in process, 6/1/94	3,000
Maintenance, factory equipment	1,300	Work in process, 6/30/94	2,500
Indirect materials	2,200	Finished goods, 6/1/94	5,000
Factory manager's salary	3,000	Finished goods, 6/30/94	6,000

Instructions
(a) Prepare a cost of goods manufactured schedule for June 1994.

(b) Prepare an income statement through gross profit for June 1994 assuming net sales are $98,100.

Prepare a cost of goods manufactured schedule and present the ending inventories of the balance sheet.
(S.O. 5, 6, 7)

E21–7   An analysis of the accounts of Waterford Manufacturing, Inc., reveals the following manufacturing cost data for the month ended June 30, 1994:

Inventories:	Beginning	Ending
Raw materials	$9,000	$12,000
Work in process	5,000	7,000
Finished goods	8,000	6,000

Costs incurred:
   Raw materials purchases $64,000, direct labor $50,000, manufacturing overhead $19,200. The specific overhead costs were: indirect labor $5,500, factory insurance $4,000, machinery de-

preciation $4,000, machinery repairs $1,800, factory utilities $2,400, miscellaneous factory costs $1,500.

Instructions

(a) Prepare the cost of goods manufactured schedule for the month ended June 30, 1994.

(b) Show the presentation of the ending inventories on the June 30, 1994 balance sheet.

E21–8 The cost of goods manufactured schedule shows each of the cost elements. Complete the following schedule for Strange Manufacturing Company:

Determine missing amounts in cost of goods manufactured schedule. (S.O. 5, 6)

STRANGE MANUFACTURING COMPANY
Cost of Goods Manufactured Schedule
For the Year Ended December 31, 1993

Work in process (1/1)			$200,000
Direct materials			
Raw materials inventory (1/1)	$?		
Add: Raw material purchases	158,000		
Less: Raw material inventory (12/31)	6,500		
Direct materials used		$190,000	
Direct labor		?	
Manufacturing overhead			
Indirect labor	$ 18,000		
Factory depreciation	36,000		
Factory utilities	68,000		
Total overhead		?	
Total manufacturing costs			?
Total cost of work in process			$?
Less: Work in process (12/31)			87,000
Cost of goods manufactured			$600,000

E21–9 Wexford Motor Company manufactures automobiles. During September 1994, the company purchased 5,000 head lamps at a cost of $8 per lamp. Wexford withdrew 4,550 lamps from the warehouse during the month. Fifty of these lamps were used to replace the head lamps in autos used by traveling sales staff. The remaining 4,500 lamps were put in autos manufactured during the month.

Determine the amount of cost to appear in various accounts and indicate in which financial statements these accounts would appear. (S.O. 5, 6, 7)

Of the autos put into production during September 1994, 95% were completed and transferred to the company's storage lot. Eighty percent of the cars completed during the month were sold by September 30.

Instructions

(a) Determine the cost of head lamps that would appear in each of the following accounts at September 30, 1994: Raw Materials, Work in Process, Finished Goods, Cost of Goods Sold, and Selling Expenses.

(b) Specify whether each of the accounts in (a) would appear on the income statement or on the balance sheet at September 30, 1994.

E21–10 Wicklow Company is a manufacturer of personal computers. Various costs and expenses associated with its operations are as follows:

Classify various costs into different cost categories. (S.O. 3, 4)

1. Sales commissions paid to sell personal computers.
2. Depreciation on the factory building.
3. Wages of workers assembling personal computers.
4. Soldering materials used on factory assembly lines.
5. Salaries for the night security guards for the factory building.
6. Property taxes on the factory building.
7. Production superintendents' salaries.
8. Memory boards and chips used in assembling computers.
9. Depreciation on the factory equipment.

The company intends to classify these costs and expenses into the following categories:

(a) direct materials, (b) direct labor, (c) manufacturing overhead, and (d) period costs.

Prepare a partial work sheet of a manufacturing firm.
(S.O. 8)

Instructions

List the items (1)–(9). For each item, indicate the cost category to which the item belongs.

*E21–11

Instructions

Using the data in Exercise 21–7, prepare a partial work sheet for Waterford Manufacturing, Inc.

PROBLEMS

Classify manufacturing costs into different categories and compute the unit cost.
(S.O. 3, 4)

P21–1   The Kilmeedy Company specializes in manufacturing motorcycles. The model is well accepted by consumers, and the company has a large number of orders to keep the factory production at 1,000 motorcycles per month. Kilmeedy's monthly manufacturing cost and other expense data are as follows.

Factory manager's salary	$ 5,000
Maintenance costs on factory building	300
Advertising for motorcycles	10,000
Sales commissions	5,000
Depreciation on factory building	700
Rent on factory equipment	5,000
Insurance on factory building	1,000
Raw materials (frames, tires, etc.)	20,000
Utility costs for factory	800
Supplies for general office	200
Wages for assembly line workers	32,000
Depreciation on office equipment	500
Miscellaneous materials (lubricants, solders, etc.)	700

Instructions

(a) Prepare an answer sheet with the following column headings:

	Product Costs					
Cost Item	Direct Materials	Direct Labor	Manufacturing Overhead	Period Costs	Prime Costs	Conversion Costs

Enter each cost item on your answer sheet, placing the dollar amount under the appropriate headings. Total the dollar amounts in each of the columns.

(b) Compute the cost to produce one motorcycle.

Classify manufacturing costs into different categories and compute the unit cost.
(S.O. 3, 4)

P21–2   Currier Company, a manufacturer of tennis rackets, started its production in November 1994. For the past five years Currier had been a retailer of sports equipment. After a thorough survey of tennis racket markets, Currier Company decided to turn its retail store into a tennis racket factory.

Raw materials cost for a tennis racket will total $20 per racket. Workers on the production lines are on average paid $10 per hour. A racket usually takes two hours to complete. In addition, the rent on the equipment used to produce rackets amounts to $1,000 per month. Additional materials such as glue, paint, and other small parts cost $4 per racket. A supervisor was hired to oversee production; her monthly salary will be $2,000.

Janitorial costs were $1,200 monthly. Advertising costs for the rackets will be $6,000 per month. The factory building depreciation expense is $8,400 per year. Property taxes on the factory building will be $3,600 per year.

Instructions

(a) Prepare an answer sheet with the following column headings:

Product Costs						
Cost Item	Direct Materials	Direct Labor	Manufacturing Overhead	Period Costs	Prime Costs	Conversion Costs

Assuming that Currier manufactures, on average, 2,000 tennis rackets per month, enter each cost item on your answer sheet, placing the dollar amount under the appropriate headings. Total the dollar amounts in each of the columns.

(b) Compute the cost to produce one racket.

P21–3 Incomplete manufacturing costs, expenses, and selling data for two different cases are as follows:

Indicate the missing amount of different cost items; prepare a condensed cost of goods manufactured schedule, an income statement, and a partial balance sheet.
(S.O. 5, 6, 7)

	Case	
	1	2
Direct Materials Used	$ 8,000	(g)
Direct Labor	3,000	4,000
Manufacturing Overhead	4,000	5,000
Total Manufacturing Costs	(a)	20,000
Beginning Work in Process Inventory	1,000	(h)
Ending Work in Process Inventory	(b)	2,000
Sales	21,500	(i)
Sales Discounts	1,500	1,200
Cost of Goods Manufactured	13,500	21,000
Beginning Finished Goods Inventory	(c)	3,500
Goods Available for Sale	16,000	(j)
Cost of Goods Sold	(d)	(k)
Ending Finished Goods Inventory	1,000	2,500
Gross Profit	(e)	6,000
Operating Expenses	2,500	(l)
Net Income	(f)	3,200

Instructions

(a) Indicate the missing amount for each letter.

(b) Prepare a condensed cost of goods manufactured schedule for Case 1.

(c) Prepare an income statement and the current assets section of the balance sheet for Case 1, assuming that in Case 1 the other items in the current assets section are as follows: Cash, $3,000, Receivables (net), $10,000, Raw Materials, $500, and Prepaid Expenses, $200.

P21–4 The following data were taken from the records of Connaught Manufacturing Company for the year ended December 31, 1994.

Prepare a cost of goods manufactured schedule, a partial income statement, and a partial balance sheet.
(S.O. 5, 6, 7)
S

Raw Materials		Factory Insurance	$ 5,400
Inventory 1/1/94	$ 43,500	Factory Machinery Depreciation	7,700
Raw Materials		Freight-in on Raw Materials Purchased	3,900
Inventory 12/31/94	46,200	Factory Utilities	15,900
Finished Goods		Office Utilities Expense	8,600
Inventory 1/1/94	85,000	Sales	475,000
Finished Goods		Sales Discounts	3,200
Inventory 12/31/94	79,800	Plant Manager's Salary	30,000
Work in Process		Factory Property Taxes	6,100
Inventory 1/1/94	10,200	Factory Repairs	800
Work in Process		Raw Materials Purchases	64,600
Inventory 12/31/94	6,500	Cash	28,000
Direct Labor	145,100		
Indirect Labor	19,100		
Accounts Receivable	27,000		

Instructions

(a) Prepare a cost of goods manufactured schedule.

(b) Prepare an income statement through gross profit.

(c) Prepare the current assets section of the balance sheet at December 31.

Prepare a cost of goods manufactured schedule and a correct income statement.
(S.O. 5, 6)

P21–5 Monaghan Company is a manufacturer of toys. Its controller, Ed Belfast, resigned in August 1994. An inexperienced assistant accountant has prepared the following income statement for the month of August 1994.

MONAGHAN COMPANY
Income Statement
For the Month Ended August 31, 1994

Sales (net)		$670,000
Less: Operating expenses		
Raw materials purchased	$200,000	
Direct labor cost	150,000	
Advertising expense	80,000	
Selling and administrative salaries	70,000	
Rent on factory facilities	60,000	
Depreciation on sales equipment	55,000	
Depreciation on factory equipment	40,000	
Indirect labor cost	20,000	
Factory utilities	10,000	
Factory insurance	5,000	690,000
Net Loss		$ (20,000)

Prior to August 1994, the company had been profitable every month. The company's president is concerned about the accuracy of the income statement above. As a friend of the president, you have been asked to review the income statement and make necessary corrections. After examining other manufacturing cost data, you have acquired additional information as follows:

1. Inventory balances at the beginning and end of August were:

	August 1	August 31
Raw materials	$18,000	$33,000
Work in process	25,000	31,000
Finished goods	40,000	60,000

2. Only 70% of the utilities expense and 80% of the insurance expense apply to factory operations; the remaining amounts should be charged to selling and administrative activities.

Instructions

(a) Prepare a cost goods manufactured schedule for August 1994.

(b) Prepare a correct income statement for August 1994.

Complete a work sheet; prepare a cost of goods manufactured schedule, an income statement, and a balance sheet; journalize and post the closing entries.
(S.O. 8)

*P21–6 Londonderry Manufacturing Company uses a simple manufacturing accounting system. At the end of its fiscal year on August 31, 1994, the adjusted trial balance contains the following accounts.

Debits		Credits	
Cash	$ 15,700	Accumulated Depreciation	$ 353,000
Accounts Receivable (net)	63,900	Notes Payable	45,000
Finished Goods Inventory	56,000	Accounts Payable	38,200
Work in Process Inventory	27,800	Income Taxes Payable	9,000
Raw Materials Inventory	37,200	Common Stock	352,000
Plant Assets	890,000	Retained Earnings	205,300
Raw Materials Purchases	236,500	Sales	996,000
Direct Labor	280,900		
Indirect Labor	27,400		
Factory Repairs	17,200		
Factory Depreciation	18,000		
Factory Manager's Salary	40,000		
Factory Insurance	12,000		
Factory Property Taxes	12,900		

Debits		Credits	
Factory Utilities	$ 13,300		
Selling Expenses	98,500		
Administrative Expenses	115,200		
Income Tax Expense	36,000		
	$1,998,500		$1,998,500

Physical inventory accounts on August 31, 1994 show the following inventory amounts: Finished Goods $49,600, Work in Process $33,400, and Raw Material $46,500.

Instructions

(a) Enter the adjusted trial balance data on a work sheet in financial statement order and complete the work sheet.

(b) Prepare a cost of goods manufactured schedule for the year.

(c) Prepare an income statement for the year and a balance sheet at August 31, 1994.

(d) Journalize the closing entries.

(e) Post the closing entries to Manufacturing Summary and to Income Summary.

ALTERNATE PROBLEMS

P21–1A Ulster Company specializes in manufacturing a unique model of bicycle helmet. The model is well accepted by consumers, and the company has a large number of orders to keep the factory production at 10,000 helmets per month (80% of its full capacity). Ulster's monthly manufacturing cost and other expense data are as follows.

Classify manufacturing costs into different categories and compute the unit cost.
(S.O. 3, 4)

Rent on factory equipment	$ 6,000
Insurance on factory building	1,500
Raw materials (plastics, polystyrene, etc.)	70,000
Utility costs for factory	900
Supplies for general office	300
Wages for assembly line workers	36,000
Depreciation on office equipment	800
Miscellaneous materials (lubricants, solders, etc.)	1,200
Factory manager's salary	5,700
Property taxes on factory building	400
Advertising for helmets	11,000
Sales commissions	7,000
Depreciation on factory building	1,500

Instructions

(a) Prepare an answer sheet with the following column headings:

	Product Costs					
Cost Item	Direct Materials	Direct Labor	Manufacturing Overhead	Period Costs	Prime Costs	Conversion Costs

Enter each cost item on your answer sheet, placing the dollar amount under the appropriate headings. Total the dollar amounts in each of the columns.

(b) Compute the cost to produce one helmet.

P21–2A Macroom Company, a manufacturer of stereo systems, started its production in October 1994. For the past three years Macroom had been a retailer of stereo systems. After a thorough survey of stereo system markets, Macroom Company decided to turn its retail store into a stereo equipment factory.

Raw materials cost for a stereo system will total $70 per unit. Workers on the production lines are on average paid $12 per hour. A stereo system usually takes five hours to complete. In addition, the rent on the equipment used to assemble stereo systems amounts to $1,200 per

Classify manufacturing costs into different categories and compute the unit cost.
(S.O. 3, 4)

month. Additional materials such as solders, paint, and other small parts, cost $5 per system. A supervisor was hired to oversee production; her monthly salary will be $2,400.

Janitorial costs were $1,300 monthly. Advertising costs for the stereo system will be $8,500 per month. The factory building depreciation expense is $7,200 per year. Property taxes on the factory building will be $4,800 per year.

Instructions

(a) Prepare an answer sheet with the following column headings:

	Product Costs					
Cost Item	Direct Materials	Direct Labor	Manufacturing Overhead	Period Costs	Prime Costs	Conversion Costs

Assuming that Macroom manufactures, on average, 1,200 stereo systems per month, enter each cost item on your answer sheet, placing the dollar amount under the appropriate headings. Total the dollar amounts in each of the columns.

(b) Compute the cost to produce one stereo system.

P21–3A Incomplete manufacturing costs, expenses, and selling data for three different cases are as follows.

Indicate the missing amount of different cost items; prepare a condensed cost of goods manufactured schedule, an income statement, and a partial balance sheet.
(S.O. 5, 6, 7)

	Case	
	1	2
Direct Materials Used	$ 7,000	(g)
Direct Labor	6,000	8,000
Manufacturing Overhead	5,000	4,000
Total Manufacturing Costs	(a)	21,000
Beginning Work in Process Inventory	1,000	(h)
Ending Work in Process Inventory	(b)	3,000
Sales	24,500	(i)
Sales Discounts	2,500	1,400
Cost of Goods Manufactured	16,500	22,000
Beginning Finished Goods Inventory	(c)	3,500
Goods Available for Sale	18,000	(j)
Cost of Goods Sold	(d)	(k)
Ending Finished Goods Inventory	2,000	2,500
Gross Profit	(e)	7,000
Operating Expenses	3,500	(l)
Net Income	(f)	2,200

Instructions

(a) Indicate the missing amount for each letter.

(b) Prepare a condensed cost of goods manufactured schedule for Case 1.

(c) Prepare an income statement and the current assets section of the balance sheet for Case 1, assuming that in Case 1 the other items in the current assets section are as follows: Cash, $4,000, Receivables (net), $15,000, Raw Materials, $600, and Prepaid Expenses, $400.

Prepare a cost of goods manufactured schedule, a partial income statement, and a partial balance sheet.
(S.O. 5, 6, 7)

P21–4A The following data were taken from the records of Caherdaniel Manufacturing Company for the fiscal year ended June 30, 1994.

Raw Materials Inventory 7/1/93	$ 46,500	Accounts Receivable	$ 27,000
		Factory Insurance	4,600
Raw Materials Inventory 6/30/94	39,600	Factory Machinery Depreciation	15,000
		Freight-in on Raw Materials Purchased	8,600
Finished Goods Inventory 7/1/93	96,000	Factory Utilities	24,600
		Office Utilities Expense	8,650
Finished Goods Inventory 6/30/94	98,900	Sales	547,000
		Sales Discounts	3,300
Work in Process Inventory 7/1/93	21,000	Plant Manager's Salary	29,000
		Factory Property Taxes	9,600
Work in Process Inventory 6/30/94	16,700	Factory Repairs	1,400
Direct Labor	147,250	Raw Materials Purchases	89,800
Indirect Labor	24,460	Cash	32,000

Instructions

(a) Prepare a cost of goods manufactured schedule.

(b) Prepare an income statement through gross profit.

(c) Prepare the current asset section of the balance sheet at June 30, 1994.

P21–5A Ballymalis Company is a manufacturer of computers. Its controller, Mike Reynolds, resigned in October 1994. An inexperienced assistant accountant has prepared the following income statement for the month of October 1994.

Prepare a cost of goods manufactured schedule and a correct income statement.
(S.O. 5, 6)

BALLYMALIS COMPANY
Income Statement
For the Month Ended October 31, 1994

Sales (net)		$780,000
Less: Operating expenses		
Raw materials purchased	$260,000	
Direct labor cost	190,000	
Advertising expense	90,000	
Selling and administrative salaries	75,000	
Rent on factory facilities	60,000	
Depreciation on sales equipment	45,000	
Depreciation on factory equipment	30,000	
Indirect labor cost	25,000	
Factory utilities	12,000	
Factory insurance	8,000	795,000
Net Loss		$ (15,000)

Prior to October 1994, the company had been profitable every month. The company's president is concerned about the accuracy of the income statement above. As a friend of the president, you have been asked to review the income statement and make necessary corrections. After examining other manufacturing cost data, you have acquired additional information as follows:

1. Inventory balances at the beginning and end of October were:

	October 1	October 31
Raw materials	$15,000	$31,000
Work in process	16,000	24,000
Finished goods	30,000	50,000

2. Only 80% of the utilities expense and 70% of the insurance expense apply to factory operations; the remaining amounts should be charged to selling and administrative activities.

Instructions

(a) Prepare a schedule of cost of goods manufactured for October 1994.

(b) Prepare a correct income statement for October 1994.

Broadening Your Perspective

DECISION CASE

Guinness Manufacturing Company specializes in producing fashion outfits. On July 31, 1993, a tornado touched down at its factory and general office. The inventories in the warehouse and the factory were totally damaged due to heavy rain and moisture. The general office nearby was completely destroyed. Next morning, through a careful search over the disaster site, however, Pete Olsmon, the company's controller, and Diana Hoffman, the cost accountant, were able to recover a small part of manufacturing cost data for the current month.

"What a horrible experience," sighed Pete. "And the worse part is that we may not have enough records to use in filing an insurance claim."

"This is the first time I have ever experienced a tornado touchdown," replied Diana. "It is indeed terrible. However, I managed to recover some of the manufacturing cost data that I was working on yesterday afternoon. The data indicate that our direct labor cost in July totaled $250,000 and that we had purchased $340,000 of raw materials. In addition, I recall that the raw materials used for July was $350,000. But I'm not sure this information will help; the rest of our records are blown away."

"Well, not exactly," said Pete. "I was working on the year-to-date income statement when the tornado warning was announced. My recollection is that our sales in July were $1,250,000 and our gross profit ratio has been 40% of sales. Also, I can remember that our cost of goods available for sale was $780,000 for July."

"Maybe we can work something out from this information!" exclaimed Diana. "My experience tells me that our manufacturing overhead is usually 60% of direct labor."

"Hey, look what I just found," cried Diana. "It's a copy of this June's balance sheet, and it shows that our inventories as of June 30 are Finished Goods, $36,000, Work in Process, $22,000, and Raw Materials, $19,000."

"Super," yelled Pete. "Let's go work something out."

In order to file an insurance claim Guinness Company must determine the amount of its inventories as of July 31, 1993, the date of the tornado touchdown.

Instructions
Determine the amount of cost in the Raw Materials, Work in Process, and Finished Goods inventory accounts as of the date of the tornado touchdown.

CRITICAL THINKING CASE

Refer to the opening vignette regarding Murray Bicycle and answer the following questions:

1. In the opening story about Murray Bicycle, the "big three domestic car companies" were contrasted to the "big three U.S. bicycle makers." Discuss the similarities and the differences in the production processes, general product cost accounts, and cost flows of the car companies and the bicycle makers.

2. Relate the management functions discussed in the chapter to the bicycle manufacturing and marketing cycle.

3. Identify some of the likely manufacturing overhead costs incurred by a bicycle manufacturer.

ETHICAL CASE

Pascal Margallas, controller for Kasmais Industries, was reviewing production cost reports for the year. One amount in these reports continued to bother him—advertising. During the year, the company had instituted an expensive advertising campaign to sell some its slower moving products. It was still too early to tell whether the advertising campaign was successful. There had been much internal debate as how to report advertising costs. The Vice-President of Finance argued that advertising costs should be reported as a cost of production, just like direct materials and direct labor. He therefore recommended that this cost be identified as manufacturing overhead and reported as part of inventory costs until sold. Others disagreed. Pascal believed that this cost should be reported as an expense of the current period based on the conservatism principle. Others argued that it should be reported as Prepaid Advertising and reported as a current asset.

The president finally had to decide the issue. He argued that these costs should be reported as inventory. His arguments were practical ones. He noted that the company was experiencing financial difficulty and expensing this amount in the current period might jeopardize a planned bond offering. Also by reporting the advertising costs as inventory rather than as prepaid advertising, less attention would be directed to it by the financial community.

Instructions

(a) Who are the stakeholders in this situation?

(b) What are the ethical issues involved in this situation?

(c) What would you do if you were Pascal Margallas?

Answers to Self-Study Questions

1. a   2. c   3. c   4. d   5. c   6. d   7. c   8. b   9. b   10. c
11. c

CONCEPTS FOR REVIEW

Before studying this chapter, you should know or, if necessary, review:

a. *How a perpetual inventory system works (Ch. 9, p. 370–2)*

b. *The three classifications of manufacturing costs. (Ch. 21, p. 861–62)*

c. *What is the difference between product and period costs? (Ch. 21, p. 863)*

d. *The form and content of a cost of goods manufactured schedule. (Ch. 21, p. 866)*

CHAPTER 22

JOB ORDER COST ACCOUNTING

Study Objectives

After studying this chapter, you should be able to:

1. *Explain the characteristics and purposes of cost accounting.*

2. *Describe the flow of costs in a job order cost accounting system.*

3. *Explain the nature and importance of a job cost sheet.*

4. *Indicate how the predetermined overhead rate is determined and used.*

5. *Prepare entries for jobs completed and sold.*

6. *Distinguish between under- and overapplied manufacturing overhead.*

Western States Fire Apparatus, Inc., of Cornelius, Oregon, is one of the few American companies that makes fire trucks. The company builds about 25 trucks per year—many of which are bought by colleges. Founded in 1941, the company is run by the children and grandchildren of the original founder.

"We buy the chassis, which is the cab and the frame," says Susan Scott, the company's bookkeeper. "In our computer, we set up an account into which all of the direct material that is purchased for that particular job is charged." Other direct materials include the fire pump—which can cost $10,000—the lights, the siren, ladders, and hoses.

As for direct labor, the production workers fill out job sheets that tell what jobs they worked on. Usually, the company is building four trucks at any one time. On payday, the controller allocates the payroll to the appropriate job record.

Indirect materials, such as aluminum, steel, nuts and bolts, and wiring are *allocated to each job in proportion to direct material dollars. Other costs, such as insurance and supervisors' salaries, are allocated based on direct labor hours. "We need to allocate overhead in order to know what kind of price we have to charge when we submit our bids," she says.*

Western gets orders through a "blind-bidding" process—the firm doesn't know what competitors are offering to build their fire trucks. "If we bid too low, we won't make a profit. If we bid too high, we don't get the job."

Regardless of the final price for the truck, the quality had better be first rate. "The fire departments let you know if they don't like what you did, and you usually end up fixing it."

You are now familiar with manufacturing costs and many of the important cost concepts in a manufacturing company. This chapter adds a vital dimension to the accumulation of manufacturing costs. The accumulated costs are assigned to and reported for specific jobs such as printing 500 wedding announcements or producing 10,000 sheets of business letter-head stationery for a company.

Data on the cost of specific jobs can be useful to management in a variety of ways. For example, in the fire trucks vignette above, job cost data can be used by the manager in:

1. Setting the selling price for the job.
2. Bidding on similar jobs in the future.
3. Evaluating worker performance by comparing the cost of the job with similar previous jobs.
4. Evaluating worker performance by comparing the cost of the job with cost estimates made when the job was accepted.
5. Developing market strategies.
6. Developing future production goals.

In sum, knowledge of job costs contributes to each of management's functions—planning, organizing and directing, and controlling.

This chapter is the first of two chapters on cost accounting systems. We begin the discussion with an overview of the flow of costs in a job order cost accounting system. We then use a case study to explain and illustrate the documents, entries, and accounts in this type of cost accounting system.

Study Objective 1

Explain the characteristics and purposes of cost accounting.

Cost Accounting Systems

Cost accounting involves the measuring, recording, and reporting of product costs. From the data accumulated, both the total cost and the unit cost of each product is determined.

A cost accounting system consists of manufacturing cost accounts that are fully integrated into the general ledger of a company. **An important feature of a cost accounting system is the use of a perpetual inventory system that provides information immediately on the cost of a product.** There are two basic types of cost accounting systems: (1) a job order cost system and (2) a process cost system. Although cost accounting systems differ widely from company to company, most are based on one of these two traditional product costing systems.

Under a job order cost system, costs are assigned to each **job**, such as the manufacture of a high-speed drilling machine, or to each **batch** of goods, such as 500 wedding invitations. Jobs or batches may be completed to fill a specific customer order or to replenish inventory. An important feature of job order costing is that each job (or batch) has its own distinguishing characteristics. For example, each house is custom built, each motion picture is unique, and each printing job is different. The objective is to compute the cost per job. At each point in the manufacturing process, the job and its associated costs can be identified. A job order cost system measures costs for each completed job, rather than for set time periods.

A process cost system is used when a series of connected manufacturing processes or departments produce a large volume of uniform or relatively homogeneous products. Production is continuous to ensure that adequate inventories of the finished product(s) are on hand. A process cost system is used in the manufacture of cereal, the refining of petroleum, and the production of automobiles. Process costing accounts for and accumulates product-related costs for a period of time (such as a week or a month) as opposed to assigning costs to specific products or job orders. In process costing, the costs are assigned to or accumulated by departments or processes for a set period of time.

A company may use both types of cost systems. For example, General Motors uses process cost accounting for its standard model cars, such as Chevrolets and Buicks, and job order cost accounting for a custom-made limousine for the President of the United States. The objective of both systems is to provide product unit cost information for product pricing, cost control, inventory valuation, and financial statement presentation. End-of-period inventory values are computed by using product unit cost data. The job order cost system will be explained in this chapter; the process cost system will be discussed in Chapter 23.

Accounting in Action · *Business Insight*

Many companies suffer from poor cost accounting. As a result, companies sometimes price some products too high and others too low. They also make some products they ought not to be selling at all and buy others, often from overseas suppliers, that they could more profitably make themselves. Moreover, inaccurate cost data lead companies to misallocate capital and frustrate efforts by plant managers to improve efficiency.

For example, consider a diversified company in the business of rebuilding diesel locomotives. The managers thought they were making money until a consulting firm determined that costs had been seriously underestimated. The company bailed out of the business, and not a moment too soon. Says the consultant who advised the company: "The more contracts it won, the more money it lost."

Before You Go On . . .

1. How may management use job order cost data in planning, organizing and directing, and controlling?

2. What is a cost accounting system?

3. How does a job order cost system differ from a process cost system?

*J*ob Order Cost Flow

Study Objective 2

Describe the flow of costs in a job order cost accounting system.

ILLUSTRATION 22-1

Job order cost accounting system

The flow of costs (direct materials, direct labor, and manufacturing overhead) in job order cost accounting parallels the physical flow of the materials as they are converted into finished goods. There are two major steps in the flow of costs: (1) **accumulating** the manufacturing costs incurred and (2) **assigning** the accumulated costs to the work done. As shown in Illustration 22-1, manufacturing costs incurred are accumulated in entries 1–3 by debits to Raw Materials Inventory, Factory Labor, and Manufacturing Overhead. No attempt is made when costs are incurred to associate the costs with specific jobs. The remaining entries (entries 4–8) pertain to the assignment of manufacturing costs incurred. First, as illustrated, costs are assigned to the Work in Process Inventory account. All debits to this account must also be assigned to specific jobs. When a job is finished,

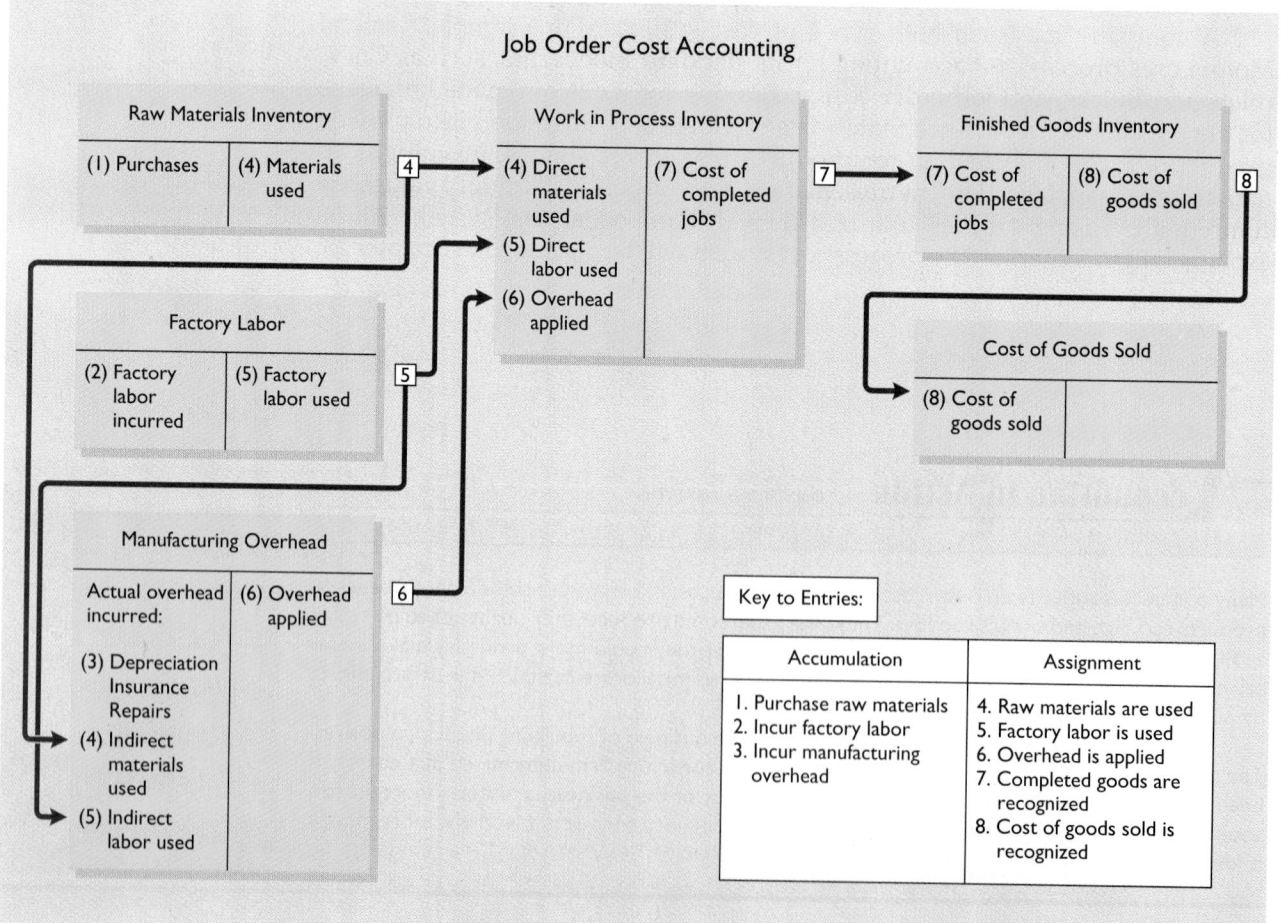

its cost is transferred to finished goods. Later, when the goods are sold, their cost is transferred to costs of goods sold. We will use a case study to explain and illustrate how a job order system operates.

Accumulating Manufacturing Costs

In a job order cost system, manufacturing costs are recorded in the period in which they are incurred. To illustrate, we will use the January transactions of Wallace Manufacturing Company, which makes tools and dies.

Raw Materials Costs

The costs of raw materials purchased are debited to Raw Materials Inventory when materials are received. This account is debited for the invoice cost and freight costs chargeable to the purchaser. It is credited for purchase discounts taken and purchase returns and allowances. No effort is made at this point to associate the cost of materials with specific jobs or orders. The procedures for ordering, receiving, recording, and paying for raw materials are similar to the purchasing procedures of a merchandising company.

To illustrate the purchase of raw materials, assume that Wallace Manufacturing Company purchases 2,000 handles (Stock No. AA2746) at $5 per unit ($10,000) and 800 modules (Stock No. AA2850) at $40 per unit ($32,000) for a total cost of $42,000 ($10,000 + $32,000). The entry to record this purchase on January 4 is:

Helpful hint How does this entry differ for a merchandising company that has a perpetual inventory system? Answer: The debit is to Merchandise Inventory.

	(1)		
Jan. 4	Raw Materials Inventory	42,000	
	Accounts Payable		42,000
	(Purchase of raw materials on account)		

Raw Materials Inventory is a control account. The subsidiary ledger consists of individual records for each item of raw materials. The records may take the form of accounts (or cards) that are manually or mechanically prepared, or data files maintained electronically on disks or magnetic tape. The records, referred to as **materials inventory records** (or **stores ledger cards**), are similar to the perpetual inventory records illustrated in Chapter 9 for a merchandising company. The card for Stock No. AA2746 following the purchase is shown in Illustration 22-2.

ILLUSTRATION 22-2

Materials inventory card

Item: Handles							Part No: AA2746			
	Receipts			Issues			Balance			
Date	Units	Cost	Total	Units	Cost	Total	Units	Cost	Total	
1/4	2,000	$5	$10,000				2,000	$5	$10,000	

After all postings have been completed, the sum of the balances in the raw materials subsidiary ledger should equal the balance in the raw materials inventory control account.

Factory Labor Costs

The procedures for accumulating factory labor costs are similar to those used in computing the payroll for a merchandising company. For example, time clocks and time cards are used to determine total hours worked; gross and net earnings for each employee are listed in a payroll register; and individual employee earnings records are maintained. To help ensure the accuracy of payroll data, a company should follow the principles of internal control for payrolls described in Chapter 12.

In a manufacturing company, the cost of factory labor consists of (1) gross earnings of factory workers, (2) employer payroll taxes on such earnings, and (3) fringe benefits (such as sick pay, pensions, and vacation pay) incurred by the employer. **Labor costs are debited to Factory Labor when they are incurred.** To illustrate, assume that Wallace Manufacturing incurs $32,000 of factory labor costs, of which $27,000 relates to wages payable and $5,000 relates to payroll taxes payable in January. The entry is:

(2)

Jan. 31	Factory Labor	32,000	
	Factory Wages Payable		27,000
	Employer Payroll Taxes Payable		5,000
	(To record factory labor costs)		

Factory labor is subsequently assigned to work in process and manufacturing overhead as explained later in the chapter.

Manufacturing Overhead Costs

A company may have many types of overhead costs. The accumulation of these costs may be recognized **daily**, as in the case of machinery repairs and the use of indirect materials and indirect labor. Alternatively, overhead costs may be recorded **periodically** through adjusting entries, as in the case of property taxes, depreciation, and insurance. Using assumed data, a summary entry for manufacturing overhead in Wallace Manufacturing Company is:

(3)

Jan. 31	Manufacturing Overhead	13,800	
	Utilities Payable		4,800
	Prepaid Insurance		2,000
	Accounts Payable (for repairs)		2,600
	Accumulated Depreciation		3,000
	Property Taxes Payable		1,400
	(To record overhead costs)		

Manufacturing Overhead is a control account. The subsidiary ledger consists of individual accounts for each type of cost, such as Utilities Expense, Insurance Expense, and Repair Expense.

Assigning Manufacturing Costs to Work in Process

Study Objective 3

Explain the nature and importance of a job cost sheet.

As shown in the flow chart in Illustration 22-1, assigning manufacturing costs to work in process results in **debits** to Work in Process Inventory and **credits** to Raw Materials Inventory, Factory Labor, and Manufacturing Overhead. Journal entries for the assignment of costs to work in process are usually made and posted monthly. An indispensable accounting record in assigning costs to jobs is the job cost sheet, shown in Illustration 22-3. A *job cost sheet* is a form used

Accounting in Action · *Business Insight*

Manufacturing overhead sometimes represents a significant portion of total manufacturing costs in government contracts, and it often is the most difficult cost for management to control. For example, one of the nation's biggest defense contractors at one time billed the government for $170 million in overhead expenses on government contracts over a three-year period. After the Defense Audit Agency challenged $63.6 million of this amount, the company withdrew $23 million of the charges.

to record the costs chargeable to a specific job and to determine the total and unit cost of the completed job. Postings to job cost sheets are made daily, directly from supporting documentation that shows the cost and job to be charged.

A separate job cost sheet is kept for each job. Job cost sheets constitute the subsidiary ledger for the Work in Process Inventory account. **Each entry to Work in Process Inventory must be accompanied by a corresponding posting to one or more job cost sheets.**

ILLUSTRATION 22-3

Job cost sheet

Job Cost Sheet

Job No. _____   Quantity _____
Item _____   Date Requested _____
For _____   Date Completed _____

Date	Direct Materials	Direct Labor	Manufacturing Overhead

Cost of completed job
  Direct materials $ _____
  Direct labor   _____
  Manufacturing overhead   _____
Total cost $ _____
Unit cost (total dollars ÷ quantity) $ _____

Raw Materials Costs

Raw materials costs are assigned when the materials are issued by the storeroom. To achieve effective internal control over the issuance of materials, the storekeeper should obtain a written authorization each time materials are released to production. The authorization for issuing raw materials is made on a prenumbered materials requisition slip signed by an authorized employee such as a department supervisor. Materials may be used directly on a job, or they may be considered to be indirect materials. As shown in Illustration 22-4, the requisition should indicate the quantity and type of materials withdrawn and the account

ILLUSTRATION 22-4

Materials requisition slip

Wallace Manufacturing Company
Materials Requisition Slip

| Deliver to: | Assembly Department | | Req. No. | R247 |
| Charge to: | Work in Process—Job No. 101 | | Date: | 1/6/93 |

Quantity	Description	Stock No.	Cost Per Unit	Total
200	Handles	AA2746	$5.00	$1,000

Requested by *Bruce Howart*   Received by *Herb Crowley*

Approved by *Kap Shin*   Costed by *Heather Remmers*

Helpful hint The internal control principle is documentation procedures which includes prenumbering to enhance subsequent accountability.

to be charged. The account is Work in Process Inventory for direct materials and Manufacturing Overhead for indirect materials.

The requisition is prepared in duplicate. A copy is retained in the storeroom as evidence of the materials released; the original is sent to accounting, where the cost per unit and total cost of the materials used are determined. Any of the inventory costing methods (FIFO, LIFO, or average cost) may be used in costing the requisitions; the method selected by management should be followed consistently. After the requisition slips have been costed, they are posted daily to the materials inventory records. In addition, requisitions for direct materials are posted daily to the individual job cost sheets.

Periodically, the requisitions are sorted, totaled, and journalized. For example, if $24,000 of direct materials and $6,000 of indirect materials are used in Wallace Manufacturing in January, the entry is:

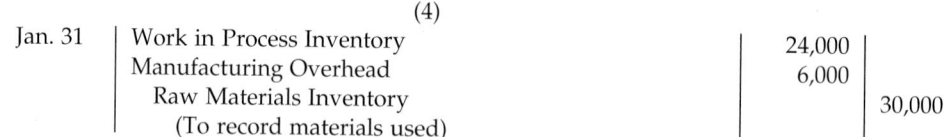

		(4)		
Jan. 31	Work in Process Inventory		24,000	
	Manufacturing Overhead		6,000	
	Raw Materials Inventory			30,000
	(To record materials used)			

The requisition slips show total direct materials costs of $12,000 for Job No. 101, $7,000 for Job No. 102, and $5,000 for Job No. 103. The posting of requisition slip R247 and other assumed postings to the job cost sheets for materials are shown in Illustration 22-5. After all postings have been completed, the sum of the totals of the direct materials columns of the job cost sheets should equal the direct materials debited to Work in Process Inventory.

The materials inventory record for Part No. AA2746, after posting requisition slip R247 and an assumed requisition slip for 760 handles costing $3,800 on January 10 for Job 102, is shown in Illustration 22-6.

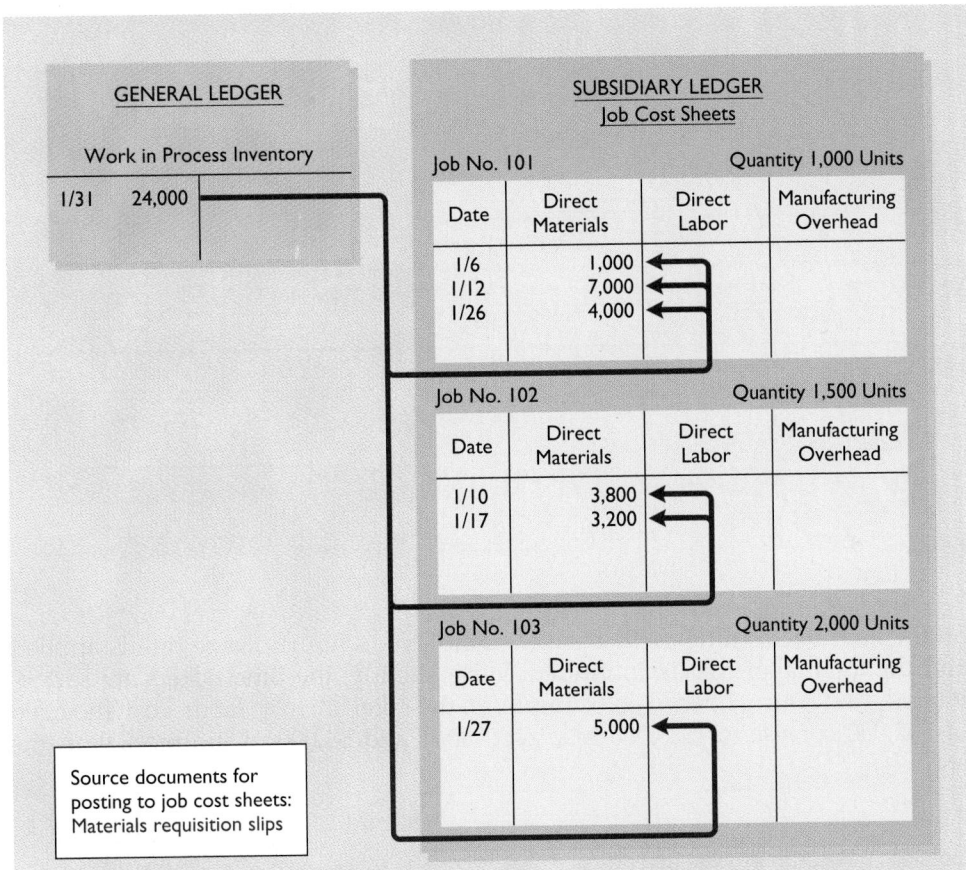

ILLUSTRATION 22-5

Job cost sheets—direct materials

ILLUSTRATION 22-6

Materials inventory card following issuances

Item: Handles						Part No: AA2746			
	Receipts			Issues			Balance		
Date	Units	Cost	Total	Units	Cost	Total	Units	Cost	Total
1/4	2,000	$5	$10,000				2,000	$5	$10,000
1/6				200	$5	$1,000	1,800	$5	9,000
1/10				760	$5	3,800	1,040	$5	5,200

Factory Labor Costs

Factory labor costs are assigned to jobs on the basis of time tickets prepared when the work is performed. The **time ticket** should indicate the employee, the hours worked, and the account to be charged. The account Work in Process Inventory is debited for direct labor, and Manufacturing Overhead is debited for indirect labor. When direct labor is involved, the job number must be indicated as shown in Illustration 22-7.

In some companies, different colored time tickets are used for direct and indirect labor. All time tickets should be approved by the employee's supervisor.

The time tickets are later sent to the payroll department where the total time reported for an employee for a pay period is reconciled with total hours, shown

ILLUSTRATION 22-7

Time ticket

Wallace Manufacturing Company
Time Ticket

Date: 1/6/93

| Employee | John Nash | Employee No. | 124 |
| Charge to: | Work in Process | Job No. | 101 |

Time			Hourly Rate	Total Cost
Start	Stop	Total Hours		
0800	1200	4	10.00	40.00

Approved by *Bob Kadler*   Costed by *S. Bono*

on the employee's time card. Then the employee's hourly wage rate is applied and the total labor cost is computed. Subsequently, the time tickets are sorted, totaled, and journalized. For example, if the total factory labor cost incurred of $32,000 consists of $28,000 of direct labor and $4,000 of indirect labor, the entry is:

(5)

Jan. 31	Work in Process Inventory	28,000	
	Manufacturing Overhead	4,000	
	Factory Labor		32,000
	(To assign factory labor to production)		

As a result of this entry, Factory Labor is left with a zero balance, and gross earnings are assigned to the appropriate manufacturing accounts. In some companies the accumulation and assignment of factory labor are combined into an entry in which Work in Process Inventory and Manufacturing Overhead are debited and Factory Wages Payable and other liabilities are credited.

We will assume that the labor costs chargeable to the three jobs are $15,000, $9,000, and $4,000. The Work in Process Inventory and job cost sheets after posting are shown in Illustration 22-8. As in the case of direct materials, the postings to the direct labor columns of the job cost sheets should equal the posting of direct labor to Work in Process Inventory.

Helpful hint Prove the $28,000 by totaling the charges by jobs:

101	$15,000
102	9,000
103	4,000
	$28,000

![Technology in Action banner]

Technology in Action

A job cost computer program provides summaries of material and labor expenses by job. The program enables the company to accumulate costs by jobs, provide data to accounts receivable for billings, assign overhead costs, and provide up-to-date management reports. The paperwork and reports generated by such systems are basically the same as shown for Wallace Manufacturing Company. The major difference between manual and computerized systems is the time involved in converting data into information and in getting feedback (reports) to management.

ILLUSTRATION 22-8

Job cost sheets—direct labor

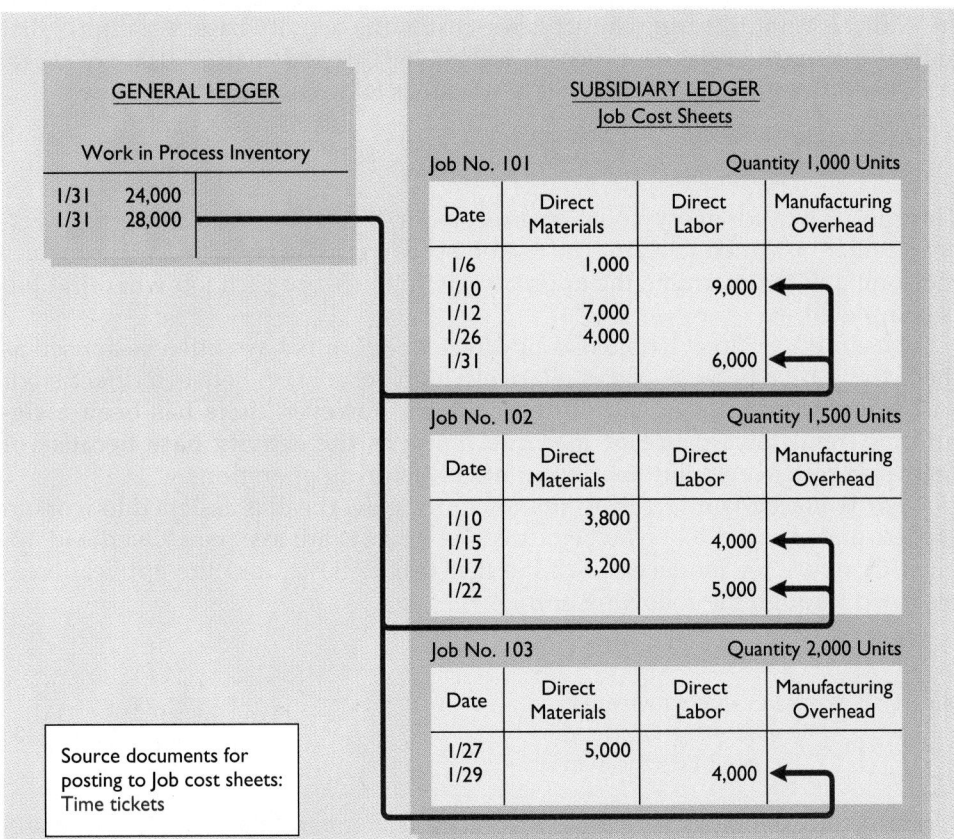

Manufacturing Overhead Costs

Unlike direct materials and direct labor that apply to specific jobs, manufacturing overhead relates to production operations as a whole. Consequently, these costs cannot be assigned to specific jobs on the basis of actual costs incurred. Instead, manufacturing overhead is assigned to work in process and to specific jobs **on an estimated basis** through the use of a predetermined overhead rate.

The predetermined overhead rate is based on the relationship between estimated annual overhead costs and expected annual operating activity, expressed in terms of a common activity base. The common activity base may be stated in terms of direct labor costs, direct labor hours, machine hours, or any other measure that will provide an equitable basis for applying overhead costs to jobs. The predetermined overhead rate is established at (or prior to) the beginning of the year. The formula for a predetermined overhead rate is:

Study Objective 4

Indicate how the predetermined overhead rate is determined and used.

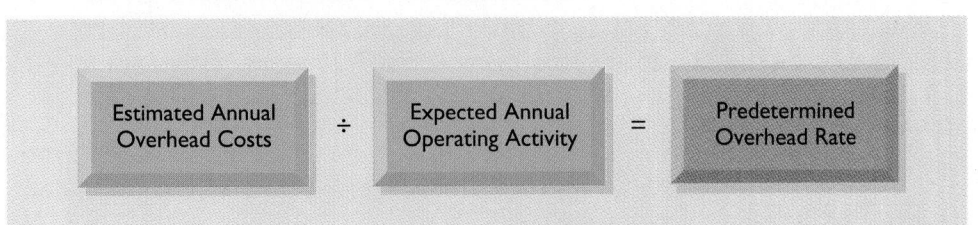

ILLUSTRATION 22-9

Formula for predetermined overhead rate

At Wallace Manufacturing, direct labor cost is the activity base. Assuming that annual overhead costs are expected to be $280,000 and that $350,000 of direct labor costs are anticipated, the overhead rate is 80%, computed as follows:

$$\$280{,}000 \div \$350{,}000 = 80\%$$

This means that for every dollar of direct labor, 80 cents of manufacturing overhead will be assigned to a job. The use of a predetermined overhead rate enables the company to determine the approximate total cost of each job **when the job is completed**.

Historically, direct labor costs or direct labor hours have often been used as the activity base because of the relatively high correlation between direct labor and manufacturing overhead. In recent years, however, **there has been a significant trend toward use of machine hours as the activity base because of increased reliance on automation in manufacturing operations**.

For Wallace Manufacturing, manufacturing overhead is assigned to work in process and charged to jobs when direct labor costs are assigned. Overhead applied therefore for January is $22,400 ($28,000 × 80%), and the application is recorded through the following entry.

Helpful hint The debit of $22,400 to Work in Process is accounted for as follows:

101	$12,000
102	7,200
103	3,200
	$22,400

(6)

Jan. 31	Work in Process Inventory	22,400	
	Manufacturing Overhead		22,400
	(To assign overhead to jobs)		

After posting, the Work in Process Inventory account and the job cost sheets will appear as shown in Illustration 22-10.

ILLUSTRATION 22-10

Job cost sheets—manufacturing overhead applied

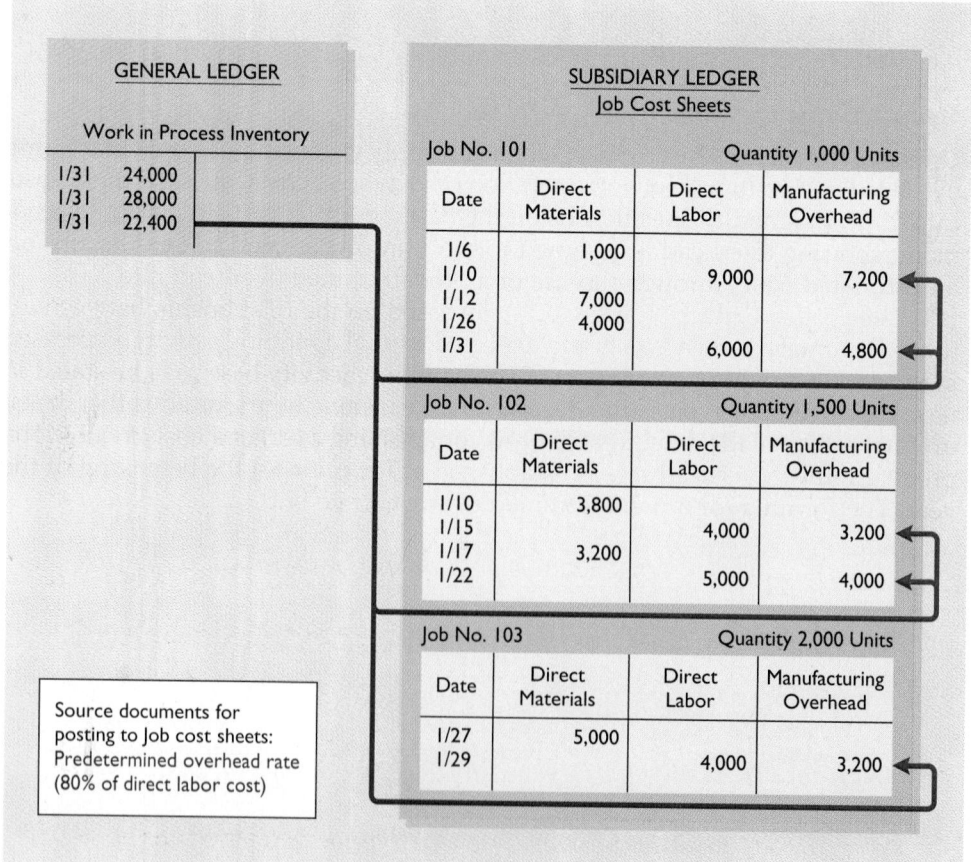

At the end of each month, the balance in Work in Process Inventory should equal the sum of the costs shown on the job cost sheets of unfinished jobs. Assuming that all jobs are unfinished, proof of the agreement of the control and subsidiary accounts in Wallace Manufacturing is shown below.

ILLUSTRATION 22-11

Proof of job cost sheets to work in process inventory

Work in Process Inventory		Job Cost Sheets	
Jan. 31	24,000	No. 101	$39,000
Jan. 31	28,000	102	23,200
Jan. 31	22,400	103	12,200
	74,400		$74,400

Before You Go On . . .

1. What accounts are debited when manufacturing costs are incurred?

2. What source documents are used in assigning manufacturing costs to Work in Process Inventory?

3. What is a job cost sheet, and what is its primary purpose?

4. What is the formula for computing a predetermined overhead rate?

Assigning Costs of Completed Jobs

When a job is completed, the costs are summarized and the lower portion of the applicable job cost sheet is completed. For example, if we assume that Job No. 101 is completed on January 31, the job cost sheet will show the following:

Study Objective 5

Prepare entries for jobs completed and sold.

ILLUSTRATION 22-12

Completed job cost sheet

Job Cost Sheet

Job No. _____ 101 _____ Quantity _____ 1,000 _____
Item _____ Magnetic Sensors _____ Date Requested _____ February 5 _____
For _____ Tanner Company _____ Date Completed _____ January 31 _____

Date	Direct Materials	Direct Labor	Manufacturing Overhead
1/6	$ 1,000		
1/10		$ 9,000	$ 7,200
1/12	7,000		
1/26	4,000		
1/31		6,000	4,800
	$12,000	$15,000	$12,000

Cost of completed job
  Direct materials $ 12,000
  Direct labor   15,000
  Manufacturing overhead   12,000
Total cost $ 39,000
Unit cost ($39,000 ÷ 1,000) $ 39.00

When a job is finished, an entry is made to transfer its total cost to finished goods inventory. The entry for Wallace Manufacturing is:

(7)

Jan. 31	Finished Goods Inventory	39,000	
	Work in Process Inventory		39,000
	(To record completion of Job No. 101)		

Finished Goods Inventory is a control account that controls individual finished goods records in a finished goods subsidiary ledger. The records are similar to the perpetual inventory records illustrated in Chapter 9. Postings to the receipts columns are made directly from completed job cost sheets. The finished goods inventory record for Job No. 101 is shown below in Illustration 22-13.

ILLUSTRATION 22-13

Finished goods record

Item: Magnetic Sensors									Job No: 101	
	Receipts			Issues			Balance			
Date	Units	Cost	Total	Units	Cost	Total	Units	Cost	Total
1/31	1,000	$39	$39,000				1,000	$39	$39,000
2/2				1000	$39	$39,000			–0–

Assigning Costs to Cost of Goods Sold

Recognition of the cost of goods sold is made when each sale occurs. The cost of goods sold is obtained from the individual finished goods inventory records. For example, if Wallace Manufacturing sells Job No. 101 for $50,000, on account on February 2, the entries are:

(8)

Feb. 2	Accounts Receivable	50,000	
	Sales		50,000
	(To record sale of Job No. 101)		
2	Cost of Goods Sold	39,000	
	Finished Goods Inventory		39,000
	(To record cost of Job No. 101)		

The units sold, the cost per unit, and the total cost of goods sold for each job sold are recorded in the issues section of the finished goods record as shown in Illustration 22-13.

Summary of Job Order Cost Flows

A completed flow chart for a job order cost accounting system is shown in Illustration 22-14. All postings are keyed to entries 1–8 in Wallace Manufacturing Company's accounts presented in the cost flow graphic in Illustration 22-1. The graphic also provides a summary of the inventory control accounts, subsidiary ledgers, and source documents for assigning costs to jobs.

ILLUSTRATION 22-14

Job order cost system—flow of costs and documents

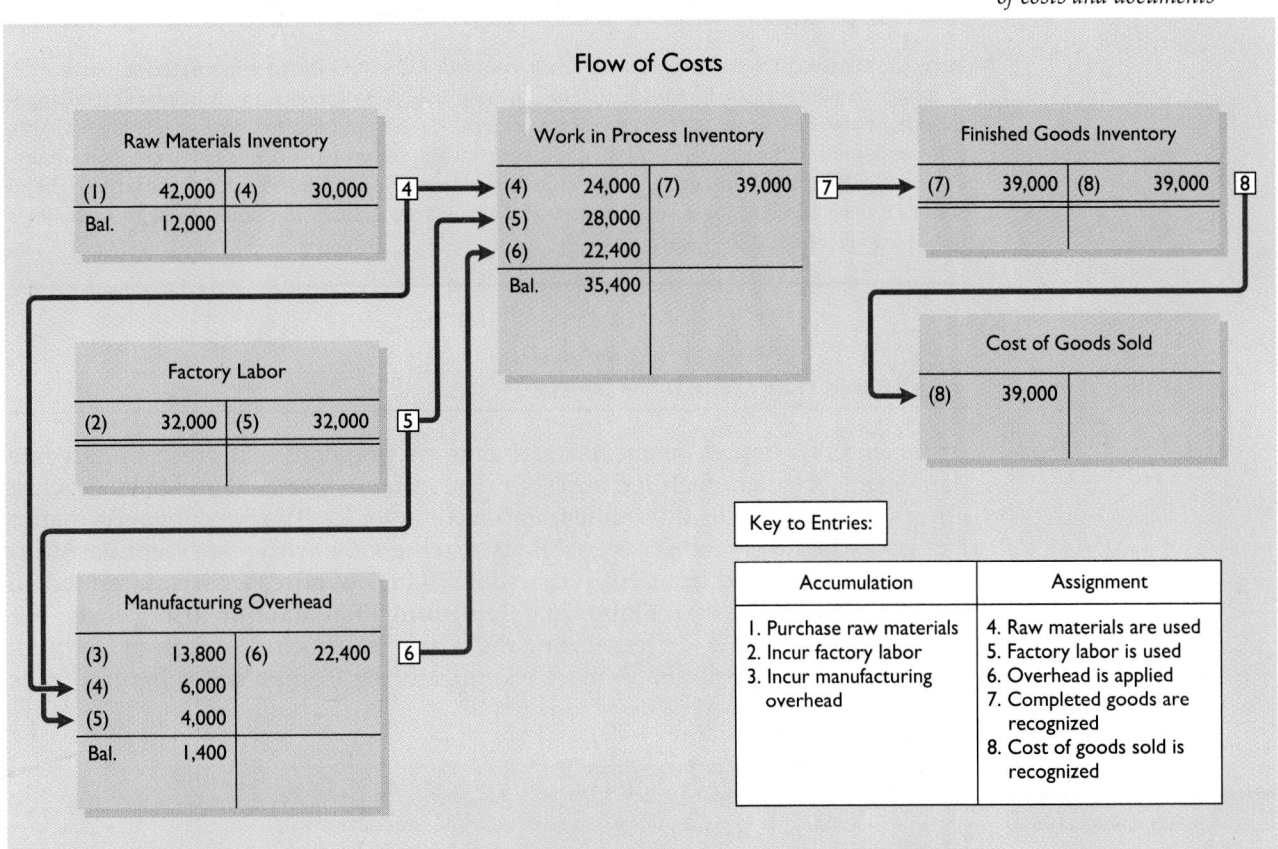

Flow of Costs

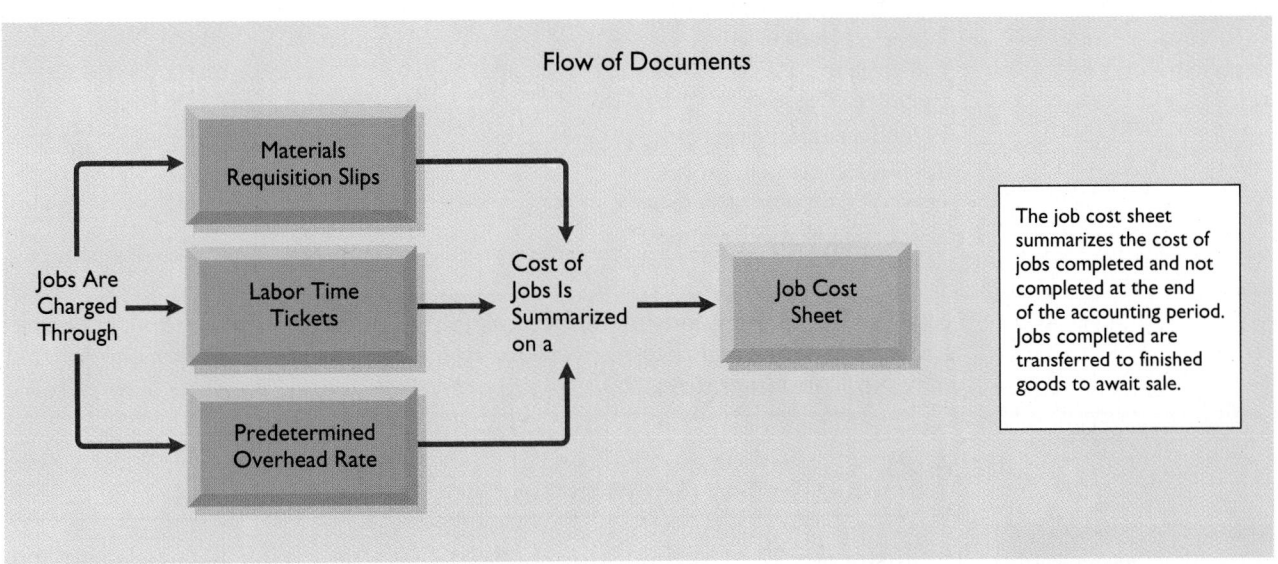

Flow of Documents

Technology in Action

Many job order cost systems are run by small manufacturers. And with the increased sophistication of micro computers, small manufacturers can now use them for extremely sophisticated applications. They can now use micros to perform (1) computer-aided manufacturing (CAM), (2) computer-aided testing (CAT), (3) computer-aided design (CAD), (4) electronic data interchange (EDI), and (5) materials requirement planning (MRP). As a result of breakthroughs in software development, for a small investment, manufacturers can use software with capabilities only dreamed about a few years ago.

Reporting Job Cost Data

At the end of a period, financial statements are prepared that present aggregate data on all jobs manufactured and sold. The income statement and balance sheet effects are the same as those illustrated in Chapter 21. The cost of goods manufactured schedule in job order costing is also the same with one exception. **Manufacturing overhead applied, rather than actual overhead costs, is added to direct materials and direct labor in determining total manufacturing costs.** The schedule is prepared directly from the Work in Process Inventory account. A condensed schedule for Wallace Manufacturing Company for January is as follows:

ILLUSTRATION 22-15

Cost of goods manufactured schedule

WALLACE MANUFACTURING COMPANY		
Cost of Goods Manufactured Schedule		
For the Month Ended January 31, 1993		
Work in process, January 1		$ –0–
Direct materials used	$24,000	
Direct labor	28,000	
Manufacturing overhead applied	22,400	
Total manufacturing costs		74,400
Total cost of work in process		74,400
Less: Work in process, January 31		35,400
Cost of goods manufactured		$39,000

Note that the cost of goods manufactured ($39,000) agrees with the amount transferred from Work in Process Inventory to Finished Goods Inventory in journal entry No. 7 in Illustration 22-14.

Under- or Overapplied Manufacturing Overhead

Study Objective 6

Distinguish between under- and overapplied manufacturing overhead.

In Illustration 22-14, Manufacturing Overhead has a debit balance of $1,400. When Manufacturing Overhead has a debit balance at the end of the month, overhead is said to be underapplied. Underapplied overhead means that the overhead assigned to work in process is less than the overhead incurred. Conversely, when manufacturing overhead has a credit balance at the end of the month, overhead is overapplied. Overapplied overhead means that the overhead assigned to work in process is greater than the overhead incurred.

The existence of under- or overapplied overhead at the end of a month usually does not require corrective action by management. If the result is attributable to normal fluctuations in costs and production, no corrective action may even be possible. In Wallace Manufacturing, the predetermined overhead rate was based on expected annual overhead costs of $280,000 and annual direct labor costs of $350,000. This does not mean that each month will have one-twelfth of both factors. For example, $48,000 of utility costs may be anticipated for the year, but variations in heating and air-conditioning costs are expected to produce higher utility costs in the winter and summer months and smaller utility costs in the spring and fall months. Thus, the January costs of $4,800 may be offset by May costs of $3,200. Similarly, January direct labor cost of $28,000, which is slightly below the average monthly cost ($29,167), may be offset by direct labor costs in other months of $30,000 or more. In sum, the existence of under- or overapplied overhead at the end of a month is often expected. It is also anticipated that monthly differences between actual and applied overhead will be offsetting over the course of the year.

When monthly financial statements are prepared, under- or overapplied overhead is reported on the balance sheet. **Underapplied overhead is shown as a prepaid expense in the current asset section. Overapplied overhead is reported as unearned revenue in the current liability section.**

At the end of the year, any balance in Manufacturing Overhead should be eliminated through an adjusting entry. Generally, under- or overapplied overhead is considered to be an adjustment of cost of goods sold. Thus, underapplied overhead is debited to Cost of Goods Sold, and overapplied overhead is credited to Cost of Goods Sold. To illustrate the adjusting entry, assume that Wallace Manufacturing has underapplied overhead of $900 on December 31. The adjusting entry is:

Dec. 31	Cost of Goods Sold	900	
	Manufacturing Overhead		900
	(To transfer underapplied overhead to cost of goods sold)		

Conceptually, it can be argued that under- or overapplied overhead at the end of the year should be allocated among ending work in process, finished goods, and cost of goods sold. However, most companies feel that the increased accuracy resulting from this allocation is not worth the cost and effort. The bulk of this amount will be allocated to cost of goods sold anyway. The reason is that

Helpful hint True or false. Underapplied overhead is reported as a current liability in an interim balance sheet. Answer: False, it is reported as a current asset.

Accounting in Action · *Business Insight*

Overhead also applies in nonmanufacturing companies. The State of Michigan found that auto dealers were charging documentary and service fees ranging from $18 to $445 per automobile and inspection fees from $88 to $360. These fees often were charged auto buyers after a base price had been negotiated. The Attorney General of the State of Michigan ruled that auto dealers cannot charge customers additional fees for routine overhead costs. The attorney general said: "Overhead is part of the sales price of a motor vehicle. Processing paper work, dealer incurred costs, and inspection fees to qualify cars for extended warranty plans are ordinary overhead expenses."

Source: The Ann Arbor News, July 18, 1989.

by the end of the year, most manufacturing costs will flow through work in process and finished goods to cost of goods sold. In addition, the amount of under- or overapplied overhead is often small.

Before You Go On . . .

1. When are entries made to record the completion and sale of a job?

2. What costs are included in total manufacturing costs in the cost of goods manufactured schedule?

3. How is under- or overapplied manufacturing overhead reported in monthly financial statements?

Summary of Study Objectives

1. *Explain the characteristics and purposes of cost accounting.* Cost accounting involves the procedures for measuring, recording, and reporting product costs. From the data accumulated, the total cost and the unit cost of each product is determined.

2. *Describe the flow of costs in a job order cost accounting system.* In job order cost accounting, manufacturing costs are first accumulated in three accounts: Raw Materials Inventory, Factory Labor, and Manufacturing Overhead. The accumulated costs are then assigned to Work in Process Inventory and eventually to Finished Goods Inventory and Cost of Goods Sold.

3. *Explain the nature and importance of a job cost sheet.* A job cost sheet is a form used to record the costs chargeable to a specific job and to determine the total and unit cost of the completed job. Job cost sheets constitute the subsidiary ledger for the Work in Process Inventory control account.

4. *Indicate how the predetermined overhead rate is determined and used.* The predetermined overhead rate is based on the relationship between estimated annual overhead costs and expected annual operating capacity expressed in terms of a common activity base, such as direct labor cost. The rate is used in assigning overhead costs to work in process and to specific jobs.

5. *Prepare entries for jobs completed and sold.* When jobs are completed, the cost is debited to Finished Goods Inventory and credited to Work in Process Inventory. When a job is sold the entries are: (a) Debit Cash or Accounts Receivable and credit Sales for the selling price and (b) Debit Cost of Goods Sold and credit Finished Goods Inventory for the cost of the goods.

6. *Distinguish between under- and overapplied manufacturing overhead.* Underapplied manufacturing overhead means that the overhead assigned to work in process is less than the overhead incurred. Conversely, overapplied overhead means that the overhead assigned to work in process is greater than the overhead incurred.

GLOSSARY

Cost accounting · An area of accounting that involves the measuring, recording, and reporting of product costs. (p. 894).

Cost accounting system · Manufacturing cost accounts that are fully integrated into the general ledger of a company. (p. 894).

Job cost sheet · A form used to record the costs chargeable to a job and to determine the total and unit cost of the completed job. (p. 898).

Job order cost system · A cost accounting system in which costs are assigned to each job or batch. (p. 895).

Materials requisition slip · A document authorizing the issuance of raw materials from the storeroom to manufacturing. (p. 899).

Overapplied overhead · A situation in which overhead assigned to work in process is greater than the overhead incurred. (p. 908).

Predetermined overhead rate · A rate based on the relationship between estimated annual overhead costs and expected annual operating activity, expressed in terms of a common activity base. (p. 903).

Process cost system · A system of accounting used by companies that manufacture relatively homogeneous products through a series of continuous processes or operations. (p. 895).

Underapplied overhead · A situation in which overhead assigned to work in process is less than the overhead incurred. (p. 908).

DEMONSTRATION PROBLEM

During February, Cardella Manufacturing works on two jobs: Numbers A16 and B17. Summary data concerning these jobs are as follows:

Manufacturing Costs Incurred:

Purchased $54,000 of raw materials on account.
Factory labor $76,000 plus $4,000 employer payroll taxes.
Manufacturing overhead exclusive of indirect materials and indirect labor $59,800.

Assignment of Costs:

Direct materials:	Job A16 $27,000, Job B17 $21,000
Indirect materials:	$3,000
Direct labor:	Job A16 $52,000, Job B17 $26,000
Indirect labor:	$2,000

Manufacturing overhead rate 80% of direct labor costs.

Job A16 was completed and sold on account for $150,000. Job B17 was only partially completed.

Instructions

(a) Journalize the February transactions in the sequence followed in the chapter.

(b) What was the amount of under- or overapplied manufacturing overhead?

Solution to Demonstration Problem

(a)

1.

Feb. 28	Raw Materials Inventory	54,000	
	Accounts Payable		54,000
	(Purchase of raw materials on account)		

2.

28	Factory Labor	80,000	
	Factory Wages Payable		76,000
	Employer Payroll Taxes Payable		4,000
	(To record factory labor costs)		

3.

28	Manufacturing Overhead	59,800	
	Accounts Payable, Accumulated Depreciation, and Prepaid Insurance		59,800
	(To record overhead costs)		

Helpful hints

1. In accumulating costs, three accounts are debited: Raw Materials Inventory, Factory Labor, and Manufacturing Overhead.
2. When Work in Process Inventory is debited, one of the three accounts in (1) must be credited.
3. Finished Goods Inventory is debited for the cost of completed jobs, and Cost of Goods Sold is debited for the cost of jobs sold.
4. Overhead is underapplied when Manufacturing Overhead has a debit balance.

4.

28	Work in Process Inventory	48,000	
	Manufacturing Overhead	3,000	
	Raw Materials Inventory		51,000
	(To assign raw materials to production)		

5.

28	Work in Process Inventory	78,000	
	Manufacturing Overhead	2,000	
	Factory Labor		80,000
	(To assign factory labor to production)		

6.

28	Work in Process Inventory	62,400	
	Manufacturing Overhead		62,400
	(To assign overhead to jobs)		

7.

28	Finished Goods Inventory	120,600	
	Work in Process Inventory		120,600
	(To record completion of Job A16: direct		
	materials, $27,000, direct labor $52,000 and		
	manufacturing overhead $41,600)		

8.

28	Accounts Receivable	150,000	
	Cost of Goods Sold	120,600	
	Sales		150,000
	Finished Goods Inventory		120,600
	(To record sale of Job A16)		

(b) Manufacturing Overhead has a debit balance of $2,400 as shown below:

Manufacturing Overhead

(3)	59,800	(6)	62,400
(4)	3,000		
(5)	2,000		
Bal.	2,400		

Thus, manufacturing overhead is underapplied for the month.

SELF-STUDY QUESTIONS

Answers are at the end of the chapter.

(S.O. 1) 1. Cost accounting involves the measuring, recording, and reporting of:
    a. future costs.
    b. product costs.
    c. manufacturing processes.
    d. managerial accounting decisions.

(S.O. 2) 2. In accumulating raw materials costs, the cost of raw materials purchased in a perpetual system is debited to:
    a. Raw Materials Inventory.
    b. Raw Material Purchases.
    c. Purchases
    d. Work in Process.

3. When incurred, factory labor costs are debited to: (S.O. 2)
    a. Work in Process.
    b. Factory Wages Expense.
    c. Factory Wages Payable.
    d. Factory Labor.

4. The source documents for assigning costs to job cost sheets are: (S.O. 3)
    a. invoices, time tickets, and the predetermined overhead rate.
    b. materials requisition slips, time tickets, and the predetermined overhead rate.
    c. materials requisition slips, payroll reg-

ister, and the predetermined overhead rate.

d. materials requisition slips, time tickets, and the actual overhead costs.

(S.O. 3) 5. In recording the issuance of raw materials in a job order cost system, it would be *incorrect* to:
a. debit Work in Process Inventory.
b. debit Manufacturing Overhead.
c. debit Finished Goods Inventory.
d. credit Raw Materials Inventory.

(S.O. 3) 6. The entry when direct factory labor is assigned to jobs is a debit to:
a. Factory Labor and a credit to Manufacturing Overhead.
b. Manufacturing Overhead and a credit to Factory Labor.
c. Work in Process Inventory and a credit to Factory Labor.
d. Factory Labor and a credit to Work in Process Inventory.

(S.O. 4) 7. The formula for computing the predetermined manufacturing overhead rate is estimated annual overhead costs divided by an expected annual operating activity, expressed as:
a. direct labor cost.
b. direct labor hours.
c. machine hours.
d. any of the above.

(S.O. 4) 8. In the Cleo Company, the predetermined overhead rate is 80% of direct labor cost.

During the month, $180,000 of factory labor costs are incurred, of which $150,000 is direct labor and $30,000 is indirect labor. Actual overhead incurred was $145,000. The amount of overhead debited to Work in Process Inventory should be:
a. $120,000.
b. $144,000.
c. $145,000.
d. $150,000.

(S.O. 5) 9. In BAC Company, Job No. 26 is completed at a cost of $4,500 and later sold for $7,000 cash. A correct entry is:
a. Debit Finished Goods Inventory $7,000 and credit Work in Process Inventory $7,000.
b. Debit Cost of Goods Sold $7,000 and credit Finished Goods Inventory $7,000.
c. Debit Accounts Receivable $7,000 and credit Sales $7,000.
d. Debit Finished Goods Inventory $4,500 and credit Work in Process Inventory $4,500.

(S.O. 6) 10. In preparing monthly financial statements, underapplied overhead is reported in the balance sheet as a(an):
a. prepaid expense.
b. unearned revenue.
c. noncurrent asset.
d. noncurrent liability.

QUESTIONS

1. How may job cost data be used by management?

2. Distinguish between cost accounting and a cost accounting system.

3. Distinguish between the two principal types of cost accounting systems.

4. What type of industry is likely to use a job order cost system? Give some examples.

5. What type of industry is likely to use a process cost system? Give some examples.

6. Describe the major steps in the flow of costs in a job order cost accounting system.

7. There are three inventory control accounts in a job order system. Identify the control accounts and their subsidiary ledgers.

8. What source documents are used in accumulating direct labor costs?

9. Entries to manufacturing overhead normally are only made daily. Do you agree? Explain.

10. Edie Monay is confused about the source documents used in assigning materials and labor costs. Identify the documents and give the entry for each document.

11. What is the purpose of a job cost sheet?

12. Indicate the source documents that are used in charging costs to specific jobs.

13. Differentiate between a "materials inventory record" and a "materials requisition slip" as used in a job order cost system.

14. Paul Abdul believes actual manufacturing overhead should be charged to jobs. Do you agree? Why or why not?

15. What relationships are involved in computing a predetermined overhead rate?

16. How can the agreement of Work in Process Inventory and job cost sheets be verified?

17. Jan Jerome believes that the cost of goods manufactured schedule in job order cost accounting is the same as in manufacturing accounting. Is Jan correct? Explain.

18. Rob Palmer is confused about under- and overapplied manufacturing overhead. Define the terms for Rob and indicate the balance in the manufacturing overhead account applicable to each term.

19. Under- or overapplied overhead is reported in the income statement when monthly financial statements are prepared. Do you agree? If not, indicate the proper presentation.

20. At the end of the year, under- or overapplied overhead is closed to Income Summary. Is this correct? If not, indicate the customary treatment of this account.

BRIEF EXERCISES

Prepare a flowchart of a job order cost accounting system, and identify transactions. (S.O. 2)

BE22–1 Precision Tool & Die begins operations on January 1. Because all work is done to customer specifications, the company decides to use a job cost accounting system. Prepare a flow chart of a typical job order system with arrows showing the flow of costs. Identify the eight transactions.

Prepare entries in accumulating manufacturing costs. (S.O. 2)

BE22–2 During the first month of operations, Precision Tool & Die accumulated the following manufacturing costs: raw materials $6,000 on account, factory labor $4,000 of which $3,500 relates to factory wages payable and $500 relates to payroll taxes payable, and utilities payable $2,000. Prepare separate journal entries for each type of manufacturing cost.

Prepare entry for the assignment of raw materials costs. (S.O. 2)

BE22–3 In January, Precision Tool & Die requisitions raw materials for production as follows: Job 1 $1,000, Job 2 $1,200, Job 3 $1,500, and general factory use $400. Prepare a summary journal entry to record raw materials used.

Prepare entry for the assignment of factory labor costs. (S.O. 2)

BE22–4 Factory labor data for Precision Tool & Die is given in BE22–2. During January, time tickets show that the factory labor of $4,000 was used as follows: Job 1 $1,200, Job 2 $1,400. Job 3 $900 and general factory use $500. Prepare a summary journal entry to record factory labor used.

Prepare job cost sheets. (S.O. 3)

BE22–5 Data pertaining to job cost sheets for Precision Tool & Die are given in BE22–3 and BE22–4. Prepare the job cost sheets for each of the three jobs. (Note: You may omit the column for Manufacturing Overhead.)

Compute predetermined overhead rates. (S.O. 4)

BE22–6 The Flora Company estimates that annual manufacturing overhead costs will be $400,000. Estimated annual operating activity bases are: direct labor cost $500,000, direct labor hours 50,000, and machine hours 80,000. Compute the predetermined overhead rate for each activity base.

Assign manufacturing overhead to production. (S.O. 4)

BE22–7 During the first quarter, Flora Company incurs the following direct labor costs: January $40,000, February $35,000, and March $50,000. For each month, prepare the entry to assign overhead to production using a predetermined rate of 80% of direct labor cost.

Prepare entries for completion and sale of completed jobs. (S.O. 5)

BE22–8 In March, Petko Company completes Jobs 10 and 11 costing $25,000 and $32,000, respectively. On March 31, Job 10 is sold to the customer for $40,000 in cash. Journalize the entries for the completion of the two jobs and the sale of Job 10.

Indicate statement classification of under- or overapplied overhead. (S.O. 6)

BE22–9 On September 30, balances in Manufacturing Overhead are: Flora Company—Debit $2,400, Petko Company—Credit $3,000. Indicate how each company should report its balance at September 30, assuming each company prepares annual financial statements on December 31.

BE22–10 At December 31, balances in Manufacturing Overhead are: Flora Company—Debit $1,800, Petko Company—Credit $1,200. Prepare the adjusting entry for each company at December 31, assuming the adjustment is made to cost of goods sold.

Prepare adjusting entries for under- and overapplied overhead.
(S.O. 6)

EXERCISES

E22–1 The gross earnings of the factory workers for the Pavar Company during the month of January is $96,000. The employer's payroll taxes for the factory payroll is $9,000 and the fringe benefits to be paid by the employer on this payroll is $4,000. Of the total accumulated cost of factory labor, 90% is related to direct labor and 10% is attributable to indirect labor.

Prepare entries for factory labor.
(S.O. 2)

Instructions

(a) Prepare the entry to record the factory labor costs for the month of January.

(b) Prepare the entry to assign factory labor to production.

E22–2 Mears Manufacturing uses a job order cost accounting system. On May 1, the company has a balance in Work in Process Inventory of $3,200 and two jobs in process: Job No. 429 $2,000, and Job No. 430 $1,200. During May, a summary of source documents reveals the following:

Prepare journal entries for manufacturing costs.
(S.O. 2, 3, 4, 5)

For	Materials Requisition Slips	Labor Time Tickets
Job No. 429	$2,500	$ 2,400
Job No. 430	2,000	3,000
Job No. 431	4,500	7,600
General Use	800	1,200
	$9,800	$14,200

Mears Manufacturing applies manufacturing overhead to jobs at an overhead rate of 80% of direct labor cost. Job No. 429 is completed during the month.

Instructions

(a) Prepare summary journal entries to record the requisition slips, time tickets, the assignment of manufacturing overhead to jobs, and the completion of Job No. 429.

(b) Post the entries to Work in Process Inventory and prove the agreement of the control account with the job cost sheets.

E22–3 A job order cost sheet for the Linx Company is shown below.

Analyze a job cost sheet and prepare entries for manufacturing costs.
(S.O. 2, 3, 4, 5)

Job No. 92			For 2,000 Units
Date	Direct Materials	Direct Labor	Manufacturing Overhead
1/ 1	5,000	6,000	4,500
8	6,000		
12		8,000	6,400
25	2,000		
27		4,000	3,200
	13,000	18,000	14,100

Cost of completed job:	
Direct materials	$13,000
Direct labor	18,000
Manufacturing overhead	14,100
Total cost	$45,100
Unit cost ($45,100 ÷ 2,000)	$22.55

Instructions

(a) On the basis of the foregoing data answer the following questions:

(1) What was the balance in Work in Process Inventory on January 1 if this was the only unfinished job?

(2) If manufacturing overhead is applied on the basis of direct labor cost, what overhead rate was used in each year?

(b) Prepare summary entries at January 31 to record the current year's transactions pertaining to Job No. 92.

Analyze costs of manufacturing and determine missing amounts.
(S.O. 2, 5)

E22–4   Manufacturing cost data for Cinder Company, which uses a job order cost system, are presented below:

	Case A	Case B	Case C
Direct materials	(a)	$83,000	$ 65,000
Direct labor used	$ 50,000	96,000	(h)
Manufacturing overhead applied	42,500	(d)	(i)
Total manufacturing costs	180,650	(e)	250,000
Work in process 1/1/93	(b)	15,500	12,000
Total cost of work in process	201,500	(f)	(j)
Work in process 12/31/93	(c)	11,800	(k)
Cost of goods manufactured	192,300	(g)	262,000

Instructions

Indicate the missing amount for each letter. Assume that in all cases manufacturing overhead is applied on the basis of direct labor cost and the rate is the same.

Compute the manufacturing overhead rate and the amount of under- or over-applied overhead.
(S.O. 4, 6)

E22–5   The Leppart Company applies manufacturing overhead to jobs on the basis of machine hours used. Overhead costs are expected to total $300,000 for the year, and machine usage is estimated at 125,000 hours.

In January, $26,000 of overhead costs are incurred and 10,000 machine hours are used. For the remainder of the year, $284,000 of overhead costs are incurred and 120,000 machine hours are worked.

Instructions

(a) Compute the manufacturing overhead rate for the year.

(b) What is the amount of under- or overapplied overhead at January 31? How should this amount be reported in the financial statements prepared on January 31?

(c) What is the amount of under- or overapplied overhead at December 31?

(d) Assuming the under- or overapplied overhead for the year is not allocated to inventory accounts, prepare the adjusting entry to assign the amount to cost of goods sold.

Analyze job cost sheet and prepare entry for completed job.
(S.O. 2, 3, 4, 5)

E22–6   A job cost sheet of the Wing Company is given below:

Job Cost Sheet

JOB NO.   469   Quantity   2,000

ITEM   White Lion Cages   Date Requested   7/2

FOR   Tesla Company   Date Completed   7/31

Date	Direct Materials	Direct Labor	Manufacturing Overhead
7/10	700		
12	900		
15		440	550
22		360	450
24	1,600		
27	1,500		
31		540	675

Cost of completed job:

   Direct materials _____

   Direct labor _____

   Manufacturing overhead _____

Total cost _____

Unit cost _____

Instructions

(a) Answer the following questions:
 (1) What are the source documents for direct materials, direct labor, and manufacturing overhead costs assigned to this job?
 (2) What is the predetermined manufacturing overhead rate?
 (3) What is the total cost and unit cost of the completed job?

(b) Prepare the entry to record the completion of the job.

E22–7 Anna Schmitt Corporation incurred the following transactions.

Prepare entries for manufacturing costs.
(S.O. 2, 4, 5)

 1. Purchased raw materials on account, $45,900.
 2. Raw Materials of $36,000 were requisitioned to the factory. An analysis of the materials requisition slips indicated that $8,800 was classified as indirect materials.
 3. Factory labor costs incurred were $64,900 of which $59,000 pertained to factory wages payable and $5,900 pertained to employer payroll taxes payable.
 4. Time tickets indicated that $60,000 was direct labor and $4,900 was indirect labor.
 5. Overhead costs incurred on account were $80,500.
 6. Manufacturing overhead was applied at the rate of 160% of direct labor cost.
 7. Goods costing $87,000 were completed and transferred to finished goods.
 8. Finished goods costing $68,000 to manufacture were sold on account for $103,000.

Instructions
Journalize the transactions. (Omit explanations.)

E22–8 Richy's Printing Corp. uses a job order cost system. The following data summarize the operations related to the first quarter's production:

Prepare entries for manufacturing costs.
(S.O. 2, 3, 4, 5)

 1. Materials purchased on account $172,000 and factory wages incurred, $87,300.
 2. Materials requisitioned and factory labor used by job:

	Materials	Factory Labor
Job A20	$ 32,240	$18,000
Job A21	40,920	26,000
Job A22	36,100	15,000
Job A23	39,270	25,000
General factory use	4,470	3,300
	$153,000	$87,300

 3. Manufacturing overhead costs incurred on account, $39,750.
 4. Depreciation on machinery and equipment, $14,550.
 5. Manufacturing overhead rate is 80% of direct labor cost.
 6. Job completed during the quarter: A20, A21, and A23.

Instructions
Prepare entries to record the operations summarized above. (Prepare a schedule showing the individual cost elements and total cost for each job in item 6.)

E22–9 At May 31, the accounts of Bayberry Manufacturing Company show the following:

Prepare a cost of goods manufactured schedule and partial financial statements.
(S.O. 2, 5)

 1. May 1 inventories—finished goods $12,600, work in process $14,700, and raw materials $8,200.
 2. May 31 inventories—finished goods $8,500, work in process $16,900, and raw materials, $7,100.
 3. Debit postings to work in process were: direct materials $72,400, direct labor $32,000, and manufacturing overhead applied $64,000.
 4. Sales totaled $200,000.

Instructions

(a) Prepare a condensed cost of goods manufactured schedule.
(b) Prepare an income statement for May through gross profit.
(c) Indicate the balance sheet presentation of the manufacturing inventories at May 31, 1993.

Compute work in process and finished goods from job cost sheets.
(S.O. 3, 5)

E22–10 The Strock Company begins operations on April 1. Information from job cost sheets shows the following:

Job Number	Manufacturing Costs Assigned		
	April	May	June
10	$5,200	$4,400	
11	3,100	3,900	$3,000
12	1,200		
13		4,700	4,500
14		2,900	3,500

Job 12 was completed in April. Job 10 was completed in May, and Jobs 11 and 13 were completed in June. Each job was sold for 50% above its cost in the month following completion.

Instructions
Answer the following questions:

1. What is the balance in Work in Process Inventory at the end of each month?
2. What is the balance in Finished Goods Inventory at the end of each month?
3. What is the gross profit for May, June, and July?

PROBLEMS

Prepare entries in a job cost system and job cost sheets.
(S.O. 2, 3, 4, 5)

P22–1 Vanessa Manufacturing uses a job order cost accounting system. On January 1, the company had Raw Materials Inventory $15,000 and Finished Goods Inventory, represented by Job No. 12, $124,000. During the month, the following summary transactions and events occurred.

1. Purchased raw materials on account $225,000.
2. Incurred factory labor $300,000 of which $276,000 relates to factory wages payable and the balance (or $24,000) pertains to employer payroll taxes payable.
3. Incurred manufacturing overhead on account $260,000.
4. Recognized $9,000 of depreciation on factory machinery.
5. Charged direct materials to jobs: No. 13 $110,000 and No. 14 $70,000, and charged indirect materials of $50,000 to manufacturing overhead. The jobs call for the production of 20,000 and 10,000 units, respectively.
6. Charged factory labor to jobs on basis of time tickets: No. 13 $180,000 and No. 14 $100,000. The remaining labor was indirect.
7. Charged overhead to jobs at the rate of 120% of direct labor cost.
8. Completed Job No. 13.
9. Sold Job No. 12 on account for $180,000.

Instructions
(a) Journalize the transactions and events.

(b) Open accounts for the beginning inventories and post the entries to the job order cost accounts and to the job cost sheets for Jobs 13 and 14.

(c) Reconcile the balance in Work in Process Inventory with the costs of unfinished jobs.

Prepare entries in a job cost system and partial income statement.
(S.O. 2, 3, 4, 5, 6)

P22–2 For the year ended December 31, 1993, the job cost sheets of the Jan Robins Company contained the following data.

Job Number	Explanation	Direct Materials	Direct Labor	Manufacturing Overhead	Total Costs
7650	Balance 1/1	$18,000	$20,000	$25,000	$ 63,000
	Current year's costs	22,000	30,000	37,500	89,500
7651	Balance 1/1	12,000	18,000	22,500	52,500
	Current year's costs	28,000	40,000	50,000	118,000
7652	Current year's costs	40,000	54,000	67,500	161,500

Other data:

1. Raw materials inventory totaled $20,000 on January 1. During the year, $100,000 of raw materials were purchased on account.

2. Finished goods on January 1 consisted of Job No. 7648 for $98,000 and Job No. 7649 for $62,000.

3. Job No. 7650 and Job No. 7651 were completed during the year.

4. Job Nos. 7648, 7649, and 7650 were sold on account for $380,000.

5. Manufacturing overhead incurred on account totaled $115,000.

6. Other manufacturing overhead consisted of indirect materials $12,000, indirect labor $18,000, and depreciation on factory machinery $6,000.

Instructions

(a) Journalize the transactions in the sequence followed in the chapter. Credit Factory Wages Payable when recording factory labor.

(b) Prove the agreement of Work in Process Inventory with job cost sheets pertaining to unfinished work.

(c) Prepare the adjusting entry for manufacturing overhead, assuming the balance is allocated entirely to cost of goods sold.

(d) Prepare an income statement for the year through gross profit. (Hint: Show cost of goods sold as one line.)

P22–3 Gene Simons is a contractor specializing in custom-built jacuzzis. On May 1, 1993, his ledger contains the following data:

Prepare entries in a job cost system and cost of goods manufactured schedule.

(S.O. 2, 3, 4, 5)

Raw Materials Inventory	$30,000
Work in Process Inventory	12,200
Manufacturing Overhead	2,500 (dr.)

The Manufacturing Overhead account has debit totals of $12,500 and credit totals of $10,000. Subsidiary data for Work in Process Inventory on May 1 include:

Job Cost Sheets

Job By Customer	Direct Materials	Direct Labor	Manufacturing Overhead
Jovi	$2,500	$2,000	$1,400
Roth	2,000	1,200	840
Nicks	900	800	560
	$5,400	$4,000	$2,800

A summary of materials requisition slips and time tickets for the month of May reveals the following:

Job by Customer	Materials Requisition Slips	Time Tickets
Jovi	$ 500	$ 400
Roth	600	1,000
Nicks	2,300	1,300
Jett	2,400	2,900
	5,800	5,600
General Use	1,500	2,600
	$7,300	$8,200

During May the following costs were incurred: (a) raw materials purchased on account, $5,000, (b) labor paid, $8,200, (c) manufacturing overhead paid $1,400. Overhead was charged to jobs on the basis of direct labor cost at the same rate as in the previous month.

The jacuzzis for customers Jovi, Roth, and Nicks were completed during May. Each jacuzzi was sold for $12,000 cash.

Instructions

(a) Prepare journal entries for the May transactions.

(b) Post the entries to Work in Process Inventory.

(c) Reconcile the balance in Work in Process Inventory with the costs of unfinished jobs.

(d) Prepare a cost of goods manufactured schedule for May.

Compute predetermined overhead rates, apply overhead, and indicate statement presentation of under- or overapplied overhead.
(S.O. 4, 6)

P22–4 Holbrock Company uses a job order cost system in each of its three manufacturing departments. Manufacturing overhead is applied to jobs on the basis of direct labor cost in Department A, direct labor hours in Department B, and machine hours in Department C.

In establishing the predetermined overhead rates for 1993 the following estimates were made for the year:

	Department		
	A	B	C
Manufacturing overhead	$900,000	$800,000	$750,000
Direct labor cost	$600,000	$100,000	$600,000
Direct labor hours	50,000	40,000	50,000
Machine hours	100,000	120,000	150,000

During January the job cost sheets showed the following costs and production data:

	Department		
	A	B	C
Direct materials used	$92,000	$86,000	$64,000
Direct labor cost	$48,000	$35,000	$50,400
Manufacturing overhead incurred	$75,000	$67,000	$64,500
Direct labor hours	4,000	3,500	4,200
Machine hours	8,000	10,500	12,600

Instructions

(a) Compute the predetermined overhead rate for each department.

(b) Compute the total manufacturing cost assigned to jobs in January in each department.

(c) Compute the under- or overapplied overhead for each department at January 31.

(d) Indicate the statement presentation of the under- or overapplied overhead at January 31.

(e) If the amount in (d) was the same at December 31, how would it be reported in the year end financial statements?

Analyze manufacturing cost accounts and determine missing amounts.
(S.O. 2, 3, 4, 5, 6)

P22–5 Tiffany Company's fiscal year ends on June 30. The following accounts are found in its job order cost accounting system for the first month of the new fiscal year.

Raw Materials Inventory

July 1	Beginning balance	19,000	July 31	Requisitions	(A)
31	Purchases	88,400			
July 31	Ending balance	(B)			

Work in Process Inventory

July 1	Beginning balance	(C)	July 31	Jobs completed	(F)
31	Direct materials	72,000			
31	Direct labor	(D)			
31	Overhead	(E)			
July 31	Ending balance	(G)			

Finished Goods Inventory

July 1	Beginning balance	(H)	July 31	Cost of goods sold	(J)
31	Completed jobs	(I)			
July 31	Ending balance	(K)			

Factory Labor

July 31	Factory wages	(L)	July 31	Wages assigned	(M)

Manufacturing Overhead

July 31	Indirect materials	8,900	July 31	Overhead applied	97,500
31	Indirect labor	16,000			
31	Other overhead	(N)			

Other data:

1. On July 1, two jobs were in process: Job No. 4085 and Job No. 4086 with costs of $17,000 and $8,200, respectively.

2. During July, Job Nos. 4087, 4088, and 4089, were started. On July 31, only Job No. 4089 was unfinished. This job had charges for direct materials $2,000, direct labor $1,500 plus manufacturing overhead.

3. On July 1, Job No. 4084, costing $135,000, was in the finished goods warehouse. On July 31, Job No. 4088, costing $143,000, was in finished goods.

4. Manufacturing overhead was applied at the rate of 130% of direct labor cost. Overhead was $2,000 underapplied in July.

Instructions

List the letters A through N and indicate the amount pertaining to each letter. Show computations.

ALTERNATE PROBLEMS

P22–1A Carlis Manufacturing uses a job order cost accounting system. On January 1, the company had Raw Materials Inventory $10,000 and Finished Goods Inventory, represented by Job No. 18, $135,000. During the month, the following summary transactions and events occurred.

Prepare entries in a job cost system and job cost sheets.
(S.O. 2, 3, 4, 5)

1. Purchased raw materials on account $270,000.

2. Incurred factory labor $340,000 of which $302,000 relates to factory wages payable and the balance (or $38,000) pertains to employer payroll taxes payable.

3. Incurred manufacturing overhead on account $350,000.

4. Recognized $10,000 of depreciation on factory machinery.

5. Charged direct materials to jobs: No. 19 $150,000 and No. 20 $110,000. The jobs call for the production of 20,000 and 10,000 units, respectively.

6. Charged factory labor to jobs on basis of time tickets: No. 19 $240,000 and No. 20 $90,000. The remaining labor was indirect.

7. Charged overhead to jobs at the rate of 110% of direct labor cost.

8. Completed Job No. 19.

9. Sold Job No. 18 on account for $200,000.

Instructions

(a) Journalize the transactions and events.

(b) Open accounts for the beginning inventories and post the entries in (a) to the job order cost accounts and to the job cost sheets.

(c) Reconcile the balance in Work in Process Inventory with the costs of unfinished jobs.

P22–2A For the year ended December 31, 1993, the job cost sheets of the Banner Company contained the following data.

Prepare entries in a job cost system and partial income statement.
(S.O. 2, 3, 4, 5, 6)

Job Number	Explanation	Direct Materials	Direct Labor	Manufacturing Overhead	Total Costs
7640	Balance 1/1	$25,000	$24,000	$28,800	$ 77,800
	Current year's costs	34,000	36,000	43,200	113,200
7641	Balance 1/1	11,000	18,000	21,600	50,600
	Current year's costs	40,000	48,000	57,600	145,600
7642	Current year's costs	48,000	60,000	72,000	180,000

Other data:

1. Raw materials inventory totaled $15,000 on January 1. During the year, $140,000 of raw materials were purchased on account.

2. Finished goods on January 1 consisted of Job No. 7638 for $87,000 and Job No. 7639 for $92,000.

3. Job No. 7640 and Job No. 7641 were completed during the year.

4. Job Nos. 7638, 7639, and 7641 were sold on account for $550,000.

5. Manufacturing overhead incurred on account totaled $135,000.

6. Other manufacturing overhead consisted of indirect materials $14,000, indirect labor $20,000, and depreciation on factory machinery $8,000.

Instructions

(a) Journalize the transactions in the sequence followed in the chapter. (Credit Factory Wages Payable when recording factory labor.)

(b) Prove the agreement of Work in Process Inventory with job cost sheets pertaining to unfinished work.

(c) Prepare the adjusting entry for manufacturing overhead, assuming the balance is allocated entirely to Cost of Goods Sold.

(d) Prepare an income statement for the year through gross profit. (Hint: Show cost of goods sold as one line.)

Prepare entries in a job cost system and cost of goods manufactured schedule.

(S.O. 2, 3, 4, 5)

P22–3A   First Addition Inc. is a construction company specializing in custom patios. The patios are constructed of concrete, brick, fiberglass, and lumber, depending upon customer preference. On June 1, 1993, the general ledger for First Addition contains the following data:

Raw Material Inventory	$4,200	Manufacturing Overhead Applied	$27,200
Work in Process Inventory	$5,540	Manufacturing Overhead Incurred	$26,375

Subsidiary data for Work in Process Inventory on June 1 are as follows:

Job Cost Sheets

	Customer Job		
Cost Element	Dion	Cole	Kix
Direct materials	$ 600	$ 800	$ 900
Direct labor	320	540	580
Manufacturing overhead	400	675	725
	$1,320	$2,015	$2,205

A summary of materials requisition slips and time tickets for June shows the following:

Customer Job	Materials Requisition Slips	Time Tickets
Dion	$ 800	$ 450
Lock	2,000	1,000
Cole	500	360
Kix	1,300	800
Dion	300	250
	4,900	2,860
General use	1,500	1,200
	$6,400	$4,060

During June, raw materials purchased on account were $3,900 and all wages were paid. Additional overhead costs consisted of depreciation on equipment $700 and miscellaneous costs of $400 incurred on account. Overhead was charged to jobs at the same rate that was used in May. The patios for customers Dion, Cole, and Kix were completed during June and sold for a total $21,700. Each customer paid in full.

Instructions

(a) Journalize the June transactions.

(b) Post the entries to Work in Process Inventory.

(c) Reconcile the balance in Work in Process Inventory with the costs of unfinished jobs.

(d) Prepare a cost of goods manufactured schedule for June.

P22–4A Whipple Manufacturing Company uses a job order cost system in each of its three manufacturing departments. Manufacturing overhead is applied to jobs on the basis of direct labor cost in Department X, direct labor hours in Department Y, and machine hours in Department Z.

In establishing the predetermined overhead rates for 1994 the following estimates were made for the year:

Compute predetermined overhead rate, apply overhead and indicate statement presentation of under- or overapplied overhead.

(S.O. 4, 6)

	Department		
	X	Y	Z
Manufacturing overhead	$1,200,000	$1,500,000	$900,000
Direct labor cost	$1,500,000	$1,250,000	$450,000
Direct labor hours	100,000	125,000	40,000
Machine hours	400,000	500,000	120,000

During January, the job cost sheets showed the following costs and production data:

	Department		
	X	Y	Z
Direct materials used	$140,000	$126,000	$78,000
Direct labor costs	$120,000	$110,000	$37,500
Manufacturing overhead incurred	$99,000	$129,000	$76,000
Direct labor hours	8,000	11,000	3,500
Machine hours	34,000	45,000	10,400

Instructions

(a) Compute the predetermined overhead rate for each department.

(b) Compute the total manufacturing costs assigned to jobs in January in each department.

(c) Compute the under- or overapplied overhead for each department at January 31.

(d) Indicate the statement presentation of the under- or overapplied overhead at January 31.

(e) If the amount in (d) was the same at December 31, how would it be reported in the year end financial statements?

P22–5A The Sting Corporation's fiscal year ends on November 30. The following accounts are found in its job order cost accounting system for the first month of the new fiscal year.

Analyze manufacturing accounts and determine missing amounts.

(S.O. 2, 3, 4, 5, 6)

Raw Materials Inventory

Dec. 1	Beginning balance	(A)	Dec. 31	Requisitions	15,850
31	Purchases	17,225			
Dec. 31	Ending balance	7,775			

Work in Process Inventory

Dec. 1	Beginning balance	(B)	Dec. 31	Jobs completed	(F)
31	Direct materials	(C)			
31	Direct labor	8,100			
31	Overhead	(D)			
Dec. 31	Ending balance	(E)			

Finished Goods Inventory

Dec. 1	Beginning balance	(G)	Dec. 31	Cost of goods sold	(I)
31	Completed jobs	(H)			
Dec. 31	Ending balance	(J)			

Factory Labor

Dec. 31	Factory wages	10,600	Dec. 31	Wages assigned	(K)

Manufacturing Overhead

Dec. 31	Indirect materials	1,900	Dec. 31	Overhead applied	(M)
31	Indirect labor	(L)			
31	Other overhead	1,850			

Other data:

1. On December 1, two jobs were in process: Job No. 154 and Job No. 155. These jobs had combined direct materials costs of $9,750 and direct labor costs of $12,000. Overhead was applied at a rate that was 80% of direct labor cost.

2. During December, Job Nos. 156, 157, and 158, were started. On December 31, Job No. 158 was unfinished. This job had charges for direct materials $3,800, direct labor $4,400 plus manufacturing overhead. All jobs, except for Job No. 158, were completed in December.

3. On December 1, Job No. 153 was in the finished goods warehouse. It had a total cost of $5,000. On December 31, Job No. 157 was the only job finished that was not sold. It had a cost of $4,000.

4. Manufacturing overhead was $230 overapplied in December.

Instructions

List the letters A through M and indicate the amount pertaining to each letter.

*B*roadening Your Perspective

DECISION CASE

The Paula Products Company uses a job order cost system. For a number of months there has been an ongoing rift between the sales department and the production department concerning a special order product, TC-1. TC-1 is a seasonal product that is manufactured in batches of 1,000 units. TC-1 is sold at cost plus a markup of 40% of cost.

The sales department is unhappy because fluctuating unit production costs significantly affect selling prices. Sales personnel complain that this has caused excessive customer complaints and the loss of considerable orders for TC-1.

The production department maintains that each job order must be fully costed on the basis of the costs incurred during the period in which the goods are produced. Production personnel maintain that the only real solution to the problem is for the sales department to increase sales in the slack periods.

Laurie Fiala, president of the company, asks you as the company accountant to collect quarterly data for the past year on TC-1. From the cost accounting system, you accumulate the following production quantity and cost data:

	Quarter			
Costs	1	2	3	4
Direct materials	$100,000	$220,000	$ 80,000	$200,000
Direct labor	60,000	132,000	48,000	120,000
Manufacturing overhead	105,000	123,000	97,000	125,000
Total	$265,000	$475,000	$225,000	$445,000
Production in batches	5	11	4	10
Unit cost (per batch)	$ 53,000	$ 43,182	$ 56,250	$ 44,500

Instructions

(a) What manufacturing cost element is responsible for the fluctuating unit costs? Why?

(b) What is your recommended solution to the problem of fluctuating unit cost?

(c) Restate the quarterly data on the basis of your recommended solution.

CRITICAL THINKING CASE

Refer to the opening vignette regarding Western States Fire Apparatus, Inc. and answer the following questions:

1. Would you expect Western States to use a job order or a process cost system? Why?

2. How is manufacturing overhead charged to production at Western States?

3. How is a job defined?

4. What steps might management take to ensure the quality of each fire truck?

ETHICAL CASE

Morgan Printing provides printing services to many different corporate clients. Although Morgan bids most jobs, some jobs, particularly new ones, are often negotiated on a cost plus basis. Cost plus means that the buyer is willing to pay the actual cost plus a return on these costs to Morgan.

Pamela Smart, controller for Morgan, has recently returned from a meeting where Morgan's president stated that he wanted her to find a way to charge most costs to any project that was on a cost plus basis. The president noted that the company needed more profits to meet its stated goals this period. By charging more costs to the cost plus projects and therefore less cost to the jobs that were bid, the company should be able to increase its profits for the current year.

Pamela knew why the president wanted to take this action. Rumors were that he was looking for a new position and if the company reported strong profits the president's opportunities would be enhanced. Pamela also recognized that she could probably increase the cost of certain jobs by changing the basis used to allocate manufacturing overhead.

Instructions

(a) Who are the stakeholders in this situation?

(b) What are the ethical issues in this situation?

(c) What would you do if you were Pamela Smart?

Answers to Self-Study Questions
1. b   2. a   3. d   4. b   5. c   6. c   7. d   8. a   9. d   10. a

CONCEPTS FOR REVIEW

Before studying this chapter, you should know or, if necessary, review:

a. *How manufacturing costs are accumulated in the accounts. (Ch. 22, p. 897–98)*

b. *How manufacturing costs are assigned to work in process, finished goods, and cost of goods sold. (Ch. 22, p. 897–906)*

c. *The flow of costs and supporting documents in a job order cost accounting system. (Ch. 22, p. 896–97 and 906–907)*

PROCESS COST ACCOUNTING

Study Objectives

After studying this chapter, you should be able to:

1. *Explain the flow of costs in process cost accounting.*

2. *State the end-of-period procedures in process cost accounting.*

3. *Compute the physical units of production.*

4. *Compute equivalent units of production.*

5. *Indicate how unit costs are computed.*

6. *Explain the method and objective of assigning costs to units of output.*

7. *Prepare a production cost report.*

8. *Apply end-of-period procedures to a second process.*

9. *Explain just-in-time (JIT) processing.*

10. *Explain the primary feature and objective of activity-based costing (ABC).*

O*ne of the fastest growing companies in the nation is Ben & Jerry's Homemade, Inc., based in Waterbury, Vt. The ice cream company that started out of a garage in 1978 is now a public company with sales reaching $97 million in fiscal 1991.*

Making ice cream is a process—a movement of product from a mixing department to a prepping department to a pint department. The mixing department is where the ice cream is created. The prep area is where extras such as cherries and walnuts are added to the ice cream. And the pint department is where the ice cream is actually put into containers. As the product is processed from one department to the next, the appropriate materials, labor, and overhead are added to it.

"The incoming ingredients from the shipping and receiving departments are stored in certain locations, either in a freezer or dry warehouse," says Beecher Eurich, staff accountant. "As ingredients get added so do the costs associated with them.

How much ice cream is actually produced? Running the plant around the clock, 24,000 pints are produced per 8-hour shift, or 72,000 pints per day.

Using a FIFO method, Eurich can tell you how much a certain batch of ice cream costs to make—its materials, labor, and overhead in each of the production departments. She generates reports for the production department heads, but makes sure not to overdo it. "You can get bogged down in numbers," says Eurich. "If you're generating a report that no one can use, then that's a waste of time." More likely, though, Ben & Jerry's production people want to know how efficient they are. Why? Many own stock in the company. Besides, the company is growing so fast that the threat of layoff is nil.

Process cost accounting is the system of accounting used by companies such as Ben & Jerry's Homemade, Inc. that manufacture products through a series of continuous processes or operations. In job order cost accounting, the focus is on the individual job. In contrast, process cost accounting focuses on the process involved in producing homogeneous products.

The major accounting differences between job order and process cost systems are highlighted first in this chapter. Then we explain and illustrate the entries, accounts, and reports associated with process cost accounting. At the end of the chapter, just-in-time processing (JIT) and activity based costing (ABC) are considered.

Characteristics of Continuous Process Manufacturing

Continuous process manufacturing, sometimes referred to as mass production operations, occurs in producing such items as steel by USX Corp., cereals by Kellogg's, petroleum products by Exxon, and paint by Sherwin-Williams. One characteristic of this type of manufacturing is that **once the production begins, it continues until the finished product emerges.** For example, in a beverage company such as Coca-Cola, the process begins with the blending of the bever-

Accounting in Action · *Business Insight*

The new General Motors Corporation assembly plants are missing a key element of traditional mass production: the assembly line. Instead, the company utilizes hundreds of automated, unmanned carriers to carry a car as it goes through the assembly process. With the carriers, each car follows a prescribed path, receiving instructions from computers through wires buried in the plant floor. Cars with extensive options are moved out of the main path until the options are installed.

age. Next, the beverage is dispensed into bottles that are moved into position by automated machinery. The bottles are then capped, packaged, and forwarded to the finished goods warehouse. A second characteristic is that **when the finished product emerges, all units will have been processed in the same manner with precisely the same amount of materials, labor, and overhead**. Each finished unit, such as a bottle of Coke, will therefore be indistinguishable one from another.

Continuous process manufacturing companies generally produce for stock (inventory) rather than for specific orders. Sherwin-Williams, for example, will produce gallons of interior latex semi-gloss paint and put them into the finished goods warehouse, ready to be shipped to paint and hardware stores when ordered. In recent years, continuous operations have become highly automated, and there has been a marked increase in the use of robotic equipment.

Features of Process Cost Accounting

In process cost accounting, as in a job order system, it is necessary to record both the accumulation and assignment of manufacturing costs. A distinctive feature of process cost accounting, however, is that **individual work in process accounts are maintained for each production department or manufacturing process**. For example, in our beverage company there would be a Work in Process account for each of the manufacturing processes, as illustrated below:

ILLUSTRATION 23-1

Manufacturing processes and work in process accounts

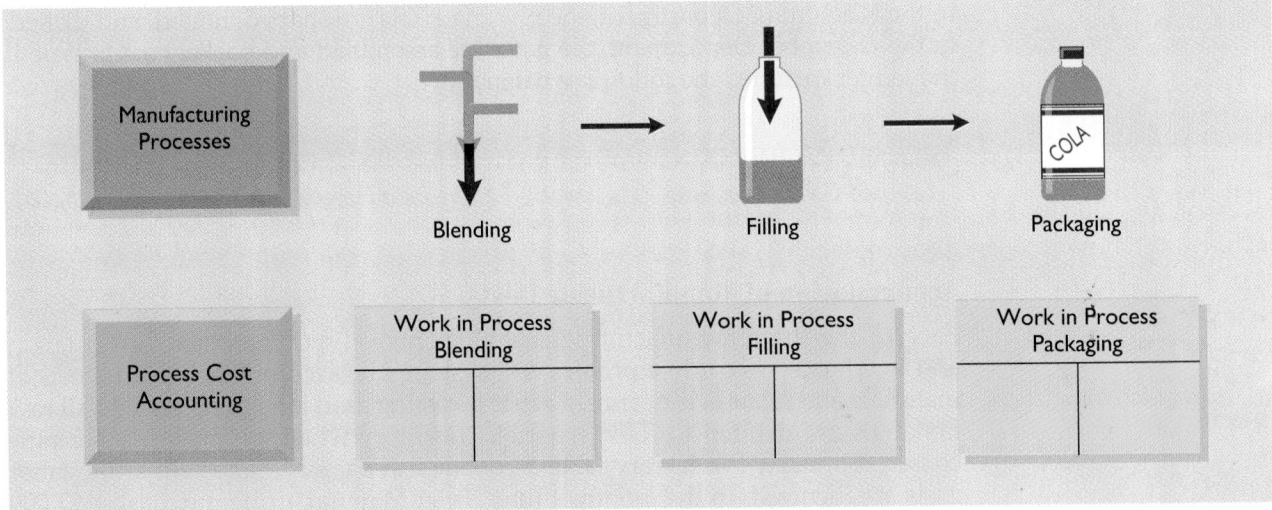

A second feature of process costing is that **costs charged to work in process are summarized in production cost reports rather than in job cost sheets**. There are also significant differences between process and job order cost accounting in determining total manufacturing costs and unit costs. In process cost accounting, **total costs are determined at the end of a period of time**, such as a month, rather than when a job is finished. **Unit costs are computed by dividing total manufacturing costs by the units produced during the period.**

The major differences between job order cost accounting and process cost accounting are summarized in Illustration 23-2.

ILLUSTRATION 23-2

Differences between job order and process cost accounting

Feature	Job Order Cost Accounting	Process Cost Accounting
Work in process accounts	One for each job	One for each process
Summary of manufacturing costs	Job cost sheets	Production cost reports
Determination of total manufacturing costs	Each job	Each period
Unit cost computation	Cost of each job ÷ Units produced for the job	Total manufacturing costs ÷ Units produced during the period

Process Cost Flow

Study Objective 1

Explain the flow of costs in process cost accounting.

The flow of costs in a process cost accounting system is shown in Illustration 23-3. Note that separate work in process accounts are provided for each producing department. The other accounts and the flow of costs are the same as in job order cost accounting. For example, manufacturing costs are accumulated by debits to Raw Materials Inventory, Factory Labor, and Manufacturing Overhead. These costs are then assigned to Work in Process, Finished Goods Inventory, and Cost of Goods Sold. The methods of assigning costs, however, differ significantly. These differences are explained and illustrated later in the chapter.

The entries pertaining to the accumulation and assignment of costs are explained in the following pages, using the June transactions of the Tyler Manufacturing Company. The entries are keyed to the numbers in Illustration 23-3. Tyler Company manufactures automatic can openers that are sold to retail outlets for $19.95. Manufacturing consists of two processes: machining and assembly. In the Machining Department, the raw materials are shaped, honed, and drilled. In the Assembly Department, the parts are assembled and packaged. On June 1, the ledger includes the following balances:

Raw Materials Inventory	$24,000	Work in Process—Machining	$ –0–
Finished Goods Inventory	6,000	Work in Process—Assembly	3,600

Accumulation of Manufacturing Costs

Each of the three manufacturing cost elements—direct materials, direct labor, and overhead—occur in a process cost system. The accumulation of the costs of materials and labor is the same in process costing as in job order costing. All raw materials are debited to Raw Materials Inventory when the materials are purchased. Similarly, all factory labor is debited to Factory Labor when the labor costs are incurred. In the month of June, Tyler Manufacturing purchases $17,000 of raw materials and incurs $20,400 of factory labor. The summary entries for these costs are as follows:

(1)

June 30	Raw Materials Inventory	17,000	
	Accounts Payable		17,000
	(To record purchases of raw materials on account)		

(2)

June 30	Factory Labor	20,400	
	Wages Payable		20,400
	(To record factory labor costs)		

ILLUSTRATION 23-3

Flow of costs in process cost accounting

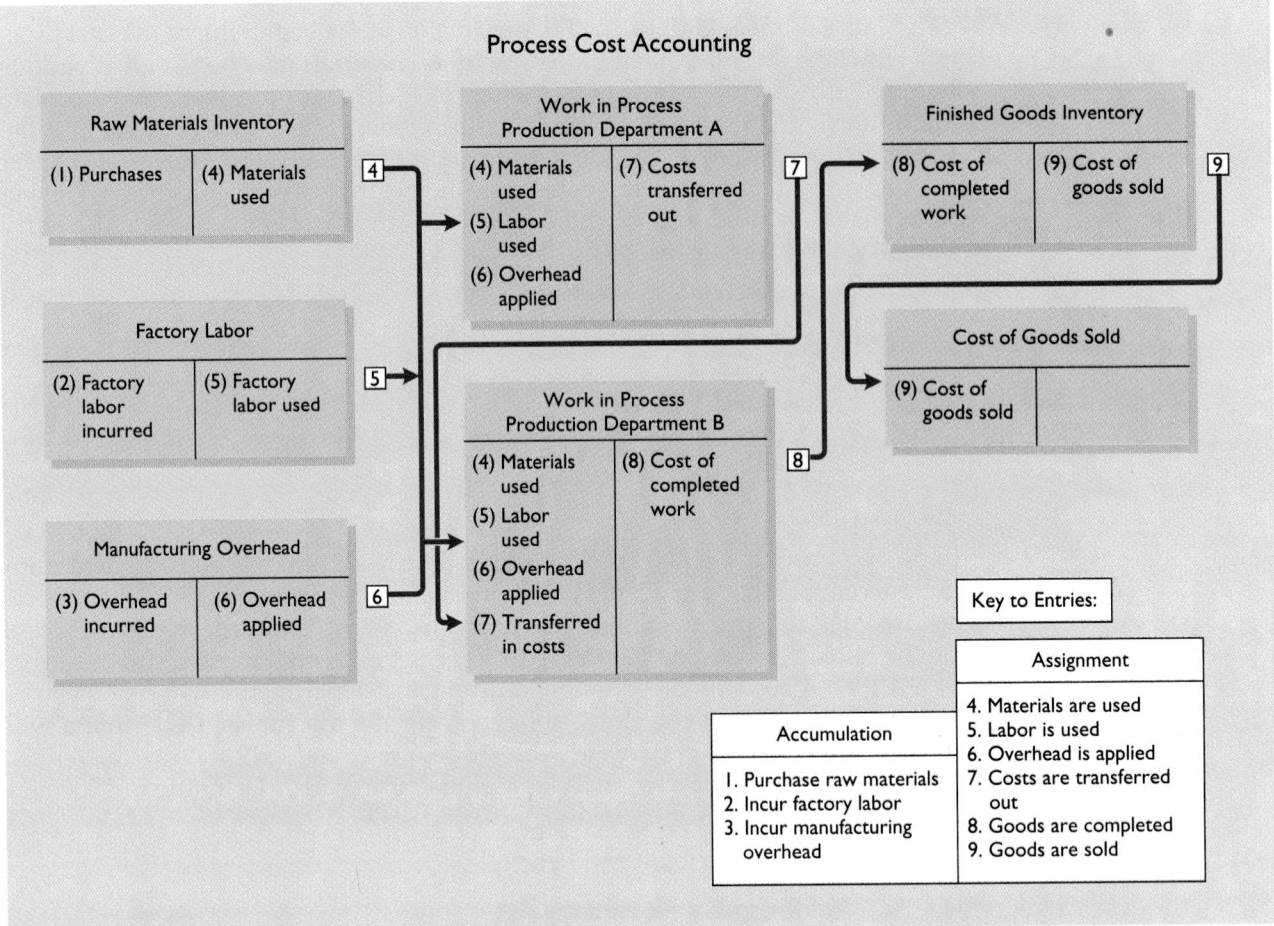

The accumulation of manufacturing overhead costs may also be the same as in job order costing. That is, overhead costs are debited to Manufacturing Overhead as they are incurred. During June, overhead costs were $41,000 in Tyler Manufacturing. The summary entry to record these costs is:

	(3)		
June 30	Manufacturing Overhead	41,000	
	Cash (Accounts Payable, etc.)		41,000
	(To record overhead incurred)		

Assignment of Manufacturing Costs

The assignment of the three manufacturing cost elements in process cost accounting is discussed below.

Materials Costs

All raw materials issued for production are a materials cost to the producing department. Materials requisition slips may be used in a process cost system, but **fewer requisitions are generally required, because the materials are used for**

processes rather than jobs. Requisitions are issued less frequently in a process cost system because the requisitions are for larger quantities. When a raw material is used by only one department, it is possible to determine the quantity used by a physical inventory count.

Materials are usually added to production at the beginning of the first process. However, in subsequent processes, other materials may be added at various points. For example, in the manufacture of Hershey candy bars, the chocolate and other ingredients are added at the beginning of the first process, and the wrappers and cartons are added at the end of the packaging process. At Tyler Manufacturing, materials are entered at the beginning of each process. During June, materials used are: Machining, $15,000, and Assembly, $4,000. The entry to record the materials used is:

	(4)		
June 30	Work in Process—Machining	15,000	
	Work in Process—Assembly	4,000	
	Raw Materials Inventory		19,000
	(To record materials used)		

Factory Labor Costs

In process costing, as in job order costing, time tickets may be used in determining the cost of labor assignable to the production departments. Since labor costs are assigned to a process rather than a job, the labor cost chargeable to a process can be obtained from the payroll register or departmental payroll summaries.

All labor costs incurred within a producing department are a cost of processing the raw materials. Thus, labor costs for the Machining Department will include the wages of employees who shape, hone, and drill the raw materials. During June, the labor costs in Tyler Manufacturing are: Machining $14,000 and Assembly $6,400. The entry to assign these costs is:

	(5)		
June 30	Work in Process—Machining	14,000	
	Work in Process—Assembly	6,400	
	Factory Labor		20,400
	(To assign factory labor to production)		

Accounting in Action · *Business Insight*

In one of Caterpillar's automated cells, work is fed into the cost center (or cell), processed by numerous robotic machines, and transferred to the next cost center without human intervention. One person tends all of the machines and spends more time on machine maintenance than operating the machines. In such cases, overhead rates based on direct labor hours may be misleading. Surprisingly, in some companies, manufacturing overhead continues to be distributed on the basis of direct labor despite the fact that there is no cause-and-effect relationship between labor and overhead.

Manufacturing Overhead Costs

The objective in assigning overhead in process cost accounting is to allocate the overhead costs to the production departments on an objective and equitable basis. In modern manufacturing, that basis is the activity that "drives" or causes the costs. For most companies, today, the primary driver of overhead costs in continuous manufacturing operations is **machine time used**, not direct labor. Thus, **machine hours are widely used** in allocating manufacturing overhead costs to processing departments.

To illustrate the assignment of overhead costs, we will assume in Tyler Manufacturing that overhead is charged to production departments at the rate of $10 per machine hour. In June, machine hours were 2,200 in the Machining Department and 1,820 in the Assembly Department. Thus, the entry to allocate overhead to the two processes is:

Helpful hint When should overhead be applied on the basis of machine hours? Answer: When machine hours "drive" overhead costs; i.e., when there is a cause and effect relationship between machine hours and overhead.

	(6)		
June 30	Work in Process—Machining	22,000	
	Work in Process—Assembly	18,200	
	Manufacturing Overhead		40,200
	(To assign overhead to processes)		

After the foregoing entries are posted, the work in process accounts of Tyler Manufacturing Company show the data indicated in Illustration 23-4. The question marks indicate that the amounts are yet to be determined. The answers to the question marks are obtained through special end-of-period procedures explained in the following sections.

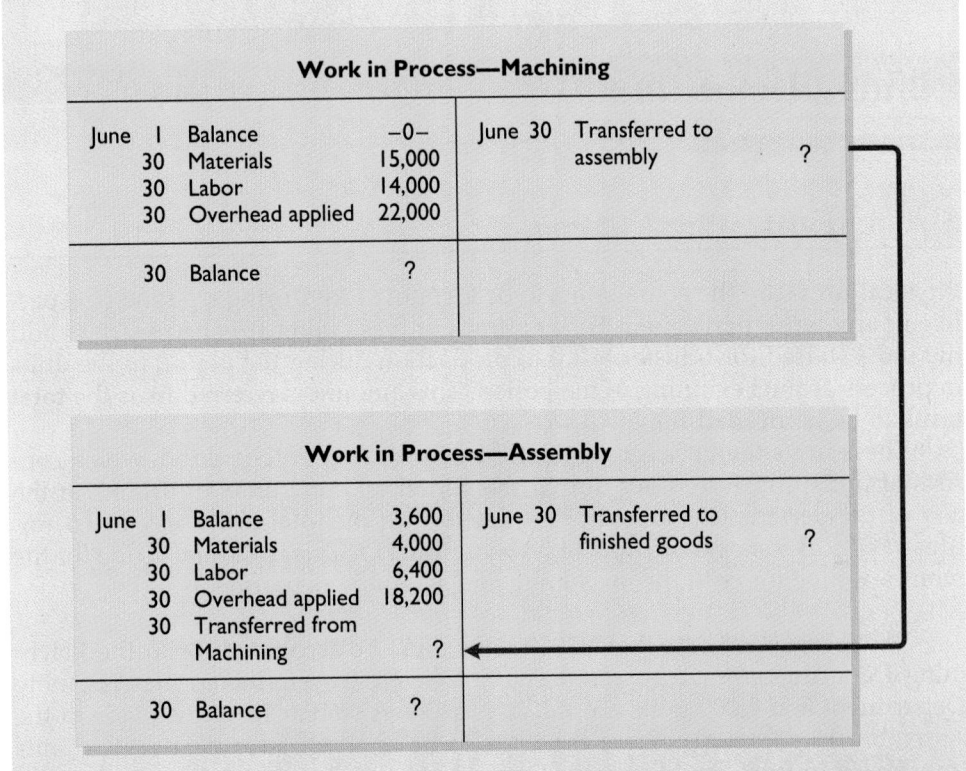

ILLUSTRATION 23-4

Work in process accounts

Before You Go On . . .

1. Who might use a process cost accounting system?

2. What are the principal differences between job order cost accounting and process cost accounting?

End-of-Period Procedures

Study Objective 2

State the end-of-period procedures in process cost accounting.

By the end of the period, Tyler Manufacturing has accumulated the materials, labor, and overhead costs in each production department's work in process account. Now Tyler must assign these accumulated costs to (1) the units transferred out of each department and (2) the units in the ending work in process in each department. The procedures used in computing and assigning the costs present the most difficult challenge to your understanding of process cost accounting. For each process, it is necessary at the end of the period to:

1. Compute the physical units.
2. Compute equivalent units of production.
3. Compute unit costs of production.
4. Assign costs to the units transferred and in process.
5. Prepare the production cost report.

In the next two sections, we will explain these procedures in detail. First, we will make all of the required computations for the Machining Department of Tyler Manufacturing. Then we will explain the computations for the Assembly Department.

SECTION I   Machining Department

Computing Physical Units

Study Objective 3

Compute the physical units of production.

Physical units are the actual units to be accounted for during a period irrespective of any work performed. To keep track of these units, it is necessary to add the units started (or transferred) into production during the period to the units in process at the beginning of the period. This amount is referred to as the **total units to be accounted for**.

These units then are accounted for by the output of the period, which consists of units transferred out during the period and any units in process at the end of the period. This amount is referred to as the **total units accounted for**. Illustration 23-5 shows the flow of physical units for Tyler Manufacturing for the month of June for both the machining and assembly departments.

The records indicate that 10,000 units must be accounted for in the Machining Department. Of this sum, 8,000 units were transferred to the Assembly Department and 2,000 units are still in process. A similar record is made in the Assembly Department, where the units to be accounted for include the units transferred in from the Machining Department.

ILLUSTRATION 23-5

Production data in units

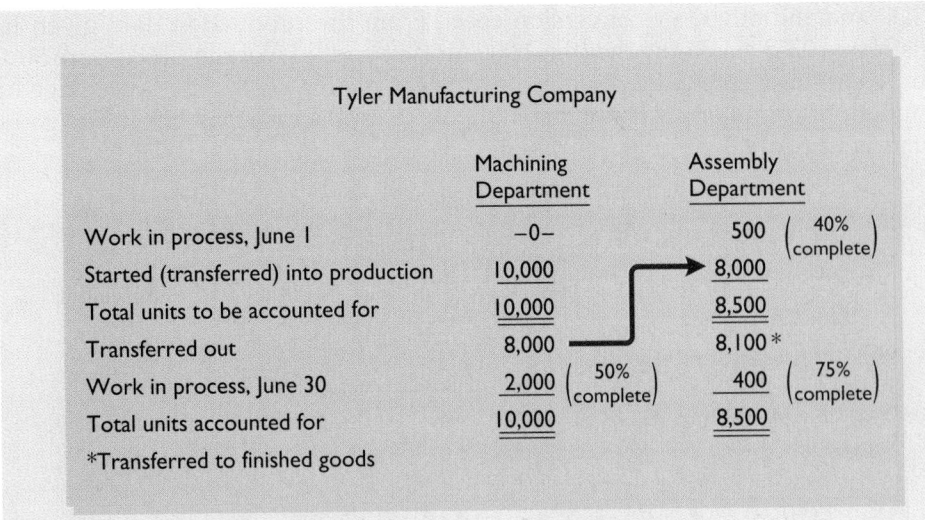

Tyler Manufacturing Company

	Machining Department	Assembly Department
Work in process, June 1	–0–	500 (40% complete)
Started (transferred) into production	10,000	8,000
Total units to be accounted for	10,000	8,500
Transferred out	8,000	8,100 *
Work in process, June 30	2,000 (50% complete)	400 (75% complete)
Total units accounted for	10,000	8,500

*Transferred to finished goods

Helpful hint Physical units are always stated in actual units irrespective of any work performed.

The percentages pertaining to the units in work in process in Illustration 23-5 refer to the percentage of completion of the units. The percentages are not relevant in accounting for physical units, but they are needed in the other end-of-period procedures.

Computing Equivalent Units of Production

Once the physical flow of the units is established, it is necessary to measure each department's productivity in terms of equivalent units of production. **Equivalent units of production are the work done during the period on the physical units of output, expressed in terms of fully completed units.** For example, if a department's output consists entirely of 4,000 units of work in process that are 60% complete, equivalent units of production are 2,400 (4,000 × 60%). The concept of equivalent units is not unique to cost accounting. For example, your university probably expresses enrollment statistics in terms of equivalent full-time students in addition to the total number of students. If taking 9 hours of course work when 15 hours is considered full-time, a student would be counted as a 60% equivalent full-time student; two half-time students would be counted as one equivalent full-time student.

Equivalent units of production are determined by applying the percentage of work done to the physical units of output. Equivalent units are the sum of the work performed to:

1. Finish the units of beginning work in process inventory.
2. Complete the units started into production during the period.
3. Start, but only partially complete, the units in ending work in process inventory.

Normally, in continuous processing, some units will always be in process at both the beginning and end of the period.

Equivalent Units for Materials

At Tyler Manufacturing, materials are entered at the beginning of each process, and conversion costs (labor and overhead) are incurred uniformly during the process. Thus, two computations of equivalent units are required: one for ma-

Study Objective 4

Compute equivalent units of production.

terials and the other for conversion costs. From the production data given in Illustration 23-5, we know that the 2,000 units in ending work in process are 50% complete. This percentage pertains only to conversion costs. The percentage of completion for materials is not stated, because in this case it is 100%. The computation of equivalent units for materials is as follows:

ILLUSTRATION 23-6

Computation of equivalent units—materials

	Machining Department		
Production Data	**Physical Units**	**Materials Added This Period**	**Equivalent Units**
Work in process, June 1	–0–	–0–	–0–
Started and finished	8,000	100%	8,000
Work in process, June 30	2,000	100%	2,000
Total	10,000		10,000

Helpful hint If 30,000 units are started into production and 5,000 units are in process at the end of the period, how many units were started and finished? Answer: 25,000 (30,000 − 5,000)

In the Machining Department, the equivalent units for materials (10,000) equal the physical units to be accounted for (10,000).

The term units started and finished may be confusing to you. **It means the number of units that were both started and completed during the period.** As a consequence, the units in work in process at the beginning and at the end of the period are not included in units "started and finished." The easiest way to compute the units started and finished is to determine the units of completed work transferred out of the department and subtract the units in work in process at the beginning of the period. The computation for the Machining Department is as follows:

ILLUSTRATION 23-7

Computation of units started and finished

Units transferred out	8,000
Less: Units of work in process, June 1	–0–
Units started and finished	8,000

Note that the units in ending work in process are ignored in determining the units started and finished.

Equivalent Units for Conversion Costs

The computation of equivalent units for conversion costs is basically the same as for material costs, as illustrated below.

ILLUSTRATION 23-8

Computation of equivalent units—conversion costs

	Machining Department		
Production Data	**Physical Units**	**Work Added This Period**	**Equivalent Units**
Work in process, June 1	–0–	–0–	–0–
Started and finished	8,000	100%	8,000
Work in process, June 30	2,000	50%	1,000
Total	10,000		9,000

Alternatively, the graphic in Illustration 23-9 may be used in computing the equivalent units of conversion costs:

ILLUSTRATION 23-9

Equivalent units for conversion costs—graphic illustration

Machining Department

Production Data	Physical Units	Work Added This Period	%	Equivalent Units
Work in process, June 1	–0–		–0–	–0–
Started and finished	8,000		100	8,000
Work in process, June 30	2,000		50	1,000
Total	10,000			9,000

0 20 40 60 80 100

Note in this case, that equivalent units (9,000), do not equal the physical units to be accounted for (10,000).

Computing Unit Costs of Production

Armed with knowledge of the equivalent units of production, we can now compute the unit production costs. Unit production costs are costs expressed in terms of equivalent units of production. When equivalent units of production are different for materials and conversion costs, three unit costs are computed: (1) materials, (2) conversion, and (3) total manufacturing. As shown in Illustration 23-4, costs in June for the Machining Department are materials $15,000 and conversion costs $36,000 (labor, $14,000 plus overhead $22,000). The formulas and computations of the unit costs are as follows:

ILLUSTRATION 23-10

Unit cost formulas and computations—Machining Department

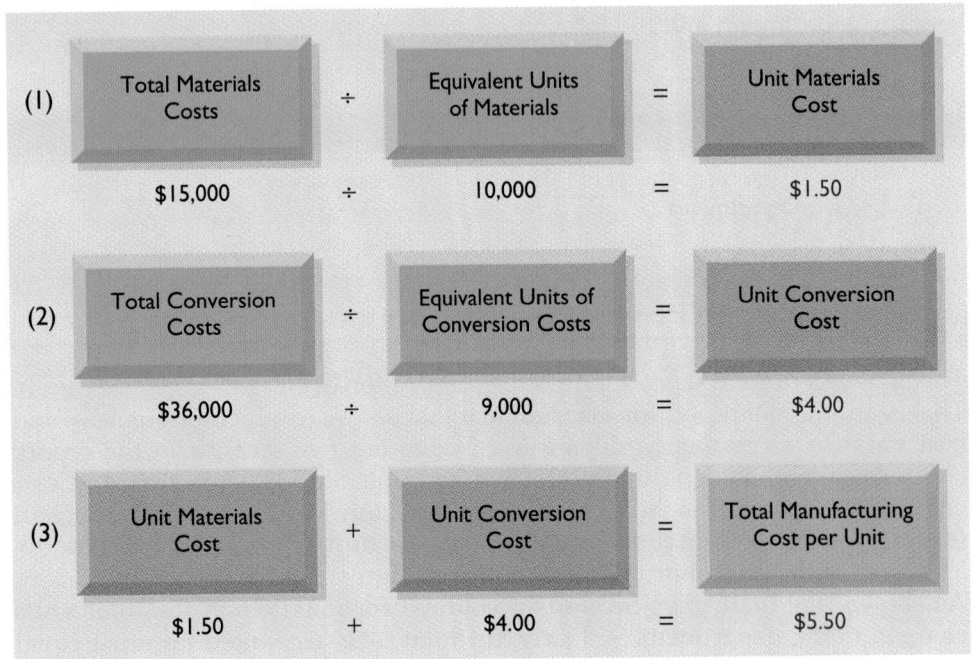

(1)	Total Materials Costs	÷	Equivalent Units of Materials	=	Unit Materials Cost
	$15,000	÷	10,000	=	$1.50
(2)	Total Conversion Costs	÷	Equivalent Units of Conversion Costs	=	Unit Conversion Cost
	$36,000	÷	9,000	=	$4.00
(3)	Unit Materials Cost	+	Unit Conversion Cost	=	Total Manufacturing Cost per Unit
	$1.50	+	$4.00	=	$5.50

When equivalent units of production are the same for materials and conversion costs, it is necessary to compute only the total manufacturing cost per unit. The computation is total manufacturing cost divided by equivalent units of production.

Assigning Costs to Units Transferred and in Process

Our next task is to determine the total cost of the units transferred out and the total cost of the units in ending work in process. To obtain these amounts, unit costs are assigned to the equivalent units of production for the period. The computations for the Machining Department are as follows:

ILLUSTRATION 23-11

Assignment of costs—Machining Department

Machining Department

Costs to be Assigned	Assignment of Costs	Equivalent Units	Unit Cost		Total Costs Assigned
Total manufacturing costs	Transferred out				
	Work in process, June 1	–0–	$–0–	$ –0–	
	Started and finished	8,000	$5.50	44,000	$44,000
$51,000	Work in process, June 30				
	Materials	2,000	$1.50	3,000	
	Conversion costs	1,000	$4.00	4,000	7,000
					$51,000

Study Objective 6

Explain the method and objective of assigning costs to units of output.

Note that total manufacturing cost per unit, $5.50, is used in costing the units started and finished. In contrast, the unit cost of materials and the unit cost of conversion are needed in costing the units in process. As indicated in the schedule, **the total costs to be assigned must equal the total costs assigned.**

When the costs have been assigned, an entry is needed to record the cost of goods transferred out of the department. In this case, the transfer is to the Assembly Department, and the following entry is made:

	(7)		
June 30	Work in Process—Assembly	44,000	
	Work in Process—Machining		44,000
	(To record transfer of 8,000 units to the Assembly Department)		

Preparing the Production Cost Report

Study Objective 7

Prepare a production cost report.

The final end-of-period procedure is the preparation of a production cost report. This is an internal report for management that shows **production quantity and cost data** for a production department. There are five sections in the report: (1) Units charged to department, (2) Units accounted for, (3) Unit costs, (4) Costs charged to department, and (5) Costs accounted for. The production cost report for the Machining Department of Tyler Manufacturing is shown in Illustration 23-12. All of the preceding end-of-period procedures are identified in the report. As shown, the **total physical units accounted for must equal the total units charged to the department.** Similarly, **the total costs accounted for must equal the total costs charged.**

Helpful hint What are the two self-checks in the report? Answer: (a) Total physical units accounted for must equal the total units charged. (2) Total costs accounted for must equal the total costs charged.

Production cost reports provide a basis for evaluating the productivity of a department. In addition, the cost data can be used to assess whether unit costs and total costs are reasonable. When the quantity and cost data are compared with predetermined goals, top management can also ascertain whether current performance is meeting planned objectives.

ILLUSTRATION 23-12

Production cost report

TYLER MANUFACTURING COMPANY
Machining Department
Production Cost Report
For the Month Ended June 30, 1993

	Physical Units (Step 1)	Equivalent Units	
		Materials	Conversion Costs (Step 2)
QUANTITIES			
Units charged to department			
In process, June 1	–0–		
Started into production	10,000		
Total units charged	10,000		
Units accounted for			
Transferred out			
In process, June 1	–0–	–0–	–0–
Started and finished	8,000	8,000	8,000
Total	8,000	8,000	8,000
In process, June 30	2,000	2,000	1,000 (2,000 × 50%)
Total units accounted for	10,000	10,000	9,000

COSTS		Materials	Conversion Costs	Total
Unit costs (Step 3)				
Costs in June	(a)	$15,000	$36,000	$51,000
Equivalent units	(b)	10,000	9,000	
Unit costs (a) ÷ (b)		$1.50	$4.00	$5.50
Costs charged to department				
In process, June 1				$ –0–
Costs in June				51,000
Total costs charged				$51,000
Costs accounted for (Step 4)				
Transferred out				
In process, June 1			$ –0–	
Started and finished (8,000 × $5.50)			44,000	$44,000
In process, June 30				
Materials (2,000 × $1.50)			3,000	
Conversion costs (1,000 × $4.00)			4,000	7,000
Total costs accounted for				$51,000

Before You Go On . . .

1. How do physical units differ from equivalent units of production?

2. What are the formulas for computing unit costs of production?

3. How are costs assigned to units transferred out and in process?

4. What are the five sections of a production cost report?

SECTION 2   Assembly Department

Study Objective 8

Apply end-of-period procedures to a second process.

Computing Physical Units

The physical units to be accounted for in the Assembly Department are determined in the same manner as in the Machining Department. From the Tyler Manufacturing production data presented earlier, the physical units for the Assembly Department are shown in Illustration 23-13.

ILLUSTRATION 23-13

Production data in physical units

Assembly Department	
	Units
Work in process, June 1 (40% complete)	500
Transferred in	8,000
Total units to be accounted for	8,500
Transferred out	8,100
Work in process, June 30 (75% complete)	400
Units accounted for	8,500

In this case the units transferred out (8,100) plus the units in ending work in process (400) equal the total units to be accounted for (8,500).

Computing Equivalent Units of Production

The equivalent units of production for the Assembly Department are computed in the same way as for the Machining Department. However, the presence of a beginning work in process adds a new dimension to process cost accounting.

When there are units in process at the beginning of the period, it is necessary to identify the cost flow assumption to be used. We will use the first-in, first-out (FIFO) costing method in this text and in homework problems. Other methods are discussed in cost accounting courses.

Under the **FIFO costing method**, the computation of equivalent units of production (as well as the computation of unit production costs and the assignment of costs to units transferred out and in process) is done on a first-in, first-out basis. The FIFO cost flow assumption usually corresponds to the actual physical flow of the goods in that beginning work in process is normally completed before new work is started. This assumption affects the determination of equivalent units as follows:

1. The first units finished during the current period are the units in beginning work in process. Thus, units started and finished during the current period are the units transferred out minus the units in beginning work in process. For the Assembly Department, units started and finished in June are 7,600 (8,100 − 500).
2. Only the work required to finish the units of beginning work in process is included in the equivalent units of production for the current period.

Equivalent Units for Materials

Since materials are entered at the beginning of the process, no additional materials costs are required to complete the beginning work in process. In addition, 100% of the materials costs has been incurred on the ending work in process. Thus, the computation of equivalent units for materials is as follows:

ILLUSTRATION 23-14

Computation of equivalent units—materials

Assembly Department

Production Data	Physical Units	Materials Added This Period	Equivalent Units
Work in process, June 1	500	–0–	–0–
Started and finished	7,600	100%	7,600
Work in process, June 30	400	100%	400
Total	8,500		8,000

Equivalent Units for Conversion Costs

The 500 units of beginning work in process were 40% complete in terms of conversion costs. Thus, 300 equivalent units (60% × 500 units) of conversion costs were required to complete the beginning inventory. In addition, the 400 units of ending work in process were 75% complete in terms of conversion costs. Thus the equivalent units for conversion costs is 8,200, computed as follows:

ILLUSTRATION 23-15

Computation of equivalent units—conversion costs

Assembly Department

Production Data	Physical Units	Work Added This Period	Equivalent Units
Work in process, June 1	500	60%	300
Started and finished	7,600	100%	7,600
Work in process, June 30	400	75%	300
Total	8,500		8,200

Computing Unit Costs of Production

The production costs chargeable to the Assembly Department in June consist of the following debits to work in process.

ILLUSTRATION 23-16

Costs charged to assembly department

Work in Process—Assembly Department

June 1 Balance	3,600	
30 Materials	4,000	
30 Labor	6,400	
30 Overhead	18,200	
30 Transferred from Machining Dept.	44,000	
Total	76,200	

Our objective is to determine the unit costs of production for the month of June.

Under the FIFO method, this determination is based entirely on the production costs incurred on work done during the month. Thus, the costs in the beginning work in process are not relevant, because they were incurred on work done in the preceding month.

Helpful hint In a second department, total materials costs equals the sum of (1) materials added in the department plus (2) costs transferred in.

The June costs for the Assembly Department include the same types of costs as in the Machining Department with one exception: the costs tranferred in from the Machining Department. Transferred-in costs **are recognized as materials cost to the receiving department.** At Tyler Manufacturing, these costs are a cost to the Assembly Department. Therefore, total materials costs are $48,000 (materials added by the Assembly Department $4,000 + the transferred-in costs $44,000). Conversion costs total $24,600 (labor $6,400 + overhead $18,200). The computations of unit costs in the Assembly Department are as follows:

ILLUSTRATION 23-17

Unit cost computations—Assembly Department

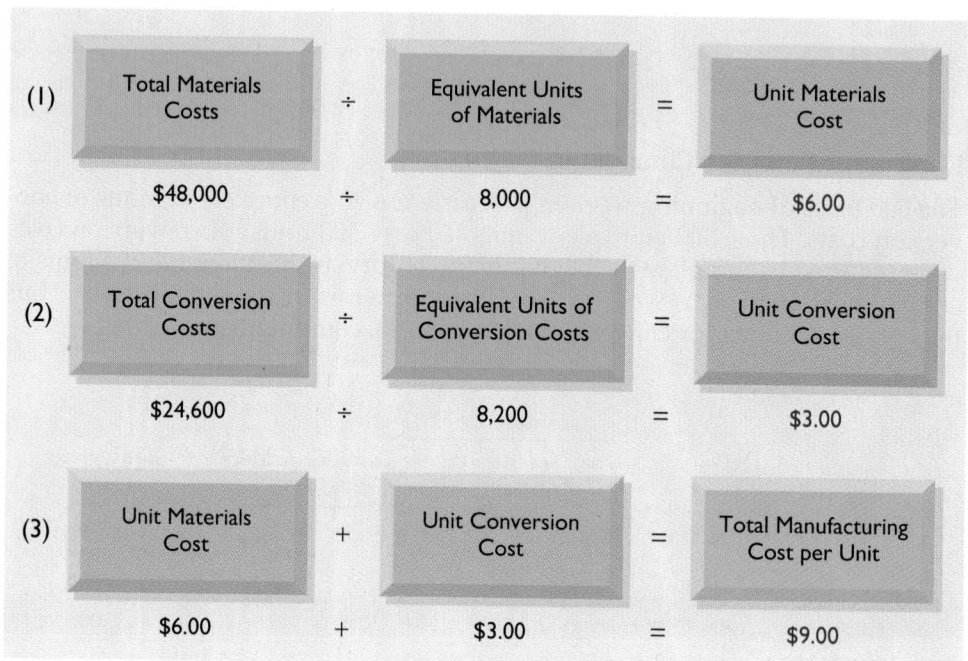

As shown, the unit costs are $6.00 for materials, $3.00 for conversion costs, and $9.00 for total manufacturing costs.

Assigning Costs to Units Transferred and in Process

Under the FIFO method, the first goods to be completed during the period are the units in beginning work in process. Thus, the cost of the beginning work in process is always assigned to the goods transferred to finished goods (or to the next department). The FIFO method also means that ending work in process will be assigned only production costs that are incurred in the current period. The assignment of the manufacturing costs in the Assembly Department is shown in Illustration 23-18.

Again, you can see that the costs assigned ($72,900 + $3,300) equal the costs to be assigned ($76,200). In this case, the total costs assigned to units transferred out can be obtained by multiplying the units (8,100) by the unit cost of the goods started and finished ($9.00). This procedure is valid only if there has been no change in unit costs between the preceding and current months. In solving homework problems, the step-by-step approach should be followed.

ILLUSTRATION 23-18

*Assignment of costs—
Assembly Department*

	Assembly Department				
Costs to be Assigned	Assignment of Costs	Equivalent Units	Unit Cost		Total Costs Assigned
Total manufacturing costs	Transferred out				
	Work in process, June 1	–0–	$–0–	$3,600	
$76,200	Conversion costs	300	$3.00	900	$ 4,500
	Started and finished	7,600	$9.00		68,400
	Ending work in process				72,900
	Materials	400	$6.00	2,400	
	Conversion costs	300	$3.00	900	3,300
					$76,200

The units completed in the Assembly Department are transferred to the finished goods warehouse. The entry for this transfer is:

(8)

June 30	Finished Goods Inventory	72,900	
	Work in Process—Assembly		72,900
	(To record transfer of 8,100 units to finished goods)		

Preparing the Production Cost Report

The procedure for preparing a production report is the same for every department. The report for the Assembly Department is shown in Illustration 23-19. As in the report for the Machining Department, **the total physical units accounted for equals the units charged to the department**. Similarly, the **total costs accounted for equals the total costs charged to the department**.

Technology in Action

Manufacturing accounting is an application that requires a great deal of internal (RAM) and external (hard disk) memory. Until recently, microcomputers with really large memories of both kinds were not available. However, manufacturing accounting programs are now available for microcomputers, having up to a megabyte of RAM and 20 megabytes of hard disk external storage capacity. For those students not familiar with megabytes, let's just say that it's a lot of memory!

Process Cost Flow Summary

The flow of costs in process cost accounting was graphically presented in Illustration 23-3 earlier in this chapter. The ledger accounts after posting the June transactions of Tyler Manufacturing Company and the flow of documents are shown in Illustration 23-20.

ILLUSTRATION 23-19

Production cost report

TYLER MANUFACTURING COMPANY
Assembly Department
Production Cost Report
For the Month Ended June 30, 1993

	Physical Units (Step 1)	Equivalent Units: Materials (Step 2)	Equivalent Units: Conversion Costs (Step 2)	
QUANTITIES				
Units charged to department				
In process, June 1	500			
Transferred in	8,000			
Total units charged	8,500			
Units accounted for				
Transferred out				
In process, June 1	500	-0-	300	(500 × 60%)
Started and finished	7,600	7,600	7,600	
Total	8,100	7,600	7,900	
In process, June 30	400	400	300	(400 × 75%)
Total units accounted for	8,500	8,000	8,200	

COSTS		Materials	Conversion Costs	Total
Unit costs (Step 3)				
Costs in June	(a)	$48,000	$24,600	$72,600
Equivalent units	(b)	8,000	8,200	
Unit costs (a) ÷ (b)		$6.00	$3.00	$9.00
Costs charged to department				
In process, June 1				$ 3,600
Costs in June				72,600
Total costs charged				$76,200
Costs accounted for (Step 4)				
Transferred out				
In process, June 1		$ 3,600		
Conversion costs (300 × $3.00)		900	$ 4,500	
Started and finished (7,600 × $9.00)			68,400	$72,900
In process, June 30				
Materials (400 × $6.00)			2,400	
Conversion costs (300 × $3.00)			900	3,300
Total costs accounted for				$76,200

ILLUSTRATION 23-20

Process cost accounts and document flow

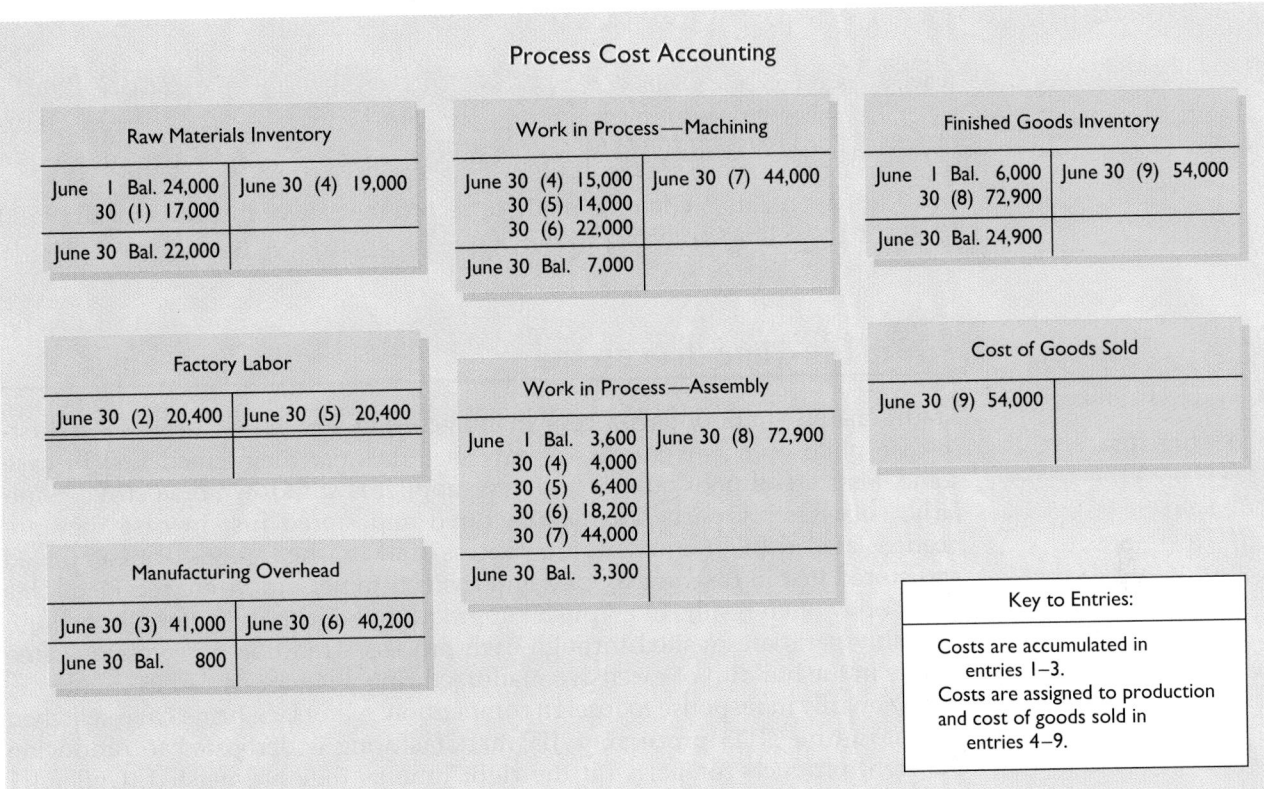

Process Cost Accounting

Raw Materials Inventory

June 1 Bal. 24,000	June 30 (4) 19,000
30 (1) 17,000	
June 30 Bal. 22,000	

Factory Labor

| June 30 (2) 20,400 | June 30 (5) 20,400 |

Manufacturing Overhead

| June 30 (3) 41,000 | June 30 (6) 40,200 |
| June 30 Bal. 800 | |

Work in Process—Machining

June 30 (4) 15,000	June 30 (7) 44,000
30 (5) 14,000	
30 (6) 22,000	
June 30 Bal. 7,000	

Work in Process—Assembly

June 1 Bal. 3,600	June 30 (8) 72,900
30 (4) 4,000	
30 (5) 6,400	
30 (6) 18,200	
30 (7) 44,000	
June 30 Bal. 3,300	

Finished Goods Inventory

June 1 Bal. 6,000	June 30 (9) 54,000
30 (8) 72,900	
June 30 Bal. 24,900	

Cost of Goods Sold

| June 30 (9) 54,000 | |

Key to Entries:

Costs are accumulated in entries 1–3.
Costs are assigned to production and cost of goods sold in entries 4–9.

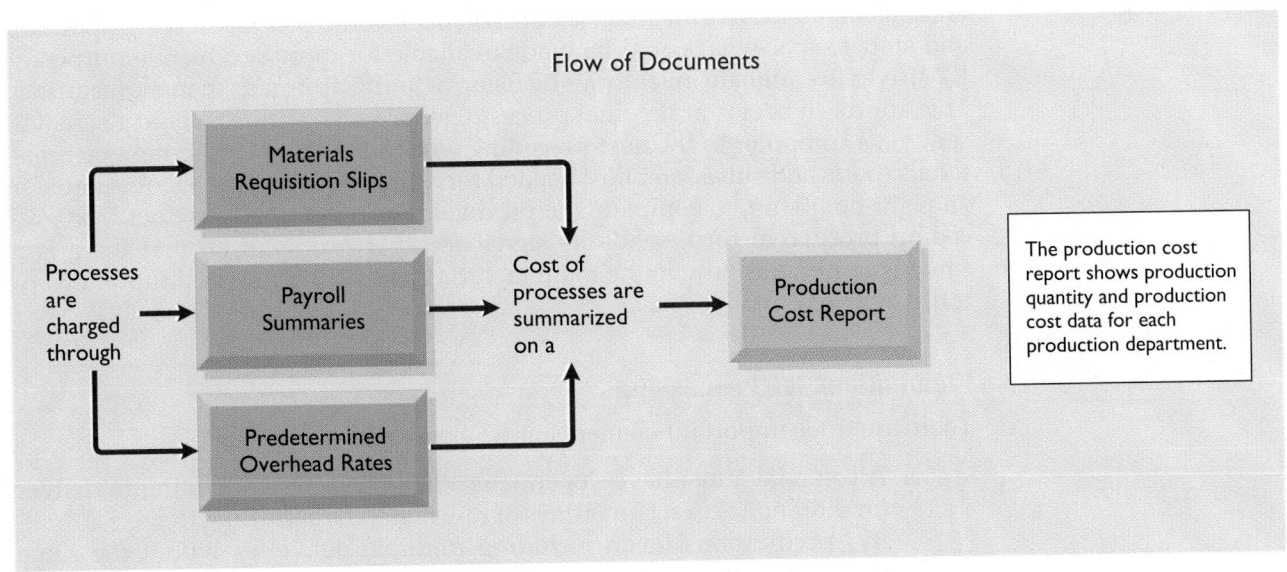

Flow of Documents

Processes are charged through →

Materials Requisition Slips

Payroll Summaries

Predetermined Overhead Rates

→ Cost of processes are summarized on a →

Production Cost Report

The production cost report shows production quantity and production cost data for each production department.

Each posting is based on journal entries illustrated earlier except for the posting pertaining to the cost of goods sold. Data for this entry are obtained from finished goods perpetual inventory records. Assuming 6,000 of the can openers costing $9.00 each are sold in June, the entry to record the cost of goods sold is as follows:

(9)

June 30	Cost of Goods Sold	54,000	
	Finished Goods Inventory		54,000
	(To record cost of 6,000 units sold)		

In addition, an entry would be made to record the sale of the units for $119,700 (6,000 × the selling price of $19.95).

Just-in-Time Processing

Traditionally, continuous process manufacturing has been based on a **just-in-case** philosophy. Inventories of raw materials are maintained **just in case** some items are of poor quality or a key supplier is shutdown by a strike. Similarly, subassembly parts are manufactured and stored **just in case** they are needed later in the manufacturing process, and finished goods are completed and stored **just in case** unexpected and rush customer orders are received. This philosophy often results in a **"push"** approach in which raw materials and subassembly parts are pushed through each process. Traditional processing often results in the buildup of extensive manufacturing inventories.

Primarily in response to foreign competition, many U.S. firms have switched to just-in-time (JIT) processing. JIT manufacturing is dedicated to producing the right products (or parts) at the right time as they are needed. Under JIT processing, raw materials are received **just in time** for use in production, subassembly parts are completed **just in time** for use in finished goods, and finished goods are completed **just in time** to be sold. As this description suggests, a primary objective of JIT is to eliminate all manufacturing inventories. Inventories are considered to have an adverse effect on net income because of tying up funds and storage space that could be made available for more productive purposes. JIT strives to eliminate inventories by using a **"pull"** approach in manufacturing. This approach begins at the final process (cell or work station) where a signal is sent via a computer to the next preceding work station indicating the exact materials (parts and subassemblies) needed for a time period, such as four hours or an eight-hour shift, to complete the production of a specified product. The preceding process, in turn, sends its signal to other processes so that there is a smooth continuous flow in the manufacturing process and no buildup of inventories at any point.

Elements of JIT Processing

There are three important elements in JIT processing.

1. A company must have dependable suppliers who are willing to deliver on short notice exact quantities of raw materials according to precise quality specifications (even including multiple deliveries within the same day). Suppliers must also be willing to deliver the raw materials at specified work stations rather than at a central receiving department. This type of purchasing requires constant and direct communication with suppliers. This is facilitated when there is on-line computer linkage between the company and its suppliers.

2. A multiskilled work force must be developed. Under JIT, machines are often strategically grouped around work cells or centers and much of the work is automated. As a result, one worker may have the responsibility to operate and maintain several different types of machines.

3. A total quality control system must be established throughout the manufacturing operations. Total quality control means **no defects**. Since only required quantities are signaled by the **pull** approach, any defects at any work station will shut down operations at subsequent work stations. Total quality control requires continuous monitoring by both employees and supervisors at each work station.

Benefits of JIT Processing

The major benefits of JIT processing are

1. Manufacturing inventories are significantly reduced or eliminated.
2. Product quality is enhanced.
3. Rework costs and inventory storage costs are reduced or eliminated.
4. Production cost savings are realized from the improved flow of goods through the processes.

One of the major accounting benefits of JIT is the elimination of raw materials and work in process inventory accounts. In place of these accounts is one account, Raw and In-Process Inventory. All materials and conversion costs are charged to this account. Because of the reduction (or elimination) of in-process inventories, the computation of equivalent units of production is simplified.

A ccounting in Action · *Business Insight*

JIT first hit the USA in the early 1980s when it was adopted by automobile companies to meet foreign competition. It is now being successfully used in many companies, including General Electric, Caterpillar, and Harley-Davidson. The effects in most cases have been dramatic. For example, after using JIT for two years, a major division of Hewlett-Packard found that work in process inventories (in dollars) were down 82%, scrap/rework costs were down 30%, space utilization was down 40%, and labor efficiency improved 50%. As indicated, JIT not only reduces inventory, but enables a manufacturer to produce a better product faster and with less waste.

A ctivity-Based Costing

Activity-based costing (ABC) is a development in product costing that has received much attention in recent years. In contrast to conventional cost systems that focus on units of production, **ABC** is a cost accounting system that focuses on the **activities** performed to produce specific products. **Costs are then traced from the activities to products, based on each product's consumption of the activities.**

Study Objective 10

Explain the primary feature and objective of activity-based costing (ABC).

In a conventional cost system, a single unit-level basis of allocation is used to allocate overhead costs to products. As explained in this text, the basis may be direct labor or machine hours used to manufacture the product. The assumption in this approach is that as volume increases, so does the cost of all inputs consumed by the product. However, distorted cost data result when input costs are unrelated to the number of units produced.

In ABC, the cost of a product is equal to the sum of the costs of all activities performed to manufacture it. The activities may extend from the ordering of the raw materials to the packaging of the finished product. ABC recognizes that to have accurate and meaningful cost data, more than one basis of allocating activity costs to products is needed. In selecting the basis, ABC seeks to identify the **cost driver** that measures the activities performed on the product. Examples of activities and possible cost drivers are as follows:

ILLUSTRATION 23-21

Activities and cost drivers in ABC

Activity	Cost driver (Basis of allocation)
Ordering raw materials	Ordering hours; number of times ordered
Receiving raw materials	Number of shipments; number of orders
Storing raw materials	Number of parts used, number of requisitions
Transporting raw materials to machines	Material-handling hours; number of times ordered
Machine set-up time	Set-up hours: number of set-ups
Product design	Number of products

Consider the case of a company that produces products in both small and large batches. ABC traces the costs of machine set-up time to each batch. The set-up cost for each batch is then allocated to the units in the batch. Assuming the same set-up cost for all batches, the per unit set-up cost will be higher for small batches than large batches. In contrast, traditional costing aggregates set-up costs and then allocates the total to units produced on the basis of direct labor hours. Assuming each unit requires the same amount of direct labor, the unit set-up cost will be the same for all batches. In such cases, inaccurate product costs will result.

Accounting in Action ▪ *Business Insight*

Activity-based costing (ABC) has become the hot topic of the early 1990s in management accounting. Articles, seminars, and consultants are all espousing the benefits of the ABC system.

As a result, more companies are attempting to use this approach. But, progress is slow. A recent survey shows that (1) the direct labor allocation approach used for overhead costs still dominates product costing, (2) these product cost numbers (developed using direct labor cost allocations) are still used for strategic and competitive decisions, and (3) nonmanufacturing costs are rarely (if ever) included as part of product costs, even though in an ABC system they often would be considered product costs. Adapted from Emore and Ness, "The Slow Pace of Meaningful Change in Cost Systems," *Journal of Cost Management* (Winter, 1991).

Two important assumptions must be met in using ABC:

1. All costs in the activity must be driven by the cost driver used to assign costs.

2. All costs in the activity should respond proportionally to changes in the activity level of the cost driver.

For example, if costs are driven by more than one factor but only one is used in allocating the costs, distorted product costs may result.

Activity-based costing may be used with either a job order or a process cost accounting system. The primary benefit of ABC is more accurate and meaningful product costing. However, improved cost data about an activity can lead to reduced costs for the activity. In sum, ABC makes managers realize that it is activities and not products that determine the profitability of a company.

Before You Go On . . .

1. How are transferred-in costs treated in computing unit costs of production?

2. How are costs assigned to units transferred out when there is beginning work in process?

3. What are the principal accounting effects of just-in-time (JIT) processing?

4. What are the primary differences between activity-based costing (ABC) and conventional costing?

Summary of Study Objectives

1. *Explain the flow of costs in process cost accounting.* The cost flow in process cost accounting is basically the same as in job order cost accounting. The accumulation of manufacturing costs (materials, labor, and overhead) is the same in process cost accounting as in job order costing. In process costing, costs are assigned to more than one work in process account, and the method of assigning costs is different.

2. *State the end-of-period procedures in process cost accounting.* End-of-period procedures are used to:
(a) Compute the physical units.
(b) Compute equivalent units of production.
(c) Compute unit costs of production.
(d) Assign costs to units transferred and in process.
(e) Prepare the production cost report.

3. *Compute the physical units of production.* Keeping track of the physical units of product consists of adding the units started into production during the period to the units in process at the beginning of the period to determine the total units to be accounted for. These units then are accounted for by the output of the period, which consists of units transferred out during the period and any units in process at the end of the period.

4. *Compute equivalent units of production.* Equivalent units of production are the sum of the work performed to (a) finish the units of beginning work in process inventory, if any; (b) complete the units started into production during the period; and (c) start, but only partially complete, the units in ending work in process inventory.

5. *Indicate how unit costs are computed.* There are two steps in determining unit costs: (a) determine the equivalent units of production, and (b) divide the appropriate costs by the equivalent units. Unit costs are computed for total manufacturing costs and generally it is also necessary to compute unit costs separately for materials and conversion costs.

6. *Explain the method and objective of assigning costs to units of output.* Costs are assigned to work done by applying unit costs to the equivalent units of work done. The objective of assigning costs is to determine the costs to be assigned to units transferred out and the units in ending work in process.

7. *Prepare a production cost report.* The production cost report contains both quantity and cost data for a production department. There are five sections in the report: (a) Units charged to department, (b) Units ac-

counted for, (c) Unit costs, (d) Costs charged to department, and (e) Costs accounted for.

8. Apply end-of-period procedures to a second process. For a second process, (a) work done to complete beginning inventory is added in computing equivalent units, (b) costs transferred in are a materials cost, and (c) costs are assigned to beginning work in process in determining the cost of units transferred out.

9. Explain just-in-time (JIT) processing. JIT is a manufacturing technique that is dedicated to producing

the right products at the right time as needed. One of the principal accounting effects is that a Raw and In-Process Inventory account replaces both the raw materials and work in process inventory accounts.

10. Explain the primary feature and objective of activity-based costing (ABC). ABC is a method of product costing that focuses on the activities performed to produce products. It then assigns the cost of the activities to products by using cost drivers that measure the activities performed. The primary objective of ABC is accurate and meaningful product costs.

GLOSSARY

Activity-based costing · A cost accounting system that focuses on the activities performed in manufacturing a specific product. (p. 947).

Equivalent units of production · The work done during the period on the physical units of output expressed in terms of fully completed units. (p. 935).

Just-in-time processing · A processing system dedicated to producing the right products (or parts) as they are needed and the elimination of manufacturing inventories. (p. 946).

Physical units · Actual units to be accounted for during a period irrespective of any work performed. (p. 934).

Production cost report · An internal report for man-

agement that shows both production quantity and cost data for a production department. (p. 938).

Process cost accounting · A system of accounting used by companies that manufacture products through a series of continuous processes or operations. (p. 928).

Transferred-in costs · Costs transferred in from a department that are considered to be a materials cost to the receiving department. (p. 942).

Unit production costs · Costs expressed in terms of equivalent units of production. (p. 937).

Units started and finished · Units both started and completed during the period. (p. 936).

DEMONSTRATION PROBLEM

Karlene Industries produces plastic ice cube trays in two processes: heating and stamping. All materials are added at the beginning of the Heating Department.

On November 1, 1,000 trays were in process in the Heating Department that were 70% complete. During November 12,000 trays were started into production. On November 30, 2,000 trays were in process that were 60% complete.

The following cost information for the Heating Department was also available:

Work in process, November 1	$1,000	Labor	$2,300
Materials	3,000	Overhead	4,600

Instructions

(a) Prepare a production cost report for the Heating Department for the month of November, 1993.

(b) Journalize the transfer of costs to the Stamping Department.

Solution to Demonstration Problem

(a)

KARLENE INDUSTRIES
Heating Department
Production Cost Report
For the Month Ended November 30, 1993

Helpful Hints
1. Remember that total units accounted for must equal total units charged.
2. Similarly, total costs accounted for must equal total costs charged.
3. Equivalent units used for unit costs must equal equivalent units shown under total units accounted for.
4. The total costs charged must equal the debit total in work in process.

	Physical Units (Step 1)	Equivalent Units	
		Materials	Conversion Costs
Quantities		(Step 2)	
Units charged to department			
In process, November 1	1,000		
Started into production	12,000		
Total units charged	13,000		
Units accounted for			
Transferred out			
In process, November 1	1,000	–0–	300 (1,000 × 30%)
Started and finished	10,000	10,000	10,000
Total	11,000	10,000	10,300
In process, November 30	2,000	2,000	1,200 (2,000 × 60%)
Total units accounted for	13,000	12,000	11,500

Costs

		Materials	Conversion Costs	Total
Unit costs (Step 3)				
Costs in November	(a)	$ 3,000	$ 6,900 (1)	$ 9,900
Equivalent units	(b)	12,000	11,500	
Unit costs (a) ÷ (b)		$.25	$.60	$.85

Costs charged to department		Total
In process, November 1		$ 1,000
Costs in November		9,900
Total costs charged		$10,900

Costs accounted for (Step 4)

Transferred out			
In process, November 1	$ 1,000		
Conversion costs (300 × $.60)	180	$ 1,180	
Started and finished (10,000 × $.85)		8,500	$ 9,680
In process, November 30			
Materials (2,000 × $.25)		500	
Conversion costs (1,200 × $.60)		720	1,220
Total costs accounted for			$10,900

(1) Labor $2,300 plus overhead of $4,600.

(b) Nov. 30   Work in Process—Stamping 9,680
               Work in Process—Heating   9,680
               (To record transfer of 11,000
               units to Stamping Department)

SELF-STUDY QUESTIONS

Answers are at the end of the chapter.

(S.O. 1)   1. Which of the following items is not a characteristic of a process production system?
   a. Once production begins, it continues until the finished product emerges.
   b. The focus is on continually producing homogeneous products.
   c. When the finished product emerges, all units have precisely the same amount of materials, labor, and overhead.
   d. The products produced are heterogeneous in nature.

(S.O. 2)   2. End-of-period procedures in process cost accounting do not include:
   a. preparing a job cost sheet.
   b. computing equivalent units of production.
   c. assigning costs to units transferred and in process.
   d. computing physical units of production.

(S.O. 3)   3. In the RYZ Company, there are 600 units in beginning work in process 60% completed, 7,000 units started into production, and 500 units in ending work in process 20% completed. The physical units to be accounted for are:
   a. 7,000.
   b. 7,360.
   c. 7,600.
   d. 7,340.

(S.O. 3)   4. A company has 1,000 units in beginning work in process, 15,000 units started into production, and 1,500 units in ending work in process. The units transferred out are:
   a. 15,000.
   b. 16,000.
   c. 14,500.
   d. 13,500.

(S.O. 4)   5. The Mora Company has 2,000 units in beginning work in process, 20% complete as to conversion costs, 25,000 units started and finished, and 3,000 units in ending work in process, 40% complete as to conversion costs. Equivalent units for materials and conversion costs are, respectively:
   a. 28,000 and 26,600.
   b. 28,000 and 27,800.
   c. 27,000 and 26,200.
   d. 27,000 and 29,600.

6. The KLM Company has no beginning   (S.O. 5)
   work in process; 9,000 units are started and finished and 3,000 units in ending work in process are one-third finished. If total material costs are $45,000, the unit materials cost is:
   a. $5.00
   b. $3.75.
   c. $4.10 (rounded).
   d. $4.50.

7. The Toney Company has unit costs of $10   (S.O. 6)
   for materials and $20 for conversion costs. If there are 2,500 units in ending work in process, 40% complete as to conversion costs, the total cost assignable to the ending inventory is:
   a. $45,000.
   b. $55,000.
   c. $30,000.
   d. $40,000.

8. A production cost report: (S.O. 7)
   a. is an external report.
   b. shows costs charged to department but not costs accounted for.
   c. shows equivalent units of production but not physical units.
   d. contains five sections.

9. In determining unit costs in a second   (S.O. 8)
   department:
   a. costs in beginning inventory are added to costs incurred during the period.
   b. only costs incurred during the period are used.
   c. only costs incurred on units transferred in are used.
   d. no correct answer is given.

10. Just-in-time processing (JIT):   (S.O. 9)
   a. strives to eliminate inventories.
   b. uses a pull approach in manufacturing.
   c. both of the above.
   d. neither (a) nor (b).

11. Activity based costing (ABC):   (S.O. 10)
   a. can only be used in a process cost system.
   b. focuses on units of production.
   c. uses only a single basis of allocation.
   d. focuses on activities performed to produce a product.

QUESTIONS

1. What are the distinguishing characteristics of continuous process manufacturing?

2. Identify the features of process cost accounting.

3. Jack Jones believes there are significant differences in the flow of costs between job order cost accounting and process cost accounting. Do you agree? Explain.

4. What source documents are used in assigning (a) materials and (b) labor to production?

5. What criterion and basis are commonly used in allocating overhead to processes?

6. Terri Turner is uncertain about the end-of-period procedures in process cost accounting. State the procedures that are required in the sequence in which they are performed.

7. Ken Kruse is confused about computing physical units. Explain to Ken how physical units to be accounted for and physical units accounted for are determined.

8. What is meant by the term "equivalent units of production"?

9. How are equivalent units computed?

10. The Marie Company had 500 units of beginning work in process. During the period, 8,000 units were completed, and there were 400 units of ending work in process. What were the units started and finished?

11. Sanders Co. has 600 units of beginning work in process two-thirds complete. During the period 9,000 units were completed, and there were 500 units of ending work in process one-fifths complete. What are the equivalent units of production?

12. Cessna Co. started and finished 1,000 units for the period. Its beginning inventory is 600 units one-fourth complete and its ending inventory is 500 units one-fifth complete. How many units were transferred out this period?

13. The Hepp Company transfers out 12,000 units and has 2,000 units of ending work in process that are 25% complete. Materials are entered at the beginning of the process and there is no beginning work in process. Assuming unit materials costs of $3 and unit conversion costs of $8, what are the costs to be assigned to units (a) transferred out and (b) in ending work in process?

14. (a) Jason Jelk believes the production cost report is an external report for stockholders. Is Jason correct? Explain.
(b) Identify the sections in a production cost report.

15. What purposes are served by a production cost report?

16. When units are transferred from one department to another, how should the receiving department handle the costs transferred in?

17. In the Grubb Company, there are 800 units of ending work in process that are 100% complete as to materials and 25% complete as to conversion costs. If the unit cost of materials is $4 and the costs assigned to the 800 units is $5,400, what is the per-unit conversion cost?

18. (a) Describe the philosophy and approach of just-in-time processing.
(b) Identify the major elements of JIT processing.

19. (a) What are the principal differences between activity-based costing (ABC) and conventional product costing?
(b) What is the primary objective of ABC?

20. What assumptions must be met in using ABC?

BRIEF EXERCISES

Journalize entries for accumulating costs.
(S.O. 1)

BE23-1 Sable Manufacturing purchases $25,000 of raw materials on account, and it incurs $30,000 of factory labor costs. Journalize the two transactions on March 31 assuming the labor costs are not paid until April.

Journalize the assignment of materials and labor costs.
(S.O. 1)

BE23-2 Data for Sable Manufacturing are given in BE23-1. Supporting records show that (a) the Assembly Department used $14,000 of raw materials and $17,000 of the factory labor, and (b) the Finishing Department used the remainder. Journalize the assignment of the costs to the processing departments on March 31.

Journalize the assignment of overhead costs.
(S.O. 1)

BE23-3 Factory labor data for Sable Manufacturing are given in BE23-2. Manufacturing overhead is assigned to departments on the basis of 200% of labor costs. Journalize the assignment of overhead to the Assembly and Finishing Departments.

Compute physical units of production.
(S.O. 3)

BE23-4 Manitee Manufacturing Company has the following production data for selected months.

Month	Beginning Work in Process	Units Started and Finished	Ending Work in Process Units	Ending Work in Process % Complete
Jan.	-0-	30,000	5,000	40%
March	-0-	50,000	4,000	75
July	-0-	60,000	3,000	30

Compute the physical units for each month.

Compute equivalent units of production. (S.O. 4)

BE23-5 Using the data in BE23-4, compute equivalent units of production for materials and conversion costs, assuming materials are entered at the beginning of the process.

Compute unit costs of production. (S.O. 5)

BE23-6 In the Carolina Company total material costs are $36,000, and total conversion costs are $50,000. Equivalent units of production are materials 12,000 and conversion costs 10,000. Compute the unit costs for materials, conversion costs, and total manufacturing costs.

Assign costs to units transferred out and in process.
(S.O. 6)

BE23-7 The Sosa Company has the following production data for April: units started and finished, 30,000, ending work in process 5,000 units that are 100% complete for materials and 20% complete for conversion costs. If unit materials cost is $8 and unit conversion cost is $12, determine the costs to be assigned to the units transferred out and the units in ending work in process. The total costs to be assigned are $652,000.

Prepare a partial production cost report. (S.O. 7)

BE23-8 Using the data in BE23-7 prepare the cost section of the production cost report for the Sosa Company.

Compute unit costs in a second processing department.
(S.O. 8)

BE23-9 Production costs chargeable to the Finishing Department in June in the Maddox Company are: materials $8,000, labor $20,000, overhead $18,000, and transferred in costs $42,000. Equivalent units of production are materials 20,000 and conversion costs 19,000. Compute the unit costs for materials and conversion costs.

Assign costs in a second processing department.
(S.O. 8)

BE23-10 Data for the Maddox Company are given in BE23-9. Production records indicate that 18,000 units were started and finished, and 2,000 units in ending work in process were 50% completed. Show the assignment of costs to the units transferred out and in process.

EXERCISES

Compute physical units and equivalent units of production.
(S.O. 3, 4)

E23-1 In the Kam Company, materials are entered at the beginning of each process. Work in process inventories, with the percentage of work done on conversion costs, and production data for its Sterilizing Department in selected months during 1993 are as follows:

	Beginning Work in Process		Units Started and Finished	Ending Work in Process	
Month	Units	Conversion Cost %		Units	Conversion Cost %
January	–0–	—	8,000	1,000	60
March	–0–	—	10,000	3,000	30
May	–0–	—	15,000	2,500	80
July	3,500	70	9,000	1,500	90

Instructions

(a) Compute the physical units for January and May.

(b) Compute the equivalent units of production for (1) materials and (2) conversion costs for each month.

E23–2 The Cutting Department of Boran Manufacturing has the following production and cost data for July.

Determine equivalent units, unit costs, and assignment of costs. (S.O. 4, 5, 6)

Production	Costs	
1. Started and finished 8,000 units.	Beginning work in process	$ –0–
2. Started 1,000 units that are 30% completed at July 31.	Materials	27,000
	Labor	14,000
	Manufacturing overhead	19,200

Materials are entered at the beginning of the process. Conversion costs are incurred uniformly during the process.

Instructions

(a) Determine the equivalent units of production for (1) materials and (2) conversion costs.

(b) Compute unit costs and show the assignment of manufacturing costs to units transferred out and in work in process.

E23–3 Data for Boran Manufacturing are presented in E23–2.

Journalize and post work in process transactions. (S.O. 1)

Instructions

(a) Journalize the transactions that affect the work in process account.

(b) Post the transactions to work in process and finished goods. (Use T-accounts.)

E23–4 The Sanding Department of the Cope Furniture Company has the following production and manufacturing cost data for March 1993.

Prepare a production cost report. (S.O. 3, 4, 5, 6, 7)

Production: 12,000 units started and finished; 4,000 units started that are 100% completed as to materials and 25% completed as to conversion costs.

Manufacturing costs: Materials $48,000; labor $26,000; overhead $52,000.

Instructions

Prepare a production cost report.

E23–5 The Smelting Department of the Beed Manufacturing Company has the following production and cost data for November.

Compute equivalent units, unit costs, and costs assigned. (S.O. 4, 5, 6)

Production: Beginning work in process 2,000 units that are 100% complete as to materials and 30% complete as to conversion costs; units started and finished 9,000 units; and ending work in process 1,000 units that are 100% complete as to materials and 60% complete as to conversion costs.

Manufacturing costs: Work in process, November 1, $15,800; materials added $50,000; labor and overhead $143,000.

Instructions

(a) Compute the equivalent units of production for (1) materials and (2) conversion costs for the month of November.

(b) Compute the unit costs for the month.

(c) Determine the costs to be assigned to the units transferred out and in process.

Answer questions on costs and production.
(S.O. 3, 4, 5, 6)

E23–6   The ledger of the Tomberk Company has the following work in process account:

Work in Process—Painting

5/1	Balance	4,000	5/31	Transferred out	?
5/31	Materials	4,400			
5/31	Labor	1,200			
5/31	Overhead	1,400			
5/31	Balance	?			

Production records show that there were 800 units in the beginning inventory, 50% complete, 1,100 units started, and 1,300 units transferred out. The units in ending inventory were 66⅔% complete. Materials are entered at the beginning of the painting process.

Instructions
Answer the following questions:

(a) How many units are in process at May 31?
(b) What is the unit materials cost for May?
(c) What is the unit conversion cost for May?
(d) What is the total cost of units started in April and completed in May?
(e) What is the total cost of units started and finished in May?
(f) What is the cost of the May 31 inventory?

Journalize transactions for two processes.
(S.O. 8)

E23–7   The Kajak Manufacturing Company has two production departments: Cutting and Assembly. July 1 inventories are Work in Process—Cutting $2,900, Work in Process—Assembly $10,600, and Finished Goods $31,000. During July, the following transactions occurred.

1. Purchased $35,600 of raw materials on account.
2. Incurred $56,000 of factory labor. (Credit Wages Payable.)
3. Incurred $70,000 of manufacturing overhead; $42,000 was paid and the remainder is unpaid.
4. Requisitioned materials for Cutting $15,700 and Assembly $8,900.
5. Used factory labor for Cutting $29,000 and Assembly $27,000.
6. Applied overhead at the rate of $20 per machine hour. Machine hours were Cutting 1,740 and Assembly 1,620.
7. Transferred goods costing $67,700 from the Cutting Department to the Assembly Department.
8. Transferred goods costing $134,900 from Assembly to Finished Goods.
9. Sold goods costing $135,000 for $200,000 on account.

Instructions
Journalize the transactions. (Omit explanations.)

Compute equivalent units, unit costs, and costs assigned.
(S.O. 4, 5, 6)

E23–8   The Polishing Department of the Keen Manufacturing Company has the following production and manufacturing cost data for September. Materials are entered at the beginning of the process.

Production: Beginning inventory 2,600 units that are 100% complete as to materials and 30% complete as to conversion costs; units started that came from a prior department 12,000; ending inventory of 3,000 units 10% complete as to conversion costs.

Manufacturing costs: Beginning inventory costs of $63,180; costs transferred into Polishing during the month, $120,000; materials costs added in Polishing during the month, $48,000; labor and overhead applied in Polishing during the month, $133,440 and $266,880, respectively.

Instructions
(a) Compute the equivalent units of production for materials and conversion costs for the month of September.
(b) Compute the unit costs for materials and conversion costs for the month.
(c) Determine the costs to be assigned to the units transferred out and in process.

E23-9 The Welding Department of the Tomlop Manufacturing Company has the following production and manufacturing cost data for February 1993. All materials are added at the beginning of the process.

Prepare a production cost report for a second process.
(S.O. 8)

Manufacturing Costs		Production Data	
Beginning work in process	$ 32,175	Beginning work in process	15,000 units
Costs transferred in	75,000		1/10 complete
Materials	45,000	Units transferred out	49,000
Labor and overhead	105,400	Units transferred in	60,000
		Ending work in process	26,000
			1/5 complete

Instructions

Prepare a production cost report for the Welding Department for the month of February.

E23-10 The Maryanne Company manufactures pizza sauce through two production departments: Cooking and Canning. In each process, materials and conversion costs are incurred evenly throughout the process. For the month of April, the work in process accounts show the following debits.

Journalize transactions and answer questions.
(S.O. 1, 6, 8)

	Cooking	Canning
Beginning work in process	$ -0-	$ 4,000
Materials	19,000	6,000
Labor	8,500	5,000
Overhead	29,500	21,800
Costs transferred in		54,000

Instructions

(a) Journalize the April transactions.

(b) If 110,000 units were started into production in Cooking and 90,000 units were transferred to Canning, what is the cost per unit of the goods transferred out.

(c) What is the total materials cost for the Canning Department in April?

PROBLEMS

P23-1 Marina Corporation manufactures water skis through two processes: Molding and Packaging. In the Molding Department fiber glass is heated and shaped into the form of a ski. In the Packaging Department, the skis are placed in cartons and sent to the finished goods warehouse. Materials are entered at the beginning of both processes. Labor and manufacturing overhead are incurred uniformly throughout each process. Production and cost data for the Molding Department for January 1993 are presented below.

Complete end-of-period procedures for first process.
(S.O. 3, 4, 5, 6, 7)

Production Data	January
Beginning work in process units	-0-
Units started into production	42,500
Ending work in process units	2,500
Percent complete—ending inventory	40%

Cost Data	
Materials	$595,000
Labor	96,400
Overhead	231,600
Total	$923,000

Instructions

(a) Compute the physical units of production.

(b) Determine the equivalent units of production for materials and conversion costs.

(c) Compute the unit costs of production.

(d) Determine the costs to be assigned to the units transferred out and in process.

(e) Prepare a production cost report for the Molding Department for the month of January.

Complete end-of-period procedures for first process.
(S.O. 3, 4, 5, 6, 7)

P23–2   The Fridge Corporation manufactures in separate processes refrigerators and freezers for homes. In each process, materials are entered at the beginning and conversion costs are incurred uniformly. Production and cost data for the first process in making two products in two different manufacturing plants are as follows:

	Stamping Department	
	Plant A	Plant B
Production Data—June	R12 Refrigerators	F24 Freezers
Work in process units, June 1	–0–	–0–
Units started into production	21,000	20,000
Work in process units, June 30	4,000	2,500
Work in process percent complete	75	60
Cost Data—June		
Work in process, June 1	$ –0–	$ –0–
Materials	840,000	760,000
Labor	200,000	240,000
Overhead	400,000	292,000
Total	$1,440,000	$1,292,000

Instructions

(a) For each plant:
  (1) Compute the physical units of production.
  (2) Compute equivalent units of production for materials and for conversion costs.
  (3) Determine the unit costs of production.
  (4) Show the assignment of costs to units transferred out and in process.

(b) Prepare the production cost report for Plant A.

Journalize and post transactions and show assignment of costs.
(S.O. 1, 3, 4, 5, 6)

P23–3   The Brazil Company manufactures a nutrient, Everlife, through two manufacturing processes: (1) Blending and (2) Packaging. All materials are entered at the beginning of each process. On August 1, 1993, inventories consisted of Raw Materials $5,000, Work in Process—Blending $–0–, Work in Process—Packaging $3,945, and Finished Goods $7,500. The beginning inventory for Packaging consisted of 500 units, 2/5 complete as to conversion costs. During August, 9,000 units were started into production in Blending and the following transactions were completed:

1. Purchased $25,000 of raw materials on account.
2. Issued raw materials for production: Blending $16,200 and Packaging $3,690.
3. Incurred labor costs of $17,880.
4. Used factory labor: Blending $13,320 and Packaging $4,560.
5. Incurred $36,500 of manufacturing overhead on account.
6. Applied manufacturing overhead at the rate of $30 per machine hour. Machine hours were Blending 900 and Packaging 300.
7. Transferred 8,200 units from Blending to Packaging at a cost of $54,120. Unfinished units in Blending are 1/4 complete as to conversion costs.
8. Transferred 8,600 units from Packaging to Finished Goods at a cost of $74,490. Unfinished units in the Packaging Department are 3/4 complete as to conversion costs.
9. Sold goods costing $62,000 for $90,000 on account.

Instructions

(a) Journalize the August transactions.

(b) Post the entries to the work in process accounts.

(c) Compute the costs assigned to units transferred out and in process in blending?

P23–4 Hodak Company has several processing departments. Costs charged to the Assembly Department for October 1993 totaled $1,305,000 as follows:

Assign costs and prepare production cost report with transferred-in costs. (S.O. 8)

Work in process inventory, October 1	$ 66,500	Overhead	$121,000
Materials added	124,500	Costs transferred in	913,000
Labor	80,000		

Production records show that 25,000 units were in beginning work in process 40% complete, 415,000 units were transferred in, and 35,000 units were in ending work in process 20% complete. Materials are entered at the beginning of each process.

Instructions

(a) Determine the equivalent units of production and the unit costs for the Assembly Department.

(b) Determine the assignment of costs to goods transferred in and in process.

(c) Prepare a production cost report for the Assembly Department.

P23–5 The work in process accounts of the Tastie Cereal Co. that pertain to the making of "Fast Pops," a new breakfast cereal, during the month of July are presented below.

Determine equivalent units and unit costs and assign costs for processes with transferred-in costs. (S.O. 8)

Work in Process—Mixing

July 31	Materials	63,000	July 31	Transferred out	100,000
31	Labor	17,000			
31	Overhead	23,800			

Work in Process—Baking

July 1	Inventory	2,200	July 31	Transferred out	122,400
31	Labor	4,000			
31	Overhead	16,200			
31	Transferred in	100,000			

Work in Process—Packaging

July 1	Inventory	6,720	July 31	To Finished Goods	?
31	Materials	40,800			
31	Labor	14,000			
31	Overhead	27,400			
31	Transferred in	122,400			

Production and inventory data for the Baking and Packaging Departments are as follows:

Department	Inventory, July 1 Units	% Complete	Inventory, July 31 Units	% Complete	Units Transferred Out
Baking	4,000	50	–0–	—	204,000
Packaging	8,000	40	6,000	70	206,000

All materials are entered at the beginning of each process.

Instructions

For the Baking and Packaging Departments:

(a) Determine the equivalent units of production for materials and conversion costs.

(b) Determine the unit cost of materials, the unit conversion costs, and the total manufacturing cost per equivalent unit.

(c) Show the assignment of costs to units transferred out and in process.

P23–6 The Zephyr Furniture Company manufactures living room furniture through two departments: Framing and Upholstering. Materials are entered at the beginning of each process. For May, the following cost data are obtained from the two work-in-process accounts.

Answer questions relating to percentage of completion, unit costs, and costs assigned. (S.O. 4, 5, 6, 8)

	Framing	Upholstering
Work in process, May 1	$–0–	$?
Materials	360,000	?

	Framing	Upholstering
Conversion costs	270,000	345,000
Costs transferred in	–0–	550,000
Costs transferred out	550,000	?
Work in process, May 31	80,000	?

Instructions

Answer the following questions:

(a) If 3,000 sofas were started into production on May 1 and 2,500 sofas were transferred to Upholstering, what was the unit cost of materials for May in the Framing Department?

(b) Using the data in (a) above, what was the per unit conversion cost of the sofas transferred to Upholstering?

(c) Continuing the assumptions in (a) above, what is the percentage of completion of the units in process at May 31 in the Framing Department?

(d) If the materials cost per unit in Upholstering is $350, what was the cost of materials added in Upholstering in May?

(e) If the conversion cost per unit in Upholstering is $150, what are the equivalent units of conversion costs for May?

(f) Assuming there is no beginning work in process in Upholstering, what is the cost of the work in process at May 31 if 800 units are 25% completed?

(g) Assuming the per unit conversion costs for Upholstering in (d) and (e), what is the percentage of completion of 1,000 units of ending work in process inventory if the total costs assigned are $380,000?

(h) If unit costs were the same in April as in May, what is the cost of the May 1 work in process inventory in Upholstering if there are 1,000 units 60% complete?

ALTERNATE PROBLEMS

Complete end-of-period procedures for first process.
(S.O. 3, 4, 5, 6, 7)

P23–1A   Bolling Company manufactures bowling balls through two processes: Molding and Packaging. In the Molding Department, the urethane, rubber, plastics, and other materials are molded into bowling balls. In the Packaging Department, the balls are placed in cartons and sent to the finished goods warehouse. All materials are entered at the beginning of each process. Labor and manufacturing overhead are incurred uniformly throughout each process. Production and cost data for the Molding Department during June 1993 are presented below.

Production Data	June
Beginning work in process units	–0–
Units started into production	22,000
Ending work in process units	2,000
Percent complete—ending inventory	45%

Cost Data	
Materials	$198,000
Labor	25,400
Overhead	141,800
Total	$365,200

Instructions

(a) Prepare a schedule showing physical units of production.

(b) Determine the equivalent units of production for materials and conversion costs.

(c) Compute the unit costs of production.

(d) Determine the costs to be assigned to the units transferred and in process for June.

(e) Prepare a production cost report for the Molding Department for the month of June only.

P23–2A Premier Industries Inc. manufactures in separate processes furniture for homes. In each process, materials are entered at the beginning, and conversion costs are incurred uniformly. Production and cost data for the first process in making two products in two different manufacturing plants are as follows:

Complete end-of-period procedures for first process.
(S.O. 3, 4, 5, 6, 7)

	Cutting Department	
	Plant 1	Plant 2
Production Data—July	T12-Tables	C10-Chairs
Work in process units, July 1	–0–	–0–
Units started into production	20,000	18,000
Work in process units, July 31	1,000	500
Work in process percent complete	60	80
Cost Data—July		
Work in process, July 1	$ –0–	$ –0–
Materials	320,000	270,000
Labor	180,000	146,000
Overhead	94,400	68,800
Total	$594,400	$484,800

Instructions

(a) For each plant:
  (1) Compute the physical units of production.
  (2) Compute equivalent units of production for materials and for conversion costs.
  (3) Determine the unit costs of production.
  (4) Show the assignment of costs to units transferred out and in process.

(b) Prepare the production cost report for Plant 1.

P23–3A The Arder Company manufactures a finished product, Vitadrink, through two manufacturing processes: (1) Mixing and (2) Packaging. All materials are entered at the beginning of each process. On October 1, 1994, inventories consisted of Raw Materials $26,000, Work in Process—Mixing $0, Work in Process—Packaging $250,000, and Finished Goods $89,000. The beginning inventory for Packaging consisted of 10,000 units that were 50% complete as to conversion costs. During October, 50,000 units were started into production in the Mixing Department and the following transactions were completed:

Journalize and post transactions and show assignment of costs.
(S.O. 1, 3, 4, 5, 6)

1. Purchased $300,000 of raw materials on account.

2. Issued raw materials for production: Mixing $200,000 and Packaging $45,000.

3. Incurred labor costs of $228,900.

4. Used factory labor: Mixing $172,500 and Packaging $56,400.

5. Incurred $820,000 of manufacturing overhead on account.

6. Applied indirect manufacturing overhead on the basis of $25 per machine hour. Machine hours were 26,400 in Mixing and 6,600 in Packaging.

7. Transferred 45,000 units from Mixing to Packaging at a cost of $990,000. Unfinished units in Mixing are 25% complete as to conversion costs.

8. Transferred 53,000 units from Packaging to Finished Goods at a cost of $1,455,000. Units unfinished in the Packaging Department are 60% complete as to conversion costs.

9. Sold goods costing $1,460,000 for $2,100,000 on account.

Instructions

(a) Journalize the October transactions.

(b) Post the entries to the work in process accounts.

(c) Compute the costs assigned to units transferred out and in process in mixing.

P23–4A Weeler Company has several processing departments. Costs charged to the Assembly Department for November 1994 totaled $2,019,500 as follows:

Assign costs and prepare production cost report with transferred in costs.
(S.O. 8)

Inventory, November 1	$ 95,300	Overhead	$ 330,880
Materials added	160,000	Costs transferred in	1,312,000
Labor	121,320		

Production records show that 30,000 units were in beginning work in process 30% complete, 640,000 units were transferred in, and 25,000 units were in ending work in process 40% complete. Materials are entered at the beginning of each process.

Instructions

(a) Determine the equivalent units of production and the units costs for the Assembly Department.

(b) Determine the assignment of costs to goods transferred out and in process.

(c) Prepare a production cost report for the Assembly Department.

Determine equivalent units and unit costs and assign costs for processes with transferred in costs. (S.O. 8)

P23–5A The work in process accounts of the Yummy Cookie Co. that pertain to the making of "Tastee Snacks," a new cookie, during the month of July are presented below.

Work in Process—Mixing

July 31	Materials	50,000	July 31	Transferred out	120,000
31	Labor	18,800			
31	Overhead	54,400			

Work in Process—Baking

July 1	Inventory	2,700	July 31	Transferred out	183,600
31	Labor	10,600			
31	Overhead	50,300			
31	Transferred in	120,000			

Work in Process—Packaging

July 1	Inventory	5,370	July 31	To Finished Goods	?
31	Materials	24,480			
31	Labor	8,740			
31	Overhead	28,310			
31	Transferred in	183,600			

Production and inventory data for the Baking and Packaging Departments are as follows:

Department	Inventory, July 1		Inventory, July 31		Units Transferred Out
	Units	% Complete	Units	% Complete	
Baking	24,000	25	–0–	—	1,224,000
Packaging	30,000	30	40,000	75	1,214,000

All materials are entered at the beginning of a process.

Instructions

For the Baking and Packaging Departments:

(a) Determine the equivalent units of production for (1) materials and (2) conversion costs.

(b) Determine (1) the unit cost of materials, (2) the unit conversion costs, and (3) the total manufacturing cost per equivalent unit.

(c) Show the assignment of costs to units transferred out and in process.

Broadening Your Perspective

DECISION CASE

The Key West Company manufactures suntan lotion called Surtan in 11-ounce plastic bottles. Surtan is sold in a very competitive market. As a result, management is very cost-conscious. Surtan is manufactured through two processes: mixing and filling. Materials are entered at the beginning of each process and labor and manufacturing overhead occur uniformly throughout each process. Unit costs are based on the cost per gallon of Surtan using FIFO costing.

On June 30, 1993, Sara Simmons, the chief accountant for the past 20 years, opted to take early retirement. Her replacement, Joe Jacobs, had extensive accounting experience with motels in the area but only limited contact with manufacturing accounting.

During July, Joe correctly accumulates the following production quantity and cost data for the Mixing Department.

Production quantities: Work in process, July 1, 8,000 gallons 75% complete; started into production 100,000 gallons; work in process, July 31, 5,000 gallons 20% complete.

Production costs: Beginning work in process $82,000; incurred in July: materials $500,000, conversion costs $686,000.

Joe proceeded to prepare a production cost report on the basis of physical units involved. His report showed a production cost of $13.35 per gallon of Surtan. The management of Key West was shocked at the high unit cost. The president comes to you, as Sara's top assistant, to review Joe's report and prepare a correct report if necessary.

Instructions

(a) Show how Joe arrived at the unit cost of $13.35 per gallon of Surtan.

(b) What error(s) did Joe make in preparing his production cost report?

(c) Prepare a correct production cost report for July.

CRITICAL THINKING CASE

Refer to the opening story about Ben & Jerry's Homemade, Inc. and answer the following questions.

1. How many processes are used by Ben & Jerry's to make ice cream? Identify the processes.

2. Why does Ben & Jerry use a process costing system rather than a job order system?

3. How does the production report satisfy the needs of the department heads?

ETHICAL CASE

R. B. Robin Company manufactures a high tech component that passes through two production processing departments, molding and assembly. Department managers are partially compensated on the basis of units of products completed and transferred out relative to units of product put into production. This was intended as encouragement to be efficient and to minimize waste.

Bob Guymer is the department head in the molding department and Wayne Dermatolis is his quality control inspector. During the month of June, Bob had three new employees who were not yet technically skilled. As a result, many of the units produced in June had minor molding defects. In order to maintain the department's normal high rate of completion, Bob told Wayne to pass through inspection and on to the assembly department all units that had defects nondetectable to the human eye. "Company and industry tolerances on this product are too high anyway," says Bob. "Less than 2% of the units we produce are subjected in the market to the stress tolerance we've designed into them. The odds of those 2% being any of this month's units are even less. Anyway, we're saving the company money."

Instructions

(a) Who are the potential stakeholders involved in this situation?

(b) What alternatives does Wayne have in this situation? What might the company do to prevent this from occurring?

Answers to Self-Study Questions
1. d   2. a   3. c   4. c   5. b   6. b   7. a   8. d   9. b   10. c
11. d

CONCEPTS FOR REVIEW

Before studying this chapter, you should know or, if necessary, review:

a. *The three manufacturing cost elements. (Ch. 21, p. 861–2)*

b. *The difference between product and period costs. (Ch. 21, p. 863)*

c. *The income statement for a manufacturing company. (Ch. 21, p. 864–5)*

COST-VOLUME-PROFIT RELATIONSHIPS

Study Objectives

After studying this chapter, you should be able to:

1. *Distinguish between variable and fixed costs.*

2. *Explain the meaning and importance of the relevant range.*

3. *Explain the concept of mixed costs.*

4. *State the five components of cost-volume-profit analysis.*

5. *Indicate the meaning of contribution margin and the ways it may be expressed.*

6. *Identify the three ways that the break-even point may be determined.*

7. *Define the term "margin of safety" and give the formulas for computing it.*

8. *Give the formulas for determining sales required to earn target net income.*

9. *Explain the term "sales mix" and its effects in determining break-even sales.*

10. *Describe the essential features of a cost-volume-profit income statement.*

11. *Explain the difference between absorption costing and variable costing.*

I

n a manufacturing company, managers tend to worry a lot. Is the price high enough to make a profit, yet low enough to compete? Are costs low enough to make a profit, yet high enough to ensure quality? Is volume high enough to cover costs and make a profit? At what point do we break-even on costs and revenues? Are we running out of capacity?

All of these questions also apply to a campus parking system. "Our parking program is self-supporting. It receives no state money. It has to break even," says Bob Seibolt, director of campus safety at Boise State University in Boise, Idaho.

Currently, the school has 4,566 spaces available to serve over 14,000 students and 2,100 employees. "We park 10 to 12 thousand cars a day," says Seibolt. "That means we've got to turn each space 3 or 4 times. And that's just daytime. This is also a major center for nighttime events. We have a 2,000 seat performing arts theatre, a 12,000 seat pavilion for basketball and concerts, and a 23,000 seat football stadium. We expect three-quarters of a million visitors this year. But we handle it."

In addition to its sale of parking permits, the Boise facility generates revenues from meters and parking tickets. In fiscal 1990–1991, revenues from these three sources totaled $323,000; in fiscal 1991–1992, the total was $375,000. Because of a rate increase and some additional spaces, Seibolt estimates that 1992–1993 revenues will be $500,000. The rate increase was granted to pay for an additional 156 spaces— which Seibolt says will cost $142,000 to develop. Even with the addition, space is tight. "We are getting to the point where we can no longer guarantee that everyone will always be able to find a parking space," he says.

As indicated above, business conditions are constantly changing. Management, therefore, is frequently faced with decisions that relate to the effects of change on the company's costs, revenues, and net income. Some typical business decisions are:

1. If American Airlines is to make a profit when it reduces all domestic fares by 50%, what reduction in costs or increase in passengers will be required?

2. What increase in sales revenue will be needed to maintain current profit levels if Ford Motor Company meets the United Auto Workers' demands for higher wages?

3. What level of sales will General Motors need to cover its costs exactly for the Saturn automobile in the next model year?

4. What will be the effect on the cost of producing one ton of steel at USX Corp. if its program to modernize plant facilities reduces the work force by 50%?

5. If McDonald's doubles its annual advertising expenditures, what increase in sales volume will be required to increase net income by 10%?

In making these decisions, management must understand how costs respond to changes in sales volume and the effect of this interaction of costs and revenues on profits. **Cost-volume-profit (CVP)** relationships apply to a company as a whole as well as to segments of a business, such as a division or department. Management looks to accounting for quantitative data that are relevant for these types of business decisions. A prerequisite to understanding CVP relationships is knowledge of the behavior of costs.

In this chapter, we first explain the considerations involved in cost behavior analysis. Then we discuss and illustrate CVP analysis and variable costing.

SECTION I Cost Behavior Analysis

Cost behavior analysis is the study of how specific costs respond to changes in the level of activity within a company. As expected, some costs change, and others remain the same. A knowledge of cost behavior is important to management in planning business operations and in deciding between alternative courses of action. Cost behavior analysis applies to all types of entities as the vignette about parking at Boise State illustrates. The essential starting point in cost behavior analysis is a consideration of the activity index.

Activity Index

There are many ways to measure business activity within a company. Activity levels may be expressed in terms of sales dollars (in a retail company), miles driven (in a trucking company), room occupancy (in a hotel), or number of customers called on (by a salesperson). Many companies use more than one measurement base. A manufacturing company, for example, may use direct labor hours or units of output for manufacturing costs and sales revenue or units sold for selling expenses.

For an activity level to be useful in cost behavior analysis, there should be correlation between changes in the level or volume of activity and changes in costs. The activity level selected is referred to as the activity (or volume) index. The **activity index** identifies the activity that causes changes in the behavior of costs. Once an appropriate activity index is selected, it is possible to classify the behavior of costs in response to changes in activity levels into three categories: variable, fixed, or mixed.

Variable Costs

Variable costs are costs that vary **in total** directly and proportionately with changes in the activity level. If the level increases 10%, total variable costs will increase 10%. If the level of activity decreases by 25%, variable costs will be reduced 25%. Examples of variable costs include direct materials and direct labor in a manufacturing company; cost of goods sold, sales commissions, and freight-out in a merchandising company; and gasoline in airline and trucking companies. A variable cost may also be defined as a cost that **remains the same per unit at every level of activity**.

To illustrate the behavior of a variable cost, assume that the Damon Company manufactures radios that contain a $10 digital clock. The activity index is the number of radios produced. For each radio manufactured, the total cost of the clocks increases by $10. As illustrated in part (a) of Illustration 24-1, total cost of the clocks will be $20,000 if 2,000 radios are manufactured, and $100,000 when 10,000 radios are produced. The digital clocks can also be used to show that a variable cost remains the same per unit as the level of activity changes. As shown in part (b) of Illustration 24-1, the unit cost of $10 for the clocks is the same whether 2,000 or 10,000 radios are produced.

Companies that rely heavily on labor to manufacture a product or to render a service are likely to have many variable costs. In contrast, companies that use a high proportion of machinery and equipment in producing revenue, such as public utilities, may have few variable costs.

> **Study Objective 1**
>
> *Distinguish between variable and fixed costs.*

ILLUSTRATION 24-1

Behavior of total and unit variable costs

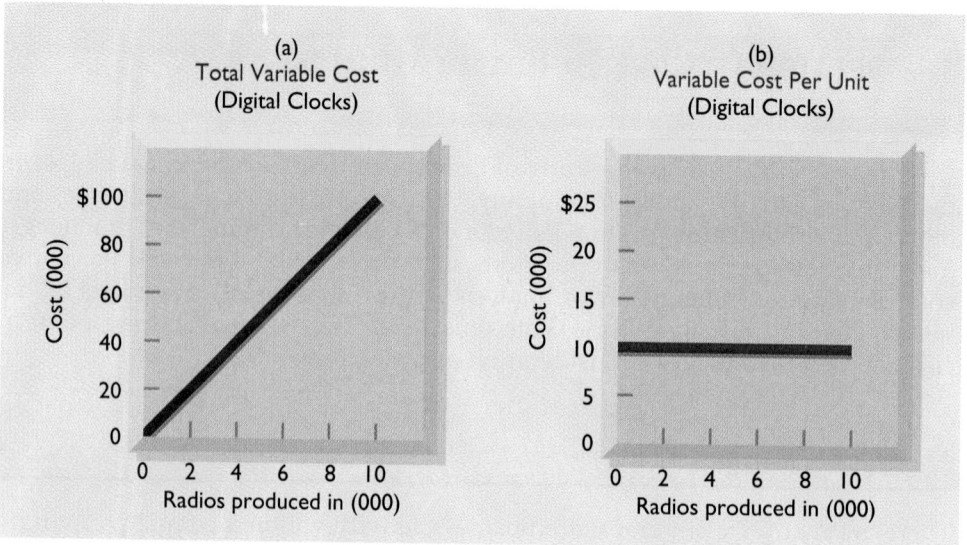

ixed Costs

Fixed costs are costs that remain the same **in total** regardless of changes in the activity level. Examples include property taxes, insurance, rent, supervisory salaries, and depreciation on buildings and equipment. Because fixed costs remain constant in total as activity changes, it follows that **fixed costs per unit vary inversely with activity. As volume increases, unit cost declines and vice versa.**

To illustrate the behavior of fixed costs, assume that the Damon Company leases all of its productive facilities at a cost of $10,000 per month. Total fixed costs will remain constant at every level of activity as shown in part (a) of Illustration 24-2. However, on a per unit basis, the cost of rent will decline as activity increases as shown in part (b) of Illustration 24-2. At 2,000 units, the unit cost is $5 ($10,000 ÷ 2,000); when 10,000 radios are produced, the unit cost is only $1 ($10,000 ÷ 10,000). The cost behavior patterns are graphically shown below.

The trend in many companies is to have more fixed costs and fewer variable costs. This development results from increased use of automation and less use

ILLUSTRATION 24-2

Behavior of total and unit fixed costs

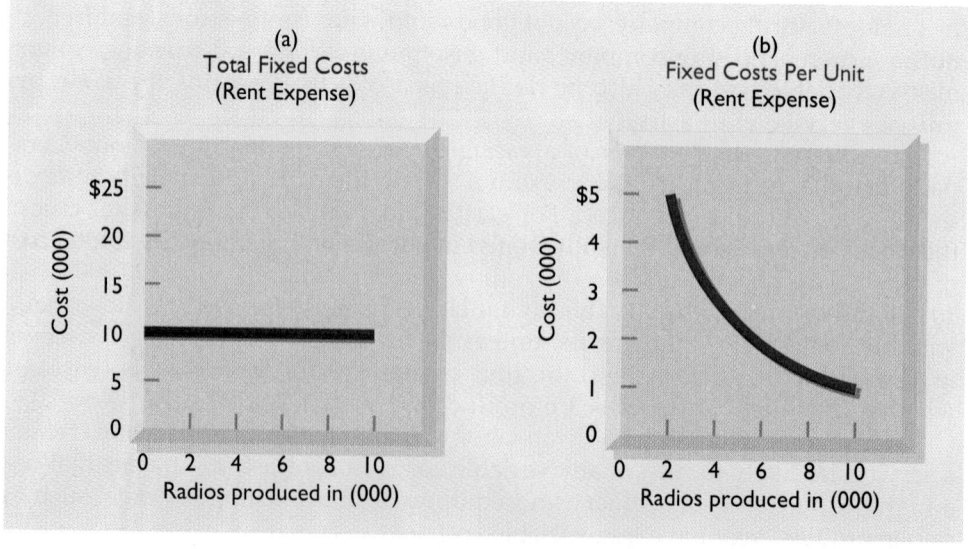

of the work force. As a result, depreciation and lease charges, which are fixed costs, increase whereas direct labor costs, which are variable costs, decrease.

Relevant Range

In Illustrations 24-1 and 24-2, straight lines were drawn throughout the entire activity index for total variable costs and total fixed costs. In essence, the assumption was made that the costs were **linear**. It is now necessary to ask: Is the straight-line relationship realistic? Can the linear assumption produce useful data for CVP analysis?

In most business situations, a straight-line relationship does not exist for variable costs throughout the entire range of activity. At abnormally low levels of activity, it may be impossible to be cost efficient, since the scale of operations may not allow the company to obtain quantity discounts in the purchase of raw materials or use specialization of labor. In contrast, at abnormally high levels of activity, labor costs may increase sharply because of overtime pay, and materials costs may jump significantly because of excess spoilage caused by worker fatigue. Consequently, in the real world, the relationship between the behavior of a variable cost and changes in the activity level is often **curvilinear**, as shown in part (a) of Illustration 24-3.

> **Study Objective 2**
>
> *Explain the meaning and importance of the relevant range.*

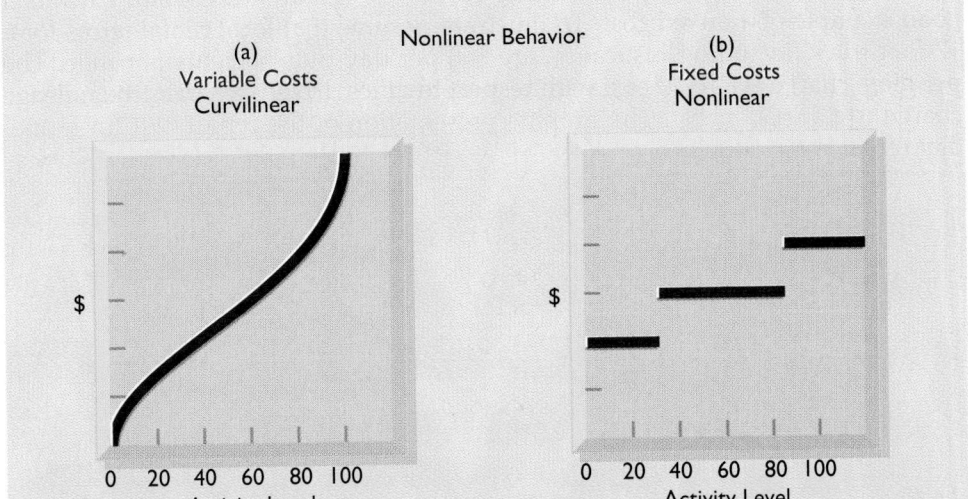

ILLUSTRATION 24-3

Nonlinear behavior

Total fixed costs also do not have a straight-line relationship over the entire range of activity. While some fixed costs will not change, it is possible for management to change other fixed costs. The behavior of total fixed costs through all levels of activity is shown in part (b) of Illustration 24-3.

For most companies, operating at almost zero or at 100% capacity is the exception rather than the rule. Instead, companies often operate over a somewhat narrower range, such as 40–80% of capacity. The range over which a company expects to operate during a year is called the relevant range of the activity index. Within this range, as shown in both diagrams in Illustration 24-4, a straight-line relationship generally exists for both variable and fixed costs.

As you can see, although the straight-line relationship may not be completely realistic, the linear assumption produces useful data for CVP analysis as long as the level of activity remains within the relevant range.

> **Helpful hint** Fixed costs that may be changeable include research such as new product development and management training programs.

ILLUSTRATION 24-4

*Linear behavior within
relevant range*

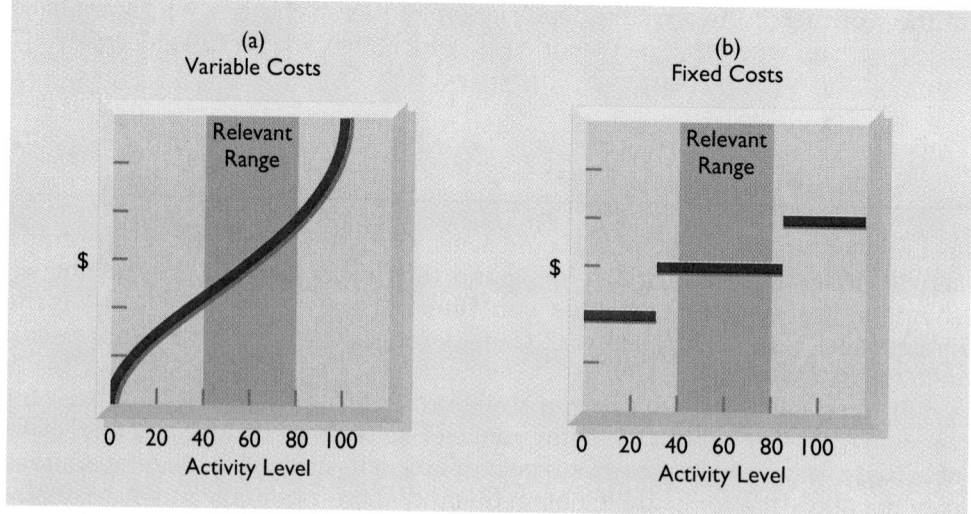

Mixed Costs

Mixed costs contain both a variable cost element and a fixed cost element. Sometimes called **semivariable costs, mixed costs increase in total but not proportionately with changes in the activity level**. The rental of a U-Haul truck is a good example of a mixed cost. To illustrate, assume that local rental terms for a 17-foot truck, including insurance, are $50 per day plus 50 cents per mile. The per diem charge is a fixed cost with respect to miles driven, whereas the mileage charge is a variable cost. The graphic presentation of the rental cost for a one-day rental is as follows:

ILLUSTRATION 24-5

Behavior of a mixed cost

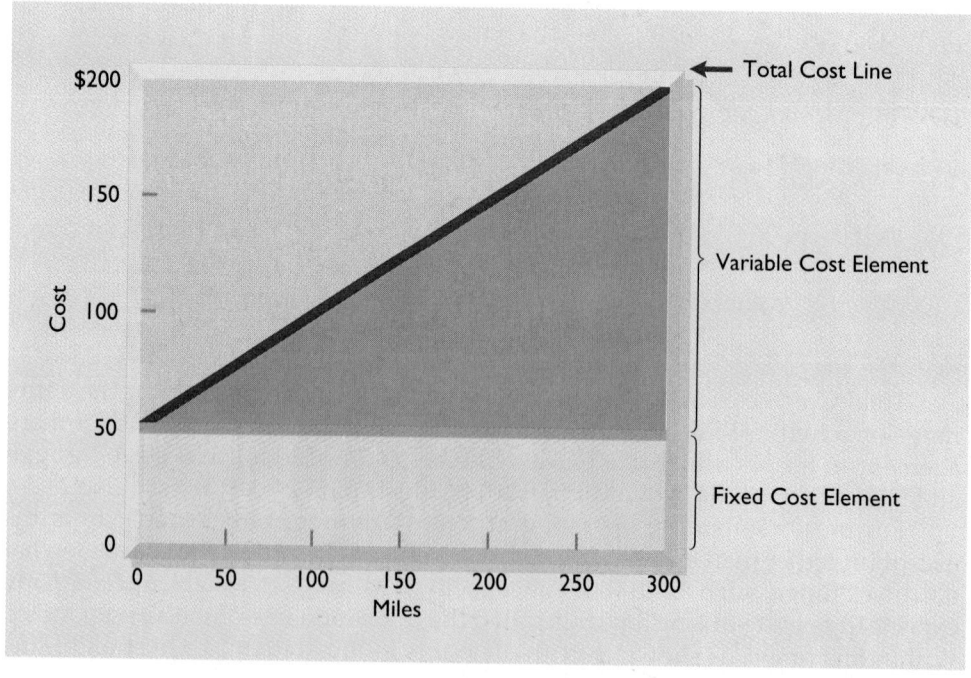

In this case, as in others, the fixed cost element is the cost of having the service available, whereas the variable cost element is the cost of actually using the service. Another example of a mixed cost is utility costs (electric, telephone, and so on), where there is a flat service fee plus a usage charge.

For purposes of CVP analysis, **mixed costs must be classified into their fixed and variable elements**. Accordingly, we must ask: How does management make the classification? One possibility is to determine the variable and fixed components each time a mixed cost is incurred. This approach is rarely followed because of time and cost constraints. Instead, the customary approach is to make the determination of variable and fixed costs on an **aggregate basis** at the end of a period of time, using the company's past experience with the behavior of the mixed cost at various levels of activity. With this approach, there are several methods that management may use in making the determination. We will explain the **high-low method**; other methods are explained in cost accounting courses.[1]

High-Low Method

The high-low method is a mathematical method that uses the total costs incurred at the high and low levels of activity. The difference in costs between the high and low levels represents variable costs, since only the variable cost element can change as activity levels change. The steps in computing fixed and variable costs under this method are as follows:

1. **Determine variable cost per unit from the following formula:**

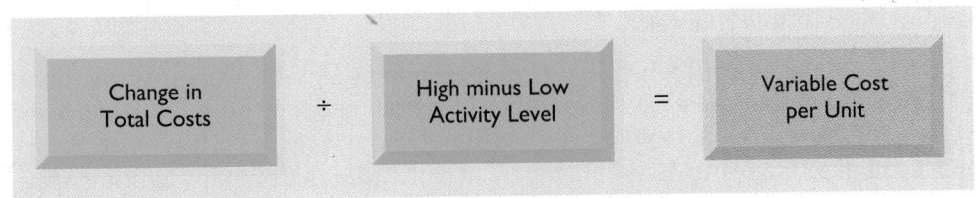

ILLUSTRATION 24-6

Formula for variable cost per unit

To illustrate, assume that Metro Transit Company has the following maintenance costs and mileage data for its fleet of buses over a four-month period:

ILLUSTRATION 24-7

Assumed maintenance costs and mileage data

Month	Miles Driven	Total Cost	Month	Miles Driven	Total Cost
January	20,000	$30,000	March	35,000	$49,000
February	40,000	48,000	April	50,000	63,000

The high and low levels of activity are 50,000 miles in April and 20,000 miles in January. The maintenance costs at these two levels are $63,000 and $30,000, respectively. The difference in maintenance costs is $33,000 ($63,000 − $30,000) and the difference in miles is 30,000 (50,000 − 20,000). Therefore, for Metro Transit, variable cost per unit is $1.10, computed as follows:

$$\$33,000 \div 30,000 = \$1.10$$

2. **Determine the fixed cost by subtracting the total variable cost at either the high or the low activity level from the total cost at that activity level.**

For Metro Transit, the computations are shown in Illustration 24-8:

---

[1]Other methods include the scatter diagram method and least squares regression analysis.

ILLUSTRATION 24-8

High-low method computation of fixed costs

	Activity Level	
	High	**Low**
Total cost	$63,000	$30,000
Less: Variable costs		
50,000 × $1.10	55,000	
20,000 × $1.10		22,000
Total fixed costs	$ 8,000	$ 8,000

Maintenance costs are therefore $8,000 per month plus $1.10 per mile. For example, at 45,000 miles, estimated maintenance costs would be $49,500 variable (45,000 × $1.10) and $8,000 fixed. The high-low method generally produces a reasonable estimate for analysis. However, it does not produce a precise measurement of the fixed and variable elements in a mixed cost because other activity levels are ignored in the computation.

Importance of Identifying Variable and Fixed Costs

Why is it important to segregate costs into variable and fixed elements? The answer may become apparent if we return to the five questions raised on the second page of this chapter.

1. To make a profit when it cuts domestic fares by 50%, American Airlines will have to increase the number of passengers or cut its variable costs for those flights. Its fixed costs will not change.

2. Higher wages to UAW members at Ford Motor Company will increase the variable costs of manufacturing automobiles. To maintain present profit levels, Ford will have to cut other variable costs or increase the price of its automobiles.

3. To cover its costs exactly on the Saturn automobile for the next model year, General Motors must determine the sales volume at which sales revenue will equal total costs, both fixed and variable.

4. The modernizing of plant facilities at USX Corp. changes the proportion of fixed and variable costs of producing one ton of steel. Fixed costs increase because of higher depreciation charges whereas variable costs decrease due to the reduction in the number of steelworkers.

5. Doubling its advertising expense increases McDonald's fixed costs. Sales volume must be increased to cover three items: (1) the increase in advertising, (2) the variable costs of the increased sales volume, and (3) the desired additional net income.

Before You Go On . . .

1. What are the effects on total cost and per unit cost due to a change in activity on (a) a variable cost and (b) a fixed cost?

2. What is the relevant range and the behavior of costs within this range?

3. What are the steps in applying the high-low method to mixed costs?

SECTION 2 Cost-Volume-Profit Analysis

Cost-volume-profit (CVP) analysis is the study of the effects of changes in costs and volume on a company's profits. CVP analysis is important in profit planning. It also is a critical factor in such management decisions as setting selling prices, determining the best product mix, and making maximum use of production facilities.

Basic Components

CVP analysis involves a consideration of the interrelationships among the following components.

1. Volume or level of activity.
2. Unit selling prices.
3. Variable cost per unit.
4. Total fixed costs.
5. Sales mix.

The following assumptions underlie each CVP application:

1. The behavior of both costs and revenues is linear throughout the relevant range of the activity index.
2. All costs can be classified as either variable or fixed with reasonable accuracy.
3. Changes in activity are the only factors that affect costs.
4. All units produced are sold.
5. When more than one type of product is sold, total sales will be in a constant sales mix.

When these assumptions are not valid, the results of CVP analysis may be inaccurate.

In applications of CVP analysis that follow, we will assume that the term "cost" includes **all** costs and expenses pertaining to production and sale of the product. That is, **cost includes manufacturing costs plus selling and administrative expenses**. We will use the Vargo Video Company as an example. Relevant data for the video-cassette recorders (VCRs) made by this company are as follows:

Unit selling price	$500
Unit variable costs	$300
Total monthly fixed costs	$200,000

ILLUSTRATION 24-9

Assumed selling price and cost data for Vargo Video

Contribution Margin

One of the key relationships in CVP analysis is contribution margin (CM). **Contribution margin is the amount of revenue remaining after deducting variable costs.** For example, if we assume that Vargo Video sold 1,000 VCRs in a given month, the contribution margin would be computed as follows:

Study Objective 4

State the five components of cost-volume-profit analysis.

Study Objective 5

Indicate the meaning of contribution margin and the ways it may be expressed.

ILLUSTRATION 24-10

Computation of contribution margin

Sales (1,000 × $500)	$500,000
Variable costs (1,000 × $300)	300,000
Contribution margin	**$200,000**

This contribution margin is then available to cover fixed costs and to produce income for the company.

Views differ as to the best way to express contribution margin (CM). Some individuals favor a per unit basis. The formula for contribution margin per unit is:

ILLUSTRATION 24-11

Formula for contribution margin per unit

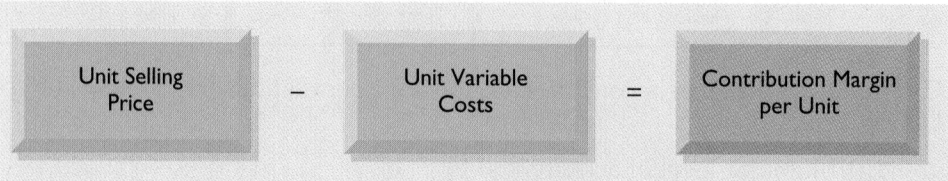

At Vargo Video, the contribution margin per unit is $200, computed as follows:

$$\$500 - \$300 = \$200$$

Contribution margin per unit indicates that for every VCR sold, Vargo will have $200 to apply to its fixed costs and contribute to income. Since fixed costs are $200,000, Vargo Video must sell 1,000 VCRs ($200,000 ÷ $200) before there is any income. Above that sales volume, every sale will contribute $200 to income. Thus, if 1,500 units are sold, income will be $100,000 (500 × $200).

Others prefer to use a contribution margin ratio. The formula for this ratio is:

ILLUSTRATION 24-12

Formula for contribution margin ratio

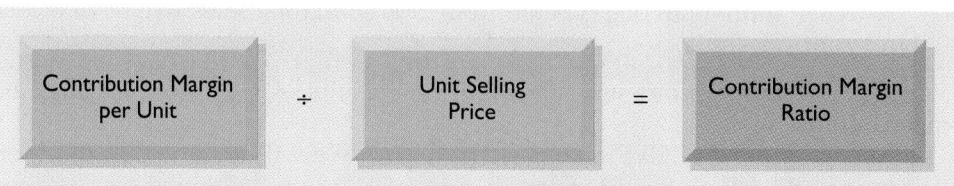

At Vargo Video, the ratio is 40%, as shown below.

$$\$200 ÷ \$500 = 40\%$$

The CM ratio of 40% means that 40 cents of each sales dollar ($1 × 40%) is available to cover fixed costs and to produce income. This expression of contribution margin is very helpful in determining the effect of changes in sales on income. To illustrate, if the management of Vargo Video wants to know the effect of a $50,000 increase in sales, they simply multiply $50,000 by the CM ratio (40%) to determine that income will increase $20,000.

Study Objective 6

Identify the three ways that the break-even point may be determined.

Break-Even Analysis

A second key relationship in CVP analysis is the level of activity at which total revenues equals total costs, both fixed and variable. This level of activity is called the break-even point. At this volume of sales, the company will realize no in-

Accounting in Action · *Business Insight*

It pays to know how break-even is defined. For example, *Flashdance*, a highly successful film, provided little to the movie producers initially because of the definitions used for profits. As one producer noted, "The studios do not cheat and they do not lie—they just have very creative accounting methods. A studio, for example, has at least four ways to define 'break-even' and 24 different types of 'gross,' and they're all legitimate." Perhaps the Hollywood bookkeeper is right when he observed, "Most of the creative work in this business is done in the accounting department."

come and suffer no loss. Since income is not involved when the break-even point is the objective, the analysis is often referred to simply as **break-even analysis**. Knowledge of the break-even point is useful to management in deciding whether to introduce new product lines, change sales prices on established products, or enter new market areas.

The break-even point can be:

1. Computed from a mathematical equation.
2. Computed by using contribution margin.
3. Derived from a cost-volume-profit (CVP) graph.

The break-even point can be expressed **either in sales dollars or sales units**.

Mathematical Equation

In its simplest form, the equation for break-even sales is:

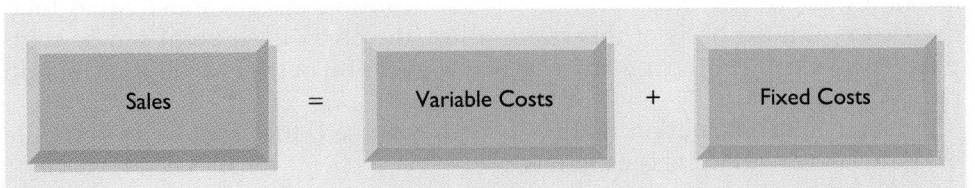

ILLUSTRATION 24-13

Break-even equation

The break-even point in dollars is found by expressing variable costs as a percentage of unit selling price. For Vargo Video, the percentage is 60% ($300 ÷ $500). The computation is:

$$X = .60X + \$200{,}000$$
$$.40X = \$200{,}000$$
$$X = \$500{,}000$$

where:

$$X = \text{sales dollars at the break-even point}$$
$$.60X = \text{variable costs as a percentage of unit selling price}$$
$$\$200{,}000 = \text{total fixed costs}$$

Sales, therefore, must be $500,000 for Vargo Video to break even.

Thus, break-even units are 1,000 ($500,000 ÷ $500). The break-even point in units can be computed directly from the mathematical equation by using unit selling prices and unit variable costs. The computation is:

$$\$500X = \$300X + \$200,000$$

$$\$200X = \$200,000$$

$$X = 1,000 \text{ units}$$

where:

$$\$500X = \text{unit selling price} \times \text{sales volume}$$

$$\$300X = \text{variable cost per unit} \times \text{sales volume}$$

$$\$200,000 = \text{total fixed costs}$$

The accuracy of the computations can be proved as follows:

ILLUSTRATION 24-14

Break-even proof

Sales (1,000 × $500)		$500,000
Total costs:		
Variable (1,000 × $300)	$300,000	
Fixed	200,000	500,000
Net income		$ –0–

Contribution Margin Technique

Since we know that contribution margin equals total revenues less variable costs, it follows that at the break-even point, **contribution margin must equal total fixed costs**. On the basis of this relationship, the break-even point can be computed by using either the contribution margin per unit or the contribution margin ratio.

When the contribution margin per unit is used, the formula to compute break-even sales in units is as follows:

ILLUSTRATION 24-15

Formula for break-even point using contribution margin per unit

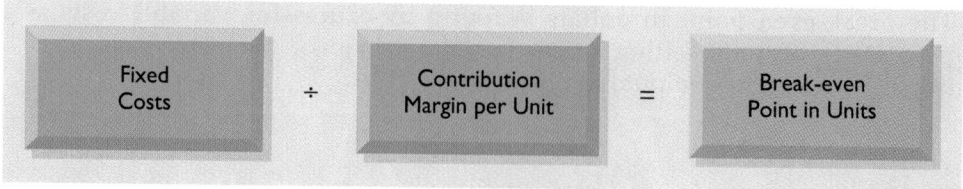

For Vargo Video, the contribution margin per unit is $200, as explained above. Thus, the computation is:

$$\$200,000 \div \$200 = 1,000 \text{ units}$$

When the contribution margin ratio is used, the formula to compute break-even sales in dollars is:

ILLUSTRATION 24-16

Formula for break-even point using contribution margin ratio

We know that the contribution margin ratio for Vargo Video is 40%. Thus, the computation is:

$$\$200,000 \div 40\% = \$500,000$$

Graphic Presentation

An effective way to derive the break-even point is to prepare a break-even graph. Because this graph also shows costs, volume, and profits, it is referred to as the cost-volume-profit (CVP) graph.

In the graph in Illustration 24-17, sales volume is recorded along the horizontal axis. This axis should extend to the maximum level of expected sales. Both total revenues (sales) and total costs (fixed plus variable) are recorded on the vertical axis.

ILLUSTRATION 24-17

CVP graph

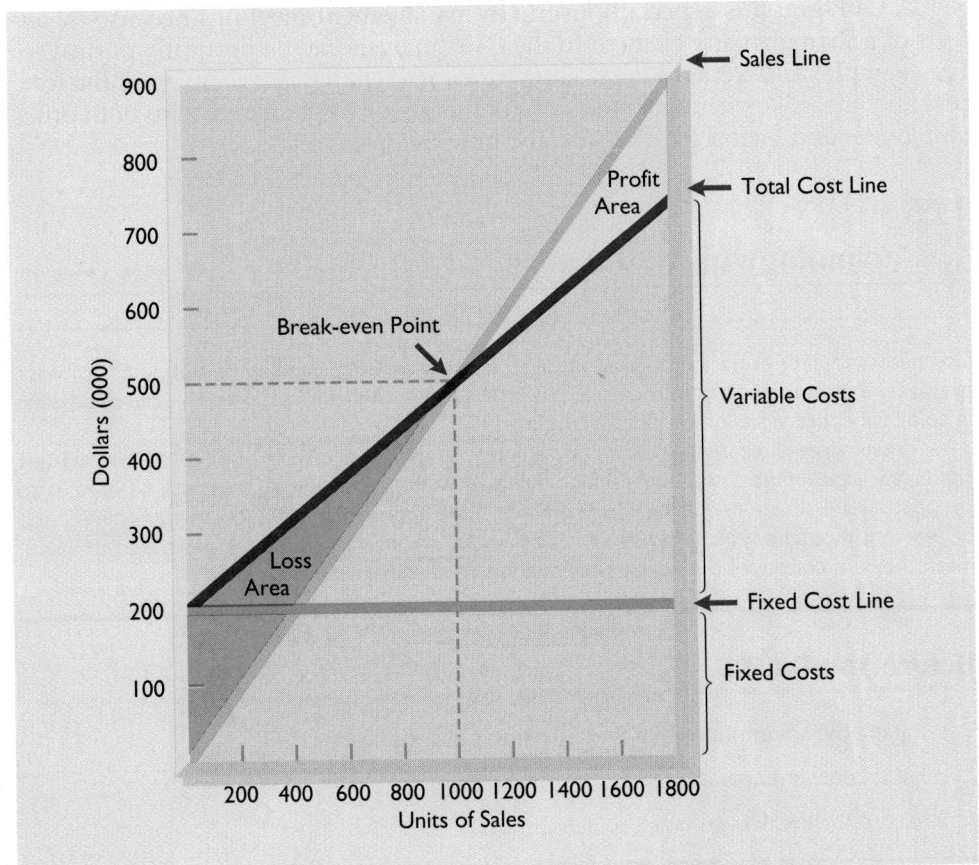

The construction of the graph, using the data for Vargo Video, is as follows:

1. Plot the total revenue line starting at the zero activity level. For every VCR sold, total revenue increases by $500. For example, at 200 units, sales are $100,000, and at the upper level of activity (1,800 units), sales are $900,000. Note that the revenue line is assumed to be linear throughout the full range of activity.

2. Plot the total fixed cost by a horizontal line. For the VCRs, this line is plotted at $200,000, and it is the same at every level of activity.

3. Plot the total cost line starting at the fixed cost line at zero activity and increasing the amount by the variable cost at each level of activity. For each VCR, variable costs are $300. Thus, at 200 units, total variable cost is $60,000 and the total cost is $260,000; at 1,800 units total variable cost is $540,000, and total cost is $740,000. On the graph, the amount of the variable cost can be derived from the difference between the total cost and fixed cost lines at each level of activity.

4. Determine the break-even point from the intersection of the total cost line and the total revenue line. The break-even point in dollars is found by drawing a horizontal line from the break-even point to the vertical axis. The break-even point in units is obtained by drawing a vertical line from the break-even point to the horizontal axis. For the VCRs, the break-even point is $500,000 of sales, or 1,000 units. At this sales level, Vargo Video will cover costs but make no profit.

In addition to identifying the break-even point, the CVP graph shows both the net income and net loss areas. Thus, the amount of income or loss at each level of sales can be derived from the total sales and total cost line.

A CVP graph is especially useful in management meetings because the effects of a change in any element in the CVP analysis can be promptly portrayed. For example, a 10% increase in selling price will change the location of the total revenue line. Likewise, the effects on total costs of wage increases to both office employees and factory workers can be quickly observed.

Technology in Action

Computer graphics are a valuable companion to an increasing number of computer software packages. Graphs can be instantly changed to provide visual "what if" analysis. This can all be done in color for either video or hard copy output.

While current technology allows for stunning graphs in a variety of different formats (pie charts, bar, stacked bar, two-dimensional, three-dimensional, etc.), care must still be used as to the appropriate situations for the use of graphs. In the appropriate situation, a graph can literally be worth a thousand words. However, just because graphs can be quickly generated does not mean they can convey all the needed information for a management decision.

Before You Go On . . .

1. What are the assumptions that underlie each CVP application?

2. What is contribution margin and how may it be expressed?

3. How can the break-even point be determined?

Margin of Safety

Study Objective 7

Define the term "margin of safety" and give the formulas for computing it.

The margin of safety is another relationship that may be used in CVP analysis. Margin of safety is the difference between actual or expected sales and sales at the break-even point. This relationship measures the "breathing room" or "cushion" that management has to break even if actual or expected sales fail to materialize. The margin of safety may be expressed in dollars or as a ratio.

The formula for stating the **margin of safety in dollars** is:

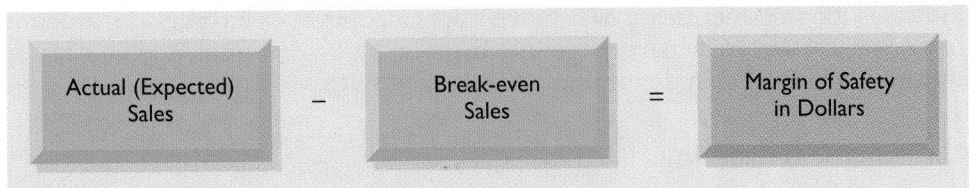

ILLUSTRATION 24-18

Formula for margin of safety in dollars

Assuming that actual (expected) sales for Vargo Video are $750,000, the computation is:

$$\$750,000 - \$500,000 = \$250,000$$

In contrast, the formula and computation for determining the **margin of safety ratio** are:

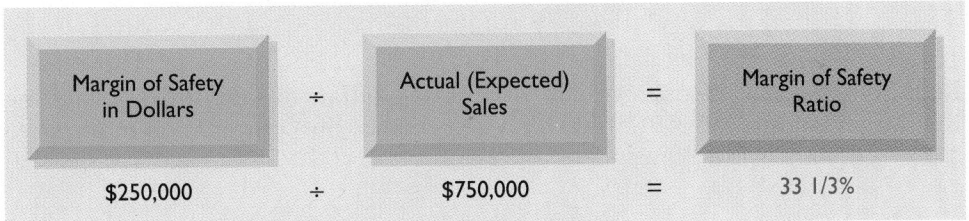

ILLUSTRATION 24-19

Formula for margin of safety ratio

Accounting in Action · *Business Insight*

Computation of break-even and margin of safety is important for various types of business. Consider how the promoter for the Rolling Stones' tour used the break-even point and margin of safety. For example, one outdoor show should bring 70,000 individuals at $35 apiece on the average for a gross of $2.45 million. The promoter guarantees $1.2 million to the Rolling Stones. In addition, 20% of gross or approximately $500,000 goes to the stadium in which the performance is staged. Add another $400,000 for other expenses such as ticket takers, parking attendants, advertising, and so on. This leaves $350,000 per show to the promoter, if it sells out. At 75%, the promoter breaks about even, and at 50%, the promoter loses hundreds of thousands of dollars. However, the promoter also shares in sales of T-shirts and memorabilia for which the promoter will net over $7 million during the tour. If the Rolling Stones' tour is a success, the promoter could make $35 million!

Source: Forbes, May 15, 1989.

The higher the dollars or the percentage, the greater the margin of safety. The adequacy of the margin of safety should be evaluated by management in terms of such factors as the vulnerability of the product to competitive pressures and to downturns in the economy.

Study Objective 8

Give the formulas for determining sales required to earn target net income.

Target Net Income

Management usually sets an income objective for individual product lines. This objective called target net income is extremely useful to management because it indicates the sales necessary to achieve a specified level of income. The amount of sales necessary to achieve target net income can be determined from each of the approaches used in determining break-even sales.

Mathematical Equation

From our consideration of the break-even point, we know that it results in no profit or loss for the company. By adding a factor for target net income to the break-even equation, we obtain the following formula for determining required sales:

ILLUSTRATION 24-20

Formula for required sales to meet target net income

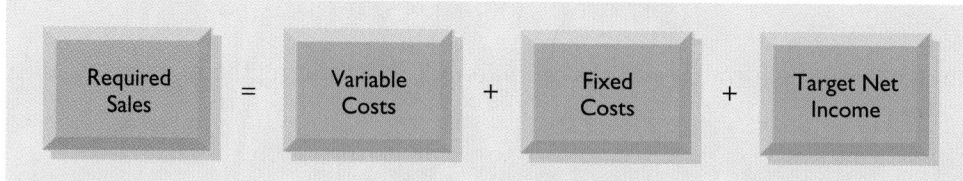

Required sales may be expressed in **either sales dollars or sales units**. Assuming that target net income is $120,000 for Vargo Video, the computation of required sales in dollars is as follows:

$$X = .60X + \$200,000 + \$120,000$$

$$.40X = \$320,000$$

$$X = \$800,000$$

where:

$$X = \text{required sales}$$

$$.60X = \text{variable costs as a percentage of unit selling price}$$

$$\$200,000 = \text{total fixed costs}$$

$$\$120,000 = \text{target net income}$$

The sales volume in units at the targeted income level is found by dividing the sales dollars by the unit selling price ($800,000 ÷ $500) = 1,600 units.[2]

Contribution Margin Technique

As in the case of break-even sales, the sales required to meet a target net income can be computed in either dollars or units. The formula using the contribution margin ratio is as follows:

---

[2]The units can be derived directly by using unit prices in the equation: $500X = $300X + $200,000 + $120,000; $200X = $320,000 or 1,600 units.

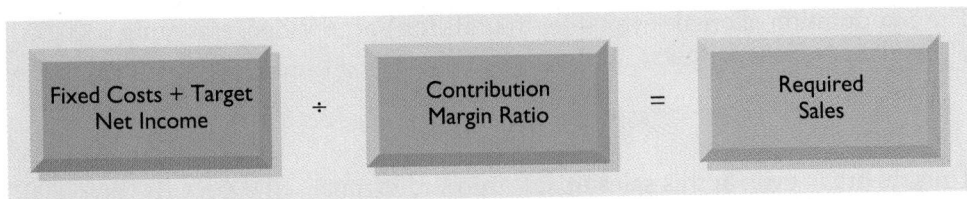

ILLUSTRATION 24-21

Formula for required sales using contribution margin ratio

The computation for Vargo Video is as follows:

$$\$320,000 \div 40\% = \$800,000$$

Graphic Presentation

The CVP graph presented in Illustration 24-17 can also be used to derive the sales required to meet target net income. In the profit area of the graph, the distance between the sales line and the total cost line at any point equals net income. Required sales are found by analyzing the differences between the two lines until the desired net income is found.

Sales Mix

In the preceding discussion, we have focused on one product, video-cassette recorders. One of the assumptions of CVP analysis is that if more than one product is involved, the sales mix of the products remains constant. **Sales mix** is the relative combination in which a company's products are sold. For example, if 2 units of Product A are sold for every 1 unit of Product B, the sales mix of the two products is 2:1. Break-even sales can be computed for a mix of two or more products by determining the **weighted average unit contribution margin of all the products**.

To illustrate, we will assume that Vargo Video sells both VCRs and television sets (TVs) at the following per unit data:

Study Objective 9

Explain the term "sales mix" and its effects in determining break-even sales.

ILLUSTRATION 24-22

Per unit data—sales mix

Unit Data	VCRs	TVs
Selling price	$500	$800
Variable costs	300	400
Contribution margin	$200	$400
Sales mix	3	1

The total contribution margin of the 4 units sold is $1,000 ($200 × 3 + $400 × 1), and the weighted average unit contribution margin is $250 ($1,000 ÷ 4). The break-even formula is as follows:

ILLUSTRATION 24-23

Break-even formula—sales mix

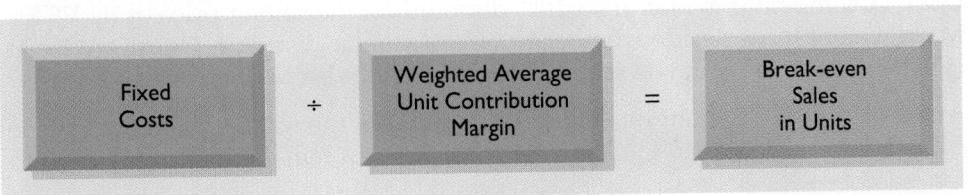

The computation of break-even sales in units for Vargo Video, assuming $200,000 of fixed costs, is as follows:

$$\$200,000 \div \$250 = 800 \text{ units}$$

Thus, to break even at this sales mix, Vargo Video must sell 600 VCRs (¾ × 800) and 200 TVs (¼ × 800). This can be verified by the following:

ILLUSTRATION 24-24

Break-even proof—sales mix

Product	Unit Sales	×	Unit CM	=	Total CM
VCRs	600	×	$200	=	$120,000
TVs	200	×	400	=	80,000
	800				$200,000

Management should continually review the company's sales mix. At any specified volume of sales, **net income will be greater if more high contribution margin units are sold than low contribution margin units**. For Vargo Video, the television sets produce the higher contribution margin. Consequently, if 300 TVs and 500 VCRs are sold, net income would be higher at the same total volume of sales than in the current sales mix. An analysis of these relationships shows that a shift from low margin sales to high margin sales may increase net income, even though there is a decline in total sales volume. Likewise, a shift from high to low margin sales may result in a decrease in net income, even though there is an increase in total sales volume.

CVP and Changes in the Business Environment

When the IBM personal computer (PC) was introduced, it sold for $2,500; today the same type of computer sells for less than $1,000. When high oil prices collapsed, the break-even point for airline and trucking companies dropped dramatically. Because of lower prices for imported steel, the demand for domestic steel dropped significantly. The point should be clear: Business conditions change rapidly and management must respond intelligently to these changes. CVP analysis can help. To illustrate how CVP analysis can be used in responding to change, we will use the following independent situations that might occur at Vargo Video. Each case is based on the original VCR sales and cost data, which were:

ILLUSTRATION 24-25

Original VCR sales and cost data

Unit selling price	$500
Unit variable cost	$300
Total fixed costs	$200,000
Break-even sales	$500,000 or 1,000 units

CASE 1 A competitor is offering a 10% discount on the selling price of its VCRs. Management must decide whether to offer a similar discount. **Question:** What effect will a 10% discount on selling price have on the break-even point for VCRs?

Answer: A 10% discount on selling price reduces the selling price per unit to $450 [$500 − ($500 × 10%)]. Variable costs per unit remain unchanged at $300.

Thus, the contribution margin per unit is $150. Assuming no change in fixed costs, break-even sales are 1,333 units, computed as follows:

ILLUSTRATION 24-26

Computation of break-even sales in units

Fixed Costs	÷	Contribution Margin per Unit	=	Break-even Sales
$200,000	÷	$150	=	1,333 units (rounded)

For Vargo Video, this change would require monthly sales to increase by 333 units or 33⅓% in order to break even. In reaching a conclusion about offering a 10% discount to customers, management must determine the likelihood of achieving the increased sales. Also, management should estimate the possible loss of sales if the competitor's discount price is not matched.

CASE II To meet the continuing threat of foreign competition, management invests in new robotic equipment that will significantly lower the amount of direct labor required to make the VCRs. It is estimated that total fixed costs will increase 30% and that variable cost per unit will decrease 30%. **Question:** What effect will the new equipment have on the sales volume required to break even?

Answer: Total fixed costs become $260,000 [$200,000 + (30% × $200,000)], and variable cost per unit is now $210 [$300 − (30% × $300)]. The new break-even point is 900 units, computed as follows:

ILLUSTRATION 24-27

Computation of break-even sales in units

Fixed Costs	÷	Contribution Margin per Unit	=	Break-even Sales
$260,000	÷	($500 − $210)	=	900 units (rounded)

These changes appear to be advantageous for Vargo Video because the break-even point is reduced by 10%, or 100 units.

CASE III The principal supplier of raw materials has just announced a price increase. It is estimated that the higher cost will increase the variable cost of VCRs by $25 per unit. Management would like to hold the line on the selling price of VCRs. It plans a cost-cutting program that will save $17,500 in fixed costs per month. Vargo is currently realizing monthly net income of $80,000 on sales of 1,400 VCRs. **Question:** What increase in sales will be needed to maintain the same level of net income?

Answer: The variable cost per unit increases to $325 ($300 + $25), and fixed costs are reduced to $182,500 ($200,000 − $17,500). Because of the change in variable cost, the variable cost becomes 65% of sales ($325 ÷ $500). Using the equation for target net income, we find that required sales are $750,000, computed as follows:

ILLUSTRATION 24-28

Computation of required sales

$$\text{Required sales} = \text{Variable Costs} + \text{Fixed Costs} + \text{Target Net Income}$$
$$X = .65X + \$182,500 + \$80,000$$
$$.35X = \$262,500$$
$$X = \$750,000$$

To achieve the required sales, 1,500 VCRs will have to be sold ($750,000 ÷ $500), an increase of 100 units. If this does not seem to be a reasonable expectation, management will either have to effect further reductions in costs or accept less net income if the selling price remains unchanged.

CVP Income Statement

Study Objective 10

Describe the essential features of a cost–volume–profit income statement.

As you have learned, cost behavior and contribution margin are key factors in CVP analysis. Because management makes its decisions on these factors, it often wants the results of these decisions reported in a similar format. This has led to the development for **internal use only** of a **CVP** or **contribution margin format** for the income statement. The CVP income statement classifies costs and expenses as variable or fixed and specifically reports contribution margin in the body of the statement. This is in contrast to the income statement traditionally prepared for external use, in which no disclosure is made of the behavior of costs and expenses. In the traditional statement, costs and expenses are classified only by function, such as cost of goods sold, selling expenses, and administrative expenses.

To illustrate the CVP income statement, we will assume that Vargo Video is successful in reaching its target net income of $120,000 (see page 980). From an analysis of the transactions, the following information is obtained on the $680,000 of costs that were incurred in June:

ILLUSTRATION 24-29

Assumed cost and expense data

	Variable	Fixed	Total
Cost of goods sold	$400,000	$120,000	$520,000
Selling expenses	60,000	40,000	100,000
Administrative expenses	20,000	40,000	60,000
	$480,000	$200,000	$680,000

The CVP income statement and the conventional income statement based on these data are shown side-by-side for comparative purposes below.

ILLUSTRATION 24-30

Traditional versus CVP income statement

VARGO VIDEO COMPANY
Income Statement
For the Month Ended June 30, 1993

Traditional Format

Sales		$800,000
Cost of goods sold		520,000
Gross profit		280,000
Operating expenses		
Selling expenses	$100,000	
Administrative expenses	60,000	
Total operating expenses		160,000
Net income		$120,000

CVP Format

Sales		$800,000
Variable expenses		
Cost of goods sold	$400,000	
Selling expenses	60,000	
Administrative expenses	20,000	
Total variable expenses		480,000
CONTRIBUTION MARGIN		320,000
Fixed expenses		
Cost of goods sold	120,000	
Selling expenses	40,000	
Administrative expenses	40,000	
Total fixed expenses		200,000
Net income		$120,000

Note that net income is the same ($120,000) in both of the statements. The major difference is the format for the expenses. As illustrated, the CVP statement classifies costs and expenses as either variable or fixed. Another difference is that the traditional statement shows gross profit, whereas the CVP statement shows contribution margin. Study the CVP form carefully. It will be used in remaining chapters, and it is often used in business in internal reporting to management.

Before You Go On . . .

1. What is the formula for computing the margin of safety (a) in dollars and (b) as a ratio?

2. State the formula for computing break-even sales in units when a company sells more than one product.

3. How does a CVP income statement differ from a traditional income statement?

SECTION 3   Variable Costing

In earlier chapters, all manufacturing costs, both variable and fixed, have been classified as product costs. In job order costing, for example, a job is assigned the costs of direct materials, direct labor, and both variable and fixed manufacturing overhead. This costing approach is referred to as full or absorption costing because all manufacturing costs are charged to, or absorbed by, the product. An alternative approach is to use variable costing. Under variable costing only direct materials, direct labor, and variable manufacturing costs are considered product costs; fixed manufacturing costs are recognized as period costs (expenses) when incurred. The difference between absorption costing and variable costing is graphically shown as follows:

Study Objective 11

Explain the difference between absorption costing and variable costing.

ILLUSTRATION 24-31

Difference between absorption costing and variable costing

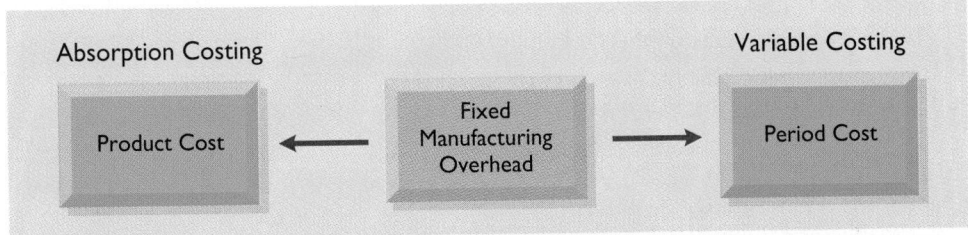

Selling and administrative expenses are period costs under both absorption and variable costing.

To illustrate the computation of unit production cost under absorption and variable costing, assume that Premium Products Corporation manufactures a polyurethane sealant called Fix-it for car windshields. Relevant data for Fix-it in January 1993, the first month of production, is as follows:

Selling Price: $20 per unit.

Units: Produced 30,000; sold 20,000; beginning inventory –0–.

Variable unit costs: Manufacturing $9 (direct materials $5, direct labor $3, and variable overhead $1), and selling and administrative expenses $2.

Fixed costs: Manufacturing overhead $120,000 and selling and administrative expenses $15,000.

The per unit production cost under each costing approach is:

ILLUSTRATION 24-32

Computation of per unit production cost

Type of Cost	Absorption Costing	Variable Costing
Direct materials	$ 5	$5
Direct labor	3	3
Variable manufacturing overhead	1	1
Fixed manufacturing overhead ($120,000 ÷ 30,000 units produced)	4	0
Total unit cost	$13	$9

The difference in total unit cost of $4 ($13 − $9) occurs because fixed manufacturing costs are a product cost under absorption costing and a period cost under variable costing. Based on these data, each unit sold and each unit remaining in inventory are costed at $13 under absorption costing and at $9 under variable costing.

Effects on Income

The income statements under the two costing approaches are shown in Illustrations 24-33 and 24-34. The conventional income statement format is used with absorption costing and the cost-volume-profit format is used with variable costing. Computations are inserted parenthetically in the statements to facilitate your understanding of the amounts.

ILLUSTRATION 24-33

Absorption costing income statement

PREMIUM PRODUCTS COMPANY
Income Statement
For the Month Ended January 31, 1993
(Absorption Costing)

Sales (20,000 units × $20)		$400,000
Cost of goods sold		
Inventory, January 1	$ −0−	
Cost of goods manufactured (30,000 units × $13)	390,000	
Cost of goods available for sale	390,000	
Inventory, January 31 (10,000 units × $13)	130,000	
Cost of goods sold (20,000 units × $13)		260,000
Gross profit		140,000
Selling and administrative expenses (Variable, 20,000 units × $2 + fixed, $15,000)		55,000
Income from operations		$ 85,000

Income from operations under absorption costing shown in Illustration 24-33 is $40,000 higher than under variable costing ($85,000 − $45,000) shown in Illustration 24-34.

As highlighted in the two income statements, there is a $40,000 difference in the ending inventories ($130,000 under absorption costing and $90,000 under variable costing). Under absorption costing, $40,000 of the fixed overhead costs (10,000 units × $4) have been deferred to a future period as a product cost. In contrast, the entire fixed manufacturing costs are expensed when incurred under variable costing.

ILLUSTRATION 24-34

Variable costing income statement

Helpful hint Note the difference in the computation of the ending inventory: $9 per unit here, $13 per unit above. students if that is sound business strategy.

PREMIUM PRODUCTS COMPANY
Income Statement
For the Month Ended January 31, 1993
(Variable Costing)

Sales (20,000 units × $20)		$400,000
Variable expenses		
Variable cost of goods sold		
Inventory, January 1	$ –0–	
Variable manufacturing costs (30,000 units × $9)	270,000	
Cost of goods available for sale	270,000	
Inventory, January 31 (10,000 units × $9)	90,000	
Variable cost of goods sold	180,000	
Variable selling and administrative expenses (20,000 units × $2)	40,000	
Total variable expenses		220,000
Contribution margin		180,000
Fixed expenses		
Manufacturing overhead	120,000	
Selling and administrative expenses	15,000	
Total fixed expenses		135,000
Income from operations		$ 45,000

As shown, when units produced exceed units sold, income under absorption costing is higher than under variable costing. Conversely, when units produced are less than units sold, income under absorption costing is lower than under variable costing. The reason is that the cost of the beginning inventory will be higher under absorption costing than under variable costing. For example, if 30,000 units of Fix-it are sold in February and only 20,000 units are produced, income from operations will be $40,000 less under absorption costing than under variable costing because of the $40,000 difference ($130,000 vs. $90,000) in the beginning inventories.

When units produced and sold are the same, income from operations will be equal under the two costing approaches. Since there is no ending inventory, there is no deferral of any fixed overhead costs of the current period to future periods through the ending inventory. The foregoing effects of the two costing approaches on income from operations may be summarized as follows:

ILLUSTRATION 24-35

Summary of income effects

Circumstance	Effects on Income From Operations
Units produced exceed units sold	Income higher under absorption costing than under variable costing
Units produced less than units sold	Income lower under absorption costing than under variable costing
Units produced equal units sold	Income same under either approach

Rationale for Variable Costing

The rationale for variable costing centers on the purpose of fixed manufacturing costs which is to have productive facilities available for use. Conceptually, these costs are incurred whether a company operates at zero or 100% of capacity. Thus, proponents of variable costing argue that these costs should be expensed in the period in which they are incurred.

Supporters of absorption costing defend the assignment of fixed manufacturing overhead costs to inventory on the basis that these costs are as much a cost of getting a product such as Fix-it ready for sale as direct materials or direct labor. Accordingly, these costs should not be matched with revenues until the product is sold.

The use of variable costing in product costing is only acceptable for internal use by management. It cannot be used in determining product costs in financial statements prepared in accordance with generally accepted accounting principles because it understates inventory costs. To comply with the matching principle, a company must use absorption costing for its work in process and finished goods inventories. Similarly, absorption costing must be used for income tax purposes.

Before You Go On . . .

1. What is variable costing?

2. What is the rationale for variable costing?

Summary of Study Objectives

1. Distinguish between variable and fixed costs. Variable costs are costs that vary in total directly and proportionately with changes in the activity index. Fixed costs are costs that remain the same in total regardless of changes in the activity index.

2. Explain the meaning and importance of the relevant range. The relevant range is the range of activity in which a company expects to operate during a year. It is important in CVP analysis because the behavior of costs is linear throughout the relevant range.

3. Explain the concept of mixed costs. Mixed costs increase in total but not proportionately with changes in the activity level. For purposes of CVP analysis, mixed costs must be classified into their fixed and variable elements. One method that management may use is the high–low method.

4. State the five components of cost–volume–profit analysis. The five components of CVP analysis are (a) volume or level of activity, (b) unit selling prices, (c) variable cost per unit, (d) total fixed costs, and (e) sales mix.

5. Indicate the meaning of contribution margin and the ways it may be expressed. Contribution margin is the amount of revenue remaining after deducting variable costs. It can be expressed as a per unit amount or as a ratio.

6. Identify the three ways that the break-even point may be determined. The break-even point can be (a) computed from a mathematical equation, (b) computed by using a contribution margin technique, and (c) derived from a CVP graph.

7. Define the term "margin of safety" and give the formulas for computing it. Margin of safety is the difference between actual or expected sales and sales at the break-even point. The formulas for margin of safety are Actual (Expected) Sales − Break-even Sales = Margin of Safety in Dollars; Margin of Safety in Dollars ÷ Actual (Expected) Sales = Margin of Safety Ratio.

8. Give the formulas for determining sales required to earn target net income. One formula is: Required Sales = Variable Costs + Fixed Costs + Target Net Income. Another formula is: Fixed Costs + Target Net Income ÷ Contribution Margin Ratio = Required Sales.

9. Explain the term "sales mix" and its effects in determining break-even sales. Sales mix is the relative combination in which a company's products are sold. Break-even sales are determined by using the weighted average unit contribution margin of all the products.

10. *Describe the essential features of a cost–volume–profit income statement.* The CVP income statement classifies costs and expenses as variable or fixed and reports contribution margin in the body of the statement.

11. *Explain the difference between absorption costing and variable costing.* Under absorption costing, fixed manufacturing costs are product costs; under variable costing, fixed manufacturing costs are period costs.

GLOSSARY

Absorption costing · A costing approach in which all manufacturing costs are charged to the product. (p. 985).

Break-even point · The level of activity at which total revenues equal total costs. (p. 974).

Contribution margin · The amount of revenue remaining after deducting variable costs. (p. 973).

Cost behavior analysis · The study of how specific costs respond to changes in the level of activity. (p. 967).

Cost–volume–profit analysis · The study of the effects of changes in costs and volume on a company's profits. (p. 973).

Cost–volume–profit graph · A graph showing the relationship between costs, volume, and profits. (p. 977).

Cost–volume–profit income statement · A statement for internal use that classifies costs and expenses as fixed or variable and reports contribution margin. (p. 984).

Fixed costs · Costs that remain the same in total regardless of changes in the activity level. (p. 968).

High–low method · A mathematical method that uses the total costs incurred at the high and low levels of activity. (p. 971).

Margin of safety · The difference between actual or expected sales and sales at the break-even point. (p. 979).

Mixed costs · Costs that contain both a variable and a fixed cost element. (p. 970).

Relevant range · The range over which the company expects to operate during the year. (p. 969).

Target net income · The income objective for individual product lines. (p. 980).

Variable costing · A costing approach in which only variable manufacturing costs are product costs and fixed manufacturing costs are period costs (expenses). (p. 985).

Variable costs · Costs that vary in total directly and proportionately with changes in the activity level. (p. 967).

DEMONSTRATION PROBLEM

The Mabo Company makes pocket calculators that sell for $20 each. For the coming year, management expects fixed costs to total $220,000 and variable costs to be $9.00 per unit.

Instructions

(a) Compute break-even sales in dollars using the mathematical equation.

(b) Compute break-even sales using the contribution margin (CM) ratio.

(c) Compute the margin of safety percentage assuming actual sales are $500,000.

(d) Compute the sales required to earn net income of $165,000.

Solution to Demonstration Problem

(a) Break-even Sales = Variable Costs + Fixed Costs

$$X = .45X + \$220,000$$
$$.55X = \$220,000$$
$$X = \$400,000$$

Helpful hints
1. Know the formulas.
2. Recognize that variable costs change with sales volume; fixed costs do not.
3. Avoid computational errors.
4. Prove your answers.

(b) Contribution Margin per Unit = Unit Selling Price − Unit Variable Costs
$$= \$11\ (\$20 - \$9)$$

Contribution Margin Ratio = Contribution Margin per Unit ÷ Unit Selling Price
$$= 55\%\ (\$11 \div \$20)$$

Break-even Sales = Fixed Cost ÷ Contribution Margin Ratio
$$X = \$220{,}000 \div 55\%$$
$$X = \$400{,}000$$

(c) Margin of Safety $= \dfrac{\text{Actual Sales} - \text{Break-even Sales}}{\text{Actual Sales}}$

$$= \dfrac{\$500{,}000 - \$400{,}000}{\$500{,}000}$$
$$= 20\%$$

(d) Required Sales = Variable Costs + Fixed Costs + Net Income
$$X = .45X + \$220{,}000 + \$165{,}000$$
$$.55X = \$385{,}000$$
$$X = \$700{,}000$$

SELF-STUDY QUESTIONS

Answers are at end of chapter.

(S.O. 1) 1. Variable costs are costs that
   a. vary in total directly and proportionately with changes in the activity level.
   b. remain the same per unit at every activity level.
   c. both of the above.
   d. none of the above.

(S.O. 2) 2. The relevant range is
   a. the range over which the company expects to operate during a year.
   b. the range of activity in which variable costs will be curvilinear.
   c. the range of activity in which fixed costs will be curvilinear.
   d. usually from zero to 100% of operating capacity.

(S.O. 3) 3. Mixed costs consist of a
   a. variable cost element and a relevant cost element.
   b. fixed cost element and a controllable cost element.
   c. relevant cost element and a controllable cost element.
   d. variable cost element and a fixed cost element.

(S.O. 4) 4. One of the following is not involved in CVP analysis. That factor is
   a. sales mix.
   b. unit selling prices.
   c. volume or level of activity.
   d. fixed costs per unit.

(S.O. 5) 5. Contribution margin
   a. is revenue remaining after deducting variable costs.
   b. may be expressed as contribution margin per unit.
   c. both of the above.
   d. none of the above.

(S.O. 6) 6. Gossen Company is planning to sell 200,000 pliers for $2.00 per unit. The contribution margin ratio is 25%. If Gossen will break even at this level of sales, what are the fixed costs?
   a. $100,000.
   b. $160,000.
   c. $200,000.
   d. $300,000.

(S.O. 7) 7. Marshall Company had actual sales of $600,000 when break-even sales were $400,000. What is the margin of safety ratio?
   a. 33%.
   b. 50%.
   c. 67%.
   d. 75%.

(S.O. 8) 8. The mathematical equation for computing required sales to obtain target net income is: Required sales =
   a. variable costs + target net income.
   b. fixed costs + target net income.
   c. variable costs + fixed costs + target net income.
   d. no correct answer is given.

(S.O. 9) 9. Keynes Company sells both radios and cassette players at the following per unit data:

Units Data	Radios	Cassette Players
Selling price	$40	$70
Variable costs	35	50
Contribution margin	5	20
Sales mix	2	1

What is the number of radios and cassette players that Keynes must sell in order to break even if fixed costs are $30,000?

	Radios	Cassette Players
a.	1,000	500
b.	1,500	750
c.	2,000	1,000
d.	3,000	1,500

(S.O. 10) 10. Cournot Company sells 100,000 wrenches for $12.00 a unit. Fixed costs are $280,000 and net income is $200,000. What should be reported as variable expenses in the CVP income statement?
  a. $480,000.
  b. $720,000.
  c. $900,000.
  d. $920,000.

(S.O. 11) 11. Under variable costing, fixed manufacturing costs are classified as:
  a. product costs.
  b. period costs.
  c. both (a) and (b).
  d. neither (a) nor (b).

QUESTIONS

1. Sally Laird argues that cost behavior analysis is a study of how specific costs (and expenses) vary between companies. Do you agree? Explain.

2. Variable costs are costs that vary in total directly and proportionately with changes in net income. Is this a true statement? Why?

3. Contrast the behavior of a variable cost and a fixed cost, both in total and on a per unit basis, in response to changes in the level of activity.

4. Sam Berg claims that the relevant range concept is not important for fixed costs. Do you agree? Explain.

5. "The relevant range is indispensable in cost behavior analysis." Is this true? Why?

6. Bill White is confused. He does not understand why rent on his apartment is a fixed cost and rent on a Hertz rental truck is a mixed cost. Explain the difference to Bill.

7. How should mixed costs be classified in CVP analysis? What approach is used to effect the appropriate classification?

8. At the high and low levels of activity during the month, direct labor hours are 90,000 and 40,000, respectively, and the related costs are $140,000 and $90,000. What are the fixed and variable costs at any level of activity?

9. "Cost–volume–profit (CVP) analysis is based entirely on unit costs." Do you agree? Explain.

10. Paula Sanchez defines contribution margin as the amount of profit available to cover operating expenses. Is there any truth in this definition? Discuss.

11. In the Warren Company, the Speedo pocket calculator sells for $40 and variable costs per unit are estimated to be $28. What is the contribution margin per unit and the contribution margin ratio?

12. "Break-even analysis is of limited use to management because a company cannot survive by just breaking even." Do you agree? Explain.

13. Assume that total fixed costs are $12,000 for Laser-Tech Inc., and it has a contribution margin per unit of $15 and a contribution margin ratio of 20%. Compute the break-even sales in dollars.

14. Laurie Rupert asks your help in constructing a CVP graph. Explain to Laurie how (a) the break-even point is plotted and (b) the level of activity and dollar sales at the break-even point are determined.

15. Define the term "margin of safety." If Molitor Company expects to sell 1,250 units of its product at $10 per unit, and break-even sales for the product is $10,000, what is the margin of safety ratio?

16. The Yount Company's break-even sales are $600,000. Assuming fixed costs are $180,000, what sales dollars are needed to achieve a target net income of $45,000?

17. The sales mix of the Crantner Company's two products is 5:2. What does 5:2 mean? What effect, if any, does a company's sales mix have on CVP analysis?

18. The Surhoff Company sells two products: X and Y. Their unit contribution margins are $55 and $70, respectively, and their sales mix is 2:1. What is the weighted average unit contribution margin if 600 units are sold?

19. What are the similarities and differences between a CVP income statement and a traditional income statement?

20. The traditional income statement for the Trenton Company shows sales $900,000, cost of goods sold $500,000, and operating expenses $300,000. Assuming all costs and expenses are 70% variable and 30% fixed, prepare a CVP income statement through contribution margin.

21. Distinguish between absorption costing and variable costing.

22. (a) What is the major rationale for the use of variable costing? (b) Discuss why variable costing may not be used for financial reporting purposes.

BRIEF EXERCISES

Classify costs as variable, fixed, or mixed.
(S.O. 1)

BE24–1 Monthly production costs in the Magen Company for two levels of production are as follows:

Cost	2,000 units	4,000 units
Indirect labor	$10,000	$20,000
Supervisory salaries	5,000	5,000
Maintenance	3,000	3,600

Indicate which costs are variable, fixed, and mixed and give the reason for each answer.

Diagram the behavior of costs within the relevant range. (S.O. 2)

BE24–2 In the Weld Company, the relevant range of production is 40–80% of capacity. At 40% of capacity, a variable cost is $2,000 and a fixed cost is $3,000. Diagram the behavior of each cost within the relevant range assuming the behavior is linear.

Diagram the behavior of a mixed cost. (S.O. 3)

BE24–3 In the Dillard Company, a mixed cost is $40,000 plus $8 per direct labor hour. Diagram the behavior of the cost using increments of 1,000 hours up to 5,000 hours on the horizontal axis and increments of $20,000 up to $80,000 on the vertical axis.

Determine variable and fixed cost elements using the high–low method.
(S.O. 3)

BE24–4 The Feldo Company accumulates the following data concerning a mixed cost using miles as the activity level.

	Miles Driven	Total Cost		Miles Driven	Total Cost
January	8,000	$14,200	March	8,500	$15,000
February	7,500	13,600	April	8,200	14,500

Compute the variable and fixed cost elements using the high-low method.

BE24–5 Determine the missing amounts.

	Unit Selling Price	Unit Variable Costs	Contribution Margin Per Unit	Contribution Margin Ratio
1.	$250	$200	(a)	(b)
2.	$500	(c)	$125	(d)
3.	(e)	(f)	$360	40%

Determine missing amounts for contribution margin. (S.O. 5)

BE24–6 The Cason Company has a unit selling price of $400, variable costs per unit of $280, and fixed costs of $120,000. Compute the break-even point using (a) a mathematical equation and (b) contribution margin per unit.

Compute the break-even point. (S.O. 6)

BE24–7 In the Michele Company actual sales are $1,200,000 and break-even sales are $900,000. Compute (a) the margin of safety in dollars and (b) the margin of safety ratio.

Compute the margin of safety and the margin of safety ratio. (S.O. 7)

BE24–8 In the Allen Company, variable costs are 70% of sales, fixed costs are $180,000, and management's net income goal is $60,000. Compute the required sales needed to achieve management's net income goal of $60,000 (Use the mathematical equation approach).

Compute sales for target net income. (S.O. 8)

BE24–9 The Largo Company sells 3 units of AA to 1 unit of BB that have contribution margins of $100 and $200, respectively. Fixed costs are $250,000. Compute the unit sales at the break-even point. How many units of each product must be sold?

Compute break-even sales units for two products. (S.O. 9)

BE24–10 Zermat Manufacturing Inc. has sales of $1,900,000 for the first quarter of 1993. In making the sales, the company incurred the following costs and expenses:

Prepare CVP income statement. (S.O. 10)

	Variable	Fixed
Cost of goods sold	$660,000	$540,000
Selling expenses	95,000	60,000
Administrative expenses	79,000	60,000

Prepare a CVP income statement for the quarter ended March 31, 1993.

BE24–11 Selle Company's fixed overhead costs are $5 per unit, and its variable overhead costs are $8 per unit. In the first month of operations, 50,000 units are produced and 45,000 units are sold. What will be the difference in income under absorption costing and variable costing? Which costing approach will produce the higher income? Why?

Compute net income under absorption and variable costing (S.O. 11)

EXERCISES

E24–1 The Miller Company manufactures a single product. Annual production costs incurred in the manufacturing process are shown below for two levels of production:

Define and classify variable, fixed, and mixed costs. (S.O. 1, 3)

	Costs Incurred			
Production in Units	5,000		10,000	
Production Costs	Total Cost	Cost/ Unit	Total Cost	Cost/ Unit
Direct materials	$8,250	$1.65	$16,500	$1.65
Direct labor	9,500	1.90	19,000	1.90
Utilities	1,400	.28	2,300	.23
Rent	4,000	.80	4,000	.40
Supervisory salaries	1,000	.20	1,000	.10
Maintenance	800	.16	1,100	.11

Instructions

(a) Define the terms "variable costs," "fixed costs," and "mixed costs."

(b) Classify each cost above as either variable, fixed, or mixed.

Determine fixed and variable costs using the high–low method and prepare graph.
(S.O. 1, 3)

E24–2 The controller of Gruber Industries has collected the following monthly expense data for use in analyzing the cost behavior of maintenance costs:

Month	Total Maintenance Costs	Total Machine Hours
January	$ 2,900	3,000
February	3,000	4,000
March	3,600	6,000
April	4,200	7,900
May	3,200	5,000
June	4,400	8,000

Instructions

(a) Determine the fixed and variable cost components using the high–low method.

(b) Prepare a graph showing the behavior of maintenance costs and identify the fixed and variable cost elements. Use 2,000 unit increments and $1,000 cost increments.

Compute contribution margin, break-even point, and margin of safety.
(S.O. 5, 6, 7) **S**

E24–3 In the month of June, Jody's Beauty Salon gave 2,000 haircuts, shampoos, and permanents at an average price of $25. During the month, fixed costs were $10,000 and variable costs were 60% of sales.

Instructions

(a) Determine the contribution margin in dollars, per unit, and as a ratio.

(b) Using the contribution margin technique, compute the break-even point in dollars and in units.

(c) Compute the margin of safety in dollars and as a ratio.

Prepare a CVP graph and compute break-even point and margin of safety.
(S.O. 6, 7)

E24–4 The Werda Company estimates that variable costs will be 50% of sales and fixed costs will total $800,000. The selling price of the product is $4.

Instructions

(a) Prepare a CVP graph, assuming maximum sales of $3,200,000. (Note: Use $400,000 increments for sales and costs and 100,000 increments for units.)

(b) Compute the break-even point in (1) units and (2) dollars.

(c) Compute the margin of safety in (1) dollars and (2) as a ratio, assuming actual sales are $2.0 million.

Compute variable cost per unit, contribution margin ratio, and increase in fixed costs. (S.O. 5)

E24–5 In 1993, the Argo Company had a break-even point of $350,000 based on a selling price of $7 per unit and fixed costs of $70,000. In 1994, the selling price and the variable cost per unit did not change, but the break-even point increased to $420,000.

Instructions

(a) Compute the variable cost per unit and the contribution margin ratio for 1993.

(b) Compute the increase in fixed costs for 1994.

Compute various components to derive target net income under different assumptions.
(S.O. 6, 8)

E24–6 The Benor Company had $90,000 of net income in 1993 when the selling price per unit was $150, the variable costs per unit were $90, and the fixed costs were $510,000. Management expects per unit data and total fixed costs to remain the same in 1994. The president of the Benor Company is under pressure by the stockholders to double profits in 1994.

Instructions

(a) Compute the number of units sold in 1993.

(b) Compute the number of units that would have to be sold in 1994 to reach the stockholders' desired profit level.

(c) Assume that the Benor Company sells the same number of units in 1994 as they did in 1993. What would the selling price have to be in order to reach the stockholders' desired profit level?

(d) Again assume that the number of units sold in 1994 will be the same as the number of units sold in 1993. If the selling price cannot be changed, by how much must the variable costs per unit be decreased to reach the stockholders' desired profit level?

E24–7 The following information is selected from the records of the Olympic Company, which produces and sells two products:

	Product A	Product B
Selling price per unit	$ 9.00	$ 17.00
Units sold	100,000	50,000
Variable manufacturing cost per unit	$ 4.00	$ 9.00

Compute sales mix, weighted average unit contribution margin, and break-even point.
(S.O. 5, 6, 9)

S

Fixed manufacturing overhead costs are $230,000, and fixed selling and administrative expenses are $94,000.

Instructions

(a) Compute the sales mix for the Olympic Company.

(b) Calculate the weighted average unit contribution margin.

(c) Compute the break-even point in units, assuming the sales mix computed in part (a).

E24–8 The Family Appliance Center sells three models of Super Clean dishwashers. Selling price and variable cost data for the models are as follows:

Compute and prove the break-even point in units with sales mix.
(S.O. 5, 6, 9)

	Economy	Standard	Deluxe
Unit selling price	$600	$750	$900
Unit variable costs	$400	$500	$600
Expected sales volume (units)	500	300	200

Instructions

(a) Compute the break-even point in units, assuming total fixed costs are $211,500.

(b) Prove the correctness of your answer.

E24–9 The Louis E. Company reports the following operating results for the month of August: Sales $300,000 (units 5,000); variable costs $210,000; and fixed costs $70,000. Management is considering the following independent courses of action to increase net income.

Compute net income under different alternatives.
(S.O. 10)

1. Increase selling price by 15% with no change in total variable costs.

2. Reduce variable costs to 60% of sales.

3. Reduce fixed costs by $10,000.

Instructions

Compute the net income to be earned under each alternative. Which course of action will produce the highest net income?

E24–10 The Hicks Company had sales in 1993 of $1,500,000 on 60,000 units. Variable costs totaled $720,000, and fixed costs totaled $480,000.

A new raw material is available that will decrease the variable costs per unit by 20% or $2.40. However, to process the new raw material, fixed operating costs will increase by $50,000. Management feels that one-half of the decline in the variable costs per unit should be passed on to the company's customers in the form of a sales price reduction. The marketing department expects that this sales price reduction will result in a 10% increase in the number of units sold.

Prepare a CVP income statement before and after changes in business environment.
(S.O. 10)

Instructions

(a) Prepare a CVP income statement for 1993 before any of the proposed changes are made.

(b) Prepare a CVP income statement, assuming the changes are made as described.

E24–11 The Ellen-Start Equipment Company manufactures and distributes industrial air compressors. The following costs are available for the year ended December 31, 1993. The company has no beginning inventory. In 1993, 1,500 units were produced, but only 1,200 units were sold. The unit selling price was $4,500. Costs and expenses were:

Compute total product cost and prepare income statement under absorption and variable costing.
(S.O. 11)

Variable costs per unit	
Direct materials	$ 500
Direct labor	1,500
Variable manufacturing overhead	300
Variable selling and administrative expenses	75
Annual fixed costs and expenses	
Manufacturing overhead	$1,200,000
Selling and administrative expenses	100,000

Instructions

(a) Compute the manufacturing cost of one unit of product using (1) absorption costing, and (2) variable costing.

(b) Prepare a 1993 income statement for the Ellen-Start Company using the variable costing approach.

PROBLEMS

Determine variable and fixed costs, compute break-even point, prepare a CVP graph, and determine net income.
(S.O. 1, 3, 5, 6)

P24–1   The Campus Barber Shop employs four barbers. One barber, who also serves as the manager, is paid a salary of $1,200 per month. The other barbers are paid $1,000 per month. In addition, each barber is paid a commission of $4 per haircut. Other monthly costs are: store rent $800 plus 60 cents per haircut, depreciation on equipment $500, barber supplies 40 cents per haircut, utilities $300, and advertising $200. The price of a haircut is $10.

Instructions

(a) Determine the variable cost per haircut and the total monthly fixed costs.

(b) Compute the break-even point in units and dollars.

(c) Prepare a CVP graph, assuming a maximum of 1,800 haircuts in a month. Use increments of 300 haircuts on the horizontal axis and $3,000 increments on the vertical axis.

(d) Determine the net income, assuming 1,500 haircuts are given in a month.

Prepare a CVP income statement, compute break-even point, contribution margin ratio, margin of safety ratio, and sales for target net income.
(S.O. 5, 6, 7, 8, 10)

P24–2   The Citrus Company bottles and distributes LOKAL, a fruit drink. The beverage is sold for 50 cents per 16-oz. bottle to retailers who charge customers 70 cents per bottle. At full (100%) plant capacity, management estimates the following revenues and costs.

Net sales	$2,000,000	Selling expenses—variable	$ 90,000
Direct materials	360,000	Selling expenses—fixed	150,000
Direct labor	450,000	Administrative expenses—	
Manufacturing overhead—		variable	30,000
variable	270,000	Administrative expenses—	
Manufacturing overhead—		fixed	70,000
fixed	280,000		

Instructions

(a) Prepare a CVP income statement for the year 1993 based on management's estimates.

(b) Compute the break-even point in (1) units and (2) dollars.

(c) Compute the contribution margin ratio and the margin of safety ratio.

(d) Determine the sales required to earn net income of $200,000.

Compute break-even point under alternative courses of action.
(S.O. 5, 6)

P24–3   ACE Manufacturing had a bad year in 1993. For the first time in its history it operated at a loss. The company's income statement showed the following results from selling 60,000 units of product: Net sales $1,500,000; total costs and expenses $1,740,000; and net loss $240,000. Costs and expenses consisted of the following:

	Total	Variable	Fixed
Cost of goods sold	$1,200,000	$780,000	$420,000
Selling expenses	420,000	75,000	345,000
Administrative expenses	120,000	45,000	75,000
	$1,740,000	$900,000	$840,000

Management is considering the following independent alternatives for 1994.

1. Increase unit selling price 20% with no change in costs, expenses, and sales volume.

2. Change the compensation of salespersons from fixed annual salaries totaling $200,000 to total salaries of $60,000 plus a 5% commission on net sales.

3. Purchase new high-tech factory machinery that will reduce total cost of goods sold by $150,000 and change the proportion between variable and fixed cost of goods sold to 50:50.

Instructions

(a) Compute the break-even point in dollars for the year 1993.

(b) Compute the break-even point in dollars under each of the alternative courses of action. Which course of action do you recommend?

P24–4 Cheryl Smith is the advertising manager for the Fashion Shoe Store. She is currently working on a major promotional campaign. Her ideas include the installation of a new lighting system and increased display space that will add $28,000 in fixed costs to the $180,000 currently spent. In addition, Cheryl is proposing that a 6⅔% price decrease from $30.00 to $28.00 will produce an increase in sales volume from 16,000 to 20,000 units. Variable costs will remain at $15.00 per pair of shoes. Management is impressed with Cheryl's ideas but concerned about the effects that these changes will have on the break-even point and the margin of safety.

Compute break-even point and margin of safety ratio and prepare a CVP income statement before and after changes in business environment.
(S.O. 6, 7, 10)

Instructions

(a) Compute the current break-even point in units and compare it to the break-even point in units if Cheryl's ideas are used.

(b) Compute the margin of safety ratio for current operations and after Cheryl's changes are introduced. (Round to nearest full percent.)

(c) Prepare a CVP income statement for current operations and after Cheryl's changes are introduced. Would you make the changes suggested?

P24–5 Precision Equipment manufactures two models of cameras: Superfast and Ultrafast. Unit data for each model are as follows:

Compute contribution margin ratio, break-even point, and sales to meet target net income and prepare a CVP income statement with a sales mix.
(S.O. 5, 6, 8, 9, 10)

	Superfast	Ultrafast
Selling price	$240	$330
Variable costs and expenses:		
Direct materials	60	60
Direct labor	40	70
Manufacturing overhead	34	36
Selling	20	25
Administrative	26	29
Total variable	$180	$220

Monthly fixed costs are: manufacturing overhead $45,000; selling expenses $33,000; and administrative expenses $22,000.

Instructions

(a) Compute the contribution margin ratio for each model.

(b) Compute the break-even point in dollars for each model using the contribution margin ratio, assuming fixed costs are divided equally between the products.

(c) Compute the sales necessary to make net income of $25,000 on Superfast and $40,000 on Ultrafast. Each model incurs 50% of the fixed costs.

(d) Assuming unit sales are 1,500 for Superfast and 1,100 for Ultrafast, prepare a CVP income statement for the month ended June 30, 1993 showing the net income on each product line and for the company as a whole. Each model incurs 50% of the fixed costs.

P24–6 The Ohio Metal Company produces the steel wire that goes into the production of paper clips. In 1993, the first year of operations, Ohio produced 40,000 miles of wire and sold 30,000 miles. In 1994, the production and sales results were exactly reversed. In each year, selling price per mile was $80, variable manufacturing costs were 25% of the sales price, variable selling expenses were $8.00 per mile sold, fixed manufacturing costs were $1,200,000 and fixed administrative expenses were $300,000.

Prepare income statements under absorption and variable costing.
(S.O. 11)

Instructions

(a) Prepare comparative income statements for each year using variable costing.

(b) Prepare comparative income statements for each year using absorption costing.

(c) Reconcile the differences each year in income from operations under the two costing approaches.

(d) Comment on the effects of production and sales on net income under the two costing approaches.

ALTERNATIVE PROBLEMS

Determine variable and fixed costs, compute break-even point, prepare a CVP graph, and determine net income.
(S.O. 1, 3, 5, 6)

P24–1A   Gary Peace owns the Peace Barber Shop. He employs five barbers and pays each a base rate of $800 per month. One of the barbers serves as the manager and receives an extra $400 per month. In addition to the base rate, each barber also receives a commission of $3.50 per haircut.

Other costs are as follows:

Advertising	$200 per month
Rent	$600 per month
Barber supplies	$.30 per haircut
Utilities	$175 per month plus $.20 per haircut
Magazines	$25 per month

Gary currently charges $10 per haircut.

Instructions

(a) Determine the variable cost per haircut and the total monthly fixed costs.

(b) Compute the break-even point in units and dollars.

(c) Prepare a CVP graph, assuming a maximum of 1,800 haircuts in a month. Use increments of 300 haircuts on the horizontal axis, and $3,000 on the vertical axis.

(d) Determine net income, assuming 1,200 haircuts are given in a month.

Prepare a CVP income statement, compute break-even point, contribution margin ratio, margin of safety ratio, and sales for target net income.
(S.O. 5, 6, 7, 8, 10)

P24–2A   The Kalon Company bottles and distributes NOKAL, a diet soft drink. The beverage is sold for 40 cents per 16-oz. bottle to retailers who charge customers 60 cents per bottle. At full (100%) plant capacity, management estimates the following revenues and costs.

Net sales	$1,800,000
Direct materials	400,000
Direct labor	460,000
Manufacturing overhead—variable	300,000
Manufacturing overhead—fixed	183,000
Selling expenses—variable	80,000
Selling expenses—fixed	65,000
Administrative expenses—variable	20,000
Administrative expenses—fixed	52,000

Instructions

(a) Prepare a CVP income statement for the year 1993 based on management's estimates.

(b) Compute the break-even point in (1) units and (2) dollars.

(c) Compute the contribution margin ratio and the margin of safety ratio. (Round to full percents.)

(d) Determine the sales required to earn net income of $180,000.

Compute break-even point under alternative courses of action.
(S.O. 5, 6)

P24–3A   Barr Manufacturing's sales slumped badly in 1993. For the first time in its history, it operated at a loss. The company's income statement showed the following results from selling 600,000 units of product: Net sales $2,400,000; total costs and expenses $2,610,000; and net loss $210,000. Costs and expenses consisted of the following:

	Total	Variable	Fixed
Cost of goods sold	$2,100,000	$1,440,000	$ 660,000
Selling expenses	310,000	72,000	238,000
Administrative expenses	200,000	48,000	152,000
	$2,610,000	$1,560,000	$1,050,000

Management is considering the following independent alternatives for 1994.

1. Increase unit selling price 25% with no change in costs, expenses, and sales volume.

2. Change the compensation of salespersons from fixed annual salaries totaling $210,000 to total salaries of $30,000 plus a 5% commission on net sales.

3. Purchase new automated equipment that will reduce total cost of goods sold by

$315,000 and change the proportion between variable and fixed cost of goods sold to 60% variable and 40% fixed.

Instructions

(a) Compute the break-even point in dollars for the year 1993.

(b) Compute the break-even point in dollars under each of the alternative courses of action. (Round to full percents.) Which course of action do you recommend?

P24–4A Cheryl Small is the advertising manager for the Model Shoe Store. She is currently working on a major promotional campaign. Her ideas include the installation of a new lighting system and increased display space that will add $25,000 in fixed costs to the $200,000 currently spent. In addition, Cheryl is proposing that a 5% price decrease ($40.00 to $38.00) will produce a 20% increase in sales volume (20,000 to 24,000). Variable costs will remain at $20.00 per pair of shoes. Management is impressed with Cheryl's ideas but concerned about the effects that these changes will have on the break-even point and the margin of safety.

Compute break-even point and margin of safety ratio and prepare a CVP income statement before and after changes in business environment.
(S.O. 6, 7, 10)

Instructions

(a) Compute the current break-even point in units and compare it to the break-even point in units if Cheryl's ideas are used.

(b) Compute the margin of safety ratio for current operations and after Cheryl's changes are introduced. (Round to nearest full percent.)

(c) Prepare a CVP income statement for current operations and after Cheryl's changes are introduced. Would you make the changes suggested?

P24–5A Powers Company manufactures two models of televisions: Superclear and Ultraclear. Unit data for each model are as follows:

Compute contribution margin ratio, break-even point, and sales to meet target net income and prepare a CVP income statement with a sales mix.
(S.O. 5, 6, 8, 9, 10)

	Superclear	Ultraclear
Selling price	$360	$480
Variable costs and expenses:		
Direct materials	90	95
Direct labor	50	60
Manufacturing overhead	60	68
Selling	32	36
Administrative	20	29
Total variable	$252	$288

Monthly fixed costs are: manufacturing overhead $72,000; selling expenses $48,000; and administrative expenses $24,000.

Instructions

(a) Compute the contribution margin ratio for each model.

(b) Compute the break-even point in dollars for each model using the contribution margin ratio, assuming fixed costs are divided equally between the products.

(c) Compute the sales necessary to make net income of $36,000 on Superclear and $48,000 on Ultraclear. Each model incurs 50% of all fixed costs.

(d) Assuming unit sales are 1,200 for Superclear and 1,000 for Ultraclear, prepare a CVP income statement for the month ended September 30, 1993 showing the net income on each product line and for the company as a whole. Each model incurs 50% of all fixed costs.

*B*roadening Your Perspective

DECISION CASE 1

Candice Company has decided to introduce a new product. The new product can be manufactured by either a capital intensive method or labor intensive method. The manufacturing method will not affect the quality of the product. The estimated manufacturing costs by the two methods are as follows:

	Capital Intensive	Labor Intensive
Raw materials	$5 per unit	$5.60 per unit
Direct labor	$6 per unit	$7.20 per unit
Variable overhead	$3 per unit	$4.80 per unit
Fixed manufacturing costs	$2,440,000	$1,320,000

Candice's market research department has recommended an introductory unit sales price of $30. The incremental selling expenses are estimated to be $500,000 annually plus $2 for each unit sold regardless of manufacturing method.

Instructions

(a) Calculate the estimated break-even point in annual unit sales of the new product if Candice Company uses the:
(1) capital intensive manufacturing method.
(2) labor intensive manufacturing method.

(b) Determine the annual unit sales volume at which Candice Company would be indifferent between the two manufacturing methods.

(c) Explain the circumstances under which Candice should employ each of the two manufacturing methods.

(d) Identify the business factors other than operating leverage that Candice must consider before selecting the capital intensive or labor intensive manufacturing method.

(CMA adapted)

DECISION CASE 2

The condensed income statement for the Rose and Simon partnership for 1993 is as follows:

ROSE AND SIMON COMPANY
Income Statement
For the Year Ended December 31, 1993

Sales (200,000 units)		$1,200,000
Cost of goods sold		800,000
Gross profit		400,000
Operating expenses		
Selling	280,000	
Administrative	160,000	440,000
Net loss		($40,000)

A cost behavior analysis indicates that 75% of the cost of goods sold are variable; 50% of the selling expenses are variable; and 25% of the administrative expenses are variable.

Instructions
(Round to nearest unit, dollar, and percentage, where necessary.)

(a) Prepare a CVP income statement for 1993.

(b) Compute the break-even point in total sales dollars and in units.

(c) Rose has proposed a plan to get the partnership "out of the red" and improve its profitability. She feels that the quality of the product could be substantially improved by spending $.55 more per unit on better raw materials. The selling price per unit could be increased to only $6.50 because of competitive pressures. Rose estimates that sales volume will increase by 30%. What effect will Rose's plan have on the profits and the break-even point in dollars of the partnership?

(d) Simon was a marketing major in college. He believes that sales volume could be increased only by intensive advertising and promotional campaigns. He, therefore, proposed the following plan as an alternative to Rose's: (1) increase variable selling expenses to $.85 per unit; (2) lower the selling price per unit by $.20; and (3) increase fixed selling expenses by $20,000. Simon quoted an old marketing research report that said that sales volume would increase by 50% if these changes were made. What effect will Simon's plan have on the profits and the break-even point in dollars of the partnership?

(e) Which plan should be accepted? Explain your answer.

CRITICAL THINKING CASE

Refer to the opening story about Boise State University and answer the following questions.

1. What costs of operating the parking system are (a) variable, (b) fixed, and (c) mixed?

2. What proportion of the total costs are likely to be (a) variable and (b) fixed?

3. What options does Seibolt have in controlling (or cutting) costs?

4. What additional sources of revenue may be available for the parking system?

ETHICAL CASE

Danny Dern is an accountant for Top-Chip Company. Early this year Danny made a highly favorable projection of sales and profits over the next three years for its hot-selling computer PLEX. He presented his projections to senior management and as a result they decided to expand production in this area. This decision led to dislocations of some plant personnel because individuals were reassigned to one of the company's newer plants in another state. However, no one was fired, and in fact the company expanded its work force slightly.

Unfortunately Danny rechecked his computations on the projections a few months later and found that he had made an error that would have reduced his projections substantially. Luckily, sales of PLEX have exceeded projections so far and management is satisfied with its decision. Danny, however, is not sure what to do. Should he confess his honest mistake and jeopardize his possible promotion? He suspects that no one will catch the error because sales of PLEX have exceeded his projections and it appears that profits will materialize close to his projections.

Instructions
(a) Who are the stakeholders in this situation?

(b) Identify the ethical issues involved in this situation.

(c) What are the possible alternative actions for Danny? What would you do if in Danny's position?

Answers to Self-Study Questions
1. c   2. a   3. d   4. d   5. c   6. a   7. a   8. c   9. c   10. b
11. b

BUDGETARY PLANNING

Study Objectives

After studying this chapter, you should be able to:

1. *State the essentials of effective budgeting.*

2. *Indicate the advantages of budgeting.*

3. *Identify the budgets that comprise the master budget.*

4. *Describe the sources for preparing the budgeted income statement.*

5. *Explain the principal sections of a cash budget.*

6. *Explain the features of long-range planning.*

7. *Indicate the applicability of budgeting in nonmanufacturing companies.*

Every university has a budget. Usually, there's a capital budget for big projects such as new buildings, and there's an operating budget for the day-to-day expenditures.

At the University of Nebraska, the operating budget request takes up four volumes totalling nearly 900 pages. Because the university is funded by the state of Nebraska, the budget must be submitted to the state legislature for approval. That means the university has to pay lobbyists to plead its case. The budget is due September 15th of every other year. The lawmakers consider it during their sessions, which begin in January.

As you might expect, increases in expenses are resisted because money is tight. "Roughly 70% of our budget goes toward salaries" says Paula Boroff, budget officer at the Omaha campus. "A university is a very labor intensive institution," she *observes. The total budget for the 1992–1993 fiscal year is about $95 million, reflecting a 1% cut in state funds from the prior year.*

One budget item that should be of interest to you is the "remission" category. That's where scholarships are funded. "This year, the budget for honor students and needy students is nearly $2 million—$1,994,488 to be exact," says Boroff, who recently received her MBA from the University of Nebraska graduate school. "Of our 16,000 students, we had 8,274 on some kind of aid," she says.

As you read through this chapter, think about some of the expenses your university incurs—and how it might save money without harming the quality of education, as the University of Nebraska had to do in finalizing its 1992–1993 operating budget.

As indicated from the opening vignette, budgeting is an integral part of our society. As students, you budget your study time and your money. Families budget income, and governmental agencies budget revenues and expenditures. Business enterprises use budgets in planning and controlling their operations.

Our primary focus in this chapter is budgeting by business enterprises. Through budgeting it should be possible for management to "run a tighter ship" and to avoid or eliminate the following situations:

From day to day, management never knows whether enough cash will be available to pay creditors.

Some product lines have excessive inventories, whereas others have inadequate inventories.

Substantial operating losses occur because management does not consider the impact of foreign competition on its product lines.

In this chapter, we consider the role of budgeting as a **planning tool** of management. We also describe the budgeting process and the types of budgets that may be developed.

Budgeting and Management

One of management's major responsibilities is planning. As explained in Chapter 21, **planning** is the process of establishing enterprise objectives. The term "goal congruence" is sometimes used in planning to indicate that there is agreement among all levels of management as to the objectives of the company and the proposed means of accomplishing them.

A budget is a formal written summary (or statement) of management's plans for a specified future time period, expressed in financial terms. It normally represents the primary means of communicating agreed-upon objectives throughout the business organization. Once adopted, a budget becomes an important basis for evaluating performance. Thus, it promotes efficiency and serves as a deterrent to waste and inefficiency. We consider the role of budgeting as a control device in Chapter 26.

A budget is an aid to management; it is not a substitute for management. A budget cannot operate or enforce itself. The benefits of budgeting will be realized only when budgets are carefully prepared and properly administered by management.

Budgeting and Accounting

Accounting information makes major contributions to the budgeting process. Past performance is often the starting point in budgeting. From the accounting records, historical data on revenues, costs, and expenses can be obtained. These data may be helpful in formulating future budget goals.

Normally, accounting has the responsibility for expressing management's budgeting goals in financial terms. In this role, it becomes the translator of management's plans, and it provides the means of communicating the budget to all areas of responsibility. Accounting also prepares periodic budget reports that provide the basis for measuring performance and comparing actual results with planned objectives. The budget itself, and the administration of the budget, however, are entirely management responsibilities.

Technology in Action

In large firms, the computer is an essential tool in the budgeting process. Entire computer programs are designed to aid in budget preparation. These systems can also be integrated into the general ledger and provide a complete reporting package for monitoring budgeted vs. actual results. Packages with similar features are available for microcomputers so even small companies can adopt the budgeting practices found in major companies.

A powerful feature of many spreadsheet packages is the ability to merge and consolidate budget data as it flows up the organizational chain of command.

Essentials of Effective Budgeting

If budgets are to be effective, there must be a sound organizational structure, research and analysis, and management acceptance of the budget program.

Study Objective 1

State the essentials of effective budgeting.

Sound Organizational Structure

Effective budgeting is dependent on an organizational structure in which authority and responsibility over all phases of operations are clearly defined. The establishment of responsibility is a prerequisite for budgeting. Budgets are prepared by departments, and managers have the responsibility for meeting their budgets. Subsequent comparisons of actual results with budget expectations are made to determine how well managers discharge their responsibilities.

Research and Analysis

A budget based entirely on past performance is ineffective. In today's highly competitive business environment, management must look ahead, or it will fall behind. Through research and analysis it is possible to determine the feasibility of new products, services, and operating techniques, as well as the market potential of new territories and branches. Research and analysis lead to careful

Accounting in Action · *Business Insight*

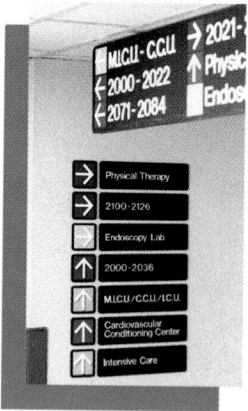

Participation does matter. Take a not-for-profit situation like University Hospital. The degree of effectiveness of managers and first-line supervisors at University Hospital—or any hospital, for that matter—depends upon many personality traits. One of the most important of these traits is the ability to be motivated by being involved. This trait is essential because the degree of decentralization typical in a hospital setting requires individuals to make timely quality decisions within the scope of established general guidelines. Furthermore, the various departments tend to be so diverse and complex that the department director is the "expert" who must relate to the vice president, a "generalist," in developing and executing a plan of operation. Therefore, the hospital setting is ideal for a high degree of participative budgeting given the diverse departments and individuals and groups of differing ranks.

The participative approach to budgeting has proven so successful at University Community Hospital that the finance committee has jokingly suggested the budget was prepared after the fact.

Source: Marvin A. Feldbush, "Participative Budgeting in a Hospital Setting," *Management Accounting,* September 1981, pp. 43–46.

investigation and informed judgments. **Budgets based on research and analysis should represent realistic goals that will contribute to the growth and profitability of a company.**

Management Acceptance

The effectiveness of the budget program is directly related to its acceptance by all levels of management. Acceptance of budgets by division managers, department heads, and supervisors is enhanced when these individuals participate fully in the preparation of the budgets. As shown in Illustration 25-1, the

ILLUSTRATION 25-1

Flow of budget data from bottom to top

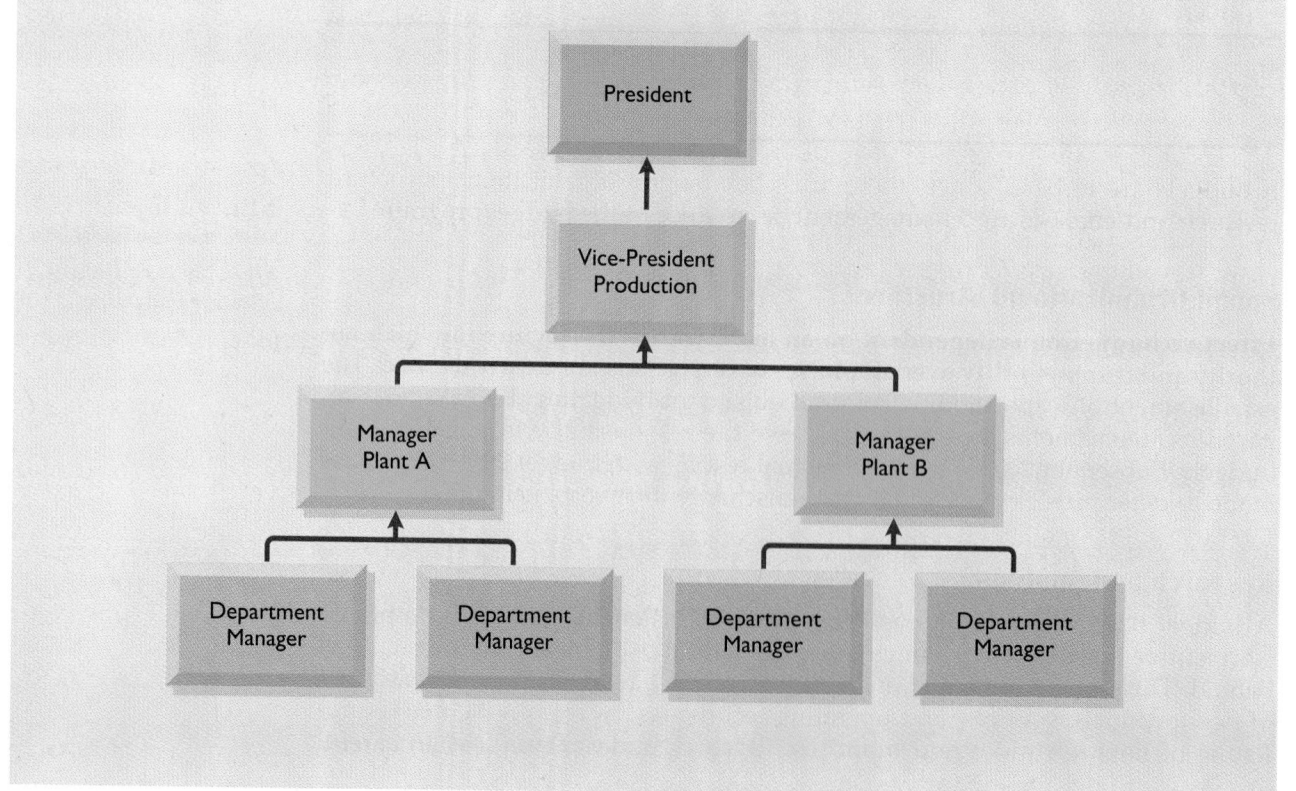

flow of input data for budgeting should be from the lowest level of responsibility to the highest. The input is reviewed and then consolidated as it moves to each higher level of management. The budget must have the support of top management.

Once the budget has been adopted, it should be an important basis for evaluating performance. Variations between actual and expected results should be systematically reviewed to determine their cause(s). However, care should be exercised to see that individuals are not held responsible for variations that are beyond their control.

Budgeting and Human Behavior

A budget can have a significant effect on human behavior. On the one hand, a budget may have a strong positive influence that inspires a manager to higher levels of performance. On the other hand, a budget may discourage additional effort and have a negative impact on the morale of a manager. Why do these diverse affects occur? The answer is found in the manner in which the budget is developed and administered.

In developing the budget, each level of management should be invited and encouraged to participate. The overall objective is to reach agreement on a budget that the manager considers to be fair and achievable. When this objective is met, the budget will have a positive effect on the manager. In contrast, if the manager views the budget as being unfair and unrealistic, he or she may become discouraged and uncommitted to the budget goals. The risk of having unrealistic budgets is generally greater when the budget is developed from top management down to lower management than vice versa.

Administering the budget relates to the manner in which the budget is used by top management. As explained earlier, the budget should have the complete support of top management. In addition, the budget should be an important basis for evaluating performance. The effect of an evaluation on a manager will be positive when top management tempers criticism with advice and assistance. In contrast, the response of a manager is likely to be negative when the budget is used exclusively to assess blame. Top management should also be sensitive to the behavioral implications of its actions. An understanding and flexible attitude has a positive influence on human behavior. Conversely, a rigid and inflexible attitude has a negative effect on the manager who is being evaluated.

A budget may be used as a pressure device to force improved performance. Alternatively, it can be used as a positive aid in the achievement of projected goals. In sum, a budget can become a friend or a foe to the manager.

The human factor is an important aspect of budgeting. When properly used, budgets can be a positive motivating force within a company.

Advantages of Budgeting

Budgeting offers many advantages to a company. The primary benefits are:

1. It requires all levels of management to **plan ahead** and to formalize their future goals on a recurring basis.
2. It provides **definite objectives** for evaluating performance at each level of responsibility.
3. It creates an **early warning system** for potential problems. With early warning, management has time to solve the problem before things get out of hand. For example, the cash budget may reveal the need for outside financing several months before an actual cash shortage occurs.

Study Objective 2

Indicate the advantages of budgeting.

4. It facilitates the **coordination of activities** within the business by correlating the goals of each segment with overall company objectives. Thus, production and sales promotion can be integrated with expected sales.

5. It results in greater **management awareness** of the entity's overall operations and the impact of external factors, such as economic trends, on the company's operations.

6. It contributes to **positive behavior patterns** throughout the organization by motivating personnel to meet planned objectives.

Length of the Budget Period

A budget may be prepared for any period of time. Such factors as the type of budget, the nature of the company, the need for periodic appraisal, and prevailing business conditions will influence the length of the budget period. For example, cash may be budgeted monthly, whereas a plant expansion program budget may cover a 10-year period.

The budget period should be long enough to provide an attainable goal under normal business conditions. Ideally, the time period should minimize the impact of seasonal and cyclical business fluctuations. On the other hand, the budget period should not be so long that reliable estimates are impossible.

The **most common budget period is one year**. The annual budget, in turn, is often supplemented by monthly and quarterly budgets. Many companies today use **continuous 12-month budgets** by dropping the month just ended and adding a future month. One advantage of continuous budgeting is that it keeps management planning a full year ahead.

Budgeting Process

The development of the budget for the coming year generally starts several months before the end of the current year. Following a formal process of input and review, the budget is put in final form and adopted before the start of the new year.

In many companies, responsibility for coordinating the preparation of the budget is assigned to a budget committee. The committee is often headed by a budget director. It ordinarily includes the president, treasurer, chief accountant (controller), and management personnel from each of the major areas of the company, such as sales, production, and research.

Accounting in Action · *Business Insight*

Congress not only approves the federal budget, it also establishes the rules of the game. Recently, it ruled that in complying with Gramm-Rudman-Hollings budget ceilings (no longer in effect, since the 1990 budget agreements), the U.S. Postal Service losses and the cost of bailing out the savings and loan industry, were "off-budget" items. This led one commentator to suggest that Congress should go all the way and proclaim the entire federal budget deficit an "off-budget" item.

Source: Forbes, May 29, 1989.

The budgeting process usually begins with the collection of data from each of the organizational units of the company. These data are then reviewed, modified if necessary, and integrated. During this part of the budgeting process, the budget committee serves as a review board where managers and supervisors can defend their budget goals and requests. After differences are reconciled, the budget is prepared by the budget committee and approved. Copies of the budget are subsequently distributed to the various levels of management who have budget responsibilities.

Before You Go On . . .

1. What are the factors essential to effective budgeting?

2. What are the advantages of budgeting?

3. How does the budget process work?

The Master Budget

The **master budget** is a set of interrelated budgets that constitutes a plan of action for a specified time period. The individual budgets included in a master budget for a manufacturing company are shown in Illustration 25-2. The master budget is developed within the framework of a **sales forecast** that shows potential sales for the industry and the company's expected share of such sales. Sales forecasting involves a consideration of such factors as (1) general economic conditions, (2) industry trends, (3) market research studies, (4) anticipated advertising and promotion, (5) previous market share, (6) changes in prices, and (7) technological developments.

> **Study Objective 3**
>
> *Identify the budgets that comprise the master budget.*

The inputs of sales personnel and top management are essential in preparing the sales forecast. Because a forecast involves many uncertainties, various approaches are taken in an effort to increase the reliability of the forecast. These include a variety of sophisticated statistical and mathematical techniques. Today, many companies use **financial planning models** to forecast sales. A model can express the effects of both internal and external factors on sales.

As shown in Illustration 25-2, there are two classes of budgets in the master budget. **Operating budgets** include the individual budgets that culminate in the preparation of the budgeted income statement. The primary objective of these budgets is to establish goals for the company's sales and production personnel. In contrast, **financial budgets** include the cash budget and the budgeted balance sheet. These budgets focus primarily on the cash resources needed to fund expected operations and planned capital expenditures.

The master budget is prepared in the sequence shown in Illustration 25-2. The operating budgets are developed first beginning with the sales budget. After these budgets have been determined, the financial budgets are prepared. We will explain and illustrate each budget shown in Illustration 25-2 except the capital expenditure budget. This budget is discussed under the topic, Capital Budgeting, in Chapter 28.

ILLUSTRATION 25-2

Components of the master budget

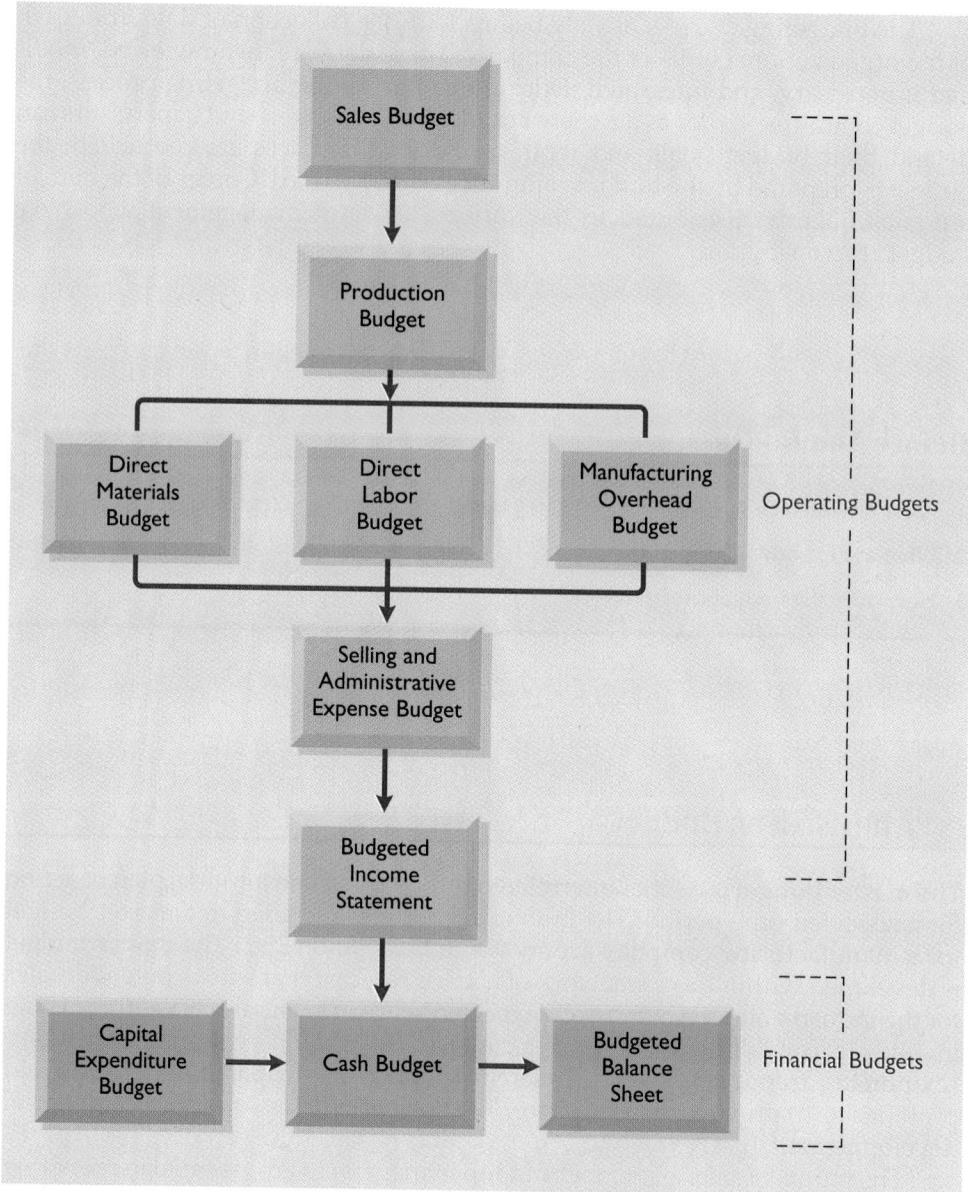

Preparing the Operating Budgets

A case study of the Hayes Company will be used in preparing the operating budgets. Hayes Company manufactures and sells a single product, Kitchen-mate. The budgets will be prepared by quarters for the year ending December 31, 1993. The Hayes Company begins its annual budgeting process on September 1, 1992, and it completes the budget for 1993 by December 1, 1992.

Helpful hint For a retail or manufacturing company, what is the starting point in preparing the master budget and why? Answer: Preparation of the sales budget is the starting point in preparing the master budget because it sets the level of activity for other functions such as production and purchasing.

Sales Budget

As shown in the master budget in Illustration 25-2, **the sales budget is the first budget prepared**. Each of the other budgets is dependent on the sales budget. The sales budget is derived from the sales forecast, and it represents management's best estimate of sales revenue for the budget period. An inaccurate sales budget may adversely affect net income. For example, an overly optimistic sales budget may result in excessive inventories that may have to be sold at reduced prices. In contrast, an unduly conservative budget may result in loss of sales revenue due to inventory shortages.

The sales budget is prepared by multiplying the expected unit sales volume for each product by its anticipated unit selling price. For the Hayes Company, sales volume is expected to be 3,000 units in the first quarter with 500-unit increments in each succeeding quarter. Based on a sales price of $60 per unit, the sales budget for the year, by quarters, is shown in Illustration 25-3 below.

ILLUSTRATION 25-3

Sales budget

HAYES COMPANY
Sales Budget
For the Year Ending December 31, 1993

	Quarter				
	1	2	3	4	Year
Expected unit sales	3,000	3,500	4,000	4,500	15,000
Unit selling price	× $60	× $60	× $60	× $60	× $60
Total sales	$180,000	$210,000	$240,000	$270,000	$900,000

The anticipated sales revenue may be classified as cash or credit sales and by geographical regions, territories, or salespersons.

Production Budget

The production budget shows the units that must be produced to meet anticipated sales. Production requirements are determined from the following formula:[1]

ILLUSTRATION 25-4

Production requirements formula

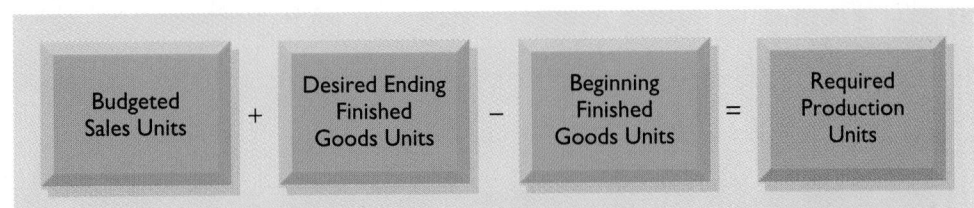

A realistic estimate of ending inventory is essential in scheduling production requirements. Excessive inventories in one quarter may lead to cutbacks in production and layoffs of employees in a subsequent quarter. Conversely, inadequate inventories may result either in added costs for overtime work or in lost sales in a later period. On the basis of past experience, the Hayes Company believes it can meet future sales requirements by maintaining an ending inventory equal to 20% of the next quarter's budgeted sales volume. For example, the ending finished goods inventory for the first quarter is 700 units (20% × anticipated second-quarter sales of 3,500 units). The production budget is shown in Illustration 25-5.

---

[1]This formula ignores any work in process inventories, which are assumed to be nonexistent in the Hayes Company.

ILLUSTRATION 25-5

Production budget

		Quarter			
HAYES COMPANY					
Production Budget					
For the Year Ending December 31, 1993					
	1	2	3	4	Year
Expected unit sales (Illustration 25-3)	3,000	3,500	4,000	4,500	
Add: Desired ending finished goods units[a]	700	800	900	1,000[b]	
Total required units	3,700	4,300	4,900	5,500	
Less: Beginning finished goods units	600[c]	700	800	900	
Required production units	3,100	3,600	4,100	4,600	15,400

[a]20% of next quarter's sales
[b]Expected 1994 first quarter sales, 5,000 units × 20%
[c]20% of estimated first quarter 1993 sales units

The production budget, in turn, provides the basis for determining the budgeted costs for each manufacturing cost element, as explained in the following pages.

Direct Materials Budget

The **direct materials budget** contains both the quantity and cost of direct materials to be purchased. The quantities of direct materials are derived from the following formula:

ILLUSTRATION 25-6

Formula for direct materials quantities

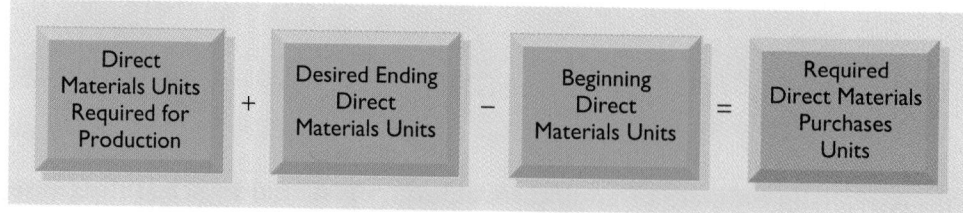

The budgeted cost of direct materials to be purchased is then computed by multiplying the required units of direct materials by the anticipated cost per unit.

The desired ending inventory is again a critical component in the budgeting process. For example, inadequate inventories could result in temporary shutdowns of production. Because of its close proximity to suppliers, Hayes Company has found that an ending inventory of raw materials equal to 10% of the next quarter's production is sufficient. The manufacture of each Kitchen-mate requires two pounds of raw materials and the expected cost per pound is $4. The direct materials budget is shown in Illustration 25-7.

ILLUSTRATION 25-7

Direct materials budget

HAYES COMPANY
Direct Materials Budget
For the Year Ending December 31, 1993

	Quarter				
	1	2	3	4	Year
Units to be produced (Illustration 25-5)	3,100	3,600	4,100	4,600	
Direct materials per unit	× 2	× 2	× 2	× 2	
Total pounds needed for production	6,200	7,200	8,200	9,200	
Add: Desired ending direct materials (pounds)[a]	720	820	920	1,020[b]	
Total materials required	6,920	8,020	9,120	10,220	
Less: Beginning direct materials (pounds)	620[c]	720	820	920	
Direct materials purchases	6,300	7,300	8,300	9,300	
Cost per pound	× $4	× $4	× $4	× $4	
Total cost of direct materials purchases	$25,200	$29,200	$33,200	$37,200	$124,800

[a]10% of next quarter's production
[b]Estimated 1994 first quarter pounds needed for production, 10,200 × 10%
[c]10% of estimated first quarter pounds needed for production

Technology in Action

The successful manufacturers of the 1990s will be fully computerized. A crucial step on the way is material requirements planning (MRP) systems. Initial MRP systems accepted a sales forecast and computed how much materials, inventory, people, and machinery a company needed to manufacture the product. Current MRP systems link the company's manufacturing resource planning with its financial management, creating a powerful system of control over the entire business planning and operating process. With MRP, management can make decisions on facts rather than on "hunches" and "instinct".

Direct Labor Budget

Like the direct materials budget, the direct labor budget contains both quantity (hours) and cost data necessary to meet production requirements. Direct labor hours are determined from the production budget. At the Hayes Company, two hours of direct labor are required to produce each unit of finished goods, and the anticipated hourly wage rate is $10. These data are shown in Illustration 25-8. The direct labor budget is critical in maintaining a labor force that can meet the expected levels of production.

Manufacturing Overhead Budget

The manufacturing overhead budget shows the expected indirect manufacturing costs for the budget period. As shown in Illustration 25-9, **this budget distinguishes between variable and fixed overhead costs**. From previous experience, the Hayes Company expects variable costs to fluctuate with production

ILLUSTRATION 25-8

Direct labor budget

Helpful hint An important assumption here is that the company can add and subtract from its work force as needed so that the $10 per hour labor cost applies to a wide range of possible production activity.

HAYES COMPANY
Direct Labor Budget
For the Year Ending December 31, 1993

| | Quarter | | | | |
	1	2	3	4	Year
Units to be produced (Illustration 25-5)	3,100	3,600	4,100	4,600	
Direct labor time (hours) per unit	× 2	× 2	× 2	× 2	
Total required direct labor hours	6,200	7,200	8,200	9,200	
Direct labor cost per hour	× $10	× $10	× $10	× $10	
Total direct labor cost	$62,000	$72,000	$82,000	$92,000	$308,000

volume on the basis of the following rates per direct labor hour: indirect materials $1.00, indirect labor $1.40, utilities $0.40, and maintenance $0.20. Thus, for 6,200 direct labor hours, budgeted indirect materials are $6,200 (6,200 × $1), and budgeted indirect labor is $8,680 (6,200 × $1.40). The Hayes Company also recognizes that some maintenance is fixed. The amounts reported for fixed costs are assumed.

In the Hayes Company, overhead is applied to production on the basis of direct labor hours. Thus, as shown in Illustration 25-9, the annual rate is $8 per hour ($246,400 ÷ 30,800).

ILLUSTRATION 25-9

Manufacturing overhead budget

HAYES COMPANY
Manufacturing Overhead Budget
For the Year Ending December 31, 1993

| | Quarter | | | | |
	1	2	3	4	Year
Variable costs					
Indirect materials	$ 6,200	$ 7,200	$ 8,200	$ 9,200	$ 30,800
Indirect labor	8,680	10,080	11,480	12,880	43,120
Utilities	2,480	2,880	3,280	3,680	12,320
Maintenance	1,240	1,440	1,640	1,840	6,160
Total variable	18,600	21,600	24,600	27,600	92,400
Fixed costs					
Supervisory salaries	20,000	20,000	20,000	20,000	80,000
Depreciation	3,800	3,800	3,800	3,800	15,200
Property taxes and insurance	9,000	9,000	9,000	9,000	36,000
Maintenance	5,700	5,700	5,700	5,700	22,800
Total fixed	38,500	38,500	38,500	38,500	154,000
Total manufacturing overhead	$57,100	$60,100	$63,100	$66,100	$246,400
Direct labor hours	6,200	7,200	8,200	9,200	30,800
Manufacturing overhead rate per direct labor hour ($246,400 ÷ 30,800)					$8.00

Selling and Administrative Expense Budget

The Hayes Company combines its operating expenses into one budget, the selling and administration expense budget. This budget is a projection of anticipated selling and administrative expenses for the budget period. In this budget, as in the preceding budget, expenses are classified as either variable or fixed. In this case, the variable expense rates per unit of sales are sales commissions, $3.00, and freight-out, $1.00. Variable expenses per quarter are based on the unit sales projected in the sales budget (Illustration 25-3). For example, sales in the first quarter are expected to be 3,000 units. Thus, Sales Commissions Expense is $9,000 (3,000 × $3), and Freight-out is $3,000 (3,000 × $1). Fixed expenses are based on assumed data. The selling and administrative expense budget is shown in Illustration 25-10.

ILLUSTRATION 25-10

Selling and administrative expense budget

HAYES COMPANY					
Selling and Administrative Expense Budget					
For the Year Ending December 31, 1993					

	Quarter				
	1	2	3	4	Year
Variable expenses					
Sales commissions	$ 9,000	$10,500	$12,000	$13,500	$ 45,000
Freight-out	3,000	3,500	4,000	4,500	15,000
Total variable	12,000	14,000	16,000	18,000	60,000
Fixed expenses					
Advertising	5,000	5,000	5,000	5,000	20,000
Sales salaries	15,000	15,000	15,000	15,000	60,000
Office salaries	7,500	7,500	7,500	7,500	30,000
Depreciation	1,000	1,000	1,000	1,000	4,000
Property taxes and insurance	1,500	1,500	1,500	1,500	6,000
Total fixed	30,000	30,000	30,000	30,000	120,000
Total selling and administrative expenses	$42,000	$44,000	$46,000	$48,000	$180,000

Budgeted Income Statement

The budgeted income statement is the important end product in preparing operating budgets. This budget indicates the expected profitability of operations for the budget period. Once established, the budgeted income statement provides the basis for evaluating company performance. As you would expect, this budget is prepared from the previous budgets. For example, to find the cost of goods sold, it is first necessary to determine the total unit cost of producing one Kitchenmate as follows:

Study Objective 4

Describe the sources for preparing the budgeted income statement.

ILLUSTRATION 25-11

Computation of total unit cost

	Cost of One Kitchen-mate			
Cost Element	**Illustration**	**Quantity**	**Unit Cost**	**Total**
Direct materials	25-7	2 pounds	$ 4.00	$ 8.00
Direct labor	25-8	2 hours	$10.00	20.00
Manufacturing overhead	25-9	2 hours	$ 8.00	16.00
Total unit cost				$44.00

Cost of goods sold can then be determined by multiplying the units sold by the unit cost. For the Hayes Company, budgeted cost of goods sold is $660,000 (15,000 × $44). All data for the statement are obtained from the individual operating budgets except the following: (1) interest expense is expected to be $100 and (2) income taxes are estimated to be $12,000. The budgeted income statement is shown below.

ILLUSTRATION 25-12

Budgeted income statement

HAYES COMPANY Budgeted Income Statement For the Year Ending December 31, 1993	
Sales (Illustration 25-3)	$900,000
Cost of goods sold (15,000 × $44)	660,000
Gross profit	240,000
Selling and administrative expenses (Illustration 25-10)	180,000
Income from operations	60,000
Interest expense	100
Income before income taxes	59,900
Income tax expense	12,000
Net income	$ 47,900

Preparing the Financial Budgets

As shown in Illustration 25-2, the financial budgets consist of the capital expenditure budget, the cash budget, and the budgeted balance sheet. The capital expenditure budget is discussed in Chapter 28; the other budgets are explained in the following sections.

Cash Budget

The cash budget shows anticipated cash flows. Because cash is so vital in a company, this budget is considered to be the most important output in preparing financial budgets. The cash budget contains three sections (cash receipts, cash disbursements, and financing) and the beginning and ending cash balances as shown in Illustration 25-13.

ILLUSTRATION 25-13

Pro forma cash budget

Cash Budget	
Beginning cash balance	$X,XXX
Add: Cash receipts (Itemized)	X,XXX
Total available cash	X,XXX
Less: Cash disbursements (Itemized)	X,XXX
Excess (deficiency) of available cash over cash disbursements	X,XXX
Financing	X,XXX
Ending cash balance	$X,XXX

The **cash receipts section** includes expected receipts from the company's principal source(s) of revenue such as cash sales and collections from customers on credit sales. This section also shows anticipated receipts of interest and dividends, and proceeds from planned sales of investments, plant assets, and the company's capital stock.

The **cash disbursements section** shows expected payments for direct materials, direct labor, manufacturing overhead, and selling and administrative expenses. This section also includes projected payments for income taxes, dividends, investments, and plant assets.

The **financing section** shows expected borrowings and the repayment of the borrowed funds plus interest. This section is needed when there is a cash deficiency or the cash balance is below management's minimum required balance.

In preparing the cash budget, data must be prepared in sequence because the ending cash balance of one period becomes the beginning cash balance for the next period. Data for preparing the cash budget are obtained from other budgets and from information provided by management. In practice, cash budgets are often prepared for the year on a monthly basis.

Helpful hint Why is the cash budget prepared after the other budgets are prepared? Answer: Because the information generated by the other budgets dictate the need for and the inflows and outflows of cash.

To minimize detail, we will assume that the Hayes Company prepares an annual cash budget by quarters. The cash budget for the Hayes Company is based on the following assumptions:

1. The January 1, 1993 cash balance is expected to be $38,000.
2. Sales (Illustration 25-3)—60% are collected in the quarter sold and 40% are collected in the following quarter. Accounts receivable of $60,000 at December 31, 1992 are expected to be collected in full in the first quarter of 1993.
3. Marketable securities are expected to be sold for $2,000 cash in the first quarter.
4. Direct materials (Illustration 25-7)—50% are paid in the quarter purchased and 50% are paid in the following quarter. Accounts payable of $10,600 at December 31, 1992 are expected to be paid in full in the first quarter of 1993.
5. Direct labor (Illustration 25-8)—100% is paid in the quarter incurred.
6. Manufacturing overhead (Illustration 25-9) and selling and administrative expenses (Illustration 25-10)—all items except depreciation are paid in the quarter incurred.
7. Management plans to purchase a new truck in the second quarter for $10,000 cash.
8. The company makes equal quarterly payments of its estimated annual income taxes.
9. Loans are repaid in the first subsequent quarter in which there is sufficient cash.

The preparation of schedules for collections from customers (assumption No. 2, above) and cash payments for direct materials (assumption No. 4, above) is useful in preparing the cash budget. The schedules are shown in Illustrations 25-14 and 25-15.

The cash budget for the Hayes Company is shown in Illustration 25-16. The budget indicates that $3,000 of financing will be needed in the second quarter to maintain a minimum cash balance of $15,000. Since there is an excess of available cash over disbursements of $22,500 at the end of the third quarter, the borrowing is repaid in this quarter plus $100 interest.

A cash budget contributes to more effective cash management. ample, it can show when additional financing will be necessary well before the actual need arises. Conversely, it can indicate when excess cash will be available for investments or other purposes.

ILLUSTRATION 25-14

Collections from customers

Schedule of Expected Collections from Customers				
	Quarter			
	1	2	3	4
Accounts receivable, 12/31/92	$ 60,000			
First quarter ($180,000)	108,000	$ 72,000		
Second quarter ($210,000)		126,000	$ 84,000	
Third quarter ($240,000)			144,000	$ 96,000
Fourth quarter ($270,000)				162,000
Total collections	$168,000	$198,000	$228,000	$258,000

ILLUSTRATION 25-15

Payments for direct materials

Schedule of Expected Payments for Direct Materials				
	Quarter			
	1	2	3	4
Accounts payable, 12/31/92	$10,600			
First quarter ($25,200)	12,600	$12,600		
Second quarter ($29,200)		14,600	$14,600	
Third quarter ($33,200)			16,600	$16,600
Fourth quarter ($37,200)				18,600
Total payments	$23,200	$27,200	$31,200	$35,200

ILLUSTRATION 25-16

Cash budget

HAYES COMPANY Cash Budget For the Year Ending December 31, 1993					
		Quarter			
	Assumption	1	2	3	4
Beginning cash balance	1	$ 38,000	$ 25,500	$ 15,000	$ 19,400
Add: Receipts					
Collections from customers	2	168,000	198,000	228,000	258,000
Sale of securities	3	2,000	0	0	0
Total receipts		170,000	198,000	228,000	258,000
Total available cash		208,000	223,500	243,000	277,400
Less: Disbursements					
Direct materials	4	23,200	27,200	31,200	35,200
Direct labor	5	62,000	72,000	82,000	92,000
Manufacturing overhead	6	53,300[1]	56,300	59,300	62,300
Selling and administrative expenses	6	41,000[2]	43,000	45,000	47,000
Purchase of truck	7	0	10,000	0	0
Income tax expense	8	3,000	3,000	3,000	3,000
Total disbursements		182,500	211,500	220,500	239,500
Excess (deficiency) of available cash over disbursements		25,500	12,000	22,500	37,900
Financing					
Borrowings		0	3,000	0	0
Repayments—plus $100 interest	9	0	0	3,100	0
Ending cash balance		$ 25,500	$ 15,000	$ 19,400	$ 37,900

[1]$57,100 − $3,800 depreciation
[2]$42,000 − $1,000 depreciation

Budgeted Balance Sheet

The budgeted balance sheet is a projection of financial position at the end of the budget period. This budget is developed from the budgeted balance sheet for the preceding year and the budgets for the current year. Pertinent data from the budgeted balance sheet at December 31, 1992 are as follows:

Building and equipment	$182,000	Common stock	$225,000
Accumulated depreciation	$ 28,800	Retained earnings	$ 46,480

The budgeted balance sheet at December 31, 1993, is shown below.

ILLUSTRATION 25-17

Budgeted balance sheet

HAYES COMPANY
Budgeted Balance Sheet
December 31, 1993

Assets

Cash		$ 37,900
Accounts receivable		108,000
Finished goods inventory		44,000
Raw materials inventory		4,080
Buildings and equipment	$192,000	
Less: Accumulated depreciation	48,000	144,000
Total assets		$337,980

Liabilities and Stockholders' Equity

Accounts payable	$ 18,600
Common stock	225,000
Retained earnings	94,380
Total liabilities and stockholders' equity	$337,980

The computations and sources of the amounts are explained below.

Cash—ending cash balance $37,900, shown in the cash budget (Illustration 25-16).

Accounts receivable—40% of fourth quarter sales $270,000, shown in the schedule of expected collections from customers (Illustration 25-14).

Finished goods inventory—desired ending inventory 1,000 units, shown in production budget (Illustration 25-5) times the total unit cost, $44, shown in Illustration 25-11).

Raw materials inventory—desired ending inventory 1,020 pounds, times the cost per pound, $4 shown in the direct materials budget (Illustration 25-7).

Buildings and equipment—December 31, 1992 balance $182,000, plus purchase of truck for $10,000.

Accumulated depreciation—December 31, 1992 balance $28,800, plus $15,200 depreciation shown in manufacturing overhead budget (Illustration 25-9) and $4,000 depreciation shown in selling and administrative expense budget (Illustration 25-10).

Accounts payable—50% of fourth quarter purchases $37,200, shown in schedule of expected payments for direct materials (Illustration 25-15).

Common stock—Unchanged from the beginning of the year.

Retained earnings—December 31, 1992 balance $46,480, plus net income, $47,900, shown in budgeted income statement in Illustration 25-12.

Technology in Action

Once the budgeting data are entered into the computer, the various budgets (sales, cash, etc.) can be prepared, as well as the budgeted financial statements. Management can also manipulate the budgets in "what if" (sensitivity) analyses based on different hypothetical assumptions. For example, suppose that sales were budgeted to be 10 percent higher in the coming quarter. What impact would the change have on the rest of the budgeting process and the financing needs of the business? The computer can quickly "play out" the impact of the various assumptions on the budgets. Armed with these analyses, management can make more informed decisions about the impact of various projects and anticipate future problems and business opportunities. Budgeting is one of the top uses of electronic spreadsheets. Template versions of every one of the Hayes Company budgets shown in this chapter could easily be prepared. This would be an outstanding learning project for anyone wanting to gain hands-on experience with spreadsheets.

Before You Go On . . .

1. How may the individual budgets in the master budget be classified?

2. What is the sequence for preparing the budgets that comprise the operating budgets?

3. What are the three principal sections of the cash budget?

Budgeting and Long-Range Planning

Study Objective 6

Explain the features of long-range planning.

Helpful hint In comparing a budget with a long-range plan: (1) Which has more detail? (2) Which is done for a longer period of time? (3) Which is more concerned with short-term goals? Answer: (1) Budget. (2) Long-range plan. (3) Budget.

Budgeting and long-range planning are not the same. One important difference is the **time period involved**. The maximum length of a budget is usually one year, and budgets are often prepared for shorter periods of time, such as a month or a quarter. In contrast, long-range planning usually encompasses a period of at least five years.

A second significant difference is **in emphasis**. Budgeting is concerned with the achievement of specific short-term goals, such as meeting annual profit objectives. Long-range planning, on the other hand, involves the selection of strategies to achieve long-term goals and the development of policies and plans to implement the strategies. In long-range planning, consideration is also given to anticipated trends in the economic and political environment and policies the company should follow to cope with them.

The final difference between budgeting and long-range planning pertains to the **amount of detail presented**. Budgets, as you have seen earlier in this chapter, can be very detailed. The detail is needed to provide a basis for control. Long-range plans contain considerably less detail, because the data are intended more for a review of progress toward long-term goals than for an evaluation of specific results to be achieved.

Long-range planning should be a systematic and formalized process. The primary objective of long-range planning is to develop the best strategy to maximize the company's performance over an extended future period. Neither budgeting nor long-range planning can solve all the problems of a manager. Nor can they guarantee the success of the company. However, the two activities should contribute to better planning, control, and decision making by management.

Budgeting in Nonmanufacturing Companies

Budgeting is not limited to manufacturing companies. Budgets may also be used in profit planning by merchandising companies, service enterprises, and not-for-profit organizations.

Merchandising Companies

As in manufacturing operations, the sales budget is both the starting point and the key factor in the development of the master budget for a merchandising company. The major differences between the master budget of a merchandising company and a manufacturing budget are that **(1) a merchandise purchases budget is used instead of a production budget, and (2) the manufacturing budgets (direct materials, direct labor, and manufacturing overhead) are not applicable**. The merchandise purchases budget shows the estimated cost of goods to be purchased to meet expected sales. The formula for determining budgeted merchandise purchases is:

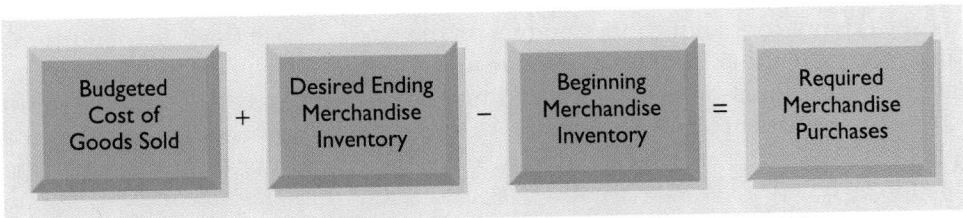

ILLUSTRATION 25-18

Merchandise purchases formula

To illustrate, assume that the budget committee of the Lima Company is preparing the merchandise purchases budget for July. It estimates that budgeted sales will be $300,000 in July and $320,000 in August. Cost of goods sold is expected to be 70% of sales, and the company's desired ending inventory is 30% of the following month's cost of goods sold. Required merchandise purchases for July are $214,200 computed as follows:

ILLUSTRATION 25-19

Computation of required merchandise purchases

Budgeted cost of goods sold (budgeted sales for July, $300,000 × 70%)	$210,000
Desired ending merchandise inventory (budgeted cost of goods sold for August, $320,000 × 70% × 30%)	67,200
Total	277,200
Less: Beginning merchandise inventory (budgeted sales for July, $300,000 × 70% × 30%)	63,000
Required merchandise purchases for July	$214,200

When the merchandising company is departmentalized, separate budgets are prepared for each department. For example, a grocery store may start by preparing sales budgets and purchases budgets for each of its major departments, such as meats, dairy, and produce. These budgets are then combined into a master budget for the store. When a retailer has branch stores, separate master budgets are prepared for each store. Then these budgets are incorporated into master budgets for the company as a whole.

Service Enterprises

In service enterprises, such as a public accounting firm, a law office, or a medical practice, the critical factor in budgeting is **coordinating professional staff needs with anticipated services**. If a firm is overstaffed, (1) labor costs will be disproportionately high, (2) profits will be lower because of the additional salaries, and (3) staff turnover may increase because of lack of challenging work. In contrast, if an enterprise is understaffed, revenue may be lost because existing and prospective client needs for service cannot be met, and professional staff may seek other positions because of excessive work loads.

Budget data for service revenue may be obtained from expected output or expected input. When output is used, it is necessary to determine the expected billings of clients for services rendered. For a public accounting firm, output would be the sum of its billings in auditing, tax, and consulting services. When service revenue is derived from input data, each professional staff member is required to project his or her billable time. Billing rates are then applied to billable time to produce expected service revenue.

Not-for-Profit Organizations

Budgeting is just as important for not-for-profit organizations as for profit-oriented enterprises. The budget process, however, is significantly different. In most cases not-for-profit entities budget **on the basis of cash flows (expenditures and receipts), rather than on a revenue and expense basis.** Further, the starting point in the process is usually expenditures, not receipts. For the not-for-profit entity, management's task generally is to find the receipts needed to support the planned expenditures. This was the case for the University of Nebraska in the opening vignette. The activity index is also likely to be significantly different. For example, in a not-for-profit entity, such as a university, budgeted faculty positions may be based on full-time equivalent students or credit hours expected to be taught in a department.

For some governmental units, the budget must be approved by voters. In other cases, such as state governments and the federal government, legislative approval is required. After the budget is adopted, it must be strictly followed, and overspending is often illegal. In governmental budgets, authorizations tend to be on a line-by-line basis. That is, the budget for a municipality may have a specified authorization for police and fire protection, garbage collection, street paving, and so on. The line item authorization of governmental budgets significantly limits the amount of discretion management can exercise. The city manager often cannot use savings in one line item, such as street paving, to cover increased spending in another line item, such as snow removal.

Before You Go On . . .

1. How does long-range planning differ from budgeting?

2. What is the formula for computing required merchandise purchases?

3. How does budgeting in service and not-for-profit organizations differ from budgeting in manufacturing and merchandising companies?

Summary of Study Objectives

1. *State the essentials of effective budgeting.* The essentials of effective budgeting are (a) sound organizational structure, (b) research and analysis, and (c) management acceptance.

2. *Identify the advantages of budgeting.* The primary advantages of budgeting are that it (a) requires management to plan ahead, (b) provides definite objectives for evaluating performance, (c) creates an early warning system for potential problems, (d) facilitates coordination of activities, (e) results in greater management awareness, and (f) contributes to positive behavior patterns.

3. *Identify the budgets that comprise the master budget.* The master budget consists of the following budgets: (a) sales, (b) production, (c) direct materials, (d) direct labor, (e) manufacturing overhead, (f) selling and administrative expense, (g) budgeted income statement, (h) capital expenditure budget, (i) cash budget, and (j) budgeted balance sheet.

4. *Describe the sources for preparing the budgeted income statement.* The budgeted income statement is prepared from (a) the sales budget, (b) the budgets for direct materials, direct labor, and manufacturing overhead, and (c) the selling and administrative expense budget.

5. *Explain the principal sections of a cash budget.* The cash budget has three sections (receipts, disbursements, and financing) and the beginning and ending cash balances.

6. *Explain the features of long-range planning.* Long-range planning usually encompasses a period of at least five years. It involves the selection of strategies to achieve long-term goals and the development of policies and plans to implement the strategies. Long-range plans contain considerably less detail than a budget.

7. *Indicate the applicability of budgeting in non-manufacturing companies.* Budgeting may be used in merchandising companies for development of a master budget. In service enterprises budgeting is a critical factor in coordinating staff needs with anticipated services. In not-for-profit organizations, the starting point in budgeting is usually expenditures, not receipts.

GLOSSARY

Budget · A formal written summary of management's plans for a specified future time period expressed in financial terms. (p. 1004).

Budget committee · A group responsible for coordinating the preparation of the budget. (p. 1008).

Budgeted balance sheet · A projection of financial position at the end of the budget period. (p. 1019).

Budgeted income statement · An estimate of the expected profitability of operations for the budget period. (p. 1015).

Cash budget · A projection of anticipated cash flows. (p. 1016).

Direct labor budget · A projection of the quantity and cost of direct labor to be incurred to meet production requirements. (p. 1013).

Direct materials budget · An estimate of the quantity and cost of direct materials to be purchased. (p. 1012).

Financial budgets · Individual budgets that indicate the cash resources needed for expected operations and planned capital expenditures. (p. 1009).

Long-range planning · The selection of strategies to achieve long-term goals and the development of policies and plans to implement the strategies. (p. 1020).

Manufacturing overhead budget · An estimate of expected indirect manufacturing costs for the budget period. (p. 1013).

Master budget · A set of interrelated budgets that constitutes a plan of action for a specific time period. (p. 1009).

Merchandise purchases budget · The estimated cost of goods to be purchased in a merchandising company to meet expected sales. (p. 1021).

Operating budgets · Individual budgets that culminate in a budgeted income statement. (p. 1009).

Production budget · A projection of production requirements to meet anticipated sales. (p. 1011).

Sales budget · An estimate of expected sales for the budget period. (p. 1010).

Sales forecast · The projection of potential sales for the industry and the company's expected share of such sales. (p. 1009).

Selling and administrative expense budget · A projection of anticipated selling and administrative expenses for the budget period. (p. 1014).

DEMONSTRATION PROBLEM

The Soroco Company is preparing its master budgets for 1993. Relevant data pertaining to its sales and production budgets are as follows:

Sales. Sales for the year are expected to total 1,200,000 units. Quarterly sales are 20%, 25%, 30%, and 25% respectively. The sales price is expected to be $50 per unit for the first three quarters and $55 per unit beginning in the fourth quarter. Sales in the first quarter of 1994 are expected to be 10% higher than the budgeted sales volume for the first quarter of 1993.

Production. Management desires to maintain ending finished goods inventories at 25% of the next quarter's budgeted sales volume.

Instructions
Prepare the sales budget and production budget by quarters for 1993.

Helpful hints
1. For the sales budget, know the form and content.
2. The sales budget is the first budget prepared.
3. Each of the other budgets is dependent on the sales budget.
4. The production budget shows the units that must be produced to meet anticipated sales.
5. The production budget provides the bases for determining the budgeted cost for each manufacturing cost element.
6. Know how to compute the beginning and ending finished goods units.

Solution to Demonstration Problem

SOROCO COMPANY
Sales Budget
For the Year Ending December 31, 1993

	Quarter				
	1	2	3	4	Year
Expected unit sales	240,000	300,000	360,000	300,000	1,200,000
Unit selling price	× $50	× $50	× $50	× $55	—
	$12,000,000	$15,000,000	$18,000,000	$16,500,000	$61,500,000

SOROCO COMPANY
Production Budget
For the Year Ending December 31, 1993

	Quarter				
	1	2	3	4	Year
Expected unit sales	240,000	300,000	360,000	300,000	
Add: Desired ending finished goods units	75,000	90,000	75,000	66,000[1]	
Total required units	315,000	390,000	435,000	366,000	
Less: Beginning finished goods units	60,000[2]	75,000	90,000	75,000	
Required production units	255,000	315,000	345,000	291,000	1,206,000

[1]Estimated first quarter 1994 sales volume 240,000 + (240,000 × 10%) = 264,000; 264,000 × 25%.
[2]25% of estimated first quarter 1993 sales units.

SELF-STUDY QUESTIONS

Answers are at the end of the chapter.

(S.O. 1)   1. The essentials of effective budgeting do not include:
a. management acceptance.
b. top down budgeting.
c. research and analysis.
d. sound organizational structure.

(S.O. 2)   2. The advantages of budgeting include all but one of the following:
a. Management can plan ahead.
b. An early warning system is provided for potential problems.
c. The coordination of activities is facilitated.
d. It enables disciplinary action to be taken at every level of responsibility.

(S.O. 3)   3. A sales budget is:
a. derived from the production budget.
b. not the starting point for the master budget.
c. management's best estimate of sales revenue for the year.
d. only prepared for credit sales.

(S.O. 3)   4. The formula for the production budget is budgeted sales in units plus:
a. desired ending finished goods units less beginning finished goods units.
b. beginning finished goods units less desired ending finished goods units.
c. desired ending direct materials units less beginning direct materials units.
d. desired ending merchandise inventory less beginning merchandise inventory.

(S.O. 3)   5. Direct materials inventories are kept in pounds in the Byrd Company and the total pounds of direct materials needed for production is 9,500. If the beginning inventory is 1,000 pounds and the desired ending inventory is 1,200 pounds, the total pounds to be purchased is:
a. 9,400.
b. 9,500.
c. 9,700.
d. 10,700.

(S.O. 3)   6. The formula for computing the direct labor cost budget is to multiply the direct labor cost per hour by the:
a. physical units to be produced.
b. total required direct labor hours.
c. equivalent units to be produced.
d. no correct answer is given.

(S.O. 4)   7. Each of the following budgets is used in preparing the budgeted income statement except the:
a. sales budget.
b. capital expenditure budget.
c. selling and administrative budget.
d. direct labor budget.

(S.O. 5)   8. Expected direct materials purchases in the Read Company are $60,000 in the first quarter and $90,000 in the second quarter. Forty percent of the purchases are paid in cash as incurred and the balance is paid in the following quarter. The budgeted cash payments for purchases in the second quarter are:
a. $96,000.
b. $60,000.
c. $90,000.
d. $72,000.

(S.O. 6)   9. Compared to budgeting, long-range planning generally has the:
a. longer time period.
b. same amount of detail.
c. same emphasis.
d. same time period.

(S.O. 7)   10. The budget for a merchandising company differs from a budget for a manufacturing company because:
a. a merchandise purchases budget replaces the production budget.
b. the manufacturing budgets are not applicable.
c. both of the above.
d. none of the above.

QUESTIONS

1. How does a budget aid management in planning?

2. "Accounting's role in budgeting is limited to expressing management's goals in financial terms." Do you agree? Explain.

3. Pedro Valdez asks your help in understanding the essentials of effective budgeting. Identify the essentials for Pedro.

4. Arsenio and Sigourney are discussing the advantages of budgeting. They ask you to identify the primary benefits for them. Comply with their request.

5. What criteria are helpful in determining the length of the budget period? What is the most common budget period?

6. Distinguish between a master budget and a sales forecast.

7. What budget is the starting point in preparing the master budget? What may result if this budget is inaccurate?

8. "The production budget shows both unit production data and unit cost data." Is this true? Explain.

9. The Peno Company has 8,000 beginning finished goods units. Budgeted sales units are 150,000. If management desires 12,000 ending finished goods units, what are the required units of production?

10. In preparing the direct materials budget for the Ramir Company, management concludes that required purchases are 50,000 units. If 46,000 direct materials units are required in production and there are 4,000 units of beginning direct materials, what is the desired units of ending direct materials?

11. The production budget of the Lukas Company calls for 90,000 units to be produced. If it takes 30 minutes to make one unit and the direct labor rate is $13 per hour, what is the total budgeted direct labor cost?

12. The Kopek Company's manufacturing overhead budget shows total variable costs of $186,000 and total fixed costs of $170,250. Total production in units is expected to be 120,000. It takes 15 minutes to make one unit, and the direct labor rate is $15 per hour. Express the manufacturing overhead rate as (a) a percentage of direct labor cost, and (b) an amount per direct labor hour.

13. Walsh Company's variable selling and administrative expenses are 10% of net sales and fixed expenses are $50,000 per quarter. The sales budget shows expected sales of $200,000 and $250,000 in the first and second quarters, respectively. What are the total budgeted selling and administrative expenses for each quarter?

14. For the Aldred Company, the budgeted cost for one unit of product is direct materials $12, direct labor $20, and manufacturing overhead 75% of direct labor cost. If 20,000 units are expected to be sold at $77 each, what is the budgeted gross profit?

15. Indicate the supporting schedules used in preparing a budgeted income statement through gross profit for a manufacturing company.

16. Identify the three sections of a cash budget. What balances are also shown in this budget?

17. Chang Company has credit sales of $300,000 in January. Past experience suggests that 40% is collected in the month of sale, 50% in the month following the sale, and 5% in the second month following the sale. Compute the cash collections from January sales in January, February, and March.

18. Kim Basing maintains that the only difference between budgeting and long-range planning is time. Do you agree? Why or why not?

19. What is the formula for determining required merchandise purchases in a merchandising company?

20. How may expected revenues in a service enterprise be computed?

BRIEF EXERCISES

Prepare a diagram of a master budget.
(S.O. 3)

BE25–1 Carla Manufacturing Company uses the following budgets: Balance Sheet, Capital Expenditure, Cash, Direct Labor, Direct Materials, Income Statement, Manufacturing Overhead, Production, Sales, and Selling and Administrative. Prepare a diagram of the interrelationships of the budgets in the master budget. Indicate whether each budget is an operating or a financial budget.

BE25–2 The Stern Company estimates that unit sales will be 10,000 in quarter 1, 12,000 in quarter 2, 14,000 in quarter 3, and 12,000 in quarter 4. Using a sales price of $50 per unit, prepare the sales budget by quarters, for the year ending December 31, 1993.

Prepare a sales budget.
(S.O. 3)

BE25–3 Sales budget data for the Stern Company are given in BE25–2. Management desires to have an ending finished goods inventory equal to 20% of the next quarter's expected unit sales. Prepare a production budget by quarters, for the first six months of 1993.

Prepare a production budget for two quarters.
(S.O. 3)

BE25–4 Siver Company has 1,200 pounds of raw materials in its December 31, 1992, ending inventory. Required production for January and February are 4,000 and 5,000 units, respectively. Three pounds of raw materials are needed for each unit and the estimated cost per pound is $5. Management desires an ending inventory equal to 10% of next month's materials requirements. Prepare the direct materials budget for January.

Prepare a direct materials budget for one month.
(S.O. 3)

BE25–5 For Kisten Company, units to be produced are 5,000 in quarter 1 and 6,000 in quarter 2. It takes 1.5 hours to make a finished unit, and the expected hourly wage rate is $10 per hour. Prepare a direct labor budget by quarters, for the six months ending June 30, 1993.

Prepare a direct labor budget for two quarters.
(S.O. 3)

BE25–6 For Morgan Marie Sondgeroth, Inc., variable manufacturing overhead costs are expected to be $28,000 in the first quarter of 1993 with $4,000 increments in each of the remaining three quarters. Fixed overhead costs are estimated to be $35,000 in each quarter. Prepare the manufacturing overhead budget by quarters, for the year.

Prepare a manufacturing overhead budget.
(S.O. 3)

BE25–7 The Marla Company classifies its selling and administrative expense budget into variable and fixed components. Variable expenses are expected to be $21,000 in the first quarter and $3,000 increments are expected in the remaining quarters of 1993. Fixed expenses are expected to be $30,000 in each quarter. Prepare the selling and administrative expense budget by quarters, for 1993.

Prepare a selling and administrative expense budget.
(S.O. 3)

BE25–8 The Mayville Company has completed all of its operating budgets. The sales budget for the year shows 50,000 units and total sales of $2,000,000. The total unit cost of making one unit of sales is $30. Selling and administrative expenses are expected to be $220,000 and income taxes are estimated to be $50,000. Prepare a budgeted income statement for the year ending December 31, 1993.

Prepare a budgeted income statement for the year.
(S.O. 4)

BE25–9 Lurial Industries expects credit sales for January, February, and March to be $200,000, $250,000, and $300,000 respectively. It is expected that 60% of the sales will be collected in the month of sale, and 40% will be collected in the following month. Compute cash collections from customers for each month.

Prepare data for cash budget.
(S.O. 5)

BE25–10 KRB Wholesalers is preparing its merchandise purchases budget. Budgeted sales are $400,000 for April and $420,000 for May. Cost of goods sold is expected to be 70% of sales, and the company's desired ending inventory is 20% of the following month's cost of goods sold. Compute the required purchases for April.

Determine required merchandise purchases for one month.
(S.O. 7)

EXERCISES

E25–1 Gazza Electronics Inc. produces and sells two models of pocket calculators: XQ-103, and XQ-104. The calculators sell for $10 and $15, respectively. Because of the intense competition Gazza faces, management budgets sales semiannually. Its projections for the first two quarters of 1993 are as follows:

Prepare sales budget for two quarters.
(S.O. 3)

| | Unit Sales | |
Product	Quarter 1	Quarter 2
XQ-103	32,000	27,000
XQ-104	12,000	13,000

No changes in selling prices are anticipated.

Instructions
Prepare a sales budget for the two quarters ending June 30, 1993. List the products and show for each quarter and for the six months, units, selling price, and total sales by product and in total.

Prepare quarterly
production budgets.
(S.O. 3)

E25–2 Stallon Company produces and sells two types of automobile batteries: the heavy-duty HD-240 and the long-life LL-250. The 1993 sales budget for the two products is as follows:

	HD-240	LL-250
1st quarter	5,000	10,000
2nd quarter	7,000	18,000
3rd quarter	8,000	20,000
4th quarter	10,000	35,000

The January 1, 1993 inventory of HD-240 and LL-250 units are 4,000 and 8,000, respectively. Management desires an ending inventory each quarter equal to 80% of the next quarter's sales. Sales in the first quarter of 1994 are expected to be 20% higher than sales in the same quarter in 1993.

Instructions
Prepare separate quarterly production budgets for each product by quarters for 1993.

Prepare direct materials
purchases budget.
(S.O. 3)

E25–3 Clover Industries has adopted the following production budget for the first four months of 1993.

Month	Units	Month	Units
January	10,000	March	6,000
February	8,000	April	4,000

Each unit requires six pounds of raw materials costing $1.25 per pound. On December 31, 1992, the ending raw materials inventory was 36,000 pounds. Management wants to have a raw materials inventory at the end of the month equal to 60% of next month's production requirements.

Instructions
Prepare a direct materials purchases budget by months for the first quarter of 1993.

Prepare production and
direct materials budgets
by quarters for six
months.
(S.O. 3)

E25–4 The Kimoy Company budget committee has reached agreement on the following data for the six months ending June 30, 1993.

Sales units (by quarters):	(1) 5,000, (2) 6,000
Ending raw materials inventory:	50% of the next quarter's production requirements
Ending finished goods inventory:	25% of the next quarter's expected sales units

The ending raw materials and finished goods inventories at December 31, 1992, follow the same percentage relationships to production and sales that occur in 1993. Three pounds of raw materials are required to make each unit of finished goods. Raw materials purchased are expected to cost $5 per pound. Sales of 7,000 units and required production of 7,250 units are expected in the third quarter of 1993.

Instructions
(a) Prepare a production budget by quarters for the six months.
(b) Prepare a direct materials budget by quarters for the six months.

Prepare direct labor
budget.
(S.O. 3)

E25–5 Meter, Inc. is preparing its direct labor budget for 1993 from the following production budget based on a calendar year:

Quarter	Units	Quarter	Units
1	20,000	3	35,000
2	25,000	4	30,000

Each unit requires 1.8 hours of direct labor.

Instructions
Prepare a direct labor cost budget for 1993. Wage rates are expected to be $14 for the first two quarters and $15.40 for quarters 3 and 4.

E25–6 Spielman Company is preparing its manufacturing overhead budget for 1993. Relevant data consist of the following:

Prepare manufacturing overhead budget for the year.
(S.O. 3)
S

Units to be produced (by quarters): 10,000; 12,000; 14,000; 16,000.

Direct labor: time—1.5 hours per unit.

Variable overhead costs per direct labor hour: indirect materials $.70; indirect labor $1.20; and maintenance $.30.

Fixed overhead costs per quarter: supervisory salaries $25,000; depreciation $9,000; and maintenance $5,000.

Instructions
Prepare the manufacturing overhead budget for the year, showing quarterly data.

E25–7 The Norvil Company combines its operating expenses for budget purposes in a selling and administrative expense budget. For the first six months of 1993, the following data are developed:

Prepare selling and administrative expense budget for two quarters.
(S.O. 3)

1. Sales: 10,000 units quarter 1; 12,000 units quarter 2.
2. Variable costs per dollar of sales: sales commissions 5%; delivery expense 2%; and advertising 3%.
3. Fixed costs per quarter: sales salaries $10,000; office salaries $6,000; depreciation $4,200; insurance $1,500; utilities $800, and repairs expense $500.
4. Unit selling price $20.

Instructions
Prepare a selling and administrative expense budget by quarters, for the first six months of 1993.

E25–8 The Smoltz Company has accumulated the following budget data for the year 1993:

Prepare budgeted income statement for the year.
(S.O. 3, 4)

1. Sales: 25,000 units; unit selling price $80.
2. Cost of one unit of finished goods: direct materials, 2 pounds at $5 per pound; direct labor, 3 hours at $12 per hour; and manufacturing overhead $6 per direct labor hour.
3. Inventories: raw materials only: beginning, 10,000 pounds; ending, 15,000 pounds.
4. Raw materials cost: $5 per pound.
5. Selling and administrative expenses: $190,000.
6. Income taxes: 30% of income before income taxes.

Instructions
Prepare a budgeted income statement for 1993. Show the computation of cost of goods sold.

E25–9 Hunt Company expects to have a cash balance of $46,000 on January 1, 1993. Relevant monthly budget data for the first two months of 1993 are as follows:

Prepare cash budget for two months.
(S.O. 5)

Collections from customers: January $70,000; February $150,000.

Payments to suppliers: January $40,000; February $75,000.

Direct labor: January $30,000; February $40,000. Wages are paid in the month they are incurred.

Manufacturing overhead: January $21,000; February $30,000. These costs include depreciation of $1,000 per month. All other overhead costs are paid as incurred.

Selling and administrative expenses: January $14,000; February $21,000. These costs are exclusive of depreciation. They are paid as incurred.

Sales of marketable securities in January are expected to realize $10,000 in cash. Hunt Company has a line of credit at a local bank that enables it to borrow up to $25,000. The Hunt Company wants to maintain a minimum monthly cash balance of $20,000.

Instructions
Prepare a cash budget for January and February.

E25–10 In May, 1993, the budget committee of Hill Co. Stores assembles the following data in preparation of budgeted merchandise purchases for the month of June.

Prepare purchases budget and budgeted income statement for a merchandising company.
(S.O. 7)

1. Expected sales: June $500,000, July $550,000.

2. Cost of goods sold is expected to be 70% of sales.

3. Desired ending merchandise inventory is 30% of the following (next) month's cost of goods sold.

4. The beginning inventory at June 1 will be the desired amount.

Instructions

(a) Compute the budgeted merchandise purchases for June.

(b) Prepare the budgeted income statement for June through gross profit on sales.

PROBLEMS

Prepare budgeted income statement and supporting budgets.
(S.O. 3, 4)

P25–1   Davic Farm Supply Company manufactures and sells a fertilizer called Basic II. The following data are developed for preparing budgets for Basic II for the first two quarters of 1993.

1. Sales: Quarter 1, 40,000 bags: quarter 2, 60,000 bags. Selling price is $50 per bag.

2. Direct materials: Each bag of Basic II requires 6 pounds of Crup at a cost of $2 per pound and 10 pounds of Dert at $1.50 per pound.

3. Desired inventory levels:

Type of Inventory	January 1	April 1	July 1
Basic II (bags)	10,000	15,000	20,000
Crup (pounds)	9,000	12,000	15,000
Dert (pounds)	15,000	20,000	25,000

4. Direct labor: direct labor time is 15 minutes per bag at an hourly rate of $10 per hour.

5. Selling and administrative expenses are expected to be 10% of sales plus $100,000 per quarter.

6. Income taxes are expected to be 30% of income from operations.

Your assistant has prepared two budgets: the manufacturing overhead budget that shows expected costs to be 100% of direct labor cost, and the direct materials budget for Dert which shows the cost of Dert to be $682,500 in quarter 1 and $982,500 in quarter 2.

Instructions

Prepare the budgeted income statement for the first six months of 1993 and all required supporting budgets by quarters. (Note: Use variable and fixed in the selling and administrative expense budget.)

Prepare sales, production, direct materials, direct labor, and income statement budgets.
(S.O. 3, 4)

P25–2   Leiter Inc. is preparing its annual budgets for the year ending December 31, 1993. Accounting assistants furnish the following data:

	Product LN 35	Product LN 40
Sales budget:		
Anticipated volume in units	400,000	180,000
Unit selling price	$15.00	$30.00
Production budget:		
Desired ending finished goods units	30,000	25,000
Beginning finished goods units	20,000	5,000
Direct materials budget:		
Direct materials per unit (pounds)	2	3
Desired ending direct materials units	50,000	20,000
Beginning direct materials units	40,000	10,000
Cost per pound	$2.00	$3.00
Direct labor budget:		
Direct labor time per unit	.5	.75
Direct labor rate per hour	$8.00	$8.00
Budgeted income statement:		
Total unit cost	$10.00	$20.00

An accounting assistant has prepared the detailed manufacturing overhead budget and the selling and administrative expense budget. The latter shows selling expenses of $460,000 for product LN 35 and $450,000 for product LN 40, and administrative expenses of $420,000 for product LN 35 and $370,000 for product LN 40. Income taxes are expected to be 30%.

Instructions
Prepare the following budgets for the year. Show data for each product. Quarterly budgets should not be prepared.

(a) Sales
(b) Production
(c) Direct materials
(d) Direct labor
(e) Income statement (Note: Income taxes are not allocated to the products.)

P25–3 Eastland Industries had sales in 1993 of $5,250,000 and gross profit of $1,587,500. Management is considering two alternative budget plans to increase its gross profit in 1994.

Plan A would increase the selling price per unit from $6.00 to $6.60. Sales volume would decrease by 10% from its 1993 level. Plan B would decrease the selling price per unit by 5%. The marketing department expects that the sales volume would increase by 100,000 units.

At the end of 1993, Eastland has 75,000 units on hand. If Plan A is accepted, the 1994 ending inventory should be equal to 87,500 units. If Plan B is accepted, the ending inventory should be equal to 100,000 units. Each unit produced will cost $2.00 in direct materials, $1.00 in direct labor, and $.50 in variable overhead. The fixed overhead for 1994 should be $600,000.

Prepare sales and production budgets and compute cost per unit under two plans.
(S.O. 3, 4)

Instructions
(a) Prepare a sales budget for 1994 under (1) Plan A and (2) Plan B.

(b) Prepare a production budget for 1994 under (1) Plan A and (2) Plan B.

(c) Compute the cost per unit under (1) Plan A and (2) Plan B. Explain why the cost per unit is different for each of the two plans. (Round to two decimals.)

(d) Which plan should be accepted? (Hint: Compute the gross profit under each plan.)

P25–4 The Kruise Company prepares monthly cash budgets. Relevant data from operating budgets are:

Prepare a cash budget for two months.
(S.O. 5)

	January	February
Sales	$360,000	$400,000
Direct materials purchases	100,000	120,000
Direct labor	80,000	95,000
Manufacturing overhead	60,000	75,000
Selling and administrative expenses	75,000	85,000

All sales are on account. Collections are expected to be 50% in the month of sale, 30% in the first month following the sale, and 20% in the second month following the sale. Forty percent (40%) of direct material purchases are paid in cash in the month of purchase, and the balance due is paid in the month following the purchase. All other items above are paid in the month incurred. Depreciation has been excluded from manufacturing overhead and selling and administrative expenses.

Other data:

(1) Credit sales—November 1992 $200,000; December 1992 $280,000.

(2) Purchases of direct materials—December 1992, $90,000.

(3) Other receipts—January: collection of December 31, 1992 interest receivable $3,000; February: proceeds from sale of securities $5,000.

(4) Other disbursements—February: payment of $20,000 for land.

The company's cash balance on January 1, 1993 is expected to be $60,000. The company wants to maintain a minimum cash balance of $50,000.

Instructions
(a) Prepare schedules for (1) expected collections from customers and (2) expected payments for direct materials purchases.

(b) Prepare a cash budget for January and February in columnar form.

Prepare purchases and income statement budgets for a merchandising company.
(S.O. 7)

P25–5 The budget committee of the Fields Company collects the following data for its West-wood Store in preparing budgeted income statements for July and August, 1993.

1. Expected sales: July $400,000, August $450,000, September $500,000.
2. Cost of goods sold is expected to be 72% of sales.
3. Company policy is to maintain ending merchandise inventory at 25% of the following month's cost of goods sold.
4. Operating expenses are estimated to be:

Sales salaries	$20,000 per month
Advertising	4% of monthly sales
Delivery expense	2% of monthly sales
Sales commissions	3% of monthly sales
Rent expense	$3,000 per month
Depreciation	$700 per month
Utilities	$500 per month
Insurance	$300 per month

5. Income taxes are estimated to be 25% of income from operations.

Instructions

(a) Prepare the merchandise purchases budget for each month in columnar form.

(b) Prepare budgeted income statements for each month in columnar form. Show the details of cost of goods sold in the statements.

Prepare budgeted income statement and balance sheet.
(S.O. 3, 4)

P25–6 Charter Industries' balance sheet at December 31, 1992, is presented below.

CHARTER INDUSTRIES
Balance Sheet
December 31, 1992

Assets

Current assets		
Cash		$ 7,500
Accounts receivable		82,500
Finished goods inventory (2,000 units)		30,000
Total current assets		120,000
Property, plant, and equipment		
Equipment	$40,000	
Less: Accumulated depreciation	10,000	30,000
Total assets		$150,000

Liabilities and Stockholders' Equity

Liabilities		
Notes payable		$ 25,000
Accounts payable		45,000
Total liabilities		70,000
Stockholders' equity		
Common stock	$50,000	
Retained earnings	30,000	
Total stockholders' equity		80,000
Total liabilities and stockholders' equity		$150,000

Budgeted data for 1993 include the following:

	Quarter 4	Total
Sales budget (8,000 units at $30)	$70,000	$240,000
Direct materials used	17,000	67,200
Direct labor	8,500	33,600
Manufacturing overhead applied	10,000	42,000
Selling and administrative expenses	18,000	76,000

To meet sales requirements and to have 2,400 units of finished goods on hand at December 31, 1993, the production budget shows 8,400 required units of output. The total unit cost of production is expected to be $17. Charter Industries uses the first-in, first out (FIFO) inventory costing method. Selling and administrative expenses include $4,000 for depreciation on equipment. Interest expense is expected to be $3,500 for the year. Income taxes are expected to be 25% of income before income taxes.

All sales and purchases are on account. It is expected that 60% of quarterly sales are paid within the quarter and the remainder is paid in the following quarter. Direct materials purchases are paid 50% in the quarter incurred and the remainder in the following quarter. Purchases in the fourth quarter were the same as the materials used. In 1993, the company expects to purchase additional equipment costing $24,000. It expects to pay $8,000 on notes payable plus all interest due and payable to December 31. Accounts payable at December 31 includes amounts due suppliers plus other accounts payable of $7,500. In 1993, the company expects to declare and pay a $2,000 cash dividend. Unpaid income taxes at December 31 will be $5,000. The company's cash budget shows an expected cash balance of $18,575 at December 31, 1993.

Instructions
Prepare a budgeted income statement for 1993 and a budgeted balance sheet at December 31, 1993.

ALTERNATE PROBLEMS

P25–1A   Howe Farm Supply Company manufactures and sells a pesticide called Snare. The following data are developed for preparing budgets for Snare for the first two quarters of 1994.

Prepare budgeted income statement and supporting budgets.
(S.O. 3, 4)

1. Sales: Quarter 1, 32,000 bags: quarter 2, 48,000 bags. Selling price is $50 per bag.
2. Direct materials: Each bag of Snare requires 6 pounds of Gumm at a cost of $2 per pound and 8 pounds of Tarr at $1.50 per pound.
3. Desired inventory levels:

Type of Inventory	January 1	April 1	July 1
Snare (bags)	8,000	12,000	18,000
Gumm (pounds)	9,000	10,000	13,000
Tarr (pounds)	14,000	20,000	25,000

4. Direct labor: direct labor time is 20 minutes per bag at an hourly rate of $12 per hour.
5. Selling and administrative expenses are expected to be 8% of sales plus $200,000 per quarter.
6. Income taxes are expected to be 30% of income from operations.

Your assistant has prepared two budgets: the manufacturing overhead budget that shows expected costs to be 150% of direct labor cost, and the direct materials budget for Tarr which shows the cost of Tarr to be $441,000 in quarter 1 and $655,500 in quarter 2.

Instructions
Prepare the budgeted income statement for the first six months and all required supporting budgets by quarters. (Note: Use variable and fixed in the selling and administrative expense budget.)

P25–2A   Connely Inc. is preparing its annual budgets for the year ending December 31, 1994. Accounting assistants furnish the following data:

Prepare sales, production, direct materials, direct labor, and income statement budgets.
(S.O. 3, 4)

	Product JB 50	Product JB 60
Sales budget:		
Anticipated volume in units	450,000	160,000
Unit selling price	$20.00	$30.00
Production budget:		
Desired ending finished goods units	25,000	15,000
Beginning finished goods units	20,000	10,000

	Product JB 50	Product JB 60
Direct materials budget:		
Direct materials per unit (pounds)	2	3
Desired ending direct materials units	30,000	15,000
Beginning direct materials units	40,000	10,000
Cost per pound	$3.00	$4.00
Direct labor budget		
Direct labor time per unit	.4	.6
Direct labor rate per hour	$10.00	$10.00
Budgeted income statement:		
Total unit cost	$12.00	$20.00

An accounting assistant has prepared the detailed manufacturing overhead budget and the selling and administrative expense budget. The latter shows selling expenses of $660,000 for product JB 50 and $340,000 for product JB 60 and administrative expenses of $420,000 for product JB 50 and $360,000 for product JB 60. Income taxes are expected to be 30%.

Instructions

Prepare the following budgets for the year. Show data for each product. Quarterly budgets should not be prepared.

(a) Sales
(b) Production
(c) Direct materials
(d) Direct labor
(e) Income statement (Note: Income taxes are not allocated to the products.)

Prepare sales and production budgets and compute cost per unit under two plans.
(S.O. 3, 4)

P25–3A   Parson Industries had sales in 1993 of $6,000,000, and gross profit of $1,500,000. Management is considering two alternative budget plans to increase its gross profit in 1994.

Plan A would increase the selling price per unit from $8.00 to $8.40. Sales volume would decrease by 5% from its 1993 level. Plan B would decrease the selling price per unit by $.50. The marketing department expects that the sales volume would increase by 150,000 units.

At the end of 1993, Parson has 30,000 units of inventory on hand. If Plan A is accepted, the 1994 ending inventory should be equal to 4% of the 1994 sales. If Plan B is accepted, the ending inventory should be equal to 40,000 units. Each unit produced will cost $1.50 in direct labor, $2.00 in direct materials, and $.90 in variable overhead. The fixed overhead for 1994 should be $1,200,000.

Instructions

(a) Prepare a sales budget for 1994 under each plan.

(b) Prepare a production budget for 1994 under each plan.

(c) Compute the production cost per unit under each plan. Why is the cost per unit different for each of the two plans? (Round to two decimals.)

(d) Which plan should be accepted? (Hint: Compute the gross profit under each plan.)

Prepare a cash budget for two months.
(S.O. 5)

P25–4A   The Kempen Company prepares monthly cash budgets. Relevant data from operating budgets are:

	January	February
Sales	$350,000	$400,000
Direct materials purchases	120,000	140,000
Direct labor	80,000	95,000
Manufacturing overhead	70,000	75,000
Selling and administrative expenses	79,000	86,000

All sales are on account. Collections are expected to be 50% in the month of sale, 40% in the first month following the sale, and 10% in the second month following the sale. Fifty percent (50%) of direct material purchases are paid in cash in the month of purchase, and the balance due is paid in the month following the purchase. All other items above are paid in the month incurred except for selling and administrative expenses that includes $1,000 of depreciation per month.

Other data:

(1) Credit sales—November 1992 $260,000; December 1992 $300,000.

(2) Purchases of direct materials—December 1992, $100,000.

(3) Other receipts—January: collection of December 31, 1992 notes receivable $15,000; February: proceeds from sale of securities $6,000.

(4) Other disbursements—February: withdrawal of $5,000 cash for personal use of owner, T. Kempen.

The company's cash balance on January 1, 1993 is expected to be $55,000. The company wants to maintain a minimum cash balance of $50,000.

Instructions

(a) Prepare schedules for (1) expected collections from customers and (2) expected payments for direct materials purchases.

(b) Prepare a cash budget for January and February in columnar form.

P25–5A The budget committee of the Felder Company collects the following data for its Lakeview Store in preparing budgeted income statements for May and June 1994.

> Prepare purchases and income statement budgets for a merchandising company.
> (S.O. 7)

1. Sales for May are expected to be $600,000. Sales in June and July are expected to be 10% higher than the preceding month.

2. Cost of goods sold is expected to be 75% of sales.

3. Company policy is to maintain ending merchandise inventory at 33⅓% of the following month's cost of goods sold.

4. Operating expenses are estimated to be:

Sales salaries	$30,000 per month
Advertising	5% of monthly sales
Delivery expense	3% of monthly sales
Sales commissions	4% of monthly sales
Rent expense	$5,000 per month
Depreciation	$800 per month
Utilities	$600 per month
Insurance	$500 per month

5. Income taxes are estimated to be 25% of income from operations.

Instructions

(a) Prepare the merchandise purchases budget for each month in columnar form.

(b) Prepare budgeted income statements for each month in columnar form. Show the details of cost of goods sold in the statements.

Broadening Your Perspective

DECISION CASE 1

Kinison Corporation operates on a calendar-year basis. It begins the annual budgeting process in late August when the president establishes targets for the total dollar sales and net income before taxes for the next year.

The sales target is given to the marketing department where the marketing manager formulates a sales budget by product line in both units and dollars. From this budget, sales quotas by product line in units and dollars are established for each of the corporation's sales districts. The marketing manager also estimates the cost of the marketing activities required to support the target sales volume and prepares a tentative marketing expense budget.

The executive vice president uses the sales and profit targets, the sales budget by product line, and the tentative marketing expense budget to determine the dollar amounts that can be devoted to manufacturing and corporate office expense. The executive vice president prepares the budget for corporate expenses, and then forwards to the production department the product-line sales budget in units and the total dollar amount that can be devoted to manufacturing.

The production manager meets with the factory managers to develop a manufacturing plan that will produce the required units when needed within the cost constraints set by the executive vice president. The budgeting process usually comes to a halt at this point because the production department does not consider the financial resources allocated to be adequate.

When this standstill occurs, the vice president of finance, the executive vice president, the marketing manager, and the production manager meet together to determine the final budgets for each of the areas. This normally results in a modest increase in the total amount available for manufacturing costs while the marketing expense and corporate office expense budgets are cut. The total sales and net income figures proposed by the president are seldom changed. Although the participants are seldom pleased with the compromise, these budgets are final. Each executive then develops a new detailed budget for the operations in his or her area.

None of the areas has achieved its budget in recent years. Sales often run below the target. When budgeted sales are not achieved, each area is expected to cut costs so that the president's profit target can still be met. However, the profit target is seldom met because costs are not cut enough. In fact, costs often run above the original budget in all functional areas (marketing, production, and corporate office). The president is disturbed that Kinison has not been able to meet the sales and profit targets. He hired a consultant with considerable experience with companies in Kinison's industry. The consultant reviewed the budgets for the past four years. He concluded that the product-line sales budgets were reasonable and that the cost and expense budgets were adequate for the budgeted sales and production levels.

Instructions

(a) Discuss how the budgeting process as employed by Kinison Corporation contributes to the failure to achieve the president's sales and profit targets.

(b) Suggest how Kinison Corporation's budgeting process could be revised to correct the problems.

(c) Should the functional areas be expected to cut their costs when sales volume falls below budget? Explain your answer.

(CMA adapted.)

DECISION CASE 2

The Triple-F Health Club (Family, Fitness, and Fun) is a nonprofit family-oriented health club. The club's Board of Directors is developing plans to acquire more equipment and expand the club facilities. The Board plans to purchase about $25,000 of new equipment each year and wants to begin a fund to purchase the adjoining property in four or five years. The adjoining property has a market value of about $300,000.

The club manager, Jan Crowe, is concerned that the Board has unrealistic goals in light of its recent financial performance. She has sought the help of a club member with an accounting background to assist her in preparing a report to the Board supporting her concerns.

The club member reviewed the club's records, including the cash basis income statements presented below. The review and discussions with Jan Crowe disclosed the additional information that follows the statement.

TRIPLE-F HEALTH CLUB
Statement of Income (Cash Basis)
For Years Ended October 31
($000 omitted)

	1993	1992
Cash revenues		
Annual membership fees	$355.0	$300.0
Lesson and class fees	234.0	180.0
Miscellaneous	2.0	1.5
Total cash received	$591.0	$481.5

	1993	1992
Cash expenses		
Manager's salary and benefits	$ 36.0	$ 36.0
Regular employees' wages and benefits	190.0	190.0
Lesson and class employee wages and benefits	195.0	150.0
Towels and supplies	16.0	15.5
Utilities (heat and light)	22.0	15.0
Mortgage interest	35.1	37.8
Miscellaneous	2.0	1.5
Total cash expenses	$496.1	$445.8
Cash income	$ 94.9	$ 35.7

Additional information:

1. Other financial information as of October 31, 1993
   (a) Cash in checking account, $7,300.
   (b) Outstanding mortgage balance, $360,000.
   (c) Accounts payable arising from invoices for supplies and utilities that are unpaid as of October 31, 1993, $2,500.

2. No unpaid bills existed on October 31, 1992.

3. The club purchased $25,000 worth of exercise equipment during the current fiscal year. Cash of $10,000 was paid on delivery and the balance was due on October 1 but has not been paid as of October 31, 1993.

4. The club began operations in 1987 in rental quarters. In October of 1989 it purchased its current property (land and building) for $600,000, paying $120,000 down and agreeing to pay $30,000 plus 9% interest annually on November 1 until the balance was paid off.

5. Membership rose 3% during 1993. This is approximately the same annual rate the club has experienced since it opened.

6. Membership fees were increased by 15% in 1993. The Board has tentative plans to increase the fees by 10% in 1994.

7. Lesson and class fees have not been increased for three years. The board policy is to encourage classes and lessons by keeping the fees low. The members have taken advantage of this policy and the number of classes and lessons have grown significantly each year. The club expects the percentage growth experienced in 1993 to be repeated in 1994.

8. Miscellaneous revenues are expected to grow at the same percentage as experienced in 1993.

9. Operating expenses are expected to increase. Hourly wage rates and the manager's salary will need to be increased 15% because no increases were granted in 1993. Towels and supplies, utilities, and miscellaneous expenses are expected to increase 25%.

Instructions

(a) Construct a cash budget for 1994 for the Triple-F Health Club.

(b) Identify any operating problem(s) that this budget discloses for the Triple-F Health Club. Explain your answer.

(c) Is Jan Crowe's concern justified that the Board's goals are unrealistic? Explain your answer. (CMA, adapted.)

CRITICAL THINKING CASE

Refer to the opening story about the University of Nebraska and answer the following questions.

1. How does the length of the budget period for the University of Nebraska compare with the guidelines given in the chapter for businesses?

2. What impact might the budget have on University administrators, faculty, and students?

3. Who do you believe comprises the budget committee at your college or university?

4. What specific types of expenses, other than salaries, might be cut in the University of Nebraska budget without harming the quality of education?

ETHICAL CASE

You are an accountant in the budgetary, projections, and special projects department of Axel-Gear Corp., a large manufacturing company. The president, Warner Daggart, asks you on very short notice to prepare some sales and income projections covering the next two years of the company's much heralded new product lines. He wants these projections for a series of speeches he is making while on a two-week trip to eight east-coast brokerage firms. The president hopes to bolster Axel-Gears' stock sales and price.

You work 23 hours in two days to compile the projections, hand deliver them to the president, and are swiftly but graciously thanked as he departs. A week later you find time to go over some of your computations and discover a miscalculation that makes the projections grossly overstated. You quickly inquire about the president's itinerary and learn that he has made half of his speeches and has half yet to make. You are in a quandry as to what to do.

Instructions

(a) What are the consequences of telling the president of your gross miscalculations?

(b) What are the consequences of **not** telling the president of your gross miscalculations?

(c) What are the ethical considerations to you and the president in this situation?

Answers to Self-Study Questions
1. b   2. d   3. c   4. a   5. c   6. b   7. b   8. d   9. a   10. c

CONCEPTS FOR REVIEW

Before studying this chapter, you should know or, if necessary, review:

a. *The meaning of the management function of controlling. (Ch. 21, p. 859–60)*

b. *The purposes and advantages of a budget. (Ch. 25, pp. 1004 and 1007–8)*

c. *The difference between variable costs and fixed costs. (Ch. 24, p. 967–8)*

CHAPTER 26

BUDGETARY CONTROL AND RESPONSIBILITY ACCOUNTING

Study Objectives

After completing the study of this chapter, you should be able to:

1. *Describe the concept of budgetary control.*

2. *Evaluate the usefulness of static budget reports.*

3. *Explain the development of flexible budgets and the usefulness of flexible budget reports.*

4. *Describe the concept of responsibility accounting.*

5. *Indicate the features of responsibility reports for cost centers.*

6. *Identify the content of responsibility reports for profit centers.*

7. *Explain the basis and formulas used in evaluating performance in investment centers.*

V*irtually every department on a college campus develops a budget and then compares that budget to the amount actually spent. As the school term progresses, the person in charge of the budget can see how well the department is doing compared to expectations.*

One of the most expensive departments on campus is the athletic department. That fact usually rankles the academic department heads. They argue that a university exists first and foremost to educate. But the money for sports is often justified because the sports teams—particularly at big schools—generate large incomes from television contracts that can then be used for a variety of educational purposes.

At the University of Nevada, Las Vegas, each athletic team has its own budget and its own financial statement. This financial information "shows what the teams have spent for the month and for the year to date, and how the actual expenditures compare to the budget,'' says Merv Gupton, athletic accounting manager. The biggest budget items: scholarships for students, payroll, and travel costs.

UNLV sports teams include men's basketball, women's basketball, men's tennis, women's tennis, men's baseball, women's softball, soccer, football, women's track and cross country, men's golf, and men's and women's swimming. Travel costs are usually the most uncontrollable item in the budget. What if you get two-thirds through the season and run out of money? ''One sports team might be able to help out another,'' says Gupton. Or more likely, ''if a coach is running low on money, the team won't fly—it'll take the bus.''

The vignette indicates that not only is it necessary for an athletic department to have budgets, it also can use budgets to control its activities. For example, if you were the athletic director at UNLV, you might require periodic updates from each coach showing actual and budgeted expenses.

As illustrated in Chapter 25, budgets are also used in business. For example, if you were the CEO of a company, you might exercise control over each business activity by using budgets to:

1. Determine whether the sales department is meeting expected sales goals.
2. Identify cost overruns in production.
3. Determine the effectiveness of each department manager in using company resources.
4. Identify the manager that is doing the best job in meeting planned budget activities.

This chapter focuses on two aspects of management control: (1) budgetary control and (2) responsibility accounting.

Concept of Budgetary Control

Study Objective 1

Describe the concept of budgetary control.

As stated at the beginning of the managerial accounting chapters, one of management's major functions is controlling the operations of the company. Control was defined as the steps taken by management to see that planned objectives are met. We now need to ask: How do budgets assist management in controlling operations?

The use of budgets in controlling operations is known as budgetary control. **The centerpiece of budgetary control is the use of budget reports that compare actual results with planned objectives.** The preparation and use of budget reports is based on the belief that planned objectives lose much of their potential value without some monitoring of progress along the way. Just as your professors give midterm examinations to evaluate your progress, so top management requires periodic reports on the progress that department managers are making toward planned annual objectives.

Budget reports provide the feedback needed by management to see whether actual operations are on course. The feedback for a crucial objective, such as having enough cash on hand to pay bills, may be made daily. For other objectives, such as meeting budgeted annual sales and operating expenses, monthly budget reports may suffice. Because of the flexibility of managerial accounting, budget reports can be prepared as frequently as needed. On the basis of the budget reports, management first analyzes any differences between actual and planned results to determine their causes. From this analysis, management may take corrective action, or it may decide to modify the future plans.

Budgetary control involves the following:

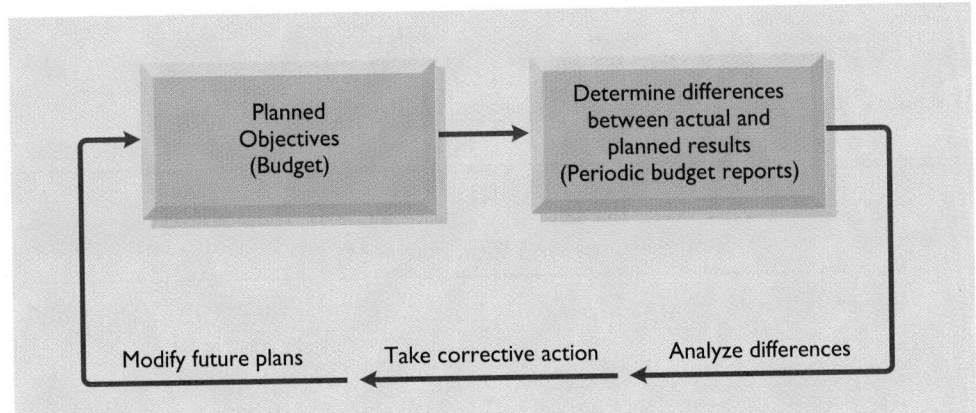

ILLUSTRATION 26-1

Budgetary control

Budgetary control works best when a company has a formalized reporting system. The system should (1) identify the name of the budget report, such as the sales budget, the manufacturing overhead budget, and so on; (2) state the frequency of the report, such as weekly, or monthly; (3) specify the purpose of the report; and (4) indicate the primary recipient(s) of the report. The following schedule illustrates a partial budgetary control system for a manufacturing company. Note the emphasis on control in the reports and the frequency of the reports. For example, there is a daily report on scrap and a weekly report on labor.

ILLUSTRATION 26-2

Budgetary control reporting system

Name of Report	Frequency	Purpose	Primary Recipient(s)
Sales	Weekly	Determine whether sales goals are being met	Top management and sales manager
Labor	Weekly	Control direct and indirect labor cost	Vice president of production and production department managers
Scrap	Daily	Determine efficient use of materials	Production manager
Departmental overhead costs	Monthly	Control overhead costs	Department manager
Selling expenses	Monthly	Control selling expenses	Sales manager
Income statement	Monthly and quarterly	Determine whether income objectives are being met	Top management

Master Budget Performance Reports

You learned in Chapter 25 that the master budget formalizes management's planned objectives for the coming year. The budgetary process also sets forth the means of achieving the financial results desired for the year. Thus, to achieve its planned net income, the company budgets sales, cost of goods sold, and operating expenses. To illustrate the role of the master budget in budgetary control, we will use the budget developed for the Hayes Company in Chapter 25. Budget

Study Objective 2

Evaluate the usefulness of static budget reports.

and actual sales data for the Kitchen-mate product in the first and second quarters of 1993 are as follows:

ILLUSTRATION 26-3

Budget and actual sales data

Sales	First Quarter	Second Quarter	Total
Budgeted	$180,000	$210,000	$390,000
Actual	179,000	199,500	378,500
Difference	$ 1,000	$ 10,500	$ 11,500

The sales budget report for the first quarter is shown below.

ILLUSTRATION 26-4

Sales budget report—first quarter

HAYES COMPANY
Sales Budget Report
For the Quarter Ended March 31, 1993

Product Line	Budget	Actual	Difference Favorable F Unfavorable U
Kitchen-mate[a]	$180,000	$179,000	$1,000 U

[a]In practice, each product line would be included in the report.

The report shows that sales are $1,000 under budget—an unfavorable result. This difference is less than 1% of budgeted sales ($1,000 ÷ $180,000 = .0056). Top management's analysis of unfavorable differences is often influenced by the materiality (significance) of the difference. Since the difference of $1,000 is immaterial in this case, we will assume that the management of the Hayes Company makes no analysis and takes no specific action.

The budget report for the second quarter presented in Illustration 26-5 contains one new feature: cumulative year-to-date information. This report indicates that sales for the second quarter were $10,500 below budget, which is 5% of budgeted sales ($10,500 ÷ $210,000). Top management may conclude that the difference between budgeted and actual sales in the second quarter merits analysis.

ILLUSTRATION 26-5

Sales budget report—second quarter

HAYES COMPANY
Sales Budget Report
For the Quarter Ended June 30, 1993

Product Line	Second Quarter			Year-to-Date		
	Budget	Actual	Difference Favorable F Unfavorable U	Budget	Actual	Difference Favorable F Unfavorable U
Kitchen-mate	$210,000	$199,500	$10,500 U	$390,000	$378,500	$11,500 U

The analysis should start by asking the sales manager the cause(s) of the shortfall. If corrective action is needed, it should be discussed. For example, management may decide to spur sales by offering sales incentives to customers or by increasing the advertising of Kitchen-mates. On the other hand, if management concludes that a downturn in the economy is responsible for the lower sales, it may decide to modify planned sales and profit goals.

From the examples above, you can see that a master sales budget is useful in evaluating the performance of a sales manager. It is now necessary to ask: How appropriate is the master budget for evaluating a manager's performance in controlling costs? The master budget for the Hayes Company was geared to one level of activity—expected annual sales of $900,000. In this case, the master budget is a static budget.

In a static budget, the data are not modified or adjusted regardless of changes in activity during the year. This means that **actual results are always compared with budget data at the original budgeted activity level**. Thus, the static budget is appropriate in evaluating a manager's effectiveness in controlling cost when:

1. The actual level of activity closely approximates the master budget activity level, and/or
2. The behavior of the costs in response to changes in activity is fixed.

A static budget report is, therefore, appropriate for fixed manufacturing costs and fixed selling and administrative expenses. However, as you will see shortly, static budget reports may not be a proper basis for evaluating a manager's performance in controlling variable costs.

Helpful hint Which of the following is likely to be of little use when costs are variable—static budget or flexible budget? Answer: static budget.

The Flexible Budget

In contrast to a static budget, which is based on one level of activity, a flexible budget projects budget data for various levels of activity. In essence, **the flexible budget is a series of static budgets at different levels of activity**. The flexible budget recognizes that the budgetary process has greater usefulness if it is adaptable to changed operating conditions.

Flexible budgets can be prepared for each of the types of budgets included in the master budget. For example, Marriott Hotels can budget revenues and net income on the basis of 60%, 80%, and 100% of room occupancy. Similarly, American Van Lines can budget its operating expenses on the basis of various levels of truck miles driven. Likewise, the bottling department of Coca-Cola can budget manufacturing costs on the basis of 70%, 80%, and 100% of direct labor costs or machine hours.

> **Study Objective 3**
>
> *Explain the development of flexible budgets and the usefulness of flexible budget reports.*

Why Flexible Budgets?

Assume that you are the manager in charge of manufacturing overhead in the Forging Department of Barton Steel. In preparing the manufacturing overhead budget for 1993, you prepare the following budget based on a production volume of 10,000 units of steel ingots.

BARTON STEEL **Manufacturing Overhead Budget (Static)** **Forging Department** **For the Year Ended December 31, 1993**	
Budgeted production in units (steel ingots)	10,000
Budgeted costs	
Indirect materials	$ 250,000
Indirect labor	260,000
Utilities	190,000
Depreciation	280,000
Property taxes	70,000
Supervision	50,000
	$1,100,000

ILLUSTRATION 26-6

Static overhead budget

Helpful hint The static budget is the master budget of Chapter 25.

Fortunately for the company, the demand for steel ingots has increased, and 12,000 units are produced during the year, rather than 10,000. You are elated because increased sales means increased profitability, which should mean a large raise for you and the employees in your department. Unfortunately, a comparison of the actual costs incurred with the budgeted costs for the year in the Forging Department has put you on the spot. The budget report is shown below.

ILLUSTRATION 26-7

Static overhead budget report

BARTON STEEL
Manufacturing Overhead Budget Report (Static)
Forging Department
For the Year Ended December 31, 1993

	Budget	Actual	Difference Favorable F Unfavorable U
Production in units	10,000	12,000	
Costs			
Indirect materials	$ 250,000	$ 295,000	$ 45,000 U
Indirect labor	260,000	312,000	52,000 U
Utilities	190,000	225,000	35,000 U
Depreciation	280,000	280,000	–0–
Property taxes	70,000	70,000	–0–
Supervision	50,000	50,000	–0–
	$1,100,000	$1,232,000	$132,000 U

Helpful hint   Emphasize that a static budget will not work if a company has substantial variable costs.

Note that this comparison is based on budget data based on the original activity level (10,000 steel ingots). The comparison indicates that the Forging Department is significantly *over budget* for three of the six overhead costs. Moreover, there is a total unfavorable difference of $132,000, which is 12% over budget ($132,000 ÷ $1,100,000). Your supervisor is very unhappy! Instead of sharing in the company's success, you may find yourself looking for another job. What would you do in this situation?

A careful examination of the manufacturing overhead budget identifies the problem: The budget data are not relevant! At the time the budget was developed, it was anticipated that only 10,000 units of steel ingots would be produced, but 12,000 ingots were manufactured. As a result, the comparison of actual variable costs with budgeted costs is meaningless. The reason is that as production increases, the budget allowances for variable costs should increase both directly and proportionately. The variable costs in this example are indirect materials, indirect labor, and utilities.

An analysis of the budget data for these costs at 10,000 units produces the following per unit results:

ILLUSTRATION 26-8

Variable costs per unit

Item	Total Cost	Per Unit
Indirect materials	$250,000	$25
Indirect labor	260,000	26
Utilities	190,000	19
	$700,000	$70

The budgeted variable costs at 12,000 units, therefore, are as follows:

ILLUSTRATION 26-9

Budgeted variable costs (12,000 units)

Item	Computation	Total
Indirect materials	$25 × 12,000	$300,000
Indirect labor	26 × 12,000	312,000
Utilities	19 × 12,000	228,000
		$840,000

The budget cost data at 12,000 units are referred to as **flexible budget data**. Since fixed costs do not change in total as activity changes, the budgeted amounts for these costs remain the same. The budget report based on the flexible budget is shown in Illustration 26-10.

ILLUSTRATION 26-10

Flexible overhead budget report

BARTON STEEL
Manufacturing Overhead Budget Report (Flexible)
Forging Department
For the Year Ended December 31, 1993

	Budget	Actual	Difference Favorable F Unfavorable U
Production in units	12,000	12,000	
Variable Costs			
Indirect materials	$ 300,000	$ 295,000	$5,000 F
Indirect labor	312,000	312,000	–0–
Utilities	228,000	225,000	3,000 F
Total variable	840,000	832,000	8,000 F
Fixed Costs			
Depreciation	280,000	280,000	–0–
Property taxes	70,000	70,000	–0–
Supervision	50,000	50,000	–0–
Total fixed	400,000	400,000	–0–
Total costs	$1,240,000	$1,232,000	$8,000 F

This report indicates that the Forging Department is below budget—a favorable difference. Instead of worrying about being fired, you may be in line for a raise or a promotion after all! As indicated from the foregoing analysis, the only appropriate comparison is between actual costs at 12,000 units of production and budgeted costs at 12,000 units of production. Flexible budget reports provide this comparison.

Developing the Flexible Budget

The flexible budget is prepared from the master budget. To develop the flexible budget, the following steps should be taken.

1. Identify the activity index and the relevant range of activity.
2. Identify the variable costs and determine the budgeted variable cost per unit of activity for each cost.
3. Identify the fixed costs and determine the budgeted amount for each cost.

4. Prepare the budget for selected increments of activity within the relevant range.

The activity index should significantly influence the costs that are being budgeted. For manufacturing overhead costs, the activity index is usually the same as the index used in developing the predetermined overhead rate, that is, direct labor hours or machine hours. For selling and administrative expenses, the activity index usually is sales or net sales.

The choice of selected increments of activity is largely a matter of expediency. For example, if the relevant range is 8,000 to 12,000 direct labor hours, increments of 1,000 hours may be selected. The flexible budget is prepared in columnar form for each increment within the relevant range.

Flexible Budget Illustrated

To illustrate the preparation of the flexible budget, we will use the Fox Manufacturing Company. The management of Fox Manufacturing wants to use the flexible budget for monthly comparisons of actual and budgeted manufacturing overhead costs of the Finishing Department. The master budget for the year ending December 31, 1993 shows expected annual operating capacity of 120,000 direct labor hours and the following overhead costs:

ILLUSTRATION 26-11

Master budget data

Variable		Fixed	
Indirect materials	$180,000	Depreciation	$180,000
Indirect labor	240,000	Supervision	120,000
Utilities	60,000	Property taxes	60,000
Total	$480,000	Total	$360,000

The application of the four steps is as follows:

Step 1. Identify the activity index and the relevant range of activity. The activity index is direct labor hours. Management concludes that the relevant range is 8,000 − 12,000 direct labor hours.

Step 2. Identify the variable costs and determine the budgeted variable cost per unit of activity for each cost. There are three variable costs. The variable cost per unit is found by dividing each total budgeted cost by the direct labor hours used (120,000) in preparing the master budget. For Fox Manufacturing, the computations are:

ILLUSTRATION 26-12

Computation of variable costs per direct labor hour

Variable Cost	Computation	Variable Cost Per Direct Labor Hour
Indirect materials	$180,000 ÷ 120,000	$1.50
Indirect labor	240,000 ÷ 120,000	2.00
Utilities	60,000 ÷ 120,000	.50
Total		$4.00

Step 3. Identify the fixed costs and determine the budgeted amount for each cost. There are three fixed costs. Since Fox Manufacturing desires monthly budget data, the budgeted amount is found by dividing each annual budgeted cost by 12. For Fox Manufacturing, the monthly budgeted fixed costs are: Depreciation $15,000, Supervision $10,000, and Property taxes $5,000.

Step 4. Prepare the budget for selected increments of activity within the

relevant range. Management requires that the budget be prepared in increments of 1,000 direct labor hours.

The flexible budget is shown in Illustration 26-13. From the budget, the following formula may be used to determine total budgeted costs at any level of activity: **Total budgeted costs = fixed costs + (total variable cost per unit × activity level).** For Fox Manufacturing, fixed costs are $30,000 and total variable cost per unit is $4.00. Thus, at 9,000 direct labor hours, total budgeted costs are $66,000 [fixed costs, $30,000 + ($4.00 × 9,000)]. Similarly, at 8,622 direct labor hours, total budgeted costs are $64,488 [$30,000 + ($4.00 × 8,622)].

Helpful hint Using the data given for the Fox Manufacturing Company, what amount of total costs would be budgeted for 10,600 direct labor hours?
Answer:

Fixed	$30,000
Variable (10,600 × $4)	42,400
Total	$72,400

ILLUSTRATION 26-13

Flexible overhead budget

FOX MANUFACTURING COMPANY
Monthly Flexible Manufacturing Overhead Budget
Finishing Department
For the Year Ended December 31, 1993

Activity level					
Direct labor hours	8,000	9,000	10,000	11,000	12,000
Variable costs					
Indirect materials	$12,000	$13,500	$15,000	$16,500	$18,000
Indirect labor	16,000	18,000	20,000	22,000	24,000
Utilities	4,000	4,500	5,000	5,500	6,000
Total variable	32,000	36,000	40,000	44,000	48,000
Fixed costs					
Depreciation	15,000	15,000	15,000	15,000	15,000
Supervision	10,000	10,000	10,000	10,000	10,000
Property taxes	5,000	5,000	5,000	5,000	5,000
Total fixed	30,000	30,000	30,000	30,000	30,000
Total costs	$62,000	$66,000	$70,000	$74,000	$78,000

Total budgeted costs can also be shown graphically as in Illustration 26-14.

ILLUSTRATION 26-14

Graphic flexible budget data highlighting 10,000 and 12,000 activity levels

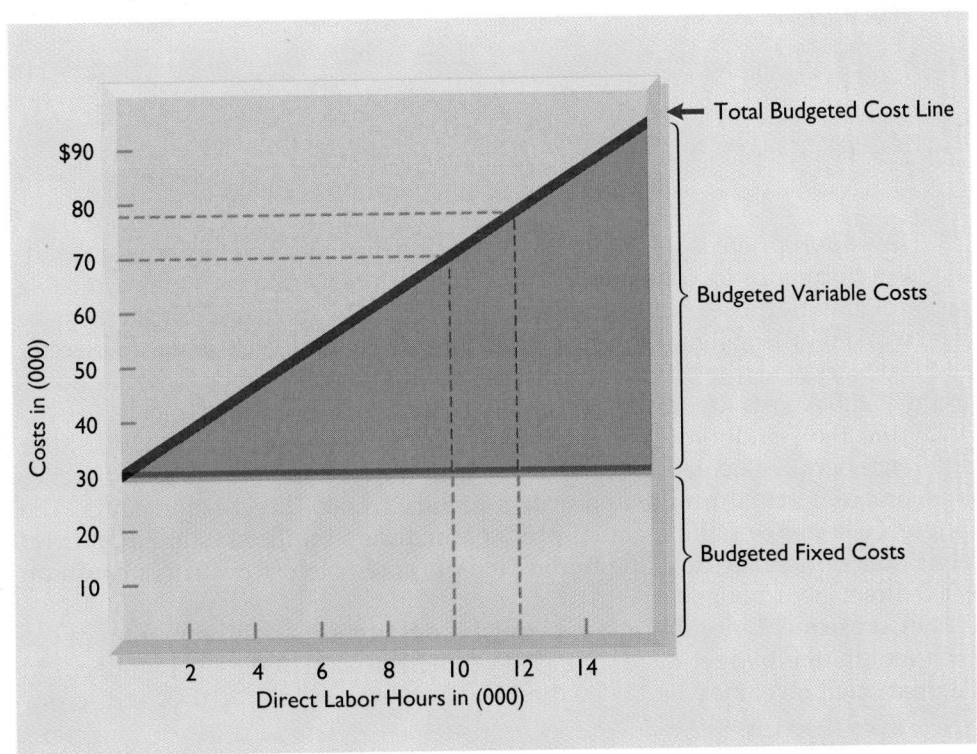

In the graph, the activity index is shown on the horizontal axis and costs are indicated on the vertical axis. The graph highlights two of the 1,000 increments (10,000 and 12,000). As shown in Illustration 26-14, total budgeted costs are $70,000 [$30,000 + ($4.00 × 10,000)] and $78,000 [$30,000 + ($4.00 × 12,000)], respectively.

Flexible Budget Reports

Flexible budget reports represent another type of internal report produced by managerial accounting. The flexible budget report consists of two sections: (1) production data and (2) cost data. Consequently, the report provides a basis for evaluating a manager's performance in two areas: production control and cost control. Flexible budgets are widely used in production and service departments. A budget report for the Finishing Department of Fox Company for the month of January is shown in Illustration 26-15. In this month, 8,800 direct labor hours were expected but 9,000 hours were worked. The budget data are based on the flexible budget for 9,000 hours in Illustration 26-13. The actual cost data are assumed.

ILLUSTRATION 26-15

Flexible overhead budget report

FOX MANUFACTURING COMPANY **Manufacturing Overhead Budget Report (Flexible)** **Finishing Department** **For the Month Ended January 31, 1993**			
Direct labor hours (DLH)			Difference
Expected 8,800	Budget at	Actual Costs	Favorable F
Actual 9,000	9,000 DLH	9,000 DLH	Unfavorable U
Variable costs			
Indirect materials	$13,500	$14,000	$ 500 U
Indirect labor	18,000	17,000	1,000 F
Utilities	4,500	4,600	100 U
Total variable	36,000	35,600	400 F
Fixed costs			
Depreciation	15,000	15,000	—
Supervision	10,000	10,000	—
Property taxes	5,000	5,000	—
Total fixed	30,000	30,000	
Total costs	$66,000	$65,600	$ 400 F

How appropriate is this report in evaluating the Finishing Department manager's performance in controlling costs? The report clearly provides a reliable basis for this purpose. Both actual and budget costs are based on the activity level worked during January. Since variable costs generally are incurred directly by the department, the difference between the budget allowance for those hours and the actual costs are the responsibility of the department manager.

From the standpoint of production control, the report shows a 200-hour difference between actual direct labor hours and expected hours. This difference is favorable if actual production orders required 9,000 direct labor hours. The difference is unfavorable if actual production orders required only 8,800 direct labor hours. In either case, the budget for purposes of cost control is based on 9,000 direct labor hours.

In subsequent months, other flexible budget reports will be prepared. For each month, the budget data are based on the actual activity level attained. In February that level may be 11,000 direct labor hours, in July, 10,000, and so on.

Management by Exception

Management by exception means that top management's review of a budget report is directed either entirely or primarily to differences between actual results and planned objectives. This approach enables top management to focus on problem areas that need attention. Management by exception does not mean that top management will investigate every difference. For this approach to be effective, there must be some guidelines for identifying an exception. The usual criteria are materiality and controllability of the item.

Materiality

Without quantitative guidelines, management would have to investigate every budget difference regardless of the amount. Materiality is usually expressed as a percentage difference from budget. For example, the percentage difference may be set at 5% for important items and 10% for other items. This means that all differences either over or under budget by the specified percentage will be investigated. Costs over budget warrant investigation to determine why they were not controlled. In contrast, costs under budget merit investigation to determine whether costs critical to the profitability of the division are being curtailed. For example, if maintenance costs are budgeted at $80,000 and only $40,000 is spent, there may be major unexpected breakdowns in productive facilities in the future.

Alternatively, a company may specify a single percentage difference from budget for all items and supplement this guideline with a minimum dollar limit. For example, the exception criteria may be stated at 5% of budget or more than $10,000.

Controllability of the Item

Exception guidelines are more restrictive for controllable items than for items that are not controllable by the manager being evaluated. In fact, there may be no guidelines for noncontrollable items. For example, a large unfavorable difference between actual and budgeted property tax expense may not be flagged by management for investigation because the only possible causes are an unexpected increase in the tax rate or in the assessed value of the property. An investigation into the difference will be useless because the manager cannot control either cause.

Before You Go On . . .

1. What is the meaning of budgetary control?

2. When is a static budget appropriate for evaluating a manager's effectiveness in controlling costs?

3. What is a flexible budget?

4. How is a flexible budget developed?

Concept of Responsibility Accounting

Like budgeting, responsibility accounting is an important part of management accounting. **Responsibility accounting** involves accumulating and reporting costs (and revenues, where relevant) on the basis of the individual manager who

Study Objective 4

Describe the concept of responsibility accounting.

has the authority to make the day-to-day decisions about the items. Under responsibility accounting, the evaluation of a manager's performance is based on matters directly under that manager's control. Responsibility accounting can be used at every level of management in which the following conditions exist:

1. Costs and revenues can be directly associated with the specific level of management responsibility.
2. The costs and revenues are controllable at the level of responsibility with which they are associated.
3. Budget data can be developed for evaluating the manager's effectiveness in controlling the costs and revenues.

Helpful hint All companies use responsibility accounting. Without some form of responsibility accounting, there would be chaos in discharging management's control function.

Responsibility accounting is based on the premise that an organization is essentially a group of individuals striving toward common goals. When individual goals are compatible with the goals established by top management there is **goal congruence** within the organization. In effect, responsibility accounting personalizes the managerial accounting system. Under responsibility accounting, any individual who has control and is accountable for a specified set of activities can be recognized as a responsibility center. Thus, responsibility accounting may extend from the lowest level of control to the top strata of management. Once responsibility has been established, the effectiveness of the individual's performance is first measured and reported for the specified activity, and it is then reported upward throughout the organization.

Responsibility accounting is especially valuable in a decentralized company. Decentralization means that the control of operations is delegated by top management to many individuals (managers) throughout the organization. The term segment is sometimes used to identify areas of responsibility in decentralized operations. Under responsibility accounting, reports are prepared periodically such as monthly, quarterly, and annually, to provide a basis for evaluating the performance of each manager.

Responsibility accounting is an essential part of any effective system of budgetary control. The reporting of costs and revenues under responsibility accounting differs from budgeting in two respects:

1. A distinction is made between controllable and noncontrollable items.
2. Performance reports either emphasize, or only include items controllable by the individual manager.

Accounting in Action · *A Business Insight*

Since devising the budgeting system, JKL, Inc., a large New York advertising agency, has become aware of which specific accounts are unprofitable and the reasons why. Since the budgeting and control system has been instituted, the agency has resigned several unprofitable accounts that otherwise would have gone unnoticed. Account managers and supervisors now feel responsible for the profitability of their accounts. They carefully monitor actual hours spent on each account to make sure the account is being managed and run as efficiently as possible. For example, an account manager noticed a large amount of supervisory creative time was being spent on an account. Further investigation showed that the supervisors, rather than the creative department, were doing the actual creative work. She pointed this out, and a junior creative team was appointed to the account, saving a great deal of money.

Source: William B. Mills, "Drawing Up a Budgeting System for an Ad Agency," *Management Accounting,* December, 1983, p. 52.

Responsibility accounting applies to both profit and not-for-profit entities. The former seek to maximize net income, whereas the latter wish to minimize the cost of providing the service.

Controllable versus Noncontrollable Revenues and Costs

All costs and revenues are controllable at some level of responsibility within a company. This truth underscores the adage by the chief executive officer of any organization that "the buck stops here." Under responsibility accounting, the critical issue is **whether the cost or revenue is controllable at the level of responsibility with which it is associated**.

A cost is considered to be controllable at a given level of managerial responsibility if that manager has the power to incur it within a given period of time. From this criterion, it follows that

Helpful hint Are there more or less controllable costs as you move to higher levels of management? Answer: More.

1. All costs are controllable by top management because of the broad range of its authority.
2. Fewer costs are controllable as one moves down to each lower level of managerial responsibility because of the manager's decreasing authority.

In general, **costs incurred directly by a level of responsibility are controllable at that level**. In contrast, costs incurred indirectly and allocated to a responsibility level are considered to be noncontrollable at that level.

Responsibility Reporting System

A responsibility reporting system involves the preparation of a report for each level of responsibility shown in the company's organization chart. To illustrate a responsibility reporting system, we will use the partial organization chart and production departments of the Francis Company in Illustration 26-16.

ILLUSTRATION 26-16

Partial organization chart

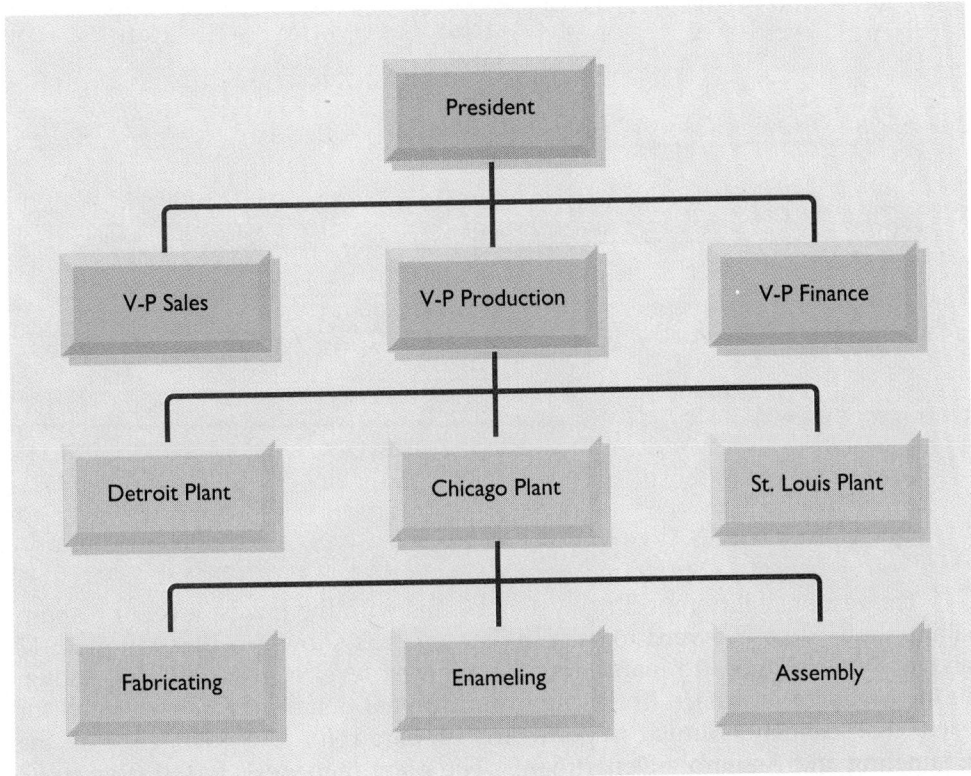

ILLUSTRATION 26-17

Responsibility reporting system

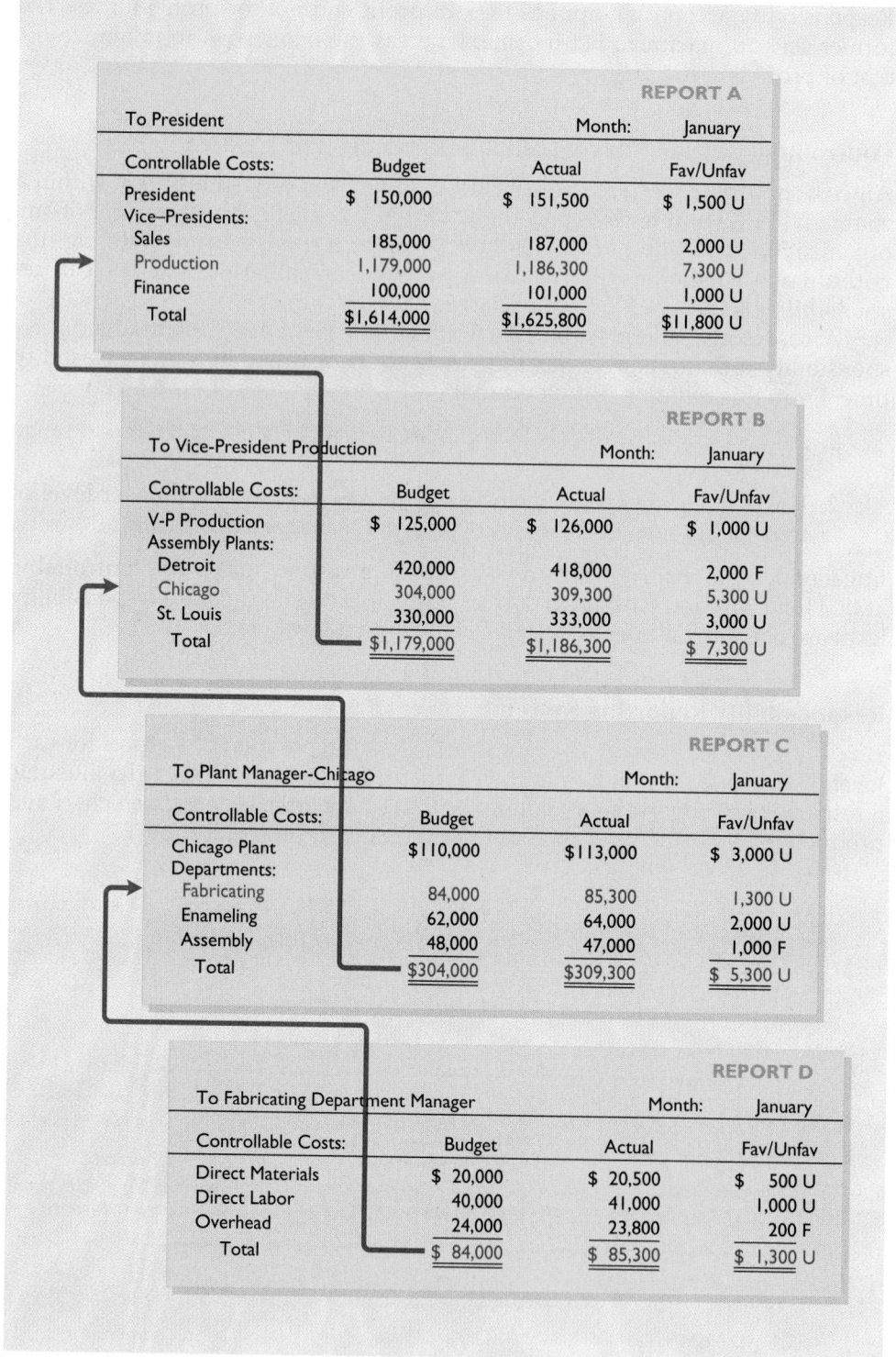

The responsibility reporting system begins with the lowest level of responsibility and moves upward to each higher level, as shown in Illustration 26-17 above. Report D goes to managers at the lowest level of responsibility shown in the organization chart. In this report additional detail may be presented for each cost element. Similar reports are prepared for the managers of the Enameling and Assembly Departments. The plant manager's report (Report C)

shows the costs of the Chicago plant that are controllable at the second level of responsibility. In addition, Report C shows summary data for each department that is accountable to the plant manager. Similar reports are prepared for the Detroit and St. Louis plant managers. Report B shows the controllable costs of the vice-president of production and summary data on the three assembly plants for which this officer is responsible. At the top level of responsibility, the president receives a report (Report A) that shows the controllable costs and expenses of this office and summary data on the vice-presidents that are accountable to the president.

A responsibility reporting system permits management by exception at each level of responsibility within the organization. In addition to the information shown in Illustration 26-17, each higher level of responsibility can obtain the detailed report for each lower level of responsibility. For example, the vice-president of production in the Francis Company may request the Chicago plant manager's report because this plant is $5,300 over budget.

This type of reporting system also permits comparative evaluations. In the illustration above, the Chicago plant manager can easily rank the department manager's effectiveness in controlling manufacturing costs. Comparative rankings provide further incentive for a manager to control costs. For example, the Detroit plant manager will want to continue to be No. 1 in the report to the vice-president of production, and the Chicago plant manager will not want to remain No. 3 in future reporting periods.

Technology in Action

Computerized accounting systems can play a major role in increasing the timeliness of performance reports. The computer's speed in processing and reorganizing information has enabled management to receive feedback reports of exceptions much sooner after the exceptions have occurred than would have been possible with a manual system. Efficiency is increased because management's attention is directed to significant deviations requiring corrective action before these deviations get too far "out of hand."

Management has also come to rely on personal computers to increase the timeliness of information receipt. When connected to the main computer system, a manager can "download" financial information and perform additional calculations and manipulations on the information for a decision at hand in a fraction of the time needed to request such information from the EDP Department. Though more timely, accuracy must not be sacrificed, and all calculations should be tested for correctness before being used for decision making.

Types of Responsibility Centers

There are three basic types of responsibility centers: cost centers, profit centers, and investment centers. These centers indicate the degree of responsibility the manager has for the performance of the center.

A cost center incurs costs (and expenses) but does not directly generate revenues. Managers of cost centers have the authority to incur costs. They are evaluated on their ability to control costs. Cost centers are usually either production departments or service departments. The former participate directly in making the product whereas the latter provide only support services. In a Ford Motor Company automobile plant, the welding, painting, and assembling departments are production departments, and the maintenance, cafeteria, and personnel departments are service departments.

Helpful hint (1) Is the jewelry department of Marshall Field's department store a profit center or a cost center? (2) Is the props department of a movie studio a profit center or a cost center? Answers: (1) profit center (2) cost center.

A profit center incurs costs (and expenses) but also generates revenues. Managers of profit centers are judged on the profitability of their centers. Examples of profit centers include the individual departments of a retail store, such as clothing, furniture, and automotive products, and branch offices of banks.

Like a profit center, an investment center incurs costs (and expenses) and generates revenues. In addition, an investment center has control over the investment funds available for use. Managers of investment centers are evaluated on the profitability of the center and on the rate of return earned on the funds invested. Investment centers are often associated with subsidiary companies. For example, PepsiCo owns Frito-Lay (potato chips) and Pizza Hut and Kentucky Fried Chicken (restaurants), whereas General Mills owns Parker Brothers (games) and Izod Lacoste (fashions). In each of these instances, the manager of the investment center (segment) is able to control or significantly influence investment decisions pertaining to such matters as plant expansion and entry into new market areas.

The evaluation of a manager's performance in each type of responsibility center is explained in the remainder of this chapter.

Before You Go On . . .

1. What conditions are essential for responsibility accounting?

2. What is involved in a responsibility reporting system?

3. Name the three types of responsibility centers and distinguish among them.

Responsibility Performance Reports for Cost Centers

Study Objective 5

Indicate the features of responsibility reports for cost centers.

The evaluation of a manager's performance for cost centers is based on the manager's ability to meet budgeted goals for controllable costs. **Performance reports for cost centers compare actual controllable costs with flexible budget data.**

A responsibility performance report is illustrated below. The report is adapted from the budget report for the Fox Manufacturing Company in Illustration 26-15 on page 1050. It assumes that the Finishing Department manager is able to control all manufacturing overhead costs except depreciation, property taxes, and his own monthly supervisory salary of $6,000. The remaining $4,000 of supervision costs are assumed to apply to other supervisory personnel within the Finishing Department whose salaries are controllable by the manager.

ILLUSTRATION 26-18

Responsibility report for a cost center

FOX MANUFACTURING COMPANY
Finishing Department
Manufacturing Overhead Cost Responsibility Report
For the Month Ended January 31, 1993

Controllable Cost	Budget	Actual	Difference Favorable F Unfavorable U
Indirect materials	$13,500	$14,000	$ 500 U
Indirect labor	18,000	17,000	1,000 F
Utilities	4,500	4,600	100 U
Supervision	4,000	4,000	–0–
	$40,000	$39,600	$ 400 F

Only controllable costs are included in the report, and no distinction is made between variable and fixed costs. As in budget reports, the responsibility report continues the concept of management by exception. In this case, top management may request an explanation of the $1,000 favorable difference in indirect labor and/or the $500 unfavorable difference in indirect materials.

Responsibility Accounting for Profit Centers

To properly evaluate the performance of a manager of a profit center, detailed information is needed about both controllable revenues and controllable costs. The operating revenues earned by a profit center such as sales are controllable by the manager. All variable costs (and expenses) incurred by the center are also controllable by the manager because they vary with sales. However, to determine the controllability of fixed costs, it is necessary to distinguish between direct and indirect fixed costs.

Direct and Indirect Fixed Costs

A profit center may have both direct and indirect fixed costs. Direct fixed costs are costs that relate specifically to one center and are incurred for the sole benefit of that center. Since these fixed costs can be traced directly to a center, they are also called **traceable costs**.

In contrast, indirect fixed costs pertain to a company's overall operating activities and they are incurred for the benefit of more than one profit center. Indirect fixed costs are allocated to profit centers on some type of equitable basis. For example, property taxes on a building occupied by more than one center may be allocated on the basis of square feet of floor space used by each center. Alternatively, the costs of a company's personnel department may be allocated to profit centers on the basis of the number of employees in each center. Because these fixed costs apply to more than one center, they are also called **common**

Accounting in Action ▪ *Business Insight*

Many companies have profit centers. However, Bell Atlantic Corp. goes one step further by charging other departments within the company for its services. The program works like this: Systems, medical services, business research, training and development, and six other departments now charge the rest of the company for their time and services. With what they earn, these so-called client-service groups must pay for all their expenses—rent, office equipment, electricity, office cleaning, and most important, salaries and benefits. Profit, if there is any, goes back to the company. And if a department fails—which hasn't happened yet—it could be given a new manager, suffer layoffs, or even be eliminated in favor of using outsiders. As one individual noted, "If you have a free lunch counter, people are going to keep lining up. Now, requesting departments have to think over carefully what projects are important to them."

Source: "At Bell Atlantic Competing Is Learned from Inside," *The Wall Street Journal*, July 12, 1989.

costs. Examples of the two types of fixed costs are:

ILLUSTRATION 26-19

Types of direct and indirect fixed costs

Direct (Traceable) Fixed Costs	Indirect (Common) Fixed Costs
Profit center manager's salary.	Company president's salary.
Other supervisory salaries.	Corporate headquarters costs.
Depreciation on center's equipment.	Depreciation on building occupied by more than one profit center.
Timekeeping for center's employees.	Company payroll department costs.

It might be presumed that (1) direct fixed costs are controllable by the profit center manager and (2) indirect fixed costs are not controllable by this manager. This is true for all indirect costs but not for all direct fixed costs. In the above list of direct fixed costs, the manager's salary and depreciation are the responsibility of higher management that authorized these costs. The other direct fixed costs are controllable by the profit center manager. Thus, under responsibility accounting the following classifications of fixed costs are recognized:

ILLUSTRATION 26-20

Fixed cost classifications

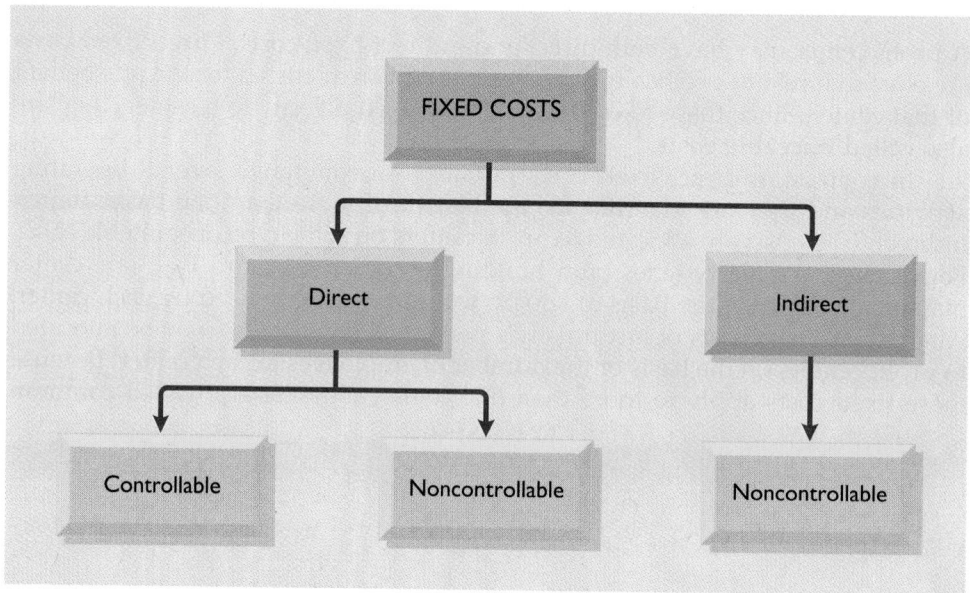

Responsibility Performance Report

Study Objective 6

Identify the content of responsibility reports for profit centers.

The responsibility performance report for a profit center shows budgeted and actual controllable revenues and costs. The report is prepared using the contribution margin income statement explained in Chapter 24. In the report:

1. Controllable fixed costs are deducted from contribution margin.
2. The excess of contribution margin over controllable fixed costs is identified as controllable margin.
3. Noncontrollable fixed costs are not reported.

The performance report for the manager of the Marine Division, a profit center of Mantle Manufacturing Company, is shown in Illustration 26-21. For the year, the Marine Division also had $60,000 of noncontrollable direct fixed costs, and Mantle Manufacturing had $150,000 of indirect fixed costs.

Controllable margin is considered to be the best measure of the manager's performance **in controlling revenues and costs**. This report shows that the manager's performance was below budgeted expectations by approximately 10%

ILLUSTRATION 26-21

Responsibility report for profit center

MANTLE MANUFACTURING COMPANY Marine Division Management Performance Report For the Year Ended December 31, 1993			
	Budget	Actual	Difference Favorable F Unfavorable U
Sales	$1,200,000	$1,150,000	$50,000 U
Variable costs			
Cost of goods sold	500,000	490,000	10,000 F
Selling and administrative	160,000	156,000	4,000 F
Total	660,000	646,000	14,000 F
Contribution margin	540,000	504,000	36,000 U
Controllable fixed costs			
Cost of goods sold	100,000	100,000	–0–
Selling and administrative	80,000	80,000	–0–
Total	180,000	180,000	–0–
Controllable margin	$ 360,000	$ 324,000	$36,000 U

($36,000 ÷ $360,000). Top management would likely investigate the causes of this unfavorable result. Note that the report does not show either the Marine Division's noncontrollable direct fixed costs or its share of the company's indirect fixed costs. These costs would be included in a report on the profitability of the profit center.

Responsibility reports for profit centers may also be prepared monthly. In addition, they may include cumulative year-to-date results.

Responsibility Accounting for Investment Centers

As explained earlier, an important characteristic of an investment center is that the manager can control or significantly influence the investment funds available for use. Thus, the primary basis for evaluating the performance of a manager of an investment center is the return on investment (ROI). The return on investment is considered to be superior to any other performance measurement because it shows the effectiveness of the manager in utilizing the assets at the manager's disposal.

Study Objective 7

Explain the basis and formulas used in evaluating performance in investment centers.

Return on Investment (ROI)

The basic formula for computing ROI for an investment center, together with assumed illustrative data, is shown in Illustration 26-22. Both factors in the formula are controllable by the investment center manager. Operating assets consist

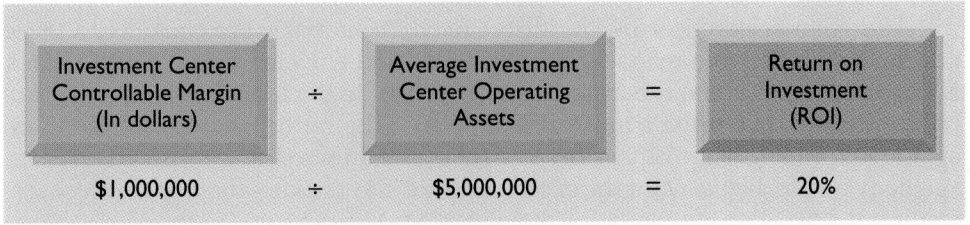

Investment Center Controllable Margin (In dollars)	÷	Average Investment Center Operating Assets	=	Return on Investment (ROI)
$1,000,000	÷	$5,000,000	=	20%

ILLUSTRATION 26-22

Basic ROI formula

of current assets and plant assets used in operations by the center and controlled by the manager. Nonoperating assets such as idle plant assets and land held for future use are excluded. Average operating assets are usually based on the cost or book value of the assets at the beginning and end of the year.

Responsibility Performance Report

The scope of the investment center manager's responsibility significantly affects the content of the performance report. Since an investment center is an independent entity for operating purposes, **direct fixed costs are most generally controllable by the investment center manager**. For example, the manager is responsible for depreciation on investment center assets. Accordingly, more fixed costs are identified as controllable in the performance report for an investment center manager. In addition, the report shows budgeted and actual ROI below controllable margin.

To illustrate the responsibility report, we will now assume that the Marine Division of Mantle Manufacturing Company is an investment center with budgeted and actual average operating assets of $2,000,000. In addition, we will assume that the manager can control the $60,000 of direct fixed costs that were not controllable when the division was a profit center. The performance report is shown in Illustration 26-23.

ILLUSTRATION 26-23

Responsibility report for investment center

MANTLE MANUFACTURING COMPANY
Marine Division
Management Performance Report
For the Year Ended December 31, 1993

	Budget	Actual	Difference Favorable F Unfavorable U
Sales	$1,200,000	$1,150,000	$50,000 U
Variable costs			
Cost of goods sold	500,000	490,000	10,000 F
Selling and administrative	160,000	156,000	4,000 F
Total	660,000	646,000	14,000 F
Contribution margin	540,000	504,000	36,000 U
Controllable fixed costs			
Cost of goods sold	100,000	100,000	–0–
Selling and administrative	80,000	80,000	–0–
Other fixed costs	60,000	60,000	–0–
Total	240,000	240,000	–0–
Controllable margin	$ 300,000	$ 264,000	$36,000 U
Return on investment	15% (a)	13.2% (b)	1.8% U

(a) $\dfrac{\$300,000}{\$2,000,000}$ (b) $\dfrac{\$264,000}{\$2,000,000}$

The other fixed costs are the direct fixed costs that were considered to be noncontrollable by the manager when the Marine Division was a profit center. Note, however, that the report still does not include the Marine Division's share of Mantle Manufacturing's indirect fixed costs. The report shows that the manager's performance was 12% below budget expectations (1.8% ÷ 15%). Top management would likely want an explanation of the reasons for this unfavorable result.

ROI—Expanded Formula

The basic formula for computing ROI for an investment center can be expanded into two separate but interrelated financial relationships: (1) the controllable margin percentage earned on sales and (2) the number of times operating assets are turned over during the period.

These relationships are computed as follows:

$$\text{Controllable margin percentage} = \frac{\text{Controllable Margin (in dollars)}}{\text{Sales}}$$

$$\text{Asset turnover} = \frac{\text{Sales}}{\text{Average Operating Assets}}$$

Thus, the expanded formula for ROI is:

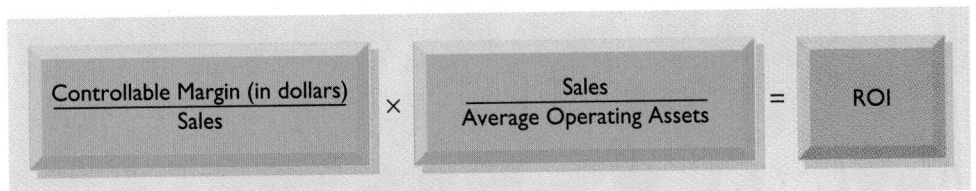

ILLUSTRATION 26-24

Expanded ROI formula

The expanded formula is based on two underlying considerations. First, the controllable margin percentage indicates the amount of such margin produced by each dollar of sales. For example, if the controllable margin percentage is 5%, five cents in margin will result from each $1 of sales. Second, asset turnover indicates the frequency that operating assets produce sales. The more frequently sales are produced, the greater the turnover. With a 5% controllable margin, ROI will be 15% if asset turnover is 3 times and 20% if asset turnover is 4 times.

Improving ROI

The manager of an investment center can improve ROI by (1) increasing sales, (2) reducing variable and/or controllable fixed costs, or (3) reducing average operating assets. To illustrate, we will use the Aero Division of Mantle Manufacturing which had a 12% ROI based on the following data: Sales $2,000,000, variable costs $1,100,000, controllable fixed costs $300,000, and average operating assets of $5,000,000. Contribution margin is $900,000 ($2,000,000 − $1,100,000), and controllable margin is $600,000 ($900,000 − $300,000).

1. **Sales are increased 10% ($200,000).** Assuming no change in the contribution margin percentage which was 45% ($900,000 ÷ $2,000,000), a $200,000 increase in sales will increase contribution margin by $90,000. It will also increase controllable margin by the same amount since controllable fixed costs will not change. Thus, controllable margin becomes $690,000 ($600,000 + $90,000). The new ROI is 13.8% computed as follows:

ILLUSTRATION 26-25

ROI computation—sales increase

$$\frac{\$690,000}{\$2,200,000} \times \frac{\$2,200,000}{\$5,000,000} = 13.8\%$$

An increase in sales benefits both the investment center and the company if it results from new business. It would not benefit the company if the increase was achieved at the expense of other investment centers.

2. **Costs are decreased 10% ($140,000).** A $140,000 reduction in variable and/or controllable fixed costs results in a corresponding increase in controllable margin. Thus, this margin is $740,000 ($600,000 + $140,000) and ROI becomes 14.8% as shown by the following:

ILLUSTRATION 26-26

ROI computation—decrease in costs

$$\frac{\$740,000}{\$2,000,000} \times \frac{\$2,000,000}{\$5,000,000} = 14.8\%$$

This course of action is clearly beneficial when "fat," waste, and inefficiencies are eliminated. However, a reduction in necessary maintenance or other vital costs for the sake of an immediate increase in ROI is not likely to be acceptable to top management.

3. **Average operating assets are decreased 10% ($500,000).** This change causes average operating assets to be $4,500,000 ($5,000,000 − $500,000). Thus, ROI becomes 13.3% as shown below:

ILLUSTRATION 26-27

ROI computation—decrease in operating assets

$$\frac{\$600,000}{\$2,000,000} \times \frac{\$2,000,000}{\$4,500,000} = 13.3\%$$

Like decreases in costs, reductions in operating assets may or may not be prudent. It is beneficial to eliminate overinvestment in inventories and to dispose of excessive plant assets. However, it is unwise to reduce inventory below current needs or to dispose of essential plant assets.

Judgmental Factors in ROI

The return on investment approach includes two judgmental factors.

1. **Valuation of operating assets.** Operating assets may be valued at acquisition cost, book value, appraised value, or market value. The first two bases are readily available from the accounting records.

2. **Margin (income) measure.** This measure may be controllable margin, income from operations, or net income.

Each of the alternative values for operating assets can provide a reliable basis for evaluating a manager's performance as long as it is consistently applied between reporting periods. However, the use of income measures other than controllable margin will not result in a valid basis for evaluating the performance of an investment center manager because they will include some noncontrollable revenues and costs.

Principles of Performance Evaluation

Performance evaluation is at the center of responsibility accounting. **Performance evaluation** is a management function that compares actual results with budget goals. It is based on internal reports prepared by the management accountant. The evaluation of performance involves much more than identifying differences (exceptions) between actual and planned results. Performance evaluation includes both behavioral and reporting principles.

Behavioral Principles

The human factor is critical in the evaluation of performance. Behavioral principles should include the following:

1. **Managers of responsibility centers should have direct input into the process of establishing budget goals of their area of responsibility.** Without such input, managers may view the goals as unrealistic or arbitrarily set by top management. Such views adversely affect the managers' motivation to meet the targeted objectives.

2. **The evaluation of performance should be based entirely on matters that are controllable by the manager being evaluated.** Criticism of a manager on matters outside his or her control reduces the effectiveness of the evaluation process. Moreover, it leads to negative reactions by a manager and to doubts about the fairness of the company's evaluation policies.

3. **Top management should support the evaluation process.** As explained earlier, the evaluation process begins at the lowest level of responsibility and extends upward to the highest level of management. Managers quickly lose faith in the process when top management ignores, overrules, or bypasses established procedures for evaluating a manager's performance.

4. **There must be provision for managers to respond to their evaluations.** An effective evaluation system is not a one-way street. Managers should have the opportunity to defend their performance. Evaluation without feedback is both impersonal and ineffective.

5. **The evaluation should identify both good and poor performance.** Praise for good performance is a powerful motivating factor for a manager. This is especially true when a manager's compensation includes rewards for meeting budget goals.

Reporting Principles

Performance evaluation under responsibility accounting also involves reporting principles. These principles pertain primarily to the internal reports that provide the basis for evaluating performance. Performance reports should

1. Contain only data that are controllable by the manager of the responsibility center.
2. Provide accurate and reliable budget data to measure performance.
3. Highlight significant differences between actual results and budget goals.
4. Be tailormade for the intended evaluation.
5. Be prepared at reasonable intervals.

Before You Go On . . .

1. What is the primary objective of a performance report for a cost center?

2. How does contribution margin differ from controllable margin in a performance report for a profit center?

3. What are the basic and the expanded formulas for computing return on investment (ROI)?

4. Identify the three actions a manager may take to improve ROI.

Summary of Study Objectives

1. Describe the concept of budgetary control. Budgetary control consists of (a) preparing periodic budget reports that compare actual results with planned objectives, (b) analyzing the differences to determine their causes, (c) taking appropriate corrective action, and (d) modifying future plans, if necessary.

2. Evaluate the usefulness of static budget reports. Static budget reports are useful in evaluating the progress toward meeting planned sales and profit goals. They are also appropriate in assessing a manager's effectiveness in controlling fixed costs and expenses when (a) actual activity closely approximates the master budget activity level and/or (b) the behavior of the costs in response to changes in activity is fixed.

3. Explain the development of flexible budgets and the usefulness of flexible budget reports. To develop the flexible budget it is necessary to
(a) Identify the activity index and the relevant range of activity.
(b) Identify the variable costs and determine the budgeted variable cost per unit of activity for each cost.
(c) Identify the fixed costs and determine the budgeted amount for each cost.
(d) Prepare the budget for selected increments of activity within the relevant range.

Flexible budget reports permit an evaluation of a manager's performance in controlling production and costs.

4. Describe the concept of responsibility accounting. Responsibility accounting involves the accumulation and reporting of revenues and costs on the basis of the individual manager who has the authority to make the day-to-day decisions about the items. Under responsibility accounting, the evaluation of a manager's performance is based on the matters directly under the manager's control. In responsibility accounting, it is necessary to distinguish between controllable and noncontrollable fixed costs and to identify three types of responsibility centers: cost, profit, and investment.

5. Indicate the features of responsibility reports for cost centers. Responsibility reports for cost centers compare actual costs with flexible budget data. The reports show only controllable costs and no distinction is made between variable and fixed costs.

6. Identify the content of responsibility reports for profit centers. Responsibility reports show contribution margin, controllable fixed costs, and controllable margin for each profit center.

7. Explain the basis and formula used in evaluating performance in investment centers. The primary basis for evaluating performance in investment centers is return on investment (ROI). The basic formula for computing ROI for investment centers is: Controllable Margin (in dollars) ÷ Average Operating Assets. The expanded ROI formula is based on two financial relationships: (1) Controllable Margin Percentage and (2) Asset Turnover, and is expressed as follows:

$$\frac{\text{Controllable Margin}}{\text{Sales}} \times \frac{\text{Sales}}{\text{Average Operating Assets}} = \text{ROI}$$

GLOSSARY

Budgetary control · The use of budgets to control operations. (p. 1042).

Controllable costs · Costs that a manager has the authority to incur within a given period of time. (p. 1053).

Controllable margin · Contribution margin less controllable fixed costs. (p. 1058).

Cost center · A responsibility center that incurs costs but does not directly generate revenues. (p. 1055).

Decentralization · Control of operations is delegated by top management to many managers throughout the organization. (p. 1052).

Direct fixed costs · Costs that relate specifically to a responsibility center and are incurred for the sole benefit of the center. (p. 1057).

Flexible budget · A projection of budget data for various levels of activity. (p. 1045).

Indirect fixed costs · Costs that are incurred for the benefit of more than one profit center. (p. 1057).

Investment center · A responsibility center that incurs costs, generates revenues, and has control over the investment funds available for use. (p. 1056).

Management by exception · The review of budget reports by top management directed entirely or primarily to differences between actual results and planned objectives. (p. 1051).

Noncontrollable costs · Costs incurred indirectly and allocated to a responsibility center that are not controllable at that level. (p. 1053).

Profit center · A responsibility center that incurs costs and also generates revenues. (p. 1056).

Responsibility accounting · A part of management accounting that involves accumulating and reporting revenues and costs on the basis of the individual manager who has the authority to make the day-to-day decisions about the items. (p. 1051).

Responsibility reporting system · The preparation of reports for each level of responsibility shown in the company's organization chart. (p. 1053).

Return on investment (ROI) · A measure of the profitability of an investment center computed by dividing controllable margin (in dollars) by average operating assets. (p. 1059).

Segment · Another name for a responsibility center. (p. 1052).

Static budget · A projection of budget data at one level of activity. (p. 1045).

DEMONSTRATION PROBLEM

The Glenda Company uses a flexible budget for manufacturing overhead based on direct labor hours. For 1993 the master overhead budget for the Packaging Department at normal capacity of 300,000 direct labor hours was as follows:

Variable Costs		Fixed Costs	
Indirect labor	$360,000	Supervision	$ 60,000
Supplies and lubricants	150,000	Depreciation	24,000
Maintenance	210,000	Property taxes	18,000
Utilities	120,000	Insurance	12,000
	$840,000		$114,000

During July, 24,000 direct labor hours were worked when 25,000 hours were expected to be worked. The company incurred the following variable costs in July: Indirect labor $30,200, supplies and lubricants $11,600, maintenance $17,500, and utilities $9,200. Actual fixed overhead costs were the same as monthly budgeted fixed costs.

Instructions
Prepare a flexible budget report for the Packaging Department for July.

Solution to Demonstration Problem

GLENDA COMPANY
Manufacturing Overhead Budget Report (Flexible)
Packaging Department
For the Month Ended July 31, 1993

Direct labor hours (DLH) Expected 25,000 Actual 24,000	Budget 24,000 DLH	Actual Costs 24,000 DLH	Difference Favorable F Unfavorable U
Variable costs			
Indirect labor	$28,800	$30,200	$1,400 U
Supplies and lubricants	12,000	11,600	400 F
Maintenance	16,800	17,500	700 U
Utilities	9,600	9,200	400 F
Total variable	67,200	68,500	1,300 U

Helpful hints
1. Use budget data for actual direct labor hours worked.
2. Classify each cost as variable or fixed.
3. Determine the difference between budgeted and actual costs.
4. Identify the difference as favorable or unfavorable.
5. Determine the difference in total variable costs, total fixed costs, and total costs.

Direct labor hours (DLH) Expected 25,000 Actual 24,000	Budget 24,000 DLH	Actual Costs 24,000 DLH	Difference Favorable F Unfavorable U
Fixed costs			
Supervision	5,000	5,000	–0–
Depreciation	2,000	2,000	–0–
Property taxes	1,500	1,500	–0–
Insurance	1,000	1,000	–0–
Total fixed	9,500	9,500	–0–
Total costs	$76,700	$78,000	$1,300 U

SELF-STUDY QUESTIONS

Answers are at the end of the chapter.

(S.O. 1) 1. Budgetary control involves all but one of the following:
a. modifying future plans.
b. analyzing differences.
c. determining differences between actual and planned results.
d. using static budgets.

(S.O. 2) 2. A static budget is useful in controlling costs when cost behavior is:
a. fixed.
b. mixed.
c. variable.
d. linear.

(S.O. 3) 3. At zero direct labor hours in a flexible budget graph, the total budgeted cost line intersects the vertical axis at $30,000. At 10,000 direct labor hours, the line drawn from the total budgeted cost line intersects the vertical axis at $90,000. Fixed and variable costs may be expressed as:
a. $30,000 fixed plus $9 per direct labor hour variable.
b. $30,000 fixed plus $6 per direct labor hour variable.
c. $60,000 fixed plus $3 per direct labor hour variable.
d. $60,000 fixed plus $6 per direct labor hour variable.

(S.O. 3) 4. At 9,000 direct labor hours the flexible budget for indirect materials is $27,000. If $28,000 of indirect materials costs are incurred at 9,200 direct labor hours, the flexible budget report should show the following difference for indirect materials:
a. $1,000 unfavorable.
b. $400 unfavorable.
c. $400 favorable.
d. $1,000 favorable.

(S.O. 4) 5. Under responsibility accounting, the evaluation of a manager's performance is based on matters that the manager:
a. has shared responsibility with another manager.
b. directly controls.
c. directly and indirectly controls.
d. indirectly controls.

6. Responsibility centers include: (S.O. 4)
a. cost centers.
b. profit centers.
c. investment centers
d. all of the above.

7. Performance reports for cost centers: (S.O. 5)
a. distinguish between fixed and variable costs.
b. use static budget data.
c. include only controllable costs.
d. include both controllable and noncontrollable costs.

8. In a responsibility report for a profit center, controllable fixed costs are deducted from contribution margin to show: (S.O. 6)
a. controllable margin.
b. profit center margin.
c. net income.
d. income from operations.

9. In the expanded formula for return on investment (ROI), the numerators for controllable margin and asset turnover are, respectively: (S.O. 7)
a. controllable margin percentage and sales.
b. controllable margin dollars and sales.
c. controllable margin dollars and average operating assets.
d. controllable margin percentage and average operating assets.

10. A manager of an investment center can improve ROI by: (S.O. 7)
a. increasing average operating assets.
b. reducing sales.
c. reducing variable and/or controllable fixed costs.
d. increasing variable costs.

QUESTIONS

1. Leslie Lane is critiquing budgetary control. What essential steps should she include in her critique?

2. Budgetary control is facilitated when a company has a formalized reporting system. List the features of such a system.

3. How may a budget report for the second quarter differ from a budget report for the first quarter?

4. Dan Draker questions the usefulness of a master sales budget in evaluating sales performance. Is there justification for Dan's concern? Explain.

5. Under what circumstances may a static budget be an appropriate basis for evaluating a manager's effectiveness in controlling costs?

6. "A flexible budget is really a series of static budgets." Is this true? Why?

7. The static manufacturing overhead budget based on 40,000 direct labor hours shows budgeted indirect labor costs of $56,000. During March, the department incurs $67,000 of indirect labor while working 50,000 direct labor hours. Is this a favorable or unfavorable performance? Why?

8. A static overhead budget based on 40,000 direct labor hours shows Factory Insurance $6,400 as a fixed cost. At the 50,000 direct labor hours worked in March, factory insurance costs were $6,800. Is this a favorable or unfavorable performance? Why?

9. Paul Kinsells is confused about how a flexible budget is prepared. Identify the steps for Paul.

10. The Barr Company has prepared a graph of flexible budget data. At zero direct labor hours, the total budgeted cost line intersects the vertical axis at $25,000. At 12,000 direct labor hours, the line drawn from the total budgeted cost line intersects the vertical axis at $85,000. How may the fixed and variable costs be expressed?

11. The flexible budget formula is fixed costs $40,000 plus variable costs of $3 per direct labor hour. What is the total budgeted cost at (a) 9,200 hours and (b) 12,345 hours?

12. What is management by exception? What criteria may be used in identifying exceptions?

13. What is responsibility accounting? Explain the purpose of responsibility accounting.

14. Alice Walcot is studying for an accounting examination. Describe for Alice what conditions are necessary for responsibility accounting to be used effectively.

15. Distinguish between controllable and noncontrollable costs.

16. How do responsibility reports differ from budget reports?

17. What is the relationship, if any, between a responsibility reporting system and a company's organization chart?

18. Distinguish among the three types of responsibility centers.

19. (a) What costs are included in a performance report for a cost center? (b) In the report, are variable and fixed costs identified?

20. How do direct fixed costs differ from indirect fixed costs? Are both types of fixed costs controllable?

21. Tracy Kolar is confused about controllable margin reported in an income statement for a profit center. How is this margin computed and what is its primary purpose?

22. What is the primary basis for evaluating the performance of the manager of an investment center? Indicate the basic formula for the basis.

23. State the expanded formula for return on investment (ROI). Indicate three ways that ROI can be improved.

24. Indicate two behavioral principles that pertain to (a) the manager being evaluated and (b) top management.

BRIEF EXERCISES

Prepare static budget report.
(S.O. 2)

BE26–1   For the quarter ended March 31, 1993, the Elba Company accumulates the following sales data for product, Garden-Tools: $320,000 budget; $305,000 actual. Prepare a static budget report for the quarter.

Prepare static budget report for two quarters.
(S.O. 2)

BE26–2   Data for the Elba Company are given in BE26–1. In the second quarter, budgeted sales were $380,000 and actual sales were $390,000. Prepare a static budget report for the second quarter and for the year to date.

Show usefulness of flexible budgets in evaluating performance.
(S.O. 3)

BE26–3   In the Debby Company, direct labor is $20 per hour, and the company expects to operate at 10,000 direct labor hours each month. In January, direct labor totaling $210,000 is incurred in working 10,700 hours. Prepare a static budget report and a flexible budget report. Evaluate the usefulness of each report.

Prepare a flexible budget for variable costs.
(S.O. 3)

BE26–4   The O'Shea Company expects to produce 1,200,000 units of Product XX in 1993. Monthly production is expected to range from 80,000 to 120,000 units. Budgeted variable manufacturing costs per unit are: direct materials $4, direct labor $6, and overhead $3. Prepare a flexible manufacturing budget for the relevant range value using 20,000 unit increments.

Prepare flexible budget report.
(S.O. 3)

BE26–5   Data for the O'Shea Company are given in BE26–4. In March, 1993, the company incurs the following costs in producing 100,000 units: direct materials $410,000, direct labor $590,000, and variable overhead $305,000. Prepare a flexible budget report for March. Were costs controlled?

Prepare a responsibility report for a cost center.
(S.O. 5)

BE26–6   In the Assembly Department of the Shane Company, budgeted and actual manufacturing overhead costs for the month of April, 1993 were as follows:

	Budget	Actual
Indirect materials	$15,000	$14,000
Indirect labor	20,000	20,800
Utilities	10,000	10,500
Supervision	5,000	5,000

All costs are controllable by the department manager. Prepare a responsibility report for April for the cost center.

Prepare a responsibility report for a profit center.
(S.O. 6)

BE26–7   Maris Manufacturing Company accumulates the following summary data for the year ending December 31, 1993 for its Aqua Division which it operates as a profit center: Sales—$2,000,000 budget, $2,100,000 actual; variable costs—$1,000,000 budget, $1,050,000 actual; and controllable fixed costs—$300,000 budget, $320,000 actual. Prepare a responsibility report for the Aqua Division.

Prepare a responsibility report for an investment center.
(S.O. 7)

BE26–8   For the year ending December 31, 1993, the Gretchen Company accumulates the following data for the Plastics Division which it operates as an investment center: contribution margin—$700,000 budget, $715,000 actual; controllable fixed costs—$300,000 budget, $295,000 actual. Average operating assets for the year were $2,000,000. Prepare a responsibility report for the Plastics Division beginning with contribution margin.

Compute return on investment using expanded formula.
(S.O. 7)

BE26–9   For its three investment centers, the Hatch Company accumulates the following data:

	I	II	III
Sales	$2,000,000	$3,000,000	$ 4,000,000
Controllable margin	1,200,000	2,000,000	3,000,000
Average operating assets	6,000,000	8,000,000	10,000,000

Compute the return on investment (ROI) for each center.

Compute return on investment under changed conditions.
(S.O. 7)

BE26–10   Data for the investment centers for the Hatch Company are given in BE26–9. The centers expect the following changes in the next year: (I) increase sales 10%; (II) decrease costs $200,000; (III) decrease operating assets $500,000. Compute the expected return on investment (ROI) for each center. Assume center I has a contribution margin percentage of 70%.

EXERCISES

E26–1 The Piana Company uses a flexible budget for manufacturing overhead based on direct labor hours. Variable manufacturing overhead costs per direct labor hour are as follows:

Indirect labor	$1.00
Indirect materials	.50
Utilities	.25

Prepare flexible manufacturing overhead budget. (S.O. 3)

Fixed overhead costs per month are: Supervision $3,000, Depreciation $1,500, and Property Taxes $700.

The company believes it will normally operate in a range of 7,000–10,000 direct labor hours per month.

Instructions
Prepare a monthly flexible manufacturing overhead budget for 1993 for the expected range of activity, using increments of 1,000 direct labor hours.

E26–2 Using the information in Exercise 26–1, assume that in July, 1993, the Piana Company incurs the following manufacturing overhead costs:

Prepare flexible budget reports for manufacturing overhead costs and comment on findings. (S.O. 3)

Variable		Fixed	
Indirect labor	$8,700	Supervision	$3,000
Indirect materials	4,300	Depreciation	1,500
Utilities	2,100	Property Taxes	700

Instructions
(a) Prepare a flexible budget performance report, assuming that the company worked 9,000 direct labor hours during the month. The company expected to work 9,000 direct labor hours.

(b) Prepare a flexible budget performance report, assuming that the company worked 8,500 direct labor hours during the month. The company expected to work 8,500 direct labor hours.

(c) Comment on your findings.

E26–3 The Lloyd Company uses flexible budgets to control its selling expenses. Monthly sales are expected to range from $170,000 to $200,000. Variable costs and their percentage relationship to sales are: Sales Commissions (6%), Advertising (5%), Traveling (3%), and Delivery (2%). Fixed selling expenses will consist of Sales Salaries $30,000, Depreciation on Delivery Equipment $5,000, and Insurance on Delivery Equipment $1,000.

Prepare flexible selling expense budget. (S.O. 3)

Instructions
Prepare a monthly flexible budget for each $10,000 increment of sales within the relevant range for the year ending December 31, 1993.

E26–4 The actual selling expenses incurred in March, 1993 by the Lloyd Company are as follows:

Prepare flexible budget reports for selling expenses. (S.O. 3)

Variable Expenses		Fixed Expenses	
Sales Commissions	$10,700	Sales Salaries	$30,000
Advertising	8,200	Depreciation	5,000
Travel	5,100	Insurance	1,000
Delivery	3,500		

Instructions
(a) Prepare a flexible budget performance report for March using the budget data in Exercise 26–3, assuming that March sales were $170,000. Expected and actual sales are the same.

(b) Prepare a flexible budget performance report, assuming that March sales were $180,000. Expected sales and actual sales are the same.

(c) Comment on the importance of using flexible budgets in evaluating the performance of the sales manager.

E26–5 The Higgins Company's manufacturing overhead budget for the first quarter of 1993 contained the following data:

Prepare flexible budget and responsibility report for manufacturing overhead.
(S.O. 3, 5)

Variable Costs		Fixed Costs	
Indirect materials	$12,000	Supervisory salaries	$30,000
Indirect labor	10,000	Depreciation	7,000
Utilities	8,000	Property taxes and insurance	8,000
Maintenance	6,000	Maintenance	5,000

Actual variable costs were: indirect materials $14,200, indirect labor $9,600, utilities $8,700, and maintenance $4,000. Actual fixed costs equaled budgeted costs except for property taxes and insurance, which were $8,100.

All costs are considered controllable by the production department manager except for depreciation, property taxes, and insurance.

Instructions

(a) Prepare a flexible overhead budget report for the first quarter.

(b) Prepare a responsibility performance report for the first quarter.

Prepare flexible budget report and answer question.
(S.O. 2, 3)

E26–6   As sales manager, Greg Penter was given the following static budget report for selling expenses in the Clothing Department of the Roark Company for the month of October.

ROARK COMPANY
Clothing Department
Budget Report
For the Month Ended October 31, 1993

			Difference
			Favorable F
	Budget	Actual	Unfavorable U
Sales in units	8,000	10,000	2,000 F
Variable costs:			
Sales commissions	$ 2,000	$ 2,250	$ 250 U
Advertising expense	800	850	50 U
Travel expense	4,000	4,900	900 U
Free samples given out	1,000	1,300	300 U
Total variable	7,800	9,300	1,500 U
Fixed costs:			
Rent	1,500	1,500	–0–
Sales salaries	1,200	1,200	–0–
Office salaries	800	800	–0–
Depreciation—autos (sales staff)	500	500	–0–
Total fixed	4,000	4,000	–0–
Total costs	$11,800	$13,300	$1,500 U

As a result of this budget report, Greg was called into the president's office and congratulated on his fine sales performance. He was reprimanded, however, for allowing his costs to get out of control. Greg knew something was wrong with the performance report that he had been given. However, he was not sure what to do, and comes to you for advice.

Instructions

(a) Prepare a budget report based on flexible budget data to help Greg.

(b) Should Greg have been reprimanded?

State total budgeted cost formulas and prepare flexible budget graph.
(S.O. 3)

E26–7   The Miranda Company has two production departments: Fabricating and Assembling. At a department managers' meeting, the controller uses flexible budget graphs to explain total budgeted costs. Separate graphs based on direct labor hours are used for each department. The graphs show the following:

1. At zero direct labor hours, the total budgeted cost line and the fixed cost line intersect the vertical axis at $40,000 in the Fabricating Department and $28,000 in the Assembling Department.

2. At normal capacity of 50,000 direct labor hours, the line drawn from the total budgeted

cost line intersects the vertical axis at $160,000 in the Fabricating Department, and $108,000 in the Assembling Department.

Instructions

(a) State the total budgeted cost formula for each department.

(b) Compute the total budgeted cost for each department, assuming actual direct labor hours worked were 53,000 and 47,000, in the Fabricating and Assembling Departments, respectively.

(c) Prepare the flexible budget graph for the Fabricating Department, assuming the maximum direct labor hours in the relevant range is 100,000. Use increments of 10,000 direct labor hours on the horizontal axis and increments of $50,000 on the vertical axis.

E26–8 The Montross Company's organization chart includes the president; the vice-president of production; three assembly plants—Dallas, Atlanta, and Tucson; and two departments within each plant—Machining and Finishing. Budget and actual manufacturing cost data for July, 1993 are as follows:

Prepare reports in a responsibility reporting system.
(S.O. 4)

> Finishing Department—Dallas: Direct materials $42,000 actual, $46,000 budget; direct labor $83,000 actual, $82,000 budget; manufacturing overhead $51,500 actual, $49,200 budget.
>
> Machining Department—Dallas: Total manufacturing costs $218,000 actual, $215,000 budget.
>
> Atlanta Plant: Total manufacturing costs $426,000 actual, $421,000 budget.
>
> Tucson Plant: Total manufacturing costs $494,000 actual, $499,000 budget.

The Dallas plant manager's office costs were $95,000 actual and $92,000 budget. The vice-president of production's office costs were $133,000 actual and $130,000 budget. Office costs are not allocated to departments and plants.

Instructions

Prepare the reports in a responsibility system for (a) the Finishing Department—Dallas, (b) the plant manager—Dallas, and (c) the vice-president of production. Use the format on page 1054.

E26–9 Sure Shoe Manufacturing Inc. has three divisions which are operated as profit centers. Operating data for the divisions listed alphabetically are as follows:

Compute missing amounts in responsibility reports for three profit centers and prepare a report.
(S.O. 6)

Operating Data	Women's Shoes	Men's Shoes	Children's Shoes
Contribution margin	$260,000	(3)	$160,000
Controllable fixed costs	100,000	(4)	(5)
Controllable margin	(1)	$ 90,000	98,000
Sales	600,000	450,000	(6)
Variable costs	(2)	300,000	240,000

Instructions

(a) Compute the missing amounts. Show computations.

(b) Prepare a management responsibility report for the Women's Shoe Division assuming (1) the data are for the month ended June 30, 1993 and (2) all data equal budget except variable costs which are $20,000 over budget.

E26–10 Data for the following subsidiaries of the L. A. Bonder Company which are operated as investment centers are as follows:

Compute missing amounts in expanded ROI formula.
(S.O. 7)

	Ace Co.	King Co.	Queen Co.
Sales	$1,200,000	(4)	(7)
Controllable margin	(1)	(5)	$ 85,500
Average operating assets	(2)	$700,000	750,000
Controllable margin percentage	10%	9%	(8)
Asset turnover	1.5	(6)	1.2
Return on investment (ROI)	(3)	12.6%	(9)

Instructions

Compute the missing amounts using the expanded ROI formula. (Round to one decimal.)

Compute ROI for current year and for possible future changes.
(S.O. 7)

E26–11   The Mastercraft Division of the Lorene Company reported the following data for the current year.

Sales	$3,000,000
Variable costs	1,800,000
Controllable fixed costs	600,000
Average operating assets	4,000,000

Top management is unhappy with the investment center's return on investment (ROI). It asks the manager of the Mastercraft Division to submit plans to improve ROI in the next year. The manager believes it is feasible to consider the following independent courses of action.

1. Increase sales by $300,000 with no change in the contribution margin percentage.
2. Reduce variable costs by $100,000.
3. Reduce average operating assets by 5%.

Instructions

(a) Compute the return on investment (ROI) for the current year.

(b) Using the expanded ROI formula, compute the ROI under each of the proposed courses of action. (Round to one decimal.)

PROBLEMS

Prepare flexible budget and budget report for manufacturing overhead.
(S.O. 3)

P26–1   The Muller Company estimates that 240,000 direct labor hours will be worked during 1993 in the Assembly Department. On this basis, the following budgeted manufacturing overhead data are computed:

Variable Overhead Costs		Fixed Overhead Costs	
Indirect labor	$ 72,000	Supervision	$ 60,000
Indirect materials	48,000	Depreciation	30,000
Repairs	24,000	Insurance	9,600
Utilities	12,000	Rent	7,200
Lubricants	9,600	Property taxes	6,000
	$165,600		$112,800

It is estimated that direct labor hours worked each month will range from 18,000 to 24,000 hours.

During January, 20,000 direct labor hours were worked and the following overhead costs were incurred.

Variable Overhead Costs		Fixed Overhead Costs	
Indirect labor	$ 6,200	Supervision	$5,000
Indirect materials	3,600	Depreciation	2,500
Repairs	1,600	Insurance	800
Utilities	900	Rent	700
Lubricants	830	Property taxes	500
	$13,130		$9,500

Instructions

(a) Prepare a monthly flexible manufacturing overhead budget for each increment of 2,000 direct labor hours over the relevant range for the year ending December 31, 1993.

(b) Prepare a manufacturing overhead budget report for January, assuming 20,500 direct labor hours were expected.

(c) Comment on management's efficiency in controlling manufacturing overhead costs in January.

P26–2 The Kenard Manufacturing Company produces one product, Kebo. Because of wide fluctuations in demand for Kebo, the Assembly Department experiences significant variations in monthly production levels.

Prepare flexible budget, budget report, and graph for manufacturing overhead.
(S.O. 3)

The master manufacturing overhead budget for the year, based on 300,000 direct labor hours, and the actual overhead costs incurred in July in which 27,500 labor hours were worked, and 27,500 hours were expected to be worked, are as follows:

Overhead Cost	Master Budget	Actual in July
Variable:		
Indirect labor	$ 360,000	$32,000
Indirect materials	210,000	17,000
Utilities	90,000	8,000
Maintenance	60,000	5,400
Fixed:		
Supervision	150,000	12,500
Depreciation	120,000	10,000
Insurance and taxes	60,000	5,000
Total	$1,050,000	$89,900

Instructions

(a) Prepare a flexible overhead budget for the year ending December 31, 1993, assuming monthly production levels range from 22,500 to 30,000 direct labor hours. Use increments of 2,500 direct labor hours.

(b) Prepare a budget performance report for July 1993 comparing actual results with budget data based on the flexible budget.

(c) Were costs effectively controlled? Explain.

(d) State the formula for computing the total monthly budgeted costs in Kenard Company.

(e) Prepare the flexible budget graph showing total budgeted costs at 25,000 and 27,500 direct labor hours. Use increments of 5,000 on the horizontal axis and increments of $10,000 on the vertical axis.

P26–3 The Boggs Company uses budgets in controlling costs. The May 1993 budget report for the company's Packaging Department is as follows:

State total budgeted cost formula and prepare flexible budget reports for two time periods.
(S.O. 2, 3)

BOGGS COMPANY
Budget Report
Packaging Department
For the Month Ended May 31, 1993

Manufacturing Costs	Budget	Actual	Difference Favorable F Unfavorable U
Variable costs:			
Direct materials	$ 30,000	$ 32,000	$2,000 U
Direct labor	40,000	43,000	3,000 U
Indirect materials	15,000	15,200	200 U
Indirect labor	12,500	13,000	500 U
Utilities	7,500	7,100	400 F
Maintenance	5,000	5,100	100 U
Total variable	110,000	115,400	5,400 U
Fixed costs:			
Rent	7,000	7,000	–0–
Supervision	8,000	8,000	–0–
Depreciation	5,000	5,000	–0–
Total fixed	20,000	20,000	–0–
Total costs	$130,000	$135,400	$5,400 U

The budget amounts in the report were on the master budget for the year, which assumed that 600,000 units would be produced. (Hint: The budget amounts above are one-twelfth of the master budget for the year.)

The company president was displeased with the department manager's performance. The department manager, who thought he had done a good job, could not understand the unfavorable results. In May, 55,000 units were produced.

Instructions

(a) State the total budgeted cost formula.

(b) Prepare a budget report for May using flexible budget data. Why does this report provide a better basis for evaluating performance than the report based on static budget data? Assume 57,000 units were expected to be produced in the Packaging Department?

(c) In June, 40,000 units were produced when 39,000 were expected. Prepare the budget report using flexible budget data, assuming (1) each variable cost was 20% less in June than its actual cost in May, and (2) fixed costs were the same in the month of June as in May.

Prepare responsibility report for a profit center.
(S.O. 6)

P26–4 Midwest Manufacturing Inc., operates the Home Appliance Division as a profit center. Operating data for this division for the year ended December 31, 1993 are as follows:

	Budget	Difference from Budget
Sales	$2,400,000	$100,000 U
Cost of goods sold		
Variable	1,200,000	80,000 U
Controllable fixed	200,000	10,000 F
Selling and administrative		
Variable	240,000	10,000 F
Controllable fixed	60,000	5,000 U
Noncontrollable fixed costs	50,000	2,000 U

In addition, Midwest Manufacturing incurs $150,000 of indirect fixed costs that were budgeted at $155,000. Twenty percent (20%) of these costs are allocated to the Home Appliance Division.

Instructions

(a) Prepare a responsibility performance report for the Home Appliance Division for the year.

(b) Comment on the manager's performance in controlling revenues and costs.

(c) Identify any costs excluded from the performance report and explain why they were excluded.

Prepare responsibility report for an investment center and compute ROI using expanded formula.
(S.O. 7)

P26–5 Mainliner Manufacturing Company manufactures a variety of garden and lawn equipment. The company operates through three divisions. Each division is an investment center. Operating data for the Lawnmower Division for the year ended December 31, 1993 and relevant budget data are as follows:

	Actual	Comparison with Budget
Sales	$2,800,000	$200,000 unfavorable
Variable cost of goods sold	1,400,000	150,000 unfavorable
Variable selling and administrative expenses	300,000	50,000 favorable
Controllable fixed cost of goods sold	270,000	On target
Controllable fixed selling and administrative expenses	80,000	On target

Average operating assets for the year for the Lawnmower Division were $5,000,000 which was also the budgeted amount.

Instructions

(a) Prepare a responsibility report (in thousands of dollars) for the Lawnmower Division.

(b) Evaluate the manager's performance. Which items will likely be investigated by top management?

(c) Compute the expected ROI in 1994 for the Lawnmower Division, using the expanded ROI formula, assuming the following changes.

1. Variable cost of goods sold is decreased by 10%.

2. Average operating assets are decreased by 10%.
3. Sales are increased by $500,000 and this increase is expected to increase contribution margin by $200,000.

P26–6 The Marti Mark Company uses a responsibility reporting system. It has divisions in Denver, Seattle, and San Diego. Each division has three production departments: Cutting, Shaping, and Finishing. The responsibility for each department rests with a manager who reports to the division production manager. Each division manager reports to the vice-president of production. There are also vice-presidents for marketing, finance, and personnel. All vice-presidents report to the president.

Prepare reports for cost centers under responsibility accounting and comment on performance of managers.
(S.O. 4)

In January 1993, controllable actual and budget manufacturing overhead cost data for the departments and divisions were as follows:

Manufacturing Overhead	Actual	Budget
Individual costs—Cutting Department—Seattle:		
Indirect labor	$ 73,000	$ 70,000
Indirect materials	46,700	46,000
Maintenance	21,500	18,000
Utilities	20,100	17,000
Supervision	20,000	20,000
	$ 181,300	$ 171,000
Total costs:		
Shaping Department—Seattle	$ 158,000	$ 148,000
Finishing Department—Seattle	210,000	208,000
Denver division	676,000	673,000
San Diego division	722,000	715,000
	$1,766,000	$1,744,000

Additional overhead costs were incurred as follows: Seattle division production manager—actual costs $52,500, budget $51,000; vice-president of production—actual costs $65,000, budget $64,000; president—actual costs $76,400, budget $74,200. These expenses are not allocated.

The vice-presidents who report to the president, other than the vice-president of production, had the following expenses:

Vice-president	Actual	Budget
Marketing	$133,600	$130,000
Finance	107,000	105,000
Personnel	116,800	114,000

Instructions
(a) Prepare the following responsibility performance reports:
   (1) Manufacturing overhead—Cutting Department manager—Seattle division.
   (2) Manufacturing overhead—Seattle division manager.
   (3) Manufacturing overhead—vice-president of production.
   (4) Manufacturing overhead and expenses—president. Use the format on page 1054.

(b) Comment on the comparative performances of
   (1) Department managers in the Seattle division.
   (2) Division managers.
   (3) Vice-presidents.

ALTERNATE PROBLEMS

Prepare flexible budget and budget report for manufacturing overhead. (S.O. 3)

P26–1A   The Hall Company estimates that 360,000 direct labor hours will be worked during the coming year, 1993, in the Packaging Department. On this basis, the following budgeted manufacturing overhead cost data are computed for the year:

Fixed Overhead Costs		Variable Overhead Costs	
Supervision	$ 90,000	Indirect labor	$144,000
Depreciation	45,000	Indirect materials	90,000
Insurance	27,000	Repairs	54,000
Rent	36,000	Utilities	72,000
Property taxes	18,000	Lubricants	18,000
	$216,000		$378,000

It is estimated that direct labor hours worked each month will range from 27,000 to 36,000 hours.

During October, 27,000 direct labor hours were worked and the following overhead costs were incurred:

Fixed overhead costs: Supervision $7,500, Depreciation $3,750, Insurance $2,225, Rent $3,000, and Property taxes $1,500.

Variable overhead costs: Indirect labor $11,760, Indirect materials, $6,400, Repairs $4,000, Utilities $5,900, and Lubricants $1,740.

Instructions

(a) Prepare a monthly flexible manufacturing overhead budget for each increment of 3,000 direct labor hours over the relevant range for the year ending December 31, 1993.

(b) Prepare a flexible budget report for October, when 27,500 direct labor hours were expected.

(c) Comment on management's efficiency in controlling manufacturing overhead costs in October.

Prepare flexible budget, budget report, and graph for manufacturing overhead. (S.O. 3)

P26–2A   The Hermal Company manufactures tablecloths. Sales have grown rapidly over the past two years. As a result, the president has installed a budgetary control system for 1993. The following data were used in developing the master manufacturing overhead budget for the Ironing Department, which is based on an activity index of direct labor hours.

Variable Costs	Rate per Direct Labor Hour	Annual Fixed Costs	
Indirect labor	$.40	Supervision	$27,000
Indirect materials	.50	Depreciation	18,000
Factory utilities	.30	Insurance	12,000
Factory repairs	.20	Rent	24,000

The master overhead budget was prepared on the expectation that 480,000 direct labor hours will be worked during the year. In June 42,000 direct labor hours were worked and 42,000 were expected. At that level of activity, actual costs were as follows:

Variable—per direct labor hour: Indirect labor $.42, Indirect materials $.50, Factory utilities $.32, and Factory repairs $.20.
Fixed: same as budgeted.

Instructions

(a) Prepare a monthly flexible manufacturing overhead budget for the year ending December 31, 1993, assuming production levels range from 35,000 to 50,000 direct labor hours. Use increments of 5,000 direct labor hours.

(b) Prepare a budget performance report for June comparing actual results with budget data based on the flexible budget.

(c) Were costs effectively controlled? Explain.

(d) State the formula for computing the total budgeted costs for the Hermal Company.

(e) Prepare the flexible budget graph, showing total budgeted costs at 35,000 and 45,000 direct labor hours. Use increments of 5,000 direct labor hours on the horizontal axis and increments of $10,000 on the vertical axis.

P26–3A The Fernando Company uses budgets in controlling costs. The August 1993 budget report for the company's Assembling Department is as follows:

State total budgeted cost formula and prepare flexible budget reports for two time periods.
(S.O. 2, 3)

FERNANDO COMPANY
Budget Report
Assembling Department
For the Month Ended August 31, 1993

Manufacturing	Budget	Actual	Difference Favorable F Unfavorable U
Variable costs:			
Direct materials	$ 48,000	$ 47,000	$1,000 F
Direct labor	72,000	68,000	4,000 F
Indirect materials	24,000	24,200	200 U
Indirect labor	18,000	17,500	500 F
Utilities	15,000	14,900	100 F
Maintenance	9,000	9,100	100 U
Total variable	186,000	180,700	5,300 F
Fixed costs:			
Rent	12,000	12,000	–0–
Supervision	15,000	15,000	–0–
Depreciation	7,000	7,000	–0–
Total fixed	34,000	34,000	–0–
Total costs	$220,000	$214,700	$5,300 F

The budget data in the report are based on the master budget for the year, which assumed that 720,000 units would be produced. The Assembling Department manager is pleased with the report and expects a raise, or at least praise for a job well done. The company president, however, is unhappy with the results for August, because only 58,000 units were produced. (Hint: The budget amounts above are one-twelfth of the master budget.)

Instructions

(a) State the total budgeted cost formula.

(b) Prepare a budget report for August using flexible budget data. Why does this report provide a better basis for evaluating performance than the report based on static budget data? Assume 62,000 units were expected to be produced.

(c) In September, 64,000 units were produced when 65,000 were expected. Prepare the budget report using flexible budget data, assuming (1) each variable cost was 10% higher than its actual cost in August, and (2) fixed costs were the same in September as in August.

P26–4A Eastern Manufacturing Inc., operates the Patio Furniture Division as a profit center. Operating data for this division for the year ended December 31, 1993 are as follows:

Prepare responsibility report for a profit center.
(S.O. 6)

	Budget	Difference from Budget
Sales	$2,500,000	$50,000 F
Cost of goods sold		
Variable	1,300,000	60,000 F
Controllable fixed	200,000	5,000 U
Selling and administrative		
Variable	220,000	5,000 U
Controllable fixed	50,000	1,000 U
Noncontrollable fixed costs	70,000	4,000 U

In addition, Eastern Manufacturing incurs $180,000 of indirect fixed costs that were budgeted at $175,000. Twenty percent (20%) of these costs are allocated to the Patio Furniture Division.

Instructions

(a) Prepare a responsibility performance report for the Patio Furniture Division for the year.

(b) Comment on the manager's performance in controlling revenues and costs.

(c) Identify any costs excluded from the performance report and explain why they were excluded.

Prepare responsibility report for an investment center and compute ROI using expanded formula. (S.O. 7)

P26–5A Hanlon Manufacturing Company manufactures a variety of tools and industrial equipment. The company operates through three divisions. Each division is an investment center. Operating data for the Home Division for the year ended December 31, 1993 and relevant budget data are as follows:

	Actual	Comparison with Budget
Sales	$1,500,000	$100,000 favorable
Variable cost of goods sold	700,000	100,000 unfavorable
Variable selling and administrative expenses	125,000	25,000 unfavorable
Controllable fixed cost of goods sold	170,000	On target
Controllable fixed selling and administrative expenses	55,000	On target

Average operating assets for the year for the Home Division were $2,500,000 which was also the budgeted amount.

Instructions

(a) Prepare a responsibility report (in thousands of dollars) for the Home Division

(b) Evaluate the manager's performance. Which items will likely be investigated by top management?

(c) Compute the expected ROI in 1994 for the Home Division, using the expanded ROI formula, assuming the following changes.
   1. Variable cost of goods sold is decreased by 10%.
   2. Average operating assets are decreased by 8%.
   3. Sales are increased by 200,000 and this increase is expected to increase contribution margin by $90,000.

*B*roadening Your Perspective

FINANCIAL REPORTING PROBLEM

PepsiCo, Inc. has three responsibility centers that are called industry segments. They are soft drinks, snack foods, and restaurants. These segments are operated as investment centers. Refer to the PepsiCo annual report in Appendix L and answer the following questions using the information provided in the Business Segments section.

1. How do the segments rank in terms of total (a) net sales and (b) operating profits? What conclusions do you draw from the rankings?

2. Does the segment data focus on controllability, profitability, or both? Explain.

3. Compute the return on investment (ROI) for each segment for 1991 and 1990. Use operating profits as the numerator and identifiable assets as the denominator in the formula. What conclusions do you draw from the rankings?

4. Are indirect company fixed costs disclosed in the segment data? Explain.

5. Within the restaurant segment, how do the chains rank in profitability?

DECISION CASE 1

Hilltop University offers continuing education programs in many cities throughout the state. For the convenience of its faculty, the school operates a motor pool. In 1993, the motor pool operated with 15 automobiles until March, when two additional vehicles were acquired. The motor pool furnishes gasoline, oil, and other supplies for its automobiles. A mechanic does routine maintenance and minor repairs. Major repairs are done at a nearby commercial garage.

Each year, the supervisor of the motor pool submits an operating budget to the university administration. Depreciation (using the straight-line method) on the automobiles is recorded in the budget in order to determine the cost per mile of operating the vehicles. The operating budget for 1993 approved by university administration is as follows:

MOTOR POOL
Operating Budget
For the Year Ended December 31, 1993

Basis: 15 automobiles

Expenses	
Gasoline	$ 18,000
Oil and minor repairs	5,400
Commercial repairs	2,700
Insurance	7,200
Salaries	36,000
Automobile depreciation	40,500
Total expenses	$109,800
Total miles	360,000
Total cost per mile	$ .3050

The annual budget was based on the following assumptions:

1. Annual mileage per car, 24,000.
2. Average miles per gallon of gasoline, 20.
3. Cost per gallon of gasoline, $1.00.
4. Cost per mile for oil and minor repairs, $0.015.
5. Annual cost per automobile for commercial repairs, $180.
6. Annual cost per automobile for insurance, $480.
7. Annual cost per automobile for depreciation, $2,700.
8. Salaries of $36,000 are the total annual cost.

In April, the 17 vehicles were driven 33,000 miles and the following budget report was prepared by the university administration.

MOTOR POOL
Operating Budget Report
For the Month Ended April 30, 1993

	Budget	Actual Costs	Difference Favorable F Unfavorable U
Activity: Mileage	30,000	33,000	3,000 F
Expenses			
Gasoline	$ 1,500	$ 1,600	$ 100 U
Oil and minor repairs	450	480	30 U
Commercial repairs	225	200	25 F
Insurance	600	680	80 U
Salaries	3,000	3,000	–0–
Depreciation	3,375	3,825	450 U
Total expenses	$ 9,150	$ 9,785	$ 635 U

The supervisor is unhappy with the budget report because it is not based on a flexible budget.

Instructions

(a) What type of budget report was prepared by the university administration? Was the supervisor's unhappiness justified? Why?

(b) Prepare a budget report for April using a flexible budget.

(c) Evaluate the supervisor's performance based on the budget report in (b) above.

(CMA adapted)

DECISION CASE 2

Blu Meadows is a 400-acre farm on the outskirts of the Kentucky Bluegrass, specializing in the boarding of broodmares and their foals. The recent economic downturn in the thoroughbred industry has led to a decline in breeding activities, and it has made the boarding business extremely competitive. To meet the competition, Blu Meadows planned in 1993 to entertain clients, advertise more extensively, and absorb expenses formerly paid by clients such as veterinary and blacksmith fees.

The budget report for 1993 is presented below. As shown, the static income statement budget for the year is based on an expected 21,900 boarding days at $25 per mare. The variable expenses per mare per day were budgeted: Feed $5, Veterinary fees $3, Blacksmith fees $.30, and Supplies $.40. All other budgeted expenses were either semifixed or fixed.

During the year, management decided not to replace a worker who quit in March, but it did issue a new advertising brochure and do more entertaining of clients.[1]

BLU MEADOWS
Static Budget Income Statement
Year Ended December 31, 1993

	Actual	Master Budget	Difference
Number of mares	52	60	8*
Number of boarding days	18,980	21,900	2,920*
Sales	$379,600	$547,500	$167,900*
Less variable expenses:			
Feed	104,390	109,500	5,110
Veterinary fees	58,838	65,700	6,862
Blacksmith fees	6,074	6,570	496
Supplies	7,402	8,760	1,358
Total variable expenses	176,704	190,530	13,826
Contribution margin	202,896	356,970	154,074*
Less fixed expenses:			
Depreciation	45,000	45,000	–0–
Insurance	11,000	11,000	–0–
Utilities	12,000	14,000	2,000
Repairs and maintenance	10,000	11,000	1,000
Labor	88,000	96,000	8,000
Advertisement	11,000	8,000	3,000*
Entertainment	8,000	5,000	3,000*
Total fixed expense	185,000	190,000	5,000
Net income	$ 17,896	$166,970	$149,074*

*Unfavorable.

Instructions

(a) Based on the static budget report,

  (1) What was the primary cause(s) of the loss in net income?

  (2) Did management do a good, average, or poor job of controlling expenses?

  (3) Were management's decisions to stay competitive sound?

---

[1]Data for this case is based on the following article: Sprohge, Hans, and Talbott, John, "New Applications for Variance Analysis," *Journal of Accountancy*, (AICPA, New York), April 1989, pages 137–141.

(b) Prepare a flexible budget report for the year.

(c) Based on the flexible budget report, answer the three questions in part (a) above.

(d) What course of action do you recommend for the management of Blu Meadows?

CRITICAL THINKING CASE

Refer to the opening case about the athletic department of the University of Nevada, Las Vegas, and answer the following questions.

1. Would you expect a static or a flexible budget to be used in comparing actual and budgeted expenditures for each team?

2. Which of the biggest budget items are variable and which are fixed?

3. What is the relationship, if any, of the budgets used at UNLV and the allocation of cash to each team?

ETHICAL CASE

American Products Corporation participates in a highly competitive industry. In order to meet this competition and achieve profit goals the company has chosen the decentralized form of organization. Each manager of a decentralized investment center is measured on the basis of profit contribution, market penetration, and return on investment. Failure to meet the objectives established by corporate management for these measures has not been acceptable and usually has resulted in demotion or dismissal of an investment center manager.

An anonymous survey of managers in the company revealed that the managers feel the pressure to compromise their personal ethical standards to achieve the corporate objectives. For example, at certain plant locations there was pressure to reduce quality control to a level which could not assure that all unsafe products would be rejected. Also, sales personnel were encouraged to use questionable sales tactics to obtain orders, including gifts and other incentives to purchasing agents.

The chief executive officer is disturbed by the survey findings. In his opinion such behavior cannot be condoned by the company. He concludes that the company should do something about this problem.

Instructions

(a) Who are the stakeholders (the affected parties) in this situation?

(b) Identify the ethical implications, conflicts, or dilemmas in the above described situation.

(c) What might the company do to reduce the pressures on managers and decrease the ethical conflicts?

(CMA adapted)

Answers to Self-Study Questions
1. d   2. a   3. b   4. b   5. b   6. d   7. c   8. a   9. b   10. c

CHAPTER 27

PERFORMANCE EVALUATION THROUGH STANDARD COSTS

Study Objectives

After studying this chapter, you should be able to:

1. Distinguish between a standard and a budget.

2. Identify the advantages of standard costs.

3. Describe how standards are set.

4. Indicate the formulas for determining direct materials and direct labor variances.

5. State the formulas for determining manufacturing overhead variances.

6. Discuss the reporting of variances.

7. Enumerate the features of a standard cost accounting system.

There's a very good chance that the highlighter you're holding in your hand was made by Sanford Corp., a maker of marking pens and other writing instruments. Sanford, based in Illinois, annually sells in excess of $100 million worth of highlighters, fine point pens, markers for overhead projectors, and other writing instruments.

Since Sanford makes literally millions of writing utensils per year, the company must keep tight control over manufacturing costs. As a result, a very important part of Sanford's manufacturing process is the determination of how much direct materials, labor and overhead should cost. These costs are then compared to actual costs to assess performance efficiency.

Raw materials for Sanford's pens include plastic, a barrel, a plug, a cap, a reservoir, and a felt tip. These parts are assembled by machine to produce thousands *of units per hour. A major component of manufacturing overhead, then, includes machine maintenance—some fixed, some variable.*

There's still a labor component, though: the machine operator. It is this person who makes or breaks Sanford's productivity. "We try to control labor efficiency the best we can," says Bob Stoltz, Sanford's controller. "But excessive labor time is often due to malfunctioning equipment—which is difficult to control."

In contrast, labor rates are more predictable since the hourly workers are covered by a union contract. The story is the same with the fringe benefits and some supervisory salaries. Even volume levels are fairly predictable—demand for the product is high— so that fixed overhead is efficiently absorbed. Raw material standard costs are based on the previous year's actual prices plus any anticipated inflation. Lately, though, inflation has been so low that the company is considering any price increase in raw material to be unfavorable.

Suppose you were assigned the responsibility of manufacturing 100,000 Sanford acetate marking pens. How would you want your performance as manager to be evaluated? An important consideration would be whether you accomplished the task of manufacturing 100,000 pens. Just as importantly would be whether or not you met the scheduled completion date and the expected quality control objectives. Collectively, these measures relate to your **effectiveness** in performing your assigned responsibility.

Your boss would want to use some additional measures to evaluate your performance. These measures would relate to the **efficiency** of your managing the whole process. Efficiency focuses on the cost of accomplishing the task. Efficiency measures are used to ascertain whether (1) the best cost was obtained in purchasing raw materials, (2) the specified quantities of raw materials were used, and (3) the anticipated amount and level of skilled labor were utilized. Because most tasks like this one are required to be accomplished with limited resources, efficiency measures are often very demanding.

In this chapter we continue the study of controlling costs by considering additional measures that permit the evaluation of performance. We first explain the performance measures called standard costs, which are predetermined unit costs. Next, we illustrate how standard costs are used. We then describe a standard cost accounting system.

Need for Standards

Standards are a fact of life. You met the admission standards for the college or university you are attending. The automobile that you drive had to meet certain governmental environment standards. The hamburgers and salads you eat in a restaurant have to meet certain health and nutritional standards before they can be sold. The reason for standards in these cases is very simple: They help to ensure that the overall quality of the product produced is high. Without standards, quality control is lost.

Standards are also common in business. Those imposed by government agencies are often called **regulations**. They include the Fair Labor Standards Act, the Equal Employment Opportunity Act, and a multitude of environmental standards. Standards established internally by a company may extend to personnel matters, such as employee absenteeism and ethical codes of conduct, quality control standards for products, and standard costs for goods and services.

Although we will focus on manufacturing operations in the remainder of this chapter, you should also recognize that standard costs are also applicable to many other types of businesses. For example, a fast-foods restaurant such as McDonald's knows not only the price it should pay for pickles, beef, buns, and other ingredients, but also how much time it should take an employee to flip hamburgers. If too much is paid for pickles or too much time is taken to prepare Big Macs, the deviations are noticed and corrective action is taken. Moreover, standard costs may be used in not-for-profit enterprises such as universities, charitable organizations, and governmental agencies.

Distinction Between Standards and Budgets

In concept, **standards** and budgets are essentially the same. Both are predetermined costs and both contribute significantly to management planning and control. There is a difference, however, in the way the terms are expressed. A standard is a **unit** amount, whereas a budget is a **total** amount. Thus, it is customary to state that the standard cost of direct labor for a unit of product is $10. However, if 5,000 units of the product are produced, the $50,000 of direct labor is the budgeted labor cost. In this context, a standard is the budgeted cost per unit of product. A standard is, therefore, concerned with each individual cost component that makes up the entire budget.

There are important accounting differences between budgets and standards. Except in the application of manufacturing overhead to jobs and processes, budget data are not journalized in cost accounting systems. In contrast, as will be illustrated later in the chapter, standard costs may be incorporated into cost accounting systems. It is also possible for a company to report its inventories at standard cost in its financial statements, but it is not possible to report inventories at budgeted costs.

> **Study Objective 1**
>
> *Distinguish between a standard and a budget.*

Why Standard Costs?

Standard costs offer the following advantages to an organization:

1. Standard costs facilitate **management planning** by establishing expected future costs.
2. When properly set, they should promote **greater economy** and efficiency of operations by making employees more "cost-conscious."
3. They may be useful in **setting selling prices** for finished goods.
4. They contribute to **management control** by providing a basis for evaluating the performance of managers responsible for controlling costs.
5. Performance may be evaluated through **management by exception**, as deviations (or variances) from standard are highlighted.
6. When standard costs are incorporated into the accounting system, they **simplify the costing of inventories** and reduce clerical costs.

> **Study Objective 2**
>
> *Identify the advantages of standard costs.*

These advantages will be realized only when standard costs are carefully established and prudently used. Using standards solely as a means of finding fault or placing blame can have a negative effect on managers and employees. In an effort to minimize this effect, many companies offer wage incentives to those who meet their standards.

Setting Standard Costs—A Difficult Task

Study Objective 3

Describe how standards are set.

The setting of standard costs to produce a unit of product is a difficult task. It requires input from all persons who have responsibility for costs and quantities. To determine the standard cost of direct materials, management may have to consult the purchasing agents, product managers, quality control engineers, and production supervisors. In setting the cost standard for direct labor, pay rate data are obtained from the payroll department, and the labor time requirements may be determined by industrial engineers. The managerial accountant provides input to the standards-setting process through the accumulation of historical cost data and knowledge of the behavior of costs in response to changes in activity levels. The decision as to what the standard cost should be is, of course, a management responsibility.

Standards may be set at one of two levels: ideal or normal. Ideal standards represent the optimum level of performance under perfect operating conditions. In contrast, normal standards represent an efficient level of performance that is attainable under expected operating conditions.

Some managers believe ideal standards will stimulate the conscientious worker to ever-increasing improvement. However, most managers believe that because these standards are so difficult, if not impossible, to meet, they discourage self-improvement and lower the morale of the entire work force. Very few companies use ideal standards.

Most companies that use standards set them at a normal level. When properly set, normal standards should be **rigorous but attainable**. Normal standards allow for rest periods, machine breakdowns, and other "normal" contingencies pertaining to the production process. It will be assumed in the remainder of this chapter that standard costs are set at a normal level.

Technology in Action

Computerized standard cost systems represent one of the most complex accounting systems to develop and maintain. The standard cost system must be fully integrated into the general ledger, allow for the creation and timely maintenance of the data base of standard usage and costs for every product, and perform various variance computations. Such systems must also produce variance reports by product, department, or employee. With the increased use of automation and robotics, the computerized standard cost system may even be tied directly into these systems to gather variance information.

To be effective in controlling costs, standard costs need to be current at all times. Thus, standards should be under continuous review and should be changed whenever it is determined that the existing standard is not a good measure of performance. Circumstances that may warrant revision of a standard include changed wage rates resulting from a new union contract, a change in product specifications, or the implementation of a new manufacturing method.

Setting Standards—A Case Study

To establish the standard cost of producing a product, it is necessary to establish standards for each manufacturing cost element—direct materials, direct labor, and manufacturing overhead. The standard for each element is derived from a consideration of the standard price to be paid and the standard quantity to be used. To illustrate, we will assume that Xonic, Inc., wishes to use standard costs to measure performance in filling an order for 1,000 gallons of Weed-O, a liquid weed killer.

Direct Materials

The direct materials price standard is the cost per unit of direct materials that should be incurred. This standard should be based on the purchasing department's best estimate of the **cost of raw materials**. This is frequently based on an analysis of current purchase prices. The price standard should also include an amount for related costs such as receiving, storing, and handling. The materials price standard per pound of material for Xonic's weed killer is:

Item	Price
Purchase price, net of discounts	$2.70
Freight	.20
Receiving and handling	.10
Standard direct materials price per pound	$3.00

ILLUSTRATION 27-1

Setting direct materials price standard

The direct materials quantity standard is the quantity of direct materials that should be used per unit of finished goods. This standard is expressed as a physical measure, such as pounds, barrels, or board feet. In setting the standard, consideration should be given to both the quality and quantity of materials required to manufacture the product. The standard should include allowances for unavoidable waste and normal spoilage. To illustrate, the standard quantity per unit for Xonic, Inc., is as follows:

Item	Quantity (Pounds)
Required materials	3.5
Allowance for waste	.4
Allowance for spoilage	.1
Standard direct materials quantity per unit	4.0

ILLUSTRATION 27-2

Setting direct materials quantity standard

The standard direct materials cost per unit is the standard direct materials price times the standard direct materials quantity. For Xonic, Inc., the standard direct material costs per gallon of Weed-O is $12.00 ($3.00 × 4.0 pounds).

Direct Labor

The direct labor price standard is the rate per hour that should be incurred for direct labor. This standard is based on current wage rates adjusted for anticipated changes, such as cost of living adjustments (COLAs) included in many union contracts. In addition, the price standard generally includes employer payroll taxes and fringe benefits, such as paid holidays and vacations. For Xonic, Inc., the direct labor price standard, often called the **standard direct labor rate**, is as follows:

ILLUSTRATION 27-3

Setting direct labor price standard

Item	Price
Hourly wage rate	$ 7.50
COLA	.25
Payroll taxes	.75
Fringe benefits	1.50
Standard direct labor rate per hour	$10.00

The direct labor quantity standard is the time that should be required to make one unit of the product. This standard, often called the **direct labor efficiency** standard, is especially critical in labor-intensive (as opposed to capital-intensive) companies. Allowances should be made in setting this standard for rest periods, cleanup, machine setup, and machine downtime. For Xonic, Inc., the direct labor quantity standard is as follows:

ILLUSTRATION 27-4

Setting direct labor quantity standard

Item	Quantity (Hours)
Actual production time	1.5
Rest periods and cleanup	.2
Setup and downtime	.3
Standard direct labor hours per unit	2.0

The standard direct labor cost per unit is the standard direct labor rate times the standard direct labor hours. For Xonic, Inc., the standard direct labor cost per gallon of Weed-O is $20 ($10.00 × 2.0 hours).

Manufacturing Overhead

For manufacturing overhead, a standard predetermined overhead rate is used in setting the standard. This overhead rate is determined by dividing budgeted overhead costs by an expected standard activity index. For example, the index may be standard direct labor hours or standard machine hours. Xonic, Inc., uses standard direct labor hours as the activity index. The company expects to produce 13,200 gallons of Weed-O during the year at normal capacity. Since it takes two direct labor hours for each gallon, total standard direct labor hours are 26,400 (13,200 × 2). At this level of activity, overhead costs are expected to be $132,000, of which $79,200 are variable and $52,800 are fixed. The standard predetermined overhead rates, therefore, are computed as shown in Illustration 27-5:

ILLUSTRATION 27-5

Computing predetermined overhead rates

Budgeted Overhead Costs	Amount	÷ Standard Direct Labor Hours =	Overhead Rate per Direct Labor Hour
Variable	$ 79,200	26,400	$3.00
Fixed	52,800	26,400	2.00
Total	$132,000	26,400	$5.00

The standard manufacturing overhead rate per unit is the predetermined overhead rate times the direct labor quantity standard. For Xonic, Inc., the standard manufacturing overhead rate per gallon of Weed-O is $10 ($5 × 2 hours).

Total Standard Cost per Unit

Now that the standard quantity and price have been established per unit of product, the total standard cost can be determined. The total standard cost per unit is the sum of the standard costs of direct materials, direct labor, and manufacturing overhead. For Xonic, Inc., the total standard cost per gallon of Weed-O is $42, as shown on the following standard cost card.

XONIC, INC. Standard Cost Card			
Product: Weed-O	**Unit Measure: Gallon**		
Manufacturing Cost Elements	Standard Quantity ×	Standard Price =	Standard Cost
Direct materials	4 pounds	$ 3.00	$12.00
Direct labor	2 hours	$10.00	20.00
Manufacturing overhead	2 hours	$ 5.00	10.00
			$42.00

ILLUSTRATION 27-6

Standard cost card

The standard cost card provides the basis for determining variances from standards.

Accounting in Action · *Business Insight*

Setting standards can be difficult. Consider Susan's Chili Factory, which manufactures and sells chili. The cost of manufacturing Susan's chili consists of the costs of raw materials, labor to convert the basic ingredients to chili, and overhead. We will use material cost as an example. Three standards need to be developed. They are: (1) What should be the formula (mix) of ingredients for one gallon of chili? (2) What should be the normal wastage (or shrinkage) for the individual ingredients? (3) What should be the standard cost for the individual ingredients that go into the chili?

Susan's Chili Factory also provides a good illustration as to how standard costs can be used by management in controlling costs. Suppose that summer droughts have reduced crop yields and, as a result, prices have doubled for beans, onions, and peppers. In such a case, actual costs will be significantly higher than standard costs, which will cause management to evaluate the situation. Such an evaluation might lead to an increase in the price charged for a gallon of chili, reexamination of the product mix to see if other types of ingredients can be used, or curtailment of production until ingredients can be purchased at or near standard costs. Similarly, assume that poor maintenance procedures caused the onion-dicing blades to become dull. As a result, usage of onions to make a gallon of chili tripled. Because this deviation is quickly highlighted through standard costs, corrective action can be taken.

Source: Adapted from David R. Beran, "Cost Reduction Through Control Reporting," *Management Accounting*, April 1982, pp. 29–33.

Before You Go On . . .

1. How do standards differ from budgets?

2. What are the advantages of standard costs to an organization?

3. Distinguish between normal standards and ideal standards. Which standard is more widely used? Why?

Determining Variances from Standards

One of the major management uses of standard costs is to identify variances from standards. Variances are the differences between total actual costs and total standard costs. To illustrate, we will assume that in producing 1,000 gallons of Weed-O in the month of June, Xonic, Inc., incurred the following costs:

ILLUSTRATION 27-7

Actual production costs

Direct materials	$13,020
Direct labor	20,580
Variable overhead	6,500
Fixed overhead	4,400
Total actual costs	$44,500

Total standard costs are determined by multiplying the units produced by the standard cost per unit. The total standard cost of Weed-O is $42,000 (1,000 gallons × $42). Thus, the total variance is $2,500, as shown below.

ILLUSTRATION 27-8

Computation of total variance

Actual costs	$44,500
Standard costs	42,000
Total variance	$ 2,500

Note that the variance is expressed in total dollars and not on a per-unit basis.

When actual costs exceed standard costs, the variance is unfavorable. Thus, the $2,500 variance is unfavorable. An unfavorable variance has a negative connotation. It suggests that too much was paid for one or more of the manufacturing cost elements or that the elements were used inefficiently.

If actual costs are less than standard costs, the variance is favorable. A favorable variance has a positive inference. It suggests efficiencies in incurring manufacturing costs and in using direct materials, direct labor, and manufacturing overhead. However, be careful: A favorable variance could be obtained by using inferior materials. In printing wedding invitations, for example, a favorable variance could result from using an inferior grade of paper. Similarly, a favorable variance might be achieved in installing tires on an automobile assembly line by tightening only half of the lug bolts. The point should be obvious: a variance is not favorable if quality control standards have been sacrificed. To properly interpret the significance of a variance, you must analyze it to determine the underlying cause(s).

Analyzing Variances

Analyzing variances begins with a determination of the cost elements that comprise the variance. **For each cost element, a total dollar variance is computed. Then this variance is analyzed into a price variance and a quantity variance.** The relationships are shown graphically as follows:

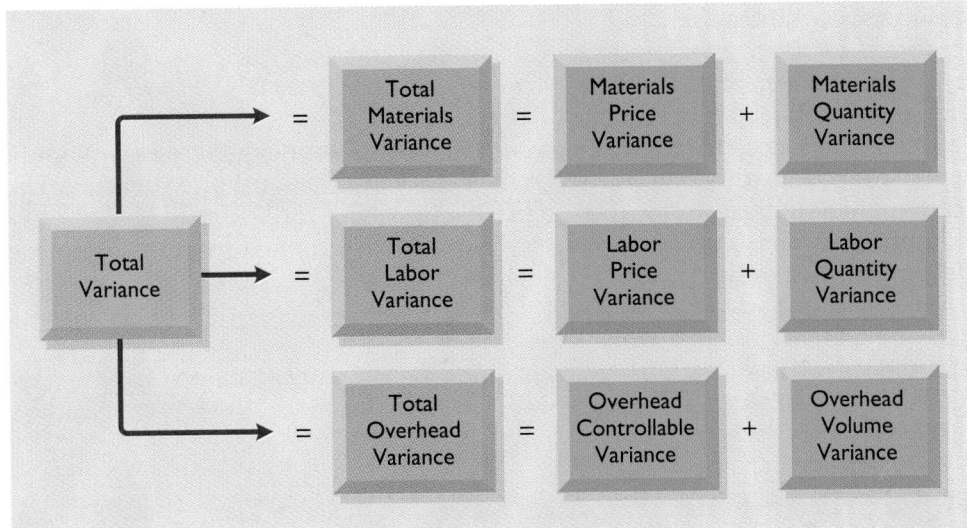

ILLUSTRATION 27-9

Relationships of variances

Each of the variances is explained below.

Study Objective 4

Indicate the formulas for determining direct materials and direct labor variances.

Direct Materials Variances

In completing the order for 1,000 gallons of Weed-O, Xonic used 4,200 pounds of direct materials purchased at a cost of $3.10 per unit. The total materials variance is computed from the following formula:

ILLUSTRATION 27-10

Formula for total materials variance

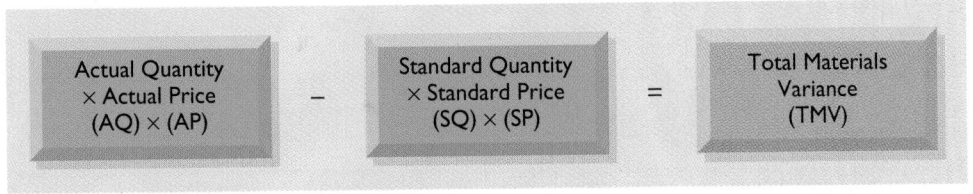

For Xonic, Inc., the total materials variance is $1,020 ($13,020 − $12,000) unfavorable as shown below:

$$(4{,}200 \times \$3.10) - (4{,}000 \times \$3.00) = \$1{,}020 \text{ U}$$

Next, the total variance is analyzed to determine the amount attributable to costs and to quantity (use). The materials price variance is computed from the formula shown in Illustration 27-11.[1]

---

[1]It will be assumed that all materials purchased during the period are used in production and no units remain in inventory at the end of the period.

ILLUSTRATION 27-11

Formula for materials price variance

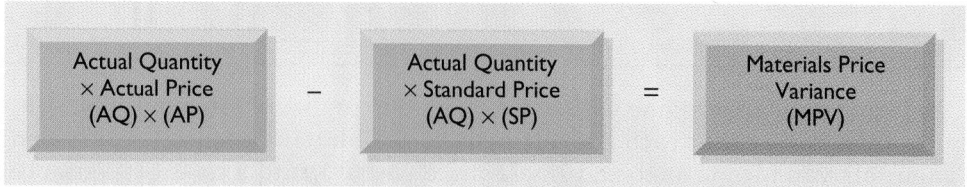

For Xonic, Inc., the materials price variance is $420 ($13,020 − $12,600) unfavorable as shown below:

$$(4{,}200 \times \$3.10) - (4{,}200 \times \$3.00) = \$420 \text{ U}$$

Helpful hint The formula is:

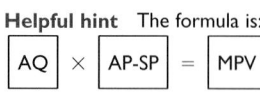

The price variance can also be computed by multiplying the actual quantity purchased by the difference between the actual and standard price per unit. The computation in this case is $4{,}200 \times (\$3.10 - \$3.00) = \$420$ U.

The materials quantity (or use) variance is determined from the following formula:

ILLUSTRATION 27-12

Formula for materials quantity variance

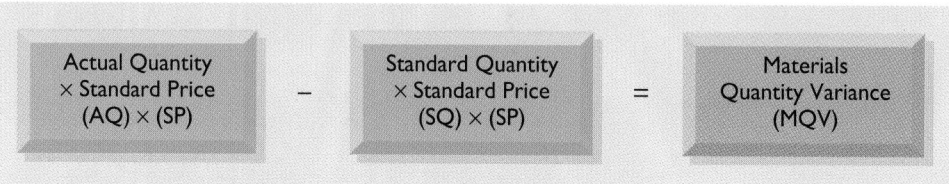

For Xonic, Inc., the materials quantity variance is $600 ($12,600 − $12,000) unfavorable, as shown below:

$$(4{,}200 \times \$3.00) - (4{,}000 \times \$3.00) = \$600 \text{ U}$$

Helpful hint The formula is:

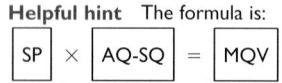

This variance can also be computed by applying the standard price to the difference between actual and standard quantitites used. The computation in this example is $\$3.00 \times (4{,}200 - 4{,}000) = \$600$ U.

The total materials variance of $1,020(U), therefore, consists of the following:

ILLUSTRATION 27-13

Summary of materials variance

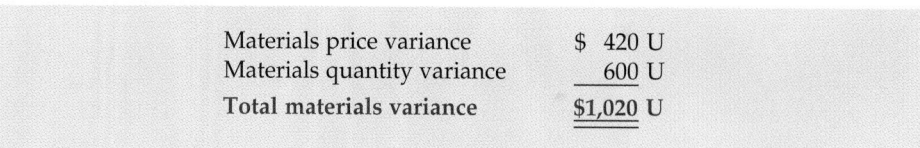

Materials price variance	$ 420 U
Materials quantity variance	600 U
Total materials variance	**$1,020 U**

Using a Variance Matrix

Some accountants favor the use of a matrix to determine and analyze a variance. **When the matrix is used, the formulas for each cost element are computed first and then the variances.** The completed matrix for the direct materials variance for Xonic, Inc. is shown in Illustration 27-14. The matrix provides a convenient structure for determining each variance.

Direct Labor Variances

The process of determining direct labor variances is the same as for determining the direct materials variances. In completing the Weed-O order, Xonic, Inc., incurred 2,100 direct labor hours at an average hourly rate of $9.80 when the standard hours allowed for the units produced was 2,000 hours (1,000 units × 2 hours)

ILLUSTRATION 27-14

Matrix for direct materials variance

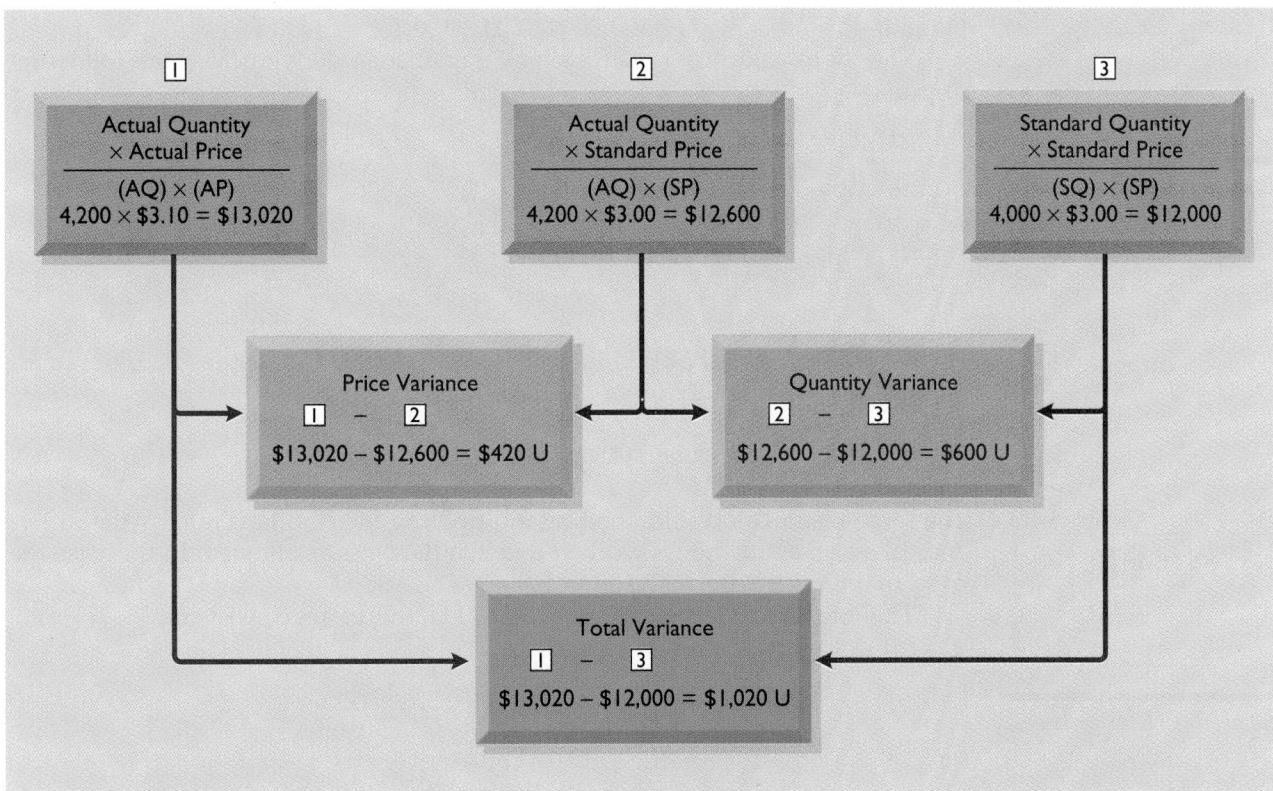

and the standard rate was $10 per hour. The **total labor variance** is obtained from the following formula:

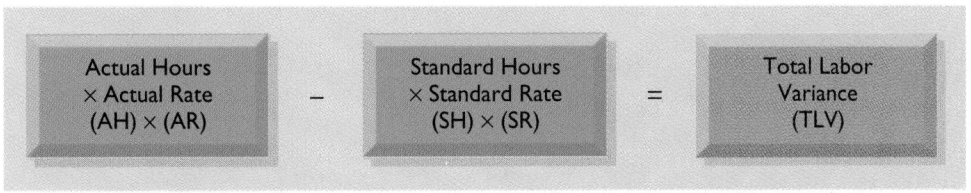

ILLUSTRATION 27-15

Formula for total labor variance

The total labor variance is $580 ($20,580 − $20,000) unfavorable, as shown below:

$$(2,100 \times \$9.80) - (2,000 \times \$10.00) = \$580 \text{ U}$$

The formula for the **labor price (or rate) variance** is:

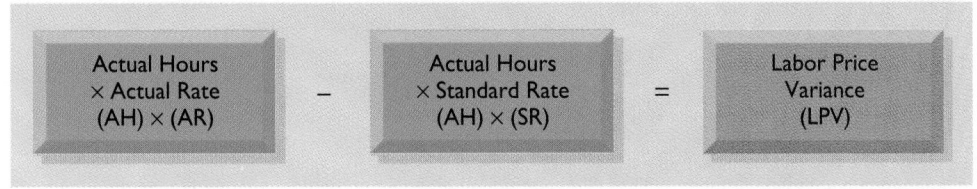

ILLUSTRATION 27-16

Formula for labor price variance

For Xonic, Inc., the labor price variance is $420 ($20,580 − $21,000) favorable as shown at the top of the next page.

$$(2,100 \times \$9.80) - (2,100 \times \$10.00) = \$420 \text{ F}$$

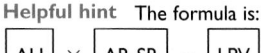

This variance can also be computed by multiplying actual hours worked by the difference between the actual pay rate and the standard pay rate. The computation in this example is $2,100 \times (\$10.00 - \$9.80) = \$420$ F.

The labor quantity (or efficiency) variance is derived from the following formula:

ILLUSTRATION 27-17

Formula for labor quantity variance

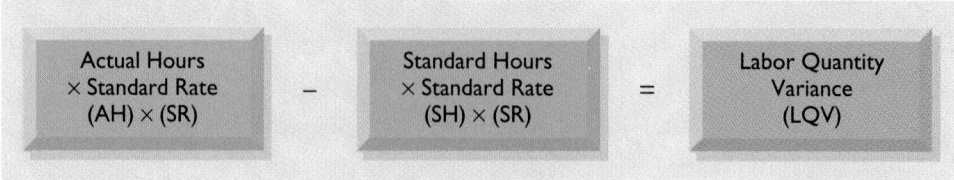

For Xonic, Inc., the labor quantity variance is $1,000 ($21,000 − $20,000) unfavorable as shown at the top of the next page.

$$(2,100 \times \$10.00) - (2,000 \times \$10.00) = \$1,000 \text{ U}$$

The same result can be obtained by multiplying the standard rate by the difference between actual hours worked and standard hours allowed. In this case the computation is $\$10.00 \times (2,100 - 2,000) = \$1,000$ U.

The total direct labor variance of $580 U, therefore, consists of:

ILLUSTRATION 27-18

Summary of labor variances

ILLUSTRATION 27-19

Labor price variance	$ 420 F
Labor quantity variance	1,000 U
Total direct labor variance	**$ 580 U**

Matrix for direct labor variances

These results can also be obtained from the matrix in Illustration 27-19.

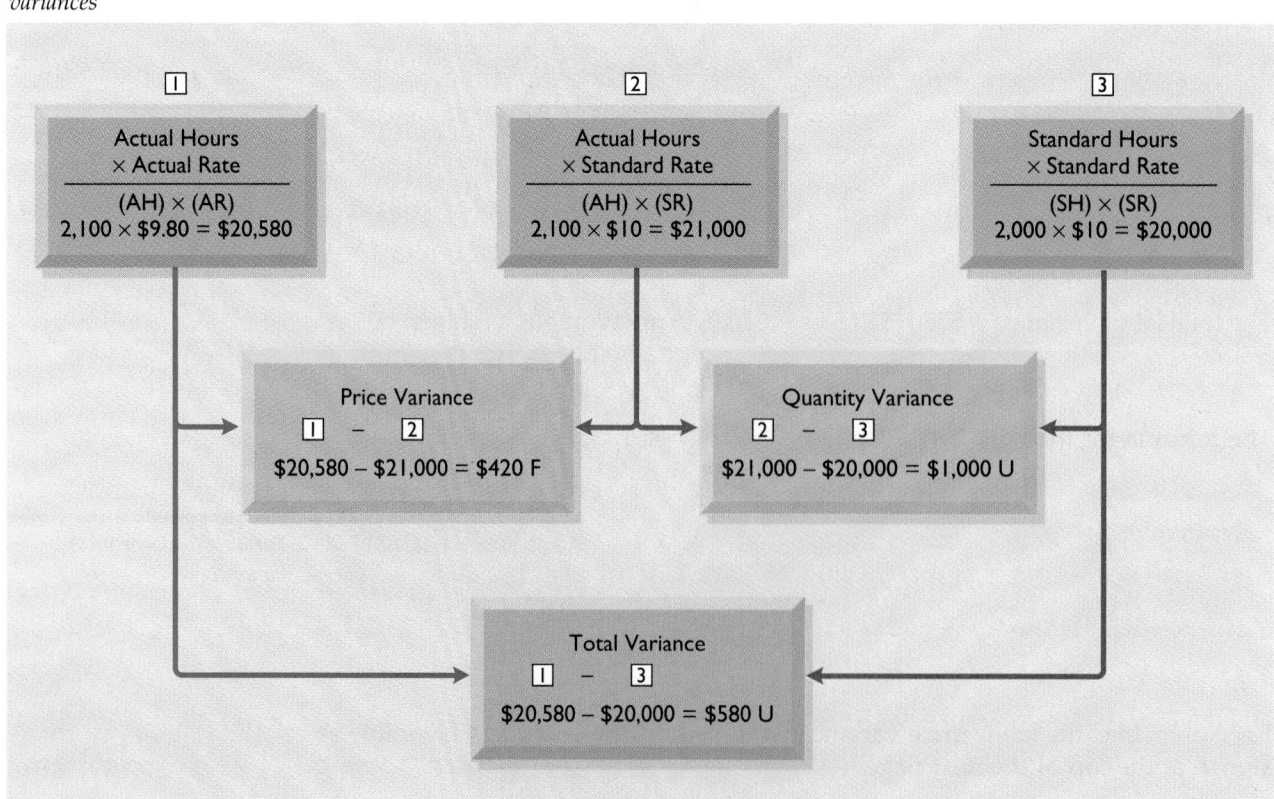

ccounting in Action · *Business Insight*

At United Parcel Service (UPS) performance standards are set by industrial engineers for many tasks performed by UPS employees. For example, according to a *Wall Street Journal* article, a UPS driver is expected to walk at a pace of three feet per second when going to a customer's door and knock rather than take the time to look for a doorbell. *The Wall Street Journal* reported that a UPS executive attributes the company's success to its ability to manage and hold labor accountable.

Source: The Wall Street Journal, April 22, 1986.

Manufacturing Overhead Variances

The computation of the manufacturing overhead variances is conceptually the same as the computation of the materials and labor variances. However, the task is more challenging for manufacturing overhead because both variable and fixed overhead costs must be considered.

> **Study Objective 5**
>
> State the formulas for determining manufacturing overhead variances.

Total Overhead Variance

The total overhead variance is the difference between actual overhead costs and overhead costs applied to work done. As indicated earlier, manufacturing overhead costs incurred were $10,900, as follows:

Variable overhead	$ 6,500
Fixed overhead	4,400
Total actual overhead	$10,900

ILLUSTRATION 27-20

Actual overhead costs

With standard costs, manufacturing overhead costs are applied to work in process on the basis of the **standard hours allowed** for the work done. Standard hours allowed are the hours that should have been worked for the units produced. For the Weed-O order, the standard hours allowed are 2,000 and the predetermined overhead rate is $5 per direct labor hour. Thus, overhead applied is $10,000 (2,000 × $5). Note that actual hours of direct labor (2,100) are not used in appyling manufacturing overhead.

The formula for the total overhead variance is:

ILLUSTRATION 27-21

Formula for total overhead variance

$$\boxed{\text{Actual Overhead}} - \boxed{\text{Overhead Applied}} = \boxed{\text{Total Overhead Variance}}$$

Thus, for Xonic, Inc., the total overhead variance is $900 unfavorable as shown below:

$$\$10,900 - \$10,000 = \$900 \text{ U}$$

The overhead variance is generally analyzed through a price variance and a quantity variance. The name usually given to the price variance is the overhead controllable variance, whereas the quantity variance is referred to as the over-head volume variance.

Overhead Controllable Variance

The overhead controllable variance (also called the **budget** or **spending variance**) is the difference between the actual overhead costs incurred and the budgeted costs for the **standard hours allowed**. The budgeted costs are determined from the flexible manufacturing overhead budget. The budget for Xonic, Inc., is as follows:

ILLUSTRATION 27-22

Flexible budget using standard direct labor hours

XONIC, INC. Flexible Manufacturing Overhead Budget				
Activity Index				
Standard direct labor hours	1,800	2,000	2,200	2,400
Costs				
Variable costs				
Indirect materials	$1,800	$ 2,000	$ 2,200	$ 2,400
Indirect labor	2,700	3,000	3,300	3,600
Utilities	900	1,000	1,100	1,200
Total variable	5,400	6,000	6,600	7,200
Fixed costs				
Supervision	3,000	3,000	3,000	3,000
Depreciation	1,400	1,400	1,400	1,400
Total fixed	4,400	4,400	4,400	4,400
Total costs	$9,800	$10,400	$11,000	$11,600

As shown, the budgeted costs for 2,000 standard hours are $10,400 ($6,000 variable and $4,400 fixed).[2]

The formula for the overhead controllable variance is:

ILLUSTRATION 27-23

Formula for overhead controllable variance

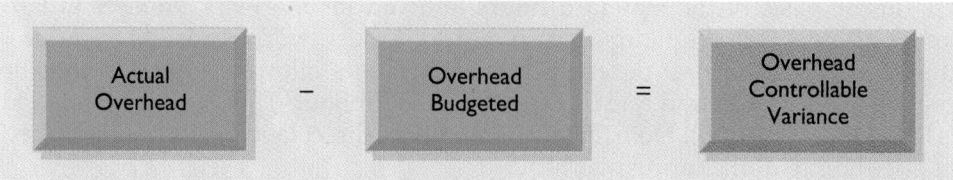

The overhead controllable variance for Xonic, Inc., is $500 unfavorable as shown below:

$$\$10,900 - \$10,400 = \$500 \text{ U}$$

Most controllable variances are associated with variable costs which are controllable costs. Fixed costs are usually known at the time the budget is prepared. In Xonic, Inc., the variance is accounted for by comparing the actual variable overhead costs ($6,500) with the budgeted variable costs ($6,000).

If management desires, actual and budgeted overhead for each manufacturing overhead cost that contributes to the controllable variance can be com-

---

[2]The flexible budget formula is: fixed costs $4,400 plus variable costs $3 per hour. Thus, total budgeted costs are $4,400 + ($3 × 2,000), or $10,400.

pared. In addition, cost and quantity variances can be developed for each overhead cost, such as indirect materials and indirect labor.

Overhead Volume Variance

The overhead volume variance indicates whether plant facilities were efficiently used during the period. The formula for computing the volume variance is as follows:

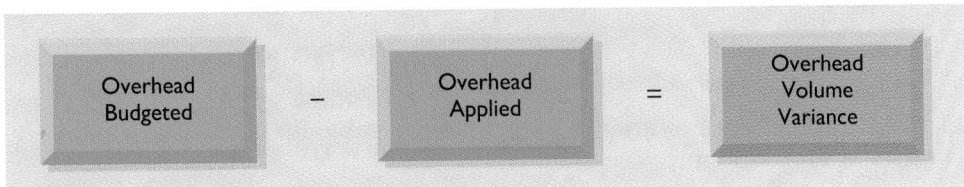

ILLUSTRATION 27-24

Formula for overhead volume variance

Both the factors in this formula have been explained above. The overhead budgeted is the same as the amount used in computing the controllable variance or $10,400 in our example. Overhead applied of $10,000 is the amount used in determining the total overhead variance. For Xonic Inc., the overhead volume variance is $400 unfavorable as shown below:

$$\$10,400 - \$10,000 = \$400 \text{ U}$$

Further insight into the volume variance can be obtained from a detailed analysis of the two factors. As shown in the flexible manufacturing overhead budget, the budgeted overhead of $10,400 consists of $6,000 variable and $4,400 fixed. As indicated in determining the predetermined overhead rate on page 1088, the rate of $5 consists of $3 variable and $2 fixed. The detailed analysis, therefore, is:

ILLUSTRATION 27-25

Detailed analysis of overhead volume variance

Overhead budgeted		
Variable costs	$6,000	
Fixed costs	4,400	$10,400
Overhead applied		
Variable costs (2,000 × $3)	6,000	
Fixed costs (2,000 × $2)	4,000	10,000
Overhead volume variance—unfavorable		$ 400

A careful examination of this analysis indicates that **the overhead volume variance relates solely to fixed costs** (fixed costs budgeted $4,400 − fixed costs applied $4,000). Thus, **the volume variance measures the amount that fixed overhead costs are under- or overapplied**.

We have already established that total fixed costs remain the same at every level of activity within the relevant range. Since a predetermined overhead rate based on normal capacity is used in applying overhead, **it follows that if the standard hours allowed are less than the standard hours at normal capacity, fixed overhead costs will be underapplied**. In contrast, **if production exceeds normal capacity, fixed overhead costs will be overapplied**.

An alternative formula for computing the overhead volume variance is shown in Illustration 27-26.

ILLUSTRATION 27-26

Alternative formula for over-head volume variance

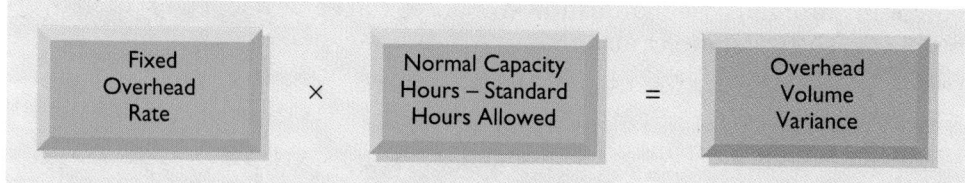

In Xonic Inc., normal capacity is 26,400 hours for the year or 2,200 hours for a month (26,400 ÷ 12), and the fixed overhead rate is $2 per hour. Thus, the volume variance is $400 unfavorable as shown below:

$$\$2 \times (2,200 - 2,000) = \$400 \text{ U}$$

The total overhead variance of $900 unfavorable for Xonic, Inc., therefore, consists of the following:

ILLUSTRATION 27-27

Summary of overhead variance

Overhead controllable variance	$500 U
Overhead volume variance	400 U
Total overhead variance	$900 U

ILLUSTRATION 27-28

Matrix for manufacturing overhead variance

The results can also be obtained from the matrix in Illustration 27-28.

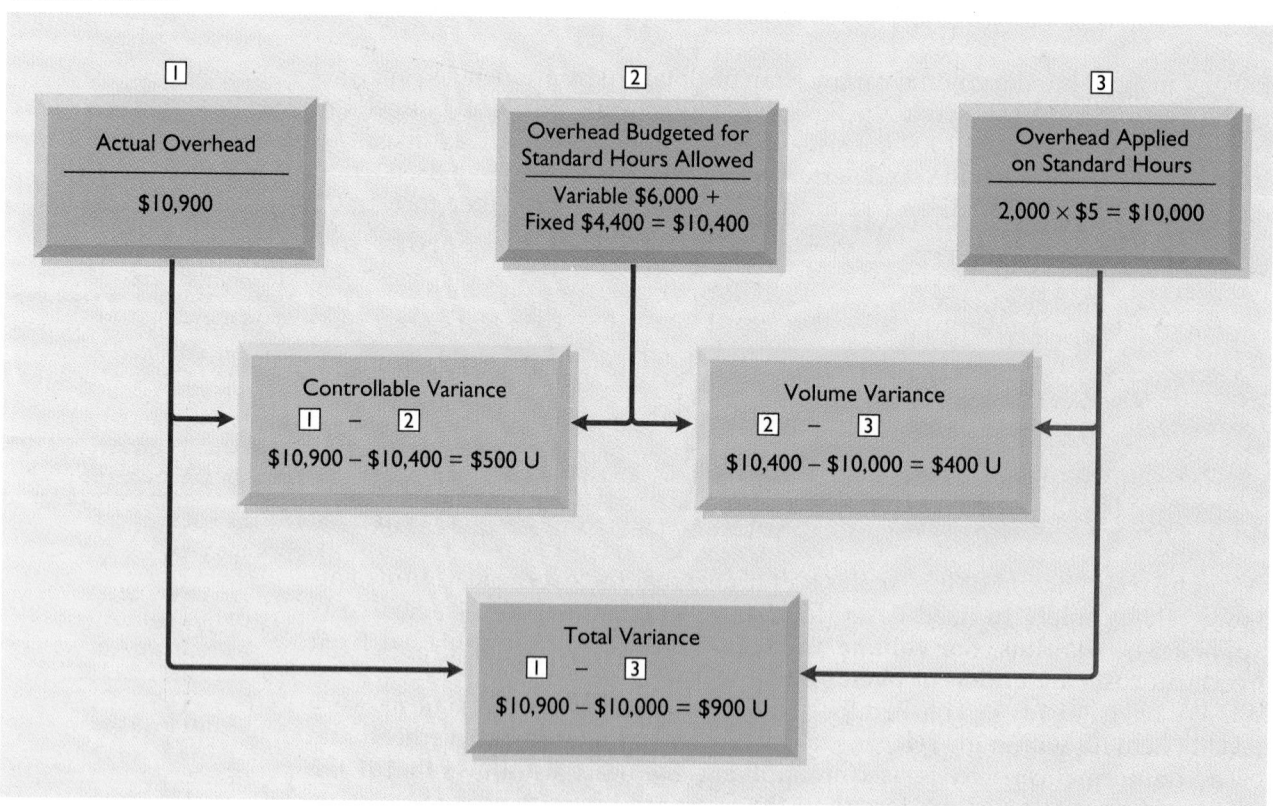

In computing the overhead variances under the two-variance approach, it is important to remember the following:

1. Standard hours allowed are used in each of the variances.

2. Budgeted costs for the controllable variance are derived from the flexible budget.
3. The controllable variance generally pertains to variable costs.
4. The volume variance pertains solely to fixed costs.

Reporting Variances

All variances should be reported to appropriate levels of management as soon as possible. The sooner management is informed, the sooner problems can be evaluated and corrective actions taken if necessary.

The form, content, and frequency of variance reports vary considerably among companies. One approach is to prepare a weekly report for each department that has primary responsibility for cost control. Under this approach, materials price variances are reported to the purchasing department, and all other variances are reported to the production department that did the work. The following report for Xonic, Inc., with the materials for the Weed-O order listed first, illustrates this approach:

Study Objective 6

Discuss the reporting of variances.

ILLUSTRATION 27-29

Materials price variance report

XONIC, INC.
Variance Report—Purchasing Department
For Week Ended June 8, 1990

Type of Materials	Quantity Purchased	Actual Price	Standard Price	Price Variance	Explanation
X 100	4,200 lbs.	$3.10	$3.00	$420 U	Rush order.
X 142	1,200 units	2.75	2.80	60 F	Quantity discount.
A 85	600 doz.	5.20	5.10	60 U	Regular supplier on strike.
Total price variance				$420 U	

The explanation column is completed after consultation with the purchasing department manager.

Variance reports facilitate the principle of "management by exception" explained in Chapter 26. For example, the vice-president of purchasing can use the report illustrated above to evaluate the effectiveness of the purchasing department manager. Similarly, the vice-president of production can use production department variance reports to determine how well each production manager is controlling costs. In using variance reports, top management normally looks for **significant variances**. The significance of a variance may be judged on the basis of some quantitative measure, such as more than 10% of the standard or more than $1,000.

Causes of Variances

What are the causes of a variance? The causes may relate to both internal and external factors as explained below.

Materials Variances

The investigation of a materials price variance usually begins in the purchasing department. Many factors affect the price paid for raw materials. These include the delivery method used, availability of quantity and cash discounts, and

Accounting in Action · *Business Insight*

If purchase price variances are used as a basis for measuring performance, purchasing departments often will continually search for the lowest cost item. However, this situation can become counterproductive if it leads to late deliveries of the goods or the purchase of inferior quality goods.

the quality of the materials requested. To the extent that these factors have been considered in setting the price standard, the purchasing department should be responsible for any variances. It should be recognized, however, that a variance may be beyond the control of the purchasing department. In a period of inflation, prices may rise faster than expected. Moreover, actions by groups over which the company has no control, such as the OPEC nations when they sharply increase oil prices, may cause an unfavorable variance. There are also times when a production department may be responsible for the price variance. This may occur when a rush order forces the company to pay a higher price for the materials.

The starting point for determining the cause(s) of an unfavorable materials quantity variance is in the production department. If the variances are due to inexperienced workers, faulty machinery, or carelessness, the production department would be responsible. However, if the materials obtained by the purchasing department were of inferior quality, then the purchasing department should be responsible.

Labor Variances

Labor price variances usually result from two factors: (1) paying workers higher wages than expected, and (2) misallocation of workers. In companies where pay rates are determined by union contracts, labor price variances should be very infrequent. When workers are not unionized, there is a much higher likelihood of such variances. The responsibility for these variances rests with the manager who authorized the wage increase. Misallocation of the work force refers to using skilled workers in place of unskilled workers and vice versa. The use of an inexperienced worker instead of an experienced one will result in a favorable price variance because of the lower pay rate of the unskilled worker. An unfavorable price variance would result if the skilled worker were substituted for the inexperienced employee. The production department generally is responsible for labor price variances resulting from misallocation of the work force.

Labor quantity variances relate to the efficiency of workers. An investigation of the causes of a quantity variance generally focuses on the production department. The causes of an unfavorable variance may be poor training, worker fatigue, faulty machinery, or carelessness. These causes are the responsibility of the production department. However, if the excess time is due to inferior materials, the responsibility falls outside the production department.

Manufacturing Overhead Variances

Since the controllable variance relates to variable manufacturing costs, the responsibility for the variance rests with the production department. The cause of a variance may be (1) higher than expected use of indirect materials, indirect labor, and factory supplies or (2) increases in indirect manufacturing costs, such as fuel and maintenance costs.

The overhead volume variance is the responsibility of the production department if the cause is inefficient use of direct labor or machine breakdowns. However, when the cause is a lack of sales orders, the responsibility rests outside the production department.

Before You Go On . . .

1. What are the formulas for computing the total, price, and quantity variances for direct materials?

2. What are the formulas for computing the total, price, and quantity variances for direct labor?

3. What are the formulas for computing the total, controllable, and volume variances for manufacturing overhead?

Standard Cost Accounting System

A standard cost accounting system is a double-entry system of accounting in which standard costs are used in making entries and standard cost variances are formally recognized in the accounts. A standard cost system may be used with either job order or process costing. At this point, we will explain and illustrate a standard cost, job order cost accounting system. The system includes two important assumptions: (1) variances from standards are recognized at the earliest opportunity, and (2) the Work in Process account is maintained exclusively on the basis of standard costs. In practice, there are many variations among standard cost systems. However, the system described here should facilitate your transition to a specific company's system.

Study Objective 7

Enumerate the features of a standard cost accounting system.

Journal Entries

The transactions of Xonic, Inc., will be used to illustrate the journal entries. Note as you study the entries that the major difference between the entries here and those for the job order cost accounting system in Chapter 22 is the variance accounts.

1. Purchase raw materials on account for $13,020 when the standard cost is $12,600.

Raw Materials Inventory	12,600	
Materials Price Variance	420	
Accounts Payable		13,020
(To record purchase of materials)		

The inventory account is debited for actual quantities at standard cost. This enables the perpetual materials records to show actual quantities. The price variance, which is unfavorable, is debited to Materials Price Variance.

2. Incur direct labor costs of $20,580 when the standard labor cost is $21,000.

Factory Labor	21,000	
Labor Price Variance		420
Wages Payable		20,580
(To record direct labor costs)		

Like the raw materials inventory account, Factory Labor is debited for actual hours worked at the standard hourly rate of pay. In this case, the labor variance is favorable. Thus, Labor Price Variance is credited.

3. Incur actual manufacturing overhead costs of $10,900.

Manufacturing Overhead	10,900	
Accounts Payable/Cash/Acc. Depreciation		10,900
(To record overhead incurred)		

The controllable overhead variance is not recorded at this time. It is dependent on standard hours applied to work in process, which is not known at the time overhead is incurred.

4. Issue raw materials for production at a cost of $12,600 when the standard cost is $12,000.

Work in Process Inventory	12,000	
Materials Quantity Variance	600	
Raw Materials Inventory		12,600
(To record issuance of raw materials)		

Work in Process Inventory is debited for standard materials quantities used at standard prices. The variance account is debited because the variance is unfavorable. Raw Materials Inventory is credited for actual quantities at standard prices.

5. Assign factory labor to production at a cost of $21,000 when standard cost is $20,000.

Work in Process Inventory	20,000	
Labor Quantity Variance	1,000	
Factory Labor		21,000
(To assign factory labor to jobs)		

Work in Process Inventory is debited for standard labor hours at standard rates, and the unfavorable variance is debited to Labor Quantity Variance. The credit to Factory Labor produces a zero balance in this account.

6. Applying manufacturing overhead to production, $10,000.

Work in Process Inventory	10,000	
Manufacturing Overhead		10,000
(To assign overhead to jobs)		

Work in Process Inventory is debited for standard hours allowed multiplied by the standard overhead rate.

7. Transfer completed work to finished goods, $42,000.

Finished Goods Inventory	42,000	
Work in Process Inventory		42,000
(To record transfer of completed work to finished goods)		

In this example, both inventory accounts are at standard cost.

8. The 1,000 gallons of Weed-O are sold for $60,000.

Accounts Receivable	60,000	
Cost of Goods Sold	42,000	
Sales		60,000
Finished Goods Inventory		42,000
(To record sale of finished goods and the cost of goods sold)		

Cost of Goods Sold is debited at standard cost. Gross profit, in turn, is the difference between sales and the standard cost of goods sold.

9. Recognize unfavorable overhead variances: controllable, $500; volume, $400.

Overhead Controllable Variance	500	
Overhead Volume Variance	400	
Manufacturing Overhead		900
(To recognize overhead variances)		

This entry recognizes the overhead variances. Prior to this entry, a debit balance of $900 existed in Manufacturing Overhead. The above entry therefore produces a zero balance in the Manufacturing Overhead account. The information needed for this entry is often not available until the end of the accounting period.

Ledger Accounts

The cost accounts for Xonic, Inc. after posting the entries are as follows:

ILLUSTRATION 27-30

Cost accounts with variances

Helpful hint All debit balances in variance accounts indicate unfavorable variances; all credit balances indicate favorable balances.

Note that six variance accounts are included in the ledger. The remaining accounts are the same as those illustrated for a job order cost system in Chapter 22 in which only actual costs were used.

Statement Presentation of Variances

In income statements prepared for management under a standard cost accounting system, **cost of goods sold is stated at standard cost and the variances are separately disclosed**, as shown in Illustration 27-31. The statement is based entirely on the production and sale of Weed-O and assumes selling and administrative costs of $3,000.

ILLUSTRATION 27-31

Variances in income statement for management

XONIC, INC. Income Statement For the Month Ended June 30, 1993		
Sales		$60,000
Cost of goods sold (at standard)		42,000
Gross profit (at standard)		18,000
Variances		
Materials price	$ 420	
Materials quantity	600	
Labor price	(420)	
Labor quantity	1,000	
Overhead controllable	500	
Overhead volume	400	
Total variance (unfavorable)		2,500
Gross profit (actual)		15,500
Selling and administrative expenses		3,000
Net income		$12,500

Observe that each variance is shown, as well as the total variances. In this example, variations from standard costs reduced net income by $2,500.

In financial statements prepared for stockholders and other external users, standard costs may be used. The costing of inventories at standard costs is in accordance with generally accepted accounting principles when there are no significant differences between actual costs and standard costs. Hewlett-Packard and Westinghouse Electric, for example, report their inventories at standard costs. However, if there are significant differences between actual and standard costs, inventories and cost of goods sold must be reported at actual costs.

It is also possible to show the variances in an income statement prepared in the contribution margin format. To do so, it is necessary to analyze the overhead variances into variable and fixed components. This type of analysis is explained in cost accounting textbooks.

Before You Go On . . .

1. Does a debit balance in a variance account indicate favorable or unfavorable performance?

2. What entry is made to recognize overhead variances in the accounts?

3. How are standard costs and variances reported in income statements prepared for management?

Summary of Study Objectives

1. *Distinguish between a standard and a budget.* Both standards and budgets are predetermined costs. The primary difference is that a standard is a unit amount, whereas a budget is a total amount. A standard may be regarded as the budgeted cost per unit of product.

2. *Identify the advantages of standard costs.* Standard costs offer a number of advantages to an organization. They (a) facilitate management planning, (b) promote greater economy and efficiency, (c) are useful in setting selling prices, (d) contribute to management control, (e) permit "management by exception," and (f) simplify the costing of inventories and reduce clerical costs.

3. *Describe how standards are set.* The direct materials price standard should be based on the delivered cost of raw materials plus an allowance for receiving and handling. The direct materials quantity standard should establish the required quantity plus an allowance for waste and spoilage.

The direct labor price standard should be based on current wage rates and anticipated adjustments such as COLAs. In addition, it generally includes payroll taxes and fringe benefits. Direct labor quantity standards should be based on required production time plus an allowance for rest periods, cleanup, machine setup, and machine downtime.

For manufacturing overhead, a standard predetermined overhead rate is used based on an expected standard activity index such as standard direct labor hours or standard direct labor cost.

4. *Indicate the formulas for determining direct materials and direct labor variances.* The formulas for the direct materials variances are:

$$\begin{pmatrix} \text{Actual quantity} \\ \times \text{ Actual price} \end{pmatrix} - \begin{pmatrix} \text{Standard quantity} \\ \times \text{ Standard price} \end{pmatrix} = \begin{matrix}\text{Total}\\\text{materials}\\\text{variance}\end{matrix}$$

$$\begin{pmatrix} \text{Actual quantity} \\ \times \text{ Actual price} \end{pmatrix} - \begin{pmatrix} \text{Actual quantity} \\ \times \text{ Standard price} \end{pmatrix} = \begin{matrix}\text{Materials}\\\text{price}\\\text{variance}\end{matrix}$$

$$\begin{pmatrix} \text{Actual quantity} \\ \times \text{ Standard price} \end{pmatrix} - \begin{pmatrix} \text{Standard quantity} \\ \times \text{ Standard price} \end{pmatrix} = \begin{matrix}\text{Materials}\\\text{quantity}\\\text{variance}\end{matrix}$$

The formulas for the direct labor variances are:

$$\begin{pmatrix} \text{Actual hours} \\ \times \text{ Actual rate} \end{pmatrix} - \begin{pmatrix} \text{Standard hours} \\ \times \text{ Standard rate} \end{pmatrix} = \begin{matrix}\text{Total}\\\text{labor}\\\text{variance}\end{matrix}$$

$$\begin{pmatrix} \text{Actual hours} \\ \times \text{ Actual rate} \end{pmatrix} - \begin{pmatrix} \text{Actual hours} \\ \times \text{ Standard rate} \end{pmatrix} = \begin{matrix}\text{Labor}\\\text{price}\\\text{variance}\end{matrix}$$

$$\begin{pmatrix} \text{Actual hours} \\ \times \text{ Standard rate} \end{pmatrix} - \begin{pmatrix} \text{Standard hours} \\ \times \text{ Standard rate} \end{pmatrix} = \begin{matrix}\text{Labor}\\\text{quantity}\\\text{variance}\end{matrix}$$

5. *State the formulas for determining manufacturing overhead variances.* The formulas for the manufacturing overhead variances are:

$$\begin{matrix}\text{Actual}\\\text{overhead}\end{matrix} - \begin{matrix}\text{Overhead}\\\text{applied}\end{matrix} = \begin{matrix}\text{Total overhead}\\\text{variance}\end{matrix}$$

$$\begin{matrix}\text{Actual}\\\text{overhead}\end{matrix} - \begin{matrix}\text{Overhead}\\\text{budgeted}\end{matrix} = \begin{matrix}\text{Overhead control-}\\\text{lable variance}\end{matrix}$$

$$\begin{matrix}\text{Overhead}\\\text{budgeted}\end{matrix} - \begin{matrix}\text{Overhead}\\\text{applied}\end{matrix} = \begin{matrix}\text{Overhead volume}\\\text{variance}\end{matrix}$$

6. *Discuss the reporting of variances.* Variances are reported to management in variance reports. The reports facilitate management by exception because significant differences can be highlighted.

7. *Enumerate the features of a standard cost accounting system.* In a standard cost accounting system, standard costs are journalized and posted and separate variance accounts are maintained in the ledger. When differences between actual costs and standard costs do not differ significantly, inventories may be reported at standard costs.

GLOSSARY

Direct labor price standard · The rate per hour that should be incurred for direct labor. (p. 1087).

Direct labor quantity standard · The time that should be required to make one unit of product. (p. 1088).

Direct materials price standard · The cost per unit of direct materials that should be incurred. (p. 1087).

Direct materials quantity standard · The quantity of direct materials that should be used per unit of finished goods. (p. 1087).

Ideal standards · Standards based on the optimum level of performance under perfect operating conditions. (p. 1086).

Labor price (rate) variance · The difference between the actual hours times the actual rate and the actual hours times the standard rate. (p. 1093).

Labor quantity (efficiency) variance · The difference between actual hours times the standard rate and standard hours times the standard rate. (p. 1094).

Materials price variance · The difference between the actual quantity times the actual price and the actual quantity times the standard price. (p. 1091).

Materials quantity (use) variance · The difference between the actual quantity times the standard price and the standard quantity times the standard price. (p. 1092).

Normal standards · Standards based on an efficient level of performance that are attainable under expected operating conditions. (p. 1086).

Overhead controllable variance · The difference between actual overhead incurred and overhead budgeted for the standard hours allowed. (p. 1096).

Overhead volume variance · The difference between overhead budgeted for the standard hours allowed and the overhead applied. (p. 1097).

Standard cost accounting system · A double-entry system of accounting in which standard costs are used in making entries and variances are recognized in the accounts. (p. 1101).

Standard costs · Predetermined unit costs that are measures of performance. (p. 1084).

Standard hours allowed · The hours that should have been worked for the units produced. (p. 1095).

Standard predetermined overhead rate · An overhead rate based on an expected standard activity index. (p. 1088).

Total labor variance · The difference between actual hours times the actual rate and standard hours times the standard rate for labor. (p. 1093).

Total materials variance · The difference between the actual quantity times the actual price and the standard quantity times the standard price of materials. (p. 1091).

Total overhead variance · The difference between actual overhead costs and overhead costs applied to work done. (p. 1095).

Variances · The difference between total actual costs and total standard costs. (p. 1090).

DEMONSTRATION PROBLEM

The Manlow Company makes a cologne called Allure. The standard cost for one bottle of Allure is as follows:

Manufacturing Cost Elements	Standard Quantity	Price	Cost
Direct materials	6 oz.	× $ .90	$ 5.40
Direct labor	0.5 hrs.	× $12.00	6.00
Manufacturing overhead	0.5 hrs.	× $ 4.80	2.40
			$13.80

During the month, the following transactions occurred in manufacturing 10,000 bottles of Allure.

1. 58,000 ounces of materials were purchased at $1.00 per ounce.
2. All the materials purchased were used to produce the 10,000 bottles of Allure.
3. 4,900 direct labor hours were worked at a total labor cost of $56,350.
4. Variable manufacturing overhead incurred was $15,000 and fixed overhead incurred was $10,400.

The manufacturing overhead rate of $4.80 is based on a normal capacity of 5,200 direct labor hours. The total budget at this capacity is $10,400 fixed and $14,560 variable.

Instructions

Compute the total variance and the variances for each of the manufacturing cost elements.

Solution to Demonstration Problem

Total Variance

Actual costs incurred:		
Direct materials		$ 58,000
Direct labor		56,350
Manufacturing overhead		25,400
		139,750
Standard cost (10,000 × $13.80)		138,000
Total variance		$ 1,750 (U)

Direct Materials Variances

Total	=	$58,000	−	$54,000	= $4,000 U
		(58,000 × $1.00)		(60,000 × $.90)	
Price	=	$58,000	−	$52,200	= $5,800 U
		(58,000 × $1.00)		(58,000 × $.90)	
Quantity	=	$52,200	−	$54,000	= $1,800 F
		(58,000 × $.90)		(60,000 × $.90)	

Direct Labor Variances

Total	=	$56,350	−	$60,000	= $3,650 F
		(4,900 × $11.50)		(5,000 × $12.00)	
Price	=	$56,350	−	$58,800	= $2,450 F
		(4,900 × $11.50)		(4,900 × $12.00)	
Quantity	=	$58,800	−	$60,000	= $1,200 F
		(4,900 × $12.00)		(5,000 × $12.00)	

Overhead variances

Total	=	$25,400	−	$24,000	= $1,400 U
		($15,000 + $10,400)		(5,000 × $4.80)	
Controllable	=	$25,400	−	$24,400	= $1,000 U
		($15,000 + $10,400)		($14,000 + $10,400)	
Volume	=	$24,400	−	$24,000	= $ 400 U
		($14,000 + $10,400)		(5,000 × $4.80)	

Helpful hints

1. Check to make sure the total variance and the sum of the individual variances are equal.
2. Find the price variance first; then the quantity variance.
3. Budgeted overhead costs are based on flexible budget data.
4. Overhead applied is based on standard hours allowed.
5. Actual hours worked is not relevant in computing overhead variances.
6. The overhead volume variance relates solely to fixed costs.

SELF-STUDY QUESTIONS

Answers are at the end of the chapter.

(S.O. 1) 1. Standards differ from budgets in that:
    a. budgets may be used in valuing inventories but not standards.
    b. budgets may be journalized and posted but not standards.
    c. only budgets contribute to management planning and control.
    d. budgets are a total amount and standards are a unit amount.

(S.O. 2) 2. The advantages of standard costs include all the following except:
    a. management by exception may be used.
    b. management planning is facilitated.

    c. management must use a static budget.
    d. they may simplify the costing of inventories.

3. The setting of standards is: (S.O. 3)
    a. a management decision.
    b. a managerial accountant decision.
    c. a worker decision.
    d. preferably set at the ideal level of performance.

4. Each of the following formulas is correct (S.O. 4) except:
    a. Materials price variance = (actual quantity × actual cost) − (standard quantity × standard cost).

b. Labor price variance = (actual hours × actual rate) − (actual hours × standard rate).

c. Overhead controllable variance = actual overhead − overhead budgeted.

d. Overhead volume variance = overhead budgeted − overhead applied.

(S.O. 4)   5. In producing product AA, 6,300 pounds of direct materials were used at a cost of $1.10 per pound when the standard was 6,000 pounds at $1 per pound. The direct materials quantity variance is:

a. $300 unfavorable.

b. $330 unfavorable.

c. $600 unfavorable.

d. $630 unfavorable.

(S.O. 4)   6. In producing product ZZ, 14,800 direct labor hours were used at a rate of $8.20 per hour when the standard was 15,000 hours at $8.00 per hour. Based on these data, the direct labor:

a. quantity variance is $1,600 unfavorable.

b. price variance is $2,960 favorable.

c. price variance is $3,000 unfavorable.

d. quantity variance is $1,600 favorable.

(S.O. 5)   7. Which of the following is correct about overhead variances?

a. The controllable variance generally pertains to fixed overhead costs.

b. The volume variance pertains solely to variable overhead costs.

c. Budgeted overhead costs are based on the flexible overhead budget.

d. Standard hours actually worked are used in each variance.

8. The formula for computing the total overhead variance is: (S.O. 5)

a. overhead budgeted less overhead applied.

b. actual overhead less overhead applied.

c. actual overhead less overhead budgeted.

d. no correct answer given.

9. Which of the following is incorrect about variance reports?   (S.O. 6)

a. They should only be sent to the top level of management.

b. They facilitate "management by exception.

c. They should be prepared as soon as possible.

d. They may vary in form, content, and frequency among companies.

10. Which of the following is incorrect about a standard cost accounting system?   (S.O. 7)

a. It is applicable to job order costing.

b. It is applicable to process costing.

c. It keeps separate accounts for each variance.

d. It is a single-entry system.

QUESTIONS

1. Marian Mota claims that standards and budgets are entirely different. Is Marian correct? Explain.

2. Mark Nero claims that there are important accounting differences between standards and budgets. Is Mark correct? Explain.

3. Standard costs facilitate management planning. What are the other advantages of standard costs?

4. Contrast the roles of the management accountant and management in setting standard costs.

5. Distinguish between an ideal standard and a normal standard.

6. What factors should be considered in setting (a) the materials price standard, and (b) the materials quantity standard?

7. The objective in setting the direct labor quantity standard is to determine the aggregate time required to make one unit of product. Do you agree? What allowances should be made in setting this standard?

8. How is the predetermined overhead rate determined when standard costs are used?

9. What is the difference between a favorable cost variance and an unfavorable cost variance?

10. In each of the following formulas, supply the words that should be inserted for each number in parentheses.
(a) (Actual quantity × (1)) − (standard quantity × (2)) = total materials variance.
(b) ((3) × actual price) − (actual quantity × (4)) = materials price variance.
(c) (Actual quantity × (5)) ((6) × standard price) = materials quantity variance.

11. In the direct labor variance matrix, there are three factors: (1) actual hours × actual rate, (2) actual hours × standard rate, and (3) standard hours × standard rate. Using the numbers, indicate the formulas for each of the direct labor variances.

12. The Dant Company's standard predetermined overhead rate is $8.00 per direct labor hour. For the month of June, 26,000 actual hours were worked and 27,000 standard hours were allowed. Normal capacity hours were 28,000. How much overhead was applied?

13. If the $8.00 per hour overhead rate in question 12 consists of $5.00 variable, and actual overhead costs were $218,000, what is the overhead controllable variance for June? Is the variance favorable or unfavorable?

14. Using the data in questions 12 and 13, what is the overhead volume variance for June? Is the variance favorable or unfavorable?

15. What is the purpose of computing the overhead volume variance? What is the basic formula for this variance?

16. Helen Hart does not understand why the overhead volume variance indicates that fixed overhead costs are under- or overapplied. Clarify this matter for Helen.

17. Stu Stone is attempting to outline the important points about overhead variances on a class examination. List four points that Stu should include in his outline.

18. How often should variances be reported to management? What principle may be used with variance reports?

19. What circumstances may cause the purchasing department to be responsible for both an unfavorable materials price variance and an unfavorable materials quantity variance?

20. (a) Explain the basic features of a standard cost accounting system. (b) What type of balance will exist in the variance account when (1) the materials price variance is unfavorable and (2) the labor quantity variance is favorable?

21. (a) How are variances reported in income statements prepared for management? (b) May standard costs be used in preparing financial statements for stockholders? Explain.

BRIEF EXERCISES

BE27–1 The Worley Company uses both standards and budgets. For the year, estimated production of Product X is 400,000 units. Total estimated cost for materials and labor are $1,200,000 and $1,600,000. Compute the estimates for (a) a standard cost and (b) a budgeted cost.

Distinguish between a standard and a budget.
(S.O. 1)

BE27–2 The Ward Company accumulates the following data concerning raw materials in making one gallon of finished product: (1) Price—net purchase price $3.20, freight-in $.20 and receiving and handling $.30; (2) quantity—required materials 2.6 pounds, allowance for waste and spoilage .4 pounds. Compute the (a) standard direct materials price per gallon; (b) standard direct materials quantity per gallon and (c) total standard material cost per gallon.

Set direct materials standard.
(S.O. 3)

BE27–3 Labor data for making one gallon of finished product in the Ward Company are as follows: (1) Price—hourly wage rate $10.00, payroll taxes $.80, and fringe benefits $1.20; (2) Quantity—actual production time 1.1 hours, rest periods and clean up .25 hours, and setup and downtime .15 hours. Compute the (a) standard direct labor rate per hour; (b) standard direct labor hours per gallon and (c) the standard labor cost per gallon.

Set direct labor standard.
(S.O. 3)

Compute direct materials variances.
(S.O. 4)

BE27–4 The Midal Company's standard materials cost per unit of output is $10 (2 pounds × $5.00). During July, the company uses 3,200 pounds of materials costing $16,640 in making 1,500 units of finished product. Compute the total, price, and quantity direct materials variances.

Compute direct labor variances.
(S.O. 4)

BE27–5 The Renown Company's standard labor cost per unit of output is $20 (2 hours × $10.00 per hour). During August, the company incurs 1,900 hours of direct labor at an hourly cost of $9.50 per hour in making 1,000 units of finished product. Compute the total, price, and quantity direct labor variances.

Compute total manufacturing overhead variance.
(S.O. 5)

BE27–6 In October, Hooper Company reports 21,000 actual direct labor hours and it incurs $102,000 of manufacturing overhead costs. Standard hours allowed for the work done is 20,000 hours and the predetermined overhead rate is $5.00 per direct labor hour. Compute the total manufacturing overhead variance.

Compute the manufacturing overhead controllable variance.
(S.O. 5)

BE27–7 Some overhead data for the Hooper Company are given in BE27–6. In addition, the flexible manufacturing overhead budget shows that budgeted costs are $4.00 variable per direct labor hour and $24,000 fixed. Compute the manufacturing overhead controllable variance.

Compute overhead volume variance. (S.O. 5)

BE27–8 Using the data in BE27–6 and BE27–7, compute the manufacturing overhead volume variance.

Journalize materials variances.
(S.O. 7)

BE27–9 Journalize the following transactions for Morey Manufacturing.

1. Purchased 6,000 units of raw materials on account for $12,600 when the standard cost was $12,000.

2. Issued 5,100 units of raw materials costing $10,710 for production when the standard units were 5,000.

Journalize labor variances.
(S.O. 7)

BE27–10 Journalize the following transactions for Hebert Manufacturing.

1. Incurred direct labor costs for 3,000 hours of $24,600 when the standard labor cost was $24,000.

2. Assigned 3,000 direct labor hours costing $24,600 to production when standard hours were 3,200.

EXERCISES

Compute standard materials costs.
(S.O. 3)

S

E27–1 Robin Renn manufactures and sells homemade wine, and she wants to develop a standard cost per gallon. The following are required for production of a 50-gallon batch:

3,000 ounces of grape concentrate at $.02 per ounce
55 pounds of granulated sugar at $.30 per pound
60 lemons at $.65 each
50 yeast tablets at $.25 each
50 nutrient tablets at $.15 each
2,500 ounces of water at $.004 per ounce

Robin estimates that 4% of the grape concentrate is wasted, 12% of the sugar is lost, and 20% of the lemons cannot be used.

Instructions
Compute the standard cost of the ingredients for one gallon of wine. (Carry computations to three decimal places.)

Compute materials price and quantity variances.
(S.O. 4)

E27–2 The standard cost of Product B manufactured by the Key Company includes 3 units of direct materials at $5.00 per unit. During June, 30,000 units of direct materials are purchased at a cost of $4.60 per unit, and 27,600 units of direct materials are used to produce 9,000 units of Product B.

Instructions

(a) Compute the materials price and quantity variances.

(b) Repeat (a), assuming the purchase price is $5.20 and the quantity used is 26,400 units.

E27–3 The Garcia Company's standard labor cost of producing one unit of Product DD is 4 hours at the rate of $12.00 per hour. During August, 40,500 hours of labor are incurred at a cost of $12.10 per hour to produce 10,000 units of Product DD.

Compute labor price and quantity variances.
(S.O. 4)

Instructions

(a) Compute the labor price and quantity variances.

(b) Repeat (a), assuming the standard is 4.2 hours of direct labor at $12.40 per hour.

E27–4 Kotton, Inc., which produces a single product, has prepared the following standard cost sheet for one unit of the product.

Compute materials and labor variances.
(S.O. 4)

Direct materials (8 pounds at $2.50 per pound)	$20.00
Direct labor (3 hours at $12.00 per hour)	$36.00

During the month of April, the company manufactures 240 units and incurs the following actual costs:

Direct materials (1,900 pounds)	$4,940
Direct labor (700 hours)	$7,700

Instructions

Compute the total, price, and quantity variances for materials and labor.

E27–5 Data for Kotten, Inc. are given in E27–4.

Journalize entries for materials and labor variances.
(S.O. 7)

Instructions

Journalize the entries to record the materials and labor variances.

E27–6 The following direct materials and direct labor data pertain to the operations of Timms Manufacturing Company for the month of August.

Compute the materials and labor variances and list reasons for unfavorable variances.
(S.O. 4, 6)

Costs		Quantities	
Actual labor rate	$13.00 per hour	Actual hours incurred and used	4,200 hours
Actual materials price	$126.00 per ton	Actual quantity of materials purchased and used	1,250 tons
Standard labor rate	$12.00 per hour	Standard hours used	4,300 hours
Standard materials price	$130.00 per ton	Standard quantity of materials used	1,200 tons

Instructions

(a) Compute the total, price, and quantity variances for materials and labor.

(b) List two possible explanations for each of the unfavorable variances calculated above and suggest where responsibility for the unfavorable result might be placed.

E27–7 The following information was taken from the annual manufacturing overhead cost budget of the Starz Company:

Compute manufacturing overhead variances and interpret findings.
(S.O. 5)

Variable manufacturing overhead costs	$33,000
Fixed manufacturing overhead costs	$20,625
Normal production level in hours	16,500
Normal production level in units	4,125

During the year, 4,000 units were produced, 16,100 hours were worked, and the actual manufacturing overhead was $53,000. Actual fixed manufacturing overhead costs equaled budgeted fixed manufacturing overhead costs. Overhead is applied on the basis of direct labor hours.

Instructions

(a) Compute the total, fixed, and variable predetermined manufacturing overhead rates.

(b) Compute the total, controllable, and volume overhead variances.

(c) Briefly interpret the overhead controllable and volume variances computed in (b).

Compute overhead variances and journalize transactions and adjusting entry.
(S.O. 5, 7)

E27–8   Manufacturing overhead data for the production of Product H by the Parker Company are as follows:

Overhead incurred for 51,000 actual direct labor hours worked	$212,000
Overhead rate (variable $3.00; fixed $1.00) at normal capacity of 54,000 direct labor hours	$ 4.00
Standard hours allowed for work done	52,000

Instructions

(a) Compute the total, controllable, and volume overhead variances.

(b) Journalize the incurrence of the overhead costs and the application of overhead to the job, assuming a standard cost accounting system is used.

(c) Prepare the adjusting entry for the overhead variances.

Prepare a variance report for direct labor.
(S.O. 4, 6)

E27–9   During March, 1993, the Tenze Tool & Die Company worked on four jobs. A review of direct labor costs reveals the following summary data:

Job Number	Actual Hours	Actual Costs	Standard Hours	Standard Costs	Total Variance
A257	220	$4,400	225	$4,500	$ 100 F
A258	450	9,900	420	8,400	1,500 U
A259	300	6,150	300	6,000	150 U
A260	116	2,088	110	2,200	112 F
Total variance					$1,438 U

Analysis reveals that Job A257 was a repeat job. Job A258 was a rush order that required overtime work at premium rates of pay. Job A259 required a more experienced replacement worker on one shift. Work on Job A260 was done for one day by a new trainee when a regular worker was absent.

Instructions
Prepare a report for the plant supervisor on direct labor cost variances for March. The report should have columns for (1) Job No., (2) Actual Hours, (3) Standard Hours, (4) Labor Quantity Variance, (5) Actual Rate, (6) Standard Rate, (7) Labor Price Variance, and (8) Explanations.

Prepare income statement for management.
(S.O. 7)

E27–10   Artis Company uses a standard cost accounting system. During January, the company reported the following manufacturing variances:

Material price variance	$1,250 debit	Labor quantity variance	$ 725 debit
Material quantity variance	700 credit	Overhead controllable	200 credit
Labor price variance	525 debit	Overhead volume	1,000 debit

In addition, 6,000 units of product were sold at $8.00 per unit. Each unit sold had a standard cost of $6.00. Selling and administrative expenses were $8,000 for the month.

Instructions
Prepare an income statement for management for the month ending January 31, 1993.

Journalize entries in a standard cost accounting system.
(S.O. 7)

E27–11   The Dutton Company installed a standard cost system on January 1. Selected transactions for the month of January are as follows:

1. Purchased 20,000 units of raw materials on account at a cost of $3.20 per unit. Standard cost was $3.00 per unit.

2. Issued 17,000 units of raw materials for jobs that required 17,500 standard units of raw materials.

3. Incurred 15,100 actual hours of direct labor at an actual rate of $4.90 per hour. The standard rate is $5.00 per hour. (Credit Wages Payable)

4. Performed 15,100 hours of direct labor on jobs when standard hours were 15,300.

5. Applied overhead to jobs at the rate of 100% of direct labor cost.

Instructions

Journalize the January transactions.

Answer questions concerning missing entries and balances. (S.O. 4, 5, 7)

E27–12 The La Rosa Company uses a standard cost accounting system. Some of the ledger accounts have been destroyed in a fire. The controller asks your help in reconstructing some missing entries and balances.

Instructions

Answer the following questions:

(a) Materials Price Variance shows a $3,400 favorable balance, and Accounts Payable shows $128,000 of raw materials purchases. What was the amount debited to Raw Materials Inventory for raw materials purchased?

(b) Materials Quantity Variance shows a $3,000 unfavorable balance, and Work in Process Inventory shows $124,000 for direct materials used. What was the amount credited to Raw Materials Inventory for direct materials used?

(c) Labor Price Variance shows a $1,500 unfavorable balance, and Factory Labor shows a debit of $151,000 for wages incurred. What was the amount credited to Wages Payable?

(d) Factory Labor shows a credit of $151,000 for direct labor used, and Labor Quantity Variance shows an $900 unfavorable balance. What was the amount debited to Work in Process for direct labor used?

(e) Overhead applied to Work in Process totaled $168,000. If the total overhead variance was $1,200 unfavorable, what was the amount of overhead costs debited to Manufacturing Overhead?

(f) Overhead Controllable Variance shows a debit balance of $1,500. What was the amount and type of balance (debit or credit) in Overhead Volume Variance?

PROBLEMS

Compute variances, and prepare income statement. (S.O. 4, 5, 7)

P27–1 Tomay Manufacturing Company uses a standard cost accounting system. In July, 1993, it accumulates the following data relative to jobs started and finished:

Cost and Production Data	Actual	Standard
Raw materials		
Units purchased	17,500	
Units used	17,500	18,000
Unit cost	$3.20	$3.00
Direct labor		
Hours worked	2,900	3,000
Hourly rate	$11.80	$12.00
Manufacturing overhead		
Incurred	$87,200	
Applied		$90,000

Manufacturing overhead was applied on the basis of direct labor hours. Normal capacity for the month was 2,800 direct labor hours. At normal capacity, budgeted overhead costs were: variable $56,000 and fixed $28,000.

Jobs finished during the month were sold for $240,000; selling and administrative expenses were $25,000.

Instructions

(a) Compute all of the variances for direct materials, direct labor, and manufacturing overhead.

(b) Prepare an income statement for management. Ignore income taxes.

Compute variances and prepare income statement. (S.O. 4, 5, 7)

P27–2 The Haft Corporation manufactures a single product. The standard cost per unit of product is as follows:

Direct materials—2 pounds of plastic at $5.00 per pound	$10.00
Direct labor—2 hours at $12.00 per hour	24.00
Variable manufacturing overhead	12.00
Fixed manufacturing overhead	6.00
Total standard cost per unit	$52.00

The master manufacturing overhead budget for the year based on normal productive capacity of 180,000 direct labor hours (90,000 units) shows total variable costs of $1,080,000 and total fixed costs of $540,000. Overhead is applied on the basis of direct labor hours. Actual costs for November in producing 7,600 units were as follows:

Direct materials (14,900 pounds)	$ 73,010
Direct labor (14,800 hours)	180,560
Variable overhead	90,700
Fixed overhead	45,000
Total manufacturing costs	$389,270

The purchasing department normally buys the quantities of raw materials that are expected to be used in production each month. Raw materials inventories, therefore, can be ignored.

Instructions

(a) Compute all of the materials, labor, and overhead variances.

(b) Prepare an income statement for management for the month ending November 30, 1993, assuming (1) 7,500 units were sold at $90 per unit and (2) selling and administrative expenses were $80,000. Ignore income taxes.

Compute variances, journalize entries, and identify significant variances.
(S.O. 4, 5, 6, 7)

P27–3 Top-Value Clothiers manufactures women's business suits. The company uses a standard cost accounting system. In March 1993, 12,000 suits were made. The following standard and actual cost data applied to the month of March when normal capacity was 15,000 direct labor hours.

Cost Element	Standard (per unit)	Actual
Direct materials	5 yards at $7.00 per yard	$416,100 for 57,000 yards ($7.30 per yard)
Direct labor	1.0 hours at $12.00 per hour	$121,000 for 11,000 hours ($11.00 per hour)
Overhead	1.0 hours at $9.00 per hour (fixed $6.00; variable $3.00)	$90,000 fixed overhead $48,000 variable overhead

Overhead is applied on the basis of direct labor hours. At normal capacity, budgeted fixed overhead costs were $90,000 and budgeted variable overhead costs were $45,000.

Instructions

(a) Compute the total, price, and quantity variances for (1) materials and (2) labor, and the total, controllable, and volume variances for manufacturing overhead.

(b) Journalize the entries to record the variances assuming (1) all purchases of materials were on account and (2) Wage Payable was credited for factory labor incurred.

(c) Which of the materials and labor variances should be investigated if management considers a variance of more than 7% from standard to be significant?

Journalize and post standard cost entries and prepare income statement.
(S.O. 4, 5, 7)

P27–4 Reid Manufacturing Company uses standard costs with its job order cost accounting system. In January, an order (Job 84) was received for 4,000 units of Product D. The standard cost of 1 unit of Product D is as follows:

Direct materials—1.5 pounds at $4.00 per pound	$ 6.00
Direct labor—1 hour at $9.00 per pound	9.00
Overhead—1 hour (variable $6.00; fixed $10.00)	16.00
Standard cost per unit	$31.00

Overhead is applied on the basis of direct labor hours. Normal capacity for the month of January was 4,500 direct labor hours. During January, the following transactions applicable to Job No. 84 occurred.

1. Purchased 6,250 pounds of raw materials on account at $3.80 per pound.
2. Requisitioned 6,250 pounds of raw materials for production.
3. Incurred 3,900 hours of direct labor at $9.20 hour.
4. Worked 3,900 hours of direct labor on Job No. 84.
5. Incurred $66,650 of manufacturing overhead on account.
6. Applied overhead to Job No. 84 on the basis of direct labor hours.
7. Transferred Job No. 84 to finished goods.
8. Billed customer for Job No. 84 at a selling price of $250,000.
9. Incurred selling and administrative expenses on account, $61,000.

Instructions

(a) Journalize the transactions.

(b) Post to the job order cost accounts.

(c) Prepare the entry to recognize the overhead variances.

(d) Prepare the income statement for management for January 1993.

P27–5 Oker Manufacturing Company uses a standard cost accounting system. In 1993, 33,000 units were produced. Each unit took several pounds of direct materials and 1⅓ standard hours of direct labor at a standard hourly rate of $12.00. Normal capacity was 42,000 direct labor hours. During the year, 130,000 pounds of raw materials were purchased at $.94 per pound. All pounds purchased were used during the year.

Answer questions about variances.
(S.O. 4, 5, 7)

Instructions

Answer the following questions:

(a) If the materials price variance was $5,200 unfavorable, what was the standard materials price per pound?

(b) If the materials quantity variance is $1,800 favorable, what was the standard materials quantity per unit?

(c) What were the standard hours allowed for the units produced?

(d) If the labor quantity variance is $9,600 unfavorable, what were the actual direct labor hours worked?

(e) If the labor price variance is $11,200 favorable, what was the actual rate per hour?

(f) If total budgeted manufacturing overhead was $315,000 at normal capacity, what was the predetermined overhead rate?

(g) What was the standard cost per unit of product?

(h) How much overhead was applied to production during the year?

(i) If the fixed overhead rate was $2.50, what was the overhead volume variance?

(j) If the overhead controllable variance is $3,000 favorable, what were the total variable overhead costs incurred?

(k) Using selected answers above, what were the total costs assigned to work in process?

ALTERNATE PROBLEMS

P27–1A The Tabler Manufacturing Corporation accumulates the following data relative to jobs started and finished during the month of June 1993:

Compute variances and prepare income statement.
(S.O. 4, 5, 7)

Costs and Production Data	Actual	Standard
Raw materials purchases, 10,400 units	$21,840	$20,000
Raw materials units used	10,400	10,000
Direct labor payroll	$122,100	$120,000
Direct labor hours worked	14,800	15,000
Manufacturing overhead incurred	$178,200	
Manufacturing overhead applied		$180,000
Machine hours expected to be used at normal capacity		42,500
Budgeted fixed overhead for June		$42,500
Variable overhead rate per hour		$3.00

Overhead is applied on the basis of standard machine hours. Three hours of machine time are required for each direct labor hour. The jobs were sold for $400,000; selling and administrative expenses were $40,000.

Instructions

(a) Compute all of the variances for direct materials, direct labor, and manufacturing overhead.

(b) Prepare an income statement for management. Ignore income taxes.

Compute variances and prepare income statement.
(S.O. 4, 5, 6, 7)

P27–2A   Carmor Corporation manufactures a single product. The standard cost per unit of product is shown below:

Direct materials—1 pound plastic at $7.00 per pound	$ 7.00
Direct labor—1.5 hours at $12.00 per hour	18.00
Variable manufacturing overhead	11.25
Fixed manufacturing overhead	3.75
Total standard cost per unit	$40.00

The predetermined manufacturing overhead rate is $10 per direct labor hour ($15.00 ÷ 1.5). This rate was computed from a master manufacturing overhead budget based on normal production of 90,000 direct labor hours (60,000 units) for the year. The master budget showed total variable costs of $675,000 and total fixed costs of $225,000. Actual costs for October in producing 4,800 units were as follows:

Direct materials (5,100 pounds)	$ 37,230
Direct labor (7,000 hours)	87,500
Variable overhead	57,170
Fixed overhead	18,750
Total manufacturing costs	$200,650

The purchasing department normally buys the quantitites of raw materials that are expected to be used in production each month. Raw materials inventories, therefore, can be ignored.

Instructions

(a) Compute all of the materials, labor, and overhead variances.

(b) Prepare an income statement for management for the month ending October 31, 1994, assuming 4,400 units were sold at $65 per unit and selling and administrative expenses were $35,000. Ignore income taxes.

Compute variances, journalize entries, and identify significant variances.
(S.O. 4, 5, 6, 7)

P27–3A   Quality Clothiers is a small company that manufactures tall men's suits. The company has used a standard cost accounting system. In May 1994, 11,250 suits were produced. The following standard and actual cost data applied to the month of May when normal capacity was 14,000 direct labor hours.

Cost Element	Standard (per unit)	Actual
Direct materials	8 yards at $4.50 per yard	$364,000 for 91,000 yards ($4.00 per yard)
Direct labor	1.2 hours at $13.00 per hour	$189,000 for 14,000 hours ($13.50 per hour)
Overhead	1.2 hours at $6.00 per hour (fixed $3.50; variable $2.50)	$49,000 fixed overhead $34,500 variable overhead

Overhead is applied on the basis of direct labor hours. At normal capacity, budgeted fixed overhead costs were $49,000 and budgeted variable overhead was $35,000.

Instructions

(a) Compute the total, price, and quantity variances for (1) materials and (2) labor, and the total, controllable, and volume variances for manufacturing overhead.

(b) Journalize the entries to record the variances assuming (1) all purchases of materials were on account and (2) Wages Payable was credited for factory labor incurred.

(c) Which of the materials and labor variances should be investigated if management considers a variance of more than 8% from standard to be significant?

P27-4A The LeMar Corporation uses standard costs with its job order cost accounting system. In January, an order (Job No. 12) for 2,000 units of Product B was received. The standard cost of 1 unit of Product B is as follows:

Journalize and post standard cost entries and prepare income statement.
(S.O. 4, 5, 7)

Direct materials	3 pounds at $1.00 per pound	$ 3.00
Direct labor	1 hour at $8.00 per hour	8.00
Overhead	2 hours (Variable $4.00 per machine hour; fixed $2.00 per machine hour)	12.00
Standard cost per unit		$23.00

Normal capacity for the month was 4,200 machine hours. During January, the following transactions applicable to Job No. 12 occurred:

1. Purchased 6,100 pounds of raw materials on account at $1.20 per pound.
2. Requisitioned 6,100 pounds of raw materials for Job No. 12.
3. Incurred 2,200 hours of direct labor at a rate of $7.80 per hour.
4. Worked 2,200 hours of direct labor on Job No. 12.
5. Incurred manufacturing overhead on account $24,300.
6. Applied overhead to Job No. 12 on basis of standard machine hours used.
7. Completed Job No. 12.
8. Billed customer for Job No. 12 at a selling price of $70,000.
9. Incurred selling and administrative expenses on account $2,000.

Instructions

(a) Journalize the transactions.

(b) Post to the job order cost accounts.

(c) Prepare the entry to recognize the overhead variances.

(d) Prepare the January 1994 income statement for management.

P27-5A Olay Manufacturing Company uses a standard cost accounting system. In 1994, 30,000 units were produced. Each unit took several pounds of direct materials and 1½ standard hours of direct labor at a standard hourly rate of $12.00. Normal capacity was 50,000 direct labor hours. During the year, 124,000 pounds of raw materials were purchased at $.96 per pound. All pounds purchased were used during the year.

Answer questions about variances.
(S.O. 4, 5, 7)

Instructions

Answer the following questions:

(a) If the materials price variance was $4,960 favorable, what was the standard materials price per pound?

(b) If the materials quantity variance is $4,000 unfavorable, what was the standard materials quantity per unit?

(c) What were the standard hours allowed for the units produced?

(d) If the labor quantity variance is $7,200 unfavorable, what were the actual direct labor hours worked?

(e) If the labor price variance is $9,120 favorable, what was the actual rate per hour?

(f) If total budgeted manufacturing overhead was $350,000 at normal capacity, what was the predetermined overhead rate?

(g) What was the standard cost per unit of product?

(h) How much overhead was applied to production during the year?

(i) If the fixed overhead rate was $2.00, what was the overhead volume variance?

(j) If the overhead controllable variance is $3,000 unfavorable, what were the total variable overhead costs incurred?

(k) Using one or more answers above, what were the total costs assigned to work in process?

Broadening Your Perspective

DECISION CASE 1

The Mason Company is going to expand its punch press department. The company is about to purchase several new punch presses from Equipment Manufacturers, Inc. Equipment Manufacturers' engineers report that their mechanical studies indicate that for Mason's intended use, the output rate for one press should be 1,000 pieces per hour. The Mason Company has similar presses now in operation. At present, production from these presses averages 600 pieces per hour.

A detailed study of the Mason Company's experience shows that the average is derived from the following individual outputs:

Worker	Output per hour (pieces)
J. Smith	750
H. Brown	750
R. Jones	600
J. Hardy	550
P. Clark	500
B. Randall	450
Total	3,600
Average	600

Mason's management also plans to institute a standard cost accounting system in the near future. The company's engineers are supporting a standard based on 1,000 pieces per hour; the accounting department is arguing for a standard of 750 pieces per hour; and the department supervisor is arguing for a standard of 600 pieces per hour.

Instructions

(a) What arguments would each proponent be likely to use to support his or her case?

(b) Which alternative best reconciles the needs of cost control and motivation for improved performance? Explain the reasons for your choice.

(CMA adapted)

DECISION CASE 2

Planning Professionals, a management consulting firm, specializes in strategic planning for financial institutions. Tom Allen and Beth Mears, partners in the firm, are assembling a new strategic planning model for use by clients. The model is designed for use on most microcomputers and replaces a rather lengthy manual model currently marketed by the firm. To market the new model Tom and Beth will need to provide clients with an estimate of the number of labor hours and computer time needed to operate the model. The model is currently being test marketed at five small financial institutions. These financial institutions are listed below, along with the number of combined computer/labor hours used by each institution to run the model one time.

Financial Institutions	Computer/Labor Hours Required
Midland National	25
First State	45
Financial Federal	40
Pacific America	30
Lakeview National	30
Total	170
Average	34

Any company that purchases the new model will need to purchase user manuals to access and operate the system. Also required are specialized computer forms that are only sold by Planning Professionals. User manuals will be sold to clients in cases of 20 at a cost of $300 per case. One manual must be used each time the model is run because each manual includes a nonreusable computer accessed password for operating the system. The specialized computer forms are sold in packages of 250 costing $50 per package. One application of the model requires the use of 50 forms. This sum includes two forms that are generally wasted in each application due to printer alignment errors. The overall cost of the strategic planning model to user clients is $12,000. Most clients will use the model four times annually.

Planning Professionals must provide its clients with estimates of ongoing costs incurred in operating the new strategic planning model. They would like to provide this information in the form of standard costs.

Instructions

(a) What factors should be considered in setting a standard for computer/labor hours?

(b) What alternatives for setting a standard for computer/labor hours might be used?

(c) What standard for computer/labor hours would you select? Justify your answer.

(d) Determine the standard material cost associated with the user manuals and computer forms for each application of the strategic planning model.

CRITICAL THINKING CASE

Refer to the data pertaining to the Sanford Corp. at the beginning of this chapter, and answer the following questions:

1. Should predetermined unit costs be based on normal or ideal manufacturing activity?

2. What factor is critical in controlling costs? How might Sanford improve its control over this factor?

3. For internal reporting to top management, should Sanford report actual costs, standard costs, or both? Why?

4. In financial statements for stockholders, should Sanford report actual costs, standard costs, or both? Why?

ETHICAL CASE

In Camden Manufacturing Company production workers in the painting department are paid on the basis of productivity. The labor time standard for a unit of product is established through periodic time studies conducted by the Manpower Management Department. In a time study, the actual time required to complete a specific task by a worker is observed. Allowances are then made for preparation time, rest periods, and clean up time. Joe Jorken is one of several veterans in the painting department.

Joe is informed by Manpower Management that he will be used in the time study for the painting of a new product. The findings will be the basis for establishing the labor time standard for the next six months. During the test, Joe deliberately slows his normal work pace in an effort to obtain a labor time standard that will be easy to meet. Because it is a new product, the Manpower Management representative who conducted the test is unaware that Joe did not give the test his best effort.

Instructions

(a) Who was benefitted and who was harmed by Joe's actions?

(b) Was Joe ethical in the way he performed the time study test?

(c) What measure(s) might the company take to obtain valid data for setting the labor time standard?

Answers to Self-Study Questions
1. d   2. c   3. a   4. a   5. a   6. d   7. c   8. b   9. a   10. d

INCREMENTAL ANALYSIS
AND CAPITAL BUDGETING

S hould radio station WLHA, the voice of the University of Wisconsin at Madison, upgrade its power from 10 to 400 watts? That's the capital budgeting decision facing not only the station but also the students—because they would foot the bill.

The station's annual operating budget is $2,000, used mostly for upkeep. The money comes from solicitation campaigns in student dormitories. Because the Federal Communications Commission classifies the station as non-commercial, it is not allowed to accept advertising. "The university already applied to the FCC to become commercial, but was denied because there wasn't room on the dial," says Scooter Pegram, the station manager. Pegram, 25, worked in commercial radio for five years— and then decided to come back to school to get a degree.

In addition to the $2,000 annual budget, the station has fundraisers to pay for items such as ceiling tiles and minor engineering equipment. "We just sold off some old transmitters," says Pegram. "For promotional purposes, we'll trade airtime for pizzas and records."

Pegram says the station provides an important source of information for the student community. "If everything goes well, we'll make an upgrade to 400 watts. We'll need to hire a consulting engineer for about $1,500, and then it will cost, say, $5,000 to upgrade our equipment. Once the FCC approves the upgrade, then we'll go to each of the dorms and ask them for money," he says. "The payback isn't primarily in dollars. There are smaller campuses that have powerful radio stations and we should have that here."

An important purpose of management accounting is to provide management with relevant information for decision making. Examples of these decisions might include:

1. WLHA's decision to upgrade the power of its radio station from 10 to 400 watts.
2. Boeing's decision to spend $5 billion to build a plane for the 21st century—the B-777.
3. RCA's decision to buy the picture tubes for its television sets rather than to manufacture them.

In this chapter we discuss a number of management decisions and consider the information that is relevant to each.

In addition, we explain management's decision-making process known as capital budgeting. This process pertains to a company's major investments in long-term productive assets.

Management's Decision-Making Process

Making decisions is an important part of management. Management's decision-making process does not always follow a set pattern, because decisions vary significantly in their scope, urgency, and importance. It is possible, however, to

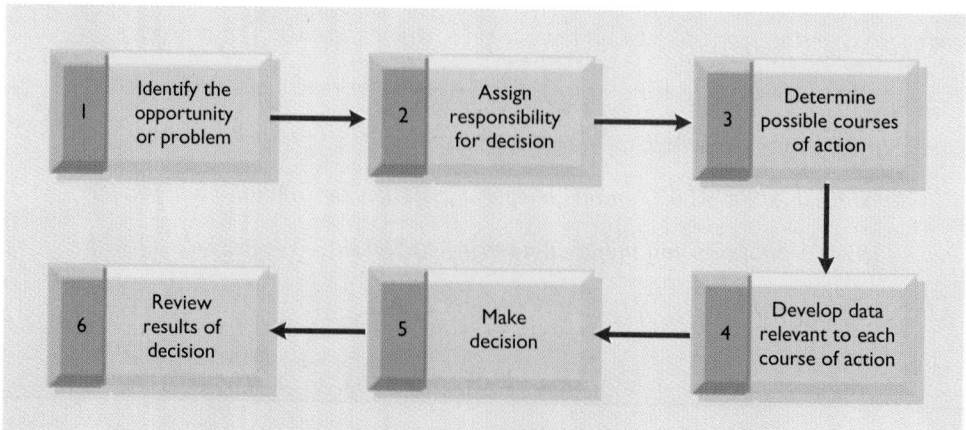

identify some steps that are frequently involved in the process. These steps are graphically shown in Illustration 28-1.

Accounting's contribution to the decision-making process occurs primarily in Steps 4 and 6. In Step 4, for each possible course of action, relevant revenue and cost data are provided to show the expected overall effect on net income. In Step 6, internal reports are prepared that review the actual impact of the decision.

SECTION 1   Incremental Analysis

In making business decisions, management ordinarily considers both financial and nonfinancial information. **Financial** information is related to revenues and costs and their effect on the company's overall profitability. **Nonfinancial** information relates to such factors as the effect of the decision on employee turnover, the environment, or the overall image of the company in the community. Although the nonfinancial information can be as important as, and in some cases more important than, the financial information, we will limit our discussion primarily to financial information that is relevant to the decision.

Study Objective 2

Describe the concept of incremental analysis.

Meaning of Incremental Analysis

Decisions involve a choice among alternative courses of action. Suppose that you were deciding whether to purchase or lease an IBM PC for your accounting homework. The financial data relate to the cost of leasing versus the cost of purchasing. For example, leasing would involve periodic lease payments; purchasing would require payment of the purchase price. In other words, the financial data relevant to the decision are the data that would vary in the future among the possible alternatives. The process used to identify the financial data that change under alternative courses of action is called incremental analysis or differential analysis. In some cases, you will find that when you use incremental analysis, both costs and revenues will change. In other cases, only costs or revenues will vary.

Since management's decision will affect the future, it follows that incremental analysis includes the probable effects of that decision on future earnings. Such data inevitably involve estimates and uncertainty. Gathering data for incremental analyses may involve market analysts, engineers, and accountants. In quantifying the data, the accountant is expected to exercise professional judgment to produce the most reliable information available at the time the decision must be made.

How Incremental Analysis Works

The basic approach in incremental analysis is illustrated in the following example.

	Alternative A	Alternative B	Net Income Increase (Decrease)
Revenues	$125,000	$110,000	$(15,000)
Costs	100,000	80,000	20,000
Net income	$ 25,000	$ 30,000	$ 5,000

ILLUSTRATION 28-2

Basic approach in incremental analysis

In this example, alternative B is being compared with alternative A.

The analysis shows that incremental revenue will be $15,000 less under alternative B than under alternative A but a $20,000 incremental cost saving will be realized.[1] Thus, alternative B will produce $5,000 more net income than alternative A.

In incremental analysis, it is also important to recognize that (1) variable costs may not change under the alternative courses of action, and (2) fixed costs may change. For example, direct labor, normally a variable cost, is not an incremental cost in deciding between two new factory machines if each asset requires the same amount of direct labor. In contrast, rent expense, normally a fixed cost, is an incremental cost in a decision to continue occupancy of a building or to purchase or lease a new building.

Types of Incremental Analysis

A number of different types of decisions involve incremental analysis. The more common types are:

1. Acceptance of an order at a special price.
2. Make or buy.
3. Sell or process further.
4. Retain or replace equipment.
5. Elimination of an unprofitable segment.
6. Allocation of limited resources.

We will consider each of these types of analysis in the following pages.

Acceptance of an Order at a Special Price

Study Objective 3

Identify the relevant costs in accepting an order at a special price.

Helpful hint This is a good example of different costs for different purposes. In the long-run all costs are relevant but for this decision only costs that change are relevant.

Sometimes, a company may have an opportunity to obtain additional business if it is willing to make a major price concession to a specific customer. To illustrate, assume that Sunbelt Company produces 100,000 automatic blenders per month, which is 80% of plant capacity. Variable manufacturing costs are $8 per unit, and fixed manufacturing costs are $400,000, or $4 per unit. The blenders are normally sold directly to retailers at $20 each. Sunbelt has an offer from Mexico Co. (a foreign wholesaler) to purchase an additional 2,000 blenders at $11 per unit. Acceptance of the offer would not affect normal sales of the product, and the additional units can be manufactured without increasing plant capacity. What should management do?

If management makes its decision on the basis of the total cost per unit of $12 ($8 + $4), the order would be rejected, because costs ($12) would exceed revenues ($11) by $1 per unit. However, since the units can be produced within existing plant capacity, the special order will not increase fixed costs. The relevant data for the decision, therefore, are the variable manufacturing costs per unit of $8 and the expected revenue of $11 per unit. Thus, as shown in Illustration 28-3, Sunbelt will increase its net income by $6,000 by accepting this special order.

Two points should be emphasized. First, it is assumed that sales of the product in other markets would not be affected by this special order. If other sales were affected, then Sunbelt would have to consider the lost sales in making the decision. Second, if Sunbelt is operating at full capacity, it is likely that the special order would be rejected. Under such circumstances, the company would have

---

[1] Although income taxes are sometimes important in incremental analysis, they are ignored in the chapter for simplicity's sake.

	Reject Order	Accept Order	Net Income Increase (Decrease)
Revenues	$-0-	$22,000	$22,000
Costs	-0-	16,000	(16,000)
Net income	$-0-	$ 6,000	$ 6,000

to expand plant capacity, and, the special order would have to absorb these additional fixed manufacturing costs, as well as the variable manufacturing costs.

Make or Buy

When a manufacturer assembles component parts in producing a finished product, management must decide whether to make or buy the components. For example, General Motors Corporation may either make or buy the batteries, tires, and radios used in its cars. Similarly, Zenith Corporation may make or buy the electronic circuitry, cabinets, and speakers for its television sets. The decision to make or buy components should be made on the basis of incremental analysis.

To illustrate the analysis, assume that Baron Company incurs the following annual costs in producing 25,000 ignition switches for motor scooters:

ILLUSTRATION 28-4

Annual product cost data

Direct materials	$ 50,000
Direct labor	75,000
Variable manufacturing overhead	40,000
Fixed manufacturing overhead	60,000
Total manufacturing costs	$225,000
Total cost per unit ($225,000 ÷ 25,000)	$9.00

Alternatively, Baron Company may purchase the ignition switches from Ignition, Inc., at a price of $8 per unit. The question again is, "What should management do?"

On the one hand, it appears that management should purchase the ignition switches for $8, rather than make them at a cost of $9. However, a review of operations indicates that if the ignition switches are purchased from Ignition, Inc., all of Baron's variable costs but only $10,000 of its fixed manufacturing costs will be eliminated. Thus, $50,000 of the fixed manufacturing costs will remain if the ignition switches are purchased. The relevant costs for incremental analysis, therefore, are as follows:

ILLUSTRATION 28-5

Incremental analysis—make or buy

	Make	Buy	Net Income Increase (Decrease)
Direct materials	$ 50,000	$ -0-	$ 50,000
Direct labor	75,000	-0-	75,000
Variable manufacturing costs	40,000	-0-	40,000
Fixed manufacturing costs	60,000	50,000	10,000
Purchase price (25,000 × $8)	-0-	200,000	(200,000)
Total annual cost	$225,000	$250,000	$ (25,000)

This analysis indicates that Baron Company will incur $25,000 of additional cost by buying the ignition switches. Therefore, Baron should continue to make the ignition switches, even though the total manufacturing cost is $1 higher than the purchase price. The reason is that if the company purchases the ignition switches, it will still have fixed costs of $50,000 to absorb.

The foregoing analysis is complete only if it is assumed that the productive capacity used to make the ignition switches cannot be converted to another purpose. If there is an opportunity to use this productive capacity in some other manner, then this opportunity cost must be considered. Opportunity cost may be defined as the potential benefit that may be obtained by following an alternative course of action. To illustrate, assume that through buying the switches, Baron Company can use the released productive capacity to generate additional income of $28,000. This lost income is an additional cost of continuing to make the switches in the make-or-buy decision. This opportunity cost therefore is added to the "Make" column, for comparison. As shown, it is now advantageous to buy the ignition switches.

ILLUSTRATION 28-6

Make or buy with opportunity cost

	Make	**Buy**	**Net Income Increase (Decrease)**
Total annual cost	$225,000	$250,000	$(25,000)
Opportunity cost	28,000	–0–	28,000
Total cost	$253,000	$250,000	$ 3,000

The qualitative factors in this decision, not considered in the numbers above, include the adverse effect on employees producing the ignition switches. In addition, management must assess how long the supplier will be able to satisfy the company's quality control standards at the quoted price per unit.

Sell or Process Further

Study Objective 5

Give the decision rule in deciding whether to sell or process materials further.

Many manufacturers have the option of selling products at a given point in the production cycle or continuing to process with the expectation of selling them at a higher price. For example, a bicycle manufacturer such as Schwinn could sell its 10-speed bicycles to retailers either unassembled or assembled, and a furniture manufacturer such as Ethan Allen could sell its dining room sets to furniture stores either unfinished or finished. The sell-or-process further decision should be made on the basis of incremental analysis. The basic decision rule is: **Process further as long as the incremental revenue from such processing exceeds the incremental processing costs.**

Assume, for example, that Woodmasters Inc. makes tables. The cost to manufacture an unfinished table is $35, computed as follows:

ILLUSTRATION 28-7

Per unit cost of unfinished table

Direct material	$15
Direct labor	10
Variable manufacturing overhead	6
Fixed manufacturing overhead	4
Manufacturing cost per unit	$35

The selling price per unfinished unit is $50. Woodmasters currently has unused productive capacity that is expected to continue indefinitely. Management concludes that some of this capacity may be used to finish the tables and sell them at $60 per unit. For a finished table, it is anticipated that direct materials and direct labor costs will increase $2 and $4, respectively. In addition, variable manufacturing overhead costs will increase by $2.40 (60% of direct labor). No increase is anticipated in fixed manufacturing overhead. The incremental analysis on a per unit basis is as follows:

	Sell	Process Further	Net Income Increase (Decrease)
Sales per unit	$50.00	$60.00	$10.00
Cost per unit			
Direct materials	15.00	17.00	(2.00)
Direct labor	10.00	14.00	(4.00)
Variable manufacturing overhead	6.00	8.40	(2.40)
Fixed manufacturing overhead	4.00	4.00	–0–
Total	$35.00	$43.40	$ (8.40)
Net income per unit	$15.00	$16.60	$ 1.60

ILLUSTRATION 28-8

Incremental analysis—sell or process further

Helpful hint Current net income is objective. Net income from processing further is an estimate. In making its decision, management could add a "risk" factor for the estimate.

As indicated from the analysis, it would be advantageous for Woodmaster to process the tables further. In this case, the incremental revenue of $10.00 from the additional processing is $1.60 higher than the incremental processing costs of $8.40.

Retain or Replace Equipment

Management often has to decide whether to continue using an asset or replace it. To illustrate, assume that the Jeffcoat Company has a factory machine with a book value of $40,000 and a remaining useful life of four years. A new machine is available that costs $120,000 and is expected to have zero salvage value at the end of its four-year useful life. If the new machine is acquired, variable manufacturing costs are expected to decrease from $160,000 to $125,000 annually and the old unit will be scrapped. The incremental analysis for the four-year period is as follows:

Study Objective 6

Identify the factors to be considered in retaining or replacing equipment.

ILLUSTRATION 28-9

Incremental analysis—retain or replace equipment

	Retain Equipment	Replace Equipment	Net Income Increase (Decrease)
Variable manufacturing costs	$640,000[a]	$500,000[b]	$140,000
New machine cost		120,000	(120,000)
Total	$640,000	$620,000	$ 20,000

[a](4 years × $160,000)
[b](4 years × $125,000)

In this case, it would be to the company's advantage to replace the equipment. The lower variable manufacturing costs due to replacement more than offset the cost of the new equipment.

One other point should be mentioned regarding Jeffcoat's decision: **The book value of the old machine does not affect the decision.** Book value is a sunk cost, which is a cost that cannot be changed by any present or future decision. Sunk costs, therefore, **are not relevant in incremental analysis**. In this example, if the asset is retained, book value will be depreciated over its remaining useful life. On the other hand, if the new unit is acquired, book value will be recognized as a loss of the current period. Thus, the effect of book value on

Accounting in Action · *Business Insight*

As an example of opportunity cost, one construction company with a heavy load of debt had several pieces of very expensive equipment that had been fully depreciated. The company's books told management that this equipment wasn't tying up any capital. Supposedly it didn't cost the company anything to keep that equipment, except for maintenance expenses. But the equipment could have been sold for a good price. Therefore that zero book value was misleading. The equipment was actually taking up a substantial amount of expensive capital and contributing to the company's weak financial position.

current and future earnings is the same regardless of the replacement decision. Any trade-in allowance or cash disposal value of the existing asset, however, is relevant to the decision, because this value will not be realized if the asset is continued in use.

Study Objective 7

Explain the factors that are relevant in deciding whether to eliminate an unprofitable segment.

Elimination of an Unprofitable Segment

Our concern here focuses on the relevant data management needs in deciding whether to eliminate an unprofitable segment. To illustrate, assume that Martina Company manufactures tennis racquets in three models: Pro, Master, and Champ. Pro and Master are profitable lines, whereas Champ (highlighted in color in the table below) operates at a loss. Condensed income statement data are:

ILLUSTRATION 28-10

Segment income data

	Pro	Master	Champ	Total
Sales	$800,000	$300,000	$100,000	$1,200,000
Variable expenses	520,000	210,000	90,000	820,000
Contribution margin	280,000	90,000	10,000	380,000
Fixed expenses	80,000	50,000	30,000	160,000
Net income	$200,000	$ 40,000	$ (20,000)	$ 220,000

It might be expected that total net income will increase by $20,000 to $240,000 if the unprofitable line of racquets is eliminated. However, it is possible for net income to decrease if the Champ line is discontinued. The reason is that the fixed expenses allocated to the Champ racquets will have to be absorbed by the other products. To illustrate, assume that the $30,000 of fixed costs applicable to the unprofitable segment are allocated ⅔ and ⅓ to the Pro and Master product lines, respectively. Fixed expenses will increase to $100,000 ($80,000 + $20,000) in the Pro line and to $60,000 ($50,000 + $10,000) in the Master line. The revised income statement is:

ILLUSTRATION 28-11

Income data after eliminating unprofitable product line

Helpful hint A decision to discontinue a segment based solely on the bottom line (net loss) is inappropriate.

	Pro	Master	Total
Sales	$800,000	$300,000	$1,100,000
Variable expenses	520,000	210,000	730,000
Contribution margin	280,000	90,000	370,000
Fixed expenses	100,000	60,000	160,000
Net income	$180,000	$ 30,000	$ 210,000

Total net income has decreased $10,000 ($220,000 − $210,000). This result is also obtained in the following incremental analysis of the Champ racquets.

	Continue	Eliminate	Net Income Increase (Decrease)
Sales	$100,000	$ –0–	$(100,000)
Variable expenses	90,000	–0–	90,000
Contribution margin	10,000	–0–	(10,000)
Fixed expenses	30,000	30,000	–0–
Net income	$ (20,000)	$(30,000)	$ (10,000)

ILLUSTRATION 28-12

Incremental analysis— eliminating an unprofitable segment

The loss in net income is attributable to the contribution margin ($10,000) that will not be realized if the segment is discontinued.

In deciding on the future status of an unprofitable segment, management should consider the effect of elimination on related product lines. It may be possible for continuing product lines to obtain some or all of the sales lost by the discontinued product line. In addition, management should consider the effect of eliminating the product line on employees who may have to be discharged or retrained.

Allocation of Limited Resources

We all have limited resources at our disposal. For a company, the limited resource may be floor space in a retail department store, or raw materials, direct labor hours, or machine capacity in a manufacturing company. When a company has limited resources, management must decide which products to make and sell.

To illustrate, assume that Collins Company manufactures deluxe and standard model pen and pencil sets. The limiting resource is machine capacity, which is 3,600 hours per month. Relevant data consist of the following:

Study Objective 8

Determine which products to make and sell when a company has limited resources.

	Deluxe Sets	Standard Sets
Contribution margin per unit	$8	$6
Machine hours required	4	2

ILLUSTRATION 28-13

Contribution margin and machine hours

The deluxe sets may appear to be more profitable since they have a higher contribution margin ($8) than the standard sets ($6). However, note that the standard sets take fewer machine hours to produce than the deluxe sets. Therefore, it is necessary to find the **contribution margin per unit of limited resource**. This is obtained by dividing the contribution margin per unit of each product by the number of units of the limited resource required for each product. The computation shows that the standard sets have a higher contribution margin per unit of limited resource.

Helpful hint CM alone is not enough in this decision. The key factor is CM per limited resource.

	Deluxe Sets	Standard Sets
Contribution margin per unit (a)	$8	$6
Machine hours required (b)	4	2
Contribution margin per unit of limited resource (a) ÷ (b)	$2	$3

ILLUSTRATION 28-14

Contribution margin per unit of limited resource

If the Collins Company is able to increase machine capacity from 3,600 hours

Accounting in Action · *Business Insight*

Incremental analysis is based on numerical computations. However, be careful. Whether you are talking about the present or the future, the key point is not the precision or the official status of numbers but the understanding of what lies behind them and what they mean. It is much better to have a crude estimate based on a good understanding than to have a precise statistic or exact calculation, however authoritative, that is conceptually flawed.

Take Xerox as an example. Some years ago the company had a bad experience as a result of projecting demand for its big copiers on the basis of a correct prediction of the overall trend on the number of copies that would be made. It failed to realize, however, that the introduction of cheaper, smaller copiers would transfer demand from big, fast machines to small, convenient machines. Another example is AMF, manufacturer of bowling equipment. AMF boomed for years because the number of bowling alleys kept increasing year after year. But then there were enough, and since bowling alleys don't wear out quickly, sales for AMF plummeted because few new alleys were being built.

Source: The Wall Street Journal, August 5, 1985.

to 4,200 hours, the additional 600 hours could be used to produce either the standard or deluxe pen and pencil sets. The total contribution margin under each alternative is found by multiplying the machine hours by the contribution margin per unit of limited resource as shown below.

ILLUSTRATION 28-15

Computation of total contribution margin

	Produce Deluxe Sets	Produce Standard Sets
Machine hours (a)	600	600
Contribution margin per unit of limited resource (b)	$2	$3
Contribution margin (a) × (b)	$1,200	$1,800

From this analysis, we can see that to maximize net income all of the increased capacity should be used to make and sell the standard sets.

Before You Go On . . .

1. Give three examples of how incremental analysis might be used.

2. What is the decision rule in deciding to sell or process products further?

3. How may the elimination of an unprofitable segment decrease the overall net income of a company?

4. What is the critical factor in allocating limited resources?

SECTION 2   Capital Budgeting

Individuals make capital expenditures when they buy a new home, car, or television set. Similarly, businesses make capital expenditures when they modernize plant facilities or expand operations. Examples include the new terminal built by United Airlines at O'Hare Airport and the Saturn automobile plant built by General Motors in Tennessee.

The amounts spent by companies on capital expenditures each year are substantial. For example, in a recent year, U.S. businesses spent approximately $375 billion on capital expenditures. More specifically, in 1990, Ford Motor Company spent $7 billion, Dow Chemical spent $1.9 billion, and General Electric spent $2.3 billion. In business enterprises, as for individuals, the amount of possible capital expenditures usually exceeds the funds available for such expenditures. Thus, the resources available must be allocated (or budgeted) among the competing alternatives. The process of making capital expenditure decisions in business is known as capital budgeting.

Many companies follow a carefully prescribed process in capital budgeting. At least once a year, proposals for projects are requested from each department and plant and from authorized personnel. The proposals are screened by a capital budgeting committee, which submits its findings to the officers of the company. The officers, in turn, select the projects they believe to be most worthy of funding and submit them to the board of directors. Ultimately, the directors approve the capital expenditure budget for the year. The involvement of top management and the board of directors in the process demonstrates the importance of capital budgeting decisions. These decisions often have a significant impact on a company's future profitability. Indeed, poor capital budgeting decisions have led to the bankruptcy of some companies. Accounting data are indispensable in assessing the probable effects of capital expenditures.

Approaches to Capital Budgeting

To provide management with relevant data for capital budgeting decisions, accountants should be familiar with the quantitative techniques that may be used. The three most common techniques are: (1) annual rate of return, (2) cash payback, and (3) discounted cash flow. To illustrate the three quantitative techniques, assume that Tappan Company is considering an investment of $130,000 in new equipment. The new equipment is expected to last 10 years and have zero salvage value at the end of its useful life. The straight-line method of depreciation is used for accounting purposes. The expected annual revenues and costs of the new product that will be produced from the investment are:

Sales		$200,000
Less: Costs and expenses		
Manufacturing costs (exclusive of depreciation)	$145,000	
Depreciation expense ($130,000 ÷ 10)	13,000	
Selling and administrative expenses	22,000	180,000
Income before income taxes		20,000
Income tax expense		7,000
Net income		$ 13,000

ILLUSTRATION 28-16

Annual net income from capital expenditure

Annual Rate of Return

The annual rate of return technique is based directly on accounting data. It indicates **the profitability of a capital expenditure** by dividing expected annual net income by the average investment. The formula for computing annual rate of return is shown in Illustration 28-17.

Study Objective 9

Contrast the annual rate of return and cash payback techniques in capital budgeting.

ILLUSTRATION 28-17

Annual rate of return formula

Expected annual net income is obtained from the income statement. Tappan Company's expected annual net income is $13,000. Average investment is based on the following:

ILLUSTRATION 28-18

Computation of average investment

$$\text{Average investment} = \frac{\text{Original investment} + \text{Investment at end of useful life}}{2}$$

The investment at the end of useful life is equal to the asset's salvage value, if any. For Tappan Company, average investment is $65,000 [($130,000 + $0) ÷ 2]. The annual rate of return for Tappan Company is therefore 20%, computed as follows:

$$\$13,000 \div \$65,000 = 20\%$$

The annual rate of return is then compared with the management's required minimum rate of return for investments of similar risk. The minimum rate of return (also called the **hurdle rate** or **cutoff rate**) is generally based on the company's **cost of capital**. The cost of capital is the rate of return that management expects to pay on all borrowed and equity funds. It does not relate to the cost of funding a specific project. The decision rule is: **A project is acceptable if its rate of return is greater than management's minimum rate of return; it is unacceptable when the reverse is true.** When the rate of return technique is used in deciding among several acceptable projects, **the higher the rate of return for a given risk, the more attractive the investment.**

Helpful hint A capital budgeting decision based on only one technique may be misleading. It is often wise to analyze the situation from a number of different perspectives.

The principal advantages of this technique of analysis are the simplicity of its calculation and management's familiarity with the accounting terms used in the computation. A major limitation of the annual rate of return approach is that it does not consider the time value of money. For example, no consideration is given as to whether cash inflows from the investment will occur early or late in the life of the investment. As explained in Appendix N, recognition of the time value of money can make a significant difference between the future value and the discounted present value of an investment.

Cash Payback

The cash payback technique identifies the time period required to recover the cost of the capital investment from the annual cash inflow produced by the investment. The formula for computing the cash payback period is:

ILLUSTRATION 28-19

Cash payback formula

Annual cash inflow, also known as net cash inflow, is approximated by taking net income and adding back depreciation expense. Depreciation expense is added back because depreciation on the capital expenditure does not involve an annual outflow of cash. Accordingly, the depreciation deducted in determining net income must be added back to determine annual cash inflows. In the Tappan Company example, annual cash inflow is $26,000, as shown below.

ILLUSTRATION 28-20

Computation of annual cash inflow

Net income	$13,000
Add: Depreciation expense	13,000
Annual cash inflow	**$26,000**

The cash payback period in this example is therefore 5 years, computed as follows:

$$\$130,000 \div \$26,000 = 5 \text{ years}$$

The evaluation of the payback period is often related to the expected useful life of the asset. For example, assume that at Tappan Company a project is unacceptable if the payback period is longer than 60% of the asset's expected useful life. The five-year payback period in this case is 50% of the project's expected useful life. Thus, the project is acceptable. It follows that when the payback technique is used to decide among acceptable alternative projects, **the shorter the payback period, the more attractive the investment**. The reason is that: (1) the earlier the investment is recovered, the sooner the cash funds can be used for other purposes, and (2) the risk of loss from obsolescence and changed economic conditions is less in a shorter payback period.

The cash payback technique may be useful as an initial screening tool. It also may be the most critical factor in the capital budgeting decision for a company that desires a fast turnaround of its investment because of a weak cash position. Like the annual rate of return technique, the cash payback technique is relatively easy to compute and understand. However, it should not ordinarily be the only basis for the capital budgeting decision because it ignores the expected profitability of the project. To illustrate, assume that Projects A and B have the same payback period, but Project A's useful life is double the useful life of Project B. Project A's earning power, therefore, is twice as long as Project B's. A further disadvantage of this technique is that it ignores the time value of money.

Discounted Cash Flow

The discounted cash flow technique is generally recognized as the most informative and best conceptual approach to making capital budgeting decisions. This technique considers both the estimated total cash inflows from the investment and the time value of money. As indicated above, consideration of the time value of money is critical because of the long-term impact of the capital budgeting decision. The expected total cash inflow consists of the sum of the annual cash inflows plus the estimated liquidation proceeds when the asset is sold for salvage at the end of its useful life. Because liquidation proceeds are generally immaterial, they are ignored in subsequent discussions. Two methods are used with the discounted cash flow technique: (1) net present value and (2) internal rate of return. Before we discuss the methods, we recommend that you examine Appendix N if you need a review of present value concepts.

Study Objective 10

Distinguish between the net present value and internal rate of return methods.

Net Present Value Method

Under the net present value method, cash inflows are discounted to their present value and then compared with the capital outlay required by the investment. The difference between these two amounts is referred to as **net present value**.

The interest rate to be used in discounting the future cash inflows is the required minimum rate of return. **A proposal is acceptable when net present value is zero or positive**, because this means the rate of return on the investment equals or exceeds the required rate of return. When net present value is negative, the project is unacceptable. The following diagram illustrates these points.

ILLUSTRATION 28-21

Net present value decision diagram

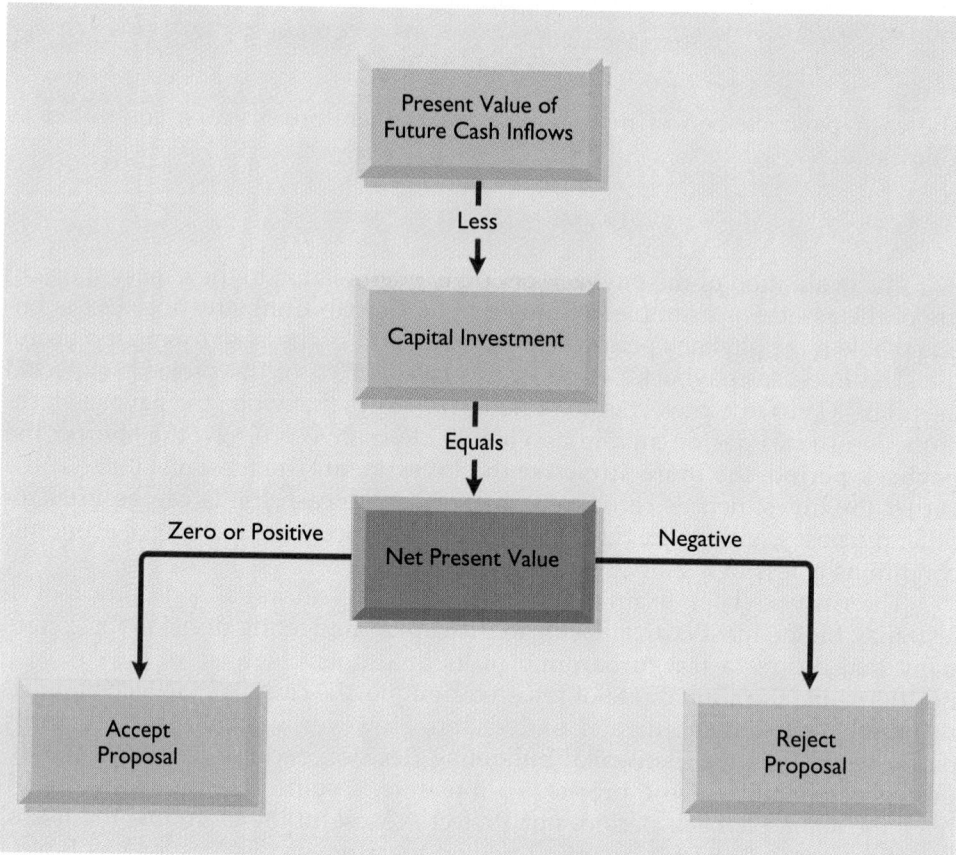

When making a selection among acceptable proposals, **the higher the positive net present value, the more attractive the investment**. The application of this method to two cases is described below. In each case, we will assume that the investment has no salvage value at the end of its useful life.

EQUAL ANNUAL CASH FLOWS. Tappan Company's annual cash inflows are $26,000. If we assume this amount is uniform over the asset's useful life, the present value of the annual cash inflows can be computed by using Table 2 in Appendix N based on the present value of an annuity of 1 for 10 periods. The computations at rates of return of 12% and 15%, respectively, are:

ILLUSTRATION 28-22

Present value of annual cash inflows

	Present Values at Different Discount Rates	
	12%	15%
Discount factor for 10 periods	5.65022	5.01877
Present value of cash inflows:		
$26,000 × 5.65022	**$146,906**	
$26,000 × 5.01877		**$130,488**

Therefore, the analysis of the proposal by the net present value method is as follows:

ILLUSTRATION 28-23

Computations of net present values

Helpful hint The ABC Co. expects equal cash flows over an asset's 5-year useful life. What discount factor should be used in determining present values if management wants (1) a 12% return or (2) a 15% return? Answer: Using Table 2, the factors are (1) 3.60478 and (2) 3.35216.

	12%	15%
Present value of future cash inflows	$146,906	$130,488
Capital investment	130,000	130,000
Positive (negative) net present value	$ 16,906	$ 488

The proposed capital expenditure is acceptable at a required rate of return of both 12% and 15% because the net present values are positive.

UNEQUAL ANNUAL CASH INFLOWS. When annual cash inflows are unequal, it is not possible to use annuity tables to calculate their present value. Instead, tables showing the present value of a single future amount must be applied to each annual cash inflow. To illustrate, assume in the Tappan Company that management expects the same aggregate annual cash inflow ($260,000) but a declining market demand for the new product over the life of the equipment. The present value of the annual cash flows is calculated as follows using Table 1 in Appendix N:

ILLUSTRATION 28-24

Computing present value of unequal annual cash inflows

Year	Assumed Annual Cash Inflows	Discount Factor 12%	Discount Factor 15%	Present Value 12%	Present Value 15%
	(1)	(2)	(3)	(1) × (2)	(1) × (3)
1	$ 36,000	.89286	.86957	$ 32,143	$ 31,305
2	32,000	.79719	.75614	25,510	24,196
3	29,000	.71178	.65752	20,642	19,068
4	27,000	.63552	.57175	17,159	15,437
5	26,000	.56743	.49718	14,753	12,927
6	24,000	.50663	.43233	12,159	10,376
7	23,000	.45235	.37594	10,404	8,647
8	22,000	.40388	.32690	8,885	7,192
9	21,000	.36061	.28426	7,573	5,969
10	20,000	.32197	.24719	6,439	4,944
	$260,000			$155,667	$140,061

Therefore, the analysis of the proposal by the net present value method is as follows:

ILLUSTRATION 28-25

Analysis of proposal using net present value method

	12%	15%
Present value of future cash inflows	$155,667	$140,061
Capital investment	130,000	130,000
Positive (negative) net present value	$ 25,667	$ 10,061

In this example, the present values of the cash inflows are greater than the $130,000 capital investment. Thus, the project is acceptable at both a 12% and 15% required rate of return. The difference between the present values using the 12% rate under equal cash inflows ($146,906) and unequal cash inflows ($155,667) is due to the pattern of the inflows.

Internal Rate of Return Method

The internal rate of return method, differs from the net present value method in that it results in finding the **interest yield** of the potential investment. The **internal rate of return** is the rate that will cause the present value of the proposed capital expenditure to equal the present value of the expected annual cash inflows. The determination of the internal rate of return involves two steps.

Step 1. Compute the internal rate of return factor. The formula for this factor is:

ILLUSTRATION 28-26

Formula for internal rate of return factor

The computation for the Tappan Company, assuming equal annual cash inflows is:

$$\$130,000 \div \$26,000 = 5.0^2$$

Step 2. Use the factor and the present value of an annuity of 1 table to find the internal rate of return. Table 2 of Appendix N is used in this step. The internal rate of return is found by locating the discount factor in the table that is closest to the internal rate of return factor for the time period covered by the annual cash flows.

In Tappan Company, the annual cash inflows are expected to continue for 10 years. Thus, it is necessary to read across the period 10 row in Table 2 to find the discount factor. Row 10 is reproduced below for your convenience.

TABLE 2 PRESENT VALUE OF AN ANNUITY OF 1								
(n) Periods	5%	6%	8%	9%	10%	11%	12%	15%
10	7.72173	7.36009	6.71008	6.41766	6.14457	5.88923	5.65022	5.01877

In this case, the closest discount factor to 5.0 is 5.01877 which represents an interest rate of approximately 15%. The approximate rate can be determined by interpolation, but since we are using estimated annual cash flows such precision is seldom required.

When the internal rate of return has been determined, it is compared to management's required minimum rate of return. The decision rule, therefore, is: **accept the project when the internal rate of return is equal to or greater than the required rate of return, and reject the project when the internal rate of return is less than the required rate.** These relationships are shown graphically in Illustration 28-27. Assuming the minimum required rate of return is 10% for Tappan Company, the project is acceptable because the 15% internal rate of return is greater than the required rate.

The internal rate of return method is widely used in practice. Most managers find the internal rate of return easy to interpret.

---

[2]When annual cash inflows are equal, the internal rate of return factor is the same as the cash payback period.

ILLUSTRATION 28-27

Internal rate of return decision diagram

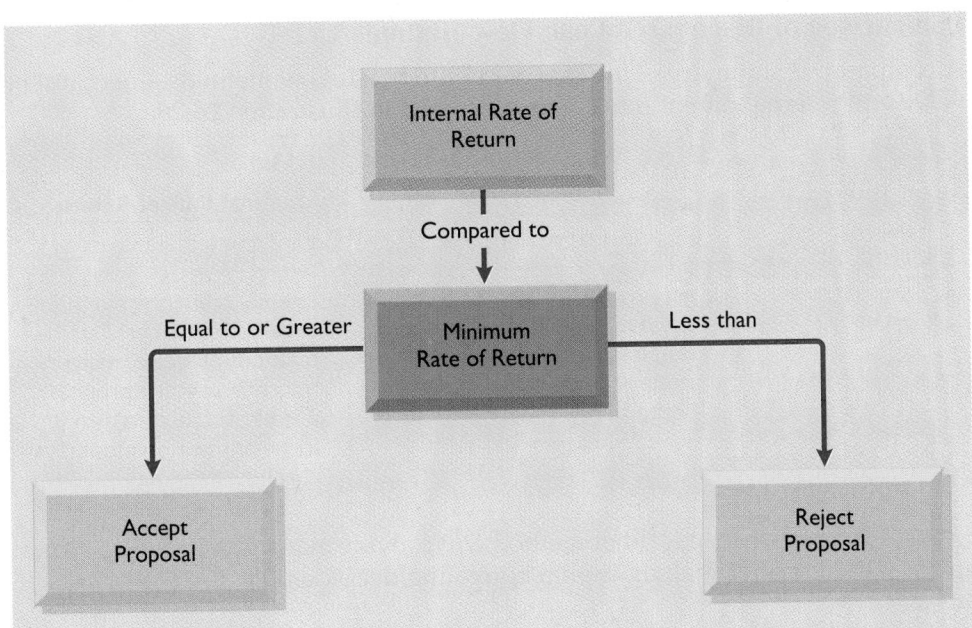

Accounting in Action · *Business Insight*

Which methods are used the most? One survey asked financial officers which method they used in considering expenditures for factory automation.

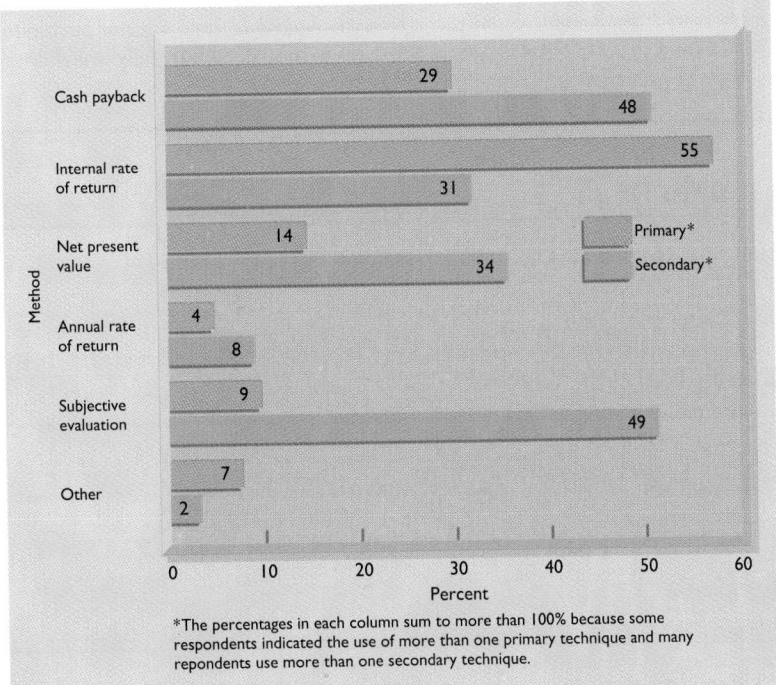

*The percentages in each column sum to more than 100% because some respondents indicated the use of more than one primary technique and many respondents use more than one secondary technique.

Note that cash payback and internal rate of return are the most popular.

Source: James A. Hendricks, "Applying Cost Accounting to Factory Automation," *Management Accounting*, December, 1988.

Comparison of Discounted Cash Flow Methods

A comparative summary of the two discounted cash flow methods—net present value and internal rate of return—is presented in Illustration 28-28.

ILLUSTRATION 28-28

Comparison of discounted cash flow methods

Item	Net Present Value	Internal Rate of Return
1. Objective	Compute net present value.	Compute internal rate of return.
2. Decision rule	If net present value is zero or positive, accept the proposal; if net present value is negative, reject the proposal.	If internal rate of return is equal to or greater than the minimum required rate of return, accept the proposal; if internal rate of return is less than the minimum rate, reject the proposal.

When properly used, either method will provide management with relevant quantitative data for making capital budgeting decisions.

Technology in Action

There are software packages available for each of the decision situations described in the incremental analysis and capital budgeting sections of this chapter. Because of their power and flexibility, spreadsheet programs can also be designed to perform any of these calculations. Thus, businesses often face another decision. Should they purchase packages dedicated only to specific tasks (called a canned approach) or will a general purpose application package, like a spreadsheet or data base program, be better? Management often turns to accountants to help answer such questions. As discussed in Chapter 6, the costs of each alternative should be carefully weighed against the benefits before any purchase is made.

Before You Go On . . .

1. What is the formula for and the decision rule in using the annual rate of return method?

2. What is the formula for the cash payback method?

3. When is a proposal acceptable under (a) the net present value method and (b) the internal rate of return method?

Summary of Study Objectives

1. Identify the steps in management's decision-making process. Management's decision-making process consists of (a) identifying the problem or opportunity, (b) assigning responsibility for the decision, (c) determining possible courses of action, (d) developing data relevant to each course of action, (e) mak-

ing the decision, and (f) reviewing the results of the decision.

2. Describe the concept of incremental analysis. Incremental analysis is the process used to identify financial data that change under alternative courses of action. These data are relevant to the decision because they will vary in the future among the possible alternatives.

3. *Identify the relevant costs in accepting an order at a special price.* The relevant information in accepting an order at a special price is the difference between the variable manufacturing costs and expected revenues.

4. *Indicate the relevant costs in a make-or-buy decision.* In a make-or-buy decision, the relevant costs are (a) the variable manufacturing costs that will be saved, (b) the purchase price, and (c) opportunity costs.

5. *Give the decision rule in deciding whether to sell or process materials further.* The decision rule in deciding whether to sell or process materials further is: process further as long as the incremental revenue from processing exceeds the incremental processing costs.

6. *Identify the factors to be considered in retaining or replacing equipment.* The factors to be considered in determining whether equipment should be retained or replaced are the effects on variable costs and the cost of the new equipment. In addition, any disposal value of the existing asset must be considered.

7. *Explain the factors that are relevant in deciding whether to eliminate an unprofitable segment.* In deciding whether to eliminate an unprofitable segment, it is necessary to determine the contribution margin, if any, produced by the segment and the disposition of the segment's fixed expenses.

8. *Determine which products to make and sell when a company has limited resources.* When a company has limited resources, it is necessary to find the contribution margin per unit of limited resource. This amount is then multiplied by the units that could be produced to determine which product maximizes net income.

9. *Contrast the annual rate of return and cash payback techniques in capital budgeting.* The annual rate of return is obtained by dividing expected annual net income by the average investment. The cash payback technique identifies the time period to recover the cost of the investment. The formula is: Cost of capital expenditure divided by estimated annual cash inflow equals cash payback period. The shorter the payback period, the more attractive the investment.

10. *Distinguish between the net present value and internal rate of return methods.* Under the net present value method, the present value of future cash inflows is compared with the capital investment to determine net present value. The decision rule is: Accept the project if net present value is zero or positive; reject the investment if net present value is negative.

Under the internal rate of return method, the objective is to find the true interest yield of the potential investment. The decision rule is: Accept the project when the internal rate of return is equal to or greater than the required rate of return; reject the project when the internal rate of return is less than the required rate.

GLOSSARY

Annual rate of return technique · The determination of the profitability of a capital expenditure by dividing expected annual net income by the average investment. (p. 1133).

Capital budgeting · The process of making capital expenditure decisions in business. (p. 1133).

Cash payback technique · A capital budgeting technique that identifies the time period required to recover the cost of a capital investment from the annual cash inflow produced by the investment. (p. 1134).

Differential analysis (same as incremental analysis) · The process of identifying the financial data that change under alternative courses of action. (p. 1125).

Discounted cash flow technique · A capital budgeting technique that considers both the estimated total cash inflows from the investment and the time value of money. (p. 1135).

Incremental analysis (same as differential analysis) · The process of identifying the financial data that change under alternative courses of action. (p. 1125).

Internal rate of return method · A method used in capital budgeting that results in finding the interest yield of the potential investment. (p. 1138).

Net present value method · A method used in capital budgeting in which cash inflows are discounted to their present value and then compared to the capital outlay required by the capital investment. (p. 1135).

Opportunity cost · The potential benefit that may be obtained from following an alternative course of action. (p. 1128).

Sunk cost · A cost that cannot be changed by any present or future decision. (p. 1129).

DEMONSTRATION PROBLEM 1

The Juanita Company must decide whether to make or buy some of its components. The costs of producing 50,000 electrical cords for its floor lamps are as follows:

Direct materials	$60,000	Variable overhead	$12,000
Direct labor	30,000	Fixed overhead	8,000

Instead of making the electrical cords at an average cost per unit of $2.20 ($110,000 ÷ 50,000), the company has an opportunity to buy the cords at $2.30 per unit. If the cords are purchased all variable costs and one-half of the fixed costs will be eliminated.

Instructions

(a) Prepare an incremental analysis showing whether the company should make or buy the electrical cords.

(b) Will your answer be different if the released productive capacity will generate additional income of $25,000?

Helpful hints:

1. Look for the costs that change.
2. Ignore the costs that do not change.
3. Use the format in the chapter for your answer.
4. Recognize that opportunity cost can make a difference.

Solution to Demonstration Problem

(a)

	Make	Buy	Net Income Increase (Decrease)
Direct materials	$ 60,000	$ –0–	$ 60,000
Direct labor	30,000	–0–	30,000
Variable manufacturing costs	12,000	–0–	12,000
Fixed manufacturing costs	8,000	4,000	4,000
Purchase price	–0–	115,000	(115,000)
Total cost	$110,000	$119,000	$ (9,000)

This analysis indicates that the Juanita Company will incur $9,000 of additional costs if it buys the electrical cords.

(b)

	Make	Buy	Net Income Increase (Decrease)
Total cost	$110,000	$119,000	$ (9,000)
Opportunity cost	25,000		25,000
Total cost	$135,000	$119,000	$ 16,000

This analysis shows that net income will be increased by $16,000 if the electrical cords are purchased.

DEMONSTRATION PROBLEM 2

The Sierra Company is considering a long-term capital investment project called ZIP. ZIP will require an investment of $120,000 and it will have a useful life of 4 years. Annual net income is expected to be: Year 1, $12,000; Year 2, $10,000; Year 3, $8,000; and Year 4, $6,000. Depreciation is computed by the straight-line method with no salvage value. The company's cost of capital is 12%.

Instructions

(Round all computations to two decimal places)

(a) Compute the annual rate of return for the project.

(b) Compute the cash payback period for the project. (Round to two decimals.)

(c) Compute the net present value for the project. (Round to nearest dollar.)

(d) Should the project be accepted? Why?

Solution to Demonstration Problem 2

(a) $9,000 ($36,000 ÷ 4) ÷ $60,000 ($120,000 ÷ 2) = 15%

(b) $120,000 ÷ $39,000 ($9,000 + $30,000) = 3.08 years

(c)

Year	Discount Factor	Cash Inflow	Present Value
1	.89286	$42,000	$ 37,500
2	.79719	40,000	31,888
3	.71178	38,000	27,048
4	.63552	36,000	22,879
			119,315
Capital investment			120,000
Negative net present value			$ (685)

(d) The annual rate of return of 15% is good. However, the cash payback period is 77% of the project's useful life and net present value is negative. The recommendation is to reject the project.

Helpful Hints

1. The formula for annual rate of return is expected annual net income divided by average investment.
2. The formula for the cash payback method is cost of the investment divided by annual cash inflows.
3. Annual cash inflow equals annual net income plus annual depreciation expense.
4. Be careful to use the correct discount factor in using the net present value method.

SELF-STUDY QUESTIONS

Answers are at the end of chapter.

(S.O. 1)
1. Three of the steps in management's decision process are (1) review results of decision, (2) develop data relevant to each course of action, and (3) make the decision. The steps are prepared in the following order:
   a. (1), (2), (3)
   b. (3), (2), (1)
   c. (2), (3), (1)
   d. (2), (1), (3)

(S.O. 2)
2. Differential analysis is the process of identifying the financial data that:
   a. change under alternative courses of action.
   b. do not change under alternative courses of action.
   c. are mixed under alternative courses of action.
   d. no correct answer given.

(S.O. 3)
3. It costs a company $14 of variable costs and $6 of fixed costs to produce product A that sells for $30. A foreign buyer offers to purchase 3,000 units at $18 each. If the special offer is accepted and produced with unused capacity, net income will:
   a. decrease $6,000.
   b. increase $6,000.
   c. increase $9,000.
   d. increase $12,000.

(S.O. 4)
4. In a make or buy decision, relevant costs are:
   a. manufacturing costs that will be saved.
   b. the purchase price of the units.

c. opportunity costs.
d. all of the above.

(S.O. 5)
5. The decision rule in a sell or process further decision is: process further as long as the incremental revenue from process exceeds:
   a. variable processing costs.
   b. incremental processing costs.
   c. fixed processing costs.
   d. no correct answer given.

(S.O. 6)
6. In a decision to retain or replace equipment, the book value of the old equipment is a (an):
   a. sunk cost.
   b. opportunity cost.
   c. incremental cost.
   d. marginal cost.

(S.O. 7)
7. If an unprofitable segment is eliminated,
   a. net income will always increase.
   b. fixed expenses allocated to the eliminated segment will have to be absorbed by other segments.
   c. variable expenses of the eliminated segment will have to be absorbed by other segments.
   d. net income will always decrease.

(S.O. 8)
8. If the contribution margin per unit is $10 and it takes 2.5 machine hours to produce the unit, the contribution margin per unit of limited resource is:
   a. $25.
   b. $5.
   c. $4.
   d. no correct answer given.

(S.O. 9) 9. Which of the following is incorrect about the annual rate of return technique?
a. The calculation is simple.
b. The accounting terms used are familiar to management.
c. The time value of money is considered.
d. The timing of the cash inflows is not considered.

10. A positive net present value means that the: (S.O. 10)
a. project's rate of return exceeds the required rate of return.
b. project's rate of return is less than the cutoff rate.
c. project's rate of return equals the required rate of return.
d. project is unacceptable.

QUESTIONS

1. Carl Lipken claims that management decisions usually follow a set pattern. Is his assertion correct? Explain.

2. How does accounting contribute to the decision-making process of management?

3. Incremental analysis involves the accumulation of information concerning a single course of action. Do you agree? Why?

4. Pam Marling asks your help concerning the relevance of variable and fixed costs in incremental analysis. Help Pam with her problem.

5. What data are relevant in deciding whether to accept an order at a special price?

6. The Partor Company has an opportunity to buy parts at $7 each that currently cost $10 to make. What manufacturing costs are relevant to this make-or-buy decision?

7. Define the term "opportunity cost." How may this cost be relevant in a make or buy decision?

8. What is the decision rule in deciding whether to sell a product or process it further?

9. Your roommate is confused about sunk costs. Explain to your roommate the meaning of sunk costs and their relevance to a decision to retain or replace equipment.

10. Diversified Inc. has one product line that is unprofitable. What circumstances may cause overall company net income to be lower if the unprofitable product line is eliminated?

11. How is the contribution margin per unit of limited resources computed?

12. Describe the process a company may use in screening and approving the capital expenditure budget.

13. Your classmate is confused about the factors that are included in the annual rate of return technique. What is the formula for this technique?

14. Stacy Kolb is trying to understand the term "cost of capital." Define the term and indicate its relevance to the decision rule under the annual rate of return technique.

15. Joe Culvar claims the formula for the cash payback technique is the same as the formula for the annual rate of return technique. Is Joe correct? What is the formula for the cash payback technique?

16. What are the advantages and disadvantages of the cash payback technique?

17. Two types of present value tables may be used with the discounted cash flow technique. Identify the tables and the circumstance(s) when each table should be used.

18. What is the decision rule under the net present value method?

19. Identify the steps required in using the internal rate of return method.

20. The Erkolay Company uses the internal rate of return method. What is the decision rule for this method?

BRIEF EXERCISES

BE28-1   The steps in management's decision making process are listed in random order below. Indicate the order in which the steps should be executed.

_____ Make decision
_____ Assign responsibility for decision
_____ Identify the opportunity or problem
_____ Determine possible courses of action
_____ Review results of decision
_____ Develop data relevant to each course of action

Identify the steps in management's decision making process.
(S.O. 1)

BE28-2   The Ash Company is considering two alternatives. Alternative A will have sales of $150,000 and costs of $100,000. Alternative B will have sales of $185,000 and costs of $120,000. Compare Alternative A to Alternative B showing incremental revenues, costs, and net income.

Determine incremental changes.
(S.O. 2)

BE28-3   In the Faford Company it costs $30 per unit ($20 variable and $10 fixed) to make a product that normally sells for $45. A foreign wholesaler offers to buy 4,000 units at $25 each. Faford will incur special shipping costs of $1 per unit. Assuming that Faford has excess operating capacity, indicate the net income (loss) Faford would realize by accepting the special order.

Determine whether to accept special order.
(S.O. 3)

BE28-4   Langlois Manufacturing incurs unit costs of $8 ($5 variable and $3 fixed) in making a sub-assembly part for its finished product. A supplier offers to make 10,000 of the assembly part at $6 per unit. If the offer is accepted, Langlois will save all variable costs but no fixed costs. Prepare an analysis showing the total cost saving, if any, Langlois will realize by buying the part.

Determine whether to make or buy a part.
(S.O. 4)

BE28-5   Woodcraft Inc., makes unfinished bookcases that it sells for $60. Production costs are $30 variable and $10 fixed. Because it has unused capacity, Woodcraft is considering finishing the bookcases and selling them for $70. Variable finishing costs are expected to be $8 per unit with no increase in fixed costs. Prepare an analysis on a per unit basis showing whether Woodcraft should sell unfinished or finished bookcases.

Determine whether to sell or process further.
(S.O. 5)

BE28-6   The Stockton Company has a factory machine with a book value of $90,000 and a remaining useful life of four years. A new machine is available at a cost of $200,000. This machine will have a four year useful life with no salvage value. The new machine will lower annual variable manufacturing costs from $600,000 to $420,000. Prepare an analysis showing whether the old machine should be retained or replaced.

Determine whether to retain or replace equipment.
(S.O. 6)

BE28-7   Trevina, Inc., manufactures golf clubs in three models. For the year, the Eagle line has a net loss of $20,000 from sales $200,000, variable expenses $180,000 and fixed expenses $40,000. If the Eagle line is eliminated, $30,000 of fixed costs will remain. Prepare an analysis showing whether the Eagle line should be eliminated.

Determine whether to eliminate an unprofitable segment.
(S.O. 7)

BE28-8   In the Graf Company, data concerning two products are: Contribution margin per unit—Product A $10, Product B $12; machine hours required for one unit—Product A 2, Product B 4. Compute the contribution margin per unit of limited resource for each product.

Show allocation of limited resources.
(S.O. 8)

BE28-9   The Grace Company is considering purchasing new equipment for $200,000. It is expected that the equipment will produce annual net income of $10,000 over its five year useful life. Annual depreciation will be $40,000. Compute the payback period.

Compute the cash payback period for a capital investment.
(S.O. 9)

BE28-10   The Willens Company accumulates the following data concerning a proposed capital investment: cash cost $210,000, annual cash inflow $40,000; present value of cash inflows for 10 years 5.65 (rounded). Determine the net present value and indicate whether the investment should be made.

Compute net present value of an investment.
(S.O. 10)

EXERCISES

Make incremental analysis for special order.
(S.O. 3)

E28–1 The Graham Company manufactures toasters. For the first eight months of 1994, the company reported the following operating results while operating at 75% of plant capacity:

Sales (400,000 units)	$4,000,000
Cost of goods sold	2,400,000
Gross profit	1,600,000
Operating expenses	900,000
Net income	$ 700,000

Cost of goods sold was 70% variable and 30% fixed; operating expenses were 60% variable and 40% fixed.

In September, Graham Company receives a special order for 15,000 toasters at $6.40 each from the Avante Company of Mexico City. Acceptance of the order would result in $3,000 of shipping costs but no increase in fixed operating expenses.

Instructions

(a) Prepare an incremental analysis for the special order.

(b) Should the Graham Company accept the special order? Why or why not?

Make incremental analysis for make or buy decision.
(S.O. 4)

E28–2 Kanable Inc. has been manufacturing its own shades for its table lamps. The company is currently operating at 100% of capacity, and variable manufacturing overhead is charged to production at the rate of 50% of direct labor cost. The direct materials and direct labor cost per unit to make the lamp shades are $4.00 and $6.00, respectively. Normal production is 30,000 table lamps per year.

A supplier offers to make the lamp shades at a price of $14.00 per unit. If Kanable Inc. accepts the supplier's offer, all variable manufacturing costs will be eliminated, but the $40,000 of fixed manufacturing overhead currently being charged to the lamp shades will have to be absorbed by other products.

Instructions

(a) Prepare the incremental analysis for the decision to make or buy the lamp shades.

(b) Should Kanable Inc. buy the lamps?

(c) Would your answer be different in (b) above if the productive capacity released by discontinuing making the lamp shades could be used to produce income of $35,000?

Make incremental analysis for further processing of materials.
(S.O. 5)

E28–3 Diana Jones recently opened her own basketweaving studio. She sells finished baskets in addition to the raw materials needed by customers to weave baskets of their own. Diana has put together a variety of raw material kits, each including materials at various stages of completion. Unfortunately, owing to space limitations, Diana is unable to carry all varieties of kits originally assembled and must choose between two basic packages.

The basic introductory kit includes undyed, uncut reeds (with dye included) for weaving one basket. This basic package costs Diana $12 and sells for $27. The second kit, called Stage 2, includes cut reeds that have already been dyed. With this kit the customer need only soak the reeds and weave the basket. Diana is able to produce the second kit by using the basic materials included in the first kit and adding one hour of her own time, which she values at $16 per hour. Because she is more efficient at cutting and dying reeds than her average customer, Diana is able to make two kits of the dyed reeds, in one hour, from one kit of undyed reeds. The kit of dyed reeds sells for $32.

Instructions

Determine whether Diana's basketweaving shop should carry the basic introductory kit with undyed reeds or the Stage 2 kit with reeds already dyed. Prepare an incremental analysis to support your answer.

Make incremental analysis for retaining or replacing equipment.
(S.O. 6)

E28–4 White Enterprises uses a word processing computer to handle its sales invoices. Lately, business has been so good that it takes an extra three hours per night, plus every third Saturday, to keep up with the volume of sales invoices. Management is considering updating its computer with a faster model that would eliminate all of the overtime processing.

	Current Machine	New Machine
Original purchase cost	$15,000	$24,000
Accumulated depreciation	6,000	—
Estimated operating costs	21,000	15,600
Useful life	5 years	5 years

If sold now, the current machine would have a salvage value of $2,000. If operated for the remainder of its useful life, the current machine would have zero salvage value. The new machine is expected to have zero salvage value after five years.

Instructions
Should the current machine be replaced? (Ignore the time value of money.)

E28–5 Lori Hamson, a recent graduate of Rolling's accounting program, evaluated the operating performance of Watkin Company's six divisions. Lori made the following presentation to Watkin's Board of Directors and suggested the Hudson Division be eliminated. "If the Hudson Division is eliminated," she said, "our total profits would increase by $16,870."

Make incremental analysis concerning elimination of division.
(S.O. 7)

	The Other Five Divisions	Hudson Division	Total
Sales	$1,664,200	$ 98,200	$1,762,400
Cost of goods sold	978,520	76,470	1,054,990
Gross profit	685,680	21,730	707,410
Operating expenses	527,940	38,600	566,540
Net income	$ 157,740	$(16,870)	$ 140,870

In the Hudson Division, cost of goods sold is $62,000 variable and $14,470 fixed, and operating expenses are $12,000 variable and $26,600 fixed. None of the Hudson Division's fixed costs will be eliminated if the division is discontinued.

Instructions
Is Lori right about eliminating the Hudson Division? Prepare a schedule to support your answer.

E28–6 Lorenson Company manufactures and sells three products. Relevant per unit data concerning each product are given below:

Compute contribution margin and determine the product to be manufactured.
(S.O. 8)

	Product		
	A	B	C
Selling price	$8	$12	$14
Variable costs and expenses	$4	$ 9	$12
Machine hours to produce	2	1	2

Instructions
(a) Compute the contribution margin per unit of the limited resource for each product.

(b) Assuming 1,200 additional machine hours are available, which product should be manufactured?

(c) Prepare an analysis showing the total contribution margin if the additional hours are (1) divided equally among the products, and (2) allocated entirely to the product identified in (b) above.

E28–7 Griven Service Center just purchased an automobile hoist for $9,000. The hoist has a five-year life and an estimated salvage value of $680. Installation costs and freight charges were $2,900 and $580, respectively. Griven uses straight-line depreciation.

Compute cash payback period and annual rate of return.
(S.O. 9)

The new hoist will be used to replace mufflers and tires on automobiles. Griven estimates that the new hoist will enable his mechanics to replace four extra mufflers per week. Each muffler sells for $65 installed. The cost of a muffler is $40 and the labor cost to install a muffler is $10.

Instructions
(a) Compute the payback period for the new hoist.

(b) Compute the annual rate of return for the new hoist. (Round to one decimal.)

Compute cash payback period and net present value.
(S.O. 9, 10)

E28-8 The Karst Manufacturing Company is considering three new projects, each requiring an equipment investment of $21,000. Each project will last for three years and produce the following cash inflows:

Year	AA	BB	CC
1	$ 6,000	$ 9,500	$13,000
2	9,000	9,500	9,000
3	15,000	9,500	11,000
Total	$30,000	$28,500	$33,000

The equipment's salvage value is zero, and Karst uses straight-line depreciation. Karst will not accept any project with a payback period over two years. Karst's minimum required rate of return is 15%.

Instructions

(a) Compute each project's payback period, indicating the most desirable project and the least desirable project using this method. (Round to two decimals.)

(b) Compute the net present value of each project. Does your evaluation change? (Round to nearest dollar.)

Compute annual rate of return, cash payback period, and net present value.
(S.O. 9, 10)

E28-9 Frenk Company is considering a capital investment of $180,000 in additional productive facilities. The new machinery is expected to have a useful life of 6 years with no salvage value. Depreciation is by the straight-line method. During the life of the investment, annual net income and cash inflows are expected to be $18,000 and $48,000 respectively. Frenk has a 15% cost of capital rate which is the minimum acceptable rate of return on the investment.

Instructions
(Round to two decimals.)

(a) Compute (1) the annual rate of return and (2) the cash payback period on the proposed capital expenditure.

(b) Using the discounted cash flow technique, compute the net present value.

Determine internal rate of return.
(S.O. 10)

E28-10 The McKnight Company is considering three capital expenditure projects. Relevant data for the projects are as follows:

Project	Investment	Annual Income	Life of Project
22A	$240,000	$18,000	6 years
23A	270,000	25,400	9 years
24A	288,000	20,000	8 years

Annual income is constant over the life of the project. Each project is expected to have zero salvage value at the end of the project. McKnight Company uses the straight-line method of depreciation.

Instructions
(a) Determine the internal rate of return for each project. Round the internal rate of return factor to three decimals.

(b) If McKnight Company's minimum required rate of return is 12%, which projects are acceptable?

PROBLEMS

Make incremental analysis for special order and identify nonfinancial factors in decision.
(S.O. 3)

P28-1 Rainbow Sports Inc. manufactures basketballs for the American Basketball Association (ABA). For the first six months of 1994, the company reported the following operating results while operating at 90% of plant capacity.

	Amount	Per Unit
Sales	$4,500,000	$50.00
Cost of goods sold	3,600,000	40.00
Selling and administrative expenses	360,000	4.00
Net income	$ 540,000	$ 6.00

Fixed costs for the period were: cost of goods sold $900,000, and selling and administrative expenses $180,000.

In July, normally a slack manufacturing month, Rainbow Sports receives a special order for 10,000 basketballs at $33 each from the Italian Basketball Association (IBA). Acceptance of the order would increase variable selling and administrative expenses $.35 per unit because of shipping costs but would not increase fixed costs and expenses.

Instructions

(a) Prepare an incremental analysis for the special order.

(b) Should Rainbow Sports Inc. accept the special order?

(c) What is the minimum selling price on the special order to produce net income of $2.25 per ball?

(d) What nonfinancial factors should management consider in making its decision?

P28–2 The management of the Pomay Manufacturing Company is trying to decide whether to continue manufacturing a part or to buy it from an outside supplier. The part, called WISCO, is a component of the company's finished product.

The following information was collected from the accounting records and production data for the year ending December 31, 1994.

Make incremental analysis related to make or buy; consider opportunity cost, and identify nonfinancial factors.
(S.O. 4)

1. 7,000 units of WISCO were produced in the Machining Department.

2. Variable manufacturing costs applicable to the production of each WISCO unit were: Direct materials $4.75, Direct labor $4.60, Indirect labor $.45, Utilities $.35.

3. Fixed manufacturing costs applicable to the production of WISCO were:

Cost Item	Direct	Allocated
Depreciation	$1,600	$ 900
Property taxes	400	200
Insurance	900	600
	$2,900	$1,700

All variable manufacturing and direct fixed costs will be eliminated if WISCO is purchased. Allocated costs will have to be absorbed by other production departments.

4. The lowest quotation for 7,000 WISCO units from a supplier is $74,000.

5. If WISCO units are purchased, freight and inspection costs would be $.30 per unit, and receiving costs totaling $750 per year would be incurred by the Machining Department.

Instructions

(a) Prepare an incremental analysis for WISCO. Your analysis should have columns for (1) Make WISCO, (2) Buy WISCO, and (3) Net Income Increase/Decrease.

(b) Based on your analysis, what decision should management make?

(c) Would the decision be different if the Pomay Company has the opportunity to produce $5,000 of net income with the facilities currently being used to manufacture WISCO? Show computations.

(d) What nonfinancial factors should management consider in making its decision?

P28–3 Barry Manufacturing Company has four operating divisions. During the first quarter of 1994, the company reported aggregate income from operations of $165,000 and the following divisional results.

Compute contribution margin and prepare incremental analysis concerning elimination of divisions. (S.O. 7)

	Division			
	I	II	III	IV
Sales	$500,000	$400,000	$300,000	$200,000
Cost of goods sold	300,000	250,000	270,000	180,000
Selling and administrative expenses	60,000	80,000	35,000	60,000
Income (loss) from operations	$140,000	$ 70,000	$ (5,000)	$ (40,000)

Analysis reveals the following percentages of variable costs in each division.

	I	II	III	IV
Cost of goods sold	70%	80%	75%	90%
Selling and administrative expenses	40	50	60	70

Discontinuance of any division would save 50% of the fixed costs and expenses for that division.

Top management is very concerned about the unprofitable divisions (III and IV). Consensus is that one or both of the divisions should be discontinued.

Instructions

(a) Compute the contribution margin for Divisions III and IV.

(b) Prepare an incremental analysis concerning the possible discontinuance of (1) Division III and (2) Division IV. What course of action do you recommend for each division?

(c) Prepare a columnar condensed income statement for Barry Manufacturing, assuming Division IV is eliminated. Use the CVP format. Division IV's unavoidable fixed costs are allocated equally to the continuing divisions.

(d) Reconcile the total income from operations ($165,000) with the total income from operations without Division IV.

Compute rate of return, cash payback, and net present value.
(S.O. 9, 10)

P28–4   The Eric and Tatum partnership is considering three long-term capital investment proposals. Each investment has a useful life of 5 years. Relevant data on each project are as follows:

	Project Tic	Project Tac	Project Toe
Capital investment	$140,000	$160,000	$200,000
Annual net income:			
year 1	12,000	18,000	27,000
2	12,000	17,000	22,000
3	12,000	16,000	21,000
4	12,000	12,000	18,000
5	12,000	9,000	7,000
Total	$ 60,000	$ 72,000	$ 95,000

Depreciation is computed by the straight-line method with no salvage value. The company's cost of capital is 15%.

Instructions

(a) Compute the annual rate of return for each project. (Round to two decimals.)

(b) Compute the cash payback period for each project. (Round to two decimals.)

(c) Compute the net present value for each project. (Round to nearest dollar.)

(d) Rank the projects on each of the foregoing bases. Which project do you recommend?

Compute annual rate of return, cash payback, and net present value.
(S.O. 9, 10)

P28–5   Jane Korrina is an accounting major at a midwestern state university located approximately 60 miles from a major city. Many of the students attending the university are from the metropolitan area and visit their homes regularly on the weekends. Jane, an entrepreneur at heart, realizes that few good commuting alternatives are available for students doing weekend travel. She believes that a weekend commuting service could be organized and run profitably from several suburban and downtown shopping mall locations. Jane has gathered the following investment information:

1. Six used vans would cost a total of $66,000 to purchase and would have a 3-year useful life with negligible salvage value. Jane plans to use straight-line depreciation.

2. Ten drivers would have to be employed at a total annual payroll expense of $48,000.

3. Other annual out of pocket expenses associated with running the commuter service would include Gasoline $12,000, Maintenance $2,800, Repairs $3,500, Insurance $3,200, Advertising $1,500.

4. Jane has visited several financial institutions to discuss funding for her new venture. The best interest rate she has been able to negotiate is 9%. Use this rate for cost of capital.

5. Jane expects each van to make 9 round trips weekly and carry an average of 5 students each trip. The service is expected to operate 30 weeks each year, and each student will be charged $12.00 for a round-trip ticket.

Instructions

(a) Determine the annual (1) net income, and (2) cash inflow for the commuter service.

(b) Compute (1) the annual rate of return, and (2) the cash payback period. (Round to two decimals.)

(c) Compute the net present value of the commuter service. (Round to the nearest dollar.)

(d) What should Jane conclude from these computations?

ALTERNATE PROBLEMS

P28–1A The Murray Company is currently producing 16,000 units per month, which is 80% of its production capacity. Variable manufacturing costs are currently $11.00 per unit, and fixed manufacturing costs are $48,000 per month. Murray pays a 9% sales commission to its sales people, has $30,000 in fixed administrative expenses per month, and is averaging $320,000 in sales per month.

Make incremental analysis for special order and identify nonfinancial factors in decisions.
(S.O. 3)

A special order received from a foreign company would enable the Murray Company to operate at 100% capacity. The foreign company offered to pay 75% of Murray's current selling price per unit. If the order is accepted, Murray will have to spend an extra $2.00 per unit to package the product for overseas shipping. Also, the Murray Company would need to lease a new stamping machine to imprint the foreign company's logo on the product, at a monthly cost of $2,500. The special order would require a sales commission of $3,000.

Instructions

(a) Compute the number of units involved in the special order and the foreign company's offered price per unit.

(b) What is the manufacturing cost of producing one unit of Murray's product for regular customers?

(c) Prepare an incremental analysis of the special order. Should management accept the order?

(d) What is the lowest price that Murray could accept for the special order to earn net income of $1.00 per unit?

(e) What nonfinancial factors should management consider in making its decision?

P28–2A The management of the Orlan Manufacturing Company has asked for your assistance in deciding whether to continue manufacturing a part or to buy it from an outside supplier. The part, called Tropica, is a component of Orlan's finished product.

Make incremental analysis related to make or buy, consider opportunity cost, and identify nonfinancial factors.
(S.O. 4)

An analysis of the accounting records and the production data revealed the following information for the year ending December 31, 1993.

1. The Machinery Department produced 36,000 units of Tropica.

2. Each Tropica unit requires 10 minutes to produce. Three people in the Machinery Department work full time (2,000 hours per year) producing Tropica. Each person is paid $10.00 per hour.

3. The cost of materials per Tropica unit is $2.00.

4. Manufacturing costs directly applicable to the production of Tropica are: Indirect la-

bor, $5,500; Utilities, $1,300; Depreciation, $1,600; Property taxes and insurance, $1,000. All of the costs will be eliminated if Tropica is purchased.

5. The lowest price for a Tropica from an outside supplier is $3.50 per unit. Freight charges will be $.30 per unit, and a part-time receiving clerk at $8,500 per year will be required.

6. If Tropica is purchased, the excess space will be used to store Orlan's finished product. Currently, Orlan rents storage space at approximately $.50 per per unit stored per year. Approximately 4,500 units per year are stored in the rented space.

Instructions

(a) Prepare an incremental analysis for the make or buy decision. Should Orlan make or buy the part? Why?

(b) Prepare an incremental analysis, assuming the released facilities can be used to produce $12,000 of net income in addition to the savings on the rental of storage space. What decision should now be made?

(c) What nonfinancial factors should be considered in the decision?

P28–3A   Western Manufacturing Company has four operating divisions. During the first quarter of 1993, the company reported total income from operations of $61,000 and the following results for the divisions:

Compute contribution margin and prepare incremental analysis concerning elimination of divisions.
(S.O. 7)

	Division			
	Denver	Helena	Portland	Seattle
Sales	$450,000	$720,000	$930,000	$520,000
Cost of goods sold	380,000	480,000	576,000	430,000
Selling and administrative expenses	120,000	207,000	246,000	120,000
Income (loss) from operations	$ (50,000)	$ 33,000	$108,000	$ (30,000)

Analysis reveals the following percentages of variable costs in each division.

	Denver	Helena	Portland	Seattle
Cost of goods sold	95%	80%	90%	90%
Selling and administrative expenses	80	60	70	60

Discontinuance of any division would save 60% of the fixed costs and expenses for that division.

Top management is deeply concerned about the unprofitable divisions (Denver and Seattle). The consensus is that one or both of the divisions should be eliminated.

Instructions

(a) Compute the contribution margin for the two unprofitable divisions.

(b) Prepare an incremental analysis concerning the possible elimination of (1) the Denver Division and (2) the Seattle Division. What course of action do you recommend for each division?

(c) Prepare a columnar condensed income statement using the CVP format for Western Manufacturing Company, assuming (1) the Denver Division is eliminated, and (2) the unavoidable fixed costs and expenses of the Denver Division are allocated 30% to Helena, 50% to Portland, and 20% to Seattle.

(d) Compare the total income from operations with the Denver Division ($61,000) to total income from operations without this division.

Compute rate of return, cash payback, and net present value.
(S.O. 9, 10)

P28–4A   The partnership of Main and Street is considering three long-term capital investment proposals. Relevant data on each project are as follows:

	Project		
	Brown	Red	Yellow
Capital investment	$180,000	$220,000	$250,000
Annual net income:			
Year 1	25,000	20,000	26,000
2	16,000	20,000	24,000

	Project		
	Brown	Red	Yellow
Capital investment	$180,000	$220,000	$250,000
Annual net income:			
Year 3	13,000	20,000	23,000
4	10,000	20,000	22,000
5	8,000	20,000	20,000
Total 6	$72,000	$100,000	$115,000

Salvage value is expected to be zero at the end of each project. Depreciation is computed by the straight-line method. The company's minimum rate of return is the company's cost of capital which is 12%.

Instructions

(a) Compute the average annual rate of return for each project. (Round to two decimals.)

(b) Compute the cash payback period for each project. (Round to two decimals.)

(c) Compute the net present value for each project. (Round to nearest dollar.)

(d) Rank the projects on each of the foregoing bases. What project do you recommend?

P28–5A Teresa Gerry is managing director of the Goodwill day care center. Goodwill is currently set up as a full-time child care facility for children between the ages of 12 months and 6 years. Teresa is trying to determine whether the center should expand its facilities to incorporate a newborn care room for infants between the ages of 6 weeks and 12 months. The necessary space already exists. An investment of $24,000 would be needed, however, to purchase cribs, high chairs, etc. The equipment purchased for the room would have a 5-year useful life with zero salvage value.

Compute annual rate of return, cash payback, and net present value.
(S.O. 9, 10)

The newborn nursery would be staffed to handle 12 infants on a full-time basis. The parents of each infant would be charged $150 weekly, and the facility would operate 52 weeks of the year. Staffing the nursery would require two full-time specialists and five part-time assistants at an annual cost of $74,000. Food, diapers, and other miscellaneous supplies are expected to total $12,500 annually.

Instructions

(a) Determine (1) annual net income, and (2) cash inflow for the new nursery.

(b) Compute (1) the annual rate of return and (2) the cash payback period for the new nursery. (Round to two decimals.)

(c) Assuming that Goodwill can borrow the money needed for expansion at 12%, compute the net present value of the new room. (Round to the nearest dollar.)

(d) What should Teresa conclude from these computations?

Broadening Your Perspective

FINANCIAL REPORTING PROBLEM

Refer to the PepsiCo, Inc. financial statements in Appendix L and answer the following questions.

1. Using the chairman's letters to "Dear Friends", what was PepsiCo's total capital spending on its segments in 1991?

2. How was the capital spending divided (a) among the segments and (b) between international and domestic?

3. How, if at all, is PepsiCo. expanding globally?

4. From the Business Segments section (or the Financial Highlights at the beginning of

the report) and your answer in question 2 above, how does the capital spending match up with total segment operating profits?

5. From the Business Segments section, what has been the trend in capital spending for each segment and in total from 1989–1991?

6. From Investing Activities under Management's Analysis-Cash Flows, what types of capital spending plans does PepsiCo have for 1992?

DECISION CASE

The Navaro Company is considering the purchase of a new machine. The invoice price of the machine is $115,000, freight charges are estimated to be $4,000, and installation costs are expected to be $6,000. Salvage value of the new equipment is expected to be zero after a useful life of 4 years. Existing equipment could be retained and used for an additional 4 years if the new machine is not purchased. At that time, the salvage value of the equipment would be zero. If the new machine is purchased now, the existing machine would have to be scrapped. Navaro's accountant, Darcy Hank, has accumulated the following data regarding annual sales and expenses with and without the new machine.

1. Without the new machine, Navaro can sell 11,000 units of product annually at a per unit selling price of $100. If the new unit is purchased, the number of units produced and sold would increase by 20%, and the selling price would remain the same.

2. The new machine is faster than the old machine, and it is more efficient in its usage of materials. With the old machine the gross profit rate will be 26.5% of sales, whereas the rate will be 28% of sales with the new machine.

3. Annual selling expenses are $180,000 with the current equipment. Because the new equipment would produce a greater number of units to be sold, annual selling expenses are expected to increase by 10% if it is purchased.

4. Annual administrative expenses are expected to be $100,000 with the old machine, and $113,000 with the new machine.

5. The current book value of the existing machine is $36,000. Navaro uses straight-line depreciation.

6. Navaro's management wants a minimum rate of return of 15% on its investment and a payback period of no more than 3 years.

Instructions
(Ignore income tax effects.)

(a) Prepare an incremental analysis for the four years showing whether Navaro should keep the existing machine or buy the new machine.

(b) Calculate the annual rate of return for the new machine. (Round to two decimals.)

(c) Compute the payback period for the new machine. (Round to two decimals.)

(d) Compute the net present value of the new machine. (Round to the nearest dollar.)

(e) On the basis of the foregoing data, would you recommend that Navaro buy the machine? Why?

CRITICAL THINKING CASE

Refer to the vignette at the beginning of this chapter and answer the following questions.

1. Should the cost of hiring a consulting engineer by WLHA be included in a capital budgeting decision? Explain.

2. Should the cost of upgrading equipment be included in a capital budgeting decision? Explain.

3. Which method of making this capital budgeting decision would you recommend to Scooter? Why?

4. Assuming an upgrade to 400 watts is approved, would you expect even or uneven cash flows from the purchase of new equipment?

ETHICAL CASE

Bristle Brush Company operates in a state where corporate taxes and workmen's compensation insurance rates have recently doubled. Bristle's president has just assigned you the task of preparing an economic analysis and making a recommendation relative to moving the company's entire operation to Missouri. The president is slightly in favor of such a move because Missouri is his boyhood home and also where he owns a fishing lodge.

You have just completed building your dream house, moved in, and sodded the lawn. Your children are all doing well in school and sports and, along with your spouse, want no part of a move to Missouri. If the company does move, so will you because the town is a one-industry community and you and your spouse will have to move to have employment. Moving, when everyone else does, will cause you to take a big loss on the sale of your house. The same hardships will be suffered by your coworkers; and, the town will be devastated.

In compiling the costs of moving versus not moving, you have latitude in the assumptions you make, the estimates you compute, and the discount rates and time periods you project. You are in a position to singlehandedly influence the decision.

Instructions

(a) Who are the stakeholders in this situation?

(b) What are the ethical issues in this situation?

(c) What would you do in this situation?

Answers to Self-Study Questions
1. c   2. a   3. d   4. d   5. b   6. a   7. b   8. c   9. c   10. a

APPENDIX L

SPECIMEN FINANCIAL STATEMENTS

The Annual Report

Once each year a corporation communicates to its stockholders and other interested parties by issuing a complete set of audited financial statements. The **annual report**, as this communication is called, summarizes the financial results of its operation for the year and its plans for the future. Many such annual reports have become attractive, multicolored, glossy public relations ad pieces containing pictures of corporate officers and directors as well as photos and descriptions of new products and new buildings. Yet the basic function of every annual report is to report financial information, almost all of which is a product of the corporation's accounting system.

The content and organization of corporate annual reports has become fairly standardized. Excluding the public relations part of the report (pictures, products, and propaganda), the following items are the traditional financial portions of the annual report:

> Financial Highlights
> Letter to the Stockholders
> Management's Report
> Auditor's Report
> Financial Statements (and Management's Analysis)
> Notes to the Financial Statements
> Supplementary Financial Information

In this appendix we illustrate current financial reporting with a comprehensive set of corporate financial statements that are prepared in accordance with generally accepted accounting principles and audited by an international independent certified public accounting firm. We are grateful for permission to use the actual financial statements and other accompanying financial information from the annual report of a large, publicly held company, PepsiCo, Inc.

Financial Highlights

The financial highlights section, called the **Financial Summary** by PepsiCo, is usually presented inside the front cover or on the first two pages of the annual report. This section generally reports the total or per share amounts for five to ten financial items for the current year and one or more previous years. Financial items from the income statement and the balance sheet that typically are presented are sales, income from continuing operations, net income, net income per share, dividends per common share, and the amount of capital expenditures. The financial highlights section from PepsiCo's **Annual Report** is shown below:

PepsiCo, Inc.

Financial Highlights

(tabular dollars in millions except per share amounts)	1991	1990	Percent Change
Net sales	$19,608	17,803	+10
Soft drinks	$ 6,915	6,523	+ 6
Snack foods	$ 5,566	5,054	+10
Restaurants	$ 7,127	6,226	+14
Segment operating profits	$ 2,227	2,224	—
Soft drinks	$ 863	768	+12
Snack foods	$ 788	934	−16
Restaurants	$ 576	522	+10
Income from continuing operations	$ 1,080	1,091	− 1
Per Share	$ 1.35	1.37	− 1
Net income	$ 1,080	1,077	—
Per Share	$ 1.35	1.35	—
Cash dividends declared	$ 363	302	+20
Per Share	$ 0.460	0.383	+20
Net cash provided by continuing operations	$ 2,430	2,110	+15
Purchases of property, plant and equipment for cash	$ 1,458	1,180	+24
Acquisitions and investments in affiliates for cash	$ 641	631	
Return on average shareholders' equity	% 20.7	24.8	

As shown above, PepsiCo chose also to present the percent change from last year to the current year for each of the reported items and net sales and operating profits by segments.

▟etter to the Stockholders

Nearly every annual report contains a letter to the stockholders from the Chairman of the Board or the President (or both). This letter typically discusses the company's accomplishments during the past year and highlights significant events such as mergers and acquisitions, new products, operating achievements, business philosophy, changes in officers or directors, financing commitments, expansion plans, and future prospects. The letter to the stockholders ("Dear Friends") signed by Wayne Calloway, Chairman of the Board and Chief Executive Officer of PepsiCo, is shown below:

Dear Friends:

Not very subtle I guess, but our pink eyed friends on the cover are the best way we know to symbolize "rapid growth," something as natural to us as it is to them.

The quest for rapid growth keeps us hopping. It also keeps us innovating, shaking things up, breaking down barriers; all in search of new opportunities.

Rapid, profitable growth is the best way we know to create shareholder wealth and employee opportunity, two essential ingredients for a successful corporation.

At PepsiCo, we've increased sales and net income at an exhilarating rate of nearly 15% for 26 years. That means we've doubled our business about every five years. But now that we're about $20 billion big, you might well ask, how long can this keep going on?

Forever, as far as we're concerned. At least, that's our intention. Because without growth, PepsiCo wouldn't be the same company you invested in…nor would it be an attractive place to work.

But how? Where will PepsiCo's future growth come from? How does a $20 billion company add another $20 billion in just five years?

That's the theme of this year's Annual Report. We'll describe some future opportunities: big, small, local and global. Whatever their size or scope, you can be sure that our 338,000 employees are committed to realizing their full potential. By the time you finish this report, I hope you share our enthusiasm.

But first, some words about last year.

1991 Results

The numbers were certainly not as good as we would have liked, somewhat below our historical trends. On a reported basis, net income and income per share were even with last year at $1.1 billion and $1.35, respectively. Given the economy and consumer spending, they were only partially indicative of the more powerful and underlying progress we made since last year.

- Sales reached nearly $20 billion, an increase of 10%.
- Dividends declared per share increased 20%.
- Earnings, excluding unusual items, were $1.50 per share, up 9%.
- All three businesses achieved solid sales growth, with soft drinks up 6%, snack foods up 10% and restaurants up 14%.
- Operating profits, excluding unusual items, grew 5%. Soft drinks were up 11%, restaurants up 12% and snack foods down 3%.
- The price of a share of PepsiCo stock increased 31%, better than S&P 400 growth of 27%.
- Cash from operations hit a record $2.4 billion, a 15% increase.

This last number is critical. Our ability to internally generate cash is one of the most important measures of our company's health because it's cash that fuels opportunity. In the last five years, our operations have provided nearly $10 billion of cash for reinvestment in our businesses and for increased dividends.

Creating Opportunities

But numbers really don't begin to describe the progress we've made. At Frito-Lay, we streamlined and decentralized our business to focus more closely on our retail customers, our consumers and the competition. In our United Kingdom snack foods operations, we consolidated facilities and our sales group. We also restructured domestic and international KFC operations. These moves will pay off in a more agile organization with increased competitiveness.

But more than just restructuring some of our businesses, over the last few years we've also identified major and long-term opportunities for future growth. We think about these opportunities in two ways: redefining our basic businesses and expanding globally. Both are big leaps forward because they change the very markets we deal in, our categories and our geography.

Net Cash Provided By Continuing Operations
($ In Millions)

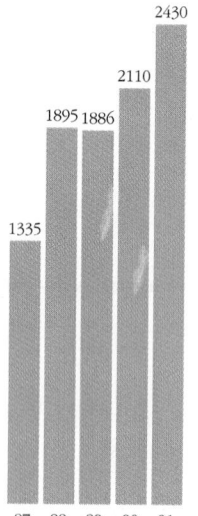

Net cash provided by continuing operations has grown at a compounded annual rate of 14.9% over the past five years.

Return On Average Shareholders' Equity*
(Percent)

*Based on income from continuing operations

When we talk about redefining our business, here's what we mean. Not too long ago, we would have described ourselves as a company in the business of soft drinks, snack chips and quick service restaurants. Today, we're in the business of beverages, snack foods and quick service food distribution.

I'm not sure if this sounds so different, but believe me it opens up huge opportunities by significantly expanding our horizons. For example, a soft drink company sells only carbonated colas and the like; a beverage company might sell things like water and tea or fruit based drinks. Also, a restaurant company is constricted to certain physical locations. A food distribution company can take its products wherever there's a customer, without necessarily making an investment in a large restaurant.

At the same time we were redefining our businesses, we also reconsidered our geographic limitations. Up until a few years ago, we were basically a strong U.S. company with a solid but limited international presence. Yes, we were doing business in nearly 150 countries, but it was primarily limited to soft drinks.

Not so today. In 1991, nearly one out of every four sales dollars came from our international operations, nearly double the level of five years ago. When you consider that 95% of the world's population is outside the U.S., you can see what that means in terms of opportunity. And this is doubly true for our kinds of products, which are in great demand everywhere on earth, with almost no economic or cultural barriers.

Let me expand on those two basic changes in our overall business proposition.

Redefining our Business

I believe there's a consumer revolution taking place across the globe and that's why we must redefine how we do business. Fueled by economics and cultural trends, the revolution involves people seeking more control of their lives, more value in the things they do and more personal freedom. The pace of change is accelerating, particularly as habits shift, lifestyles evolve and the Baby Boomers step into middle age.

Understanding this change is key to future growth and it adds up to a mandate for even higher quality products at far better prices and far more convenient locations—within an arm's reach if possible. That's why we're distributing our products in new ways, adding thousands of points of distribution in the form of delivery and kiosks and finding new outlets for our snack foods and soft drinks.

At Pizza Hut, for example, in 1977, virtually all our pizzas were sold from traditional restaurants. A few years ago, we added delivery and then express units. Now you can find Pizza Hut pizza in school lunchrooms, shopping malls, airports, hotels and sports arenas. You can even order our pizza from room service at Marriott Hotels. Taco Bell is right in there, too. Our self-contained kiosks are starting to multiply like…well, like rabbits. When you consider that the airport terminal foodservice market alone is $1.3 billion in sales, you can see why we're popping up in unexpected places.

In snack foods and soft drinks, we're just as active in expanding our traditional businesses. We've introduced new products like Doritos brand cracker crisps, a cross between a cracker and a chip that may create a whole new snack food category. And we're moving into other beverage products with our new partners at Lipton Tea and Ocean Spray.

Expanding Globally

We're also breaking out geographically. Although our products are famous and widespread, they are vastly underrepresented with the 95% of the world's population outside the U.S. So opportunity flashes before our eyes everywhere we look.

We're off to a good start. For example, we've more than doubled the number of countries where we sell snack foods from nine in 1986 to 23 in 1991. But even that's hardly a dent when you think of the whole world.

The number of our restaurants outside the U.S. has gone from about 2,500 in 1986 to more than 5,000 today. But we've hardly begun. In the U.S., there's one of our quick service restaurants for about every 16,000 people. Internationally, there's only one for every 1,000,000 people. That's what we mean by potential.

I'll talk more about our opportunities in each of our businesses later in this report under the sections we headline "Chairman's Outlook."

Getting Bigger to Get Better

Growth without purpose is pointless. We don't seek growth just to be bigger. Our goal is to get better.

Rapid growth creates an exciting, turned-on environment that's very attractive for recruiting high potential employees. It also creates new and far bigger opportunities for current employees, allowing them to seek bigger challenges and grow personally. In that way, rapid growth links the aspirations of employees with the requirements of shareholders in a way that is very satisfying to both.

One interesting PepsiCo program symbolizes this linkage very clearly. It's called PepsiCo SharePower and it allows our full-time employees to become shareholders by giving them stock options. If the price of the stock climbs, employees benefit right along with shareholders. This means that the interests

Net Sales
($ In Billions)

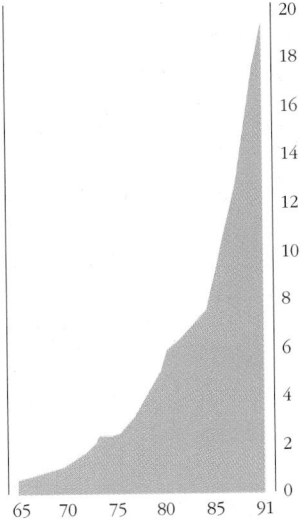

**Segment Net Sales
Total: $19,608**
($ In Millions)

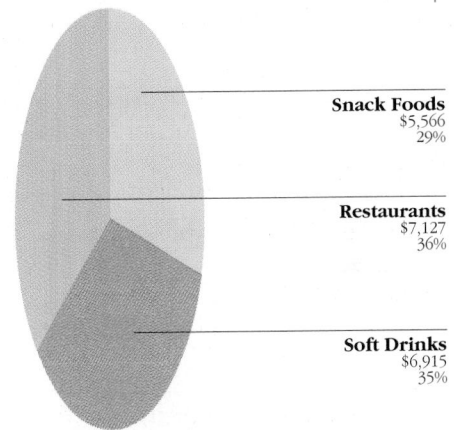

Snack Foods
$5,566
29%

Restaurants
$7,127
36%

Soft Drinks
$6,915
35%

Segment Operating Profits
Total: $2,227
($ In Millions)

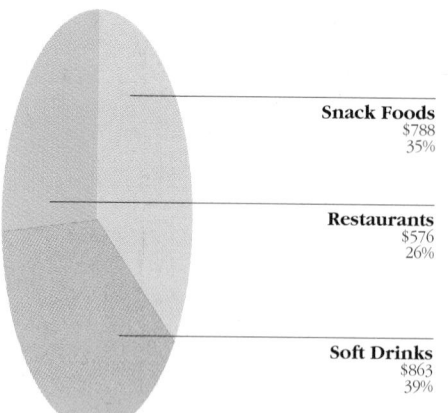

Snack Foods
$788
35%

Restaurants
$576
26%

Soft Drinks
$863
39%

Segment Capital Spending
Total: $1,480
($ In Millions)

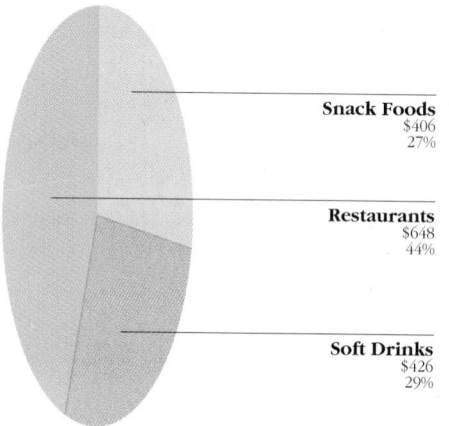

Snack Foods
$406
27%

Restaurants
$648
44%

Soft Drinks
$426
29%

Segment Capital Spending
Total: $1,480
($ In Millions)

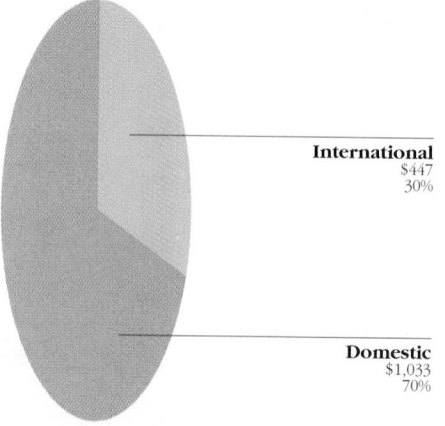

International
$447
30%

Domestic
$1,033
70%

of shareholders and employees are tied tightly together and everyone associated with the corporation shares a strong and clear vision of the future. Since we began SharePower, PepsiCo people have stepped forward with thousands of ideas to increase the financial performance of your company.

Public Commitment

Of course, a commitment to our shareholders includes a commitment to our communities and society at large. We don't do business in a vacuum.

In regard to the environment, for example, today more soft drink containers are recycled than any other container for any other product, anywhere in the U.S. The reusable plastic bottle we're developing is another giant step forward. Each of our divisions has a long-standing commitment to finding ways to help protect the environment. Frito-Lay, for example, has been reusing cartons since the 1950s.

In these challenging times, we're also reaching out to our communities in powerful economic ways. As just one example, we have a major commitment to develop business with minority-owned suppliers. Since 1982, PepsiCo has purchased well over $1 billion of goods and services from minority vendors. Thus a strong, growing company can have impact far beyond its own businesses.

Looking Forward

The future looks good. As I think you'll see, PepsiCo has all the elements in place to make our vision come true. That's not to say the future is without challenge. But with great products, dedicated people and strong financial resources, we believe we're up to it. And, most importantly, we're absolutely committed to achieving high returns for you, our shareholders.

In this quest we will miss the wise counsel of Cliff Garvin, who retires after 17 years on our Board of Directors. Cliff's far-reaching experience has been extremely valuable and we thank him for all he did on behalf of PepsiCo. Despite Cliff's departure, we still have one of the strongest boards in all corporate America, and we have their full dedication and commitment to helping us reach our goals.

So read on. You'll find this year's report full of facts, figures, statistics and strategies. Mostly, we hope you'll find it full of promise. All of us at PepsiCo look forward to the future with great enthusiasm and excitement.

Wayne Calloway

Wayne Calloway
Chairman of the Board and Chief Executive Officer

Management's Report

A relatively recent addition to corporate annual reports is the statement made by management about its role in and responsibility for the accuracy and integrity of the financial statements. PepsiCo's management letter is entitled **Management's Responsibility for Financial Statements**. In it the Chairman of the Board and Chief Executive Officer along with the Chief Financial Officer and the Controller, on behalf of management: (1) assume primary responsibility for the financial statements and the related notes, (2) outline and assess the company's internal control system, (3) declare the financial statements in conformity with generally accepted accounting principles, and (4) comment on the audit by the certified public accountant and the composition and role of the Audit Committee of the Board of Directors. PepsiCo's management report is presented below:

Management's Responsibility for Financial Statements

To Our Shareholders:

Management is responsible for the reliability of the consolidated financial statements and related notes. To help meet this responsibility, we maintain a system of internal control, supported by formal policies and procedures, which include an active Code of Conduct program intended to ensure key employees adhere to the highest standards of personal and professional integrity. PepsiCo's internal audit function monitors and reports on the adequacy of and compliance with our internal controls, policies and procedures. Although no cost effective internal control system will preclude all errors and irregularities, we believe our system of internal control provides reasonable assurance that assets are safeguarded, transactions are recorded in accordance with our policies and the financial information is reliable.

The consolidated financial statements have been prepared in conformity with generally accepted accounting principles and include amounts based upon our estimates and judgments, as required. The consolidated financial statements have been audited by our independent auditors who have expressed their opinions with respect to the fairness of the statements. Their audits included a review of the system of internal control and tests of transactions to the extent they considered necessary to render their opinions.

The Audit Committee of the Board of Directors is composed solely of outside directors. The Audit Committee meets periodically with our independent auditors, PepsiCo internal auditors and management to review accounting, auditing, internal control and financial reporting matters. Both our independent auditors and internal auditors have free access to the Audit Committee.

Wayne Calloway
Chairman of the Board and Chief Executive Officer

Robert G. Dettmer
Executive Vice President and Chief Financial Officer

Robert L. Carleton
Senior Vice President and Controller

Auditor's Report

All publicly held corporations, as well as many other enterprises and organizations (both profit and not-for-profit, large and small) engage the services of independent certified public accountants for the purpose of obtaining an objective, expert report on their financial statements. Based on a comprehensive examination of the company's accounting system and records, and the financial statements, the outside CPA issues the auditor's report.

The standard auditor's report consists of three paragraphs: (1) an introductory paragraph, (2) a scope paragraph, and (3) the opinion paragraph. In the introductory paragraph, the auditor identifies who and what was audited and indicates the responsibilities of management and the auditor relative to the financial statements. In the scope paragraph the auditor states that the audit was conducted in accordance with generally accepted auditing standards and discusses the nature and limitations of the audit. In the opinion paragraph, the auditor expresses an informed opinion as to (1) the fairness of the financial statements and (2) their conformity with generally accepted accounting principles. The **Report of KPMG Peat Marwick Independent Auditors** appearing in PepsiCo's Annual Report is shown below:

Report of KPMG Peat Marwick Independent Auditors

Board of Directors and Shareholders
PepsiCo, Inc.

We have audited the accompanying consolidated balance sheet of PepsiCo, Inc. and subsidiaries as of December 28, 1991 and December 29, 1990, and the related consolidated statements of income, shareholders' equity, and cash flows for the years then ended. These financial statements are the responsibility of PepsiCo, Inc.'s management. Our responsibility is to express an opinion on these financial statements based on our audits. The consolidated financial statements of PepsiCo, Inc. and subsidiaries as of December 30, 1989 and for the year then ended were audited by other auditors whose report dated February 6, 1990, expressed an unqualified opinion on those statements.

We conducted our audits in accordance with generally accepted auditing standards. Those standards require that we plan and perform the audit to obtain reasonable assurance about whether the financial statements are free of material misstatement. An audit includes examining, on a test basis, evidence supporting the amounts and disclosures in the financial statements. An audit also includes assessing the accounting principles used and significant estimates made by management, as well as evaluating the overall financial statement presentation. We believe that our audits provide a reasonable basis for our opinion.

In our opinion, the financial statements referred to above present fairly, in all material respects, the consolidated financial position of PepsiCo, Inc. and subsidiaries as of December 28, 1991 and December 29, 1990, and the results of its operations and its cash flows for the years then ended in conformity with generally accepted accounting principles.

KPMG Peat Marwick

New York, New York
February 4, 1992

The auditor's report issued on PepsiCo's financial statements is "unqualified" or "clean"; that is, it contains no qualifications or exceptions. In other words, the auditor conformed completely with generally accepted auditing standards in performing the audit, and the financial statements conformed in all material respects with generally accepted accounting principles.

When the financial statements do not conform with generally accepted accounting principles, the auditor must issue a "qualified" opinion and describe the exception. If the lack of confirmity with GAAP is sufficiently material, the auditor is compelled to issue an "adverse" or negative opinion. An adverse opinion means that the financial statements do not present fairly the company's financial condition and/or the results of the company's operations at the dates and for the periods reported.

In circumstances where the auditor is unable to perform all the auditing procedures necessary to reach a conclusion as to the fairness of the financial statements, a "disclaimer" must be issued. In these rare instances, the auditor must report the reason for failure to reach a conclusion on the fairness of the financial statements.

Companies strive to obtain an unqualified auditor's report. Hence, only infrequently are you likely to encounter anything other than this type of opinion on the financial statements.

Financial Statements and Accompanying Notes

The standard set of financial statements consists of: (1) a comparative income statement for three years, (2) a comparative balance sheet for two years, (3) a comparative statement of cash flows for three years, (4) a statement of retained earnings (or stockholders' equity) for three years, and (5) a set of accompanying notes that are considered an integral part of the financial statements. The auditor's report, unless stated otherwise, covers the financial statements and the accompanying notes. The financial statements and accompanying notes plus some supplementary data and analyses for PepsiCo, Inc., appear on the following pages.

Note to the student: For purposes of consistency PepsiCo uses 52 weeks as its fiscal year in preparing its financial statement. For six years in a row 52 weeks is used; every seventh year a 53-week year is adopted to catch up.

Consolidated Statement of Income

PepsiCo, Inc.

(in millions except per share amounts)
PepsiCo, Inc. and Subsidiaries
Fifty-two weeks ended December 28, 1991, December 29, 1990 and December 30, 1989

	1991	1990	1989
Net Sales	**$19,607.9**	$17,802.7	$15,242.4
Costs and Expenses, net			
Cost of sales	**9,395.5**	8,549.4	7,421.7
Selling, general and administrative expenses	**7,880.8**	7,008.6	5,887.4
Amortization of goodwill and other intangibles	**208.7**	189.1	150.4
Gain on joint venture stock offering	**–**	(118.2)	–
Interest expense	**615.9**	688.5	609.6
Interest income	**(163.3)**	(182.1)	(177.2)
	17,937.6	16,135.3	13,891.9
Income from Continuing Operations Before Income Taxes	**1,670.3**	1,667.4	1,350.5
Provision for Income Taxes	**590.1**	576.8	449.1
Income from Continuing Operations	**1,080.2**	1,090.6	901.4
Discontinued Operation Charge (net of income tax benefit of $0.3)	**–**	(13.7)	–
Net Income	**$ 1,080.2**	$ 1,076.9	$ 901.4
Income (Charge) Per Share			
Continuing operations	**$ 1.35**	$ 1.37	$ 1.13
Discontinued operation	**–**	(0.02)	–
Net Income Per Share	**$ 1.35**	$ 1.35	$ 1.13
Average shares outstanding used to calculate income (charge) per share	**802.5**	798.7	796.0

See accompanying Notes to Consolidated Financial Statements.

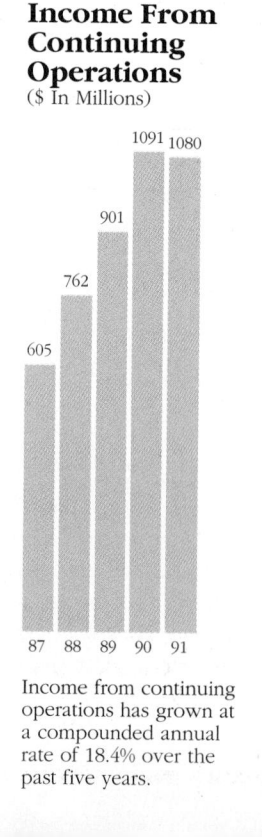

Net Sales
($ In Millions)

Net sales have grown at a compounded annual rate of 16.8% over the past five years.

LIO

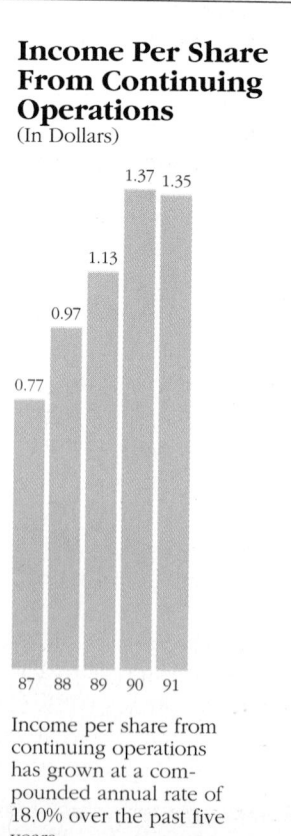

Income From Continuing Operations
($ In Millions)

Income from continuing operations has grown at a compounded annual rate of 18.4% over the past five years.

Income Per Share From Continuing Operations
(In Dollars)

Income per share from continuing operations has grown at a compounded annual rate of 18.0% over the past five years.

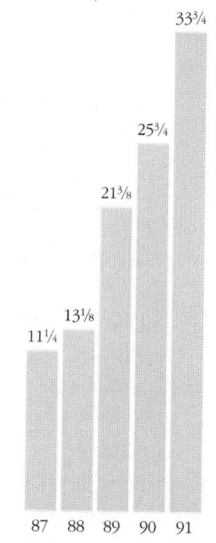

Year-End Market Price Of Stock
(In Dollars)

The market price of PepsiCo Capital Stock has grown at a compounded annual rate of 31.0% over the past five years.

Management's Analysis–Results of Operations

PepsiCo's domestic and international businesses operate in markets that are highly competitive and subject to local economic influences such as inflation, commodity cost movements and tax and wage legislation. Further, many of its businesses are currently affected by recessionary pressures. PepsiCo will continue to mitigate these factors by enhancing the appeal and value of its products through brand promotion, product innovation and quality improvement and prudent pricing actions, as well as increasing the worldwide availability of its products. Costs will continue to be contained through more efficient and effective purchasing, manufacturing, distribution and administrative processes. Acquisitions also provide opportunities to expand the businesses and achieve even more efficient resource utilization. The extent to which these and other strategies continue to be successful will substantially determine future growth rates.

The Financial Accounting Standards Board has issued new accounting rules for postretirement benefits other than pensions and is expected to issue new rules for accounting for income taxes. See Notes to Consolidated Financial Statements.

Because of the significant impact of the 1989 acquisitions of several franchised bottling operations and two snack chip companies in the United Kingdom (the U.K. operations), as well as the 1989 reconsolidation of a bottling operation in Japan previously held for sale, the analysis of 1990 vs. 1989 results provides certain comparisons excluding the 1990 results of such operations (collectively, the Acquisitions) for the corresponding periods that the operations were not reflected in 1989 results.

Net Sales rose 10% in 1991, driven by additional restaurant units (constructed or acquired from franchisees, net of units closed or sold) and volume growth in the snack foods and restaurants segments. Higher sales also reflected acquisitions of domestic and international franchised bottling operations and increased international pricing that was partially offset by lower net prices in domestic restaurants. Sales rose 17% in 1990. Excluding the impact of the Acquisitions, sales increased 14%, driven by volume growth in all three segments and additional restaurant units, and aided by higher prices. International sales represented 23%, 21% and 18% of total sales in 1991, 1990 and 1989, respectively, reflecting double-digit growth in all three industry segments, with the acquisition of the U.K. operations also contributing to the 1990 increase. The trend of an increasing international component of sales and operating profits is expected to continue.

Cost of sales as a percentage of net sales was 47.9%, 48.0% and 48.7% in 1991, 1990 and 1989, respectively. In 1991, the impact in soft drinks of higher concentrate pricing and lower domestic ingredient costs was largely offset in snack foods by a higher rate of manufacturing cost increases than international price advances. The 1990 decrease principally reflected higher pricing and lower ingredient costs in domestic soft drinks and snack foods.

Selling, general and administrative expenses rose 12% in 1991 and 19% in 1990. Unusual items accounted for one point of the growth in both years. Higher sales volumes, increased marketing costs and additional restaurant units led the increase in both years, with the 1990 growth also due to additional operating expenses of the Acquisitions.

Amortization of goodwill and other intangibles rose in 1991 and 1990 due to acquisition activity. A portion of the amortization expense is deductible for income tax purposes, and the after-tax expense amounts per share were $0.22, $0.20 and $0.16 in 1991, 1990 and 1989, respectively.

Gain on joint venture stock offering of $118.2 million relates to the 1990 initial public offering (IPO) of shares of PepsiCo's KFC joint venture in Japan (KFC-J). See Note to Consolidated Financial Statements.

Interest expense decreased 11% in 1991 but grew 13% in 1990. The decrease in 1991 reflected lower average interest rates, partially offset by higher average borrowings. The increase in 1990 reflected higher average borrowings to finance the Acquisitions, partially offset by a decline in average interest rates.

Interest income decreased 10% in 1991 but grew 3% in 1990. In 1991, lower average interest rates were partially offset by higher average balances of offshore short-term investment portfolios, but in 1990, higher portfolio balances exceeded the impact of lower rates.

Income from Continuing Operations Before Income Taxes was even with 1990 and posted 23% growth over 1989. Excluding unusual items, the KFC-J IPO gain and the impact of the Acquisitions (with related financing costs), the increases were 13% and 26% in 1991 and 1990, respectively. The growth in both years reflected operating profit advances driven by higher volumes and additional restaurant units. Operating profits grew at a slower rate in 1991 due largely to a profit decline in snack foods, but this impact was partially offset by lower net interest expense. Excluding unusual items, international operating profits represented 18%, 16% and 14% of combined segment operating profits in 1991, 1990 and 1989, respectively, reflecting base business growth, with the increase over 1989 also due to the acquisition of the U.K. operations.

Provision for Income Taxes as a percentage of income from continuing operations was 35.3%, 34.6% and 33.3% in 1991, 1990 and 1989, respectively. A current tax benefit was not available on substantially all of the international unusual charges in 1991 and 1990, and the KFC-J IPO gain had an unusually high tax rate. See Note to Consolidated Financial Statements. Excluding the impact of these items, the effective rates were 34.6% in 1991 and 32.7% in 1990, with the increase over 1990 due primarily to higher taxes on foreign income.

Income and Income Per Share from Continuing Operations in 1991 declined 1% to $1.08 billion and $1.35, respectively, but grew 21% in 1990. Unusual charges in 1991 totaled $119.8 million after-tax or $0.15 per share, and the net impact in 1990 of unusual charges and the KFC-J IPO gain was a $4.2 million charge after-tax or $0.01 per share. Excluding these items, income and income per share from continuing operations rose 10% and 9% in 1991, and grew 21% and 22% in 1990, respectively.

Consolidated Balance Sheet

PepsiCo, Inc.

(in millions except per share amount)
PepsiCo, Inc. and Subsidiaries
December 28, 1991 and December 29, 1990

	1991	1990
ASSETS		
Current Assets		
Cash and cash equivalents	$ 186.7	$ 170.8
Short-term investments, at cost which approximates market	1,849.3	1,644.9
	2,036.0	1,815.7
Accounts and notes receivable, less allowance: $97.5 in 1991 and $90.8 in 1990	1,481.7	1,414.7
Inventories	661.5	585.8
Prepaid expenses and other current assets	386.9	265.2
Total Current Assets	4,566.1	4,081.4
Investments in Affiliates and Other Assets	1,681.9	1,505.9
Property, Plant and Equipment, net	6,594.7	5,710.9
Goodwill and Other Intangibles, net	5,932.4	5,845.2
Total Assets	$18,775.1	$17,143.4
LIABILITIES AND SHAREHOLDERS' EQUITY		
Current Liabilities		
Short-term borrowings	$ 228.2	$ 1,626.5
Accounts payable	1,196.6	1,116.3
Income taxes payable	492.4	443.7
Other current liabilities	1,804.9	1,584.0
Total Current Liabilities	3,722.1	4,770.5
Long-term Debt	7,806.2	5,600.1
Nonrecourse Obligation	–	299.5
Other Liabilities and Deferred Credits	631.3	626.3
Deferred Income Taxes	1,070.1	942.8
Shareholders' Equity		
Capital stock, par value 1⅔¢ per share: authorized 1,800.0 shares, issued 863.1 shares	14.4	14.4
Capital in excess of par value	476.6	365.0
Retained earnings	5,470.0	4,753.0
Currency translation adjustment	330.3	383.2
	6,291.3	5,515.6
Less: Treasury stock, at cost: 74.0 shares in 1991, 74.7 shares in 1990	(745.9)	(611.4)
Total Shareholders' Equity	5,545.4	4,904.2
Total Liabilities and Shareholders' Equity	$18,775.1	$17,143.4

See accompanying Notes to Consolidated Financial Statements.

Management's Analysis—Financial Condition

PepsiCo's principal objective is to increase the value of its shareholders' investment through integrated operating, investing and financing strategies that maximize cash returns on investments and optimize the cost of capital. The cost of capital is a weighting of cost of debt and cost of equity, with the latter representing a measure of expected return to investors in PepsiCo's stock. PepsiCo estimates its cost of capital to be approximately 11%. PepsiCo's strong financial condition provides continued access to capital markets throughout the world.

Assets increased $1.6 billion or 10% over 1990. This increase reflected purchases of property, plant and equipment (PP&E), acquisition and affiliate investment activity and growth in the base businesses.

Short-term investments, substantially all of which consist of high-grade marketable securities portfolios held offshore, rose $204 million or 12% over 1990. This increase reflected higher portfolios from operations or to support financing of certain international businesses. The portfolio in Puerto Rico represents the significant majority of the investments, reflecting the strong operating cash flows of the centralized soft drink concentrate manufacturing facilities that operate there under a tax incentive grant. The grant provides that the portfolio funds may be remitted to the U.S. without any tax. In 1991, PepsiCo liquidated $500 million of the Puerto Rico portfolio, with a portion used to refinance an international investment and the remainder remitted to the U.S. PepsiCo continually reassesses its alternatives to redeploy these and other offshore portfolios, considering other investment opportunities, tax consequences and overall financing strategies.

The $122 million or 46% increase in prepaid expenses and other current assets over 1990 was due principally to increased prefunding of employee benefit expenses and higher prepaid media advertising costs.

PepsiCo's purchases of PP&E totaled $1.5 billion in 1991 and $1.2 billion in 1990. The purchases were led in both years by new unit additions in the restaurants segment. The 1991 growth also reflected increased investments in international soft drinks and additional production capacity in domestic snack foods.

Liabilities rose $991 million or 8% over 1990, reflecting a $508 million net increase in total debt (including the nonrecourse obligation) to fund investing and other financing activities. The growth also reflected a $221 million or 14% increase in other current liabilities over 1990, due primarily to restructuring charges accrued in 1991 and higher accrued interest expense.

PepsiCo's unused credit facilities with lending institutions, which exist largely to support the issuances of short-term borrowings, were $3.5 billion at year-end 1991 and 1990. This amount of short-term borrowings was classified as long-term at year-end 1991 and 1990, reflecting PepsiCo's intent and ability, through the existence of the credit facilities, to refinance these borrowings.

Financial Leverage is utilized by PepsiCo in managing its capital structure to optimize the overall cost of capital, considering the favorable tax treatment of debt, while maintaining operating and financial flexibility.

PepsiCo measures leverage on a net basis, which takes into account its large offshore short-term investment portfolios. These portfolios are managed as part of PepsiCo's overall financing strategy and are not required to support day-to-day operations. Therefore, PepsiCo believes its net debt position, which reflects the pro forma remittance of the portfolios, net of related taxes, as a reduction of total debt (excluding the nonrecourse obligation outstanding at year-end 1990), is the most meaningful historical cost measure of financial leverage used in its business. PepsiCo's ratio of net debt to net capital employed (defined as net debt, other liabilities and deferred credits, deferred income taxes and shareholders' equity) was 47% at both year-end 1991 and 1990.

PepsiCo also measures financial leverage on a market value basis. Management believes that market leverage (defined as net debt as a percent of net debt plus the market value of equity, based on the year-end stock price) better measures PepsiCo's financial leverage from the perspective of investors in its securities, as it reflects the portion of the current value of PepsiCo that is financed with debt. Unlike historical cost measures, the market value of equity is based primarily on the expected future cash flows that will both support debt and provide returns to shareholders. The market net debt ratio was 19% and 22% at year-end 1991 and 1990, respectively. The decline in the ratio was due to a 31% increase in PepsiCo's stock price, partially offset by a 12% increase in net debt. PepsiCo has established a target range for its market net debt ratio of 20-25%. PepsiCo believes that it can safely exceed this range on a short-term basis to take advantage of strategic acquisition opportunities.

Because of its strong cash generating capability, PepsiCo believes that its current leverage level does not significantly affect its overall cost of debt or reduce its flexibility to invest in the business.

PepsiCo's negative operating working capital position, which principally reflects the cash sales nature of its restaurant operations, effectively provides additional capital for investment. Operating working capital, which excludes short-term investments and short-term borrowings, was a negative $777 million and $708 million at year-end 1991 and 1990, respectively.

Shareholders' Equity rose $641 million or 13% over 1990, reflecting 1991 net income of $1.08 billion partially offset by dividends declared of $363 million. The decrease in the currency translation adjustment, which relates principally to net assets in the U.K., reflected a stronger U.S. dollar against the pound sterling. Issuances of treasury stock for acquisitions, which drove the increase in capital in excess of par value, were more than offset by purchases of stock for treasury on the open market.

Based on income from continuing operations, PepsiCo's return on average shareholders' equity was 20.7% in 1991 compared to 24.8% in 1990. Excluding the impact of 1991 and 1990 unusual charges and the 1990 gain on joint venture stock offering, the return on average shareholders' equity was 22.7% in 1991 and 24.9% in 1990.

Consolidated Statement of Cash Flows

(in millions)
PepsiCo, Inc. and Subsidiaries
Fifty-two weeks ended December 28, 1991, December 29, 1990 and December 30, 1989

PepsiCo, Inc.

	1991	1990	1989
Cash Flows from Continuing Operations:			
Income from continuing operations	$1,080.2	$1,090.6	$ 901.4
Adjustments to reconcile income from continuing operations to net cash provided by continuing operations:			
Gain on joint venture stock offering	–	(118.2)	–
Depreciation and amortization	1,034.5	884.0	772.0
Deferred income taxes	122.6	106.1	71.2
Other noncash charges and credits, net	227.2	120.3	128.4
Changes in operating working capital, excluding effect of acquisitions:			
Accounts and notes receivable	(55.9)	(124.8)	(149.9)
Inventories	(54.8)	(20.9)	(50.1)
Prepaid expenses and other current assets	(100.2)	(61.6)	6.5
Accounts payable	57.8	25.4	134.9
Income taxes payable	(3.4)	136.3	80.9
Other current liabilities	122.3	72.8	(9.4)
Net change in operating working capital	(34.2)	27.2	12.9
Net Cash Provided by Continuing Operations	2,430.3	2,110.0	1,885.9
Cash Flows–Investing Activities:			
Acquisitions and investments in affiliates	(640.9)	(630.6)	(3,296.6)
Purchases of property, plant and equipment	(1,457.8)	(1,180.1)	(943.8)
Proceeds from joint venture stock offering	–	129.6	–
Proceeds from sales of property, plant and equipment	69.6	45.3	69.7
Short-term investments, by original maturity:			
More than three months–purchases	(1,849.2)	(2,093.2)	(2,131.1)
More than three months–sales	1,873.2	2,139.4	1,476.4
Three months or less, net	(164.9)	(228.0)	667.0
Other, net	(105.8)	(119.7)	(97.9)
Net Cash Used for Investing Activities	(2,275.8)	(1,937.3)	(4,256.3)
Cash Flows–Financing Activities:			
Proceeds from issuances of long-term debt	2,799.6	777.3	71.7
Payments of long-term debt	(1,048.2)	(298.0)	(405.4)
Retirement of nonrecourse obligation	(300.3)	–	–
Short-term borrowings, by original maturity:			
More than three months–proceeds	2,551.9	4,041.9	1,109.5
More than three months–payments	(3,097.4)	(2,647.4)	(476.2)
Three months or less, net	(467.1)	(1,480.7)	2,292.2
Cash dividends paid	(343.2)	(293.9)	(241.9)
Purchases of treasury stock	(195.2)	(147.7)	–
Other, net	(31.2)	(28.6)	(28.9)
Net Cash Provided by (Used for) Financing Activities	(131.1)	(77.1)	2,321.0
Effect of Exchange Rate Changes on Cash and Cash Equivalents	(7.5)	(1.0)	(17.1)
Net Increase (Decrease) in Cash and Cash Equivalents	15.9	94.6	(66.5)
Cash and Cash Equivalents–Beginning of Year	170.8	76.2	142.7
Cash and Cash Equivalents–End of Year	$ 186.7	$ 170.8	$ 76.2
Supplemental Cash Flow Information:			
Cash Flow Data			
Interest paid	$ 490.1	656.9	591.1
Income taxes paid	$ 385.9	375.0	239.7
Schedule of Noncash Investing and Financing Activities			
Liabilities assumed in connection with acquisitions	$ 70.9	126.7	342.9
Issuance of treasury stock and debt for acquisitions	$ 162.7	105.1	103.9
Issuance of treasury stock for compensation awards and conversion of debentures	$ 14.7	13.5	9.3
Additions of capital leases	$ 26.5	18.1	15.7

See accompanying Notes to Consolidated Financial Statements.

Management's Analysis–Cash Flows

Cash flow activity in 1991 reflected strong cash flows from continuing operations of $2.4 billion and net proceeds of $439 million from activity in total debt (including the nonrecourse obligation). Major funding needs included purchases of property, plant and equipment (PP&E) of $1.5 billion, acquisitions and investments in affiliates of $641 million and dividends of $343 million.

One of PepsiCo's most significant financial strengths is its internal cash generation capability. In 1991, the snack foods and soft drinks segments provided particularly strong cash flows after PP&E purchases and acquisitions. A cash use in the restaurants segment reflected funding of additional units, both constructed and acquired from franchisees. Net cash flows from PepsiCo's domestic businesses were partially offset by international uses of cash, reflecting strategies to grow international operations. As the chart below illustrates, in both 1991 and 1990, net cash provided by continuing operations substantially funded purchases of PP&E, dividend payments and acquisitions and affiliate investments.

Net Cash Provided by Continuing Operations vs. PP&E Purchases, Dividends Paid and Acquisitions/Affiliate Investments
($ In Millions)

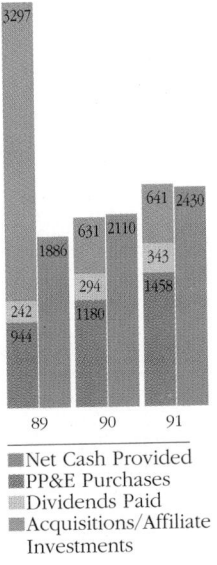

Legend:
■ Net Cash Provided
■ PP&E Purchases
□ Dividends Paid
■ Acquisitions/Affiliate Investments

Net Cash Provided by Continuing Operations in 1991 rose $320 million or 15% over 1990, and in 1990 grew $224 million or 12% over 1989. The joint venture stock offering gain in 1990 relates to the initial public offering of a KFC joint venture in Japan. See Note to Consolidated Financial Statements on page 43. The comparison of the 1991 net change in operating working capital to 1990 reflects the timing of income tax payments and higher prefunded employee benefit expenses, partially offset by modest growth in accounts receivable due to slower volume growth in domestic bottling operations as well as the impact of accrued restructuring charges. The 1990 to 1989 comparison of operating working capital changes was also affected by several increases and decreases in various accounts, the net of which was not significant. The increases in depreciation and amortization noncash charges of $151 million in 1991 and $112 million in 1990 reflected increased PP&E investment as well as goodwill and other intangibles and PP&E associated with recent acquisitions. The other net noncash charges and credits reflect increased accruals of noncurrent liabilities in 1991.

Investing Activities over the past three years reflected strategic spending in all three industry segments through acquisitions, investments in affiliates and purchases of PP&E. Acquisition and affiliate investment activity in 1991 included cash and noncash (primarily treasury stock issuance) transactions of $641 million and $163 million, respectively, and was led by acquisitions of franchised domestic restaurant operations. The number of probable transactions as of February 1992 indicates that acquisitions and affiliate investments in 1992 will likely exceed the total 1991 activity. PepsiCo continues to seek opportunities to strengthen its position in its domestic and international industry segments through such strategic acquisition activity. Purchases of PP&E are expected to increase to approximately $1.7 billion in 1992 from $1.5 billion in 1991, with almost half of the 1992 amount targeted for the restaurants segment and the balance evenly divided between the soft drinks and snack foods segments. The 1992 planned spending is led by new restaurant units, productive capacity expansion in snack foods and soft drinks as well as additional vending equipment in soft drinks. Approximately 30% of the planned 1992 PP&E spending relates to international businesses, about the same as 1991 and 1990.

Financing Activities resulted in an increase in net cash used of $54 million over 1990, principally reflecting higher payments of dividends and purchases of treasury stock, partially offset by increased net proceeds from total debt activity.

During 1991, PepsiCo issued $3.9 billion of notes and used the proceeds to refinance short-term borrowings, a portion of which funded investing and other financing activities including retirement of the nonrecourse obligation. Substantially all of the issuances were under a $2.5 billion shelf registration statement filed with the Securities and Exchange Commission in March 1991 and a $1.5 billion shelf registration statement filed in 1990. In December 1991, PepsiCo filed a shelf registration statement covering potential debt issuances of $3.3 billion, all of which was available for future issuances as of February 1992. As a result of the refinancings and interest rate swap transactions, at year-end 1991 the majority of PepsiCo's debt was effectively at fixed interest rates as compared to year-end 1990 when the majority was effectively at variable rates.

Cash dividends declared were a record $363 million in 1991 and $302 million in 1990. PepsiCo targets a dividend payout of approximately one-third of the prior year's income from continuing operations, thus retaining sufficient earnings to enhance productive capability and provide financial resources for growth opportunities.

Share repurchase decisions are evaluated considering the target capital structure and other investment opportunities. In 1991, PepsiCo repurchased 6.4 million shares at a cost of $195 million. Including these repurchases, 20.8 million shares have been purchased under the 45 million share repurchase authority granted by PepsiCo's Board of Directors in 1987.

Consolidated Statement of Shareholders' Equity

PepsiCo, Inc.

(shares in thousands, dollars in millions except per share amounts)
PepsiCo, Inc. and Subsidiaries
Fifty-two weeks ended December 28, 1991, December 29, 1990 and December 30, 1989

	Capital Stock				Capital in Excess of Par Value	Retained Earnings	Currency Translation Adjustment	Total
	Issued		Treasury					
	Shares	Amount	Shares	Amount				
Shareholders' Equity, December 31, 1988	863,083	$ 14.4	(74,649)	$ (509.7)	$ 302.6	$ 3,329.7	$ 24.0	$ 3,161.0
1989 Net income						901.4		901.4
Cash dividends declared (per share-$0.32)						(252.7)		(252.7)
Currency translation adjustment							42.2	42.2
Shares issued in connection with an acquisition			1,266	8.6	17.9			26.5
Payment of compensation awards and exercise of stock options			901	6.2	2.6			8.8
Conversion of debentures			456	3.1	0.8			3.9
Shareholders' Equity, December 30, 1989	863,083	$ 14.4	(72,026)	$ (491.8)	$ 323.9	$ 3,978.4	$ 66.2	$ 3,891.1
1990 Net income						1,076.9		1,076.9
Cash dividends declared (per share-$0.38)						(302.3)		(302.3)
Currency translation adjustment							317.0	317.0
Purchase of treasury stock			(6,310)	(147.7)				(147.7)
Shares issued in connection with acquisitions			2,013	16.3	30.1			46.4
Payment of compensation awards and exercise of stock options			1,072	7.8	9.1			16.9
Conversion of debentures			549	3.9	1.7			5.6
Shares reissued to Employee Stock Ownership Plan			8	0.1	0.2			0.3
Shareholders' Equity, December 29, 1990	863,083	$ 14.4	(74,694)	$ (611.4)	$ 365.0	$ 4,753.0	$ 383.2	$ 4,904.2
1991 Net income						1,080.2		1,080.2
Cash dividends declared (per share-$0.46)						(363.2)		(363.2)
Currency translation adjustment							(52.9)	(52.9)
Purchase of treasury stock			(6,392)	(195.2)				(195.2)
Shares issued in connection with acquisitions			5,613	46.7	95.0			141.7
Payment of compensation awards and exercise of stock options			1,446	13.6	16.4			30.0
Conversion of debentures			44	0.4	0.2			0.6
Shares reissued to Employee Stock Ownership Plan			1					
Shareholders' Equity, December 28, 1991	**863,083**	**$14.4**	**(73,982)**	**$(745.9)**	**$476.6**	**$5,470.0**	**$330.3**	**$5,545.4**

See accompanying Notes to Consolidated Financial Statements.

Notes to Consolidated Financial Statements

(tabular dollars in millions except per share amounts)

Summary of Significant Accounting Policies

Principles of Consolidation. The financial statements reflect the consolidated accounts of PepsiCo, Inc. and its wholly-owned subsidiaries. Intercompany accounts and transactions have been eliminated. Investments in affiliates in which PepsiCo exercises significant influence but not control are accounted for by the equity method, and the equity in net income is included in the Consolidated Statement of Income under the caption "Selling, general and administrative expenses." Certain reclassifications were made to 1990 and 1989 amounts to conform with the 1991 presentation.

Goodwill and Other Intangibles. Goodwill and other intangibles represent the excess of the purchase price over the fair market value of net tangible assets of businesses acquired, with the largest portion attributable to the value of Pepsi-Cola franchise rights reacquired in the acquisitions of franchised bottling operations. Goodwill and other intangibles are amortized on a straight-line basis over appropriate periods generally ranging from 20 to 40 years. Accumulated amortization was $757 million and $548 million at year-end 1991 and 1990, respectively.

Marketing Costs. Marketing costs are reported in the Consolidated Statement of Income under the caption "Selling, general and administrative expenses" and include costs of advertising, marketing and promotional programs. Promotional discounts are expensed as incurred, and other marketing costs not deferred are charged to expense ratably in relation to sales over the year in which incurred. Marketing costs deferred consist of media and personal service advertising prepayments, materials in inventory and production costs of future media advertising; these assets are expensed in the year used.

Classification of Restaurant Operating Expenses. Operating expenses incurred at the restaurant unit level consist primarily of food and related packaging costs, labor associated with food preparation and customer service, and overhead expenses. For purposes of the Consolidated Statement of Income, food and packaging costs as well as all labor-related expenses are classified as "Cost of sales," and all other unit level expenses are classified as "Selling, general and administrative expenses."

Cash Equivalents. Cash equivalents are comprised of funds temporarily invested (with original maturities not exceeding three months) as part of PepsiCo's management of day-to-day operating cash receipts and disbursements. All other investment portfolios, primarily held offshore, are classified as short-term investments.

Net Income Per Share. Net income per share is computed by dividing net income by the weighted average number of shares and share equivalents outstanding during each year.

Research and Development Expenses. Research and development expenses, which are expensed as incurred, were $99 million, $101 million and $91 million in 1991, 1990 and 1989, respectively.

Business Segments

Information regarding industry segments and geographic areas of operations is provided on pages L23 and L24.

Acquisitions and Investments in Affiliates

During 1991, acquisition and affiliate investment activity, led by acquisitions of franchised domestic restaurant operations, aggregated $804 million, comprised of $641 million in cash, $142 million in PepsiCo Capital Stock and $21 million in notes. All of the activity was within PepsiCo's three industry segments.

During 1990, acquisition and affiliate investment activity aggregated $736 million, principally for cash, and included an equity interest in a Mexican cookie business as well as acquisitions of franchised bottling and restaurant operations.

During 1989, acquisitions aggregated $3.4 billion, principally for cash, and included the franchised domestic bottling operations of General Cinema Corporation (GC Beverage), acquired in March 1989 for $1.77 billion, and two snack chip companies in the United Kingdom, Smiths Crisps Limited and Walkers Crisps Holdings Limited (the U.K. operations), acquired in July 1989 for $1.34 billion. The remaining activity consisted primarily of acquisitions of franchised domestic bottling and restaurant operations.

The acquisitions have been accounted for by the purchase method; accordingly, their results are included in the Consolidated Financial Statements from their respective dates of acquisition.

Assuming the acquisitions of GC Beverage and the U.K. operations had occurred at the beginning of 1989, the unaudited pro forma combined 1989 net sales, net income and net income per share of PepsiCo and these acquisitions were computed to be $15.6 billion, $859 million and $1.08, respectively. The aggregate impact of acquisitions in 1991 and 1990 and all other acquisitions in 1989 was not material to PepsiCo's net sales, net income or net income per share; accordingly, no related pro forma information is provided. The pro forma information does not necessarily represent what the actual consolidated results would have been for 1989.

Joint Venture Stock Offering

In 1990, PepsiCo recorded an unusual gain of $118.2 million ($53.0 after-tax or $0.07 per share) related to an initial public offering (IPO) to Japanese investors by PepsiCo's KFC joint venture in Japan (KFC-J). KFC-J's principal shareholders are Mitsubishi Corporation and PepsiCo. The IPO consisted of 6.5 million shares of stock in KFC-J. Each principal shareholder sold 2.25 million shares, and KFC-J sold an additional two million new shares. PepsiCo's sale of 2.25 million shares generated pretax cash proceeds of $129.6 million.

The gain from the IPO consisted of a $94.3 million gain ($42.3 after-tax) from PepsiCo's sale of the 2.25 million shares and a $23.9 million ($10.7 after-tax) noncash equity gain from the sale of the two million new shares by KFC-J. As a result of these transactions, each principal shareholder's interest declined from 48.7% to 30.5%. The effective tax rate on the gain was 55.2%, reflecting the relatively low U.S. tax basis of PepsiCo's investment in KFC-J compared to its book value, which included nondeductible goodwill and other intangibles.

Discontinued Operation Charge

The discontinued operation charge of $14.0 million ($13.7 after-tax or $0.02 per share) represents additional amounts provided in 1990 for various pending lawsuits and claims relating to a business sold in a prior year. Substantially all of the charge is a capital loss for which PepsiCo has derived no tax benefit.

Inventories

Inventories are valued at the lower of cost (computed on the average, first-in, first-out or last-in, first-out methods) or net realizable value. Inventories computed on the last-in, first-out (LIFO) method comprised 49% and 54% of inventories at year-end 1991 and 1990, respectively.

	1991	1990
Raw materials, supplies and in-process .	$350.7	$315.4
Finished goods	324.2	285.3
Total (approximates current cost)	674.9	600.7
Excess of current cost over LIFO cost. . .	(13.4)	(14.9)
	$661.5	$585.8

PepsiCo hedges certain of its domestic raw material purchases through commodity futures contracts to reduce its exposure to market price fluctuations. Gains and losses on these contracts are included in the cost of the raw materials.

Property, Plant and Equipment

Property, plant and equipment are stated at cost. Depreciation is calculated principally on a straight-line basis over the estimated useful lives of the assets. Depreciation expense in 1991, 1990 and 1989 was $800 million, $686 million and $610 million, respectively.

	1991	1990
Land.	$ 880.1	$ 785.4
Buildings and improvements	3,707.1	3,173.7
Capital leases, primarily buildings	288.2	265.4
Machinery and equipment	5,626.3	4,753.2
	10,501.7	8,977.7
Accumulated depreciation.	(3,907.0)	(3,266.8)
	$ 6,594.7	$ 5,710.9

Short-term Borrowings and Long-term Debt

	1991	1990

Short-term Borrowings

	1991	1990
Commercial paper (6.1% and 7.9% weighted average interest rate at year-end 1991 and 1990, respectively)	$ 1,616.7	$ 3,168.8
Current maturities of long-term debt issuances	619.2	1,085.0
Notes (A)	1,100.0	624.8
Other borrowings.	342.3	247.9
Amount reclassified to long-term debt (B)	(3,450.0)	(3,500.0)
	$ 228.2	$ 1,626.5

Long-term Debt

	1991	1990
Short-term borrowings, reclassified (B)	$3,450.0	$ 3,500.0
Notes due 1992 through 1998 (7.1% and 7.9% weighted average interest rate at year-end 1991 and 1990, respectively) (A)	3,381.0	1,513.7
Zero coupon notes, $1.1 billion due 1992-2012 (14.1% and 14.0% semi-annual weighted average yield to maturity at year-end 1991 and 1990, respectively)	365.6	348.1
Swiss franc perpetual Foreign Interest Payment bonds (C)	210.7	209.9
European Currency Units 7⅜% notes due 1992 (D)	134.2	135.2
Pound sterling 9⅛% notes due 1993 (D)	112.5	115.5
Swiss franc 5¼% bearer bonds due 1995 (D)	99.5	104.7
Italian lire 10½% notes due 1991 (D) . . .	–	88.8
Swiss franc 7⅛% notes due 1994 (D) . . .	74.1	
Canadian dollar 8¾% notes due 1991 (A).	–	64.6
Capital lease obligations (See Note on page L19.)	213.3	193.8
Other, due 1992-2020 (7.7% and 8.9% weighted average interest rate at year-end 1991 and 1990, respectively)	384.5	410.8
	8,425.4	6,685.1
Less current maturities of long-term debt issuances.	(619.2)	(1,085.0)
Total long-term debt.	$7,806.2	$ 5,600.1

Long-term debt is carried net of any related discount or premium and unamortized debt issuance costs. The debt agreements include various restrictions, none of which is presently significant to PepsiCo.

The annual maturities of long-term debt through 1996, excluding capital lease obligations and the reclassified short-term borrowings, are: 1992-$600 million, 1993-$1.05 billion, 1994-$883 million, 1995-$400 million and 1996-$834 million.

(A) PepsiCo has entered into interest rate swap agreements to effectively convert $865 million and $679 million of fixed interest rate debt issuances to variable rate debt with a weighted average interest rate of 4.6% and 7.8% at year-end 1991 and 1990, respectively, as well as effectively convert $164 million of variable interest rate debt to fixed rate debt with an interest rate of 7.8% at year-end 1991. The differential to be paid or received on interest rate swaps is accrued as interest rates change and is charged or credited to interest expense over the life of the agreements.

(B) At year-end 1991 and 1990, $3.5 billion of short-term borrowings were classified as long-term, reflecting PepsiCo's intent and ability to refinance these borrowings on a long-term basis, through either long-term debt issuances or rollover of existing short-term borrowings. At year-end 1991 and 1990, PepsiCo had revolving credit agreements covering potential borrowings aggregating $3.5 billion, with the current agreements expiring 1995 through 1997. These unused credit facilities provide the ability to refinance short-term borrowings.

(C) The coupon rate of the Swiss franc 400 million perpetual Foreign Interest Payment bonds issued in 1986 is 7½% through 1996. The interest payments are made in U.S. dollars at a fixed contractual exchange rate. The bonds have no stated maturity date. At the end of each 10-year period after the issuance of the bonds, PepsiCo and the bondholders each have the right to cause redemption of the bonds. If not redeemed, the coupon rate will be adjusted based on the prevailing yield of 10-year U.S. Treasury Securities. The principal of the bonds is denominated in Swiss francs. PepsiCo can, and intends to, limit the ultimate redemption amount to the U.S. dollar proceeds at issuance, which is the basis of the carrying value in both years.

(D) PepsiCo has entered into currency exchange agreements to hedge its foreign currency exposure on these issues of non-U.S. dollar denominated debt. At year-end 1991, the carrying value of this debt aggregated $420 million and the net receivable under related currency exchange agreements aggregated $77 million, resulting in a net effective U.S. dollar liability of $343 million with a weighted average fixed interest rate of 7.3%. At year-end 1990, the aggregate carrying values of the debt and the receivable under related currency exchange agreements were $444 million and $101 million, respectively, resulting in a net effective U.S. dollar liability of $343 million consisting of $294 million with a weighted average variable interest rate of 7.5% and $49 million with a weighted average fixed interest rate of 9.9%. The gross receivables and payables under the currency exchange agreements are reflected in the Consolidated Balance Sheet under the appropriate current and noncurrent asset and liability captions. Changes in the value of a currency exchange agreement resulting from exchange rate movements are offset by changes in the carrying value of the related non-U.S. dollar denominated debt, as both values are based on current exchange rates.

PepsiCo has entered into several interest rate swap agreements, which are effective in early 1992 and terminate in twelve to sixteen months, to effectively fix the interest rates on $1.1 billion of commercial paper borrowings.

Except for these commercial paper swaps, the maturity dates of interest rate swaps and currency exchange agreements correspond with those of the related debt instruments. The counterparties to PepsiCo's interest rate swaps and currency exchange agreements consist of a diversified group of financial institutions. PepsiCo is exposed to credit risk to the extent of nonperformance by these counterparties; however, PepsiCo regularly monitors its positions and the credit ratings of these counterparties and considers the risk of default to be remote. Additionally, due to the frequency of interest payments and receipts, PepsiCo's credit risk related to interest rate swaps is not significant.

Nonrecourse Obligation

In 1987, PepsiCo received net proceeds of $299 million under a nonrecourse obligation agreement whereby this principal amount and related interest were payable solely from future royalty payments from certain independent franchisees of one of PepsiCo's restaurant chains for a period not to exceed 10 years. The variable interest rate, based on a commercial paper rate, was 8.4% at year-end 1990. The agreement provided that principal repayments during the first five years could be readvanced. As PepsiCo had intended to elect this provision, the entire obligation had been classified as noncurrent in 1990. Because of the increased costs of the arrangement, PepsiCo decided to prepay the entire principal in May 1991.

Leases

PepsiCo has noncancelable commitments under both capital and operating leases, primarily for restaurant units. Certain of these units have been subleased to restaurant franchisees. Commitments on capital and operating leases expire at various dates through 2032.

Future minimum commitments and sublease receivables under noncancelable leases are as follows:

| | Commitments | | Sublease Receivables | |
	Capital	Operating	Direct Financing	Operating
1992	$ 41.8	$ 204.6	$ 4.5	$ 8.6
1993	39.0	179.3	4.4	8.2
1994	37.5	156.5	4.2	7.6
1995	34.2	144.9	4.0	6.9
1996	30.0	127.0	3.7	6.1
Later years ..	182.5	650.4	14.4	25.5
	$365.0	$1,462.7	$35.2	$62.9

At year-end 1991, the present value of minimum payments under capital leases was $213 million, after deducting $2 million for estimated executory costs (taxes, maintenance and insurance) and $150 million representing imputed interest. The present value of minimum receivables under direct financing subleases was $21 million, after deducting $14 million of unearned interest income.

Total rental expense and income and the contingent portions of these totals were as follows:

	1991	1990	1989
Total rental expense	**$323.2**	272.7	236.9
Contingent portion of expense	**$ 22.3**	21.4	20.8
Total rental income	**$ 13.0**	10.5	14.2
Contingent portion of income	**$ 4.8**	4.9	4.5

Contingent rentals are based on sales by restaurants in excess of levels stipulated in the lease agreements.

Income Taxes

Detail of the provision for income taxes on income from continuing operations:

		1991	1990	1989
Current–	Federal.....	**$315.5**	$301.5	$221.7
	Foreign.....	**125.0**	126.6	89.5
	State.......	**51.5**	62.3	38.0
		492.0	490.4	349.2
Deferred–	Federal.....	**63.5**	66.0	95.7
	Foreign.....	**25.2**	12.5	1.2
	State.......	**9.4**	7.9	3.0
		98.1	86.4	99.9
		$590.1	$576.8	$449.1

The deferred provision, which results principally from differences in the timing of expense recognition for financial reporting and tax purposes, included amounts related to depreciation of property, plant and equipment of $56.2 million, $40.6 million and $36.3 million and amortization of intangibles of $49.0 million, $46.0 million and $47.3 million in 1991, 1990 and 1989, respectively. Also included was $23.3 million in 1991 related to increased prefunding of employee benefit expenses. In 1991, the deferred provision was reduced by $41.7 million related to restructuring charges.

U.S. and foreign income from continuing operations before income taxes:

	1991	1990	1989
U.S.	**$1,054.3**	$ 915.5	$ 843.4
Foreign	**616.0**	751.9	507.1
	$1,670.3	$1,667.4	$1,350.5

PepsiCo operates centralized soft drink concentrate manufacturing facilities in Puerto Rico and Ireland under long-term tax incentives. The foreign amount in the above table includes approximately 50% (consistent with the allocation for tax purposes) of the income from sales of concentrate manufactured in Puerto Rico.

Deferred taxes were not provided on unremitted earnings of foreign subsidiaries that are intended to be indefinitely reinvested. These unremitted earnings aggregated approximately $945 million at year-end 1991, exclusive of amounts that if remitted in the future would result in little or no tax under current tax laws and the Puerto Rico tax incentive grant.

Reconciliation of the U.S. federal statutory tax rate to PepsiCo's effective tax rate on income from continuing operations, based on the dollar impact of these major components on the provision for income taxes:

	1991	1990	1989
U.S. federal statutory tax rate........	**34.0%**	34.0%	34.0%
State income tax, net of federal tax benefit.....................	**2.4**	1.9	2.0
Effect of lower taxes on foreign income (including Puerto Rico and Ireland).....................	**(2.3)**	(3.9)	(3.9)
Nondeductible amortization of domestic goodwill and other intangibles....................	**1.8**	1.6	2.0
Tax basis difference related to joint venture stock offering	**–**	1.6	–
Other, net	**(0.6)**	(0.6)	(0.8)
Effective tax rate	**35.3%**	34.6%	33.3%

Deferred taxes reported in the Consolidated Balance Sheet include $174.0 million and $200.9 million in 1991 and 1990, respectively, related to Safe Harbor Leases (the Leases) in which PepsiCo invested in 1981 and 1982. These amounts are based on the current U.S. federal statutory tax rate. These transactions, which do not impact the provision for income taxes, decrease income taxes payable over the initial years of the Leases and increase them over the later years. Taxes payable related to the Leases are estimated to be $30.1 million over the next five years.

PepsiCo has not adopted Statement No. 96 (SFAS 96) "Accounting for Income Taxes" that was issued in 1987, as the Financial Accounting Standards Board (the FASB) has been deliberating revisions and now anticipates issuing a new standard in 1992 that supersedes SFAS 96. Based on an Exposure Draft issued by the FASB in June of 1991, the new standard is expected to retain the basic principles of SFAS 96 to account for deferred income taxes under the liability method, as well as permit adoption on either a prospective or retroactive basis. It is probable that PepsiCo will account for the adoption on a prospective basis as a change in accounting principle. While simplifying certain provisions of SFAS 96, the Exposure Draft changed, among other things, the transition rules relating to acquisitions completed prior to the adoption date of the new standard, possibly requiring restatement of certain assets and liabilities recorded in allocating the purchase prices of these acquisitions. PepsiCo has not expended the significant effort to evaluate the impact of the Exposure Draft, because of PepsiCo's substantial past acquisition activity and the likelihood that the new standard will reflect revisions to the Exposure Draft. The new standard is expected to require adoption by 1993.

Postretirement Benefits Other Than Pensions

PepsiCo provides health care and life insurance benefits to certain retired domestic employees, the costs of which are expensed as incurred. The 1991, 1990 and 1989 expense for retiree health care claims incurred and life insurance premiums paid was $23.9 million, $20.4 million and $15.4 million, respectively. In December 1990, the FASB issued Statement of Financial Accounting Standards No. 106 (SFAS 106) "Employers' Accounting for Postretirement Benefits Other Than Pensions." SFAS 106 requires employers to accrue the cost of postretirement benefits (principally health care) over the years employees provide services to the date of their full eligibility for such benefits. SFAS 106 is required to be adopted by 1993.

Upon adoption, SFAS 106 requires the recognition of a transition obligation that represents future retirement benefit costs related to services already provided by active and retired employees to the date of adoption. Employers have the option to expense the transition obligation immediately or amortize it over a period of up to 20 years.

PepsiCo's preliminary estimates of its pretax transition obligation, which PepsiCo intends to expense immediately upon adoption of SFAS 106, range from $500 million to $700 million ($310 million to $430 million after-tax, or $0.38 to $0.55 per share). PepsiCo's estimated annual pretax expense to be accrued under SFAS 106 would exceed the amount of estimated benefit costs to be incurred by a range of $30 million to $50 million ($20 million to $30 million after-tax, or $0.02 to $0.04 per share). These preliminary estimates are based upon the benefit plans expected to be in place upon adoption. The actual expense to be recorded will depend on certain factors, including the final health care inflation rates assumed and the discount rate used when recording the transition obligation.

Based on the current accounting standard used by PepsiCo in recording income taxes, as well as a proposed new FASB standard for accounting for income taxes expected to be required for 1993 reporting, the amounts presented parenthetically above reflect a tax benefit for these expenses. PepsiCo's cash flows will be unaffected by this accounting change because PepsiCo intends to continue its current practice of paying the costs of these postretirement benefits as incurred.

Pension Plans

PepsiCo has noncontributory defined benefit pension plans covering substantially all full-time domestic employees as well as contributory and noncontributory defined benefit pension plans covering certain international employees. Benefits generally are based on years of service and compensation or stated amounts for each year of service. PepsiCo funds the domestic plans in amounts not less than minimum statutory funding requirements nor more than the maximum amount that can be deducted for federal income tax purposes. International plans are funded in amounts sufficient to comply with local statutory requirements. The plans' assets consist principally of equity securities, government and corporate debt securities and other fixed income obligations. Capital Stock of PepsiCo accounted for approximately 19% and 18% of the total market value of the plans' assets at year-end 1991 and 1990, respectively.

In 1989, PepsiCo acquired the U.K. operations, the employees of which were covered by various plans including multiemployer plans. As the preliminary allocation of these plans' assets and the transfer of relevant employees to separate plans were not completed until late 1990, the 1991 and 1990 information presented below includes both the domestic plans and the U.K. operations' plans, while the 1989 information includes only the domestic plans. Other international plans are not significant in the aggregate and therefore are not included in the following disclosures.

The net pension expense (credit) for company-sponsored plans (the Plans) included the following components:

	1991	1990	1989
Service cost of benefits earned	$ 46.8	$ 48.1	$ 32.0
Interest cost on projected benefit obligations	69.2	63.3	47.1
Return on Plan assets:			
Actual	(224.1)	(27.0)	(154.6)
Deferred gain (loss)	134.2	(55.9)	89.9
	(89.9)	(82.9)	(64.7)
Amortization of net transition gain	(19.0)	(19.0)	(19.0)
Pension expense (credit)	$ 7.1	$ 9.5	$ (4.6)

The disclosures below have been aggregated for all Plans, as the amounts for certain small plans with accumulated benefit obligations exceeding the assets were not significant. Reconciliations of the funded status of the Plans to the prepaid pension liability included in the Consolidated Balance Sheet are as follows:

	1991	1990
Actuarial present value of benefit obligations:		
Vested benefits	$ (717.1)	$(549.9)
Nonvested benefits	(96.8)	(90.8)
Accumulated benefit obligation	(813.9)	(640.7)
Effect of projected compensation increases	(133.0)	(101.9)
Projected benefit obligation	(946.9)	(742.6)
Plan assets at fair value	1,199.3	985.7
Plan assets in excess of projected benefit obligation	252.4	243.1
Unrecognized prior service cost	48.7	42.4
Unrecognized net gain	(103.4)	(84.6)
Unrecognized net transition gain	(129.1)	(148.1)
Prepaid pension liability	$ 68.6	$ 52.8
Included in:		
"Investments in Affiliates and Other Assets"	$ 106.5	$ 85.3
"Other current liabilities"	(22.6)	(17.0)
"Other Liabilities and Deferred Credits"	(15.3)	(15.5)
	$ 68.6	$ 52.8

The assumptions used in computing the information above were as follows:

	1991	1990	1989
Discount rate-pension expense (credit)	9.5%	9.1	10.1
Expected long-term rate of return on plan assets	10.2%	10.2	10.0
Discount rate-projected benefit obligation	8.6%	9.5	9.0
Future compensation growth rate	3.3%-7.4%	5.0-7.0	5.0-7.0

The 1991 and 1990 discount rates and rates of return represent weighted averages, reflecting the combined assumptions for domestic and the U.K. operations' plans.

Full-time domestic employees not covered by the Plans generally are covered by multiemployer plans as part of collective-bargaining agreements. Pension expense for these multiemployer plans was not significant in the aggregate.

Employee Incentive Plans

PepsiCo has established certain employee incentive plans under which stock options are granted. A stock option allows an employee to purchase a share of PepsiCo Capital Stock (Stock) in the future at the fair market value on the date of the grant.

Under the PepsiCo SharePower Stock Option Plan, approved by the Board of Directors and effective in 1989, essentially all employees other than executive officers, part-time and short-service employees may be granted stock options annually. The number of options granted is based on each employee's annual earnings. The options generally become exercisable ratably over five years from the grant date and must be exercised within 10 years of the grant date. SharePower options were granted to approximately 107,000 employees in 1991 and 91,000 in 1990.

The shareholder-approved 1987 Long-Term Incentive Plan (the Plan), which has provisions similar to plans in place in prior years, provides incentives to eligible senior and middle management employees. In addition to grants of stock options, which are generally exercisable between 1 and 15 years from the grant date, the Plan allows for grants of performance share units (PSUs), stock appreciation rights (SARs) and incentive stock units (ISUs).

A PSU is equivalent in value to a share of Stock at the grant date and vests for payment four years from the grant date, contingent upon attainment of prescribed performance goals. Prior to 1988, PSUs were granted to eligible senior management employees together with an equal number of stock options. Since 1988, PSUs are not directly granted, but additional stock options are granted that may be surrendered for a specified number of PSUs within 60 days of the grant date. During 1991, 50,208 stock options were surrendered for 16,736 PSUs. Total PSUs outstanding at year-end 1991 and 1990 were 809,099 and 795,732, respectively. Prior to 1991, SARs were granted to eligible senior management employees in connection with stock options becoming exercisable. A SAR allowed these employees to surrender an option for a payment representing the difference between the fair market value of Stock on the SAR exercise date and the option exercise price. Of the 272,568 SARs outstanding at year-end 1990, 15,203 were exercised and the remainder were canceled at no cost in 1991. Prior to 1989, eligible middle management employees were granted ISUs rather than stock options. ISUs vest for payment at specified dates over a six year period, and each ISU is equivalent in value to a share of Stock at those respective dates. ISUs outstanding at year-end 1991 and 1990 were 162,591 and 585,149, respectively. Amounts expensed for PSUs, SARs and ISUs were $15 million, $13 million and $25 million in 1991, 1990 and 1989, respectively.

Grants under the Plan are approved by the Compensation Committee of the Board of Directors (the Committee), which is composed of outside directors. Payment of awards other than stock options is made in cash and/or Stock as approved by the Committee. Under the Plan, a maximum of 54 million shares of Stock can be purchased or paid pursuant to grants. There were 32 million and 34 million shares available for future grants at year-end 1991 and 1990, respectively.

Stock Option activity for 1991 and 1990 was as follows:

	SharePower Plan	Long-Term Incentive Plan
	(in thousands)	
Outstanding at December 30, 1989	10,045	18,325
Granted	8,808	12,179
Exercised	(37)	(868)
Surrendered for PSUs	–	(1,228)
Surrendered for SARs	–	(44)
Canceled	(1,589)	(1,490)
Outstanding at December 29, 1990	17,227	26,874
Granted	9,249	2,195
Exercised	(325)	(950)
Surrendered for PSUs	–	(50)
Surrendered for SARs	–	(15)
Canceled	(2,350)	(220)
Outstanding at December 28, 1991	23,801	27,834
Exercisable at December 28, 1991	4,836	4,206
Option prices per share:		
Exercised during 1991	$17.58 to $29.25	$4.11 to $26.44
Exercised during 1990	$17.58	$4.11 to $20.00
Outstanding at year-end 1991	$17.58 to $29.25	$4.11 to $33.94

Contingencies

PepsiCo is subject to various claims and contingencies related to lawsuits, taxes and other matters arising out of the normal course of business. Management believes that the ultimate liability, if any, arising from such claims or contingencies is not likely to have a material adverse effect on PepsiCo's annual results of operations or financial condition.

At year-end 1991 and 1990, PepsiCo was contingently liable under direct and indirect guarantees aggregating $86 million and $97 million, respectively. The guarantees are primarily issued to support financial arrangements of certain restaurant and bottling franchisees and PepsiCo joint ventures. PepsiCo manages the risk associated with these guarantees by performing appropriate credit reviews in addition to retaining certain rights as a franchisor or joint venture partner.

Supplementary Financial Information

In addition to the financial statements and the accompanying notes, three items of supplementary financial information typically are presented: business segment information, five- (or ten-) year summary of related financial data, and quarterly financial data.

Business Segment Information

To help financial statement users assess the performance of diversified companies that operate in several different industries and lines of business, segmented financial information is required. The required information for each significant segment includes: revenues, income from operations, capital expenditures, identifiable assets, and depreciation and amortization. This information is generally included in the form of notes and schedules in the notes accompanying the financial statements. PepsiCo's note summarizing its business segment information is shown below:

Business Segments

This information constitutes a Note to the Consolidated Financial Statements. (tabular dollars in millions)

PepsiCo operates on a worldwide basis within three industry segments: soft drinks, snack foods and restaurants.

The soft drinks segment markets Pepsi-Cola, Mountain Dew, Slice and other brands worldwide and 7UP internationally. The segment manufactures concentrates sold to franchised bottlers worldwide and operates bottling plants located principally in the United States and Canada.

The snack foods segment manufactures and markets snack chips worldwide, with Frito-Lay representing the domestic business. The international snack foods business includes major operations in Mexico, the United Kingdom and Spain.

The restaurants segment data include operations of the worldwide Pizza Hut, Taco Bell and KFC chains. Also included in the results for each chain are the operations of PFS, PepsiCo's restaurant distribution operation, which supplies principally domestic company-owned and franchised restaurants. Restaurant net sales include net sales by company-owned restaurants, initial franchise fees, royalty and rental payments from restaurants operated by franchisees and net wholesale sales to franchisees by PFS.

The segment data reflect a number of businesses acquired in all three years presented. The largest acquisitions, which occurred in 1989, were a franchised domestic bottling operation and two snack chip companies in the United Kingdom. The remaining acquisitions consisted primarily of franchised domestic and international bottling and restaurant operations.

The caption "Interest and Other Corporate Expenses, Net" includes interest expense, interest income, equity in net income of affiliates and other corporate items that are not allocated to the business segments. PepsiCo has invested in about 50 joint ventures, principally international and all within PepsiCo's three industry segments, in which it exercises significant influence but not control. Equity in net income of these affiliates was $12.3 million, $2.0 million and $13.4 million in 1991, 1990 and 1989, respectively. The decline in 1990 reflects a $15.9 million unusual charge to reduce the carrying value of a Pizza Hut international joint venture investment.

Corporate identifiable assets consist principally of offshore short-term investments and investments in affiliates. PepsiCo's investments in affiliates totaled $1.1 billion at both year-end 1991 and 1990 and $676 million at year-end 1989. At year-end 1991, the largest of these investments consisted of $337 million in a Mexican cookie business acquired in late 1990. Other major affiliate investments included $208 million in a domestic franchised bottler, $124 million in the KFC Japan joint venture and $76 million in a Canadian snack foods operation. The level of these investments has not changed materially over the last three years.

In determining geographic area data, the results of operations of PepsiCo's centralized soft drink concentrate manufacturing facilities in Puerto Rico and Ireland have been allocated based upon concentrate sales to the respective geographic areas. Certain centralized international administrative expenses in each of the three industry segments have been allocated based upon sales volumes or number of restaurants in the respective geographic areas.

Industry Segments:	Net Sales 1991	1990	1989	Operating Profits[a] 1991	1990	1989	Identifiable Assets 1991	1990	1989
Soft Drinks: Domestic	$ 5,171.5	$ 5,034.5	$ 4,623.3	$ 746.2	$ 673.8	$ 577.6			
International	1,743.7	1,488.5	1,153.4	117.1	93.8	98.6			
	6,915.2	6,523.0	5,776.7	863.3	767.6	676.2	$ 6,832.6	$ 6,465.2	$ 6,198.1
Snack Foods: Domestic	3,737.9	3,471.5	3,211.3	616.6	732.3	667.8			
International	1,827.9	1,582.5	1,003.7	171.0	202.1	137.4			
	5,565.8	5,054.0	4,215.0	787.6	934.4	805.2	4,114.3	3,892.4	3,310.0
Restaurants: Domestic	6,258.4	5,540.9	4,684.8	479.4	447.2	356.5			
International	868.5	684.8	565.9	96.2	75.2	57.8			
	7,126.9	6,225.7	5,250.7	575.6	522.4	414.3	4,254.2	3,448.9	3,070.6
Total: Domestic	15,167.8	14,046.9	12,519.4	1,842.2	1,853.3	1,601.9			
International	4,440.1	3,755.8	2,723.0	384.3	371.1	293.8			
	$19,607.9	$17,802.7	$15,242.4	$2,226.5	$2,224.4	$1,895.7	$15,201.1	$13,806.5	$12,578.7

Geographic Areas:	Net Sales 1991	1990	1989	Operating Profits[a] 1991	1990	1989	Identifiable Assets 1991	1990	1989
United States	$15,167.8	$14,046.9	$12,519.4	$1,842.2	$1,853.3	$1,601.9	$10,777.8	$ 9,980.7	$ 9,593.4
Europe	1,486.0	1,344.7	771.7	61.8	108.5	53.8	2,367.3	2,255.2	1,767.2
Canada and Mexico	1,434.7	1,089.2	899.0	198.7	164.2	117.1	917.3	689.5	409.5
Other	1,519.4	1,321.9	1,052.3	123.8	98.4	122.9	1,138.7	881.1	808.6
							15,201.1	13,806.5	12,578.7
Corporate Assets							3,574.0	3,336.9	2,548.0
Total	$19,607.9	$17,802.7	$15,242.4	2,226.5	2,224.4	1,895.7	$18,775.1	$17,143.4	$15,126.7
Interest and Other Corporate Expenses, Net[a]				(556.2)	(557.0)	(545.2)			
Income from Continuing Operations Before Income Taxes				$1,670.3	$1,667.4	$1,350.5			

	Capital Spending 1991	1990	1989	Depreciation and Amortization Expense 1991	1990	1989
Soft Drinks	$ 425.8	$ 334.1	$ 267.8	$ 393.2	$338.1	$306.3
Snack Foods	406.0	381.6	257.9	253.5	232.5	189.3
Restaurants	648.4	460.6	424.6	379.6	306.5	269.9
Corporate	4.1	21.9	9.2	8.2	6.9	6.5
	$1,484.3	$1,198.2	$ 959.5	$1,034.5	$884.0	$772.0

Results by Restaurant Chain:	Net Sales 1991	1990	1989	Operating Profits[a] 1991	1990	1989
Pizza Hut	$3,258.3	$2,949.9	$2,453.5	$314.5	$245.9	$205.5
Taco Bell	2,038.1	1,745.5	1,465.9	180.6	149.6	109.4
KFC	1,830.5	1,530.3	1,331.3	80.5	126.9	99.4
	$7,126.9	$6,225.7	$5,250.7	$575.6	$522.4	$414.3

(a) **Unusual Items:** (dollars in millions, except per share data) Profits for the years presented included several unusual charges and credits, resulting in a 1991 total charge of $170.0 ($119.8 after-tax or $0.15 per share), a 1990 net credit of $35.2 ($4.2 charge after-tax or $0.01 per share) and a 1989 net credit of $4.4 ($1.8 after-tax). The unusual items were as follows:

Soft Drinks: 1990 included $10.5 in domestic charges for receivables exposures related to highly leveraged retail customers. 1989 included a $32.5 credit resulting from a decision to retain a bottling operation in Japan previously held for sale and a $12.3 reorganization charge to decentralize international operations.

Snack Foods: 1991 included $127.0 in charges consisting of a $91.4 domestic restructuring charge to streamline operations, as well as a $35.6 international restructuring charge, consisting of $23.6 to streamline operations in the United Kingdom and $12.0 to dispose of or reduce ownership in a small, unprofitable business. 1990 included $10.6 in domestic charges for receivables exposures related to highly leveraged retail customers. 1989 included a $6.6 reorganization charge to decentralize domestic operations and a $4.3 credit resulting from a decision to retain a domestic cookie production facility previously held for sale.

Restaurants: 1991 included $43.0 in charges at KFC consisting of domestic and international restructuring charges of $32.8 and $1.2, respectively, to streamline operations and a $9.0 domestic charge related to a delay in the national roll-out of the new Skinfree Crispy chicken product. 1990 included a $17.6 charge for closures of certain underperforming restaurants as follows: $9.0 at Pizza Hut, $4.0 at Taco Bell and $4.6 ($0.6 internationally) at KFC. 1990 also included Pizza Hut charges of $8.0 to consolidate domestic field operations and $2.4 to relocate international headquarters. 1989 included reorganization charges of $8.0 at KFC and $5.5 at Taco Bell to consolidate domestic field operations.

Corporate: 1990 included a $118.2 gain from an initial public stock offering by PepsiCo's KFC joint venture in Japan, an $18.0 charge for accelerated contributions to the PepsiCo Foundation and a $15.9 charge to reduce the carrying value of a Pizza Hut international joint venture investment.

Quarterly Financial Data and Capital Stock Information

Nearly all publicly held companies and many nonpublic companies issue financial information on a quarterly basis to stockholders, regulatory agencies, and others. These quarterly reports are referred to as interim financial reports, for which there are prescribed accounting standards. Quarterly financial data along with capital stock information are frequently summarized in the Annual Report. PepsiCo summarizes its quarterly data and capital stock information as shown below and on page L28.

Quarterly Financial Data

(in millions except per share amounts, unaudited)

	First Quarter (12 Weeks)		Second Quarter (12 Weeks)		Third Quarter (12 Weeks)		Fourth Quarter (16 Weeks)		Full Year (52 Weeks)	
	1991	1990	**1991**	1990	**1991**	1990	**1991**	1990	**1991**	1990
Net sales	**$4,117.0**	3,677.7	**4,679.8**	4,204.7	**4,881.3**	4,475.7	**5,929.8**	5,444.6	**19,607.9**	17,802.7
Gross profit	**$2,153.1**	1,888.2	**2,445.1**	2,216.0	**2,531.9**	2,323.5	**3,082.3**	2,825.6	**10,212.4**	9,253.3
Income from continuing operations before income taxes	**$ 316.0**	275.6	**489.7**	438.9[a]	**433.4[b]**	566.0[c]	**431.2[d]**	386.9[e]	**1,670.3**	1,667.4
Provision for income taxes	**$ 110.6**	93.7	**171.4**	146.4	**148.0**	215.7	**160.1**	121.0	**590.1**	576.8
Income from continuing operations	**$ 205.4**	181.9	**318.3**	292.5	**285.4**	350.3	**271.1**	265.9	**1,080.2**	1,090.6
Discontinued operation charge	**$ –**	–	**–**	–	**–**	(13.7)	**–**	–	**–**	(13.7)
Net income	**$ 205.4**	181.9	**318.3**	292.5	**285.4**	336.6	**271.1**	265.9	**1,080.2**	1,076.9
Income (charge) per share:										
Continuing operations	**$ 0.26**	0.23	**0.39**	0.36	**0.36**	0.44[c]	**0.34**	0.34	**1.35**	1.37
Discontinued operation	**$ –**	–	**–**	–	**–**	(0.02)	**–**	–	**–**	(0.02)
Net income per share	**$ 0.26**	0.23	**0.39**	0.36[a]	**0.36[b]**	0.42	**0.34[d]**	0.34[e]	**1.35**	1.35

Stock Performance

PepsiCo was formed through the 1965 merger of Pepsi-Cola Company and Frito-Lay, Inc. A $1,000 investment in our stock made in 1965 was worth approximately $51,000 on December 28, 1991, assuming the reinvestment of dividends. Past performance is not necessarily indicative of future returns on investments in PepsiCo Capital Stock.

As the chart at the far right illustrates, the return on PepsiCo Capital Stock compares favorably with the performance of the Standard & Poor's 400 over the past five years.

Year-End Market Price Of Stock
(In Dollars)

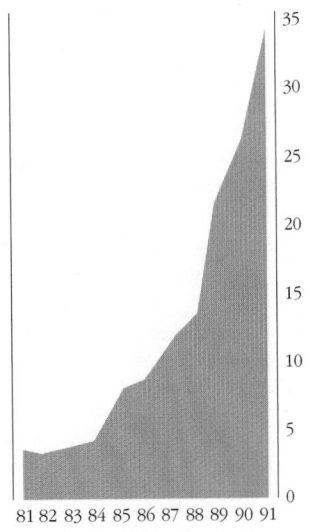

81 82 83 84 85 86 87 88 89 90 91

Comparison Of Monthly Market Price Performance
(Closing Price Indexed At 12/31/86)

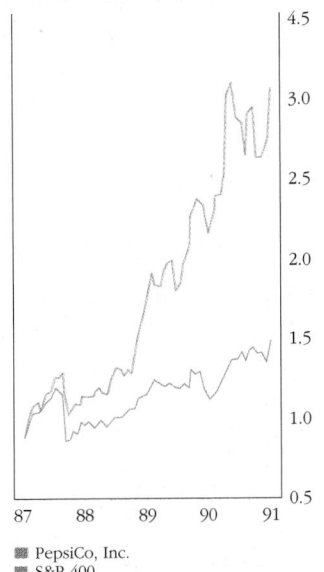

87 88 89 90 91

▪ PepsiCo, Inc.
▪ S&P 400

Five- or Ten-Year Summary

Usually presented in close proximity to the audited financial statements is a five- or ten-year summary of selected financial data. From such a summary, one can determine trends and growth patterns over a fairly long period of time. PepsiCo presented the following summary that includes operating data, financial position data, and selected statistics and ratios:

Selected Financial Data

(in millions except per share and employee amounts, unaudited) PepsiCo, Inc. and Subsidiaries	Growth Rates				
	Compounded		Annual		
	10-Year 1981-91	5-Year 1986-91	1-Year 1990-91	**1991**(a)	1990
Summary of Operations					
Net Sales.	12.8%	16.8%	10.1%	**$19,607.9**	17,802.7
Cost of sales and operating expenses.				**17,485.0**	15,628.9
Interest expense.				**615.9**	688.5
Interest income				**(163.3)**	(182.1)
				17,937.6	16,135.3
Income from continuing operations before income taxes	13.2%	19.3%	0.2%	**1,670.3**	1,667.4
Provision for income taxes				**590.1**	576.8
Income from continuing operations	14.9%	18.4%	(1.0)%	**$ 1,080.2**	1,090.6
Net income.	13.8%	18.7%	0.3%	**$ 1,080.2**	1,076.9
Income per share from continuing operations	15.5%	18.0%	(1.5)%	**$ 1.35**	1.37
Net income per share	14.1%	18.4%	–	**$ 1.35**	1.35
Cash dividends declared per share.	11.3%	17.1%	20.1%	**$ 0.460**	0.383
Average shares and equivalents outstanding				**802.5**	798.7
Cash Flow Data(e)					
Net cash provided by continuing operations.	16.8%	14.9%	15.2%	**$ 2,430.3**	2,110.0
Acquisitions and investments in affiliates for cash				**$ 640.9**	630.6
Purchases of property, plant and equipment for cash.	13.4%	11.2%	23.5%	**$ 1,457.8**	1,180.1
Cash dividends paid.	10.5%	16.4%	16.8%	**$ 343.2**	293.9
Year-End Position					
Total assets	16.8%	18.5%	9.5%	**$18,775.1**	17,143.4
Long-term debt(f).	25.5%	24.3%	32.3%	**$ 7,806.2**	5,899.6
Total debt(f)	20.8%	22.9%	6.8%	**$ 8,034.4**	7,526.1
Shareholders' equity				**$ 5,545.4**	4,904.2
Per share.	14.0%	21.6%	13.0%	**$ 7.03**	6.22
Market price per share	23.4%	31.0%	31.1%	**$ 33¾**	25¾
Shares outstanding				**789.1**	788.4
Employees	10.9%	9.6%	9.7%	**338,000**	308,000
Statistics					
Return on average shareholders' equity (g)				**20.7%**	24.8
Historical cost net debt ratio (h)				**47%**	47
Market net debt ratio (i).				**19%**	22

PepsiCo, Inc.

1989	1988[b]	1987	1986	1985	1984[c]	1983[b]	1982[d]	1981
15,242.4	12,533.2	11,018.1	9,017.1	7,584.5	7,058.6	6,568.6	6,232.4	5,873.3
13,459.5	11,184.0	9,890.5	8,187.9	6,802.4	6,479.3	5,995.7	5,684.7	5,278.8
609.6	344.2	294.6	261.4	195.2	204.9	175.0	163.5	147.7
(177.2)	(122.2)	(112.6)	(122.7)	(96.4)	(86.1)	(53.6)	(49.1)	(35.8)
13,891.9	11,406.0	10,072.5	8,326.6	6,901.2	6,598.1	6,117.1	5,799.1	5,390.7
1,350.5	1,127.2	945.6	690.5	683.3	460.5	451.5	433.3	482.6
449.1	365.0	340.5	226.7	256.7	180.5	169.5	229.7	213.7
901.4	762.2	605.1	463.8	426.6	280.0	282.0	203.6	268.9
901.4	762.2	594.8	457.8	543.7	212.5	284.1	224.3	297.5
1.13	0.97	0.77	0.59	0.51	0.33	0.33	0.24	0.32
1.13	0.97	0.76	0.58	0.65	0.25	0.33	0.27	0.36
0.320	0.267	0.223	0.209	0.195	0.185	0.180	0.176	0.158
796.0	790.4	789.3	786.5	842.1	862.4	859.3	854.1	837.5
1,885.9	1,894.5	1,334.5	1,212.2	817.3	981.5	670.2	661.5	515.0
3,296.6	1,415.5	371.5	1,679.9	160.0	–	–	130.3	–
943.8	725.8	770.5	858.5	770.3	555.8	503.4	447.4	414.4
241.9	199.0	172.0	160.4	161.1	154.6	151.3	142.5	126.2
15,126.7	11,135.3	9,022.7	8,027.1	5,889.3	4,876.9	4,446.3	4,052.2	3,960.2
6,076.5	2,656.0	2,579.2	2,632.6	1,162.0	668.1	797.8	843.2	804.6
6,942.8	4,107.0	3,225.1	2,865.3	1,506.1	948.9	1,073.9	1,033.5	1,214.0
3,891.1	3,161.0	2,508.6	2,059.1	1,837.7	1,853.4	1,794.2	1,650.5	1,556.3
4.92	4.01	3.21	2.64	2.33	2.19	2.13	1.96	1.89
21⅜	13⅛	11¼	8¾	7⅞	4⅝	4¼	3¾	4⅛
791.1	788.4	781.2	781.0	789.4	845.2	842.0	840.4	824.4
266,000	235,000	225,000	214,000	150,000	150,000	154,000	133,000	120,000
25.6	26.9	26.5	23.8	23.1	15.4	16.4	12.7	17.5
51	37	35	40	24	11	23	30	38
24	20	18	23	12	7	16	20	23

Capital Stock Information

Stock Trading Symbol

PEP

Stock Exchange Listings

The New York Stock Exchange is the principal market for PepsiCo Capital Stock, which is also listed on the Midwest, Basel, Geneva, Zurich, Amsterdam and Tokyo Stock Exchanges.

Shareholders

At year-end 1991, there were approximately 135,000 shareholders of record.

Dividend Policy

Cash dividends are declared quarterly. Quarterly cash dividends have been paid since PepsiCo was formed in 1965, and dividends have increased for 20 consecutive years.

Consistent with PepsiCo's current payout target of approximately one-third of the prior year's income from continuing operations, the 1991 dividends declared represented 34% of 1990 income from continuing operations.

Dividends Declared Per Share (in cents)

Quarter	1991	1990
1	10	8⅓
2	12	10
3	12	10
4	12	10
Total	46	38⅓

Dividend Reinvestment Plan

Shareholders may increase their investment in our stock by enrolling in PepsiCo's Dividend Reinvestment Plan. A brochure explaining this convenient plan, for which PepsiCo pays all fees, is available from our transfer agent:

Manufacturers Hanover Trust Company
450 West 33rd Street
New York, New York 10001

PepsiCo has recently added a stock certificate safekeeping feature to its current Dividend Reinvestment Plan. For details, write to the transfer agent listed above.

Stock Prices

The high, low and closing prices for a share of PepsiCo Capital Stock on the New York Stock Exchange, as reported by The Dow Jones News/Retrieval Service, for each fiscal quarter of 1991 and 1990 were as follows (in dollars):

1991	High	Low	Close
Fourth Quarter	**33⅞**	**27**	**33¾**
Third Quarter	**33½**	**27¾**	**29⅛**
Second Quarter	**35⅝**	**29½**	**30⅞**
First Quarter	**35⅛**	**23½**	**32⅞**
1990			
Fourth Quarter	27⅞	21	25¾
Third Quarter	27⅞	21¾	25¼
Second Quarter	25½	20⅝	24⅝
First Quarter	21½	18	20½

Net Sales
($ In Millions)

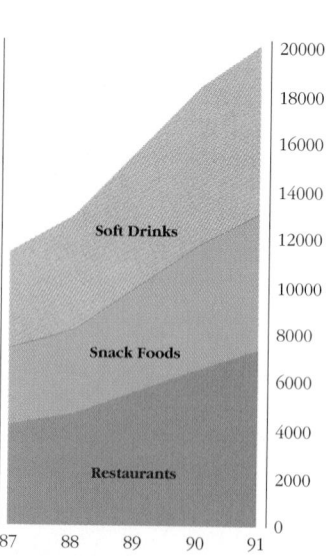

Segment Operating Profits
($ In Millions)

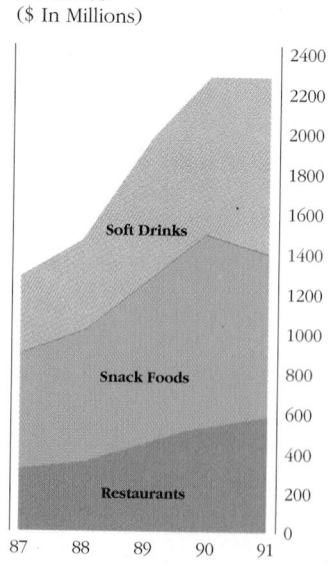

Net Sales
($ In Millions)

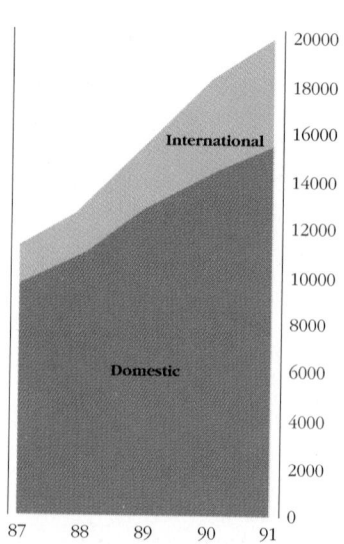

Segment Operating Profits
($ In Millions)

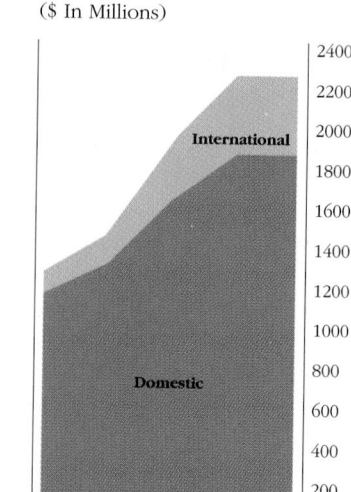

APPENDIX M

INCOME TAXES AND MANAGEMENT DECISIONS

Study Objectives

After studying this chapter, you should be able to:

1. *Contrast the importance of an average tax rate and a marginal tax rate.*

2. *Identify the filing status that an individual may elect.*

3. *Give the formula for determining taxable income.*

4. *Distinguish between the standard deduction and itemized deductions.*

5. *State the formula for determining the tax refund or balance due.*

6. *Indicate the principal components in determining taxable income for a corporation.*

7. *List circumstances in which income taxes may affect management decisions.*

8. *Describe the accounting for deferred income taxes.*

CONCEPTS FOR REVIEW

Before studying this appendix you should know, or if necessary review, the following concepts.

1. *The economic entity assumption (Ch. 1, p. 13–15)*
2. *The difference between the cash and accrual bases of accounting (Ch. 3, p. 106–7)*

They say there are only two certainties in life: death and taxes. The only difference, according to one senator, is that death doesn't get worse every time Congress meets.[1] The federal government, most states, and many cities levy an income tax. It follows that income taxes can be a significant expense for individual and corporate taxpayers. It is important, therefore, to recognize the tax consequences of business decisions.

In 1986, Congress passed the Tax Reform Act (TRA), the most sweeping federal tax legislation in more than 40 years. The Tax Reform Act of 1986, hereinafter referred to as the Act, dramatically lowered income tax rates, significantly broadened the tax base, and shifted the tax burden from individuals to corporations. It also renamed the tax law The Internal Revenue Code of 1986. Since then, the Act has been subject to minor revision.

In this chapter, we first explain the basic structure of the federal income tax system and the major provisions of the Act and revisions to it that pertain to individuals and corporations. Then we consider the effect of income taxes on business decisions.

Federal Income Tax System

Federal income taxes originated in the Sixteenth Amendment to the Constitution, which was passed in 1913. Since that date, numerous tax acts have been passed by Congress, and these acts (or laws) are summarized in the Internal Revenue Code. Primary responsibility for administering and interpreting the federal income tax laws rests with the Treasury Department, and a division of this department, the **Internal Revenue Service (IRS)**. The IRS is charged with the collection of taxes and enforcement of the tax regulations. Final authority for resolving disputes between the federal government and a taxpayer rests with the federal courts.

Originally levied solely to raise revenue for the federal government, income taxes have become a powerful economic and social force. Considerable reliance is placed on income taxes in fighting inflation and deflation, in attaining full employment, and in redistributing income for various social purposes.

Taxable Entities

Income taxes are imposed on taxable entities. A taxable entity and an accounting entity need not be identical. The three major classes of taxable entities are (1) individuals, (2) corporations, and (3) fiduciaries (estates and trusts). **A business operated as a proprietorship or a partnership is an accounting entity but not a taxable entity.** Net income from such a source is reported as income on the proprietor's or partners' individual tax return(s), regardless of whether the net income is actually withdrawn from the business. In contrast, a corporation is both an accounting and a taxable entity. A corporation must file a tax return and pay income taxes on its taxable income.

Study Objective 1

Contrast the importance of an average tax rate and a marginal tax rate.

Tax Relationships

A tax may be proportional, regressive, or progressive. A proportional tax occurs when a constant rate (or percentage) is applied regardless of changes in the

[1]"Current Accounts," *Money*, October 1986, p. 11.

amount of the tax base. Sales taxes are proportional because the same tax rate is applied irrespective of the amount of the sale. A regressive tax is one in which the amount of the tax remains unchanged or the tax rate decreases with increases in the tax base. For example, license taxes imposed for the privilege of engaging in a business, occupation, or profession are usually regressive, since they are not related to sales or net income. A small company will pay as much in license taxes as a giant corporation; the taxes for the small company represent a greater proportion of income than they do for the giant. A progressive tax results when the tax rate becomes higher as the amount of tax base increases. Federal income taxes and most state income taxes are progressive with respect to income.

In considering the effect of income taxes, it is necessary to distinguish between an average rate and a marginal rate. They are determined as follows:

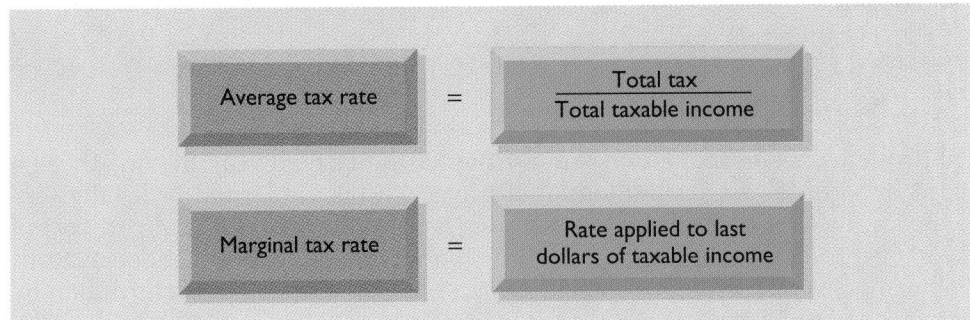

For example, if the tax rate is 28% on taxable income from $35,801 to $86,500 and 31% on all taxable income in excess of $86,500, the marginal tax rate is 31% if the taxpayer has taxable income in excess of $86,500. The highest marginal rate in 1992 was 31% for most individuals and 34% for most corporations.

The marginal tax rate is usually more significant than the average tax rate in making business decisions. For example, in both incremental analysis and in capital budgeting, the anticipated income will be subject to the marginal tax rate.

Helpful hint If you as an individual are considering taking a second job and are analyzing its effect on your net-of-tax income, which rate is relevant to your analysis—your average rate or your marginal rate? Answer: Marginal rate.

Tax Accounting Methods

For tax purposes, individual taxpayers generally have the option to use either the cash method or the accrual method in determining taxable income. **Most corporations, however, are required to use the accrual method.** The choice between the methods relates to the timing of revenues and expenses. Changes from one method to another must be approved by the Internal Revenue Service. The essential features of each method are described below.

Accrual Method

The accrual method of accounting has been stressed throughout this textbook. Under this method, revenues are recognized when they are earned, and expenses are recognized when they are incurred. The accrual method is normally used when taxable income is based on business net income.

Cash Method

Under the cash method, revenues are recognized when they are realized in cash, and expenses are recognized when they are paid. The cash method requires a minimum of record-keeping. When taxable income consists primarily of salaries, interest, and dividends, the results under this method may approximate the results under the accrual method. The cash method is normally used by individual taxpayers.

ECTION I   Individuals

Study Objective 2

Identify the filing status that an individual may elect.

Individual taxpayers must elect one filing status from the following options:

1. Single.
2. Head of household.
3. Married filing a joint return.[2]
4. Married filing a separate return.

Filing status is determined on the last day of the taxable year. To qualify as a head of a household, an individual taxpayer who is unmarried or legally separated at the end of the taxable year must have paid more than half the cost of keeping up a home that has been the principal residence of his or her dependents. In most cases, married couples will pay less tax by filing a joint return than by filing separate returns.

The Internal Revenue Service provides specific tax forms and instructions for filing an income tax return. Taxable income for an individual taxpayer is computed as follows:

ILLUSTRATION M-1

Taxable income formula for an individual

Study Objective 3

Give the formula for determining taxable income.

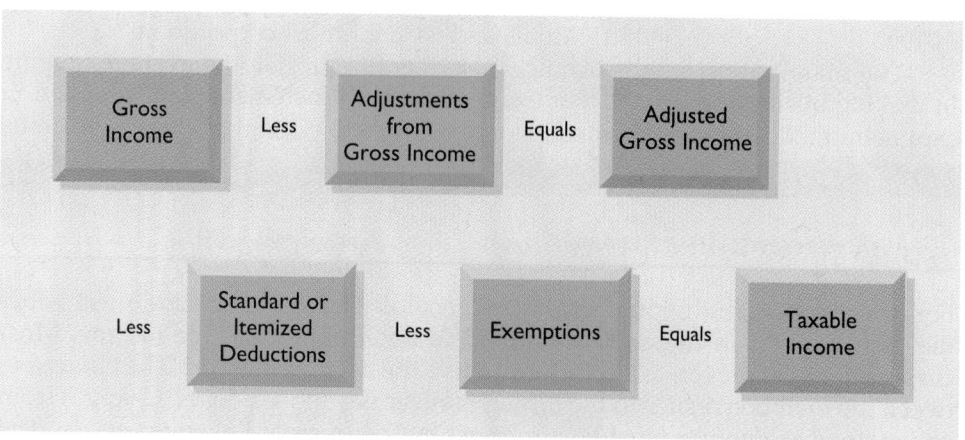

Each of the steps in the formula is explained below.

Gross Income

Gross income is "all income from whatever source derived." Gross income may be received in the form of cash, property, or services. When cash is not involved, income is measured by the fair market value of the property or services received. The Act identifies both inclusions and exclusions from gross income. A representative listing of items in each category is presented in Illustration M-2.

---

[2]This status includes qualifying widows and widowers.

Although most of the items included in gross income are self-evident, three concepts need additional explanation: (1) business income, (2) passive income, and (3) capital gains and losses.

ILLUSTRATION M-2

Gross income inclusions and exclusions

Gross Income	
Inclusions	**Exclusions**
Wages, including salaries, bonuses, commissions, fees, and tips	Interest on certain state and municipal bonds
Dividends, rents, and royalties	State and federal welfare benefits
Interest on bank deposits, bonds, and notes	Gifts, inheritances, and bequests
Business and farm income	Life insurance proceeds received from a person's death
Pensions, annuities, and endowments	Dividends on veterans' life insurance
Gains from sale or exchange of real estate, securities, and personal residence	Child support
Prizes and awards from contests, raffles, and lotteries	
Artistic, scientific, and employee productivity awards	
Unemployment compensation	
Reimbursed business expenses	
Alimony received	

Helpful hint The list of inclusions is longer than the list of exclusions. For federal income tax purposes, "gross income" means all income from whatever source, except for those items specifically excluded by the Code.

Business Income

Net income from a proprietorship and an individual's share of the net income of a partnership are included in gross income. Conversely, a net loss from a business in which the taxpayer actively participates can be offset against gross income.

Business net income or net loss determined in conformity with generally accepted accounting principles **need not be in accord with tax provisions for determining business income**. In determining net income for tax purposes, the taxpayer should take advantage of as many favorable tax provisions as possible. For example, a taxpayer would likely adopt the Tax Code's Modified Accelerated Cost Recovery System (MACRS), which provides for rapid write-off of the cost of depreciable assets.

Passive Income

The Act distinguishes between active and passive income, depending on the nature of the activity and the taxpayer's involvement in generating the income. Active income includes salaries and wages earned by the taxpayer, and business and farm income when the taxpayer materially participated in producing the income. Passive income relates to income obtained from activities in which the taxpayer does not participate on a regular, continuous, and substantial basis. An example is an individual who invests in a commercial real-estate development but does not become involved in the day to day activities of the development. The Act also recognizes portfolio income which includes interest and dividends from securities held as an investment.

All income is reported in gross income and is taxed at regular rates. Losses from a business in which the taxpayer actively participates can be offset against gross income. However, the Act prohibits the taxpayer from using net passive losses to offset the other types of income until the taxpayer's entire interest in the passive activity is terminated. At that time, net passive losses can offset active and portfolio income.

The provisions applicable to passive income and losses substantially reduce the use of tax shelters. A tax shelter is an investment that is designed to take advantage of various tax benefits. One objective of the investment is to use losses from the investment as immediate offsets against gross income. In terms of real dollars, the return on a tax shelter was often very high. Typically, investments in rental properties, equipment leasing, and oil and gas ventures have been used as tax shelters. These types of investments are generally considered to be passive activities. Thus, losses from tax shelters must now be deferred, as described above.

Capital Gains and Losses

A capital gain or loss occurs when property classified under tax law as a capital asset is sold or exchanged. A capital asset is any item of property other than (1) inventories, (2) trade receivables, (3) plant assets used in a trade or business, and (4) certain intangible assets such as copyrights and artistic compositions.[3] For an individual, capital assets include all property held for investment and for personal use.

When a capital asset is sold, gain or loss is determined by the difference between the proceeds from the sale and the **tax basis** of the property, which is generally cost or cost less accumulated depreciation. A net capital gain results when capital gains exceed capital losses. Net capital gains are included in gross income and are taxed in the same manner as other types of gross income.[4] A net capital loss occurs when capital losses exceed capital gains. Net capital losses are offset against gross income on a dollar-for-dollar basis up to a maximum of $3,000 per year. Losses in excess of $3,000 can be carried forward to future years with the same $3,000 limitation.

To illustrate a net capital gain, assume that Thomas Robinson sold the following securities in 1993:

ILLUSTRATION M-3

Computation of net capital gain

Type of Security	Tax Basis	Selling Price	Capital Gain	Capital Loss
Burlington common stock	$ 4,200	$ 6,000	$1,800	
Newport preferred stock	5,000	5,500	500	
Pacific common stock	2,600	2,000		$600
Totals	$11,800	$13,500	$2,300	$600

Thomas Robinson has realized a net capital gain of $1,700 (capital gains of $2,300 less capital losses of $600), which is reported under gross income.

Computation of Gross Income

To illustrate the computation of gross income, we will assume the following data for Thomas Robinson:

---

[3]In some cases, plant assets used in a trade or business may qualify as capital assets.

[4]If the net capital gain, however, is long-term (resulting from a capital asset held longer than one year), the maximum tax rate is 28% for individuals in the 31% tax bracket.

ILLUSTRATION M-4

Assumed income data

Salary and commissions as sales representative for Standard Manufacturing Company	$45,000
Net capital gains (see above)	1,700
Interest from tax-exempt municipal bonds	3,600
Dividends from investments	2,400
Net income from a limited partnership	5,000

Thomas Robinson's gross income is $54,100, computed as follows:

ILLUSTRATION M-5

Computation of gross income

Salaries and commissions	$45,000
Net capital gains	1,700
Dividends	2,400
Partnership income	5,000
Total gross income	$54,100

All of the items except the interest from the tax-exempt municipal bonds must be reported under gross income.

 Accounting in Action · *Business Insight*

The issue of the proper tax rate to assign to capital gains is hotly debated by our politicians and financial experts. Some contend that lower tax rates on capital gains encourage investment in businesses and spur U.S. economic growth. In recent years, those who support business interests have favored a reduction in the capital gains tax. Others argue that long-term capital gains are the same as any other type of income and therefore should be taxed at the same rate. Presently, there is a modest difference between the tax rates on capital gains and other types of income. The issue is like a leaf that gets blown about in the political winds every fall when Congress works on the federal budget for the coming year. Which way is the wind blowing as you read this book?

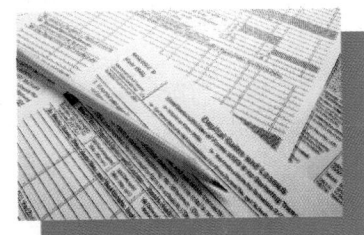

Adjustments From Gross Income

Adjustments from gross income include (1) reimbursed business expenses, (2) payments to retirement plans, and (3) alimony payments.

Reimbursed Business Expenses

Reimbursed business expenses are business expenses initially paid by the taxpayer that are subsequently reimbursed by the taxpayer's employer. Reimbursed business expenses are an adjustment to gross income to the extent that they are included in gross income. Consequently, these business expenses are offset to the extent of gross income and have no effect on the amount of adjusted gross income.

Payments to Retirement Plans

To encourage individuals to save for retirement, certain types of payments to retirement plans are deductible for tax purposes. In addition, the income earned on the assets invested is not taxed until it is withdrawn. Two of the most common types of personal retirement plans are:

1. Payments to an Individual Retirement Arrangement plan (IRA).
2. Payments to a Keogh H. R. 10 plan (Keogh).

IRAs

All individuals who work are allowed to contribute up to $2,000 annually to an IRA. However, restrictions apply as to the amount the individual may claim as an allowable deduction from gross income. **For individuals who are not covered by a company-sponsored pension plan, the allowable deduction is $2,000.** Married taxpayers filing a joint return may each deduct $2,000 if both individuals work. However, **if one spouse does not work**, the allowable deduction for the spouse is $250 per year, or a total deduction of $2,250 for the couple.

For taxpayers covered by a company-sponsored retirement plan, a deduction is permitted if income levels are below certain minimums. For example, when adjusted gross income before an IRA deduction exceeds $25,000 for a single taxpayer and $40,000 for married taxpayers filing jointly, the allowable deduction is phased out proportionately. The deductible amount becomes zero at adjusted gross income of $35,000 for a single taxpayer and at $50,000 for married taxpayers filing jointly.

Keogh Plans

Self-employed individuals can also make retirement payments to a Keogh H. R. 10 plan. The amount deductible for Keogh payments is significantly higher than the amount for IRA payments. Under a defined contribution plan, for example, the maximum deduction is $30,000. The Keogh plan enables self-employed individuals to accumulate retirement funds similar to pension funds for employed taxpayers provided by many employers.

Alimony Payments

Alimony payments made by an individual are an adjustment to gross income. To qualify as alimony, the payment must be made under a divorce or separation instrument and meet certain requirements. For example, (1) the payment must be in cash, (2) the parties must live in separate households, and (3) the payment cannot be treated as child support. Alimony payments represent gross income to the recipient.

Adjusted Gross Income

Adjusted gross income is the difference between gross income and adjustments from gross income. To illustrate the computation of adjusted gross income, assume that Jane and Carl Baker are married and filing a joint return. Jane works as a word processor for Hi-Tech Inc., which does not have a company-sponsored retirement plan, and Carl is a self-employed building contractor. In 1992, Jane earned $24,000 in salary and Carl's business income was $40,000. Both individuals made the maximum $2,000 contribution to an IRA plan. In addition, Carl made an allowable contribution to a Keogh plan of $8,000. Adjusted gross income is $52,000, computed as follows:

Gross income		
Salary	$24,000	
Business income	40,000	
Total gross income	64,000	
Deductions from gross income		
IRA contributions	$4,000	
Keogh contribution	8,000	
Total deductions		12,000
Adjusted gross income		$52,000

ILLUSTRATION M-6

Computation of adjusted gross income

Helpful hint The amounts deducted for retirement plans (IRA and Keogh) will be taxable in the future years in which the amounts are withdrawn. Most likely this will be upon retirement when the taxpayer may be in a lower tax bracket.

Deductions From Adjusted Gross Income

Deductions from adjusted gross income consist of either a standard deduction or itemized deductions.

Study Objective 4

Distinguish between the standard deduction and itemized deductions.

Standard Deduction

The standard deduction is the amount a taxpayer can claim without supporting documentation. It is the floor for determining whether or not it would be advantageous to itemize deductions. The standard deduction also helps to determine whether an individual must file a tax return. If gross income is equal to or less than the standard deduction and personal exemptions (discussed later), it is not necessary to file a tax return.

The standard deduction varies for each filing status. The deductions for 1992 are generally as follows:

Filing Status	Standard Deduction
Single	$3,600
Head of household	5,250
Married filing a joint return	6,000
Married filing a separate return	3,000

ILLUSTRATION M-7

Standard deductions, 1992

Itemized Deductions

Instead of claiming the standard deduction, the taxpayer may elect to claim itemized deductions. These deductions represent actual expenditures made by the taxpayer during the year. They are itemized in a separate tax schedule, and the taxpayer must be able to provide documentary evidence of each deduction. Itemized deductions are grouped into the following categories:

(1) Medical expenses and health insurance
(2) State and local taxes
(3) Interest expense
(4) Charitable contributions
(5) Casualty and theft losses
(6) Employee business expenses and miscellaneous deductions

ILLUSTRATION M-8

Itemized deduction categories

Medical Expenses and Health Insurance

Medical expenses consist of (1) prescription drugs and insulin, and (2) other medical and dental expenses including doctors' fees, hospital care, medical examinations, X-rays, nursing help, medical aids, ambulance service, and other travel costs to obtain medical care. This itemized deduction pertains only to expenses paid by the taxpayer that are not reimbursed by insurance or paid by others. In addition, premiums paid for hospital, doctor, and dental insurance plans are deductible.

The amount of deduction for medical expenses and health insurance is limited to payments in excess of 7.5% of adjusted gross income. The computation of this itemized deduction for Paula Coffin, using assumed data, is shown below:

ILLUSTRATION M-9

Computation of medical expenses and health insurance deduction

Prescription drugs	$ 450
Orthodontic fees	1,200
Blue Cross/Blue Shield premiums	600
Other medical and dental expenses	1,300
Total	3,550
Less: 7.5% of $30,000 adjusted gross income	2,250
Deduction for medical expenses and health insurance	**$1,300**

Basically, the Act permits the taxpayer to deduct all legitimate major medical and health care expenses above a certain minimum.

State and Local Taxes

The list of state and local taxes that are deductible is much shorter than the taxes that are disallowed. The allowable taxes and examples of taxes that are not allowable are as follows:

ILLUSTRATION M-10

Allowable and not allowable taxes

Allowable Taxes	**Not Allowable Taxes**
State and local income taxes	Federal income, estate, and excise taxes
Real estate taxes	FICA (social security) taxes
Personal property taxes	Sales taxes
	Gasoline taxes
	Automobile, driver's, and marriage license fees

Interest Expense

The Act classifies interest expense as either (1) mortgage interest on a qualified residence, (2) consumer (or personal) interest such as interest on car loans and credit cards, and (3) investment interest. The rules are:

ILLUSTRATION M-11

Interest rules

Type of Interest	**Tax Rule**
Mortgage	Fully deductible for most taxpayers
Consumer	Nondeductible
Investment	Generally deductible to extent of investment income

A qualified residence is the taxpayer's principal residence and one other residence. If a loan is secured by a principal or second residence and with the funds being used to buy, build, or improve that residence, the interest on $1,000,000 of such loans is deductible. In addition, interest on $100,000 or less of loans secured by the principal or second home are deductible regardless of the use of the proceeds.

The rules on interest expense may affect a taxpayer's use of credit. From a tax standpoint, it is advantageous to maximize the borrowing of money on one's personal residence and to minimize the use of credit for other purposes.

Charitable Contributions

An individual can deduct amounts given to qualified organizations operated for religious, charitable, educational, scientific, or literary purposes. Contributions can be in the form of cash or property (such as clothing, furniture, and equipment). The annual deduction for charitable contributions generally cannot exceed 50% of adjusted gross income. Any contributions in excess of this amount in any year can be carried forward to future years.

Casualty and Theft Losses

A taxpayer generally is allowed to deduct losses caused by vandalism, fire, storm, theft, car and boating accidents, and similar causes (often referred to as *casualties*). The deductible amount is limited to the uninsured loss, and the taxpayer must file timely insurance claims. If a taxpayer fails to pursue a claim to avoid a rate increase, no deduction is allowed. To determine the amount deductible, two tests have to be performed: First, only casualty losses in excess of $100 per loss are deductible. Second, the casualty loss (after subtracting the $100 deduction) is limited to an amount that exceeds 10% of adjusted gross income.

Employee Business Expenses and Miscellaneous Deductions

Unreimbursed business expenses and miscellaneous deductions are allowed as itemized deductions. Some items in this category are not subject to any floor (minimum amount). These include moving expenses, certain work expenses incurred by handicapped employees, and gambling losses to the extent of gambling winnings. All other items in this category are allowed only to the extent they (in the aggregate) exceed 2% of adjusted gross income. These items include the following:

TRAVEL. Travel expenses include transportation, lodging, and meals incurred on trips away from home for business purposes. No deduction is allowed for travel expenses incurred (1) as a form of education, (2) for charitable purposes that provide personal, recreational, or vacation benefits, and (3) to attend seminars for investment purposes.

ENTERTAINMENT AND MEALS. Deductions for entertainment and meals incurred for business purposes are limited to 80% of the amount paid. Further monetary restrictions apply to entertainment expenses. For example, the deduction for theater tickets is 80% of the face value of the tickets, and the deduction for the use of luxury skyboxes at a sports arena is limited to 80% of the cost of regular tickets. However, amounts paid for tickets to charitable events are generally fully deductible as charitable contributions.

Helpful hint Prior to 1987, consumer interest was deductible. When the law changed, some taxpayers who had a lot of consumer debt took out additional loans against their homes (home equity loans) to pay the consumer debt, thus changing the consumer debt to home equity debt and thereby converting the interest from nondeductible to deductible.

Meals (and other entertainment) are deductible only if (1) business is discussed before, during, or after the meal, and (2) the meal has a clear business purpose directly related to the active conduct of the taxpayer's trade or business.

Deductible travel, entertainment, and meal expenses must be aggregated with miscellaneous deductions. This total is then deductible only to the extent that it exceeds 2% of adjusted gross income. From a tax standpoint, it is better for an individual to have all business expenses reimbursed by the company. As explained earlier, reimbursed expenses have no effect on adjusted gross income. Moreover, the individual will not be required to defend the deductions for reimbursed business expenses.

OTHER INDIVIDUAL ITEMS. Expenses for union dues, tools, and uniforms are examples of items included under miscellaneous deductions. These deductions also include subscriptions to trade magazines, membership dues in professional organizations, tax counsel and tax preparation fees, and the cost of pursuing a business that is considered to be a hobby under tax law.

To illustrate the computation of employee business expenses and miscellaneous deductions, we will assume that Mary Norton incurred the following expenses when her adjusted gross income was $36,000: (1) business entertainment, $500 (paid $500 for theater tickets having a face value of $450); (2) business meals, $400; (3) income tax preparation fee, $250; and (4) membership dues in professional organization, $50. The allowable deduction is $260 computed as follows:

ILLUSTRATION M-12

Computation of allowable business expenses and miscellaneous deductions

Entertainment (80% × $450)	$360
Meals (80% × $400)	320
Income tax preparation fee	250
Membership dues in professional organization	50
Total expenses	980
Less: 2% of adjusted gross income ($36,000 × 2%)	720
Allowable deduction for business expenses and miscellaneous deductions	**$260**

Personal and Dependency Exemptions

A taxpayer is allowed a personal exemption for himself or herself, his or her spouse, and a dependency exemption for each dependent. Specific requirements must be met to qualify as a dependent. In general, a dependent must:

Helpful hint Can you as a student claim a personal exemption on your own tax return if you are already claimed as a dependent on your parents' return? Answer: No.

1. Receive less than $2,300 of gross income unless he or she is a child of the taxpayer and under 19 years of age or a full-time student under the age of 24.
2. Receive over one-half of his or her support from the taxpayer.
3. If married, not be filing a joint return with his or her spouse.
4. Be a citizen or a resident of the United States.
5. Be related to the taxpayer by marriage or by blood or have lived in the taxpayer's home for the entire taxable year.

The personal exemption is $2,300 for 1992. The amount of the personal exemption is adjusted annually for inflation. High-income taxpayers will lose part or all of this exemption if their taxable income reaches a certain level, as discussed later. In all homework assignments we will assume personal and dependency exemptions of $2,300.

An individual who is eligible to be claimed as a dependent on another taxpayer's return is not permitted a personal exemption on his or her own return. This means, for example, that students who have summer or part-time jobs during the school year cannot claim personal exemptions on their returns if they can be claimed as a dependent on their parents' return.

Taxable Income and Computation of the Tax

Taxable income is determined by subtracting deductions and exemptions from adjusted gross income. The amount of the tax is derived from two computations: (1) determining the regular tax, and (2) determining the alternative minimum tax. The taxpayer must pay the higher of the two amounts.

Determining the Regular Tax

The regular tax is computed by applying the appropriate tax rate to taxable income. The tax rates are:

Taxable Income—Dollars			
Single Taxpayer	**Head of Household**	**Married Jointly**	**Tax rate**
Up to $21,450	Up to $28,750	Up to $35,800	15%
Above $21,450 to $51,900	Above $28,750 to $74,150	Above $35,800 to $86,500	28%
Above $51,900	Above $74,150	Above $86,500	31%

ILLUSTRATION M-13

Current tax rates

The computation of the tax on $60,000 of taxable income for a single taxpayer and a married taxpayer filing a joint return are as follows:

Single Taxpayer			Married Taxpayer Filing a Joint Return		
Taxable income	Tax rate	Tax amount	Taxable income	Tax rate	Tax amount
$21,450	15%	$ 3,218	$35,800	15%	$ 5,370
30,450	28%	8,526	24,200	28%	6,776
8,100	31%	2,511	$60,000		$12,146
$60,000		$14,255			

ILLUSTRATION M-14

Computation of tax—single and married taxpayers

Alternative Minimum Tax

The alternative minimum tax is designed to ensure that all taxpayers who have economic resources will pay some income taxes. The minimum tax liability is 24% of the individual taxpayer's alternative minimum taxable income reduced by an allowable exemption. The Act prescribes numerous adjustments and preferences to taxable income in determining alternative minimum taxable income. The computation of the alternative minimum tax is deferred to a tax accounting course.

Accounting in Action · *Business Insight*

Two thirds of your fellow Americans don't like doing their taxes (although, according to a Gallup poll, 24 percent actually think it is fine). But do we have it so bad?

In Denmark, the world's leading taxer, the government takes more than the nation's income. In Belgium, taxes equal 45 percent of output; in Australia, 31 percent. Americans, in contrast, send less than 28 percent of their national income to federal, state, and local tax collectors. For example, here is total tax revenue as a percentage of GDP (Gross Domestic Product) for many of the industrialized countries.

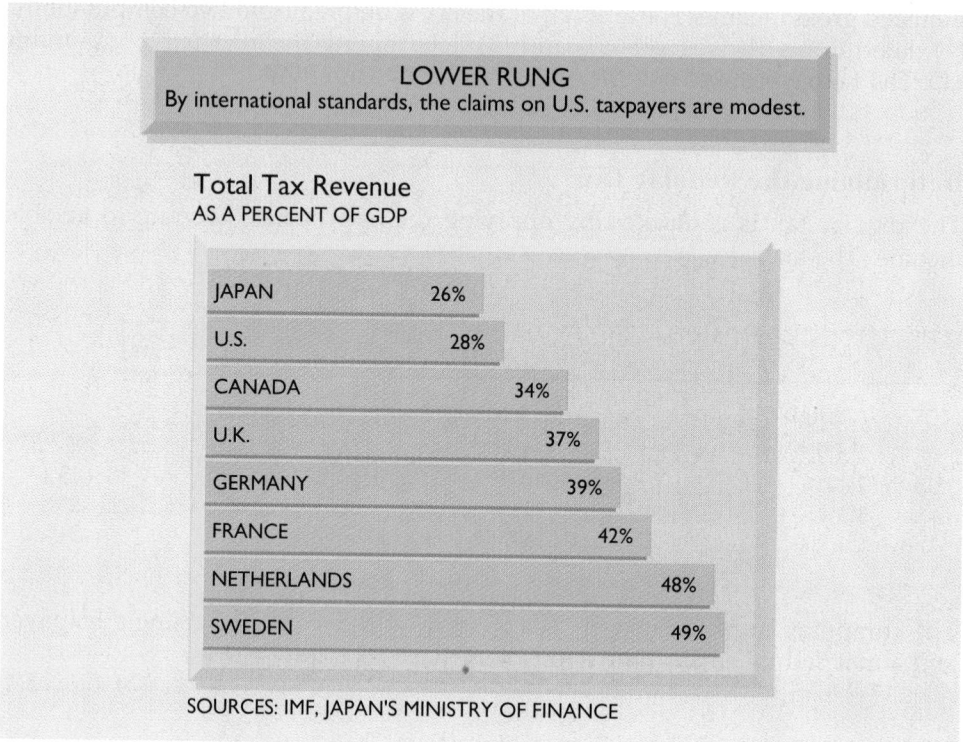

Why, then, do individuals complain about taxes? Add income, property, sales and social security taxes, and the tax rate jumps. What do you think is a proper tax rate for all your taxes?

Source: Adapted from *Newsweek,* April 13, 1992.

Study Objective 5

State the formula for determining the tax refund or balance due.

Determining Tax Refund or Balance Due

The remaining steps in the filing of an income tax return result in determining either the tax refund or the balance due. The steps consist of subtracting tax credits and tax payments from the amount of the tax as diagrammed below:

ILLUSTRATION M-15

Steps required to determine tax refund or balance due

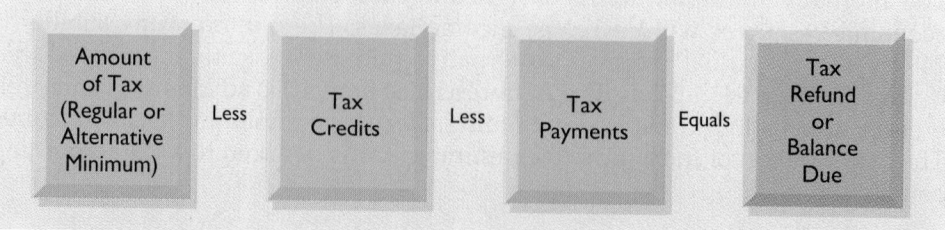

Each of these steps is explained below.

Tax Credits

Tax credits are reductions in the tax liability computed on taxable income. They are more beneficial to a taxpayer than a deduction or an exemption because they are **deducted directly** from the amount of the tax. A $100 tax credit reduces the tax liability by $100, whereas the effect of a $100 tax deduction on the tax liability depends on the taxpayer's marginal tax rate. For individuals, tax credits may be claimed for (1) child and dependent care, and (2) earned income.

The child and dependent care credit helps certain working parents to defray the cost of caring for children and elderly dependents. The earned-income credit allows low-income families with children to keep more of their earnings. The Act specifies maximum amounts for each type of tax credit.

Tax Payments

As explained in Chapter 12, employers are required to withhold income taxes from employees. In addition, a taxpayer with gross income that is not subject to withholding (e.g., dividends and interest) is required to make quarterly estimated tax payments. The withholdings and estimated payments are subtracted from the amount of the tax (less tax credits, if any) to determine either the amount payable to the Internal Revenue Service or the amount to be refunded to the taxpayer. When a refund results, the taxpayer has the option of applying the amount to the estimated tax in the following year.

Individual taxpayers are required to file a tax return on or before the 15th day of the fourth month following the close of the tax year. For individual taxpayers the tax year is generally the calendar year.

Technology in Action

This computer note is in the form of a story with a not too futuristic scenario.

It is 5 o'clock in the evening of April 15th, and you decide that you had better file your income taxes. After dinner, you sit down at your computer terminal and link into your confidential IRS file maintained at the National Computer Center. On January 3rd, your employer transmitted your earnings (Form W-2) data to your IRS file. Also, on January 4th, all banks and brokerage firms that you do business with transmitted your other income data (Form 1099) into your IRS file, so all you have to do now is make the transfer from your home accounting system, containing your itemized deductions into the IRS file.

You do this, and the video display shows that you owe $100. The display also prompts you to accept this sad fact or asks if you would like a hard copy printout of the return computations to review.

You decide to edit the hard copy and find, much to your joy, that, somehow, you failed to get a major deduction into your home accounting software. You enter the change and your IRS file is updated accordingly. The CRT now says that you have a $100 refund coming.

You push the proper function key on your computer terminal and accept the refund. In 1/10,000 of a second, $100 is electronically transferred from the IRS depository account at your local bank into your checking account. Your home accounting package is also updated to reflect the additional $100 in your account. You are happy to see, on the screen, that the IRS has accepted all of your return input and does not anticipate the need to request any other input for audit verification. The session is closed when you acknowledge acceptance of your filed return and refund. This entire process took less than 15 minutes, and you decide to enjoy the rest of your evening celebrating your refund.

Illustration of Determining Tax Refund or Balance Due

To illustrate the determination of the tax liability or the amount of the refund, we will make the computation for Reena and Greg Rhoda who are married and filing jointly. They have two children who are claimed as dependents. Reena has part-time employment. Greg and Reena are not covered by an employee-sponsored retirement plan. The couple has made the maximum payment to IRA. Their federal income tax computation for the year 1992 is shown in Illustration M-17.

SECTION 2   Partnerships

Helpful hint A partner's share of partnership income must be reported as a component of gross income on the partner's individual income tax return even if the share is not distributed to the partner.

Although a partnership is not a taxable entity, it is required to file an information return for each taxable year, regardless of the amount of partnership income. The return must state specifically the items composing gross income and the allowable deductions. In addition, the return must include the name of each partner who would be entitled to share in taxable income if distributed, and the dollar amount of the distributive share of each individual.

The tax law requires that certain specified income, deductions, and credits be **separately stated on the partnership return**. Segregated presentation is required, because these items may be subject to special treatment on the partners' individual returns. Some of the special items include tax-free interest income, charitable contributions, and capital gains and losses. Details about filing partnership tax returns are explained in a tax accounting course.

SECTION 3   Corporations

Study Objective 6

Indicate the principal components in determining taxable income for a corporation.

As a taxable entity, a corporation is required to file an income tax return annually within 2½ months of the close of its fiscal year. The provisions of the Act for corporations are extensive; many special provisions apply to certain types of corporations, such as banks and insurance companies. Corporation tax law contains no provisions for a standard deduction and personal exemptions. Moreover, the concept of adjusted gross income is not applicable to corporations.

The determination of taxable income for a corporation consists of (1) computing gross income and (2) subtracting allowable business expenses, as shown below:

ILLUSTRATION M-16

Taxable income formula for a corporation

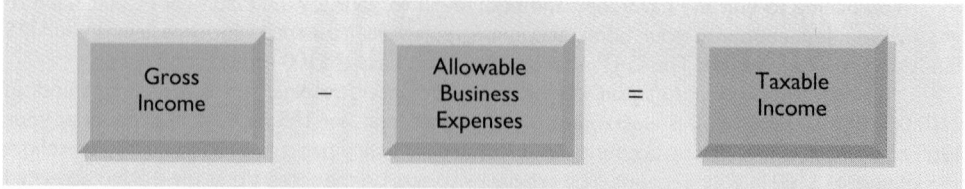

A corporation's income statement is the primary source of information for determining taxable income. As mentioned earlier, most corporations are required to use the accrual method of accounting in determining taxable income.

REENA AND GREG RHODA
Federal Income Tax Computation

GROSS INCOME			
Reena and Greg Rhoda salaries	$71,000		
Interest and dividends	3,000		
Total gross income		$74,000	
ADJUSTMENTS FROM GROSS INCOME			
Payments to IRA (Reena $2,000, Greg $2,000)		4,000	
ADJUSTED GROSS INCOME		70,000	
ITEMIZED DEDUCTIONS			
Medical expenses and health insurance			
St. Theresa Hospital—surgery	$5,250		
Orthodontic fees	2,500		
Other medical expenses	500		
Total expenses	8,250		
Less: 7.5% of adjusted gross income			
(7.5% × $70,000)	5,250		
Deductible amount		3,000	
Taxes			
State income taxes	1,200		
Real estate taxes	2,800	4,000	
Interest			
Interest on home mortgage		2,400	
Charitable contributions			
Church	1,100		
United Fund	200	1,300	
Casualty and theft loss			
Uninsured loss from boat accident	7,500		
Less: Floor ($100 per loss)	100		
	7,400		
Less: 10% of adjusted gross income	7,000	400	
Employee business expenses and miscellaneous deductions			
Income tax preparation fee	200		
Professional dues	50		
Total	250		
Less 2% of adjusted gross income			
($70,000 × 2%)	1,400	–0–	
Total itemized deductions		11,100	
Adjusted gross income less itemized deductions		58,900	
PERSONAL AND DEPENDENCY EXEMPTIONS			
($2,300 × 4)		9,200	
TAXABLE INCOME		$49,700	
COMPUTATION OF INCOME TAX			
$35,800 × 15%	$ 5,370		
13,900 × 28%	3,892	$ 9,262	
TAX PAYMENTS			
Income tax withholdings		9,000	
TAX DUE		$ 262	

The Act restricts the use of the cash method to specifically identified types of corporations.

Two areas that merit special attention in discussing corporate taxes are:

1. Tax rates
2. Effects on management decisions

Tax Rates

The Code provides for a graduated rate with a three-bracket rate structure as follows:

ILLUSTRATION M-18

Corporation tax rate structure

Taxable Income	Tax Rate
$50,000 or less	15%
$50,001–$75,000	25
Above $75,000	34

Helpful hint Even though the current law provides for lower rates, it is less lenient regarding deductions and tax credits allowed. Therefore, it is said to be increasing the income taxes paid by many corporations.

An additional 5% tax is imposed on taxable income between $100,000 and $335,000, which results in a 39% marginal rate on taxable income between $100,000 and $335,000. The 5% surtax in effect creates a flat tax rate of 34% for corporations with taxable income of $335,000 or more. The surtax is designed to recapture the revenue lost by the lower tax rates applicable to the first two tax brackets.

Effects of Taxation on Management Decisions

With a 34% marginal tax rate for most corporations, each $1 deduction saves the company 34 cents. That is probably why business decision makers typically ask, "What are the tax consequences?" in evaluating alternative actions. Thus, tax planning is important in business decision making.

The purpose of tax planning is to reduce or delay the payment of legally owed taxes. Tax planning results in tax avoidance, that is, the structuring of business decisions and transactions so that the least amount of tax is paid at the latest possible time permitted by the law. Tax evasion, not to be confused with tax avoidance, is the **illegal misstatement** of a tax liability by failing to report revenue or income received or by claiming fraudulent deductions.

The timing of business transactions is one of the simplest tax planning techniques commonly used. Business managers seeking to minimize taxable income can move discretionary expenses intended for next year into the current year and defer sales transactions near the end of the current year to the next year.

Because of the significance of taxes to both corporations and individuals and the complexity of the tax laws, specialized knowledge and experience is required in tax planning and tax return preparation. Large corporations employ tax specialists to advise them on tax matters. Individuals, proprietorships, partnerships, and many corporations engage certified public accountants for tax advice and assistance. The tax practice of many accountants and CPAs provides a major part of their revenue. Some of the tax effects and implications on management decisions are explained in the remainder of this chapter.

Determining the Form of Business Organization

A business enterprise may be either unincorporated or incorporated. Income taxes are a significant factor in deciding whether to incorporate. As previously indicated, proprietorships and partnerships are not taxable entities, whereas a corporation is a taxable entity. Moreover, the net income of an unincorporated enterprise is taxable to the owner (or owners), regardless of whether it is withdrawn from the business. In contrast, corporate earnings are taxable to the owners **only when they are received in the form of dividends**. In addition, salaries paid to owners for services rendered are a business expense only to a corporation. From a tax standpoint, the decision regarding the best form of business organization rests in part on the dividend policy that is expected to be followed by the corporation.

For tax purposes, another alternative is to form an S Corporation. An S Corporation has the legal advantages of a corporation, such as limited liability and transferability of shares. However, its tax liability is similar to that of a partnership under tax law. Thus, the taxable income of an S Corporation is subject to the maximum individual marginal tax rate of 31%, rather than the 34% marginal corporate tax rate.

> ### Study Objective 7
> List circumstances in which income taxes may affect management decisions.

Deciding on the Type of External Financing

A corporation has three primary sources of external funds: (1) bonds, (2) preferred stock, and (3) common stock. Income taxes may have a significant effect on the choice of external financing: Interest on bonds is fully deductible on the tax return, whereas dividends on preferred and common stock are not deductible. In making the decision, management should recognize that at the marginal tax rate of 34%, the after-tax expense of issuing 10% bonds is only 6.6% [10% $\times$ (1 − 34%)]. A tabular comparison of the cost of financing bonds and common stock is presented in Chapter 17.

The Choice of Accounting Basis

Tax-paying corporations generally use the same basis for computing taxable income that they use for computing accounting net income. For example, many service-oriented small businesses prepare their tax returns and keep their accounting records on the cash basis. In taxation, however, a modified cash basis that includes depreciation accounting is used. The costs of long-lived assets (buildings, machinery, automotive equipment, etc.) are capitalized and depreciated in the same manner as accrual accounting. Large corporations use the accrual basis for accounting purposes and if their gross receipts exceed $5 million, corporations (other than S Corporations) are required to use the accrual basis for tax purposes.

The cash basis allows the taxpayer a greater measure of control over the timing of revenue and deductions. For example, by delaying his or her billing, a dentist can move revenue from the current year to the next year when the tax rate or the income may be lower. The same dentist can pay business expenses and charitable contributions on December 31 of the current year and receive an immediate deduction. Or, if it is to the dentist's advantage, these expenses and contributions can be paid on January 1 and thereby be tax deductions in the next year.

Once adopted, the accounting basis—cash or accrual—must be used consistently from period to period and the basis may be changed only with the approval of the Internal Revenue Service.

Accounting in Action · *Business Insight*

In 1988, the state of Indiana started a trend by becoming the first state in the nation to require electronic income tax payments from corporate taxpayers. By 1990, another 14 states had followed the Hoosier State's lead, and in the next few years, analysts predict that over half of all state governments will require corporate tax payments via electronic funds transfer (EFT).

Why the sudden interest in electronic tax payments? "It's a real dollars-and-cents, cash flow thing," explains Richard Sessions, manager of cash and banking at Quaker Oats Company in Chicago. Since electronic funds transfer payments reach state coffers after a single day's lag, tax revenue flows far more quickly to the government in EFT states than in states using the mail to collect taxes.

From the corporate taxpayer's perspective, however, electronic tax payments aren't entirely painless. The major problem taxpayers face with EFT taxes is deciphering various state formatting requirements that spell out how and when to forward tax information and taxes due to different taxing authorities. The problem is particularly challenging for firms that do business in a number of states, because different states use different standards.

Source: David Bernstein, "Electronic Tax Explosion," *CFO Magazine,* November 1990, p. 12.

Study Objective 8

Describe the accounting for deferred income taxes.

Deferred Income Taxes

A company's **taxable income** is computed in accordance with prescribed tax regulations, whereas a company's **accounting income** (i.e., income before income taxes) is measured in accordance with generally accepted accounting principles (GAAP). Differences between tax regulations and GAAP often exist because the former are designed to raise revenue and the latter are designed to provide useful financial statements. Therefore, taxable income and accounting income often differ.

To illustrate, assume that at the beginning of 1993, you purchase a new copying machine for your business at a total cost of $4,000. **For tax purposes,** you may expense the equipment in the period of purchase. However, **for accounting purposes,** the equipment is depreciated over two years. Assuming that your company had income before depreciation and taxes in these two years of $50,000, your taxable and accounting income (using a 30% tax rate) are as follows:

	Taxable Income		Accounting Income	
	1993	1994	1993	1994
Income before depreciation	$50,000	$50,000	$50,000	$50,000
Depreciation expense				
Tax	(4,000)	–0–		
Book ($4,000 ÷ 2)			(2,000)	(2,000)
Income before income taxes	46,000	50,000	48,000	48,000
Income tax expense (30%)	(13,800)	(15,000)	(14,400)	(14,400)
Total income	$32,200	$35,000	$33,600	$33,600

→ $67,200 ←   → $67,200 ←

Total same for two years

ILLUSTRATION M-19

Computation of taxable and accounting income

In this illustration, accounting income and taxable income differ each year but are the same in total for the two years. These results are attributable in part to the amounts shown for income taxes in the two years. For example, in 1993, income taxes for accounting purposes were $600 higher than the income taxes for tax purposes ($14,400 − $13,800); in 1994, the reverse was true ($15,000 − $14,400).

Differences between income taxes based on taxable income and accounting income result in deferred income taxes—taxes that are deferred to another tax year. There are two reasons: First, Income Tax Expense is debited for the taxes based on accounting income in accordance with the matching of revenues and expenses. Thus, for 1993, Income Tax Expense is debited for 30% of accounting income before income taxes, or $14,400 (30% × $48,000). Second, Income Taxes Payable is credited for the taxes based on taxable income to show the correct tax liability. For 1993, the tax liability is $13,800 (30% × $46,000). Therefore, the deferred income taxes are $600 ($14,400 − $13,800). The entry for 1993 is as follows:

Dec. 31	Income Tax Expense	14,400	
	Income Taxes Payable		13,800
	Deferred Income Taxes		600
	(To record 1993 income taxes)		

For 1994, Income Tax Expense is again $14,400 (30% × $48,000) and Income Taxes Payable is $15,000 (30% × $50,000). The entry, therefore, is as follows:

Dec. 31	Income Tax Expense	14,400	
	Deferred Income Taxes	600	
	Income Taxes Payable		15,000
	(To record 1994 income taxes)		

Note that in 1993 Deferred Income Taxes is credited and that the account has a zero balance at the end of 1994. Normally, Deferred Income Taxes has a credit balance and is reported under long-term liabilities.

In practice, many corporations experience extended time periods when the credits to deferred income taxes exceed the debits to deferred income taxes. This is true because most companies attempt to defer the payment of their income taxes as long as possible. Therefore, accounting income is usually higher than taxable income. Consequently, the cumulative balance in deferred income taxes may be substantial, as shown by the $529 million recently reported by Dow Chemical Company and the $1,927 million reported by IBM Corp. For a growth company, deferred income taxes are often considered to be a tax saving of infinite duration.

*S*ummary of Study Objectives

1. Contrast the importance of an average tax rate and a marginal tax rate. The average tax rate is determined by dividing the total tax paid by total taxable income. The marginal tax rate is the rate applicable to the last dollars of taxable income. The marginal tax rate is usually more significant than the average tax rate in making business decisions.

2. Identify the filing status that an individual may elect. An individual must elect one filing status from the following options: (a) single, (b) head of household, (c) married and filing a joint return, and (d) married and filing a separate return.

3. Give the formula for determining taxable income. The formula for computing taxable income is: gross income less adjustments from gross income equals adjusted gross income less the standard or itemized deductions and exemptions equals taxable income.

4. *Distinguish between the standard deduction and itemized deductions.* The standard deduction is the amount a taxpayer can claim without supporting documentation. Itemized deductions represent actual expenditures made by the taxpayer during the year.

5. *State the formula for determining the tax refund or balance due.* The formula for determining the tax refund or balance due is: amount of tax (regular or alternative minimum) less tax credits and tax payments equals tax refund or balance due.

6. *Indicate the principal components in determining taxable income for a corporation.* The components in determining taxable income for a corporation are gross income and business expenses.

7. *List circumstances in which income taxes may affect management decisions.* Income taxes may affect management's decisions concerning (1) the form of business organization, (2) the type of external financing, and (3) the choice of accounting basis.

8. *Describe the accounting for deferred income taxes.* Deferred income taxes arise because of differences between accounting income computed under GAAP and taxable income determined in accordance with tax regulations. When deferred income taxes are recorded, Income Tax Expense is debited for the tax on accounting income; Income Taxes Payable is credited for the tax on taxable income, and the difference is recognized as deferred income taxes.

GLOSSARY

Active income · Income that the taxpayer has materially participated in producing. (p. M5).

Adjusted gross income · The difference between gross income and adjustments from gross income. (p. M8).

Average tax rate · The total tax paid divided by taxable income. (p. M3).

Capital gain or loss · The gain or loss resulting from the sale or exchange of property classified under tax law as a capital asset. (p. M6).

Deferred income taxes · Taxes deferred because of differences between accounting income and taxable income. (p. M21).

Gross income · All income from whatever source derived. (p. M4).

Itemized deductions · Certain actual expenditures made by the taxpayer during the year, claimed as a deduction. (p. M9).

Marginal tax rate · The tax rate applicable to the last dollars of taxable income. (p. M3).

Passive income · Income obtained from activities in which the taxpayer did not participate on a regular, continuous, and substantial basis. (p. M5).

Personal exemptions · Exemptions allowed a taxpayer for himself or herself, his or her spouse, and for each dependent. (p. M12).

Portfolio income · Income in the form of interest and dividends from securities held as an investment. (p. M5).

Proportional tax · A tax applied at a constant rate regardless of changes in the amount of the tax base. (p. M2).

Progressive tax · A tax whose rate becomes higher as the amount of the tax base increases. (p. M3).

Regressive tax · A tax whereby the amount of the tax remains unchanged or the tax rate decreases with an increase in the tax base. (p. M3).

Standard deduction · The amount a taxpayer may claim without supporting documentation. (p. M9).

Tax avoidance · Structuring business decisions and transactions so that the least amount of tax is paid at the latest possible time permitted by law. (p. M18).

Tax credits · Direct reductions in the tax liability. (p. M15).

Tax evasion · The illegal misstatement of a tax liability by failing to report revenue or income received or by claiming fraudulent deductions. (p. M18).

Tax shelter · An investment designed to take advantage of various tax benefits. (p. M6).

Taxable entities · May be either individuals, corporations, or fiduciaries (estates and trusts). (p. M2).

Taxable income · The excess of adjusted gross income over the sum of deductions and exemptions. (p. M13).

DEMONSTRATION PROBLEM

Renee and Manuel Ortiz are married and have two children in grade school. Manuel is employed by Baldwin Digital, Inc. as a salesman and he is not covered by the company's retirement plan. Renee is a housewife with no income.

In 1992, Manuel received $62,000 in salary and Renee won $1,000 in the state lottery. The Ortizes made the maximum $2,250 payment to an IRA. Because they had few itemized deductions, the Ortizes elected to use the standard deduction in filing a joint tax return for 1992. Federal income taxes withheld from Manuel's earnings totaled $7,500.

Instructions
Prepare a schedule showing taxable income and income taxes payable or refundable.

Solution to Demonstration Problem

RENEE AND MANUEL ORTIZ
Federal Income Tax Computation
For the Year 1992

Gross income		
Manuel Ortiz salary	$62,000	
Renee Ortiz lottery winnings	1,000	
Total gross income		$63,000
Adjustments from gross income		
Payments to IRA (Renee $250, Manuel $2,000)		2,250
Adjusted gross income		60,750
Standard deduction		6,000
Adjusted gross income less standard deduction		54,750
Personal exemptions ($2,300 × 4)		9,200
Taxable income		$45,550
Computation of income tax		
$35,800 × 15%	$ 5,370	
$9,750 × 28%	2,730	8,100
Tax payments		
Income tax withholdings		7,500
Tax due		$ 600

SELF-STUDY QUESTIONS

Answers are at the end of the appendix.

(S.O. 1) 1. A tax that results in a higher tax rate as the tax base increases is called a (an)
   a. proportional tax.
   b. regressive tax.
   c. average tax.
   d. progressive tax.

(S.O. 3) 2. Gross income includes all of the following except
   a. dividends, rents, and royalties.
   b. unemployment compensation.
   c. prizes from a state lottery.
   d. life insurance proceeds from a death.

(S.O. 4) 3. The categories of itemized deductions do not include

   a. state and local taxes.
   b. payments to retirement plans.
   c. interest expense.
   d. casualty and theft losses.

(S.O. 4) 4. Geri Dee paid $500 for prescription drugs, $750 for health insurance, $2,500 for orthodontic fees, and $4,000 for hospital surgery of which $3,000 was reimbursed by insurance. If Geri's adjusted gross income is $28,000, the allowable deduction for medical expenses and health insurance is:
   a. $2,650.
   b. $5,650.
   c. $2,150.
   d. $1,900.

(S.O. 6) 5. One of the following statements about corporation income taxes is true. That statement is:

a. Corporation tax rates are the same as for individual tax payers.
b. Taxable income is gross income less allowable business expenses.
c. Few corporations are required to use the accrual method of accounting in determining taxable income.
d. The concept of adjusted gross income is applicable.

6. The formula for determining a tax refund (S.O. 5) or balance due is the amount of the tax less:

a. tax credits only
b. tax payments only
c. tax credits and tax payments
d. none of the above.

7. Deferred Income Taxes is credited when (S.O. 8) accounting income is:

a. less than taxable income
b. equal to taxable income
c. greater than taxable income
d. none of the above.

QUESTIONS

1. Laurie Fiala claims that taxable entities and accounting entities may not be identical. Is Laurie correct? What are the major classes of taxable entities?

2. Distinguish between an average and a marginal income tax rate. Which rate is more significant in management decisions?

3. Identify and explain the tax methods that may be elected by a taxpayer in determining taxable income.

4. What filing status may be elected by an individual taxpayer?

5. Indicate the formula for computing taxable income.

6. Which of the following items should be included in gross revenue?
(a) Dividends, rents, and royalties
(b) State and federal welfare benefits
(c) Child support
(d) Business and farm income
(e) Unemployment compensation
(f) Gifts, inheritances, and bequests

7. Distinguish between a standard deduction and itemized deductions. Is the standard deduction the same for each filing status?

8. Identify the categories that are used for itemized deductions.

9. What steps are required to determine the tax refund or the tax due?

10. Jeff Parsons claims that an itemized deduction and a tax credit are basically the same. Is Jeff correct? Why or why not?

11. How is taxable income determined for a corporation? Where is the information generally found to determine taxable income for a corporation?

12. Lori Plunkett says that the tax brackets and tax rates for a corporation are different than they are for an individual taxpayer. Is Lori correct? Explain.

13. Identify three circumstances in which income taxes may affect management decisions.

14. Will tax considerations increase the attractiveness of bonds over stock as a source of external financing? Why?

15. What relationship exists between accounting income and taxable income when Deferred Income Taxes is credited?

EXERCISES

EM–1 Clark Pierce is single and has no dependents. Clark compiles the following information for his tax return. Clark's employer has no pension plan.

Gross income	$39,500
Payments to IRA	2,000
Itemized deductions	2,800
Income taxes withheld from salary	6,500

Compute tax refund (liability).
(S.O. 2, 3, 4, 5)

Instructions
(a) Determine the tax refund or liability
(b) Repeat (a), assuming that Clark is the head of a household with one dependent.

EM–2 Chad Young has the following sources of income in 1992.

Salary	$50,000
Income from rental properties (passive income)	8,000
Capital gain from sale of bonds	10,000
Loss from passive investment in oil and gas properties	6,000
Capital loss from sale of common stock	7,000

Compute gross income.
(S.O. 3)

Chad continues to have an interest in the oil and gas properties.

Instructions
(a) Compute gross income for the year.
(b) Repeat (a), assuming that both losses are $5,000 higher.

EM–3 Gross income and other tax data for four taxpayers are presented below:

Compute adjusted gross income.
(S.O. 3)

	Orcas	Strepp	Chen	Wanda
Gross income	$35,000	$74,000	$41,000	$53,000
IRA contribution	2,000	4,000	–0–	2,250
Keogh contribution	–0–	–0–	5,000	–0–
Reimbursed business expenses	3,000	–0–	–0–	2,300
Unreimbursed business expenses	800	500	600	–0–

Orcas is single; the other taxpayers are married and filing jointly. Orcas and Wanda are covered by company-sponsored retirement plans. Strepp and his spouse are not covered by company retirement plans; they both have income over $20,000. Chen is self-employed. Wanda's spouse has no income. Reimbursed business expenses are included in gross income.

Instructions
Compute the adjusted gross income for each taxpayer.

EM–4 Adjusted gross income and other tax data for four taxpayers are presented below:

Compute tax liability or refund
(S.O. 3, 4, 5)

	Sancho	Cho	Polly	Greg
Adjusted gross income	$28,000	$42,000	$54,000	$65,000
Itemized deductions	3,500	4,000	4,500	7,000
Exemptions	1	3	3	4
Income taxes withheld	3,700	6,000	8,125	9,600

Sancho is single with no dependents. Cho is the head of a household with two dependents. Polly is married, has one child, and is filing a joint return. Greg is married, has two children, and is filing a joint return.

Instructions
Compute the tax due or the tax refund for each taxpayer.

EM–5 Brian Trepto is a CPA who specializes in the preparation of tax returns for individuals. For 1992, four clients submit the following information:

Compute amount of tax.
(S.O. 5)

Client	Filing Status	Taxable Income
Burton Kushner	Single taxpayer	$ 89,560
Sally Mahoney	Head of household	123,790
Holly Powell	Married and filing jointly	130,200

Instructions

Compute the tax amount for each client.

Compute total of itemized deductions and compute tax liability.
(S.O. 3, 4, 5)

EM–6   Leah and Michael Nelson are married and are filing a joint income tax return for 1992. The couple's adjusted gross income is $39,000, and they have no children or dependent relatives. The Nelsons had the following tax-related activities during the year:

1. Contributions to church and United Fund	$ 850
2. Membership dues in professional associations	100
3. Interest on home mortgage	3,700
4. State sales tax	600
5. Medical and dental expenses	1,900
6. Unreimbursed business travel and entertainment	2,500
7. CPA fee for tax counseling	200
8. Blue Cross/Blue Shield premiums	800
9. Real estate taxes	2,300
10. Casualty loss in excess of insurance settlement	3,700
11. State income taxes	1,200
12. Interest on car loan	700

Instructions

(a) List the allowable itemized deductions by categories, together with any limitations on the amount deductible.

(b) Compute the tax liability for Leah and Michael Nelson.

Journal entries to record income tax expense, income tax liability, and deferred income taxes.
(S.O. 8)

EM–7   Due to the difference in treatment of an expense item for taxable and accounting income, Morgan Company reported the following taxable and accounting income figure for the three years given below:

	1991	1992	1993
Taxable income	$530,000	$540,000	$710,000
Accounting income	580,000	510,000	690,000

The company's income is taxed at 30%.

Instructions

Prepare the journal entry to record income tax expense, income tax liability, and deferred income taxes at the end of each of the three years.

PROBLEMS

Compute taxable income and amount of taxes due or refundable (joint return).
(S.O. 3, 4, 5)

PM–1   William Glassgow is a college professor. His dependents consist of his wife Jan, his mother, who is 65 years of age, and two children, Don and Donna. Don is in law school; he earned $1,200 from a summer job. Donna is a 19-year-old junior in the school of nursing. She earned $700 during the year. The Glassgows file a joint tax return. William Glassgow provides the following data from his records for the 1992 taxable year:

Income:

University salary ($62,000 less income taxes withheld $13,000)	$49,000
Dividends from stock investments	700
Consulting fees from business enterprises	21,500
Gain on sale of stock investments	800
Interest on tax-exempt municipal bonds	600

Expenses:

Unreimbursed business travel expenses	1,000
Medical expenses for mother and health insurance	5,700
Interest on home mortgage	1,200
Interest on purchase of automobile	1,000
State and local income taxes	2,300
Sales taxes on purchase of automobile	600

Charitable contributions	3,000
Income tax preparation fee	200
Membership dues to professional organizations	300

In 1992, Professor Glassgow made a $2,000 contribution to a Keogh plan on the basis of his consulting income.

Instructions
Prepare a schedule showing the computation of taxable income and the amount of taxes due or refundable. (Round to the nearest dollar.)

PM–2 Mary Ann Benson owns and operates a small proprietorship. She and her husband Robert have three children: Lori, 9 years old, Shari, 6 years old, and Dave, 20 years old. Dave receives over half of his support from his parents. He is a full-time college student who earned $1,000 during the year. Bob and Mary Ann Benson file a joint tax return for 1992. The following cash receipts and disbursements were obtained from Mary Ann's personal records.

Prepare a schedule showing taxable income and taxes due or refundable (small proprietorship and joint return).
(S.O. 3, 4, 5)

Cash receipts:

Withdrawals of income from the business	$18,000
Proceeds from sale of stock purchased as an investment for $800	1,400
Dividends from Mrs. Benson's investments	500
Interest on corporate bonds	300
Inheritance from Mr. Benson's mother's estate	5,000

Cash disbursements:

Hospitalization insurance premiums	900
Personal property taxes	1,600
Charitable contributions	1,500
Unreimbursed medical and dental expenses	2,600
Interest on home mortgage	1,100
Real estate taxes	900
State income taxes	1,200
State and local sales taxes	500
Payment to Keogh retirement plan	5,000
Estimated current year's federal income tax payments	4,400

The accounting records of the proprietorship show sales $462,000, cost of goods sold $304,000, operating expenses $108,000, and net income $50,000.

Instructions
Prepare a schedule showing taxable income and income taxes payable or refundable.

PM–3 An inexperienced tax accountant prepared the following tentative 1992 joint tax return for Seth and Joanne Reader:

Compute taxable income and taxes due (partnership and joint return).
(S.O. 3, 4, 5)

SETH AND JOANNE READER
Federal Income Tax Computation

Gross income:		
Partnership drawings	$10,000	
Interest on tax-exempt municipal bonds	200	
Prize from church raffle	400	
Dividends from investments	600	
Rents received from rental property	4,200	
Total gross income		$15,400
Deductible expenses:		
Medical expenses	1,200	
Charitable contributions	1,500	
Property taxes	3,200	
Other taxes	300	
Utilities	4,000	
Depreciation	2,000	
Total deductible expenses		12,200
Taxable income		$ 3,200

Analysis reveals the following additional data.

1. The distribution schedule for partnership income in which Seth is an active partner showed:

	SETH READER Capital
Salaries	$ 7,200
Interest on capital	1,200
Remainder	4,600
Total net income	$13,000
Less: Drawings	10,000
Increase in capital	$ 3,000

2. Some items listed under deductible expenses pertained to several activities:

	Partnership Property	Personal Residence
Property taxes	$1,200	$2,000
Utilities	1,000	3,000
Depreciation	1,000	1,000

The partnership expenses were properly recorded on the partnership books.

3. Other taxes consisted of state income taxes $250 and state sales taxes $50.

4. The Readers have one child, Lynn, who is 6 years old.

Instructions

Prepare a schedule showing the computation of taxable income and the amount of taxes due or refundable. (Round to the nearest dollar.)

Determine the balance in deferred income taxes over a series of years. Prepare journal entries to record income taxes. (S.O. 8)

PM–4   The financial information for Krueger Industries Inc. includes the following:

1.

Year	Income Taxes Payable
1992	$160,000
1993	85,000

2. On January 1, 1992, equipment costing $350,000 was purchased. For accounting purposes, the company uses straight-line depreciation over a 10-year life. For tax purposes, the company uses an accelerated method that results in depreciation of $77,000 in 1992 and $52,500 in 1993, respectively.

3. In January 1993, $245,000 was collected in advance rentals on a building for a three-year period. The entire $245,000 was reported as taxable income in 1993, but $160,000 of the $245,000 was reported as unearned revenue in 1993 for accounting purposes.

4. The tax rate is 30% in both 1992 and 1993.

Instructions

(a) Determine the amount entered in the Deferred Income tax account for 1992 and whether the amount is a debit or credit.

(b) Determine the amount entered in the Deferred Income tax account for 1993 and whether the amount is a debit or credit.

(c) Determine the balance in the Deferred Income tax account at December 31, 1993, and whether it is a debit or a credit balance.

(d) Prepare the entries for income taxes for both 1992 and 1993.

DECISION CASE 1

Jerry's RV Sales Co. sold 50 self-contained recreational vehicles for $31,000 each during 1992, its first year of business. The vehicles were purchased at the following dates and unit costs.

	Quantity	Unit Cost
January 5	10	$25,000
March 17	7	25,750
April 21	18	26,200
June 3	13	26,500
August 10	7	27,000
October 7	5	27,300

The sale of RVs is Jerry's only source of income. Business operating expenses attributable to 1992 totaled $150,000.

Instructions

(a) Compute taxable income for 1992 using the first-in, first-out (FIFO) inventory costing method.

(b) Compute taxable income for 1992 using the last-in, first-out (LIFO) inventory costing method.

(c) Which method of inventory costing, FIFO or LIFO, do you recommend be used for tax purposes? Explain and discuss.

DECISION CASE 2

Truax Corporation must raise $8,000,000 to finance a plant expansion program. Management has narrowed its choices to the issuance of either one million shares of $5 par value common stock at the current market price of $8 per share or $8 million ten-year 10% bonds. The new plant is expected to produce income before taxes of $2.5 million, and income taxes are expected to be 34%. Truax Corporation currently has 1 million shares of common stock outstanding.

Instructions

(a) Which method of financing will produce the higher net income after income taxes?

(b) Which method of financing will produce the higher earnings per share? (Hint: For both (a) and (b) prepare a tabular schedule beginning with income before interest expense and taxes.) Carry per share figures to three decimals.

Answers to Self-Study Questions
1. d   2. d   3. b   4. a   5. b   6. c   7. c

APPENDIX N

PRESENT VALUE CONCEPTS

Business enterprises borrow and invest large sums of money. Both of these types of transactions involve the use of **present value computations**. A present value computation is based on the concept of the **time value of money**. For example, would you rather be given $1,000 today or be given $1,000 a year from today? If you get the $1,000 today and invest it to earn 10% per year, the $1,000 will accumulate to $1,100 ($1,000 plus the $100 interest) one year from today. The $1,000 received today is the present value amount that is equivalent to $1,100 one year from now. The present value, therefore, is based on three variables: (1) the dollar amount to be received (future amount), (2) the length of time until the amount is received (number of periods), and (3) the interest rate (the discount rate). The process of determining the present value is referred to as **discounting the future amount**. The relationship of these fundamental variables is depicted in the following time diagram:

ILLUSTRATION N-1

Time diagram

To better understand the variables involved in present value analysis, we encourage you to use time diagrams such as the one in Illustration N-1.

In this textbook, present value computations are used in measuring several items. For example, in Chapter 17, to determine the market price of a bond, the present value of the principal and interest payments is computed. In addition, the determination of the amount to be reported for notes payable and lease liability involves present value computations. And, in Chapter 28, the discounted cash flow technique and the net present value method are used to make capital budget decisions.

Present Value of a Single Future Amount

To illustrate present value concepts, assume that you are willing to invest a sum of money that will yield $1,000 at the end of one year. In other words, what amount would you need to invest today to have $1,000 one year from now? If you want a 10% rate of return, the investment or present value is $909.09 ($1,000 ÷ 1.10). The computation of this amount is shown in Illustration N-2.

Present value computation—
$1,000 discounted at 10%
for 1 year

Present value × (1 + interest rate) = Future Value
Present value × (1 + 10%)   = $1,000
Present value   = $1,000 ÷ 1.10
Present value   = $909.09

The future amount ($1,000), the discount rate (10%), and the number of periods (1) are known. The variables in this situation can be depicted in the following time diagram:

Finding present value if dis-
counted for one period

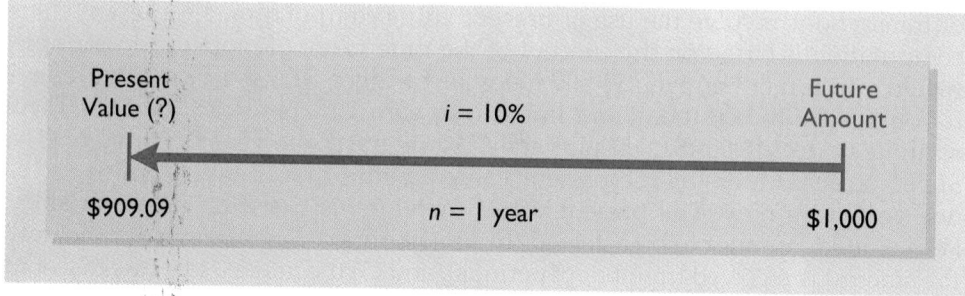

If the single future amount of $1,000 is to be received **in 2 years** and discounted at 10%, its present value is $826.45 [($1,000 ÷ 1.10) ÷ 1.10], depicted as follows:

Finding present value if dis-
counted for two periods

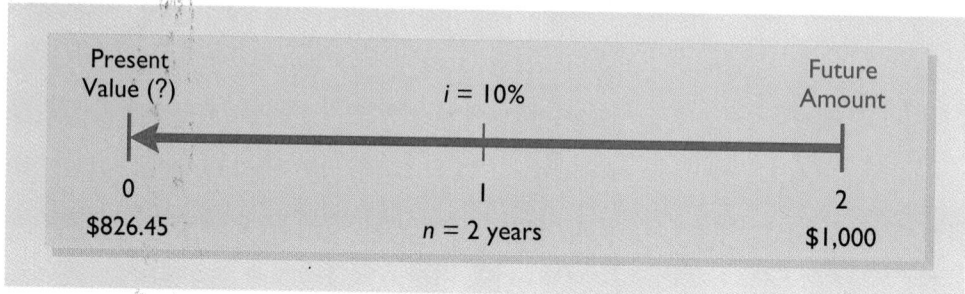

The present value of 1 may also be determined through tables that show the present value of 1 for *n* periods. In Table 1 on page N3, *n* is the number of discounting periods involved. The percentages are the periodic interest rates or discount rates, and the 5-digit decimal numbers in the respective columns are the present value of 1 factors.

When Table 1 is used, the future amount is multiplied by the present value factor specified at the intersection of the number of periods and the discount rate. For example, the present value factor for 1 period at a discount rate of 10% is .90909, which equals the $909.09 ($1,000 × .90909) computed in Illustration N-2. For 2 periods at a discount rate of 10%, the present value factor is .82645, which equals the $826.45 ($1,000 × .82645) computed previously.

Note that a higher discount rate produces a smaller present value. For example, using a 15% discount rate, the present value of $1,000 due one year from now is $869.57 versus $909.09 at 10%. It should also be recognized that the further removed from the present the future amount is, the smaller the present value. For example, using the same discount rate of 10%, the present value of $1,000 due in **five** years is $620.92 versus $1,000 due in **one** year is $909.09.

TABLE I
PRESENT VALUE OF 1

(n) Periods	4%	5%	6%	8%	9%	10%	11%	12%	15%
1	.96154	.95238	.94340	.92593	.91743	.90909	.90090	.89286	.86957
2	.92456	.90703	.89000	.85734	.84168	.82645	.81162	.79719	.75614
3	.88900	.86384	.83962	.79383	.77218	.75132	.73119	.71178	.65752
4	.85480	.82270	.79209	.73503	.70843	.68301	.65873	.63552	.57175
5	.82193	.78353	.74726	.68058	.64993	.62092	.59345	.56743	.49718
6	.79031	.74622	.70496	.63017	.59627	.56447	.53464	.50663	.43233
7	.75992	.71068	.66506	.58349	.54703	.51316	.48166	.45235	.37594
8	.73069	.67684	.62741	.54027	.50187	.46651	.43393	.40388	.32690
9	.70259	.64461	.59190	.50025	.46043	.42410	.39092	.36061	.28426
10	.67556	.61391	.55839	.46319	.42241	.38554	.35218	.32197	.24719
11	.64958	.58468	.52679	.42888	.38753	.35049	.31728	.28748	.21494
12	.62460	.55684	.49697	.39711	.35554	.31863	.28584	.25668	.18691
13	.60057	.53032	.46884	.36770	.32618	.28966	.25751	.22917	.16253
14	.57748	.50507	.44230	.34046	.29925	.26333	.23199	.20462	.14133
15	.55526	.48102	.41727	.31524	.27454	.23939	.20900	.18270	.12289
16	.53391	.45811	.39365	.29189	.25187	.21763	.18829	.16312	.10687
17	.51337	.43630	.37136	.27027	.23107	.19785	.16963	.14564	.09293
18	.49363	.41552	.35034	.25025	.21199	.17986	.15282	.13004	.08081
19	.47464	.39573	.33051	.23171	.19449	.16351	.13768	.11611	.07027
20	.45639	.37689	.31180	.21455	.17843	.14864	.12403	.10367	.06110

The following two demonstration problems (Illustrations N-5, N-6) illustrate how to use Table 1.

ILLUSTRATION N-5

Demonstration Problem—
Using Table 1 for PV of 1

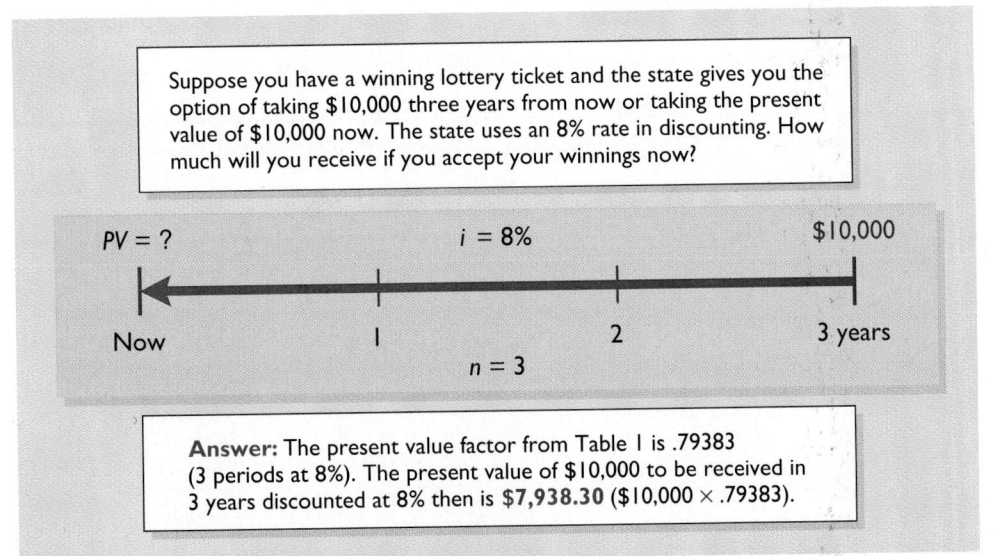

Suppose you have a winning lottery ticket and the state gives you the option of taking $10,000 three years from now or taking the present value of $10,000 now. The state uses an 8% rate in discounting. How much will you receive if you accept your winnings now?

PV = ?   i = 8% $10,000

Now   1   2   3 years

n = 3

Answer: The present value factor from Table 1 is .79383 (3 periods at 8%). The present value of $10,000 to be received in 3 years discounted at 8% then is **$7,938.30** ($10,000 × .79383).

ILLUSTRATION N-6

Demonstration Problem__
Using Table 1 for PV of 1

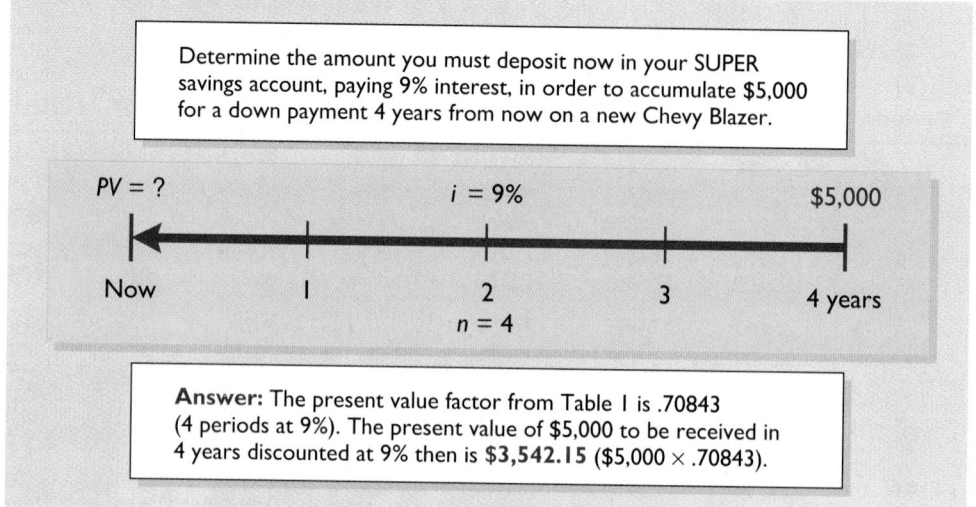

Determine the amount you must deposit now in your SUPER savings account, paying 9% interest, in order to accumulate $5,000 for a down payment 4 years from now on a new Chevy Blazer.

Answer: The present value factor from Table 1 is .70843 (4 periods at 9%). The present value of $5,000 to be received in 4 years discounted at 9% then is **$3,542.15** ($5,000 × .70843).

Present Value of a Series of Future Amounts (Annuities)

The preceding discussion involved the discounting of only a single future amount. Businesses and individuals frequently engage in transactions in which a series of equal dollar amounts are to be received or paid periodically. Examples of a series of periodic receipts or payments are loan agreements, installment sales, mortgage notes, lease (rental) contracts, and pension obligations. These series of periodic receipts or payments are called **annuities**. In computing the present value of an annuity, it is necessary to know the (1) discount rate, (2) the number of discount periods, and (3) the amount of the periodic receipts or payments. To illustrate the computation of the present value of an annuity, assume that you will receive $1,000 cash annually for three years when the discount rate is 10%. This situation is depicted in the following time diagram:

ILLUSTRATION N-7

Time diagram for a 3-year annuity

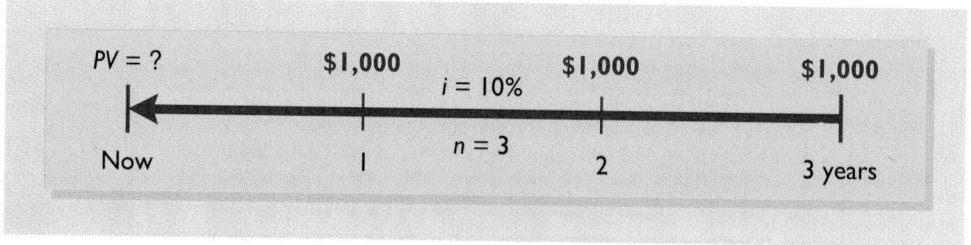

The present value in this situation may be computed as follows:

ILLUSTRATION N-8

Present value of a series of future amounts computation

Future Amount	×	Present Value of 1 Factor at 10%	=	Present Value
$1,000 (One year away)		.90909		$ 909.09
1,000 (Two years away)		.82645		826.45
1,000 (Three years away)		.75132		751.32
		2.48686		**$2,486.86**

This method of calculation is required when the periodic cash flows are not uniform in each period. However, when the future receipts are the same in each period, there are two other ways to compute present value. First, the annual cash flow can be multiplied by the sum of the three present value factors. In the example above, $1,000 × 2.48686 equals $2,486.86. Second, annuity tables may be used. As illustrated in Table 2 below, these tables show the present value of 1 to be received periodically for a given number of periods.

TABLE 2
PRESENT VALUE OF AN ANNUITY OF 1

(n) Periods	4%	5%	6%	8%	9%	10%	11%	12%	15%
1	.96154	.95238	.94340	.92593	.91743	.90909	.90090	.89286	.86957
2	1.88609	1.85941	1.83339	1.78326	1.75911	1.73554	1.71252	1.69005	1.62571
3	2.77509	2.72325	2.67301	2.57710	2.53130	2.48685	2.44371	2.40183	2.28323
4	3.62990	3.54595	3.46511	3.31213	3.23972	3.16986	3.10245	3.03735	2.85498
5	4.45182	4.32948	4.21236	3.99271	3.88965	3.79079	3.69590	3.60478	3.35216
6	5.24214	5.07569	4.91732	4.62288	4.48592	4.35526	4.23054	4.11141	3.78448
7	6.00205	5.78637	5.58238	5.20637	5.03295	4.86842	4.71220	4.56376	4.16042
8	6.73274	6.46321	6.20979	5.74664	5.53482	5.33493	5.14612	4.96764	4.48732
9	7.43533	7.10782	6.80169	6.24689	5.99525	5.75902	5.53705	5 32825	4.77158
10	8.11090	7.72173	7.36009	6.71008	6.41766	6.14457	5.88923	5.65022	5.01877
11	8.76048	8.30641	7.88687	7.13896	6.80519	6.49506	6.20652	5.93770	5.23371
12	9.38507	8.86325	8.38384	7.53608	7.16073	6.81369	6.49236	6.19437	5.42062
13	9.98565	9.39357	8.85268	7.90378	7.48690	7.10336	6.74987	6.42355	5.58315
14	10.56312	9.89864	9.29498	8.24424	7.78615	7.36669	6.98187	6.62817	5.72448
15	11.11839	10.37966	9.71225	8.55948	8.06069	7.60608	7.19087	6.81086	5.84737
16	11.65230	10.83777	10.10590	8.85137	8.31256	7.82371	7.37916	6.97399	5.95424
17	12.16567	11.27407	10.47726	9.12164	8.54363	8.02155	7.54879	7.11963	6.04716
18	12.65930	11.68959	10.82760	9.37189	8.75563	8.20141	7.70162	7.24967	6.12797
19	13.13394	12.08532	11.15812	9.60360	8.95012	8.36492	7.83929	7.36578	6.19823
20	13.59033	12.46221	11.46992	9.81815	9.12855	8.51356	7.96333	7.46944	6.25933

From Table 2 it can be seen that the present value of an annuity of 1 factor for three periods at 10% is 2.48685.[2] This present value factor is the total of the three individual present value factors as shown in Illustration N-8. Applying this amount to the annual cash flow of $1,000 produces a present value of $2,486.85.

The following demonstration problem (Illustration N-9) illustrates how to use Table 2.

---

[2]The difference of .00001 between 2.48686 and 2.48685 is due to rounding.

ILLUSTRATION N-9

Demonstration Problem—
Using Table 2 for PV of an
annuity of 1

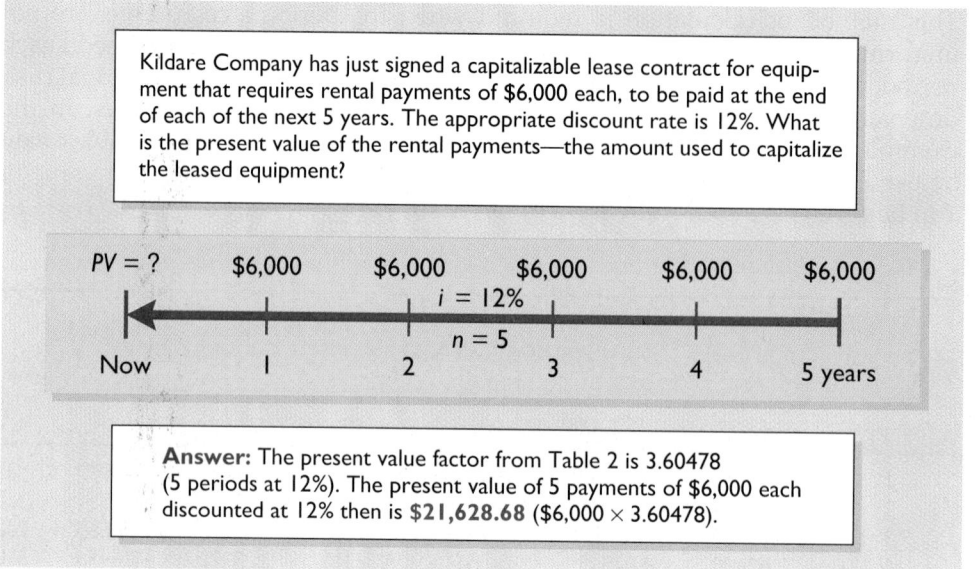

Kildare Company has just signed a capitalizable lease contract for equipment that requires rental payments of $6,000 each, to be paid at the end of each of the next 5 years. The appropriate discount rate is 12%. What is the present value of the rental payments—the amount used to capitalize the leased equipment?

Answer: The present value factor from Table 2 is 3.60478 (5 periods at 12%). The present value of 5 payments of $6,000 each discounted at 12% then is **$21,628.68** ($6,000 × 3.60478).

Time Periods and Discounting

In the preceding calculations, the discounting has been done on an annual basis using an annual interest rate. Discounting may also be done over shorter periods of time such as monthly, quarterly, or semiannually. When the time frame is less than one year, it is necessary to convert the annual interest rate to the applicable time frame. Assume, for example, that the investor in Illustration N-8 received $500 **semiannually** for three years instead of $1,000 annually. In this case, the number of periods becomes 6 (3 × 2), the discount rate is 5% (10% ÷ 2), the present value factor from Table 2 is 5.07569, and the present value of the future cash flows is $2,537.85 (5.07569 × $500). This amount is slightly higher than the $2,486.86 computed in Illustration N-8 because interest is computed twice during the same year; therefore interest is earned on the first half year's interest.

Computing the Present Value of a Bond

The present value (or market price) of a bond is a function of three variables: (1) the payment amounts, (2) the length of time until the amounts are paid, and (3) the discount rate.

The first variable (dollars to be paid) is made up of two elements: (1) a series of interest payments (an annuity) and (2) the principal amount (a single sum). To compute the present value of the bond, both the interest payments and the principal amount must be discounted—two different computations. The time diagrams for a bond due in 5 years are shown in Illustration N-10.

When the investor's discount rate is equal to the bond's contractual interest rate, the present value of the bonds will equal the face value of the bonds. To illustrate, assume a bond issue of 10%, 5-year bonds with a face value of $100,000 with interest payable **semiannually** on January 1 and July 1. If the discount rate is the same as the contractual rate, the bonds will sell at face value. In this case,

ILLUSTRATION N-10

Present value of a bond time diagram

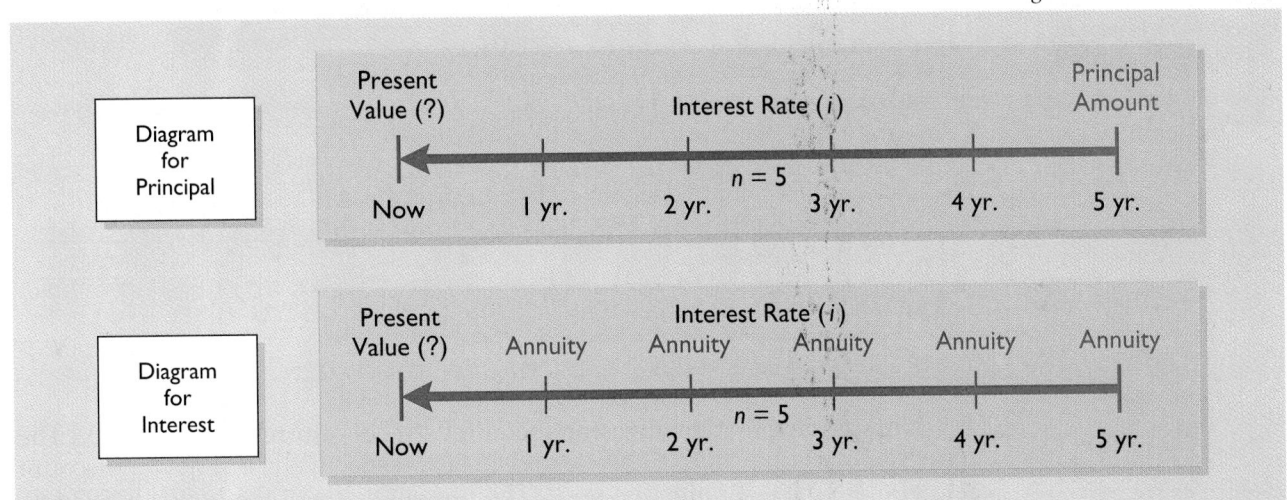

the investor will receive (1) $100,000 at maturity and (2) a series of ten $5,000 interest payments [($100,000 × 10%) ÷ 2] over the term of the bonds. The length of time is expressed in terms of interest periods, in this case, 10, and the discount rate per interest period, 5%. The following time diagram (Illustration N-11) depicts the variables involved in this discounting situation:

ILLUSTRATION N-11

Time diagram for present value of a 10%, 5-year bond paying interest semiannually

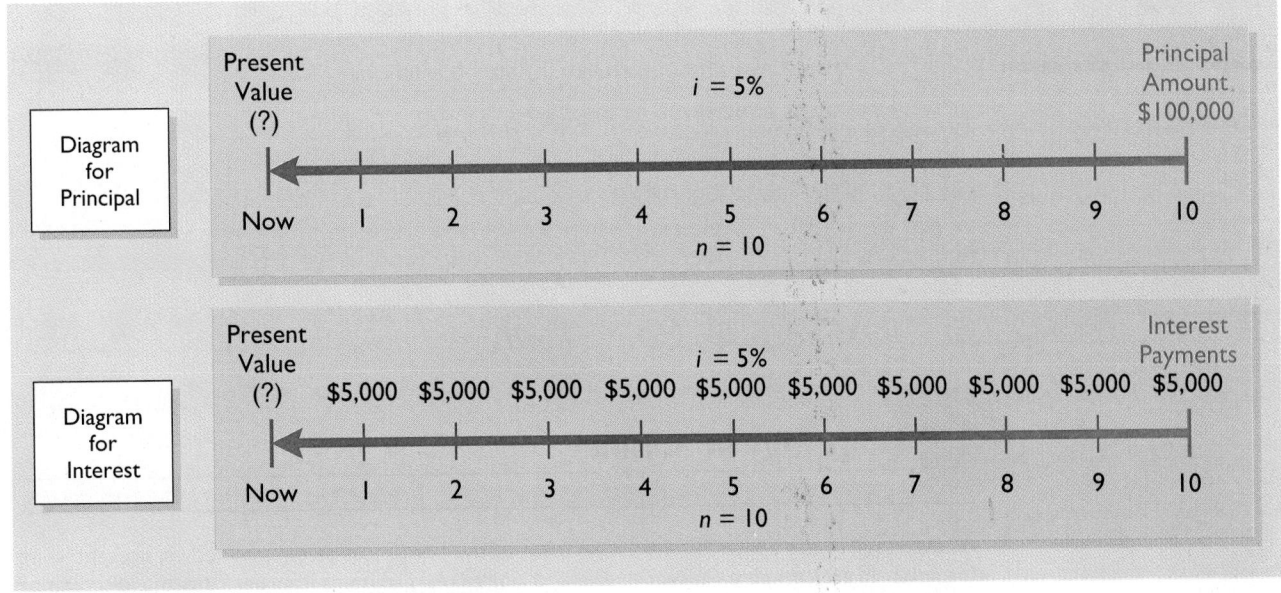

The computation of the present value of these bonds is shown below.

ILLUSTRATION N-12

Present value of principal and interest (face value)

10% Contractual Rate—10% Discount Rate	
Present value of principal to be received at maturity	
$100,000 × PV of 1 due in 10 periods at 5%	
$100,000 × .61391 (Table 1)	$ 61,391
Present value of interest to be received periodically	
over the term of the bonds	
$5,000 × PV of 1 due periodically for 10 periods at 5%	
$5,000 × 7.72173 (Table 2)	38,609*
Present value of bonds	$100,000

*(Rounded).

Now assume that the investor's required rate of return is 12%, not 10%. The future amounts are again $100,000 and $5,000, respectively, but now a discount rate of 6% (12% ÷ 2) must be used. The present value of the bonds is $92,639, as computed below:

ILLUSTRATION N-13

Present value of principal and interest (discount)

10% Contractual Rate—12% Discount Rate	
Present value of principal to be received at maturity	
$100,000 × .55839 (Table 1)	$55,839
Present value of interest to be received periodically	
over the term of the bonds	
$5,000 × 7.36009 (Table 2)	36,800
Present value of bonds	$92,639

Conversely, if the discount rate is 8% and the contractual rate is 10%, the present value of the bonds is $108,111, computed as follows:

ILLUSTRATION N-14

Present value of principal and interest (premium)

10% Contractual Rate—8% Discount Rate	
Present value of principal to be received at maturity	
$100,000 × .67556 (Table 1)	$ 67,556
Present value of interest to be received periodically	
over the term of the bonds	
$5,000 × 8.11090 (Table 2)	40,555
Present value of bonds	$108,111

Technology in Action

As discussed in this appendix, the selling price of the bonds can be determined via present value formulas. Many computer spreadsheets and computer programs can perform the discounting functions given the basic information of the situation.

The above discussion relied on present value tables in solving present value problems. Electronic hand-held calculators may also be used to compute present values without the use of these tables. Some calculators, especially the "business" or "MBA" type calculators, have present value (PV) functions that allow you to calculate present values by merely inputing the proper amount, discount rate, periods, and pressing the PV key.

BRIEF EXERCISES (Use Tables to Solve Exercises)

BEN–1 For each of the following cases, indicate (a) to what interest rate columns and (b) to what number of periods you would refer in looking up the discount rate.

Using present-value tables.

1. In Table 1 (present value of 1):

	Annual Rate	Number of Years Involved	Discounts Per Year
a.	12%	6	Annually
b.	10%	15	Annually
c.	8%	8	Semiannually

2. In Table 2 (present value of an annuity of 1):

	Annual Rate	Number of Years Involved	Number of Payments Involved	Frequency of Payments
a.	12%	20	20	Annually
b.	10%	5	5	Annually
c.	8%	4	8	Semiannually

BEN–2 (a) What is the present value of $10,000 due 8 periods from now, discounted at 8%? (b) What is the present value of $10,000 to be received at the end of each of 6 periods, discounted at 9%?

Determining present values.

BEN–3 Smolinski Company is considering an investment which will return a lump sum of $500,000 five years from now. What amount should Smolinski Company pay for this investment to earn a 15% return?

Compute the present value of a single-sum investment.

BEN–4 Pizzeria Company earns 11% on an investment that will return $875,000 eight years from now. What is the amount Pizzeria should invest now to earn this rate of return?

Compute the present value of a single-sum investment.

BEN–5 Shake-A-Soda Company sold a 5-year, noninterest-bearing $27,000 note receivable to Valley Inc. Valley Inc. wishes to earn 12% over the remaining 4 years of the note. How much cash will Shake-A-Soda receive upon sale of the note?

Compute the present value of a single-sum non-interest bearing note.

BEN–6 Roberto Company issues a three-year zero interest bearing $66,000 note. The interest rate used to discount the zero interest bearing note is 8%. What are the cash proceeds that Roberto Company should receive?

Compute the present value of a single-sum non-interest bearing note.

BEN–7 Kilarny Company is considering investing in an annuity contract that will return $20,000 annually at the end of each year for 15 years. What amount should Kilarny Company pay for this investment if it earns a 6% return?

Compute the present value of an annuity investment.

BEN–8 Zarita Enterprises earns 11% on an investment that pays back $110,000 at the end of each of the next four years. What is the amount Zarita Enterprises invested to earn the 11% rate of return?

Compute the present value of an annuity investment.

BEN–9 Hernandez Railroad Co. is about to issue $100,000 of 10-year bonds paying a 12% interest rate, with interest payable semiannually. The discount rate for such securities is 10%. How much can Hernandez expect to receive for the sale of these bonds?

Compute the present value of bonds.

BEN–10 Assume the same information as BEN–9 except that the discount rate was 12% instead of 10%. In this case, how much can Hernandez expect to receive from the sale of these bonds?

Compute the present value of bonds.

Compute the present value of a note.	**BEN–11** Caledonian Taco Company receives a $50,000, 6-year note bearing interest of 11% (paid annually) from a customer at a time when the discount rate is 12%. What is the present value of the note received by Caledonian?
Compute the present value of bonds.	**BEN–12** Galway Bay Enterprises issued 10%, 8-year, $2,000,000 par value bonds that pay interest semiannually on October 1 and April 1. The bonds are dated April 1, 1993, and are issued on that date. The discount rate of interest for such bonds on April 1, 1993, is 12%. What cash proceeds did Galway Bay receive from issuance of the bonds?
Compute the value of a machine for purposes of making a purchase decision.	**BEN–13** Barney Googal owns a garage and is contemplating purchasing a tire retreading machine for $16,280. After estimating costs and revenues, Barney projects a net cash flow from the retreading machine of $2,790 annually for 8 years. Barney hopes to earn a return of 11% percent on such investments. What is the present value of the retreading operation? Should Barney Googal purchase the retreading machine?
Compute the present value of a note.	**BEN–14** Hung-Chao Yu Company issues a 10%, 6-year mortgage note on January 1, 1993 to obtain financing for new equipment. Land is used as collateral for the note. The terms provide for semiannual installment payments, of $112,825. What were the cash proceeds received from the issuance of the note?
Compute the maximum price to pay for a machine.	**BEN–15** Ramos Company is considering purchasing equipment. The equipment will produce the following cash flows: Year 1, $30,000; Year 2, $40,000; Year 3, $50,000. Ramos requires a minimum rate of return of 15%. What is the maximum price Ramos should pay for this equipment?
Compute the interest rate on a single sum.	**BEN–16** If Kerry Rodriquez invests $1,827 now and she will receive $10,000 at the end of 15 years. What annual rate of interest will Kerry earn on her investment? (Hint: Use Table 1.)
Compute the number of periods of a single sum.	**BEN–17** Maloney Cork has been offered the opportunity of investing $24,719 now. The investment will earn 15% per year and will at the end of that time return Maloney $100,000. How many years must Maloney wait to receive $100,000? (Hint: Use Table 1.)
Compute the interest rate on an annuity.	**BEN–18** Annie Dublin purchased an investment for $11,469.92. From this investment, she will receive $1,000 annually for the next 20 years starting one year from now. What rate of interest will Annie's investment be earning for her? (Hint: Use Table 2.)
Compute the number of periods of an annuity.	**BEN–19** Andy Sanchez invests $8,851.37 now for a series of $1,000 annual returns beginning one year from now. Andy will earn a return of 8% on the initial investment. How many annual payments of $1,000 will Andy receive? (Hint: Use Table 2.)

PHOTO CREDITS

Chapter 1
Opener: William Whitehurst / The Stock Market. Page 7: Stephen Johnson / Tony Stone World Wide. Page 9: Ann States / SABA. Page 14: Bill Gallery / Stock, Boston. Page 24: John Lamb / Tony Stone World Wide.

Chapter 2
Opener: Stephen Johnson / Tony Stone World Wide. Page 49: Wes Thompson / The Stock Market. Page 50: Mitchell Layton / Duomo. Page 57: Arthur Meyerson / The Image Bank. Page 66: Romilly Lockyer / The Image Bank.

Chapter 3
Opener: Gerald French / FPG International. Page 89: Jerry Ohlinger. Page 94: Romilly Lockyer / The Image Bank. Page 107: G&G Design / The Stock Market.

Chapter 4
Opener: Flip Chalfant / The Image Bank. Page 132: Steve Proehl / The Image Bank. Page 148: Michael R. Schneps / The Image Bank. Page 151: Guy Marché / FPG International.

Chapter 5
Opener: Robert Tinney / The Stock Market. Page 184: Suzanne Murphy / Tony Stone World Wide. Page 190: Mark Antman / The Image Works. Page 192: R. Llewellyn / Superstock. Page 200: Comstock, Inc. Page 203: A. T. Willett / The Image Bank.

Chapter 6
Opener: Comstock, Inc.

Chapter 7
Opener: Stephen Marks / Stockphotos, Inc. Page 278: Tom Campbell / FPG International. Page 280: Rivera Collection / Superstock. Page 283: Courtesy of American Express Company. Page 292: Comstock, Inc. Page 294: Michel Tcherevkoff / The Image Bank.

Chapter 8
Opener: Superstock. Page 326: William Adams / FPG International. Page 333: Gary Gladstone / The Image Bank. Page 338: Superstock.

Chapter 9
Opener: Comstock, Inc. Page 360: Michael A. Keller / The Stock Market. Page 361: Tom Tracy / FPG International. Page 369: R. Rathe / FPG International. Page 371: Charlie Westerman / Liaison International.

Chapter 10
Opener: Marianne Sullivan / Index Stock. Page 402: Dave Davidson / The Stock Market. Page 403: Frank Grant / International Stock Photo. Page 408: Bob Pizaro / Comstock, Inc. Page 410: A. Boccaccio / The Image Bank. Page 417: Murray Alcosser / The Image Bank.

Chapter 11
Opener: Geoffrey Gove / The Image Bank. Page 435: Zarember / The Stock Shop. Page 441: N. Cotton / International Stock Photo. Page 444: Courtesy Lotus. Page 445: Courtesy RJR Nabisco. Page 446 (top): Miguel / The Image Bank. Page 448: Courtesy Grand Met. Page 446 (bottom): Photofest. Page 450: Courtesy IBM.

Chapter 12
Opener: Stephen Marks / The Image Bank. Page 472: Marv Lyons / The Image Bank. Page 474: Robert Keeling / FPG International. Page 479: Gabe Palmer / The Stock Market. Page 481: Griffiths / Magnum. Page 488: John Neubauer / FPG International.

Chapter 13
Opener: The Telegraph Colour Library / FPG International. Page 510: R&S Michaud / Woodfin Camp & Associates. Page 514: Comstock, Inc. Page 518: Comstock, Inc. Page 519: Edward Young / The Stock Market. Page 527: Daniel MacDonald / The Stock Shop. Page 530: Comstock, Inc.

Chapter 14
Opener: Greg Pease / Tony Stone World Wide. Page 550: Michael Neveux / WestLight. Page 554: Patrick Doherty / Stockphotos, Inc.

Chapter 15
Opener: C. Orrico / Superstock. Page 589: Jacques Chenet / Woodfin Camp & Associates. Page 590: Courtesy Delaware State Travel Service. Page 593: Roger Tully / Tony Stone World Wide. Page 604: Robert George Young / Masterfile.

Chapter 16
Opener: Anthony Johnson / The Image Bank. Page 627: Ralph Mercer / Tony Stone World Wide. Page 637: Robert Kristofik / The Image Bank. Page 640: Rob Nelson / Black Star. Page 641: Marc Vaughn / Sharp Shooters.

Chapter 17
Opener: Andy Washnik / The Stock Market. Page 666: E. Salem Krieger / The Image Bank. Page 669: Peter

Gridley/FPG International. Page 671: G. Marche/FPG International. Page 683: Dick Luria/FPG International.

Chapter 18
Opener: David Ball/The Stock Market. Page 714: Michael Simpson/FPG International. Page 722: Courtesy Borden. Page 730: Ron Chapple/FPG International. Page 733: Capital Cities/ABC, Inc.

Chapter 19
Opener: Henryk T. Kaiser/The Picture Cube. Page 753: Jim Pickerell/Stock, Boston. Page 754: Bill Gallery/Stock, Boston. Page 768 and 781: N. Tully/Sygma.

Chapter 20
Opener: Charly Franklin/FPG International. Page 818: Nora Good/Masterfile. Page 820: Courtesy J. C. Penney. Page 821: Michael Melford/The Image Bank. Page 826 (top): Comstock, Inc. Page 826 (bottom): Sepp Seitz/Woodfin Camp & Associates. Page 828: Thomas Craig/FPG International.

Chapter 21
Opener: Index Stock. Page 859: Jon Feingersh/The Stock Market. Page 862: H. R. Bramaz/Peter Arnold, Inc. Page 863: M. Simpson/FPG International.

Chapter 22
Opener: Tom Tracy/FPG International. Page 895: Chris Michaels/FPG International. Page 899: Courtesy McDonnell Douglas, St. Louis, Page 909: Bob Daemmrich/The Image Works.

Chapter 23
Opener: Steve Hanson/Stock, Boston. Page 928: Mike Dobel/Masterfile. Page 932: Paul Steel/The Stock Market. Page 947: Scott Schraft/The Stock Market. Page 948: Joseph Palmieri/Index Stock.

Chapter 24
Opener: Brett H. Froomer/The Image Bank. Page 975: Travelpix/FPG International. Page 979: F. Garcia/Stills/Retna.

Chapter 25
Opener: Spencer Grant/Stock, Boston. Page 1006: John Riley/MediChrome. Page 1008: Tom Tracy/The Stock Shop.

Chapter 26
Opener: Steve Brown/Leo de Wys, Inc. Page 1052: Comstock, Inc. Page 1057: Courtesy Bell Atlantic.

Chapter 27
Opener: Dick Luria/FPG International. Page 1089: Frederic Stein/FPG International. Page 1095: Courtesy UPS. Page 1100: A. A. Montes de Oca/FPG International.

Chapter 28
Opener: The Stock Market. Page 1130: The Telegraph Colour Library/FPG International. Page 1132: David McGlynn/FPG International.

Appendix
M7: Joe Bator/The Stock Market. M20: Walter Bibikow/The Image Bank.

COMPANY INDEX

SUBJECT INDEX

---

*Page numbers preceded by a capital letter refer to appendix sections.